Instructor's Annotated Edition

PROTAGONISTAS

A COMMUNICATIVE APPROACH

Charo Cuadrado
Pilar Melero
Enrique Sacristán

Jan Underwood
Portland Community College

VISTA HIGHER LEARNING
Boston, Massachusetts

The **PROTAGONISTAS** cover features a doorway in San Miguel de Allende, Mexico; the sculpture *Floralis Generica* by Eduardo Catalano, in Buenos Aires, Argentina; and *L'Hemisfèric* planetarium, by Santiago Calatrava, in Valencia, Spain.

Publisher: José A. Blanco
Executive Editor: Sarah Kenney
Managing Editors: María Eugenia Corbo, Paola Ríos Schaaf (Technology)
Senior Project Manager: Katie Wade
Editors: Gabriela Ferland, Paula A. Orrego, Patricia Ravetto, Carolina Zapata Pérez, Christian Biagetti (Technology), John DeCarli (Technology)
Production and Design Director: Marta Kimball
Senior Designer: Sarah Cole
Production and Design Team: Manuela Arango, Oscar Díez, Paula Díez, Mauricio Henao, Susan Prentiss, Andrés F. Vanegas García, Nick Ventullo

Student Text ISBN: 978-1-60576-977-6

Instructor's Annotated Edition ISBN: 978-1-60576-978-3

1 2 3 4 5 6 7 8 9 RW 16 15 14 13 12 11

Instructor's Annotated Edition

Table of Contents

The Vista Higher Learning Story

Your Specialized Foreign Language Publisher

Independent, specialized, and privately owned, Vista Higher Learning was founded in 2000 with one mission: to raise the teaching and learning of world languages to a higher level. This mission is based on the following beliefs:

- It is essential to prepare students for a world in which learning another language is a necessity, not a luxury.
- Language learning should be fun and rewarding, and all students should have the tools necessary for achieving success.
- Students who experience success learning a language will be more likely to continue their language studies both inside and outside the classroom.

With this in mind, we decided to take a fresh look at all aspects of language instructional materials. Because we are specialized, we dedicate 100 percent of our resources to this goal and base every decision on how well it supports language learning.

That is where you come in. Since our founding, we have relied on the continuous and invaluable feedback from language instructors and students nationwide. This partnership has proved to be the cornerstone of our success by allowing us to constantly improve our programs to meet your instructional needs.

The result? Programs that make language learning exciting, relevant, and effective through:

- an unprecedented access to resources
- a wide variety of contemporary, authentic materials
- the integration of text, technology, and media, and
- a bold and engaging textbook design

By focusing on our singular passion, we let you focus on yours.

The Vista Higher Learning Team

VISTA
HIGHER LEARNING

31 St. James Avenue, Boston, MA 02116-4104 TOLLFREE: 800-618-7375
TELEPHONE: 617-426-4910 FAX: 617-426-5209 www.vistahigherlearning.com

Getting to Know PROTAGONISTAS

Allow us to introduce **PROTAGONISTAS**, a new introductory Spanish program, and the "protagonists" from the Spanish-speaking world who bring the program to life.

Developed in Spain and adapted for use in the North American college market, **PROTAGONISTAS** takes a unique approach to beginning Spanish. The program is explicitly driven by the goal of cultivating students' intercultural communication skills. Each lesson introduces students to a **protagonista,** an individual from the Spanish-speaking world; the **protagonista** is the basis for exploring aspects of culture and daily life, all the while modeling language. This fresh approach imparts cultural and linguistic information to students not as ends in and of themselves, but as the means to an end: communication. At the same time, because of its immediacy, relevance, and authenticity, the **PROTAGONISTAS** approach keeps the goal of intercultural communicative competence in clear view.

PROTAGONISTAS' approach to the linguistic aspects of interaction is both communicative and functional-notional. This accessible text emphasizes task-driven communication within meaningful, pragmatic contexts of everyday life. The four skills are taught through a series of short, interactive activities. Vocabulary and grammar are presented at several levels, from immediate, hands-on, contextualized references to more expansive explanations.

PROTAGONISTAS offers several features that make it truly different:

- Culture is much more than an add-on, a side-bar, or even an "integrated component." In **PROTAGONISTAS**, cultural awareness is the medium through which new vocabulary and grammar are presented and practiced. Thus every language lesson is also a cultural lesson, and vice versa. This unique approach allows students to develop both the linguistic and interpersonal skills that they will need to communicate effectively with Spanish speakers from many parts of the world.
- Vocabulary and grammatical structures are presented through multiple contact points, from immediate, hands-on examples to complete and contextualized explanations. Students are given ample practice opportunities at all of these levels.
- **PROTAGONISTAS** also incorporates graphic design—page layout, use of colors, typefaces, and other graphic elements—as an integral part of the learning process. To enhance learning and make navigation easy, lesson sections are consistent throughout the book and appear either completely on one page or on a spread of two facing pages. The textbook pages themselves are also visually dramatic.
- Engaging graphics model and guide students' communication throughout the book, helping them become aware of, comprehend, and use language structures in a hands-on way.
- The **PROTAGONISTAS** program comes with a full range of print and technology ancillaries: all these materials are based on the same communicative, functional-notional approach as the book itself.

Getting to Know Your Instructor's Annotated Edition

The Instructor's Annotated Edition (IAE) of **PROTAGONISTAS** features student text pages overprinted with answers to all activities that have discrete responses. It also provides on-page guidance and support for using the materials. The annotations were written to complement and support varied teaching styles, to extend the already rich content of the student textbook, and to save you time in class preparation and course management. As you familiarize yourself with them, it is important to know that the annotations are suggestions only. Any Spanish questions, sentences, models, or simulated instructor-student exchanges are not meant to be prescriptive or limiting. You are encouraged to view these suggested "scripts" as flexible points of departure that will help you achieve your instructional goals.

Instructor annotations include a wide variety of suggestions for opening questions you can pose to get students thinking about certain topics; background information on cultural topics that you may wish to share; ideas for activities to prepare students to tackle textbook activities or to follow them up; additional, related activity ideas to expand on textbook learning; tips for making grammatical complexities more accessible to students; alternative approaches to individual textbook activities; language-acquisition strategies; strategies to help students manage the vocabulary load and presentation in the text; notes on lexical variation in the Spanish-speaking world; and additional activities for further practice or to enchance student learning.

Culture and communication are emphasized up-front, but the text offers several layers of support for new vocabulary and grammatical structures so that you can shape the course as you see fit.

Depending on your preference, class time available to you, and the needs of your students, you may ask students to prepare the **Gramática funcional** reference section at home before completing the functional spreads in class, or you may have them do so after having been exposed to new vocabulary and structures in context.

In addition to the teaching suggestions found in your Instructor's Annotated Edition, comprehensive lesson plans for each unit are available on the instructor **Supersite**. Lesson Plans include presentation and teaching suggestions for every activity in the lesson, as well as additional cultural information, expansion activities, and suggestions for differentiated instruction.

General Teaching Considerations

As students begin learning Spanish with **PROTAGONISTAS**, take some time to show them the features of the text. You will want students to notice that culture is the medium of teaching and learning in **PROTAGONISTAS,** both because it will be important that students become aware of the concept of intercultural communication early on in the course, and because they are likely to be inspired by this approach. Point out that the people featured in **PROTAGONISTAS** represent individuals from all parts of the Spanish-speaking world, and that the text allows students to peek into their lives, see what they are like, and reflect on them as they are learning the language.

Encourage students to look through the **Unidad preliminar,** where they will get a first glimpse of the protagonists they will meet throughout the text. You may also find it useful to talk to students at the beginning of your course about communicative language-learning and about the functional-notional approach. Explain to students that the Spanish they will be learning will be extremely practical and that they can expect to be able to put it to use in real-life situations quickly. Also explain that each lesson is based on a "notion"—a context, such as grocery shopping or doing housework—and a few "functions" within that notion, such as asking for prices of food items or dividing up household chores with a roommate.

Students will probably be glad to learn that the lessons in this text are "bite-sized" and that grammar explanations are lean, providing just the information needed to accomplish the task at hand. Although many students enjoy grammar, many do not see it as an end in itself, but rather as a means to an end; **PROTAGONISTAS** accommodates that view. **PROTAGONISTAS** first models language and gives students a concrete task to accomplish with new vocabulary and grammar, and then places that new information in a broader linguistic context.

Introduce the two-lesson unit format and the reading and video components that appear in the **Avance** section of each unit. Let students know that they will get built-in opportunities to review and recycle previously learned material at the end of each lesson and again at the end of every other unit.

Show students the spreads and point out that each lesson is organized in exactly the same way: three presentation spreads where vocabulary and communicative functions are presented through readings and activities, followed by the **Tarea final** and **Yo puedo...** review and self-evaluation activities and the **Gramática funcional** and **Vocabulario** reference sections at the end. Understanding the structure of the text will help students to navigate the text readily. Language students are often concerned about the study of vocabulary and grammar, so point out the **Gramática funcional** and **Vocabulario** sections, as well as the Grammar reference and bilingual glossary in the appendix, and give students a sense of what they can expect during their homework and study time. The **Tarea final** and **Yo puedo...** features of each lesson may represent an approach that is new to students, so draw their attention to those as well. These features help students assess their own level of understanding of the material and identify areas where they need additional review and practice.

Because **PROTAGONISTAS** treats graphic design as an integral part of students' language-learning experience, you may want to take a few minutes to orient students to the design of the student textbook. Call students' attention to the use of elements such as charts, diagrams, word lists, activity **modelos,** titles, and sidebars.

Finally, you will also want to give students a tour of the **Supersite** and explain your expectations for how this tool will be used throughout the course.

PROTAGONISTAS and the *Standards for Foreign Language Learning*

PROTAGONISTAS' pedagogy was informed by the ACTFL Proficiency Guidelines and the *Standards for Foreign Language Learning in the 21st Century*. Since **PROTAGONISTAS** takes a communicative approach to the teaching and learning of Spanish, the Communication goal is also central to the student text. For example, the diverse formats used in classroom activities—pair work, small group work, class circulation, information gap, task-based, and so forth—engage students in genuine exchanges of information, both providing and obtaining data, conversing, and expressing feelings and emotions. Students are also given ample opportunities to interact using spoken and written language. The functional-notional approach keeps language-learning concrete and relevant; everything presented in the text is at the service of communication.

In addition, it is worth noting that **PROTAGONISTAS** not only meets the high standards set by the U.S.'s most important national body of foreign-language teachers; this text also meets those of ACTFL's European counterpart. **PROTAGONISTAS** was developed in Spain to meet the guidelines established by the Common European Framework of Reference for Languages (CEFR). As the CEFR recommends, the text and its ancillaries develop both students' understanding of a broad variety of cultural norms from various Spanish-speaking environments, and their meta-cultural awareness of cross-cultural communication practices, as well as developing their communicative language skills.

PROTAGONISTAS

A COMMUNICATIVE APPROACH

Charo Cuadrado
Pilar Melero
Enrique Sacristán
▪
Jan Underwood
Portland Community College

VISTA
HIGHER LEARNING
Boston, Massachusetts

The **PROTAGONISTAS** cover features a doorway in San Miguel de Allende, Mexico; the sculpture *Floralis Generica* by Eduardo Catalano, in Buenos Aires, Argentina; and *L'Hemisfèric* planetarium, by Santiago Calatrava, in Valencia, Spain.

Publisher: José A. Blanco
Executive Editor: Sarah Kenney
Managing Editors: María Eugenia Corbo, Paola Ríos Schaaf (Technology)
Senior Project Manager: Katie Wade
Editors: Gabriela Ferland, Paula A. Orrego, Patricia Ravetto, Carolina Zapata Pérez, Christian Biagetti (Technology), John DeCarli (Technology)
Production and Design Director: Marta Kimball
Senior Designer: Sarah Cole
Production and Design Team: Manuela Arango, Oscar Díez, Paula Díez, Mauricio Henao, Susan Prentiss, Andrés F. Vanegas García, Nick Ventullo

Student Text ISBN: 978-1-60576-977-6

Instructor's Annotated Edition ISBN: 978-1-60576-978-3

Library of Congress Control Number: 2010940766

1 2 3 4 5 6 7 8 9 RW 16 15 14 13 12 11

Introduction

Welcome to **PROTAGONISTAS**, your gateway to the Spanish language and the vibrant cultures of the Spanish-speaking world. **PROTAGONISTAS** is adapted for North American college students from an innovative text used in Spain. It includes ground-breaking features to keep you engaged and motivated, and to make language-learning accessible. Here are just some of the original, hallmark features you will encounter in this text:

- A curriculum built around individuals from all over the Spanish-speaking world, presenting vocabulary and grammar through the context of their daily lives
- Coverage of the entire Spanish-speaking world
- An emphasis on real-life language use
- Practical, high-frequency vocabulary in meaningful contexts
- Clear, concise grammar explanations with high-impact graphics and other special features that make structures easier to learn and use
- Ample guided, focused practice to reinforce the vocabulary and grammar you are learning
- Abundant opportunities to interact with a classmate, small group, the full class, and your instructor
- Thirty-six "bite-sized" lessons, each of which is organized exactly the same way
- Careful development of your reading, writing, and listening skills, incorporating learning strategies and a process approach
- Integration of an appealing video series
- An easy-to-navigate design built around recurring sections that appear either completely on one page or on spreads of two facing pages
- Thorough learning support through on-the-spot sidebars and suggestions, models and guides to conversation, grammar clarifications, and language-learning tips
- A complete set of print and electronic supplements to help you learn Spanish

To familiarize yourself with the program's organization, turn to page xii and take the **PROTAGONISTAS** at-a-glance tour.

Apéndice

Grammar Reference Table of Contents

The Appendix includes a thorough grammar reference section, conveniently cross-referenced with the **Gramática funcional** presentations in each lesson.

The **Unit Opener** presents the protagonists you will encounter and the communicative functions you will learn in the two lessons of the unit.

Every unit includes audio and video content available on the **PROTAGONISTAS** Supersite.

Communicative functions are summarized at the beginning of the unit, so you know from the start what you will be able to accomplish by the end of each lesson.

S Audio: Activities, Vocabulary
Video: *Flash Cultura*

Unidad 4

Paco, amigo del Rastro

Lección 4A

BARRIOS CON CARÁCTER

Lección 4B

CON VISTAS AL MAR

Carmen Abreu, fundadora de Caribe Propiedades

Comprar en los mercados

AVANCE

Every unit concludes with **Avance,** a section containing review strategies and activities or readings, as well as the **Flash Cultura** cultural video series.

Each lesson features a protagonist from the Spanish-speaking world, someone who will show you how Spanish is used in real-world situations.

Each lesson begins with two functional spreads, where vocabulary and structures are presented in their functional context.

Mouse icons indicate activities that are also available on the Supersite with auto-grading.

Mi experiencia activities provide conversation outlines that guide you to use lesson vocabulary and structures for meaningful, personalized communication.

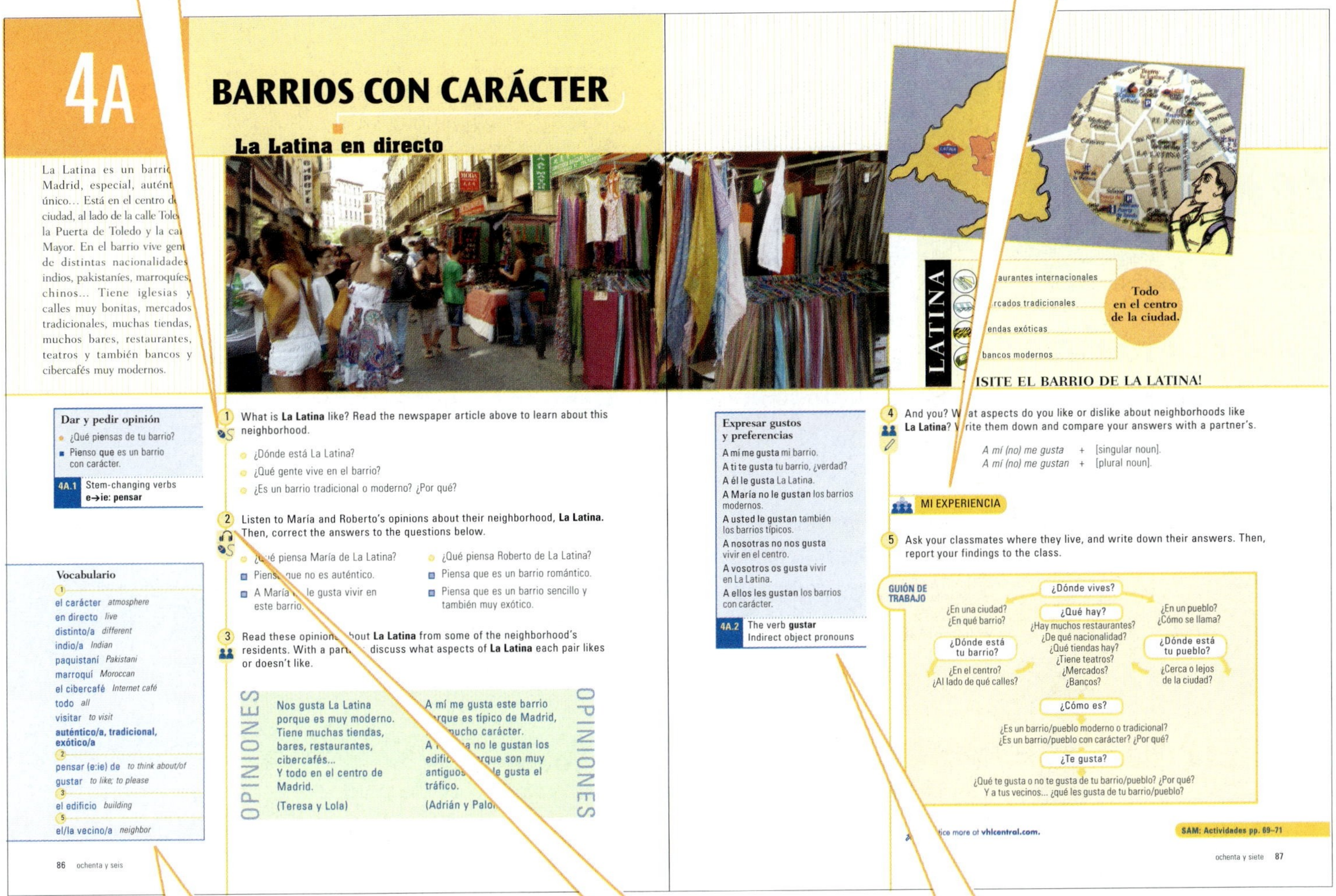

Active vocabulary is presented in **Vocabulario** sidebars, organized in order of appearance, with reference to the relevant activity. Cognates are provided without translation. Active vocabulary is also summarized at the end of the lesson.

Headset icons call out listening activities with available audio recordings.

Communicative functions are summarized in sidebars throughout the lesson. Cross-references guide you to the **Gramática funcional** reference section at the end of each lesson.

Each functional spread is self-contained, providing you with the tools and references you need to communicate in Spanish in specific real-world contexts.

Photos, colorful graphics, and varied activity formats expose you to different cultural contexts and ways of using the language.

Pair and group icons highlight communicative activities.

Writing icons indicate activities with a focus on writing.

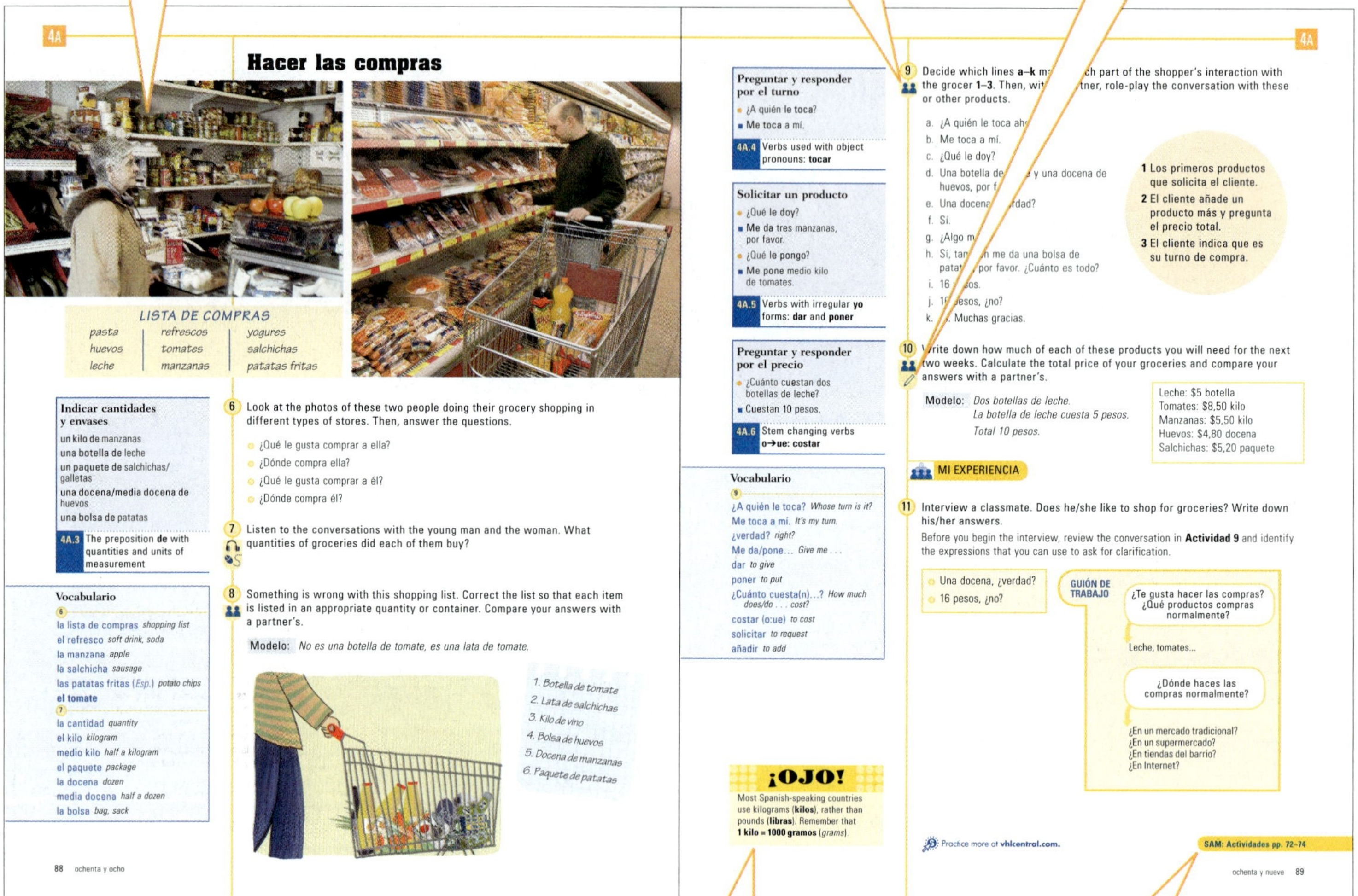

4A

Hacer las compras

LISTA DE COMPRAS

pasta	*refrescos*	*yogures*
huevos	*tomates*	*salchichas*
leche	*manzanas*	*patatas fritas*

Indicar cantidades y envases
un kilo de manzanas
una botella de leche
un paquete de salchichas/galletas
una docena/media docena de huevos
una bolsa de patatas
4A.3 The preposition **de** with quantities and units of measurement

Vocabulario
6
la lista de compras *shopping list*
el refresco *soft drink, soda*
la manzana *apple*
la salchicha *sausage*
las patatas fritas (*Esp.*) *potato chips*
el tomate
7
la cantidad *quantity*
el kilo *kilogram*
medio kilo *half a kilogram*
el paquete *package*
la docena *dozen*
media docena *half a dozen*
la bolsa *bag, sack*

6 Look at the photos of these two people doing their grocery shopping in different types of stores. Then, answer the questions.
- ¿Qué le gusta comprar a ella?
- ¿Dónde compra ella?
- ¿Qué le gusta comprar a él?
- ¿Dónde compra él?

7 Listen to the conversations with the young man and the woman. What quantities of groceries did each of them buy?

8 Something is wrong with this shopping list. Correct the list so that each item is listed in an appropriate quantity or container. Compare your answers with a partner's.

Modelo: *No es una botella de tomate, es una lata de tomate.*

1. Botella de tomate
2. Lata de salchichas
3. Kilo de vino
4. Bolsa de huevos
5. Docena de manzanas
6. Paquete de patatas

88 ochenta y ocho

Preguntar y responder por el turno
- ¿A quién le toca?
- Me toca a mí.

4A.4 Verbs used with object pronouns: **tocar**

Solicitar un producto
- ¿Qué le doy?
- Me da tres manzanas, por favor.
- ¿Qué le pongo?
- Me pone medio kilo de tomates.

4A.5 Verbs with irregular **yo** forms: **dar** and **poner**

Preguntar y responder por el precio
- ¿Cuánto cuestan dos botellas de leche?
- Cuestan 10 pesos.

4A.6 Stem changing verbs **o→ue: costar**

Vocabulario
9
¿A quién le toca? *Whose turn is it?*
Me toca a mí. *It's my turn.*
¿verdad? *right?*
Me da/pone... *Give me . . .*
dar *to give*
poner *to put*
¿Cuánto cuesta(n)...? *How much does/do . . . cost?*
costar (o:ue) *to cost*
solicitar *to request*
añadir *to add*

¡OJO!
Most Spanish-speaking countries use kilograms (**kilos**), rather than pounds (**libras**). Remember that **1 kilo = 1000 gramos** (*grams*).

9 Decide which lines **a–k** m… ch part of the shopper's interaction with the grocer **1–3**. Then, wit… tner, role-play the conversation with these or other products.

a. ¿A quién le toca ah…
b. Me toca a mí.
c. ¿Qué le doy?
d. Una botella de… y una docena de huevos, por f…
e. Una docena… rdad?
f. Sí.
g. ¿Algo m…
h. Sí, tam… n me da una bolsa de patat… por favor. ¿Cuánto es todo?
i. 16 … sos.
j. 16 pesos, ¿no?
k. … Muchas gracias.

1 Los primeros productos que solicita el cliente.
2 El cliente añade un producto más y pregunta el precio total.
3 El cliente indica que es su turno de compra.

10 …rite down how much of each of these products you will need for the next two weeks. Calculate the total price of your groceries and compare your answers with a partner's.

Modelo: *Dos botellas de leche.*
La botella de leche cuesta 5 pesos.
Total 10 pesos.

Leche: $5 botella
Tomates: $8,50 kilo
Manzanas: $5,50 kilo
Huevos: $4,80 docena
Salchichas: $5,20 paquete

MI EXPERIENCIA

11 Interview a classmate. Does he/she like to shop for groceries? Write down his/her answers.

Before you begin the interview, review the conversation in **Actividad 9** and identify the expressions that you can use to ask for clarification.

- Una docena, ¿verdad?
- 16 pesos, ¿no?

GUIÓN DE TRABAJO
¿Te gusta hacer las compras? ¿Qué productos compras normalmente?
Leche, tomates...
¿Dónde haces las compras normalmente?
¿En un mercado tradicional?
¿En un supermercado?
¿En tiendas del barrio?
¿En Internet?

Practice more at **vhlcentral.com.**

SAM: Actividades pp. 72–74

ochenta y nueve 89

¡OJO! sidebars offer further explanation or clarification about structures and usage.

References in the footer show you exactly which pages in the **Student Activities Manual** correspond to each presentation.

The third spread of each lesson features a **protagonista** from the Spanish-speaking world whose job or lifestyle ties in to the lesson themes.

Protagonists come from all countries in the Spanish-speaking world. They provide a personal connection and a practical application for the language you are learning.

4A

Paco, amigo del Rastro

Vives en La Latina, ¿verdad?
Sí, vivo en la calle Toledo.

¿Te gusta este barrio?
¡Me gusta mucho! Está en el centro y es muy típico.

El domingo trabajas en el Rastro. ¿Y los otros días de la semana?
Trabajo en el Mercado de la Cebada, en una tienda de alimentación.

¿Qué tienes en tu puesto del Rastro?
Pues muchas cosas típicas de Madrid: pósters, abanicos, postales, libros...

¿Qué te gusta del Rastro?
Me gusta todo: la gente, las calles, las tiendas, los puestos...

¿Piensas que el Rastro es un lugar único?
Sí. ¡Es un lugar único y especial!

[...]

Paco Suárez García, 38 años. Tiene un puesto en el Rastro de Madrid.

El Rastro
El Rastro es un mercado al aire libre muy popular de Madrid. Está en el barrio de La Latina. Las tiendas del Rastro generalmente están en la calle y se llaman "puestos".

Vocabulario
12
la tienda de alimentación *grocery store*
el puesto *stand (in a market)*
la cosa *thing*
el póster
13
la edad *age*

12 Indicate whether each statement is true (**verdadero**) or false (**falso**).

1. Paco no vive en La Latina.
2. Paco trabaja todos los días en el Rastro.
3. Paco no vende libros.
4. A Paco le gustan la gente, las calles y las tiendas.
5. Paco piensa que el Rastro es único y especial.

13 Fill in this information sheet about Paco.

- Nombre y apellidos: ....
- Edad: ....
- Domicilio: ....
- Lugar de trabajo (lunes a sábado): ....
- Lugar de trabajo (domingos): ....

14 In pairs, discuss what you have learned about Paco. What is he like? What things does he like? Do you know anyone like Paco?

15 Imagine that you and your partner have a stand at a street market, like Paco. What typical products from your city or region would you sell?

OPINIÓN
¿Le gusta ir a mercados como el Rastro? ¿Por qué?
¿Qué venden en estos mercados?
¿Qué compra cuando va a estos mercados?
¿Hay un mercado como el Rastro en su ciudad/pueblo? ¿Cómo es?

90 noventa

Vocabulario
16
probablemente *probably*
al aire libre *outdoor*
más conocido/a *best-known*
se celebra *is held*
encontrar (o:ue) *to find*
la antigüedad *antique*
el objeto curioso *curiosity, nicknack*
el espectáculo *show*
en general *generally*
es posible *it's possible*
regatear *to barter, to haggle*
conseguir (e:i) *to get, to obtain*
el precio *price*
bajo/a *low*
el lugar clave *landmark*
disfrutar (de) *to enjoy*
la confitería (*Arg.*) *café*
el medio de transporte *means of transportation*
el subte(rráneo) (*Arg.*) *subway*
la estación *station*
recomendado/a *recommended*
la nota, el souvenir, la línea

Internet
Cada vez son más los hispanos, sobre todo los jóvenes, que hacen la compra por Internet. Entre los productos más vendidos en la red están los de alimentación, discos y libros. ¿Y en su país? ¿Compra usted a través de Internet? ¿Qué productos?

Vocabulario
18
el agromercado *produce market*
la yuca *yucca*
el frijol *bean*
la noticia *news*
el mundo *world*

4A

16 Read this information from a Buenos Aires guidebook and fill in the notes below. Then, compare your answers with a partner's.

La feria de San Telmo
Probablemente es la feria al aire libre más conocida de Argentina. Se celebra todos los domingos en la plaza Dorrego en el barrio de San Telmo. Encuentras de todo: artesanía, antigüedades, objetos curiosos, souvenirs... También puedes ver espectáculos de tango y turistas de muchas nacionalidades.
Los vendedores en general son muy simpáticos y amables. A veces es posible regatear y conseguir precios más bajos.
La Plaza de Mayo, uno de los lugares clave de Buenos Aires, está muy cerca. En San Telmo también puedes disfrutar comidas muy ricas y puedes tomar un café en una de las tradicionales confiterías de la zona.
El mejor medio de transporte es el subte. Para llegar a San Telmo, toma la línea A (estación: Plaza de Mayo) o la línea E (estación: Belgrano).

Horario y lugar: los domingos en ____
Productos: ____
Vendedores: ____
Cómo llegar: ____
Actividades recomendadas: ____
Lugares cerca: Plaza de Mayo

[r] [rr]

17 a. Listen to these series of words. Which sound do you hear: [r] or [rr]?
a. barrio, ricas, Dorrego [ ]
b. bar, carácter, mercado [ ]

b. Read aloud the names of these neighborhoods in Buenos Aires. Which words have the [r] and [rr] sounds?
Puerto Madero Retiro Montserrat Recoleta Palermo

18 Read this paragraph about Cuban produce markets. Can you find the[se] foods where you live? Work with a partner to write a list of typical produc[t]s from your region. Then, present your list to the class.

El agromercado cuba[n]o
En Cuba es muy típico hacer la [co]mpra en los agromercados. Los cubanos [co]mpran en estos mercados papayas, yu[ca,] frijoles y papas, entre otras cosas. Es [tamb]ién un lugar donde a la gente le gusta [hab]lar de la calidad de los productos, de [los p]recios y de las noticias del mundo.

A veces la fruta y los alimentos tienen nombres diferentes en España y América Latina. Por ejemplo:
• papa (patata) • frijol (alubia)

Practice more at **vhlcentral.com**.

SAM: Activid[ades] ...5–78

nove[nta y uno] 91

Green and yellow sidebars provide additional cultural information, conversation topics, and communication strategies.

There are additional practice activities available on the Supersite for each presentation spread.

Units 1–6 include pronunciation practice. Units 7–18 feature expanded reading and writing practice.

Tarea final and **Yo puedo...** bring together the lesson's cultural and communicative goals.

Tarea final group projects give you the opportunity to apply the lesson structures and vocabulary in meaningful, real-life situations.

4A

TAREA FINAL

Un mercado en la clase

Make a list of five items you have at home that you would like to sell.
Discos, sellos...

Tell the other members of your group which products you are selling.
Un disco de Shakira. Me gusta, pero quiero comprar un CD nuevo.

Set a price for your products.
Disco, $6

Ask about at least four products being sold by another group. Try to bargain for a lower price.

Share with the class the items that you bought, as well as the purchase price.
Una camiseta de Plaza Sésamo, $20

YO PUEDO...

- Puedo hablar de mi barrio.
  Write a letter to a friend, giving him/her information about your neighborhood.
  ¿Dónde está? ¿Qué actividades puedes hacer? ¿Qué opiniones hay sobre el barrio? ¿Qué le gusta a la gente de esta zona? ¿Qué no le gusta?
- Puedo escribir una lista de compras.
  Add containers and units of measurement to this shopping list.
- Puedo mantener un diálogo en español en una tienda.
  Complete the dialogue.
- Puedo describir tres aspectos de mercados del mundo hispanohablante.
  Answer these questions.
  ¿Dónde está el Rastro? ¿Qué puedes comprar en la feria de San Telmo? ¿Qué puedes comprar en un agromercado cubano?

3 .... de patatas
1 .... de azúcar
1 .... de huevos
2 .... de leche

- ¿A quién le toca?
- ....
- ¿Qué le doy/pongo?
- ....
- ¿Algo más?
- ....
- 14 pesos. Gracias.

92 noventa y dos

Yo puedo... self-assessment gives you the opportunity to check your understanding of the lesson's communicative functions, and identify any areas where you need further review and practice.

Gramática funcional offers contextualized explanations of the structures behind the lesson's communicative functions.

Grammar explanations are organized according to the related communicative function in the lesson.

¡Póngalo en práctica! activities give you a chance to practice these structures right away. All of these activities are also available on the Supersite with auto-grading.

GRAMÁTICA FUNCIONAL

4A

4A.1 Ask for and give opinions

Stem-changing verbs **e→ie: pensar** 5.1.1

- Use the verb **pensar** (*to think*) to ask for and give opinions. **Pensar** is an **e→ie** stem-changing verb. You saw the same stem-changing pattern with **querer** in **3B.6**. Remember that the **nosotros/as** and **vosotros/as** forms don't have a stem change.

  ¿Qué **piensan** ustedes de Valparaíso?
  *What **do you think** of Valparaíso?*

  Pensamos que es una ciudad encantadora.
  ***We think** it is a charming city.*

- To ask someone's opinion about something or someone, use **pensar** + **de** + [*noun*].

  ¿Qué **piensas del** mercado de la fruta?
  *What **do you think of** the fruit market?*

- To give an opinion about something or someone, use **pensar** + **que** + [*verb*].

  Pienso que es exótico.
  *I **think** it's exotic.*

PENSAR			
(yo)	pienso	(nosotros/as)	pensamos
(tú)	piensas	(vosotros/as)	pensáis
(usted, él, ella)	piensa	(ustedes, ellos/as)	piensan

4A.2 Express tastes and preferences

The verb **gustar** 5.11
Indirect object pronouns 6.2.2

- Use the verb **gustar** (*to like; to please*) to express likes and dislikes. Unlike in English, the person or thing that is liked is the grammatical subject of the sentence in Spanish. Therefore, **gustar** is most commonly used in the 3rd person singular or plural.

  ¿Te **gusta** mi barrio?
  Do you like my neighborhood?

- Use **gusta** with a singular noun or a verb in the infinitive; use **gustan** with a plural noun.

  Sí, me **gusta** vivir en el centro; me **gustan** los barrios dinámicos.
  Yes, I like living downtown; I like lively neighborhoods.

- Always use an indirect object pronoun (**me, te, le, nos, os,** or **les**) before **gusta(n)** to indicate who likes a certain object or activity.

  ¿**Les** gusta la feria de San Telmo?
  Do you like the San Telmo market?

  Sí, **nos** gusta muchísimo.
  Yes, we like it a lot.

¡Póngalo en práctica!

G1 Complete the conversation.

- ¿Qué piensas (1) .... Buenos Aires?
- (2) .... (3) .... Buenos Aires es una ciudad muy interesante.
- ¿Y Andrea y Sebastián?
- Los dos (4) .... que Buenos Aires tiene barrios muy especiales.
- ¡Bien! ¡Todos (5) .... igual!
- ¿Cuándo vamos a Argentina?

G2 Answer the questions using the cues.

1. ¿Qué piensa Ramón del mercado? (divertido)
2. ¿Qué piensan los vecinos de este barrio? (dinámico)
3. ¿Qué piensan ustedes del museo? (interesante)
4. ¿Qué piensas tú de los edificios? (tradicionales)

G3 Complete the conversation.

¿Te (1)........................ mi barrio?

¿Tu barrio? Sí, mucho. Me (2)........................ los edificios, las calles, las tiendas...

Y a Brenda?

A Brenda y a mí (3)........................ gusta vivir en el centro de la ciudad.

¿Pero (4)........................ gusta a los dos este ambiente?

(5)........................ me gusta, pero a Brenda no. Y a ti, ¿qué (6)........................ de tu barrio?

Practice more at **vhlcentral.com.**

noventa y tres 93

Explanations in English, abundant examples, and graphics like charts and tables make the grammatical structures accessible.

If you need further support, Grammar Reference numbers direct you to traditional grammar explanations in the appendix.

Vocabulario summarizes all active vocabulary in the lesson.

Audio recordings for all active vocabulary are available on the Supersite.

Vocabulary is grouped by functional spread, and listed in alphabetical order by part of speech.

VOCABULARIO

4A

La Latina en directo

el carácter	atmosphere
el cibercafé	Internet café
el edificio	building
el/la vecino/a	neighbor
todo	all
gustar	to like; to please
pensar (e:ie) de	to think about/of
visitar	to visit
auténtico/a	authentic
distinto/a	different
en directo	live
exótico/a	exotic
indio/a	Indian
marroquí	Morroccan
paquistaní	Pakistani
tradicional	traditional

Hacer las compras

¿A quién le toca?	Whose turn is it?
¿Cuánto cuesta(n)...?	How much does/do . . . cost?
Me da/pone...	I'd like . . .
Me toca a mí.	It's my turn.
¿verdad?	right?
la bolsa	bag, sack
la cantidad	quantity
la docena	dozen
el kilo	kilogram
la lista de compras	shopping list
la manzana	apple
media docena	half a dozen
medio kilo	half a kilogram
el paquete	package
las patatas fritas (Esp.)	potato chips
el refresco	soft drink, soda
la salchicha	sausage
el tomate	tomato
añadir	to add
costar (o:ue)	to cost
dar	to give
poner	to put
solicitar	to request

Paco, amigo del Rastro

es posible	it's possible
se celebra	is held
el agromercado	produce market
la antigüedad	antique
la confitería (Arg.)	café
la cosa	thing
la edad	age
el espectáculo	show
la estación	station
el frijol	bean
la línea	line
el lugar clave	landmark
el medio de transporte	means of transportation
el mundo	world
la nota	note
la noticia	news
el objeto curioso	curiosity, nicknack
el póster	poster
el precio	price
el puesto	stand (in a market)
el souvenir	souvenir
el subte(rráneo) (Arg.)	subway
la tienda de alimentación	grocery store
la yuca	yucca
conseguir (e:i)	to get, to obtain
disfrutar (de)	to enjoy
encontrar (o:ue)	to find
regatear	to haggle, to bargain
bajo/a	low
más conocido/a	best-known
recomendado/a	recommended
al aire libre	outdoors
en general	generally
probablemente	probably

Variación léxica

¿Me da...? ↔ ¿Me pone...? (*Esp.*)

la confitería (*Arg.*) ↔ la terraza (*Esp.*)

el frijol ↔ la alubia (*Esp.*) ↔ el poroto (*Cono S.*)

hacer las compras ↔ hacer la compra (*Esp.*) ↔ hacer la despensa (*Méx.*)

la lista de compras ↔ la lista de la compra (*Esp.*)

las patatas fritas (*Esp.*) ↔ las papas fritas

el mercado ↔ la feria ↔ el mercadillo (*Esp.*) ↔ el mercado de pulgas

el subte (*Arg.*) ↔ el metro

el refresco ↔ la gaseosa ↔ la soda (*Amér. L.*)

el souvenir ↔ el recuerdo

noventa y siete 97

Variación léxica highlights alternate words and expressions used throughout the Spanish-speaking world. Active vocabulary is indicated in blue type, while the most high-frequency word or expression is listed first.

Vocabulary is listed in convenient column format that allows for easy studying.

Even-numbered units include **Estrategias** and **Competencias** activities in the **Avance** section.

Estrategias' tiered presentation reviews language-learning and communication strategies from the preceding two units.

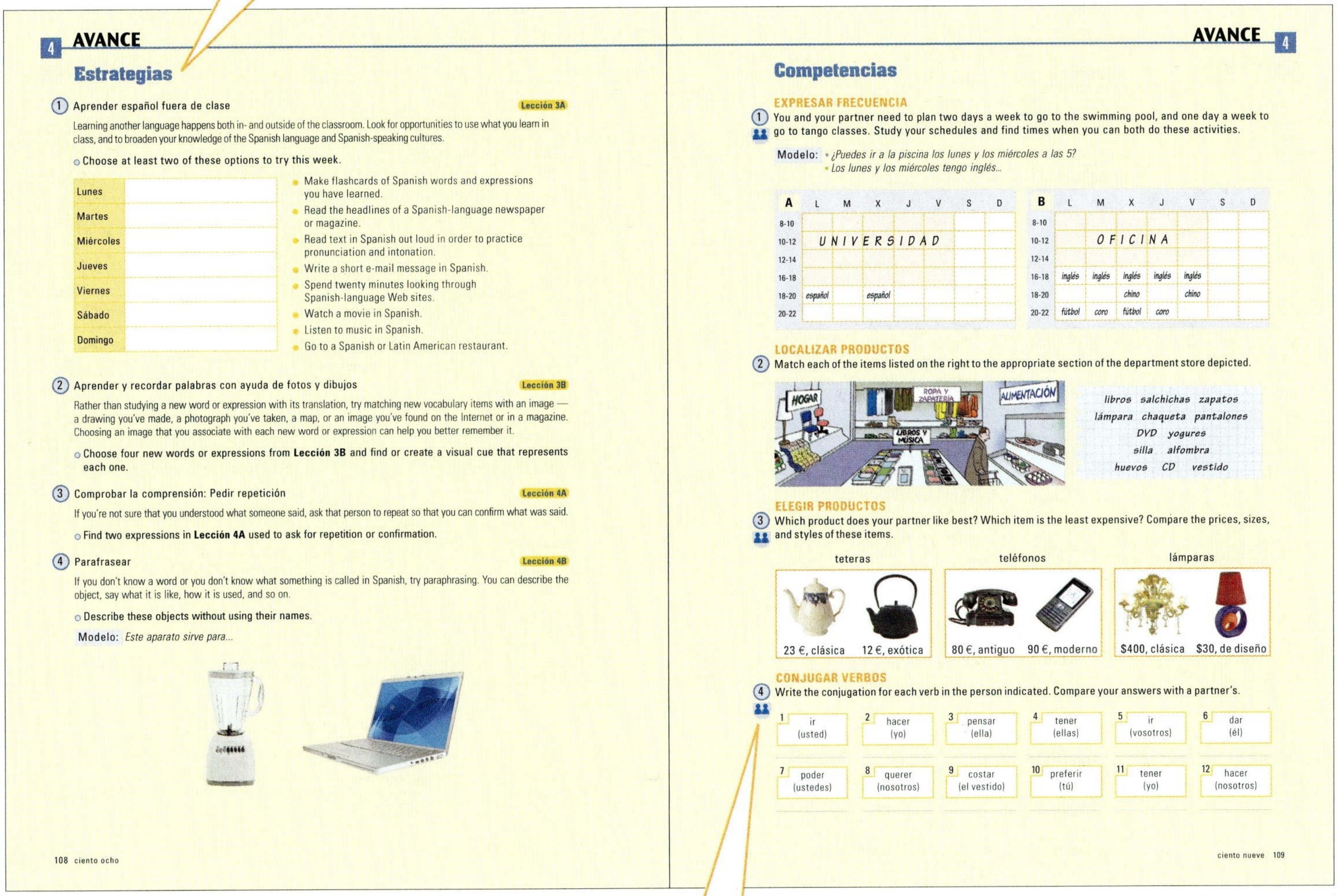

4 **AVANCE**

Estrategias

① Aprender español fuera de clase — Lección 3A

Learning another language happens both in- and outside of the classroom. Look for opportunities to use what you learn in class, and to broaden your knowledge of the Spanish language and Spanish-speaking cultures.

○ Choose at least two of these options to try this week.

Lunes	
Martes	
Miércoles	
Jueves	
Viernes	
Sábado	
Domingo	

- Make flashcards of Spanish words and expressions you have learned.
- Read the headlines of a Spanish-language newspaper or magazine.
- Read text in Spanish out loud in order to practice pronunciation and intonation.
- Write a short e-mail message in Spanish.
- Spend twenty minutes looking through Spanish-language Web sites.
- Watch a movie in Spanish.
- Listen to music in Spanish.
- Go to a Spanish or Latin American restaurant.

② Aprender y recordar palabras con ayuda de fotos y dibujos — Lección 3B

Rather than studying a new word or expression with its translation, try matching new vocabulary items with an image — a drawing you've made, a photograph you've taken, a map, or an image you've found on the Internet or in a magazine. Choosing an image that you associate with each new word or expression can help you better remember it.

○ Choose four new words or expressions from **Lección 3B** and find or create a visual cue that represents each one.

③ Comprobar la comprensión: Pedir repetición — Lección 4A

If you're not sure that you understood what someone said, ask that person to repeat so that you can confirm what was said.

○ Find two expressions in **Lección 4A** used to ask for repetition or confirmation.

④ Parafrasear — Lección 4B

If you don't know a word or you don't know what something is called in Spanish, try paraphrasing. You can describe the object, say what it is like, how it is used, and so on.

○ Describe these objects without using their names.

Modelo: *Este aparato sirve para...*

108 ciento ocho

AVANCE 4

Competencias

EXPRESAR FRECUENCIA

① You and your partner need to plan two days a week to go to the swimming pool, and one day a week to go to tango classes. Study your schedules and find times when you can both do these activities.

Modelo: • *¿Puedes ir a la piscina los lunes y los miércoles a las 5?*
• *Los lunes y los miércoles tengo inglés...*

A	L	M	X	J	V	S	D
8-10							
10-12	UNIVERSIDAD						
12-14							
16-18							
18-20	español		español				
20-22							

B	L	M	X	J	V	S	D
8-10							
10-12	OFICINA						
12-14							
16-18	inglés	inglés	inglés	inglés	inglés		
18-20			chino		chino		
20-22	fútbol	coro	fútbol	coro			

LOCALIZAR PRODUCTOS

② Match each of the items listed on the right to the appropriate section of the department store depicted.

HOGAR
ROPA Y ZAPATERÍA
ALIMENTACIÓN
LIBROS Y MÚSICA

libros salchichas zapatos lámpara chaqueta pantalones DVD yogures silla alfombra huevos CD vestido

ELEGIR PRODUCTOS

③ Which product does your partner like best? Which item is the least expensive? Compare the prices, sizes, and styles of these items.

teteras: 23 €, clásica; 12 €, exótica
teléfonos: 80 €, antiguo; 90 €, moderno
lámparas: $400, clásica; $30, de diseño

CONJUGAR VERBOS

④ Write the conjugation for each verb in the person indicated. Compare your answers with a partner's.

1 ir (usted); 2 hacer (yo); 3 pensar (ella); 4 tener (ellas); 5 ir (vosotros); 6 dar (él)
7 poder (ustedes); 8 querer (nosotros); 9 costar (el vestido); 10 preferir (tú); 11 tener (yo); 12 hacer (nosotros)

ciento nueve 109

Competencias activities review vocabulary and structures presented in the preceding two units.

Odd-numbered units feature **Lectura**, which presents literary and cultural readings that gradually increase in length and difficulty.

Vocabulario útil provides words and expressions to help you understand and talk about the reading.

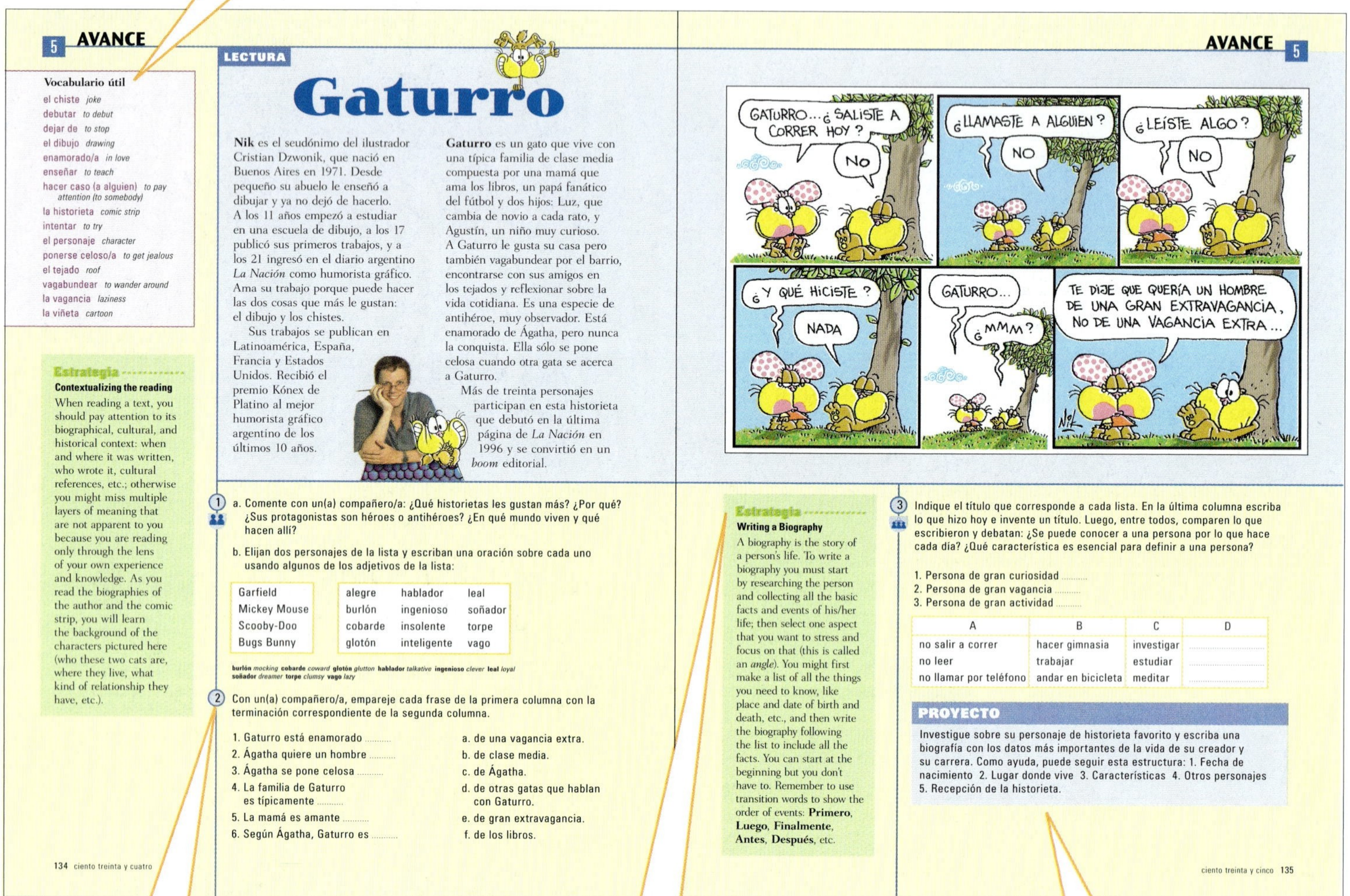

5 **AVANCE**

Vocabulario útil

el chiste *joke*
debutar *to debut*
dejar de *to stop*
el dibujo *drawing*
enamorado/a *in love*
enseñar *to teach*
hacer caso (a alguien) *to pay attention (to somebody)*
la historieta *comic strip*
intentar *to try*
el personaje *character*
ponerse celoso/a *to get jealous*
el tejado *roof*
vagabundear *to wander around*
la vagancia *laziness*
la viñeta *cartoon*

Estrategia

Contextualizing the reading

When reading a text, you should pay attention to its biographical, cultural, and historical context: when and where it was written, who wrote it, cultural references, etc.; otherwise you might miss multiple layers of meaning that are not apparent to you because you are reading only through the lens of your own experience and knowledge. As you read the biographies of the author and the comic strip, you will learn the background of the characters pictured here (who these two cats are, where they live, what kind of relationship they have, etc.).

LECTURA

Gaturro

Nik es el seudónimo del ilustrador Cristian Dzwonik, que nació en Buenos Aires en 1971. Desde pequeño su abuelo le enseñó a dibujar y ya no dejó de hacerlo. A los 11 años empezó a estudiar en una escuela de dibujo, a los 17 publicó sus primeros trabajos, y a los 21 ingresó en el diario argentino *La Nación* como humorista gráfico. Ama su trabajo porque puede hacer las dos cosas que más le gustan: el dibujo y los chistes.

Sus trabajos se publican en Latinoamérica, España, Francia y Estados Unidos. Recibió el premio Kónex de Platino al mejor humorista gráfico argentino de los últimos 10 años.

Gaturro es un gato que vive con una típica familia de clase media compuesta por una mamá que ama los libros, un papá fanático del fútbol y dos hijos: Luz, que cambia de novio a cada rato, y Agustín, un niño muy curioso. A Gaturro le gusta su casa pero también vagabundear por el barrio, encontrarse con sus amigos en los tejados y reflexionar sobre la vida cotidiana. Es una especie de antihéroe, muy observador. Está enamorado de Ágatha, pero nunca la conquista. Ella sólo se pone celosa cuando otra gata se acerca a Gaturro.

Más de treinta personajes participan en esta historieta que debutó en la última página de *La Nación* en 1996 y se convirtió en un *boom* editorial.

1 a. Comente con un(a) compañero/a: ¿Qué historietas les gustan más? ¿Por qué? ¿Sus protagonistas son héroes o antihéroes? ¿En qué mundo viven y qué hacen allí?

b. Elijan dos personajes de la lista y escriban una oración sobre cada uno usando algunos de los adjetivos de la lista:

Personajes
Garfield
Mickey Mouse
Scooby-Doo
Bugs Bunny

alegre	hablador	leal
burlón	ingenioso	soñador
cobarde	insolente	torpe
glotón	inteligente	vago

burlón *mocking* **cobarde** *coward* **glotón** *glutton* **hablador** *talkative* **ingenioso** *clever* **leal** *loyal* **soñador** *dreamer* **torpe** *clumsy* **vago** *lazy*

2 Con un(a) compañero/a, empareje cada frase de la primera columna con la terminación correspondiente de la segunda columna.

1. Gaturro está enamorado ....
2. Ágatha quiere un hombre ....
3. Ágatha se pone celosa ....
4. La familia de Gaturro es típicamente ....
5. La mamá es amante ....
6. Según Ágatha, Gaturro es ....

a. de una vagancia extra.
b. de clase media.
c. de Ágatha.
d. de otras gatas que hablan con Gaturro.
e. de gran extravagancia.
f. de los libros.

134 ciento treinta y cuatro

AVANCE 5

Estrategia

Writing a Biography

A biography is the story of a person's life. To write a biography you must start by researching the person and collecting all the basic facts and events of his/her life; then select one aspect that you want to stress and focus on that (this is called an *angle*). You might first make a list of all the things you need to know, like place and date of birth and death, etc., and then write the biography following the list to include all the facts. You can start at the beginning but you don't have to. Remember to use transition words to show the order of events: **Primero**, **Luego**, **Finalmente**, **Antes**, **Después**, etc.

3 Indique el título que corresponde a cada lista. En la última columna escriba lo que hizo hoy e invente un título. Luego, entre todos, comparen lo que escribieron y debatan: ¿Se puede conocer a una persona por lo que hace cada día? ¿Qué característica es esencial para definir a una persona?

1. Persona de gran curiosidad ....
2. Persona de gran vagancia ....
3. Persona de gran actividad ....

A	B	C	D
no salir a correr	hacer gimnasia	investigar	....
no leer	trabajar	estudiar	....
no llamar por teléfono	andar en bicicleta	meditar	....

PROYECTO

Investigue sobre su personaje de historieta favorito y escriba una biografía con los datos más importantes de la vida de su creador y su carrera. Como ayuda, puede seguir esta estructura: 1. Fecha de nacimiento 2. Lugar donde vive 3. Características 4. Otros personajes 5. Recepción de la historieta.

ciento treinta y cinco 135

Pre-reading and reading comprehension activities help you better understand the text.

Strategies give you tools to aid in reading comprehension, and written and oral expression.

Proyecto gives you the opportunity to apply oral or written presentation strategies in the context of the reading and the unit themes.

Each unit ends with a **Flash Cultura** video episode featuring fun and entertaining cultural information from around the Spanish-speaking world.

Listening and viewing strategies help you get the most out of the videos.

Flash Cultura episodes address unit themes from a different cultural perspective.

4

Flash CULTURA

Estrategia

Using visual cues

When you are watching a video in Spanish, be sure to look for visual cues that will orient you to the content and purpose of the video. Before viewing Flash Cultura, look at the video stills. What do you think this episode will be about? What Spanish words do you think they will use?

Vocabulario útil

el camarón (*Amér. L.*) *shrimp*
colones (*pl.*) *currency from Costa Rica*
¿Cuánto vale? *How much does it cost?*
el descuento *discount*
No hay problema. *No problem.*
¡Pura vida! (*C.R.*) *Cool!, Alright!*
el regateo *bargaining*
suave *soft*
el/la tico/a *person from Costa Rica*

Comprar en los mercados

You have learned how to talk about and shop for food in Spanish. In this episode of **Flash Cultura**, you will learn about shopping in the markets in San José, Costa Rica.

1. Have you ever been to an open-air market? What did you buy? Have you ever negotiated a price? What did you say? What words and expressions do you already know in Spanish that you could use for bargaining? Discuss your experiences with a partner.

2. Watch this **Flash Cultura** episode. While you watch the video, pay attention to the on-screen labels.

1 **...pero me hace un buen descuento.**

2 **¿Qué compran en el Mercado Central?**

3. Select the description that best summarizes this episode.

A. Randy Cruz va al mercado al aire libre para comprar papayas. Luego va al Mercado Central. Les pregunta a los clientes qué compran, prueba platos típicos y busca la heladería.

B. Randy Cruz va al mercado al aire libre para comprar papayas y pedir un descuento. Luego va al Mercado Central para preguntarles a los clientes qué compran en los mercados.

Estrategia

Making polite requests

When asking someone for directions, use expressions such as **Disculpe** or **Perdón** (*Excuse me*) before making your request, and be sure to say **¡Gracias!** at the end. If you do not understand, ask for confirmation using expressions such as **¿no?** and **¿verdad?**

4. With a partner, prepare a brief dialogue in which one person asks for directions to an ice cream shop (**una heladería**). Then, present your dialogue to the class.

Modelo: • *Disculpe, ¿dónde está la heladería?*
▪ *A ver... la heladería está a la derecha de...*

Practice more at **vhlcentral.com.**

Communicative activities relate previously learned vocabulary and structures to the **Flash Cultura** video.

Every **Flash Cultura** episode is available on the **PROTAGONISTAS** Supersite, along with additional comprehension activities.

The **Grammar Reference** in your textbook appendix provides additional support in the form of traditional explanations organized by grammar topics.

Grammatical structures are grouped and presented by part-of-speech.

Examples that highlight the target structure provide ample models of proper usage.

Convenient cross-references direct you to the lessons where these structures are introduced.

- Another way to refer to a group of people in general terms is **la mayoría** (*the majority; most people*). When **la mayoría** is followed by **de** + [*plural noun*], the verb can agree with **mayoría** (singular) or with the other noun (plural).

  La mayoría de los estudiantes **habla(n)** un poco de español.
  Most *students* ***speak*** *a little Spanish.*

- The plural verb must be used with the verbs **ser, estar,** and **parecer**.

  La mayoría de los profesores **son** latinoamericanos.
  The majority *of the professors* ***are*** *Latin American.*

- You can also use **los/las** + [*plural noun*] to make generalizing statements. Use the third-person plural verb form with this construction.

  Los actores son personas abiertas.
  Actors are *outgoing people.*

4 Adjectives (Los adjetivos) L1B, L2A

- An adjective always agrees with the corresponding noun in both gender and number, even when the noun and the adjective are found in separate sentences.

  Granada es un**a** ciudad fantástic**a**. Está llen**a** de impresionantes monumentos históricos.
  Granada is a fantastic city. It is full of impressive historic monuments.

4.1 Gender (El género) L2A, L12A

- As with nouns, the gender of adjectives is often signaled by the final letter. Some adjectives have distinct masculine and feminine forms; most adjectives ending in **-e**, **-ista**, or a consonant use the same form for masculine and feminine.

masculine		feminine	
-o	divertid**o**, content**o**	**-a**	divertid**a**, content**a**
-e	responsabl**e**, trist**e**	**-e**	responsabl**e**, trist**e**
-consonant	feliz	*-consonant*	feliz
-ista	optim**ista**	**-ista**	optim**ista**

- You have seen that the ending **-ista** is used in certain nouns (**taxista**, **periodista**). In adjectives, this ending remains unchanged when describing both masculine and feminine nouns.

  Clara es siempre muy optim**ista**.
  Clara is always very optimistic.

  Su novio Pedro es pesim**ista**.
  Her boyfriend Pedro is pessimistic.

⚠ Adjectives that describe colors and end in **-o** change to the ending **-a** in the feminine form: blanc**o/a**, negr**o/a**, etc. As with all adjectives, adjectives of color that end in **-e** or a consonant, such as **verde**, **azul**, **marrón**, and **gris**, can be masculine or feminine. In addition, some nouns, such as **café**, **rosa**, and **naranja**, can be used as invariable adjectives. L3B

⚠ Note that the adjectives **otro/a** and **medio/a** are used without an indefinite article.

Otra botella de agua, por favor. L2B
Another *bottle of water, please.*

¿Me da **medio** kilo de tomates? L4A
Would you give me a ***half*** *kilogram of tomatoes?*

A25

Attention icons highlight exceptions and structures that are often difficult for beginning Spanish students.

Charts and tables consolidate information for easy reference.

Learning Spanish with PROTAGONISTAS

While many elements contribute to the quality and success of learning experiences, two factors are particularly relevant to language learning. One is your beliefs about how language is learned; the other is language-learning anxiety.

As studies show, students often come to modern language courses unsure of how to approach language learning or with mistaken notions about how to do so. For example, many students believe that making mistakes when speaking the target language must be avoided because doing so will lead to permanent errors. Others are convinced that learning another language is like learning any other academic subject. In other words, they believe that success is guaranteed, provided they attend class regularly, learn the assigned vocabulary words and grammar rules, and study for exams. In fact, in a study of college-level beginning language learners in the United States, over one-third of the participants thought that they could become fluent if they studied the language for only one hour a day for two years or less. Mistaken and unrealistic beliefs such as these can cause frustration and affect motivation, thereby undermining your ability to have a successful and enjoyable language-learning experience.

Another factor that can negatively impact students' experiences is language-learning anxiety. As Professor Elaine K. Horwitz, of The University of Texas at Austin, wrote, "Surveys indicate that up to one-third of American foreign-language students feel moderately to highly anxious about studying another language. Physical symptoms of foreign-language anxiety can include heart-pounding or palpitations, sweating, trembling, fast breathing, and general feelings of unease."

PROTAGONISTAS contains several features aimed at reducing anxiety and supporting successful language learning. Its highly structured, visually dramatic interior design was conceived as a learning tool to make you feel comfortable with the content and confident about navigating the lessons. In addition, easy-to-identify cross-references and repeated features provide support at every step of the process.

Sidebars

Vocabulario sidebars list the active vocabulary presented on that spread with English translations.

Communicative functions are called out in convenient sidebars, including examples of usage and reference to the grammatical structures being practiced.

¡OJO! notes provide clarification or further linguistic or cultural information to help you better use the new structures in context.

Cultural notes offer supplementary cultural readings to help you contextualize the lesson themes.

Estrategias provide you with linguistic tools and learning strategies to help you navigate reading, writing, listening to, and conversing in Spanish.

Opinión sidebars present questions geared towards stimulating personalized conversation about the lesson themes.

Studying Vocabulary

PROTAGONISTAS takes an innovative approach to teaching vocabulary. You learn the words that you need in order to complete the communicative task at hand.

Vocabulary is presented at three different levels. First, convenient **Vocabulario** sidebars list the active words on the spread where they are used, in the order in which they are used. English translations are provided for easy reference, and cognates are listed in bold without translations, to help you see the connections between Spanish and English.

> **Vocabulario**
>
> 12
>
> la tienda de alimentación *grocery store*
>
> el puesto *stand (in a market)*
>
> la cosa *thing*
>
> **el póster**
>
> 13
>
> la edad *age*

The **Vocabulario** page at the end of each lesson summarizes the active vocabulary presented in that lesson. Here, all words are listed with their English translation, and words are grouped alphabetically by part of speech.

Finally, the Spanish-English and English-Spanish glossaries in your textbook appendix list all the text's active vocabulary with convenient references to the lesson where each word is presented.

> **Variación léxica**
>
> la alfombra ↔ **el tapete** (*Méx.*)
>
> el alquiler ↔ **la renta** (*Méx.*)
>
> amueblado/a ↔ **amoblado/a** (*Arg.*)

In addition, most lessons include a **Variación léxica** feature that provides alternate words and expressions used throughout the Spanish-speaking world. Note that only those terms listed in blue are considered active vocabulary.

Studying Grammar

Grammar structures are also presented at three levels in **PROTAGONISTAS**.

Sidebars in the lesson provide examples of the language structures you need in order to complete the communicative function presented on the page.

> **Dar y pedir opinión**
>
> - ¿Qué piensas de tu barrio?
> - Pienso que es un barrio con carácter.
>
> **4A.1** Stem-changing verbs **e→ie: pensar**

These structures are explained in their functional context in the **Gramática funcional** reference section at the end of each lesson, together with examples of usage and practice activities to reinforce what you have learned.

> **4A.1 Ask for and give opinions**
>
> Stem-changing verbs **e→ie: pensar** 5.1.1
>
> - Use the verb **pensar** (*to think*) to ask for and give opinions. **Pensar** is an **e→ie** stem-changing verb. You saw the same stem-changing pattern with **querer** in 3B.6. Remember that the **nosotros/as** and **vosotros/as** forms don't have a stem change.

Finally, the **Grammar Reference** in your textbook appendix offers a thorough traditional grammar reference where topics are organized by part of speech.

- Stem-changing verbs (**Verbos con cambio en la raíz**) L2B, L3B, L4A, L4B, L10B, L11A, L12A, L12B

	e > ie (querer)	o > ue (poder)	e > i (servir)
(yo)	quiero	puedo	sirvo
(tú)	quieres	puedes	sirves
(usted, él, ella)	quiere	puede	sirve
(nosotros/as)	queremos	podemos	servimos
(vosotros/as)	queréis	podéis	servís
(ustedes, ellos/as)	quieren	pueden	sirven

⚠ The **nosotros/as** and **vosotros/as** forms of these verbs do not have changes in the stem vowel.

Yo quiero ir al cine, pero vosotras queréis salir a cenar.
I want to go to the movies, but you want to go out to dinner.

⚠ Some verbs have irregular forms in the first-person singular conjugation in order to maintain the original pronunciation of the verb stem, e.g., **g → j**: **recoger (recojo)** or **gu → g**: **seguir (sigo)**.

Flash Cultura Video Program

The dynamic, engaging **Flash Cultura** video program draws from the cultural themes addressed in the text and provides an entertaining conclusion to the **Avance** section of each unit. Young people from all over the Spanish-speaking world share aspects of life in their countries with each other. The similarities and differences among Spanish-speaking countries that come up through their exchanges will challenge you to think about your own cultural practices and values.

The segments provide valuable cultural insights as well as linguistic input; the episodes will expose you to a wide variety of accents and vocabulary.

Here are the **Flash Cultura** episodes featured in PROTAGONISTAS.

Unidad 1: **Encuentros en la plaza** (Argentina)
Unidad 2: **Los estudios** (Mexico)
Unidad 3: **¡Fútbol en España!** (Spain)
Unidad 4: **Comprar en los mercados** (Costa Rica)
Unidad 5: **La casa de Frida** (Mexico)
Unidad 6: **¿Estrés? ¿Qué estrés?** (Spain)
Unidad 7: **El mundo del trabajo** (Ecuador)
Unidad 8: **Arquitectura modernista** (Spain)
Unidad 9: **Las fiestas** (Puerto Rico)
Unidad 10: **La salud** (Argentina)
Unidad 11: **Machu Picchu: encanto y misterio** (Peru)
Unidad 12: **Las relaciones personales** (Spain)
Unidad 13: **Inventos argentinos** (Argentina)
Unidad 14: **La comida latina** (U.S.A.)
Unidad 15: **Las alpacas** (Peru)
Unidad 16: **Puerto Rico, ¿nación o estado?** (Puerto Rico)
Unidad 17: **Lo mejor de Argentina** (Argentina)
Unidad 18: **Palacios del arte** (Spain)

Icons and Resources

Familiarize yourself with these icons that appear throughout **PROTAGONISTAS**.

Supersite content available	Listening activity/section	Writing activity
Activity available on Supersite	Pair activity	Re-entry activity
Additional activities available on Supersite	Group activity	

The SAM Activities tab on each presentation spread shows you exactly which pages in your Student Activities Manual practice the topics presented on that spread.

SAM: Actividades pp. 69–71

Student Ancillaries

- **Student Activities Manual**

  The Student Activities Manual (SAM) provides additional practice of the vocabulary and grammar in each textbook lesson. The SAM integrates written and audio activities, as well as reading comprehension and self-assessment for every lesson. Audio activities build listening comprehension, speaking, and pronunciation skills.

- **SAM MP3s**

  The SAM MP3s provide the recordings to be used in conjunction with the audio activities in the Student Activities Manual. These recordings are available on the **PROTAGONISTAS** Supersite.

- **Textbook MP3s**

  The Textbook MP3s are the recordings for the listening activities in each lesson of **PROTAGONISTAS**, as well as the active vocabulary in each end-of-lesson **Vocabulario** list. These recordings are available on the **PROTAGONISTAS** Supersite.

- **Supersite**

  Practice from the textbook, additional practice, as well as all audio and **Flash Cultura** video materials related to the **PROTAGONISTAS** program are available on the Supersite. Access is free with the purchase of a new student text. See page xxvii for additional information on the **PROTAGONISTAS** Supersite.

- **Supersite Plus**

  This option provides additional resources integrated in the Supersite: an online Student Activities Manual (WebSAM) and Wimba PRONTO.

Instructor Ancillaries

- **Instructor's Annotated Edition**

  The IAE contains a wealth of information and resources to support classroom teaching.

- ***Flash Cultura* DVD**

  The **Flash Cultura** episodes integrated in the **Avance** section of every unit are provided on DVD with subtitles in English and Spanish.

- **SAM Answer Key**

  This supplement contains the answers to all activities with discrete responses in the Student Activities Manual (available in print and on the Supersite).

- **PROTAGONISTAS Instructor Supersite**

  In addition to full access to the student Supersite, the password-protected Instructor Supersite offers a robust course-management system that allows instructors to assign activities and track student progress. Instructor Supersite access includes:

- Gradebook and course management
- Wimba Voice Board
- Textbook and SAM audio MP3s
- **Flash Cultura** episodes in streaming video
- Video scripts and translations
- Audio scripts
- Testing Program RTFs, PDFs, MP3s
- Detailed Lesson Plans
- Interactive Worksheets
- Answer Keys

- On the instructor side, Supersite Plus integrates the WebSAM into the same gradebook. Wimba PRONTO allows instructors to generate even more activities to support students.

Supersite

The **PROTAGONISTAS** Supersite provides a wealth of resources for both students and instructors. Icons indicate exactly which resources are available on the Supersite for each section of every lesson.

For Students

Student resources, available through an access code, are provided free-of-charge with the purchase of a new student text. Here is an example of what you will find at **vhlcentral.com:**

- Activities from the student text, with auto-grading
- Additional practice for all textbook sections
- Record & Compare audio activities
- All audio material related to the **PROTAGONISTAS** program
- The **Flash Cultura** video program, in streaming video
- MP3 files for the complete **PROTAGONISTAS** textbook and SAM Audio Program
- Oxford Spanish Mini Dictionary
- Flashcards with audio
- Wimba Voice Board

For Instructors

Instructors have access to the entire student site, as well as these key resources:

- The entire Instructor Ancillary package, including Testing Program and Lesson Plans, in downloadable and printable formats
- A robust course management system
- Voice Board capabilities for you to create additional activities
- And much, much more...

Supersiteplus

In addition to the resources on the **PROTAGONISTAS** Supersite, this option offers:

- **WebSAM** The online, interactive Student Activities Manual includes audio record submit activities, auto-grading for select activities, and a single gradebook for Supersite and WebSAM activities.
- **Wimba Pronto** Extend communication beyond the classroom with this powerful tool that features synchronous chat, online tutoring, online office hours capability, and more.

Acknowledgments

On behalf of its writers and editors, Vista Higher Learning expresses its sincere appreciation to the many professors nationwide who reviewed materials from **PROTAGONISTAS** and provided invaluable feedback.

We extend a special thank-you to the advisory board, who provided in-depth reviews of **PROTAGONISTAS** throughout the development of the program. Their insights, ideas, and detailed comments played a critical role in shaping the final product.

Advisory Board

M. Pilar Asensio-Manrique
Yale University, CT

Barbara Avila-Shah
University at Buffalo, SUNY, NY

María José Cabrera-Puche
West Chester University of Pennsylvania, PA

An Chung Cheng
University of Toledo, OH

Norma Corrales-Martin
Temple University, PA

Renee Craig-Odders
University of Wisconsin-Stevens Point, WI

Pablo García Loaeza
West Virginia University, WV

Judith García-Quismondo
Seton Hill University, PA

Amy George-Hirons
Tulane University, LA

Sue Griffin
Boston University, MA

Luisa Kou
University of Hawaii at Manoa, HI

Ornella Lepri Mazzuca
Dutchess Community College, NY

Lynn Loewen
Carthage College, WI

José M. López-Marrón
Bronx Community College-City University of New York, NY

Pascal Rollet
Carthage College, WI

Stacy D. Southerland
University of Central Oklahoma, OK

Reviewers

Stacy Amling
Des Moines Area Community College, IA

Carlos Andres
California State University, CA

Carlos Baez
North Hennepin Community College, MN

Christina Barnes
Valdosta State University, GA

Josephine Books
Inver Hills Community College, MN

Dennis Bricault
North Park University, IL

Carole Cloutier
University of Massachusetts-Amherst, MA

Ava Conley
Harding University, AR

Krista Croghan
Iowa Western Community College, IA

Veronica Dantan
Allegheny College, PA

Jackie Daughton
University of North Carolina
at Greensboro, NC

Beatriz DeSantiago-Fjelstad
Metropolitan State University, MN

Wendy Dodge
University of Central Arkansas, AR

María Dorantes
University of Michigan, OH

Hayden D. Duncan
Gustavus Adolphus College, MN

Kenya C. Dworkin
Carnegie Mellon University, PA

Eddy Enríquez Arana
Pennsylvania State University, PA

Angela Erickson-Grussing
College of Saint Benedict, MN

Ronna Feit
Nassau Community College, NY

Leah Fonder-Solano
University of Southern Mississippi, MS

Ryan Furness
University of Minnesota-Rochester, MN

Jennifer Garson
Pasadena City College, CA

Amy Ginck
Messiah College, PA

Jesse Gleason
Iowa State University, IA

Julie Gloss
Augsburg College, MN

Yolanda L. González
Valencia Community College, FL

Jorge González del Pozo
University of Michigan-Dearborn, MI

Marlene Gottlieb
Manhattan College, NY

Charlene M. Grant
Skidmore College, NY

Kate Grovergrys
Madison Area Technical College, WI

Nancy Hanway
Gustavus Adolphus College, MN

Michael Harrison
Monmouth College, IL

Luz Hernández
Luther College, IA

Amy Hueser
Western Iowa Tech Community College, IA

Casilde Isabelli
University of Nevada, NV

Stewart James-Lejarcegui
Iowa Wesleyan College, IA

Valerie Job
South Plains College, TX

Sister Kashuba
Chesnut Hill College, PA

Stephanie Katz
Lehigh University, PA

Kyle Kendall
University of Wisconsin, WI

Mary Ellen Kohn-Buday
Mount Mary College, WI

Mary Kuzma
Moraine Valley Community College, IL

Suzanne LaVenture
Davidson County Community College, NC

Denis R. Leahy
St. Joseph's College, NY

Kathy Leonard
Iowa State University, IA

Nelson López
Bellarmine University, KY

Paula Luteran
Hutchinson Community College, KS

Margot Maclaren
Langara College, BC, Canada

Celeste Mann
Georgian Court University, PA

Anne-Marie Martin
Portland Community College, OR

Marina Martin
St. John's University, MN

Mark J. Mascia
Sacred Heart University, CT

Carmen P. McSweeney
Pennsylvania State University, PA

Luis Millan-Mateos
Globe University/Minnesota School of Business, MN

Don Miller
University of St. Thomas, WI

Elaine Miller
Christopher Newport University, VA

Charles H. Molano
Lehigh Carbon Community College, PA

Lisa Nalbone
University of Central Florida, FL

Carla Naranjo
Montgomery College, MD

Eric Narvaez
Normandale Community College, MN

Sue Pechter
Northwestern University, IL

Pablo Pintado-Casas
Kean University, NJ

Kathryn Quinn-Sánchez
Georgian Court University, NJ

Timothy Reed
Ripon College, WI

Alice S. Reyes
Marywood University, PA

Nelly Ríos-Freund
University of St. Thomas, MN

Gladys Robalino
Messiah College, PA

Amy Rossomondo
University of Kansas, KS

Christine Sabin
Sierra College, CA

Ruth Sánchez Imizcoz
The University of the South, TN

Gabriel T. Saxton-Ruiz
University of Wisconsin-Green Bay, WI

Dave Schuettler
College of St. Scholastica, MN

Iñigo Serna
Washington State University, WA

Nancy Smith
Allegheny College, PA

Andrew Snustad
University of Minnesota, MN

Irena Stefanova
Contra Costa College, CA

Michael Tallon
University of the Incarnate Word, TX

Rita Tejada
Luther College, IA

Joshua Thomas
Louisiana State University, LA

David Thompson
Luther College, IA

Mary Thrond
Minnesota State University Moorhead, MN

Daniel G. Tight
University of St. Thomas, MN

Phyllis E. VanBuren
St. Cloud State University, MN

Melanie Waters
University of Illinois, IL

Stacey Weber-Feve
Iowa State University, IA

Julie Wilhelm
Iowa State University, IA

Jerome Williams
West Chester University, PA

James R. Wilson
Madison Area Technical College, WI

U. Theresa Zmurkwycz
St. Joseph's University, PA

Eve Zyzik
University of California, CA

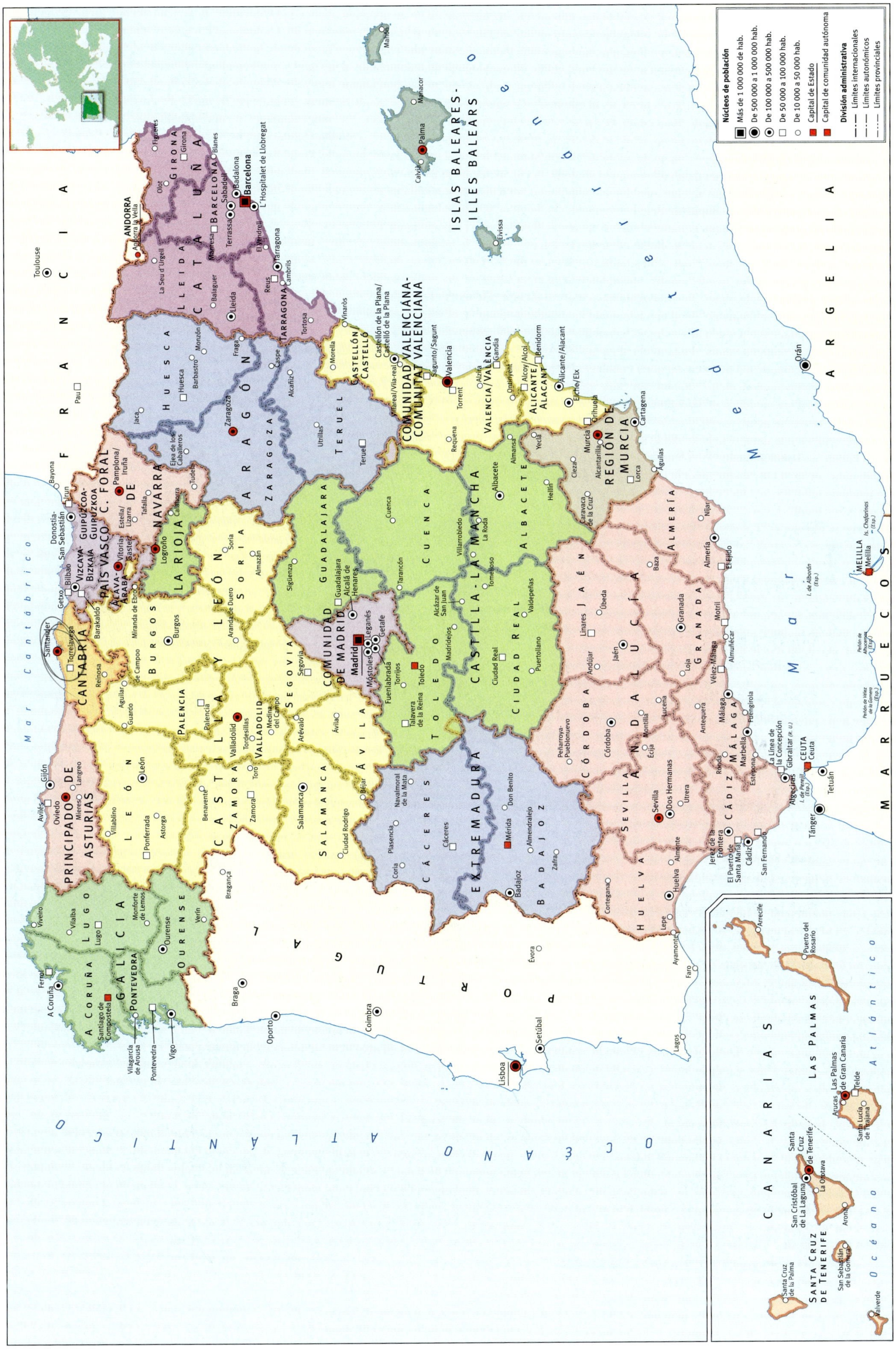
Núcleos de población
Más de 1 000 000 de hab.
De 500 000 a 1 000 000 hab.
De 100 000 a 500 000 hab.
De 50 000 a 100 000 hab.
De 10 000 a 50 000 hab.
Capital de Estado
Capital de comunidad autónoma
División administrativa
Límites internacionales
Límites autonómicos
Límites provinciales
FRANCIA
PORTUGAL
MARRUECOS
ARGELIA
ANDORRA
Mar Cantábrico
OCÉANO ATLÁNTICO
Mar Mediterráneo
GALICIA
PRINCIPADO DE ASTURIAS
CANTABRIA
PAÍS VASCO
NAVARRA
C. FORAL DE NAVARRA
LA RIOJA
ARAGÓN
CATALUÑA
CASTILLA Y LEÓN
COMUNIDAD DE MADRID
CASTILLA-LA MANCHA
EXTREMADURA
COMUNIDAD VALENCIANA-COMUNITAT VALENCIANA
REGIÓN DE MURCIA
ANDALUCÍA
ISLAS BALEARES-ILLES BALEARS
CANARIAS
LAS PALMAS
SANTA CRUZ DE TENERIFE
CEUTA
MELILLA
Madrid
Barcelona
Valencia
Sevilla
Zaragoza
Lisboa
Palma
Toulouse
Oporto
Tánger
Orán

Map of Latin America

PROTAGONISTAS

Have students look at the photos across pages 1–5 and identify famous people with whom they are familiar. Students may know: Benicio del Toro (actor); Olga Piedrahita (fashion designer); Salma Hayek (actress); Jorge Drexler (singer-songwriter); Ingrid Betancourt (politician); Jorge Edwards (writer); Salvador Moncada (scientist); Rafael Nadal (tennis player). Tell students that some of the **protagonistas** they will meet in this text are famous and others are everyday people they might meet on the street.

Benicio del Toro, San Juan (Puerto Rico) ✓

1A

Joan Fusté, Barcelona (España) ✓

1B

Juan Tomás Álvarez, Ciudad de Panamá (Panamá) ✓

2A

Rosa Iglesias, Haro (España)

2B

Pablo Linares, Colonia (Uruguay)

3A

Carmen Abreu, La Romana (República Dominicana) ✓

4B

Olga Piedrahita, Bogotá (Colombia) ✓

3B

Paco Sánchez, Madrid (España)

4A

Greet people

- ¡Hola!
- ¡Buenos días!
- ¡Buenas tardes!
- ¿Qué tal?
- ¡Buenas noches!
- ¡Buenas noches!

0.1 Greetings

Vocabulario

1

Buenos días. *Hello.; Good morning.*
Hola. *Hi.*
¿Qué tal? *How are you?; How's it going?*
Buenas tardes. *Good afternoon.*
Buenas. (*fam.*) *Hi.*
¿Qué pasa? *What's up?*
Buenas noches. *Good evening.; Good night.*

Estrategia

Vocabulario lists the active vocabulary that you learn and use in each activity, in the order in which it is presented. These words and expressions are summarized on the last page of each lesson.

1 Listen to these greetings and indicate the order in which you hear them.

3 ¡HOLA!   2 ¿QUÉ TAL?

1 BUENOS DÍAS.   4 HOLA, BUENAS TARDES.

2 In this lesson, you will meet the **protagonistas** (*protagonists*) you will encounter throughout this text. Look at the photos and read the labels. Now, listen to the recording. You will hear the names of five **protagonistas.** Check off the names you hear.

3 The **protagonistas** come from all over the Spanish-speaking world. Look at their hometowns. Then, with a partner, take turns matching these cities and towns to the corresponding country. **3 Expansion** Have students locate these places on the maps on pp. xxxi–xxxii.

1. Bogotá .... Colombia
2. Haro .... España
3. San Juan .... Puerto Rico
4. Madrid .... España
5. La Romana .... República Dominicana
6. Ciudad de Panamá .... Panamá
7. Barcelona .... España
8. Colonia .... Uruguay

Practice more at **vhlcentral.com.**

Suggestion You may want to give students a few simple ways to answer the questions **¿Qué pasa? (Nada.)** and **¿Qué tal? (Bien./Regular./Mal.)**.

¿Cómo te llamas?

Read aloud the caption for photo 5B. Briefly explain Hispanic naming conventions and that although women retain their maiden names after marriage they may use **de** + [*husband's last name*] in social situations, as in **de Maldonado.**

Salma Hayek, Coatzacoalcos (México)

Bernardo Maldonado y Juanita Rodríguez de Maldonado, McAllen, Texas (Estados Unidos)

Domingo Buendía, Quito (Ecuador)

Felipe Daza, Santiago de Chile (Chile) y Julia Navarro, Vancouver (Canadá)

Jorge Drexler, Montevideo (Uruguay)

Guadalupe Rodríguez Young, Córdoba (Argentina)

Justo Gallego, Mejorada del Campo (España)

Introduce yourself

- ¿Cómo te llamas?
- **Me llamo** Andrés Rodríguez Sánchez. **Encantado.**
- **Encantada.**
- ¿Cómo **se llama** usted?
- **Me llamo** Emiliana. **Mucho gusto.**

0.2 The verb **llamarse**

Vocabulario

4

¿Cómo te llamas? (*fam.*) *What is your name?*
(Yo) soy... *I am . . .*
(Yo) me llamo... *My name is . . .*
(Él/Ella) se llama... *His/Her name is . . .*
Encantado/a. *Pleased to meet you.*
Mucho gusto. *Pleased to meet you.*
Él/Ella es... *He/She is . . .*
¿Y tú? (*fam.*) *And you?*
¿Y usted? (*form.*) *And you?*
¿Cómo se llama? (*form.*) *What is your name?*

4 Match words from the two categories to show the different ways of telling people's names.

se *me* *te*

te *llamas*
me *llamo*
se *llama*

5 Decide whether these **protagonistas** would say **encantado**, **encantada**, or **encantados**. Check your answers with a partner.

1. Salma Hayek ....Encantada.
2. Felipe Daza ....Encantado.
3. Héctor y Gabriela ....Encantados.
4. Jorge Edwards ....Encantado.
5. Carlos y Lola ....Encantados.
6. Juanita Rodríguez de Maldonado ....Encantada.

6 a. Greet a partner and introduce yourself. Then, switch partners and introduce yourself to another classmate.

Modelo:
- ¡Hola! Me llamo Juan Domínguez. ¿Cómo se llama usted?
- Lisa Scanlon.
- Encantado.
- Encantada.
- ...

b. Now introduce yourself and your classmates to the rest of the class. Listen carefully so you can remember the names of those who were introduced before you. **6b Suggestion** Alternatively, have students do this activity in groups.

Me llamo Fabricio. → Se llama Fabricio, me llamo Alice. → Se llama Fabricio, se llama Alice, me llamo Didier...

Fernanda Pimentel y Alberto Tapia,
San Salvador (El Salvador)

Luis Soriano,
La Gloria (Colombia)

Lola Sanz,
Oviedo (España)

Carlos Salazar,
La Habana (Cuba)

Jorge Edwards,
Santiago de Chile (Chile)

José Carlos Prados,
San Juan (Puerto Rico)

Gabriela Bettini y Héctor Varela,
El Calafate (Argentina)

Spell

A (a)	Ñ (eñe)
B (be)	O (o)
C (ce)	P (pe)
D (de)	Q (cu)
E (e)	R (erre)
F (efe)	S (ese)
G (ge)	T (te)
H (hache)	U (u)
I (i)	V (ve)
J (jota)	W (doble ve)
K (ka)	X (equis)
L (ele)	Y (i griega)
M (eme)	Z (zeta)
N (ene)	

0.3 The Spanish alphabet

You may want to point out that the letters **ch (che), ll (elle),** and the letter combination **rr (doble erre)** are not included in this list. Model their pronunciations for the class.

hotel	aeropuerto	señorita	taxi	jamón
café	bar	mercado	paella	España
metro	restaurante	banco	leche	moneda
mañana	museo	policía	azúcar	chocolate

7 a. Look at these Spanish words. Which ones are similar in English? Do you know the English equivalent of any of these words? Discuss your answers with a partner. Sample answers: hotel, café, aeropuerto, bar, restaurante, museo, banco, policía, taxi, chocolate

b. Now look at the letters of the Spanish alphabet. Which letter doesn't exist in English? Which of the words above use this letter? Ñ; mañana, señorita, España

8 a. Listen to the pronunciation of each letter of the Spanish alphabet. Repeat the letters after the speaker.

b. Now listen to the pronunciation of the words listed above. Which pronunciations surprise you? Listen again and say each word aloud after you hear it.

c. Listen to the pronunciation of these words, and pay close attention to the letters marked in red. Repeat the words after the speaker.

La Habana   paella   Chile   Ibiza   jamón   Toledo

Estrategia

Mi experiencia activities guide you through conversations with your classmates that will help you review and reinforce the lesson vocabulary and structures in a meaningful, personalized context.

MI EXPERIENCIA

9 Greet and introduce yourself to your classmates.

GUIÓN DE TRABAJO

Hola.
Buenos días.
Buenas tardes.
Buenas noches.
¿Qué tal?
¿Qué pasa?

→ Me llamo...
(Yo) soy...

→ ¿Y tú?
¿Y usted?

→ Encantado/a.
Mucho gusto.

Practice more at **vhlcentral.com.**

¡Hasta pronto!

Ricardo Hernández, México, D.F. (México)

Marifé Cester, Salamanca (España)

Nelson Morales, Lima (Perú) y Edgar Hugo Torrico, La Paz (Bolivia)

Cristina Rubio, Monterrey (México)

Acacio Maye Ocomo, Malabo (Guinea Ecuatorial)

Macarena Berlín, Madrid (España)

Evaristo Acebedo, Miami, Florida (Estados Unidos)

Ask for clarification

- ¿Cómo se escribe *Acebedo*?
- A-ce-e-be-e-de-o.

0.4 Questions for clarification

Say good-bye

- Hasta luego!
- ¡Adiós!
- ¡Hasta mañana!

0.5 Leave-takings

Vocabulario

(10)

Hasta pronto. *See you soon.*
¿Cómo se escribe...? *How do you spell . . . ?*
con acento *with an accent*
¡Gracias! *Thank you!*
Adiós. *Good-bye.*
Hasta mañana. *See you tomorrow.*
¡Nos vemos! *See you!*
Hasta la vista. *See you later.*
Chau. *Bye.*
Hasta luego. *See you later.*
el saludo *greeting*
la despedida *leave-taking*

(12)

el nombre *name*
el país *country*
la ciudad *city*
el burro *donkey*
la vaca *cow*

10 Listen to the recordings and decide whether each person is saying hello (**saludos**) or good-bye (**despedidas**).

	saludos	despedidas
1	✓	☐
2	☐	✓
3	☐	✓
4	✓	☐

Suggestion You may want to teach students the expressions **De nada.** and **No hay de qué.** as responses for **¡Gracias!**

11 a. With a partner, look at the maps of Spain and Latin America on pages xxxi–xxxii. Find where each of the **protagonistas** is from, and take turns asking each other how to spell the names of different cities and countries.

Modelo:
- ¿Cómo se escribe *Arequipa*?
- A-erre-e...

11b Expansion Have pairs read over their lists and try to guess whether the names are of Spanish origin or an indigenous language.

b. Together, make a list of city and country names for five letters in the alphabet. Are there any letters for which you can't find examples?

12 As a class, try to come up with a name (**nombre**), a country (**país**), or a city (**ciudad**) that starts with or contains each letter in the alphabet.

Modelo: *Eñe... ¡España!*

LETRA	NOMBRE	PAÍS	CIUDAD

Suggestion Have pairs of students introduce themselves using their full names and ask each other how their names are spelled. Have them verify the correct spelling. Then have them find a new partner and repeat the activity.

Marina Sánchez,
Caracas (Venezuela)

Ingrid Betancourt,
Bogotá (Colombia)

Estela Salvador, Ciudad de Guatemala (Guatemala)
y Mario Martínez, Managua (Nicaragua)

Marián Rico,
San José (Costa Rica)

Salvador Moncada,
Tegucigalpa (Honduras)

Rubén Sosa, Buenos Aires (Argentina)
y Amanda Roa, Asunción (Paraguay)

Rafael Nadal,
Mallorca (España)

¡OJO!

In Spanish, the letters *b* (**be**) and *v* (**ve**) are pronounced the same. To distinguish between the two, many Spanish speakers call *b* **be de burro** (*donkey*) and *v* **ve de vaca** (*cow*). In Spain, the letter *v* is called **uve**, so this distinction is not necessary in Spain.

Estrategia

Yo puedo activities at the end of each lesson help you review the communicative functions you have learned in the lesson. These activities show you how much you learned and can help you identify which functions you need to review.

You may want to provide these alternative names for letters: **b: be grande/be larga; v: ve chica/ve corta; w: doble uve; y: ye.**

YO PUEDO...

Expansion Have students review the expressions they wrote for the first bullet and state whether they can be used in formal or informal contexts, or both.

- **Puedo saludar a la gente.**

  Write three expressions you have learned to greet people.

  ....

- **Puedo presentarme y responder a una presentación.**

  Complete this conversation.

  - ¿Cómo te ...llamas...?
  - Me ...llamo... Javier.
  - Mucho gusto.
  - ...Encantado./Mucho gusto....

- **Puedo deletrear en español.**

  Practice spelling these words in Spanish.

• chocolate	• mañana
• México	• encantado

- **Puedo preguntar cómo se escribe una palabra o un nombre.**
  - ¿ ...Cómo se escribe... *hotel*?
  - Con hache.

- **Puedo despedirme de la gente.**

  Write three expressions you have learned to say good-bye.

  ....

Practice more at **vhlcentral.com.**

SAM: Actividades pp. 1–4

GRAMÁTICA FUNCIONAL

0.1 Greet people

Greetings; Interrogative pronouns 9

- Use expressions such as **Hola**, **¿Qué tal?**, and **¿Qué pasa?** to greet people in an informal context. Note that Spanish uses both opening and closing question marks.

  - Hola, Ana, ¿qué pasa?
    Hi, Ana, what's up?
  - Hola, Jaime, ¿qué tal?
    Hi, Jaime, how's it going?

- In both formal and informal contexts, use the expressions **Buenos días** (*Good morning*), **Buenas tardes** (*Good afternoon*), or **Buenas noches** (*Good evening*) to greet people according to the time of day.

  - Buenos días, señor Martínez.
    Good morning, Mr. Martínez.
  - Buenos días.
    Good morning.

0.2 Introduce yourself

The verb **llamarse** 5.7 Reflexive pronouns 5.7.1

- To ask someone's name, say **¿Cómo te llamas?** in an informal context or **¿Cómo se llama (usted)?** in a formal context.
- To answer, say **Me llamo** + [*name*] or **(Yo) soy** + [*name*].

  - Hola, **¿cómo te llamas?**
    Hi. What's your name?
  - Hola, **soy Marta.**
    Hi, I'm Marta.
  - Buenas tardes. **¿Cómo se llama usted?**
    Good afternoon. What is your name?
  - **Me llamo** Jorge García.
    ***My name is** Jorge García.*

- When meeting someone for the first time, say **Encantado** if you are male or **Encantada** if you are female. Both men and women can also say **Mucho gusto**.

0.3 Spell

The Spanish alphabet 1.1

- Review the Spanish alphabet on page 3. Note that the letter **ñ** does not appear in the English alphabet and the letters **k** and **w** are used only in words of foreign origin.
- **Ch** (**che**) and **ll** (**elle**) are officially letters in the Spanish alphabet, although they are included under **c** and **l** in alphabetized lists. When spelling aloud, **ch**/**c-h** and **ll**/**doble l** will be equally understood.

0.4 Ask for clarification

Questions for clarification
Prepositions: **con** 10.4 Interrogative pronouns 9

- To ask how a word is spelled in Spanish, say **¿Cómo se escribe** + [*word*]? Be sure to say **¡Gracias!** (*Thank you!*) when someone helps you.

  ¿Cómo se escribe *Montevideo?*
  How do you spell Montevideo?

- To explain that a word is spelled with a certain letter, or that a letter takes a written accent, use the word **con** (*with*).

  con hache
  with an h

  a con acento
  with an accent on the a

¡Póngalo en práctica!

G1 Complete the dialogues with appropriate words or expressions.

- Hola, María, ¿(1) ...qué... tal?
- ¡(2) ...Hola..., Teresa!

- (3) ...Buenas... noches, señora Gutiérrez.
- Buenas (4) ...noches..., señor Ríos.

- Buenos (5) ...días..., Martín.
- Hola, Gladys, ¿qué (6) ...pasa/tal...?

G2 Complete the conversation.

¿Cómo (1) ...te... llamas?

Me (2) ...llamo... Raúl Soria. ¿Y tú?

Yo (3) ...soy... Clara, Clara Esteban.

(4) ...Encantado/Mucho gusto...

G3 Practice spelling these words in Spanish.

¿Cómo se ...escribe... ...?

paella	café
jamón	azúcar
Canadá	taxi
señorita	hotel
chocolate	Guatemala
aeropuerto	restaurante

¡ ...Gracias... !

G3 Expansion Have students group the words into these categories: places, people, food, and transportation. Do any words fit more than one category?

0.3 Tell students that all letters are feminine and should be used with the feminine definite article **la**: **la a, la b,** etc.

Practice more at **vhlcentral.com.**

GRAMÁTICA FUNCIONAL

0.5 Say good-bye

Leave-takings; Exclamation marks 1.5

- Use expressions such as ¡Adiós! (*Good-bye!*), ¡Hasta luego! (*See you later!*), ¡Chau! (*Bye!*), and ¡Hasta pronto! (*See you soon!*) to say good-bye in Spanish. Note that Spanish uses both opening and closing exclamation marks.

¡Hasta luego, Luisa! *See you later, Luisa!*	Adiós. ¡Hasta mañana! *Good-bye. See you tomorrow!*

- ¡Buenas noches! (*Good evening; Good night*) can be used as both a greeting and a leave-taking.

¡Póngalo en práctica!

G4 Write the missing words or punctuation.

1. ¡.....Hasta..... luego!
2. ¡.....Buenas..... noches!
3. ¡.....Hasta..... pronto!
4. .....¡..... Adiós!

Practice more at **vhlcentral.com.**

VOCABULARIO

Protagonistas

Buenas. (*fam.*)	*Hi.*
Buenas noches.	*Good evening.; Good night.*
Buenas tardes.	*Good afternoon.*
Buenos días.	*Hello.; Good morning.*
Hola.	*Hi.*
¿Qué pasa?	*What's up?*
¿Qué tal?	*How are you?; How's it going?*

¿Cómo te llamas?

¿Cómo te llamas? (*fam.*)	*What is your name?*
¿Y tú? (*fam.*)	*And you?*
¿Cómo se llama? (*form.*)	*What is your name?*
¿Y usted? (*form.*)	*And you?*
(Yo) me llamo...	*My name is . . .*
(Yo) soy...	*I am . . .*
(Él/Ella) se llama...	*His/Her name is . . .*
Él/Ella es...	*He/She is . . .*
Encantado/a.	*Pleased to meet you.*
Mucho gusto.	*Pleased to meet you.*
el aeropuerto	*airport*
el azúcar	*sugar*
el banco	*bank; bench*
el bar	*bar; café*
el café	*coffee; café*
el chocolate	*chocolate*
el hotel	*hotel*
el jamón	*ham*
la leche	*milk*
el mercado	*market*
el metro	*subway*
la moneda	*coin*
el museo	*museum*
la paella	*paella*
la policía	*police*
el restaurante	*restaurant*
la señorita	*young lady; Miss*
el taxi	*taxi*
mañana	*tomorrow*

¡Hasta pronto!

Adiós.	*Good-bye.*
Chau.	*Bye.*
Hasta la vista.	*See you later.*
Hasta luego.	*See you later.*
Hasta mañana.	*See you tomorrow.*
Hasta pronto.	*See you soon.*
¡Nos vemos!	*See you!*
¿Cómo se escribe...?	*How do you spell . . . ?*
con acento	*with an accent*
¡Gracias!	*Thank you!*
el burro	*donkey*
la ciudad	*city*
la despedida	*leave-taking*
el nombre	*name*
el país	*country*
el saludo	*greeting*
la vaca	*cow*

Países y ciudades

Argentina	*Argentina*
Bolivia	*Bolivia*
Canadá	*Canada*
Chile	*Chile*
Ciudad de Guatemala	*Guatemala City*
Ciudad de Panamá	*Panama City*
Colombia	*Colombia*
Costa Rica	*Costa Rica*
Cuba	*Cuba*
Ecuador	*Ecuador*
El Salvador	*El Salvador*
España	*Spain*
Estados Unidos (EE.UU.)	*United States (U.S.A.)*
Guatemala	*Guatemala*
Guinea Ecuatorial	*Equatorial Guinea*
Honduras	*Honduras*
La Habana	*Havana*
México	*Mexico*
México, D.F.	*Mexico City*
Nicaragua	*Nicaragua*
Panamá	*Panama*
Paraguay	*Paraguay*
Perú	*Peru*
Puerto Rico	*Puerto Rico*
República Dominicana	*Dominican Republic*
Uruguay	*Uruguay*
Venezuela	*Venezuela*

Explain that **D.F.** stands for **Distrito Federal.**

Tell students that audio recordings of all vocabulary words and expressions listed on the **Vocabulario** page are included in the Textbook Audio Program. Encourage students to study new vocabulary together with the audio and to pay close attention to the pronunciation of cognates.

SPANISH TERMS for direction lines and classroom use

Below is a list of useful words and expressions that appear in the direction lines of your text, as well as expressions your instructor might use in class.

Tell students that they are not expected to memorize these terms at this point. Rather, encourage students to refer to this list as they progress through the text and encounter these terms in activities and directions.

¿Cómo se dice...?	*How do you say . . . ?*
¿Qué significa...?	*What does . . . mean?*
No entiendo.	*I don't understand.*
Más despacio, por favor.	*Slower, please.*
Competencia	*Competence; Ability*
Estrategia	*Strategy*
Lectura	*Reading*
Mi experiencia	*My experience*
¡Ojo!	*Be careful!*
Protagonistas	*Protagonists*
Yo puedo...	*I can . . .*
el acontecimiento	*event*
la actividad	*activity*
el/la alumno/a	*student*
el anuncio	*ad(vertisement)*
el cartel/el póster	*poster*
la casilla	*(check) box*
el/la compañero/a	*colleague; classmate*
los datos	*information; data*
el diálogo/ la conversación	*dialogue/ conversation*
el ejemplo	*example*
la entrevista	*interview*
la fecha	*date*
el final	*end, ending*
el folleto	*pamphlet/brochure*
la foto(grafía)	*photo(graph)*
la frase	*phrase*
la hoja (de papel)	*sheet (of paper)*
la imagen	*picture, image*
el juego	*game*
el libro	*book*
la lista	*list*
el modelo	*model*
el número	*number*
la oración	*sentence*
la página	*page*
la palabra	*word*
el párrafo	*paragraph*
la pregunta	*question*
la prueba	*test*
el recuadro	*box*
la respuesta	*answer*
(el resto de) la clase	*(the rest of) the class*
la tabla	*table/chart*
la tarea	*homework*
la terminación	*ending*
el texto	*textbook; reading*
el titular	*title/headline*
la viñeta (cómica)	*cartoon*
el/la/los/las siguiente(s)...	*the next/following . . .*
que falta(n)	*missing*
(in)correcto/a	*(in)correct*
¿Verdadero o falso?	*True or false?*
¿Masculino o femenino?	*Masculine or feminine?*
antes	*before*
después	*after*
luego...	*then . . .*
de nuevo/otra vez	*again*
¿Cómo...?	*How . . . ?*
¿Cuál(es)...?	*Which . . . ?*
¿Cuándo...?	*When . . . ?*
¿Dónde...?	*Where . . . ?*
¿Por qué...?	*Why . . . ?*
¿Qué...?	*What . . . ?*
¿Quién(es)...?	*Who . . . ?*
En parejas/grupos...	*In pairs/groups . . .*
Adivine(n)...	*Guess . . .*
Agrupe(n)...	*Group/Organize . . .*
Anote(n)...	*Write down . . .*
Añada(n)...	*Add . . .*
Averigüe(n)...	*Find out . . .*
Busque(n)...	*Look for . . .*
Calcule(n)...	*Calculate . . .*
Clasifique(n)...	*Classify . . .*
Coloque(n)...	*Place . . .*
Comente(n)...	*Discuss . . .*
Compare(n)....	*Compare . . .*
Comparta(n)...	*Share . . .*
Complete(n)...	*Complete . . .*
Compruebe(n)...	*Check/Verify . . .*
Conjugue(n)...	*Conjugate . . .*
Construya(n)...	*Create/Build . . .*
Conteste(n)/ Responda(n) (a)...	*Answer . . .*
Cuente(n)...	*Tell . . .*
Decida(n)...	*Decide . . .*
Describa(n)...	*Describe . . .*
Descubra(n)...	*Discover/Learn . . .*
Dibuje(n)...	*Draw . . .*
Diga(n)...	*Say . . .*
Diseñe(n)...	*Design . . .*
Elabore(n)...	*Create/Make . . .*
Elija(n)...	*Choose . . .*
Escriba(n)...	*Write . . .*
Escuche(n)...	*Listen . . .*
Exponga(n)...	*Display/Post . . .*
Fíje(n)se en...	*Look at . . .*
Forme(n)...	*Form/Create . . .*
Haga(n)...	*Do/Make . . .*
Imagíne(n)se que...	*Imagine that . . .*
Informe(n)...	*Tell/Inform . . .*
Lea(n)...	*Read . . .*
Localice(n)...	*Locate/Find . . .*
Marque(n)...	*Mark/Check off . . .*
Mencione(n)...	*Mention . . .*
Mire(n)...	*Look at . . .*
Muestre(n)...	*Show . . .*
Nombre(n)...	*Name . . .*
Observe(n)...	*Observe . . .*
Obtenga(n)...	*Get/Obtain . . .*
Ordene(n) ...	*Put in order . . .*
Organice(n)...	*Organize . . .*
Piense(n) en...	*Think of/about . . .*
Ponga(n) atención (a)...	*Pay attention (to) . . .*
Practique(n)...	*Practice . . .*
Pregunte(n)...	*Ask . . .*
Presente(n)...	*Present/Introduce . . .*
Pronuncie(n)...	*Pronounce . . .*
Recuerde(n)...	*Remember . . .*
Redacte(n)...	*Write . . .*
Relacione(n)...	*Relate/Match . . .*
Rellene(n)...	*Fill in . . .*
Repita(n)...	*Repeat . . .*
Represente(n)/ Escenifique(n)...	*Role-play . . .*
Resuma(n)...	*Summarize . . .*
Reúna(n)...	*Gather . . .*
Revise(n)...	*Review . . .*
Rodee(n)...	*Circle . . .*
Seleccione(n)...	*Select . . .*
Señale(n)...	*Indicate . . .*
Subraye(n)...	*Underline . . .*
Sustituya(n)...	*Substitute . . .*
Tache(n)...	*Cross out . . .*
Transforme(n)...	*Transform . . .*
Use(n)/Utilice(n)...	*Use . . .*

Explain to students that for the commands listed, the form ending in **n** is used to address two or more people (**Escuchen**), while the form without an **n** addresses a single person (**Escuche**).

Instructor note All instructions in **PROTAGONISTAS** address the student as **usted**.

All terms on this page are also listed in the glossary in the appendix of this text.

Audio: Activities, Vocabulary
Video: *Flash Cultura*

Unidad 1

Benicio del Toro, un actor puertorriqueño

Lección 1A

¡BIENVENIDOS!

Lección 1B

LENGUAS

Joan, un catalán políglota

Encuentros en la plaza

AVANCE

1A ¡Bienvenidos!

Imágenes y palabras

Suggestion Ask students if they are familiar with any of the people, places, or things in the photographs. Give them more details as needed. Ex: Vargas Llosa is a Peruvian writer, famous worldwide for novels such as *La ciudad y los perros* (1963) and *La fiesta del chivo* (2000), and recipient of the 2010 Nobel Prize in Literature.

Numerar

0	cero	7	siete
1	uno	8	ocho
2	dos	9	nueve
3	tres	10	diez
4	cuatro	11	once
5	cinco	12	doce
6	seis		

1A.1 Numbers 0–12

Identificar y especificar

- ¿Qué es?
- Es Madrid. Es una ciudad.
- ¿Quién es?
- Es Isabel Allende. Es una escritora.

1A.2 Indefinite article **un(a)**
Interrogatives **¿qué?, ¿quién?**
The verb **ser** (3rd person sing.)

Vocabulario

1

la imagen *picture, image*
¿Quién es? *Who is it?*
¿quién? *who?*
¿Qué es? *What is it?*
el/la arquitecto/a *architect*
la comida *food*
la isla *island*
el pueblo *town*
el/la escritor(a) *writer*

1 a. Match each photo to a section of the wheel on page 11. Write the number of the photo in the corresponding section of the wheel.

b. Write out the numbers.

1	5	4	3	2	6
uno	cinco	cuatro	tres	dos	seis

c. Check your answers with a partner.

Modelo:
- *"Uno." ¿Quién es?*
- *Es Vargas Llosa. Es un escritor.*

2 a. Add the numbers showing on each pair of dice and write out the sum.

ocho — siete — diez — doce — nueve — once

b. Now use real dice. With a partner, take turns rolling the dice and giving the sum of the numbers showing.

Modelo: *Seis más dos, ¡ocho!*

3 **¿Un o una?** Write the correct indefinite article. Refer to the sections of the game wheel and pay attention to the last letter of each word.

1. un hotel	5. una playa	9. una biblioteca
2. una música	6. un metro	10. una arquitecta
3. una comida	7. una isla	11. un escritor
4. un monumento	8. un pueblo	12. un personaje

Successful Language Learning Point out that flash cards are a useful tool when learning vocabulary. Encourage students to make flash cards that contain associations that are meaningful to them (Ex: **el/la arquitecto/a -** Frank Lloyd Wright; **la comida -** Arby's), rather than simply English translations. As they move through a unit, their stack of cards will grow; encourage students to review them often, even daily. Once they feel confident that they have mastered a word, have them remove it from the stack.

¿Quién es?

Suggestion Ask students if they are familiar with Barcelona's most famous church (**La Sagrada Familia**). Then have them identify the related section of the wheel (**Antoni Gaudí**).

6

¿Qué es?

Deletrear

- ¿Cómo se escribe *Toledo*?
- Te, o, ele, e, de, o.
- ¿Cómo se escribe *Ana*? ¿Con una ene o con dos enes?
- Con una ene.
- ¿Cómo se escribe *música*?
- Con acento en la *u*.

1A.3 Interrogative **¿cómo?**

Vocabulario

③
la playa *beach*
la biblioteca *library*
el monumento, la música
⑥
el personaje *important figure; character*

4 a. Listen to the conversation and write down the place names that are mentioned. Use letters from the boxes.

A – Z – G – H – A – R – K – A – O – T – Z – U

Z A R A G O Z A

T – H – I – N – F – A – E – E – S – R – U – E

T E N E R I F E

b. Study the map in your text on page xxxii and write out the names of two cities in Latin America.

5 Choose two names from the wheel and spell them out loud. Your partner will write them out.

5 Expansion Have students form different pairs, and ask them to take turns spelling names of places on your campus for their partner to write out.

MI EXPERIENCIA

6 Think of a city, food, or person from a Spanish-speaking country. Your partner must guess whom or what you are thinking about.

GUIÓN DE TRABAJO

comida / ciudad / personaje

¿Es una comida? ¿Es una ciudad?

¿Es un personaje?

Es .... → ¿Cómo se escribe?

6 Suggestion Before forming pairs, have students brainstorm a few items for each category.

Practice more at **vhlcentral.com.**

SAM: Actividades pp. 5–7

Yo soy de Madrid, ¿y tú?

NEIL: Hola, soy Neil, ¿y tú?
AMÉLIE: Hola, yo soy Amélie. ¿Qué tal?
NEIL: Muy bien. ¿De dónde eres, Amélie?
AMÉLIE: Soy de París, ¿y tú?
NEIL: Yo soy de Mánchester.
CRISTINA: ¡Hola! Yo soy Cristina.
NEIL: Hola, Cristina, ¿qué tal? ¿Eres de Portugal?
CRISTINA: No, no soy de Portugal. Soy de Brasil, de São Paulo.
AMÉLIE:

7 Read this chat between Spanish students from all over the world and write whether each statement is true. Correct any false statements.

1. Amélie es de Londres.	*No, Amélie no es de Londres. Es de París.*
2. Neil es de Mánchester.	Sí, Neil es de Mánchester.
3. Cristina es de Portugal.	No, Cristina no es de Portugal. Es de Brasil.

8 Fill in the table with the missing form or subject pronoun.

yo	soy
tú	eres
usted	es
él/ella	es

9 a. Read this information card for a language exchange and answer the questions. Which words do you know already? How do you know them?

- ¿De dónde es esta persona?
  Es de Pamplona.
- ¿Cómo se llama?
  Se llama Raúl.

Nombre: Raúl
Origen: Pamplona
Intereses: fútbol, tenis, esquí, música (salsa, hip-hop), teatro y conciertos

b. Listen to the conversation between Raúl and the person he meets. What is his exchange partner's name? Where is she from? Se llama Carla. Es de Berlín.

10 Look at the comic and fill in the missing words. Then, act out the conversation with a partner.

Vocabulario

7

Yo soy de Madrid. *I'm from Madrid.*
¿y tú? *and you?*
muy bien *very well*
bien *well*
¿De dónde eres? *Where are you from? (fam.)*
¿De dónde es usted? *Where are you from? (form.)*
sí *yes*
Portugal, Brasil, no

9

el origen *origin*
el interés *interest*
el fútbol *soccer*
el esquí *skiing*
el tenis, la salsa, el hip-hop, el teatro, el concierto

Hablar del origen

(familiar)

- ¿De dónde eres?
- Soy de España, de Bilbao. ¿Y tú?
- Yo soy de Chile.
- ¿Eres de Bogotá?
- No, no soy de Bogotá. Soy de Cali y Ana María es de Quito, Ecuador.

(formal)

- ¿De dónde es usted?
- Soy de Zaragoza. ¿Y usted?

1A.4 Interrogative **¿de dónde?**
The verb **ser** (singular)
ser + de

Afirmar y negar

Sí, soy de León.
No, no soy de Cuenca. Soy de Córdoba.

1A.5 **sí /no, no** + [*verb*]

10 Suggestion After students complete the activity, ask if they are familiar with the soccer teams **Real Madrid** and **F.C. Barcelona**. Explain that the man on the left is wearing a **Real Madrid** jersey and the man on the right is wearing one from Barcelona. Then ask if either person supports the team from their home city.

Tú o usted

In Spanish, you can address an individual as **tú** or **usted**. Use **usted** with people who are older than you, people you don't know, and authority figures. Use **tú** with close friends and family, and with children. The informal **tú** is used much more widely in Spain than in Latin America. In Spain, **tú** is often used among people of all ages, in the workplace, at stores, etc.

Suggestion Tell students to write *same age* on one piece of paper and *older* on another. Read aloud some expressions and have students hold up *same age* if the expression is used with a peer, or *older* if it is used with someone older than the speaker. Ex: **Soy Carmen, ¿y tú?** (*same age*)

11 a. Look at the photos and decide in which situation people are using **tú** and in which situation they are using **usted**. Which situation is more formal? Which is more informal? foto A: tú, informal; foto B: usted, formal

A

B

b. Listen to the recording and complete the questions.

¿De dónde ....eres.... ?

¿De dónde ....es.... ....usted....?

12 Which question should be used in each situation? Write the appropriate question under each photo.

¿De dónde eres?
¿De dónde es usted?

A

¿De dónde eres?

B

¿De dónde es usted?

C

¿De dónde eres?

MI EXPERIENCIA

13 a. Listen to the names of these cities. How are they similar in English?

b. Use both **tú** and **usted** to ask your classmates where they are from. Before you begin, study the maps on pages xxxi and xxxii in your text to find the Spanish names of several cities.

NUEVA YORK
OTTAWA
BERLÍN
FLORENCIA
FILADELFIA
LONDRES
NUEVA ORLEANS

GUIÓN DE TRABAJO

¿De dónde eres? →
¿De dónde es usted? →

Soy...
de Nueva York.
de Ottawa.
de Filadelfia.
de Florencia.
de Berlín.
de Nueva Orleans.
de Londres.

Vocabulario

13

Nueva York *New York*
Nueva Orleans *New Orleans*
Filadelfia *Philadelphia*
Los Ángeles *Los Angeles*
Londres *London*
Ottawa, Toledo

13 Suggestion Bring in neckties for half of the class to wear. Tell students to use **usted** to address those with neckties.

Practice more at **vhlcentral.com.**

SAM: Actividades pp. 8–10

Benicio del Toro, un referente de la comunidad latina.

Benicio del Toro, un actor puertorriqueño

Los Ángeles

una mallorca

Puerto Rico

Santurce

MINUTO-TEST a... Benicio del Toro

- Una ciudad: Los Ángeles
- Una isla: Puerto Rico
- Una comida: Mallorcas
- Un barrio: Santurce
- Un personaje: Luis Buñuel

Película *Traffic*

Películas

- *Che, el argentino* (2008), director: Steven Soderbergh
- *La ciudad del pecado* (2005), directores: Frank Miller, Robert Rodríguez
- *21 gramos* (2003), director: Alejandro González Iñárritu
- *El juramento* (2001), director: Sean Penn
- *Traffic* (2000), director: Steven Soderbergh

Ask students if they have seen any of the movies listed.

Vocabulario

14

- puertorriqueño/a *Puerto Rican*
- el actor/la actriz *actor/actress*
- el minuto *minute*
- la mallorca *Puerto Rican pastry*
- el barrio *neighborhood*
- la comunidad *community*
- la película *movie*
- **el test, el/la director(a)**

15

- ¿Qué... eliges? *Which . . . do you choose?*

Mallorca pastries originated in the Balearic Islands of Spain, and derive their name from the island of Majorca (**Mallorca** in Spanish). In Puerto Rico, **mallorcas** are served for breakfast or as an afternoon snack.

14 a. Look at the photo of this lesson's protagonist and answer the questions.

Sample answers:

- ¿Quién es? Es Benicio del Toro.
- ¿De dónde es? Es de Puerto Rico.

b. Read Benicio del Toro's Minute Test and add a caption to each photo.

c. Now it's your turn to take the Minute Test. What people, places, and things do you associate with Spanish-speaking countries?

MINUTO-TEST a ____________________

- Una ciudad: ....
- Una isla: ....
- Una comida: ....
- Un pueblo: ....
- Un personaje: ....
- Un barrio: ....

15 Ask two classmates what people, places, and things they chose in the Minute Test, and write their answers in the chart.

Modelo: *¿Qué ciudad/isla/comida/pueblo/personaje/barrio eliges?*

REFERENTES CULTURALES		....	....
	una ciudad	Córdoba	
	una isla	Cuba	
	una comida	milanesas	
	un pueblo	Tarabuco	
	un personaje	Dr. Favaloro	
	un barrio	alto Perú	

OPINIÓN

What people, places, and foods do your classmates associate with Spanish-speaking countries? Discuss your ideas with a partner.

16 Choose a photograph. Your partner has to guess which photo you chose.

comida • paella • España

ciudad • Santiago de Chile • Chile

isla • Ibiza • España

comida • asado • Argentina

Modelo: *¿Es de España? ¿Es una isla? ¿Es ....?*

Expansion In Argentina, another word for **asado** is **parrillada.**

[c] [g]

17 a. Listen to these words. Is the letter *c* always pronounced the same?

Caracas - comida - Cuba / centro - ciudad

b. Now listen to how the letter *g* is pronounced.

Galápagos - golf - guacamole / Gerona - Gibraltar

c. Which vowels come after *c* and *g* in each case?
hard sound: *a, o,* and *u;* soft sound: *e* and *i*

Although **k** produces the same sound as a hard **c**, in Spanish the letter **k** is only used in words of foreign origin.

Vocabulario

16
la paella *Spanish rice dish*
el asado *barbecue*

17
el centro *center; downtown*
el golf, el guacamole

18
el referente latino *Hispanic icon*
el ceviche *marinated seafood dish*

Referentes latinos

18 What do you know about Latin America? Complete the sentences about these photos, then match the photos to the corresponding descriptions.

Caracas es una ....ciudad.... A
El ceviche ....es una comida.... C
Salma Hayek ....es una actriz.... D
Cuba ....es una isla.... B

Practice more at **vhlcentral.com.**

SAM: Actividades pp. 11–14

TAREA FINAL

Palabras, palabras...

Create a portfolio of your Spanish vocabulary!

First, brainstorm ideas with the class. What Spanish words do you know for each letter of the Spanish alphabet?

A ....

B ....

C ....

D ....

Find photos to represent your words and assemble them in a notebook or online portfolio. Add words, photos, and other materials to your portfolio throughout the Spanish course.

Suggestion Have students work in pairs to take turns spelling aloud the names they wrote for the first bullet. Their partner should write each one down and identify the category to which it belongs.

YO PUEDO...

- Puedo nombrar y especificar ciudades, comidas y personajes.
  Name two cities, foods, and people.
- Puedo preguntar cómo se escribe una palabra y deletrearla (*spell it*).
  Spell out the names of these two cities.
- Puedo decir cómo me llamo y de dónde soy.
  Write out your personal information.
- Puedo preguntar a alguien de dónde es, en situaciones formales e informales.
  Look at the photo and complete the question.

Oviedo
o - ve - i - e - de - o

Santo Domingo ese - a - ene - te - o - de - o - eme - i - ene - ge - o

....

....

....

¿De dónde eres/es usted?

GRAMÁTICA FUNCIONAL

1A.1 Use numbers 0–12

Numbers 0–12 13.1

0 **cero**	4 **cuatro**	7 **siete**	10 **diez**
1 **uno**	5 **cinco**	8 **ocho**	11 **once**
2 **dos**	6 **seis**	9 **nueve**	12 **doce**
3 **tres**			

- Use **uno** (*one*) when counting or after a noun. Use **un** before masculine nouns and **una** before feminine nouns.

la Unidad uno	un hombre	una mujer
Unit one	*one man*	*one woman*

- Use **más** (*plus*) to give sums.

Tres más siete: diez. (3 + 7 = 10)

Suggestion You may want to introduce the word **son** for students to use in addition problems. Ex: **Tres más siete son diez**. Students will learn the form **son** on p. 22.

1A.2 Identify and specify

Singular indefinite article **un(a)** 3.2
Interrogatives **¿qué?, ¿quién?** 9

- All Spanish nouns are either masculine or feminine. To say *a, an,* or *one,* use **un** with masculine nouns (which usually end in **-o**) and **una** with feminine nouns (which usually end in **-a**). Pay attention to gender as you learn nouns, as there are many exceptions.

un pueblo	una comida	un hotel	una ciudad
a/one town	*a/one food*	*a/one hotel*	*a/one city*

- To ask what something is, say **¿Qué es?** To answer, use **Es** + [*indefinite article*] + [*noun*]. **Es** is the 3rd person singular form of the verb **ser** (*to be*). There is no Spanish equivalent to the subject pronoun *it*. To say *It is,* use **Es**.

¿Qué es?	Es una isla.	Es un barrio.
What is it?	*It's an island.*	*It is a neighborhood.*

- To ask who someone is, say **¿Quién es?** To respond, use **Es** + [*name*].

¿Quién es?	Es Luis Buñuel.
Who is it?	*It's Luis Buñuel.*

1A.3 Spell

Interrogative **¿cómo?** 9

- To ask how a Spanish word is spelled, say **¿Cómo se escribe?**

¿Cómo se escribe Albarracín?
How do you spell Albarracín?

- Use the word **con** (*with*) to clarify spellings.

Con be.	Con dos erres.	Con acento en la i.
With a b.	*With two* r*'s.*	*With an accent on the* i.

- Note that Spanish questions use both opening (¿) and closing (?) question marks and that all interrogatives take a written accent.

¿Qué es?	¿Quién es?	¿Cómo se escribe?
What is it?	*Who is it?*	*How do you spell it?*

¡Póngalo en práctica!

G1 Write out these sums.

Modelo: 3 + 4 *Tres más cuatro: siete.*

1. 5 + 3 Cinco más tres: ocho.
2. 9 + 0 Nueve más cero: nueve.
3. 2 + 2 Dos más dos: cuatro.
4. 3 + 8 Tres más ocho: once.
5. 4 + 6 Cuatro más seis: diez.
6. 10 + 2 Diez más dos: doce.
7. 1 + 6 Uno más seis: siete.
8. 2 + 3 Dos más tres: cinco.

G2 Use the cues to answer the questions.

¿Qué es?

1. biblioteca Es una biblioteca.
2. monumento Es un monumento.
3. playa Es una playa.
4. barrio Es un barrio.
5. pueblo Es un pueblo.
6. comida Es una comida.
7. personaje Es un personaje.

¿Quién es?

8. Benicio del Toro Es Benicio del Toro.
9. Penélope Cruz Es Penélope Cruz.
10. Mario Vargas Llosa Es Mario Vargas Llosa.

G2 Expansion Bring in photos of places, things, and famous people and have students say what or who they see in each photo.

G3 Match each word in the box to the clarification about its spelling.

¿Cómo se escribe?

ceviche	esquí	Brasil
Ottawa	hip-hop	fútbol

1. Con acento en la i. esquí
2. Con ce. ceviche
3. Con dos tes. Ottawa
4. Con acento en la u. fútbol
5. Con ese. Brasil
6. Con hache. hip-hop

Practice more at **vhlcentral.com.**

GRAMÁTICA FUNCIONAL

1A.4 Talk about where people are from

Interrogative **¿de dónde?** 9
The verb **ser** (singular forms) 5.8.1

- To ask where someone is from, say ¿**De dónde** + [*form of* **ser**] + [*subject*]?

¿De dónde eres tú?	¿De dónde es Carolina?
Where are you from?	*Where is Carolina from?*

- To tell where someone is from, say [*subject*] + [*form of* **ser**] + **de** + [*city/country*].

Yo **soy de** Guayaquil.	Ella **es de** Paraguay.
I am from Guayaquil.	*She is from Paraguay.*

- The singular subject pronouns in Spanish are **yo** (*I*), **tú** (*you*, fam.), **usted** (*you*, form.), **él** (*he*), and **ella** (*she*). As with all verbs, **ser** (*to be*) has a set of forms corresponding to the different subjects.

SER (Formas singulares)	
(yo)	**soy**
(tú)	**eres**
(usted, él, ella)	**es**

- Unlike in English, subject pronouns are not required in Spanish and are usually omitted.

¿De dónde eres?	Soy de Miami.
*Where are **you** from?*	*I'm from Miami.*

¡OJO! Both **tú** and **usted** mean *you*. Use **tú** when addressing a friend, a family member, or someone younger than you. Use **usted** to address a person with whom you have a more formal relationship. Note that **usted** is used with the same verb forms as **él** and **ella**.

1A.5 Answer yes-or-no questions

sí/no, no + [*verb*] 12.1, 12.2

- To answer a question in the affirmative, say **Sí,** + [*verb*].

¿Es usted Antonio García?	**Sí, soy** Antonio García.
Are you Antonio García?	***Yes, I am** Antonio García.*

- To answer a question negatively, say **No, no** + [*verb*]. To make a negative statement, always place the word **no** directly before the verb.

¿Es usted de Canadá?	**No, no soy** de Canadá.
Are you from Canada?	***No, I am not** from Canada.*
¿Te llamas Pablo?	**No, no me llamo** Pablo.
Is your name Pablo?	***No, my name is not** Pablo.*

- To answer negatively and provide the correct information, you can also say **No,** + [*correct information*]: **No, me llamo Pedro.** (*No, my name is Pedro.*)

¡Póngalo en práctica!

G4 Ask where each of these people is from.

1. usted ¿De dónde es usted?
2. Gustavo ¿De dónde es Gustavo?
3. el escritor ¿De dónde es el escritor?
4. tú ¿De dónde eres tú?
5. ella ¿De dónde es ella?
6. Gabriela ¿De dónde es Gabriela?
7. él ¿De dónde es él?
8. la arquitecta ¿De dónde es la arquitecta?

G5 Complete the conversation.

Inés, ¿de (1) dónde eres?

Yo (2) soy de Cartagena. Y (3) tú, ¿de dónde eres?

Soy (4) de Barranquilla.

¡Qué lindo! Shakira (5) es de Barranquilla, ¿no?

Sí, (6) ella es de Barranquilla.

G6 Answer these questions about yourself.

1. ¿Es usted estudiante?
   Sí, soy estudiante./No, no soy estudiante.
2. ¿Es usted de Estados Unidos?
   Sí, soy de Estados Unidos./No, no soy de Estados Unidos.
3. ¿Eres escritor(a)?
   Sí, soy escritor(a)./No, no soy escritor(a).
4. ¿Eres María?
   Sí, soy María./No, no soy María.
5. ¿Eres de Puerto Rico?
   Sí, soy de Puerto Rico./No, no soy de Puerto Rico.
6. ¿Es usted arquitecto/a?
   Sí, soy arquitecto/a./No, no soy arquitecto/a.

Practice more at vhlcentral.com.

VOCABULARIO

Imágenes y palabras

¿Qué es?	*What is it?*
¿Quién es?	*Who is it?*
¿quién?	*who?*
el/la arquitecto/a	*architect*
la biblioteca	*library*
la comida	*food*
el/la escritor(a)	*writer*
la imagen	*picture, image*
la isla	*island*
el monumento	*monument*
la música	*music*
el personaje	*important figure; character*
la playa	*beach*
el pueblo	*town*

Vocabulario Explain to students that active vocabulary from the lesson is listed here in alphabetical order, divided by part of speech. Encourage students to use these lists to help them study; they can cover either the Spanish or English side of the column and quiz themselves on the appropriate translation. Remind students that all of these words and expressions are also listed in alphabetical order in the glossary at the end of their text.

Yo soy de Madrid, ¿y tú?

¿De dónde eres?	*Where are you from? (fam.)*
¿De dónde es usted?	*Where are you from? (form.)*
Yo soy de Madrid.	*I'm from Madrid.*
¿y tú?	*and you?*
el concierto	*concert*
el esquí	*skiing*
el fútbol	*soccer*
el hip-hop	*hip-hop*
el interés	*interest*
el origen	*origin*
la salsa	*salsa*
el teatro	*theater*
el tenis	*tennis*
Brasil	*Brazil*
Filadelfia	*Philadelphia*
Londres	*London*
Los Ángeles	*Los Angeles*
Nueva Orleans	*New Orleans*
Nueva York	*New York*
Ottawa	*Ottawa*
Portugal	*Portugal*
Toledo	*Toledo*
bien	*well*
muy bien	*very well*
sí	*yes*
no	*no; not*

Benicio del Toro

¿Qué... eliges?	*What . . . do you choose?*
el actor/la actriz	*actor/actress*
el asado	*barbecue*
el barrio	*neighborhood*
el ceviche	*marinated seafood dish*
el centro	*center; downtown*
la comunidad	*community*
el/la director(a)	*director*
el golf	*golf*
el guacamole	*guacamole*
la mallorca	*Puerto Rican pastry*
el minuto	*minute*
la paella	*Spanish rice dish*
la película	*movie*
el referente latino	*Hispanic icon*
el test	*test*
puertorriqueño/a	*Puerto Rican*

Suggestion Show students that common nouns are listed with their corresponding definite article (students will learn more about definite articles in **2A.4**). Tell students that studying the noun with its article will help them remember the noun's gender as they expand their vocabulary.

Variación léxica

el barrio ⟷ **el vecindario** ⟷ **la vecindad** ⟷ **la colonia** (*Méx.*)

el fútbol ⟷ **el futbol** (*Amér. C., Méx.*)

la mallorca (*P.R.*) ⟷ **la ensaimada** (*Esp.*)

el test ⟷ **la prueba**

Variación léxica Explain to students that many English words have several equivalents in Spanish. Some words are used in different regions of the Spanish-speaking world, some are used in different contexts depending on the level of formality, and some are near perfect synonyms. Only those terms marked in blue are considered active vocabulary in this text. Encourage heritage speakers to suggest additional terms based on their background.

1B LENGUAS

Hablamos

Informar sobre las lenguas que uno habla y estudia

- ¿Tú **hablas** francés?
- No, no **hablo** francés. Yo **hablo** español.
- Fernando **no habla** inglés.
- ¿Qué lenguas **estudiáis** vosotros?
- **Estudiamos** español y japonés.
- Jaime y Lola **hablan** italiano y alemán.

1B.1 Regular **-ar** verbs: **estudiar, hablar**

Vocabulario

1

hablar *to speak*
¿Qué lenguas hablas? *What languages do you speak?*
el inglés *English*
estudiar *to study*
el español *Spanish*
el italiano *Italian*
el alemán *German*
el francés *French*
el chino *Chinese*
el portugués *Portuguese*
el coreano *Korean*
el japonés *Japanese*

1 Look at the photo and listen to the conversation. In the chart, indicate which languages the students speak or study.

	ESPAÑOL	INGLÉS	FRANCÉS	ALEMÁN	ITALIANO
hablan	✓	✓	✓	✓	
estudian	✓				✓

2 Match each subject to a verb ending.

2 Suggestion Write each subject pronoun and verb ending on a separate piece of paper and shuffle them. Distribute a set to each student and have them match the items.

-AR

yo	-o
tú	-as
él/ella	-a
nosotros/as	-amos
vosotros/as	-áis
ellos/as	-an

3 Write the correct form of each verb. Compare your answers with a partner's.

(yo) **hablar**	(tú) **hablar**	(él) **estudiar**	(ella) **estudiar**	(nosotros) **estudiar**	(vosotros) **hablar**	(ellos) **hablar**
hablo	hablas	estudia	estudia	estudiamos	habláis	hablan

4 Interview your partner. What languages does he/she speak and study?

Modelo: *¿Hablas chino? ¿Estudias francés?*

4 Suggestion Have students take notes about their partner's answers and report back to the class.

Suggestion Provide city names and have students say the language that is spoken there. Ex: **Berlín (el alemán)** Then reverse the activity.

Tell students that they may also hear **americano/a** or **norteamericano/a** used to talk about Americans. Explain that **americano/a** refers to people from throughout the Americas, and that **estadounidense** is therefore a more precise term to refer to people from the U.S.

INTERCAMBIO DE CONVERSACIÓN
en la CAFETERÍA BABEL
Plaza San Juan, 6. Barcelona
Día 28 de abril a las 18:00 h

Suggestion Read aloud names of famous people and have students supply the correct adjective of nationality. Ex: **David Beckham (inglés)**

Vocabulario

5

estadounidense *American*
canadiense *Canadian*
el intercambio *exchange*
la cafetería *café*
la plaza *square*
abril *April*
18:00 h *6:00 p.m.*
chino/a *Chinese*
alemán/alemana *German*
inglés/inglesa *English*
coreano/a *Korean*
portugués/portuguesa *Portuguese*
francés/francesa *French*
e *and (before* **i** *or* **hi** *+ consonant)*
la nacionalidad *nationality*
la conversación, italiano/a

6

se habla(n) *is/are spoken*
el catalán *Catalan*
el idioma *language*

7

Pekín *Beijing*

Indicar la nacionalidad

- ¿Eres alemana?
- No, soy estadounidense.
- ¿Y él? ¿Es francés?
- No, es canadiense.

1B.2 **ser** + [*nationality*]

Informar sobre las lenguas que se hablan en un país

En México se habla español.

En Canadá se hablan dos lenguas.

1B.3 **en** + [*country/city/place*] **se habla(n)** + [*language(s)*]

5 a. Indicate each person's nationality in the photo captions.

chino alemana inglés coreana portugués francesa italiano

b. Yumi enters the cafeteria. Read the conversation and fill in the information.

- ¡Buenas tardes! ¿Cómo te llamas?
- Yumi.
- ¿Y de dónde eres, Yumi?
- Soy de Tokio, Japón.
- Muy bien. ¿Qué lenguas hablas?
- Hablo japonés e inglés. Y bueno, estudio español y francés.

Nombre: Yumi Nacionalidad: japonesa Lenguas: japonés, inglés, español, francés

c. Now you enter the cafeteria. Practice the conversation with a partner.

6 Listen to Yumi and Jordi, and indicate whether each statement is true (**verdadero**) or false (**falso**).

1. Yumi habla japonés. V
2. Jordi estudia francés. F
3. En Barcelona se hablan español y catalán. V
4. En Tokio se habla japonés. V

7 Have you been to any of these cities? What languages are spoken there?

Modelo: *En Montevideo se habla...*

PEKÍN MONTREAL
MONTEVIDEO BUENOS AIRES

MI EXPERIENCIA

8 Ask your classmates what languages they speak and study.

GUIÓN DE TRABAJO

¿Eres...?
¿Qué lenguas hablas?
¿Hablas...?
alemán, inglés, francés, italiano | español, chino, coreano, portugués
¿Qué lenguas estudias?
¿Qué lengua se habla en tu país/familia?

Practice more at **vhlcentral.com.**

SAM: Actividades pp. 15–16

Hablar de la profesión

- Antonio, ¿a qué te dedicas? ¿Eres arquitecto?
- No, soy ingeniero.
- ¿Y usted? ¿A qué se dedica?
- No trabajo. Soy jubilada.
- Nosotras somos médicas. Y vosotros, ¿sois psicólogos?
- Paloma y Miguel son abogados.

médico — médicos
ingeniera — ingenieras

1B.4 The verb **ser** (plural forms)
ser + [*profession*]
Plural of nouns

Valorar el trabajo y las carreras

- ¿Es una profesión **interesante**?
- Sí, sí, es muy **interesante**.

aburrido/a
divertido/a
estresante
interesante

1B.5 **ser** + [*opinion*]

Vocabulario

9

la guía *guide(book)*
el trabajo *job*
el sumario *table of contents*
el amo/a de casa *homemaker*
el/la abogado/a *lawyer*
el/la ingeniero/a *engineer*
el/la profesor(a) *teacher*
el/la técnico/a informático/a *computer technician*
el/la psicólogo/a *psychologist*
el/la médico/a *doctor*
el/la cajero/a *cashier*
la profesión, el/la secretario/a

10

trabajar *to work*
¿A qué te dedicas? *What do you do (for work)?*
también *too, as well*
¡Qué interesante! *How interesting!*
el hospital

11

divertido/a *fun*
estresante *stressful*
aburrido/a *boring*

Profesiones y trabajos

Suggestion Read through the list of professions and have students rate each one with one or more of the adjectives from **1B.5**.

http://www.profesiones.es

GUÍA DE PROFESIONES Y TRABAJOS
Sumario

arquitecto/a	técnico/a informático/a
amo/a de casa	psicólogo/a
abogado/a	secretario/a
ingeniero/a	médico/a
profesor(a)	cajero/a

9 Read the guide to jobs and identify which occupations are centered around interacting with people. Discuss your answers with a partner.

Contacto con personas: Answers may vary. Sample answers: arquitecto/a, abogado/a, ingeniero/a, profesor(a), psicólogo/a, secretario/a, médico/a, cajero/a

10 Read this conversation and decide whether each statement below is true (**verdadero**) or false (**falso**).

- Somos Blanca y Juana. Trabajamos en un hospital. Blanca es psicóloga y yo, médica. ¿Y tú? ¿A qué te dedicas? ¿También eres médica?
- No, yo soy secretaria.
- ¡Qué interesante! ¿Y vosotros?
- Nosotros somos arquitectos.

	V	F
1. Blanca y Juana son ingenieras.	☐	✓
2. Ellos son arquitectos.	✓	☐
3. Juana es médica.	✓	☐

11 Listen to the radio program. What do these people do for work, and how do they describe their profession?

La medicina es .... | una profesión... | ... divertida / ... estresante (circled) / ... interesante (circled) / ... aburrida

12 In pairs, take turns using words from each group to form sentences.

Modelo: *Ellos son profesores.*

12 Suggestion Remind students to pay attention to the gender of the nouns in the third column.

vosotras	somos	cajeros
nosotros	sois	profesores
ellos	son	psicólogas
ellas		amas de casa
nosotras		secretarios
vosotros		abogadas

Numerar

- ¿Cuál es tu número de teléfono/celular?
- Es el seis, noventa y nueve, trece, cuarenta, treinta y uno. (6 99 13 40 31)

12	doce	33	treinta y tres
13	trece	...	
14	catorce	40	cuarenta
15	quince	41	cuarenta y uno
16	dieciséis	42	cuarenta y dos
17	diecisiete	43	cuarenta y tres
18	dieciocho	...	
19	diecinueve	50	cincuenta
20	veinte	60	sesenta
21	veintiuno	70	setenta
22	veintidós	80	ochenta
...		90	noventa
30	treinta	100	cien
31	treinta y uno		
32	treinta y dos		

1B.6 Numbers 12–100

Vocabulario

(14)
¿Cuál es tu número de teléfono? *What is your phone number?*
el (teléfono) celular *cell phone*

(15)
la biología *biology*
las ciencias políticas *political science*
la economía *economics*
la historia *history*
la informática *computer science*
la literatura *literature*
la química *chemistry*
la carrera *major*

13 a. Choose three photos and say the numbers you see aloud. Your partner should then identify which photo you are talking about.

Modelo: *Es la foto...*

Suggestion Have a volunteer read aloud the sign in the middle photo of the top row. Explain that in Argentina, **palomita** is a cut of beef (chuck).

b. Write out the numbers you see in each photo on the line below.

1 noventa y nueve

2 veintidós

3 cero, cero, cero, setenta y ocho, veintisiete, ocho

4 veinte

5 diecinueve

6 setenta y nueve

14 a. Listen to the recording of these phone numbers and write them down. Pay close attention to how the numbers are grouped.

Irene: 676 100 929 Daniel: 629 43 31 60 Cristina: 626 87 26 30

alternate combination

b. Exchange phone numbers with a partner.

Modelo:
- *¿Cuál es tu número de teléfono?*
- *0160-4458679: cero, uno, seis...*

14 If students do not feel comfortable sharing their phone number, tell them to invent one or simply invert a few of the digits.

MI EXPERIENCIA

15 Ask your classmates about their studies and their jobs.

GUIÓN DE TRABAJO

¿A qué te dedicas?/¿Qué estudias?

Estudio... → biología, ciencias políticas, economía, historia, informática, literatura, química...

Soy... → arquitecto/a, secretario/a, psicólogo/a, ingeniero/a..., médico/a...

¿Es una carrera/profesión... → interesante? aburrida? divertida? estresante?

cuál es tu Nº de tel?

Practice more at **vhlcentral.com.**

SAM: Actividades pp. 17–19

Joan, un catalán políglota

FORO DE LENGUAS

Joan	Título del mensaje: **Intercambios de conversación** Citar
Registrado: 20-Sep Mensajes: 1	Publicado: 20-Sep ¡Hola! Me llamo Joan Fusté. Soy de Barcelona. Hablo catalán y español. Trabajo en el Museo Picasso. Soy guía y, claro, con los turistas hablo inglés, francés, italiano... Es un trabajo muy interesante, ¡y divertido! También estudio alemán. Busco personas para practicar idiomas...

LENGUAS

Like many countries in the Spanish-speaking world, parts of Spain have two official languages: Spanish and the regional language. For example, **catalán** is spoken in Cataluña, **euskera** is spoken in **País Vasco,** and **gallego** is spoken in Galicia.

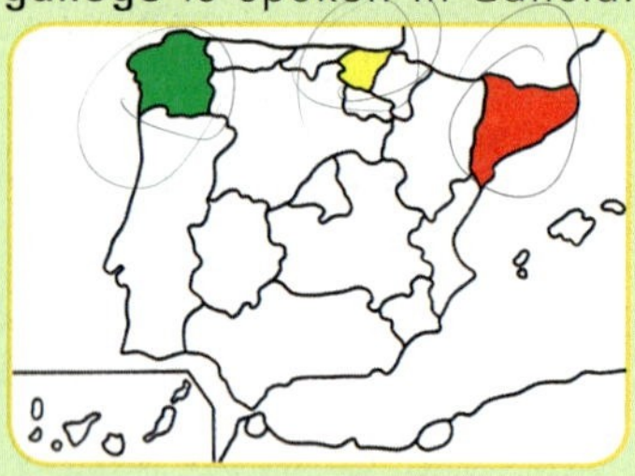

16 Look at the photo of Joan and his name tag. What city does he live in? Where does he work? Have you ever been there?

Barcelona; el Museo Picasso

17 Read Joan's post on the language forum and complete the information below.

- Nombre y apellido: Joan Fusté
- Ciudad: Barcelona
- Profesión: Guía (turístico)

18 Answer the questions.

1. ¿Qué lenguas habla Joan? ¿Qué lenguas estudia?
   Habla catalán, español, inglés, francés e italiano. Estudia alemán.
2. ¿Ser guía turístico es un trabajo interesante para Joan?
   Sí, ser guía turístico es un trabajo muy interesante para Joan.

19 Write an answer to Joan's posting. Include your name, nationality, job, major, and any languages you speak or study.

FORO DE LENGUAS

Respuesta	Título del mensaje: **Intercambios de conversación** Citar
Registrado: 20-Sep Mensajes: 1	Publicado: 20-Sep ¡Hola, Joan! ....

Euskera does not have any genealogical relationship to any other language.

Have students research the Basque or Galician equivalents of a few Spanish phrases or words they know. Have them describe the similarities and differences.

Vocabulario

17

- **políglota** *polyglot, multilingual*
- **el foro** *forum*
- **el/la guía (turístico/a)** *(tour) guide*
- **claro** *of course*
- **el/la turista** *tourist*
- **buscar** *to look for*
- **la persona** *person*
- **País Vasco** *Basque Country*
- **el euskera** *Basque (language)*
- **el gallego** *Galician (language)*

Vocabulario ***cont.***

el nombre *name*
el apellido *last name*

(20)

la clase *class*
la foto(grafía) *photo(graph)*
internacional *international*
el banco *bank*

20 Have a volunteer read Anna's e-mail out loud. Ask students what they think the phrase **te envío** (*I'm sending you*) means. Show students that they can still understand the overall message of a text even if they don't know all of the words.

OPINIÓN

¿Qué lenguas se estudian más en su país?
Se estudian más...

¿Qué lenguas se estudian en su universidad?
Se estudian...

¿Qué otras lenguas o dialectos se hablan en su país?
Se habla(n)...

20 a. Look at the photo next to the e-mail message. What do you think the e-mail will say? Read it.

Mensaje nuevo

Enviar | Chat | Adjuntar | Agenda | Tipo de letra | Colores | Borrador

De: Anna
Para: Pablo Fernández
Asunto: CLASES DE ESPAÑOL

Hola, Pablo, ¿qué tal?
Te envío una foto de mi clase de español. ¡Sí, estudio español! Es una clase muy divertida y muy internacional. Somos seis: un inglés, una francesa, dos italianas, un portugués y yo. En clase hablamos español. Carla y Paola, las italianas, trabajan en un banco. Son abogadas.

b. Fill in the missing information about the students mentioned in the e-mail.

Nombre: Valérie Renoir
Profesión: técnica informática
Nacionalidad: ......francesa......
Idiomas: francés, inglés

Nombre: Carla Conte
Profesión: ......abogada......
Nacionalidad: ......italiana......
Idiomas: ......italiano......, inglés

Entonación

21 a. Listen to these sentences and repeat after the speaker. Pay special attention to the intonation.

Estudio español. ¿Hablas inglés? ¿Estudias idiomas?

b. Listen to these sentences and draw the intonation you hear on a separate sheet of paper. Sentence 1: rising intonation; Sentence 2: falling intonation

Vocabulario

(22)

indígena *indigenous, native*
el quechua *Quechua*
el guaraní *Guarani*

22 a. You have read about the variety of languages spoken in Spain. Now think about where Spanish is spoken in the Americas. In which of these countries is Spanish not an official language? Circle it/them.

☐ Ecuador	☐ (Estados Unidos)	✓ Perú	☐ (Brasil)
✓ México	✓ Chile	✓ Argentina	✓ Venezuela
✓ Colombia	✓ Uruguay	☐ Cuba	☐ Guatemala

b. Listen to the recording and check off the countries that are mentioned. These are the most populous countries in Latin America.

c. Now listen to the recording to learn in which countries **quechua** and **guaraní** are spoken in addition to Spanish.

El quechua se habla en ......Perú......, Ecuador, Bolivia, Colombia, Argentina y Chile.
El guaraní se habla en Paraguay, ...Argentina...... y Bolivia.

Machu Picchu, Perú

Practice more at **vhlcentral.com.**

SAM: Actividades pp. 20–24

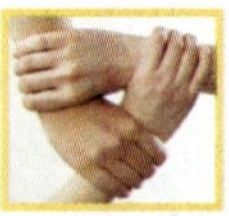

TAREA FINAL

Suggestion Have students interview two classmates. Tell them to address one classmate with **tú** and the other with **usted.**

Compañeros de clase

Gather information about a classmate.
Answer his/her questions as well.

¿Cómo te llamas? ¿De dónde eres?
¿Qué lenguas hablas/estudias?
¿A qué te dedicas? ¿Cuál es tu número de teléfono? ...

Fill in your partner's information on this card.

- Nombre: ....
- Nacionalidad: ....
- Lenguas que habla y estudia: ....
- Profesión/Carrera: ....
- Teléfono: ....

Share your partner's information with the rest of the class.

YO PUEDO...

- **Puedo decir el nombre de distintas lenguas.**
  List five languages.
- **Puedo informar sobre las lenguas que hablo y estudio.**
  Answer these questions.
- **Puedo rellenar una ficha de inscripción con mis datos.**
  Complete this card with your information.
- **Puedo nombrar diferentes profesiones y carreras.**
  List four professions and four academic majors.
- **Puedo comprender y dar números de teléfono.**
  Write out your phone number(s).

¿Qué lenguas hablas? ....

¿Qué lenguas estudias? ....

Nombre: ....
Nacionalidad: ....
Profesión/Carrera: ....

Mi número de teléfono es: ....

Celular: ....

GRAMÁTICA FUNCIONAL

1B.1 Talk about the languages you speak and study

Regular **-ar** verbs 5.1.1

- Use the verbs **hablar** (*to speak*) and **estudiar** (*to study*) to talk about the languages people speak and study.

  ¿Qué lenguas **hablas**?
  *What languages **do you speak**?*

  Hablo inglés y **estudio** español.
  ***I speak** English and **I study** Spanish.*

- **Estudiar** and **hablar** are regular **-ar** verbs. In order to conjugate these verbs, drop the **-ar** ending from the infinitive and add the endings that correspond to the different subject pronouns. All regular **-ar** verbs use the same set of endings.

	ESTUDIAR	HABLAR
(yo)	estudi**o**	habl**o**
(tú)	estudi**as**	habl**as**
(usted, él, ella)	estudi**a**	habl**a**
(nosotros/as)	estudi**amos**	habl**amos**
(vosotros/as)	estudi**áis**	habl**áis**
(ustedes, ellos/as)	estudi**an**	habl**an**

- Since all regular **-ar** verbs follow this pattern, you can tell the subject of the verb by looking at the ending. As you saw in 1A.4, this allows you to omit the subject pronoun.

  Hablas portugués e inglés, ¿no?
  ***You speak** Portuguese and English, right?*

- In 1A.4, you learned the singular subject pronouns **yo**, **tú**, **usted**, **él**, and **ella**. The plural subject pronouns are **nosotros/as** (*we*), **vosotros/as** (*you*, fam.), **ustedes** (*you*, form. and fam.), and **ellos/as** (*they*).

  Nosotros estudiamos español y **ellos** estudian chino.
  ***We** study Spanish and **they** study Chinese.*

- The feminine forms **nosotras**, **vosotras**, and **ellas** are used only when all members of the group are female. For groups of mixed gender or groups that are all male, use the masculine forms **nosotros**, **vosotros**, and **ellos**.

  Clara y Mónica = **ellas**

  Clara y Roberto = **ellos**

  Roberto y Daniel = **ellos**

¡OJO!

Both **vosotros/as** and **ustedes** mean *you* and are used to address a group of people. In Spain, **vosotros/as** is used in familiar contexts, similar to when **tú** is used. However, in Latin America, **ustedes** is used to address groups in both formal and familiar contexts.

¡Póngalo en práctica!

G1 Decide whether each group should be called **ellos** or **ellas**.

1. Rubén y Carlos ellos
2. Raquel y Daniel ellos
3. Ana y Rosa ellas
4. Tomás y David ellos
5. Gloria, Teresa y Ramón ellos

G2 Match each form of **hablar** to its corresponding subject pronoun.

d	1. usted	a. hablas
e	2. nosotras	b. hablan
b	3. ellos	c. hablo
a	4. tú	d. habla
f	5. vosotros	e. hablamos
c	6. yo	f. habláis

G2 Expand the second column by adding forms of **trabajar** and **estudiar**. Explain that each item will have three answers.

G3 Use the cues to state what languages these people study.

Modelo: Eduardo / chino
Eduardo estudia chino.

1. nosotros / coreano
   Nosotros estudiamos coreano.
2. ustedes / francés
   Ustedes estudian francés.
3. yo / español
   Yo estudio español.
4. vosotras / italiano
   Vosotras estudiáis italiano.
5. tú / japonés
   Tú estudias japonés.
6. tú y yo / alemán
   Tú y yo estudiamos alemán.
7. Miguel y Elena / catalán
   Miguel y Elena estudian catalán.
8. Mauricio y tú / portugués
   Mauricio y tú estudian/estudiáis portugués.

Practice more at **vhlcentral.com.**

GRAMÁTICA FUNCIONAL

1B.2 Identify nationalities

ser + [*nationality*] 4.1; 5.8.1

- To indicate a person's nationality, use **ser** + [*nationality*]. Unlike in English, adjectives of nationality are not capitalized in Spanish.

Nuno **es portugués.**	Chiara **es italiana.**
*Nuno **is Portuguese**.*	*Chiara **is Italian.***

- Most Spanish adjectives have multiple forms. An adjective must match the person it describes in gender and number. When the masculine form ends in **-o**, form the feminine by changing the **-o** to **-a**.

  Iván es colombian**o** y Eugenia es colombian**a**.
  Iván is Colombian and Eugenia is Colombian.

- When the masculine form ends in **-e**, there is no change for the feminine form.

  Scott es canadiens**e** y Laura es canadiens**e**.
  Scott is Canadian and Laura is Canadian.

- When the masculine form ends in a consonant, form the feminine by adding **-a**. If the masculine form has a written accent on the final syllable, drop the accent mark for the feminine form.

  Pierre es franc**és** y Julie es franc**esa**.
  Pierre is French and Julie is French.

1B.3 Indicate the languages spoken in a country

en + [*country/city/place*] 10.11

se habla(n) + [*language(s)*] 5.12.1

- To ask which languages are spoken in a given place, say **¿Qué lenguas se hablan en** [*place*]?

  ¿Qué lenguas se hablan en Chile?
  *What languages are spoken **in** Chile?*

- Use **en** (*in*) before the name of a city, country, or other place to talk about what happens there.

  ¿Qué lenguas se hablan **en** Barcelona/**en** clase?
  *What languages are spoken **in** Barcelona/**in** class?*

- To tell what languages are spoken in a place, say **En** + [*place*] + **se habla(n)** + [*language(s)*]. Use **habla** for one language and **hablan** for more than one.

  En Santiago de Chile **se habla** español.
  *In Santiago, Chile, Spanish **is spoken**.*

  En Santiago de Compostela **se hablan** español y gallego.
  *In Santiago de Compostela, Spanish and Galician **are spoken**.*

- Use only the 3rd-person forms of a verb (**habla, hablan**) after **se**.

¡Póngalo en práctica!

G4 Give the missing form of each adjective.

masculino	femenino
1. japonés	japonesa
2. alemán	alemana
3. canadiense	canadiense
4. italiano	italiana
5. coreano	coreana
6. inglés	inglesa
7. francés	francesa
8. portugués	portuguesa

G5 Use the cues to tell people's nationalities.

1. Sonia / Portugal Sonia es portuguesa.
2. Rafael / Estados Unidos Rafael es estadounidense.
3. Pierre / Francia Pierre es francés.
4. Carmen y Carlos / España Carmen y Carlos son españoles.
5. James / Canadá James es canadiense.
6. Ángela y Valentina / Colombia Ángela y Valentina son colombianas.
7. Ming / China Ming es chino.
8. Josef y Konrad / Alemania Josef y Konrad son alemanes.

G6 Say what language(s) is/are spoken in each place.

Modelo: Marruecos / árabe
En Marruecos se habla árabe.

1. Bolivia / español
   En Bolivia se habla español.
2. Canadá / inglés y francés
   En Canadá se hablan inglés y francés.
3. Corea / coreano
   En Corea se habla coreano.
4. Alemania / alemán
   En Alemania se habla alemán.
5. Suiza / alemán, italiano y francés
   En Suiza se hablan alemán, italiano y francés.
6. Hong Kong / chino e inglés
   En Hong Kong se hablan chino e inglés.

G5 Expansion Have students make all necessary changes and rewrite the sentences so that the adjectives are of the opposite gender. Ex: **Felipe es portugués.**

Practice more at **vhlcentral.com.**

GRAMÁTICA FUNCIONAL

1B.4 Talk about professions

ser + [*profession*] 5.8.1

Plural of nouns 2.2

The verb **ser** (plural forms)

- Use the question **¿A qué se dedica?** (*form.*) or **¿A qué te dedicas?** (*fam.*) to inquire about a person's job or profession.

  ¿A qué te dedicas, Manuela?
  What do you do, Manuela?

- To answer, use **ser** + [*profession*].

  Soy profesora de español.
  I'm a Spanish teacher.

- Most names of professions have different masculine and feminine forms.

masculino	femenino
el arquitecto	la arquitecta
el ingeniero	la ingeniera
el profesor	la profesora
el técnico informático	la técnica informática

  José Luis es ingeniero y Claudia es ingeniera.
  José Luis is an engineer and Claudia is an engineer.

- Use the plural forms of **ser** to talk about more than one person. Unlike **hablar** and **estudiar**, **ser** is an irregular verb. This means it does not follow a regular conjugation pattern and you must memorize the forms.

SER			
(yo)	**soy**	(nosotros/as)	**somos**
(tú)	**eres**	(vosotros/as)	**sois**
(usted, él, ella)	**es**	(ustedes, ellos/as)	**son**

- Use plural nouns with the plural forms of a verb. When a noun ends in an unaccented vowel, form the plural by adding **-s**.

  Somos ingenieros, arquitectos y médicos.
  We are engineers, architects, and doctors.

- When a noun ends in a consonant, form the plural by adding **-es**. If the final syllable has a written accent, drop the accent mark when forming the plural.

  profesor - profesores / *teacher - teachers*
  profesión - profesiones / *profession - professions*

- As with adjectives, when a noun represents a group of mixed gender, use the masculine form.

  Darío es psicólogo y Cati es psicóloga. Darío y Cati son psicólogos.
  Darío is a psychologist and Cati is a psychologist.
  Darío and Cati are psychologists.

G9 In Spain, October 12th is known as the **Fiesta Nacional de España,** which commemorates Columbus' arrival to the Americas. In Latin America, however, it is known as **el Día de la Raza** and represents the birth of a new identity.

¡Póngalo en práctica!

G7 Write the plural of each noun.

1. idioma ...idiomas...
2. trabajo ...trabajos...
3. carrera ...carreras...
4. nacionalidad ...nacionalidades...
5. psicóloga ...psicólogas...
6. celular ...celulares...
7. turista ...turistas...
8. cafetería ...cafeterías...

G8 Complete the sentences with the appropriate forms of **ser**.

G8 Point out the tag question in item 3. Explain that with negative statements, **¿verdad?** must be used instead of **¿no?**

1. Luis ...es... técnico informático.
2. David y yo ...somos... ingenieros.
3. Ustedes ...son... médicos, ¿no?
4. Luis Miguel y Alberto ...son... secretarios.
5. Yo ...soy... médico.
6. Esteban y tú ...son/sois... abogados.

G9 Complete the conversation using appropriate words and expressions.

Jorge, ¿a qué (1) ...te... dedicas?

Soy (2) ...médico... en el Hospital 12 de Octubre. Y tú, ¿a qué te (3) ...dedicas... ?

(4) ...Soy... profesora de biología.

¡Qué interesante! Mi amigo David también es (5) ...profesor... de biología.

¿David Ramírez?

¡Sí!

¡Qué casualidad! David y yo (6) ...somos... colegas en el Instituto La Paz.

Practice more at **vhlcentral.com.**

GRAMÁTICA FUNCIONAL

1B.5 Give opinions about professions and majors

ser + [*adjective*] 5.8.2

- Use **ser** + [*adjective*] to give your opinion about a profession, class, or other experience.

aburrido/a	estresante
divertido/a	interesante

Eres ingeniero, ¿no? ¿Es una profesión **aburrida**?
*You're an engineer, right? Is that a **boring** profession?*

No, no **es** una profesión **aburrida**. **Es interesante**.
*No, **it's** not a **boring** profession. **It's interesting**.*

1B.6 Use numbers 12–100

Numbers 12–100 13.1

12 doce	**17** diecisiete	**40** cuarenta	**90** noventa
13 trece	**18** dieciocho	**50** cincuenta	**100** cien
14 catorce	**19** diecinueve	**60** sesenta	
15 quince	**20** veinte	**70** setenta	
16 dieciséis	**30** treinta	**80** ochenta	

- Form numbers 21–29 by combining **veinti-** + [*numbers 1–9*]: **veintiuno**, **veintidós**, etc. Note that **veintidós** (*twenty-two*), **veintitrés** (*twenty-three*), and **veintiséis** (*twenty-six*) have a written accent.

Hay **veinticinco** estudiantes en la clase.
*There are **twenty-five** students in the class.*

- Form numbers 30 and higher as three separate words: **treinta/cuarenta**, etc. + **y** + [*numbers 1–9*]: **treinta y uno**, **treinta y dos**, etc.

- For numbers that end in **uno**, use **un** before masculine nouns and **una** before feminine nouns.

cuarenta y **un** abogados — *forty-one lawyers*
cincuenta y **una** cajeras — *fifty-one cashiers*

- Use **cien** before nouns or when counting. For numbers over one hundred, use **ciento**.

Hay **cien** técnicos y **ciento cinco** arquitectos.
*There are **one hundred** technicians and **one hundred five** architects.*

¡OJO! In Spanish, phone numbers are frequently given in pairs of numbers, such that the number **616 23 45 18** would be pronounced **seis, dieciséis, veintitrés, cuarenta y cinco, dieciocho.**

Share with students this easy way to remember which numbers have a written accent: any number from 16 to 29 that ends in **-s** carries an accent.
Although it is not as common, the numbers 16 through 19 and 21 through 29 can be written as three words: **diez y seis, veinte y uno,** etc.

G10 Remind students that the adjectives **interesante** and **estresante** have only two forms (singular and plural) and do not have distinct masculine and feminine forms.

¡Póngalo en práctica!

G10 Use adjectives to give your opinion of these majors.

Modelo: ciencias políticas
Ciencias políticas es una carrera estresante.

1. química
2. historia
3. economía
4. literatura
5. biología
6. informática

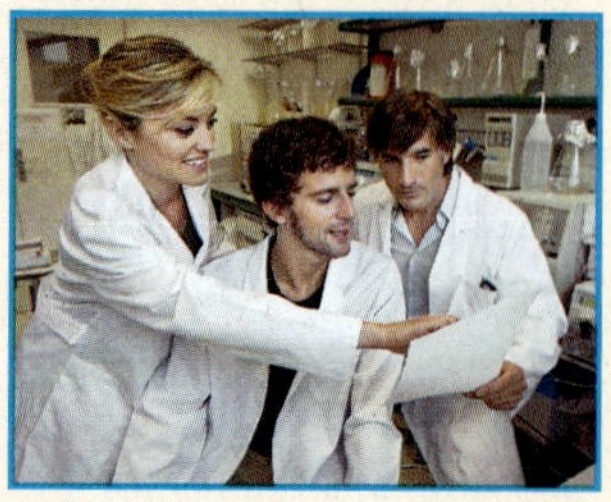

G11 Write out these numbers.

1. **48** cuarenta y ocho
2. **72** setenta y dos
3. **28** veintiocho
4. **81** ochenta y uno
5. **55** cincuenta y cinco
6. **63** sesenta y tres

G12 Practice giving these phone numbers.
Suggested answers:

915 44 24 13	nueve, quince, cuarenta y cuatro, veinticuatro, trece
614 81 90 90	seis, catorce, ochenta y uno, noventa, noventa
523 68 55 26	cinco, ventitrés, sesenta y ocho, cincuenta y cinco, veintiséis
937 70 33 51	nueve, treinta y siete, setenta, treinta y tres, cincuenta y uno
802 22 18 04	ocho, cero, dos, veintidós, dieciocho, cero, cuatro
025 70 20 90	cero, venticinco, setenta, veinte, noventa

Practice more at **vhlcentral.com.**

VOCABULARIO

Hablamos

¿Qué lenguas hablas?	*What languages do you speak?*
se habla(n)	*is/are spoken*
18:00 h	*6:00 p.m.*
abril	*April*
el alemán	*German*
la cafetería	*café; cafeteria*
el catalán	*Catalan*
el chino	*Chinese*
la conversación	*conversation*
el coreano	*Korean*
el español	*Spanish*
el francés	*French*
el idioma	*language*
el inglés	*English*
el intercambio	*exchange*
el italiano	*Italian*
el japonés	*Japanese*
la nacionalidad	*nationality*
Pekín	*Beijing*
la plaza	*square*
el portugués	*Portuguese*
estudiar	*to study*
hablar	*to speak*
alemán/alemana	*German*
canadiense	*Canadian*
chino/a	*Chinese*
coreano/a	*Korean*
estadounidense	*American*
francés/francesa	*French*
inglés/inglesa	*English*
italiano/a	*Italian*
portugués/ portuguesa	*Portuguese*
e	*and* (before **i** *or* **hi** + consonant)

Profesiones y trabajos

¿A qué te dedicas?	*What do you do (for work)?*
¿Cuál es tu número de teléfono?	*What is your phone number?*
¡Qué interesante!	*How interesting!*
el/la abogado/a	*lawyer*
el amo/a de casa	*homemaker*
el banco	*bank*
la biología	*biology*
el/la cajero/a	*cashier*
la carrera	*major*
las ciencias políticas	*political science*
la economía	*economics*
la guía	*guide(book)*
la historia	*history*
el hospital	*hospital*
la informática	*computer science*
el/la ingeniero/a	*engineer*
la literatura	*literature*
el/la médico/a	*doctor*
la profesión	*profession*
el/la profesor(a)	*teacher*
el/la psicólogo/a	*psychologist*
la química	*chemistry*
el/la secretario/a	*secretary*
el sumario	*table of contents*
el/la técnico/a informático/a	*computer technician*
el (teléfono) celular	*cell phone*
el trabajo	*job*
trabajar	*to work*
aburrido/a	*boring*
divertido/a	*fun*
estresante	*stressful*
interesante	*interesting*
también	*too, as well*

Joan, un catalán políglota

el apellido	*last name*
la clase	*class*
el euskera	*Basque (language)*
el foro	*forum*
la foto(grafía)	*photo(graph)*
el gallego	*Galician (language)*
el guaraní	*Guarani*
el/la guía (turístico/a)	*(tour) guide*
el nombre	*name*
País Vasco	*Basque Country*
la persona	*person*
el quechua	*Quechua*
el/la turista	*tourist*
buscar	*to look for*
indígena	*indigenous, native*
internacional	*international*
políglota	*polyglot, multilingual*
claro	*of course*

Point out that the word **e** (*and*) is used instead of **y** in order to avoid the repetition of the **i** sound. Ask students to come up with phrases that would require them to use **e** instead of **y**. (Ex: **divertido e interesante**; **francés e inglés**)

Variación léxica

claro ↔ **por supuesto** ↔ **desde luego**

el euskera ↔ **el vasco**

la lengua ↔ **el idioma**

el/la médico/a ↔ **el/la doctor(a)**

políglota ↔ **plurilingüe**

Tell students that they may encounter the alternate feminine form **la médico**. However, **la médica** or **la doctora** are the preferred words used to refer to a female doctor.

Vocabulario útil

Chao./Chau. *Bye.*
¿Qué onda? *What's up?*
¿Cómo te va? *How are you doing? (fam.)*
¿Cómo le va? *How are you doing? (form.)*
el/la amigo/a *friend*
el abrazo *hug*
el apretón de manos *handshake*
el beso *kiss*

el ayuntamiento *city hall*
la plaza *square*

Suggestion Have students read through the **Vocabulario útil** and ask them to identify which sayings they would use to greet a friend. Encourage them to refer to the preliminary lesson for additional ideas.

Suggestion Ask heritage speakers to share their experiences with certain elements described in the article, such as decreased personal space and air kisses.

LECTURA

Saludos y besos en los países hispanos

In Spanish-speaking countries, kissing on the cheek is a customary way to greet friends and family members. Even when people are introduced for the first time, it is common for them to kiss, particularly in non-business settings. Whereas North Americans maintain considerable personal space when greeting, Spaniards and Latin Americans tend to decrease their personal space and give one or two kisses (**besos**) on the cheek, sometimes accompanied by a handshake (**apretón de manos**) or a hug (**abrazo**). In formal business settings, where associates do not know one another on a personal level, a simple handshake is appropriate.

Greeting someone with a **beso** varies according to gender and region. Men generally greet each other with a hug or warm handshake, with the exception of Argentina, where male friends and relatives lightly kiss on the cheek. Greetings between men and women, and between women, generally include kissing, but can differ depending on the country and context.

Estrategia

Using charts and tables

Charts and tables are a helpful way to organize and summarize information in an easy-to-reference format. They allow you to see patterns in data and can provide interesting supplementary information to a reading. Creating your own tables can also be a useful study method. For this reading, you can create a table with the countries mentioned and list the common greetings next to the country names. You can later use the table you created to study and review the readings.

1 How do you greet different people?

	beso	abrazo	apretón de manos
un amigo			
una amiga			
un abogado			
una profesora			

2 Indicate how these people are likely to greet each other according to the reading.

un abrazo	un beso
un apretón de manos	dos besos

Matías y Marcos, amigos (Argentina)
un beso

Marta y Eduardo, abogados (Bolivia)
un apretón de manos

John y Lauren, amigos (EE.UU.)
un abrazo/un beso

Suggestion Ask students to research a famous plaza in Latin America or Spain. Have them prepare a brief oral report about the plaza's key features, including its location, when it was built, what it is used for today, and important surrounding landmarks. Encourage them to include a photo.

In Spain, it is customary to give **dos besos**, starting with the right cheek first. In Latin American countries, including Mexico, Costa Rica, Colombia, and Chile, a greeting consists of a single "air kiss" on the right cheek. Peruvians also "air kiss," but strangers will simply shake hands. In Colombia, female acquaintances tend to simply pat each other on the right forearm or shoulder.

Tendencias

País	Beso	País	Beso
Argentina	💋	España	💋 💋
Bolivia	~~💋~~	México	💋
Chile	💋	Paraguay	💋 💋
Colombia	💋	Puerto Rico	💋
El Salvador	💋	Venezuela	💋 / 💋 💋

► La plaza principal

In the Spanish-speaking world, public space is treasured. Small city and town life revolves around the **plaza principal**. Often surrounded by cathedrals or municipal buildings like the **ayuntamiento,** the pedestrian **plaza** is designated as a central meeting place for family and friends. During warmer months, when outdoor cafés usually line the **plaza**, it is a popular spot to have a leisurely cup of coffee, chat, and people watch. One of the most famous town squares is the **Plaza Mayor** in the university town of Salamanca, Spain. Students gather underneath its famous clock tower to meet up with friends or simply take a coffee break.

Estrategia

Doing Internet research in Spanish

When you do Internet research in Spanish, in addition to using Spanish search words, you can adjust the settings of your browser so that it only searches sites that contain Spanish content. If you do not know the Spanish for the keywords you are looking for, use a good online dictionary. Avoid conducting your search in English and using an automatic translator to get the information in Spanish.

3 Two of the people in the photos in **Actividad 2** meet in a **plaza.** With a partner, write a brief conversation between them and act it out.

PROYECTO

Mapa de saludos

As you have learned, greetings can vary quite a bit from country to country. Prepare a greetings map to share with the class.

- Choose the region you will focus on (the world, Latin America, etc.).
- Research greetings in countries other than those in the reading.
- Add labels in Spanish for countries and greetings.
- Include a photo of two people from one of the countries greeting each other.

Flash Cultura

Encuentros en la plaza

You have learned about greetings and **plazas**. In this episode of **Flash Cultura**, you will learn more about how people greet each other in Argentina and about the plazas in Buenos Aires.

Suggestion Before viewing, ask students to predict what they will see and hear in a video about people meeting up in city squares in Buenos Aires.

Estrategia

Looking at labels

When you are watching **Flash Cultura** episodes, pay attention to the labels that appear on the screen. These will point out important information and names of places and monuments. You can pause the video and write down the labels. This video is about socializing in the city squares in Buenos Aires. As the different squares appear on the screen, what labels do you expect to see?

Vocabulario útil

la aventura *adventure*
Hasta pronto. *See you later.*
Mucho gusto. *Nice to meet you.*
el/la presentador(a) *presenter, host*
¡Qué bueno verte! *So good to see you!*
¡Cuánto tiempo! *Long time no see.*

Suggestion Ask students to think of expressions they already know that are similar to **Hasta pronto.**

1. Where do you and your friends meet up? Are there public places where you get together? How do you greet people when you first meet them? Discuss your experiences with a partner.

2. Watch this **Flash Cultura** episode. While you watch the video, pay attention to the on-screen labels.

1 **Today we are at the Plaza de Mayo.**

2 **—Hola.**
—¿Cómo estás?
—¡Cuánto tiempo!

3. Mark the greetings that you heard in the video.

1. Chau.	☐	4. Buenos días.	☐
2. Hola.	☑	5. Mucho gusto.	☑
3. ¿Qué tal?	☑	6. Adiós.	☐

4. Indicate whether each statement is true (**verdadero**) or false (**falso**).

	V	F
1. La presentadora habla inglés.	☑	☐
2. Gonzalo es de Estados Unidos.	☐	☑
3. Mark es de Estados Unidos.	☑	☐
4. Gonzalo estudia en la Universidad de Buenos Aires.	☐	☑

5. With a partner, prepare a brief dialogue in which two people who have not seen each other in a while meet in a **plaza**.

Modelo:
• *¡Pedro!*
■ *Hola, Martín. ¡Cuánto tiempo! ¿Qué...?*

Estrategia

Using synonyms

When greeting someone or saying goodbye, use a variety of expressions. If the other person asks **¿Cómo estás?**, after responding, you can ask him/her **¿Qué tal?** instead of repeating the original question. If you have learned colloquial expressions from different countries, remember to use them in an appropriate context!

Practice more at **vhlcentral.com.**

Audio: Activities, Vocabulary
Video: *Flash Cultura*

Unidad 2

Juan Tomás, un taxista de Panamá

Lección 2A

ENTRE EL NORTE Y EL SUR

Lección 2B

ESPECIALIDAD DE LA CASA

Rosa, camarera del bar El rey de la tapa

Los estudios

AVANCE

2A

Suggestion Point out the map and ask students what region is highlighted (Central America). Then explain that, although there are areas where Spanish is spoken in Belize, English is the official language as it is a former British colony.

ENTRE EL NORTE Y EL SUR

¡Viva Guatemala!

Distancias Entre Capitales de América Central

Km	BE	CG	SS	TE	MA	SJ	CP
BE	—	347	395	386	625	955	1357
CG	347	—	175	362	536	872	1351
SS	395	175	—	219	362	697	1178
TE	386	362	219	—	239	575	1013
MA	625	536	362	239	—	344	819
SJ	955	872	697	575	344	—	510
CP	1357	1351	1178	1013	819	510	—

Remind students that 1.6 kilometers are equivalent to one mile.

Plaza de la Constitución, Ciudad de Guatemala

Situar lugares

- ¿Dónde está Tegucigalpa?
- Está en el sur de Honduras.

2A.1 Interrogative **¿dónde?**
The verb **estar**

Expresar cantidades

100	cien
121	ciento veintiuno/a
200	doscientos/as
300	trescientos/as
400	cuatrocientos/as
500	quinientos/as
600	seiscientos/as
700	setecientos/as
800	ochocientos/as
900	novecientos/as
1000	mil

2A.2 Numbers 100–1,000

Vocabulario

1

entre *between*
el norte *north*
el sur *south*
¡Viva! *Long live . . . !*
el este *east*
el oeste *west*
la distancia *distance*
¿Dónde (está)...? *Where (is) . . . ?*

2

estar a... kilómetros de... *to be . . . kilometers from . . .*

4

cerca de *near*
lejos de *far from*
muy *very*

1 Look at the map and circle the option that best completes each statement.

1. Guatemala está en el (norte) / sur / este / oeste de América Central.
2. Panamá está en el norte / (sur) / este / oeste de América Central.
3. Managua está en el norte / sur / este / (oeste) de Nicaragua.

2 Listen to the recording and complete each statement with the missing city and distance.

1. San Salvador está a 362 kilómetros de Managua.
2. Ciudad de Panamá está a 1013 kilómetros de Tegucigalpa.
3. Managua está a 344 kilómetros de San José.
4. Belmopán está a 955 kilómetros de San José.
5. Ciudad de Guatemala está a 536 kilómetros de Managua.
6. San José está a 697 kilómetros de San Salvador.

Suggestion Emphasize that when expressing one thousand, the article **un** is never used. Write these numbers on the board and have volunteers read them aloud: 1000, 1039, 1500.

3 Refer to the distance chart and ask your partner about distances between pairs of cities in Central America.

Modelo:
- *¿Cuál es la distancia entre Managua y Belmopán?*
- *Seiscientos veinticinco kilómetros.*

3 Suggestion Before forming pairs, have volunteers identify the capital city that corresponds to each abbreviation in the chart.

4 Read these statements and check the ones that are true.

1. El Salvador está muy cerca de Honduras. ✓
2. Ciudad de Guatemala está muy lejos de Ciudad de Panamá. ✓
3. Panamá está muy cerca de Belice. ☐
4. Tegucigalpa está cerca de Ciudad de Guatemala. ✓

Indicar distancias e intensificar

San Salvador **está cerca de** Guatemala.

San Salvador **está lejos de** Belmopán.

San Salvador **está muy lejos** de San José.

San Salvador **está a** 897 km **de** San José.

2A.3 **estar cerca/lejos de muy** + [*adjective/adverb*]

Presentar y describir lugares

Ciudad de Guatemala es una ciudad fantástica.

El Palacio Nacional de la Cultura es **un** edificio famoso.

Los guatemaltecos son simpáticos.

2A.4 Article-noun-adjective agreement

2A.5 **ser/estar**
ser + [*descriptive adjective*]
estar + [*adverbs of place*]

Vocabulario

5

mayo *May*
señora (Sra.) *Mrs.*
la avenida *avenue*
la paz *peace*
México, D.F. *Mexico City*
bonito/a *pretty*
el lugar *place*
el parque *park*
la catedral *cathedral*
el edificio *building*
agradable *pleasant*
el barrio *neighborhood*
típico/a *typical*
antiguo/a *old*
el corazón *heart*
precioso/a *lovely*
el/la guatemalteco/a *Guatemalan*
simpático/a *nice*
el beso *kiss*
la capital, fantástico/a, la plaza, moderno/a

7

famoso/a, romántico/a

Ciudad de Guatemala, 26 de mayo

Hola, Lupe: Estoy en el sur de Guatemala, en la Ciudad de Guatemala, la capital. Está lejos de México, D.F., a 1060 kilómetros. Es una ciudad muy bonita, con lugares fantásticos: la Plaza de la Constitución (o Parque Central), la catedral y grandes edificios como el Palacio Nacional de la Cultura. El hotel es muy agradable y está en el Centro Histórico, un barrio típico muy antiguo en el centro. ¡Es una pequeña ciudad antigua en el corazón de una ciudad moderna! El centro de la ciudad es precioso. ¡Ah! Y los guatemaltecos ¡son muy simpáticos!

Un beso, Hugo

Sra. Guadalupe Henríquez
Avenida de la Paz, 4564
34453 México, D.F.
MÉXICO

5 Read the postcard and indicate whether each statement is true (**verdadero**) or false (**falso**). Compare your answers to a partner's.

5 Expansion Have students correct the false statements.

	V	F
1. Hugo está en la Ciudad de Guatemala.	✓	
2. El Centro Histórico es precioso.	✓	
3. La Plaza de la Constitución y el Parque Central son dos parques.		✓
4. El hotel está en un barrio moderno.		✓
5. Los guatemaltecos son muy simpáticos.	✓	

6 Choose the correct form of **ser** or **estar** to complete each sentence.

1. Antigua **es/está** una ciudad bonita.
2. Chichicastenango **es/está** cerca de la Ciudad de Guatemala.
3. Tikal **es/está** en Guatemala.
4. Cobán **es/está** una ciudad histórica.

7 Use these elements to write complete sentences with forms of **ser**.

Modelo: *El parque es romántico.*

el *la* *los* *las*

parque *hotel* *ciudad* *guatemaltecos* *plazas* *barrios*

es *son*

agradables *famoso* *simpáticos* *preciosa* *romántico* *bonitas*

MI EXPERIENCIA

8 Tell a classmate about your city or town.

GUIÓN DE TRABAJO

Se llama...

Está... → en el... (N/S/E/O)
a... kilómetros de...
cerca/lejos de...

Es (muy) ... → típico/a, romántico/a, fantástico/a, famoso/a, moderno/a, bonito/a, agradable, interesante, precioso/a, antiguo/a

Practice more at **vhlcentral.com.**

SAM: Actividades pp. 25–27

Cerca de casa

SAN JOSÉ HOY

CARTAS AL DIRECTOR

Vivo en el centro de la ciudad, cerca de la catedral. Mi barrio tiene unos lugares preciosos: museos, el ayuntamiento, la plaza, iglesias. Mi calle tiene bares y cafeterías... Todo es muy bonito y muy romántico, pero vivir en el centro también tiene problemas. Tenemos pocos parques y el tráfico es horrible. Mi casa está cerca de una discoteca y tenemos un ruido insoportable. Mi familia vive muy lejos, en la periferia, y su barrio es muy diferente: tiene parques, centros comerciales, polideportivos... y es tranquilo. ¡Mi esposo y yo vivimos en el centro, pero no somos unos privilegiados!

Lucía Olivas Gómez, San José

(Editorial de *SAN JOSÉ HOY*, 26 de mayo)

Hablar del lugar de residencia

- ¿**Vives** en el centro?
- No, **vivo** en la periferia.
- Nosotros **vivimos** en el centro y ellos **viven** en la periferia.

2A.6 Regular **-ir** verbs: **vivir**

Expresar posesión

Tengo **unas** postales de Nicoya.

San José **tiene unos** barrios muy bonitos.

2A.7 The verb **tener**
Indefinite articles (plural)

Vocabulario

9

- la carta al director *letter to the editor*
- el ayuntamiento *city hall*
- la iglesia *church*
- todo *everything*
- pocos/as *few*
- pero *but*
- vivir *to live*
- tiene *it has*
- la calle *street*
- la discoteca *disco, night club*
- el ruido *noise*
- insoportable *unbearable*
- la periferia *suburbs*
- el centro comercial *shopping mall*
- el polideportivo *sports center*

9 Read Lucía's letter to the editor and choose a title for it. Propose another title for the letter.

"EL CENTRO DE LA CIUDAD" **"VIVIR EN EL CENTRO"**

"BARRIOS CON PROBLEMAS"

10 a. Answer the questions using complete sentences. Sample answers:

- ¿Dónde vive Lucía? Vive en el centro de San José.
- ¿Dónde vive la familia de Lucía? Vive lejos, en la periferia de San José.

b. Now ask your partner about his/her neighborhood.

Modelo: • *¿Dónde vives?*
• *Vivo en... Vivo cerca/lejos de...*

11 Complete the chart with the missing forms of **vivir** from the letter.

yo	tú	usted, él, ella	nosotros/as	vosotros/as	ustedes, ellos/as
vivo	vives	vive	vivimos	vivís	viven

12 a. What problems does Lucía describe in her letter? Sample answer: El centro tiene pocos parques, tráfico horrible y ruido insoportable. No tiene centros comerciales o polideportivos.

Modelo: *El centro tiene... / no tiene...*

b. Underline all the forms of **tener** used in the letter. tiene, tenemos

13 Read the summary of Lucía's letter and circle the appropriate articles.

El centro de San José tiene (1) unos/los lugares muy románticos, pero (2) un/el centro tiene también (3) el/un tráfico horrible y las calles con discotecas tienen (4) el/un ruido insoportable. La periferia es muy diferente; tiene (5) los/unos centros comerciales y polideportivos. Está lejos, pero no tiene (6) un/el ruido del centro.

13 Expansion Have students work in pairs and reread the letter to the editor. Have them write a list of the city's features that are unique to Latin American cities. Have pairs share their lists with the class and write a master list on the board. Lastly, have pairs identify the problems that Lucía mentions and discuss whether these problems are universal or specific to Latin America.

Iglesias

Parques

Cafeterías y restaurantes

Museos

Centros comerciales

Polideportivos

Expresar posesión

Mi barrio no tiene parques.

¿Tu barrio está en el centro?

Su ciudad es preciosa.

2A.8 Possessives (singular)

Vocabulario ***cont.***

el/la privilegiado/a *lucky person*

el problema, el tráfico, horrible, la familia, diferente, tranquilo/a

12

tener *to have*

16

la tranquilidad *peace, tranquility*

ideal

14 a. Look at the photos and ask your partner what attractions his/her neighborhood has. Then, tell your partner about your neighborhood.

Modelo: *¿Tu barrio tiene...?*

b. Now tell the class about your partner's neighborhood.

Modelo: *Su barrio tiene... / no tiene...*

15 Work with a partner to write a letter to the editor of your local paper about two problems in your neighborhood. Share your letter with the class.

Sr. Director:

15 Draw attention to the greeting used in the model letter. Ask students what form of punctuation is used (a colon, or **dos puntos**). Explain that a colon is always used to open formal and informal written communication in Spanish, be it a letter, postcard, e-mail, etc.

Lugares de encuentro

Most cities in Spanish-speaking countries have a central **plaza,** where important government and religious buildings are located, where official ceremonies and celebrations are held, and where people gather to socialize or hold markets. Famous **plazas** in San José include Plaza de la Cultura and Plaza de la Democracia.

Have each student choose a Central American capital and research the names of major plazas in that city. Ask them to research what notable monuments, statues, buildings, etc., are located in each plaza.

MI EXPERIENCIA

16 Describe your ideal neighborhood or town.

Before completing the activity, decide whether each of the words listed is masculine or feminine, and list them under the appropriate definite articles.

museo, iglesia, parque, plaza, discoteca, centro comercial, polideportivo, catedral, ayuntamiento

el	la

GUIÓN DE TRABAJO

Mi barrio ideal

tiene...	no tiene...
museos	ruido
parques	tráfico
plazas	problemas
centros comerciales	tranquilidad
polideportivos	discotecas
ayuntamiento	monumentos

Practice more at **vhlcentral.com.**

SAM: Actividades pp. 28–30

Juan Tomás, taxista en la Ciudad de Panamá desde 2001, enamorado de su ciudad y su profesión.

Juan Tomás, un taxista de Panamá

Juan Tomás: *El tráfico en la Ciudad de Panamá no es muy bueno, la verdad. El centro de la ciudad tiene problemas de tráfico, de ruidos, de obras... pero es muy bonito y tiene de todo: restaurantes, monumentos, paseos, tiendas... Vivir en Panamá es fantástico, con sus fiestas, su gente, su buen tiempo... La vida aquí es muy cómoda; tienes mucha calidad de vida.*

Entrevistador: Juan Tomás, ¿y cómo es el trabajo de taxista en la Ciudad de Panamá?

Juan Tomás: *Bueno... Es un trabajo agradable, muy bonito. Escucho la radio, hablo con la gente, panameños, turistas...*

Entrevistador: ¿Y tienes clientes extranjeros?

Juan Tomás: ¡Claro! Un abrazo a todos los extranjeros y para los panameños y las panameñas. ¡Viva Panamá!

Successful Language Learning Remind students to scan an unfamiliar text for cognates to determine the type of information it contains. Have volunteers scan the taxi license for cognates; write them on the board.

Draw attention to the license number and point out the abbreviation for **número.**

Vocabulario

17

desde *since*
enamorado/a de *in love with*
..., la verdad *to tell the truth*
las obras *construction*
el paseo *walkway, path*
la tienda *store*
la fiesta *festival*
la gente *people*
el buen tiempo *good weather*
cómodo/a *comfortable*
mucho/a *much, a lot*
la calidad de vida *quality of life*
¿Cómo es...? *What is . . . like?*
el trabajo *work*
bueno... *well . . .*
escuchar la radio *to listen to the radio*
hablar con la gente *to talk to people*
el/la panameño/a *Panamanian*
extranjero/a *foreign*
el abrazo *hug*
la central *main office*
n.º (el número) *number*
el domicilio *home address*
el/la cliente, la licencia

19

ocupado/a *busy*
allí *there*

17 Look at Juan Tomás's taxi license and answer these questions. Suggested answers:

1. ¿Dónde vive? Vive en Calle Colón, 3.
2. ¿Dónde trabaja? Trabaja en (la Ciudad de) Panamá.
3. ¿Cuál es el número de su licencia? El número de su licencia es 00-BA-957.

MUNICIPIO DE PANAMÁ

CENTRAL DE RADIO-TAXI

LICENCIA DE TAXISTA:
N.º 00-BA-957

Nombre:
Juan Tomás Álvarez

Domicilio:
Calle Colón, 3
Panamá, Ciudad Capital

18 Read the interview and answer the questions.
Suggested answers:

1. ¿Qué problemas tiene el centro de la ciudad?
   Tiene problemas de tráfico, de ruidos y de obras.
2. ¿Qué lugares interesantes tiene?
   Tiene restaurantes, monumentos, paseos y tiendas.
3. ¿Cómo es vivir en la Ciudad de Panamá?
   La vida es muy cómoda; la gente tiene mucha calidad de vida.

19 Listen to the call from the Radio-Taxi dispatch and answer the questions.

Central: Central de Radio-Taxi. ¿Dónde estás?
Taxista: Estoy en el centro, muy cerca de la Universidad, en la Avenida José de Fábrega.
Central: ¿Estás ocupado?
Taxista: No.
Central: Hay un cliente en la calle 53 Oeste, número 43.
Taxista: Estoy cerca; estoy allí en tres minutos.
Central: Perfecto. Gracias.

1. ¿Dónde está el taxista? Está en el centro, muy cerca de la Universidad, en la Avenida José de Fábrega.
2. ¿Dónde está el cliente? Está en la calle 53 Oeste, número 43.

20 In pairs, practice reading the interview aloud, taking turns with the different roles. Then role-play a similar conversation for the class.

21 Panamanians are very proud of their city. Interview a classmate to find out what he/she thinks about his/her city or region. Also answer his/her questions.

Modelo: *¿La gente de tu ciudad está orgullosa de ella? ¿Y tú?*

Show students that **ella** in this sentence means *it*, referring to **tu ciudad**.

Vocabulario *cont.*

perfecto/a

(21)

orgulloso/a *proud*

(22)

la población *population*
el/la habitante *inhabitant*
el clima *climate*
el calor *heat*
el verano *summer*
el frío *cold*
el invierno *winter*
la superficie *area*
la universidad *university*
el ambiente *atmosphere*
único/a *unique*
el/la universitario/a *college student*
joven (*pl.* jóvenes) *young*
los jóvenes *young people*
además *in addition*
importante, la pirámide, las ruinas

Ask students if they know what UNAM stands for (**Universidad Nacional Autónoma de México**). Tell them that it is one of the largest univerisities in the world, with an enrollment exceeding 300,000.

Point out that Mexico City metropolitan area has a population of approximately 20 million.

22 a. Read the excerpt from a tourbook about Mexico City. Underline the key pieces of information.

MÉXICO, D.F.

Draw attention to the population statistic for Mexico City. Point out the use of spaces instead of commas, as in English.

Ciudad: *México, D.F.*
Población: *8 842 000 habitantes*
Clima: *calor en verano y frío en invierno*
Superficie: *1485 km²*
País: *México*

Tell students that km² is **kilómetros cuadrados.**

México, D.F. es la capital de México. Está en en el centro del país, al este del océano Pacífico y al oeste del golfo de México. Tiene barrios muy típicos, como Coyoacán, San Ángel y Chapultepec, y una universidad muy antigua, la UNAM. También tiene monumentos importantes: el Ángel de la Independencia, el Monumento a Benito Juárez, el Monumento a la Revolución Mexicana y el Monumento a los Niños Héroes. El ambiente es único: universitarios, jóvenes, turistas, etc. La gente es muy agradable. Además, muy cerca de la ciudad están las pirámides de Teotihuacán, y se pueden visitar las ruinas.

b. How does this guide describe Mexico City? List the adjectives used in the description. típicos, antigua, importantes, único, agradable

c. Imagine you work in a travel agency. Choose a city you know well and describe it to a client. Tell him/her where it is and follow the model description of Mexico City to describe your preferences and any places of interest.

- *La ciudad es...*
- *Tiene...*
- *Está...*
- *La gente es...*

[b] [v]

23 a. Listen to these place names. What sound do they have in common?

Parque **B**erlín	A**v**enida de **B**uenos Aires	Hotel Se**v**illa
Plaza de **B**ogotá	Catedral de **V**alencia	**B**arrio de Río A**b**ajo

- In Spanish, **b** and **v** are pronounced the same.

b. Now repeat the words to practice their pronunciation.

24 **Expansion** Have students choose one of the pairs of cities and research them. Ask them to prepare a brief report about each city, using the guidebook excerpt on this page as a model.

24 a. Many city names are repeated in several Spanish-speaking countries. Use the maps on pages xxxi–xxxii of your text and the Internet to identify at least two countries where you can find cities with each of these names.

Sample answers: Córdoba: España, Argentina; Santiago: España, Chile; Guadalajara: México, España; Toledo: España, Colombia, Estados Unidos; Mérida: México, España; San José: Costa Rica, Estados Unidos; Trujillo: República Dominicana, España; Santa Cruz: Estados Unidos, Bolivia; Trinidad: Cuba, Uruguay

Córdoba	Toledo	Trujillo
Santiago	Mérida	Santa Cruz
Guadalajara	San José	Trinidad

b. Ask a partner questions about the information he/she found.

Modelo:
- *¿Dónde está Córdoba?*
- *Córdoba está en .... y ....*

Practice more at **vhlcentral.com.**

SAM: Actividades pp. 31–34

For step 3, have students cross off any elements from their lists that are in conflict with each other. Also tell them to give their city a name that reflects its most prominent feature or some part of its history.

TAREA FINAL

Su ciudad ideal

Think: what is your ideal city like?

Es... Tiene... Está... Las personas son/La gente es...

List the characteristics of the city and describe what it does and does not have.

Compare your list with a partner's, and create a combined list.

Draw a map of your city, including labels for the sites and features you chose.

Write a description of your city and present your map to the class. Have students proofread their descriptions.

YO PUEDO...

- Puedo hablar de la localización geográfica de una ciudad.
  Think of a city in your country and say how far it is from other cities or towns.
- Puedo indicar la localización de mi vivienda.
  Tell where your home is.
- Puedo hablar de diferentes aspectos de una ciudad o un lugar.
  Talk about a city. Describe three interesting aspects.
- Puedo indicar posesión o pertenencia.
  Name three of your favorite things in your city or neighborhood.

Write three sentences.

Mi casa ....

....

....

....

Mis lugares preferidos:

....

....

....

GRAMÁTICA FUNCIONAL

2A.1 Indicate places

Interrogative **¿dónde?** 9
The verb **estar** 5.8.1

- To ask where a city or place is located, say ¿**Dónde está** + [*place*]? To answer, say [*place*] **está** + **en** + [*location*].

¿**Dónde está** Santander?	Santander **está en** el norte.
Where is Santander?	*Santander is in the North.*

- Use the verb **estar** (*to be*) to express location. **Estar** is an irregular verb, so you must memorize its forms.

ESTAR			
(yo)	estoy	(nosotros/as)	estamos
(tú)	estás	(vosotros/as)	estáis
(usted, él, ella)	está	(ustedes, ellos/as)	están

Fernando, ¿**dónde estás**?	**Estoy** en Antigua.
*Fernando, where **are** you?*	***I'm** in Antigua.*

2A.2 Express quantities

Numbers 100–1000 13.1

- These are the hundreds 100 to 1000. Note the spelling changes in 500, 700, and 900.

Números del 100 al 1000			
100	cien, 121 ciento...	**600**	seiscientos/as
200	doscientos/as	**700**	setecientos/as
300	trescientos/as	**800**	ochocientos/as
400	cuatrocientos/as	**900**	novecientos/as
500	quinientos/as	**1000**	mil

- The numbers 200 through 999 agree in gender with the noun they modify.

San José está a trescient**os** cuarenta y cuatro kilómetr**os** (doscient**as** catorce mill**as**) de Managua.

San José is three hundred forty-four kilometers (two hundred fourteen miles) from Managua.

2A.3 Indicate distances and intensify

estar + **cerca/lejos** + **de** 5.8.1, 11.7
muy + [*adverb/adjective*] 11.4

- Use **estar** + **cerca/lejos** + **de** to express relative distance.

Colón **está cerca de** la Ciudad de Panamá.
*Colón **is near** Panama City.*

Canadá **está lejos de** *Guatemala.*
*Canada **is far from** Guatemala.*

Point out the contraction **de + el = del**. Write a few cloze sentences on the board and have volunteers complete them. Ex: **Panamá está cerca .... Colombia. (de) La universidad está lejos .... centro. (del)**

- To intensify the meaning of an adjective or adverb, place **muy** (*very*) immediately in front of the adjective or adverb.

La playa es **muy** bonita y está **muy cerca** de la ciudad.
*The beach is **very** pretty and it is **very close** to the city.*

¡Póngalo en práctica!

G1 Complete each sentence with the appropriate form of **estar**.

1. Managua y León ...están... en el oeste de Nicaragua.
2. Puntarenas ...está... en Costa Rica.
3. Yo ...estoy... en San Diego.
4. ¿Dónde ...está... el Lago de Nicaragua?
5. Magdalena y tú ...están/estáis... en Colón.
6. Tú ...estás... en Panamá.
7. ¿Dónde ...están... Miguel y Jesús?
8. Ricardo y yo ...estamos... en California.

G2 Write out these numbers.

1. 339 trescientos treinta y nueve
2. 437 cuatrocientos treinta y siete
3. 555 quinientos cincuenta y cinco
4. 738 setecientos treinta y ocho
5. 945 novecientos cuarenta y cinco
6. 226 doscientos veintiséis

G3 Write out these distances in **millas** or **kilómetros**.

1. 222 km doscientos veintidós kilómetros
2. 333 mi trescientas treinta y tres millas
3. 500 mi quinientas millas
4. 780 km setecientos ochenta kilómetros
5. 850 km ochocientos cincuenta kilómetros
6. 160 mi ciento sesenta millas

G4 Use the cues to write complete sentences.

1. Puebla / cerca / la Ciudad de México
   Puebla está cerca de la Ciudad de México.
2. Cuba / muy lejos / España
   Cuba está muy lejos de España.
3. Maracaibo / lejos / Arequipa
   Maracaibo está lejos de Arequipa.
4. Ciudad Juárez / muy cerca / El Paso
   Ciudad Juárez está muy cerca de El Paso.

Practice more at **vhlcentral.com.**

GRAMÁTICA FUNCIONAL

2A.4 2A.5 Present and describe places

Definite articles 3.1 **ser** + [*adjective*] 5.8.1
Gender agreement with articles and adjectives 3.1, 4.1

- Use a definite article (**el**, **la**, **los**, or **las**) to refer to a specific noun. The definite article must correspond to the gender and number of the noun it modifies.

	singular	plural
masculino	el parque	los parques
femenino	la plaza	las plazas

- Adjectives must also agree with nouns in gender and number.

La plaza es bonita.
The square is pretty.

Los barrios son bonitos.
The neighborhoods are pretty.

- Use **ser** + [*adjective*] to describe the characteristics of a person, place or thing.

2A.6 Talk about your place of residence

Regular **-ir** verbs: **vivir** 5.1.1 Prepositions: **en** 10.11

- Use the regular verb **vivir** (*to live*) to talk about where people live. Other regular **-ir** verbs follow this same conjugation pattern.

VIVIR			
(yo)	vivo	(nosotros/as)	vivimos
(tú)	vives	(vosotros/as)	vivís
(usted, él, ella)	vive	(ustedes, ellos/as)	viven

- Use **¿Dónde** + [**vivir**]? to ask where someone lives. To answer, say [**vivir**] + **en** + [*place*].

¿Dónde vives, Ángel?
Where do you live, Ángel?

Vivo en San Juan.
I live in San Juan.

2A.7 2A.8 Express possession

The verb **tener** 5.1.2 Indefinite articles (plural) 3.2
Possessive adjectives (singular) 8.1

- Use the irregular verb **tener** (*to have*) to express possession.

TENER			
(yo)	tengo	(nosotros/as)	tenemos
(tú)	tienes	(vosotros/as)	tenéis
(usted, él, ella)	tiene	(ustedes, ellos/as)	tienen

- Use the plural indefinite article **unos/as** to express the idea *some*.

Madrid tiene **unas** plazas bonitas y **unos** parques tranquilos.
*Madrid has **some** pretty squares and **some** quiet parks.*

- Use the possessive adjectives **mi** (*my*), **tu** (*your*), and **su** (*your* [form.]/*his/her/its*) with singular nouns to indicate to whom something belongs.

mi barrio
my neighborhood

tu ciudad
your city

su pueblo
your/his/her/its town

¡Póngalo en práctica!

G5 Form sentences with the words provided. Remember to include a definite article and the correct form of the verb **ser**.

1. chicos / simpáticos
   Los chicos son simpáticos.
2. ciudad / única
   La ciudad es única.
3. monumentos / antiguos
   Los monumentos son antiguos.
4. plaza / agradable
   La plaza es agradable.
5. tráfico / horrible
   El tráfico es horrible.

G6 Complete the conversation using the appropriate forms of **vivir**.

- ¿Dónde (1)...vive... María José?
- (2)...Vive... en Sevilla.
- Y tú, ¿dónde (3)...vives...?
- (4)...Vivo... en Dublín. Vosotros, ¿dónde (5)...vivís... ?
- (6)...Vivimos... en Córdoba.
- ¡Qué bien! Es una ciudad preciosa.

Suggestion Write names of famous people on the board whom you know are not at home or in their home city (Ex: **el Presidente de este país, tu familia y tú**). Have volunteers make statements. Ex: **El Presidente vive en Washington, pero ahora está en Berlín. Mi familia y yo vivimos en Boston, pero ahora mis padres están en Miami y yo estoy en Nueva York.**

G7 Complete each sentence with the appropriate possessive adjective.

1. Vivo aquí; es ...mi... casa.
2. Usted vive aquí; es ...su... ciudad.
3. Tú vives aquí; es ...tu... calle.
4. José vive aquí; es ...su... pueblo.

G8 Complete the conversation with the appropriate form of **tener** and indefinite articles.

- Yo (1)...tengo... una casa en Miami.
- Mi amigo Antonio también (2)...tiene... una casa en Miami. Es una ciudad fascinante.
- Sí, tiene (3)...unos... barrios muy interesantes y (4)...unas... playas preciosas.

Practice more at **vhlcentral.com.**

VOCABULARIO

¡Viva Guatemala!

¿Dónde?	*where?*
¿Dónde está...?	*Where is . . . ?*
estar a... kilómetros de...	*to be . . . kilometers from . . .*
señora (Sra.)	*Mrs.*
¡Viva!	*Long live . . . !*
la avenida	*avenue*
el barrio	*neighborhood*
el beso	*kiss*
la capital	*capital*
la catedral	*cathedral*
el corazón	*heart*
la distancia	*distance*
el edificio	*building*
el este	*east*
el/la guatemalteco/a	*Guatemalan*
el kilómetro	*kilometer*
el lugar	*place*
mayo	*May*
México, D.F.	*Mexico City*
el norte	*north*
el oeste	*west*
el parque	*park*
la paz	*peace*
la plaza	*plaza, square*
el sur	*south*
agradable	*pleasant*
antiguo/a	*old*
bonito/a	*pretty*
famoso/a	*famous*
fantástico/a	*fantastic*
moderno/a	*modern*
precioso/a	*lovely*
romántico/a	*romantic*
simpático/a	*nice*
típico/a	*typical*
cerca de	*near*
entre	*between*
lejos de	*far from*
muy	*very*

Cerca de casa

tiene	*it has*
el ayuntamiento	*city hall*
la calle	*street*
la carta al director	*letter to the editor*
el centro comercial	*shopping mall*
la discoteca	*disco, night club*
la familia	*family*
la iglesia	*church*
la periferia	*suburbs*
el polideportivo	*sports center*
el/la privilegiado/a	*lucky person*
el problema	*problem*
el ruido	*noise*
el tráfico	*traffic*
la tranquilidad	*peace, tranquility*
todo	*everything*
tener	*to have*
vivir	*to live*
diferente	*different*
horrible	*horrible*
ideal	*ideal*
insoportable	*unbearable*
pocos/as	*few*
tranquilo/a	*calm, quiet*
pero	*but*

Successful Language Learning Encourage students to write sentences about their own lives using the vocabulary words they have learned.

Suggestion Point out the words **joven** and **jóvenes**. Explain to students that the written accent on the plural form is necessary in order to maintain the spoken stress on the first syllable of the word. Remind students that written accent marks are an important part of a word's spelling.

Juan Tomás

bueno...	*well . . .*
..., la verdad	*to tell you the truth*
¿Cómo es...?	*What is . . . like?*
escuchar la radio	*to listen to the radio*
enamorado/a de	*in love with*
hablar con la gente	*to talk to people*
el abrazo	*hug*
el ambiente	*atmosphere*
el buen tiempo	*good weather*
la calidad de vida	*quality of life*
el calor	*heat*
la central	*main office*
el/la cliente	*client*
el clima	*climate*
el domicilio	*home address*
la fiesta	*festival*
el frío	*cold*
la gente	*people*
el/la habitante	*inhabitant*
el invierno	*winter*
los jóvenes	*young people*
la licencia	*license*
n.º (el número)	*number*
las obras	*construction*
el/la panameño/a	*Panamanian*
el paseo	*walkway, path*
la pirámide	*pyramid*
la población	*population*
las ruinas	*ruins*
la superficie	*area*
la tienda	*store*
el trabajo	*work*
la universidad	*university*
el/la universitario/a	*college student*
el verano	*summer*
cómodo/a	*comfortable*
extranjero/a	*foreign*
importante	*important*
joven (*pl.* jóvenes)	*young*
mucho/a	*much, a lot*
ocupado/a	*busy*
orgulloso/a	*proud*
perfecto/a	*perfect*
único/a	*unique*
allí	*there*
además	*in addition*
desde	*since*

Variación léxica

el ayuntamiento ⟷ **la intendencia** (*Arg., Uru.*) ⟷ **la municipalidad**

la periferia ⟷ **las afueras**

el polideportivo ⟷ **el complejo deportivo** ⟷ **el parque de recreación y deportes**

2B ESPECIALIDAD DE LA CASA

At the time of publication, one U.S. dollar is equivalent to .77 euro. Encourage students to research the current value of the euro.

Café con leche

Pedir y pagar en una cafetería

- ¿Qué desea tomar?
- Un té y un cruasán.
- ¿Cuánto es?
- Son 3 euros.

2B.1 Interrogative **¿cuánto?**

Vocabulario

(1)
la cafetería *café*
el té *tea*
el desayuno *breakfast*
la tostada *toast*
la mantequilla *butter*
por favor *please*
el cruasán *croissant*
el zumo/jugo de naranja (*Esp./Amér. L.*) *orange juice*
natural *fresh*
¿Qué desean tomar? *What would you like (to have)?*
el café solo *black coffee*
¿Cuánto es? *How much is it?*
Son 9 euros. *It's 9 euros.*
el queso *cheese*
el pan *bread*
el aceite de oliva *olive oil*
el/la compañero/a *partner*
los cereales, los churros, el sándwich, el yogur

(2)
el/la camarero/a *waiter/waitress*

1 a. Alicia and Carmen are having breakfast at a café in Alicante, Spain. Read their conversation with the waitress, and check off the items they order.

un café solo	✓
un té	
un café con leche	
un chocolate	✓
un zumo de naranja	✓

un sándwich de jamón y queso	
churros	✓
cereales	
un yogur	
un cruasán	
una tostada con mantequilla y mermelada	✓
pan tostado con aceite de oliva	

b. What would you order for breakfast at **Cafetería Levante**? And your partner?

- YO:
- MI COMPAÑERO/A:

2 Look at the menu and read each mini-conversation; then fill in the blanks to tell what each person ordered at **Cafetería Levante**.

- Por favor, camarero, ¿cuánto es?
- Son 3 euros.

Café con ....leche.... y tostada con ....mantequilla.... y ....mermelada.... .

- ¿Cuánto es, por favor?
- Son 6 euros.

....Chocolate.... con ....churros.... y zumo de ....naranja natural.... .

3 In groups of three, role-play a conversation at a café.

Hola, ¿qué...?

Yo ....

Yo ....

¿Cuánto ....?

Son ....

Ask students which breakfast items they find most appealing.

1001 Cafés

Normalmente, los españoles desayunan poco; beben una taza de café o té y siempre comen algo dulce: *galletas*, *bollería* o una *tostada* con *mantequilla y mermelada*. A veces desayunan una tostada con *aceite de oliva*, *cereales*, *yogur*.... También beben *zumo de naranja natural*. Tienen muchas formas de tomar café: café solo, café con leche, largo de café (el doble de café), corto de café (poco café), descafeinado (sin cafeína), cortado (con unas gotas de leche), café con hielo... El fin de semana es frecuente desayunar algo especial. Por ejemplo, en Madrid, chocolate con *churros* y, en Andalucía, *pan tostado con aceite y tomate*.

Hablar de las comidas del día y expresar frecuencia

- Nosotros **bebemos** té. ¿Y vosotros?
- Yo **bebo** café y ella **bebe** jugo de naranja.
- **Pedro, ¿dónde desayunas?**
- **Siempre** desayuno en casa.
- ¿Usted almuerza en casa?
- **Normalmente** almuerzo en un restaurante. A veces, ceno fuera.

2B.2 Regular **-er** verbs: **beber**

2B.3 Adverbs of frequency **almorzar** (o:ue)

Vocabulario

(4)

normalmente *normally*
desayunar *to eat breakfast*
poco/a *little*
beber *to drink*
la taza *mug, coffee cup*
siempre *always*
comer *to eat; to eat lunch (Esp.)*
algo *something*
dulce *sweet*
la galleta *cookie*
la bollería (Esp.) *pastries*
la gota *drop*
el hielo *ice*
(el fin de) semana (f.) *week(end)*
frecuente *common*
el doble, la cafeína, el descafeinado, especial

(6)

a veces *sometimes*
almorzar (o:ue) *to eat lunch*
cenar *to eat supper*
en casa *at home*
fuera *out*

4 a. What types of coffee are listed in the reading?

1. café solo
2. café con leche
3. largo de café
4. corto de café
5. descafeinado
6. cortado
7. café con hielo

b. Match the words in italics to the items shown in the photo.

1. yogur
2. pan tostado con aceite y tomate
3. churros
4. tostada
5. bollería
6. mantequilla
7. cereales
8. aceite de oliva
9. mermelada
10. galletas
11. zumo de naranja natural

5 Find the forms of the verb **beber** and write the missing verb endings on the coffee cups.

BEB-

-O -ES -E -emos -ÉIS -en

6 Listen to the interview and connect items from each column to show what you learned about Lucía's dining habits.

Siempre	desayuna	en casa.
Normalmente	almuerza	fuera.
A veces	cena	

MI EXPERIENCIA

7 Ask your classmates about their eating habits and report your findings to the class.

GUIÓN DE TRABAJO

Siempre.... Normalmente... A veces...

¿Desayunas en casa o en una cafetería?

¿Bebes café, té, jugo...? ¿Qué comes: una tostada, cereales, un huevo, un sándwich de jamón/queso...?

¿Cenas en casa o fuera?

El fin de semana...

¿Dónde almuerzas?

En un restaurante, en casa, en el trabajo...

Practice more at **vhlcentral.com.**

SAM: Actividades pp. 35–37

Pedir y pagar en un restaurante

- ¿Qué desea?
- De **primer plato**, lentejas, y de **plato principal**, dorada, por favor.
- ¿De beber?
- Agua.

...

- ¡Camarero!, por favor, **otra** botella de agua.

...

- **De postre**, un flan.
- ¿Desea **algo más**?
- No, **nada más**, gracias. La cuenta, por favor.

2B.4 **otro/a; algo/nada más**

Vocabulario

8

- **¿Algo más?** *Anything else?*
- **Nada más, gracias.** *Nothing else, thanks.*
- **la cuenta** *bill*
- **el menú del día** *fixed-price menu*
- **el primer plato** *first course*
- **el plato principal** *main course*
- **el postre** *dessert*
- **la bebida** *beverage*
- **la ensalada de la casa** *house salad*
- **las lentejas con chorizo** *lentils with chorizo (sausage)*
- **el arroz con verduras** *rice with vegetables*
- **la sopa de pescado** *fish soup*
- **la dorada** *sea bream (type of fish)*
- **el filete de ternera** *filet of veal*
- **la patata (*Esp.*)** *potato*
- **la albóndiga** *meatball*
- **el bacalao en salsa** *cod with sauce*
- **el helado** *ice cream*
- **la fruta** *fruit*
- **el flan** *flan (custard)*
- **IVA incluido** *tax included*

9

- **las verduras** *vegetables*
- **las legumbres** *legumes*
- **el pescado** *fish*
- **la carne** *meat*

10

- **el vino** *wine*
- **la cerveza** *beer*
- **la botella** *bottle*
- **vale (*Esp.*)** *OK*

Menú del día

Tell students that many restaurants in Spain offer a fixed-price **menú del día** that includes two courses, bread, dessert, and a beverage. The **menú del día** is generally more economical than ordering items á la carte.

Restaurante Casa del Pescador

Calle del Puerto, 4 (Santander)

Menú del día

PRIMER PLATO

- Ensalada de la casa
- Lentejas con chorizo
- Arroz con verduras
- Sopa de pescado

PLATO PRINCIPAL

- Dorada con ensalada
- Filete de ternera con patatas
- Albóndigas
- Bacalao en salsa

POSTRE

- Helado
- Fruta
- Flan

PAN Y BEBIDA

15 € (**IVA incluido**)

Explain that **IVA** stands for **Impuesto sobre el Valor Añadido** (Spain) and **Impuesto sobre el Valor Agregado** (Latin America). In English this is known as a *value-added tax.*

8 a. Which of the dishes at **Casa del Pescador** have you tried? What other Spanish dishes do you know? Share your answers with a partner.

b. *¿Dónde está la* **Casa del Pescador***?* Está en calle del Puerto, 4.

9 With a partner, categorize the foods on the menu as vegetables and legumes, fish, or meat. Ask your instructor if you aren't sure.

Modelo: *¿Las albóndigas son pescado o carne?*

VERDURAS Y LEGUMBRES 	PESCADOS 	CARNES 
ensalada lentejas arroz con verduras patatas	sopa de pescado dorada bacalao	filete de ternera albóndigas chorizo

10 a. Listen to Laura and Enrique's conversation with the waiter. Circle the items they order.

1. De primer plato, Laura come lentejas con chorizo/ensalada de la casa y Enrique, sopa de pescado/arroz con verduras.
2. De plato principal, Laura come albóndigas/dorada con ensalada y Enrique, bacalao en salsa/filete de ternera.
3. Bebidas: Laura y Enrique beben vino/agua/cerveza.
4. De postre, Laura come flan/helado y Enrique, flan/fruta.

b. Now listen to the rest of their conversation and circle what else they order.

5. otra cerveza/una botella de agua
6. un café/té

TAPAS Y RACIONES

Jamón serrano 14 €

Aceitunas 5 €

Queso 8 €

Gambas 9 €

Pulpo 15 €

Calamares 9 €

Valorar la comida

- ¿Qué tal está el pulpo?
- (Está) un poco picante, pero muy rico.

Adjetivos:

rico/a   salado/a
picante   soso/a

2B.5 **estar** + **muy/un poco** + [*adjective*]

Vocabulario

(11)
la ración *portion*
el jamón serrano *Serrano ham*
la aceituna *olive*
la gamba *shrimp*
el pulpo *octopus*
los calamares *calamari, squid*
¿Qué tal está(n)...? *How is/are . . . ?*
un poco *a little*
rico/a *tasty*
picante *spicy*
salado/a *salty*
soso/a *bland, lacking salt*
la tapa, positivo/a, negativo/a

11 a. Listen to these customers' opinions of **Casa del Pescador** and match each question to the response you hear.

1. ¿Qué tal está el pulpo?   a. Un poco soso.
2. ¿Qué tal está el queso?   b. Están un poco saladas.
3. ¿Qué tal están las gambas?   c. Muy ricos.
4. Y los calamares, ¿qué tal están?   d. Está un poco picante.

b. Categorize the opinions as positive or negative.

positivo: muy ricos   negativo: soso, saladas, picante

12 Mónica and Cristián are having tapas at **Casa del Pescador**. What do they order? Work with a partner to complete this conversation creatively, including the waiter's lines from the box at the right. Sample answers:

- ¿Tomamos unas tapas?
- Vale. ¡Camarero, por favor!
- ¿Qué desean?
- Una ración de pulpo y una de gambas.
- Y una ración de jamón serrano.
- ¿Y para beber?
- Dos cervezas, por favor.

[...]

- Camarero, otra ración de pulpo, ¡está muy rico!
- ¿Algo más?
- No, nada más, gracias. La cuenta, por favor.

¿Qué desean?
¿Y para beber?
¿Algo más?

13 With a partner, role-play a similar situation at **Casa del Pescador**.

Modelo:
- *¡Hola, buenas tardes!*
- *Hola, ¿qué desean?*

MI EXPERIENCIA

Tell students that the octopus shown here is **pulpo a la gallega**, or Galician-style octopus, a traditional dish in Spanish tapas bars.

14 What do you normally eat and drink at restaurants? Ask your classmates. Before you begin, use an idea web to organize your thoughts.

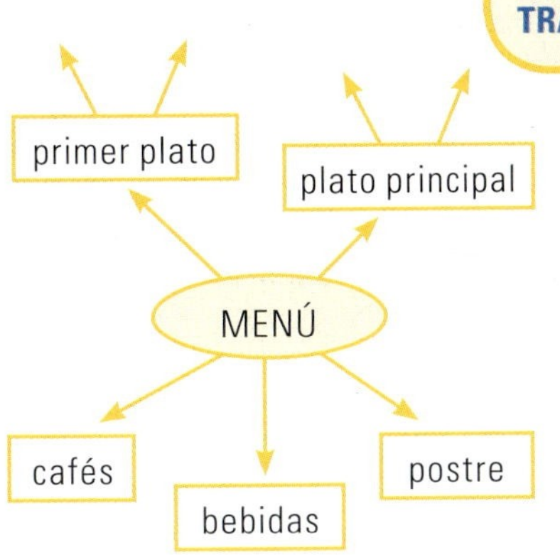

GUIÓN DE TRABAJO

En un restaurante, ¿comes normalmente el menú del día?
¿Almuerzas un primer plato, plato principal y postre?
¿Y para cenar?
¿Qué bebes normalmente?
¿Tomas postre o café?

Practice more at **vhlcentral.com.**

SAM: Actividades pp. 38–40

Rosa, camarera del bar El rey de la tapa

Have students turn to page 51 to see a photo of **tortilla española**. Tell them that in Spain, this dish is also called **tortilla de patatas**.

DIARIO
LA RIOJA

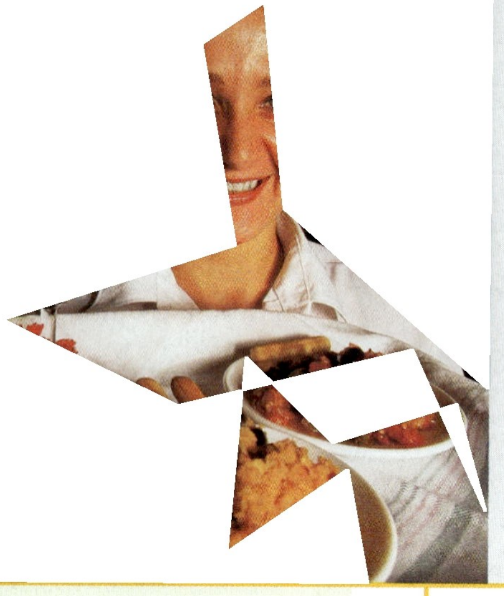

PREMIO A "LA CAMARERA DE LA RIOJA" MÁS PROFESIONAL Y SIMPÁTICA

Rosa Iglesias tiene 35 años y vive en Haro (La Rioja, España). Trabaja como camarera en el popular bar El rey de la tapa en la calle Mayor, 4. Rosa recibe este premio por su profesionalidad y simpatía. El rey de la tapa es un bar especializado en tapas y vinos: la tortilla española, los pimientos, el jamón, el pulpo y los caracoles están muy ricos, los vinos de La Rioja son excelentes... pero para los clientes, la especialidad de la casa es la simpatía de Rosa.

Tapear

Going out for **tapas** is a Spanish tradition; it's an opportunity to get together with friends and have a good time. According to legend, **tapas** get their name from the piece of bread that bartenders used to put over a glass of wine to cover (**tapar**) and protect it. Over time, these slices of bread were served with a piece of ham, **chorizo**, or cheese, and that's how **tapas** were born.

Vocabulario

(17)
- **el premio** *award*
- **el año** *year*
- **recibir** *to receive*
- **la profesionalidad** *professionalism*
- **la simpatía** *friendliness*
- **especializado/a en** *specializing in*
- **la tortilla española** *Spanish potato omelet*
- **el pimiento** *(bell) pepper*
- **el caracol** *snail, escargot*
- **tapear** *to eat tapas*
- **el bar, profesional, popular**

(18)
- **económico/a** *affordable*

15 a. What product is commonly associated with the region of La Rioja?

Aceitunas — *Pescado* — *Vino* — *Jamón*

b. Find La Rioja on a map of Spain. Then, take turns asking a partner: *¿Está lejos o cerca de ....?*

16 Look at the photo of Rosa and answer the questions. Suggested answers:

- ¿Dónde está? Está en un restaurante/bar.
- ¿Toma tapas con amigos o trabaja? Trabaja.

17 Read the article from the local paper and take notes on information about Rosa and the bar where she works. Suggested answers:

Rosa
- Tiene 35 años.
- Vive en Haro. Es camarera. Es simpática. Es
- muy profesional.
- ....
- ....

El rey de la tapa
- Está en la calle Mayor, 4.
- Su especialidad son los vinos y las tapas:
- tortilla española, pimientos, jamón, pulpo y
- caracoles. La especialidad de la casa es la
- simpatía de Rosa.

18 Why did Rosa receive an award? Check off the correct answer.

- Por la tapa más rica: la tortilla de patatas. ☐
- Por el restaurante más económico de La Rioja. ☐
- Por ser la camarera más simpática y profesional. ☑

19 Read the paragraph about tapas and discuss these questions with a partner.

- ¿Existe esta costumbre en su país?
- ¿Hay bares de tapas en su ciudad?

Vocabulario

20

el dulce *sweet, candy*
el huevo *egg*
el arroz *rice*
los alimentos *food*
la pasta

22

mexicano/a *Mexican*
gastronómico/a *gastronomic, culinary*
el maíz *corn*
la naranja *orange*
la papa (*Amér. L.*) *potato*
el taco, la tradición

OPINIÓN

¿Tiene usted una cafetería, un bar o restaurante habitual?

¿Conoce restaurantes españoles en su ciudad?

- ¿Tienen menú del día?
- ¿Tienen tapas?
- ¿Los camareros son profesionales y simpáticos?

tortilla mexicana

tortilla española

20 Study this food pyramid and write down how many times per week you eat each of these foods.

Modelo:
- Alimentos: *leche*
- Veces por semana: *siete*

21 In Spanish, the terms for these types of words are: **aguda** (stressed on the last syllable), **llana** (second-to-last), and **esdrújula** (third-to-last). There is a fourth category—**sobresdrújula**—in which the stress falls on a syllable before the third-to-last.

Stressed syllable

21 a. Listen to these words and underline the stressed syllable.

mantequilla filete bacalao postre arroz lentejas tostada
patata dorada jamón helado churro ternera albóndigas chorizo

b. Which syllable is most often stressed: the last, the second-to-last, or the third-to-last? the second-to-last syllable

22 Read the text about **tortillas** and answer the question.

América Latina tiene muchas tradiciones gastronómicas. Por ejemplo, en México son muy típicos los tacos, las tortillas de maíz con carne o verduras y la salsa muy picante. Las tortillas mexicanas y las tortillas españolas son muy diferentes. Una palabra, dos comidas distintas.

- What are the names for these foods in Spain?

AMÉRICA LATINA	ESPAÑA
jugo de naranja	zumo de naranja
papas	patatas

22 Expansion Have students research other foods that have the same name but refer to different dishes according to the region or country.

23 Find a recipe for **tortilla española** and one for **tortilla mexicana** and write a list of the ingredients in Spanish. Compare your recipes with a partner's.

Modelo: *La tortilla española tiene...*

Practice more at **vhlcentral.com.**

SAM: Actividades pp. 41–46

TAREA FINAL

Un restaurante español

Open a Spanish restaurant! Working with a partner, first choose a name.

Bar La tortilla española, Bar El pulpo...

Tell students that **El Museo del Jamón** is a popular chain of tapas bars in Madrid specializing in Spanish ham.

Create a menu of breakfast items and **tapas**.

Desayunos	Precio	Tapas	Precio
Café + tostada	*$4*		

Write a dialogue between a client placing an order and a waiter/waitress who tells the client about the dishes.

Role-play your dialogue for the class.

Encourage groups to rehearse their script several times before role-playing their dialogues for the class. Suggest that they use props.

YO PUEDO...

- Puedo pedir un desayuno y preguntar por el precio.
  In groups of three, use the menu you created in Tarea final to practice ordering food.
- Puedo hablar de costumbres en relación con la comida y expresar frecuencia.
  Write a blog posting about your eating habits.
- Puedo pedir un menú del día y la cuenta.
  De bebida, ...
  De primer plato, ...
  De plato principal, ...
  De postre, ...
  Por favor, ...
- Puedo valorar la comida.
  Use these words: salado/a, soso/a, rico/a

- ¿Dónde y qué desayuna normalmente?
- ¿Almuerza en el trabajo, en casa, en un restaurante?
- ¿Cena el fin de semana en casa o en un restaurante?

En el restaurante Casa del Pescador normalmente:

- la ensalada está ......rica......
- los calamares están ......salados......
- la carne está ......sosa......

GRAMÁTICA FUNCIONAL

Point out that, even though **almorzar** is a stem-changing verb, the endings are the same as for other **-ar** verbs students know.

2B.1 Order and pay at a café

Interrogative **¿cuánto?** 9 Regular **-ar** verbs: **desear** 5.1.1

- To take someone's order at a restaurant or café, ask **¿Qué desea?** if there is one client or **¿Qué desean?** for more than one.

¿Qué desea, señorita? *What would you like, miss?*	**¿Qué desean**, señores? *What would you like, gentlemen?*

- To ask how much you owe at a café, say **¿Cuánto es?** *(How much is it?)* To answer, say **Son X euros/dólares/pesos**, etc.

2B.2 Talk about daily meals

Regular **-er** verbs: **beber, comer** 5.1.1

- Use the verbs **comer** *(to eat)* and **beber** *(to drink)* to talk about your meals. **Comer** and **beber** are regular **-er** verbs; all regular **-er** verbs follow the same conjugation pattern.

	COMER	BEBER
(yo)	como	bebo
(tú)	comes	bebes
(usted, él, ella)	come	bebe
(nosotros/as)	comemos	bebemos
(vosotros/as)	coméis	bebéis
(ustedes, ellos/as)	comen	beben

Yo normalmente **bebo** un café por las mañanas y **como** unas galletas.
*I usually **drink** a coffee in the morning and **I eat** some cookies.*

2B.3 Express frequency

Adverbs of frequency 11.8
Stem-changing verbs **o→ue: almorzar** 5.1.1

- Use the adverbs **siempre** *(always)*, **normalmente** *(normally)*, and **a veces** *(sometimes)* to talk about frequency. Place the adverbs directly before the verb.

Normalmente desayuno en casa; **siempre** almuerzo fuera.
***Normally**, I have breakfast at home; I **always** have lunch out.*

- To discuss the meals of the day, use **desayunar** to talk about breakfast (**el desayuno**), **almorzar** to talk about lunch (**el almuerzo**), and **cenar** to talk about supper (**la cena**). **Desayunar** and **cenar** follow the regular **-ar** conjugation pattern.

Tú desayun**as** galletas y Ramón desayun**a** tostada.
You have cookies for breakfast and Ramón has toast.

- **Almorzar** is an **o→ue** stem-changing verb; this means that the stressed **-o-** in the stem changes to **-ue-** in every form except the **nosotros/as** and **vosotros/as** forms. Note that the endings still follow the conjugation pattern of regular **-ar** verbs.

ALMORZAR			
(yo)	almuerzo	(nosotros/as)	almorzamos
(tú)	almuerzas	(vosotros/as)	almorzáis
(usted, él, ella)	almuerza	(ustedes, ellos/as)	almuerzan

Successful Language Learning Write the forms of **almorzar** on the board, draw a line around the stem-changing forms, and point out the boot-like shape. Explain that this is a good visual tool that students can use for all stem-changing verbs.

¡Póngalo en práctica!

G1 Complete the conversation logically.

- Buenos días.
- Buenos días. ¿(1) Qué desea ?
- Un café con leche y un cruasán.
- Muy bien. Aquí tiene.
- ¿(2) Cuánto es ?
- (3) Son tres euros.
- ¡Muchas gracias!

G2 Complete the sentences with the appropriate forms of **beber** or **comer**.

1. Lorenzo come pan tostado.
2. Tú bebes zumo de naranja natural.
3. Mateo y yo bebemos café con leche.
4. ¿ Comen ustedes los churros?
5. Vosotras bebéis un café cortado.
6. Adela bebe una taza de chocolate.
7. Yo siempre como flan de postre.
8. Antonio y Jorge beben té con el desayuno.
9. Gabriela y yo comemos pan con mermelada.
10. ¿ Comes (tú) las galletas?

G3 Unscramble the words to write complete sentences. Remember to conjugate the verbs.

1. a veces / desayunar / café / Joaquín
Joaquín a veces desayuna café.
2. en casa / almorzar / siempre / mis amigos
Mis amigos siempre almuerzan en casa.
3. nosotros / fuera / a veces / cenar
Nosotros a veces cenamos fuera.
4. almorzar / en la cafetería / tú y Manolo / siempre
Tú y Manolo siempre almuerzan/almorzáis en la cafetería.
5. yogur / normalmente / yo / desayunar
Yo normalmente desayuno yogur.

Practice more at **vhlcentral.com.**

GRAMÁTICA FUNCIONAL

You may want to tell students that when ordering in a restaurant, they may also say **Como primer plato/plato principal/postre**, etc.

2B.4 Order and pay at a restaurant

otro/a 6.5 **algo/nada más** 6.5

- To inquire about specials or items on a menu at a restaurant, ask **¿Qué tienen de** + [**menú/primer plato/postre**, etc.]?

  ¿Qué tienen de primer plato?
  What do you have as a starter?

- When ordering, say **De primer plato/plato principal/postre...** for food, and **Para beber...** for drinks.

  De plato principal, el arroz con pollo, y **para beber**, una botella de agua.
  ***As a main dish**, the rice with chicken, and **to drink**, a bottle of water.*

- Use **otro/a** (*another*) to request more items. **Otro/a** must agree in gender and number with the noun it modifies, and is never used with an indefinite article.

  Otro café y **otra** botella de agua, por favor.
  ***Another** coffee and **another** bottle of water, please.*

- To ask clients if they would like anything else, say **¿Desea(n) algo más?** If you do not want anything more, say **No, nada más.**

¿Desea algo más?	**No, nada más.**
Would you like anything else?	***No, nothing else.***

2B.5 Give your opinion on food

estar + muy/un poco + [*adjective*] 5.8.1, 11.4

- To inquire about the quality of food that someone is eating, ask **¿Qué tal está(n)** + [*food*]?

  ¿Qué tal están las lentejas?
  ***How are** the lentils?*

- To explain how the food is, say **Está(n)** + [*adjective*]. Remember, the adjective must agree in gender and number with the food you are describing.

  La sopa **está rica**, pero el arroz **está soso**.
  *The soup **is tasty**, but the rice **is bland**.*

- Use **muy** to intensify a description, and use **un poco** to soften the impact of negative opinions.

  Los pimientos están **muy ricos**, pero los calamares están **un poco salados**.
  *The peppers are **delicious**, but the calamari is a **bit salty**.*

¡OJO!

Use **estar** + [*adjective*] to describe how food tastes on a specific occasion: **El queso está muy salado.** (*The (This) cheese is really salty.*) Use **ser** + [*adjective*] to describe the general characteristics of a food: **Los jalapeños son picantes.** (*Jalapeño peppers are spicy.*)

¡Póngalo en práctica!

G4 Complete the dialogue.

¿Qué (1) desea ?

¿Qué tienen como (2) menú ?

(3) De primer plato, tenemos arroz con verduras, ensalada o sopa de pescado. De (4) plato principal , bacalao en salsa o filete de ternera.

De (5) primer plato , sopa de pescado, y de (6) plato principal , filete de ternera.

¿Desea (7) algo más?

Sí, (8) un café y la (9) cuenta , por favor.

G5 Use the cues to write complete sentences with **estar**. Change adjectives when necessary for agreement.

1. el pescado / un poco / soso
   El pescado está un poco soso.
2. los calamares / muy / rico
   Los calamares están muy ricos.
3. el pulpo / un poco / picante
   El pulpo está un poco picante.
4. las albóndigas / un poco / salado
   Las albóndigas están un poco saladas.
5. el queso / un poco / salado / pero / rico
   El queso está un poco salado, pero está rico.
6. las gambas / muy / rico
   Las gambas están muy ricas.
7. el chorizo / un poco / picante
   El chorizo está un poco picante.
8. todo / muy / rico
   Todo está muy rico.

Give students other adjectives for critiquing food, such as **delicioso/a, frío/a, grasiento/a, sabroso/a,** and **simple**.

Practice more at vhlcentral.com.

VOCABULARIO

Café con leche

¿Qué desean tomar?	*What would you like (to have)?*
por favor	*please*
¿Cuánto es?	*How much is it?*
Son 9 euros.	*It's 9 euros.*
el aceite de oliva	*olive oil*
la bollería (*Esp.*)	*pastries*
el café solo	*black coffee*
la cafeína	*caffeine*
la cafetería	*café*
el/la camarero/a	*waiter/waitress*
los cereales	*cereal*
los churros	*churros*
el/la compañero/a	*partner*
el cruasán	*croissant*
el desayuno	*breakfast*
el descafeinado	*decaf coffee*
el doble	*double*
el fin de semana	*weekend*
la galleta	*cookie*
la gota	*drop*
el hielo	*ice*
el jugo de naranja (*Amér. L.*)	*orange juice*
la mantequilla	*butter*
la mermelada	*jam, marmalade*
el pan	*bread*
el queso	*cheese*
el sándwich	*sandwich*
la semana	*week*
la taza	*mug, coffee cup*
el té	*tea*
la tostada	*toast*
el yogur	*yogurt*
el zumo de naranja (*Esp.*)	*orange juice*
algo	*something*
almorzar (o:ue)	*to eat lunch*
beber	*to drink*
cenar	*to eat supper*
comer	*to eat; to eat lunch (Esp., Méx.)*
desayunar	*to eat breakfast*
dulce	*sweet*
especial	*special*
frecuente	*common*
natural	*fresh*
poco/a	*little*
a veces	*sometimes*
en casa	*at home*
fuera	*out*
normalmente	*normally*
siempre	*always*

Menú del día

¿Algo más?	*Anything else?*
Nada más, gracias.	*Nothing else, thanks.*
¿Qué tal está(n)...?	*How is/are . . . ?*
un poco	*a little*
IVA incluido	*tax included*
vale (*Esp.*)	*OK*
la aceituna	*olive*
la albóndiga	*meatball*
el arroz con verduras	*rice with vegetables*
el bacalao en salsa	*cod with sauce*
la bebida	*beverage*
la botella	*bottle*
los calamares	*calamari, squid*
la carne	*meat*
la cerveza	*beer*
la cuenta	*bill*
la dorada	*sea bream (type of fish)*
la ensalada de la casa	*house salad*
el filete de ternera	*filet of veal*
el flan	*flan (custard)*
la fruta	*fruit*
la gamba	*shrimp*
el helado	*ice cream*
el jamón serrano	*Serrano ham*
las legumbres	*legumes*
las lentejas con chorizo	*lentils with chorizo (sausage)*
el menú del día	*fixed-price menu*
la patata (*Esp.*)	*potato*
el pescado	*fish*
el plato principal	*main course*
el postre	*dessert*
el primer plato	*first course*
el pulpo	*octopus*
la ración	*portion*
la sopa de pescado	*fish soup*
la tapa	*tapa*
las verduras	*vegetables*
el vino	*wine*
negativo/a	*negative*
picante	*spicy*
positivo/a	*positive*
rico/a	*tasty*
salado/a	*salty*
soso/a	*bland, lacking salt*

Rosa Iglesias

los alimentos	*food*
el año	*year*
el arroz	*rice*
el bar	*bar*
el caracol	*snail, escargot*
el dulce	*sweet, candy*
el huevo	*egg*
el maíz	*corn*
la naranja	*orange*
la papa (*Amér. L.*)	*potato*
la pasta	*pasta*
el pimiento	*(bell) pepper*
el premio	*award*
la profesionalidad	*professionalism*
la simpatía	*friendliness*
el taco	*taco*
la tortilla española	*Spanish potato omelet*
la tradición	*tradition*
recibir	*to receive*
tapear	*to eat tapas*
económico/a	*affordable*
especializado/a en	*specializing in*
gastronómico/a	*gastronomic, culinary*
mexicano/a	*Mexican*
popular	*popular*
profesional	*professional*

Variación léxica

almorzar ⟷ **comer** (*Esp., Méx.*)	**el jugo** (*Amér. L.*) ⟷ **el zumo** (*Esp.*)
la bollería (*Esp.*) ⟷ **la pastelería** (*Amér. L.*) ⟷ **las facturas** (*Arg.*)	**el sándwich** ⟷ **el bocadillo** (*Esp.*) ⟷ **la torta** (*Méx.*)
el/la camarero/a ⟷ **el/la mesero/a** (*Amér. L.*)	**la tortilla española** ⟷ **la tortilla de patatas** (*Esp.*)
el cruasán ⟷ **la medialuna** (*Arg.*)	**De acuerdo** ⟷ **¡Vale!** (*Esp.*)

Suggestion Tell students to group vocabulary from this lesson into categories, such as breakfast foods, dinner foods, drinks, etc.

Suggestion Draw a large food pyramid on the board. Have volunteers write words they have learned in the lesson in the appropriate sections.

2 AVANCE

Estrategias

1 Deducir nuevas palabras a través de cognados — Lección 1A

Recognizing Spanish words that are similar to words you already know in English or another language can help you expand your vocabulary.

- Read these words and identify the English cognates.

aeropuerto	restaurante	idea	radio	música	teléfono

- Make a list of other cognates you have learned in **Unidades 1 y 2**.

2 Crear palabras a partir de reglas de formación — Lección 1B

You can use patterns of word formation to recognize the relationships between words and help expand your vocabulary. For example, if you know that **pintar** means to *paint* and that the suffix **-or(a)** can be added to a verb stem to create the name of a profession, you can see that **un(a) pintor(a)** is a painter.

- Match words from the word bank to the related words below to see how the names for some professions are formed. Use a dictionary if necessary.

cartero/a	periodista	recepcionista	trabajador(a)	zapatero/a
librero/a	pescador(a)	taxista	vendedor(a)	

+ -ista	+ -ero/a	+ -dor(a)
el periódico periodista	la carta cartero/a	pescar pescador(a)
la recepción recepcionista	el libro librero/a	trabajar trabajador(a)
el taxi taxista	el zapato zapatero/a	vender vendedor(a)

3 Hacer listas y fichas de palabras — Lección 2A

Creating vocabulary lists and flashcards can be a helpful way to study new words and expressions. Think of different ways to organize the words: in alphabetical order, by part of speech, or by where and how you use them.

- Make flashcards for the words you learned in **Lección 2A**.

Encourage students to use images or word associations rather than English translations on their flashcards.

4 Hacer redes de palabras — Lección 2B

Making word maps is a helpful way to organize and learn vocabulary. They allow you to visually organize words into thematically-related groups to help you learn words in context.

- Fill in this word map about breakfast Sample answers:

DESAYUNOS
- cruasán/bollería
- mermelada
- tostada
- café con leche
- fruta

Competencias

LENGUAS

(1) What languages are spoken in these five countries? Find their names in the word search (**sopa de letras**).

C	T	I	E	S	P	A	Ñ	O	L	I
M	U	P	É	S	Y	S	B	U	S	T
F	R	R	A	L	E	M	Á	N	U	A
Y	R	A	Z	H	R	T	E	I	G	L
G	O	A	N	X	K	Ñ	R	A	T	I
A	V	Z	N	I	N	G	L	É	S	A
U	R	U	R	C	A	E	Z	G	S	N
K	R	M	O	R	É	T	X	Á	P	O
Ñ	O	W	B	C	U	S	V	S	H	D

REINO UNIDO

inglés

FRANCIA

francés

ALEMANIA

alemán

ITALIA

italiano

ESPAÑA

español

CIFRAS

(2) Write out the numbers in words and the words in numerals.

diecinueve años	555 pesos	los años ochenta	Madrid-Barcelona 630 km
19 años	quinientos cincuenta y cinco pesos	los años 80	Madrid-Barcelona seiscientos treinta km

HABLAR DE REFERENTES DE UNA CULTURA CONCRETA

(3) Complete these sentences with the appropriate indefinite article and adjective ending.

- El guacamole es ...una... comida mexican...a... .
- Cuba es ...una... isla muy bonit...a... .
- La puerta de Alcalá es ...un... monumento muy famos...o... de Madrid.
- Varadero es ...una... playa fantástic...a... de Cuba.

4 Suggestion Make sure that students only look at the card that corresponds to them. If needed, hand out photocopies of the cards.

DAR DATOS PERSONALES

(4) Choose card A or B, and ask your partner questions to fill in the missing information.

A

Nombre: Mario Fernández García
Nacionalidad: ...español...
Dirección: calle Postas, 35, Bilbao
Profesión: ...arquitecto...

B

Nombre: ...Mario Fernández García...
Nacionalidad: español
Dirección: ...calle Postas, 35, Bilbao...
Profesión: arquitecto

PEDIR Y PAGAR EN UN CAFÉ

(5) Look at the illustration and work with a partner to create a dialogue about this situation.

HABLAR DE UN LUGAR

(6) Complete each sentence with an appropriate form of **ser** or **estar.**

- ¿Dónde ...está... Sucre?
- ¿...Es... una ciudad boliviana?
- ¿...Está... lejos o cerca de La Paz?
- Sucre ...es... una ciudad histórica.

5 Suggestion Before beginning pair work, brainstorm with the class a list of words and expressions related to ordering in a restaurant.

Flash CULTURA

Estrategia

Brainstorming questions before viewing

Before you watch a cultural video, think about what information you expect to learn and what questions you would like to have answered. What do you already know about Mexico City? What do you know about the university system in Mexico? In what ways is the UNAM similar to your school or university? Write down your questions, and as you watch this Flash Cultura, take notes on the answers you see and hear.

Vocabulario útil

- ¿Cuál es tu materia favorita? *What it is your favorite subject?*
- ¿Cuántos años tienes? *How old are you?*
- la carrera de medicina *medical degree program, major*
- las ciencias de la comunicación *communications*
- el derecho *law*
- la facultad *(academic) department*
- ofrecer (zc) *to offer*
- la residencia estudiantil *dorm(itory)*

Estrategia

Using idea webs to make comparisons

An idea web is a useful way to graphically summarize information relating to a given topic. When you take notes, try not to write out complete sentences. Instead, write only key facts, words, and phrases, and use circles, lines, and arrows to show the relationships between ideas. Later, you can use these categories to make comparisons.

Los estudios

You have learned about several Latin American cities, including **México, D.F.** Now you will learn about the **UNAM**, Mexico's largest university. You will meet several students, learn about their majors, and about some of the **UNAM**'s most famous alumni.

1. What is the name of your school or university? What degree program are you in? What are your favorite classes? Share your experiences with a partner.

2. Watch this **Flash Cultura** episode.

1 **Estudio derecho en la UNAM.**

After showing the video, ask students to describe a few facts about the UNAM that were surprising to them.

Have the class scan through the **Vocabulario útil** to look for cognates. Then point out the false cognates (**carrera, facultad**).

2 **¿Conoces algún profesor famoso que dé clases en la UNAM?**

3. Match each sentence starter with the appropriate ending.

1. Los estudiantes de la UNAM no viven ___c___
2. México, D.F. es ___d___
3. La UNAM es ___a___
4. La UNAM ofrece ___b___

a. una universidad muy grande.
b. 74 carreras de estudio.
c. en residencias estudiantiles.
d. la ciudad más grande de América Latina.

4. Create an idea web to summarize what you learned about the **UNAM**. Then, create another idea web about your school or college and write a paragraph comparing and contrasting the two institutions. Use the word **pero** in your contrasts and the word **también** in your comparisons.

Modelo: *La UNAM está en una ciudad muy grande, pero mi universidad está...*

Practice more at **vhlcentral.com.**

Audio: Activities, Vocabulary
Video: *Flash Cultura*

Unidad 3

Pablo Linares, dos ritmos de vida

Lección 3A

RITMO DE VIDA

Lección 3B

CENTRO COMERCIAL

Olga Piedrahita, la moda en Colombia

Fútbol en España

AVANCE

3A

Ask students what day is considered bad luck in this country (Friday the 13th). Point out the red square and tell students that in the Spanish-speaking world, **martes 13** is considered an unlucky day. Share with the class this expression: **Martes 13: ni te cases, ni te embarques, ni de tu casa te apartes.**

RITMO DE VIDA

Point out the times given on the flyer and explain that it is common in Spanish-speaking countries to use the 24-hour clock, especially for events and schedules.

Horarios

Have students look at the calendar. Explain that, unlike in English, the days of the week are not capitalized in Spanish.

ABRIL

lunes	martes	miércoles	jueves	viernes	sábado	domingo
			1	2	3	4
5	6	7	8	9	10	11
12	13	14	15	16	17	18
19	20	21	22	23	24	25
26	27	28	29	30		

Atención: personas del mundo de las finanzas, profesionales, jóvenes, niños...

La Bolsa de Comercio de Buenos Aires les invita al

DÍA DE PUERTAS ABIERTAS

el 13 de abril
de 08:30 h a 18:00 h

Visitas con guía cada 20 minutos

Sarmiento 299
C1041AAE Buenos Aires

Contacto:
visitasguiadas@bcba.sba.com.ar

Hablar de horarios y días de la semana

Abre de diez de la mañana a ocho y media de la noche.

- ¿Qué hora es? (14:20)
- Son las dos y veinte de la tarde.
- ¿Y en Santiago? (13:20)
- Es la una y veinte de la tarde.
- ¿Qué día abre la Bolsa?
- El martes 13 de abril.

01:00 h-11:00 h: 1-11 de la mañana
12:00 h: 12 del mediodía
13:00 h-19:00 h: 1-7 de la tarde
20:00 h-00:00 h: 8-12 de la noche

El lunes/martes/miércoles...

3A.1 Telling time
Days of the week

Vocabulario

1

el horario *schedule*
el mundo de las finanzas *world of finance*
el/la niño/a *boy/girl*
la bolsa (de comercio) *stock exchange*
abierto/a *open*
el 13 de abril *April 13*

1 Look at the calendar. What day of the week is the **Día de Puertas Abiertas**?
martes

2 a. What are the opening hours of the Buenos Aires stock exchange?

La Bolsa abre de 8:30 h / 8:30 de la mañana a 18:00 h / 6 de la tarde .

b. When the Buenos Aires stock exchange opens, what time is it in these other financial capitals? Mark the times on the clocks and write them out in words.

1. Nueva York (-1 hora) 2. Tokio (+12 horas) 3. Londres (+4 horas) 4. Madrid (+5 horas)

Son las siete y media de la mañana. | Son las ocho y media de la noche. | Son las doce y media del mediodía. | Es la una y media de la tarde.

3 Write the time displayed on each clock.

18:25 Son las seis y veinticinco de la tarde.
12:45 Es la una menos cuarto de la tarde.
06:40 Son las siete menos veinte de la mañana.
22:00 Son las diez de la noche.

4 Match each day to its common abbreviation.

L M Mi J V S D

lunes • jueves • martes • miércoles • sábado • domingo • viernes

Explain that Monday is considered the first day of the week in Spanish-speaking countries; thus, the calendar starts with **lunes**.

Suggestion Practice days of the week by giving series of days and having students supply the missing day. Ex: **domingo, lunes... (martes)**

Vicente, músico

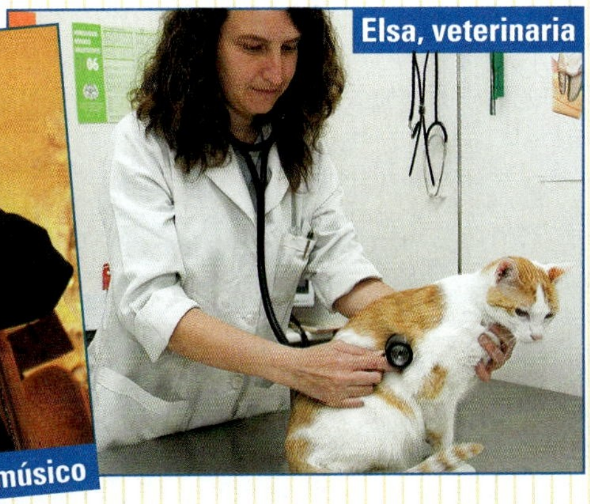
Elsa, veterinaria

Vocabulario *cont.*

el día de la semana *day of the week*
el lunes *Monday*
el martes *Tuesday*
el miércoles *Wednesday*
el jueves *Thursday*
el viernes *Friday*
el sábado *Saturday*
el domingo *Sunday*
el/la profesional, el calendario

2
abrir *to open*

3
¿Qué hora es? *What time is it?*
el reloj *clock; watch*
de la mañana *a.m., in the morning*
de la tarde *p.m., in the afternoon*
de la noche *p.m., in the evening/night*

Hablar de rutinas

- ¿Cuándo vas al gimnasio?
- Voy los lunes por la mañana y los jueves por la tarde.
- ¿A qué hora va Marta a clase?
- Va a clase a las 8:00 h.

Por la mañana/tarde/noche...
Los lunes/jueves/sábados...

3A.2 Time expressions
The verb **ir; a + el = al**

Vocabulario

5
la rutina diaria *daily routine*
¿A qué hora...? *At what time . . . ?*
hacer *to do; to make*
ir a trabajar *to go to work*
llegar a casa *to arrive home*
por la mañana *in the morning*
por la tarde *in the afternoon*
por la noche *in the evening, at night*
el programa de radio, el/la veterinario/a, el/la músico/a, el gimnasio

6
el cine *movie theater*

7
una persona de 80 años *an 80-year-old person*
el/la vigilante nocturno/a *night security guard*

5 a. A Spanish radio program interviews Vicente and Elsa about their daily routines. Before you listen, look at their photos and guess at what time they do each activity.

Vicente	Rutinas	Elsa
10:00 h	desayunar	8:00 h
16:00 h	ir a trabajar	9:00 h
15:00 h	comer	13:30 h
00:00 h	llegar a casa	19:30 h
23:30 h ó 21:30 h/22:00 h	cenar	20:30 h – 21:00 h

Before playing the audio, introduce **¿A qué hora...?** by contrasting it with **¿Qué hora es?** Ex: **¿Qué hora es? ¿A qué hora es la clase de español?**

b. Now listen to the recording and check the accuracy of your guesses.

6 Suggestion Ask a volunteer to read through the model sentence. Explain that **los sábados** means *on Saturdays*. Ask how one would say *on Saturday* (**el sábado**).

6 Use elements from each column to create original questions.

(usted)	*¿Vais*	*los sábados*	*por la mañana*	*al cine?*
(vosotros)	*¿Van*	*los martes*	*por la tarde*	*a la disco?*
(ustedes)	*¿Va*	*los lunes*	*por la noche*	*al mercado?*

7 Choose one of the three people listed below and describe his/her daily routine. Your partner should guess whom you are describing.

- Un(a) niño/a
- Una persona de 80 años
- Un(a) vigilante nocturno/a

MI EXPERIENCIA

8 Suggestion Before they interview a partner, have students write out their own schedules in a chart format.

8 What are your classmates' daily routines like? Interview a partner and report your findings to the class. Whose routines are most similar?

GUIÓN DE TRABAJO

¿A qué hora desayunas/almuerzas/comes?
¿Cenas a las ocho/nueve de la noche...?
¿Vas al gimnasio? ¿Cuándo?
¿Trabajas?
¿Estudias?
¿A qué hora vas al trabajo/a la universidad?
¿A qué hora llegas a casa?

Por la...
mañana
tarde
noche

los lunes
los martes
los miércoles
los jueves
los viernes

los sábados
los domingos
el fin de semana

Practice more at **vhlcentral.com.**

SAM: Actividades pp. 47–49

Agenda semanal

- Verónica, ¿qué haces después de clases?
- Todos los días tengo una o dos actividades. Los lunes por la tarde, a las ocho, hago yoga. Los martes colaboro en una asociación del barrio de nueve a diez o diez y media de la noche.
- ¿Todos los martes?
- Sí, todos, y los miércoles de ocho a nueve y media, Ana y yo hacemos un curso de informática. ¡Ah!, y los jueves de ocho a nueve tengo clase de francés...
- ¿Qué haces los viernes?
- Los viernes por la noche, Emilio y yo salimos; vamos al cine.
- ¿Salís todos los viernes?
- Sí, normalmente sí. El sábado por la mañana hago las compras en el centro comercial y el domingo salimos a pasear con la familia... ¿Y tú?

Expresar frecuencia

- Jorge, ¿qué **haces** por la tarde?
- **Salgo** con los niños y voy al parque.
- ¿Todos los días?
- Sí, **todas las tardes**. Después **hago** deporte.
- ¿Y no **vas** al cine o a un restaurante...?
- Sí, los viernes mi mujer y yo **hacemos** algo especial o **salimos** con amigos.
- Yo **nunca salgo** los viernes.

Todos los días, todas las tardes, todos los jueves...

3A.3 Verbs with irregular **yo** forms: **hacer, salir**
Expressions of frequency

9 a. Verónica and Nuria are college students. Read and listen to their conversation over coffee. Write down the missing information in Verónica's weekly planner.

	lunes	martes	miércoles	jueves	viernes	sábado	domingo
POR LA MAÑANA	clases	clases	clases	clases	clases	hacer las compras	día familiar
POR LA TARDE/ NOCHE	yoga	asociación	informática	francés	cine		salir a pasear

b. Underline the forms of **hacer** and **salir** in the conversation above and complete the chart with the missing forms.

	yo	tú	usted, él, ella	nosotros/as	vosotros/as	ustedes, ellos/as
HACER	hago	haces	hace	hacemos	hacéis	hacen
SALIR	salgo	sales	sale	salimos	salís	salen

10 a. Listen to this interview with a teenager on the street in Madrid. How often does he do each activity?

1. Hacer deporte: los lunes y los miércoles
2. Salir con amigos: todos los fines de semana
3. Hacer algo en casa: Todos los días hace la cama. A veces hace la compra con su padre.

b. How often do you do these activities? Ask a partner about his/her habits.

Modelo: *¿Con qué frecuencia vas al cine? ¿Tienes clases todos los días?*

- hacer deporte
- cenar afuera
- ir al teatro o al cine
- hacer las compras
- salir con amigos

10b Suggestion Have students ask follow-up questions, such as where or at what time(s) their partner does the activities.

Vocabulario

9

la agenda (semanal) *(weekly) planner*
la mujer *woman; wife*
todos los días *every day*
colaborar *to participate*
el curso *class, course*
tener clase *to have class*
salir (con amigos) *to go out (with friends)*
hacer las compras *to go grocery shopping*
pasear *to go for a walk*
el yoga

Cultural Note Explain that going grocery shopping tends to be a more frequent activity in the Spanish-speaking world than in the U.S., since many people still buy perishable items such as bread and fruit at specialty shops.

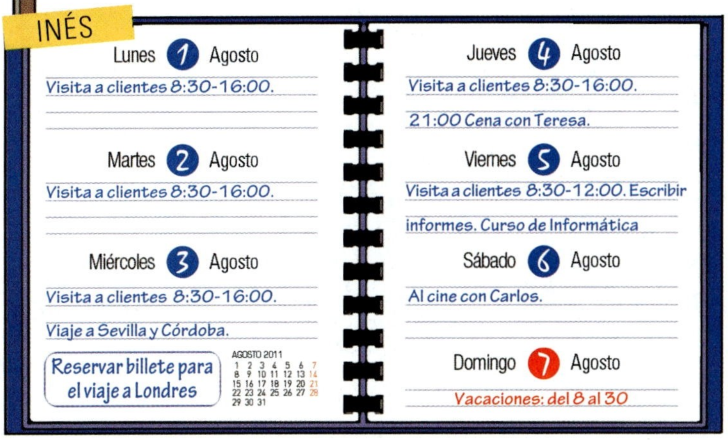

Comparar

- ¿Dónde trabajas?
- En un gimnasio; trabajo por la mañana y por la tarde.
- ¡Trabajas **más** horas **que** yo!
- Sí, ¡y hago **menos** deporte **que** tú!

3A.4 Comparatives **más/menos + que**

11 Read Andrés and Inés's schedules and compare them.

Modelo: *Inés hace más viajes que Andrés.*

11 Suggestion Tell students to find at least five points of comparison.

12 Now compare your answers to **Actividad 10b** with your partner's.

Modelo: *Hago deporte todos los días y tú haces deporte los sábados.*
→ Hago más deporte que tú.

13 Compare this information about Spain with your country.

EN ESPAÑA

- Los trabajadores tienen 22 días de vacaciones al año.
- El calendario tiene 14 días festivos.
- En julio y agosto los niños no van al colegio.
- El horario de trabajo es normalmente de 8:00/9:00 h a 18:00/20:00 h.

MI EXPERIENCIA

14 Ask your partner about his/her activities. Compare your schedules and present your findings to the class.

GUIÓN DE TRABAJO

¿A qué hora vas a la universidad /a trabajar? → A la(s)...

¿A qué hora sales de clases/ trabajar? → A la(s)...

¿Qué haces por las tardes? → Hago teatro. Voy a clase de... Salgo con...

¿Con qué frecuencia? → Todos los días. Todos los martes. Todas las tardes.

Mi compañero/a:
trabaja más/menos horas que yo.
hace más/menos deporte que yo.

Vocabulario

10
la entrevista *interview*
el ritmo de vida *pace of life*
¿Con qué frecuencia? *How often?*
hacer deporte *to exercise*
hacer algo en casa *to do something at home*
hacer la cama *to make the bed*
el horario de trabajo *work schedule*
terminar *to end*

11
el viaje de negocios *business trip*
las vacaciones *vacation*
tres veces al año *three times a year*
la vez (*pl.* veces) *time*
más que *more than*
menos que *less than*

13
el/la trabajador(a) *worker*
el día festivo *holiday*
julio *July*
agosto *August*
el colegio *school*

14
salir de *to leave*

Practice more at **vhlcentral.com.**

SAM: Actividades pp. 50–52

Pablo Linares, dos ritmos de vida

EL **BLOG** DE Pablo

Nombre: Pablo Linares
Edad: 35 años
Ciudad: Buenos Aires/Colonia
Ver datos completos

HOME | COMENTARIOS | DATOS

"Trabajo y descanso" **Lunes, 8 de diciembre, 22:30 h.**

Escribir este blog es terapia; trabajo mucho y no hablo con otras personas.

Soy de Colonia, Uruguay, pero vivo en Buenos Aires porque trabajo en la bolsa. Salgo de casa a las siete y media de la mañana, desayuno en una cafetería y a las ocho en punto entro en el trabajo. Por la noche llego a casa a las nueve. Hago aproximadamente 50 llamadas de teléfono al día. El ritmo de vida es muy intenso, ¡no paro un segundo! Todos los días hago lo mismo: trabajar, leer prensa económica, comer en diez minutos y media hora de deporte por la noche en el gimnasio. Los miércoles ceno con compañeros en un restaurante y hablamos, naturalmente, de la bolsa.

Los viernes por la tarde salgo de la bolsa a las seis, tomo el ferry y a las ocho y media estoy en Colonia. Soy persona de campo y quiero estar al aire libre. Mi familia tiene una estancia muy tranquila cerca de Colonia.

En la estancia, el celular no funciona, no tengo tele, no tengo Internet...

Tengo el río, mis libros, amigos, más tiempo que en la ciudad, menos estrés que de lunes a viernes y más paz. ¡Los sábados y domingos tengo otro ritmo de vida!

Bolsa de Comercio de Buenos Aires
Nombre: Pablo
Apellidos: Linares García
D.N.I.: 22.756.240

15 What type of text does Pablo Linares write? Choose the best category for this type of blog.

☐ Biografía ☐ Informe profesional ☑ Diario personal

16 Which photos represent Pablo during the week? And on the weekends?

A

B

C

- Durante la semana: foto A
- Los fines de semana: fotos B y C

17 Reread the blog and write your answer to the question on a separate piece of paper.

17 Expansion Have students work in pairs to brainstorm a list of activities they enjoy on the weekends.

- ¿Qué hace Pablo Linares normalmente los fines de semana?
  va a Colonia, está al aire libre, lee libros, está con la familia y amigos

18 Relate each of the words from Pablo's blog with the corresponding day(s) of the week. **18 Suggestion** Have students make a calendar of Pablo's activities.

bolsa, paz, gimnasio, estancia, celular, río, Buenos Aires, Colonia, estrés, prensa económica, blog, compañeros

lunes
martes
miércoles
jueves
viernes
el fin de semana

de lunes a viernes: bolsa, Buenos Aires, celular, estrés, gimnasio, blog, prensa económica, compañeros; el fin de semana: estancia, paz, río, Colonia

Vocabulario

(15)

- el descanso *rest*
- diciembre *December*
- la terapia *therapy*
- entrar en *to enter*
- aproximadamente *approximately*
- la llamada de teléfono *telephone call*
- parar *to stop*
- la prensa económica *financial press*
- el deporte *sport(s)*
- tomar el ferry *to take the ferry*
- el campo *country(side)*
- al aire libre *outdoors*
- la estancia (*Cono S.*) *ranch*
- la tele(visión) *television*
- el río *river*
- el tiempo *time*
- el estrés *stress*
- el DNI (Documento Nacional de Identidad) *national identity card*
- **el blog, intenso/a**

Vocabulario

19

el/la empleado/a *employee*
llevar a los niños al colegio *to take the kids to school*
cocinar *to cook*
limpiar *to clean*
programar *to plan*
tiempo para uno/a mismo/a *time for oneself*
la clase de música *music class*
la piscina *swimming pool*
la pintura *painting*
el karate

20

el coche (*Esp.*) *car*
la montaña *mountain*
llegar *to arrive*

21

ir en coche *to go by car*

22

relajado/a *relaxed*
la zona colonial *the colonial area*
aprender español *to learn Spanish*
fuera de clase *outside of class*
participar en *to participate in*
ver películas *to watch movies*
viajar *to travel*
el chat

OPINIÓN

¿Le interesan los blogs?

¿Usted lee o escribe blogs?

¿Tiene usted diferentes ritmos de vida?

Estrategia

Consider ways that you can learn Spanish outside of class. Which options are most interesting to you?

- ☐ hacer un intercambio
- ☐ participar en un chat en español
- ☐ ver películas en español
- ☐ hacer un blog en español
- ☐ viajar a países hispanohablantes
- ☐ escuchar música en español
- ☐ ....

19 a. Many families have an intense daily schedule. Read this magazine article and write down the activities that homemakers and children do. Compare notes with a partner. Amos/as de casa: llevar a los niños al colegio, hacer las compras, cocinar, limpiar Niños: clases, música, piscina, karate, pintura, informática

¡RITMOS DE VIDA DIFERENTES, PERO TODOS INTENSOS!

Un empleado de bolsa tiene un ritmo de trabajo muy intenso, pero no es el único caso. Otro ejemplo de ritmo de vida intenso son las amas y los amos de casa. En su agenda semanal está: llevar a los niños al colegio, hacer las compras, cocinar, limpiar... Son muchas horas y todos los días. Es importante programar la vida y tener tiempo para uno mismo, hacer deporte, salir con amigos, etc. ¿Y los niños? Muchos niños también tienen un ritmo de vida intenso: clases de 8:00 a 16:00 h (una hora de pausa para comer de 12:00 a 13:00 h) y por la tarde mil actividades: los lunes y los martes clase de música, los miércoles, piscina, los jueves, clase de karate, los viernes, pintura, informática...

b. What other professions tend to require an intense daily schedule? Think of the professions you learned in **Lección 1B.** Suggested answers: abogado/a, ingeniero/a, técnico/a informático/a, secretario/a, médico/a

ch ll ñ

20 a. Listen to these words; pay attention to the pronunciation of **ch**, **ll**, and **ñ**.

mañana ocho llegar montaña ellos chocolate
noche llamada coche La Coruña niño

b. Write three more words you have learned with these letters.
Possible answers: panameño, chorizo, mantequilla

21 Listen to these sentences and repeat them after the speaker.

1. En La Coruña voy a la montaña por la mañana.
2. Ellos llaman porque llegan a las ocho.
3. Por la noche, muchos van en coche.

Language Note Note that **ch** and and **ll** are digraphs (two letters that together make one sound). Conventionally they are considered part of the Spanish alphabet, but **ch** and **ll** do not have their own entries in a glossary.

22 Listen to the recording and match the comments with these photos.

1. "El ritmo de vida aquí es muy relajado" (C)
2. "Después de la cena, la zona colonial tiene otro ritmo" (A)
3. "El ritmo de vida es muy acelerado" (B)

A — Santo Domingo, República Dominicana

B — Santiago, Chile

C — Costa Rica

Have students do an Internet search for **blogs en español** and share with the class the ones they found the funniest or most interesting.

Practice more at **vhlcentral.com.**

SAM: Actividades pp. 53–56

Encourage students to think in detail about the person they chose (where they live, how far they live from work, their interests and hobbies, whether they have children, etc.). Encourage students to create a "backstory" for their character.

TAREA FINAL

Un plan para la semana

Choose a profession or a type of person and think about his/her lifestyle.

Un(a) ejecutivo/a, un(a) universitario/a, un(a) niño/a...

Discuss your person with a partner. Choose either your partner's person or yours.

Take notes on the weekly activities of that person and create a schedule for him/her.

Trabaja/Estudia todos los días de 9:00 h a 18:00 h.

Por las tardes...

Por las noches...

Share the schedule you created for that person with the class.

Va a trabajar a las diez de la noche. Todos los meses viaja al extranjero...

Listen to your classmates' presentations and guess what type of person or profession they chose.

YO PUEDO...

- Puedo preguntar e informar sobre la hora.
  Complete the conversation.
- Puedo hablar de horas y rutinas.
  Write an e-mail message to a Spanish-speaking friend and tell him/her about your typical day. Answer these questions.
- Puedo rellenar una agenda.
  Write a schedule of the things you have planned for next week.
- Puedo hacer una comparación.
  Think of a friend of yours and write three comparisons between your life and his/hers.

Sample answers:

- Perdone, ¿...qué... ...hora... ...es...?
- ...Es... la una y media. / ...Son... las dos menos ...cuarto... .

- ¿Estudia/Trabaja por la mañana, por la tarde, por la noche?
  ¿A qué hora va a clases/al trabajo?
- ¿Hace deporte? ¿Sale con sus amigos?

- ¿Estudia/Trabaja más o menos horas que yo?
- ¿Hace más o menos deporte?

GRAMÁTICA FUNCIONAL

You may also want to give students the expressions **Son las doce del día** for *12 p.m.* and **Son las doce de la noche** for *12 a.m.*

3A.1 Talk about schedules and days of the week

Telling time, days of the week 2.1, 5.8.1

- To ask what time it is, say **¿Qué hora es?** To answer, say **Es** + [**la una/el mediodía/la medianoche**] or **Son** + [*other times*]. To specify, use **en punto** (*sharp*), **de la mañana** (*a.m.; in the morning*), **de la tarde** (*p.m.; in the afternoon*), and **de la noche** (*p.m.; in the evening/night*).

Es la una.	Son las dos en punto.	Son las seis de la tarde.
It's 1 o'clock.	*It's 2 o'clock sharp.*	*It's six p.m.*

- For times up to the half-hour, say **y** + [*minutes*]. For other times, subtract minutes from the next hour: **menos** + [*minutes*].

Son la siete **y diez**.	Son las diez **menos veinte**.
It's 7:10.	*It's 9:40.*

- Use **y quince** or **y cuarto** to say *quarter past*, use **menos cuarto** to say *quarter to*, and **y treinta** or **y media** to refer to a half-hour.

Son las tres **y media**.	Son las dos **menos cuarto**.
It's 3:30.	*It's 1:45.*

- The 24-hour clock is commonly used in writing, though you should not use it when speaking. Instead, use the 12-hour clock and specify **de la mañana, de la tarde,** etc.

- The week on most Spanish calendars begins on Monday (**lunes**). All days of the week are masculine, and they are not capitalized.

lunes	martes	miércoles	jueves	viernes	sábado	domingo

3A.2 Talk about times of day and routines

The verb **ir** 5.1.2 The contraction **al** 10.1
The preposition **por** 10.16

- Use the irregular verb **ir** (*to go*) to talk about your daily routine.

IR			
(yo)	voy	(nosotros/as)	vamos
(tú)	vas	(vosotros/as)	vais
(usted, él, ella)	va	(ustedes, ellos/as)	van

- **Ir** is often used with the preposition **a** (*to*). When **a** precedes the masculine article **el**, the words combine to form the contraction **al**.

Vamos **al** gimnasio a las tres.
*We're going **to the** gym at three.*

- To ask what time an event takes place, say **¿A qué hora...?** To tell what time an event takes place, say **a la(s)** + [*time*].

- **¿A qué hora** vas a clases? *What time do you go to class?*
- Voy a clases **a las ocho**. *I go to class **at eight**.*

- To indicate a general time of day, use **por** + [**la mañana/la tarde/la noche**].

Van a la universidad **por la mañana**.
*They go to the university **in the morning**.*

¡Póngalo en práctica!

G1 Write what time it is. Sample answers:

1. **4:00 a.m.** Son las cuatro (en punto) de la mañana.
2. **7:20 p.m.** Son las siete y veinte de la tarde.
3. **12:45 p.m.** Es la una menos cuarto de la tarde.
4. **9:30 p.m.** Son las nueve y media/treinta de la noche.
5. **10:35 a.m.** Son las once menos veinticinco de la mañana.
6. **3:30 p.m.** Son las tres y media/treinta de la tarde.
7. **12:00 a.m.** Es la medianoche /Son las doce de la noche (en punto).

G2 Unscramble the cues to tell the time using complete sentences.

1. cuarto / mañana / menos / cinco
   Son las cinco menos cuarto de la mañana.
2. ocho / punto / noche
   Son las ocho en punto de la noche.
3. tarde / seis / media
   Son las seis y media de la tarde.
4. once / noche / catorce / y
   Son las once y catorce de la noche.
5. menos / una / mañana / veinte
   Es la una menos veinte de la mañana.
6. nueve / noche / y / quince
   Son las nueve y quince de la noche.

G3 Complete each sentence with the appropriate form of **ir**.

1. Pedro ....va.... a la universidad en coche.
2. Gonzalo y Analía ....van.... al centro por la mañana.
3. Claudia y yo ....vamos.... a trabajar.
4. Mariana y tú ....van/vais.... al cine.
5. Tú ....vas.... a la discoteca.

G4 Complete the conversation.

- Gloria, ¿vas (1)....al.... cine esta noche?
- Sí, José María y yo (2)....vamos.... a ver una película.
- ¡Qué bien! ¿(3)....A.... qué hora es la película?
- A (4)....las.... ocho (5)....y.... media. ¿Tienes planes?
- Sí, hoy tengo la clase de yoga (6)....por.... la noche.

3A.2 Suggestion Have students write out their weekly schedules. Then, have students work in pairs to ask each other about where they go at certain times. **Ex: —Es jueves y son las tres de la tarde. ¿Adónde vas? —Voy al edificio Sherman. —¿Por qué? —Porque voy a la clase de literatura.**

Practice more at **vhlcentral.com.**

GRAMÁTICA FUNCIONAL

Contrast **el** + [*day of the week*] and **los** + [*day of the week*] by talking about sporting events. Ex: **¿Cuándo son los partidos de fútbol americano de la universidad? (Son *los* sábados.) ¿Y cuándo es el partido entre Notre Dame y Boston College? (Es *el* sábado.)**

- Use **el** + [*day of the week*] to say that something will happen on that day. Use **los** + [*day of the week (plural form)*] to talk about recurring events that happen on that day of the week. Note that only **sábado** and **domingo** add an **-s** to form the plural; the other days are invariable.

Voy a Cali **el martes.** *I'm going to Cali **on Tuesday.***	Tengo yoga **los jueves.** *I have yoga **on Thursdays.***

3A.3 Express frequency

Verbs with irregular **yo** forms: **hacer, salir** 5.1.2
Expressions of frequency 13.3

- Use the verbs **hacer** (*to make; to do*) and **salir** (*to go out*) to talk about activities. Both verbs have irregular **yo** forms ending in **-go**; the rest of the forms follow the regular conjugation patterns for **-er** and **-ir** verbs, respectively.

	HACER	SALIR
(yo)	hago	salgo
(tú)	haces	sales
(usted, él, ella)	hace	sale
(nosotros/as)	hacemos	salimos
(vosotros/as)	hacéis	salís
(ustedes, ellos/as)	hacen	salen

Los domingos **hago** la tarea o **salgo** con los amigos.
*On Sundays, **I do** homework or **go out** with friends.*

- To indicate that something happens every day/week/morning, etc., use **todos/as** + **los/las** + [*time designation*]. Always use a plural noun with this construction.

Elena hace deporte **todos los días** y sale **todos los fines de semana.**
*Elena works out **every day** and goes out **every weekend.***

3A.4 Compare

Comparatives: **más/menos + que/de** 12.7

- To compare two experiences, use the construction **más/menos** + [*noun*] + **que**. Use **más** (*more*) to indicate a greater degree and **menos** (*less*) to indicate a lesser degree.

Trabajas **más horas que** yo, pero tengo **menos vacaciones que** tú.
*You work **more hours than** I do, but I have **less vacation than** you do.*

- To compare two actions or activities, use the construction [*verb*] + **más/menos** + **que**.

Laura **estudia menos que** Jaime, y Jaime **sale más que** ella.
*Laura **studies less than** Jaime, and Jaime **goes out more** than she does.*

- To express *more/less than* a number, use **más/menos** + **de**.

Julia estudia **más de cuatro** horas al día.
*Julia studies **more than four** hours a day.*

Antonio va al gimnasio **menos de una** vez al mes.
*Antonio goes to the gym **less than once** a month.*

¡Póngalo en práctica!

G5 Complete the conversation.

- ¿Qúe planes tienes para (1) ......el...... jueves?
- Normalmente, voy al gimnasio (2) ......los...... martes y los jueves. ¿Por qué?
- Ah, (3) ......el...... jueves voy a un concierto de jazz con Lucía y Guillermo.

G6 Choose the correct ending to complete each sentence.

b	1. Tomás y yo	a. hacéis deporte.
d	2. Clara	b. hacemos las compras.
a	3. Beatriz y tú	c. sales de casa.
f	4. Yo	d. sale con amigos.
e	5. Ustedes	e. hacen planes.
c	6. Tú	f. salgo el viernes.

G7 Use the cues to form sentences with **todos/as**.

1. Raquel / hacer deporte / fin de semana
   Raquel hace deporte todos los fines de semana.
2. David y Jorge / hacer las compras / semana
   David y Jorge hacen las compras todas las semanas.
3. tú / salir de casa / mañana
   Tú sales de casa todas las mañanas.
4. yo / salir con amigos / viernes
   Yo salgo con amigos todos los viernes.

G8 Complete the conversation.

Yo tengo quince días de vacaciones y tú tienes diez, ¿no?

Sí, tú tienes (1) ......más...... días de vacaciones (2) ......que...... yo.

Bueno, pero yo trabajo todas las tardes y tú no. Trabajas menos (3) ......de...... treinta horas por semana.

Es verdad, yo trabajo (4) ......menos...... (5) ......que...... tú.

Practice more at **vhlcentral.com.**

VOCABULARIO

Horarios

¿Qué hora es?	*What time is it?*
¿A qué hora...?	*At what time . . . ?*
una persona de 80 años	*an 80-year-old person*
el día de la semana	*day of the week*
el lunes	*Monday*
el martes	*Tuesday*
el miércoles	*Wednesday*
el jueves	*Thursday*
el viernes	*Friday*
el sábado	*Saturday*
el domingo	*Sunday*
el 13 de abril	*April 13*
la bolsa (de comercio)	*stock exchange*
el calendario	*calendar; schedule*
el cine	*movie theater*
el gimnasio	*gym*
el horario	*schedule*
el mundo de las finanzas	*world of finance*
el/la músico/a	*musician*
el/la niño/a	*boy/girl*
el/la profesional	*professional*
el programa de radio	*radio program*
el reloj	*clock; watch*
la rutina diaria	*daily routine*
el/la veterinario/a	*veterinarian*
el/la vigilante nocturno/a	*night security guard*
abrir	*to open*
hacer	*to do; to make*
ir a trabajar	*to go to work*
llegar a casa	*to arrive home*
abierto/a	*open*
de la mañana	*a.m., in the morning*
de la tarde	*p.m., in the afternoon*
de la noche	*p.m., in the evening/night*
por la mañana	*in the morning*
por la tarde	*in the afternoon*
por la noche	*in the evening, at night*

Agenda semanal

¿Con qué frecuencia?	*How often?*
todos los días	*every day*
tres veces al año	*three times a year*
más que	*more than*
menos que	*less than*
la agenda (semanal)	*(weekly) planner*
agosto	*August*
el colegio	*school*
el curso	*class, course*
el día festivo	*holiday*
la entrevista	*interview*
el horario de trabajo	*work schedule*
julio	*July*
la mujer	*woman; wife*
el ritmo de vida	*pace of life*
el/la trabajador(a)	*worker*
las vacaciones	*vacation*
la vez (*pl.* veces)	*time*
el viaje de negocios	*business trip*
el yoga	*yoga*
colaborar	*to participate*
hacer algo en casa	*to do something at home*
hacer deporte	*to exercise*
hacer la cama	*to make the bed*
hacer las compras	*to go grocery shopping*
pasear	*to go for a walk*
salir (con amigos)	*to go out (with friends)*
salir de	*to leave*
tener clase	*to have class*
terminar	*to end*

Pablo Linares

tiempo para uno/a mismo/a	*time for oneself*
el blog	*blog*
el campo	*country(side)*
el chat	*chat room*
la clase de música	*music class*
el coche (*Esp.*)	*car*
el deporte	*sport(s)*
el descanso	*rest*
diciembre	*December*
el DNI (Documento Nacional de Identidad)	*national identity card*
el/la empleado/a	*employee*
la estancia (*Cono S.*)	*ranch*
el estrés	*stress*
el karate	*karate*
la llamada (de teléfono)	*(telephone) call*
la montaña	*mountain*
la pintura	*painting*
la piscina	*swimming pool*
la prensa económica	*financial press*
el río	*river*
la tele(visión)	*television*
la terapia	*therapy*
el tiempo	*time*
la zona colonial	*the colonial area*
aprender español	*to learn Spanish*
cocinar	*to cook*
entrar en	*to enter*
ir en coche	*to go by car*
limpiar	*to clean*
llegar	*to arrive*
llevar a los niños al colegio	*to take the kids to school*
parar	*to stop*
participar en	*to participate in*
programar	*to plan*
tomar el ferry	*to take the ferry*
ver películas	*to watch movies*
viajar	*to travel*
intenso/a	*intense*
relajado/a	*relaxed*
al aire libre	*outdoors*
aproximadamente	*approximately*
fuera de clase	*outside of class*

Variación léxica

el carro (*Amér. L.*) ↔ **el coche** (*Esp.*) ↔ **el auto** (*Cono S.*)

el colegio ↔ **la escuela**

la finca ↔ **la hacienda** ↔ **la estancia** (*Cono S.*)

la mujer ↔ **la esposa**

el DNI ↔ **la cédula de identidad** ↔ **la cédula de ciudadanía** (*Méx.*)

As a warm-up, ask students if they prefer to receive gifts or gift cards. Then point out the **cheque-regalo** and ask students which items they would pick.

3B CENTRO COMERCIAL

¡Regalos fantásticos!

Identificar y especificar

- ¿**Este** libro de **aquí** es de fotografía?
- No, **ese** libro de **ahí** es de fotografía.

3B.1 Demonstratives and adverbs of location

Hablar de la existencia

- ¿Qué tiendas **hay** en la calle comercial?
- **Hay** una librería y una zapatería.

3B.2 The verb **haber: hay**

Vocabulario

1

el regalo *present*
el centro comercial *shopping mall*
la perfumería *perfume/cosmetics shop*
la librería *bookstore*
el cheque-regalo *gift voucher*
la chaqueta *jacket*
caro/a *expensive*
la colección, original, el perfume, personal

2

el abanico *(hand-held) fan*
las gafas *glasses*
práctico/a *practical*
feo/a *ugly*

1 a. Carmela and Jorge are buying a present for a friend. Listen to their conversation with the sales clerk and answer the questions.

1. ¿De qué regalos hablan Carmela y Jorge? Hablan de una colección de CD, una chaqueta, un libro y un perfume.
2. ¿De qué regalo habla el vendedor? Habla del cheque-regalo.

b. Listen to their conversation again and associate the words in each column.

este/esta → cerca/aquí	ese/esa → lejos/ahí	estos/estas → cerca/aquí	esos/esas → lejos/ahí

2 a. Look at the **cheque-regalo** and circle the items available this week.

Hay... *(libros)* *abanicos* *(perfumes)* *coches* *(colección de CD)* *teléfonos celulares* *gafas*

b. Use these adjectives to discuss the **cheque-regalo** in pairs.

bonito/a • original • personal • diferente • práctico/a • moderno/a • feo/a

2 **Expansion** Have students work in pairs to look around the room and state what there is and is not. Then have them do the same for places in the community.

3 Match each item to the store where it is sold.

1. libros ...c...
2. perfume ...d...
3. chaqueta ...b...
4. zapatos ...a...
5. CD ...e...

a. zapatería
b. tienda de ropa
c. librería
d. perfumería
e. tienda de discos

Explain to students that the plural of **el CD** (pronounced **el cedé**) is written **los CD**.

Localizar

¿Dónde está el bolígrafo?

Está **en** la mesa, **al lado del** libro.

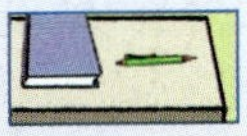

Está **a la derecha del** libro.

Está **a la izquierda del** libro.

Está **debajo del** libro.

Está **detrás del** libro.

Está **delante del** libro.

Está **entre** el libro y el teléfono.

Está **encima del** libro.

3B.3 **estar** + [*prepositional phrase*]; **de + el = del**

Vocabulario *cont.*

(3)

el zapato *shoe*
la zapatería *shoe store*
la tienda de ropa *clothing store*
la tienda de discos *music store*

(4)

el bolígrafo *pen*
la mesa *table*
al lado de *next to*
a la derecha de *to the right of*
a la izquierda de *to the left of*
debajo de *under*
detrás de *behind*
delante de *in front of*
encima de *on (top of)*
del (= de + el) *of the*
el despertador *alarm clock*
el pañuelo *scarf; handkerchief*
la lámpara *lamp*
las gafas de sol *sunglasses*
el marco *picture frame*
el paraguas *umbrella*
la tienda de regalos *gift shop*
el objeto *object*

(5)

el reloj (de pulsera) *(wrist)watch*

Explain that the prices in the drawing are in **pesos**, which use the same symbol (**$**) as dollars.

4 a. Look at the gift shop window and identify the items described.

1. Están a la derecha de los libros: *las gafas de sol*
2. Está encima de la agenda: el pañuelo
3. Está a la izquierda de los CD: el despertador
4. Están a la derecha de la lámpara: los libros
5. Está detrás de los zapatos: el perfume
6. Está delante de la chaqueta: el paraguas

b. Choose three items in the store and tell your partner where they are.

Modelo:
- *Está entre el perfume y el paraguas.*
- *¿El marco?*

5 Expansion Have pairs tell each other about items in their own rooms and their relative location. Ex: **En mi cuarto hay... Está al lado de...**

5 In pairs, use the adjectives from **Actividad 2b** to describe these gifts.

Modelo: *El reloj es muy práctico.*

MI EXPERIENCIA

6 Create a **cheque-regalo**. Choose two gifts for this week, the stores that will participate in the promotion, and a price. Explain your offer to the class.

GUIÓN DE TRABAJO

¿Qué regalos hay? → Hay... libros, despertadores, paraguas... → ¿Cómo son? → originales, prácticos/as, interesantes ...

¿Qué tiendas hay? → Hay... perfumerías, librerías, tiendas de ropa...

.... pesos

Practice more at **vhlcentral.com.**

SAM: Actividades pp. 57–59

Prendas de moda

SECCIÓN MODA

Leticia lleva una camiseta anaranjada, una falda negra y unas zapatillas de deporte rojas.

Carlos lleva una chaqueta anaranjada, una camiseta amarilla y unos pantalones azules.

Sara lleva una camiseta verde y unos pantalones grises. Ángel lleva una camiseta anaranjada y unos jeans azules.

Juanjo lleva un traje marrón, una camisa azul y una corbata roja, y Mireia lleva un vestido blanco con unas botas marrones.

For additional practice with colors and clothing, have students write a description of what they are wearing today.

7 a. Read the descriptions and write the photo number that corresponds to each person or pair.

[2] Leticia [3] Sara y Ángel [1] Carlos [4] Juanjo y Mireia

7b Suggestion Challenge students by asking them to study each photo for a minute or two, then cover it and try to fill in the chart from memory.

b. For each color, list the articles of clothing that appear in the description.

marrón	gris	blanco/a	negro/a
traje, botas	pantalones	vestido	falda

rojo/a	verde	azul	amarillo/a	anaranjado/a
zapatillas de deporte, corbata	camiseta	jeans, pantalones, camisa	camiseta	chaqueta, camiseta

8 Write down the colors of the clothes your classmates are wearing.

Modelo: *Anne lleva unos pantalones azules...*

9 a. Listen to these conversations in a clothing store and circle the three items mentioned.

vestido	(falda)	traje	pantalones	(zapatos)	(suéter)

b. Listen to the recording again and match items in each column.

1. Quiero ...c... a. suéteres?
2. ¿Tienen ...a... b. talla tiene?
3. Quería ...d... c. una falda, por favor.
4. ¿Qué ...b... d. esos zapatos del escaparate.
5. ¿De qué ...e... e. color?

10 With a partner, role-play a conversation between a shopper and a salesperson. Choose three items from the store front and ask for them, specifying the size and color you want.

Modelo: *Quiero el vestido verde, los zapatos...*

Indicar el color

Una chaqueta **blanca**.

Un bolso **blanco**.

Unas zapatillas **blancas**.

Unos pantalones **blancos**.

3B.4 Colors

Hablar de la ropa

Marta **lleva** un vestido verde y unos zapatos verdes.

3B.5 The verb **llevar**

Solicitar productos

Quiero una camisa azul.

Quería unos zapatos negros.

¿**Tienen** jeans de señora?

3B.6 Stem-changing verbs **e→ie: querer**

Vocabulario

7

la prenda *garment*
llevar *to wear*
la camiseta *T-shirt*
anaranjado/a *orange*
la falda *skirt*
negro/a *black*
las zapatillas de deporte *running shoes, sneakers*
rojo/a *red*
amarillo/a *yellow*
los pantalones *pants*
azul *blue*

Vocabulario ***cont.***

- **verde** *green*
- **gris** *gray*
- **el traje** *suit*
- **marrón** *brown*
- **la camisa** *shirt*
- **la corbata** *tie*
- **el vestido** *dress*
- **blanco/a** *white*
- **la bota** *boot*
- **el bolso** *bag*
- **la marca** *brand*
- **el color, los jeans**

(9)

- **el suéter** *sweater*
- **querer (e:ie)** *to want*
- **el escaparate** *shop window*
- **¿De qué color (*m.*)?** *What color?*
- **¿De qué talla (*f.*)?** *What size?*

Referirse a un objeto ya mencionado

Lo llevo siempre. (el reloj)

La quería marrón. (la falda)

Los tengo en azul. (los pantalones)

¿Las puedo ver? (las camisetas)

3B.7 Direct object pronouns

Pedir permiso y aceptar

- ¿Puedo ver esos pantalones?
- Por supuesto.
- ¿Puedo pagar con tarjeta?
- Sí, claro.

3B.8 Stem-changing verbs **o→ue: poder** Affirmative statements

Vocabulario

(11)

- **¿Los puedo ver?** *Can I see them?*
- **ver** *to see*
- **Lo siento.** *I'm sorry.*
- **con tarjeta** *with a credit card*

(12)

- **en efectivo** *in cash*

(13)

- **preferido/a** *favorite*
- **el dibujo** *drawing*
- **la escuela** *school*

Have two volunteers role-play the conversation for the class.

Cliente: Hola, quería esta camisa.
Vendedora: ¿Qué talla tiene?
Cliente: La talla L. ¿La tiene blanca?
Vendedora: Sí, aquí está.
Cliente: También quería estos pantalones, ¿los puedo ver?
Vendedora: Sí, claro, aquí los tiene.
Cliente: Y estas gafas de sol... ¿Las tiene marrones?
Vendedora: No, las tengo negras.
Cliente: Ese suéter, ¿lo tiene verde?
Vendedora: No, lo siento. Lo tenemos en azul.
Cliente: Gracias, ¿puedo pagar con tarjeta?
Vendedora: Sí, por supuesto.

11 a. Read the conversation and write the clothing item each question refers to.

1. ¿La tienen blanca? *la camisa*
2. ¿Los puedo ver? los pantalones
3. ¿Las tiene marrones? las gafas de sol
4. ¿Lo tiene verde? el suéter

b. Rewrite the questions, substituting the underlined words with **lo**, **la**, **los**, or **las**.

1. Quería este suéter negro. ¿Tienen el suéter negro en la talla M?
   ¿Lo tienen en la talla M?
2. Quería estas gafas. ¿Tienen estas gafas en otro color? ¿Las tienen en otro color?
3. Quería unos pantalones. ¿Tiene pantalones negros? ¿Los tiene negros?
4. Me gusta esta camiseta. ¿Tienen esta camiseta en la talla L? ¿La tienen en la talla L?

12 Now it's time to pay. Match the expressions with the method of payment.

- en efectivo ..B..
- con tarjeta ..A..

A 

B 

MI EXPERIENCIA

12 Expansion Ask students which method of payment they prefer. As a class, come up with a list of advantages and disadvantages for each.

13 What are your favorite colors and clothes?

First, review clothing vocabulary and associate words with pictures. Then draw a picture of your favorite clothing item.

zapatos

camisa

jeans/pantalones

vestido

GUIÓN DE TRABAJO

Mi ropa favorita es...

Aquí su dibujo

una falda
unos pantalones
una camisa
un vestido
unos zapatos
un suéter...

verde
azul
rojo/a
anaranjado/a
negro/a
blanco/a

Lo, la, los, las, **llevo** en...

el trabajo, la escuela, una fiesta, casa...

Mi color favorito es el ....

Practice more at **vhlcentral.com.**

SAM: Actividades pp. 60–62

Invite students to talk about their favorite designers.

Olga Piedrahita, la moda en Colombia

ESCAPARATE **Suggestion** Before students read the text, have them scan the magazine cover and article for cognates.

"Para mí, la moda es comunicación. La moda es arte."

Moda colombiana

Olga Piedrahita es una importante diseñadora colombiana. Estudió Bellas Artes en Estados Unidos y ahora trabaja en Colombia. Pertenece a un grupo de diseñadores llamados "intelectuales" que hacen moda artística y creativa. La diseñadora colombiana representa a Colombia en la **LatinoAmérica Fashion** en el marco del Salón Internacional de la Moda de Madrid.

Olga Piedrahita presenta una interesante colección para la mujer contemporánea. Sus trabajos son personales y prácticos; su lema, "arte para llevar". Sus camisas, faldas, vestidos o pantalones reflejan magia, poesía y humor, y los colores son verdes, marrones, azules y grises.

Vocabulario

14
- la edición especial *special edition*
- la moda *fashion*
- el/la diseñador(a) *designer*
- colombiano/a *Colombian*
- estudió *she/he studied*
- pertenecer (zc) *to belong*
- el Salón Internacional de la Moda *International Fashion Fair*
- contemporáneo/a *contemporary*
- el lema *motto*
- la moda infantil *children's fashion*
- la portada *cover*
- el viaje *trip*
- **la comunicación, el arte, la decoración**

16
- el/la modelo *(fashion) model*

Expansion Have students work in small groups to rate these clothing characteristics in order of greatest to least importance: quality, low price, designer name, trendy, artistic/avant-garde. What other characteristics do they consider when shopping for clothing?

14 Look at this magazine cover and answer the questions.

1. ¿Qué tipo de revista es?

   ☑ de moda ☐ de decoración ☐ de viajes

2. ¿Cuándo sale la revista?

   ☐ todos los días ☐ todas las semanas ☑ todos los meses

3. ¿Cuáles son los temas de la revista?

   ☑ moda ☑ viajes ☐ cine ☑ regalos ☑ decoración

15 a. Answer these questions about Olga Piedrahita.

- ¿De dónde es? Es de Colombia.
- ¿Cuál es su profesión? Es diseñadora.

b. With a partner, reread the article and answer these questions.

- ¿Cuál es la opinión de Olga Piedrahita sobre la moda? ¿Están ustedes de acuerdo? La moda es "arte para llevar".

16 Look at the photo of Olga Piedrahita and write a brief description of what she is wearing.

Modelo: *Olga Piedrahita lleva...*

17 Listen to the radio ad and answer the question.

- ¿De qué habla? Suggested answer: Habla de la revista "Escaparate".

Vocabulario

(18)

el consumo *consumption*
los complementos *accessories*
la artesanía *crafts*
venir *to come*
en vías de desarrollo *developing*
el comercio justo *fair trade*
garantizar *to guarantee*
el sueldo *wage*
digno/a *decent*
el/la productor(a) *producer*
proteger (j) *to protect*
el derecho *right*
el objetivo *goal, objective*
hacer consciente *to make aware*
el/la consumidor(a) *consumer*
comprar *to buy*
responsable, el producto, la organización

OPINIÓN

¿Sigue usted la moda?

¿Cree que la moda es una forma de arte?

¿Compra usted por Internet? ¿Qué tipo de productos?¿Por qué prefiere esta opción?

Vocabulario

(19)

la rebaja *discount*

(20)

el puro habano *Cuban cigar*
la yerba mate *mate (infusion)*
el tapiz (*pl.* tapices) *tapestry*

20a Suggestion Ask students if they have ever come across any of these products in this country.

CONSUMO RESPONSABLE

Muchos productos que compramos todos los días, como por ejemplo, la ropa, los complementos, la comida y la artesanía, vienen de países en vías de desarrollo. Las organizaciones internacionales de comercio justo quieren garantizar un sueldo digno al productor y proteger los derechos de los niños y de las mujeres en estos países. Otro objetivo de estas organizaciones es hacer conscientes a los consumidores del origen de los productos que compran.

Have students examine the labels of the clothes they are wearing and accessories they brought with them to class, and write down where each item was made. Have them share their lists with the class and discuss the information.

18 a. Read the text and answer these questions. Sample answers:

1. ¿De qué productos habla el texto? Habla de la ropa, los complementos, la comida y la artesanía.
2. ¿De dónde vienen los productos de este tipo de comercio? Vienen de países en vías de desarrollo.
3. ¿Cuál es el objetivo del comercio justo? El objetivo es garantizar un sueldo digno al productor, proteger los derechos de los niños y las mujeres y hacer conscientes a los consumidores del origen de los productos.

b. Discuss your answer to question 3 with a partner. Do you agree?

[j] [g]

19 a. Listen to these words. Underline the sound they have in common.

gimnasio	traje	joven	agenda	rebajas	objetivo
origen	ecológica	jirafa	tarjeta	mujeres	justo

b. Now organize the words according to how this sound is spelled.

ja	je/ge	ji/gi	jo	ju
rebajas	traje origen mujeres	ecológica gimnasio jirafa	joven	justo

20 a. These are some typical products from Latin America. Match each product to its country of origin.

A 
puros habanos

B 
yerba mate

C 
tapices

D 
café

(C) Perú (A) Cuba (D) Colombia (B) Argentina

b. What other products from Latin America can you name?

Practice more at **vhlcentral.com.**

SAM: Actividades pp. 63–68

TAREA FINAL

Tienda de regalos

You may wish to add to students' lists by giving them additional vocabulary.

Have students look at the photos and say what is sold at each store.

- Make a list of the types of stores you have seen in this lesson.
- With a partner, choose a type of store. Give the store a name and decide what products it will sell.
- Come up with a special of the month and make a poster advertising the items and their prices.
- Hang the posters in your classroom, and, as a class, vote on who has the best promotion.

YO PUEDO...

- Puedo hablar sobre las tiendas y los artículos que hay en ellas.
  Choose a store you know and list what items are sold there.

Tienda: ....
Artículos: ....
....
....
....

- Puedo localizar objetos en el espacio.
  Choose an item near you and say where it is located, using prepositions of location.
- Puedo identificar diferentes prendas de ropa y especificar su color.
  Write the name and color of each article of clothing.

pantalones/jeans grises

vestido anaranjado

camiseta verde

falda azul

- Puedo pedir un artículo en una tienda y solicitar información sobre la forma de pago.
  Complete this dialogue.

- Buenos días, ...querría... unos pantalones azules.
- Por supuesto.
- ¿...Puedo... pagar ...con... ...tarjeta...?

GRAMÁTICA FUNCIONAL

Tell students that they may occasionally see **este/a/os/as** or **ese/a/os/as** written with an accent mark when these words are used as pronouns. Contemporary usage states that this diacritical mark should be used only in case of ambiguity.

3B.1 Identify and specify items

Demonstratives and adverbs of location 7.1, 7.2, 11.7

- When referring to specific objects, use the adjectives **este/a/os/as** (*this/these*), and **ese/a/os/as** (*that/those*) to identify precisely which object(s) you are talking about.

  Este pañuelo cuesta $50, pero **ese** pañuelo cuesta $30.
  *This scarf costs $50, but **that** scarf costs $30.*

- **Este/a/os/as** and **ese/a/os/as** must agree in gender and number with the nouns they modify. Place these adjectives before nouns.

(aquí)		(ahí)	
este libro estos libros	esta lámpara estas lámparas	ese libro esos libros	esa lámpara esas lámparas

- For added emphasis and precision, use the expressions **de aquí** (*over here*) and **de ahí** (*over there*) to specify which item(s) you are talking about.

  Esta agenda **de aquí** es muy práctica.
  *This planner **(over) here** is very practical.*

  Ese paraguas **de ahí** es muy original.
  *That umbrella **(over) there** is very original.*

- **Este/a/os/as** and **ese/a/os/as** can also be used on their own, as pronouns. Remember that the pronoun should match the gender and number of the noun or person it represents.

  Esta es la vendedora.
  This is the saleswoman.

  Esos son los libros de García Márquez.
  Those are the books by García Márquez.

3B.2 Express existence

The verb **haber: hay** 5.1.2, 5.9

- Use the verb **hay** (*there is/are*) to express that something exists.

  Hay tres libros encima de la mesa.
  ***There are** three books on the table.*

- Note that **hay** is invariable; it is used both for a single items and for multiple items.

  Hay una lámpara. *There is a lamp.*
  Hay cuatro marcos. *There are four picture frames.*

- Use **hay** in questions to mean *is/are there.*

  ¿**Hay** discos de Juanes?
  Are there (any) CDs by Juanes?

  ¿Qué **hay** en la tienda de regalos?
  *What **is there** in the gift shop?*

Point out that to say that *there isn't* or *aren't* any, one uses **no hay. No** is always placed before the verb.

3B.1 You may wish to introduce the neuter forms **esto** and **eso**, which refer to unidentified or unspecified nouns, situations, or ideas. Point out that they do not change in gender. Practice them by pretending to be unfamiliar with objects in the room; have students explain what they are. Ex: **¿Qué es esto? (Es un mapa. Tiene los países del mundo.)**

¡Póngalo en práctica!

G1 Write the appropriate form of **este/a/os/as** or **ese/a/os/as** for each item.

(de aquí)	(de ahí)
1. estos regalos	6. ese marco
2. esta tienda	7. esos libros
3. estas perfumerías	8. esas chaquetas
4. este abanico	9. ese escaparate
5. esta colección	10. esa librería

G2 Write a sentence identifying each person or object.

Modelo: (aquí) Juan
Este es Juan.

1. (ahí) las gafas
   Esas son las gafas.
2. (aquí) los paraguas
   Estos son los paraguas.
3. (aquí) Ana y Jorge
   Estos son Ana y Jorge.
4. (ahí) el perfume
   Ese es el perfume.
5. (ahí) la zapatería
   Esa es la zapatería.
6. (aquí) el cheque-regalo
   Este es el cheque-regalo.

G3 Look at the inventory for the gift shop and write four sentences describing what can be found there.

OBJETO	CANTIDAD
abanico	32
pañuelo	14
marco	21
lámpara	8
libro	55
gafas de sol	10

Sample answers: Hay treinta y dos abanicos. Hay catorce pañuelos. Hay veintiún marcos. Hay ocho lámparas. Hay cincuenta y cinco libros. Hay diez gafas de sol.

Practice more at **vhlcentral.com.**

3B

GRAMÁTICA FUNCIONAL

Point out that the icons express the relative location of the circle or the darker square.

3B.3 Identify relative location

estar + [*preposition/prepositional phrase*] 5.1.2, 5.8.1, 10.11, 10.17
de + el = del

en / encima de		debajo de	
a la derecha de		delante de	
a la izquierda de		detrás de	

Have students devise their own icons for **al lado de** and **entre**.

- To describe where something is in relation to something else, use **estar** + [*preposition/prepositional phrase*].

Las gafas de sol **están al lado de** la lámpara.
*The sunglasses **are next to** the lamp.*

El coche **está delante de la** librería.
*The car **is in front of the** bookstore.*

- When **de** is followed by the masculine article **el**, combine the words to form the contraction **del**.

Los CD están a la derecha **del** despertador.
*The CDs are to the right **of the** alarm clock.*

3B.4 Indicate colors

Colors 4.1 The plural 4.2

- Use colors to specify and add detail to a description. Place adjectives of color after the nouns they modify.

rojo/a/os/as	anaranjado/a/os/as	amarillo/a/os/as
verde(s)	azul(es)	blanco/a/os/as
negro/a/os/as	gris(es)	marrón/marrones

- Some nouns, such as **café, rosa,** and **naranja,** can be used as invariable adjectives to refer to the colors brown, pink, and orange, respectively. They are most commonly used with the noun **color**.

Irene lleva un suéter **color naranja** y unos pantalones **rosa**.
*Irene is wearing an **orange** sweater and **pink** pants.*

3B.5 Talk about clothing

The verb **llevar** 5.1.1

- Use the verb **llevar** (*to wear; to take*) to talk about the clothes people wear. **Llevar** is a regular **-ar** verb.

LLEVAR			
(yo)	llevo	(nosotros/as)	llevamos
(tú)	llevas	(vosotros/as)	lleváis
(usted, él, ella)	lleva	(ustedes, ellos/as)	llevan

Héctor y Lourdes **llevan** unas zapatillas de deporte blancas.
*Héctor and Lourdes **are wearing** white sneakers.*

- As you saw in **Lección 3A**, **llevar** can also mean *to take*.

Llevo mis libros a clase.
*I **take** my books to class.*

Tell students they can also use the verbs **usar** and **traer** to talk about wearing clothing.

¡Póngalo en práctica!

G4 Say where each item is in relation to the other.

Modelo: *la tienda de regalos* *la librería*

Modelo: *La tienda de regalos está a la derecha de la librería.*

1. el CD el libro
   El CD está debajo del libro.
2. el despertador la lámpara
   El despertador está detrás de la lámpara.
3. el marco el pañuelo
   El marco está en el/encima del pañuelo.
4. el abanico los CD
   El abanico está a la derecha de los CD.
5. el celular la chaqueta
   El celular está a la izquierda de la chaqueta.
6. los jeans los suéteres
   Los jeans están delante de los suéteres.

G5 Complete the paragraph using the correct form of each adjective.

En el escaparate de la tienda hay unos pantalones (1) azules (azul), un suéter (2) verde (verde), una camisa (3) roja (rojo) y unos zapatos (4) marrones (marrón). También hay un bonito vestido (5) rosa (rosa), unas faldas (6) amarillas (amarillo) y una corbata (7) negra (negro).

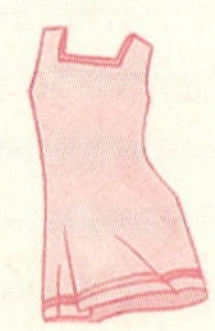

G6 Complete each sentence with the appropriate form of **llevar.**

1. Manolo siempre lleva una corbata.
2. Celia y Rebeca llevan unas camisetas verdes.
3. Yo llevo un suéter bonito.
4. Tú llevas unos jeans negros.
5. Ustedes llevan unas gafas de sol elegantes.
6. Carlos y yo llevamos unos zapatos nuevos.
7. Mi madre siempre lleva prendas de marca.
8. El cajero y tú lleváis/llevan el mismo suéter.

Practice more at **vhlcentral.com.**

GRAMÁTICA FUNCIONAL

3B.6 Request products

Stem-changing verbs e→ie: querer 5.1.1
Demonstrative adjectives and pronouns 7.1, 7.2

- Use the verb **querer** (*to want*) to request products.

  Hola, **quiero** estos zapatos, por favor.
  *Hello, **I want** these shoes, please.*

- **Querer** is an **e→ie** stem-changing verb; the **e** in the stem changes to **ie** in all forms except for the **nosotros/as** and **vosotros/as** forms. You saw a similar pattern with **almorzar** in 2B.3.

3B.6 Remind students of "boot verbs". Ask a volunteer to write the forms of **querer** on the board and another to draw the boot formation and explain what it means.

QUERER			
(yo)	quiero	(nosotros/as)	queremos
(tú)	quieres	(vosotros/as)	queréis
(usted, él, ella)	quiere	(ustedes, ellos/as)	quieren

¿**Quieres** el vestido verde o este azul?
***Do you want** the green dress or this blue one?*

Quiero este de aquí, por favor.
***I want** this one here, please.*

- To make a polite request, use **quería** (*I wanted*) instead of **quiero**.

3B.7 Refer to a previously mentioned object

Direct object pronouns 6.2.1

- To avoid unnecessary repetition, use a direct object pronoun to refer to an object that has been mentioned previously.

  Quería esta falda. ¿**La** tienen verde?
  *I'd like this skirt. Do you have **it** in green?*

- A direct object is a noun that receives the action of a verb. In the statement *I'm wearing jeans,* the direct object is *jeans*; it answers the question *What am I wearing?*

SUBJECT	VERB	DIRECT OBJECT
Esperanza	lleva	una camiseta azul.
Esperanza	*is wearing*	*a blue T-shirt.*

- Direct object pronouns agree with the nouns they replace.

	singular	plural
masculino	lo	los
femenino	la	las

Luis compra **los zapatos**. ↔ Luis **los** compra.
*Luis buys **the shoes**. ↔ Luis buys **them**.*

Queremos **la lámpara**. ↔ **La** queremos.
*We want **the lamp**. ↔ We want **it**.*

Successful Language Learning Emphasize that using direct object pronouns will make students' speech sound more natural.

- Place a direct object pronoun directly before the conjugated verb.

  Lo tengo y **lo** llevo siempre.
  *I have **it** and I wear **it** all the time.*

¡Póngalo en práctica!

G7 Complete the conversation with the appropriate forms of **querer**.

Buenos días, nosotras (1) queremos unos vestidos de fiesta.

Muy bien. ¿De qué colores los (2) quieren/queréis ?

Yo (3) quiero/quería un vestido azul. Manuela (4) quiere ese vestido negro de ahí.

Lo siento mucho; no tenemos vestidos azules. ¿(5) Quiere usted ver otro color?

Ay, no, gracias. Yo realmente (6) quiero uno azul.

G8 Complete the conversations with the appropriate direct object pronouns.

- Hola, quería unos zapatos marrones.
- ¿De qué número (1) los quiere?
- (2) Los quiero del número 42, por favor.

- Buenas tardes, quería una falda nueva.
- ¿De qué color (3) la quiere?
- ¿(4) La tienen roja?
- Sí, (5) la tenemos roja y negra también.

G9 Rewrite each sentence using a direct object pronoun.

1. Concepción lleva la camiseta.
   Concepción la lleva.
2. Germán y tú queréis las gafas negras.
   Germán y tú las queréis.
3. Claudia y yo queremos los zapatos elegantes.
   Claudia y yo los queremos.
4. La tienda tiene los jeans nuevos.
   La tienda los tiene.
5. ¿De qué talla quiere la camiseta?
   ¿De qué talla la quiere?
6. Quiero el suéter gris.
   Lo quiero gris

Practice more at **vhlcentral.com.**

GRAMÁTICA FUNCIONAL

3B.8 Request and grant permission

Stem-changing verbs **o→ue: poder** 5.1.1
Infinitive constructions 5.10
Affirmative expressions 14.19

- Use the verb **poder** (*to be able to*) to request and grant permission.

  ¿**Podemos** ver ese reloj?
  Can we see that watch?

- **Poder** is an **o→ue** stem-changing verb. As with other stem-changing verbs, the stem change occurs in all forms except the **nosotros/as** and **vosotros/as** forms.

PODER			
(yo)	puedo	(nosotros/as)	podemos
(tú)	puedes	(vosotros/as)	podéis
(usted, él, ella)	puede	(ustedes, ellos/as)	pueden

  ¿**Puedo** pagar con tarjeta?
  Can I pay with a credit card?

- **Poder** is often used in combination with another verb; in this construction, use the conjugated form of **poder** followed by the infinitive of the second verb.

  Sí, usted **puede pagar** con tarjeta.
  *Yes, you **can pay** with a credit card.*

- **Querer** is also frequently used in combination with an infinitive.

  Quiero ver esa camiseta.
  ***I want to see** that T-shirt.*

- When you use a direct object pronoun with an infinitive construction, the direct object pronoun can be placed before the conjugated verb or it can be attached to the end of the infinitive.

  ¿**La** puedo ver? / ¿Puedo ver**la**?
  *Can I see **it**?*

- Use affirmative expressions such as **claro** and **por supuesto** (*of course*) to add emphasis and variety to your conversations.

• ¿Puedo pagar con tarjeta? ▪ Sí, por supuesto.

¡Póngalo en práctica!

G10 Match each sentence starter with the appropriate ending.

1. Silvia y yo...
2. El vendedor...
3. Tú...
4. Yo...
5. Gabriel y Daniel...

a. ...3... puedes pagar con tarjeta.
b. ...2... puede vender los regalos.
c. ...5... pueden comprar las gafas.
d. ...1... podemos hacer las compras.
e. ...4... puedo llevar mi nuevo vestido.

G11 Rewrite each sentence using a direct object pronoun.

1. ¿Puedo ver el paraguas?
   ¿Lo puedo ver?/¿Puedo verlo?
2. ¿Quiere comprar los CD?
   ¿Los quiere comprar?/¿Quiere comprarlos?
3. Puedes llevar los zapatos negros.
   Los puedes llevar./Puedes llevarlos.
4. Los niños pueden llevar jeans al restaurante.
   Los niños los pueden llevar al restaurante./Los niños pueden llevarlos al restaurante.

G12 Use phrases from the word bank to complete this conversation.

Claro, aquí tiene.	Sí, por supuesto.
Solo en efectivo.	¿Lo puedo ver?
¿Puedo pagar con tarjeta?	

• Buenos días. Quería este suéter. (1) ¿Lo puedo ver?
▪ (2) Sí, por supuesto. Aquí está.
• ¿Lo tienen en la talla M?
▪ (3) Claro, aquí tiene.
• Muchas gracias. Es muy elegante; lo quiero comprar. (4) ¿Puedo pagar con tarjeta?
▪ Lo siento, no. (5) Solo en efectivo.

Practice more at **vhlcentral.com.**

VOCABULARIO

¡Regalos fantásticos!

el abanico	(hand-held) fan
el bolígrafo	pen
el centro comercial	shopping mall
la chaqueta	jacket
el cheque-regalo	gift voucher
la colección	collection
el despertador	alarm clock
las gafas (de sol)	(sun)glasses
la lámpara	lamp
la librería	bookstore
el marco	picture frame
la mesa	table
el objeto	object
el pañuelo	scarf; handkerchief
el paraguas	umbrella
el perfume	perfume
la perfumería	perfume/cosmetics shop
el regalo	present
el reloj (de pulsera)	(wrist)watch
la tienda de discos	music store
la tienda de regalos	gift shop
la tienda de ropa	clothing store
el zapato	shoe
la zapatería	shoe store
caro/a	expensive
feo/a	ugly
original	original
personal	personal
práctico/a	practical
a la derecha de	to the right of
a la izquierda de	to the left of
al lado de	next to
debajo de	under
delante de	in front of
detrás de	behind
encima de	on (top of)
del (= de + el)	of the

Prendas de moda

¿De qué color (*m.*)?	What color?
¿De qué talla (*f.*)?	What size?
Lo siento.	I'm sorry.
¿Los puedo ver?	Can I see them?
la bota	boot
el bolso	bag
la camisa	shirt
la camiseta	T-shirt
el color	color
la corbata	tie
el dibujo	drawing
el escaparate	shop window
la escuela	school
la falda	skirt
los jeans	jeans
la marca	brand
los pantalones	pants
la prenda	garment
la talla	size
el traje	suit
el suéter	sweater
el vestido	dress
las zapatillas (de deporte)	running shoes, sneakers
llevar	to wear
querer (e:ie)	to want
ver	to see
amarillo/a	yellow
anaranjado/a	orange
azul	blue
blanco/a	white
gris	gray
marrón	brown
negro/a	black
preferido/a	favorite
rojo/a	red
verde	green
en efectivo	cash
con tarjeta	with a credit card

Olga Piedrahita

estudió	he/she studied
el arte	art
la artesanía	crafts
el comercio justo	fair trade
los complementos	accessories
la comunicación	communication
el/la consumidor(a)	consumer
el consumo	consumption
la decoración	decoration
el derecho	right
el/la diseñador(a)	designer
la edición especial	special edition
el lema	motto
la moda	fashion
la moda infantil	children's fashion
el/la modelo	(fashion) model
el objetivo	goal, objective
la organización	organization
la portada	cover
el producto	product
el/la productor(a)	producer
el puro habano	Cuban cigar
la rebaja	discount
el Salón Internacional de la Moda	International Fashion Fair
el sueldo	wage
el tapiz (*pl.* tapices)	tapestry
el viaje	trip
la yerba mate	mate (infusion)
comprar	to buy
garantizar	to guarantee
hacer consciente	to make aware
pertenecer (zc)	to belong
proteger (j)	to protect
venir	to come
colombiano/a	Colombian
contemporáneo/a	contemporary
digno/a	decent; worthy
en vías de desarrollo	developing
responsable	responsible

Review clothing vocabulary by having students see if they can find classmates who are wearing each of the clothing items listed on this page.

Variación léxica

la camiseta ↔ el polo (*Ven.*) ↔ la playera (*Méx.*) ↔ la remera (*Arg.*) ↔ la polera (*Chi.*)

la falda ↔ la pollera (*Cono S.*) ↔ la saya (*Cub.*)

las gafas ↔ los lentes ↔ los anteojos ↔ los espejuelos (*Cub.*)

los jeans ↔ los vaqueros (*Esp.*) ↔ los bluyines (*Cub.*)

el suéter ↔ el jersey (*Esp.*) ↔ el pulóver ↔ la chompa (*Per.*)

las zapatillas (de deporte) ↔ los (zapatos de) tenis ↔ las deportivas (*Esp.*)

Vocabulario útil

alentar (e:ie) *to cheer, to root for*
el campeón/la campeona *champion*
la Copa Mundial *World Cup*
la cuna *cradle*
el deporte *sport*
entre *between*
el equipo *team*
ganador(a) *winning*
el/la jugador(a) *player*
junto/a *together*
el país *country*
paralizar *to paralize*
el partido *game*
el pasatiempo *pastime*
el/la seguidor(a) *follower*

Estrategia

Using a bilingual dictionary

Language-learners often make the mistake of using the first option given in a bilingual dictionary without consulting the other options. Always pay attention to the examples and information provided to differentiate word meanings in your dictionary. Look at the photo in the article on the right. What is it about? Which meaning of the word **partido** will apply in this case?

1 *Pol* party
2 *Dep* match, game

2 Expansion Have students correct the false statements.

LECTURA

Dos idiomas, dos camisetas, un campeón

El fútbol en España es pasión de multitudes. Los dos equipos más conocidos de este país son el Real Madrid y el Barça (que oficialmente se llama Fútbol Club Barcelona). Un partido entre estos dos equipos paraliza Madrid y Barcelona. Los seguidores del Real Madrid llevan camisetas blancas y alientan

1 Discuss these questions with a partner.

¿Qué deportes practicas? ¿Qué deportes miras en la televisión? ¿Vas al estadio para ver algún deporte? ¿Qué rivalidades deportivas importantes conoces? ¿De qué color es la camiseta de tu equipo favorito?
Also ask students about sports teams at your school.

2 Indicate whether each statement is **verdadero** or **falso**.

1. El fútbol no es muy popular en España. Falso.
2. En Madrid, la gente habla catalán. Falso.
3. Los jugadores del Real Madrid llevan camisetas blancas. Verdadero.
4. El equipo nacional español no tiene jugadores del Barça. Falso.
5. España es el país ganador de la Copa Mundial 2010. Verdadero.
6. En México, el hockey sobre césped es popular entre las chicas de escuela secundaria. Falso.
7. En el mundo hispanohablante, los deportes son parte del programa de estudios universitario. Falso.
8. Las estudiantes argentinas y españolas practican hockey habitualmente. Verdadero.

Rivalidades del fútbol

Argentina:	Boca Juniors vs River Plate
Perú:	Universitario vs Alianza
México:	Águilas del América vs Chivas del Guadalajara
Chile:	Colo colo vs Universidad de Chile
Guatemala:	Comunicaciones vs Municipal
Uruguay:	Peñarol vs Nacional
Colombia:	Millonarios vs Independiente Santa Fe

a su equipo en español. Los seguidores del Barça llevan camisetas rojas y azules y alientan a su equipo en catalán.

Trece jugadores del Barça y diez del Real Madrid participaron° en la Copa Mundial de 2010 (seis del Barça y cinco del Real Madrid en el equipo nacional español; el resto en equipos de otros países). España es hoy el campeón mundial. Madrid y Barcelona hablan idiomas diferentes y son rivales en el fútbol, pero juntas son cuna de campeones.

participaron *participated*

► Los estudiantes y el deporte

En los países hispanohablantes no es común practicar deportes como parte del programa de estudios universitario. Algunas universidades tienen equipos deportivos, pero esto no es muy habitual. En general, los estudiantes practican deportes como pasatiempo fuera de la universidad.

En la escuela secundaria, los estudiantes practican deportes en la escuela y fuera de la escuela. En Argentina, los chicos practican fútbol y rugby, mientras que° entre las chicas es muy popular el hockey sobre césped°. En México, Colombia y España, el fútbol y el baloncesto° son populares entre los chicos. Las chicas mexicanas y colombianas practican baloncesto y vóleibol, mientras que las españolas practican vóleibol y hockey. En América Central y el Caribe, el béisbol es muy popular entre los estudiantes.

mientras que *while*
hockey sobre césped *field hockey*
baloncesto *basketball*

Estrategia

Conducting interviews

When conducting an interview, start by introducing yourself (**Hola, soy Pedro Gómez de Conexión Deportiva**). Then introduce the person you are interviewing (**Hoy estamos con Juan Ramírez, estudiante de.../Hoy entrevistamos a.../Hoy está con nosotros Juan Ramírez, estudiante de..., para hablar de...**). After asking all the questions you need to ask, thank your interviewee (**Juan, gracias por participar en esta entrevista./Gracias por hablar con nosotros.**)

3 In pairs, improvise an interview with a high school student about the sports he/she practices at school and out of school. Use some of the words and expressions in the box. Alternatively, have students write out the dialogue, but encourage them to improvise as they play their roles.

deporte	favorito/a	partido
en la escuela	fuera de la escuela	practicar

PROYECTO

Rivalidades

Choose two sports rivals and prepare a poster or a presentation about them to show in class.

- Choose two sports rivals (it can be two professional teams, two college teams, etc.)
- Introduce each of the teams (what sport they play, what city/state/country they are from).
- Include other relevant information: their stadiums, their jersey colors, etc.
- Illustrate your presentation with photos.

Flash Cultura

¡Fútbol en España!

Many famous players have played for **Real Madrid** and **Barça** over the years. In this **Flash Cultura**, you will learn about David Beckham and Ronaldinho, who used to play for **Real Madrid** and **Barça**, respectively. Did you know that Lionel Messi, one of the stars of the 2010 World Cup, currently plays for **Barça**?

Argentine Lionel Messi began playing soccer at a young age. He won both the **Ballon d'Or** and FIFA World Player awards by the age of 22. In 2006, he became the youngest Argentine to play in the FIFA World Cup. At the 2008 Beijing Olympics, Messi won an Olympic gold medal with the Argentina Olympic soccer team.

Estrategia

Reviewing useful vocabulary

Look at the questions in **Actividad 1.** From these questions, you can guess that three of the topics that will be addressed in this **Flash Cultura** are snacks eaten during sporting events, famous soccer players, and how fans celebrate. Review all the words you have learned about these topics to be better prepared to watch the video and talk about it.

Vocabulario útil

la afición *fans*
el/la aficionado/a *follower, fan*
celebrar *to celebrate*
la estrella *star*
ganar *to win*
el/la jugador(a) *player*
perder (e:ie) *to lose*
preferido/a *favorite*

1 Discuss these questions with a partner.

¿Qué comen cuando van a un estadio a ver deportes? ¿Qué jugadores de fútbol famosos conoces? ¿Cómo celebran los aficionados las victorias en tu país?

2 Watch this **Flash Cultura** episode. While you watch the video, listen for the Spanish words you have already learned.

(Hay mucha afición al fútbol en España.)

¿Y cuál es vuestro jugador favorito?

3 Mark the statements you hear in the video.

1. El fútbol en España es muy importante. ✓
2. Nunca pierde el Real Madrid. ☐
3. ¿Quieres sal? ☐
4. Sí, un poquito. Muchas gracias. ✓
5. También quiero palomitas de maíz. ☐
6. ¿Y quién va a ganar? ✓

3 Suggestion Have students read through the statements. Then have them watch the video and complete the activity.

4 With a partner, prepare a brief interview with a sports fan in a stadium.

Modelo:
- *¿Quién gana hoy?*
- *Los Red Sox, por supuesto.*
- *¿Qué comes?*

Practice more at **vhlcentral.com.**

Audio: Activities, Vocabulary
Video: *Flash Cultura*

Unidad 4

Paco, amigo del Rastro

Lección 4A

BARRIOS CON CARÁCTER

Lección 4B

CON VISTAS AL MAR

Carmen Abreu, fundadora de Caribe Propiedades

Comprar en los mercados

AVANCE

4A

Suggestion Show students photographs of neighborhoods, monuments, markets, and landmarks in Madrid or other cities in Spanish-speaking countries. Encourage them to talk about their own towns or neighborhoods and any cities they have traveled to in Spanish-speaking countries.

BARRIOS CON CARÁCTER

La Latina en directo

La Latina es un barrio de Madrid, especial, auténtico, único... Está en el centro de la ciudad, al lado de la calle Toledo, la Puerta de Toledo y la calle Mayor. En el barrio vive gente de distintas nacionalidades: indios, pakistaníes, marroquíes, chinos... Tiene iglesias y calles muy bonitas, mercados tradicionales, muchas tiendas, muchos bares, restaurantes, teatros y también bancos y cibercafés muy modernos.

Dar y pedir opinión

- ¿Qué piensas de tu barrio?
- Pienso que es un barrio con carácter.

4A.1 Stem-changing verbs **e→ie: pensar**

2 Suggestion Review the **Dar y pedir opinión** sidebar with students before you play the audio for Activity 2.

Vocabulario

1
- el carácter *atmosphere*
- en directo *live*
- distinto/a *different*
- indio/a *Indian*
- paquistaní *Pakistani*
- marroquí *Moroccan*
- el cibercafé *Internet café*
- todo *all*
- visitar *to visit*
- **auténtico/a, tradicional, exótico/a**

2
- pensar (e:ie) de *to think about/of*
- gustar *to like; to please*

3
- el edificio *building*

5
- el/la vecino/a *neighbor*

1 What is **La Latina** like? Read the newspaper article above to learn about this neighborhood. Suggested answers.

- ¿Dónde está La Latina? La Latina está en el centro de Madrid.
- ¿Qué gente vive en el barrio? Vive gente de distintas nacionalidades.
- ¿Es un barrio tradicional o moderno? ¿Por qué? Es un barrio tradicional y moderno.

2 Listen to María and Roberto's opinions about their neighborhood, **La Latina**. Then, correct the answers to the questions below.

- ¿Qué piensa María de La Latina?
  - Piensa que no es auténtico. Piensa que es especial.
  - A María no le gusta vivir en este barrio. A María le gusta vivir en este barrio.
- ¿Qué piensa Roberto de La Latina?
  - Piensa que es un barrio romántico. Piensa que es un barrio con carácter.
  - Piensa que es un barrio sencillo y también muy exótico. Piensa que es un barrio tradicional y también muy internacional.

3 Read these opinions about **La Latina** from some of the neighborhood's residents. With a partner, discuss what aspects of **La Latina** each pair likes or doesn't like.

OPINIONES

Nos gusta La Latina porque es muy moderno. Tiene muchas tiendas, bares, restaurantes, cibercafés... Y todo en el centro de Madrid.

(Teresa y Lola)

A mí me gusta este barrio porque es típico de Madrid, con mucho carácter. A Paloma no le gustan los edificios porque son muy antiguos y no le gusta el tráfico.

(Adrián y Paloma)

OPINIONES

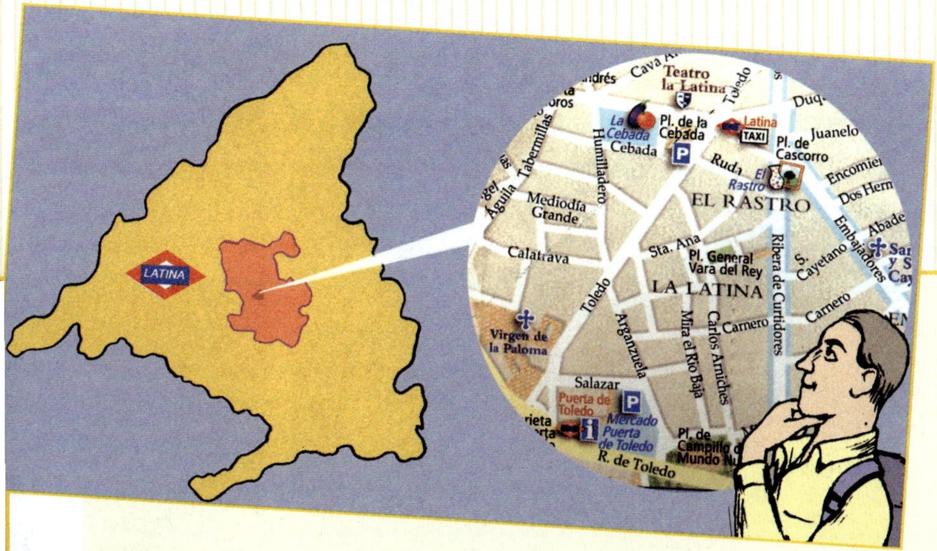

LATINA

- restaurantes internacionales
- mercados tradicionales
- tiendas exóticas
- bancos modernos

Todo en el centro de la ciudad.

¡VISITE EL BARRIO DE LA LATINA!

Expresar gustos y preferencias

A mí me gusta mi barrio.
A ti te gusta tu barrio, ¿verdad?
A él le gusta La Latina.
A María no le gustan los barrios modernos.
A usted le gustan también los barrios típicos.
A nosotras no nos gusta vivir en el centro.
A vosotros os gusta vivir en La Latina.
A ellos les gustan los barrios con carácter.

4A.2 The verb **gustar**
Indirect object pronouns

Expansion Have students research a city in a Spanish-speaking country and identify the major neighborhoods. Are any of these neighborhoods similar to **La Latina**?

4 And you? What aspects do you like or dislike about neighborhoods like **La Latina**? Write them down and compare your answers with a partner's.

A mí (no) me gusta + [singular noun].
A mí (no) me gustan + [plural noun].

MI EXPERIENCIA

5 Ask your classmates where they live, and write down their answers. Then, report your findings to the class.

GUIÓN DE TRABAJO

¿Dónde vives?

¿En una ciudad?
¿En qué barrio?

¿Dónde está tu barrio?
¿En el centro?
¿Al lado de qué calles?

¿En un pueblo?
¿Cómo se llama?

¿Dónde está tu pueblo?
¿Cerca o lejos de la ciudad?

¿Qué hay?
¿Hay muchos restaurantes?
¿De qué nacionalidad?
¿Qué tiendas hay?
¿Tiene teatros?
¿Mercados?
¿Bancos?

¿Cómo es?
¿Es un barrio/pueblo moderno o tradicional?
¿Es un barrio/pueblo con carácter? ¿Por qué?

¿Te gusta?
¿Qué te gusta o no te gusta de tu barrio/pueblo? ¿Por qué?
Y a tus vecinos... ¿qué les gusta de tu barrio/pueblo?

Practice more at **vhlcentral.com.**

SAM: Actividades pp. 69–71

Hacer las compras

LISTA DE COMPRAS

pasta	refrescos	yogures
huevos	tomates	salchichas
leche	manzanas	patatas fritas

Indicar cantidades y envases

un kilo de manzanas
una botella de leche
un paquete de salchichas/galletas
una docena/media docena de huevos
una bolsa de patatas

4A.3 The preposition **de** with quantities and units of measurement

Vocabulario

6

la lista de compras *shopping list*
el refresco *soft drink, soda*
la manzana *apple*
la salchicha *sausage*
las patatas fritas (*Esp.*) *potato chips*
el tomate

7

la cantidad *quantity*
el kilo *kilogram*
medio kilo *half a kilogram*
el paquete *package*
la docena *dozen*
media docena *half a dozen*
la bolsa *bag, sack*

6 Look at the photos of these two people doing their grocery shopping in different types of stores. Then, answer the questions.

- ¿Qué le gusta comprar a ella?
- ¿Dónde compra ella?
- ¿Qué le gusta comprar a él?
- ¿Dónde compra él?

Suggestion Review the units of measurement presented in sidebar 4A.3 with students before they complete Activity 6. Ask students to name other products they typically purchase in these quantities.

7 Listen to the conversations with the young man and the woman. What quantities of groceries did each of them buy?

Joven: un paquete de salchichas, dos botellas de refrescos, una bolsa de patatas fritas, dos paquetes de pasta. Carmen: un kilo de tomates, dos kilos de manzanas, una docena de huevos, una botella de leche.

8 Something is wrong with this shopping list. Correct the list so that each item is listed in an appropriate quantity or container. Compare your answers with a partner's.

Modelo: *No es una botella de tomate, es una lata de tomate.*

1. Botella de tomate
2. Lata de salchichas
3. Kilo de vino
4. Bolsa de huevos
5. Docena de manzanas
6. Paquete de patatas

Suggested answers. 1. botella de vino 2. lata de tomate 3. kilo de manzanas 4. bolsa de patatas 5. docena de huevos 6. paquete de salchichas

Preguntar y responder por el turno

- ¿A quién **le toca**?
- **Me toca** a mí.

4A.4 Verbs used with object pronouns: **tocar**

Solicitar un producto

- ¿Qué **le doy**?
- **Me da** tres manzanas, por favor.
- ¿Qué **le pongo**?
- **Me pone** medio kilo de tomates.

4A.5 Verbs with irregular **yo** forms: **dar** and **poner**

Preguntar y responder por el precio

- ¿Cuánto **cuestan** dos botellas de leche?
- **Cuestan** 10 pesos.

4A.6 Stem changing verbs **o→ue: costar**

Vocabulario

9

¿A quién le toca? *Whose turn is it?*
Me toca a mí. *It's my turn.*
¿verdad? *right?*
Me da/pone... *Give me . . .*
dar *to give*
poner *to put*
¿Cuánto cuesta(n)...? *How much does/do . . . cost?*
costar (o:ue) *to cost*
solicitar *to request*
añadir *to add*

¡OJO!

Most Spanish-speaking countries use kilograms (**kilos**), rather than pounds (**libras**). Remember that **1 kilo = 1000 gramos** (*grams*).

9 Decide which lines **a–k** match each part of the shopper's interaction with the grocer **1–3**. Then, with a partner, role-play the conversation with these or other products.

a. ¿A quién le toca ahora?
b. Me toca a mí.
c. ¿Qué le doy?
d. Una botella de leche y una docena de huevos, por favor.
e. Una docena, ¿verdad?
f. Sí.
g. ¿Algo más?
h. Sí, también me da una bolsa de patatas, por favor. ¿Cuánto es todo?
i. 16 pesos.
j. 16 pesos, ¿no?
k. Sí. Muchas gracias.

1 Los primeros productos que solicita el cliente. d
2 El cliente añade un producto más y pregunta el precio total. h
3 El cliente indica que es su turno de compra. b

10 Write down how much of each of these products you will need for the next two weeks. Calculate the total price of your groceries and compare your answers with a partner's.

Modelo: *Dos botellas de leche.*
La botella de leche cuesta 5 pesos.
Total 10 pesos.

Leche: $5 botella
Tomates: $8,50 kilo
Manzanas: $5,50 kilo
Huevos: $4,80 docena
Salchichas: $5,20 paquete

MI EXPERIENCIA

11 Interview a classmate. Does he/she like to shop for groceries? Write down his/her answers.

Before you begin the interview, review the conversation in **Actividad 9** and identify the expressions that you can use to ask for clarification.

- Una docena, ¿verdad?
- 16 pesos, ¿no?

GUIÓN DE TRABAJO

¿Te gusta hacer las compras? ¿Qué productos compras normalmente?

Leche, tomates...

¿Dónde haces las compras normalmente?

¿En un mercado tradicional?
¿En un supermercado?
¿En tiendas del barrio?
¿En Internet?

Successful Language Learning
Encourage students to use questions such as **¿no?** and **¿verdad?** to ask for confirmation if they are unsure about information.

Practice more at **vhlcentral.com.**

SAM: Actividades pp. 72–74

Paco, amigo del Rastro

Vives en La Latina, ¿verdad?
Sí, vivo en la calle Toledo.

¿Te gusta este barrio?
¡Me gusta mucho! Está en el centro y es muy típico.

El domingo trabajas en el Rastro. ¿Y los otros días de la semana?
Trabajo en el Mercado de la Cebada, en una tienda de alimentación.

¿Qué tienes en tu puesto del Rastro?
Pues muchas cosas típicas de Madrid: pósters, abanicos, postales, libros...

¿Qué te gusta del Rastro?
Me gusta todo: la gente, las calles, las tiendas, los puestos...

¿Piensas que el Rastro es un lugar único?
Sí. ¡Es un lugar único y especial!

[...]

El Rastro
El Rastro es un mercado al aire libre muy popular de Madrid. Está en el barrio de La Latina. Las tiendas del Rastro generalmente están en la calle y se llaman "puestos".

Vocabulario

(12)

la tienda de alimentación *grocery store*
el puesto *stand (in a market)*
la cosa *thing*
el póster

(13)

la edad *age*

OPINIÓN

¿Le gusta ir a mercados como el Rastro? ¿Por qué?

¿Qué venden en estos mercados?

¿Qué compra cuando va a estos mercados?

¿Hay un mercado como el Rastro en su ciudad/pueblo? ¿Cómo es?

12 Indicate whether each statement is true (**verdadero**) or false (**falso**).

1. Paco no vive en La Latina. Falso.
2. Paco trabaja todos los días en el Rastro. Falso.
3. Paco no vende libros. Falso.
4. A Paco le gustan la gente, las calles y las tiendas. Verdadero.
5. Paco piensa que el Rastro es único y especial. Verdadero.

13 Fill in this information sheet about Paco.

- Nombre y apellidos: Paco Suárez García
- Edad: 38 años
- Domicilio: calle Toledo, La Latina
- Lugar de trabajo (lunes a sábado): Mercado de la Cebada
- Lugar de trabajo (domingos): el Rastro

14 In pairs, discuss what you have learned about Paco. What is he like? What things does he like? Do you know anyone like Paco?

15 Imagine that you and your partner have a stand at a street market, like Paco. What typical products from your city or region would you sell?

Suggestion As a class, brainstorm what other products students expect to find at an open-air market. Have a volunteer record these ideas on the board.

16 Read this information from a Buenos Aires guidebook and fill in the notes below. Then, compare your answers with a partner's.

La feria de San Telmo

Probablemente es la feria al aire libre más conocida de Argentina. Se celebra todos los domingos en la plaza Dorrego en el barrio de San Telmo. Encuentras de todo: artesanía, antigüedades, objetos curiosos, souvenirs... También puedes ver espectáculos de tango y turistas de muchas nacionalidades.

Los vendedores en general son muy simpáticos y amables. A veces es posible regatear y conseguir precios más bajos.

La Plaza de Mayo, uno de los lugares clave de Buenos Aires, está muy cerca. En San Telmo también puedes disfrutar comidas muy ricas y puedes tomar un café en una de las tradicionales confiterías de la zona.

El mejor medio de transporte es el subte. Para llegar a San Telmo, toma la línea A (estación: Plaza de Mayo) o la línea E (estación: Belgrano).

Horario y lugar: *los domingos en* la plaza Dorrego

Productos: artesanía, antigüedades, objetos curiosos, souvenirs

Vendedores: muy simpáticos y amables

Cómo llegar: subte, líneas A y E

Actividades recomendadas: espectáculos de tango, comidas y confiterías

Lugares cerca: *Plaza de Mayo*

Vocabulario

16

probablemente *probably*
al aire libre *outdoor*
más conocido/a *best-known*
se celebra *is held*
encontrar (o:ue) *to find*
la antigüedad *antique*
el objeto curioso *curiosity, nicknack*
el espectáculo *show*
en general *generally*
es posible *it's possible*
regatear *to barter, to haggle*
conseguir (e:i) *to get, to obtain*
el precio *price*
bajo/a *low*
el lugar clave *landmark*
disfrutar (de) *to enjoy*
la confitería (*Arg.*) *café*
el medio de transporte *means of transportation*
el subte(rráneo) (*Arg.*) *subway*
la estación *station*
recomendado/a *recommended*
la nota, el souvenir, la línea

[r] [rr]

17 a. Listen to these series of words. Which sound do you hear: **[r]** or **[rr]**?

a. barrio, ricas, Dorrego [rr]
b. bar, carácter, mercado [r]

Suggestion Ask students to give additional examples of words with the **[r]** or **[rr]** sounds and model pronunciation for the class.

b. Read aloud the names of these neighborhoods in Buenos Aires. Which words have the **[r]** and **[rr]** sounds?

Puerto Madero *Retiro* *Montserrat* *Recoleta* *Palermo*

Internet
Cada vez son más los hispanos, sobre todo los jóvenes, que hacen la compra por Internet. Entre los productos más vendidos en la red están los de alimentación, discos y libros. ¿Y en su país? ¿Compra usted a través de Internet? ¿Qué productos?

18 Read this paragraph about Cuban produce markets. Can you find these foods where you live? Work with a partner to write a list of typical products from your region. Then, present your list to the class.

El agromercado cubano

En Cuba es muy típico hacer la compra en los agromercados. Los cubanos compran en estos mercados papayas, yucas, frijoles y papas, entre otras cosas. Es también un lugar donde a la gente le gusta hablar de la calidad de los productos, de los precios y de las noticias del mundo.

A veces la fruta y los alimentos tienen nombres diferentes en España y América Latina. Por ejemplo:
- papa (patata)
- frijol (alubia)

Vocabulario

18

el agromercado *produce market*
la yuca *yucca*
el frijol *bean*
la noticia *news*
el mundo *world*

Practice more at **vhlcentral.com.**

SAM: Actividades pp. 75–78

TAREA FINAL

Un mercado en la clase

Suggestion Encourage students to bring in photos or magazine cut-outs of different products to "sell". Have students set out a budget of how much money they can spend at the virtual market before they begin the activity.

Make a list of five items you have at home that you would like to sell.

Discos, sellos...

Tell the other members of your group which products you are selling.

Un disco de Shakira. Me gusta, pero quiero comprar un CD nuevo.

Set a price for your products.

Disco, $6

Ask about at least four products being sold by another group. Try to bargain for a lower price.

Share with the class the items that you bought, as well as the purchase price.

Una camiseta de Plaza Sésamo, $20

Expansion Have students research the exchange rates between the dollar, the euro, and different Latin American currencies. Encourage groups to convert their prices to one of these currencies and present their findings to the class.

YO PUEDO...

- **Puedo hablar de mi barrio.**

  Write a letter to a friend, giving him/her information about your neighborhood.

  ¿Dónde está? ¿Qué actividades puedes hacer? ¿Qué opiniones hay sobre el barrio? ¿Qué le gusta a la gente de esta zona? ¿Qué no le gusta?

- **Puedo escribir una lista de compras.**

  Add containers and units of measurement to this shopping list.

- **Puedo mantener un diálogo en español en una tienda.**

  Complete the dialogue.

- **Puedo describir tres aspectos de mercados del mundo hispanohablante.**

  Answer these questions.

  ¿Dónde está el Rastro? ¿Qué puedes comprar en la feria de San Telmo? ¿Qué puedes comprar en un agromercado cubano?

3 .... de patatas
1 .... de azúcar
1 .... de huevos
2 .... de leche

- ¿A quién le toca?
- ....
- ¿Qué le doy/pongo?
- ....
- ¿Algo más?
- ....
- 14 pesos. Gracias.

GRAMÁTICA FUNCIONAL

4A.1 Ask for and give opinions

Stem-changing verbs e→ie: pensar 5.1.1

- Use the verb **pensar** (*to think*) to ask for and give opinions. **Pensar** is an **e→ie** stem-changing verb. You saw the same stem-changing pattern with **querer** in 3B.6. Remember that the **nosotros/as** and **vosotros/as** forms don't have a stem change.

¿Qué **piensan** ustedes de Valparaíso?
*What **do you think** of Valparaíso?*

Pensamos que es una ciudad encantadora.
***We think** it is a charming city.*

- To ask someone's opinion about something or someone, use **pensar** + **de** + [*noun*].

¿Qué **piensas del** mercado de la fruta?
*What **do you think of** the fruit market?*

- To give an opinion about something or someone, use **pensar** + **que** + [*verb*].

Pienso que es exótico.
***I think** it's exotic.*

PENSAR

(yo)	**pie**nso	(nosotros/as)	pensamos
(tú)	**pie**nsas	(vosotros/as)	pensáis
(usted, él, ella)	**pie**nsa	(ustedes, ellos/as)	**pie**nsan

4A.2 Express tastes and preferences

The verb gustar 5.11
Indirect object pronouns 6.2.2

- Use the verb **gustar** (*to like; to please*) to express likes and dislikes. Unlike in English, the person or thing that is liked is the grammatical subject of the sentence in Spanish. Therefore, **gustar** is most commonly used in the 3rd person singular or plural.

¿Te **gusta** mi barrio?
Do you like my neighborhood?

- Use **gusta** with a singular noun or a verb in the infinitive; use **gustan** with a plural noun.

Sí, me **gusta** vivir en el centro; me **gustan** los barrios dinámicos.
Yes, I like living downtown; I like lively neighborhoods.

- Always use an indirect object pronoun (**me**, **te**, **le**, **nos**, **os**, or **les**) before **gusta**(**n**) to indicate who likes a certain object or activity.

¿**Les** gusta la feria de San Telmo?
Do you like the San Telmo market?

Sí, **nos** gusta muchísimo.
Yes, we like it a lot.

¡Póngalo en práctica!

G1 Complete the conversation.

- ¿Qué piensas (1) ....de.... Buenos Aires?
- (2) ....Pienso.... (3) ....que.... Buenos Aires es una ciudad muy interesante.
- ¿Y Andrea y Sebastián?
- Los dos (4) ....piensan.... que Buenos Aires tiene barrios muy especiales.
- ¡Bien! ¡Todos (5) ....pensamos.... igual!
- ¿Cuándo vamos a Argentina?

G2 Answer the questions using the cues.

1. ¿Qué piensa Ramón del mercado? (divertido) Ramón piensa que el mercado es divertido.
2. ¿Qué piensan los vecinos de este barrio? (dinámico) Los vecinos piensan que este barrio es dinámico.
3. ¿Qué piensan ustedes del museo? (interesante) Nosotros/as pensamos que el museo es interesante.
4. ¿Qué piensas tú de los edificios? (tradicionales) Yo pienso que los edificios son tradicionales.

G3 Complete the conversation.

¿Te (1)....gusta.... mi barrio?

¿Tu barrio? Sí, mucho. Me (2)....gustan.... los edificios, las calles, las tiendas...

Y a Brenda?

A Brenda y a mí (3)....nos.... gusta vivir en el centro de la ciudad.

¿Pero (4)....os/les.... gusta a los dos este ambiente?

(5)....A mí.... me gusta, pero a Brenda no. Y a ti, ¿qué (6)....te gusta.... de tu barrio?

Practice more at **vhlcentral.com.**

GRAMÁTICA FUNCIONAL

- For emphasis or clarification, use **a** + **mí, ti, usted, él, ella, nosotros/as, vosotros/as, ustedes, ellos/as**, or a person's name.

A mí me gusta hacer las compras en el mercado, pero a Martín no le gusta. ¿Y a ti?
I like to shop at the market, but Martín doesn't. How about you?

a mí	**me**	
a ti	**te**	
a usted, a él, a ella	**le**	**gusta(n)**
a nosotros/as	**nos**	
a vosotros/as	**os**	
a ustedes, a ellos/as	**les**	

Me gust**a** mi barrio.
Me gust**an** las tiendas.
Me gust**a** vivir aquí.

gust**a**	+ [*singular noun*]
gust**an**	+ [*plural noun*]
gust**a**	+ [*infinitive*]

4A.3 Indicate quantities and units of measurement

The preposition **de** with quantities and units of measurement 10.5

- Use the preposition **de** when indicating quantities. Use the formula [*number*] + [*unit of measurement*] + **de** + [*item or product*].

Quiero **dos kilos de naranjas.**
*I want **two kilograms of oranges**.*

- These are some common units of measurement.

una **bolsa de** patatas fritas
un **paquete de** azúcar
una **botella de** leche
un **kilo / medio kilo de** manzanas, tomates...
una **docena / media docena de** huevos

4A.4 Ask and tell whose turn it is

Verbs used with object pronouns: **tocar** 6.2.3

- To indicate whose turn it is in a line or a game, use the idiomatic construction [*indirect object pronoun*] + **toca** + **a** + [**mí, ti,** etc., or a *person's name*].

¡Me toca a mí!
It's my turn!

¡Nos toca a nosotros!
It's our turn!

- **Toca** is the 3rd person singular form of the verb **tocar** (*to touch*).

¿Te toca a ti ahora?
Is it your turn now?

No, le toca a María Jesús.
No, it's María Jesús's turn.

me		**(a mí)**
te		**(a ti)**
le	**toca**	**(a usted, a él, a ella)**
nos		**(a nosotros/as)**
os		**(a vosotros/as)**
les		**(a ustedes, a ellos/as)**

Explain that idiomatic expressions (such as **tocarle a alguien**) are set expressions whose meaning does not necessarily correspond to the literal meaning of the component words. Encourage students to practice using these constructions in context and separately from the individual words.

¡Póngalo en práctica!

G4 Answer the questions using the cues.

1. ¿A Mauricio le gustan los barrios con carácter? (sí) Sí, (a él) le gustan los barrios con carácter.
2. ¿A Valeria y a Diego les gusta la comida marroquí? (no) No, (a ellos) no les gusta la comida marroquí.
3. ¿A ustedes les gusta vivir en el centro? (no) No, (a nosotros) no nos gusta vivir en el centro.
4. ¿A los vecinos les gustan las tiendas exóticas? (sí) Sí, (a ellos) les gustan las tiendas exóticas.
5. ¿A vosotros os gusta hacer las compras en el mercado? (no) No, (a nosotros) no nos gusta hacer las compras en el mercado.
6. ¿Te gusta ir al centro comercial? (no) No, (a mí) no me gusta ir al centro comercial.
7. ¿Al señor Martínez le gusta la pasta con tomate? (sí) Sí, (al señor Martínez/a él) le gusta la pasta con tomate.

G5 Complete the conversations.

Por favor, me pone una (1) ....bolsa.... de patatas fritas, un (2) ....paquete.... de azúcar, una (3) ....botella.... de vino y una (4) ....docena.... de huevos.

Buenos días. Quiero (5) ....medio kilo.... (500 gr) de tomates y (6) ....media/una docena.... de huevos.

Muy buenas. Queremos dos (7) ....paquetes/libras.... de pasta, dos (8) ....botellas/latas.... de refresco y un (9) ....kilo.... de cebollas, por favor.

G6 Complete the conversation.

- Buenos días. ¿A quién le toca ahora?
- Me (1) ....toca.... a mí.
- Perdone, pero (2) ....nos.... toca a nosotros.
- Es verdad, (3) ....les.... toca a ellos.

G7 Match each sentence starter with the correct ending.

c	1. Nos toca	a. a mí.
d	2. Te toca	b. a ustedes.
b	3. Les toca	c. a nosotras.
f	4. Le toca	d. a ti.
a	5. Me toca	e. a vosotros.
e	6. Os toca	f. a Marcos.

Practice more at **vhlcentral.com.**

GRAMÁTICA FUNCIONAL

4A.5 Ask for a product

Verbs with irregular **yo** forms: **dar** and **poner** 5.1.2

- Use the verbs **dar** (*to give*) and **poner** (*to put*) to ask for items. Both **dar** and **poner** have irregular **yo** forms.

¿Me **da/pone** una botella de agua, por favor?
*Would you **give me** a bottle of water, please?*

¡OJO! **¿Qué le doy?** is the most commonly used expression for orders. **¿Qué le pongo?** is used primarily in Spain.

- The **yo** form of **dar** is **doy**. The other present-tense forms follow the regular pattern for **-ar** verbs.

¿Qué le **doy**?
What would you like?

DAR			
(yo)	doy	(nosotros/as)	damos
(tú)	das	(vosotros/as)	dais
(usted, él, ella)	da	(ustedes, ellos/as)	dan

- As you saw with **hacer** and **salir** in **3A.3**, some verbs have irregular **yo** forms ending in **-go**. The **yo** form of **poner** is **pongo**. The other present-tense forms follow the regular pattern for **-er** verbs.

¿Qué le **pongo**?
What would you like?

PONER			
(yo)	pongo	(nosotros/as)	ponemos
(tú)	pones	(vosotros/as)	ponéis
(usted, él, ella)	pone	(ustedes, ellos/as)	ponen

- When you use **dar** or **poner** to ask for items, use an indirect object pronoun to specify *to* or *for whom* the items are being requested. As you have seen in **4A.2** and **4A.4**, the Spanish indirect object pronouns are **me, te, le, nos, os,** and **les**. These pronouns correspond to *to/for me, you, him/her, us, you (pl., fam.), them/you (pl.)* in English.

¿**Te** doy algo más, Dani?
*Would **you** like anything else, Dani?*

- Place indirect object pronouns before the conjugated form of the verb.

Sí, **me** das medio kilo de arroz, por favor.
*Yes, please give **me** half a kilogram of rice.*

¡Póngalo en práctica!

G8 Complete the conversation.

¿Qué (1) le (2) doy/pongo?

(3) Me (4) da/pone un kilo de tomates, por favor.

¿Qué (5) les pongo, señoritas?

(6) Nos (7) pone dos botellas de agua fría, por favor.

G9 Unscramble the words to write complete sentences.

1. un paquete de salchichas / me / pone / por favor
   Me pone un paquete de salchichas, por favor.
2. doy / les / algo más / ¿?
   ¿Les doy algo más?
3. nos / por favor / una botella de leche / pone
   Nos pone una botella de leche, por favor.
4. un paquete de pasta / me / por favor / da
   Me da un paquete de pasta, por favor.

G10 Complete the statements with the correct form of **dar** or **poner**.

1. El vendedor me da (dar) dos kilos de tomates.
2. Tú me das (dar) un paquete de galletas.
3. Yo les doy (dar) los refrescos.
4. Ustedes nos dan (dar) las papas fritas.
5. Nosotros te ponemos (poner) las bebidas.
6. El camarero nos pone (poner) el desayuno.

Practice more at **vhlcentral.com.**

GRAMÁTICA FUNCIONAL

4A.6 Ask and tell how much something costs

Stem-changing verbs o→ue: costar 5.1.1

- Use the verb **costar** (*to cost*) to request and give information about prices. Like **poder** (see 3B.8), **costar** is an **o→ue** stem-changing verb.

  ¿Cuánto **cuesta** el pañuelo?
  *How much **does** the scarf **cost**?*

- Use **costar** only in the 3rd person singular (to talk about one item) or the 3rd person plural (to talk about more than one item).

  Los zapatos **cuestan** 300 pesos.
  *The shoes **cost** 300 pesos.*

¡Póngalo en práctica!

G11 Complete the conversation.

- Por favor, ¿cuánto cuesta este abanico?
- El abanico (1)......cuesta...... 50 euros.
- Y ¿(2)......cuánto...... cuestan estas postales?
- Las postales (3)......cuestan...... 2 euros.

Practice more at **vhlcentral.com.**

SÍNTESIS

Look at the photographs and write a short conversation for each of them using the words and expressions provided.

1. 

barrio	calle	gustar	tradicional

- ______________________________
- ______________________________
- ______________________________
- ______________________________

2. 

Me da...	más	kilo	tomates

- ______________________________
- ______________________________
- ______________________________
- ______________________________

3. 

costar	euros	pasta	todo

- ______________________________
- ______________________________
- ______________________________
- ______________________________

VOCABULARIO

La Latina en directo

el carácter	*atmosphere*
el cibercafé	*Internet café*
el edificio	*building*
el/la vecino/a	*neighbor*
todo	*all*
gustar	*to like; to please*
pensar (e:ie) de	*to think about/of*
visitar	*to visit*
auténtico/a	*authentic*
distinto/a	*different*
en directo	*live*
exótico/a	*exotic*
indio/a	*Indian*
marroquí	*Morroccan*
paquistaní	*Pakistani*
tradicional	*traditional*

Hacer las compras

¿A quién le toca?	*Whose turn is it?*
¿Cuánto cuesta(n)...?	*How much does/do . . . cost?*
Me da/pone...	*I'd like . . .*
Me toca a mí.	*It's my turn.*
¿verdad?	*right?*
la bolsa	*bag, sack*
la cantidad	*quantity*
la docena	*dozen*
el kilo	*kilogram*
la lista de compras	*shopping list*
la manzana	*apple*
media docena	*half a dozen*
medio kilo	*half a kilogram*
el paquete	*package*
las patatas fritas (*Esp.*)	*potato chips*
el refresco	*soft drink, soda*
la salchicha	*sausage*
el tomate	*tomato*
añadir	*to add*
costar (o:ue)	*to cost*
dar	*to give*
poner	*to put*
solicitar	*to request*

Paco, amigo del Rastro

es posible	*it's possible*
se celebra	*is held*
el agromercado	*produce market*
la antigüedad	*antique*
la confitería (*Arg.*)	*café*
la cosa	*thing*
la edad	*age*
el espectáculo	*show*
la estación	*station*
el frijol	*bean*
la línea	*line*
el lugar clave	*landmark*
el medio de transporte	*means of transportation*
el mundo	*world*
la nota	*note*
la noticia	*news*
el objeto curioso	*curiosity, nicknack*
el póster	*poster*
el precio	*price*
el puesto	*stand (in a market)*
el souvenir	*souvenir*
el subte(rráneo) (*Arg.*)	*subway*
la tienda de alimentación	*grocery store*
la yuca	*yucca*
conseguir (e:i)	*to get, to obtain*
disfrutar (de)	*to enjoy*
encontrar (o:ue)	*to find*
regatear	*to haggle, to bargain*
bajo/a	*low*
más conocido/a	*best-known*
recomendado/a	*recommended*
al aire libre	*outdoors*
en general	*generally*
probablemente	*probably*

Variación léxica

¿Me da...? ↔ **¿Me pone...?** (*Esp.*)

la confitería (*Arg.*) ↔ **la terraza** (*Esp.*)

el frijol ↔ **la alubia** (*Esp.*) ↔ **el poroto** (*Cono S.*)

hacer las compras ↔ **hacer la compra** (*Esp.*) ↔ **hacer la despensa** (*Méx.*)

la lista de compras ↔ **la lista de la compra** (*Esp.*)

las patatas fritas (*Esp.*) ↔ **las papas fritas**

el mercado ↔ **la feria** ↔ **el mercadillo** (*Esp.*) ↔ **el mercado de pulgas**

el subte (*Arg.*) ↔ **el metro**

el refresco ↔ **la gaseosa** ↔ **la soda** (*Amér. L.*)

el souvenir ↔ **el recuerdo**

4B

Suggestion Bring in real-estate listings from a Spanish-speaking country, and ask students to identify words they already know in the listings. Point out any vocabulary variation specific to that country; see **Variación léxica** on page 107 for suggestions. Encourage students to provide the full word for any abbreviated terms.

CON VISTAS AL MAR

Apartamento de alquiler

1 **Alquiler.** Apartamento 60 m^2. 1 dormitorio, salón, cocina y 1 baño. Amueblado. Terraza. Vistas al mar. Piscina a 5 minutos. **Precio: $1200 /mes**

2 **Alquiler.** Casa 190 m^2. 4 dormitorios, 3 baños, salón, cocina. 2 terrazas. Vacía. Jardín y garaje. Bien comunicada. Playa a 2 kilómetros. **Precio: $2000 /mes**

3 **Venta.** Apartamento 90 m^2. 1 dormitorio principal y 2 dormitorios más, 2 baños, salón-comedor, cocina. Vacío. Terraza. Garaje. Mucho sol. Centro de La Libertad. Estación de autobús a 3 minutos. **Precio: $270 500**

La Libertad, El Salvador

Hablar de viviendas

- ¿Cuántos dormitorios tiene?
- Tiene tres.
- ¿Qué **hay** cerca del apartamento?
- **Hay** un colegio, un parque...
- ¿**Está** bien comunicado?
- Sí, el metro **está** a 5 minutos.

4B.1 **hay/estar ¿cuántos/as?**

Informar del precio

El precio del apartamento **es** $456 000.

1000	mil
10 000	diez mil
100 000	cien mil
200 000	doscientos/as mil
1 000 000	un millón
2 000 000	dos millones

4B.2 Numbers 1,000 and higher

Vocabulario

1

- el alquiler *rental; rent*
- el dormitorio *bedroom*
- el salón *living room*
- el comedor *dining room*
- la cocina *kitchen*
- el baño *bathroom*
- amueblado/a *furnished*
- la terraza *balcony*
- la piscina *swimming pool*

1 Find these rooms on the floor plan.

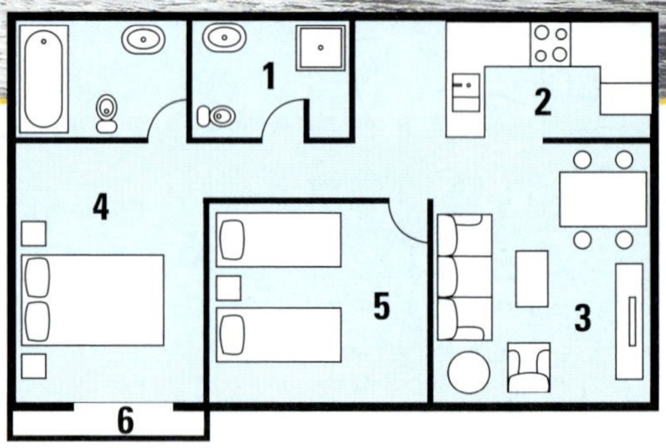

baño	salón
dormitorio principal con baño	cocina
	dormitorio
	balcón

Modelo: *El 1 es el baño...*

el 2 es la cocina; el 3 es el salón; el 4 es el dormitorio principal con baño; el 5 es el dormitorio; el 6 es el balcón

2 a. Read the real-estate listings and choose one of the homes. Then, try to figure out which listing your partner chose. Ask him/her what the home has, where it is, and what is close by.

- ¿Cuántos/as .... tiene?
- ¿Dónde está?
- ¿Qué hay cerca?

- Tiene...
- Está...
- Hay...

Suggestion Tell students that homes in most Spanish-speaking countries are measured in square meters (**metros cuadrados**). 1 m^2 equals about 11 ft^2.

b. Which home would be appropriate for a family with three children? And a couple with no children?

- Una familia con tres niños puede alquilar .... porque ....
- Una pareja sin hijos puede alquilar .... porque ....

3 Match each price to one of the homes listed.

1. El precio del apartamento 1 es ..a..
2. El precio del apartamento 3 es ..c..
3. El precio de la casa es ..b..

a. mil doscientos dólares al mes.
b. dos mil dólares al mes.
c. doscientos setenta mil quinientos dólares.

Expansion Have students write real-estate listings without prices. Then, have them work in small groups to decide what an appropriate rental and sale price for each home would be. Encourage students to look up exchange rates and price the homes in **euros, pesos mexicanos, colones,** etc.

A

B

C

4 a. Mercedes and Luis are looking for a home in **La Libertad**. Look at the available homes in photos A, B, and C. What types of homes are they?

1. apartamento ....C.... 2. estudio ....B.... 3. casa ....A....

b. Listen to the recording and complete the questions with **qué** or **cuál**.

- ¿....Qué.... tipo de vivienda es: un estudio, un apartamento, una casa?
- ¿....Cuál.... es la otra oferta?
- Perfecto. Calle Mayor, ¿....qué.... número?

c. Listen to the recording again and take notes about each home.
Sample answers.

- A: *La casa está* vacía. 3 dormitorios, 2 baños, salón, cocina, jardín, 5 cuadras de la playa
- B: El estudio no está en el centro. grande, vistas al mar, amueblado, terraza
- C: El apartamento está en el centro. 2 dormitorios, salón, baño, garaje

5 Write your own real estate listing. Compare your ad with a partner's, and answer these questions.

- ¿Qué vivienda es de alquiler? ¿Cuál está a la venta?
- ¿Qué vivienda tiene más habitaciones? ¿Cuál es más cara?

MI EXPERIENCIA

6 Ask your partner about his/her ideal home. Then, share your findings with the class.

GUIÓN DE TRABAJO

¿Cómo es tu vivienda ideal?

- ¿Está cerca de la playa? ¿Está cerca de la montaña?
- ¿Cuántos dormitorios tiene? ¿Cuántos metros cuadrados tiene?
- ¿Tiene garaje, terraza, jardín…?
- ¿Qué hay cerca?
- ¿Cuál es el precio del alquiler/de venta?

Practice more at **vhlcentral.com.**

SAM: Actividades pp. 79–81

Vocabulario *cont.*

- la casa *house*
- vacío/a *empty*
- el jardín *yard*
- bien comunicado/a *easily accessible*
- la venta *sale*
- principal *main*
- el salón-comedor *living room-dining room*
- el sol *sun*
- el autobús *bus*
- ¿Cuántos/as? *How many?*
- el balcón *balcony*
- **el apartamento, el garaje**

Identificar

¿**Qué** casas le gustan?
¿**Cuál** es de alquiler?
¿Y **cuáles** tienen piscina?

4B.3 **¿qué?** + [*noun*] + [*verb*]
¿cuál/cuáles? + [*verb*]

Vocabulario

2
- el anuncio *ad*

4
- la inmobiliaria *real-estate agency*
- el estudio *studio apartment*
- ¿Cuál(es)? *Which one(s)?*

5
- a la venta *for sale*
- la habitación *room*
- caro/a *expensive*

6
- la vivienda ideal *ideal home*
- los metros cuadrados (m^2) *square meters*

6 **Successful Language Learning** Ask students what verb they already know is similar to **vivienda** (**vivir**). Encourage them to identify the relationship between **vivir** (*to live*) and **vivienda** (*the place where one lives*).

Su casa, su estilo

1. Mesa funcional: $480
2. Sillón cómodo: $530
3. Silla sencilla: $150
4. Sofá de diseño: $2000
5. Lámpara moderna: $310
6. Armario práctico: $950
7. Cama clásica: $2675
8. Alfombra elegante: $370

Describir objetos, tamaños y cualidades

- ¿Cómo es la cama?
- Es una cama de matrimonio **ancha, larga** y muy **moderna**.

Tamaño: pequeño/a, grande, ancho/a, largo/a

Cualidades: sencillo/a, práctico/a, clásico/a, cómodo/a, moderno/a, elegante, antiguo/a, funcional, de diseño

4B.4 **ser** + (**muy**) + [*adjective*]

Hablar de preferencias

- ¿Qué estilo **prefieren**?
- **Preferimos** el estilo clásico.
- ¿Te gusta esta silla negra?
- **Prefiero** la silla blanca.

4B.5 Stem-changing verbs **e→ie: preferir**

Vocabulario

7

¿Cómo es? *What is it like?*
el estilo *style*
los objetos domésticos *furnishings*
la mesa *table*
el sillón *armchair*
la silla *chair*
el diseño *design*
el armario *closet*
la cama *bed*
la alfombra *carpet*
funcional, el sofá, clásico/a

7 Look at the furnishings listed in this catalogue. Where do you have each of these items in your home? Compare your answers with a partner's.
Suggested answers.

en la cocina	en el salón	en el dormitorio
una mesa una silla	un sofá, un sillón, una alfombra, una lámpara	una cama, un armario

8 Choose three objects from the photo of the living room and write a sentence to describe each one.

Modelo: *La lámpara es roja, sencilla y funcional.*

Expansion Ask students to describe their own living rooms. Have them share their descriptions with the class.

9 a. Listen to these three young people as they choose furnishings for their apartment. Then, decide whether each statement is **verdadero** or **falso**.

	V	F
1. Las chicas prefieren las sillas rojas.	✓	
2. El chico prefiere las sillas negras.	✓	
3. El chico prefiere una alfombra moderna, de colores alegres.		✓
4. Los tres prefieren una alfombra clásica.		✓

b. Listen to the end of the conversation and answer the question.

- ¿Qué compran? Compran las sillas rojas y la alfombra clásica.

10 Which furnishings do you like? What is your style? Interview your partner to find out his/her preferences.

- ¿Qué muebles y objetos prefieres?
- ¿Cuál es tu estilo?

ESTE TELEVISOR SIRVE PARA TODO

 +  +  = 

Ahora tiene tres aparatos en uno.

¡COMPRE AHORA SU TELEVISOR!

Expresar utilidad

- ¿Para qué **sirve** este aparato?
- Es muy práctico, **sirve para** hacer pan en casa.
- ¿Y estos botones?
- **Sirven para** encender el aparato.

4B.6 Stem-changing verbs
e→i: servir
servir para + [*infinitive*]

¡OJO!

Note that **el televisor** is a television set, while **la televisión** refers to broadcasting.

Vocabulario

(8)
grande *big*
pequeño/a *small*
la cama de matrimonio *double bed*
ancho/a *wide*
elegante

(9)
alegre *bright*

(11)
¿Para qué sirve? *What is it used for?*
servir (e:i) para... *to be good for . . .*
el televisor *television (set)*
la televisión *television*
el aparato *device*
la función *function*
la película en DVD *movie on DVD*
el correo electrónico *e-mail*
el botón *button*
encender (e:ie) *to turn on*

(13)
la computadora, la radio

11 Look at this ad. What can this television set do?

Sirve para...

1. ver la televisión. ☑
2. ver películas en DVD. ☑
3. escribir correos electrónicos. ☐
4. escuchar música. ☑

12 Match each form of the verb **servir** to the corresponding subject(s). Then, underline the forms with an **e→i** stem change.

sirve	servís	sirves	sirven	sirvo	servimos
nosotros/as	ustedes	yo	tú	vosotros/as	él/ella

yo sirvo, tú sirves, él/ella sirve, nosotros/as servimos, vosotros/as servís, ustedes sirven

13 Choose one of these objects and write several sentences describing its characteristics and function(s). Then, switch papers with a partner and try to figure out which object he/she chose.

MI EXPERIENCIA

Suggestion Tell students that **servir** is an **e:i** stem-changing verb. Remind students that, while the vowel change is different, the conjugation follows the same pattern as other stem-changing verbs they have learned, i.e., there is no stem-change in the **nosotros/as** or **vosotros/as** forms.

14 What is your partner's home style? Write down his/her answers, and share your findings with the class.

Before you begin the activity, read the definition on the left and write the word being defined.

Es un mueble.
Está en el dormitorio.
Es para una o dos personas y es muy cómoda. Sirve para dormir, leer y ver la tele.
Es ...una cama...

Escriba las definiciones de:
ARMARIO LÁMPARA

GUIÓN DE TRABAJO TEST DE ESTILO

1. ¿Cómo son los muebles de su apartamento/casa?
   a. funcionales
   b. modernos
   c. antiguos
2. Prefiere los muebles y objetos porque...
   a. sirven para algo y son económicos.
   b. son de diseño.
   c. son elegantes.
3. ¿Cómo es su salón?
   a. blanco
   b. azul
   c. amarillo
4. ¿Qué estilo prefiere?
   a. práctico y sencillo
   b. de diseño y diferente
   c. elegante y tradicional

Muchas a: Su casa es funcional.
Muchas b: Tiene una casa moderna.
Muchas c: Su casa es clásica.

Practice more at **vhlcentral.com.**

SAM: Actividades pp. 82–84

Carmen Abreu, fundadora de Caribe Propiedades

Carmen Abreu, 34 años. Directora de una inmobiliaria.

CARIBE PROPIEDADES

Esta agencia inmobiliaria nace en un bonito pueblo de la costa dominicana: La Romana. Carmen Abreu, su fundadora y directora, explica el origen de Caribe: "Me gusta vivir cerca del mar, pero también viajo mucho por el mundo. En vacaciones, no me gustan los hoteles, todos son iguales; prefiero los apartamentos: es más cómodo, privado y barato. Esta es la idea de mi proyecto. Hay muchos turistas que también prefieren pasar las vacaciones en un buen apartamento en la costa caribeña, un apartamento con muebles funcionales, cómodo, bien comunicado, económico y, naturalmente, con terraza y vistas al mar."

¿Cuál es su opción: estudio, apartamento o casa? ¿Alquiler o compra?

CARIBE OFRECE LO MEJOR

CARIBE PROPIEDADES

Carmen Abreu
Directora

Trinitaria esq. Santa Rosa
Bayahibe, La Romana
Tel.: 809-688-1234
c.abreu@caribeprop.com.do

Vocabulario

(15)
- **el/la fundador(a)** *founder*
- **el mar Caribe** *Caribbean Sea*
- **privado/a** *private*
- **barato/a** *cheap*
- **el proyecto** *project*
- **pasar las vacaciones** *spend one's vacation*
- **caribeño/a** *Caribbean*
- **ofrecer (c:z)** *to offer*
- **lo mejor** *the best*
- **la isla** *island*
- **la playa** *beach*
- **la idea, la costa, el mapa**

(16)
- **el puesto** *job, position*

15 Look at the map and find La Romana. What is the name of the beach nearby?

- Isla Catalina
- Playa Caleta (circled)
- Rancho Arriba

16 What is Carmen's position at the agency? How can she be reached?

Sample answers.

- Puesto: Es la directora de la inmobiliaria.
- Información de contacto: por teléfono, por correo electrónico, en persona

17 Choose the option that best completes this statement.

El proyecto de Carmen, la agencia inmobiliaria, nace porque...

- ☐ su familia tiene muchos apartamentos en La Romana y los quiere alquilar.
- ☐ los hoteles de la costa dominicana no tienen muchas habitaciones.
- ☑ para Carmen, alquilar un apartamento tiene muchas ventajas.

18 What characteristics does Carmen consider important in an apartment? Underline relevant words and phrases in the reading. Do you agree?

19 You are looking for an apartment by the beach. Fill in this form for Carmen's real estate agency.

Busco:

Lugar:

Características:

Nombre:

Teléfono:

Vocabulario

20

los destinos turísticos *tourist destinations*
la Familia Real *the royal family*
la temporada alta *peak season*
los atractivos *attractions*
la gastronomía *gastronomy, cuisine*
la naturaleza *nature*
la belleza *beauty*
el paraíso *paradise*
el medio ambiente *environment*
las Islas Baleares *Balearic Islands*
el impuesto *tax*
financiar *to finance*
el mantenimiento *maintenance*
la presión *pressure*
el/la hotelero/a *hotel manager*
la agencia de viajes *travel agency*
la experiencia *experience*

OPINIÓN

¿Busca su apartamento de vacaciones por Internet?

¿Cree que las buenas ofertas están en Internet o en las agencias de viajes?

¿Tiene experiencias de alquiler en España o América Latina?

Suggestion Tell students that an apartment is commonly called **departamento** in many parts of Latin America. Ask heritage speakers to provide additional lexical variants.

Suggestion Point out the title of the apartment listing. Explain to students that the construction **Se alquila** or **Se vende** is commonly used when an object or home is for rent/sale. Students learned a similar construction in **1B.3: Se habla español.**

20 a. Read these texts and choose the best headline for each paragraph.

La isla de Mallorca es uno de los principales destinos turísticos. También la Familia Real pasa allí las vacaciones de verano. Al aeropuerto de su capital, Palma, llegan en la temporada alta más de 100 000 personas al día. Los atractivos de las islas son el clima, la cultura, el arte y la gastronomía. Otro atractivo turístico es su naturaleza, y la calidad y belleza de sus playas. Mallorca también es un paraíso ecológico, por eso es necesario proteger el medio ambiente.

En el año 2001 nace la "ecotasa" en las Islas Baleares. Es un impuesto que pagan los hoteles y apartamentos para financiar el mantenimiento del medio ambiente. Unos meses más tarde, en octubre de 2003, se elimina por la presión de los hoteleros.

Suggestion Before students read the headline options below, ask them to suggest possible titles for each paragraph.

"Un destino turístico... y ecológico" primer párrafo

"Todos a Mallorca"

"Mallorca: la isla preferida de los turistas"

"Impuesto ecológico: ¿Sí o no?" segundo párrafo

b. Match each word with its nearest synonym or definition.

1. destino ...c...
2. atractivo ...d...
3. proteger ...b...
4. medio ambiente ...a...
5. impuesto ...e...

a. naturaleza
b. defender del peligro
c. lugar de viaje o de vacaciones
d. elemento interesante
e. dinero que se paga al Estado

c. Are you in favor of an ecotax? Do you consider Mallorca a vacation destination? What about your classmates?

Modelo: *Yo pienso que la ecotasa...*

[c] [qu] [k]

21 The [k] sound is represented by these consonants. Listen to the words and fill in the table with other words you have learned with the [k] sound.

- c + a, o, u: casa, cosas, cualidad
- qu + e, i: pequeño, quiero
- k in foreign words: kiwi, karate, kilómetro

c	qu	k
casa *cocina*	*alquiler* *parque*	*kilómetro*

22 Compare these listings from Argentina and Mexico to the listings on page 98. Which words are different? Write the equivalent term you have learned.

SE ALQUILA DEPARTAMENTO

Buenos Aires, zona centro. Departamento de 3 ambientes. Amoblado. Living de 20 m². 2 baños. Cochera. $4200

Argentina	Equivalente
departamento	*apartamento*
ambiente	habitación
amoblado	amueblado
living	salón
cochera	garaje

CASA EN EL D.F.

Casa con 5 recámaras. Sala de 30 m². Alberca y jardín. $45 000 000

México	Equivalente
recámara	dormitorio
sala	salón
alberca	piscina

Practice more at vhlcentral.com.

SAM: Actividades pp. 85–90

TAREA FINAL

Intercambio de casa

Write two descriptions, one of your home, and one of a home you would like to rent somewhere in Spain or Latin America.

Apartamento, 90 m², centro de la ciudad...

Choose which home you are going to offer for the house exchange.

Tu apartamento porque tiene vistas al parque...

Tell the class about the house you are offering.

Es una casa...

Choose your favorite home exchange destination.

Suggestions

- Divide the class into two groups. One group are people looking to rent an apartment in a Spanish-speaking country; the other group are real-estate agents. The potential renters must prepare a list of questions and preferences, and the real-estate agents must prepare descriptions of the apartments they have available.
- Have students brainstorm a list of undesirable characteristics for an apartment (**lejos de la playa, con vistas al aeropuerto**, etc.), and encourage groups to write an ad for an apartment they would NOT want to rent.

YO PUEDO...

Suggestion Show students photos of different pieces of furniture, rooms, apartments, and houses, and ask them to describe each, then state their preferences.

- Puedo hablar de mi vivienda.

  Write to a friend and describe your home: number of rooms, size, nearby attractions, price, etc.

- Puedo identificar algo a través de preguntas.

  Look at the illustration and ask questions to identify one piece of furniture.

¿..................?

- Puedo describir un mueble y preguntar por sus características.

  Describe your favorite sofa.

¿Qué tamaño, características y estilo tiene?

....

....

- Puedo hablar de mis preferencias.

  Which of the homes pictured on page 99 is your favorite?

- Puedo referirme a la utilidad de algo.

  What are these items used for?

Un libro

....

Un televisor

....

GRAMÁTICA FUNCIONAL

4B.1 Talk about houses and homes

hay/estar; ¿cuántos/as? 5.9; 9

- Use **hay** to talk about the existence of something. As you learned in 3B.2, **hay** can be followed by a singular or plural noun.

  En mi barrio, no **hay** muchos apartamentos de alquiler.
  *In my neighborhood, **there are** not many apartments for rent.*

- Use **estar** to describe where something is located.

  La casa de mi tía **está** a cinco minutos de la playa.
  *My aunt's house **is** five minutes from the beach.*

- Use **¿cuántos/as?** to ask how many of something there are. Remember to use **cuántos** with masculine nouns and **cuántas** with feminine nouns. To answer, say **Tiene...**

  ¿**Cuántas** habitaciones tiene el apartamento?
  ***How many** rooms does the apartment have?*

4B.2 Talk about prices

Numbers 1,000 and higher 13.1

- Use multiples of one thousand (**mil**) and one million (**un millón**) to talk about housing prices.

1000	mil
10 000	diez mil
100 000	cien mil
200 000	doscientos/as mil
1 000 000	un millón
2 000 000	dos millones

Note:
EE.UU. = 1,000,000.00
México = 1,000,000.00
España = 1.000.000,00
Este texto = 1 000 000,00

- Numbers ending in **-cientos/as** agree in gender with the nouns they modify, even when followed by **mil**.

  Setecientas mil libras son **ochocientos mil** euros.
  ***700,000** pounds are **800,000** euros.*

- When **millón/millones** is followed by a noun, use **de** before the noun.

  La casa de Coyoacán cuesta **cinco millones de pesos**.
  *The house in Coyoacán costs **five million pesos**.*

4B.3 Identify which item you are talking about

¿qué? vs. ¿cuál(es)? 9

- Use **¿qué?** or **¿cuál(es)?** to identify which item(s) a person is talking about. Remember that question words take an accent.

  ¿**Qué** casa tiene piscina? ¿**Cuál** es la más grande?
  ***Which** house has a swimming pool? **Which one** is the biggest?*

- Use **qué** + [*noun*] + [*verb*] to ask *which*.

  ¿**Qué apartamento** te gusta?
  ***Which apartment** do you like?*

Expansion Model alternative phrasing of questions for students: **¿Cuál de estas casas tiene garaje?**

- Use **cuál** + [*verb*] to ask *which one* and **cuáles** + [*verb*] to ask *which ones*. Never use a noun immediately following **cuál(es)**.

  De estas casas, ¿**cuáles** tienen garaje?
  *Of these houses, **which ones** have a garage?*

¡Póngalo en práctica!

G1 Complete each sentence with **hay** or the correct form of **estar**.

1. ...Hay... tres casas a la venta.
2. El estudio ...está... cerca del centro.
3. Estas casas ...están... lejos de la estación.
4. En tu barrio, ¿...hay... muchas casas grandes?

G2 Complete the conversation.

- Lola, ¿(1) ...hay... un parque cerca de tu casa?
- No, pero tenemos un jardín.
- ¿Dónde (2) ...está... tu casa?
- (3) ...Está... a diez minutos de la playa.
- ¿(4) ...Cuántos... dormitorios tiene?
- (5) ...Tiene... dos, un salón, baño y cocina.

G3 Say how much each of these homes costs.

Modelo: *La casa en El Paso cuesta trescientos veinte mil dólares.*

CASA
Santa Bárbara:
$2 100 000

La casa en Santa Bárbara cuesta dos millones cien mil dólares.

APARTAMENTO
Nueva York:
$5 000 000

El apartamento en Nueva York cuesta cinco millones de dólares.

ESTUDIO
Miami:
$150 000

El estudio en Miami cuesta ciento cincuenta mil dólares.

APARTAMENTO
Santa Fe:
$400 000

El apartamento en Santa Fe cuesta cuatrocientos mil dólares.

APARTAMENTO
Londres:
£530 000

El apartamento en Londres cuesta quinientas treinta mil libras.

G4 Complete the questions.

¿cuál? ¿qué? ¿cuáles?

1. De estas casas, ¿...cuál... es de alquiler?
2. ¿...Qué... apartamento está en el centro?
3. ¿...Cuáles... os gustan más: los modernos o los clásicos?
4. ¿...Qué... barrio te gusta?
5. ¿...Qué... estilo les gusta a ustedes?
6. ¿...Cuál... es más caro?

Practice more at **vhlcentral.com.**

GRAMÁTICA FUNCIONAL

4B.4 Describe objects, sizes, and characteristics

ser + (muy) + [*adjective*] 5.8.2

- Use **ser** + [*adjective*] to describe the size and characteristics of an object. Remember that adjectives must agree in gender and number with the noun they modify.

Suggestion Before they complete Activity G5, ask students to list as many adjectives as they can think of that they could use to describe homes, and write them on the board.

La mesa es **grande** y **moderna**.
*The table is **large** and **modern**.*

- Add **muy** before an adjective to intensify its meaning.

El sofá es **muy cómodo**.
*The sofa is **very comfortable**.*

4B.5 Talk about preferences

Stem-changing verbs e→ie: preferir 5.1.1

- Use the verb **preferir** (*to prefer*) to talk about preferences. As with **querer** (3B.6) and **pensar** (4A.1), **preferir** is an **e→ie** stem-changing verb.

¿Ustedes **prefieren** los sillones verdes o los azules?
*Do you **prefer** the green armchairs or the blue ones?*

- Remember that the **nosotros/as** and **vosotros/as** forms don't have a stem change.

Nosotros **preferimos** las lámparas modernas.
*We **prefer** modern lamps.*

PREFERIR			
(yo)	prefiero	(nosotros/as)	preferimos
(tú)	prefieres	(vosotros/as)	preferís
(usted, él, ella)	prefiere	(ustedes, ellos/as)	prefieren

4B.6 Explain how things are used

Stem-changing verbs e→i: servir 5.1.1
servir + para + [*infinitive*] 10.15

- Use the verb **servir** (*to serve*) to ask and explain how something is used. **Servir** is an **e→i** stem-changing verb. As with other stem-changing verbs, the **nosotros/as** and **vosotros/as** forms don't have a stem change.

Los teléfonos **sirven** para hacer llamadas.
*Telephones **are used** to make calls.*

- To ask what something is used for, say, **¿Para qué sirve(n)?** To answer, use **sirve(n)** + **para** + [*infinitive*].

¿**Para qué sirve** este aparato?
What is this device for?

Expansion Tell students to place prepositions before interrogatives when forming questions: **¿Para qué sirven? ¿De dónde vienes?**

SERVIR			
(yo)	sirvo	(nosotros/as)	servimos
(tú)	sirves	(vosotros/as)	servís
(usted, él, ella)	sirve	(ustedes, ellos/as)	sirven

¡Póngalo en práctica!

G5 Use words from the list and other adjectives to write two sentences describing each house.

muy	cómodo/a	pequeño/a
no	moderno/a	sencillo/a

G6 Complete the conversation with the correct forms of **preferir**.

¿Qué (1) prefiere usted: un sofá o tres sillones?

(2) Prefiero un sofá.

Y ustedes, ¿(3) prefieren las sillas blancas o negras?

(4) Preferimos el color blanco.

G7 Match each sentence starter with the most logical ending, and write the correct form of **servir**.

1. Los televisores sirven
2. El dinero sirve
3. El metro y el autobús sirven
4. La taza sirve
5. La radio sirve
6. Las camas sirven

a. 3 para ir al centro.
b. 1 para ver películas.
c. 4 para tomar el café.
d. 2 para comprar.
e. 6 para dormir.
f. 5 para escuchar música.

Practice more at **vhlcentral.com.**

VOCABULARIO

Apartamento de alquiler

¿Cuál(es)?	*Which one(s)?*
¿Cuántos/as?	*How many?*
el alquiler	*rental; rent*
el anuncio	*ad*
el apartamento	*apartment*
el autobús	*bus*
el balcón	*balcony*
el baño	*bathroom*
la casa	*house*
la cocina	*kitchen*
el comedor	*dining room*
el dormitorio	*bedroom*
el estudio	*studio apartment*
el garaje	*garage*
la habitación	*room*
la inmobiliaria	*real-estate agency*
el jardín	*yard*
los metros cuadrados (m^2)	*square meters*
la piscina	*swimming pool*
el salón	*living room*
el salón-comedor	*living room-dining room*
el sol	*sun*
la terraza	*balcony*
la venta	*sale*
la vivienda ideal	*ideal home*
a la venta	*for sale*
amueblado/a	*furnished*
bien comunicado/a	*easily accessible*
caro/a	*expensive*
principal	*main*
vacío/a	*empty*

Su casa, su estilo

¿Cómo es?	*What is it like?*
¿Para qué sirve?	*What is it used for?*
la alfombra	*carpet*
el aparato	*device*
el armario	*closet*
el botón	*button*
la cama	*bed*
la cama de matrimonio	*double bed*
la computadora	*computer*
el correo electrónico	*e-mail*
el diseño	*design*
el estilo	*style*
la función	*function*
la mesa	*table*
los objetos domésticos	*furnishings*
la película en DVD	*movie on DVD*
la radio	*radio*
la silla	*chair*
el sillón	*armchair*
el sofá	*sofa*
la televisión	*television*
el televisor	*television (set)*
encender (e:ie)	*to turn on*
servir (e:i) para...	*to be good for . . .*
alegre	*bright*
ancho/a	*wide*
clásico/a	*classic*
elegante	*elegant*
funcional	*functional*
grande	*big*
pequeño/a	*small*

Expansion Draw students' attention to the words **el sofá** and **el mapa**. Remind them that, although both words end in **-a**, they are both masculine nouns and must be used with masculine articles and adjectives. **La radio**, on the other hand, is feminine.

Carmen Abreu

la agencia de viajes	*travel agency*
los atractivos	*attractions*
la belleza	*beauty*
la costa	*coast*
los destinos turísticos	*tourist destinations*
la experiencia	*experience*
la Familia Real	*the royal family*
el/la fundador(a)	*founder*
la gastronomía	*gastronomy, cuisine*
el/la hotelero/a	*hotel manager*
la idea	*idea*
el impuesto	*tax*
la isla	*island*
las Islas Baleares	*Balearic Islands*
el mantenimiento	*maintenance*
el mapa	*map*
el mar Caribe	*Caribbean Sea*
el medio ambiente	*environment*
lo mejor	*the best (thing)*
la naturaleza	*nature*
el paraíso	*paradise*
la playa	*beach*
la presión	*pressure*
el proyecto	*project*
el puesto	*job, position*
la temporada alta	*peak season*
financiar	*to finance*
ofrecer (zc)	*to offer*
pasar las vacaciones	*to spend one's vacation*
barato/a	*cheap*
caribeño/a	*Caribbean*
privado/a	*private*

Variación léxica

la alfombra ⟷ **el tapete** (*Méx.*)

el alquiler ⟷ **la renta** (*Méx.*)

amueblado/a ⟷ **amoblado/a** (*Arg.*)

el apartamento ⟷ **el departamento** (*Amér. L.*) ⟷ **el piso** (*Esp.*)

el dormitorio ⟷ **la recámara** (*Méx.*) ⟷ **la pieza** (*Arg.*)

el garaje ⟷ **la cochera** (*Arg.*)

la habitación ⟷ **el ambiente** (*Arg.*)

la piscina ⟷ **la alberca** (*Méx.*) ⟷ **la pileta** (*Arg.*)

el salón (*Esp.*) ⟷ **la sala (de estar)** (*Amér. L.*) ⟷ **el living** (*Arg.*)

Estrategias

Suggestion Encourage heritage speakers to share with the class specific Spanish-language restaurants, musicians, newspapers, Web sites, television programs, etc., that they know.

1 Aprender español fuera de clase

Lección 3A

Learning another language happens both in- and outside of the classroom. Look for opportunities to use what you learn in class, and to broaden your knowledge of the Spanish language and Spanish-speaking cultures.

- Choose at least two of these options to try this week.

Lunes	
Martes	
Miércoles	
Jueves	
Viernes	
Sábado	
Domingo	

- Make flashcards of Spanish words and expressions you have learned.
- Read the headlines of a Spanish-language newspaper or magazine.
- Read text in Spanish out loud in order to practice pronunciation and intonation.
- Write a short e-mail message in Spanish.
- Spend twenty minutes looking through Spanish-language Web sites.
- Watch a movie in Spanish.
- Listen to music in Spanish.
- Go to a Spanish or Latin American restaurant.

2 Aprender y recordar palabras con ayuda de fotos y dibujos

Lección 3B

Rather than studying a new word or expression with its translation, try matching new vocabulary items with an image — a drawing you've made, a photograph you've taken, a map, or an image you've found on the Internet or in a magazine. Choosing an image that you associate with each new word or expression can help you better remember it.

- Choose four new words or expressions from **Lección 3B** and find or create a visual cue that represents each one.

3 Comprobar la comprensión: Pedir repetición

Lección 4A

If you're not sure that you understood what someone said, ask that person to repeat so that you can confirm what was said.

- Find two expressions in **Lección 4A** used to ask for repetition or confirmation.

4 Parafrasear

Lección 4B

If you don't know a word or you don't know what something is called in Spanish, try paraphrasing. You can describe the object, say what it is like, how it is used, and so on.

- Describe these objects without using their names.

Modelo: *Este aparato sirve para...*

Expansion Bring to class photos of additional objects and ask students to repeat the activity in pairs.

Competencias

Suggestion Point out the day headings on the Spanish weekly calendars. Ask students to guess which day is labeled X. Tell students that in order to distinguish between **martes** and **miércoles**, **miércoles** is often abbreviated with an **X** on calendars and schedules in Spain.

EXPRESAR FRECUENCIA

1 You and your partner need to plan two days a week to go to the swimming pool, and one day a week to go to tango classes. Study your schedules and find times when you can both do these activities.

Modelo: • *¿Puedes ir a la piscina los lunes y los miércoles a las 5?*
• *Los lunes y los miércoles tengo inglés...*

A	L	M	X	J	V	S	D
8-10							
10-12	U N I V E R S I D A D						
12-14							
16-18							
18-20	español		español				
20-22							

B	L	M	X	J	V	S	D
8-10							
10-12	O F I C I N A						
12-14							
16-18	inglés	inglés	inglés	inglés	inglés		
18-20			chino		chino		
20-22	fútbol	coro	fútbol	coro			

LOCALIZAR PRODUCTOS

2 Match each of the items listed on the right to the appropriate section of the department store depicted.

libros salchichas zapatos
lámpara chaqueta pantalones
DVD yogures
silla alfombra
huevos CD vestido

Hogar: lámpara, silla, alfombra / Libros y música: libros, DVD, CD / Ropa y zapatería: zapatos, chaqueta, pantalones, vestido / Alimentación: salchichas, yogures, huevos

ELEGIR PRODUCTOS

3 Which product does your partner like best? Which item is the least expensive? Compare the prices, sizes, and styles of these items.

teteras

23 €, clásica

12 €, exótica

teléfonos

80 €, antiguo

90 €, moderno

lámparas

$400, clásica

$30, de diseño

CONJUGAR VERBOS

4 Write the conjugation for each verb in the person indicated. Compare your answers with a partner's.

1 ir (usted) — va
2 hacer (yo) — hago
3 pensar (ella) — piensa
4 tener (ellas) — tienen
5 ir (vosotros) — vais
6 dar (él) — da
7 poder (ustedes) — pueden
8 querer (nosotros) — queremos
9 costar (el vestido) — cuesta
10 preferir (tú) — prefieres
11 tener (yo) — tengo
12 hacer (nosotros) — hacemos

Comprar en los mercados

You have learned how to talk about and shop for food in Spanish. In this episode of **Flash Cultura**, you will learn about shopping in the markets in San José, Costa Rica.

Estrategia

Using visual cues

When you are watching a video in Spanish, be sure to look for visual cues that will orient you to the content and purpose of the video. Before viewing **Flash Cultura**, look at the video stills. What do you think this episode will be about? What Spanish words do you think they will use?

Vocabulario útil

- **el camarón (*Amér. L.*)** *shrimp*
- **colones (*pl.*)** *currency from Costa Rica*
- **¿Cuánto vale?** *How much does it cost?*
- **el descuento** *discount*
- **No hay problema.** *No problem.*
- **¡Pura vida! (*C.R.*)** *Cool!, Alright!*
- **el regateo** *bargaining*
- **suave** *soft*
- **el/la tico/a** *person from Costa Rica*

Successful Language Learning Ask students to identify the question they already know that has the same meaning as **¿Cuánto vale?** (**¿Cuánto cuesta?**). Explain that **vale** comes from the verb **valer** (*to be worth*).

1. Have you ever been to an open-air market? What did you buy? Have you ever negotiated a price? What did you say? What words and expressions do you already know in Spanish that you could use for bargaining? Discuss your experiences with a partner.

2. Watch this **Flash Cultura** episode. While you watch the video, pay attention to the on-screen labels.

1 **...pero me hace un buen descuento.**

Suggestion Encourage students to share with the class any experiences they have had in Costa Rica or at open-air markets.

Suggestion After students have watched **Flash Cultura**, encourage them to discuss any aspects of Costa Rican markets that they found surprising. What elements were similar to markets in their community?

2 **¿Qué compran en el Mercado Central?**

3. Select the description that best summarizes this episode.

   (A.) Randy Cruz va al mercado al aire libre para comprar papayas. Luego va al Mercado Central. Les pregunta a los clientes qué compran, prueba platos típicos y busca la heladería.

   B. Randy Cruz va al mercado al aire libre para comprar papayas y pedir un descuento. Luego va al Mercado Central para preguntarles a los clientes qué compran en los mercados.

Estrategia

Making polite requests

When asking someone for directions, use expressions such as **Disculpe** or **Perdón** (*Excuse me*) before making your request, and be sure to say **¡Gracias!** at the end. If you do not understand, ask for confirmation using expressions such as **¿no?** and **¿verdad?**

4. With a partner, prepare a brief dialogue in which one person asks for directions to an ice cream shop (**una heladería**). Then, present your dialogue to the class.

   Modelo:
   - *Disculpe, ¿dónde está la heladería?*
   - *A ver... la heladería está a la derecha de...*

Practice more at **vhlcentral.com.**

Audio: Activities, Vocabulary
Video: *Flash Cultura*

Unidad 5

Salma Hayek, más que una cara bonita

Lección 5A

EXPERIENCIAS PERSONALES

Lección 5B

MI GENTE

Juanita y Bernardo, dos abuelos muy activos

La casa de Frida

AVANCE

Point out the word **cumpleaños** and its relationship to the verb **cumplir** (*to achieve; to turn*). Tell students to use the construction **cumplir** + [*number*] + **años** to talk about turning a certain age: **Hoy Manuela cumple 50 años.**

5A EXPERIENCIAS PERSONALES

¡Felicidades, Manuela!

Estudiamos juntos en la universidad en Montevideo.

Celebraste tu boda.

¡FELIZ CUMPLEAÑOS!

Tus amigos queremos recordar y compartir contigo momentos felices de tu vida.

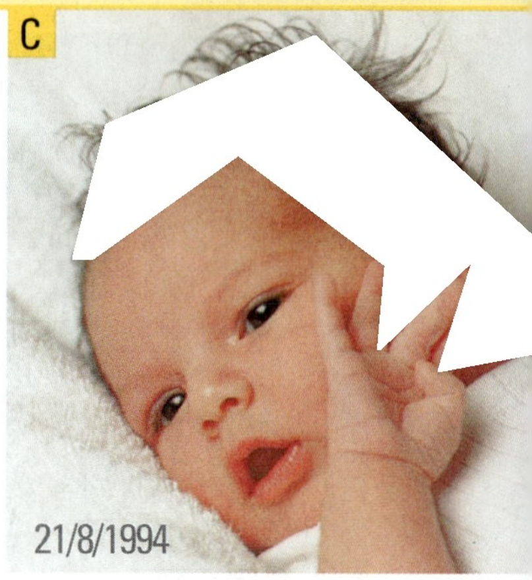

Nació tu hija Celia.

Hablar del pasado

- ¿Dónde **naciste**?
- **Nací** en Montevideo y **viví** allí 20 años.
- ¿Cuándo **terminaste** los estudios?
- **Terminé** en 1999.

5A.1 Interrogative **¿cuándo?** Preterite of regular verbs

Dar fechas en el pasado

El 7 **de** abril **de** 1958 nació Alberto y **el** 21 **de** agosto **de** 1990 nacieron sus hijos.

5A.2 Dates

Vocabulario

1

¡Felicidades! *Congratulations!*
feliz (*pl.* felices) *happy*
el cumpleaños (*invar.*) *birthday*
recordar (o:ue) *to remember*
compartir *to share*
contigo *with you*
la tarjeta de felicitación *greeting card*
los estudios *studies*
el momento

2

el pie de foto *caption*
la boda *wedding*
juntos/as *together*

1 Observe las fotos de la tarjeta de felicitación (A–D) y clasifíquelas.

- Estudios: A
- Trabajo: D
- Familia: B, C

2 Complete la felicitación con los pies de foto correspondientes.

"Celebraste tu boda." "Estudiamos juntos en la universidad en Montevideo."
"Carolina y tú abrieron la tienda." "Nació tu hija Celia."

3 Fíjese en la tarjeta de felicitación (A–D). Indique si las oraciones son verdaderas (V) o falsas (F).

	V	F
1. El 8 de mayo de 1988 Manuela celebró su boda.	✓	
2. El 21 de agosto de 1994 nació Celia, la hija de Manuela.	✓	
3. El 30 de julio de 1998 Manuela y Carolina abrieron la tienda.		✓

4 a. Manuela habla de los días más importantes de su vida. ¿Cuáles son?

el 21 de agosto de 1994 | el 2 de agosto de 1998 | el 8 de mayo de 1988

b. Escuche de nuevo y compruebe las fechas con su compañero/a.

Modelo: • *¿Cuándo abrió la tienda/nació su hija/celebró su boda?* • *El...*

5 Complete la tabla con las formas del pretérito indefinido.

	-AR	-ER	-IR
yo	terminé	nací	abrí
tú	terminaste	naciste	abriste
usted, él, ella	terminó	nació	abrió
nosotros/as	terminamos	nacimos	abrimos
vosotros/as	terminasteis	nacisteis	abristeis
ustedes, ellos/as	terminaron	nacieron	abrieron

Carolina y tú abrieron la tienda.

Mont Blanc is the highest mountain in the Alps, Western Europe, and the European Union.

UNA MUJER ACTIVA

En marzo de 1997 Manuela y sus amigos subieron al Mont Blanc durante la Semana Santa. En junio del 2000 Manuela viajó a Guatemala y trabajó en una escuela con mujeres indígenas, en un proyecto de una organización no gubernamental. Visitó muchos pueblos.

En abril de 2008 recibió el premio a la mujer empresaria del barrio por su tienda de comercio justo.

ENERO	FEBRERO	MARZO
ABRIL	MAYO	JUNIO
JULIO	AGOSTO	SEPTIEMBRE
OCTUBRE	NOVIEMBRE	DICIEMBRE

Indicar el tiempo con los meses del año

En agosto Manuela abrió la tienda.

5A.3 en + [*month/year*]

Vocabulario *cont.*

nacer (zc) *to be born*
el/la hijo/a *son/daughter*
celebrar

4

la fecha *date*

6

marzo *March*
subir *to climb*
la Semana Santa *Easter/Holy Week*
la ONG (organización no gubernamental) *NGO (non-governmental organization)*
junio *June*
la mujer empresaria *businesswoman*
enero *January*
el acontecimiento *event*
activo/a, febrero, septiembre, noviembre

8

el carro (*Amér. L.*) *car*
cambiar de casa *to move*

6 After students read **Una mujer activa,** explain that a non-governmental organization (**organización no gubernamental, ONG**) is a non-profit entity that provides various services, such as humanitarian support. Ask students if they can name any examples (Amnesty International, Greenpeace, the Red Cross). Explain that the plural of **la ONG** is **las ONG.**

6 Observe las imágenes de los viajes y el trabajo de Manuela y lea el texto. Anote cuándo ocurrieron estos acontecimientos.

¿Qué pasó?	¿Cuándo pasó?
Manuela subió al Mont Blanc.	en marzo de 1997
Manuela trabajó con una ONG.	en junio del 2000
Manuela recibió el premio a la mujer empresaria del barrio.	en abril de 2008

7 Y usted, ¿qué vivió en estas fechas? ¿Empezó un proyecto? ¿Cambió de casa? ¿Y su compañero/a?

Modelo: *En marzo de 1997,...*

Abrí...	Cambié...	Celebré...
Empecé...	Terminé...	Viajé...

MI EXPERIENCIA

7 Expansion Have students report to the class about their partner's experiences.

8 Pregunte a sus compañeros por momentos importantes de su pasado: estudios, trabajo, casa, viajes, proyectos... Cuente sus respuestas a la clase.

GUIÓN DE TRABAJO

¿Cuándo empezaste/terminaste...?
el colegio
los estudios
tu trabajo
...

¿Qué pasó?
¿En enero?
¿En octubre?
¿El 3 de agosto de 1995?
...

Compré un carro.
Cambié de casa.
Visité otro país.
...

Practice more at **vhlcentral.com.**

SAM: Actividades pp. 91–93

Diario de viaje

Explain that this photo is of Santa Marta. Have students name some activities that they could do there.

12 de abril

Hace dos meses empecé el viaje. El mes pasado viajé a Santa Marta. Conocí a mucha gente y pasé momentos fantásticos. Después viajé en autobús hacia el sur de Colombia, al departamento del Meta. Descubrí una naturaleza impresionante: zonas desérticas, bosques, jungla... La semana pasada volé a Leticia. Allí recorrí el río Amazonas en barco y ¡ayer nadé con delfines! Este país es maravilloso.

9 a. Lea el diario de viaje de Alberto. ¿De qué país habla? Hable con su compañero/a de las aventuras de Alberto. Colombia. Answers will vary.

Modelo: *Alberto empezó el viaje...*

b. Subraye los momentos específicos que Alberto mencionó en su diario el 12 de abril y anótelos en el calendario.

hace dos meses → FEBRERO

L	M	Mi	J	V	S	D
			1	2	3	4
5	6	7	8	9	10	11
12	13	14	15	16	17	18
19	20	21	22	23	24	25
26	27	28				

el mes pasado → MARZO

L	M	Mi	J	V	S	D
			1	2	3	4
5	6	7	8	9	10	11
12	13	14	15	16	17	18
19	20	21	22	23	24	25
26	27	28	29	30	31	

ABRIL (ayer → 11; hoy → 12; la semana pasada → 2–8)

L	M	Mi	J	V	S	D
						1
2	3	4	5	6	7	8
9	10	11	12	13	14	15
16	17	18	19	20	21	22
23 30	24	25	26	27	28	29

Indicar momentos puntuales en el pasado

El año pasado trabajé mucho.

Hace 2 años abrí mi negocio.

La semana pasada viajé a Argentina.

anoche = ayer por la noche

5A.4 Time expressions

10 a. Usted es el/la protagonista de estas imágenes. Relaciónelas con las actividades de la lista.

- A salir con mis amigos
- D cenar en un restaurante
- C ver una película
- E lavar los platos
- F escuchar un concierto
- B ver una exposición

b. Anote cuándo realizó usted estas actividades.

1. ....
2. ....
3. *Anoche salí con mis amigos.*
4. ....
5. ....
6. ....

c. Haga preguntas a sus compañeros/as acerca de las actividades que realizaron.

Modelo: *¿Cuándo saliste con tus amigos? ¿Qué lugares visitaste?*

Vocabulario

9

- **el diario** *diary, journal*
- **hace dos meses** *two months ago*
- **empezar (e:ie)** *to start*
- **el mes pasado** *last month*
- **pasado/a** *last*
- **conocer (zc)** *to meet; to know (people)*
- **el autobús** *bus*
- **impresionante** *impressive*

Vocabulario *cont.*

la zona *region*
el bosque *forest*
la semana pasada *last week*
volar (o:ue) *to fly*
ayer *yesterday*
recorrer *to travel*
el río *river*
en barco *by boat*
nadar *to swim*
el delfín *dolphin*
maravilloso/a *wonderful*
desértico/a, la jungla, el Amazonas

10

lavar los platos *to do the dishes*
realizar *to do; to perform*
anoche *last night*

Expresar secuencias temporales

De 2003 a 2004 viajé por Asia.

5A.5 **de... a...**

Estructurar un relato

- ¿Dónde trabajó **primero**?
- **Primero** trabajé en Berlín, **luego** volví a España y **después** trabajé en una organización no gubernamental.

5A.6 Transition words

Vocabulario

14

el/la novio/a *boyfriend/girlfriend*
Perdona,... *Excuse me, . . .*
el aniversario

11 a. Escuche la entrevista a Alberto en el programa de radio *La ventana abierta*. ¿Cuál es el motivo de la entrevista?

☐ su viaje a Brasil ☑ su blog de Internet ☐ su viaje a Centroamérica

b. Escuche de nuevo y anote cuándo viajó Alberto a estos lugares.

Centroamérica	Indonesia	África
de enero a junio de 2006	hace 3 años	en 2001

12 Escriba su propia secuencia temporal sobre estos temas.

estudios viajes vivienda

Modelo: *Estudié en la escuela secundaria de 2004 a 2009.*

1. ....
2. ....
3. ....

13 Describa sus actividades de la semana pasada. Use las palabras del recuadro.

primero	de... a....
luego	hace...
después	

MI EXPERIENCIA

14 Haga preguntas a sus compañeros para conocer momentos importantes de sus vidas. Recuerde cómo reaccionar y mostrar interés. Presente la información a la clase.

Elija las expresiones más adecuadas en cada momento para mostrar interés.

- ¿Ah, sí? ¡Qué interesante!
- ¿Y qué pasó?
- ¿Y qué tal?

Viví en la India tres años.

La semana pasada celebré mi aniversario de boda en el restaurante que me recomendaste.

Ayer vi a mi primer novio.

GUIÓN DE TRABAJO

¿Cuándo...?

estudiaste
viajaste
cambiaste
empezaste
...

Primero...
Luego...

de...
a...

anoche
ayer
la semana pasada
el mes pasado
hace dos años

Perdona, ¿qué estudiaste...?
¿Dónde...?
¿Cuándo...?

Practice more at **vhlcentral.com.**

SAM: Actividades pp. 94–96

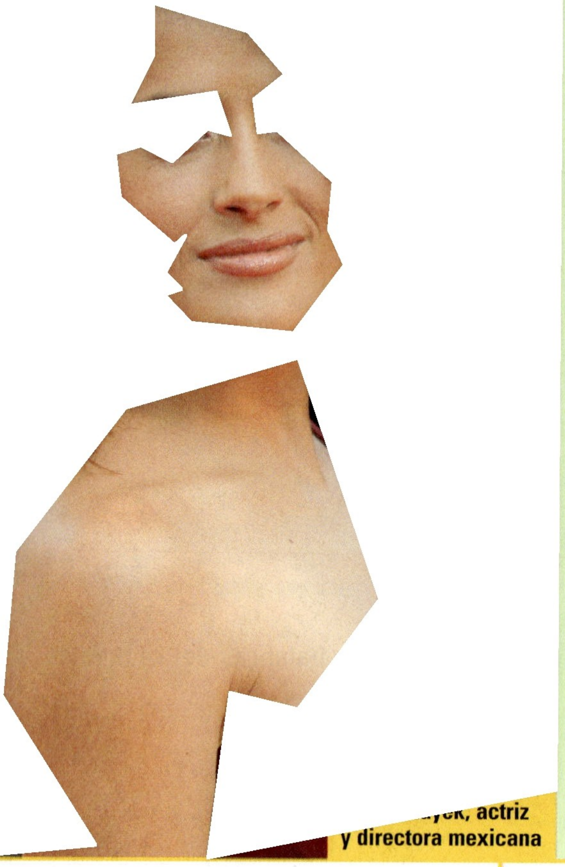

...yek, actriz y directora mexicana

Salma Hayek, más que una cara bonita

Have students name the films and/or shows in which they have seen Salma Hayek act.

Salma Hayek nació en México el 2 de septiembre de 1966. Hija de un empresario y una cantante de ópera, hoy es una famosa actriz, modelo, productora y directora.

Estudió Relaciones Internacionales, pero dejó la universidad para dedicarse a la actuación. Pronto se transformó en una estrella de las telenovelas. Sin embargo, abandonó su exitosa carrera en México para probar suerte en los Estados Unidos.

Participó en muchas películas. Una de las más destacadas es *Frida*, la biografía de la pintora mexicana Frida Kahlo. En 2002 quedó nominada al premio Oscar por esa interpretación. En *Bandidas* actuó con Penélope Cruz, una amiga que es como su hermana.

Después de que nació su hija Valentina, pasó dos años sin trabajar. En 2009 regresó al cine con *El aprendiz de vampiro*, una historia de terror y fantasía.

Salma Hayek es más que una cara bonita. Es un símbolo de mujer luchadora e independiente, conocida por su compromiso social y defensa de la cultura mexicana.

Vocabulario

15

- **la cara** *face*
- **el/la cantante** *singer*
- **dejar** *to quit; to give up*
- **la actuación** *acting*
- **la estrella** *star*
- **la telenovela** *soap opera*
- **sin embargo** *however*
- **exitoso/a** *successful*
- **la carrera** *career*
- **probar (o:ue) suerte** *to try one's luck*
- **destacado/a** *notable*
- **el premio** *award; prize*
- **la interpretación** *performance*
- **actuar** *to act*
- **el/la hermano/a** *brother/sister*
- **la historia** *story*
- **luchador(a)** *fighter*
- **Filosofía y Letras** *Arts*
- **el compromiso** *commitment*

Show students that when dates are written out in numerals in Spanish, the day comes before the month. Thus, 2/9/1966 = September 2, 1966.

15 Lea el texto y diga qué carrera estudió Salma Hayek en la universidad.

- ☐ Filosofía y Letras
- ☐ Actuación
- ☑ Relaciones Internacionales

16 Ordene los acontecimientos según la información del texto.

16 Suggestion Alternatively, have students make a time line of Salma Hayek's life.

- [1] NACIÓ EL 02/09/1966.
- [6] NACIÓ SU HIJA VALENTINA.
- [3] SE TRANSFORMÓ EN ACTRIZ DE TELENOVELAS.
- [4] VIAJÓ A LOS ESTADOS UNIDOS.
- [2] EMPEZÓ A ESTUDIAR RELACIONES INTERNACIONALES.
- [5] QUEDÓ NOMINADA AL PREMIO OSCAR POR SU PELÍCULA *FRIDA*.

17 Fíjese en el póster de la película que aparece en la imagen e indique a qué trabajo de Salma Hayek corresponde. *Frida*

18 ¿Qué otros actores y actrices latinoamericanos conoce? Escriba un párrafo sobre un actor o una actriz y preséntelo a la clase. Incluya al menos cinco acontecimientos de su pasado.

Cine latinoamericano

En la actualidad, el cine latinoamericano cuenta con profesionales de trayectoria internacional. Algunos de ellos son los directores mexicanos Alfonso Cuarón y Guillermo del Toro, y la actriz América Ferrera, de origen hondureño.

OPINIÓN

¿Qué premios de cine son más conocidos en su país? ¿Qué actores los recibieron?

Vocabulario

19

ganar *to win*

20

la pata *paw*
la bata *robe*
el par *pair*

21

la quinceañera *fifteen-year-old girl*
el banquete *reception*
el baile *dance, ball*
la caravana de coches *motorcade*
el/la novio/a *groom/bride*
del brazo *arm in arm*
la misa *Mass*
católico/a *Catholic*
algunos/as *some*
la vela *candle*
cumplir 15 años *to turn 15 years old*
la manera *way*

21 Expansion Ask students what similar traditions exist in this country (*sweet sixteen, Bar/Bat Mitzvah*). Have students mention any **quinceañera**-themed products they have seen in this country, such as Hallmark cards or Barbie dolls. If any students have seen the 2006 film **Quinceañera,** have a volunteer summarize the plot for the class and discuss the traditional and non-traditional elements of the **quinceañera** as shown in the movie.

19 ¿A cuáles de estos personajes hispanos conoce? Escoja dos de ellos e investigue su historia personal. Escriba tres datos sobre cada uno y comparta la información con su compañero/a.

Shakira *Rafael Nadal* *Benicio del Toro*

Felipe de Borbón *Isabel Allende* *Rigoberta Menchú*

¿Trabajó en...?
¿Escribió...?
¿Ganó...?
¿Nació en...?
¿Vivió con.../en...?

19 Expansion Have students research one of the people pictured and write a brief biography.

[b] [p]

20 a. Escuche estas palabras y diga qué sonido es más fuerte: [b] o [p]. [p]

biografía viaje pasado presente

b. Escuche y marque cómo se escribe, con **b** o **p**.

pata bata

beso peso

bar par

c. Escuche de nuevo y escriba la palabra debajo de la imagen.

d. Pronuncie las siguientes palabras. Después escuche y compruebe sus respuestas.

universidad abril primero después

21 a. Lea el texto y señale la opción correcta.

La fiesta de los 15 años o fiesta de la quinceañera

En muchos países latinoamericanos, las jóvenes celebran sus 15 años con grandes fiestas, banquetes, bailes y hasta caravanas de coches. Llevan vestidos blancos similares a los de las novias y entran al salón del brazo de su padre. En México, antes de la fiesta se celebra una misa católica. En Argentina, algunas quinceañeras regalan 15 velas a las personas más importantes de su vida.

¿Qué se celebra?

- [ ] una boda
- [x] un cumpleaños

¿Quién lo celebra?

- [ ] los jóvenes de 15 años
- [x] solo las chicas que cumplen 15 años

b. ¿Se celebra en su país de manera especial este día?

Practice more at **vhlcentral.com.**

SAM: Actividades pp. 97–100

TAREA FINAL

Biografía de la clase

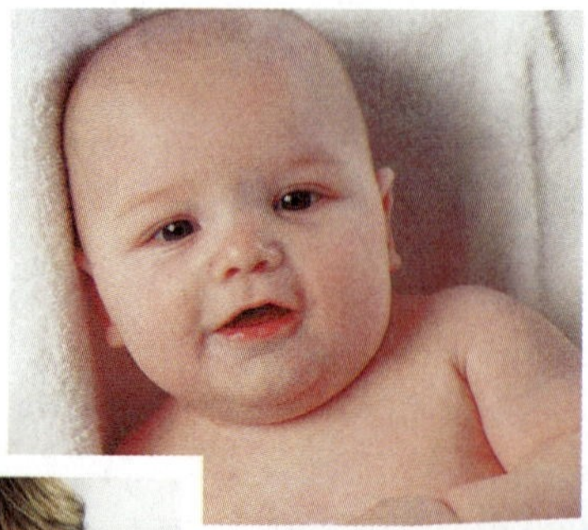

Escriba cinco momentos importantes de su vida e indique cuándo ocurrieron.

- *estudiar*
- *cambiar de casa/de ciudad*
- *empezar un proyecto*
- *viajar*
- *trabajar*
- *comprar una casa/un coche*

Pregunte por los momentos importantes de la vida de su compañero/a.

¿Qué momentos importantes recuerdas de tu vida?
¿Cuándo...?

Comente con su compañero/a si hay algunas coincidencias en sus datos.

Elijan tres fechas y averigüen qué pasó en la vida de tres o cuatro compañeros de clase en esas fechas.

Expansion Have students write ten statements comparing the events of different students' lives. Ex: **Jessica viajó a más países que David.**

YO PUEDO...

- Puedo hablar de mi vida y de la de otras personas en el pasado.
  Escriba tres datos sobre su pasado con sus referencias personales.
- Puedo referirme a fechas en el pasado para contar acontecimientos.
  Escriba dos fechas sobre otras personas y qué pasó.

  ....

  ....
- Puedo nombrar los meses del año.
  Nombre tres meses.

  ....
- Puedo hablar de etapas en la vida.
  Describa brevemente dos etapas de su vida.

El año pasado ....
....
Hace ....
....
La semana pasada ....
....

De ....
a ....
....
De ....
a ....
....

GRAMÁTICA FUNCIONAL

5A.1 Talk about the past

Interrogative **¿cuándo?** 9
The preterite of regular verbs 5.2.1

- Use the interrogative **¿Cuándo?** to ask when an event occurred in the past.

  ¿Cuándo terminaste la escuela secundaria?
  When did you finish high school?

- Note that **¿Cuándo?** asks *When?* in a general sense, whereas **¿A qué hora?** prompts you to answer with a specific time of day.

- Use the preterite (**pretérito indefinido**) to express actions or states completed in the past. Spanish uses two simple tenses, the preterite and the imperfect, to talk about events in the past.

- **Viajar** (*to travel*), **nacer** (*to be born*), and **vivir** exemplify the conjugation patterns of regular **-ar**, **-er**, and **-ir** verbs in the **pretérito indefinido**.

	VIAJAR	NACER	VIVIR
(yo)	viaj**é**	nac**í**	viv**í**
(tú)	viaj**aste**	nac**iste**	viv**iste**
(usted, él, ella)	viaj**ó**	nac**ió**	viv**ió**
(nosotros/as)	viaj**amos**	nac**imos**	viv**imos**
(vosotros/as)	viaj**asteis**	nac**isteis**	viv**isteis**
(ustedes, ellos/as)	viaj**aron**	nac**ieron**	viv**ieron**

¿Cuándo **viajaste** a El Salvador?
*When **did you travel** to El Salvador?*

Mi hermana **nació** en 2002.
*My sister **was born** in 2002.*

- The endings for regular **-er** and **-ir** verbs are identical in the preterite.

  Nadia **conoció** a su novio el día que **cumplió** 18 años.
  *Nadia **met** her boyfriend the day **she turned** 18.*

¡OJO! Note that the **yo** and **usted/él/ella** forms of all three conjugations have written accents on the last syllable to show that it is stressed. If you forget to include the accent, it can change the meaning of the word entirely! **viajo** = *I travel*
viajó = *you/he/she traveled*

- The preterite **nosotros/as** forms of regular **-ar** and **-ir** verbs are identical to their present-tense forms. The context can indicate which tense is being used.

  Cada año **pasamos** las vacaciones en Puerto Vallarta.
  *Every year, **we spend** our vacation in Puerto Vallarta.*

  Pasamos cuatro noches en Puerto Vallarta en mayo.
  ***We spent** four nights in Puerto Vallarta in May.*

Game Create a *Bingo-style* sheet, with a different infinitive phrase (Ex: **empezar un proyecto**) in each square. Have students circulate around the classroom and try to find students that did these activities last week; when they find someone who did, they write that person's initials in the corresponding square. The winner is the first student to get five names in a horizontal, vertical, or diagonal row.

¡Póngalo en práctica!

G1 Elija la forma del pretérito indefinido que corresponde a cada sujeto.

celebrar		
b	1. ellas	a. celebrasteis
e	2. nosotros	b. celebraron
a	3. vosotros	c. celebraste
f	4. usted	d. celebré
c	5. tú	e. celebramos
d	6. yo	f. celebró

subir		
d	1. ustedes	a. subió
c	2. yo	b. subisteis
f	3. tú	c. subí
a	4. él	d. subieron
e	5. nosotros	e. subimos
b	6. vosotras	f. subiste

G2 Complete las oraciones con la forma correcta del verbo.

1. ¿Cuándo ...nació... (nacer) tu hermana?
2. Nosotros ...vivimos... (vivir) en Cuernavaca diez años.
3. Gonzalo ...terminó... (terminar) sus estudios en 2005.
4. Tú ...recibiste... (recibir) el premio de poesía.
5. Mis padres ...abrieron... (abrir) una tienda.
6. Gabriela y tú ...viajaron/viajasteis... (viajar) a Lima en diciembre.

G3 Escriba oraciones completas usando el pretérito indefinido. **G3 Expansion** Have students create three additional items for a partner to complete.

1. Damián / trabajar / para una ONG
   Damián trabajó para una ONG.
2. Laura y Beatriz / estudiar / en la UNAM
   Laura y Beatriz estudiaron en la UNAM.
3. Analía y tú / abrir / una tienda de ropa
   Analía y tú abrieron/abristeis una tienda de ropa.
4. yo / subir / el Aconcagua
   Yo subí el Aconcagua.
5. nosotros / visitar / muchos pueblos bonitos
   Nosotros visitamos muchos pueblos bonitos.
6. tú / comprar / unas gafas de sol
   Tú compraste unas gafas de sol.

Practice more at **vhlcentral.com.**

GRAMÁTICA FUNCIONAL

- -Ar and -er verbs with a present-tense stem change are regular in the preterite. That is, they do *not* have a stem change.

	PRESENTE	PRETÉRITO INDEFINIDO
recordar (o:ue)	Recuerdo tu boda.	Recordé tu boda.
	I remember your wedding.	*I remembered your wedding.*
encender (e:ie)	Encienden las luces.	Encendieron las luces.
	They turn on the lights.	*They turned on the lights.*

- However, -ir verbs with a stem change in the present do have a stem change in the preterite in the **usted/él/ella** and **ustedes/ellos/ellas** forms only.

- Verbs with an **e→i** stem change, such as **servir**, maintain the **e→i** stem change in these two forms of the preterite. Verbs with an **o→ue** stem change, such as **dormir** (*to sleep*), have an **o→u** stem change in the preterite.

	SERVIR	DORMIR
(yo)	serví	dormí
(tú)	serviste	dormiste
(usted, él, ella)	sirvió	durmió
(nosotros/as)	servimos	dormimos
(vosotros/as)	servisteis	dormisteis
(ustedes, ellos/as)	sirvieron	durmieron

- Verbs ending in **-car, -gar,** and **-zar** have a spelling change in the **yo** form of the preterite.

	PRACTICAR	LLEGAR	EMPEZAR
(yo)	practi**qué**	lle**gué**	empe**cé**

- The verbs **creer** (*to believe*), **leer** (*to read*), and **oír** (*to hear*) follow the same pattern of spelling changes in the preterite: the **i** in the ending carries an accent, and changes to **y** in the **usted/él/ella** and **ustedes/ellos/ellas forms.**

	CREER	LEER	OÍR
(yo)	creí	leí	oí
(tú)	creíste	leíste	oíste
(usted, él, ella)	cre**y**ó	le**y**ó	o**y**ó
(nosotros/as)	creímos	leímos	oímos
(vosotros/as)	creísteis	leísteis	oísteis
(ustedes, ellos/as)	cre**y**eron	le**y**eron	o**y**eron

- The verb **ver** is regular in the preterite, but its forms do not take a written accent.

  Vi la nueva película de Almodóvar.
  I saw Almodóvar's new film.

- Note that several common verbs, such as **ir, ser, estar, hacer, tener, poder, poner,** and **querer**, have irregular preterite forms. You will learn these forms in coming lessons.

¡Póngalo en práctica!

G4 Escriba las formas del pretérito indefinido que faltan.

1. Juan	empezó	pensó
2. Lourdes y yo	empezamos	pensamos
3. tú	empezaste	pensaste
4. ustedes	empezaron	pensaron
5. yo	empecé	pensé
6. vosotras	empezasteis	pensasteis

G5 Complete el párrafo con el pretérito indefinido de los verbos.

En marzo de este año, Luis (1) viajó (viajar) a México. Antes del viaje, (2) leyó (leer) la guía de viajes entera. (3) Compró (comprar) el pasaje en la agencia de viajes y (4) llamó (llamar) al hotel para hacer la reserva. El día del vuelo, (5) salió (salir) de su casa a las ocho, (6) tomó (tomar) un taxi y (7) llegó (llegar) al aeropuerto a las nueve. (8) Entró (entrar) en el aeropuerto, (9) tomó (tomar) un café en el bar y (10) pagó (pagar) en efectivo. Luego (11) subió (subir) al avión, la azafata le (12) sirvió (servir) un refresco y Luis (13) empezó (empezar) su maravilloso viaje.

G5 Suggestion Challenge students by removing the words in parentheses and providing them in a word bank instead.

G6 Use las expresiones para escribir oraciones originales sobre usted mismo/a.

1. nacer Nací...
2. terminar la escuela secundaria Terminé...
3. empezar la universidad Empecé...
4. cumplir 10 años Cumplí...
5. viajar a otro estado por primera vez Viajé...
6. visitar un museo Visité...

G6 Expansion After students write their sentences, have them get together with a partner and take turns guessing what their partner wrote for each item.

Practice more at **vhlcentral.com.**

GRAMÁTICA FUNCIONAL

5A.2 **Suggestion** Tell students that they may also see dates written with Roman numerals for the month: **el 15 de septiembre de 1999 → 15/IX/1999**.

5A.2 Give dates in the past

Dates 10.5

- When answering the question **¿Cuándo?**, you will often need to provide a date. To give the date in Spanish, say **el** + [*day*] + **de** + [*month*] + **de** + [*year*].

¿Cuándo naciste? — El veintitrés de marzo de 1995.
When were you born? — *March twenty-third, 1995.*

Suggestion Write a list of historical events on the board and have students say on what date they occurred.

- When referring to the first of the month, use **el primero** (*the first*); for all other days, use the cardinal numbers you have already learned (**dos, tres, cuatro,** etc.)
- In Spanish, always pronounce the year as a single number; do not separate it into two pairs. Use the article **el** for the year 2000 (**el dos mil**).

El **primero** de julio de **mil novecientos noventa.**
*July **first, nineteen ninety.***

- Unlike in English, when dates are written in numerical format in Spanish, the day precedes the month.

Español:	17/2/1982	El 17 de febrero de 1982.
English:	*2/17/1982*	*February 17, 1982.*

5A.3 Specify with months and years

en + [*month/year*] 10.11

- Months are not capitalized in Spanish.

enero	abril	julio	octubre
febrero	mayo	agosto	noviembre
marzo	junio	septiembre	diciembre

- To tell when something happened by specifying the month or the year, use **en** + [*month*] or **en** + [*year*].

¿Cuándo empezaste a estudiar español?
When did you start studying Spanish?

En septiembre. / En 2009.
In September. / In 2009.

5A.4 Specify moments in the past

Time expressions 5.2.3, 11.6

- Use these expressions to tell when events happened in the past.

el año **pasado**	ayer
el mes **pasado**	anoche
la semana **pasada**	**hace** dos días/un año...
el jueves **pasado**	el 3 **de** agosto **de** 1995

- Use **el/la** + [*time designation*] + **pasado/a** to say *last week/month*, etc. Use **hace** + [*time period*] to express *ago*.

Silvia abrió la tienda **hace tres años.**
*Silvia opened the store **three years ago.***

¡Póngalo en práctica!

G7 Escriba estas fechas con palabras.

1. 3/5/1988 — El tres de mayo de mil novecientos ochenta y ocho.
2. 20/6/2000 — El veinte de junio del dos mil.
3. 12/12/2002 — El doce de diciembre de dos mil dos.
4. 1/9/1860 — El primero de septiembre de mil ochocientos sesenta.
5. 12/10/1492 — El doce de octubre de mil cuatrocientos noventa y dos.
6. 30/7/1997 — El treinta de julio de mil novecientos noventa y siete.
7. 18/8/1932 — El dieciocho de agosto de mil novecientos treinta y dos.
8. 6/11/1808 — El seis de noviembre de mil ochocientos ocho.

G8 Escriba oraciones completas en el pretérito indefinido.

1. Ana / terminar los estudios / junio
   Ana terminó los estudios en junio.
2. David y Marcos / viajar a Texas / enero
   David y Marcos viajaron a Texas en enero.
3. tú / recibir el premio / 2002
   Tú recibiste el premio en 2002.
4. Laura y yo / abrir la tienda / 1999
   Laura y yo abrimos la tienda en 1999.
5. yo / cambiar de casa / mayo
   Yo cambié de casa en mayo.

G9 Complete la conversación con palabras y expresiones adecuadas.

- Jaime, ¿saliste (1) anoche? Te llamé (2) ayer, pero no contestaste.
- Sí, Raquel y yo cenamos en el restaurante mexicano de la calle Limón. Mi padre comió allí el mes (3) pasado y nos lo recomendó. Cenamos allí la semana (4) pasada, y nos gustó tanto que volvimos.
- ¡Es muy bueno ese restaurante! Cené allí (5) hace dos semanas.

Practice more at **vhlcentral.com.**

5A

GRAMÁTICA FUNCIONAL

G10 **Expansion** Have students rephrase the items to say how long ago these people did these things. Ex: **Ramón vivió en Quito hace... años**.

5A.5 Express time sequences

de... a... 10.1, 10.5

- To specify the timing of an event or activity, use **de** + [*starting point*] + **a** + [*end point*].

Estudié en la UNAM **de** 2005 **a** 2009.
I studied at the UNAM ***from*** *2005* ***to*** *2009.*

Trabajé en la heladería **de** junio **a** agosto de 2008.
I worked at the ice cream shop ***from*** *June* ***through*** *August, 2008.*

5A.6 Structure a narrative

Transition words 11.6, 14.12

- Use transition words such as **primero** (*first*), **luego** (*then*), and **después** (*then, afterward*) to show the time relationship between events.

Pilar estudió biología **primero, luego** hizo el doctorado y **después** consiguió trabajo en un hospital.

First*, Pilar studied biology,* ***then*** *she got her Ph.D., and* ***later*** *she got a job at a hospital.*

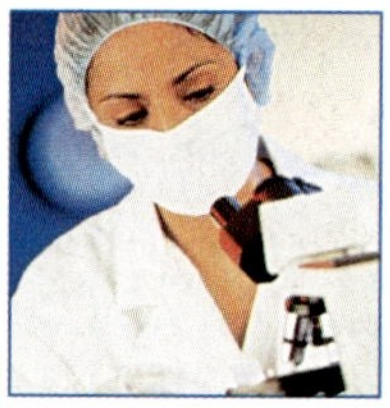

¡Póngalo en práctica!

G10 Escriba oraciones completas.

1. Ramón / vivir en Quito / 1998–2000
   Ramón vivió en Quito de 1998 al 2000.
2. tú / estudiar francés / septiembre–diciembre
   Tú estudiaste francés de septiembre a diciembre.
3. los chicos / viajar por Europa / julio–octubre
   Los chicos viajaron por Europa de julio a octubre.
4. nosotros / trabajar en el banco / 2003–2007
   Nosotros trabajamos en el banco de 2003 a 2007.

G11 Use **primero, luego** y **después** para combinar estas oraciones.

1. Juan estudió literatura.
2. Escribió una novela.
3. Ganó un premio.

Sample answer: Primero, Juan estudió literatura, luego escribió una novela y después ganó un premio.

Practice more at **vhlcentral.com.**

SÍNTESIS

Mire las fotos y escriba una breve conversación para cada una usando las palabras y expresiones del recuadro.

Suggestion Have students peer-edit their dialogues.

1. 

nacer	2008	hijo	celebrar tu boda	2005

- ______________________
- ______________________
- ______________________
- ______________________

2. 

de... a...	estudiar	trabajar	primero	después

- ______________________
- ______________________
- ______________________
- ______________________

VOCABULARIO

¡Felicidades, Manuela!

¡Felicidades!	*Congratulations!*
el acontecimiento	*event*
la boda	*wedding*
el carro (*Amér. L.*)	*car*
el cumpleaños (*invar.*)	*birthday*
enero	*January*
los estudios	*studies*
febrero	*February*
la fecha	*date*
el/la hijo/a	*son/daughter*
junio	*June*
marzo	*March*
el momento	*moment*
la mujer empresaria	*businesswoman*
noviembre	*November*
la ONG (organización no gubernamental)	*NGO (non-governmental organization)*
el pie de foto	*caption*
la Semana Santa	*Easter/Holy Week*
septiembre	*September*
la tarjeta de felicitación	*greeting card*
contigo	*with you*
cambiar de casa	*to move*
celebrar	*celebrate*
compartir	*to share*
nacer (zc)	*to be born*
recordar (o:ue)	*to remember*
subir	*to climb*
activo/a	*active*
feliz (*pl.* felices)	*happy*
juntos/as	*together*

Diario de viaje

en barco	*by boat*
hace dos meses	*two months ago*
Perdona, ...	*Excuse me, . . .*
el Amazonas	*Amazon River*
el aniversario	*anniversary*
el autobús	*bus*
el bosque	*forest*
el delfín	*dolphin*
el diario	*diary, journal*
la jungla	*jungle*
el mes pasado	*last month*
el/la novio/a	*boyfriend/girlfriend*
el río	*river*
la semana pasada	*last week*
la zona	*region*
conocer (zc)	*to meet; to know (people)*
empezar (e:ie)	*to start*
lavar los platos	*to do the dishes*
nadar	*to swim*
realizar	*to do; to perform*
recorrer	*to travel*
volar (o:ue)	*to fly*
desértico/a	*desert-like*
impresionante	*impressive*
maravilloso/a	*wonderful*
pasado/a	*last*
anoche	*last night*
ayer	*yesterday*

Salma Hayek

del brazo	*arm in arm*
la actuación	*acting*
el baile	*dance, ball*
el banquete	*reception*
la bata	*robe*
el/la cantante	*singer*
la cara	*face*
la caravana de coches	*motorcade*
la carrera	*career*
el compromiso	*commitment*
la estrella	*star*
Filosofía y Letras	*Arts*
el/la hermano/a	*brother/sister*
la historia	*story*
la interpretación	*performance*
la manera	*way*
la misa	*Mass*
el/la novio/a	*groom/bride*
el par	*pair*
la pata	*paw*
el premio	*award; prize*
la quinceañera	*fifteen-year-old girl*
la telenovela	*soap opera*
la vela	*candle*
actuar	*to act*
cumplir 15 años	*to turn 15 years old*
dejar	*to quit; to give up*
ganar	*to win*
probar (o:ue) suerte	*to try one's luck*
algunos/as	*some*
católico/a	*Catholic*
destacado/a	*notable*
exitoso/a	*successful*
luchador(a)	*fighter*
sin embargo	*however*

Variación léxica

el autobús ⟷ **el colectivo** (*Arg.*) ⟷ **la guagua** (*Car.*) ⟷ **el bus** (*Amér. L.*)

el carro (*Amér. L.*) ⟷ **el coche** (*Esp.*) ⟷ **el auto (móvil)** (*Amér. L.*)

el/la chico/a ⟷ **el/la chavo/a** (*Méx.*) ⟷ **el/la chaval(a)** (*Esp.*) ⟷ **el/la botija** (*Uru.*) ⟷ **el/la chamo/a** (*Ven.*) ⟷ **el/la chamaco/a** (*Amér. L.*)

la telenovela ⟷ **el culebrón** (*Esp.*) ⟷ **la novela** (*Arg.*) ⟷ **la teleserie** (*Chi.*)

5B MI GENTE

Suggestion Have students create their own family tree. Have them introduce their families and explain the relationships to a partner. Provide additional vocabulary as needed.

Foto de familia

Una pareja feliz

Dolores y Ramón están casados. El próximo mes celebran ¡40 años de matrimonio! Son una pareja feliz; están jubilados y ahora tienen mucho tiempo libre. Tienen tres hijos maravillosos: Manuel, Mario y Marisa.

Manuel está soltero. Mario está casado con Paula y juntos tienen una hija, Lucía, de 5 años. Marisa está divorciada y vive con su hijo Sergio, de 3 años.

Los fines de semana, Dolores hace una rica comida para sus hijos y nietos. A los dos nietos les gusta mucho ir a casa de sus abuelos.

padre + madre = padres
abuelo + abuela = abuelos
nieto + nieta = nietos
hermano + hermana = hermanos
tío + tía = tíos
primo + prima = primos
hijo(s) + hija(s) = hijos

Ramón .... Dolores
Manuel .... Mario / Paula .... Marisa
Lucía .... Sergio

Hablar del estado civil

- ¿Estás soltera o casada?
- Estoy divorciada.

5B.1 **estar** + [*marital status*]

Vocabulario

1

- mi gente *my folks*
- casado/a *married*
- el próximo mes *next month*
- el matrimonio *marriage*
- la pareja *couple; partner*
- jubilado/a *retired*
- el tiempo libre *free time*
- el/la hijo/a *son/daughter*
- soltero/a *single*
- divorciado/a *divorced*
- los fines de semana *on weekends*
- los nietos *grandchildren*
- los abuelos *grandparents*
- el árbol genealógico *family tree*
- los padres *parents*
- el/la abuelo/a *grandfather/ grandmother*
- el/la nieto/a *grandson/ granddaughter*
- el/la hermano/a *brother/sister*
- los hermanos *siblings*
- el/la tío/a *uncle/aunt*
- el/la primo/a *cousin*

1 a. Fíjese en la fotografía. ¿Cuál es el tema de este artículo? Después lea el texto y complete el árbol genealógico.

b. ¿Quién es quién?

1. Manuel, Mario y Marisa son ....hermanos.... .
2. Paula y Mario son los ....padres.... de Lucía.
3. Lucía y Sergio son los ....nietos.... de Ramón y Dolores.

Suggestion Ask heritage speakers what family-related terms are most commonly used in their families.

2 Agrupe a los miembros de esta familia según su estado civil. Compruebe las respuestas con su compañero/a.

Está soltero/a.	Está casado/a.	Está divorciado/a.
Manuel	*Dolores,* Ramón, Mario, Paula	Marisa

3 Laura habla sobre su familia con una compañera de trabajo. Anote cuántos hermanos tiene y cuántos nietos tienen sus padres.

Tiene ....dos.... hermanos y sus padres tienen ....cinco.... nietos.

4 Observe la ilustración. ¿Cuál es el estado civil de Enrique? Está casado.

1

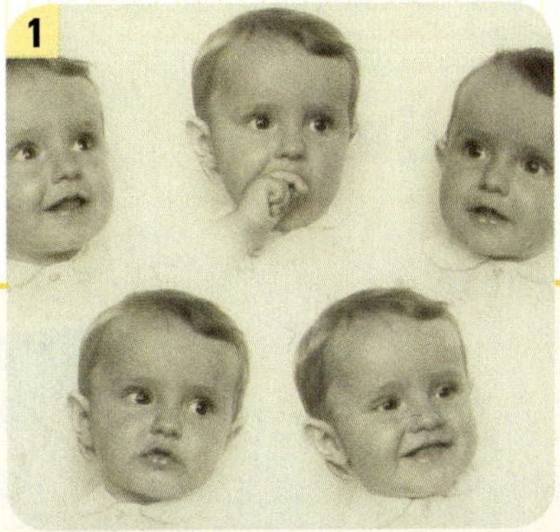

2

3

Recuerdos de familia

Suggestion Have students bring in a few family photos. Have pairs of students talk about the people in the photos.

4

"Aquí estamos el abuelo y yo con vuestros padres y el hijo de mi hermana." 2
"Este es nuestro hijo Mario con dos años. Lucía, éste es tu padre." 1
"Estos son mis hermanos, los tíos de vuestros padres." 4
"Sergio, esta es tu madre con sus compañeros de clase en el colegio." 3

Hablar de los familiares

¿**Su marido** trabaja mucho?
¿**Tus padres** están jubilados?
Nuestras nietas son pequeñas.
Vuestros hermanos, ¿dónde viven?
Sus abuelos son de Bogotá.

5B.2 Plural possessives

Vocabulario

2
el miembro *member*
el estado civil *marital status*
4
mañana *tomorrow*
5
el recuerdo *memory; souvenir*
enseñar *to show; to teach*
el marido *husband*
el álbum
7
el nacimiento *birth*
último/a *last*
la adopción, adoptar

Hijos

La mayoría de las parejas españolas tienen un solo hijo. Hay pocos nacimientos, pero el número de adopciones aumentó. El 80% de los niños que se adoptaron durante los últimos años nacieron en otros países, como China, Rusia y Ucrania.

5 a. Dolores enseña a sus nietos el álbum de familia. Relacione las frases con las fotografías antiguas.

b. Diga quién aparece en cada una de las fotografías. Suggested answers:

1. *Es su hijo.* 2. Son su marido, sus hijos y el hijo de su hermana. 3. Es su hija con sus compañeros de clase. 4. Son sus hermanos.

c. Revise las formas de los posesivos.

1. (yo) *mis* hijos / mis hijas
2. (tú) tus tíos / tus tías
3. (usted, él, ella) sus hermanos / sus hermanas
4. (nosotros/as) nuestros padres / nuestras madres
5. (vosotros/as) vuestros abuelos / vuestras abuelas
6. (ustedes, ellos/as) sus nietos / sus nietas

6 ¿Quién es para Dolores su familia? ¿Y para usted?

Modelo: *Para Dolores, su familia son los padres, los hijos...* los nietos, los abuelos y los hermanos.

Suggestion Tell students a few family-related **refranes** (Ex: **Entre marido y mujer nadie se debe meter**) and have students identify any English equivalents. Have them state which expressions they feel are true and why.

MI EXPERIENCIA

7 ¿Cómo son las familias de sus compañeros? Anote sus respuestas. Luego cuente al resto de la clase sus averiguaciones.

GUIÓN DE TRABAJO

¿Cómo es tu familia? ¿Es una familia grande/pequeña?
¿Tienes hermanos? ¿Están casados, solteros, divorciados...?

Descríbela.

¿Y tú? ¿Estás casado/a? ¿Soltero/a? ¿Divorciado/a?
¿Tienes pareja? ¿Tienes hijos?

Para mí, una familia es...

...una pareja con o sin hijos.
...una madre o un padre y su hijo....

Practice more at **vhlcentral.com.**

SAM: Actividades pp. 101–103

Mis amigos, mi otra familia

MI CUMPLEAÑOS

Mis amigos de la universidad en el día de mi cumpleaños

EN LA OFICINA

Mis compañeros de trabajo, mi otra familia

Suggestion Have students write a description of their best friend.

Hablar de conocidos

- ¿Conoces a Laura? Es una amiga de Montevideo. La conozco **desde** pequeña.
- No, no la **conozco**.
- Este es Pedro, un amigo del trabajo, ¿lo **conoces**?
- Sí, lo **conozco desde hace** unos días.

5B.3 Irregular verbs **-zc-**
conocer a + [*people*]
conocer + [*places/things*]

5B.4 **desde**
desde hace

Vocabulario

8
el/la compañero/a de trabajo *coworker*
desde *since; from*
desde hace *for (and until now)*
desde pequeño/a *since childhood*

10
cronológicamente *chronologically*

Suggestion Have pairs of students take turns asking each other if they know certain people (professors, students, or staff) at the university.

8 a. Escuche a Jaime hablar con su hija sobre sus amigos. ¿Cómo se llaman? Escriba sus nombres en la foto.

b. ¿De dónde los conoce y desde cuándo?

trabajo colegio universidad barrio	Mario Silvio Luisa Cris	desde hace 3 semanas desde hace 2 años desde hace 20 años desde hace unos meses desde 1980

Modelo: *A Mario lo conoce de la universidad, desde hace 20 años.*

A Silvio lo conoce del trabajo, desde hace unos meses.
A Luisa la conoce del trabajo, desde hace dos años.
A Cris la conoce de la universidad, desde hace 20 años.

9 Complete la conversación. ¿Cuándo se usa *conocer a*?

- Luisa, yo no (1)...conozco... el Museo Nacional, ¿tú lo (2)...conoces...?
- No, pero mi amigo Julio lo (3)...conoce... muy bien. ¿(4)...Conoces... a Julio?
- Sí, lo (5)...conozco... de la universidad.
- ¿Ah, sí?

10 a. Escriba el nombre de dos amigos. Su compañero/a le pregunta de dónde y desde cuándo los conoce.

Modelo: *A tu amigo Sebastián, ¿lo conoces del colegio?*

b. ¿Dónde conocemos normalmente a los amigos? Ordene los lugares cronológicamente. Suggested answer:

trabajo	colegio	barrio	universidad	...

barrio - colegio - universidad - trabajo

Hablar de viajes y de experiencias en momentos concretos

- ¿Adónde **fuiste** el año pasado?
- **Fui** a Argentina con un amigo.
- ¿Dónde **estuviste**?
- **Estuvimos** una semana en Buenos Aires y desde allí **fuimos** en avión a la Patagonia. **Fue** un viaje inolvidable.

5B.5 Irregular preterite forms **ir, ser, estar**

Vocabulario

11

las memorias *memoirs*
parecer (c:zc) *to seem*
adecuado/a *appropriate; suitable*
la relación *relationship*
la amistad *friendship*
olvidar *to forget*
¡Qué tiempos aquellos! *Those were the days!*
la Navidad *Christmas*
increíble *incredible*
el punto en común *point in common*
gran (grande) *great*
inolvidable *unforgettable*
la economía

12

la aventura *adventure*

13

la mujer *wife; woman*

¡OJO!

The adjective **grande** drops the final **-de** before a singular noun. **Gran** before a noun means *great*. **Grande** following a noun means *large* or *big*. So, **un gran país** refers to *a great country*, whereas **un país grande** refers to *a big country*.

1. soltero ...e...	a. madre
2. padre ...a...	b. hijo
3. tíos ...d...	c. mujer
4. marido ...c...	d. primos
5. hija ...b...	e. casado

11 a. Este es un fragmento de las "memorias" de Marisa. ¿Qué título le parece más adecuado? "Laura, una amiga muy especial"

"Laura, una amiga muy especial"

"Laura, mi hermana"

"Viajar con amigos"

[...] Mi amiga Laura es como una hermana. La veo poco; ella vive en Veracruz con su marido y su hija. Hablamos mucho por teléfono; es una relación de amistad muy especial. No olvidamos los momentos que vivimos juntas. De 1994 a 1999, estudiamos Economía en la Universidad de Guadalajara. ¡Qué tiempos aquellos! En la Navidad de 2002 fuimos de viaje a Perú y estuvimos en muchas ciudades. ¡Fue una experiencia increíble! Un año más tarde yo estuve de profesora en Lima y ella estuvo en Chile. Mi hijo nació tres años más tarde y cuatro años después de eso nació su hija. Nuestras vidas tienen muchos puntos en común. ¡Es una gran amiga!

b. ¿Qué pasó según las memorias de Marisa en las siguientes fechas?

1994–1999: Estudiaron Economía en la Universidad de Guadalajara. 2002: Fueron de viaje a Perú. 2003: Marisa trabajó de profesora en Lima, Laura estuvo en Chile. 2006: Nació el hijo de Marisa. 2010: Nació el hijo de Laura.

1994–1999 | 2002 | 2003 | 2006 | 2010

c. Fíjese en el texto y complete la terminación de estos verbos.

ella est..uvo.. / nosotras fui..mos.. / ellas fue..ron.. / yo est..uve..

12 Piensen en experiencias con amigos. ¿Qué pasó? ¿Cuándo?

En 19...
De 20... a...

fuimos a...
estuvimos en...

viaje
universidad
América Latina
aventura

MI EXPERIENCIA

13 Primero relacione las palabras de las dos listas de la izquierda para repasar el vocabulario. Luego presente sus amigos a sus compañeros de clase.

GUIÓN DE TRABAJO

¿Quiénes son tus amigos?
Compañeros de estudios, de trabajo, hermanos, ...
¿De dónde conoces a tus amigos?
Del trabajo, de los viajes, del barrio,...
¿Desde cuándo conoces a tus amigos?
Desde hace...

¿Están casados, solteros...? ¿Tienen pareja?
¿Qué momentos importantes viviste con ellos?
Fui con .... a ....
Estuve con .... en ....

Practice more at vhlcentral.com.

SAM: Actividades pp. 104–106

Suggestion As a reading aid, have students draw a simple weekly calendar and, as they read the paragraphs, have them fill in Juanita and Bernardo's activities.

Bernardo y Juanita, abuelos a tiempo completo

Suggestion Have students compare and contrast Juanita and Bernardo with their own grandparents.

Juanita y Bernardo, dos abuelos muy activos

Juanita y Bernardo son una pareja de jubilados de 81 y 84 años, respectivamente. Viven en el estado de Texas; Bernardo es de Texas y Juanita nació en el estado de Tamaulipas, México. Hace mucho tiempo, decidieron formar una familia grande... ¡y lo lograron! Tienen 6 hijos y 21 nietos.

Juanita, ¿en qué ocupan su tiempo de lunes a viernes?
Yo hago las compras, cocino y limpio la casa. Mi marido me ayuda y además cuida el jardín. También cuidamos a nuestro nieto más pequeño: lo recogemos del kínder y lo llevamos a la alberca.

¿Y por la noche?
Miramos la televisión. ¡Nos encantan las películas viejas y las telenovelas! Algunas noches cenamos con amigos. Bernardo pasa horas contando chistes. ¡Es una persona muy alegre!

¿Y los fines de semana?
Los sábados paseamos y caminamos en el parque. ¡Nos mantiene sanos! Los domingos descansamos y vamos a la iglesia. También tenemos diversos acontecimientos familiares. ¡En los últimos dos años celebramos 5 bodas, 4 fiestas de quinceañera y 6 bautizos!

Vocabulario

(14)
- el estado *state*
- lograr *to manage*
- ocupar *to spend; to take up*
- ayudar *to help*
- cuidar a *to take care of*
- recoger *to pick up*
- el kínder (*Méx.*) *kindergarten*
- llevar *to take*
- la alberca (*Méx.*) *pool*
- encantar *to love, to get a kick out of*
- viejo/a *old*
- el chiste *joke*
- alegre *happy*
- pasear *to take a walk*
- caminar *to walk*
- mantener (e:ie) *to keep*
- sano/a *healthy*
- descansar *to rest*
- diverso/a *various*
- el bautizo *baptism*

(17)
- el placer *pleasure*
- **la obligación, compatible**

14 a. Mire la foto. ¿Qué relación familiar tienen estas personas?
Sample answer: Son marido y mujer.

b. Ahora lea el texto. ¿Qué hacen Juanita y Bernardo de lunes a viernes?

1. Están en la cama hasta las once de la mañana. ☐
2. Recogen al nieto del kinder. ☑
3. Comen con amigos. ☐
4. Hacen las compras. ☑
5. Van a la iglesia. ☐
6. Limpian la casa. ☑

15 Con un(a) compañero/a, imaginen una entrevista con Juanita o Bernardo. Hagan preguntas sobre el fin de semana pasado. Luego presenten su entrevista a la clase.

16 Pregunte a su compañero/a si tiene abuelos, hermanos o primos. ¿Pasa mucho tiempo con ellos? ¿Pasó usted mucho tiempo con sus abuelos u otros familiares?

17 **¿Obligación o placer?** ¿Conoce a abuelos como Juanita y Bernardo? ¿Cree usted que para Juanita y Bernardo es una obligación estar con su nieto? ¿Por qué?

¡Gracias, abuelos!
Cada vez más familias funcionan gracias a los abuelos: **llevan a sus nietos al colegio, los cuidan cuando están enfermos y en verano pasan con ellos las vacaciones si los padres trabajan.**

Vocabulario

(17)

estar de acuerdo *to agree*
bastante *quite a lot*
alguien *someone*
valerse *to be self-sufficient*
pedir (e:i) ayuda *to ask for help*
la ayuda *help*
los Servicios Sociales *Social Services*
pedir (e:i) un crédito *to ask for a loan*
la guardería *day care*
el familiar *relative*
estar en desacuerdo *to disagree*
tener confianza en *to trust in*
el papel de *role of*
gracias a... *thanks to. . .*
enfermo/a *sick*

(20)

la mamá (*fam.*) *mom*
el papá (*fam.*) *dad*
el/la esposo/a (*Amér. L.*) *husband/wife*
la mayoría *most*
el/la inmigrante *immigrant*

¡OJO!

The letters *c* (before *e* and *i*) and *z* are pronounced as [s] in southern Spain and in Latin America (**seseo**), but as [z] (like the *th* in *think*) in most of Spain (**ceceo**).

El 36,21% de los inmigrantes que viven en España nacieron en América Latina. Los países más destacados son Ecuador (11,13%), Colombia (6,40%), Argentina (3,63%), Bolivia (3,37%) y Perú (2,31%).

20 Spain has seen a large increase in immigrants from Latin America, due to the so-called "law of the grandchildren," by which grandchildren of Spanish citizens who live in former colonies may apply for Spanish citizenship.

18 Mire el siguiente estudio del Centro de Investigaciones Sociológicas (CIS) de España sobre la familia. ¿Está de acuerdo con estas afirmaciones? Marque después si las oraciones que aparecen más abajo son verdaderas (**V**) o falsas (**F**).

¿Está usted muy, bastante, poco o nada de acuerdo?

	Muy de acuerdo	Bastante de acuerdo	Ni de acuerdo ni en desacuerdo	Poco de acuerdo	Nada de acuerdo
Cuando alguien no puede valerse, es mejor pedir ayuda a los Servicios Sociales que a la familia.	10,4 %	19,6 %	14,7 %	38,0 %	16,4 %
Si necesita dinero, pide un crédito a un banco, no a la familia.	14,7 %	29,7 %	14,3 %	28,3 %	11,6 %
Prefiere llevar a los hijos a una guardería a llevarlos con los abuelos o familiares.	16,1 %	32,3 %	16,1 %	25,0 %	8,9 %

www.cis.es

18 Expansion Have students use the questionnaire to survey three classmates.

	V	F
1. Muchos españoles tienen más confianza en la familia que en los Servicios Sociales.	✓	
2. Pocos españoles prefieren pedir créditos al banco.		✓
3. La mayoría de los españoles están de acuerdo con el papel de abuelos de Juanita y Bernardo.		✓

[c] [z]

19 a. Luis busca el número de teléfono y la dirección de un amigo. Fíjese: **c** + **e, i** y **z** + **a, o, u** representan el mismo sonido. Escuche y marque ese sonido en estas palabras.

Cela, Cerezo, Cid... Aquí está: Cifuentes Cubero, Zulma.
Su dirección es: calle Zárraga, 8, Villa Ortúzar

b. Ahora escuche a Marcelo repetir las mismas frases. ¿Qué diferencia nota entre las dos formas de pronunciar la **c** y la **z**?
Suggested answer: Luis pronuncia la **c** y la **z** de diferente manera. Marcelo las pronuncia igual.

20 a. La comunidad latinoamericana más numerosa en España es la ecuatoriana. Doris llegó con su marido hace un año. Escuche la entrevista y escriba los términos que ella usa para hablar de su familia y amigos.

Una familia ecuatoriana

España	Ecuador
padres	mamá y papá
marido	esposo
hermano	ñaño
amigos	pana

b. Pregunte a su compañero/a y compare con el resto de la clase.

¿Conoces a familias latinoamericanas? ¿De qué países son?

Practice more at **vhlcentral.com.**

SAM: Actividades pp. 107–112

TAREA FINAL

Nuestro álbum de amigos y familiares

Piense en un familiar o amigo/a.
Hermano/a, amigo/a de la universidad, del barrio...

Escriba un texto breve con la información más importante.
Nombre, relación, experiencias vividas en el pasado...

Presente su familiar o amigo/a a sus compañeros de grupo.
Se llama..., lo conozco de..., es..., estuvimos en...

Organicen un álbum de fotos de amigos y familiares del grupo y escriban los datos sobre ellos.
Este es Nelson...

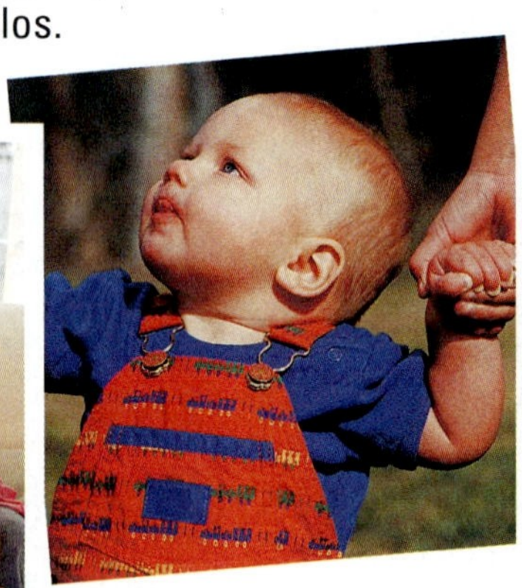

YO PUEDO...

- **Puedo hablar de mi familia.**
  Dibuje un árbol genealógico de su familia y descríbalo en un pequeño texto. Hable del estado civil de sus hermanos, primos...
- **Puedo hablar sobre conocidos.**
  Complete la conversación.
- **Puedo contar una experiencia compartida con amigos o familia.**
  Complete las oraciones, anotando una experiencia del pasado.
- **Puedo hablar de distintos modelos de familia.**
  ¿Qué modelos de familia son especialmente frecuentes en su país?

- ¿Conoces a Marta?
- Sí, es una amiga del colegio.
- Ah, yo no la ....

Estuve en ....
Fui a ....
Fui ....

GRAMÁTICA FUNCIONAL

5B.1 Talk about marital status

estar + [*marital status*] 5.8.1

- Use **estar** + **soltero/a** (*single*), **casado/a** (*married*), or **divorciado/a** (*divorced*) to tell someone's marital status.

Yo **estoy soltera**, mi hermano **está casado** y mi hermana **está divorciada**.
I **am single**, *my brother* **is married**, *and my sister* **is divorced**.

¡OJO! In many Spanish-speaking countries, it is also possible to use **ser** with marital status (**Soy casado/a**).

5B.2 Talk about family relationships

Possessive adjectives (plural) 8.1

- In 2A.8, you learned to use the possessive adjectives **mi**, **tu**, and **su** to express possession of individual objects. Here are the possessive adjectives to use with all combinations of people and things.

	singular	plural
(yo)	**mi** hijo/hija	**mis** hijos/hijas
(tú)	**tu** amigo/amiga	**tus** amigos/amigas
(usted, él, ella)	**su** hermano/hermana	**sus** hermanos/hermanas
(nosotros/as)	**nuestro** padre **nuestra** madre	**nuestros** padres **nuestras** madres
(vosotros/as)	**vuestro** tío **vuestra** tía	**vuestros** tíos **vuestras** tías
(ustedes, ellos/as)	**su** abuelo/abuela	**sus** abuelos/abuelas

- Possessive adjectives match the person or thing *possessed* in gender and number, not the *possessor*.

Nuestr**a** tí**a** vive en San Diego y nuestr**os** prim**os**, aquí.
Our aunt lives in San Diego and our cousins live here.

- Note that **su(s)** can mean *your*, *his*, *her*, *its*, or *their*. Use context to determine who the possessor is, and be sure to provide enough information to ensure that your meaning is clear.

Está con **sus** *tías.*
She's with **her** *aunts.*

Los padres hablan con **su** hijo.
The parents talk to **their** *son.*

5B.3 5B.4 Talk about people you know

Irregular verbs **c→zc** 5.1.2 **a personal** 10.1

- Use the verb **conocer** (*to know*) to talk about people, places, or things you are familiar with. **Conocer** has an irregular **yo** form.

CONOCER			
(yo)	conozco	(nosotros/as)	conocemos
(tú)	conoces	(vosotros/as)	conocéis
(usted, él, ella)	conoce	(ustedes, ellos/as)	conocen

Conozco bien la Ciudad de Guatemala.
I **know** *Guatemala City well.*

¿**Conoces** a mi primo, Marcos?
Do you **know** *my cousin, Marcos?*

¡Póngalo en práctica!

G1 Complete la conversación.

- ¿(1) Está/Estás casado?
- No, tengo pareja, pero no estamos (2) casados.
- ¿Y Juana?
- Está (3) soltera; le gusta vivir sola.
- María (4) está casada y tiene dos hijos, ¿no?
- No, está (5) divorciada y, sí, tiene dos hijos; viven con ella. El ex marido está (6) casado. La nueva esposa se llama Marcela.

G2 Suggestion Challenge students by giving them the chart only with the nouns; they should provide all possessive adjectives.

G2 Complete la tabla con las formas que faltan.

	singular	plural
1.	su nieto	sus nietos
2.	mi prima	mis primas
3.	nuestro amigo	nuestros amigos
4.	vuestra abuela	vuestras abuelas
5.	tu vecino	tus vecinos
6.	su hijo	sus hijos

G3 Complete las conversaciones de forma lógica.
Sample answers:

- (1) mis/nuestros tíos, los hermanos de mi padre, se llaman Roberto y Paz, como (2) sus padres.
- ¡Qué coincidencia! (3) Mi tía también se llama Paz, igual que mi abuela materna.
- (4) Nuestros padres no nos comprenden.
- ¡Uf! ¡(5) Nuestra madre piensa que tenemos cinco años!
- Pero, por lo menos (*at least*), (6) vuestro padre trabaja con jóvenes como nosotros y entiende (7) nuestros problemas.

G4 Complete las oraciones con la forma adecuada de **conocer**.

1. Guillermo conoce a mi hermana.
2. Claudia y yo conocemos el Museo del Prado.
3. Julieta y tú conocen/conocéis al hermano de Germán.
4. Tú conoces la ciudad, ¿verdad?
5. Yo conozco a Javier desde pequeño.
6. Mi padres conocen al arquitecto.

Practice more at **vhlcentral.com.**

5B GRAMÁTICA FUNCIONAL

- To express that a person is known, use **conocer** + **a** + [*person*]. This usage is called the **a personal**, and is required whenever a person is the direct object of a verb.

  Conocemos **a** la directora. ¿Conocen ustedes **a** María?
  We know the director. Do you know María?

¡OJO! Spanish has two words that mean *to know*: **conocer** and **saber**. You will learn to use the verb **saber** in **6B.1**.

desde, desde hace, hace + que 10.7, 10.8

- Use **desde**, **desde hace**, or **hace** + **que** with a present-tense verb to tell how long something has been happening.
  Use **desde** + [*specific time in the past*] to mean *since*.

  Conozco a Luisa **desde** 2002/el año pasado/pequeña.
  *I've known Luisa **since** 2002/last year/I was little.*

- To specify the length of time something has been going on, use **desde hace** + [*span of time*].

  Conocemos a su madre **desde hace** una semana/dos años.
  *We've known her mother **for** a week/two years.*

- Express the same meaning with the construction **hace** + [*span of time*] + **que**.

  Hace una semana/dos años **que** conocemos a su madre.
  *We've known her mother **for** a week/two years.*

- Use **hace** with a verb in the **pretérito indefinido** to mean *ago*.

  Conocí a Mireia **hace** tres semanas.
  *I met Mireia three weeks **ago**.*

Tell students that the construction **hace** + [*span of time*] + **que** + [*preterite*] can also be used to mean *ago*.

5B.5 Talk about trips and experiences at specific times

Irregular preterite: ir, ser, estar 5.2.2, 5.2.3

- The verbs **ir**, **ser**, and **estar** are irregular in the **pretérito indefinido**. Note that these irregular forms do not have written accents.

	IR/SER	ESTAR
(yo)	**fui**	**estuv**e
(tú)	**fuiste**	**estuv**iste
(usted, él, ella)	**fue**	**estuv**o
(nosotros/as)	**fuimos**	**estuv**imos
(vosotros/as)	**fuisteis**	**estuv**isteis
(ustedes, ellos/as)	**fueron**	**estuv**ieron

- **Ir** and **ser** have the same conjugation in the preterite, so you must use context to clarify meaning. Remember that the verb **ir** is often followed by **a**.

  Fuimos a una fiesta en casa de Pedro. **Fue** una noche divertida.
  *We **went** to a party at Pedro's house. **It was** a fun evening.*

¡Póngalo en práctica!

G5 Complete las oraciones con **desde, desde hace** o **hace**.

1. Miguel conoce a Elena desde hace quince años.
2. Nosotros conocemos a Patricia desde el año pasado.
3. Mi tío trabaja aquí desde el martes.
4. Hace muchos años que Magda y Carlos conocen Londres.
5. Valeria vive en Colón desde hace tres meses.

G6 Complete las oraciones con **desde** o **hace**.

1. Vivimos en Guayaquil desde mayo.
2. Viajaron a Puebla hace cinco años.
3. Escribe poesía desde la universidad.
4. Mi tío terminó sus estudios hace 20 años.
5. Raúl conoció a Verónica hace tres semanas.

G7 Escriba oraciones completas. Fíjese en el uso del **a personal**. Sample answers:

1. Tomás / junio / conocer / Juanita / desde
   Tomás conoce a Juanita desde junio.
2. desde hace / yo / 5 años / Acapulco / conocer
   Conozco Acapulco desde hace cinco años.
3. conocer / nosotras / Felipe / hace 2 semanas
   Nosotras conocimos a Felipe hace dos semanas.
4. Pablo / conocer / desde pequeño / las vecinas
   Pablo conoce a las vecinas desde pequeño.

G8 Elija el final correcto para cada oración.

b	**1.** Claudio y tú...	**a.** fui a México en mayo.
e	**2.** María...	**b.** estuvisteis juntos en Oaxaca.
d	**3.** Mis sobrinos...	**c.** fuiste la ganadora del concurso.
a	**4.** Yo...	**d.** estuvieron en la fiesta anoche.
c	**5.** Tú...	**e.** fue al mercado por la mañana.

G8 Expansion For items a, c, and e, have students state whether the verb is **ser** or **ir**, and how they know.

G9 Indique si el verbo conjugado es una forma de **ser** o de **ir**.

SER	IR	
☐	☑	1. Juan fue al parque con sus hermanos.
☑	☐	2. Mario y yo siempre fuimos buenos amigos.
☐	☑	3. ¿Ustedes fueron a la fiesta de cumpleaños?
☑	☐	4. Carla y tú fuisteis buenas estudiantes.

Practice more at vhlcentral.com.

VOCABULARIO

Foto de familia

los fines de semana	*(on) weekends*
mi gente	*my folks*
el próximo mes	*next month*
el/la abuelo/a	*grandfather/ grandmother*
los abuelos	*grandparents*
la adopción	*adoption*
el álbum	*album*
el árbol genealógico	*family tree*
el estado civil	*marital status*
el/la hermano/a	*brother/sister*
los hermanos	*siblings*
el/la hijo/a	*son/daughter*
el marido	*husband*
el matrimonio	*marriage*
el miembro	*member*
el nacimiento	*birth*
el/la nieto/a	*grandson/ granddaughter*
los nietos	*grandchildren*
los padres	*parents*
la pareja	*couple; partner*
el/la primo/a	*cousin*
el recuerdo	*memory; souvenir*
el tiempo libre	*free time*
el/la tío/a	*uncle/aunt*
adoptar	*to adopt*
enseñar	*to show; to teach*
casado/a	*married*
divorciado/a	*divorced*
jubilado/a	*retired*
soltero/a	*single*
último/a	*last*
mañana	*tomorrow*

Mis amigos, mi otra familia

desde pequeño/a	*since childhood*
¡Qué tiempos aquellos!	*Those were the days!*
la amistad	*friendship*
la aventura	*adventure*
el/la compañero/a de trabajo	*coworker*
la economía	*Economics*
las memorias	*memoirs; memories*
la mujer	*wife; woman*
la Navidad	*Christmas*
el punto en común	*point in common*
la relación	*relationship*
olvidar	*to forget*
parecer (zc)	*to seem*
adecuado/a	*appropriate; suitable*
gran (grande)	*great*
increíble	*incredible*
inolvidable	*unforgettable*
cronológicamente	*chronologically*
desde	*since; from*
desde hace	*for (and until now)*

Juanita y Bernardo

gracias a..	*thanks to. . .*
la alberca (*Méx.*)	*pool*
la ayuda	*help*
el bautizo	*baptism*
el chiste	*joke*
el/la esposo/a (*Amér. L.*)	*husband/wife*
el estado	*state*
el familiar	*relative*
la guardería	*day care*
el/la inmigrante	*immigrant*
el kínder (*Méx.*)	*kindergarten*
la mamá (*fam.*)	*mom*
la mayoría	*most, majority*
la obligación	*obligation*
el papá (*fam.*)	*dad*
el papel de	*role of*
el placer	*pleasure*
los Servicios Sociales	*Social Services*
alguien	*someone*
ayudar	*to help*
caminar	*to walk*
cuidar a	*to take care of*
descansar	*to rest*
encantar	*to love, to get a kick out of*
estar de acuerdo	*to agree*
estar en desacuerdo	*to disagree*
llevar	*to take*
lograr	*to manage*
mantener (e:ie)	*to keep*
ocupar	*to spend; to take up*
pasear	*to take a walk*
pedir (e:i) ayuda	*to ask for help*
pedir (e:i) un crédito	*to ask for a loan*
recoger (j)	*to pick up*
tener confianza en	*to trust in*
valerse	*to be self-sufficient*
alegre	*happy*
compatible	*compatible*
diverso/a	*various*
enfermo/a	*sick*
sano/a	*healthy*
viejo/a	*old*
bastante	*quite a lot*

Variación léxica

el/la amigo/a ⟷ **el/la pana** (*Ven., Ecua.*) ⟷ **el cuate** (*Méx.*)

el bautizo ⟷ **el bautismo** (*Arg.*)

el colegio secundario ⟷ **la escuela secundaria** ⟷ **el liceo** (*Amér. L.*) ⟷ **el instituto** (*Esp.*) ⟷ **la prepa** (*Méx.*)

la guardería ⟷ **la sala cuna** (*Chi.*)

el kínder (*Méx.*) ⟷ **el jardín de la infancia** (*Esp.*) ⟷ **el jardín de infantes** (*Arg.*) ⟷ **el jardín infantil** (*Chi.*) ⟷ **el jardín de niños** (*Méx. central*)

Vocabulario útil

el chiste *joke*
debutar *to debut*
dejar de *to stop*
el dibujo *drawing*
enamorado/a *in love*
enseñar *to teach*
hacer caso (a alguien) *to pay attention (to somebody)*
la historieta *comic strip*
intentar *to try*
el personaje *character*
ponerse celoso/a *to get jealous*
el tejado *roof*
vagabundear *to wander around*
la vagancia *laziness*
la viñeta *cartoon*

Estrategia

Contextualizing the reading

When reading a text, you should pay attention to its biographical, cultural, and historical context: when and where it was written, who wrote it, cultural references, etc.; otherwise you might miss multiple layers of meaning that are not apparent to you because you are reading only through the lens of your own experience and knowledge. As you read the biographies of the author and the comic strip, you will learn the background of the characters pictured here (who these two cats are, where they live, what kind of relationship they have, etc.).

Suggestion
Have students make comparisons between Gaturro and Garfield.

LECTURA

Gaturro

Nik es el seudónimo del ilustrador Cristian Dzwonik, que nació en Buenos Aires en 1971. Desde pequeño su abuelo le enseñó a dibujar y ya no dejó de hacerlo. A los 11 años empezó a estudiar en una escuela de dibujo, a los 17 publicó sus primeros trabajos, y a los 21 ingresó en el diario argentino *La Nación* como humorista gráfico. Ama su trabajo porque puede hacer las dos cosas que más le gustan: el dibujo y los chistes.

Sus trabajos se publican en Latinoamérica, España, Francia y Estados Unidos. Recibió el premio Kónex de Platino al mejor humorista gráfico argentino de los últimos 10 años.

Gaturro es un gato que vive con una típica familia de clase media compuesta por una mamá que ama los libros, un papá fanático del fútbol y dos hijos: Luz, que cambia de novio a cada rato, y Agustín, un niño muy curioso. A Gaturro le gusta su casa pero también vagabundear por el barrio, encontrarse con sus amigos en los tejados y reflexionar sobre la vida cotidiana. Es una especie de antihéroe, muy observador. Está enamorado de Ágatha, pero nunca la conquista. Ella sólo se pone celosa cuando otra gata se acerca a Gaturro.

Más de treinta personajes participan en esta historieta que debutó en la última página de *La Nación* en 1996 y se convirtió en un *boom* editorial.

1 a. Comente con un(a) compañero/a: ¿Qué historietas les gustan más? ¿Por qué? ¿Sus protagonistas son héroes o antihéroes? ¿En qué mundo viven y qué hacen allí?

b. Elijan dos personajes de la lista y escriban una oración sobre cada uno usando algunos de los adjetivos de la lista:

Garfield
Mickey Mouse
Scooby-Doo
Bugs Bunny

alegre	hablador	leal
burlón	ingenioso	soñador
cobarde	insolente	torpe
glotón	inteligente	vago

burlón *mocking* **cobarde** *coward* **glotón** *glutton* **hablador** *talkative* **ingenioso** *clever* **leal** *loyal* **soñador** *dreamer* **torpe** *clumsy* **vago** *lazy*

2 Con un(a) compañero/a, empareje cada frase de la primera columna con la terminación correspondiente de la segunda columna.

1. Gaturro está enamorado ...c...
2. Ágatha quiere un hombre ...e...
3. Ágatha se pone celosa ...d...
4. La familia de Gaturro es típicamente ...b...
5. La mamá es amante ...f...
6. Según Ágatha, Gaturro es ...a...

a. de una vagancia extra.
b. de clase media.
c. de Ágatha.
d. de otras gatas que hablan con Gaturro.
e. de gran extravagancia.
f. de los libros.

Have a volunteer explain the play on words in the last panel (**extravagancia, vagancia extra**).

Estrategia

Writing a Biography

A biography is the story of a person's life. To write a biography you must start by researching the person and collecting all the basic facts and events of his/her life; then select one aspect that you want to stress and focus on that (this is called an *angle*). You might first make a list of all the things you need to know, like place and date of birth and death, etc., and then write the biography following the list to include all the facts. You can start at the beginning but you don't have to. Remember to use transition words to show the order of events: **Primero**, **Luego**, **Finalmente**, **Antes**, **Después**, etc.

3 Indique el título que corresponde a cada lista. En la última columna escriba lo que hizo hoy e invente un título. Luego, entre todos, comparen lo que escribieron y debatan: ¿Se puede conocer a una persona por lo que hace cada día? ¿Qué característica es esencial para definir a una persona?

1. Persona de gran curiosidad ......C......
2. Persona de gran vagancia ......A......
3. Persona de gran actividad ......B......

A	B	C	D
no salir a correr	hacer gimnasia	investigar	....
no leer	trabajar	estudiar	....
no llamar por teléfono	andar en bicicleta	meditar	....

PROYECTO

Investigue sobre su personaje de historieta favorito y escriba una biografía con los datos más importantes de la vida de su creador y su carrera. Como ayuda, puede seguir esta estructura: 1. Fecha de nacimiento 2. Lugar donde vive 3. Características 4. Otros personajes 5. Recepción de la historieta.

Suggestion Have students include a copy of one of their favorite cartoons.

Estrategia

Doing background research

Before watching the video, you can perform some basic research about the people mentioned in it, so you have a context for what you will see. In this **Flash Cultura**, you will learn about Frida Kalho and Diego Rivera. What do you already know about them? When did they live? What was their artistic style? What kind of relationship did they have?

Vocabulario útil

apreciar *to observe*
la artesanía *crafts*
la bendición *blessing*
el/la jardinero/a *gardener*
la mascota *pet*
el muro *wall*
el recorrido *tour*
resguardar *to shelter*
la silla de ruedas *wheelchair*

Successful Language Learning You may ask students to guess the lexical family for the word **jardín** (**jardinero**, **jardinería**, etc.) and also tell them about special meanings as in **jardín de infantes** (*kindergarten*) or the **jardín** (*outfield*) in baseball.

Estrategia

Expressing your opinion

Remember that when someone asks your opinion on something, you can soften the force of your words by using expressions that stress this is your point of view and not a value judgment, such as **yo creo/pienso que, para mí, a mí me gusta/me encanta/me asombra** (*it amazes me*), or **lo que más/menos me gusta...**

Flash Cultura

La casa de Frida

Ya leyó sobre la carrera de Salma Hayek y sobre las familias en el mundo hispano. En este episodio de **Flash Cultura** va a ver la casa de la artista mexicana que Hayek interpretó en el cine: Frida Kalho, una mujer que vivió una vida de película y tuvo un matrimonio inusual.

1. Con un(a) compañero/a, hable de las siguientes preguntas: ¿Es importante el lugar donde vivimos? ¿Qué cosas expresa la decoración de una casa sobre sus habitantes? ¿Cuál puede ser el lugar más personal de una casa? ¿Por qué es interesante conocer la casa de los artistas? ¿Qué esperan encontrar en la casa de Frida? **Suggestion** Ask students about their experiences visiting different kinds of museums, especially atypical ones.

2. Mire este episodio de **Flash Cultura**. Recuerde que el museo que va a ver es en realidad una casa, por lo que la visita empieza en la puerta principal y termina en el dormitorio de Frida.

Suggestion After watching the video, discuss with students whether they would prefer to live in an old house already decorated by someone else or a brand-new apartment.

1 **¿Y te gustaría vivir en una casa así?**

2 **Y es muy divertido... encontrarse un gatito...**

3. Indique si las oraciones son verdaderas (**V**) o falsas (**F**). Después, en parejas, corrijan las falsas.

   1. Diego Rivera se casó dos veces con Frida. V
   2. Frida nunca tuvo una mascota en su casa. F. Frida tuvo gatos en su casa.
   3. El jardinero conoció a Diego. V
   4. El museo de Frida se llama Casa Amarilla. F. El museo se llama Casa Azul.
   5. Frida usó silla de ruedas varias veces. V

4. Con un(a) compañero/a, escriba una breve guía de recorrido para el museo de Frida Kalho. Luego lean su guía a la clase.

   Modelo: *La casa es de color... El patio está en el centro de la casa y tiene... El jardinero trabaja allí desde hace... Frida pintó... En la cocina hay... Finalmente, llegamos al...*

Practice more at **vhlcentral.com.**

Audio: Activities, Vocabulary
Video: *Flash Cultura*

Unidad 6

Lección 6A

EL ARTE DE VIVIR

Domingo Buendía, maestro de yoga

Lección 6B

AMOR A DISTANCIA

Julia y Felipe, amor a distancia

¿Estrés? ¿Qué estrés?

AVANCE

6A EL ARTE DE VIVIR

Ask students to study these promotional materials for a retreat for the elderly. Ask students which of these activities they would be interested in. What other activities would students add in a program designed for young adults?

Suggestion Ask students to look at the list of places and leisure activities. For each entry in the list, have them name at least three examples of these places and activities in your community or region.

Tiempo libre

¡Bienvenidos todos!

Colaboramos un año más con el Instituto Nacional de las Personas Adultas Mayores (INAPAM) para ofrecer el mejor viaje.

Este año estamos en San Miguel de Allende, en el centro de nuestro país, México.

Con esta carta les entregamos un folleto con los lugares y actividades más interesantes de la ciudad para disfrutar al máximo de su tiempo libre.

¡Gracias por su participación!

	página
Tiendas	2
Bares	7
Restaurantes	9
Cines	10
Conciertos	12
Exposiciones	14
Teatros	15
Monumentos	16
Museos	17
Mercados de artesanías	18
Deportes	19
Excursiones	20
Fiestas populares	21
Actividades con descuento para mayores	24

Cuantificar

- ¿Vas **mucho** al cine?
- Sí, voy **mucho**. ¿Y tú?
- Yo voy **bastante**.

- ¿Miras **mucho** la televisión?
- No, **poco**. ¿Y tú?
- Yo **casi nada**.

6A.1 Adverbs of quantity

Negar

- Yo estudio alemán y bailo tango. ¿Y tú?
- Yo **no** estudio alemán **ni** bailo tango, pero leo mucho.
- Yo **no** practico deporte **nunca**.

6A.2 Double negatives

Vocabulario

1
las personas mayores *the elderly*
la fiesta popular *festival*
el descuento *discount*
la exposición *exhibition*
estar dirigido a *to be aimed at*
la excursión

2
el ocio *leisure*

1 Lea el texto de la carta. ¿A quiénes están dirigidas las actividades de tiempo libre? ¿Qué edad cree que tienen los participantes?
Suggested answers: Están dirigidas a personas mayores. Tienen más de 60 años.

2 a. Clasifique las actividades y los lugares de ocio en estos grupos y compare sus respuestas con las de su compañero/a. Sample answer: actividades culturales: cines, conciertos, exposiciones, teatros, monumentos, museos; actividades gastronómicas: bares, restaurantes; actividades de diversión: tiendas, mercados de artesanías, deportes, excursiones, fiestas populares

- actividades culturales
- actividades gastronómicas
- actividades de diversión

b. ¿Hay alguna actividad o lugar de ocio en dos o más grupos? ¿Cuál?

3 a. Seleccione en la lista las tres actividades que usted realiza con más frecuencia y pregunte por ellas a su compañero/a.

Modelo:
- *¿Vas mucho al teatro?*
- *Sí, voy bastante.*

b. ¿Cuáles son las actividades que usted no hace nunca?

4 a. Escuche la encuesta a los participantes del viaje y marque cuántas veces mencionan estas actividades.

estar con la familia	XXX	mirar la televisión	XXXX
salir con los amigos	XXX	navegar por Internet	XX
cocinar	XX	ir al cine	XX
ir de compras	XX	practicar deporte	X

b. ¿Cuál es la actividad que más realizan estas personas? ¿Y la que menos realizan? la actividad que más realizan: mirar la televisión; la actividad que menos realizan: practicar deporte

2

3

4

5

6

¿Te gusta…
- cocinar?
- pintar?
- bailar?
- hacer cerámica?
- hacer yoga?
- hacer excursiones?

HORARIOS DE LAS ACTIVIDADES

HORA	L	M	Mi	J	V	S
16:00–17:30	Yoga	Pintura	Excursión	Cocina	Yoga	Excursión
17:30–19:00	Pintura	Baile	Salsa	Baile	Pintura	Baile
19:00–20:30	Cocina	Cerámica	Cocina	Cerámica	Cerámica	Visita ciudad

Preguntar e indicar frecuencia

- ¿Cuántas **veces al mes** van de excursión?
- Yo, **dos veces al mes**.
- Yo, **una vez a la semana**.
- Yo no voy **nunca**.
- Yo **a veces**...

6A.3 Expressions of frequency

Vocabulario ***cont.***

la diversión *fun*

3
mucho *a lot*
nunca *never*
casi nunca *hardly ever*

4
mirar *to watch; to look at*
navegar por Internet *to surf the Internet*

5
pintar *to paint*
bailar *to dance*
hacer cerámica *to make pottery*
el yoga

6
una vez a la semana *once a week*
dos veces al mes *twice a month*
organizar

8
pasivo/a

5 Indique la actividad de cada foto.

1. bailar
2. pintar
3. cocinar
4. hacer yoga
5. hacer cerámica
6. hacer excursiones

6 ¿Qué actividades se organizan con estas frecuencias?

una vez a la semana	salsa, visita ciudad
dos veces a la semana	yoga, excursión
tres veces a la semana	pintura, cocina, baile, cerámica

7 ¿Realiza usted o alguna persona que conoce estas actividades? ¿Con qué frecuencia? Hable con su compañero/a. **7** **Suggestion** Have students brainstorm a few more activities to discuss.

Modelo: *Tengo una amiga que hace yoga dos veces a la semana.*

8 Una de las principales actividades de ocio de la gente es mirar la tele. ¿Mira usted mucho la tele? ¿Cree que es una buena manera de ocupar su tiempo? Comente con su compañero/a los aspectos positivos y negativos de esta actividad de ocio pasiva.

MI EXPERIENCIA

9 Encuentre a compañeros de clase que practican las mismas actividades de ocio que usted. Presenten el resultado al grupo.

GUIÓN DE TRABAJO

¿Qué haces en tu tiempo libre? → ¿Viajas mucho? ¿Vas mucho al cine?

bailar
hacer yoga
viajar
estar con la familia
estar con los amigos
ir al cine
hacer deporte
...

una vez...
dos veces...

a la semana
al mes
al año
...

Practice more at **vhlcentral.com.**

SAM: Actividades pp. 113–115

Un día perfecto

CUESTIONARIO DE BIENESTAR

	Sí	No
1 ¿Ha dormido bien hoy?	☐	☐
2 ¿Ha tomado un buen desayuno hoy?	☐	☐
3 ¿Ha dado un paseo esta semana?	☐	☐
4 ¿Ha hablado con un amigo hoy?	☐	☐
5 ¿Ha reído en su trabajo o en casa?	☐	☐
6 ¿Ha leído un libro interesante este mes?	☐	☐
7 ¿Ha comido bien hoy?	☐	☐
8 ¿Ha aprendido algo este año?	☐	☐

- 8 veces Sí: ¡Felicitaciones!
- De 5 a 7 veces Sí: No está mal.
- Menos de 5 veces Sí: Un consejo: menos trabajo y más tiempo para usted.

Describir su día

- ¿Hoy has dormido bien?
- Sí, gracias, **he dormido** muy bien.
- Mi hija hoy no **ha dormido** nada.

- ¿Habéis tomado **ya** un café esta mañana?
- No, **todavía no** hemos tomado café.

6A.4 Present perfect
Expressions of time
hoy, esta semana, este mes, este año, ya/todavía no

Vocabulario

10

el bienestar *well-being*
hoy *today*
dar un paseo *to take a walk*
esta semana *this week*
reír (e:i) *to laugh*
este mes *this month*
este año *this year*
¡Felicitaciones! *Congratulations!*
el consejo *piece of advice*
el cuestionario *questionnaire*

12

ya *already*
todavía no *not yet*

Suggestion In pairs, have students take turns thinking of a celebrity and saying three things that he/she has done recently. Their partner has to guess who it is.

10 a. Responda al cuestionario y comente los resultados con el grupo.

b. Mencione tres actividades que hace usted para tener un "día perfecto". Compare su lista con las de sus compañeros y elaboren una lista común.

Modelo: *leer un libro, dar un paseo, salir con amigos...*

10 Expansion Have students make a list of all the verbs they have learned recently in Spanish class.

11 a. Elija la forma del verbo **haber** que corresponde a cada persona.

ha	habéis	han	has	he	hemos

1. yo ....he.... reído
2. tú ....has.... reído
3. usted, él, ella ....ha.... reído
4. nosotros/as ....hemos.... reído
5. vosotros/as ....habéis.... reído
6. ustedes, ellos/as ....han.... reído

b. Relacione cada participio con su infinitivo.

1. hablado ....c....
2. leído ....a....
3. dormido ....b....

a. leer
b. dormir
c. hablar

12 a. ¿Qué actividades de la lista de la **Actividad 10B** ya ha realizado o todavía no ha realizado hoy?

b. Anote cuándo las ha realizado. Compare sus respuestas con las de su compañero/a.

hoy | esta semana | este mes

13 Escuche el mensaje telefónico y marque en la columna adecuada.

Susana ...	ya	todavía no
ha llamado a Antonio.	✔	
ha recibido el correo electrónico.	✓	
ha contestado el correo electrónico.		✓
ha leído el libro.	✓	
ha hablado con Antonio.		✓

14 Expansion In pairs, have students create a comic like the one on the right, with a similar "twist," but in a different context (such as a father and his son).

Dar consejos

- Estoy muy cansado...
- **Tienes que** descansar un poco más.
- ✦ **¿Por qué no** trabajas menos?

6A.5 Expressions to give advice

Vocabulario

(14)

¿Por qué no...? *Why don't you . . .?*
tener (e:ie) que *to have to*
cansado/a *tired*

(15)

todo el día *all day*
hacer (g) ejercicio *to exercise, to work out*
reservar *to set aside*
dormir (o:ue) la siesta *to take a nap*
la siesta *nap*

(17)

pues *well*
a ver *let's see*

Suggestion Have students make a list of obligations that they have for this week, using **tener que.** Have pairs of students ask each other what they have to do. Then have them share with the class any obligations that they have in common.

14 Fíjese en la imagen. ¿Es una situación normal? ¿Quién tiene problemas y cuáles son? ¿Qué consejos recibe? Añada otros consejos.
Sample answers: Tiene que tomarse más tiempo para usted. ¿Por qué no hace yoga?

15 a. Relacione cada situación con su consejo correspondiente.

Hoy he dormido muy poco.
¿Por qué no duermes la siesta?

He trabajado todo el día.
¿Por qué no organizas el día para tener tiempo libre?

Esta semana no he practicado deporte.
Tienes que reservar un día a la semana para hacer ejercicio.

¿Por qué no organizas el día para tener tiempo libre?

Tienes que reservar un día a la semana para hacer ejercicio.

¿Por qué no duermes la siesta?

b. Proponga un consejo para estas situaciones. Sample answers:

1. Su amigo solo come carne. Tienes que comer algunas frutas y verduras.
2. Su amiga siempre va a todos los lugares en coche. ¿Por qué no caminas un poco?
3. Su hijo mira mucho la tele. Tienes que hacer deporte, salir al aire libre.

16 Ofrezca a su compañero/a tres consejos para tener un día perfecto a partir de sus respuestas al cuestionario de la **Actividad 10**.

Modelo: *Tienes que... / ¿Por qué no...?*

MI EXPERIENCIA

17 ¿Cómo ha sido su semana? Primero, aprenda recursos para controlar una conversación. Escriba las respuestas de sus compañeros.

Palabras para ganar tiempo:

- Bueno...
- Pues...
- A ver...

Responda a las siguientes preguntas:

- ¿Hoy ha escuchado música?
- ¿Hoy ha dormido bien?
- ¿Esta semana ha recibido una buena noticia?

GUIÓN DE TRABAJO

¿Esta semana ha sido perfecta? → (Bueno...) Esta semana...

¿Qué tengo que hacer para tener un día perfecto? → (Pues...) Tienes que...

Hoy... ↓ Ya... Todavía no... → dormir (bien) / desayunar (fruta) / hablar con un(a) amigo/a / leer un buen libro / comer (bien) / recibir una buena noticia

Practice more at **vhlcentral.com.**

SAM: Actividades pp. 116–118

Domingo Buendía, maestro de yoga

TU PERIÓDICO.com Los internautas preguntan

Lunes, 19 de noviembre

Domingo Buendía (Quito, Ecuador, 1948) es médico y psicólogo, y dirige desde 1981 en Quito uno de los centros de yoga más importantes de América Latina. Ha viajado a muchos países orientales, principalmente a la India, y ha entrevistado a los principales maestros de psicología oriental y relajación. Ha publicado muchos libros sobre la meditación, el yoga y la autoayuda.

El maestro Buendía ha participado en la sección "Los internautas preguntan" del blog de *Tu Periódico* y ha hablado con ellos.

18:08 Matías

Maestro, he leído muchos de sus libros y todos me han encantado. Soy director de una empresa, trabajo muchas horas al día y practico yoga desde hace unos años, pero no encuentro equilibrio ni tranquilidad. ¿Qué me aconseja?

Before discussing the reading, survey the class to find out what they know about yoga and meditation. Then ask them to name any self-help books that they have read or with which they are familiar.

18:10 Maestro Buendía

¿Por qué no organizas tu ocio? Hay tiempo para todo. Tiempo para trabajar y tiempo para descansar. Tienes que aprender a decir "no".

18:13 Alejandro

Practico mucho yoga y hago mis ejercicios todos los días, pero no duermo casi nada.

18:14 Maestro Buendía

El yoga no es solo una serie de ejercicios físicos relajantes. Es una ciencia del alma que busca la paz del espíritu. El cuerpo y la mente tienen que estar en conexión.

18:20 Luz

Voy a clase de yoga dos veces a la semana. ¿Cuál es el mejor momento del día para practicar?

18:30 Maestro Buendía

Cada persona es un mundo diferente y el momento del día no es muy importante. Es más importante encontrar un lugar tranquilo y en silencio para escuchar la voz de nuestra mente.

Vocabulario

18

- el/la maestro/a *master; teacher*
- el/la internauta *Internet user*
- dirigir (j) *to run; to manage*
- la autoayuda *self-help*
- la empresa *company*
- el equilibrio *balance*
- aconsejar *to advise*
- relajante *relaxing*
- la ciencia *science*
- el alma (*f.*) *soul*
- el espíritu *spirit*
- el cuerpo *body*
- la mente *mind*
- estar en conexión *to be connected*
- **la relajación, físico/a**

18 Observe el texto en el que participa el maestro Buendía. ¿Dónde encuentra normalmente este tipo de textos? ¿Participa usted en foros como este?

☐ libros ☑ Internet ☐ televisión

19 Lea la nota biográfica del maestro Buendía. ¿Cuál ha sido su formación? ¿Dónde ha viajado? Sample answer: Es médico y psicólogo. Ha viajado a muchos países orientales, principalmente a la India.

20 a. Revise las respuestas del maestro Buendía a los internautas y escriba una lista de consejos para relajarse. organizar el ocio, aprender a decir "no", conectar el cuerpo y la mente, encontrar un lugar tranquilo y en silencio para escuchar la voz de nuestra mente

b. ¿Tiene usted alguna pregunta para Domingo Buendía? Escríbala.

21 ¿Usted o algún conocido practica yoga? ¿Qué efectos positivos tiene? Comente con sus compañeros. ¿Qué hace usted para mantener equilibrio en su vida?

Point out the word **el alma**. Explain that the masculine article is used solely to avoid repetition of the [a] sound; the noun itself remains feminine, and therefore adjectives that modify it remain feminine. Ex: **el alma tranquila**.

22 a. Lea el artículo sobre la jornada laboral en España. ¿Qué es la jornada flexible? ¿Existe en su país? ¿Cuál es el horario laboral de su país?

Suggested answer: La jornada flexible permite a los trabajadores decidir la hora de entrada y de salida.

TIEMPO PARA TODO

España es uno de los países europeos que más horas dedica al trabajo. ¿Cómo se puede mejorar la productividad sin trabajar tanto tiempo? Algunas de las recomendaciones son flexibilizar los horarios y limitar las horas de trabajo en la oficina.

La flexibilidad horaria permite a los trabajadores decidir la hora de entrada y salida del trabajo para conciliar la vida personal y la profesional.

Limitar las horas de trabajo es otra posibilidad. Un ejemplo es la política de "luces apagadas". Establece una hora de salida exacta, y el trabajador tiene que organizarse mejor para hacer su trabajo antes de esa hora.

Para muchos trabajadores tener un buen horario es más importante que tener un buen sueldo. No tener el suficiente tiempo libre es un factor de estrés muy importante que nos hace rendir menos en el trabajo.

22 **Suggestion** Before students read the article, have them read the information on the Spanish workday in Lesson **3A**, page 63.

b. Anote las conclusiones del artículo.

1. Algunas recomendaciones para mejorar el horario laboral son...
   flexibilizar los horarios y limitar las horas de trabajo en la oficina
2. La política de "luces apagadas" establece...
   una hora de salida exacta y el trabajador tiene que organizarse para hacer su trabajo antes de esa hora.
3. Para muchos trabajadores es más importante...
   tener un buen horario que tener un buen sueldo.

c. Marque en el calendario su tiempo de ocio y de trabajo. Compare su calendario semanal con el de un(a) compañero/a. ¿Quién tiene mayor equilibrio?

	lunes	martes	miércoles	jueves	viernes	sábado	domingo
9:00 h–17:00 h							
17:00 h–22:00 h							

[p] [t]

23 La *p* y la *t* en español tienen los siguientes sonidos. Escuche estos trabalenguas y después intente repetirlos.

"Tres tristes tigres comen trigo en un trigal."
"El que poca papa gasta, poca papa paga."

24 a. Lea el texto e indique qué tipo de actividad de ocio describe.

☐ cultural ☐ deportiva ☑ social

Reunirse con la familia y los amigos a tomar mate es una costumbre social en varios países de América Latina, especialmente Argentina y Uruguay. La yerba mate es una hierba que se bebe en infusión, su origen es muy antiguo y tiene propiedades estimulantes.

El mate es una hierba que se bebe en infusión. Se toma en Argentina y Uruguay.

b. ¿Qué es el mate? ¿En qué países se toma especialmente? ¿Conoce otros ritos sociales particulares del mundo hispano?

Practice more at vhlcentral.com.

SAM: Actividades pp. 119–122

Vocabulario *cont.*

la voz (*pl.* voces) *voice*
el encuentro *meeting*
oriental, la India, la psicología, la meditación, el silencio

19
la formación *education*

21
el efecto

22
la jornada flexible *flexible workday*
mejorar *to improve*
flexibilizar *to make flexible*
la flexibilidad horaria *schedule flexibility*
la entrada *arrival*
la salida *departure*
conciliar *to reconcile*
la política *policy*
la luz apagada *lights off*
establecer (zc) *to establish*
mejor *better*
suficiente *enough*
rendir (e:i) *to perform*
menos *less*
europeo/a, dedicar, la productividad, la recomendación, limitar, la oficina, decidir, la posibilidad, exacto/a, el factor

Comparar experiencias

- Para ti, ¿es **mejor** tener un buen sueldo o un buen horario?
- Para mí, el horario flexible es **más importante que** el dinero.

6A.6 Comparatives: adjectives/ adverbs

Vocabulario

23
el trabalenguas *tongue-twister*

24
deportivo/a *sporting*
reunirse *to meet, to gather*
el mate *mate*
la hierba *herb*
la propiedad *property*
estimulante *stimulating*
el rito *ritual*
la lluvia *rain*
cultural, social, la infusión

24 Tell students that **mate** is the name for the beverage and also for the container in which it is served. The metal straw, which also works as a sieve, is called **la bombilla.** Explain that drinking **mate** is a social activity in which everyone shares the same **mate.**

TAREA FINAL

Vivir el arte

Escriba una lista de tres actividades de ocio cultural que ha realizado últimamente.

Teatro, cine, libros, música...

Pregunte a su compañero/a por las actividades de su lista.

¿Has ido al cine a ver...?

Encourage students to ask follow-up questions, such as **¿Cuándo y adónde fuiste a verla?**

Recomiende a su compañero/a alguna de las actividades de su lista.

Tienes que leer...

Elijan tres actividades ideales para un fin de semana con lluvia.

YO PUEDO...

- Puedo hablar de mis actividades de ocio.

  Complete el horario semanal con sus actividades de ocio.

	lunes	martes	miércoles	jueves	viernes	sábado	domingo
por la mañana							
por la tarde							
por la noche							

- Puedo expresar frecuencia.

  Escriba con qué frecuencia realiza las siguientes actividades.

Ir al cine.
....
Estar con los amigos.
....
Ir a la montaña.
....

- Puedo describir mi día.

  Relate en un diario sus actividades de esta semana.

- Puedo dar consejos.

  Responda con un consejo.

"He comido muy mal."
....
"Esta semana he dormido poco."
....

GRAMÁTICA FUNCIONAL

6A.1 **Suggestion** Contrast **mucho** and **mucho/a** by writing on the board these sentences: **—¿Estudias mucho? —Sí, tengo mucha tarea. —¿Comen mucho en restaurantes? —No, no tenemos mucho dinero para esas cosas.** Have volunteers identify which are adverbs and which are adjectives and explain how they know this.

6A.1 Express quantity

Adverbs of quantity 11.4

- Use the adverbs **mucho** (*a lot*), **bastante** (*enough; quite a bit*), and **poco** (*little, seldom*) to say how often people perform different activities.

  Corro **bastante**, pero voy **poco** al gimnasio.
  I run ***quite a bit****, but I* ***rarely*** *go to the gym.*

- Place these adverbs immediately following the verb they modify. Remember that adverbs are invariable, so they never change form.

  ¿Vas **mucho** a ese restaurante?
  Do you ***often*** *go to that restaurant?*

- Use **no** + [*verb*] + (**casi**) **nada** to express *not at all*.

¿Bailas mucho?	No, no bailo **casi nada**.
Do you dance a lot?	*No, I* ***hardly*** *dance* ***at all****.*

6A.2 Express negation

Double negatives 12.3

- Use the expressions **ni... ni...** (*neither . . . nor . . .*), **nunca** (*never*), and **nada** (*nothing*) to make negative statements. Say **no** + [*verb*] + [*negative expression*].

  No me gusta **ni** el cine **ni** el teatro.
  I ***don't*** *like the movies* ***or*** *the theater.*

¡OJO! Unlike in English, you must use double (or sometimes triple!) negatives in this construction. This means you might use a negative expression in Spanish (**nunca, nada**) in cases where you would use an indefinite word in English (*ever, anything*).

- When making a negative statement, always place a negative word before the conjugated verb. Remember that when a statement begins with **no**, **nunca**, etc., all elements of that statement must be negative.

  ¡**No** le gusta hacer **nada**!
  He ***doesn't*** *like to do* ***anything****!*

  Pedro **no** termina **nunca** la tarea.
  Pedro ***doesn't ever*** *finish the homework.*

- You can also place the negative expression at the beginning of a sentence, before the verb.

  Nunca vamos a la playa.
  We ***never*** *go to the beach.*

- Use **ni... ni...** when listing several items, activities, etc.

  No quiero **ni** bailar **ni** cantar **ni** escuchar música.
  I don't want to dance, sing, ***or*** *listen to music.*

6A.2 **Suggestion** Present these negative words by using them in complaints, using a whiny tone. Ex: **Mis estudiantes no vienen nunca a las horas de oficina.** Contrast them with "opposite" statements (**Mis estudiantes siempre vienen a las horas de oficina**), using an upbeat tone.

¡Póngalo en práctica!

G1 Ordene las palabras para escribir oraciones completas.

1. bastante / Juan / viajar
   Juan viaja bastante.
2. poco / bailar / nosotros
   Nosotros bailamos poco.
3. trabajar / Mariela y tú / mucho
   Mariela y tú trabajan/trabajáis mucho.
4. casi nada / tú / comer
   Tú no comes casi nada.
5. ir a clase de yoga / poco / yo
   Yo voy poco a clase de yoga.
6. practicar deporte / ustedes / mucho
   Ustedes practican mucho deporte.

G2 Complete las oraciones.

no | ni | nada | nunca

1. Maite ...no... va ...nunca... a la biblioteca.
2. Tú ...no... comes ...ni... fruta ...ni... verduras.
3. El profesor ...nunca... llega tarde.
4. Juliancito ...no... come ...nada/nunca... .
5. ...No... vamos ...ni... al museo ...ni... al concierto.
6. Ramón ...no... sale ...nunca... los jueves.
7. ¡Mi madre ...no... entiende ...nada...!
8. ...No... quiero comprar ...ni... este suéter ...ni... ese otro.

G3 Responda a las preguntas con negaciones dobles.

1. ¿Te gusta el tango o la salsa?
   No me gusta ni el tango ni la salsa.
2. ¿Haces deporte con frecuencia?
   No hago deporte nunca./No hago nada de deporte.
3. ¿Bebes té o café en el desayuno?
   No bebo nada en el desayuno./No bebo ni té ni café en el desayuno.
4. ¿Pedro trabaja o estudia?
   Pedro no trabaja ni estudia.
5. ¿Vosotros vais de excursión con frecuencia?
   (Nosotros) no vamos de excursión nunca.
6. ¿Ustedes saben mucho de informática?
   No, no sabemos nada de informática.

Practice more at vhlcentral.com.

GRAMÁTICA FUNCIONAL

6A.3 Ask about and indicate frequency

Expressions of frequency 11.8

- Use the word **vez** (*time*) to talk about frequency. Note the spelling change in the plural, **veces**.

  Roberto va a yoga tres **veces** a la semana.
  *Roberto goes to yoga three **times** a week.*

- Use the construction [*number*] + **vez/veces** + **al/a la** + [**día/semana/mes/año**, *etc.*] to say how often something happens.

  Viajamos a México **dos veces al año**.
  *We travel to Mexico **twice (two times) a year**.*

- As you learned in **2B.3**, **a veces** means *sometimes*.

  A veces vamos a la playa, pero nunca vamos a la piscina.
  ***Sometimes** we go to the beach, but we never go to the pool.*

¡OJO!

You have learned three words in Spanish to say *time*: **el tiempo**, **la hora**, and **la vez**. Use **el tiempo** to discuss time in a general sense: **¿Qué haces en tu tiempo libre?** Use **la hora** to refer to a time of day: **¿Qué hora es?** Use **la vez** to talk about an instance or occasion: **¿Cuántas veces has visto** *El Señor de los Anillos?*

6A.4 Describe your day

Present perfect 5.3, 5.3.1

Expressions of time 11.6

- Use the present perfect (**el pretérito perfecto**) to talk about past actions that are connected to the present. The **pretérito perfecto** tells what a person *has done*.

  ¿Alguna vez **has leído** *Cien años de soledad*?
  *Have you ever **read*** One Hundred Years of Solitude?

- The **pretérito perfecto** is a compound tense composed of two parts: **haber** + [*past participle*]. **Haber** is an irregular verb.

HABER			
(yo)	he	(nosotros/as)	hemos
(tú)	has	(vosotros/as)	habéis
(usted, él, ella)	ha	(ustedes, ellos/as)	han

- Form the past participle of regular verbs by adding **-ado** to the stem of **-ar** verbs and **-ido** to the stem of **-er** and **-ir** verbs.

hablar	→	habl**ado**
comer	→	com**ido**
vivir	→	viv**ido**

6A.4 Suggestion Ask students to write down three things that they have to do before the next class period, using **tener que** (Ex: **Tengo que comprar papel**). Then, as a warm-up during the next class, have them pair up and exchange lists; they should take turns asking about the activities (**¿Has comprado papel?**).

¡Póngalo en práctica!

G4 Escriba oraciones completas usando las pistas. Agregue **al** o **a la** para formar expresiones de frecuencia.

1. Ángeles / 4 veces / ir a la piscina / semana
   Ángeles va a la piscina cuatro veces a la semana.
2. 1 vez / tú y yo / mes / ver una película
   Tú y yo vemos una película una vez al mes.
3. comer verduras / mis padres / 2 veces / día
   Mis padres comen verduras dos veces al día.
4. año / tú y Luis / viajar a Caracas / 3 veces
   Tú y Luis viajan/viajáis a Caracas tres veces al año.
5. mes / yo / ir de excursión / 2 veces
   Yo voy de excursión dos veces al mes.

G5 Elija la opción correcta para completar cada oración. **G5 Expansion** Reverse the activity by giving students the past participle; they have to supply the infinitive.

1. Mi hermana y yo...
2. Tus vecinos...
3. Tú...
4. Usted...
5. Yo...
6. Tú y Elena...

4	**a.** ha conocido al presidente.
6	**b.** habéis estudiado química.
2/6	**c.** han viajado a Canadá.
1	**d.** hemos alquilado esta película tres veces.
5	**e.** he comido dos platos de arroz.
3	**f.** has dormido la siesta hoy.

G6 Escriba el participio de cada verbo.

1. tomar ......tomado......
2. recibir ......recibido......
3. aprender ......aprendido......
4. dar ......dado......
5. hablar ......hablado......
6. leer ......leído......

Practice more at **vhlcentral.com.**

GRAMÁTICA FUNCIONAL

- When the stem of an **-er** or **-ir** verb ends in **-a**, **-e**, or **-o**, add a written accent mark to the **i** of the **-ido** ending.

  Hemos **reído** mucho.
  *We have **laughed** a lot.*

- You will learn irregular past participles in **7B.1**.
- The past participle does not change in form depending on the subject, only the form of **haber**.

  Ustedes **han ido** a Puerto Rico y yo también **he ido** a Puerto Rico.
  *You **have gone** to Puerto Rico and I **have gone** to Puerto Rico, too.*

- Use the **pretérito perfecto** with time expressions such as **alguna vez** (*ever*), **ya** (*already*), and **todavía no** (*not yet*) to talk about things people have or have not done.

  ¿**Alguna vez** has estado en San Miguel de Allende?
  *Have you **ever** been to San Miguel de Allende?*

  Yo **ya** he estado, pero Beatriz **todavía no** ha ido.
  *I've **already** been, but Beatriz has **not** gone **yet**.*

- Never place these expressions between **haber** and the past participle; unlike in English, the two components of the **pretérito perfecto** cannot be separated.

  Ya hemos conocido a la novia de Luis.
  *We have **already** met Luis's girlfriend.*

- The **pretérito perfecto** can also be used to refer to the recent past, especially in a context that is still connected to the present (*this morning, this week*, etc.). Expressions such as **hoy**, **esta semana**, **este mes**, and **este año** often accompany this usage.

  ¿Dónde **has estado** hoy?
  Te **he llamado** y no **has contestado**.
  *Where **were you** today?*
  ***I called** you and **you didn't answer**.*

  Ay, **he dejado** el móvil en casa.
  Esta tarde **he ido** al médico.
  *Oh, **I left** my cell phone at home.*
  *This afternoon **I went** to the doctor.*

- To form the present perfect of **hay**, use **ha habido**.

  Ha habido algunos problemas con la productividad del equipo.
  ***There have been** some problems with the team's productivity.*

¡OJO!

The **pretérito perfecto** is widely used in Spain, especially in reference to the recent past. However, its use is limited in Latin America, and in some countries the **pretérito indefinido** exclusively is used in all contexts presented here.

G7 Expansion For items 1, 4, and 5, have students write logical responses to the questions. For items 2 and 3, have them write questions that could have elicited the statements.

¡Póngalo en práctica!

G7 Complete las conversaciones con **ya, alguna vez,** o **todavía no.**

- Silvia, ¿(1) ....alguna vez.... has ido a Bolivia?
- No, (2) ....todavía no.... he ido, pero me gustaría ir.
- ¿Ustedes (3) ....ya.... han ido a ver la exposición de Chillida?
- Sí, la vimos ayer. ¿Tú no?
- No, (4) ....todavía no.... he ido.

G8 Escriba oraciones completas usando el pretérito perfecto. Suggested answers:

1. ¿? / alguna vez / (usted) / estudiar física
   ¿Alguna vez ha estudiado física?
2. cenar en ese restaurante / esta semana / (nosotros) / ya
   Ya hemos cenado en ese restaurante esta semana.
3. Gloria / conocer al amor de su vida / todavía no
   Gloria todavía no ha conocido al amor de su vida.
4. (tú) / ya / ¿? / estar en México
   ¿Ya has estado en México?
5. ir al dentista / ya / ¿? / (tú y Carlos) / este año
   ¿Ya han/habéis ido al dentista este año?

G9 Complete el párrafo de manera lógica.

Hoy (yo) (1) ....he.... llamado a Antonio y (2) ....hemos.... comido juntos. Después Antonio ha (3) ....ido.... (ir) a trabajar y yo (4) ....he.... comprado el periódico y he (5) ....leído.... (leer) todas las noticias. A la seis, mis hermanos (6) ....han.... llegado y hemos (7) ....preparado.... (preparar) la cena para la familia. Luego a las siete y media (8) ....hemos.... cenado todos juntos.

G8 Suggestion Before assigning the activity, explain that they will fill in the blanks with a form of **haber** or a past participle.

Practice more at **vhlcentral.com.**

GRAMÁTICA FUNCIONAL

6A.5 Give advice

Expressions to give advice 5.10, 9

- Use the question **¿Por qué no** + [*verb*]? to offer someone advice.

  ¿**Por qué no** descansas un poco?
  Why don't you rest for a bit?

- To be more assertive in your recommendation, use the construction **tener** + **que** + [*infinitive*].

  Tienes que descansar.
  You have to rest.

- Use **tener** + **que** + [*infinitive*] to express other sorts of obligations.

  Tengo que pasar por el banco esta tarde.
  I have to go by the bank this afternoon.

6A.6 Compare experiences

Comparatives: adjectives/adverbs 4.4.2, 12.7

- Use the construction **más/menos** + [*adjective/adverb*] + **que** to compare some characteristic of two people, items, or experiences.

  La salud es **más importante que** el dinero.
  *Health is **more important than** money.*

  Ariel corre **menos a menudo que** Ramón.
  *Ariel runs **less often than** Ramón.*

- When comparing two nouns, make sure the adjective agrees in gender and number with the first noun.

  Mi tía es **más seria que** mi tío.
  *My aunt is **more serious than** my uncle.*

- Some adjectives have irregular comparative forms. Use these forms instead of **más** + [*adjective*].

ADJETIVO	COMPARATIVO
bueno/a	**mejor**
malo/a	**peor**
grande	**mayor**
pequeño/a	**menor**
joven	**menor**
viejo/a	**mayor**

Este hotel es **mejor que** ese hotel.
*This hotel is **better than** that hotel.*

- When **grande** and **pequeño/a** refer to age, use the irregular comparatives **mayor** and **menor**; for size, use the regular comparatives.

  Yo soy **mayor que** Carlos.
  *I'm **older than** Carlos.*

  Esta casa es **más grande que** esa.
  *This house is **bigger than** that one.*

- The adverbs **bien** (*well*) and **mal** (*badly*) have the irregular comparative forms **mejor** and **peor**.

  Marisol baila **peor** que yo, pero canta **mejor**.
  *Marisol dances **worse** than I (do), but she sings **better**.*

¡Póngalo en práctica!

G10 Transforme las oraciones usando **¿Por qué no...?** o **tener + que**.

1. Tienes que dormir más.
   ¿Por qué no duermes más?
2. ¿Por qué no estudia en la biblioteca?
   Tiene que estudiar en la biblioteca.
3. Tienen que comer más verduras.
   ¿Por qué no comen más verduras?

4. ¿Por qué no tomáis unas vacaciones?
   Tenéis que tomar unas vacaciones.

6A.6 Suggestion Have students write statements comparing themselves to different family members.

G11 Escriba oraciones comparativas con **más** o **menos**.

1. el tren / económico / el avión
   El tren es más/menos económico que el avión.
2. bailar / divertido / pintar
   Bailar es más/menos divertido que pintar.
3. mis padres / serios / yo
   Mis padres son más/menos serios que yo.
4. practico deporte / frecuentemente / tú
   Practico deporte más/menos frecuentemente que tú.
5. haces yoga / a menudo / Ignacio
   Haces yoga más/menos a menudo que Ignacio.
6. llegamos / temprano / los vecinos
   Llegamos más/menos temprano que los vecinos.

G12 Complete las oraciones con comparativos irregulares.

1. El profesor habla ....mejor.... (bien) que yo.
2. Su hermano es ....menor.... (joven) que yo.
3. Mis abuelos son ....mayores.... (viejo) que ese hombre.
4. Clara baila ....peor.... (mal) que Daniel.
5. Los calamares son ....peores.... (malo) que las gambas.
6. Estas naranjas son ....mejores.... (bueno) que esas.
7. Tengo dos hermanos ....mayores.... (grande).
8. En este restaurante sirven ....mejores.... (bueno) tapas que en el otro.

6A.6 Suggestion Have students write a description of a famous person, using comparatives to compare them to other people in their field. Tell them not to use the person's name. Then, in small groups, have students read their descriptions aloud for the others to guess who it is.

Practice more at **vhlcentral.com.**

VOCABULARIO

Tiempo libre

estar dirigido/a a	*to be aimed at*
el descuento	*discount*
la diversión	*fun*
la excursión	*excursion*
la exposición	*exhibition*
la fiesta popular	*festival*
el ocio	*leisure*
las personas mayores	*the elderly*
el yoga	*yoga*
bailar	*to dance*
hacer cerámica	*to do pottery*
mirar	*to watch; to look at*
navegar por Internet	*to surf the Internet*
organizar	*to organize*
pintar	*to paint*
pasivo/a	*passive*
casi nunca	*hardly ever*
dos veces al mes	*twice a month*
mucho	*a lot*
nunca	*never*
una vez a la semana	*once a week*

Un día perfecto

a ver	*let's see*
¡Felicitaciones!	*Congratulations!*
¿Por qué no...?	*Why don't you...?*
pues	*well*
el bienestar	*well-being*
el consejo	*piece of advice*
el cuestionario	*questionnaire*
la siesta	*nap*
dar un paseo	*to take a walk*
dormir (o:ue) la siesta	*to take a nap*
hacer (g) ejercicio	*to exercise, to work out*
reír (e:i)	*to laugh*
reservar	*to set aside*
tener (e:ie) que	*to have to*
cansado/a	*tired*
esta semana	*this week*
este año	*this year*
este mes	*this month*
hoy	*today*
todavía no	*not yet*
todo el día	*all day*
ya	*already*

Domingo Buendía

el alma (*f.*)	*soul*
la autoayuda	*self-help*
la ciencia	*science*
el cuerpo	*body*
el efecto	*effect*
la empresa	*company*
el encuentro	*meeting*
la entrada	*arrival*
el equilibrio	*balance*
el espíritu	*spirit*
el factor	*factor*
la flexibilidad horaria	*schedule flexibility*
la formación	*education*
la hierba	*herb*
la India	*India*
la infusión	*infusion*
el/la internauta	*Internet user*
la jornada flexible	*flexible workday*
la luz apagada	*lights off*
la lluvia	*rain*
el/la maestro/a	*master; teacher*
el mate	*mate*
la meditación	*meditation*
la mente	*mind*
la oficina	*office*
la política	*policy*
la posibilidad	*possibility*
la productividad	*productivity*
la propiedad	*property*
la psicología	*psychology*
la recomendación	*recommendation*
la relajación	*relaxation*
el rito	*ritual*
la salida	*departure*
el silencio	*silence*
el trabalenguas	*tongue-twister*
la voz (*pl.* voces)	*voice*
aconsejar	*to advise*
conciliar	*to reconcile*
decidir	*to decide*
dedicar	*to dedicate*
dirigir (j)	*to run; to manage*
establecer (zc)	*to establish*
estar en conexión	*to be connected*
flexibilizar	*to make flexible*
limitar	*to limit*
mejorar	*to improve*
rendir (e:i)	*to perform*
reunirse	*to meet, to gather*
cultural	*cultural*
deportivo/a	*sporting*
estimulante	*stimulating*
europeo/a	*European*
exacto/a	*exact*
físico/a	*physical*
oriental	*oriental*
relajante	*relaxing*
social	*social*
suficiente	*enough*
mejor	*better*
menos	*less*

Variación léxica

la siesta ⟷ **el camarón** (*fam. Ven.*) ⟷ **el motoso** (*fam., Col.*)

el trabajo ⟷ **el camello** (*fam. Col.*) ⟷ **el curro** (*fam. Esp.*) ⟷ **el laburo** (*fam. Arg.*) ⟷ **la pega** (*Chi.*)

mirar la televisión (*Amér. L.*) ⟷ **ver la televisión** (*Esp.*)

¡Felicitaciones! (*Amér. L.*) ⟷ **¡Felicidades!** ⟷ **¡Enhorabuena!** (*Esp.*)

6B

AMOR A DISTANCIA

Planes de viaje

Suggestion Have students identify all possible modes of transportation they can use to travel from the university to their parents' house.

Suggestion For each question below, have students rate the options from the least to most expensive and from the least to most comfortable (if applicable).

Viajes de ida y vuelta

- ¿Viaja usted en...? ☐ avión ☐ tren ☐ coche ☐ bici
- ¿Compra billete de...? ☐ ida ☐ ida y vuelta
- ¿Pasa la noche en un...? ☐ camping ☐ hotel ☐ apartamento ☐ albergue
- ¿Reserva el hotel y el vuelo en...? ☐ Internet ☐ una agencia de viajes
- ¿Va usted a...? ☐ ciudades ☐ pueblos ☐ playas
- ¿Qué hace usted? ☐ hacer deporte ☐ ver monumentos ☐ tomar fotos

Hacer planes

- ¿Qué **vas a hacer** estas vacaciones?
- **Voy a viajar.** Tengo unos amigos en Caracas pero no **sé** si voy a ir allí. Y, después, **voy a ir** a la playa. Y tú, ¿qué planes tienes?
- No sé...

6B.1 **ir + a + [*infinitive*]** **saber**

Vocabulario

1
ida y vuelta *round-trip*
el avión *airplane*
el tren *train*
la bici(cleta) *bike (bicycle)*
el billete *ticket*
pasar la noche *to spend the night*
el camping *campsite*
el albergue *hostel*
el vuelo *flight*
tomar fotos *to take pictures*

2
el castillo *castle*
el paseo a caballo *horseback ride*
el caballo *horse*
con encanto *charming*

3
el puente (*Esp.*) *long weekend*
el dinero *money*

1 ¿Qué tipo de viajes hace usted normalmente? Complete el cuestionario y compare sus respuestas con las de su compañero/a.

Modelo: *Yo normalmente viajo en avión y él/ella en coche...*

2 Fíjese en la oferta de la agencia Ida y vuelta. ¿Qué actividades le gustan?

Pueblos de Castilla
Fines de semana con encanto

Viajes
IDA y VUELTA

Información y reservas:
Agencia de viajes **IDA Y VUELTA:**
C/ Alcalá, 51.
Teléfono: 91 435 06 88
www.idayvuelta.com

- Paseos por el campo
- Excursión a los castillos (Sepúlveda, Pedraza, Turégano)
- Paseos a caballo
- Hoteles con encanto

3 Escuche la conversación de estas tres personas. ¿Qué planes tienen?

	Jaime	Elisa	Tomás
Va a ir a unos pueblos de Segovia con una amiga.	✓		
Va a hacer un viaje por Europa en verano.			✓
Va a descansar.			✓
Va a dar un paseo a caballo.	✓		
Va a comer con su familia.		✓	
No va a salir de Madrid.		✓	

4 Imagine que tiene una semana de vacaciones. Pregunte a su compañero/a qué planes tiene. Puede decir *Voy a..., No sé si...*

Hablar de viajes y medios de transporte

- ¿Cómo vais a ir a España?
- Vamos a ir **en** coche porque no me gusta el tren. Vamos **de** París **a** Lyon. Después vamos **de** Lyon **a** Madrid y pasamos **por** Barcelona.

6B.2 **porque**
Prepositions with verbs of movement

a ➡	⊙ de ...... a ➡
en 🚗	por ...Ⓧ...

Vocabulario

(5)
¿Cómo vas? *How are you going there?*
ir en... *to go by (means of transportation)*
pasar por *to go via*
la ruta *route*
(8)
volver (o:ue) *to come back*

¡OJO!

The preposition **en** is used to talk about means of transportation, as in **en avión, en coche/carro, en tren**. An important exception is **a pie** *(on/by foot)*.

5 Lea la conversación entre Ana y Tomás y observe el mapa. ¿Adónde van Ana y su prima? ¿Por qué pueblos pasan en su ruta? Pedraza; Segovia, Turégano, Sepúlveda

6 Observe la ruta del mapa y escriba las preposiciones que faltan.

Vamos ...de... Madrid ...a... Santander ...por... Burgos.

Vamos ...en... coche.

6 Expansion Have students write similar sentences describing a route they are going to take in the community the next time they have to do an errand or go out. Ex: **Voy de la universidad a la calle Fisher. Voy a la casa de mi amiga Kristen. Paso por la tienda de discos. Voy a pie.**

7 Organice una ruta interesante por su país para una persona que está de visita por una semana. Su compañero/a le pregunta cómo ir y qué lugares visitar.

MI EXPERIENCIA

Suggestion Write different locations on the board and have the class reach a consensus on the best way (**en avión, en coche, en tren, en bici, a pie**) to get to each destination, starting from your university.

8 Pregunte a sus compañeros sus planes para los próximos viajes. ¿Tienen planes similares?

GUIÓN DE TRABAJO

¿Qué planes tienes para...? ¿Qué vas a hacer...? ➡ estas vacaciones / este fin de semana ➡ No sé si... / Voy a...

¿Vas a salir? ¿Vas a hacer un viaje? ➡ ¿Cómo vas a ir? ¿Cómo vas a volver? ➡ ¿En coche? ¿En avión? ¿En tren?

¿Vas a visitar museos? ¿Vas a hacer deporte? ⬅ ¿Cuál es la ruta? ➡ De .... a .... por ....

Practice more at **vhlcentral.com.**

SAM: Actividades pp. 123–125

Reservas

Enviar ahora | Enviar más tarde | Mensaje instantáneo | Vínculo | Eliminar | Firma | Opciones | Reajustar | Insertar | Categorías | Proyectos

De: Jaime Regidor
Para: Viajes Ida y vuelta
CC:
Asunto: Puente de la Constitución
Datos adjuntos: *ninguno*

Estimados señores:

He recibido su oferta "Pueblos de Castilla" y me gustaría reservar una habitación doble del jueves 6 al domingo 9 de este mes. También quería recibir más información sobre las excursiones a los castillos y los paseos a caballo y sus precios.

Atentamente,
Jaime Regidor

Suggestion Have students draft a response e-mail to Jaime from **Viajes Ida y vuelta**.

Empezar y terminar una carta

Estimados/as señores/as:
Atentamente,

6B.3 Formulas for written correspondence

Solicitar información o un servicio

- Hola, buenos días. **Me gustaría reservar** una habitación.
- Muy bien. **¿Quería** una habitación doble o individual?
- Doble, por favor.

6B.4 me gustaría + [*infinitive*]
quería + [*noun/infinitive*]

Vocabulario

9

el reencuentro *reunion*
Estimados señores: *Dear Sirs,*
estimado/a *dear*
el/la señor(a) *sir/madam*
reservar *to make a reservation*
la habitación doble *double room*
Atentamente, *Sincerely,*
la reserva *reservation*
la habitación individual *single room*
confirmar

6B.3 Tell students that the formulas used in written correspondence (**Estimados, Atentamente**) are equivalents, but not translations, of the English expressions (*Dear, Sincerely*).

9 Lea el correo electrónico de Jaime y señale en la tabla las respuestas correctas.

Jaime escribe para...	reservar un billete.	reservar una habitación. ✓	confirmar la reserva.
Quiere una habitación...	individual.	doble. ✓	triple.
Quiere información sobre...	excursiones. ✓	ofertas para el verano.	hoteles.

10 Relacione las frases con la información de los recuadros.

1. EMPEZAR EL CORREO
2. HACER LA RESERVA
3. ESPECIFICAR LA FECHA
4. PEDIR INFORMACIÓN
5. TERMINAR EL CORREO

Estimados señores: (1)
...del jueves 6 al domingo 9 de diciembre 3
Atentamente, 5
Me gustaría reservar... 2
Me gustaría recibir más... 4

11 Escriba un correo a uno de estos hoteles para reservar una habitación. Indique fechas, tipo de habitación, y pida información de precios.

HOTEL AGUADULCE (ALMERÍA)

HOTEL VISTANEVADA (CANDANCHÚ, PIRINEOS)

HOTEL TOLEDO (TOLEDO)

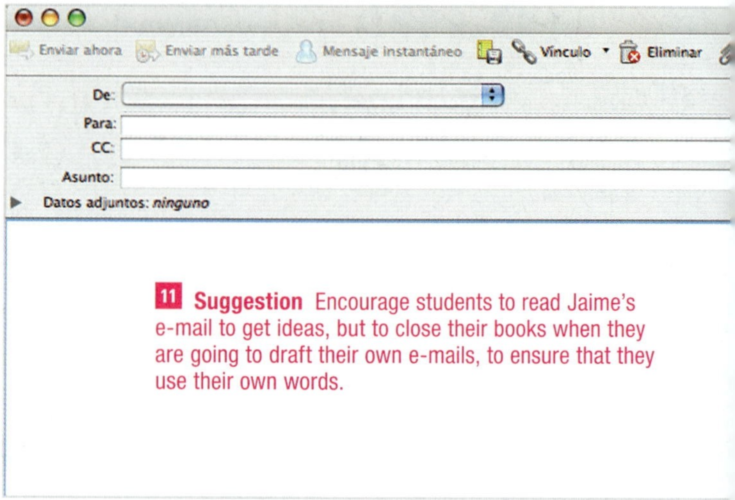

11 Suggestion Encourage students to read Jaime's e-mail to get ideas, but to close their books when they are going to draft their own e-mails, to ensure that they use their own words.

Hablar por teléfono
Proponer un plan y aceptar una propuesta

- ¿Diga/Dígame/Hola/Bueno?
- ¿Está Carmen, por favor?
- Sí, soy yo./Sí, (con) él/ella habla.
- ¿Vamos a cenar el jueves?
- Vale/De acuerdo, perfecto.
- ¡Genial!

6B.5 Expressions for phone conversations

6B.6 ir + a + [*infinitive/noun*]

Vocabulario

(12)

¿Diga?/¿Dígame?/¿Hola?/¿Bueno? *Hello?*

¿Está Carmen? *Is Carmen there?*

genial *great*

estupendo/a *wonderful*

(13)

el alojamiento *lodging*

el parador nacional *state-run hotel in a Spanish historic building*

el convento *convent*

histórico/a *historical*

el paisaje *landscape*

a pesar de *despite*

acondicionado/a *equipped*

asequible *affordable*

Paradores nacionales

Son hoteles con mucho encanto. Algunos son antiguos castillos o conventos. Están situados en lugares históricos o con paisajes impresionantes. Son muy populares, porque a pesar de ser hoteles muy bien acondicionados, los precios son asequibles.

14 Suggestion Have students look at the ticket and ask basic comprehension questions. Ex: **¿Para qué tipo de transporte es? ¿Es un billete de ida?**

12 a. Ana llama a su amiga Carmen que está en Galicia. Ordene el diálogo. Luego escuche la conversación y compruebe si el orden es correcto.

- ¿Diga? 1
- ¡Ah, perfecto! Bueno, pues nada. Nos vemos pronto. 9
- ¡Buen viaje! 10
- Genial. Oye, una cosa... ¿Ya has reservado la habitación? 7
- Hola, Carmen, soy Ana. ¿Qué tal? ¿Tienes ya el billete? 4
- Sí, soy yo. 3
- ¿Está Carmen, por favor? 2
- Sí, ya lo he comprado. Voy a llegar a las nueve y media de la noche. 5
- Sí, he reservado una habitación doble. 8
- Estupendo. Voy a buscarte a la estación y vamos a cenar. 6

b. Subraye cómo se contesta el teléfono y cómo se pregunta por alguien.

13 Imagine que tiene tres días de vacaciones. Llame a un(a) amigo/a por teléfono para organizar el transporte y el alojamiento de un fin de semana en Barcelona. Represente la conversación con un(a) compañero/a.

13 Suggestion Encourage students to sit back to back to better simulate a phone conversation.

MI EXPERIENCIA

14 Prepare un viaje con un(a) amigo/a para el fin de semana. Llame a una agencia de viajes para reservar todo.
Su compañero/a es el/la empleado/a de la agencia.

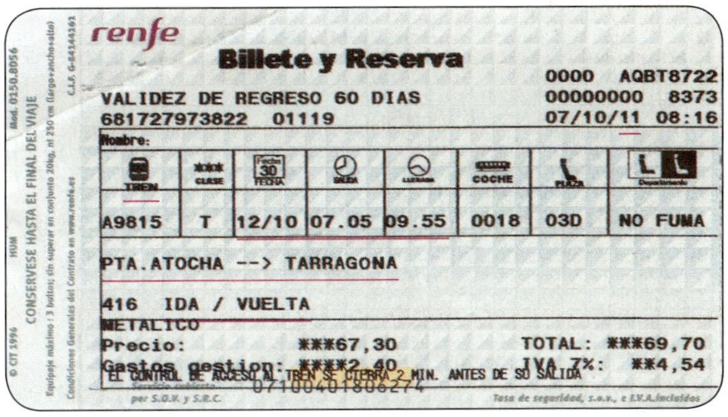
renfe
Billete y Reserva
0000 AQBT8722
VALIDEZ DE REGRESO 60 DIAS 00000000 8373
681727973822 01119 07/10/11 08:16
Nombre:

TREN	CLASE	FECHA	SALIDA	LLEGADA	COCHE	PLAZA	Departamento
A9815	T	12/10	07.05	09.55	0018	03D	NO FUMA

PTA.ATOCHA --> TARRAGONA
416 IDA / VUELTA
METALICO
Precio: ***67,30 TOTAL: ***69,70
Gastos gestion: ****2,40 IVA 7%: **4,54
EL CONTROL DE ACCESO AL TREN SE CIERRA 2 MIN. ANTES DE SU SALIDA
07100401806274
por S.O.V. y S.R.C. Tasa de seguridad, s.o.v., e I.V.A. incluidos
CONSERVESE HASTA EL FINAL DEL VIAJE

Observe el billete y subraye la información clave del viaje.

GUIÓN DE TRABAJO

¡RING RING...!

"Viajes El Mundo", buenas tardes.

Quería información sobre viajes a...

¿Cómo va a ir?

Quería reservar...

¿Adónde va a viajar?

¿Cuántas noches?

¿Billete de ida o de ida y vuelta?

Practice more at **vhlcentral.com.**

SAM: Actividades pp. 126–128

Felipe Daza y Julia Navarro, muy enamorados, en el aeropuerto de Santiago de Chile.

Julia y Felipe, amor a distancia

Felipe y Julia son novios pero viven en países diferentes, a miles de kilómetros. Él es chileno, vive en Santiago y trabaja en un banco. Julia vive en Vancouver y trabaja en un colegio. Los dos buscan la manera de estar juntos, pero no es fácil. Remind students that **colegio** is a false cognate.

Entrevistador: *Felipe, ¿dónde conociste a Julia?*

Felipe: En Canadá, en Vancouver. Fue el año pasado en un viaje de trabajo. La conocí allá en una cena, con mis compañeros... Así pasó.

Entrevistador: *Entonces, desde el año pasado no están juntos. Es mucho tiempo, ¿no?*

Julia: Sí, sí, mucho tiempo.

Entrevistador: *¿Y cómo es una relación a esta distancia?*

Felipe: Pues... chateamos, hablamos por teléfono, nos comunicamos con la cámara web, pero no siempre es fácil por la diferencia de horario. Pero tenemos planes para esta Navidad.

Entrevistador: *¿Ah, sí? ¿Qué planes tienen para estas vacaciones?*

Felipe: Vamos a estar acá, en Chile, tres semanas porque Julia tiene vacaciones en el colegio. Claro, es un viaje muy largo.

Entrevistador: *¿Van a viajar por Chile o van a estar todo el tiempo en Santiago?*

Felipe: Para Julia es la primera vez en Chile y acá es verano, un tiempo fantástico para viajar. Vamos a ir a la playa, a Viña del Mar con mi familia y después, vamos a ir al sur, a visitar los lagos y el volcán Osorno.

Julia: Y a mí me gustaría también ir al parque Pumalín, pero está un poco lejos. Vamos a ver...

Vocabulario

15

- **el amor a distancia** *long-distance love*
- **el amor** *love*
- **los novios** *sweethearts*
- **los miles** *thousands*
- **los dos** *both*
- **fácil** *easy*
- **allá** *there*
- **chatear** *to chat (on the Internet)*
- **la cámara web** *webcam*
- **acá** *here*
- **el lago** *lake*
- **el volcán**

OPINIÓN

¿Alguna vez ha tenido un(a) novio/a a distancia?

¿Qué es lo más importante para mantener una relación a distancia?

15 ¿De qué habla Felipe en esta entrevista?

1. de las tradiciones navideñas en Chile ☐
2. de sus planes para la visita de Julia ☑
3. del paisaje de Chile ☐

Direct attention to the interviewer's last question and have students read Felipe's answer. Remind students that Christmas occurs during the summer months in the Southern Hemisphere.

16 Responda a las preguntas. Suggested answers:

1. ¿Cuándo y dónde conoció Felipe a Julia? el año pasado; en Vancouver, en un viaje de trabajo, en una cena
2. ¿Tienen planes para estas vacaciones? ¿Qué van a hacer? Van a viajar, van a ir a la playa, a Viña del Mar, y después van a ir al sur, a los lagos y al volcán Osorno.
3. ¿Cuánto tiempo va a estar Julia en Chile? Va a estar tres semanas.
4. ¿Por qué se titula la entrevista "Amor a distancia"? porque Felipe y Julia viven en países diferentes
5. ¿Cómo se comunican Felipe y Julia? Se comunican por chat, hablan por teléfono y usan la cámara web.

17 ¿Tiene usted amistades o relaciones familiares a distancia? ¿Cuándo y dónde se ven? ¿Cómo se comunican? Hable con su compañero/a.

Modelo:
- *¿Tienes familiares que viven muy lejos?*
- *Sí, mis primos viven en Tokio.*
- *¿Ah, sí? ¡Qué interesante! ¿Y cómo te comunicas con ellos?*
- *Pues, ...*

Suggestion Tell students to imagine that Julia is halfway through her trip to Chile. Have them write a postcard from Julia to a friend back in Vancouver, mentioning what she and Felipe have done so far.

Suggestion Have students read the **Vocabulario** words. Ask them which words are likely of foreign origin (**trekking**, **kayak**). Remind them that *k* is used in words of foreign origin.

PARQUE PUMALÍN, CHILE

El parque tiene una extensión de unas 325 mil hectáreas. Allí están los últimos bosques vírgenes del sur de Chile. Nuestra excursión en kayak nos permite entrar en una parte del parque, correspondiente a la zona de Chiloé Continental, que tiene fiordos rodeados de vegetación, cascadas, termas a orillas del mar y lagos escondidos.

Duración: *5 días / 4 noches*
Lugar: *Patagonia Norte, Chile*
Dificultad: *moderada*
Época: *octubre a abril*
Salida: *Puerto Montt*
Alojamiento: *cabañas y campamento*
Actividades del viaje: *kayak de mar, trekking, observación de flora y fauna*
Fechas: *del 23 al 27 de enero*
del 01 al 05 de febrero
del 01 al 05 de marzo
del 31 de marzo al 03 de abril
Otros viajes:

CONSULTAS RESERVAS

Vocabulario

18

- **la extensión** *area*
- **el bosque virgen** *virgin forest*
- **permitir** *to allow*
- **rodeado/a de** *surrounded by*
- **la cascada** *waterfall*
- **las termas** *hot springs*
- **la orilla** *shore*
- **escondido/a** *hidden*
- **la dificultad** *difficulty*
- **moderado/a** *moderate*
- **la época** *time of year*
- **la salida** *departure*
- **la cabaña** *cabin*
- **el campamento** *campsite*
- **el trekking** *hiking*
- **la observación de flora y fauna** *wildlife viewing*
- **las consultas** *questions*
- **la publicidad** *advertisement*
- **la hectárea, el kayak, el fiordo, la vegetación, la duración, la Patagonia**

19

- **relajado/a** *relaxed*

20

- **el pasaje de avión** *plane ticket*
- **el auto** *car*
- **regalarse** *to give oneself*

18 Lea la publicidad de Internet y responda a las preguntas.

1. ¿De qué lugar habla esta publicidad? del parque Pumalín
2. ¿Qué tipo de turismo ofrece?
   ☑ turismo natural ☐ turismo monumental ☐ turismo de aventuras
3. ¿Dónde podría realizarse este tipo de turismo en su país?

[d] y [j] finales

19 a. Algunos hablantes de español pronuncian las [d] y [j] finales muy relajadas. Escuche las palabras terminadas en [d] y [j] y repítalas.

Madrid *ciudad* *reloj*

b. Al formar los plurales o cuando la palabra siguiente empieza con vocal, la [d] y la [j] deben pronunciarse claramente. Escuche las palabras y repítalas.

ciudades *Madrid está en España.* *El reloj es bonito.*

c. Practique esta conversación con su compañero/a.

He dejado el reloj en el hotel de Madrid.

Yo también olvidé un reloj en un viaje a Valladolid.

19 Suggestion Write these additional words on the board: **David, libertad, merced, juventud.** Say the words aloud and have students repeat after you.

20 ¿Cómo se dice? Complete esta actividad con las palabras relacionadas con el transporte que figuran en el recuadro.

auto	coche
autobús	colectivo
billete	guagua
carro	pasaje

coche ...... España
carro ...... México
auto ...... Argentina

autobús ...... España
guagua ...... Caribe
colectivo ...... Argentina

billete ...... España
pasaje ...... América Latina

Practice more at **vhlcentral.com.**

SAM: Actividades pp. 129–134

TAREA FINAL

Remind students to consider the time of year in which they will be traveling. Also, if they choose a destination in the Southern Hemisphere, they should think about what season it will be there.

Un viaje con la clase

¿Por qué no se regala un viaje con sus compañeros de clase?

¿Qué lugares de interés van a visitar? ¿Qué actividades van a hacer? Hable con un(a) compañero/a.

Vamos a ir...
Vamos a ver...
Vamos a...

Hablen de sus viajes y elijan uno. A continuación piensen en cómo llegar (transporte y ruta). Organicen la reserva de los billetes y de las habitaciones.

¿Vamos a ir en bici? ¿En avión?
¿Vamos a ir de... a...?
¿Vamos a pasar por...?

Pregunten por sus planes de viaje y juntos decidan cuál es el mejor.

¿Qué planes tienen para el viaje con la clase?

YO PUEDO...

- Puedo hablar de mis planes de viajes con otras personas.
  Anote sus planes para las próximas vacaciones.

  Las próximas vacaciones ......
  ....
  ....
  ....

- Puedo decir cómo llegar a un destino, con qué tipo de transporte y a través de qué ruta.
  Describa una ruta por su país.
- Puedo escribir un correo electrónico para reservar una habitación en un hotel.
  Escriba un breve correo electrónico indicando sus datos de viaje.

  ....
  ....
  ....
  ....

- Puedo hablar por teléfono.
  ¿Cómo se contesta el teléfono y se pregunta por alguien? Escríbalo.

  Sample answer:
  ¿.......Diga.......?
  ¿...Está Carmen, por favor...?

GRAMÁTICA FUNCIONAL

6B.1 Suggestion Have students write down three pieces of factual information about your school (Ex: **el número de teléfono de la clínica**). Have pairs take turns asking each other if they know this information. If their partner doesn't know, they should give them the information.

6B.1 Make plans

ir + a + [*infinitive*] 5.16.1
saber 5.1.2

- To ask someone what he/she is going to do, say **¿Qué va(s) a hacer?** Answer using the construction **ir + a +** [*infinitive*] to talk about plans.

  Maribel, ¿qué **vas a hacer** este verano?
  *Maribel, **what are you going to do** this summer?*

  En agosto, **voy a viajar** a Acapulco.
  *In August, **I'm going to travel** to Acapulco.*

- As with other infinitive constructions, remember to conjugate the first verb (**ir**), and use the second verb in the infinitive.

- Use the verb **saber** (*to know*) to express your degree of certainty about plans. **Saber** has an irregular **yo** form.

SABER			
(yo)	**sé**	(nosotros/as)	sabemos
(tú)	sabes	(vosotros/as)	sabéis
(usted, él, ella)	sabe	(ustedes, ellos/as)	saben

  ¿**Sabes** si vienen Juana y Pepe?
  ***Do you know** if Juana and Pepe are coming?*

- Use **no + saber + si** + [*verb*] to express uncertainty.

  Cristián quiere ir a la fiesta, pero **no sabe si puede.**
  *Cristián wants to go to the party, but **he doesn't know if he can.***

- Use **saber** to talk about knowledge of facts and **conocer** to talk about familiarity with people, places, and things.

  Conozco a Julián, pero **no sé** si viene hoy.
  ***I know** Julián, but **I don't know** if he's coming today.*

6B.2 Talk about trips and means of transportation

Prepositions with verbs of movement 10.1, 10.5, 10.11, 10.16

a ➡ | ⊙ de ...... a ➡ | en 🚗 | por.. ⓧ ..

- Use the prepositions **a** (*to*), **de** (*from*), **en** (*in; by*), and **por** (*via, through*) with verbs of movement to add detail.

  Vamos **de** Boston **a** Chicago **en** autobús y pasamos **por** Buffalo.
  *We go **from** Boston **to** Chicago **by** bus and we pass **through** Buffalo.*

- Common verbs of movement are **ir, viajar, pasar,** and **volver** (*to return*). **Volver** has an **o→ue** stem change.

- Use **porque** (*because*) to give explanations.

  Vamos en autobús **porque** es caro viajar en avión.
  *We're going by bus **because** it's expensive to travel by plane.*

¡Póngalo en práctica!

G1 Complete las oraciones para contar qué va a hacer cada persona.

1. Luisa ...va a comprar... (comprar) un carro nuevo.
2. Ignacio y Teresa ...van a visitar... (visitar) a Iván.
3. Yo ...voy a ir... (ir) a la boda de mi prima.
4. Laura y yo ...vamos a pasar... (pasar) el día en la playa.
5. Tú ...vas a trabajar... (trabajar) en esa heladería.
6. ¿Ustedes ...van a salir... (salir) esta noche?
7. Julia ...va a hacer... (hacer) un viaje en avión.
8. Ricardo y tú ...van/vais a tomar... (tomar) el ferry para Menorca.

G2 Complete la conversación con las formas correctas de **saber**.

Armando, ¿(1)...sabes... si Sara viene a la cena esta noche?

Mmm, no (2)...sé... . Me ha explicado que no (3)...sabe... si tiene que trabajar esta noche.

¿Y Carla y Alberto (4)...saben... a qué hora vamos a empezar?

Mmm, no (5)...sé... . Ahora llamo a Carla para preguntarle.

G3 Complete las oraciones con **a, de, en** o **por.**

1. Mis padres siempre viajan ...en... tren.
2. Compramos un billete para ir ...a... Lima.
3. ¿Vas a pasar ...por... Miami?
4. Ana viaja ...en... autobús porque cuesta menos.
5. Voy a salir ...de... Guadalajara por la mañana.
6. ¿Van a ir ...en... coche o ...a... pie?
7. Felipe vuelve ...a... casa el viernes.
8. Nuria y yo vamos a pasar ...por... la farmacia.
9. Todos los miércoles voy ...de... Buenos Aires ...a... Montevideo.

G3 Expansion Have students write three additional sentences for a partner to complete.

Practice more at **vhlcentral.com.**

GRAMÁTICA FUNCIONAL

6B.3 Point out the use of the colon (**dos puntos**) in salutations. Tell students that in Spanish this punctuation is used for all types of written correspondence, both formal and informal.

6B.3 Begin and end a letter

Formulas for written correspondence

- Begin a formal letter with **Estimado/a(s)** + [*name*].

Estimados Álvaro y Eva:	**Estimada** Sra. Martínez:
Dear Álvaro and Eva,	*Dear Mrs. Martínez,*

- If you are writing to an unknown or unspecified recipient, write **Estimados señores**: (*Dear sirs,*).

- Close a letter by writing **Atentamente**, (*Sincerely,*).

6B.4 Request information or services

Formulas of courtesy 5.10, 5.11

- Use the formulas **Me gustaría** + [*infinitive*] and **Quería** + [*noun/infinitive*] to request services and information.

Me gustaría reservar una habitación doble. También **quería** información sobre excursiones al Parque Pumalín.
I'd like to reserve a double room. I'd also like information about trips to Pumalín Park.

- These expressions are considered more polite than saying **Quiero** (*I want*).

6B.5 Talk on the phone

Expressions for phone conversations

- Use the expressions **¿Diga?**, **¿Dígame?** (primarily in Spain), **¿Hola?**, or **¿Bueno?** to answer the phone.
- To ask if someone is home or available, say **¿Está** + [*name*], + **por favor?**
- To answer *Speaking/This is (s)he*, say **Sí, soy yo** or **Sí, (con) él/ella habla.** You may want to tell students these additional ways of answering the phone: **¿Sí?** (Spain) and **¿Aló?** (Latin America).

• ¿Hola?	• *Hello?*
▪ ¿Está Gladys, por favor?	▪ *Is Gladys there, please?*
• Sí, soy yo. / Sí, con ella habla.	• *Yes, this is she.*

6B.6 Propose a plan and accept

Irregular verbs 5.1.2 ir a + [*infinitive*] 5.16.1

- Use **ir** + **a** + [*noun/infinitive*] to propose a plan.

¿**Vamos al** Museo Picasso?	¿**Vamos a esquiar**?
Shall we go to the Picasso Museum?	*Shall we go skiing?*

- Use affirmative expressions such as **De acuerdo**, **Perfecto**, **Genial**, **Estupendo**, **Vale**, or **Muy bien** to agree.

¡OJO!
In **3A.2**, you learned to use **ir** + **a** + [*place*] to talk about physically going to a place. Use **ir** + **a** + [*infinitive*] to say what you are *going to do*.

¡Póngalo en práctica!

G4 Complete el correo electrónico.

(1) Estimados señores:

Quería información sobre sus visitas guiadas a Valparaíso porque voy a viajar a Chile en agosto.

(2) Atentamente ,

Joaquín Ramírez

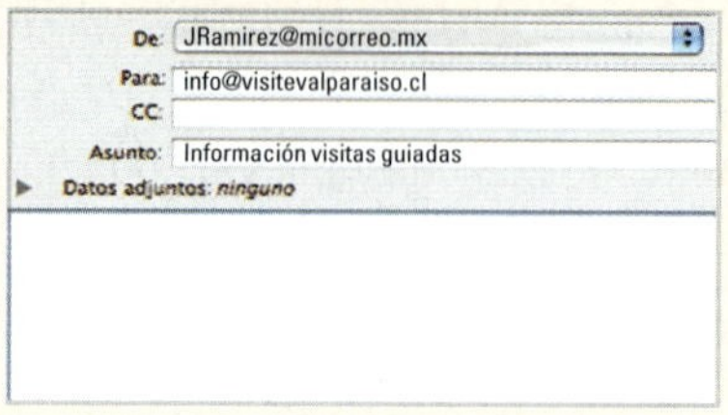

G5 Pida información o ayuda para cada situación.

Suggested answers:

1. comprar un billete
   Quería/Me gustaría comprar un billete.
2. información sobre paseos a caballo
   Quería información sobre los paseos a caballo.
3. reservar una habitación doble
   Quería/Me gustaría reservar una habitación doble.
4. un mapa de Chile
   Quería un mapa de Chile.
5. tomar el ferry
   Quería/Me gustaría tomar el ferry.

G6 Complete la conversación telefónica.

a	estupendo	vamos
de acuerdo	Hola	vas
está	soy yo	

- ¿(1) Hola ?
- Hola, ¿(2) está Verónica, por favor?
- Sí, (3) soy yo .
- Verónica, soy Carolina. ¿Qué tal?
- Muy bien, ¿y tú?
- Bien. Oye, ¿a qué hora (4) vas a llegar esta noche?
- El autobús llega a las 7:20.
- Genial. Voy (5) a buscarte a la estación y luego vamos a cenar, ¿de acuerdo?
- (6) De acuerdo/Estupendo , pero ¿(7) vamos a casa primero? Así me cambio de ropa.
- Muy bien. Nos vemos a las 7:20 en la estación.
- (8) Estupendo/De acuerdo ¡Hasta luego!

Remind students to use the contraction **al** when **a** precedes the masculine definite article **el**.

Practice more at **vhlcentral.com.**

VOCABULARIO

Planes de viaje

¿Cómo vas?	*How are you going there?*
ida y vuelta	*round-trip*
el albergue	*hostel*
el avión	*plane*
la bici(cleta)	*bike (bicycle)*
el billete	*ticket*
el caballo	*horse*
el camping	*campsite*
el castillo	*castle*
el dinero	*money*
el paseo a caballo	*horseback ride*
el puente	*long weekend*
la ruta	*route*
el tren	*train*
el vuelo	*flight*
ir en...	*to go by (means of transportation)*
pasar la noche	*to spend the night*
pasar por	*to go via*
tomar fotos	*to take pictures*
volver (o:ue)	*to come back*
con encanto	*charming*

Reservas

Atentamente,	*Sincerely,*
¿Diga?/¿Dígame?/ ¿Hola?/¿Bueno?	*Hello?*
¿Está Carmen?	*Is Carmen there?*
Estimados señores:	*Dear Sirs,*
el alojamiento	*lodging*
el convento	*convent*
la habitación doble	*double room*
la habitación individual	*single room*
el paisaje	*landscape*
el parador nacional	*state-run hotel in Spanish historic building*
el reencuentro	*reunion*
la reserva	*reservation*
el/la señor(a)	*sir/madam*
confirmar	*to confirm*
reservar	*to make a reservation*
acondicionado/a	*equipped*
asequible	*affordable*
estimado/a	*dear*
estupendo/a	*wonderful*
genial	*great*
histórico/a	*historic*
a pesar de	*despite*

Julia y Felipe

el amor a distancia	*long-distance love*
el amor	*love*
el auto	*car*
el bosque virgen	*virgin forest*
la cabaña	*cabin*
la cámara web	*webcam*
el campamento	*campsite*
la cascada	*waterfall*
las consultas	*questions*
la dificultad	*difficulty*
los dos	*both*
la duración	*duration*
la época	*time of year*
la extensión	*area*
el fiordo	*fiord*
la hectárea	*hectare*
el kayak	*kayak*
el lago	*lake*
los miles	*thousands*
los novios	*sweethearts*
la observación de flora y fauna	*wildlife viewing*
la orilla	*shore*
el pasaje de avión	*plane ticket*
la Patagonia	*Patagonia*
la publicidad	*advertisement*
la salida	*departure*
las termas	*hot springs*
el trekking	*hiking*
la vegetación	*vegetation*
el volcán	*volcano*
chatear	*to chat (on the Internet)*
permitir	*to allow*
regalarse	*to give oneself*
escondido/a	*hidden*
fácil	*easy*
moderado/a	*moderate*
relajado/a	*relaxed*
rodeado/a de	*surrounded by*
acá	*here*
allá	*there*

Variación léxica

el billete ⟷ **el boleto** (*Méx.*) ⟷ **el pasaje** (*Amér. L.*)

el camping ⟷ **el campamento**

¡De acuerdo! ⟷ **¡Vale!** (*Esp.*)

¡Genial! ⟷ **¡Chévere!** (*Amér. C.*) ⟷ **¡Chido!** (*Méx.*) ⟷ **¡Fenomenal!**

la reserva (*Esp., Arg.*) ⟷ **la reservación** (*Amér. L.*)

tomar una foto ⟷ **hacer una foto** (*Esp.*) ⟷ **sacar una foto** (*Amér. L.*)

Suggestion Have students write a conversation using as many words from **Variación léxica** as they can.

AVANCE

Estrategias

1 Mostrar interés en la conversación

Lección 5A

If you want to improve your conversational skills, show interest in what the other person is saying! Use expressions such as **¿Ah, sí?**, **¡Qué interesante!**, or **¿Y qué pasó?** to improve communication and make the conversation more interesting.

- Un(a) amigo/a le cuenta lo siguiente. Reaccione. Muestre interés.

Sample answers:

La semana pasada no fui al curso de español. — ¿Y qué pasó?

Ayer tuve la primera clase de salsa. — ¿Y qué tal?

El mes pasado fui de vacaciones a Guatemala. — ¡Qué interesante!

Trabajé en un restaurante ruso dos meses. — ¿Ah, sí?

Suggestion In pairs, have students take turns reading the statements in the speech bubbles for their partner to react.

2 Aprender vocabulario con ayuda de grupos de palabras

Lección 5B

One strategy for learning and remembering new vocabulary is to study pairs or groups of words together: antonyms, masculine and feminine forms, synonyms, or related words.

- Revise el vocabulario nuevo que ha aprendido en la Lección 5B y cree grupos de palabras para retenerlas mejor.

3 Ganar tiempo para pensar

Lección 6A

Sometimes it is helpful to hesitate or "buy time" in a conversation in order to give a more thoughtful response. In these cases, you can use filler words or expressions, such as **bueno**, **pues**, and **a ver**, that give you time to formulate your answer.

- Escuche de nuevo la conversación de la **Actividad 4a** de la **Lección 6A** y fíjese cómo usan palabras de relleno los interlocutores para ganar tiempo.

4 Subrayar palabras clave

Lección 6B

You don't need to know every word and detail in a text in order to understand its meaning. Focus on the words and expressions you already know and then look up the key words that are central to the text's meaning.

- Marque las palabras y la información clave en este texto.

> **HOTEL LA BARRANCA (ESCAPADA ROMÁNTICA)**
>
> **Pase un fin de semana romántico en un entorno natural muy especial.**
>
> Fines de semana de mayo y junio descuentos en habitaciones dobles.
> La Barranca es un acogedor hotel a solo 30 minutos de Madrid, en un valle al pie de La Maliciosa, en plena Sierra de Guadarrama, donde podrá disfrutar de un ambiente tranquilo en compañía de su pareja. El hotel se encuentra a 40 minutos del aeropuerto Madrid-Barajas, a 30 de Segovia, a 15 del Monasterio de El Escorial y a 15 minutos de las pistas de esquí. Aquí puede disfrutar de unos días de relax en un hotel de montaña rodeado de naturaleza.
> Organizamos excursiones por la sierra y visitas a las localidades cercanas.

Competencias

3 Ask students if they know Almodóvar and Amenábar's first names (Pedro, Alejandro) and if they can name the movies for which they are most famous. Then ask them for what Cohen brothers movie Javier Bardem won the 2008 Oscar (*No Country for Old Men*).

HABLAR DE PARENTESCOS

1 Responda: ¿Quién es...?

1. El padre de mi madre: ....mi abuelo....
2. La hermana de mi padre: ....mi tía....
3. La hija de mi hijo: ....mi nieta....
4. El hijo de mi madre: ....mi hermano....
5. La madre de mi padre: ....mi abuela....

1 Suggestion Have students write three more sentences for a partner to complete.

HABLAR DEL PASADO Y FUTURO

2 Clasifique las formas verbales en el siguiente cuadro.

he estado
voy a ir
fui
estuve
he ido
voy a ser
voy a estar
he sido
fui

	Pretérito perfecto	Pretérito indefinido	Futuro
ser	he sido	fui	voy a ser
estar	he estado	estuve	voy a estar
ir	he ido	fui	voy a ir

NARRAR BIOGRAFÍAS

3 Elija el texto A o el texto B y pregunte los datos que faltan a su compañero/a.

A

Javier Bardem nació en Las Palmas (Islas Canarias, España) en (1)....1969.... . Antes de trabajar en el cine, estudió (2)....pintura.... y jugó al rugby en la selección nacional. Sus primeras películas fueron *Jamón, jamón* y (3)....Huevos de oro.... . En (4)....1997.... recibió el premio del público al mejor actor europeo. Ha trabajado con importantes directores como Almodóvar y (5)....Amenábar.... . En febrero de 2008 ganó un Oscar por su actuación en una película de (6)....los hermanos Cohen.... .

B

Javier Bardem nació en (1)....Las Palmas.... ....(Islas Canarias, España).... en 1969. Antes de trabajar en el cine, estudió pintura y jugó (2)....al rugby.... en la selección nacional. Sus primeras películas fueron (3)....Jamón, jamón.... y *Huevos de oro*. En 1997 recibió el premio del (4)....público al mejor actor.... ....europeo.... . Ha trabajado con importantes directores como (5)....Almodóvar.... y Amenábar. En febrero de (6)....2008.... ganó un Oscar por su actuación en una película de los hermanos Cohen.

HABLAR DE VIAJES EN PASADO

4 Complete el texto con la preposición apropiada.

El verano pasado estuvimos (1) ....en.... Mallorca de vacaciones. Primero fuimos (2) ....a.... Valencia (3) ....en.... tren y allí tomamos un barco (4) ....a.... la isla. La vuelta fue (5) ....en.... avión, directamente (6) ....de.... Mallorca (7) ....a.... Ginebra. ¡Fue fantástico!

HACER PLANES

5 Señale qué actividades van a hacer mañana. Pregunte a su compañero/a por sus planes y anótelos en la tabla.

Actividades	Yo	Mi compañero/a
ir al cine		
estudiar español		
cenar con amigos		
trabajar		
estar en casa		
hacer las compras		
ir de viaje		
leer un libro		

¿Estrés? ¿Qué estrés?

Ya ha visto cómo aprovechar el tiempo libre y buscar el bienestar cada día en actividades de ocio y con sus amigos. En este episodio de **Flash Cultura** va a conocer cómo el estrés afecta la vida de los madrileños y qué opciones tienen para relajarse.

Estrategia

False cognates

From time to time you will come across some *false friends* or *false cognates* (words that appear to mean the same in English and Spanish but actually don't) such as **librería**, which means *bookstore* in Spanish, not *library*. So be very careful or you might misinterpret the whole sentence! Can you think of another example of a false friend?

Vocabulario útil

- el bullicio *hubbub*
- la cola *line*
- combatir *to fight*
- con prisa *in a hurry*
- mantenerse sano/a *to stay healthy*
- remar *to row*
- el retiro *getaway*
- el ruido *noise*
- trotar *to jog*

1. Hable con un(a) compañero/a de las siguientes preguntas. ¿Durante las vacaciones les gusta viajar a ciudades grandes para visitar museos y teatros o a lugares pequeños para disfrutar de la naturaleza? ¿Cuál es su lugar de retiro favorito para descansar del trabajo y el estrés?

2. Mire este episodio de **Flash Cultura**. No se distraiga (*Don't get distracted*) cuando escuche muchas voces al mismo tiempo. Concéntrese en las preguntas del presentador y en las respuestas.

Siempre hay cola para todo.

Suggestion: Ask students if they have to wait in long lines often and whether they dislike it or don't mind it. What sort of event would be important enough that they would wait in line for several hours or even a whole night?

Suggestion: Survey the class about the worst causes of stress in everyday life. Encourage students to discuss whether stress is exclusive to big cities. Do people from small towns ever feel stress?

Para mantenerse sano es importante aprender a luchar contra el estrés.

3. A partir de lo que vio en el video, ordene las siguientes actividades en la columna correspondiente.

caminar por la calle · conseguir entradas para un espectáculo · ir al trabajo · pasear con tu perro · recibir un mensaje · remar en el Retiro · tomar una siesta · tomar un baño árabe · trotar · viajar en autobús · visitar un museo

Da estrés	Combate el estrés
Sample answers: caminar por la calle, conseguir entradas para un espectáculo, ir al trabajo, recibir un mensaje, viajar en autobús	Sample answers: caminar por la calle, pasear con tu perro, recibir un mensaje, remar en el Retiro, tomar una siesta, tomar un baño árabe, trotar, visitar un museo

4. Con un(a) compañero/a, escriba una conversación entre dos amigos que planean visitar Madrid; uno/a está muy entusiasmado/a, el/la otro/a es pesimista.

Modelo: • *¿Por qué no vamos al museo?*

Estrategia

Filler words

In Spanish, as in English, many people use filler words (*muletillas*) when they speak: when you don't know how to continue in a sentence you may use **este, o sea,** or **es/quiero decir.** Also, when you need to get your thoughts together or want to rephrase a sentence you may use **pues,** or **a ver/veamos/vamos a ver.**

Practice more at **vhlcentral.com.**

Audio: Activities, Vocabulary
Video: *Flash Cultura*

Unidad 7

Jorge Drexler, cantautor uruguayo

Lección 7A

HOY POR HOY

Lección 7B

CAMBIO DE VIDA

Guadalupe Rodríguez, una nueva etapa

El mundo del trabajo

AVANCE

7A HOY POR HOY

El día a día

Explain that the word **bailaores** is used only for flamenco dancers. All other dancers (ballet, tap, jazz, etc.) are referred to as **bailarines**.

Profesión y vocación

"Me dedico a llevar fruta en camión desde México. Conduzco muchas horas al día. Estoy solo, lejos de mi familia y eso no es calidad de vida. Escucho mucha música; me hace compañía."

Carlos. San Antonio, Texas (EE.UU)

"Soy bombero; es mi vocación desde pequeño. El trabajo en equipo y la preparación física y psicológica son muy necesarios. Es una profesión de riesgo."

Pedro. A Coruña (España)

"Enseño inglés a niños, pero mi verdadera vocación es la traducción. Por las tardes traduzco literatura juvenil inglesa. Me gusta trabajar sola."

Gabriela. Santa Fe (Argentina)

"Nuestros espectáculos son el motor de nuestras vidas. El trabajo de bailaoras es el trabajo de un gran equipo, pero viajamos mucho y es difícil compaginar familia y trabajo."

Ana y Carmela. Granada (España)

Hablar del trabajo

- ¿A qué **te dedicas**?
- **Me dedico** a la traducción. **Traduzco** textos literarios.

7A.1 **dedicarse a** + [*noun/infinitive*]
Verbs with irregular **yo** forms: **traducir**, **conducir**

Vocabulario

(1)

- el día a día *daily life*
- dedicarse a (hacer) algo *to do something (for a living)*
- el camión *truck*
- conducir (zc) *to drive*
- solo/a *alone*
- (hacer) compañía *(to keep) company*
- el/la bombero/a *firefighter*
- en equipo *as a team*
- el riesgo *risk*
- enseñar *to teach*
- traducir (zc) *to translate*
- juvenil *for young people*
- el espectáculo *show*
- el/la bailaor(a) *flamenco dancer*
- difícil *hard; difficult*
- compaginar *to combine*

1 a. El trabajo marca nuestro día a día. ¿Qué profesiones representan las fotografías del reportaje? Carlos es camionero. Pedro es bombero. Gabriela es profesora/maestra. Ana y Carmela son bailaoras.

b. Compruebe sus hipótesis. Lea los textos y relacione las frases.

1. Soy camionero. ..b..
2. Son bailaoras. ..c..
3. Es profesora. ..d..
4. Soy bombero. ..a..

a. Me dedico a apagar incendios.
b. Me dedico a transportar fruta en camión.
c. Se dedican al baile flamenco.
d. Se dedica a la enseñanza.

c. ¿Con qué profesiones del texto asocia estas características?

Lejos de la familia	Trabajar en equipo	Profesión de riesgo	Preparación física	Trabajar solo/a
camionero bailaoras	bailaoras bombero	bombero	bombero bailaoras	camionero traductora

1c Expansion Have students list personality traits typical of someone who practices these professions.

2 Transforme estas oraciones como en el ejemplo.

Modelo: Estoy jubilado, cuido de mis nietos, leo...
Me dedico a cuidar de mis nietos, leer...

1. Es bailarina, baila tango.
Se dedica a bailar tango.
2. Eres diseñador, haces diseño gráfico.
Te dedicas a diseñar.

3 a. ¿A qué se dedican Gabriela y Carlos? Complete las oraciones.

1. Gabriela: "También ....traduzco.... (traducir) textos del inglés al español."
2. Carlos: " ....Conduzco.... (Conducir) un camión de 14 toneladas."

b. ¿Quiénes de los entrevistados cree usted que trabajan por vocación? ¿Quiénes no, y por qué? Pedro, Ana y Carmela. Carlos, porque está solo y lejos de su familia, y Gabriela, porque su verdadera vocación es la traducción.

Un día de espectáculo

3 "A las 21:00 h me visto y me maquillo para el espectáculo."

2 "El ensayo es a las 18:00 h. Después descanso un poco y me ducho."

4 "Después del espectáculo cenamos y a medianoche me acuesto."

1 "Me despierto a las 7:00 h, el resto del grupo se despierta más tarde."

1

2

3

4

Suggestion Ask volunteers to identify the **tapas** in the photo.

Describir hábitos

- ¿A qué hora **se acuesta** usted?
- **Me acuesto** tarde y **me despierto** temprano. **Me visto** en cinco minutos.

7A.2 **despertarse (e:ie)** **acostarse (o:ue)** **vestirse (e:i)**

Vocabulario ***cont.***

el/la camionero/a *truck driver*
apagar *to put out*
el incendio *fire*
el baile flamenco *flamenco dance*
la enseñanza *teaching*
la vocación, transportar

2

cuidar (a/de) alguien *to take care of someone*
el bailarín/la bailarina *dancer*
el diseño gráfico *graphic design*

3

por vocación *by vocation*

4

vestirse (e:i) *to get dressed*
maquillarse *to put makeup on*
el ensayo *rehearsal*
ducharse *to shower*
acostarse (o:ue) *to go to bed*
despertarse (e:ie) *to wake up*
tarde *late*
temprano *early*
levantarse *to get up*
el hábito

5

la rutina

4 Observe la vida de la bailaora Carmela un día de espectáculo. Asocie las oraciones con las imágenes y compare sus respuestas con las de su compañero/a.

5 a. ¿Cuál es la rutina de un bombero? ¿Cree que ve mucho a su familia?

b. Escuche a la mujer de Pedro, el bombero, en un programa de radio. Lea el texto y seleccione la opción correcta.

> Los horarios de mi marido son diferentes de los del resto de la familia. Cuando los niños se acuestan/se despiertan, mi marido se acuesta/se despierta. A veces los niños ven a su padre cuando se viste de bombero/desayuna. ¡Les gusta mucho!

6 Describa la rutina de uno de los entrevistados. Su compañero/a debe adivinar de quién se trata.

6 Expansion Have students write descriptions of daily routines of people in other occupations, such as a night watchman (**vigilante**) or college student. Collect the descriptions, write the professions on the board, and, as you read each description aloud, have students identify the correct profession.

MI EXPERIENCIA

7 Describa su día a día a sus compañeros/as.

GUIÓN DE TRABAJO

¿Qué estudias?/¿A qué te dedicas?
Estudio... biología. lenguas. economía.
Soy... empleado/a.

¿Por qué estudias esa carrera?/¿Es tu trabajo una vocación?

¿Cuál es tu rutina?
Me despierto a las...

¿Qué características tiene tu trabajo/futura profesión?
Trabajo/Es necesario trabajar... en equipo. solo/a. en casa.

Practice more at **vhlcentral.com.**

SAM: Actividades pp. 135–137

Intereses

8 Expansion In pairs, have students come up with another description of what the people in the photos are doing. Have volunteers read their descriptions for the class, who will identify the photo. Ex: **Estoy aprendiendo algo. (4) Estoy caminando en la playa. (1)**

Hablar de acciones que ocurren en este momento

- ¡Hola, Carmela! ¿Qué **estás haciendo**?
- ¡Hola, Ana! **Me estoy vistiendo**. ¿Y tú?
- **Estoy desayunando**. ¿Salimos a correr más tarde?

7A.3 **estar** + [*present participle*]

Have two volunteers role-play the conversation in box **7A.3** as if they were on the phone. Emphasize that **estar** + [*present participle*] is used for actions that are happening *at this moment*.

8 a. ¿Qué están haciendo en estas fotos el bombero, el camionero, las bailaoras y la profesora de inglés de la Actividad 1 (pág. 164)?

"Aquí estoy leyendo con mi hijo. Le estoy enseñando inglés." 4

"Aquí estoy durmiendo la siesta en el jardín de mi casa." 2

"Ahora mismo estamos haciendo deporte." 3

"En este momento estoy jugando con mi hija." 1

b. Complete las formas del gerundio regular.

1. jugar - jug*ando* 2. hacer - hac*iendo* 3. conducir - conduc*iendo*

Vocabulario

8

estar haciendo algo *to be doing something*
hacer deporte *to exercise*
jugar (u:ue) *to play*
al mismo tiempo *at the same time*

10

atender (e:ie) *to attend to*
el pasatiempo *pastime*
el trabajo voluntario *volunteer work*

9 a. ¿Qué están haciendo las personas en estas imágenes?

Está durmiendo. [1]
Están leyendo. [3]
Está yendo a clase. [2]

b. Ahora, complete las formas del gerundio irregular.

1. ir - .... *yendo* 2. dormir - durmiendo 3. leer leyendo

10 Un cliente llama a una empresa. ¿Por qué está ocupada la Sra. Aguilera? Escuche al secretario y ordene sus respuestas.

[2] Está atendiendo a un cliente. [3] Está saliendo de la oficina. [1] Está hablando por otra línea.

11 a. Fíjese en la viñeta cómica. Observe la segunda viñeta. ¿Qué cinco cosas está haciendo la persona al mismo tiempo? Compare sus respuestas con las de su compañero/a.

• beber • comer • conducir • dormir • escribir una carta • escuchar la radio • hablar por teléfono • leer el periódico • mirar la tele • tocar la guitarra

Está mirando la tele, ... bebiendo, comiendo, leyendo el periódico y hablando por teléfono.

b. Y usted, ¿puede hacer muchas cosas a la vez? ¿Qué está haciendo ahora?

- **le(s) encanta(n)...**
- **le(s) interesa(n)...**
- **le(s) preocupa(n)...**

estar en forma | los riesgos de su profesión | la música | la literatura juvenil | jugar con sus hijos | estar lejos de la familia | dormir la siesta | traducir

Hablar de intereses

- ¿Qué **te interesa** y qué **te preocupa**?
- **Me interesa** la literatura. **Me encantan** las siestas y **me preocupa** estar lejos de casa.
- Y a tu madre, ¿qué **le interesa** y **le preocupa**?

7A.4 Verbs like **gustar: encantar, interesar, preocupar**

Estrategia

Dar ejemplos

Me encanta la música, **por ejemplo**, el flamenco, la rumba...

Vocabulario

12

interesar *to be of interest*

estar en forma *to be fit, in (good) shape*

preocupar *to worry; to concern*

13

la preocupación *worry; concern*

dar un ejemplo *to give an example*

el tailandés *Thai*

Tailandia *Thailand*

la trompeta *trumpet*

la salud *health*

el jazz, clásico/a, los cómics

Suggestion Remind students of the conjugation of **gustar**. Have a few volunteers make statements using **gustar** with the items listed here. Then have restate their ideas using **encantar, interesar**, and **preocupar**. Ex: **No me gustan los riesgos de su profesión. Me preocupan los riesgos de su profesión.**

12 ¿Qué cree usted que les encanta, les interesa y les preocupa a nuestros profesionales?

1. A Pedro, el bombero, le preocupan... los riesgos de su profesión.
2. A Carmela y a Ana, las bailaoras, les interesa... estar en forma.
3. A Carlos, el camionero, le gusta... la música y dormir la siesta.
4. A Gabriela, la profesora, le encanta... la literatura juvenil y traducir.

13 a. Escuche la encuesta que le hacen a un joven universitario en la calle y anote la información.

Gustos	Intereses	Preocupaciones
el tailandés, ... tocar la trompeta, los cómics	la cultura de Tailandia, la literatura clásica	la salud, su futuro profesional, los problemas de los países en vías de desarrollo, los derechos humanos

b. ¿Qué le encanta, le interesa y le preocupa a usted? ¿Y a su compañero/a?

14 Termine las oraciones con ejemplos. Pregunte a su compañero/a qué ejemplos usó y por qué.

1. Me interesan todos los deportes, por ejemplo...
2. Una comida latinoamericana que me encanta es, por ejemplo...
3. Me preocupan muchas cosas, por ejemplo...

15 ¿Qué está haciendo su profesor(a)? ¿Qué cree que le interesa/preocupa?

MI EXPERIENCIA

16 ¿Qué es lo que más le gusta de aprender español? ¿Qué aspecto le parece más interesante? ¿Qué es lo más difícil de aprender una lengua? Compare sus respuestas con las de sus compañeros/as.

GUIÓN DE TRABAJO

¿Qué te interesa, preocupa, encanta? → Me interesa(n) / preocupa(n) / encanta(n) → mi acento extranjero, la música, el cine, la literatura... → Por ejemplo...

¿Qué le(s) interesa, preocupa, encanta? → A Paul le encantan las canciones... A nosotros nos interesa... → Por ejemplo...

Practice more at **vhlcentral.com.**

SAM: Actividades pp. 138–140

tocando la guitarra

Suggestion Ask students to give their opinions about Drexler's career change.

Jorge Drexler, cantautor uruguayo

Jorge Drexler nació en Montevideo en 1964. Como él dice, es hijo de un judío alemán y de una uruguaya. Estudió medicina como sus padres y hermanos, pero su verdadera vocación siempre fue la música. Desde los 30 años escribe letras de canciones y compone música.

En 1995 llegó a España, donde vive desde entonces. Ha editado una decena de discos, ha escrito canciones para otros músicos y también para el cine. Ganó un Oscar en 2005 por la canción *Al otro lado del río,* compuesta especialmente para la película *Diarios de motocicleta* de Walter Salles. Actualmente está preparando un nuevo disco y está dando conciertos por muchos países europeos y americanos.

Su día a día cambia si tiene conciertos o se dedica a componer en casa. Cuando no está de viaje, se despierta temprano y lleva a su hijo al colegio. Eso sí, siempre se acuesta tarde.

Últimamente está colaborando con una ONG, Puente al sur, que se dedica a proyectos culturales y solidarios para el desarrollo en Uruguay.

Expresar acciones en desarrollo

- ¿Qué estás haciendo ahora?
- **Actualmente** estoy escribiendo nuevas canciones.

7A.5 actualmente, últimamente

Vocabulario

17

- el/la cantautor(a) *singer-songwriter*
- decir (g) (e:i) *to say; to tell*
- el/la judío/a *Jew*
- uruguayo/a *Uruguayan*
- la letra *lyrics*
- la canción *song*
- componer (ng) *to compose*
- desde entonces *since then*
- entonces *then; so*
- editar *to edit; to release*
- el disco *album*
- especialmente *specially*
- actualmente *currently*
- dar un concierto *to give a concert*
- estar de viaje *to be away*
- últimamente *lately*
- el actor/la actriz *actor/actress*
- **preparar**

18

- madrugar *to get up early*
- la variedad *variety*

17 a. Observe la foto. ¿Conoce a nuestro protagonista? ¿Es actor? Lea su biografía y compruébelo. No es actor, es cantautor.

b. **¿Verdadero** o **falso**?

	V	F
1. A Jorge Drexler le encanta la música, pero se dedica a la medicina.	☐	☑
2. Jorge Drexler, médico de profesión, se dedica a la música.	☑	☐
3. Es un cantautor uruguayo, pero actualmente vive en España.	☑	☐
4. Colabora con una ONG porque le interesan los temas sociales.	☑	☐

c. ¿Qué representan estos tres años en su vida?

1. 2005 Ganó un Oscar.
2. 1995 Llegó a España.
3. 1994 Comenzó a escribir canciones y componer música.

18 Escuche la entrevista a Jorge Drexler del año 2009 y complete su ficha. Escuchará la entrevista dos veces.

Profesión: la medicina

Vocación: la música

Día a día: Si tiene que llevar a su hijo al colegio, se levanta temprano. Si no, prefiere no madrugar y quedarse por la noche a leer y dar vueltas por la casa.

De España le gustan: la energía vital y la gran variedad (de geografías, costumbres, gastronomías y paisajes).

Actualmente está: leyendo, escribiendo, descansando, viendo amigos y viendo películas.

Idiomas: Habla bien inglés, hebreo, portugués y castellano, y un poco de francés e italiano.

Suggestion Print the lyrics of a song by Jorge Drexler that uses vocabulary or grammatical structures from this lesson, such as *Eco*, which uses many present participles. White out key words from the lyrics in order to make a master for a cloze activity. Play the song for students and have them fill in the missing words.

Vocabulario *cont.*

la diversidad *diversity*
rico/a *rich*
el hebreo *Hebrew*
la energía, vital

20
el/la guitarrista *guitarist*
el/la trovador(a) *troubadour*
a pesar de (que) *despite*
asustar *to frighten*
la frontera *border*
tanto... como *both . . . and*
interpretar *to perform*
convertirse (e:ie) en *to become*
el/la (ingeniero/a) agrónomo/a *agronomist*
de hecho *in fact*
influyente *influential*

OPINIÓN

¿Qué profesión valora usted más: médico o cantante? ¿Por qué?

19 **Suggestion** Have volunteers read the quoted material aloud.

19 ¿Recuerda qué dice Jorge Drexler sobre su acento uruguayo? Escuche de nuevo estos fragmentos de la entrevista y fíjese cómo pronuncia las palabras marcadas.

"Yo **empecé** a estudiar música con **cinco** años y luego estudié otra carrera. Estudié **medicina**."

"Estoy sobre todo descansando, viendo amigos, **leyendo**, viendo películas."

20 a. Lea estos reportajes sobre tres artistas hispanos.

Silvio Rodríguez is a leader of the **nueva trova** movement. He currently holds a ministerial post in the Cuban parliament.

Silvio Rodríguez es un cantautor, guitarrista y compositor cubano. A él le gusta llamarse "trovador". A pesar de que su carrera comenzó hace unos 45 años, dice que todavía le asustan las luces y las cámaras. Este artista participa de manera activa en la política. En muchas ocasiones ha usado su arte para defender los ideales en los que cree.

Julieta Venegas es una de las cantautoras más famosas de América Latina. Nació el 24 de noviembre de 1970 en Tijuana, una ciudad mexicana que queda muy cerca de la frontera con los Estados Unidos. Por eso habla desde pequeña tanto español como inglés y tiene un gran conocimiento de las dos culturas. Toca varios instrumentos e interpreta diferentes estilos musicales.

Julieta Venegas has won four Latin Grammys and one Grammy.

Joan Manuel Serrat, el Nano, es un cantautor de origen catalán. Siempre le gustó tocar la guitarra, pero nunca pensó en convertirse en músico profesional. De hecho, ¡es ingeniero agrónomo! Al comienzo de su carrera sólo interpretaba canciones catalanas, pero luego decidió escribir canciones en español. Con el tiempo, se convirtió en uno de los artistas más influyentes del mundo hispano.

b. ¿Qué tienen en común estos artistas?

1. Tienen aproximadamente la misma edad. ☐
2. Son cantautores. ☑
3. Hablan varios idiomas. ☐

21 Elija otro cantautor hispano y escriba un breve reportaje sobre su vida. Si lo desea, puede llevar a la clase una de sus canciones y compartirla con sus compañeros/as.

Vocabulario

21
elegir (j) (e:i) *to choose*

22
el periódico *newspaper*
el conflicto *conflict*

Practice more at **vhlcentral.com.**

SAM: Actividades pp. 141–144

22 En grupos, formen oraciones lógicas con los siguientes elementos. Gana el grupo que consigue hacer más oraciones en menos tiempo.

22 Expansion Have students create three additional sentences about their own lives.

Estamos (dormir) poco...	ÚLTIMAMENTE	... porque nos (interesar) la actualidad.
Estamos (colaborar) con la Cruz Roja...		... porque nos (preocupar) los países en conflicto.
Estamos (aprender) español...		... porque nos (encantar) la música latina.
Estamos (leer) el periódico...	ACTUALMENTE	... porque nos (preocupar) muchas cosas.
Estamos (buscar) una casa en Acapulco...		... porque nos (interesar) los países hispanos.
Estamos (escuchar) música...		... porque nos (encantar) ir allí en verano.

TAREA FINAL

¿Qué estamos haciendo?

Lleve fotos u objetos a clase relacionados con la carrera que está estudiando, sus intereses y sus preocupaciones actuales.

Hable de ello con su compañero/a.

Quiero ser guía turístico/a porque me encanta viajar. En esta foto estoy visitando las pirámides mayas.

Compartan con la clase lo que aprendieron sobre su compañero/a.

Preparen un cartel o una presentación sobre las profesiones, vocaciones, gustos e intereses de la clase.

YO PUEDO...

- Puedo hablar del trabajo.
  ¿A qué se dedican sus familiares?
- Puedo describir hábitos.
  Describa hábitos característicos de una profesión.
- Puedo expresar lo que estoy haciendo y lo que está pasando en este momento.
  Imagine qué están haciendo ahora sus familiares o amigos.
- Puedo hablar de gustos, intereses y preocupaciones.
  ¿Qué le interesa, preocupa, encanta...?
- Puedo expresar lo que hago actualmente.
  ¿Está haciendo algo especial últimamente?

GRAMÁTICA FUNCIONAL

7A.1 Talk about work

dedicarse a + [*noun/infinitive*] 5.7.1
Verbs with irregular **yo** forms: **traducir, conducir** 5.1.2

- In 1B.4, you learned how to inquire about a person's job or profession using the question **¿A qué se/te dedica(s)?** (*form./fam.*). To answer, use **dedicarse a** + [*noun/infinitive*].
- The verb **dedicarse** is reflexive, so a reflexive pronoun (**me, te, se,** etc.) must be used; this is placed directly in front of the conjugated verb. You will learn more about reflexive verbs in 7A.2.

DEDICARSE			
(yo)	**me** dedico	(nosotros/as)	**nos** dedicamos
(tú)	**te** dedicas	(vosotros/as)	**os** dedicáis
(usted, él, ella)	**se** dedica	(ustedes, ellos/as)	**se** dedican

- You have already learned to talk about someone's profession using **ser** + [*profession*]. With **dedicarse a,** use an infinitive or the noun that describes the profession.

¿A qué se dedica tu tío?
What does your uncle do?

Se dedica a pintar casas.
He paints houses.

Y tú, **¿a qué te dedicas?**
And you, what do you do?

Me dedico al diseño gráfico.
I work in graphic design.

- In 5B.3, you learned the verb **conocer** (*to know*). **Conocer** has an irregular **yo** form, **conozco**. The verb **traducir** (*to translate*) also has an irregular **yo** form that undergoes the same **c→zc** change; the rest of the forms follow the regular conjugation pattern for **-ir** verbs.

TRADUCIR			
(yo)	tradu**zc**o	(nosotros/as)	traducimos
(tú)	traduces	(vosotros/as)	traducís
(usted, él, ella)	traduce	(ustedes, ellos/as)	traducen

¿Qué lenguas **traduces**?
What languages do you translate?

Traduzco del francés al español.
I translate from French into Spanish.

- The verb **conducir** (*to drive*) has the same **c→zc** change in the **yo** form as **traducir.**

CONDUCIR			
(yo)	condu**zc**o	(nosotros/as)	conducimos
(tú)	conduces	(vosotros/as)	conducís
(usted, él, ella)	conduce	(ustedes, ellos/as)	conducen

Conduzco un camión todos los días.
I drive a truck every day.

7A.1 Give students the verb **producir** and have them conjugate it.

G1 **Expansion** In small groups, have students take turns naming people at your school or celebrities. The other group members should call out what that person does for a living.

¡Póngalo en práctica!

G1 Elija la opción correcta para completar cada oración.

1. Nosotros...
2. Inés...
3. Yo...
4. Tú y Marcelo...
5. Tú...

3 a. me dedico a la enseñanza.
5 b. te dedicas a la arquitectura.
1 c. nos dedicamos a apagar incendios.
4 d. os dedicáis al baile flamenco.
2 e. se dedica a cuidar niños.

G2 Complete las oraciones con la forma correcta de **traducir**.

G2 **Suggestion** To simplify, tell students that some items may take the infinitive.

1. Los estudiantes ...traducen... las oraciones del inglés al español.
2. En mi trabajo, a veces ...traduzco... cartas para mi jefe.
3. Nosotros ...traducimos... mucho en la clase de latín.
4. Luciana quiere ...traducir... este documento del español al portugués.
5. Iván se dedica a ...traducir... artículos académicos.
6. ¿Qué lengua ...traduces... tú?

G3 Complete la conversación con las formas correctas de **dedicarse, traducir** y **conducir**.

¿A qué (1)...se dedica... usted?

(2)...Me dedico... a la literatura: soy escritor y traductor.

¿Qué lenguas (3)...traduce... usted?

(4)...Traduzco... textos del portugués al español. Y usted, ¿a qué se dedica?

Soy camionero. (5)...Conduzco... un camión para una empresa multinacional. (6)...Me dedico... a transportar cereales.

Practice more at **vhlcentral.com.**

7A

GRAMÁTICA FUNCIONAL

7A.2 Describe daily habits

Reflexive verbs: **despertarse, acostarse, vestirse** 5.7
Reflexive pronouns 5.7.1

- Use the reflexive verbs **despertarse** (*to wake up*), **acostarse** (*to go to bed*), and **vestirse** (*to get dressed*) to describe daily habits. You will know a verb is reflexive when you see the pronoun **se** attached to the infinitive.

	DESPERTARSE	ACOSTARSE	VESTIRSE
(yo)	**me** desp**ie**rto	**me** ac**ue**sto	**me** v**i**sto
(tú)	**te** desp**ie**rtas	**te** ac**ue**stas	**te** v**i**stes
(usted, él, ella)	**se** desp**ie**rta	**se** ac**ue**sta	**se** v**i**ste
(nosotros/as)	**nos** despertamos	**nos** acostamos	**nos** vestimos
(vosotros/as)	**os** despertáis	**os** acostáis	**os** vestís
(ustedes, ellos/as)	**se** desp**ie**rtan	**se** ac**ue**stan	**se** v**i**sten

- **Despertarse, acostarse,** and **vestirse** are stem-changing verbs with **e→ie, o→ue,** and **e→i** changes, respectively.

  Nos acostamos a la misma hora, pero (yo) **me despierto** más temprano.
  *We **go to bed** at the same time, but **I wake up** earlier.*

- Reflexive verbs indicate that the subject both performs and receives the action of the verb, showing that the subject is doing something for or to himself, herself, or itself. Place the reflexive pronoun (**me, te, se,** etc.) directly in front of the conjugated verb.

  Me visto en cinco minutos y preparo el desayuno.
  ***I get dressed (I dress myself)** in five minutes and I prepare breakfast.*

- Note that **se** is the reflexive pronoun for both the third-person singular and plural forms of reflexive verbs.

  Raquel **se** acuesta a las 22:00 h, y sus padres **se** acuestan a las 23:00 h.
  Raquel goes to bed at 10:00 p.m., and her parents go to bed at 11:00 p.m.

- You can also use other reflexive pronouns with the infinitive in appropriate contexts.

  Después de **despertarme**, me visto.
  After I wake up, I get dressed.

- Many reflexive verbs can also be used non-reflexively, but with slightly different meanings. **Me despierto** means *I wake up*, but **despierto a mi hermano** means *I wake my brother up*. Since the person doing the waking is not the recipient of the action, the reflexive pronoun is not used.

  Mi amiga Carla **se despierta** a las 7:00 h durante la semana.
  *My friend Carla **wakes up** at 7:00 a.m. during the week.*

  Despierto a mi hermano porque tiene clase a las 8:00 h.
  ***I wake up** my brother because he has class at 8:00 a.m.*

Suggestion Emphasize the difference between reflexive and non-reflexive verbs by bringing in a doll and acting out the three verbs presented here. For example, act out waking up and say **me despierto**; then act out waking up the doll and say **despierto a mi hija**. Repeat with **acostar(se)** and **vestir(se)**.

G6 Expansion Have students circulate around the room and ask each other what time they wake up and what time they go to bed. Have make note of the answers and try to find someone who has the same routine. Have students report back to the class.

¡Póngalo en práctica!

G4 Escriba el pronombre reflexivo que corresponde a cada verbo conjugado.

1. nos vestimos
2. me acuesto
3. se despierta
4. os vestís
5. te despiertas
6. se visten
7. se acuesta
8. me visto

G5 Complete las oraciones con las formas correctas de los verbos reflexivos.

1. Pablo se despierta (despertarse) temprano todos los días.
2. En general, nosotros nos despertamos (despertarse) a las 7:30 h.
3. Cuando trabajan de noche en el hospital, Adriana y Carmen se acuestan (acostarse) a las 6:00 h de la mañana.
4. Rafael siempre se acuesta (acostarse) muy tarde los viernes.
5. ¿A qué hora te acuestas (acostarse) tú?
6. Los lunes por la mañana me visto (vestirse), tomo el desayuno y salgo temprano para clase.

G6 Complete la conversación con la forma correcta del verbo reflexivo.

- ¿A qué hora (1) te acuestas (acostarse, tú) los sábados?
- (2) Me acuesto (Acostarse, yo) muy tarde y los domingos (3) me despierto (despertarse, yo) a las 11:00 h. (4) Me ducho (ducharse, yo) y después (5) me visto (vestirse, yo) y voy a dar un paseo. ¿Y tú?
- (6) Me acuesto (acostarse, yo) tarde también los sábados, pero los domingos (7) me levanto (levantarse, yo) temprano para estudiar. Mi hermana siempre (8) se despierta (despertarse) más tarde que yo.

G7 Complete las oraciones con la forma correcta de los verbos reflexivos ilustrados.

1. Mario se despierta temprano.

2. Yo me ducho y canto.

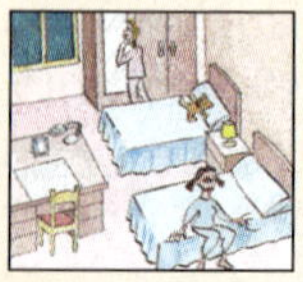

3. Marta y Raquel se levantan a la misma hora.

4. Tú te vistes para ir a la escuela.

Practice more at **vhlcentral.com.**

GRAMÁTICA FUNCIONAL

Explain that the use of the present progressive in Spanish is not identical to its use in English. The present progressive in Spanish is used to describe an action that is in progress at the time of speaking. The simple present is often the best equivalent to the English present progressive.

7A.3 Talk about actions that are happening right now

The present progressive 5.14

- Use the present progressive (**el presente progresivo**) to talk about an action that is currently in progress.

Estoy **preparando** la cena.
I am preparing dinner.

Suggestion In pairs, have students practice the present progressive by miming actions for their partner to describe.

- The **presente progresivo** is a compound tense that consists of two parts: **estar** + [*present participle*]. The present participle (**el gerundio**) of regular verbs is formed by adding **-ando** to the stem of **-ar** verbs and **-iendo** to the stem of **-er** and **-ir** verbs.

habl**ar**	→	habl**ando**
com**er**		com**iendo**
viv**ir**		viv**iendo**

- Verbs that end in **-ir** and have a stem change in the present tense also undergo a change in the present participle.

Infinitive	Present tense	Present participle
referir	e:ie ref**ie**ro	e:i ref**i**riendo
conseguir	e:i cons**i**go	e:i cons**i**guiendo
dormir	o:ue d**ue**rmo	o:u d**u**rmiendo

- If the stem of an **-er** or **-ir** verb ends in a vowel, the present participle ends in **-yendo**. For example: **leer→leyendo; oír→oyendo; traer→trayendo.**

- **Ser**, **tener**, and **ir** are rarely used in the present progressive. The present participle of the verb **ir** is **yendo**; the present participles of **ser** and **tener** are regular.

7A.4 Talk about interests

Verbs like gustar: encantar, interesar, preocupar 5.11.1

- In 4A.2, you learned to use **gustar** to express likes. The verbs **encantar** (*to love; to enjoy*), **interesar** (*to be of interest*), and **preocupar** (*to worry*) follow the same pattern. Like **gustar**, they are also used most commonly in the third-person singular and plural with indirect object pronouns.

(a mí)	**me**	encanta	→	+ [*singular noun/ infinitive(s)*]
(a ti)	**te**	interesa		
(a usted, a él, a ella)	**le**	preocupa		
(a nosotros/as)	**nos** +	encantan	→	+ [*plural noun*]
(a vosotros/as)	**os**	interesan		
(a ustedes, a ellos/as)	**les**	preocupan		

A mí **me encanta** el flamenco, pero a mis padres no **les interesa**.
I love flamenco, but my parents aren't interested in it.

You may want to point out that **gerundio** (*present participle*) is a false cognate. Although in English it is identical in form to the present participle, a gerund functions as a noun.

¡Póngalo en práctica!

G8 Escriba el gerundio de cada verbo.

1. reír ...riendo...
2. dar ...dando...
3. tomar ...tomando...
4. leer ...leyendo...
5. viajar ...viajando...
6. conducir ...conduciendo...
7. compartir ...compartiendo...
8. servir ...sirviendo...

G8 Suggestion Reverse the activity by giving students present participles and having them provide the infinitive.

G9 Complete las oraciones con las formas correctas del presente progresivo.

1. Los niños ...están jugando... (jugar) en la sala.
2. Tomás ...está comiendo... (comer) un sándwich.
3. Yo ...estoy leyendo... (leer) una novela.
4. Raquel y yo ...estamos escuchando... (escuchar) la radio.
5. Mi jefa ...está traduciendo... (traducir) el documento.
6. Tú y Gustavo ...estáis/están haciendo... (hacer) deporte.

G10 Complete las conversaciones con la forma correcta del verbo y un pronombre de objeto indirecto.

- Nuria, ¿te interesa la política?
- No, pero (1) ...me encanta... (encantar) la historia.

- ¿Les preocupa estar lejos de la familia?
- Sí, (2) ...nos preocupa... (preocupar) bastante.

- ¿A Vicente (3) ...le interesa... (interesar) la música clásica?
- No, no (4) ...le gusta... (gustar) mucho.

- ¿A José (5) ...le interesan... (interesar) los deportes?
- No, no (6) ...le preocupa... (preocupar) estar en buen estado físico.

Practice more at **vhlcentral.com.**

7A

GRAMÁTICA FUNCIONAL

Suggestion Point out that not all adverbs end in **-mente**; have students name a few that they already know (**bien, mal**). Then explain that some adverbs can take either the **-mente** ending or remain in the masculine form (**lento, rápido, bajo, suave**).

- Remember that in this construction, the object or activity that is *liked/of interest/worrisome* is the subject of the verb.

  Me interesa **el cine**, pero me encantan **las telenovelas**.
  *I'm interested in **film**, but I love **soap operas**.*

- As you learned in 4A.2 with **gustar**, use **a + mí, ti, usted, él, ella, nosotros/as, vosotros/as, ustedes, ellos/as**, or **a** + [*person's name*] for emphasis or clarification.

  A Samuel le interesa la política internacional,
  pero **a su hermana**, no.
  ***Samuel** is interested in international politics,*
  *but **his sister** isn't.*

  (A mis amigos y a mí) **nos interesan** los deportes.
  *Sports **are of interest to** us.*

- Note that the third-person singular is used with an infinitive or a series of infinitives.

  A Susana **le encanta** jugar con su hijo.
  *Susana **loves** playing with her son.*

  Me encanta cantar, bailar y escuchar música.
  ***I love** to sing, dance, and listen to music.*

7A.5 Describe ongoing actions

Adverbs 11

- Adverbs (**adverbios**) modify verbs, adjectives, or other adverbs, and are invariable. Many adverbs in Spanish are formed by adding **-mente** to the feminine form of the adjective, much like the English ending *-ly*.

adjective (*fem. sing.*)		adverb
exacta		**exactamente**
preferible	+ **mente**	**preferiblemente**
difícil		**difícilmente**

Actualmente estoy componiendo canciones.
***Currently** I am composing songs.*

- When the adjective has a written accent, the accent is maintained in the adverb as well.

  Últimamente estoy trabajando hasta muy tarde.
  ***Lately** I am working very late.*

- Some common adverbs ending in **-mente** have an equivalent form in the construction **en** + [*adjective*].

en concreto	concretamente
en general	generalmente
en especial	especialmente
en particular	particularmente

¡Póngalo en práctica!

G11 Escriba oraciones completas.

1. a Federico y a Delia / interesar / los edificios modernos
   (A Federico y a Delia) les interesan los edificios modernos.
2. a ti / preocupar / el examen de matemáticas
   (A ti) te preocupa el examen de matemáticas.
3. a Consuelo y a Rodrigo / encantar / ir a la playa
   (A Consuelo y a Rodrigo) les encanta ir a la playa.
4. a nosotros / interesar / las novelas inglesas
   (A nosotros) nos interesan las novelas inglesas.
5. a mí / encantar / la clase de yoga
   (A mí) me encanta la clase de yoga.
6. a Esteban / preocupar / las decisiones importantes
   (A Esteban) le preocupan las decisiones importantes.
7. a Paco / interesar / estudiar otras lenguas
   (A Paco) le interesa estudiar otras lenguas.
8. a vosotros / encantar / viajar
   (A vosotros) os encanta viajar.

G12 Escriba el adverbio que corresponde a cada adjetivo. **G12 Expansion** Have students create sentences using these adverbs.

1.	práctico	prácticamente
2.	triste	tristemente
3.	fácil	fácilmente
4.	seguro	seguramente
5.	frecuente	frecuentemente

G13 Cambie los adjetivos a adverbios y complete las oraciones con el adverbio apropiado. Use cada adverbio una sola vez.

general · paciente · lento · inmediato · actual

1. Esperé al doctor ....pacientemente.......... por una hora.
2. Leo ....lentamente.......... cuando estudio porque quiero entender bien el material.
3. ....Actualmente.......... estoy trabajando en el restaurante de mi tío, pero me interesa el teatro.
4. ..En general / Generalmente.. la gente de mi pueblo va a trabajar en autobús, pero algunas personas van en coche.
5. Cuando Juan escuchó la alarma de incendio, llamó ....inmediatamente.......... a los bomberos.

Practice more at **vhlcentral.com.**

VOCABULARIO

El día a día

el día a día	daily life
el/la bailaor(a)	flamenco dancer
el bailarín/la bailarina	dancer
el baile flamenco	flamenco dance
el/la bombero/a	firefighter
el camión	truck
el/la camionero/a	truck driver
el diseño gráfico	graphic design
el ensayo	rehearsal
la enseñanza	teaching
el espectáculo	show
el hábito	habit
el incendio	fire
el riesgo	risk
la rutina	routine
la vocación	vocation
acostarse (o:ue)	to go to bed
apagar	to put out
compaginar	to combine
(hacer) compañía	(to keep) company
conducir (zc)	to drive
cuidar (a/de) alguien	to take care of someone
dedicarse a (hacer) algo	to do something (for a living)
despertarse (e:ie)	to wake up
ducharse	to shower
enseñar	to teach
levantarse	to get up
maquillarse	to put makeup on
traducir (zc)	to translate
transportar	to transport
vestirse (e:i)	to get dressed
difícil	hard; difficult
juvenil	for young people
solo/a	alone
en equipo	as a team
por vocación	by vocation
tarde	late
temprano	early

Intereses

los cómics	comics
el jazz	jazz
el pasatiempo	pastime
la preocupación	worry; concern
la salud	health
el tailandés	Thai
Tailandia	Thailand
el trabajo voluntario	volunteer work
la trompeta	trumpet
atender (e:ie)	to attend to
dar un ejemplo	to give an example
estar en forma	to be fit, in (good) shape
estar haciendo algo	to be doing something
hacer deporte	to exercise
interesar	to be of interest
jugar (u:ue)	to play
preocupar	to worry; to concern
clásico/a	classic
al mismo tiempo	at the same time

Successful Language Learning Have students group vocabulary words from this lesson into word families. Have them add other words they know or look up a few in a dictionary. Ex: **el/la bailaor(a), el/la bailarín/bailarina, el baile;** additional words: **bailar, bailable**

Jorge Drexler

tanto... como	both . . . and
el actor/la actriz	actor/actress
el/la (ingeniero/a) agrónomo/a	agronomist
la canción	song
el/la cantautor(a)	singer-songwriter
el conflicto	conflict
el disco	album
la diversidad	diversity
la energía	energy
la frontera	border
el/la guitarrista	guitarist
el hebreo	Hebrew
el/la judío/a	Jew
la letra	lyrics
el periódico	newspaper
el/la trovador(a)	troubadour
la variedad	variety
asustar	to frighten
componer (ng)	to compose
convertirse (e:ie) en	to become
dar un concierto	to give a concert
decir (g) (e:i)	to say; to tell
editar	to edit; to release
elegir (j) (e:i)	to choose
estar de viaje	to be away
interpretar	to perform
madrugar	to get up early
preparar	to make; to prepare
influyente	influential
rico/a	rich
uruguayo/a	Uruguayan
vital	vital
actualmente	currently
de hecho	in fact
desde entonces	since then
entonces	then; so
especialmente	specially
últimamente	lately
a pesar de (que)	despite

Variación léxica

conducir ↔ **manejar** (*Amér. L.*)

dar un ejemplo ↔ **poner un ejemplo**

elegir (e:i) ↔ **escoger**

vestirse ↔ **ponerse la ropa**

7B CAMBIO DE VIDA

Madre trabajadora

Suggestion After completing the activities on this page, ask students to draft a response to Carla's e-mail.

Mensaje nuevo

Enviar | Chat | Adjuntar | Agenda | Tipo de letra | Colores | Borrador

De: Carla
Para: Marta
Asunto: Vuelta al trabajo

Folleto sobre ruedas

Querida Marta:

¿Cómo estás? He estado cuatro meses de baja por maternidad y esta semana he vuelto al trabajo. ¡Cuántos cambios! Me ha gustado ver a mis compañeros. Los he visto estupendos. Esta semana he tenido mucho trabajo, así que he dejado al niño con mis padres... He puesto al día mi agenda y ¡hoy he escrito más de cincuenta correos!

Te envío el nuevo folleto de mi empresa. Lo hemos actualizado.

¿Qué has hecho tú esta semana? Me ha dicho Rosa que has estado de vacaciones fuera de España.

Un beso,

Carla

Hablar de experiencias recientes

- ¿Qué has **hecho** hoy? ¿Has **visto** a Carla?
- No, no **la** he visto. Pero he hablado con ella.

7B.1 Present perfect with direct object pronouns
Irregular past participles

Vocabulario

1

la madre trabajadora *working mother*
traer *to bring*
el paquete *package*
la baja por maternidad (*Esp.*) *maternity leave*
dejar *to leave; to quit*
poner al día *to bring up to date*
enviar *to send*
actualizar *to update*
estar de vacaciones *to be on vacation*
la mensajería *courier company, messenger company*

3

la entrada *ticket*
el taller (mecánico) *repair shop*
el frigorífico (*Esp.*) *refrigerator*

1 a. Fíjese en la imagen del folleto. ¿A qué cree que se dedica esta empresa? ¿Conoce una empresa similar? Es una empresa de mensajería ecológica.

b. Lea el correo de Carla. ¿Por qué ha sido una semana especial?
Porque ha vuelto al trabajo después de cuatro meses de baja por maternidad.

2 Subraye en el texto qué ha hecho Carla esta semana. Relacione las formas irregulares con su infinitivo.

1. vuelto ..e..	4. escrito ..b..	a. hacer	d. decir
2. visto ..c..	5. hecho ..a..	b. escribir	e. volver
3. puesto ..f..	6. dicho ..d..	c. ver	f. poner

3 a. Carla habla por la noche con su marido sobre lo que han hecho en el día. Escuche la conversación. ¿Qué ha hecho cada uno?

	Carla	Ángel
- sacar las entradas para el teatro		
- llamar a sus padres	✓	
- llevar el coche al taller	✓	
- hacer las compras		✓

b. Represente con su compañero/a este fragmento de la conversación.

- ¿Has sacado las entradas para el teatro?
- Sí, las he sacado para el sábado por la noche. He pasado un momento por allí después del trabajo y antes de llevar el coche al taller.
- ¿Lo has llevado? ¡Menos mal! ¡Ah! ¿Y has llamado a tus padres? Yo no he podido llamar...
- Pues yo sí, los he llamado esta mañana.

c. Indique a qué se refieren las palabras subrayadas. las: las entradas; lo: el coche; los: sus padres

d. Con un(a) compañero/a, represente una conversación sobre lo que han hecho durante el día. Usen *la, las, lo* y *los* para referirse a cosas o personas ya mencionadas.

Suggestion Point out that **enviar** carries a written accent on all conjugated forms in the present indicative, except **nosotros/as.**

QUIÉNES SOMOS

Hacer hipótesis

- Quizás Carla tiene trabajo y ha olvidado enviar el correo.
- Creo que sí, es posible.

7B.2 **creo que sí/no, quizás, es posible**

Vocabulario

(4)
repartir *to deliver*
Creo que sí./no. *I think so./not.*
el/la auxiliar *assistant*
el/la mecánico, administrativo/a

(7)
la actividad laboral *job*
la licencia por maternidad (*Amér. L.*) *maternity leave*
el/la reportero/a

Baja por maternidad

En España las mujeres tienen 4 meses de licencia por maternidad. Los hombres casi no toman licencias para cuidar a los hijos. En muchos casos lo hacen los abuelos. En otros, se buscan trabajos que dejan más tiempo para la familia.

4 a. Fíjese en la imagen. ¿A qué se dedican los empleados de Sobre ruedas?
Silvio Villa y Pedro Simón son mensajeros, Sara Santos es directora, Manolo García es mecánico y Carla López es auxiliar administrativa.
b. Lea lo que están pensando los empleados y subraye las expresiones para hacer hipótesis.

5 Lea lo que están pensando Manolo y Sara. ¿Qué relación existe entre ellos? Con un(a) compañero/a, haga hipótesis.

Modelo: • *Quizás a Manolo le gusta Sara.* • *Es posible.*

6 ¿Cree que sus compañeros/as han hecho algo especial esta semana? Reaccione ante las hipótesis de sus compañeros/as.

Modelo: • *Yo creo que John ha ido a un concierto...* • *No sé, quizás...*

MI EXPERIENCIA

Suggestion Have students work in pairs to write mini-conversations between the employees, using the vocabulary from these pages.

7 Piense en una actividad laboral ideal y explique a sus compañeros/as qué ha hecho esta semana. Sus compañeros/as adivinan qué profesión es.

GUIÓN DE TRABAJO

¿Qué has hecho esta semana?

¿Has escrito un artículo?
Sí, sí lo he escrito.

¿Dónde trabajas?
Trabajo en una oficina pero viajo mucho.

Creo que eres reportero.

Practice more at **vhlcentral.com.**

SAM: Actividades pp. 145–147

Un día negro

EL BLOG DE SILVIO

Mi perfil
Nombre: Silvio Villa
Nacionalidad: colombiano
Edad: 32 años

Un día negro

Hoy he tenido un día negro en la oficina, de esos en los que todo va mal.

La copiadora...... no funciona, la computadora.... va muy lenta y la impresora..... no puede imprimir. No puedes recibir ni enviar correos........., un virus ha invadido la red y todos los archivos....... han desaparecido. El ratón............. está bloqueado y tampoco puedes llamar al servicio técnico porque el teléfono no funciona, pero... ¡no hay problema!, para eso tienes tu celular............ ...sin batería.

He perdido mucho tiempo y ¡no he podido entregar los paquetes a tiempo!

Pedir y ofrecer ayuda

- ¿Puedes ayudarme?
- Sí, claro. ¿Qué necesitas?
- ¿Me ayudas?
- ¡Claro! Por supuesto.
- ¿Te puedo ayudar?
- Sí, por favor.
- ¿Te ayudo?
- No, gracias. Estoy bien.

7B.3 **poder** + [*infinitive*]
ayudar, necesitar

Vocabulario

8

ir mal *to go wrong*
la (foto)copiadora *photocopier*
funcionar *to function, to work*
lento/a *slow*
la impresora *printer*
imprimir *to print*
el archivo *file*
el ratón *mouse*
bloqueado/a *locked; blocked*
¡No hay problema! *No problem!*
perder (e:ie) *to lose*
a tiempo *in/on time*
el ordenador (*Esp.*) *computer*
la computadora, la batería

9

Estoy bien. *I'm OK.*

10

mandar *to send*
guardar *to save*
el fax

8 a. Lea el blog de Silvio Villa y busque en el recuadro las palabras que faltan.

archivos • celular • computadora • copiadora • correo • impresora • ratón

b. ¿Sabe qué palabras se usan en España (*Esp.*) y cuáles en Latinoamérica (LA.)? Márquelas.

	Esp.	(LA.)		Esp.	(LA.)		Esp.	(LA.)
la computadora		✓	el móvil	✓		la copiadora		✓
el ordenador	✓		el celular		✓	la fotocopiadora	✓	

8b Suggestion As a class, reword Silvio's blog using synonyms from this page (**ordenador, mandar,** etc.).

9 a. Escuche las conversaciones y ordénelas.

1

A. Silvio, ¿puedo ayudarte? [1]
B. ¡Por supuesto! [3]
C. Sí, por favor. En esta oficina no funciona nada y tengo mucho trabajo: mi computadora está loca... ¿puedes venir un momento, por favor? [2]

2

A. Sí, claro. ¿Necesita el móvil o el fijo? [2]
B. Perdone, ¿puede decirme el teléfono del Sr. Mur? [1]
C. El móvil, por favor. [3]

9 Expansion Have students role-play the conversations in pairs.

b. Relacione las preguntas con las respuestas.

1. ¿Puedes decirme el teléfono de Sonia? ..b....
2. Perdone, ¿puedo ayudarlo? ..d...
3. ¿Puedes ayudarme un momento? ..c/a..
4. ¿Me ayudas? ..a/c..

a. Sí, ¿qué necesitas?
b. Sí, claro. Es el 897 38 97.
c. Por supuesto.
d. Sí, por favor.

10 Pida ayuda a su compañero/a para hacer las siguientes cosas. Su compañero/a reacciona usando las expresiones de la actividad anterior.

1. mandar un fax
2. guardar un archivo
3. escribir un correo en español
4. usar la impresora
5. llamar al servicio técnico

Cuando trabajé por primera vez con españoles, me llamó la atención una cosa en concreto: la costumbre del tuteo. La gente en el trabajo se habla de *tú*, especialmente los colegas, y muchas veces el jefe y sus empleados también se hablan de *tú*.

Eso es imposible en mi país, Colombia, donde incluso los colegas se hablan de *usted*.

En España, en general la gente se habla de *tú* con los vecinos, en la calle y en las tiendas. Con las personas mayores, sin embargo, normalmente se habla de *usted*. Yo ahora ya me he acostumbrado, y me gusta.

Have students state which register they would prefer to use in these situations.

Vocabulario

11

- **en concreto** *in particular*
- **el tuteo** *use of* tú
- **hablarse de *tú*** *to address somebody as* tú
- **el/la colega** *colleague*
- **hablarse de *usted*** *to address somebody as* usted
- **el/la vecino/a** *neighbor*
- **concretamente** *specifically*
- **generalmente** *generally*
- **en especial** *especially*

13

- **la reunión** *meeting*
- **laboral** *working*

Estrategia

Generalizar y matizar

Generalmente la gente se habla de *tú*, especialmente en el trabajo. El trato es, en general, informal.

Horarios laborales

En los países hispanos la jornada laboral es normalmente partida, es decir, con una parada para comer de una o dos horas. En América Latina la pausa de la comida es normalmente a las 12:00 o las 13:00 h. En España, descansan entre las 13:00 y las 15:00 h. En las empresas españolas existe generalmente la jornada reducida en verano.

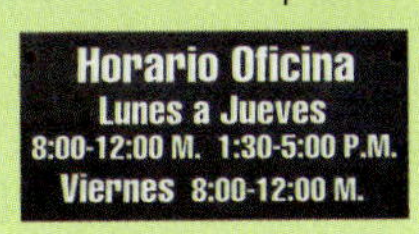

Suggestion Have students read the sign and ask them if it is from Latin America or Spain and explain how they can tell.

11 a. Lea el blog de Silvio. ¿Qué le llamó la atención en España?

la costumbre del tuteo

b. Observe las siguientes expresiones y complete el recuadro.

en concreto	concretamente
en general	generalmente
en especial	especialmente
en particular	particularmente

12 a. Una española y dos latinoamericanos hablan sobre las formas de tratamiento (*forms of adresss*) que usan generalmente. Observe el resumen y comente las diferencias con un(a) compañero/a.

Con.... hablo de...	Sara, española	Lucas, colombiano	Marta, uruguaya
los compañeros de clase	tú	tú	vos*
el jefe	usted	usted	usted
los vecinos	tú	tú	vos*
mis padres	tú	usted	vos*
las personas mayores	usted	usted	vos*

* El uso de *vos* en lugar de *tú* es común en varios países de Sudamérica y América Central, en particular en Uruguay y Argentina.

b. Lea la nota sobre los horarios laborales en España. ¿Son iguales en su país?

12 Ask students if they know native Spanish speakers and have them fill out a table indicating the forms of address that their friends and acquaintances generally use.

MI EXPERIENCIA

13 Piense en un día de trabajo en una oficina y anote las situaciones o problemas que ocurren. Pida y ofrezca ayuda en estas situaciones.

GUIÓN DE TRABAJO

La impresora no funciona. Esto es un problema, especialmente si tienes una reunión urgente porque...

→ ¿Puedes ayudarme? ¿Me puedes ayudar?
Sí, ¿qué necesitas?

→ ¿Puedo ayudarte? ¿Te puedo ayudar?
Sí, por favor.

Generalmente es difícil...
Especialmente...
En concreto...

Practice more at vhlcentral.com.

SAM: Actividades pp. 148–150

Guadalupe Rodríguez, una nueva etapa

En Villahermosa del Río, un pueblo ubicado en las montañas de la provincia de Castellón, vive y trabaja desde hace cuatro años Guadalupe Rodríguez con su familia. La vida de esta mujer argentina nacida en Córdoba y su marido escocés ha cambiado completamente desde que se mudaron de un apartamento céntrico en Londres a una masía en España.

"En algunos aspectos vivimos como hace cien años."

Guadalupe habla de su experiencia: "El invierno es muy duro y a veces no se puede salir de la masía para llegar al pueblo por la nieve. La casa es muy antigua y hemos abandonado muchas de las comodidades de la ciudad, pero esto nos gusta.

¿Estamos locos? Quizás... Aquí se puede respirar aire puro, tener animales, vivir en contacto con la naturaleza y ser autosuficiente. Esto no se puede hacer en la ciudad.

"Tengo más tiempo para mis hijas."

Este año ha sido muy intenso. Hemos hecho muchas cosas nuevas: hemos arreglado la casa, la hemos pintado... Además hemos empezado nuestro proyecto: La Ecocesta, un sistema de reparto de productos ecológicos a domicilio. Trabajamos con otros agricultores de la zona."

Guadalupe Rodríguez y sus dos hijas en su casa de Villahermosa del Río Ask students if they or anyone they know has made a major life change like Guadalupe's, either from the city to the country or vice versa, or from one country or region to another.

Expresar posibilidad

Aquí **no se puede** ir al cine o salir a cenar... pero sí **se puede** tener una vida más saludable.

7B.4 **(no) se puede**

Vocabulario

14

- **escocés/escocesa** *Scottish*
- **cambiar** *to change*
- **mudarse** *to move (from home)*
- **céntrico/a** *in the centre of town*
- **la masía** *country house (Cataluña)*
- **duro/a** *hard; tough*
- **No se puede...** *You/One can't...*
- **abandonar** *to leave; to give up*
- **las comodidades** *comforts*
- **loco/a** *crazy*
- **respirar** *to breathe*
- **autosuficiente** *self-sufficient*
- **ecológico/a** (*Esp.*) *organic*
- **arreglar** *to repair*
- **el reparto a domicilio** *home delivery*
- **el/la agricultor(a)** *farmer*
- **el negocio** *business; store*
- **la provincia, el aspecto, el aire, puro/a, el animal**

14 a. ¿Cómo ha cambiado la vida de Guadalupe? ¿Por qué es una nueva etapa?
Ya no vive en la ciudad. Vive en una masía.
b. ¿En qué consiste el negocio de Guadalupe? Es un sistema de reparto de productos ecológicos a domicilio.

15 ¿Qué se puede y qué no se puede hacer en el pueblo de Guadalupe?
No se puede: salir de la masía para llegar al pueblo en invierno; se puede: respirar aire puro, tener animales, vivir en contacto con la naturaleza, ser autosuficiente.

16 Escuche a Guadalupe y marque **verdadero (V)** o **falso (F)**.

	V	F
1. A las niñas les gusta más vivir en el pueblo que en la ciudad.	✓	
2. En el pueblo donde viven hay muchos niños.		✓
3. Sus padres no tienen tiempo para estar con ellas.		✓

17 ¿Cómo es la vida en el lugar donde usted vive? Haga una lista de las posibilidades que ofrece y coméntelas con su compañero/a.

Modelo: • *En mi ciudad/pueblo se puede vivir tranquilo.*
• *En mi ciudad/pueblo no se puede ir al cine.*

18 ¿Cuál de estos cambios de vida prefiere? Explique por qué.

mudarse a otro país — cambiar de trabajo — cambiar de carrera — hacerse vegetariano/a — desconectarse de la tecnología

Modelo: *Prefiero cambiar de trabajo porque se puede conocer gente nueva.*

Vocabulario *cont.*

18

cambiar de vida *to change one's life*
cambiar de trabajo *to change jobs*
hacerse vegetariano/a *to become a vegetarian*
desconectarse *to disconnect (oneself)*

19

sano/a *healthy*
equilibrado/a *balanced*
la cesta *basket*
el pedido *order; request*
la entrega *delivery*
a tu servicio *at your service*
variado/a *assorted*
el pago *payment*
la transferencia bancaria *bank transfer*
la dieta, la manipulación genética, estándar

22

crecer (zc) *to grow*
cultivar *to grow; to cultivate*
mundial *global, worldwide*
la miel *honey*
la hortaliza *vegetable*
orgánico/a, exportar

OPINIÓN

¿Qué piensa de la opción que eligieron Guadalupe Rodríguez y su familia? ¿Cree que se puede cambiar de vida fácilmente?

¡OJO!

Primero and **tercero** drop their final **o** when used before masculine singular nouns, as in **el primer capítulo** or **el tercer año**. This rule does not apply to **primera** and **tercera**. So you should say, for example, **la primera vez** and **la tercera calle**.

20 Suggestion Ask students if there are any services in your region similar to **Ecocesta,** such as a CSA (Community Supported Agriculture). If possible, bring in brochures or information from CSA websites and have students compare and contrast the products, prices, and services.

19 Lea el folleto de La Ecocesta y complete la información.

La Ecocesta

Una dieta ecológica es mejor para el medio ambiente y para tu salud. En La Ecocesta hay todo lo que se necesita para una alimentación sana y equilibrada: verduras, frutas y otros productos naturales (leche, pan, huevos, queso). Nuestros alimentos son totalmente ecológicos, sin productos químicos y sin manipulación genética. Nuestro servicio a domicilio lleva la ecocesta a tu casa. Se puede elegir entre tres tipos diferentes de cesta y cambiar el pedido hasta 24 horas antes de la entrega. Escríbenos un correo electrónico o llámanos. ¡Estamos a tu servicio!

TIPOS DE CESTA		PRECIOS
Estándar:	3 kg de fruta y otros productos variados	30 €
Frutimix:	4 kg de fruta	12 €
Verdumix:	4 kg de verdura	10 €

FORMAS DE PAGO
Transferencia bancaria o en efectivo.

Remind students that 1 kilogram is equivalent to 2.2 pounds, and 1 euro is worth about 1.30 U.S. dollars. Ask students if they think Ecocesta's prices are low or high.

1. Las formas de pago son transferencia bancaria o en efectivo.
2. Las posibilidades que ofrece el servicio son servicio a domicilio, posibilidad de elegir entre tres tipos de cesta y cambiar el pedido hasta 24 horas antes de la entrega
3. Los productos ecológicos son los que no llevan productos químicos ni manipulación genética.

20 a. Observe la foto. ¿Conoce el nombre de estos productos en español?
maíz, piña, pimiento, tomate, pepino, calabaza, aguacate, papaya, papa, frutos secos

b. ¿Cree que los productos ecológicos son mejores para la salud? ¿Conoce un sistema de compra parecido en su país? ¿Lo utiliza?

21 Escriba un correo a La Ecocesta para hacer un pedido. Detalle su listado de alimentos, cantidad y forma de pago. Recuerde estas expresiones útiles.

Estimados señores: | Quería solicitar... | Un saludo,

22 a. Lea esta información sobre la agricultura ecológica en México. ¿Cómo es la situación en su país?

La agricultura ecológica crece en el mundo entre el 20% y el 25% al año. En México en los últimos 15 años, el área cultivada aumentó de 25 000 a unas 400 000 hectáreas, y es el primer productor y exportador mundial de café orgánico. También produce miel, bebidas, frutas y hortalizas, carne, leche y queso. Casi el 85% de los alimentos orgánicos que se producen en México se exportan a Europa, los Estados Unidos y Japón.

b. ¿En qué tipo de países se consume la mayor parte de los alimentos ecológicos producidos en México? ¿Por qué cree que esto es así?

22 Suggestion Have students report to the class about their classmates' answers.

Practice more at **vhlcentral.com.**

SAM: Actividades pp. 151–156

23 Juegue con sus compañeros/as. Tiren dos dados para decidir qué grupo empieza la serie de preguntas y respondan a la pregunta de la casilla correspondiente.

1. ¿A qué te dedicas?
2. ¿Qué has estudiado en esta lección?
3. ¿Qué has hecho hoy?
4. No sabes el teléfono de tu profesor(a). Pregunta a tus compañeros/as.
5. ¿Qué actividades has practicado en el último año?
6. ¿Qué cosas se pueden hacer en un pueblo? ¿Y en una ciudad?
7. ¿Qué cosas no se pueden hacer en tu trabajo?
8. ¿Has comprado alguna vez productos ecológicos?
9. ¿En España generalmente la gente se habla de *tú* en el trabajo?
10. No sabes enviar un fax. Pide ayuda a tu compañero/a.
11. Tu compañero/a no encuentra un archivo. Ofrécele ayuda.
12. ¿Qué cosas crees que necesitas mejorar de tu español?

¿Tienes otras preguntas? Es tu turno. Pregunta a tus compañeros/as.

TAREA FINAL

Una nueva vida

- Hagan una lista de lugares conocidos (pueblos, ciudades...). Elijan uno de ellos.
- Decidan a qué se quieren dedicar y dónde quieren vivir.
- Hagan una pequeña descripción de su nueva vida. Cuenten al grupo, por ejemplo, lo que han hecho los últimos días.
- Elijan la alternativa más original.

YO PUEDO...

- **Puedo hablar sobre experiencias recientes.**
  Escriba una lista de todo lo que ha hecho hoy antes de ir a la clase de español.
- **Puedo hacer hipótesis.**
  Piense en una hipótesis sobre algo dudoso.
- **Puedo pedir y ofrecer ayuda.**
  Cree una conversación. Alguien le pide ayuda y otro la ofrece.
- **Puedo expresar posibilidad.**
  Escriba una lista de cosas que se puede y no se puede hacer en su trabajo.

GRAMÁTICA FUNCIONAL

7B.1 Talk about recent experiences

Irregular past participles 5.3.2
Present perfect with direct object pronouns 5.3.3

- In 6A.4, you learned to use the present perfect (**el pretérito perfecto**) to talk about past actions that are connected to the present. Remember that the **pretérito perfecto** is a compound tense composed of two parts: **haber** + [*past participle*]. You have already learned how to form the past participle with regular verbs. Several common verbs have irregular past participles.

abrir	→	**abierto**	poner	→	**puesto**
decir		**dicho**	ver		**visto**
escribir		**escrito**	volver		**vuelto**
hacer		**hecho**			

Marta ya ha **vuelto** a casa, pero no ha **hecho** la tarea.
Marta already came home, but she hasn't done her homework.

- The two components of the **pretérito perfecto** always appear together and cannot be separated by another word. When you use a direct object pronoun, place it before the conjugated form of **haber**. As you saw in 3B.7, direct object pronouns (**lo, la, los, las**) are used to refer to people or things that have been mentioned previously.

¿Has hecho la comida? Sí, **la** he hecho.
*Have you made the food? Yes, I have made **it**.*

- Likewise, when you use a reflexive verb in the **pretérito perfecto**, place the reflexive pronoun before the conjugated form of **haber**.

Yo ya **me** he duchado, pero Julia no **se** ha levantado todavía.
I have already showered, but Julia hasn't gotten up yet.

- Note that past participles may also be used as adjectives, in which case the normal rules of agreement apply.

Las ventanas están **abiertas**.
The windows are open.

Suggestion In pairs, have students discuss three things they have already done today and three things they have not done yet.

7B.2 Make hypotheses

creo que sí/no; quizás; es posible 11.5

- Use **quizás** (*perhaps; maybe*) to speculate or make hypotheses.

Quizás Manolo ya ha hecho las compras.
***Maybe** Manolo has already done the shopping.*

- To agree with someone's speculation, say **creo que sí** (*I think so*); to show some agreement, say **es posible** (*it's possible*); and to disagree, say **creo que no** (*I don't think so; I think not*).

Quizás Analía tiene un nuevo novio.
Maybe Analía has a new boyfriend.

Creo que sí./Es posible./Creo que no.
I think so./It's possible./I don't think so.

Suggestion Have students write five sentences about themselves or people they know; three of the statements should be true and two should be false. Then, have groups of students read their statements aloud; the other group members should react with **creo que sí, es posible,** and **creo que no.**

7B.1 You may want to explain that the Spanish equivalent of *to have just [done something]* is [present tense of **acabar**] + **de** + [infinitive].

¡Póngalo en práctica!

G1 Complete la conversación con las formas correctas del pretérito perfecto.

- ¡Hola, Paula! ¿Qué (1) has hecho (hacer) este verano?
- Bueno, este verano (2) he vuelto (volver) al pueblo y (3) he visto (ver) a mis amigos de la infancia.
- ¿Y qué (4) han hecho (hacer) Antonio y Clara esta semana?
- Esta semana (5) han vuelto (volver) de sus vacaciones. (6) Han escrito (Escribir) un blog sobre su viaje al Caribe.
- ¡Qué bien! Mi tía me (7) ha dicho (decir) que quiere hablar con ellos sobre su viaje.
- Sí, ellos me (8) han comentado (comentar) lo mismo. La van a llamar pronto.

G2 Complete las oraciones con un pronombre de objeto directo.

1. ● ¿Has comprado los billetes?
   ■ No, no los he comprado.
2. El reportero ha escrito un artículo y lo ha enviado a su jefe.
3. ● ¿Habéis visto a Carla?
   ■ Sí, la hemos visto.
4. La torta está muy rica. ¿La has probado?
5. ● ¿Ha comprado Toño el libro de español?
   ■ No, no lo ha comprado.
6. Has hecho una comida muy rica. La hemos comido con mucho gusto.

G3 Complete las conversaciones de manera lógica.
Suggested answers:

creo que sí **quizás** **creo que no** **es posible**

- ¿Crees que Marisa dejó su trabajo?
- No, (1) creo que no
- Paula es de Colombia, ¿no?
- Sí, (2) creo que sí
- ¿Dónde está Raquel? No la he visto hoy.
- (3) Quizás está enferma.
- Sí, (4) es posible

Practice more at **vhlcentral.com.**

GRAMÁTICA FUNCIONAL

7B.3 Ask for and offer help

poder + [*infinitive*]; **ayudar**; **necesitar** 5.1.1, 5.10
Placement of object pronouns 6.2.4

- Use the construction **poder** + [*infinitive*] (*to be able to; can*) to ask for and offer help.

  ¿**Puedes imprimir** estos documentos?
  ***Can you print** these documents?*

  Por supuesto, los **puedo imprimir**.
  *Of course, **I can print** them.*

- **Poder** is often used with the regular **-ar** verb **ayudar** (*to help*) to ask for or offer help.

  ¿Te puedo **ayudar**? — *Can I **help** you?*
  ¿Me puede **ayudar**? — *Can you **help** me?*

- When using an object pronoun with an infinitive construction, the object pronoun may be placed before the conjugated verb or attached to the end of the infinitive.

  ¿**Nos** puedes ayudar?/¿Puedes ayudar**nos**?
  *Can you help **us**?*

- **Ayudar** can also be used on its own in a question or a statement offering or asking for help. Place the object pronoun before the conjugated verb.

  ¿Te **ayudo**? — *Can **I help you**?*
  ¿Me **ayudas**? — *Can **you help** me?*

- Use the verb **necesitar** (*to need*) to ask what a person needs. **Necesitar** is a regular **-ar** verb.

  ¿Me puedes ayudar? — *Can you help me?*
  Sí, ¿qué **necesitas**? — *Yes, what **do you need**?*

7B.4 Express possibility

(no) se puede 5.12.1

- Use the expressions **se puede** (*you/one can*) + [*infinitive*] and **no se puede** (*you/one can't*) + [*infinitive*] to tell what can and cannot be done or what is or is not allowed.

  Aquí **se puede esquiar**, pero **no se puede patinar**.
  *Here **you can ski**, but **you can't skate**.*

- Use this construction to talk about possibilities in general, not tied to a specific person. As with other infinitive constructions, the second verb is always in the infinitive.

  En un pueblo pequeño **se puede** jugar en la calle, pero normalmente **no se puede** hacer compras en un centro comercial.
  *In a small town, **you can** play in the street, but generally **you can't** go shopping at a mall.*

Suggestion As a class, make a list of things that are and are not permitted on campus.

¡Póngalo en práctica!

G4 Complete las conversaciones con la forma correcta de **poder, ayudar** o **necesitar**.

- ¿(1) Puedes venir un momento?
- Sí, ¿qué (2) necesitas?
- ¿Me (3) ayudas con la traducción de esta carta?
- Claro, te puedo (4) ayudar.
- ¡Muchas gracias por tu ayuda!

- ¿Los puedo (5) ayudar?
- Sí, por favor.
- ¿Qué (6) necesitan?
- ¿(7) Puede decirnos la dirección?
- Sí, claro.

G5 Escriba preguntas completas.

Modelo: yo / ayudar / (a ustedes) / ¿?
¿Les ayudo?

1. yo / ayudar / (a ti) / ¿?
   ¿Te ayudo?
2. usted / ayudar / (a mí) / ¿?
   ¿Me ayuda?
3. nosotros / ayudar / (a vosotros) / ¿?
   ¿Os ayudamos?
4. tú / ayudar / (a nosotros) / ¿?
   ¿Nos ayudas?
5. ustedes / ayudar / (a mí) / ¿?
   ¿Me ayudan?

G6 Transforme las oraciones usando **se puede** y **no se puede**.

1. No podemos fumar (*smoke*) aquí.
   No se puede fumar aquí.
2. Podemos imprimir en esta oficina.
   Se puede imprimir en esta oficina.
3. Puedes cenar tarde en este restaurante.
   Se puede cenar tarde en este restaurante.
4. No podemos usar esta computadora.
   No se puede usar esta computadora.
5. Puedo ir en autobús.
   Se puede ir en autobús.
6. No podemos comer en la clase.
   No se puede comer en la clase.
7. Puedes mirar televisión en español.
   Se puede mirar televisión en español.

Suggestion Draw attention to the example questions that use **ayudar** and explain that it is used with direct object pronouns. Have them convert **¿Te ayudo?** to the formal register (**¿Lo/La ayudo?**).

Practice more at **vhlcentral.com.**

VOCABULARIO

Madre trabajadora

Creo que sí./no.	*I think so./not.*
la actividad laboral	*job*
el/la auxiliar	*assistant*
la baja por maternidad (*Esp.*)	*maternity leave*
la entrada	*ticket*
el frigorífico (*Esp.*)	*refrigerator*
la licencia por maternidad (*Amér. L.*)	*maternity leave*
la madre trabajadora	*working mother*
el/la mecánico/a	*mechanic*
la mensajería	*courier company, messenger company*
el paquete	*package*
el/la reportero/a	*reporter*
el taller (mecánico)	*repair shop*
actualizar	*to update*
dejar	*to leave; to quit*
enviar	*to send*
estar de vacaciones	*to be on vacation*
poner al día	*to bring up to date*
repartir	*to deliver*
traer	*to bring*
administrativo/a	*administrative*

Un día negro

Estoy bien.	*I'm OK.*
¡No hay problema!	*No problem!*
el archivo	*file*
la batería	*battery*
el/la colega	*colleague*
la computadora (*Amér. L.*)	*computer*
el fax	*fax*
la (foto)copiadora	*photocopier*
la impresora	*printer*
el ordenador (*Esp.*)	*computer*
el ratón	*mouse*
la reunión	*meeting*
el tuteo	*use of* **tú**
el/la vecino/a	*neighbor*
funcionar	*to function, to work*
guardar	*to save*
hablarse de *tú/usted*	*to address somebody as* **tú/usted**
imprimir	*to print*
ir mal	*to go wrong*
mandar	*to send*
perder (e:ie)	*to lose*
bloqueado/a	*locked; blocked*
laboral	*working*
lento/a	*slow*
a tiempo	*in/on time*
concretamente	*specifically*
en concreto	*in particular*
en especial	*especially*
generalmente	*generally*

Guadalupe Rodríguez

No se puede...	*You/One can't . . .*
el/la agricultor(a)	*farmer*
el aire	*air*
el animal	*animal*
el aspecto	*aspect*
la cesta	*basket*
las comodidades	*comforts*
la dieta	*diet*
la entrega	*delivery*
la hortaliza	*vegetable*
la manipulación genética	*genetic modification*
la masía	*country house (Cataluña)*
la miel	*honey*
el negocio	*business; store*
el pago	*payment*
el pedido	*order; request*
la provincia	*province*
el reparto a domicilio	*home delivery*
la transferencia bancaria	*bank transfer*
abandonar	*to leave; to give up*
arreglar	*to repair*
cambiar	*to change*
cambiar de trabajo	*to change jobs*
cambiar de vida	*to change one's life*
crecer (zc)	*to grow*
cultivar	*to grow; to cultivate*
desconectarse	*to disconnect (oneself)*
exportar	*to export*
hacerse vegetariano/a	*to become a vegetarian*
mudarse	*to move (from home)*
respirar	*to breathe*
autosuficiente	*self-sufficient*
céntrico/a	*in the centre of town*
duro/a	*hard; tough*
ecológico/a (*Esp.*)	*organic*
equilibrado/a	*balanced*
escocés/escocesa	*Scottish*
estándar	*standard*
loco/a	*crazy*
mundial	*global, worldwide*
orgánico/a (*Amér. L.*)	*organic*
puro/a	*pure*
sano/a	*healthy*
variado/a	*assorted*
a tu servicio	*at your service*

Variación léxica

los alimentos ecológicos (*Esp.*) ⟷ **los alimentos orgánicos** (*Amér. L.*)

la baja por maternidad (*Esp.*) ⟷ **la licencia por maternidad** (*Amér. L.*) ⟷ **el permiso por maternidad**

la cesta (*Esp.*) ⟷ **la canasta** (*Amér. L.*)

la computadora (*Amér. L.*) ⟷ **el ordenador** (*Esp.*)

la copiadora (*Cub., Méx.*) ⟷ **la fotocopiadora** (*Esp., Arg.*)

poner al día ⟷ **actualizar**

el ratón ⟷ **el mouse** (*Arg.*)

el refrigerador ⟷ **la nevera** (*Esp.*) ⟷ **el frigorífico** (*Esp.*) ⟷ **la refrigeradora** ⟷ **la heladera** (*Arg.*)

Vocabulario útil

la baja (*Esp.*)/el permiso/la licencia por enfermedad *sick leave*
el día libre *day off*
disfrutar (de) *to enjoy*
faltar (al trabajo) *to be absent, to take time off work*
los feriados (*Amér. L.*)/los días festivos (*Esp.*) *holidays*
librar (*Esp.*) *to have the day off work*
los logros *achievements*
estar en el paro (*Esp.*); estar desocupado/a *to be unemployed*
el paro (*Amér. L.*)/la huelga *strike*
el sindicato *union*
tomarse (las vacaciones) *to take (a vacation)*

Estrategia

Types of information

When reading a text, start by identifying what type of information is provided: definitions, problems and solutions, cause and effect, or comparison and contrast. Then, you can list the facts using a diagram, chart, or graphic organizer in order to compare or match the different concepts; organizing ideas this way will help you make sense of the information. In the article above, what type of information do you find? What are the important pieces of information in the text? Are there numbers, names, and specific terms?

Suggestion Read through the **Estrategia** with students and have them decide what type of visual would best organize the information. Create one on board and add to it as you go through the reading as a class.

LECTURA

Beneficios en los empleos

Alguien dijo que lo mejor del trabajo son las vacaciones... En algunos países hay más días libres y beneficios laborales° que en otros. En Estados Unidos se otorga° una licencia por maternidad de doce semanas, pero puede ser pagada o no: eso depende de cada empresa. En algunos países latinoamericanos, la ley° se ocupa de que esta licencia sea pagada°. Por ejemplo, Chile y Venezuela ofrecen dieciocho semanas de licencia a las madres trabajadoras y les pagan el 100% de su salario durante° ese tiempo. En el otro extremo se encuentra Paraguay, que concede° sólo la mitad° del salario y únicamente durante nueve de las doce semanas de licencia por maternidad.

1 Converse con un(a) compañero/a: ¿Todos los años usted se toma vacaciones? ¿Qué prefiere: un trabajo interesante con pocas vacaciones o un trabajo aburrido con más vacaciones? ¿Alguna vez se tomó un día libre con la excusa de estar enfermo/a? ¿Ha participado en alguna huelga o manifestación laboral o estudiantil?

2 A partir de la lectura, identifique el país de origen de las personas que dicen estas oraciones.

1. Estoy disfrutando cuatro meses de licencia por maternidad. Chile y Venezuela
2. Ella está preocupada porque recibe la mitad de su salario durante la licencia y ahora tiene un bebé. Paraguay
3. Me interesa festejar Navidad porque para mí este feriado es algo nuevo. Cuba
4. Hoy he terminado mis treinta días de vacaciones anuales. España
5. En mi país, tenemos licencia por maternidad, pero mi empresa no me paga el salario durante ese tiempo. Estados Unidos
6. Estamos planeando las vacaciones para los veintidós días feriados de este año. Puerto Rico

2 Suggestion Have students point out the sentence(s) in the reading where they found the corresponding information.

También es importante considerar las fiestas nacionales y religiosas que suman días de vacaciones en distintos momentos del año. En España los empleados típicamente tienen treinta días de vacaciones pagadas y otros catorce días festivos al año. Puerto Rico disfruta de veintidós días feriados en su calendario porque celebra los días no laborables de Estados Unidos, los días festivos del calendario católico y algunas fiestas exclusivas del país. En México, en cambio, hay ocho feriados nacionales, uno más que en Cuba, donde el día de Navidad es fiesta sólo desde la visita del papa Juan Pablo II a la isla en 1998.

beneficios laborales *job benefits* **se otorga** *is given* **ley** *law* **sea pagada** *is paid* **durante** *throughout* **concede** *it grants* **mitad** *half*

El currículum vítae

- El currículum vítae° contiene información personal y tiene que ser muy detallado°.
- Normalmente incluye° la educación completa, todos los trabajos que ha tenido e incluso sus gustos personales y pasatiempos.
- También puede incluir detalles que no se suele incluir° en los Estados Unidos: una foto, su estado civil e incluso si tiene coche y de qué tipo.

DATOS PERSONALES
Nombre y apellidos: **Carmelo Roca**
Fecha de nacimiento: **14 de diciembre de 1978**
Lugar de nacimiento: **Salamanca**
D.N.I.: **7885270-R**
Dirección: **Calle Ferrara 17, 5 37500 Salamanca**
Teléfono: **923 270 118**
Correo electrónico: **rocac@teleline.com**

FORMACIÓN ACADÉMICA
- 2001-2002 Máster en Administración y Dirección de Empresas, Universidad Autónoma de Madrid
- 1996-2001 Licenciado en Administración y Dirección de Empresas por la Universidad de Salamanca

CURSOS Y SEMINARIOS
- 2001 "Gestión y Creación de Empresas", Universidad de Córdoba

EXPERIENCIA PROFESIONAL
- 1999-2000 Contrato de un año en la empresa RAMA S.L., realizando tareas administrativas
- 1998-1999 Contrato de trabajo haciendo prácticas en Banco Sol

IDIOMAS
- INGLÉS Nivel alto. Título de la Escuela Oficial de Idiomas
- ITALIANO Nivel medio

INFORMÁTICA/COMPUTACIÓN
- Conocimientos de usuario de Mac / Windows
- MS Office

currículum vítae *résumé* **detallado** *detailed* **incluye** *it includes* **no se suele incluir** *aren't usually included*

► Igualdad° laboral

- **United Fruit Company** fue, por casi cien años, la mayor corporación estadounidense que monopolizó° las exportaciones de frutas de América Latina. Influenció enormemente la economía y la política de la región hasta 1970.
- **Fair Trade Coffee** trabaja para proteger° a los agricultores de café de los abusos de las grandes compañías multinacionales. Ahora, en lugares como Centroamérica, los agricultores pueden obtener mejores ganancias° a través del comercio justo.
- **Oxfam International** trabaja en países como Guatemala, Ecuador, Nicaragua y Perú para concientizar a la opinión pública de que la igualdad entre las personas es tan importante como el crecimiento° económico de las naciones.

Igualdad *Equality* **monopolizó** *monopolized* **proteger** *to protect* **ganancias** *earnings* **crecimiento** *growth*

Suggestion Have students research one of the organizations under **Igualdad laboral** and prepare a brief written report.

Estrategia

Possibilities

There are several ways to express possibility in Spanish, but they generally require complex grammatical structures. A simple way to express probability is to use the indicative mood with **quizás** (**Quizás ella te puede ayudar**), **tal vez** (**Tal vez compré demasiadas cosas**), **posiblemente** (**Posiblemente le dijo la verdad**) and **a lo mejor** (**A lo mejor, fui un tonto**). Remember that, in this phrase, **mejor** means *maybe*, not *best/better*.

Have students compare their own résumés to the description provided.

3 Se está entrevistando gente para cubrir puestos de trabajo. Hable de hipótesis y posibilidades con un(a) compañero/a.

Modelo:
- *¿Crees que ella puede obtener ese trabajo?*
- *Creo que no. No se puede trabajar en Oxfam con ropa de diseñador.*

1. Puesto vacante: recepcionista en la United Fruit Company
   Candidata: una mujer muy tímida a la que no le gusta hablar por teléfono
2. Puesto vacante: domador de leones (*lion tamer*)
   Candidato: un hombre valiente que trabajó en un zoológico por 20 años
3. Puesto vacante: niñera (*babysitter*)
   Candidata: una joven maestra que tiene dos hermanos pequeños
4. Puesto vacante: asistente en el Ministerio de Salud
   Candidato: un hombre que fuma (*smokes*) todos los días

PROYECTO

Escriba su currículum vítae siguiendo el esquema. Luego intercambie lo que escribió con su compañero/a y corrijan los errores.

1. Datos personales: nombre y apellido, edad, dirección, etc.
2. Antecedentes: qué ha estudiado, dónde ha trabajado, qué sabe hacer.
3. Información adicional: describir pasatiempos, deportes que practica, intereses personales, logros importantes (trofeos, concursos), etc.

Flash Cultura

Estrategia

Pay attention to context

When watching a video, pay attention to the context, the parts of the message that surround a given word or phrase, because there you may find clues to the meaning of unknown words and phrases. Try to identify the speaker's tone of voice and mood. Does the speaker sound angry, confused, happy, nervous, sad, or scared? Is he/she really speaking his/her mind, using irony, or joking?

Vocabulario útil

el andinismo *hiking; mountain climbing*
dar a conocer *to make known*
demostrar (o:ue) *to show*
el desarrollo *development*
el descanso *break*
desenvolverse (o:ue) *to manage*
divertido/a *fun*
exigente *demanding*
fastidioso/a *fussy*
realizar *to make*
el sombrerazo *big hat*

Estrategia

Saying *You're welcome*

When someone says **Gracias** to you, you might answer back either **De nada** or **No hay de qué**; also, you may say **Un placer** or **Encantado/a**, meaning that you are pleased to have done whatever the person is thanking you for. When there's been a reciprocal service (for example, when you buy something) the answer should be **Gracias a ti/usted** or **A ti/usted**.

El mundo del trabajo

Ya han leído sobre las profesiones, los intereses y las actividades en el mundo hispano; este episodio de **Flash Cultura** muestra a qué se dedican cada día los habitantes de Quito, Ecuador, y cómo a veces pueden unir el trabajo con el placer… y a veces no.

1 Hable con un(a) compañero/a. ¿Prefiere un trabajo con mucha rutina en una oficina o una actividad variada en contacto con la gente? ¿Le interesa trabajar ayudando a los demás? ¿Qué trabajo le parece horrible? ¿Puede ser divertido trabajar en la calle o viajando?

2 Mire este episodio de **Flash Cultura**. Mucha gente opina en el video; preste atención al contexto para poder interpretar correctamente las palabras de cada uno. ¿Quiénes no dicen la verdad? ¿Por qué?

1 **¿Cuántos años lleva usted en la profesión?**

Suggestion: After watching the episode of ***Flash Cultura***, ask students why it's no longer normal to work in the same job for one's entire career. Why do people change jobs so often?

Successful language learning: Explain that in Spain you normally say **Me corto el pelo** when you cut your own hair but also when you go to a hairdresser to have your hair cut. The same happens with **pintar la casa** and **sacarse una muela.**

2 **¿Te gusta tu trabajo?**

3 Complete las oraciones sobre el video.

1. Los policías sólo tienen tres horas de descanso diario.
2. Todos los jefes pueden ser muy amables o muy fastidiosos .
3. A través del turismo es posible dar a conocer las maravillas de Ecuador.
4. El trabajo de cada persona ayuda al desarrollo del país.
5. En Klein Tours se realizan excursiones de andinismo y viajes de exploración.

4 **Suggestion** To simplify, before students begin writing, have them brainstorm a list of phrases for each role.

4 En parejas, escriban un diálogo entre un(a) consejero/a (*adviser*) escolar que propone alternativas profesionales y un(a) alumno/a que debe decidir a qué se quiere dedicar. Luego compartan el diálogo con la clase.

Modelo:
- *A ti te interesa la gimnasia… quizás puedes ser policía.*
- *No me gusta ese trabajo porque los horarios son muy complicados y no puedo tener novio/a.*

Practice more at **vhlcentral.com.**

Audio: Activities, Vocabulary
Video: *Flash Cultura*

Unidad 8

Justo Gallego, manos a la obra

Lección 8A

HECHO A MANO

Lección 8B

HORIZONTES

Fernanda y Alberto, dueños de un negocio salvadoreño

Arquitectura modernista

AVANCE

Suggestion Explain that the boxed items are ads on a web site. Read the first box aloud and explain that **Ref.** stands for **referencia**.

8A HECHO A MANO

Habilidades

BANCO DE TIEMPO Córdoba INTERCAMBIO DE HABILIDADES

Categorías

- Música y baile
- Cuidado de personas
- Educación: clases
- Bricolaje: hogar y jardín
- Cocina
- Tecnología
- Motor
- Salud

Ref. 1: Pepe y Juanjo

Sabemos bastante de mecánica y queremos practicar taichí. ¿Puedes ayudarnos?

Motor | Salud

Ref. 2: Beatriz

¿Sabes un poco de electricidad? Yo sé algo de carpintería.

Bricolaje-hogar y jardín | Bricolaje-hogar y jardín

Emphasize to students that **saber de** is used with nouns; **de** is not used with verbs.

Hablar de habilidades

- ¿Sabes tocar la guitarra?
- Sé un poco. ¿Y tú?
- Yo **nada**, pero **sé bastante de** música y mis hijos **saben** tocar el piano **muy bien**.

8A.1 saber (de) algo, bastante...

Vocabulario

1

el intercambio *exchange*
el bricolaje *do-it-yourself*
el hogar *home*
la cocina *cooking*
saber (algo) de *to know (something) about*
la carpintería *carpentry*
bastante *quite a bit*
la habilidad, la educación, la tecnología, la electricidad, la mecánica, el taichí

2

saber *to know*
regular *so-so*
nada *at all*
tocar (un instrumento) *to play (an instrument)*
el piano

1 a. Observe la página web. ¿Qué servicio ofrece? un intercambio de habilidades

b. Relacione las categorías con los anuncios de las dos páginas. Compare sus respuestas con las de su compañero/a.

2 a. ¿Qué habilidades tiene usted? Fíjese en las estructuras e indique su grado de habilidad.

Sé...	algo/un poco, bastante, mucho de... cocina. cocinar... algo/un poco, (muy) bien, regular.
No sé...	nada, mucho de... cocina. cocinar bien, nada.

Modelo: *Sé tocar el piano muy bien pero no sé mucho de cocina.*

b. Comparta sus habilidades con su compañero/a.

Modelo:
- *Yo sé cocinar muy bien. Y tú, ¿sabes cocinar?*
- *Sí, sé un poco.*

3 ¿Quiere hacer un intercambio? Escriba un anuncio para la página web Banco de tiempo. Pregunte a su compañero/a por su anuncio.

Ref.: ....

2 Suggestion Refer students to the pictures and readings at the top of the page as models.

Ref. 3: Antonio

Sé tocar el piano y la guitarra. ¿Quién sabe informática?

Música y baile | Tecnología

Ref. 5: Felipe

¿Sabéis hacer muebles de madera? Consejos de jardinería a cambio.

Bricolaje-hogar y jardín | Bricolaje-hogar y jardín

Ref. 6: Silvia

¿Sabes cocinar? Yo sé bailar flamenco muy bien.

Música y baile | Cocina

Ref. 4: Estelle

Doy clases de francés a cambio de cuidado de niños (4 y 7 años).

Educación-clases | Cuidado de personas

Quedar

¿**Quedamos a** las 18:00 h **para** nuestro intercambio?

Quedamos con Martín **en** la plaza.

8A.2 **quedar**
para, en, a, con

Hacer propuestas; Aceptar y rechazar propuestas

- **Si queréis**, quedamos esta tarde.
- **Lo siento**, no puedo. **Es que** tengo una clase.
- **Si puedes**, quedamos a las 14:00 h.
- **De acuerdo./Vale.**

8A.3 **si quieres/puedes...**
vale; lo siento, es que...

Vocabulario

④

dar clases (de algo) *to give [subject] classes*
a cambio de *in exchange for*
el mueble *piece of furniture*
la madera *wood*
la jardinería *gardening*
quedar *to (arrange to) meet*
la guitarra

⑦

intercambiar *to exchange*

4 a. Escuche la conversación entre Estelle e Inés y lea los anuncios. ¿Con cuál de los anuncios la relaciona? anuncio referencia 4 del Banco de tiempo

b. Escuche de nuevo y corrija las informaciones falsas.

Estelle ha quedado con Inés... para ir al cine/en la plaza de las Tendillas/ el martes/a las 17:00 h. Han quedado para tomar un café en la plaza de las Tendillas, el miércoles a las 16:00 h.

5 Suggestion Have students brainstorm additional activities to propose. Write some models on the board.

5 Escriba propuestas con los elementos de los recuadros.

Si → querer / poder → ir al cine / hacer un intercambio / tomar un café / estudiar español

6 Responda a los siguientes mensajes de texto. Usted tiene clase de español hasta las 21:00 h.

¿Quedamos para ir al cine esta noche?

Si quieres, vamos a cenar mañana.

6 Suggestion Have students use all four prepositions (**para**, **en**, **a**, **con**) when making their plans.

MI EXPERIENCIA

7 Busque a una persona para intercambiar habilidades y quede con ella.

GUIÓN DE TRABAJO

¿Sabes/Saben...?
→ Sé un poco/algo, bastante, mucho de...
→ Sé cocinar/bailar muy bien, regular...
→ No sé... nada/mucho de informática.

¿Quedamos para... en... a las...? Si quieres/puedes,...
→ De acuerdo./Vale. Lo siento, es que...

Practice more at **vhlcentral.com.**

SAM: Actividades pp. 157–159

Suggestion Have volunteers describe other household tips using these items or others; for example, coffee grounds can be used to scrub greasy pots and pans, and olive oil can be used to disguise scratches on wood floors.

Trucos para el hogar

¿Los electrodomésticos no funcionan?

¿Tienes que montar o arreglar un mueble?

¿No sabes qué hacer con las plantas del jardín?

Si las actividades con las manos son muy difíciles para ti, si eres un *manazas*, estos consejos prácticos te pueden ayudar.

Para limpiar los vidrios...

utiliza agua con limón.

Para abonar tus plantas...

guarda los posos del café.

Para eliminar los parásitos...

mete cerillas en las macetas.

Dar instrucciones

Utiliza agua con limón para limpiar los vidrios.

Mete cerillas en las macetas.

Añade limón a las verduras.

8A.4 Regular imperative (**tú**)

Hablar de materiales

- ¿De qué es este cinturón?
- Es de metal y de cuero.
- ¿Y esta lámpara?
- Es de tela y de plástico.

8A.5 **ser** + **de** + [*material*]

Vocabulario

8

el truco *trick*
el electrodoméstico *appliance*
montar *to assemble*
el/la manazas (*Esp.*) *clumsy person*
el vidrio *(pane of) glass*
abonar *to fertilize*
guardar *to keep, to put away*
meter *to put*
la cerilla *match*
la maceta *flower pot*
el jabón *soap*
añadir *to add*
conservar *to keep*
sujetar *to hold*
clavar *to nail down*
el clavo *nail*
el peine *comb*
el cajón *drawer*
la planta, el parásito

8 Los trucos se han desordenado. Ordénelos y reescriba las oraciones.

1. Usa ~~cerillas~~ para limpiar los vidrios. → *Usa agua con limón para limpiar los vidrios.*
2. Mete agua con limón en las macetas para eliminar los parásitos. → Mete cerillas en las macetas para eliminar los parásitos.
3. Guarda jabón para abonar tus plantas. → Guarda los posos del café para abonar tus plantas.
4. Añade los posos del café a las verduras para conservar su color natural. → Añade limón a las verduras para conservar su color natural.
5. Sujeta con limón para clavar un clavo. → Sujeta con un peine para clavar un clavo.
6. Usa un peine para abrir los cajones. → Usa jabón para abrir los cajones.

9 a. Relacione los objetos con el material y compare sus respuestas con las de su compañero/a.

1	papel
3	cerámica
2	madera
5	plástico
7	tela
4	cuero
6	metal
8	vidrio

Modelo: • *¿De qué es la hoja?* • *Es de papel.*

b. Piense en otros objetos y pregunte a su compañero/a de qué material son.

9b Suggestion Have students describe items in the classroom.

10 Complete las instrucciones de esta receta de gazpacho.

(Pelar) los tomates y el pepino y (cortar) el pimiento.

Pela, corta

(Añadir) sal, aceite de oliva, ajo y pan duro.

Añade

(Batir) bien la mezcla.

Bate

Y (meter) la sopa en el refrigerador. ¡Buen provecho!

mete

Para conservar el color natural de las verduras...

añade limón.

Para clavar clavos...

sujeta el clavo con un peine.

Para abrir los cajones de madera fácilmente...

usa jabón.

Estrategia

Introducir una explicación y animar

- Mira, te voy a explicar algo.
- ¡Dale!/¡Venga! (*Esp.*)/ ¡Sale! (*Méx.*)

11 ¿Sabe usted algún truco? Consulte primero con su grupo y después compartan sus trucos con la clase.

de bricolaje	de limpieza	de decoración
de jardinería	de cocina	de belleza

12 a. Observe y escuche a estas dos personas. ¿Cuál es el problema?

Una de las personas no puede abrir un frasco.

Mira...

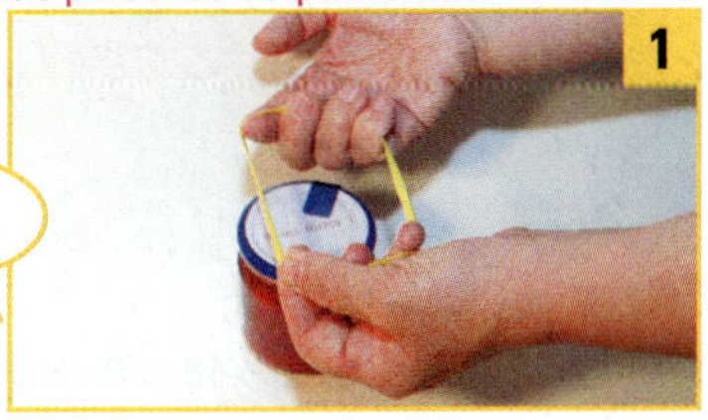

¡Dale!

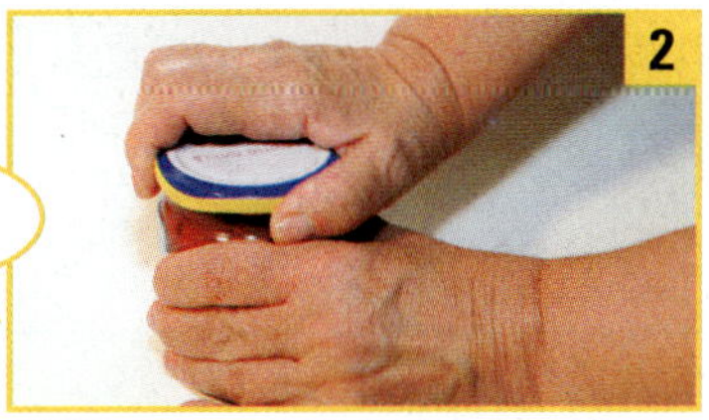

b. Escuche de nuevo. ¿Para qué se usan las expresiones anteriores?

para animar a la acción [2] para introducir la explicación [1]

c. *Manitas* y *manazas* son palabras que se usan en España para describir diferentes grados de habilidad de una persona. En su casa, ¿quién es un(a) *manitas*? ¿Quién es un(a) *manazas*?

13 Pida ayuda y dé instrucciones a su compañero/a para estas situaciones.

Su computadora no funciona. Su celular no se oye.

MI EXPERIENCIA

12C Suggestion Discuss the suffixes **-aza** and **-ita** and the connotations they provide. Have students think of possible colloquial English equivalents for **manazas** (*all fingers and thumbs; butterfingers*) and **manitas** (*jack of all trades*).

14 Comparta con sus compañeros los trucos que sabe.

GUIÓN DE TRABAJO

¿Qué sabes hacer? → Sé bricolaje, cocinar, decorar...

¿Sabes algún truco de bricolaje? → Utiliza aceite para abrir las puertas fácilmente.

Vocabulario

9

la hoja *sheet; leaf*
la caja *box*
el cinturón *belt*
el bolígrafo *ballpoint pen*
la tela *(piece of) cloth, fabric*
el cuero *leather*
el material, el plástico, el metal

10

el plato *dish; plate*
la receta (de cocina) *recipe*
pelar *to peel*
el pepino *cucumber*
la sal *salt*
el aceite *oil*
el ajo *garlic*
batir *to beat*
¡Buen provecho! *Enjoy your meal!*
el refrigerador

12

Mira... *Look...*
¡Dale!/¡Venga! (*Esp.*)/¡Sale! (*Méx.*) *Come on!*
el frasco *jar*
el/la manitas (*Esp.*) *handyman/ handywoman*
la goma elástica *rubber band*
alrededor *around*
la tapa de rosca *screw top*

Practice more at **vhlcentral.com.**

SAM: Actividades pp. 160–162

8A Justo Gallego is a former monk. After he survived the tuberculosis that forced him to leave monastic life, he vowed to build a shrine to **Nuestra Señora del Pilar** (an apparition of the Virgin Mary), to whom he had prayed.

Justo Gallego, manos a la obra

Justo Gallego (n. 1925) construye desde hace cincuenta años una catedral con sus propias manos. Está en Mejorada del Campo (Madrid) y su cúpula tiene 40 metros° de alto.

Utiliza materiales reciclados que recoge de la basura. No sabe nada de construcción, no tiene planos ni proyecto y no recibe dinero de la administración. Lo ha hecho casi todo solo, sin ayuda de nadie. Ha cumplido su sueño: construir una catedral para Nuestra Señora del Pilar. Justo explica que "es un acto de fe°".

Es increíble pensar que alguien puede hacer algo así, pero Justo lo ha logrado y ahora es famoso: su obra se ha expuesto en el MoMA de Nueva York y una marca de refrescos ha usado la imagen de Justo para una exitosa campaña de publicidad. El mensaje es claro: "Las posibilidades del ser humano son ilimitadas".

Si alguien quiere ver la catedral, puede visitar Mejorada del Campo. La construcción es el mayor interés turístico de este lugar. "Ahora soy famoso", dice Justo Gallego, pero no tiene celular, y su coche es una bicicleta. ¡Nadie ha visto nunca nada igual!

40 metros *131 feet* **fe** *faith*

Aquarius, a sports drink manufactured by Coca-Cola, featured Justo Gallego in a 2005 Spanish ad campaign.

Justo Gallego delante de la catedral que ha construido.

Hablar de personas o cosas indeterminadas

¿**Alguien** que ha construido una catedral solo? ¡Es **algo** increíble! **Nadie** ha visto nunca **nada** igual.

8A.6 alguien/nadie, algo/nada

Vocabulario

15

- **manos a la obra** *(Let's) Get to work!*
- **la mano** *hand*
- **alto/a** *high; tall*
- **reciclado/a** *recycled*
- **recoger (j)** *to collect, to pick up*
- **la basura** *garbage*
- **el dinero** *money*
- **nadie** *nobody*
- **el acto de fe** *matter of faith*
- **alguien** *somebody*
- **algo** *something*
- **lograr** *to achieve*
- **la obra (de arte)** *work of art*
- **exitoso/a** *successful*
- **el ser humano** *human being*
- **ilimitado/a** *unlimited*
- **el plano, la administración**

15 Observe la imagen de la construcción. ¿Qué tipo de edificio es?

castillo ☐ iglesia ☐ catedral ☑ museo ☐

16 a. Mire al protagonista. ¿A qué cree que se dedica? ¿Qué relación tiene con la construcción? Lea el texto y compruebe. Se dedica a construir una catedral.

b. ¿Cómo cree que Justo Gallego ha podido construir esta catedral solo?

17 Elija palabras o frases clave de cada párrafo y explique a su compañero/a por qué las eligió.

18 Elija la opción correcta.

Justo ha hecho **algo/nada** increíble. **Alguien/Nadie** ha visto **nada/algo** igual. Si **nadie/alguien** no lo cree, sólo tiene que visitar la catedral.

19 a. Escuche la entrevista a Justo Gallego. ¿Cuál de estos refranes resume mejor el mensaje de la entrevista? ¿Por qué?

Nadie es profeta en su tierra°.

Querer es poder.

A quien madruga, Dios lo ayuda.

No man is a prophet in his own land.

b. Con su compañero/a, escriban tres preguntas para hacerle a Justo.

20 ¿Alguien de su familia o amigos ha hecho algo especial o importante? ¿Conoce a un artista como Justo Gallego?

Vocabulario

19

Dios *God*

21

el esfuerzo *effort*
colectivo/a *collective*
el lugar de culto *place of worship*
el símbolo, religioso/a, respetar, la religión

24

el Patrimonio de la Humanidad *World Heritage (Site)*
el piso *floor, story*
la ingeniería *engineering*
la arquitectura

When visiting some churches, especially in rural areas, it is also recommended to dress modestly, i.e., cover one's shoulders and legs.

21 Lea el texto y relacione los títulos con los párrafos.

Catedrales

2 Las catedrales antiguas se realizaron con pocos medios técnicos gracias a un gran esfuerzo colectivo. Además de su valor religioso, fueron símbolos sociales y culturales de nuestras ciudades y hoy en día son monumentos históricos.

1 Actualmente las catedrales son lugares de culto, pero también tienen un valor artístico y turístico. Para visitar las catedrales, hay que respetar ciertas normas, por ejemplo estar en silencio y apagar el celular.

4 En España se destacan° las catedrales de Sevilla, Burgos, Toledo, León y Santiago de Compostela, donde termina la famosa ruta del Camino de Santiago.

3 Las catedrales europeas han sido modelos para la construcción de las grandes catedrales de América Latina. Algunas de las más importantes son las de Santo Domingo, México, D.F., Lima y Buenos Aires.

se destacan *stand out*

1. Religión y arte
2. Maravillas arquitectónicas
3. Influencia europea
4. La ruta de las catedrales

22 Suggestion Solicit a list of question words from students to get them started.

22 Haga preguntas a su compañero/a sobre las frases subrayadas en el texto.

Modelo: *¿Cuál es tu monumento histórico preferido y por qué? ¿De qué estilo arquitectónico es?*

23 ¿Conoce las catedrales que menciona el texto? ¿Y otras? ¿Qué monumentos famosos o importantes hay en su ciudad?

24 Suggestion If students are familiar with Calatrava's completed and proposed works in the U.S. and Canada, have them describe the constructions.

24 Expansion In groups, have students research one of the architects and prepare a brief oral report.

24 Aquí tiene algunas muestras de la arquitectura del mundo hispano. Lea las características de las obras. ¿Qué imagen las representa?

1. **Luis Barragán** (Guadalajara, México). Su casa estudio, en México, D.F. es una de las obras arquitectónicas contemporáneas más importantes en el contexto internacional y es también Patrimonio de la Humanidad de la UNESCO.
2. **Bernardo Fort-Brescia** (Lima, Perú). Es el autor junto con su esposa, Laurinda Apear, del Hotel Westin en Manhattan, Nueva York. Tiene 45 pisos y 863 habitaciones.
3. **Santiago Calatrava** (Valencia, España). Sus creaciones son mitad arquitectura, mitad ingeniería. Están en ciudades de todo el mundo como Valencia, Mérida, Bilbao, Buenos Aires y Venecia.

Practice more at **vhlcentral.com.**

SAM: Actividades pp. 163–166

25 a. Complete y ordene las instrucciones para hacer una tortilla de patata. El grupo más rápido gana. Después escuche el audio y compruebe sus respuestas.

......Da...... (Dar) la vuelta° a la tortilla. Unos minutos y ¡lista! ¡Buen provecho!

8
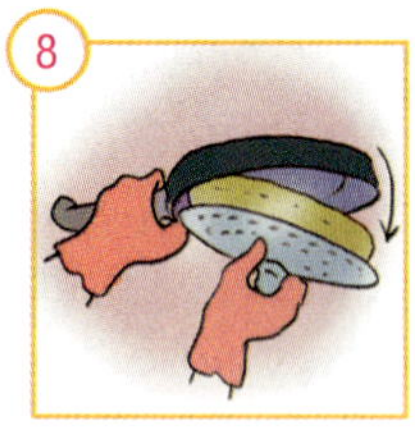

6

......Añade...... (Añadir) sal a la mezcla.

......Pela...... (Pelar) y ......corta...... (cortar) las patatas.

1

3

......Bate...... (Batir) los huevos.

......Echa......(Echar) la mezcla en la sartén° y déjala unos minutos al fuego°.

7

4

......Saca...... (Sacar) las patatas del aceite.

......Mezcla...... (Mezclar) las patatas con los huevos.

5

2

......Echa...... (Echar) las patatas en aceite.

dar la vuelta *to flip; to turn over* **la sartén** *frying pan* **el fuego** *heat; fire*

25 **Expansion** Write the steps of the recipe on the board in infinitive form. In pairs, have students take turns giving each other commands; their partner should act out the step.

b. Con su grupo, elijan una receta de cocina y escriban las instrucciones en diferentes tiras de papel. Otro grupo debe ponerlas en orden. Luego comprueben si el orden es correcto.

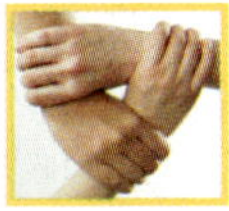

TAREA FINAL

Banco de tiempo del español

- Elabore un cuestionario sobre habilidades y conocimientos relacionados con el español. (gramática, pronunciación, cultura...)
- Conteste el cuestionario y complételo con la información de sus compañeros.
- Organicen un intercambio de habilidades en español. Creen una tabla con las habilidades y los nombres de los alumnos.
- Quede con uno o varios compañeros para intercambiar sus habilidades.

YO PUEDO...

- **Puedo hablar de habilidades.**
  Describa una de sus habilidades.
- **Puedo quedar con alguien.**
  Cree una conversación para realizar alguna actividad relacionada con la clase de español.
- **Puedo hacer preguntas.**
  Escriba un mensaje de texto con una propuesta de actividad.
- **Puedo dar instrucciones.**
  Explique a un(a) amigo/a las instrucciones de un truco para el hogar.
- **Puedo hablar de objetos y materiales.**
  Elija tres objetos de su aula y diga de qué materiales son.
- **Puedo hablar de personas o cosas indeterminadas.**
  Escriba oraciones sobre personas o cosas que no conoce.

GRAMÁTICA FUNCIONAL

8A.1 **Suggestion** Name different groups (Ex: **los políticos, los hispanos, los norteamericanos, los niños de 5 años, los estudiantes de esta universidad,** etc.) and have the class make generalized statements about what they do or do not know. Then have a brief discussion about stereotypes.

8A.1 Talk about skills

saber (de) 5.10
Adverbs of quantity and negation 11.1, 11.4, 12.3

- Use the verb **saber** (*to know [how]*) to talk about skills or abilities. **Saber** has an irregular **yo** form: **sé**.

 Sé tocar muy bien la guitarra.
 I know how *to play the guitar very well.*

- Use **saber** + [*infinitive*] to tell what someone knows how to do. Use adverbs like **algo**, **un poco**, and **(muy) bien** to indicate skill.

 Luisa **sabe** tocar **un poco** el piano.
 Luisa ***knows how to play*** *the piano* ***a bit****.*

- To indicate what someone knows *about* a topic, use **saber** + [**algo/un poco/bastante/mucho**] + **de** + [*noun*].

 Sabemos bastante de política.
 We know a lot about *politics.*

- Use **no saber** + [**nada/mucho**] + **de** + [*noun*] or **no saber** + [*infinitive*] + [**bien/nada**] to express what someone does not know how to do, or do well.

 No sé nadar **bien**.
 I don't know how *to swim* ***well****.*

8A.2 Meet with people

quedar + a/con/en/para 10.1, 10.4, 10.11, 10.15

- Use the verb **quedar** (*to meet up*) to make plans to meet people. **Quedar** is a regular verb.

 Quedamos en la parada de autobuses a las ocho.
 Let's meet *at the bus stop at eight.*

- Give more information about your meeting using **en** + [*place*], **con** + [*person*], **a** + [*time*], or **para** + [*activity* (*infinitive*)].

 Quedamos **con** mis primos **para** ir al cine.
 We're meeting ***(with)*** *my cousins* ***to*** *go to the movies.*

Point out that quedar **en** + [*activity* (*infinitive*)] is also possible. E.g. Quedamos **en** ir a su casa.

8A.3 Propose, accept, and decline plans

Si quieres/puedes... 12.9
De acuerdo./Lo siento, es que... 14.6, 14.14

- To propose plans, say **Si quieres/puedes** + [*plan*]. Be sure to match the form of **querer** or **poder** to your listener(s).

 Si quieren, pueden cenar en mi casa esta noche.
 If you want*, you can have supper at my house tonight.*

- To accept, say **¡De acuerdo!** or **¡Vale!** (*Esp.*). To politely decline, say **Lo siento, es que** + [*excuse*].

 Lo siento, es que tengo que lavarme el pelo.
 I'm sorry*, I have to wash my hair.*

¡Póngalo en práctica!

G1 Escriba oraciones completas con los elementos dados. Haga todos los cambios necesarios.

1. Pedro / algo / saber / tango
 Pedro sabe algo de tango.
2. muy bien / saber / jugar al tenis / Miriam y Laura
 Miriam y Laura saben jugar muy bien al tenis.
3. saber / vosotras / hacer adornos preciosos
 Vosotras sabéis hacer adornos preciosos.
4. (tú) / no / jardinería / ¿? / saber / mucho
 ¿No sabes mucho de jardinería?
5. cocinar / regular / yo / saber
 Yo sé cocinar regular.

G2 Empareje cada comienzo de oración con el final apropiado.

f	1. Pedro quedó con Ana para	a. las tres en la oficina.
c	2. Quedé con	b. ayudarme a estudiar.
e	3. Quedamos para	c. Manuel para cenar.
a	4. Usted quedó a	d. un restaurante.
b	5. Quedaste conmigo para	e. vernos pronto.
d	6. Quedaron en	f. llevarla a bailar.

G3 Complete la conversación.

- Sofía, si (1)..........quieres.........., vamos a cenar.
- (2)..........Lo siento.........., es que tengo que estudiar español.
- Yo sé mucho español. Si (3)..........quieres.........., puedo ayudarte.
- (4)..¡Vale!/De acuerdo... Podemos hacer un intercambio. Yo sé cocinar muy bien.
- (5)..........Si.......... quieres, puedo estar en tu casa a las 7, ¿de acuerdo?
- Sí, genial.

Suggestion Have students write down two things they know how to do well and one thing they don't know anything about at all. Collect the papers, shuffle them, and read the statements aloud for the class to guess the identity of the writer.

Practice more at **vhlcentral.com.**

8A

GRAMÁTICA FUNCIONAL

8A.4 Suggestion Give the class different scenarios and have them write commands that might be heard in that situation. Then, in groups of three, have them read the commands for their classmates to act out.

8A.4 Give instructions

Regular imperative (tú) 5.18.2

- Use commands to give someone instructions.

  Sujeta la puerta con una madera.
  ***Hold** the door with a piece of wood.*

- Regular **tú** commands have the same form as the present-tense **usted/él/ella** form of the verb.

  Usted **lava** los platos con jabón. ➔ **Lava** (tú) los platos.
  *You **wash** the plates with soap.* *Wash the plates.*

- You will learn other command forms, including irregular and negative **tú** commands, in 9B.2, 10A.1, and 16B.1.

8A.5 Talk about materials

ser + de + [*material*] 10.5

- Use **ser** + **de** + [*material*] to tell what an object is made of.

  La mesa **es de madera** y las sillas **son de metal**.
  *The table **is made of wood** and the chairs **are made of metal**.*

- Use **de** + [*material*] as an invariable adjective.

  Las botellas **de vidrio** son muy frágiles.
  ***Glass** bottles are very fragile.*

8A.6 Talk about unidentified people or things

alguien/nadie, algo/nada 6.5, 12.3

- Use the indefinite pronouns **alguien** (*someone; anyone*) and **algo** (*something; anything*) to refer to people or objects that are unspecified.

  ¿Hay **alguien** en casa? — *Is there **anyone** at home?*
  Quiero comer **algo**. — *I want to eat **something**.*

- Use **alguien** and **algo** in affirmative statements. For negative statements, use **nadie** (*nobody; anybody*) and **nada** (*nothing; anything*). As you saw in **5A.2**, all indefinite words in a negative statement must be negative (**no, nada, nadie, nunca...**).

  No veo a **nadie**. — *I **don't** see **anyone**.*
  No queremos beber **nada**. — *We **don't** want to drink **anything**.*

- Remember to use the **a personal** when **alguien** or **nadie** is the direct object of a verb. (See 5B.3.)

  ¿Viste **a alguien** cuando entraste?
  *Did you see **anyone** when you came in?*

- These pronouns can also be used as the subject of a sentence.

  ¿**Alguien** sabe **algo** de informática?
  *Does **anyone** know **anything** about computing?*

  No, **nadie** sabe **nada**.
  *No, **nobody** knows **anything**.*

¡Póngalo en práctica!

G4 Complete las oraciones con el verbo en imperativo.

1. ...Bate... (Batir) los huevos.
2. ...Añade... (Añadir) la harina y el azúcar.
3. ...Revuelve... (Revolver) bien la mezcla.
4. ...Utiliza... (Utilizar) un molde grande.
5. ...Mete... (Meter) la fuente al horno.
6. ...Espera... (Esperar) que se enfríe.

G4 Suggestion To challenge students, give them these sentences in random order. Have them first arrange them in the correct sequence and then conjugate the verbs.

G5 Escriba oraciones completas para indicar de qué material es cada objeto. Sample answers:

1. las tazas Las tazas son de cerámica.
2. la sartén La sartén es de metal.
3. las ventanas Las ventanas son de vidrio.
4. el periódico El periódico es de papel.
5. los zapatos Los zapatos son de cuero.
6. el vestido El vestido es de tela.

G6 Complete la conversación.

- ¿Llamaste a (1) ...alguien... ayer?
- No, ayer no llamé (2) ...a... (3) ...nadie...
- ¿Miraste (4) ...algo... en la televisión?
- No, (5) ...nunca... miro (6) ...nada... en la televisión.
- ¡Yo siempre encuentro (7) ...algo... interesante en la tele!
- ¿En serio? Yo nunca encuentro (8) ...nada... divertido.

G7 Responda a las preguntas con una negación o escriba las preguntas para las respuestas.
Answers may vary. Suggested answers:

1. ¿Te ha ocurrido algo? No, no me ha ocurrido nada.
2. No, no llegó nadie todavía. ¿Ya llegó alguien?
3. ¿Sabe tu hermano algo de música? No, no sabe nada (de música).
4. ¿Quieres algo? No, gracias, no quiero nada.
5. No, no conozco a nadie aquí. ¿Conoces a alguien?
6. ¿Alguien te ofreció algo? No, nadie me ofreció nada.
7. ¿Le contaste algo a alguien? No, no le conté nada a nadie.
8. No, no leí nada interesante. ¿Leíste algo interesante?

Practice more at **vhlcentral.com.**

VOCABULARIO

Habilidades

el bricolaje	*do-it-yourself*
la carpintería	*carpentry*
la cocina	*cooking*
la educación	*education*
la electricidad	*electricity*
la guitarra	*guitar*
la habilidad	*ability*
el hogar	*home*
el intercambio	*exchange*
la jardinería	*gardening*
la madera	*wood*
la mecánica	*mechanics*
el mueble	*piece of furniture*
el piano	*piano*
el taichí	*tai chi*
la tecnología	*technology*
dar clases (de algo)	*to give [subject] classes*
intercambiar	*to exchange*
quedar	*to (arrange to) meet*
saber (algo) (de)	*to know (something) (about)*
tocar (un instrumento)	*to play (an instrument)*
a cambio de	*in exchange for*
bastante	*quite a bit*
nada	*at all*
regular	*so-so*

Trucos para el hogar

¡Buen provecho!	*Enjoy your meal!*
¡Dale!/¡Venga! (*Esp.*)/**¡Sale!** (*Méx.*)	*Come on!*
Mira...	*Look...*
el aceite	*oil*
el ajo	*garlic*
el bolígrafo	*ballpoint pen*
la caja	*box*
el cajón	*drawer*
la cerilla	*match*
el cinturón	*belt*
el clavo	*nail*
el cuero	*leather*
el electrodoméstico	*appliance*
el frasco	*jar*
la goma elástica	*rubber band*
la hoja	*sheet; leaf*
el jabón	*soap*
la maceta	*flower pot*
el/la manazas (*Esp.*)	*clumsy person*
el/la manitas (*Esp.*)	*handyman/ handywoman*
el material	*material*
el metal	*metal*
el parásito	*parasite*
el peine	*comb*
el pepino	*cucumber*
la planta	*plant*
el plástico	*plastic*
el plato	*dish; plate*
la receta (de cocina)	*recipe*
el refrigerador	*refrigerator*
la sal	*salt*
la tapa de rosca	*screw top*
la tela	*(piece of) cloth, fabric*
el truco	*trick*
el vidrio	*(pane of) glass*
abonar	*to fertilize*
añadir	*to add*
batir	*to beat*
clavar	*to nail down*
conservar	*to keep*
guardar	*to keep, to put away*
meter	*to put*
montar	*to assemble*
pelar	*to peel*
sujetar	*to hold*
alrededor	*around*

Justo Gallego

manos a la obra	*(Let's) Get to work!*
el acto de fe	*matter of faith*
la administración	*administration*
la arquitectura	*architecture*
la basura	*garbage*
el dinero	*money*
Dios	*God*
el esfuerzo	*effort*
el fuego	*heat; fire*
la ingeniería	*engineering*
el lugar de culto	*place of worship*
la mano	*hand*
la obra (de arte)	*work of art*
el Patrimonio de la Humanidad	*World Heritage (Site)*
el piso	*floor, story*
el plano	*plan*
la religión	*religion*
la sartén	*frying pan*
el ser humano	*human being*
el símbolo	*symbol*
dar la vuelta	*to flip; to turn over*
lograr	*to achieve*
recoger (j)	*to collect, to pick up*
respetar	*to respect*
alto/a	*high; tall*
colectivo/a	*collective*
exitoso/a	*successful*
ilimitado/a	*unlimited*
reciclado/a	*recycled*
religioso/a	*religious*
algo	*something*
alguien	*somebody*
nadie	*nobody; anybody*

Variación léxica

el anuncio ⟷ **el aviso** (*Amér. L.*)

el bolígrafo ⟷ **la pluma** (*Méx.*) ⟷ **la birome** (*Arg.*) ⟷ **la lapicera** (*Uru., Arg.*) ⟷ **el lápiz de pasta** (*Chi.*)

la cerilla (*Esp.*) ⟷ **el fósforo** (*Amér. L.*) ⟷ **el cerillo** (*Méx.*)

¡Dale! ⟷ **¡Venga!** (*Esp.*) ⟷ **¡Sale!** (*Méx.*)

el intercambio ⟷ **el trueque** ⟷ **el canje**

el refrigerador ⟷ **la nevera** (*Esp.*) ⟷ **la heladera** (*Arg.*) ⟷ **el frigo** (*fam.*)

el vidrio ⟷ **el cristal** (*Esp.*)

8B HORIZONTES

Suggestion Introduce this section by briefly telling the class about your own family's immigrant experiences. Ask students if they can identify the home country and the conflict referred to by the speaker in the last quote. (Spain; Spanish Civil War). Students may know little about the Spanish Civil War, but may be familiar with it if they have seen Guillermo del Toro's film *El laberinto del fauno.*

Emigrantes

1

4 *"En 1905 mis abuelos fueron desde Canarias a Caracas en barco, como muchos otros españoles. Ellos se quedaron en Caracas, otros hicieron fortuna y volvieron."*

2 *"Somos salvadoreños, de Intipucá. En 1980, cuando comenzó la guerra en nuestro país, hicimos las maletas y vinimos a California. Aquí tuvimos a nuestros hijos. Ellos hablan inglés desde niños."*

5 *"En los años 60 dejé mi finca en Bolivia para buscar trabajo en Chimbote, una ciudad industrial de Perú. Mi señora y mis hijos se quedaron en el campo por un tiempo. Luego vinieron conmigo."*

3 *"Soy química. En 2001 vine a Londres con una beca de investigación. Tuve suerte y me quedé."*

1 *"En 1937, con 6 años, vine a Veracruz como niño de la guerra. Hubo españoles que volvieron de mayores, otros no quisimos o no pudimos, mi vida está aquí, en México."*

Hablar de experiencias

- Tu padre **vino** a México y ¿qué **hizo**?
- **Tuvo** suerte y **pudo** trabajar de camionero.

8B.1 Preterite of irregular verbs

Vocabulario

1

- **quedarse** *to stay*
- **hacer fortuna** *to make fortune*
- **volver (o:ue)** *to go back, to return*
- **salvadoreño/a** *Salvadoran*
- **hacer las maletas** *to pack*
- **la maleta** *suitcase*
- **tener (e:ie) un hijo** *to have a child*
- **desde niño(s)** *since childhood*
- **los años 60** *the sixties*
- **la finca** *farm*
- **el/la químico/a** *chemist*
- **la beca** *scholarship*
- **la investigación** *research*
- **la suerte** *(good) luck*
- **la guerra** *war*
- **a finales del siglo XIX** *towards the end of the 19th century*
- **a principios del siglo XX** *at the beginning of the 20th century*
- **la guerra civil** *civil war*

1 a. Lea los testimonios de la exposición *Emigrantes* y escriba el número de la foto correspondiente.

1 The Salvadoran Civil War (1980 to 1992) was a conflict between the military government and an organization of left-wing militias known as the **Frente Farabundo Martí para la Liberación Nacional (FMLN).**

b. Relacione las fotos con los siguientes titulares.

(Europa: finales del siglo XIX–principios del siglo XX) Emigración a Latinoamérica.	4
(España: 1936–1939) Exilio a Europa y Latinoamérica por la guerra civil española.	1
(Latinoamérica: años 60 y 70) Migración del campo a la ciudad.	5
(El Salvador: años 80) Exilio a los Estados Unidos y otros países de América por la guerra civil salvadoreña.	2
(Latinoamérica: 2000–actualidad) Nietos de inmigrantes vuelven al país de sus abuelos.	3

2 Marque en los textos los verbos en pretérito indefinido y clasifíquelos.

Regulares	Irregulares
se quedaron,... volvieron, comenzó, dejé, me quedé	*fueron,...* hicieron, hicimos, vinimos, tuvimos, vinieron, vine, tuve, hubo, quisimos, pudimos

3 Complete el testimonio de una visitante a la exposición usando el pretérito de estos verbos.

casarse • emigrar • poder • tener • venir

Soy argentina y ahora vivo en España. En 1920 mi abuelo (1)......emigró...... a Buenos Aires. Allá (2)......se casó...... con mi abuela y (3)......tuvieron...... dos hijos: mi mamá y mi tío Alfonso. Nunca (4)......vinieron...... a España; no (5)......pudieron...... regresar a su querida Galicia.

2

3

4

5

Suggestion Ask students simple questions about their own lives to discuss duration of important life events. Write models and their English equivalents on the board.

Indicar duración

- ¿Desde cuándo/Cuánto tiempo hace que vives aquí?
- Viví en Bogotá **durante** cinco años. **Desde** 1965 **hasta** 1970.
- ¿Desde cuándo vives aquí en Belice?
- **Desde que** me jubilé hace diez años.

8B.2 **durante, desde/de... hasta/a, desde que**

Vocabulario *cont.*

el/la obrero/a *worker*
en la actualidad *today; nowadays*
el horizonte, el/la emigrante, el testimonio, industrial, la emigración, el exilio, la migración, el/la inmigrante

3
el/la visitante *visitor*
casarse *to get married*
regresar *to go back, to return*

4
la chimenea *chimney*
la fábrica *factory*

5
¿cuánto tiempo (hace)? *how long (have/has)?*
desde/de... hasta/a *from... until/to*
desde que *since*
pasar *to happen*

¡OJO!

Usually, when the preposition **de** is followed by the article **el**, the two words combine to form the contraction **del**. However, if the article **el** is part of a proper name (**El Salvador**), this contraction does not occur: **Somos de El Salvador**.

4 a. Antes de escuchar a Faustino, un boliviano que emigró a Perú en los años sesenta, fíjese en la foto 5. ¿Por qué hay tantas chimeneas? Porque aumentó el trabajo en las fábricas y la gente migró a las ciudades.

b. Escuche a Faustino y a su mujer, y marque la opción correcta.

1. Hace casi cincuenta años desde que...
   (a) Faustino emigró a Perú. b. Faustino vino de Perú.
2. Desde 1962 hasta 1965...
   a. estuvo con su familia en Bolivia. (b) vivió solo en Perú.
3. Estuvieron juntos en Perú durante...
   a. cuarenta años. (b) treinta y siete años.

c. ¿Conoce a otros emigrantes como Faustino? ¿Qué pasó en sus vidas?

5 Lea de nuevo los titulares de la **Actividad 1b** y complete estas oraciones con *desde, hasta, durante* y *desde que.*

1. ...Desde que... los primeros emigrantes fueron a Latinoamérica han pasado más de cien años.
2. ...Desde... el año 1960 ...hasta... el año 1973 hubo migraciones del campo a la ciudad.
3. ...Durante... la guerra civil, muchas personas salieron de El Salvador.

6 ¿Desde cuándo vive en su ciudad o pueblo? ¿Cuánto tiempo hace que estudia español? Pregunte a su compañero/a.

MI EXPERIENCIA

7 ¿Ha vivido usted, su familia o un(a) amigo/a en el extranjero? Hable con sus compañeros de la experiencia.

GUIÓN DE TRABAJO

¿Dónde estuviste/estuvo...? → ¿Qué hiciste/hizo? → Hice/Hizo... Vine/Vino...

¿Cuánto tiempo estuviste/estuvo? → ¿Cuánto tiempo hace que...? ¿Desde cuándo...?

Durante... Desde/De... hasta/a...

Hace...

Point out that proper names may include restaurants, stores, or other establishments. Ex: **Los empleados de El Chalán...**

Practice more at **vhlcentral.com.**

SAM: Actividades pp. 167–169

Nuevas formas de vida

Suggestion Have students compare and contrast the immigration situation in Spain with that of this country.

España tuvo un pasado emigrante y actualmente recibe personas de todo el mundo. Aproximadamente el 10% de la población es de otros países.
Entre los colectivos de inmigrantes más numerosos en España están los marroquíes, rumanos, ecuatorianos, colombianos, británicos, alemanes y argentinos.
Muchos quieren estar en España temporalmente y enviar dinero a sus familias. Otros quieren vivir allí para siempre. Los nuevos ciudadanos trabajan en la agricultura, el servicio doméstico, el comercio, los transportes, la hostelería o la construcción, y muchos abren su propio negocio. También hay médicos, profesores de idiomas o directivos de empresas. Otros no trabajan; son inmigrantes jubilados que quieren disfrutar del buen clima y el estilo de vida todo el año.

8 a. Busque en el texto cómo se llaman los ciudadanos de estos países. Escríbalos al lado del país correspondiente.

1. Marruecos *marroquíes*
2. Rumania rumanos
3. Ecuador ecuatorianos
4. Reino Unido británicos
5. Colombia colombianos
6. Alemania alemanes
7. Argentina argentinos

b. Las banderas representan la procedencia de la población migrante más numerosa en España. Relaciónelas con los países.

9 a. ¿A qué se dedican estos nuevos ciudadanos? ¿De dónde es la población migrante que vive en su país? ¿A qué se dedica? agricultura, servicio doméstico, comercio, transportes, hostelería, construcción, enseñanza de idiomas, medicina, dirección de empresas

b. ¿A qué cree usted que se dedica la gente de su país cuando emigra?

10 a. Escuche a estas dos personas en una clase de español para extranjeros. ¿Cuáles son sus intenciones de futuro? Amina quiere vivir mucho tiempo en España, conocer otras ciudades y ayudar económicamente a su familia. Neil quiere disfrutar del sol y vivir mucho tiempo en España.

1. Amina quiere...
2. Neil quiere...

- vivir mucho tiempo en España.
- disfrutar del sol.
- conocer otras ciudades.
- ayudar económicamente a su familia.

b. ¿En qué coinciden Amina y Neil? Los dos quieren quedarse mucho tiempo en España

c. Fíjese en el acento y la entonación de Liuba, la profesora cubana. ¿Son diferentes a los de su profesor(a)?

11 Hable con su compañero/a de tres cosas que quiere lograr en su vida laboral y personal. Usen estas palabras como ayuda.

casa • hijo/a • horario • mujer/marido • sueldo • viajar

12 ¿Qué creen que representa la viñeta cómica? ¿En qué país o países creen que se encuentra esta frontera?

Vocabulario

8

- **temporalmente** *temporarily*
- **para siempre** *for ever*
- **el/la ciudadano/a** *citizen*
- **el servicio doméstico** *domestic service*
- **el comercio** *commerce*
- **el/la directivo/a** *manager*
- **la bandera** *flag*
- **la procedencia** *origin*
- **la población migrante** *migrant population*
- **el Reino Unido** *United Kingdom*

10

- **el futuro**

Expresar intenciones

- ¿Qué **quiere** hacer en los próximos años?
- **Quiero ganar** dinero para viajar por el mundo.

8B.3 **querer** + [*infinitive*]

EL ROTO

Have students express their intentions for the rest of this semester.

Suggestion Read through the list of immigrant-run businesses and ask students if any exist in their region. Then discuss what types of businesses are typically run by certain immigrant groups in this country. Ask students if they frequent these businesses and what types of goods or services they provide.

una peluquería dominicana

una tienda china

un locutorio latino

un bazar marroquí

una panadería ecuatoriana

una tetería turca

un restaurante indio

Estrategia

Reformular

¿Hay un cíber cerca? **O sea,** ¿un locutorio? **Es decir,** ¿un sitio donde pueda hacer llamadas al extranjero y usar Internet?

Vocabulario

(13)

la peluquería *hair salon*
el locutorio *call center; Internet café*
la panadería *bakery*
la tetería *tea room*
reformular *to restate*
o sea *that is*
es decir *in other words*
el juguete *toy*
el bazar

(15)

la comunidad inmigrante *immigrant community*

13 Observe las imágenes. ¿A qué negocios corresponden?

1. un bazar marroquí
2. una tienda china
3. una peluquería dominicana

14 Escuche a esta persona que habla sobre un tipo de tienda que abre la comunidad china en España. ¿Qué características tiene?

1. Muchas veces no tienen nombre, es decir, sólo tienen un letrero que dice *alimentación.*
2. Tienen un horario amplio, es decir, de 10:00 h a 03:00 h de la mañana, por ejemplo.
3. Venden de todo, o sea, artículos para la casa, juguetes, ropa, alimentación...

15 a. Reformule con su compañero/a estas oraciones usando **o sea** o **es decir.**

1. En las zonas donde viven inmigrantes hispanos hay muchos negocios latinos, o sea,...
2. Los locutorios ofrecen distintos servicios, es decir,...

b. ¿Hay restaurantes típicos de otros países en su barrio? ¿Cuáles son los negocios más comunes de comunidades inmigrantes?

MI EXPERIENCIA

16 Usted quiere abrir un negocio diferente en su país. Descríbalo.

GUIÓN DE TRABAJO

¿Qué negocio quieres abrir?

Quiero abrir...

un bar de tapas, una tetería turca, ...

¿Cómo? ¿Una tetería?

Sí, o sea, un lugar para tomar té.

Practice more at **vhlcentral.com.**

SAM: Actividades pp. 170–172

Fernanda y Alberto, dueños de un negocio salvadoreño

http://www.redempresariosmigrantes.com

El portal de los empresarios migrantes

REGISTRO | EMPRESAS | FORO | NOTICIAS | CONTACTO

- Hostelería
- Comercio
- Servicios
- Construcción

Fecha: 24 de julio
Título: Un sueño hecho realidad

Mi nombre es Fernanda Pimentel y soy de San Salvador. Mis abuelos llegaron de España a El Salvador en los años 30. Yo emigré igual que ellos. Vivo en East Boston, Massachusetts, desde hace seis años. Acá hay oportunidades, pero no es tan fácil encontrar un buen trabajo inmediatamente. Estuve en el servicio doméstico durante dos años y también cuidé a niños y a ancianos.

Mi esposo vino hace cuatro años y comenzó en la construcción. Hace seis meses, con todos los ahorros de estos años y mucho esfuerzo, hicimos realidad nuestro sueño: pudimos abrir una pequeña tienda-pupusería.

El negocio funciona bien; en la zona viven muchos salvadoreños y a los estadounidenses también les gustan nuestras pupusas. Tenemos muchos clientes estadounidenses que practican su español con nosotros cuando vienen a comprar. Además tenemos otros productos como leche, arroz, pasta... Ahora queremos traer a nuestros tres hijos. ¡El esfuerzo tiene su recompensa!

Vocabulario

17

el/la dueño/a *owner*
el/la empresario/a *businessperson*
el sueño *dream*
la oportunidad *opportunity*
hacer realidad *to make something happen*
comenzar (e:ie) *to begin, to start*
los ahorros *savings*
la pupusería *store where **pupusas** are sold*
la pupusa *Salvadoran filled tortilla*
la recompensa *reward*
tantos/as *as many*
tan/tanto... como *as much/many... as*
la tienda de alimentación *grocery store*
vender *to sell*
la sección

Comparar formas de vida

- ¿Hay muchas diferencias entre San Salvador y Boston?
- Allá hay **tantas** panaderías **como** acá, pero no hay **tanto** dinero y no es **tan** fácil abrir un negocio.

8B.4 **tan/tanto... como**

17 a. Observe el portal de Internet. ¿Qué secciones tiene? ¿Qué información cree que da? ¿Qué países están representados? Registro, empresas, foro, noticias, contacto. Estados Unidos, Canadá, México, El Salvador, Honduras, República Dominicana.

b. Lea el texto y fíjese en la foto. ¿Qué tipo de negocio es?

1. una tetería ☐
2. una pupusería y tienda de alimentación ☑
3. un bar ☐

Explain that **pupusas** are hand-made corn **tortillas**, usually filled with cheese, pork, beans, or a mixture of the three. **Pupusas** are traditionally served with **curtido**, a type of slaw with red chilies and vinegar.

c. ¿Qué productos vende? Vende pupusas y otros productos de alimentación (leche, arroz, pasta, etc.).

18 Busque en el texto estos datos de Fernanda y Alberto.

1. ¿En qué trabajó Fernanda al principio? Trabajó en el servicio doméstico y cuidó a niños y a ancianos.
2. ¿Cuánto tiempo hace que Fernanda vino a los Estados Unidos? Hace seis años.
3. ¿Desde cuándo vive con su esposo en Boston? Desde hace cuatro años.

19 San Salvador y Boston: dos formas de vida. Relacione y compare.

1. Fernanda trabaja tanto ....b....
2. En San Salvador no tuvieron tantas oportunidades de trabajo ....c....
3. Con sus hijos en Boston, la familia va a ser tan feliz ....a....

a. como en San Salvador.
b. como Alberto.
c. como en Boston.

20 ¿Cree que Fernanda y Alberto están felices con su nueva vida? ¿Qué intenciones tienen para el futuro? Sample answer: Quieren traer a sus tres hijos.

Vocabulario

21

la igualdad *equality*
al parecer *apparently*
emprendedor(a) *enterprising*
el/la propietario/a *owner*
el entretenimiento *entertainment*
el millón, el sector, la presencia

23

hacerse *to become*
el país receptor *host country*

OPINIÓN

¿Cree que es fácil encontrar trabajo en su país? ¿Hay oportunidades profesionales para las personas de procedencia extranjera?

21 a. Lea el texto y observe la gráfica.

Información para la igualdad

Cada año, llegan a los Estados Unidos aproximadamente 1,2 millones de inmigrantes. Estas personas tienen una gran importancia para la economía nacional y, al parecer, son muy emprendedoras. Según informes recientes, los inmigrantes son propietarios del 12,5% de los negocios que hay en los Estados Unidos. Los sectores más elegidos para trabajar son el entretenimiento, el transporte, el comercio, la educación y la salud.

La presencia de los inmigrantes no es igual en todos los estados. En la gráfica siguiente se ve cuáles son los estados que los inmigrantes eligen para abrir sus negocios.

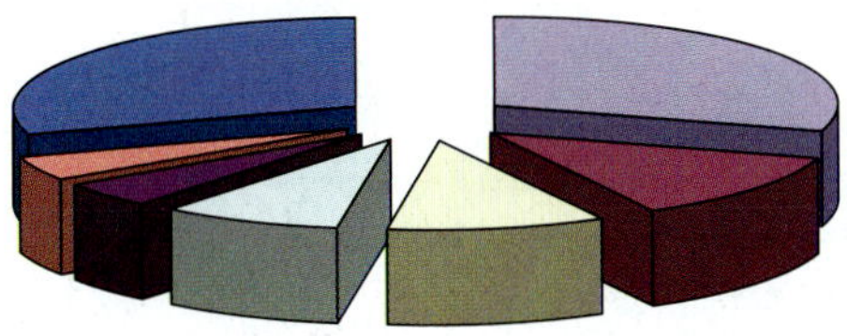

b. Complete las oraciones con las palabras del recuadro. Puede usarlas más de una vez.

más	más de	más que

1. Cada año, los Estados Unidos reciben ......más de...... 1 millón de inmigrantes.
2. California es el estado que ......más...... inmigrantes eligen para abrir sus negocios.
3. Los inmigrantes que eligen Texas para abrir sus negocios son ......más que...... los que eligen Nueva Jersey.
4. Los negocios de inmigrantes de Nueva York son casi tres veces ......más que...... los de Illinois.

c. ¿Cuál cree usted que es la procedencia de la mayoría de los inmigrantes que tienen negocios en su ciudad? ¿Por qué?

22 Participe en el foro. Escriba sus comentarios y preguntas para Fernanda y Alberto.

Comidas latinoamericanas

Cuando las personas migran de un país a otro, llevan sus costumbres, sus tradiciones ¡y sus recetas! Muchas veces, esos alimentos se hacen populares en el país receptor. Estas son algunas de las muchas comidas conocidas en los Estados Unidos:

Argentina: empanadas
Colombia: arepas, pan de bono
El Salvador: pupusas
México: enchiladas, tacos, tamales
Perú: ceviche

23 a. Lea el recuadro de la izquierda y observe las fotos. ¿Conoce alguno de estos alimentos?

empanada arepa pupusa tamal

b. ¿Ha probado alguno de ellos? ¿Qué otros alimentos extranjeros son populares en su país?

23 **Suggestion** Ask students if they have tried the foods pictured, and if and where in your university town they can be found.

Practice more at **vhlcentral.com.**

SAM: Actividades pp. 173–178

24 Suggestion Have students specify their intentions about their stay in the country, using **querer** + [infinitive]. Also have them justify their choices by making comparisons with the other countries.

24 Imagine que participará en un programa de estudios en el extranjero. Diga a sus compañeros qué país eligió y por qué.

Modelo: *Elegí Ecuador porque quiero estudiar las tortugas de las islas Galápagos.*

Argentina

China

Ecuador

Reino Unido

Colombia

Chile

Alemania

España

Cuba

México

Emphasize that every family is different, and that it's fine whether students' families have moved a great deal or not at all, and whether or not students know the history of their ancestors.

TAREA FINAL

El origen de mi familia

Piense en el origen de su familia y en los lugares donde han vivido ustedes hasta ahora, y complete esta ficha.

familiar	procedencia	destino
....	....	....

Presente la historia personal de migraciones de su familia al grupo. Haga un esquema y marque los itinerarios y etapas.

Haga preguntas a sus compañeros sobre los motivos de sus migraciones.

Reflexione con sus compañeros acerca de las causas principales que motivan estas migraciones.

YO PUEDO...

- **Puedo hablar sobre experiencias pasadas.**
  Cuente en qué lugares ha vivido o hable de la última vez que viajó a un país extranjero.
- **Puedo indicar la duración de una experiencia.**
  Indique la duración de las experiencias anteriores.
- **Puedo expresar intenciones.**
  Exprese sus intenciones sobre su lugar de residencia y su trabajo.
- **Puedo comparar formas de vida.**
  Compare las formas de vida de los diferentes lugares donde ha vivido, o los diferentes trabajos que ha tenido.

GRAMÁTICA FUNCIONAL

8B.1 Talk about experiences

Preterite of irregular verbs 5.2.2

- Many common verbs are irregular in the preterite. These verbs use an irregular preterite stem and a common set of endings.

VENIR			
(yo)	**vin**e	(nosotros/as)	**vin**imos
(tú)	**vin**iste	(vosotros/as)	**vin**isteis
(usted, él, ella)	**vin**o	(ustedes, ellos/as)	**vin**ieron

- These are the preterite stems and conjugations of some common irregular verbs.

estar →	**estuv-** →	estuve, estuviste, estuvo, estuvimos, estuvisteis, estuvieron
poder →	**pud-** →	pude, pudiste, pudo, pudimos, pudisteis, pudieron
poner →	**pus-** →	puse, pusiste, puso, pusimos, pusisteis, pusieron
saber →	**sup-** →	supe, supiste, supo, supimos, supisteis, supieron
tener →	**tuv-** →	tuve, tuviste, tuvo, tuvimos, tuvisteis, tuvieron
hacer →	**hic-** →	hice, hiciste, **hizo**, hicimos, hicisteis, hicieron
querer →	**quis-** →	quise, quisiste, quiso, quisimos, quisisteis, quisieron
conducir →	**conduj-** →	conduje, condujiste, condujo, condujimos, condujisteis, **condujeron**
decir →	**dij-** →	dije, dijiste, dijo, dijimos, dijisteis, **dijeron**
traducir →	**traduj-** →	traduje, tradujiste, tradujo, tradujimos, tradujisteis, **tradujeron**
traer →	**traj-** →	traje, trajiste, trajo, trajimos, trajisteis, **trajeron**

- Note that the **c** in the stem of **hacer** changes to **z** in the **usted/él/ella** form, in order to maintain the soft *c* sound.

  Yo **hice** la ensalada y Ramón **hizo** el pastel.
  *I **made** the salad and Ramón **made** the cake.*

- For j-stem verbs such as **conducir** and **traducir**, drop the **i** from the ending of the **ustedes/ellos/ellas** form.

  Ustedes **condujeron** desde San Salvador, ¿verdad?
  *You **drove** from San Salvador, right?*

- The preterite form of **hay** is **hubo**. As with **hay**, use **hubo** with both singular and plural objects.

  Hubo tormentas anoche y el vuelo no salió.
  ***There were** storms last night and the flight didn't leave.*

8B.2 Indicate duration

Prepositions of duration 10.5, 10.7, 10.8, 10.9, 10.14

- To ask how long something has been happening, say **¿Desde cuándo** + [*present-tense verb*]?, **¿Desde hace cuánto tiempo** + [*present-tense verb*]? or **¿Cuánto tiempo hace que** + [*present-tense verb*]?

  ¿Desde cuándo viven en Boston?
  ***How long** have you lived in Boston?*

- To say *since* some prior action or event, use **desde que** + [*verb in preterite*].

  Vivo aquí **desde que** me casé.
  *I've lived here **since** I got married.*

8B.1 Suggestion Point out that the preterite forms of **estar** and **tener** are identical except for the initial **es-** of the **estar** forms.

¡Póngalo en práctica!

G1 Complete las oraciones con la forma correcta del verbo.

1. ¿...Pudiste... (Poder) resolver el problema tú solo?
2. Mi amigo y yo ...condujimos... (conducir) por turnos durante el viaje.
3. Mis padres ...supieron... (saber) aprovechar las oportunidades.
4. Yo siempre ...quise... (querer) viajar por Latinoamérica.
5. Sonia ...hizo... (hacer) realidad su deseo de poner un negocio.
6. ¿Ustedes ...vinieron... (venir) en autobús?
7. Dos expertos ...tradujeron... (traducir) el libro al español.
8. Tú ...estuviste... (estar) en Guadalajara, ¿no es cierto?

G2 Vuelva a escribir la oración en el pretérito, sobre el día de ayer. **G2 Expansion** Have students write four additional sentences for a classmate to convert.

Modelo: Tengo que ir al médico.
Tuve que ir al médico ayer.

1. Hay un descuento en este producto hoy.
   Hubo un descuento en este producto ayer.
2. Jimena se pone la chaqueta.
   Jimena se puso la chaqueta ayer.
3. Ellos conducen muchos kilómetros.
   Ellos condujeron muchos kilómetros ayer.
4. Tú haces unos postres deliciosos.
   Tú hiciste unos postres deliciosos ayer.
5. Hay mucho tráfico.
   Hubo mucho tráfico ayer.
6. Estamos paseando en el campo.
   Estuvimos paseando en el campo ayer.
7. Vosotros podéis salir temprano hoy.
   Vosotros pudisteis salir temprano ayer.

G3 Complete la conversación.

- ¿Desde cuándo (1)...vives... (vivir, tú) en California?
- Desde que (2)...me casé... (casarse) en 2005.
- ¿Y cuánto tiempo hace que (3)...pusiste... (poner) tu propio negocio?
- (4)...Hace... tres años.
- ¿Por qué crees que tienes tanto éxito?
- Tal vez porque (5)...desde que... llegué no paro de trabajar.

Practice more at **vhlcentral.com.**

GRAMÁTICA FUNCIONAL

- Use **durante** to indicate duration.

  Durante diez años viví en el extranjero.
  For ten years I lived abroad.

- To specify the beginning and end of a time period, use **desde/de** + [*start time*] + **hasta/a** + [*end time*]. Be sure to use **desde** and **hasta** together and **de** and **a** together, and remember to form the contractions **del** and **al** when necessary.

  Trabajé en esa empresa **desde** 2003 **hasta** 2007.
  I worked for that company ***from*** *2003* ***to*** *2007.*

  Estuve de viaje **del** primero de julio **al** primero de agosto.
  I was traveling ***from*** *July first* ***to*** *August first.*

8B.3 Express intentions

querer + [*infinitive*] 5.7.1, 5.10

- Use **querer** + [*infinitive*] to express desires or intentions. Remember to conjugate only the first verb (**querer**) in infinitive constructions.

  Quiero mirar la tele esta noche. ¿Qué **quieres hacer** tú?
  I ***want to watch*** *TV tonight. What* ***do you want to do****?*

- When you use a reflexive pronoun or other object pronoun with this construction, place the pronoun before the conjugated verb or attach it to the end of the infinitive. You saw this pattern with direct object pronouns in 3B.8.

  Mañana quiero levantar**me** más tarde.
  Mañana **me** quiero levantar más tarde.
  I want to ***get up*** *later tomorrow.*

8B.4 Compare lifestyles

Comparisons of equality 4.4.3, 12.7

- Comparisons of equality express the degree to which two people, items, or experiences are similar. Use **tan** + [*adjective/adverb*] + **como** to compare descriptions with adjectives and adverbs.

  Las pupusas son **tan ricas como** las empanadas.
  Pupusas are ***as tasty as*** *empanadas.*

- Use **tanto/a(s)** + [*noun*] + **como** to compare amounts or quantities. **Tanto/a** must agree in gender and number with the noun it modifies.

  Preparé **tantos tamales como** Alberto.
  I made ***as many tamales as*** *Alberto.*

- Use [*verb*] + **tanto como** for comparisons with verbs. Note that **tanto** is invariable in this construction.

  Martín trabaja **tanto como** Eduardo.
  Martín works ***as much as*** *Eduardo (does).*

- Use **tan** and **tanto/a(s)** for emphasis when the second point of comparison is not specified.

  ¡Trabajo **tantas** horas, preparo **tanta** comida y estoy **tan** cansada!
  I work ***so many*** *hours, I make* ***so much*** *food, and I am* ***so*** *tired!*

8B.4 Suggestion Have students write four statements comparing themselves to different famous people, using comparisons of equality. Collect their papers and read the sentences aloud for the class to guess who wrote them.

8B.2 Suggestion Draw a time line of key events in your life on the board and ask questions about it, using prepositions of duration.

¡Póngalo en práctica!

G4 Escriba oraciones completas en pasado usando **desde/de..., hasta/a** o **durante.** Answers will vary. Sample answers:

1. nosotros / no poder viajar / enero–julio
   Nosotros no pudimos viajar desde/de enero hasta/a julio.
2. yo / conducir / dos días
   Yo conduje durante dos días.
3. ellos / estar casados / 1999–2006 /
   Ellos estuvieron casados desde/de 1999 hasta/a 2006.
4. tú / tener el mismo carro / cinco años
   Tú tuviste el mismo carro durante cinco años.
5. él /hacer las entrevistas / lunes–jueves
   Él hizo las entrevistas del lunes al jueves.
6. ustedes /querer tener su propia casa / 20 años
   Ustedes quisieron tener su propia casa durante 20 años.
7. Marcelo / estudiar inglés / tres años
   Marcelo estudió inglés durante tres años.

G5 Escriba oraciones completas para expresar deseos o intenciones.

1. Juan / conseguir un buen trabajo
   Juan quiere conseguir un buen trabajo.
2. tú / nunca / levantarse / temprano
   Tú nunca quieres levantarte/te quieres levantar temprano.
3. ustedes / hacer fortuna con este invento
   Ustedes quieren hacer fortuna con este invento.
4. nosotros / tener un hijo el año próximo
   Nosotros queremos tener un hijo el año próximo.
5. ellos / dedicarse más al estudio
   Ellos quieren dedicarse/se quieren dedicar más al estudio.
6. yo / acostarse temprano
   Yo quiero acostarme/me quiero acostar temprano.

G6 Complete la conversación.

- Tomás, ¿tú trabajas (1) tantas horas como Pedro?
- No, yo no trabajo (2) tanto.
- Pero su trabajo no es (3) tan cansador (4) como el tuyo.
- Es cierto, él no camina (5) tanto como yo.

G7 Escriba oraciones completas usando **tan** o **tanto/a(s)**. Suggested answers:

1. inmigrantes / Florida / establecerse / Nueva York
   En Florida se establecen tantos inmigrantes como en Nueva York.
2. ¡! / los inmigrantes / emprendedores
   ¡Los inmigrantes son tan emprendedores!
3. (yo) / viajar / ahora / no / para ir al trabajo
   Ahora no viajo tanto para ir al trabajo.
4. Isabel / dedicarse al trabajo / Diana
   Isabel se dedica al trabajo tanto como Diana.
5. Mauricio / Mariana / conducir / rápido
   Mauricio conduce tan rápido como Mariana.

Practice more at **vhlcentral.com.**

VOCABULARIO

Emigrantes

a finales del siglo XIX	*towards the end of the 19th century*
a principios del siglo XX	*at the beginning of the 20th century*
¿cuánto tiempo (hace)?	*how long (have/has)?*
los años 60	*the sixties*
la beca	*scholarship*
la chimenea	*chimney*
la emigración	*emigration*
el/la emigrante	*emigrant*
el exilio	*exile*
la fábrica	*factory*
la finca	*farm*
la guerra	*war*
la guerra civil	*civil war*
el horizonte	*horizon*
el/la inmigrante	*immigrant*
la investigación	*research*
la maleta	*suitcase*
la migración	*migration*
el/la obrero/a	*worker*
el/la químico/a	*chemist*
la suerte	*(good) luck*
el testimonio	*testimony*
el/la visitante	*visitor*
casarse	*to get married*
hacer fortuna	*to make fortune*
hacer las maletas	*to pack*
pasar	*to happen*
quedarse	*to stay*
regresar	*to go back, to return*
tener (e:ie) un hijo	*to have a child*
volver (o:ue)	*to go back, to return*
industrial	*industrial*
salvadoreño/a	*Salvadoran*
desde/de... hasta/a	*from... until/to*
desde niño(s)	*since childhood*
desde que	*since*
en la actualidad	*today; nowadays*

Nuevas formas de vida

es decir	*in other words*
o sea	*that is*
la bandera	*flag*
el bazar	*bazaar*
el/la ciudadano/a	*citizen*
el comercio	*commerce*
la comunidad inmigrante	*immigrant community*
el/la directivo/a	*manager*
el futuro	*future*
el juguete	*toy*
el locutorio	*call center; Internet café*
la panadería	*bakery*
la peluquería	*hair salon*
la población migrante	*migrant population*
la procedencia	*origin*
el Reino Unido	*United Kingdom*
el servicio doméstico	*domestic service*
la tetería	*tea room*
reformular	*to restate*
para siempre	*forever*
temporalmente	*temporarily*

Fernanda y Alberto

los ahorros	*savings*
el/la dueño/a	*owner*
el/la empresario/a	*businessperson*
el entretenimiento	*entertainment*
la igualdad	*equality*
el millón	*million*
la oportunidad	*opportunity*
el país receptor	*host country*
la presencia	*presence*
el/la propietario/a	*owner*
la pupusa	*Salvadoran filled tortilla*
la pupusería	*store where* ***pupusas*** *are sold*
la recompensa	*reward*
la sección	*section*
el sector	*sector*
el sueño	*dream*
la tienda de alimentación	*grocery store*
comenzar (e:ie)	*to begin, to start*
hacer realidad	*to make something happen*
hacerse	*to become*
vender	*to sell*
emprendedor(a)	*enterprising*
al parecer	*apparently*
tan/tanto...como	*as much/many...as*
tantos/as	*as many*

Variación léxica

el/la dueño/a ↔ **el/la propietario/a**

la maleta ↔ **la valija** (*Arg.*)

regresar ↔ **volver** (*o:ue*)

Rumania (*Amér. L.*) ↔ **Rumanía** (*Esp.*)

la tienda de alimentación ↔ **la tienda de abarrotes** (*Méx.*) ↔ **el almacén** (*Arg.*) ↔ **la tienda de abasto(s)** (*Ven.*)

Estrategias

① Dar ejemplos

Lección 7A

Including examples in a conversation allows you to explain your ideas more clearly.

○ **Añada ejemplos donde corresponda en estas conversaciones.**

1 Expansion have volunteers role-play conversations for the class.

- ¿Quedamos mañana por la noche?
- Dale, ¿qué quieres hacer?
- Si quieres, podemos ir a cenar a un restaurante exótico...
- ¡Buena idea!

- La vida en el campo me encanta.
- ¿No es un poco aburrida?
- No, es posible hacer muchas cosas...

② Generalizar y matizar

Lección 7B

Making generalizations (**generalmente/en general**) and explaining nuances (**especialmente/en especial, particularmente/en particular**) help you to be more precise in your communication.

○ **Sustituya los iconos ⬭ por expresiones para generalizar o matizar según convenga.**

En mi país, la gente en el trabajo (generalmente/en general) se tutea, (en especial/especialmente) los colegas de la misma categoría. Hay otros contextos que son más formales (en general). Por ejemplo, si hablas con una persona que no conoces, (generalmente/en general) usas el *usted*, (en especial/especialmente/en particular/particularmente) si la persona es mayor.

③ Introducir una explicación y animar

Lección 8A

Expressions such as **¡Mira!** to begin an explanation and **¡Dale!** to offer encouragement let you communicate more naturally.

○ **Complete el texto con *¡Mira!* o *¡Dale!* y ordene las ilustraciones.**

- ¡ Mira ! Así se hace un álbum de fotografías. Corta° la cartulina de las tapas°. Forra° las tapas con el papel deseado. Corta° las hojas del álbum. Realiza agujeros° y une las hojas con el cordón°. Por último, pega° el interior del álbum a la tapa interior.
- Parece fácil...
- ¡ Dale ! Ahora tú.

corta *cut* **la tapa** *cover* **forra** *cover (v.)* **agujero** *hole* **cordón** *string* **pega** *glue*

④ Reformular

Lección 8B

Restating ideas in mid-conversation will help you gain fluency and confidence in your communication.

○ **Reformule las informaciones correctas o inexactas.** Sample answers:

- ¿Qué hora es?
- Son las 10:00 h.

O sea, las diez menos cinco.

- ¿Qué día es hoy?
- Es casi fin de semana.

Es decir, hoy es viernes.

JUNIO

L	M	M	J	V	S	D
					1	2
3	4	5	6	7	8	9
10	11	12	13	(14)	15	16
17	18	19	20	21	22	23
24	25	26	27	28	29	30

4 Expansion Have students write two more brief dialogues using **o sea** and **es decir.**

Competencias

HABLAR DE TRABAJO, HÁBITOS Y ACCIONES QUE OCURREN EN EL MOMENTO

1 Forme oraciones con estas palabras. Sample answers:

Modelo: *colegio, todos los días, madrugo, niños, llevo*
Todos los días madrugo y llevo a los niños al colegio.

a. dedicarse, cantautora, escribir canciones, o sea, yo Soy cantautora; o sea, me dedico a escribir canciones.

b. vestimos, levantamos, 15 minutos, duchamos Nos levantamos, nos duchamos y nos vestimos en 15 minutos.

c. conduce un camión, filosofía, verdadera vocación, Carlos Carlos conduce un camión, pero su verdadera vocación es la filosofía.

d. leyendo el periódico, Sandro, este momento Sandro está leyendo el periódico en este momento.

HABLAR DE EXPERIENCIAS RECIENTES

2 Javier y Fernando se encuentran en el Zócalo, en México, D.F. Complete la conversación con un verbo de la lista en la forma correcta del pretérito perfecto.

decir • dejar • escribir • hacer • leer • olvidar • pasar • traer • ver • volver

- ¡Hola! Esta mañana te (1) he escrito un mensaje de texto para quedar más temprano. ¿No lo (2) has leído? Hace casi media hora que espero.
- Lo siento, Javier. Mi celular está sin batería y lo (3) he dejado en casa.
- No hay problema. ¿(4) Has traído las entradas para el concierto?
- Oh, no, ¡las (5) he olvidado! Es que (6) he hecho muchas cosas hoy y no (7) he pasado por casa.
- Pero te (8) he dicho que las necesito. El concierto es hoy.
- Perdona, por favor. Apenas esta mañana (9) he vuelto de mis vacaciones. ¿(10) Has visto un bar donde tomar algo? Yo invito.

DAR INSTRUCCIONES

3 Con su compañero/a, escriban algunos consejos para ayudar a estas personas.

3 Expansion For the second illustration, have students develop separate lists of advice for the man and for the woman.

1. entrevista de trabajo

2. primera cita

3. viaje a un país extranjero

Modelo: • *Llega temprano a una entrevista de trabajo*

HABLAR DE EXPERIENCIAS E INDICAR DURACIÓN

4 Expansion Tell students to imagine that they are 35 years old and they have been asked to write a retrospective. Have them write a paragraph using Tania's description as a model.

4 Complete el testimonio de Tania.

abrí	aprendo	cantautor	cuidé	desde hace	doméstico	exótico
fue	mi	nuestros	panadería	soy	vivo	vocación

Soy dominicana, pero (1) vivo en Barcelona (2) desde hace cuatro años. Mi primer trabajo (3) fue en el servicio (4) doméstico. Después (5) cuidé a ancianos. Pude ahorrar algo de dinero y (6) abrí una peluquería con una amiga. ¡(7) Soy tan feliz! Esta es (8) mi verdadera vocación.

Flash CULTURA

Estrategia

Getting the gist

When watching a video,try to get the gist by listening first for a statement about the general topic. Concentrate on words you know instead of fixating on unfamiliar words. The title is a good clue for predicting what the video will be about. Before watching this **Flash Cultura** episode, make one or two hypotheses based on the title **Arquitectura modernista.**

Vocabulario útil

el baldosín *ceramic tile*
brillar *to shine*
la calavera *skull*
el encargo *job, assignment*
la escama *scale*
la escalera *staircase*
la fachada *front of building*
el hierro forjado *wrought iron*
el hueso *bone*
inacabado/a *unfinished*
el tejado *tile roof*

Estrategia

Connotations

Remember that in Spanish, as in English, some words may have figurative uses. Metaphors, similes, and personifications appear not only in poetry, but also in everyday language. For example, **(Está que) se lo/la lleva el diablo** or **(Está que) echa chispas,** do not mean that a person is about to be taken away by the devil or to explode; these phrases express (colloquially) that the person is extremely angry.

Arquitectura modernista

Para todas las personas es importante cumplir sus sueños: algunas construyen cosas bellas para hacer un mundo mejor. Este episodio de **Flash Cultura** presenta las creaciones de los arquitectos catalanes que hicieron realidad sus sueños en la ciudad de Barcelona.

1 Hable con un(a) compañero/a: ¿Cuáles son los edificios más famosos de su país? ¿Dónde están? ¿Han visitado o conocen ciudades con edificios importantes? ¿Creen que un edificio solamente tiene que ser útil y cómodo o también debe ser bonito? ¿Qué es más importante?

2 Mire este episodio de **Flash Cultura.** Trate de identificar cada lugar concentrándose en una característica o en un detalle; no se preocupe por entender toda la descripción.

1 **Antonio Gaudí... también creó un extraordinario espacio público donde la gente puede disfrutar...**

Suggestion: Explain that **cuatro gatos** means *an insignificant number of people,* as in **Vinieron cuatro gatos** *(Only a few [unimportant] people came).* Ask your class to guess the meaning of other Spanish sayings like **Dar gato por liebre, Buscarle tres pies al gato,** and **Hay gato encerrado.**

Suggestion: After watching the video, discuss with students whether they would prefer to live in **Casa Batlló, Casa Amatller,** or **Casa Lleó-Morera.**

2 **La Sagrada Familia es el edificio más visitado y emblemático de la ciudad.**

3 Expansion To challenge students, eliminate the first column; have them read the phrases in the second column and identify the site.

3 Una la primera columna con la segunda para completar las oraciones.

1. La zona del Paseo de Gracia...	...3... a. fue encargo de un chocolatero.
2. La Casa Batlló de Gaudí...	...5... b. es una obra inacabada de Gaudí.
3. La Casa Amatller...	...1... c. se conoce como *La manzana de la discordia.*
4. El banco ondulado del Parque Güell...	...6... d. fue punto de encuentro de jóvenes artistas modernistas.
5. La Sagrada Familia...	...2... e. representa la leyenda de San Jorge y el dragón.
6. El café Los cuatro gatos...	...4... f. tiene forma de serpiente colorida.

4 Con un(a) compañero/a, hable de propuestas para hacer un mundo mejor; acepte o rechace cada una y escriba las que aprobó. Después, comparta el resultado con la clase.

Practice more at **vhlcentral.com.**

Audio: Activities, Vocabulary
Video: *Flash Cultura*

Unidad 9

Luis Soriano, creador del Biblioburro

Lección 9A

ETAPAS DE LA VIDA

Lección 9B

HISTORIAS DE LA CALLE

Lola, la del quiosco del barrio

Las fiestas

AVANCE

9A ETAPAS DE LA VIDA

¡Qué tiempos!

¿Dónde estabas en 2005?
¿Estudiabas en la Escuela Primaria N.º 3?
¿Qué hacías cuando estudiabas?
¿Qué hacían tus compañeros de curso?
¿Conocían el club El progreso?
¿Compartían otras actividades además de la escuela?
Si la respuesta es sí, eres uno de los compañeros de Cristina y Carlos.
En Punto de encuentro *puedes volver a ver a tus compañeros de la promoción de 2005.*
Sábado 12 de febrero. 22:00 h.

Punto de encuentro

Un programa de TV para el pasado y para el presente.
Para reencontrar a amigos de la infancia
y a compañeros de la escuela primaria.

Describir hábitos y situaciones del pasado

- ¿Qué **hacías** en la época de la escuela primaria?
- **Tenía** clases por la mañana. **Compartía** el autobús escolar de regreso a casa con Nico y Mario. **Estaba** siempre con ellos: **estudiábamos** juntos y **jugábamos** en el mismo equipo de fútbol.

9A.1 Imperfect

Vocabulario

1
la etapa *stage*
la escuela primaria *elementary school*
el punto de encuentro *meeting point*
la promoción *graduating class*
reencontrar (o:ue) *to meet again*
la infancia *childhood*
la época *time, period*
egresar *to graduate*
el programa, la TV
3
estar callado/a *to be silent, not to talk*

4 Expansion Have students say with which childhood friends they did these activities. Ex: **Jessica y yo hacíamos la tarea juntas.**

1 a. Lea el anuncio. ¿Qué es *Punto de encuentro*? Suggested answer: Es un programa de TV que tiene como objetivo reencontrar a amigos de la infancia y compañeros de la escuela primaria.

b. Localice en los textos las formas del pretérito imperfecto y complete la tabla.

	ESTAR	HACER	COMPARTIR
yo	*estaba*	*hacía*	*compartía*
tú	estabas	hacías	*compartías*
usted, él, ella	*estaba*	*hacía*	*compartía*
nosotros/as	*estábamos*	*hacíamos*	*compartíamos*
vosotros/as	*estabais*	*hacíais*	*compartíais*
ustedes, ellos/as	*estaban*	hacían	compartían

c. Localice otros verbos en pretérito imperfecto. ¿Cuál es su infinitivo? Escriba su conjugación. estudiar: estudiaba, estudiabas, estudiaba, estudiábamos, estudiabais, estudiaban; conocer: conocía, conocías, conocía, conocíamos, conocíais, conocían

2 ¿A quiénes buscan Cristina y Carlos? ¿Qué características identifican a los compañeros de su curso? Buscan a compañeros de la promoción de 2005 de la Escuela N.º 3. Conocían el club El progreso.

3 a. Escuche a Cristina y a Carlos en el programa. ¿Quién hacía estas cosas?

1. Tomaba clases de guitarra. Su hermano tenía un grupo de música y ella soñaba con tocar con ellos. Cristina
2. Vivía cerca de Juan y muchas veces salían en bici a la hora de la siesta. Jugaba al fútbol con sus amigos en el club El progreso. Carlos

b. Escuche otra vez y marque qué hacían ellos juntos.

- [ ] Hacían la tarea juntos.
- [x] Tomaban el mismo autobús escolar.
- [ ] Veían películas juntos.
- [ ] Estudiaban francés juntos.

4 ¿Qué hacía usted hace cinco o diez años? ¿Cuántos años tenía? ¿Dónde vivía? ¿Qué estudiaba? ¿A qué jugaba? ¿Qué música le gustaba?

Los invitamos este sábado a compartir el antes y el ahora.

Cuando éramos pequeños, nos reuníamos en alguna casa a jugar o caminábamos juntos a la escuela. ¡Hasta llevábamos a nuestra vecinita al jardín! Vivíamos muchas cosas juntos…

Ahora ya somos jóvenes hechos y derechos, con nuevas responsabilidades, pero si lo queremos ¡podemos vivir juntos muchas cosas más!

Comparar el pasado con el presente

- Yo antes **era** más inseguro. Ahora sé lo que quiero.
- Pues yo antes **iba** a conciertos de rock, y ahora también voy.

9A.2 Irregular imperfect forms

Vocabulario

5

- **el antes** *before; the past*
- **el/la joven hecho/a y derecho/a** *all grown-up*
- **antes** *before*
- **la responsabilidad** *responsibility*

6

- **la mochila** *backpack*
- **la carpa** *tent*
- **aventurero/a** *adventurous*
- **guapo/a** *good-looking*
- **el pelo** *hair*
- **el canal** *channel*

La televisión en el mundo hispano

Dos de los grupos audiovisuales hispánicos más importantes son Televisión española (TVE), y Televisa, en México. Ambos tienen canales de proyección internacional.

8 Suggestion Have students think about childhood games, technology, eating and exercise habits, family time, etc., and make comparisons.

5 Observe las imágenes y lea los textos. ¿Cómo eran antes y cómo son ahora estas personas? En las dos primeras fotos eran niños y en la tercera foto son jóvenes.

5 Suggestion Also have students compare what these people used to do and what they do now.

6 Escuche a un compañero que llama al programa. ¿Cómo era antes? ¿Adónde iba? ¿Y ahora? Tenía el pelo largo, y era simpático y aventurero. Ahora no tiene el pelo largo, pero es el mismo chico simpático y aventurero. Iba mucho a los campamentos organizados por la escuela. Los fines de semana va a conocer lugares nuevos con su mochila y su carpa.

7 Fíjese en las formas de los verbos regulares. Luego escriba los sujetos para las formas del pretérito imperfecto de estos dos verbos irregulares.

SER	
1. nosotros/as éramos	4. usted, él, ella era
2. vosotros/as erais	5. ustedes, ellos/as eran
3. yo era	6. tú eras

IR	
1. nosotros/as íbamos	4. vosotros/as ibais
2. yo iba	5. usted, él, ella iba
3. tú ibas	6. ustedes, ellos/as iban

8 ¿Ha cambiado mucho la vida desde que usted era pequeño/a? ¿Cómo era antes y cómo es ahora? Dé algunos ejemplos.

8 Expansion Have students compare childhood now with that of their grandparents' generation.

MI EXPERIENCIA

9 Expansion Tell students to imagine that they are organizing a reunion party of former classmates. Have them compose an ad similar to the one on page 214.

9 ¿Cómo era su vida hace cinco o diez años? Pregunte a sus compañeros.

GUIÓN DE TRABAJO

	Hace 5/10 años…	Ahora…
vivienda	*vivía*	*vivo*
edad		
estudios		
aficiones		

¿Dónde estudiabas? ¿Qué hacías? ¿Cómo eras?

Y ahora… ¿Qué haces? ¿Cómo eres?

Practice more at **vhlcentral.com.**

SAM: Actividades pp. 179–181

Segunda juventud

Suggestion Have students observe the older people in the photographs and, using their imaginations, describe what they were like and what they used to do when they were teenagers.

Seguro que tienes muchas cosas interesantes que compartir:

algún viaje, alguna canción, alguna noticia, algún amor...

Queremos escucharte.

somos-todo-oídos

Televisión para mayores de 65

Referirse a cantidades indefinidas

- ¿Hay **algún** documental en la tele?
- Sí, creo que hay **alguno**.
- ¿Hay **alguna** serie hoy?
- Sí, creo que hay **alguna**.
- ¿No hay **ningún** debate ahora?
- No, **ninguno**.
- ¿No hay **ninguna** entrevista?
- No, **ninguna**.

9A.3 **algún, ningún alguno/a, ninguno/a**

Vocabulario

(10)

la juventud *youth*
Seguro que... *I'm sure (that)...*
algún *some, any*
alguno/a *some, any*
ser todo oídos *to be all ears*
mayor de *older than*
el/la reportero/a *reporter*
el/la camarógrafo/a *cameraman/camerawoman*
el documental

(12)

ninguno/a *no, none*
ningún *no*

Estrategia

Ganar tiempo mientras pensamos

- ¿Sabe alguna canción?
- ¿Alguna canción? Mmm... bueno, pues, no sé... a ver... ¿cómo era?

10 a. Observe la imagen de la izquierda. Describa qué está pasando. Una reportera está entrevistando a un hombre mayor en la calle.
b. ¿Qué anuncia la publicidad? un programa de televisión
c. ¿Mira usted la televisión? ¿Algún programa en especial?

11 Fíjese en el texto del anuncio. Relacione los elementos de los grupos. algún amor, algún viaje; alguna canción, alguna noticia

algún, alguna — amor, canción, viaje, noticia

12 a. Escuche a esta persona a la que han entrevistado en directo en el programa de televisión y marque los temas que menciona.

¿Algún/Alguna...?	Sí, alguno/a.	No, ninguno/a.
viaje	✓	
canción	✓	
noticia		✓
amor	✓	
persona	✓	

b. Escuche de nuevo y localice las formas para ganar tiempo antes de responder. Eh... bueno...; Mmm... pues, no sé... este...; A ver... cómo era..., Mmm... pues, ahora mismo no sé...

13 Comparta con el grupo alguna información sobre estos temas para colaborar con el programa.

algún viaje | alguna canción | alguna noticia | algún amor | alguna persona | alguna experiencia con el español | otros...

Modelo:
- *¿Sabes alguna canción?*
- *Pues, no sé... a ver...*

Have students name ways that they "buy time" while speaking.

TV Hoy — Programación

9:00 h Informativo *¡Buen día, país!*
10:00 h Tertulia política en *Todas las voces.*
11:00 h La información deportiva en *Charlas de fútbol.*
12:00 h *El magacín de la tele* con informativos, pronóstico del tiempo y temas de sociedad.
14:00 h *Los jóvenes tienen la palabra* con la participación de los televidentes.
15:00 h *Trotamundos* Viajes y ritmos del mundo.
16:00 h *Somos todo oídos* para mayores de 65.

Suggestion Have students read through the programs and name titles of similar programs that currently air in this country.

14 Deporte: *Charlas de fútbol.* Música: *Trotamundos.* Noticias: *¡Buen día, país!, El magacín de la tele.* Política: *Todas las voces.* Sociedad: *El magacín de la tele, Los jóvenes tienen la palabra* y *Somos todo oídos.* Viajes: *Trotamundos.*

Expresar preferencias

- ¿Qué programa de televisión prefieres?
- Para mí, **el más interesante** es la tertulia política.
- Ese es **el más aburrido**. Para mí, **el mejor** es el programa de viajes.
- ¿Y **el peor**?
- **El peor**, las charlas de fútbol.

9A.4 **el más/menos... el mejor/peor...**

Vocabulario

14
el informativo *news (program)*
la tertulia *roundtable; talk show*
la charla (*fam.*) *conversation*
el magacín *news and talk show*
el pronóstico *weather forecast*
la sociedad *society*
el/la televidente *TV viewer*
el/la trotamundos *globetrotter*

15
el/la más/menos *the most/least*
el/la mejor/peor *the best/worst*
útil *useful*
completo/a

16
acompañar *to keep company*

17
los medios (de comunicación) *media*
entretenerse (e:ie) *to amuse oneself*
sentirse (e:ie) acompañado/a *to feel accompanied*

14 Lea la programación de televisión y clasifique los programas de acuerdo a estas categorías.

deporte • música • noticias • política • sociedad • viajes

15 a. Dé su opinión de los programas. **15 Suggestion** Have students explain their opinions.

El más... El menos...

aburrido • completo • divertido • interesante • útil

b. Con un(a) compañero/a, elija el mejor y el peor tipo de programa.

El mejor... El peor...

16 La televisión acompaña la vida de muchas personas. ¿Qué programas son los más vistos en su país? ¿Cuáles son sus preferidos? ¿Por qué?

MI EXPERIENCIA

17 Piense en los medios de comunicación que prefiere para estas situaciones, y qué programas le parecen los más interesantes en cada caso.

GUIÓN DE TRABAJO

Situaciones	Programas	Medios
entretenerse	documentales	Internet
escuchar música	información deportiva	radio
informarse	informativos	televisión
participar en debates	programas musicales	
sentirse acompañado/a	pronóstico del tiempo	

Para mí, la televisión es el mejor medio para informarse.

¿Conoces algún programa/alguna página web para escuchar música?

No, ninguno.
Sí, hay algunas muy buenas en Internet.

Practice more at **vhlcentral.com.**

SAM: Actividades pp. 182–184

9A

Luis Soriano, creador del Biblioburro

Cada fin de semana, el profesor Luis Soriano lleva su biblioteca ambulante Biblioburro a pequeñas aldeas rurales del departamento del Magdalena (Colombia). Montado en sus burros, Alfa y Beto, recorre hasta once kilómetros cargando unos 120 libros, entre cuentos infantiles, novelas, diccionarios y enciclopedias.

Luis lleva más de diez años con este proyecto. "Tuve la idea del Biblioburro cuando mis alumnos de las veredas cercanas llegaban a la escuela sin hacer la tarea porque no tenían libros en la casa. No podían investigar, ¡no podían hacer nada!", dice el profesor. Pero su proyecto es también a largo plazo: estos niños van a ser los futuros adolescentes y es importante despertarles la inquietud de la lectura para formar mentes constructivas e imaginativas.

Cuando comenzó, tenía dos burros y setenta libros. Ahora su colección cuenta con más de 4800 títulos. En esta biblioteca hay que respetar dos reglas: tocar los libros con las manos limpias y no escribir en las páginas. Para Luis, lo mejor de todo es cuando algún niño le pregunta "¿Cuándo va a regresar, maestro?" Lo peor es que algunas veces los libros que presta nunca vuelven.

Hoy el Biblioburro ya es parte de la red nacional de bibliotecas. Además, el proyecto se extendió a otras zonas y desde 2006 también funciona en la Sierra Nevada de Santa Marta.

El profesor Luis Soriano con su burro cargado de libros

Hablar de la cantidad de tiempo

Luis Soriano lleva toda una vida como maestro.

Lleva más de diez años con el Biblioburro.

El proyecto también lleva cinco años funcionando en la Sierra Nevada de Santa Marta.

9A.5 **llevar** + [*length of time*]

Vocabulario

(18)

- la biblioteca ambulante *traveling library*
- la aldea *village*
- el/la burro/a *donkey*
- cargar *to load; to carry*
- montar *to ride*
- la vereda (*Col.*) *rural neighborhood*
- a largo plazo *in the long term*
- despertar (e:ie) la inquietud *to stir up interest*
- la inquietud *interest*
- contar (o:ue) con *to include*
- prestar *to lend*
- la red *network*
- gracioso/a *funny*
- **el/la adolescente**

(19)

- la sede *headquarters*
- la devolución *return*

18 Lea el texto. Describa la actividad que realiza Luis Soriano. ¿Por qué realiza esta actividad? ¿Qué es gracioso acerca del nombre de los burros?
Lleva su biblioteca ambulante a las aldeas. Así ayuda a los niños que no tienen libros a hacer la tarea. La combinación de los dos nombres forma la palabra "alfabeto".

19 a. Conozca más detalles del profesor Luis Soriano. Escuche qué dice de estos temas y anótelo. Luego compruebe las respuestas con su compañero/a.

La sede de la biblioteca: Antes era en su casa. Ahora funciona en un edificio que construyó con la ayuda de donaciones.

Su criterio para elegir qué lugares visita con el Biblioburro: Ayudar a los niños que viven a muchos kilómetros de distancia de las carreteras.

La recepción en los pueblos: Las personas salen y se paran en las puertas a mirarlo pasar. Los niños corren detrás de los burros.

Los libros más pedidos: la literatura infantil

La devolución de los libros: Hay algunas personas que no devuelven los libros.

b. Escuche nuevamente y diga si la entrevistadora y el profesor hablan de *usted* o de *tú*. ¿Por qué cree que esto es así? Suggested answer: La entrevistadora habla de *usted*. El profesor habla de *tú*. La entrevistadora quiere mostrar respeto.

c. Lea estas oraciones de la entrevista. Las palabras subrayadas se usan en Colombia. Relaciónelas con su significado.

a. niño, muchacho (*fam.*)   b. llevar   c. barrio rural

1. Es una biblioteca para los niños que viven en esta vereda. c
2. Los peladitos que viven al lado de la carretera ven gente que pasa y eso les va dejando algo de enseñanza. a
3. *La Ilíada* no lo devolvieron porque les gustó mucho y dijeron "Este me lo cargo". b

Point out that the meaning of **pelado/a** can vary widely according to country or region. In Mexico, for example, it has pejorative connotations and it is used to describe someone poor, uneducated, vulgar, or with low social standing.

Explain that **la devolución** refers to the return of an object; to talk about a person's return, students should use **el regreso** or **la vuelta**.

Vocabulario ***cont.***
el/la campesino/a *peasant*
la donación
20
tierno/a *affectionate*
peludo/a *furry*
la tierra *land, dirt*
el prado *meadow*
la boca *mouth*
la nariz *nose*
blando/a *soft*
el algodón *cotton*
el hueso *bone*
el espejo *mirror*
el ojo *eye*
acariciar *to caress*
celeste *light blue*
el clásico, trotar
21
brillante *bright*
duro/a *hard*
transparente
23
la reseña *summary; review*
la lancha *boat*
flotante *floating*

Promover la lectura

Todo sirve para promover la lectura. Hay bibliobuses en España, un biblioavión interactivo en México, bibliolanchas en Argentina y bibliotecas flotantes en el Amazonas. ¿Hay alguna biblioteca no convencional en su ciudad o región?

Have students research one of these special libraries and write a brief summary of their findings to report to the class.

20 Juan Ramón Jiménez was a Spanish poet and writer who advocated the concept of **poesía pura.** He was awarded the Nobel Prize for Literature in 1956.

20 a. Uno de los libros que Luis Soriano lleva a veces en su Biblioburro es *Platero y yo.* En este clásico de la literatura infantil y juvenil, el escritor español Juan Ramón Jiménez narra su tierna relación con un burrito. Lea el texto y busque las palabras que tienen estos significados.

1. con mucho pelo ......peludo......
2. tierra con hierba para alimentar a los animales ......prado......
3. parte de la cabeza de algunos animales donde están la boca y la nariz ......hocico......
4. forma de caminar del caballo o del burro ......trotecillo......

Platero es pequeño, peludo, suave; tan blando por fuera, que se diría° todo de algodón, que no lleva huesos. Sólo los espejos de azabache° de sus ojos son duros cual dos escarabajos° de cristal negros.

Lo dejo suelto°, y se va al prado, y acaricia tibiamente con su hocico°, rozándolas apenas, las florecillas rosas, celestes y gualdas°... Lo llamo dulcemente: "¿Platero?", y viene a mí con un trotecillo alegre que parece que se ríe, en no sé qué cascabeleo° ideal...

que se diría *you would say he's* **azabache** *jet (black stone)* **cual dos escarabajos** *like two beetles* **suelto** *loose* **hocico** *snout* **rozándolas** *gently touching them* **gualdas** *yellow* **cascabeleo** *jingle*

Juan Ramón Jiménez (1881–1958)

b. ¿Qué actividades hace Platero y cuáles hace su dueño? Sample answer: Platero: se va al prado, acaricia las flores con su hocico, viene con un trote alegre; su dueño: lo deja suelto, lo llama.

21 Según el autor, Platero es tan blando como el algodón. Complete las comparaciones con sus propias ideas. Use un diccionario si lo necesita.

Sample answers:
1. tan transparente como ......el cristal, el agua......
2. tan negro como ......la noche, el carbón......
3. tan brillante como ......la luna, un diamante......
4. tan alto como ......una jirafa, un rascacielos......
5. tan duro como ......el metal, una piedra......

21 Expansion Have students describe a favorite pet or cartoon character, using similes.

22 ¿Por qué son importantes los animales para los seres humanos? ¿Y los seres humanos para los animales? Describa a su mascota o a algún animal. ¿Cómo es físicamente? ¿Cómo es su personalidad?

23 ¿Cuáles son los cuentos que más le gustaban en su infancia? ¿Por qué? Escriba una breve reseña de uno de sus cuentos preferidos en esa época.

24 Escuche el segundo párrafo de *Platero y yo* leído por un español y un argentino. Fíjese en cómo pronuncian estas palabras y apunte las diferencias.
acaricia, hocico, rozándolas, florecillas, llamo, dulcemente, trotecillo, parece

acaricia	rozándolas	llamo	trotecillo
hocico	florecillas	dulcemente	parece

Practice more at **vhlcentral.com.**

SAM: Actividades pp. 185–188

25 Expansion Brainstorm a few additional categories and have students continue the activity in pairs.

25 Descubra más sobre usted mismo/a. Anote el número de las tres actividades que más le interesan. Comparta el resultado con sus compañeros. ¿Hay alguna coincidencia?

1 jardín

2 viajes

3 lectura

4 deporte

5 ONG

6 actividades artísticas

7 familiares y amigos

8 cursos

Resultados:

2, 4, 5: Le encanta descubrir lugares nuevos y conocer a personas nuevas.
4, 2, 1: Tiene mucha energía física.
3, 8, 6: Siempre quiere aprender más.
5, 7, 8: Le gusta compartir su tiempo con otros.
6, 1, 3: Lo que más le gusta es expresarse.

Mi resultado:
Para mí, las más interesantes son
....
....
....

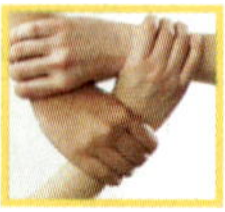

TAREA FINAL

Un programa de televisión

Definan qué tipo de programa de TV quieren hacer. Dividan el programa en secciones y trabajen en grupos pequeños o en parejas.

Escriban el guión del programa: redacción de noticias, canciones, anuncios, etc.

Presenten los contenidos al grupo.

Suggestion For students who live in the same place as they did 10 years ago, have them compare the place now with what it was like a decade ago.

YO PUEDO...

- Puedo describir hábitos del pasado.
  ¿Dónde vivía hace diez años?
- Puedo comparar el pasado con el presente.
  Compare su vida de hace cinco o diez años con la de ahora en estos aspectos: vivienda, estudios, familia.
- Puedo referirme a cantidades indefinidas.
  ¿Hay algún estudiante en clase que vive cerca de usted?
- Puedo expresar preferencias.
  Anote cuál es la mejor y la peor noticia del año según su opinión.
- Puedo hablar de la cantidad de tiempo.
  Indique cuánto tiempo lleva con esta autoevaluación.

GRAMÁTICA FUNCIONAL

9A.1 Describe habits and situations in the past

Imperfect of regular verbs 5.4.1, 5.4.3

- You have learned that Spanish uses two simple tenses, the preterite and the imperfect, to talk about events in the past. Use the imperfect (**el pretérito imperfecto**) to express repeated or habitual actions in the past, or to describe past situations.

  Cuando **estaba** en la escuela primaria, **jugaba** al fútbol.
  *When **I was** in primary school, **I played** soccer.*

- **Estudiar**, **tener**, and **vivir** exemplify the conjugation patterns of regular **-ar**, **-er**, and **-ir** verbs in the **pretérito imperfecto**.

	ESTUDIAR	TENER	VIVIR
(yo)	estudi**aba**	ten**ía**	viv**ía**
(tú)	estudi**abas**	ten**ías**	viv**ías**
(usted, él, ella)	estudi**aba**	ten**ía**	viv**ía**
(nosotros/as)	estudi**ábamos**	ten**íamos**	viv**íamos**
(vosotros/as)	estudi**abais**	ten**íais**	viv**íais**
(ustedes, ellos/as)	estudi**aban**	ten**ían**	viv**ían**

- The **yo** and **usted/él/ella** forms are the same in all conjugations of the imperfect, so you should use context to clarify. Additionally, the endings of **-er** and **-ir** verbs in the imperfect are the same.

  Yo **estudiaba** periodismo y Juan **estudiaba** biología.
  ***I studied** journalism and Juan **studied** biology.*

- Use the imperfect to describe habitual or repeated actions, actions that were in progress, physical characteristics, mental or emotional states, age, and to tell time.

  ¿Cuántos años **tenías** cuando **tomabas** clases de francés?
  *How old **were you** when **you took** French classes?*

- Use the imperfect of **haber** (**había**) to talk about the existence of things. As with **hay** in the present, **había** is used with singular or plural objects. **Suggestion** List the uses of the imperfect on the board and work with the class to come up with an example sentence for each one.

9A.2 Compare the past with the present

Imperfect of irregular verbs 5.4.2

- The verbs **ser**, **ir**, and **ver** have irregular forms in the **pretérito imperfecto**.

	SER	IR	VER
(yo)	**era**	**iba**	**veía**
(tú)	**eras**	**ibas**	**veías**
(usted, él, ella)	**era**	**iba**	**veía**
(nosotros/as)	**éramos**	**íbamos**	**veíamos**
(vosotros/as)	**erais**	**ibais**	**veíais**
(ustedes, ellos/as)	**eran**	**iban**	**veían**

  En la universidad mis amigos y yo **íbamos** todos los domingos al cine.
  *In college, my friends and I **used to go** to the movies every Sunday.*

- All other verbs are regular in the imperfect. Note that there are no stem changes in the imperfect.

¡Póngalo en práctica!

G1 Elija la forma del pretérito imperfecto que corresponde con cada sujeto.

viajar		
c	1. ella	a. viajabas
d	2. nosotros	b. viajabais
a	3. tú	c. viajaba
b	4. vosotras	d. viajábamos
e	5. ellos	e. viajaban

escribir		
c	1. ustedes	a. escribías
d	2. él	b. escribíamos
b	3. nosotras	c. escribían
e	4. vosotros	d. escribía
a	5. tú	e. escribíais

G2 Complete las oraciones con la forma correcta del verbo en el pretérito imperfecto.

Cuando mi madre (1) ....tenía.... (tener) diez años, (2) ....vivía.... (vivir) en un pueblo pequeño cerca de la costa. Ella y sus dos hermanos (3) caminaban (caminar) a la escuela todos los días y (4) ...volvían... (volver) a casa para almorzar. Mis abuelos (5) trabajaban (trabajar) en un café y todos los veranos la familia entera (6) ...pasaba... (pasar) mucho tiempo en la playa. Mi hermana y yo siempre (7) queríamos (querer) visitar el pueblo porque nuestra madre nos (8) ..contaba.. (contar) historias interesantes de su infancia.

G3 Complete las oraciones con la forma correcta del verbo en el pretérito imperfecto.

1. Cuando ......éramos...... (ser) pequeños, vivíamos con nuestra familia en las montañas.
2. Francisco y Manuel ....iban........ (ir) a la costa todos los veranos cuando vivían en Buenos Aires.
3. Yo ....iba.......... (ir) a la biblioteca después de clases.
4. La casa de campo de los abuelos de Maribel ....era.......... (ser) amplia y luminosa.
5. Durante la universidad, tú y yo nos ......veíamos...... (ver) todos los días.
6. Tú y Javier .....eran/erais..... (ser) muy tímidos durante la secundaria.

Suggestion Brainstorm a list of activities with the class and have them write them down. Tell students to check off the ones that they used to do in elementary school. Then have them circulate around the room and find other students who used to do the same activities.

Practice more at **vhlcentral.com.**

GRAMÁTICA FUNCIONAL

9A.3 Refer to undefined quantities

algún; ningún; alguno/a(s); ninguno/a 6.5

- Use **algún, alguno/a(s)** (*a/an; one; some*) and **ningún, ninguno/a** (*no; none; not any*) to talk about undefined quantities. These adjectives must agree with the nouns they modify. Always use a negative expression (**ningún, ninguno/a**) in a negative sentence.

¿Tienes **alguna** película para recomendarme?
*Do you have **a** movie to recommend to me?*

No hay **ninguna** canción buena en este CD.
*There are **no** good songs on this CD.*

- Use **algún** and **ningún** in front of singular masculine nouns.

¿Miras **algún** programa de noticias por la mañana?
*Do you watch **a** news program in the morning?*

- **Alguno/a(s)** and **ninguno/a** can also function as pronouns.

Ayer había un buen programa, pero hoy no hay **ninguno**.
*Yesterday there was a good show on, but today there aren't **any**.*

9A.4 Express preferences

Superlatives: adjectives 4.4.1, 4.4.2

- Use **el/la/los/las** + **más/menos** + [*adjective*] to describe a characteristic that surpasses all others (**el superlativo**).

El Aconcagua es **la** montaña **más alta** de las Américas.
*Aconcagua is **the highest** mountain in the Americas.*

Los programas **menos interesantes** son los concursos.
***The least interesting** programs are game shows.*

- Use the preposition **de** + [*group*] to mean *in/of* + [*group*].

Miguel es el más listo **de la clase**.
*Miguel is the smartest **in the class**.*

Suggestion Name famous people or places and have students use superlatives to talk about their most prominent characteristics.

- Some adjectives have irregular superlative forms.

bueno/a(s) →	**el/la mejor; los/las mejores**
malo/a(s) →	**el/la peor; los/las peores**

El perro es **el mejor** amigo del hombre.
*Dog is man's **best** friend.*

9A.5 Talk about length of time

llevar + [*length of time*] 5.1.1

- Use the construction **llevar** + [*length of time*] to tell how long you have been doing something.

llevar + [*length of time*]
- en + [*place*]
- como + [*profession*]
- + [*present participle*]
- con + [*other noun*]

Llevo dos años en Canarias.
I have been in the Canaries for two years.

Llevo cinco años como traductor.
I have been a translator for five years.

¡Póngalo en práctica!

G4 Complete las conversaciones.

- ¿Hay (1) ___algún___ documental en la tele esta noche?
- Sí, creo que hay (2) ___alguno(s)___
- ¿No hay (3) ___ningún___ programa de música clásica en la radio?
- No, no hay (4) ___ninguno___
- ¿Escuchaste (5) ___alguna___ noticia interesante hoy por la tele?
- No, no escuché (6) ___ninguna___
- ¿Conoces (7) ___alguna___ canción popular de España?
- Sí, conozco (8) ___alguna(s)___

Suggestion Have pairs of students write a conversation between two students at your university; one of them is a transfer student who wants to get familiar with the campus and the community. Have a few volunteers role-play their conversations for the class.

G5 Escriba oraciones completas usando el superlativo.

1. Rhode Island / estado / + pequeño / Estados Unidos
Rhode Island es el estado más pequeño de los Estados Unidos.
2. lunes / día / + malo / semana
El lunes es el peor día de la semana.
3. tertulia política / programa / – divertido / canal
La tertulia política es el programa menos divertido del canal.
4. María y Ana / + bueno / estudiante / clase
María y Ana son las mejores estudiantes de la clase.
5. el Amazonas / río / + largo / mundo
El Amazonas es el río más largo del mundo.

G6 Complete la conversación.

- ¿Cuánto tiempo (1) ___lleva___ Carmela (2) ___con___ la danza?
- (3) ___Lleva___ casi quince años (4) ___como___ bailarina.
- ¿Y sus padres viven aquí hace mucho tiempo?
- Sí, (5) ___llevan___ diez años (6) ___en___ Caracas.
- Yo (7) ___llevo___ solo cinco años en la capital.

Practice more at **vhlcentral.com.**

VOCABULARIO

¡Qué tiempos!

el antes	*before; the past*
el canal	*channel*
la carpa	*tent*
la época	*time, period*
la escuela primaria	*elementary school*
la etapa	*stage*
la infancia	*childhood*
la mochila	*backpack*
el pelo	*hair*
el programa	*program*
la promoción	*graduating class*
el punto de encuentro	*meeting point*
la responsabilidad	*responsibility*
la TV	*TV*
egresar	*to graduate*
estar callado/a	*to be silent, not to talk*
reencontrar (o:ue)	*to meet again*
aventurero/a	*adventurous*
guapo/a	*good-looking*
el/la joven hecho/a y derecho/a	*all grown-up*
antes	*before*

Segunda juventud

el/la más/menos	*the most/least*
el/la mejor/peor	*the best/worst*
Seguro que...	*I'm sure (that)...*
el/la camarógrafo/a	*cameraman/ camerawoman*
la charla (*fam.*)	*conversation*
el documental	*documentary*
el informativo	*news (program)*
la juventud	*youth*
el magacín	*news and talk show*
los medios (de comunicación)	*media*
el pronóstico	*weather forecast*
el/la reportero/a	*reporter*
la sociedad	*society*
el/la televidente	*TV viewer*
la tertulia	*roundtable; talk show*
el/la trotamundos	*globetrotter*
acompañar	*to keep company*
entretenerse (e:ie)	*to amuse oneself*
sentirse (e:ie) acompañado/a	*to feel accompanied*
ser todo oídos	*to be all ears*
algún	*some, any*
alguno/a	*some, any*
completo/a	*complete*
mayor de	*older than*
ningún	*no*
ninguno/a	*no, none*
útil	*useful*

Luis Soriano

el/la adolescente	*adolescent, teenager*
la aldea	*village*
el algodón	*cotton*
la boca	*mouth*
la biblioteca ambulante	*traveling library*
el/la burro/a	*donkey*
el/la campesino/a	*peasant*
el clásico	*classic*
la devolución	*return*
la donación	*donation*
el espejo	*mirror*
el hueso	*bone*
la inquietud	*interest*
la lancha	*boat*
la nariz	*nose*
el ojo	*eye*
el prado	*meadow*
la red	*network*
la reseña	*summary; review*
la sede	*headquarters*
la tierra	*land, dirt*
la vereda (*Col.*)	*rural neighborhood*
acariciar	*to caress*
cargar	*to load; to carry*
contar (o:ue) con	*to include*
despertar (e:ie) la inquietud	*to stir up interest*
montar	*to ride*
prestar	*to lend*
trotar	*to trot*
a largo plazo	*in the long term*
blando/a	*soft*
brillante	*bright*
celeste	*light blue*
duro/a	*hard*
flotante	*floating*
gracioso/a	*funny*
peludo/a	*furry*
tierno/a	*affectionate*
transparente	*transparent*

Variación léxica

la biblioteca ambulante ⟷ **la biblioteca itinerante** ⟷ **la biblioteca móvil**

el informativo ⟷ **el noticiero** (*Amér. L.*) ⟷ **el telediario** (*Esp.*) ⟷ **el noticiario**

egresar ⟷ **graduarse** (*Amér. L.*)

el magacín ⟷ **el programa de variedades**

gracioso/a ⟷ **divertido/a** ⟷ **chistoso/a**

el/la niño/a ⟷ **el/la peladito/a** (*fam., Col.*)

la tarea ⟷ **los deberes**

Suggestion Ask students to write a few cloze sentences using words from **Variación léxica**. Have students exchange papers with a classmate and complete the activity.

Spaniards spend an average of about 73 euros on the **Gordo de Navidad** lottery draw, which is one of the largest prizes in the world (over two billion euros in prizes and over 13,000 winning tickets). Prizes are paid immediately and are tax-free.

9B HISTORIAS DE LA CALLE

Caras del barrio

EL UNIVERSO DEL BARRIO

Su periódico semanal gratuito Viernes, 3 de diciembre

Concurso "LAS CARAS MÁS POPULARES DEL BARRIO" ¡AQUÍ ESTÁN LOS FINALISTAS!

Algunos de ellos llevan toda la vida en el barrio, como Paqui la vendedora de lotería, la de la calle Palma, la que reparte suerte y simpatía desde hace muchos años, ¡casi cincuenta! Otros viven con nosotros desde hace poco tiempo, como Hugo Valdez, el del locutorio de la calle Paloma, que llegó de República Dominicana en busca de nuevas experiencias.

¡VOTEN POR SU FAVORITO O FAVORITA!

1

"El negocio era de mis padres, y antes de mis abuelos."
—Antonio Campos

2

"He repartido muchos premios y ¡dos gordos!"
—Paqui Ruiz

Suggestion Work with the class to come up with a list of characteristics that make a good shopkeeper.

Identificar por una característica

El de la frutería se llama Antonio.
Norma es **la que** tiene el estanco.
Los de la panadería son ecuatorianos.

9B.1 el/la/los/las + de/que

Vocabulario

1
- la cara *face*
- gratuito/a *free (of charge)*
- el/la vendedor(a) de lotería *lottery ticket seller*
- el gordo *jackpot; first prize*
- gordo/a *fat*
- **el universo, popular, el/la finalista, el/la favorito/a**

2
- la agencia de lotería *lottery ticket booth*
- el estanco (*Esp.*) *tobacconist shop*
- la frutería *fruit shop*
- la juguetería *toy store*
- la papelería *stationery store*

3
- el sorteo *draw*
- la telefonía *telephone service*
- el establecimiento *store; establishment*

1 Observe el documento. ¿Qué tipo de publicación es? ¿En qué consiste el concurso? Suggested answer: Es un periódico de barrio gratuito que se publica una vez a la semana. Los vecinos tienen que elegir a la persona con el negocio más popular del barrio.

2 a. ¿Qué negocios representan la vida de este barrio? Márquelos.

agencia de lotería • bar • estanco • frutería • juguetería
locutorio • panadería • papelería • tienda de alimentación

b. Identifique a los finalistas del concurso por el negocio que tienen.
Norma es la del estanco. Hugo es el del locutorio. Paqui es la que tiene la agencia de lotería. Antonio es el que vende fruta.

Norma Hugo Paqui Antonio	es	el que vende fruta. la que tiene la agencia de lotería. la del estanco. el del locutorio.

3 Relacione estas explicaciones con las declaraciones de los finalistas.

2 El gordo es el mayor premio del sorteo de la lotería de Navidad.

4 Los locutorios ofrecen servicios de telefonía, Internet o envío de dinero, especialmente para las comunidades de extranjeros.

1 En los mercados de barrio, los negocios pasan muchas veces de padres a hijos.

3 Los estancos son los establecimientos oficiales para vender tabaco en España.

4 a. Identifique a las personas del barrio y adivine de quién habla su compañero/a.

b. ¿Quién es su favorito para ganar el concurso? ¿Por qué?

Los 10 establecimientos imprescindibles del barrio

"La ley antitabaco ha afectado mucho a mi negocio. ¡Ahora necesito vender más chicles y regalitos!"—Norma Sánchez

"Llegué a España y abrí este negocio. Muchos extranjeros llaman desde aquí a sus familias."—Hugo Valdez

Indicar el camino

- Perdone, ¿hay una cafetería cerca?
- Sí, siga usted todo recto y gire la segunda a la derecha. Vaya hasta el final de la calle y allí, al lado del gimnasio, hay una...

9B.2 Affirmative imperative (singular forms) **ve/vaya,** directions

Vocabulario

5

el chicle *chewing gum*
la floristería *florist (shop)*
el quiosco *kiosk*
recorrer *to cover (a distance)*

6

perdone (*form.*) *excuse me*
tomar *to take*
seguir (e:i) *to continue, to keep going*
recto *straight*
girar *to turn*
a la derecha *(to the) right*
a la izquierda *(to the) left*

Estrategia

Llamar la atención

- Perdona, ¿sabes dónde está la parada de autobús?
- Perdone, ¿sabe dónde hay un locutorio?

Suggestion Ask students to write mini-dialogues that one would hear at one of these establishments. Collect the papers, shuffle them, and read the exchanges aloud. Have the class guess the place.

5 Escuche la conversación. ¿Qué dos establecimientos busca una de las personas? Señale en el plano el camino que debe recorrer. la panadería y el quiosco

6 a. Marque las formas verbales del imperativo. ¿Se hablan de *tú* o de *usted*?

usted

- Perdone, ¿hay una librería cerca?
- Sí, mire, tome esta calle, siga todo recto y vaya hasta la plaza, luego gire la tercera a la derecha.

tú

- Perdona, ¿sabes dónde está el restaurante La Habana?
- Mira, toma esta calle, sigue recto y ve hasta la plaza. Después, gira a la izquierda.

b. Observe los ejemplos anteriores y complete la tabla. ¿Qué verbo es irregular? El verbo *ir* es irregular.

	GIRAR	RECORRER	SEGUIR	IR
tú	*gira*	recorre	sigue	*ve*
usted	gire	*recorra*	*siga*	vaya

MI EXPERIENCIA

7 Suggestion Have half the class set up stores in different parts of the classroom and post signs showing what kind of shop they have. The other half of the class should circulate around the classroom asking for directions and clarification.

7 Sitúe en el plano un nuevo establecimiento e indique la dirección. Identifique a sus compañeros por el establecimiento que tienen.

GUIÓN DE TRABAJO

¿Cuál es el establecimiento?	¿Dónde está?	¿Quién es Dimitri?
Es la papelería Papiro.	Sigue recto y...	El de la papelería...

Suggestion In groups, have students write down the directions to places and establishments close to your campus. Have groups read their directions aloud for the class to guess.

Practice more at **vhlcentral.com.**

SAM: Actividades pp. 189–191

Anécdotas

Suggestion To further contrast the preterite and imperfect in past narration, tell students another anecdote from your own experiences on campus.

Escriba la historia más divertida, curiosa o increíble del barrio

Participe en el concurso

1 "Era el día antes del sorteo de Navidad. Había un número 'feo' que nadie quería: el 00.101. De repente llegó un autobús de turistas y compraron todos los billetes de este número y les tocó el gordo." increíble

Francisca (Paqui) Ruiz, vendedora de lotería de la calle Palma

2 "Una vez intentaron comprar el tradicional Mercado de San Miguel para hacer oficinas. Entonces había crisis y los negocios no funcionaban. Todos vendieron, menos dos que decidieron no vender y salvaron el mercado." interesante

Antonio Campos, frutero del Mercado de San Miguel

3 "El otro día estábamos en la plaza tomando un café. De repente apareció mucha gente y empezaron a rodar la escena de una película. Necesitaban extras para el rodaje y participamos. Entonces conocimos al director y a todos los actores. Fue muy curioso ser actores por un día." curiosa/divertida

Ana López, vecina de la plaza del Carmen

Relatar en pasado

El otro día **era** mi cumpleaños. **Estaba** en mi oficina y, de repente, ¡**vinieron** todos mis compañeros con un ramo de flores!

9B.3 Preterite vs. imperfect **el otro día, de repente...**

Vocabulario

8

salvar *to save, to rescue*
el/la frutero/a *fruit seller*
el otro día *the other day*
de repente *suddenly*
rodar (o:ue) *to shoot, to film*
entonces *then*
el ramo *bouquet*
la anécdota

¡OJO!

December 28 is the Feast of the Holy Innocents, which began as a religious observation but now is a prank-filled day known as **Día de los Inocentes**, similar to April Fool's Day. The prankster usually ends his joke by exclaiming "**¡Inocente palomita!**"

8 a. Relacione las anécdotas con alguna de estas características.
Sample answers above.

curiosa • divertida • increíble • interesante

b. Localice los verbos de las anécdotas y clasifíquelos.

Pretérito indefinido	Pretérito imperfecto
llegó, ... compraron, tocó; intentaron, vendieron, decidieron, salvaron; apareció, empezaron, participamos, conocimos, fue	*era, ...* había, quería; había, funcionaban; estábamos, necesitaban

c. ¿Pretérito imperfecto o pretérito indefinido? Indique qué tiempo usamos en cada caso.

- Para describir situaciones pasadas usamos... el pretérito imperfecto.
- Para relatar acciones pasadas usamos... el pretérito indefinido.

9 Fíjese en las imágenes y construya estas anécdotas.

SITUACIONES

El otro día...
Una vez...

..........era.......... (ser) de noche, ...hacía......... (hacer) calor y yo no ....podía......... (poder) dormir.

Entonces...
De repente...

ACCIONES

..........Me levanté.......... (levantarse) de la cama y ....fui......... (ir) a dormir en el parque.

El otro día/Una vez

yo ....Iba......... (ir) por la calle solo. Todo el mundo me ....miraba......... (mirar) y yo no ....sabía......... (saber) por qué.

.........Entonces.........

Una persona ....señaló......... (señalar) el muñeco de papel de mi espalda. ¡Claro, era el 28 de diciembre, Día de los Inocentes!

9 Suggestion To simplify, first have students look only at the images and narrate the scenes in English, telling whether they would use preterite or imperfect in each case. Ex: It was one o'clock in the morning. (imperfect)

11 Expansion Have students work in pairs to ad-lib one of the conversations. Then tell them to write a similar conversation, ending with the phrase **¡No me digas!**

Suggestion Have volunteers read the conversation aloud for the class.

10 Lea la viñeta cómica. ¿Conoce al personaje famoso? ¿Conoce usted a alguien famoso? ¿A quién?

11 a. Escuche las dos anécdotas. ¿En cuál de las dos la persona se sorprende positivamente? en la primera

b. Escuche de nuevo y ordene las anécdotas.

1

¿Ah, sí? ¿Y qué pasó?	2
Yo una vez iba a casa y me encontré un billete de lotería.	1
¿De verdad? ¡Increíble! ¡Qué suerte!	4
¡Al día siguiente gané el premio!	3

2

¡Anda ya!	4
No, ¿qué te pasó?	2
¿Sabéis qué me pasó el otro día?	1
¡Llegué a la oficina y no había nadie... ¡Era domingo!	3

12 En parejas, lean las frases y reaccionen.

- En San Valentín recibí una nota anónima.
- Gané un viaje a Europa.
- Conocí a un chico muy guapo.
- Mi padre me regaló un coche.

MI EXPERIENCIA

13 Piense en una anécdota real o inventada y cuéntesela a su compañero/a.

GUIÓN DE TRABAJO

- ¿Sabes qué me pasó/ a quién conocí/ con quién estuve...? → Un día/El otro día/ Una vez estaba... y de repente/entonces...
- ¿Qué te pasó? ¿A quién conociste? → ¿De verdad? ¡No me digas! ¡Increíble!

Contar anécdotas

- ¿Sabes qué me pasó el otro día?
- No, ¿qué te pasó?
- Participé en un concurso de radio y gané un viaje al Caribe.
- ¿De verdad? ¡Increíble! ¿Cuándo debes recoger los pasajes?

9B.4 **¡Sabes/Sabe/Saben/ Sabéis qué...? ¿De verdad?...**

Vocabulario

10

comprar (billetes de) lotería *to buy lottery tickets*
¿De verdad? *Really?*
¡No me digas! *You don't say!*
¡Increíble! *Unbelievable!*
recoger (j) *to pick up*

11

¡Anda ya! (Esp.) *Come on!*

12

jugar (u:ue) a la lotería *to play the lottery*

Juegos de azar

Jugar a la lotería es una costumbre muy extendida en el mundo hispano. En España, de todos los sorteos, el de Navidad es el más popular. Se celebra el 22 de diciembre. Existe la creencia de que algunas agencias traen suerte y la gente hace cola durante horas para comprar el número de la suerte. El mejor premio se llama **el gordo**.

Practice more at **vhlcentral.com.**

SAM: Actividades pp. 192–194

9B

Lola, la del quiosco del barrio

You may want to explain that **prensa gratuita** refers to publications that are free of charge, while **prensa libre** refers to publications that do not suffer censorship.

Lola Sanz, 35 años. Quiosquera, como su madre y su abuela

Lola, tú eres una de las "caras" del barrio. ¿Cuándo empezaste a trabajar en el quiosco?
Desde pequeña, lo normal en un negocio familiar, pero hace cinco años empecé a llevarlo sola porque mi madre se jubiló.

¿Ha habido muchos cambios desde que se abrió el quiosco?
Sí, antes mi madre y mi abuela vendían sólo prensa. Ahora vendo muchas cosas más: películas, libros, postales, souvenirs, chicles... especialmente desde que hay periódicos gratuitos.

¿Y cómo es tu jornada laboral?
Empiezo a trabajar a las 6:30 h de la mañana; recibo la prensa diaria y la coloco en el puesto. Abro el quiosco de 7:00 h a 14:00 h, voy a comer a casa y por la tarde abro de 16:30 h a 20:00 h. Los domingos abro sólo por la mañana.

¿Qué se vende más: periódicos, revistas, cómics...?
Aquí hay gente que compra el periódico todos los días, pero el del domingo es el que más se vende. Muchas mujeres compran las revistas del corazón todas las semanas.

¿Y las colecciones?
Las de los niños sí se venden: los cromos de fútbol, los cuentos, los DVD... pero la gente se cansa de coleccionar y, al final, es caro.

Y con tanta promoción, ¿te falta sitio en el quiosco?
Bueno, yo tengo uno de los grandes, tengo suerte. Los quioscos aquí en Oviedo ahora son más pequeños.

¿Te gusta este barrio?
Sí, es mi barrio de toda la vida, nací y crecí aquí. Vivo muy cerca; cruzo esta calle, sigo recto cien metros y a la derecha está mi piso.

Oviedo (population: 224,000) is the capital of Asturias province in Spain. Have students locate this city on a map.

Expresar el inicio de una acción

- ¿Cuándo **empezaste a** trabajar en el quiosco?
- Hace cinco años.

9B.5 **empezar** + **a** + [*infinitive*]

Vocabulario

14

llevar (un negocio) *to run (a business)*
la prensa *press*
la postal *postcard*
colocar *to place*
la revista (del corazón) *(gossip) magazine*
el corazón *heart*
el cromo (de fútbol) (*Esp.*) *(soccer) trading card*
el cuento *short story*

14 Observe la foto y conteste las preguntas. Coméntelas con su compañero/a.

1. ¿Qué vende Lola en el quiosco? periódicos, revistas, cuentos, DVD, postales, chicles, souvenirs
2. ¿Dónde está el quiosco: en una ciudad, en un pueblo, en un lugar turístico...? en una ciudad
3. ¿Hay quioscos así en su ciudad?

15 a. Lea la entrevista a Lola y complete estas oraciones. Suggested answers:

Hace cinco años... la madre de Lola se jubiló y ella empezó a llevar sola el negocio.

A las 6:30 de la mañana... empieza a trabajar.

b. ¿Cómo es la jornada laboral de Lola? ¿Es similar a la suya?
Su jornada laboral es partida/larga. No tiene días libres, sólo la tarde del domingo.

16 Lola sabe qué productos compra más la gente de su barrio. ¿Pueden imaginar ustedes cómo son sus clientes?

17 a. Escuche la anécdota que cuenta una clienta de Lola y elija un título.

a. Visita real b. Nuevo vecino c. Vida cotidiana

b. ¿En qué establecimiento estaba esta persona? ¿Qué quería comprar? ¿Qué pasó? Reaccione a esta anécdota. En la floristería. Una plantita. El Príncipe Felipe entró a la floristería.

Vocabulario *cont.*

cansarse de (algo) *to get tired/ bored of (something)*
el sitio *room; space*
crecer (zc) *to grow up*
el/la quiosquero/a *kiosk attendant*
el souvenir, el cómic, el DVD, coleccionar, la promoción, el dispensador

18

en línea *online*
la prensa rosa *gossip press*
el suplemento dominical *Sunday supplement*
la versión, digital, multimedia, informado/a

19

la ventaja *advantage*
la desventaja *disadvantage*

21

heredar *to inherit*

OPINIÓN

¿Cómo compra la prensa: en el quiosco, en un dispensador de periódicos, por suscripción? ¿Por qué? ¿Hay prensa gratuita en su país?

Suggestion Have students name a publication in this country for each type of newspaper or magazine named in the article.

18c Sí. La prensa deportiva es la que más se lee y las revistas del corazón las que menos se leen en Internet. Además, permiten a las personas que viven fuera de su país mantenerse informadas.

Muchos negocios o empresas familiares se heredan de padres a hijos. Los hijos, desde pequeños, aprenden la profesión de los padres y continúan el negocio. Esta costumbre ya no es tan frecuente como antes, pero todavía hay muchos casos.

18 a. Lea el título de este artículo. ¿Qué significa *prensa digital* y *prensa en papel*? Prensa en papel son periódicos, revistas, etc., y prensa digital es la que se lee en Internet.

¿Prensa digital o en papel?

Leer la prensa en Internet es hoy una práctica habitual. Los principales periódicos tienen versiones en línea. Los que más se leen en español son los periódicos de deportes, como *Marca* (España) y *Ovaciones* (México). También se pueden leer en Internet periódicos de economía, como *Portafolio* (Colombia) y *Diario Financiero* (Chile). Y si se busca información general, se pueden visitar diarios como *El País* (España), *La República* (Perú) y *La Prensa* (Bolivia).

La prensa rosa o las revistas del corazón como *TVAquí* (Puerto Rico) o *Gente* (Argentina) también tienen una versión en línea pero se visitan menos, quizás porque el periódico se lee con rapidez para informarse de las noticias del día, y las revistas se leen con más tiempo.

Los periódicos digitales aprovechan las posibilidades multimedia: voz, música, video... y las noticias se actualizan varias veces al día como en la radio o la televisión. Además, permiten a las personas que viven fuera de su país mantenerse informados.

La prensa en papel se puede leer en el metro, en el sofá en casa o en un parque y no sólo delante de la computadora. Además, los periódicos del domingo traen muchos suplementos, y para muchas personas es un ritual desayunar en casa o en una cafetería con la prensa dominical.

LA PRENSA
Periodismo interactivo
Bolivia y Chile pasan a la etapa de las propuestas en el tema del mar

información general

1-0
¡QUE SÍ, QUE SOMOS CAMPEONES!

deportes

PORTAFOLIO
EL DIARIO DE ECONOMÍA Y NEGOCIOS
Nuevo plan de Ecopetrol hace subir la acción
'El verdadero lujo sobrevive'

economía

b. Anote los tipos de prensa en las imágenes correspondientes.

deportes • economía • información general

c. ¿Tienen todas las publicaciones versión digital? ¿Cuáles son las más leídas? ¿Cuáles no? ¿Por qué?

19 Busque en el texto los aspectos positivos de la prensa digital y la prensa en papel. ¿Qué otras ventajas y desventajas tienen? Comente con su compañero/a.

20 ¿Qué tipo de prensa lee usted? ¿Por qué? Explique.

21 a. Lea la información sobre profesiones que se heredan. ¿Existe esta costumbre en su país?

b. ¿Conoce algún caso? ¿Cuál es su opinión al respecto?

Practice more at **vhlcentral.com.**

SAM: Actividades pp. 195–200

22a Suggestion Have groups of three students role-play the situation. Tell them to ad-lib the dialogue, or have students write notes to prepare for their roles. Have a couple of groups act out the situation for the class.

22 a. Elija el tiempo verbal adecuado (pretérito indefinido o imperfecto) y complete la anécdota. Gana el grupo que termina primero la anécdota correctamente.

El año pasado... → yo buscaba (buscar) otro trabajo, → y envié (enviar) mi currículum a muchas empresas. → Un día recibí (recibir) la llamada de una empresa. → Era (ser) una empresa muy importante. → Yo estaba (estar) muy interesado. → Empecé (empezar) a hacer entrevistas... → y superé (superar) todas las pruebas. → La última entrevista era (ser) con el director general en un restaurante. → Todo iba (ir) bien y... → de repente yo vi (ver) que en la mesa de al lado estaba (estar) mi jefa. → No sabía (saber) qué hacer... → entonces decidí (decidir) contar la verdad. → Y al final los tres hablamos (hablar) animadamente. → Yo conseguí (conseguir) el trabajo y mi antigua jefa empezó (empezar) a colaborar con nosotros. ¡Cosas de la vida!

b. Forme un círculo con todos sus compañeros. Escriba en una hoja las primeras dos oraciones de una anécdota. Doble la hoja para que sólo se vean las últimas palabras. Luego, pásela a su compañero/a de la derecha. Esa persona debe continuar la anécdota con otras dos oraciones y doblar la hoja antes de pasarla. Al completar el círculo, lean la anécdota en voz alta.

22b Suggestion Set a time limit of one minute for each student.

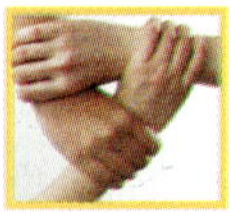

TAREA FINAL

Nuestro periódico

Hablen de anécdotas o noticias que ocurrieron ayer. La información puede ser real o no, con noticias del mundo exterior o de la clase.

Elijan un tipo de publicación y elaboren la portada (titular, noticias más importantes, imágenes, etc).

Presenten su portada a la clase.

YO PUEDO...

Suggestion Alternatively, have students identify people on campus and in the surrounding community.

- **Puedo identificar a alguien por una característica.**
  Identifique a personas de su barrio.
- **Puedo indicar el camino.**
  Explique cómo ir de su casa a un establecimiento cercano.
- **Puedo relatar en pasado.**
  Cuente una historia que le ocurrió hace tiempo.
- **Puedo contar anécdotas.**
  Escriba una conversación o una anécdota real o inventada.
- **Puedo expresar el inicio de una actividad.**
  Hable de cuándo empezó a estudiar español.

GRAMÁTICA FUNCIONAL

9B.1 Identify with a characteristic

el/la/los/las + de/que 3.1.1

- Use the construction **el/la/los/las de** + [*noun*] or **el/la/los/las que** + [*verb*] to refer to people or things based on some other point of reference.

> Jorge es **el del** restaurante cubano.
> *Jorge is **the man (the one) from** the Cuban restaurant.*
>
> Gabriela y Elena son **las que** trabajan en la librería.
> *Gabriela and Elena are **the women (the ones) who** work in the bookstore.*

- The definite article in this construction (**el/la/los/las**) must agree in gender and number with the people or things that are being identified.

9B.2 Give directions

Affirmative imperative (singular forms) 5.18.2a, 5.18.3a
Prepositional phrases of place 10.17

- Use the affirmative to give directions.

> **Gira** a la derecha. *Turn right.*
> **Gire** (usted) a la izquierda. *Turn left.*

- As you learned in **8A.4**, regular **tú** commands have the same form as the third-person form of the present. The affirmative **usted** command is formed by dropping the final **-o** of the **yo** form of the present tense. For **-ar** verbs, add **-e**; for **-er** and **-ir** verbs, add **-a**.

	GIRAR	RECOGER	SEGUIR
(tú)	gir**a**	recog**e**	sigu**e**
(usted)	gir**e**	recoj**a**	sig**a**

- The formal and informal imperatives undergo the same stem changes as verbs in the present tense. (Yo **sigo** → **Siga** usted.)

> **Sigue/Siga** todo recto.
> *Continue straight ahead.*

- The verb **ir** has irregular forms in both the formal and informal commands.

	IR
(tú)	**ve**
(usted)	**vaya**

> **Vaya** hasta el cine y gire a la derecha.
> ***Go** to the movie theater and turn right.*

- Use expressions such as **todo recto** (*straight ahead*), **la primera/segunda calle** (*the first/second street*), **a la derecha/izquierda**, (*to/on the right/left*), **al final de** (*at the end of*), and **enfrente de** (*across from*) when giving directions.

> Sigue **todo recto** y gira **a la derecha al final de** esta calle.
> La panadería está **enfrente del** restaurante.
> *Continue **straight ahead** and **turn right at the end of** this street. The bakery **is in front of** the restaurant.*

¡Póngalo en práctica!

G1 Complete las oraciones.

1. Juana es ....la que.... trabaja en la frutería.
2. Hugo es ....el del.... locutorio.
3. • ¿Qué bar ofrece el mejor café del barrio?
   ▪ Creo que ....el que.... ofrece el mejor café es ....el de.... la plaza, el bar Colombia.
4. • ¿Quién es Marina?
   ▪ Es ....la que.... tiene el bar El Rincón.
5. Héctor es ....el de.... la panadería.

Suggestion Read aloud a series of affirmative singular imperatives, both formal and informal. Some should be commands that a parent would say to a child, and some should be commands that a child would say to a parent. Have students identify the speaker of each statement.

G2 Escriba las formas correctas del imperativo afirmativo.

	tú	usted
1. pasar	pasa	pase
2. compartir	comparte	comparta
3. volver	vuelve	vuelva
4. mirar	mira	mire
5. escuchar	escucha	escuche
6. pensar	piensa	piense

G3 Complete las conversaciones con la forma correcta del imperativo formal o informal. Seleccione el verbo apropiado.

seguir · girar · ir

• Perdone, ¿sabe dónde hay una librería?
▪ Sí, mire, (1)....siga.... todo recto y (2)....gire.... a la izquierda. (3)....Vaya.... hasta la plaza. Enfrente hay una librería.

tomar · seguir · girar

• Hola, ¿sabes dónde hay un restaurante por aquí cerca?
▪ En este barrio hay muchos. Mira, (4)....sigue/toma.... esta calle hasta la floristería, (5)....gira.... a la derecha y allí hay una pizzería y un restaurante tailandés. También, Casa Lucía tiene menú del día y está cerca. (6)....Toma/Sigue.... la primera calle a la izquierda y el restaurante está enfrente del quiosco.

Practice more at **vhlcentral.com.**

GRAMÁTICA FUNCIONAL

9B.3 Narrate in the past

Preterite vs. imperfect 5.2.3, 5.4.3, 5.6

- Use the **pretérito indefinido** to narrate past actions that belong to a period of time that has ended.

  Hugo **llegó** a España hace cinco años.
  *Hugo **arrived** in Spain five years ago.*

- Use time expressions such as **el otro día** (*the other day*), **una vez** (*once*), **de repente** (*suddenly*), and **[y] entonces** (*[and] then*) with the **pretérito indefinido**.

  Una vez viajamos a Portugal en autobús.
  ***Once** we traveled to Portugal by bus.*

- Use the **préterito imperfecto** to tell about habitual or repeated actions in the past.

  Cuando **vivía** en ese barrio, siempre **compraba** el periódico en el quiosco de la plaza.
  *When **I lived** in that neighborhood, **I** always **bought** the newspaper at the kiosk in the square.*

- Use the **préterito imperfecto** to describe past situations, causes, and circumstances that establish the background details of a past event. The **préterito imperfecto** and the **pretérito indefinido** are often used together to narrate in the past.

  Hacía frío y **llovía** mucho, así que **decidimos** ir al cine.
  ***It was** cold and **it was raining** a lot, so **we decided** to go to the movies.*

- Use **mientras** (*while*) with the imperfect to describe what was happening at the same time as another action (imperfect) or when an interrupting action occurred (preterite).

9B.4 Tell anecdotes

Questions and interjections 14.6

- To introduce an anecdote, say **¿Sabe(s) qué (me pasó)?** or **¿Sabéis/Saben qué?** (*Guess what!*)
- Use expressions such as **¿Y qué pasó?** (*And what happened?*) or **¿A quién viste?** (*Who did you see?*) to show interest in the anecdote and encourage the speaker to continue.
- **¡No me digas!**, **¡Increíble!**, **¿De verdad?**, and **¿Ah, sí?** express surprise or skepticism.

9B.5 Express the beginning of an action

empezar + a + [*infinitive*] 5.10

- Use the construction **empezar + a +** [*infinitive*] to indicate the beginning of an action or an event. **Empezar** has an **e→ie** stem change in the present, and the **yo** form of the **pretérito indefinido** has a **z→c** spelling change to maintain the soft *c* pronunciation.

  Ayer **empecé a trabajar** en el restaurante; mi hermana **empieza** mañana.
  ***I started working** in the restaurant yesterday; my sister **starts** tomorrow.*

- Use **empezar** in the **pretérito indefinido** to tell when past actions began.

Suggestion Tell students that **comenzar** has the same meaning and also requires **a** when used with an infinitive.

Suggestion Have pairs of students talk about the most interesting, embarrassing, or difficult thing that happened to them in the last week.

¡Póngalo en práctica!

G4 Complete las oraciones con la forma correcta del pretérito indefinido o el pretérito imperfecto.

1. Yo ...estaba... (estar) en casa limpiando el salón y entonces ...encontré... (encontrar) debajo de la alfombra unas cartas de amor del año 1920.
2. Ayer Sabrina ...caminaba... (caminar) a la frutería cuando, de repente, ...vio... (ver) a una amiga de la infancia.
3. Tío Ramón nos ...llamó... (llamar) mientras ...preparábamos... (preparar, nosotros) la cena.
4. Alejandro ...tenía... (tener) dieciocho años cuando ...conoció... (conocer) a Celia.
5. ...Eran... (ser) las doce de la noche cuando Pedro y Alicia ...volvieron... (volver) del teatro.
6. De niña, Leila siempre ...leía... (leer) un poco en la cama y ...se acostaba... (acostarse) temprano.
7. El otro día mi abuela ...escuchó... (escuchar) una anécdota curiosa del barrio cuando ...estaba... (estar) en el mercado.
8. De joven, yo ...quería... (querer) ser astronauta y tú siempre ...hablabas... (hablar) de trabajar con animales.

Remind students that interrupted actions often are signalled by the use of words like **cuando, de repente,** and **entonces.**

G5 Empareje cada oración con su respuesta lógica.

c	1. ¿Sabes qué me pasó ayer?	a. ¿Y qué pasó?
a	2. El otro día estaba viajando en tren cuando subió Benicio del Toro.	b. ¡No me digas!
b	3. ¡Mi hermano ganó el gordo de Navidad!	c. No, ¿qué te pasó?

G6 Complete las oraciones.

- ¿Cuándo (1) ...empezasteis... (vosotros) a trabajar en el mercado?
- (2) ...Empezamos... en 1991, pero mi padre (3) ...empezó... a vender fruta en el barrio hace cincuenta años.
- ¿Cuándo (4) ...empezaste... (tú) a trabajar en el quiosco?
- (5) ...Empecé... a ayudar a mis padres a los dieciséis años y la semana que viene (6) ...empiezo... a trabajar sola.

Practice more at **vhlcentral.com.**

VOCABULARIO

Caras del barrio

perdone (*form.*)	*excuse me*
la agencia de lotería	*lottery ticket booth*
la cara	*face*
el chicle	*chewing gum*
el establecimiento	*store; establishment*
el estanco (*Esp.*)	*tobacconist shop*
el/la favorito/a	*favorite*
el/la finalista	*finalist*
la floristería	*florist (shop)*
la frutería	*fruit shop*
el gordo	*jackpot; first prize*
la juguetería	*toy store*
la papelería	*stationery store*
el quiosco	*kiosk*
el sorteo	*draw*
la telefonía	*telephone service*
el universo	*universe*
el/la vendedor(a) de lotería	*lottery ticket seller*
girar	*to turn*
recorrer	*to cover (a distance)*
seguir (e:i)	*to continue, to keep going*
tomar	*to take*
gordo/a	*fat*
gratuito/a	*free (of charge)*
popular	*popular*
a la derecha	*(to the) right*
a la izquierda	*(to the) left*
recto	*straight*

Anécdotas

¡Anda ya! (*Esp.*)	*Come on!*
¿De verdad?	*Really?*
¡Increíble!	*Unbelievable!*
¡No me digas!	*You don't say!*
la anécdota	*anecdote*
el/la frutero/a	*fruit seller*
el ramo	*bouquet*
comprar (billetes de) lotería	*to buy lottery tickets*
jugar (u:ue) a la lotería	*to play the lottery*
recoger (j)	*to pick up*
rodar (o:ue)	*to shoot, to film*
salvar	*to save, to rescue*
de repente	*suddenly*
el otro día	*the other day*
entonces	*then*

Successful Language Learning Have students group the words into categories, such as **Personas** and **Lugares**.

Lola

el cómic	*comic book*
el corazón	*heart*
el cromo (de fútbol) (*Esp.*)	*(soccer) trading card*
el cuento	*short story*
la desventaja	*disadvantage*
el dispensador	*dispenser*
el DVD	*DVD*
la postal	*postcard*
la prensa	*press*
la prensa rosa	*gossip press*
la promoción	*promotion*
el/la quiosquero/a	*kiosk attendant*
la revista (del corazón)	*(gossip) magazine*
el sitio	*room; space*
el souvenir	*souvenir*
el suplemento dominical	*Sunday supplement*
la ventaja	*advantage*
la versión	*version*
cansarse de (algo)	*to get tired/bored of (something)*
coleccionar	*to collect*
colocar	*to place*
crecer (zc)	*to grow up*
heredar	*to inherit*
llevar (un negocio)	*to run (a business)*
digital	*digital*
en línea	*online*
informado/a	*informed*
multimedia (*invar.*)	*multimedia*

Variación léxica

la agencia de lotería ⟷ **la administración de lotería** (*Esp.*) ⟷ **el expendio de lotería**	**multimedia** ⟷ **multimediático/a**
la cara ⟷ **el rostro**	**perdone** ⟷ **disculpe**
el chicle ⟷ **la goma de mascar**	**el quiosco** ⟷ **el kiosco**
el cómic ⟷ **la historieta**	**el/la quiosquero/a** ⟷ **el/la kiosquero/a**
el cromo ⟷ **la figurita** (*Amér. L.*)	**recto** ⟷ **derecho**
la floristería ⟷ **la florería** (*Arg., Cub.*)	**tomar** ⟷ **coger** (*Esp.*)
girar ⟷ **doblar**	**el/la vendedor(a) de lotería** ⟷ **el/la lotero/a** (*Esp.*)

Vocabulario útil

castigado/a *punished*
la creencia *belief*
los desfiles *parades*
festejar *to celebrate*
el fiel *faithful (person)*
hoy en día *nowadays*
mismo/a *same*
el pedido *request*
perdurar *to remain*
por entonces *in those days*
rezar *to pray*

Estrategia

Making the connection

When reading a text about traditions in another country, try to connect what you read with what you already know about that culture and related traditions. Start by building your background knowledge of the place: Where are celebrations held? What kind of culture is this? What words and expressions do you expect to encounter? Compare your traditions and your own experiences in similar situations, and ask yourself: What do I already know about this topic?

Suggestion Present the vocabulary by giving definitions and having students name the word. Ex: **La gente va a la iglesia para hacer esto. (rezar)**

LECTURA

Semana Santa: vacaciones y tradición

Procesión en Sevilla, España

Hay muchas celebraciones importantes en España, pero la Semana Santa° es una de las más espectaculares. Se festeja la semana antes de Pascua°, cuando los cristianos recuerdan la Pasión de Jesucristo. Generalmente, la gente tiene unos días de vacaciones en esa semana. Algunas personas aprovechan° estos días para viajar, pero otras prefieren participar en los desfiles en la calle y ver a los "capuchones". Esta antigua tradición perdura desde la época de la Inquisición: por entonces las personas castigadas° por motivos religiosos debían usar túnicas y sombreros°

Although the article refers to domestic tourists, the festivals in Seville and Antigua are also major draws for international tourists.

1 ¿Ha participado de alguna fiesta religiosa? ¿Se celebra alguna fiesta parecida a las de España y Guatemala en su país? ¿Qué tradiciones populares festejaban sus padres de jóvenes? ¿Qué tradiciones están vivas hoy en su país?

2 Indique si las oraciones son **verdaderas** o **falsas**. Luego, en parejas, corrija las falsas.

1. En Semana Santa, la gente puede disfrutar toda esa semana de vacaciones.
   Falso. Hay sólo algunos días de vacaciones esa semana.
2. La tradición de los capuchones perdura desde la época de la Inquisición.
   Verdadero.
3. Por entonces, la gente debía usar todo el tiempo grandes sombreros cónicos.
   Falso. Sólo la gente castigada por motivos religiosos debía llevar esos sombreros.
4. En las procesiones, los fieles desfilan con imágenes y faroles.
   Verdadero.
5. Unos elementos importantes para las celebraciones religiosas son las flores y las velas.
   Verdadero.
6. La tradición del Vía Crucis es original de Guatemala.
   Falso. La tradición llegó a Guatemala con los misioneros de Sevilla.

Suggestion After reading the article, ask students which celebrations and traditions are most interesting to them and why.

cónicos que les cubrían° la cara. Hoy en día, los miembros de las cofradías° de Semana Santa usan esos mismos sombreros mientras desfilan el Viernes Santo°. Los fieles llevan faroles° o velas° encendidas y sacan imágenes religiosas a las calles. Estas imágenes van sobre plataformas decoradas con muchas flores y velas.

Alfombra de flores en Antigua, Guatemala

En **Antigua, Guatemala**, las personas hacen alfombras° de flores y altares; también organizan Vía Crucis° y danzas°. La tradición llegó con los misioneros españoles de Sevilla y luego evolucionó° a lo largo de los años.

En **Ayacucho, Perú**, además de alfombras de flores y procesiones, hay una antigua tradición llamada "quema de la chamiza"°.

En **Iztapalapa, Ciudad de México**, el famoso Vía Crucis del cerro° de la Estrella es una representación del recorrido° de Jesucristo con la cruz°.

En **Popayán, Colombia**, en las procesiones "chiquitas", los niños llevan copias pequeñas de las imágenes que llevan las personas mayores.

Si visitas algún país hispano durante la Semana Santa, debes ver un desfile. Las playas pueden esperar hasta la semana siguiente.

Semana Santa *Holy Week* **Pascua** *Easter* **aprovechan** *take advantage of* **sombreros** *hats* **cubrían** *covered* **cofradías** *brotherhoods* **Viernes Santo** *Good Friday* **faroles** *lamps* **velas** *candles* **alfombras** *carpets* **Vía Crucis** *Stations of the Cross* **danzas** *dances* **evolucionó** *evolved* **quema de la chamiza** *burning of brushwood* **cerro** *hill* **recorrido** *route* **cruz** *cross*

Otras celebraciones famosas

- ***Oruro, Bolivia***: Durante el carnaval de Oruro se realiza la famosa Diablada, una antigua danza° que muestra la lucha° entre el bien y el mal: ángeles contra° demonios.
- ***Panchimalco, El Salvador***: La primera semana de mayo, Panchimalco se cubre de flores y de color. También hacen el Desfile de las palmas° y bailan danzas antiguas.
- ***Quito, Ecuador***: El mes de agosto es el Mes de las Artes. Danza, teatro, música, cine, artesanías y otros eventos culturales inundan° la ciudad.
- ***San Pedro Sula, Honduras***: En junio se celebra la Feria Juniana. Hay comida típica, bailes, desfiles, conciertos, rodeos, exposiciones ganaderas° y eventos deportivos y culturales.

danza *dance* **lucha** *fight* **contra** *versus* **palmas** *palm leaves* **inundan** *flood* **exposiciones ganaderas** *cattle shows*

Estrategia

Descriptive text

The main purpose of a descriptive text is to give information about a place, an event, an object, or a person. You must make use of your five senses to explain how it looks, smells, and tastes, to show the noises and textures involved. You might take an objective point of view and give facts (accurate and precise information) or you might take a subjective point of view and give opinions (expressing your own feelings, likes, and dislikes).

3 En parejas, armen un cartel de promoción turística de alguna de las fiestas mencionadas en esta página para presentar en la clase. Deben señalar los datos importantes (pueden buscar más información en Internet):

lugar • época del año • qué se celebra • cómo se celebra

Usen frases de esta lista:

Venga a disfrutar...	Viva la fiesta en...	Anímese a conocer...
No se puede perder...	Visite...	

PROYECTO

Elija una fiesta popular que se celebre en su país (el desfile del Día de San Patricio, el del Día de Acción de Gracias, Carnaval en Nueva Orleans, etc.) y escriba una breve descripción desde un punto de vista subjetivo. Luego preséntelo a la clase. Puede guiarse por estas preguntas:

1. ¿Cuándo se celebra?
2. ¿Cómo y cuándo se inició la costumbre?
3. ¿Tiene el mismo significado hoy en día?
4. ¿Cuáles son las características más importantes del festejo?
5. ¿Tiene influencias de otros países?

Flash CULTURA

Las fiestas

Ya ha visto que algunas cosas cambian con el tiempo; pero otras se hacen siempre de la misma manera: las fiestas populares de Latinoamérica reviven cada año la tradición de todo el pueblo. Este episodio de **Flash Cultura** presenta la fiesta de San Sebastián que se realiza en Puerto Rico.

Estrategia

Recognizing cognates

When you are watching a video, it helps to identify cognates. Many cognate pairs between Spanish and English happen to be high-frequency words. Focus your attention on those words that sound familiar, then try to guess their meanings based on context and your own experience.

Vocabulario útil

- **el cabezudo** *large head made of papier-mâché*
- **el cartel** *poster*
- **llevar (el nombre)** *to be named after*
- **en lugar de** *instead of*
- **la misa** *Mass*
- **el palo** *stick*
- **la parranda** *party*
- **revivir** *to revive*
- **el tambor** *drum*
- **los tres santos reyes** *The Three Wise Men*

1 ¿Se hacen desfiles y ferias en las calles de su ciudad? ¿Cómo se festejan la Navidad y el Año Nuevo en su país? ¿Qué otras fiestas importantes hay? ¿Cuánto tiempo duran los festejos? Coméntenlo en parejas.

2 Mire el video. Preste atención a las palabras que suenan conocidas, como **máscaras, procesión, competir,** etc. ¿Adivina su significado?

1

La fiesta comienza con una misa (...) y una procesión...

Expansion: Explain that there are many Spanish words other than **parranda** one can use to say *party*: **farra, juerga, jarana, jolgorio, verbena** (Spain), **guateque** (Mexico), etc.

Successful Language Learning: Tell students that progressive tenses in Spanish can be formed with verbs other than **estar**. Verbs such as **llevar, seguir,** and **ir** are also frequently used with the **gerundio** to express actions in progress.

Llevo viniendo como quince años.

2

Estrategia

Asking for clarification

When in a conversation you need to reaffirm, check, or clarify something, you might say: **¿Quieres decir que...?** *(Do you mean that...?)* **¿En qué sentido lo dices?** *(How do you mean?)*, or **¿Podrías darme un ejemplo?/¿Por ejemplo?** *(Could you give me an example?/ For example?)*

3 Complete las oraciones.

1. San Sebastián fue un soldado y ahora es un...
   (a.) mártir cristiano. b. cabezudo.
2. Las estatuas de los tres santos reyes son...
   (a.) las más populares. b. las más coloridas.
3. La fiesta de San Sebastián es...
   a. antes de Navidad. (b.) al final de Navidad.
4. En lugar de ser totalmente religiosas, las fiestas son...
   (a.) eventos de pueblo. b. misas.

3 Suggestion To challenge students, eliminate the lettered options.

4 Dos personas conversan en la fiesta: una cuenta anécdotas y la otra quiere contar algo más impresionante. Con un(a) compañero/a, escriban la conversación. Luego, preséntenla a la clase.

Modelo:
- *¿Sabes qué me pasó una vez? ¡Me encontré con el fantasma de Elvis Presley! Yo iba en la procesión y él me saludó desde el balcón.*
- *¡No me digas! Yo tengo una historia más interesante. Llevo años viniendo, y...*

4 Suggestion Assign pairs of different types of people, such as two children, or two elderly ladies.

Practice more at **vhlcentral.com.**

Audio: Activities, Vocabulary
Video: *Flash Cultura*

Unidad 10

Carlos Salazar, médico de familia en La Habana

Lección 10A

AL MAL TIEMPO BUENA CARA

Lección 10B

MEMORIAS

Jorge Edwards, recuerdos de un escritor

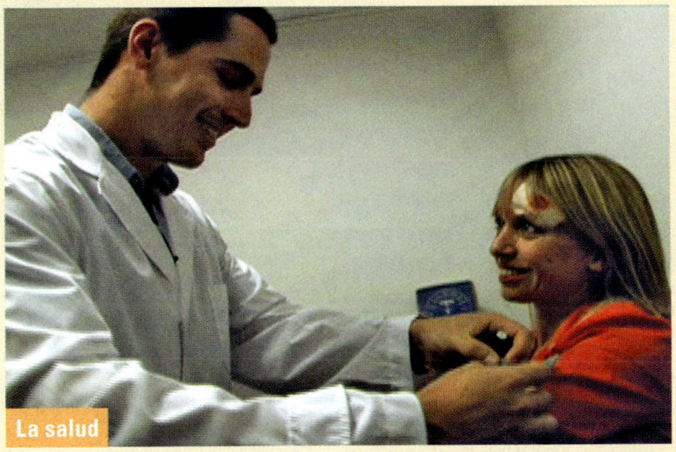

La salud

AVANCE

10A AL MAL TIEMPO BUENA CARA

Draw attention to the map and explain that it shows the political divisions of Venezuela. Tell students that there is a border dispute between Venezuela and Guayana (a former British colony) that dates back to the 19th century. Venezuela claims the territory that lies to the west of the Essequibo River, or roughly 60% of Guyana's land.

Point out the **Distrito Federal** on the map and ask a volunteer to name Venezuela's capital. (Caracas)

El tiempo y la salud

El tiempo en Venezuela hoy

sábado 30 de abril

Hace sol y buen tiempo en el norte del país, como en Sucre y en Isla Margarita, con temperaturas entre los 23 °C y 30 °C.

Está nublado en los estados del oeste como Táchira y Apure, y hace 15 °C de temperatura.

Nieva en el Pico Bolívar en Mérida. Llueve y hace frío en el estado de Bolívar.

Última actualización a las 13:36 h

Hablar del tiempo

- ¿Qué tiempo hace?
- En el norte **hace sol y buen tiempo. Hace 30 °C de temperatura.** En el sur **llueve, está nublado y hace frío.**

10A.1 hace, llueve, nieva, está nublado

Vocabulario

1

- el tiempo *weather*
- hacer sol *to be sunny*
- hacer buen/mal tiempo *there is good/bad weather*
- nublado/a *cloudy*
- nevar (e:ie) *to snow*
- llover (o:ue) *to rain*
- hacer frío/calor *to be cold/hot*
- ¿Qué tiempo hace? *What's the weather like?*
- hace 30 °C de temperatura *the temperature is 30 °C*
- **la temperatura**

2

- tomar el sol *to sunbathe*
- menos mal *thank goodness*
- por fin *at last*

4

- la estación (del año) *season*
- la primavera *spring*
- el otoño *fall*

1 a. Observe el mapa de Venezuela. ¿Qué información da? Relacione los símbolos que aparecen en el mapa con las expresiones para hablar del tiempo. Da información sobre el tiempo.

 Hace sol.
 Nieva.
 Está nublado.
 Llueve.

Hace sol.
Está nublado.
Llueve.
Nieva.

b. ¿Qué tiempo hace en Sucre? ¿Y en el Pico Bolívar?
Hace sol y buen tiempo en Sucre. Nieva en el Pico Bolívar.

2 Escuche estas conversaciones sobre el tiempo que hace hoy. ¿Qué tiempo hace en Caracas?

- *Hace...* sol.

3 ¿Qué tiempo hace en España un 16 de febrero? Mire el mapa y pregunte a su compañero/a.

Modelo:
- *¿Qué tiempo hace en el sur?*
- *Hace...*

You may want to give students the present progressive forms **está nevando** and **está lloviendo**.

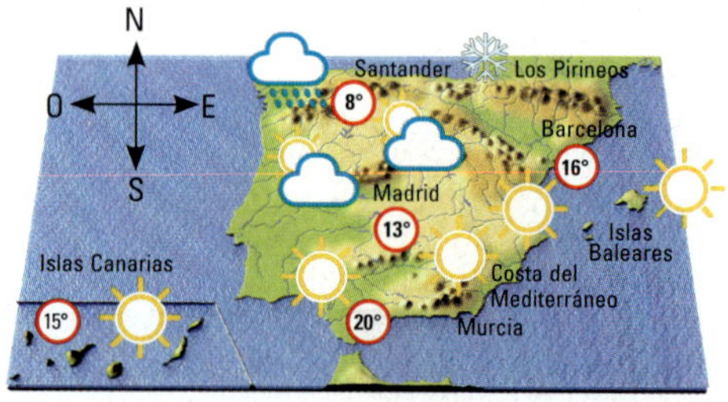

4 ¿Qué tiempo hace hoy en su ciudad o región? ¿Y en las diferentes estaciones del año? **4 Suggestion** You may also want to introduce the phrases **hacer fresco** and **hacer viento**.

En primavera	En verano	En otoño	En invierno

....	....	....	....

Encourage students to refer to **Lección 2A**, where they learned related expressions such as el **verano**, **el invierno**, **el norte**, **el sur**, etc.

¿CÓMO SE ENCUENTRA? Tome este test para saber cómo le afecta el tiempo.

En primavera

a. Me encuentro muy bien.
b. Tengo alergia y estoy cansado/a.
c. Depende, algunos días bien y otros mal.

Cuando hace calor

a. Tengo que beber mucha agua, pero me encuentro bien.
b. Estoy muy cansado/a y no tengo energía.
c. Me encuentro muy bien. Me encanta el verano.

En un día de lluvia

a. Me encanta, es muy romántico.
b. Me duelen la cabeza y los huesos.
c. Me encuentro mal. Salgo sólo si es necesario.

En otoño

a. Me encuentro bien después del verano.
b. Tengo frío y estoy siempre resfriado/a.
c. Me gusta salir y disfrutar de los colores del otoño.

Mayoría de respuestas *a*
Usted se encuentra bien en todos los climas. ¡Felicidades!

Mayoría de respuestas *b*
Usted es muy sensible al tiempo y a los cambios en general, pero piense que el clima no es lo más importante para ser feliz.

Mayoría de respuestas *c*
Usted necesita sol y calor para ser feliz. Prefiere el buen tiempo, pero se adapta cuando hace mal tiempo.

Point out that **sensible** is a false cognate. Explain that **sensible** = *sensitive* and **sensato/a** = *sensible*.

Describir síntomas y dolencias

- ¿Qué te pasa?
- Estoy enfermo. Me duele la garganta y tengo frío.
- ¿Tienes fiebre?
- No sé, me encuentro mal. Estoy resfriado.

10A.2 **doler, encontrarse (o→ue)**
tener + [*noun*]
estar + [*adjective*]

Vocabulario

5
- **encontrarse (o:ue)** *to be; to feel*
- **cansado/a** *tired*
- **depender (de)** *to depend (on)*
- **doler (o:ue)** *to hurt, to ache*
- **la cabeza** *head*
- **tener frío/calor** *to be cold/hot*
- **estar resfriado/a** *to have a cold*
- **ser sensible a** *to be sensitive to*
- **el estado físico** *physical condition*
- **el estado anímico** *state of mind*
- **la alergia, adaptarse**

6
- **la dolencia** *ailment*
- **el síntoma** *symptom*
- **la garganta** *throat*
- **la fiebre** *fever*
- **la muela** *molar*
- **el estómago** *stomach*

7
- **la manzanilla** *chamomile tea*
- **darse un baño** *to take a bath*
- **el remedio, el antibiótico, la aspirina, el/la dentista, la infección**

5 Responda al test. ¿Influye el tiempo en su estado físico y anímico? ¿Qué tiempo es mejor para usted? Hable con un(a) compañero/a.

6 Observe las imágenes. ¿Cómo se encuentran estas personas?

1. Le duele la cabeza. F
2. Le duelen las muelas. B
3. Le duele el estómago. A
4. Le duele la garganta. C
5. Está resfriado. E
6. Tiene fiebre. D

7 ¿Para qué casos son más adecuados estos remedios? ¿Conoce algún otro remedio?

- TOMAR leche con miel / antibióticos / una aspirina / una manzanilla
- IR al dentista / al médico
- OTROS: descansar / darse un baño / dormir

7 Expansion Ask volunteers to name additional remedies and identify the situations in which they would be used.

MI EXPERIENCIA

8 Piense en cómo se encuentra en las diferentes estaciones del año. Pregunte a su compañero/a y compartan los remedios más adecuados para cada síntoma o dolencia.

GUIÓN DE TRABAJO

¿Cómo te encuentras en primavera, verano...? → Si hace buen tiempo, me encuentro... En primavera siempre estoy...

¿Qué remedios conoces? → Si tengo gripe, tomo té con miel...

Practice more at **vhlcentral.com.**

SAM: Actividades pp. 201–203

Salud, divino tesoro

Consultorio de salud

1

Desde hace meses me duele mucho la espalda. A veces tomo dos aspirinas diarias durante tres o cuatro días y me encuentro mejor, pero después me duele otra vez. Otras veces me duelen las piernas; trabajo muchas horas sentada. ¿Qué puedo hacer?

Raquel García, 40 años, Montevideo

2

Trabajo con mi marido desde hace unos meses y últimamente discutimos mucho. Creo que esto afecta mi salud. Me encuentro mal y me duele el estómago. ¿Es una buena idea trabajar con la pareja? ¿Qué debería hacer?

Carmen Jiménez, 33 años, Las Palmas de Gran Canaria

3

Dirijo una pequeña empresa y siempre he disfrutado mucho con mi trabajo. Pero ahora no me gusta ir a trabajar; estoy nervioso y tenso. Me duele la cabeza muy frecuentemente. ¿Qué me aconseja?

Joaquín Simón, 58 años, San José

Pedir consejos

- Tengo estrés en el trabajo. ¿Qué puedo hacer?
- Trabaja menos horas.
- Me duele la cabeza. ¿Qué me aconseja? ¿Qué debería hacer?
- Tome una aspirina.

10A.3 **¿Qué puedo/debería hacer? ¿Qué me aconseja(s)?**

Vocabulario

9
- la espalda *back*
- la pierna *leg*
- el dolor *pain*
- **afectar, nervioso/a, tenso/a**

10
- el ojo *eye*
- el oído *ear*
- el brazo *arm*
- el pie *foot*

11
- ¿Qué te/le pasa? (*fam./form.*) *What's wrong?*
- el analgésico *painkiller*
- por cierto *by the way*
- a propósito *incidentally; by the way*
- el/la paciente *patient*

Estrategia

Añadir información a una conversación

Por cierto, el otro día escribí a un consultorio.
A propósito, ¿habéis escrito alguna vez a uno?

Estrategia Another way to add a topic to a conversation is to say **A todo esto...**

9 Lea las consultas en este consultorio de salud y elija un título para cada una.
1: Dolores de espalda; 2: Problemas de pareja; 3: Estrés en el trabajo

Estrés en el trabajo | Dolores de espalda | Problemas de pareja

10 a. ¿Qué partes del cuerpo mencionan los textos? Sitúelas en la imagen. Sitúe después el resto de las palabras del recuadro.

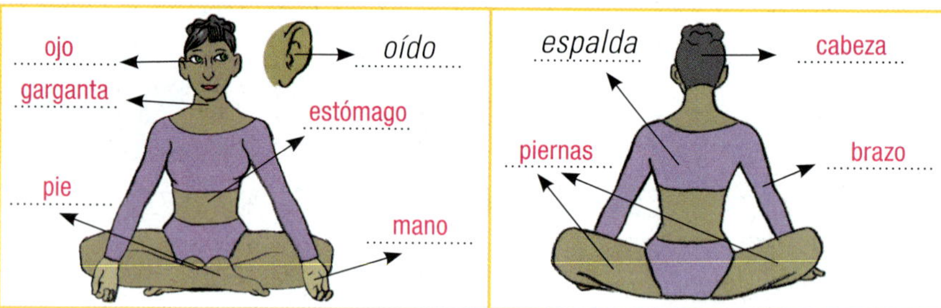

garganta • brazo(s) • pie(s) • mano(s) • ojo(s) • oído(s)

b. Busque y subraye en los textos las formas para pedir consejo.

11 a. Escuche la llamada a este programa de televisión sobre la salud. ¿Cuál de las tres personas del consultorio llama? Raquel García

b. Escuche y relacione las preguntas del especialista con las respuestas.

1. ¿Qué le pasa? ..b..
2. ¿Ha intentado hacer ejercicio? ..a..
3. Ya... Por cierto, ¿duerme bien? ..c..
4. ¿Hay algo que le preocupa? ..e..
5. A propósito, ¿ha probado algún remedio natural contra el estrés? ..d..

a. Sí, pero no me ayuda.
b. Me duele mucho la espalda.
c. No, no mucho.
d. La verdad es que no.
e. He tenido problemas con mi pareja.

c. Fíjese en las preguntas y apunte las expresiones para añadir información nueva a la conversación. Por cierto...; A propósito...

d. Haga sus propias preguntas a la paciente.

11d Suggestion You may want to introduce the terms **el/la quiropráctico/a** and **el estiramiento.**

Modelo:
- *Por cierto, ¿ha probado con la natación?*
- *A propósito,...*

Suggestion Read through the **Consejos para una vida sana** and ask students which habits from the list they practice. Are any of them incompatible with university life?

Consejos para una vida sana

1. Levántate media hora antes para hacer un poco de gimnasia.
2. Dúchate con agua fría. Es bueno para la circulación y para tu piel.
3. Desayuna alimentos con mucha fibra y toma jugos naturales.
4. ¿Tienes bicicleta? Utilízala para ir al trabajo o a clases.
5. Toma té y no café. Tómalo por las mañanas en el desayuno.
6. Come despacio y siempre a la misma hora. ¡Olvida la comida basura!
7. Trabaja menos. Deberías disfrutar más de tu familia y de tus amigos.
8. Acuéstate temprano. Deberías dormir por lo menos ocho horas.

Dar consejos

¿Llevas una vida sana?

Levántate temprano y disfruta de la vida.

También **deberías hacer** ejercicio.

Si tienes bicicleta, **utilízala**.

10A.4 The imperative with pronouns
deberías + [*infinitive*]

Vocabulario *cont.*

la natación *swimming*
el consultorio *problem page; (medical) practice*
el/la especialista, el ejercicio

(12)
hacer gimnasia *to exercise*
la piel *skin*
la fibra *fiber*
despacio *slowly*
la comida basura *junk food*
llevar una vida... *to lead a . . . life*
la circulación

¡OJO!

Spanish uses different words to talk about the inner ear and the outer ear. Use **el oído** to refer to the inner ear and your sense of hearing: **Tengo fiebre y me duelen los oídos.** Use **la oreja** to talk about the outer ear: **Mi abuelo tiene las orejas muy grandes.**

12 a. Lea los consejos de arriba. ¿Lee usted este tipo de artículos sobre la salud? ¿Qué consejos asocia con las imágenes? Lea el texto y compruebe.

b. Lea los consejos y pregunte a su compañero/a por estos y otros hábitos saludables.

13 a. Fíjese en la formación del imperativo informal de los verbos reflexivos y complete la tabla.

	Presente	Imperativo
LEVANTARSE	*te levantas*	*levántate*
DUCHARSE	te duchas	dúchate
ACOSTARSE	te acuestas	acuéstate

b. Lea estas frases del texto y diga a qué se refieren. la bicicleta; el té

- Utilízala para ir al trabajo.
- Tómalo por las mañanas.

c. Piense en un problema y anote consejos para solucionarlo. Su compañero/a debe adivinar de qué problema es.

MI EXPERIENCIA

14 Piense en sus hábitos de vida y haga una lista de cosas positivas y cosas no tan positivas. Compárela con las de sus compañeros y ofrezca consejos.

GUIÓN DE TRABAJO

¿Llevas una vida sana? → Bueno... como sano, pero no duermo mucho...

¿Qué me aconsejas?
¿Qué puedo/debería hacer? → Acuéstate pronto.
Deberías hacer ejercicio.
Por cierto, prueba el yoga.

Suggestion Prepare a list of health problems and, for each one, a few pieces of advice. Some of the advice should be logical and some should be illogical. Read aloud each health problem and advice; have students raise one hand if the statements are logical and two hands if they are not.

Practice more at **vhlcentral.com.**

SAM: Actividades pp. 204–206

10A Discuss Cuban health care. Cuba provides a doctor for every 170 residents, one of the highest doctor-to-patient ratios in the world. However, doctors' salaries remain relatively low.

Carlos Salazar, médico de familia en La Habana

Carlos Salazar, médico de familia en el Hospital Salvador Allende en La Habana

La Habana, 26 de enero

Carlos Salazar, médico de familia en La Habana, nos habla de su día a día

La sala de Medicina General del hospital es uno de los servicios que atiende a más personas.

En este servicio trabaja Carlos Salazar como médico de familia desde hace un año porque, como él mismo dice: "Me gusta poder ayudar donde es más necesario."

Hace cinco años, Carlos participó en un programa de intercambio con Venezuela y trabajó dos años en la Clínica Popular El Valle, en Caracas. Su misión era enseñar nuevas técnicas de prevención a un grupo de médicos venezolanos.

"La medicina cubana es muy prestigiosa. Por eso, nuestro país recibe a pacientes de todo el mundo. Hay que atender a más de ochenta pacientes en un día. No podemos dedicarles mucho tiempo, y a veces es difícil; por eso también hay que educar en salud. Las medicinas no son siempre la única solución, y hay que informar a los pacientes sobre hábitos de vida sanos y remedios naturales para cuidarse y sentirse bien de salud."

Cuando le preguntamos sobre el aspecto más importante de su trabajo, Carlos responde con una gran sonrisa: "Sin duda la gente, las personas... el aspecto humano. En mi trabajo hay que saber escuchar. Esto llega a las personas. Mi trabajo es duro a veces, pero me encanta."

Expresar obligación

En un día normal **hay que solucionar** muchos problemas y **hay que hacerlo** con rapidez.

10A.5 **hay que** + [*infinitive*]

Vocabulario

15

el/la médico/a de familia *family doctor*
la sala *ward*
atender (e:ie) *to see (a patient), to examine*
la sonrisa *smile*
solucionar *to solve*
el hospital, la clínica, la misión, la prevención, prestigioso/a, la medicina, la obligación

17

el/la doctor(a)

17 Suggestion Ask students what types of bland foods they eat when experiencing stomach upset.

15 a. Fíjese en la imagen del protagonista y en el título del artículo. ¿Qué sabe del sistema de salud en Cuba?

b. ¿Sabe qué es un "médico de familia"? Haga sus hipótesis. ¿Existe un equivalente en su país?

c. Ahora lea el texto y elija un título para el artículo. Justifique su elección.

"Mejor prevenir que curar"

"Programas de intercambio profesional" **"Tu médico, tu amigo"**

16 Marque en el texto con un color los problemas que Carlos tiene a diario y con otro color las soluciones que encuentra. ¿Tiene alguna otra idea para solucionar sus problemas? Hable con su compañero/a. Problemas: Muchos pacientes; Los médicos no pueden dedicarles mucho tiempo a los pacientes. Soluciones: Hay que educar en salud: informar a los pacientes sobre hábitos de vida sanos y remedios naturales.

17 Escuche la conversación entre este compañero venezolano de Carlos Salazar en la Clínica Popular El Valle y una de sus pacientes, y complete la tabla.

Síntomas	Tratamiento
dolor de cabeza y de estómago	infusión de manzanilla y comida ligera (una tortilla con un poco de arroz)

17 In the 1990s, the Cuban government officially began integrating natural medicine, such as homeopathy and acupuncture, in clinics and hospitals. Additionally, state-run radio and television programs instruct people on how to use the body's pressure points to relieve common stomach upset and headaches.

Vocabulario

18

el calzado *shoes*
el gorro *cap*
el impermeable *raincoat*
la asistencia sanitaria *health care*
la enfermedad *illness; disease*
la picazón *itch*
bañarse *to swim*
el/la salvavidas (*invar.*) *lifeguard*
vacunar *to vaccinate*
peligroso/a *dangerous*
la fiebre amarilla *yellow fever*
el paludismo *malaria*
el botiquín *first-aid kit*
el medicamento *medicine*
la herida *injury*
la crema solar protectora *sunscreen*
la diarrea, la hepatitis, la medicación, el desinfectante, el repelente, el mosquito

OPINIÓN

Piense en el sistema de asistencia sanitaria de su país. ¿Qué aspectos positivos y negativos tiene?

19 enfermedades: fiebre amarilla, hepatitis, paludismo; síntomas: fiebre, diarrea, dolor de cabeza, picazón; medicamentos: repelente de mosquitos, desinfectante para heridas, crema solar protectora; ropa: calzado, botas de *trekking*, chaqueta, pantalones largos, pantalones cortos, gorro, impermeable

21 **Expansion** Have students exchange papers and write a response.

18 Lea estas recomendaciones de viaje de la revista *Excursionista* y clasifíquelas.

ANTES DEL VIAJE: 1, 2, 3, 8, 10 DURANTE EL VIAJE: 5, 6, 7, 9
DESPUÉS DEL VIAJE: 4

RECOMENDACIONES PARA UN VIAJE DE AVENTURA

1. Visite a su médico de familia e infórmese de los medicamentos que necesita.
2. Lleve ropa y calzado adecuados al clima del país de destino. Lleve calzado cómodo, botas de *trekking*, ropa para el frío (chaqueta, pantalón largo...), para el calor (pantalones cortos, gorro), y para la lluvia (impermeable).
3. Infórmese sobre el sistema de asistencia sanitaria del país de destino.
4. Algunas enfermedades tropicales no se manifiestan inmediatamente. Si tiene síntomas como fiebre, diarrea, dolor de cabeza, picazón, etc., informe a su médico.

5. Coma solo alimentos cocinados.
6. Báñese en zonas de la playa donde haya un salvavidas.
7. Beba mucha agua. Bébala en botella, sin hielo.
8. Vacúnese contra las enfermedades peligrosas de los países de destino (fiebre amarilla, hepatitis...) y tome la medicación contra el paludismo si es necesario.
9. Cuando coma fruta, siempre lávela y pélela antes.
10. Prepare un botiquín con medicamentos básicos: desinfectante para heridas, crema solar protectora, repelente de mosquitos, etc.

19 Busque en el texto palabras relacionadas con estas categorías.

enfermedades • síntomas • medicamentos • ropa

20 Para usted, ¿cuáles son los tres consejos más importantes ofrecidos en el artículo? ¿Le sorprende alguno? ¿Ha viajado alguna vez a algún destino que ha requerido precauciones especiales?

21 Escriba al consultorio de salud, exponga un problema que tiene y pida consejo.

Nombre: .... Edad: ....
Enfermedades: ....
Alergias: ....
Comentarios: *Últimamente duermo poco, y me duele la espalda...*

22 Escuche de nuevo al doctor y a su paciente, y fíjese en estas expresiones propias del habla venezolana. ¿Qué cree que significan? ¿Ha escuchado alguna vez un acento similar en español?

○ Ahorita. ○ ¿Cómo anda? ○ ¿Cómo me la tratan? ○ ¡A la orden!

Practice more at **vhlcentral.com.**

SAM: Actividades pp. 207–210

23 Formen dos grupos y viajen por América Latina. Tiren el dado° y avancen por los países. Si contestan correctamente, pueden seguir el viaje.

1 ¿Qué tiempo hace en Isla Margarita?

2 Viajan al Amazonas. ¿Qué hay que hacer contra el paludismo?

3 Viajan de Belém (Brasil) a Montevideo (Uruguay). ¿Qué transporte utilizan? Pidan consejo.

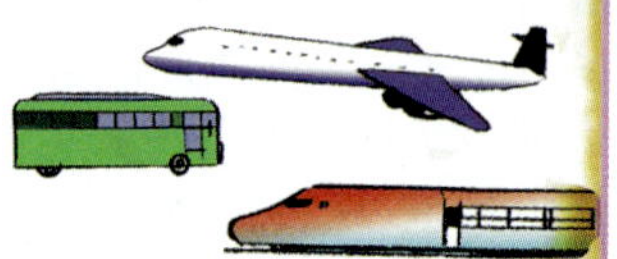

4 Aconsejen actividades interesantes para hacer en Buenos Aires (Argentina).

5 ¿Qué ropa hay que llevar a los Andes?

6 Están en Chile. Un compañero tiene gripe. Describan los síntomas.

7 ¿Qué tiempo hace en La Paz (Bolivia)?

8 Están en Perú y una compañera se encuentra mal. Piensen en remedios para el dolor de estómago.

9 Están en Colombia. Una compañera perdió su pasaporte. ¿Qué pueden hacer?

tiren el dado *roll the die* **la embajada** *embassy*

23 Suggestion Have a volunteer create a question about Ecuador for the class to answer.

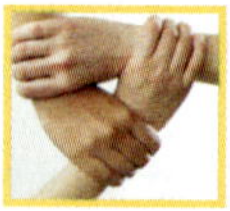

TAREA FINAL

Receta para ser feliz

Haga una lista de seis recomendaciones para ser feliz.

Disfruta de tu familia.
Acepta los cambios.
....

Compare su lista con la de su compañero/a y elijan diez recomendaciones.

Compártanlas con sus compañeros. Escojan las recomendaciones más brillantes y escriban la receta para ser feliz.

YO PUEDO...

- Puedo hablar del tiempo.
  ¿Qué tiempo hace hoy?
- Puedo expresar dolencias y síntomas.
  ¿Cómo se siente si tiene gripe?
- Puedo pedir consejos.
  Usted tiene fiebre: pida consejo.
- Puedo dar consejos.
  Escriba consejos para un amigo que tiene estrés.
- Puedo expresar obligación.
  ¿Qué hay que hacer para llevar una vida sana?

GRAMÁTICA FUNCIONAL

10A.1 Talk about the weather

hace; llueve; nieva; está nublado 5.12.2

- To inquire about the weather, say **¿Qué tiempo hace?** or **¿Qué tal (está) el tiempo?** (*How's the weather?*).
- To describe the weather, use these impersonal expressions, which do not have an expressed subject (equivalent to *it* in English).

Hace frío.	**Hace buen tiempo.**	**Nieva.**
Hace calor.	**Hace mal tiempo.**	**Está nublado.**
Hace sol.	**Llueve.**	

- To ask the temperature, say **¿Qué temperatura hace?** To answer, say **Hace** + [*number*] + **grados (centígrados/Fahrenheit).**

10A.2 Describe symptoms and ailments

doler; encontrarse/estar + bien/mal/[*adjective*], tener + [*noun*] 5.8.2, 5.11.2

- The verb **doler** (*to hurt, to ache*) undergoes an **o→ue** stem change. Like **gustar**, it is conjugated in the third person and used with indirect object pronouns. Use the verb in the singular or plural form in order to make it agree with the subject.

DOLER		
(a mí)	**me**	
(a ti)	**te**	
(a usted/él/ella)	**le**	**due**le(n)
(a nosotros/as)	**nos**	
(a vosotros/as)	**os**	
(a ustedes, a ellos/as)	**les**	

- As with **gustar** (4A.2), use **a** + **mí, ti, usted, él, ella, nosotros/as, vosotros/as, ustedes, ellos/as,** or a person's name for clarification.
- Unlike in English, use the definite article (**el, la, los, las**) and not the possessive adjective with parts of the body.

Me duele **la** cabeza. A Hugo le duelen **los** hombros.
My head hurts. *Hugo's shoulders hurt.*

- Use the reflexive verb **encontrarse** (*to be; to feel*) to express how someone is feeling. **Encontrarse** has an **o→ue** stem change.

Estoy cansada hoy, pero **me encuentro** bien.
*I am tired today, but **I feel** well.*

- When **encontrar** is used non-reflexively, it means *to find*.
- Use the construction **tener** + [*noun*] to express certain states. Remember to use **tener** + **frío/calor** to say that someone feels hot or cold and **hace** + **frío/calor** to talk about the weather.

tener calor	*to be hot*	**tener hambre**	*to be hungry*
tener frío	*to be cold*	**tener sed**	*to be thirsty*
tener fiebre	*to have a fever*	**tener sueño**	*to be sleepy*
tener gripe	*to have the flu*	**tener dolor de. . .**	*to have a . . . ache*

- Use **estar** + **bien/mal/[*adjective*]** to describe other states, as in **estoy resfriado/a** (*I have a cold*) or **estoy enfermo/a** (*I am sick*).

¡Póngalo en práctica!

G1 Complete el diálogo.

- ¿Qué tiempo (1)...hace... hoy en Caracas?
- (2)...Hace... sol y buen tiempo. ¿Qué tal el (3)...tiempo... en Mérida?
- (4)...Hace... mal tiempo. (5)...Está... nublado y (6)...hace... mucho frío.
- ¿Qué (7)...temperatura... hace?
- Hace tres (8)...grados... centígrados.

G1 Expansion Write a list of countries and months (Ex: **Argentina/agosto**) on the board and have pairs of students write a mini-dialogue for each one. Ask a few pairs to read their dialogues for the class.

G2 Complete las conversaciones con la forma correcta de **doler, encontrarse** y **tener**. Incluya el pronombre reflexivo o el pronombre de objeto indirecto si es necesario.

- ¿Qué te pasa? ¿Cómo (1)...te encuentras...?
- Me encuentro mal. (2)...Me duelen... las muelas.
- ¿Cómo está María?
- Pues no muy bien; (3)...tiene... gripe, (4)...le duele... la cabeza y (5)...tiene... fiebre.
- ¿Y a usted qué le pasa? ¿Cómo (6)...se encuentra...?
- Mal; (7)...tengo... calor y (8)...me duele... el estómago.

G3 Empareje el comienzo de cada oración con el final apropiado.

c	1. Gabriela está un poco	a. enfermo.
e	2. Leo tiene	b. piernas.
a	3. Mi hermano está	c. resfriada.
b	4. Me duelen las	d. garganta.
d	5. A Marcela le duele la	e. frío.

Suggestion Describe situations and have students say what part of the body hurts. Ex: **Lola pasó diez horas leyendo páginas web. (A ella le duelen los ojos. / Le duele la cabeza.)**

Explain that with body parts, the possessive adjective is not needed because the verb construction makes it clear to whom the speaker is referring.

Practice more at **vhlcentral.com.**

GRAMÁTICA FUNCIONAL

10A.3 Ask for advice

¿Qué puedo/debería hacer?; ¿Qué me aconseja(s)? 5.17.3

- Say **¿Qué puedo hacer?** (*What can I do?*) or **¿Qué debería hacer?** (*What should I do?*) to ask for advice.

Doctor, tengo fiebre. ¿Qué **debería** hacer?
*Doctor, I have a fever. What **should** I do?*

You may want to point out that **¿Qué debo hacer?** is also possible.

- You can also use the verb **aconsejar** (*to advise*) with an indirect object pronoun to ask someone's advice.

Tengo un problema. **¿Qué me aconseja?**
*I have a problem. **What would you advise me to do?***

You may want to give students the option of using **recomendar,** which has a similar usage to **aconsejar.**

10A.4 Give advice

The imperative with pronouns; debería(s) + *[infinitive]* 5.17.3, 5.18.4a, 5.18.5a

- You learned how to form singular affirmative commands, both formal and familiar, in 8A.4 and 9B.2. With affirmative commands, reflexive and object pronouns are always attached to the end of the imperative form. When a pronoun is attached to an affirmative command with two or more syllables, add an accent mark to maintain the original stress.

Dúch**ate** y víst**ete**. *Shower and get dressed.*	Bebe el agua. Bébe**la**. *Drink the water. Drink **it**.*

- You can also give advice using the construction **deberías** + [*infinitive*] in familiar contexts (**tú**) and **debería** + [*infinitive*] in formal situations (**usted**).

Deberías hacer deporte. ***You should** play sports.*	**Usted debería** descansar. ***You should** rest.*

- **Debería** is the conditional form of the verb **deber** (*must; to have to*). Use **debería** + [*infinitive*] to express what you should do.

- Use **deber** in the present tense to express an obligation or strong suggestion.

Tienes un examen mañana y **debes** estudiar.
*You have an exam tomorrow and you **must** study.*

10A.5 Express obligation

tener que + [*infinitive*]; **hay que** + [*infinitive*] 5.10

- In 6A.5, you learned the construction **tener** + **que** + [*infinitive*] to express obligation.

Tengo que hacer algunas llamadas.
***I have to make** some phone calls.*

- Another way to express obligation is the construction **hay que** + [*infinitive*]. **Hay que** expresses an impersonal obligation and it is invariable.

Hay que repartir las tareas.
We/One must distribute the tasks.

Suggestion Have students use **hay que** and **tener que** to talk about what a student must do to get a good grade in Spanish class.

¡Póngalo en práctica!

G4 Complete las preguntas.

1. ¿Qué me ...aconseja(s)... para llevar una vida sana?
2. Estoy muy estresada. ¿Qué ...debería/puedo... hacer?
3. No duermo bien. ¿Qué puedo ...hacer...?
4. ¿Qué ...me... aconsejas para sacar mejores notas?
5. Doctor, mi hermano siempre tiene sueño. ¿Qué le ...aconseja...?
6. Quiero comer bien, pero no tengo tiempo para preparar la comida todos los días. ¿Qué ...debería/puedo... hacer?

G5 Escriba el imperativo informal de cada verbo.

(1) ...Cambia... (Cambiar) tus hábitos de vida; (2) ...levántate... (levantarse) temprano, (3) ...practica... (practicar) deportes y (4) ...come... (comer) sano. (5) ...Acuéstate... (Acostarse) temprano y (6) ...duerme... (dormir) ocho horas como mínimo.

G6 Transforme cada oración al imperativo usando el pronombre de objeto directo apropiado.

Modelo: *Deberías beber la leche. Bébela.*

1. Deberías utilizar la bicicleta para ir al trabajo. ...Utilízala...
2. Deberías comer las verduras. ...Cómelas...
3. Toma el jugo. ...Tómalo...
4. Deberías leer estos libros. ...Léelos...
5. Deberías probar el yoga. ...Pruébalo...
6. Usted debería tomar la manzanilla. ...Tómela...
7. Usted debería levantarse temprano. ...Levántese temprano...
8. Usted debería evitar la comida basura. ...Evítela...

G7 Complete las oraciones usando **hay que** o la forma correcta de **tener que**. Suggested answers.

1. Para llevar una vida sana, ...hay que... hacer ejercicio.
2. Un médico ...tiene que... atender a muchos pacientes.
3. Lucas e Iván ...tienen que... terminar el proyecto.
4. ...Hay que... meter goles para ganar el partido.
5. ¿Qué ...hay que... hacer para aprender un idioma?
6. El paciente ...tiene que... hablar con el médico ahora.

Suggestion Ask students to write a series of affirmative commands, some with pronouns and some without, that would be used in a particular context. Have students read their lists to a partner, who will guess the context.

Practice more at **vhlcentral.com.**

VOCABULARIO

El tiempo y la salud

menos mal	*thank goodness*
por fin	*at last*
estar resfriado/a	*to have a cold*
hace 30 °C de temperatura	*the temperature is 30°C*
hacer buen/mal tiempo	*there is good/bad weather*
hacer frío/calor	*to be cold/hot*
hacer sol	*to be sunny*
¿Qué tiempo hace?	*What's the weather like?*
la alergia	*allergy*
el antibiótico	*antibiotic*
la aspirina	*aspirin*
la cabeza	*head*
el/la dentista	*dentist*
la dolencia	*ailment*
la estación (del año)	*season*
el estado anímico	*state of mind*
el estado físico	*physical condition*
el estómago	*stomach*
la fiebre	*fever*
la garganta	*throat*
la infección	*infection*
la manzanilla	*chamomile tea*
la muela	*molar*
el otoño	*fall*
la primavera	*spring*
el remedio	*remedy, cure*
el síntoma	*symptom*
la temperatura	*temperature*
el tiempo	*weather*
adaptarse	*to adapt*
darse un baño	*to take a bath*
depender (de)	*to depend (on)*
doler (o:ue)	*to hurt, to ache*
encontrarse (o:ue)	*to be; to feel*
llover (o:ue)	*to rain*
nevar (e:ie)	*to snow*
ser sensible a	*to be sensitive to*
tener frío/calor	*to be cold/hot*
tomar el sol	*to sunbathe*
cansado/a	*tired*
nublado/a	*cloudy*

Salud, divino tesoro

a propósito	*incidentally; by the way*
llevar una vida...	*to lead a . . . life*
por cierto	*by the way*
¿Qué te/le pasa? (*fam./form.*)	*What's wrong?*
el analgésico	*painkiller*
el brazo	*arm*
la circulación	*circulation*
la comida basura	*junk food*
el consultorio	*problem page; (medical) practice*
el dolor	*pain*
el ejercicio	*exercise*
la espalda	*back*
el/la especialista	*specialist*
la fibra	*fiber*
la natación	*swimming*
el oído	*ear*
el ojo	*eye*
el/la paciente	*patient*
el pie	*foot*
la piel	*skin*
la pierna	*leg*
afectar	*to affect*
hacer gimnasia	*to exercise*
nervioso/a	*nervous*
tenso/a	*tense*
despacio	*slowly*

Carlos Salazar

tiren el dado	*roll the die*
la asistencia sanitaria	*health care*
el botiquín	*first-aid kit*
el calzado	*shoes*
la clínica	*clinic*
la crema solar protectora	*sunscreen*
el desinfectante	*disinfectant*
la diarrea	*diarrhea*
el/la doctor(a)	*doctor*
la embajada	*embassy*
la enfermedad	*illness; disease*
la fiebre amarilla	*yellow fever*
el gorro	*cap*
la hepatitis	*hepatitis*
la herida	*injury*
el hospital	*hospital*
el impermeable	*raincoat*
la medicación	*medication*
el medicamento	*medicine*
la medicina	*medicine*
el/la médico/a de familia	*family doctor*
la misión	*mission*
el mosquito	*mosquito*
la obligación	*obligation*
el paludismo	*malaria*
la picazón	*itch*
la prevención	*prevention*
el repelente	*repellent*
la sala	*ward*
el/la salvavidas (*invar.*)	*lifeguard*
la sonrisa	*smile*
atender (e:ie)	*to see (a patient), to examine*
bañarse	*to swim*
solucionar	*to solve*
vacunar	*to vaccinate*
peligroso/a	*dangerous*
prestigioso/a	*prestigious*

Successful Language Learning Encourage students to try a variety of memorization techniques until they find the ones that work best for them. When studying vocabulary, some may have greater success by writing out the words, others may prefer to make flash cards, and some students learn best when they listen to a recording of the words as they read through the lists.

Variación léxica

centígrados ⟷ **grados Celsius**

la comida basura ⟷ **la comida chatarra** (*Arg., Méx.*)

el consultorio ⟷ **la consulta** (*Esp.*)

la crema solar protectora ⟷ **el protector solar** (*Amér. L.*)

la malaria ⟷ **el paludismo**

el medicamento ⟷ **la medicina** (*Amér. L.*) ⟷ **el remedio** (*Arg.*)

la picazón ⟷ **el picor** (*Esp.*) ⟷ **la comezón**

el/la salvavidas ⟷ **el/la guardavidas** (*Arg.*) ⟷ **el/la socorrista** (*Esp.*)

solucionar ⟷ **resolver**

10B MEMORIAS

Imágenes de la memoria

Madrid, 16 de junio de 1977

Primeras elecciones democráticas

Los españoles votaron ayer, 15 de junio, en las primeras elecciones democráticas de los últimos 40 años. Fue un día histórico y la gente estaba emocionada.

Bogotá, 21 de octubre de 1982

Premio Nobel de Literatura para García Márquez

Anoche estaba en su casa de Ciudad de México y un periodista lo llamó para entrevistarlo. Así recibió la noticia.

García Márquez has houses in Cartagena, Colombia, and also in Mexico City, where he and his wife settled in 1961.

Hablar de memorias

García Márquez **estaba** en su casa y **recibió** la noticia por teléfono.

Hoy **hemos votado** por primera vez. La gente **estaba** emocionada.

10B.1 Preterite
Present perfect
Imperfect

Vocabulario

1

el Premio Nobel *Nobel Prize; Nobel laureate*
el/la periodista *journalist, reporter*
emocionado/a *excited*
votar, la memoria, las elecciones, democrático/a

3

el/la testigo *witness*
el entusiasmo *enthusiasm*
emocionante *exciting; moving*
el optimismo *optimism*
decisivo/a, la generación

4

la moneda *currency*
dejar de *to stop, to cease*
desaparecer (zc) *to disappear*
el torneo *tournament*

1 a. Tome unos momentos para observar las imágenes de las dos páginas. Cierre el libro. ¿Qué imagen recuerda en primer lugar? ¿Recuerda las otras?

b. ¿Qué otra imagen quiere añadir a la exposición *Imágenes de la memoria*?

2 a. Lea las noticias de las dos páginas y anote ejemplos para cada tiempo verbal. 1: llamó, recibió, votaron, Fue, se reunieron, dejó, se usó, logró; 2: ha entrado; ha ganado; 3: estaba

1 pretérito indefinido | 2 pretérito perfecto | 3 pretérito imperfecto

b. Indique cuál de los tiempos anteriores usamos para:

- expresar acciones pasadas. 1
- describir situaciones en el pasado. 3
- expresar acciones pasadas conectadas con el presente. 2

3 a. Escuche a estos españoles que hablan de un momento importante de la historia de España. ¿De qué momento hablan?
Hablan de las primeras elecciones democráticas.

b. Escuche de nuevo y anote estos datos.

	¿Dónde y con quién estaban?
Mateo	Estaba en Salamanca con sus padres.
Celia	Estaba en Cuenca con su marido y sus hijos.
Julián	Estaba en Zaragoza.

c. ¿Ha vivido alguno de los momentos de las fotografías? ¿Cuál? ¿Dónde estaba y qué hacía cuando sucedió?

1.° de enero de 2000

Cambio de milenio

Varias horas antes de la medianoche, cientos de miles de personas de todo el mundo se reunieron frente a los monumentos representativos de cada ciudad para celebrar.

1.° de enero de 2002

El euro (EUR o €) ha entrado hoy en circulación como moneda única de la Unión Europea

En España, la peseta dejó de ser la moneda oficial hace tres años, pero se usó hasta ayer. Va a desaparecer como moneda física el 28 de febrero de 2002.

11 de julio de 2010

España ha ganado la Copa Mundial de Fútbol

Después de participar trece veces en el campeonato, la selección española (La Roja) ha ganado su primera copa del mundo en Sudáfrica.

Relacionar momentos pasados

El Muro de Berlín se derribó veintiocho años después de su construcción.

Antes de retirarse, el ciclista español Miguel Ángel Indurain ganó el Tour de Francia cinco veces.

10B.2 **antes/después de** + [*infinitive/noun*]

Vocabulario *cont.*

- morir (o:ue) *to die*
- la muerte *death*
- el hecho *event*
- el Muro de Berlín *Berlin Wall*
- derribar *to knock down, to demolish*
- **el milenio, la Unión Europea**

4 a. Lea estas informaciones. ¿Ocurrieron antes o después de los momentos de las imágenes? Complete las oraciones. Suggested answers:

Gabriel García Márquez publicó *Cien años de soledad* en 1967.
El escritor colombiano recibió el Nobel quince años después de publicar *Cien años de soledad*.

El dictador español Francisco Franco murió el 20 de noviembre de 1975.
Las primeras elecciones democráticas se celebraron dos años después de la muerte de Franco.

La peseta dejó de ser la moneda oficial de España el 1.° de enero de 1999.
La peseta dejó de ser la moneda oficial de España tres años antes de la entrada en circulación del euro.

b. Añada otros hechos que ocurrieron antes y después de los que se representan en las cinco fotografías.

4b Suggestion For homework, have students write a brief description and find a photo for each additional event. In class, make a time line of events by hanging up the descriptions in chronological order around the room.

MI EXPERIENCIA

5 Piense en un hecho histórico que ha vivido. Cuente a sus compañeros qué recuerdos tiene de ese día. Exprese las acciones y describa las situaciones.

GUIÓN DE TRABAJO

- ¿Has vivido algún momento histórico especial para ti?
- ¿Cuándo? En 2004...
- ¿Dónde estabas cuando pasó? Ese día estaba en... Vivía en... Tenía 9 años...
- ¿Qué ocurrió?
- ¿Qué pasó antes/después? Antes de... Después de...
- ¿Con quién estabas? Estaba con mi familia...

MERCOSUR

En 1985, Argentina y Brasil firmaron un acuerdo que dio origen al Mercosur (Mercado Común del Sur), creado oficialmente en 1991 por Argentina, Brasil, Paraguay y Uruguay. Este mercado integra económica, política y culturalmente países muy diferentes y, al mismo tiempo, muy cercanos. Es el mayor productor de alimentos del mundo. Los miembros asociados son: Bolivia, Chile, Colombia, Ecuador, Perú y Venezuela.

Read through the note about **Mercosur**. In the second sentence, you may want to point out the series of adverbs and explain that in a series such as this, **-mente** is only used with the last adverb.

Practice more at **vhlcentral.com.**

SAM: Actividades pp. 211–213

Chile en la memoria

Tan lejos y tan cerca

Hola a todos los chilenos y chilenas. Soy Elizabeth. Vivo y trabajo en Europa, en Bélgica. Estoy contenta acá. Solo tengo un problema: todavía no he conocido a ningún chileno para hablar de nuestro país. Quiero estar en contacto con otros compatriotas y creo que esta es una bonita oportunidad. ¿Creen que es posible?

Espero sus noticias. ¡Hasta pronto!

¡Hablamos!

Explain that **opinar** can be translated as *to opine*, but a more colloquial way would be *to think*.

Comentarios recientes

Hernán ¡Hola, Elizabeth y compatriotas chilenos en el mundo! Opino que este blog es fantástico. Llevo en París diez años. Llegué por trabajo y todavía no he vuelto a mi tierra. Para mí es un poco difícil estar lejos de mis familiares. ¿Y para ustedes?

Carolina Yo salí en momentos muy duros en mi país, por motivos políticos. Los años pasan rápido... Ya soy abuela y estoy en paz, pero mi corazón está todavía en Chile. En mi opinión, el propio país no puede olvidarse nunca. Y ustedes, ¿qué opinan? ¿Están de acuerdo?

Pedir y dar opiniones

- ¿Creen que vivir afuera es difícil?
- Yo creo que sí.
- Para mí, tiene muchas ventajas. ¿Están de acuerdo?
- En mi opinión, es mejor estar en tu propio país. ¿Qué opinan?

10B.3 **creer/opinar que..., para mí; en mi opinión...**

Vocabulario

6

- **vivir afuera** *to live abroad*
- **Bélgica** *Belgium*
- **el/la compatriota** *fellow countryman/countrywoman*
- **estar en paz** *to be at peace*
- **no puede olvidarse** *cannot be forgotten*
- **estar de acuerdo** *to agree*
- **la esperanza** *hope*
- **la nostalgia** *homesickness; nostalgia*
- **la tristeza** *sadness*
- **la decepción** *disappointment*
- **En mi opinión,...**

Point out that **decepción** is a false cognate.

Estrategia

Minimizar el desacuerdo

- Es duro estar lejos, **pero bueno, depende**... para mí es una oportunidad.
- **Claro que** es difícil, **pero** no imposible.

6 a. Fíjese en el blog y lea los textos. ¿Qué tienen en común los testimonios de estos chilenos? Márquelo.

Sienten... esperanza • nostalgia • tristeza • decepción

b. Para Hernán y Carolina, ¿cuáles fueron los motivos para salir de Chile?
trabajo y política

7 a. Marque en el texto las formas para pedir una opinión.
¿Creen que es posible?, ¿Y para ustedes?, ¿qué opinan?, ¿Están de acuerdo?

b. Complete estas opiniones a partir del texto. Identifique quién dice cada una.

- Opino que este blog es fantástico (Hernán)
- Creo que esta es una bonita oportunidad (Elizabeth)
- En mi opinión, el propio país no puede olvidarse nunca (Carolina)
- Para mí es un poco difícil estar lejos de mis familiares (Hernán)

8 a. Escuche a dos chilenos que hablan de sus experiencias en otros países. ¿A quién corresponden estas intervenciones?

	Diego	Sofía
1. Para mí es muy duro estar acá, lejos de mi país.	✓	
2. Es duro estar lejos, pero bueno, depende... Para mí ha sido una oportunidad para encontrar un trabajo mejor.		✓
3. En mi opinión, cuando sales y estás lejos tanto tiempo, es muy difícil volver.	✓	
4. Claro que es difícil volver a veces, pero no imposible. Yo quiero regresar un día.		✓

b. ¿Diego y Sofía opinan lo mismo de su experiencia? ¿Cómo expresan su desacuerdo? No.

de un modo suave ☑ de un modo fuerte ☐

9 ¿Qué opina usted de vivir y trabajar afuera? ¿Cuáles cree que son los aspectos positivos y negativos?

Expansion Ask students to think of other reasons why a person might emigrate from their country of origin. Then have them discuss with a partner under what circumstances they would emigrate from their country of origin, where they would go, and how they might feel in their new country.

FORO CHILE EN LA MEMORIA

Entrada: Carlos Vallejo **23-09**

Amigos, quiero compartir con ustedes algunas reflexiones de nuestros queridos escritores chilenos.

«La experiencia es como un billete de lotería comprado después del sorteo. No creo en ella.»

(GABRIELA MISTRAL)

«Vengo del llamado tercer mundo. (¿Cuál es el segundo?)»

(ISABEL ALLENDE)

«Algún día en algún lugar vas a encontrarte a ti mismo, y esa puede ser la más feliz o la más amarga de tus horas.»

(PABLO NERUDA)

Carolina: No estoy de acuerdo con Gabriela Mistral. Para mí la experiencia es esencial. ¿No creen?

Leonardo: Yo tampoco estoy de acuerdo con Gabriela Mistral. Creo que no tiene razón. La experiencia enseña muchas cosas.

Sandra: Pues yo sí estoy de acuerdo con ella. Yo tampoco creo en la experiencia.

Pablo: Es verdad, Sandra, tienes razón. La experiencia no sirve para nada.

Carolina: Para mí la frase de Isabel Allende es la mejor. Es la mejor escritora de Chile.

Pablo: ¡Ah! En esto no estoy de acuerdo. No es verdad. Neruda es el mejor.

Expresar acuerdo y desacuerdo

- Neruda tiene razón.
- Estoy de acuerdo.
- Sí, yo también.
- Neruda es el mejor escritor chileno.
- No es verdad. No estoy de acuerdo.
- Yo tampoco.

10B.4 **(no) estar de acuerdo, (no) tener razón, (no) ser verdad también, tampoco**

Vocabulario

8
recordar (o:ue) *to remember*
el desacuerdo *disagreement*

10
amargo/a *bitter; painful*
tampoco *not… either, neither*
tener razón *to be right*
ser verdad *to be true*

12
la tormenta *storm*

10 a. ¿Conoce a estos escritores? Lea sus frases. ¿Le gustan? ¿Por qué?

b. Lea los comentarios del foro. ¿Cuáles muestran estar de acuerdo y cuáles en desacuerdo? Subráyelos con colores distintos.

c. Complete las oraciones con **también** o **tampoco**.

- Estoy de acuerdo.
- Yo también.

- No estoy de acuerdo.
- Yo tampoco.

Acuerdo: Sandra, Pablo (primera intervención) y Carolina (segunda intervención). Desacuerdo: Carolina (primera intervención), Leonardo y Pablo (segunda intervención).

11 ¿Con qué opiniones del foro está usted de acuerdo y con cuáles no?

12 ¿Está de acuerdo con el mensaje que transmite cada uno de estos refranes? ¿Por qué? Explíquelo por escrito, dando ejemplos concretos de momentos pasados de su vida en los que estos refranes se aplicaron o no.

Mejor malo conocido que bueno por conocer. | El que guarda siempre tiene. | Después de la tormenta viene la calma.

12 Suggestion You may want to add one or two of these sayings: **Al que madruga, Dios lo ayuda; El tiempo lo cura todo; No hay mejor maestra que la necesidad.**

MI EXPERIENCIA

13 Vote con el resto de sus compañeros para elegir los tres personajes más representativos y carismáticos de la historia.

GUIÓN DE TRABAJO

Yo creo que Teresa de Calcuta es la más representativa... En mi opinión,...

Estoy de acuerdo. Para mí también es... Tienes razón.

No estoy de acuerdo. No es verdad. Yo tampoco estoy de acuerdo.

Practice more at **vhlcentral.com.**

SAM: Actividades pp. 214–216

10B

Jorge Edwards, recuerdos de un escritor

At the time of Edwards' diplomatic post in Cuba, the president of Chile was Salvador Allende, a democratically elected president and member of the Socialist party. After just three months in Cuba, Castro accused the Chilean of "conduct hostile to the revolution" and declared Edwards persona non grata; from his experiences in Cuba he wrote and entitled the book of the same name.

"El hombre es historia, es memoria y es, a la vez, como se sabe, desmemoria."

Jorge Edwards, escritor chileno

Buenos Aires, 1.° de abril de 2008

El escritor chileno Jorge Edwards ha ganado el II Premio de Narrativa Iberoamericana Planeta-Casamérica

"*La casa de Dostoievski* toma el nombre de un edificio en ruinas de Santiago de Chile donde vivía un grupo de poetas y pintores a mediados del siglo XX", ha declarado el feliz autor después de conocer la noticia.

Jorge Edwards es uno de los principales representantes de la narrativa chilena. Ha ganado el Premio Nacional de Literatura de Chile en 1994 y el Premio Cervantes en 1999.

Estudió Derecho y representó a Chile como diplomático en Cuba y París. Allí se relacionó con algunos grandes del *boom* de la literatura latinoamericana, como Gabriel García Márquez, Julio Cortázar y Mario Vargas Llosa. Después del golpe de estado de Pinochet, abandonó su vida diplomática y se exilió en Barcelona, donde empezó su labor editorial. Actualmente, Jorge Edwards es escritor, editor y también colabora en diversos periódicos de Europa y América Latina como crítico literario.

Entre sus obras principales se encuentra la biografía *Adiós, poeta...* (1990). En esta obra, el escritor recuerda una parte de la vida de Pablo Neruda en el contexto cultural, social y político de la historia de Chile.

También ha publicado, entre otras muchas obras: *Persona non grata* (1973), donde el autor recuerda su período como representante del gobierno chileno en La Habana; *Machado de Assis* (2002), sobre el escritor brasileño Joaquim Machado de Assis, y *El sueño de la historia,* (2000) de gran éxito entre la crítica, en la que recuerda la historia de Chile.

Expresar qué se recuerda

El escritor **recuerda** la historia de Chile.

10B.5 **recordar (o→ue)**

Vocabulario

14

- **recordar (o:ue)** *to remember*
- **el/la representante** *representative*
- **la narrativa** *fiction*
- **relacionarse** *to run in the same circles*
- **el golpe de estado** *coup d'état*
- **abandonar** *to quit*
- **exiliarse** *to go into exile*
- **la nota de prensa** *press release*
- **representar, colaborar, el/la crítico/a literario/a**

OPINIÓN

¿Ha leído alguna obra de algún escritor latinoamericano o español? ¿Cuál? ¿Le ha gustado? ¿Por qué?

14 a. Observe la imagen y lea el titular. ¿A qué se dedica nuestro protagonista?
Es escritor.

b. Lea la nota de prensa sobre Jorge Edwards. ¿Cuál es el motivo de la información que se publica sobre él?
Jorge Edwards recibió el II Premio de Narrativa Iberoamericana Planeta-Casamérica.

15 Anote otros datos de su biografía que se mencionan.

- Países donde ha vivido. ¿Por qué motivos?: Cuba y Francia (diplomático); España (exilio)
- Actividad profesional: diplomático, editor, crítico literario, escritor
- Libros publicados: *Adiós, poeta; Persona non grata; Machado de Assis; El sueño de la historia; La casa de Dostoievski*

16 a. Indique qué recuerda el autor en algunas de sus obras. Recuerda la vida de Pablo Neruda como personaje clave en la historia de Chile (*Adiós, poeta*). Recuerda su período como representante del gobierno chileno en La Habana (*Persona non grata*). Recuerda la historia de Chile (*El sueño de la historia*).

Modelo: *Recuerda...*

b. ¿Y usted qué recuerda? Piense en un período pasado de su vida. ¿Dónde vivía? ¿Con quién? ¿Qué hacía?

Modelo: *Recuerdo que...*

17 a. Lea la cita de Jorge Edwards y explique con otras palabras su significado.

b. ¿Qué datos de la biografía del protagonista le han llamado la atención? ¿Le parece un personaje interesante? ¿Están sus compañeros de acuerdo?

17a Suggestion Guide students to understanding the quote by helping them to uncover the meaning of **desmemoria (falta de memoria)**.

Roberto Matta is one of Chile's most famous painters and an important figure in the surrealist movement.

Vocabulario

18

el encuentro *encounter*
el/la poeta/la poetisa *poet*
el piano de cola *grand piano*
cuyo/a *whose*
el miedo *fear*
nasal, el poema

20

el soneto

21

la dictadura *dictatorship*

Estrategia

Using a monolingual dictionary

When you come across a new word in Spanish, consult a monolingual dictionary. A monolingual Spanish dictionary describes meaning using descriptions, synonyms, and examples in Spanish rather than translations. Reading Spanish definitions will help you learn related words, and will keep you thinking in Spanish only.

El *boom* latinoamericano

En las décadas de 1960 y 1970, Gabriel García Márquez, Mario Vargas Llosa, Guillermo Cabrera Infante, Julio Cortázar, José Donoso y Carlos Fuentes, entre otros escritores latinoamericanos, revolucionaron la manera de contar historias. En las novelas del *boom*, las cosas irreales se describen como reales, los hechos no siempre están en orden cronológico, hay una mezcla de narradores y abunda el interés en la historia y la política.

18 a. Lea este discurso de Jorge Edwards. ¿Qué suceso relata?

- una aventura
- un encuentro
- un recuerdo de Chile

«Tres o cuatro años después, en una casa de lo que ya se llamaba el barrio alto, el dueño, un arquitecto avanzado para el Chile de esos tiempos, se acercó al grupo de adolescentes del que yo formaba parte y nos presentó a un poeta de voz nasal, de tez aceitunada, vestido con un traje de gabardina de color verde botella. Era una casa diferente de todas las que había visto antes, con un cuadro del entonces joven Roberto Matta encima de un piano de cola negro, con dos dibujos de Pablo Picasso en una esquina.

"A la edad de ustedes", nos dijo el poeta, cuyo nombre, Pablo Neruda, sonaba tan extraño como su voz, "yo estudiaba matemáticas en un banco del Cementerio General, debajo de grandes magnolias, y le tenía un miedo pánico a los exámenes...". Ya conocía el primero de sus *Veinte poemas de amor*, otro de mis textos de iniciación, y devoré cada una de sus palabras como un maná.»

EDWARDS, Jorge:
Discurso en la recepción del Premio Cervantes.

voz:	Para hablar. Hablar en voz alta o en voz baja. Voz nasal, de nariz.
tez:	Cara. Tez aceitunada: Cara de color aceituna, verdoso.
gabardina:	Tipo de tela.
banco:	Asiento en que pueden sentarse varias personas, en un parque, por ejemplo.
cementerio:	Lugar donde se entierran los muertos.
magnolias:	Flores de un gran árbol, el magnolio.
devorar:	Comer con mucha hambre.
maná:	Alimento sagrado, según la Biblia.

b. Escriba una definición o descripción para estas palabras.

1. acercarse: ....
2. verde botella: ....
3. el miedo pánico: ....

19 Escriba un relato breve sobre un encuentro. Use estos elementos del texto anterior.

Hace tres o cuatro años... era... conocí a... dijo... y...

19 Expansion Collect students' papers, shuffle them, and read the stories aloud. Have the class guess who wrote each one.

20 a. ¿Conoce a Gabriela Mistral y a Pablo Neruda? Lea el texto y busque más información sobre estos escritores chilenos en Internet.

Gabriela Mistral

Gabriela Mistral, poetisa chilena, fue la primera escritora de América Latina que ganó el Nobel de Literatura, en 1945. Algunas de sus obras son *Sonetos de la muerte* (1914) y *Lagar* (1954).

Pablo Neruda ganó el Nobel en 1971. Algunas de sus obras son, por ejemplo, *Veinte poemas de amor y una canción desesperada* (1924), o *Confieso que he vivido* (1974), un libro de memorias donde el escritor recuerda hechos históricos de Chile.

Pablo Neruda

b. ¿Qué otros escritores latinoamericanos conoce? ¿De dónde son? ¿Qué obras han escrito? Comparta sus conocimientos con su compañero/a.

Practice more at **vhlcentral.com.**

SAM: Actividades pp. 217–222

21 a. Tiren el dado y decidan quién empieza el juego. Hagan la pregunta con **qué, cuándo, dónde** o **quién** al equipo contrario, según el color. Si la respuesta no es correcta, pasa el turno al equipo contrario.

1. ¿La Roja ganó la Copa Mundial?
2. ¿Huracán° Katrina?
3. ¿España 1977?
4. ¿Reforma° del sistema de salud de los EE.UU.?
5. ¿*Cien años de soledad*?
6. ¿Juegos Olímpicos de 1992?
7. ¿1.° de enero de 2000 en el mundo?
8. ¿Neruda, *Veinte poemas de amor...*?
9. ¿Dictadura militar de Pinochet?
10. ¿Nobel de Literatura 1971?
11. ¿Ganó Edwards en 1999?
12. ¿Primera poetisa chilena Nobel de Literatura?
13. ¿Entrada en circulación del euro?
14. ¿*Boom* de la literatura latinoamericana?
15. ¿Primera presidenta en Chile?

¿Qué? ¿Cuándo? ¿Dónde? ¿Quién?

Respuestas

2010 2010 1924 Décadas de 1960 y 1970	Primeras elecciones democráticas Cambio de milenio El Premio Cervantes	EE.UU. Barcelona Chile Unión Europea	Gabriel García Márquez Pablo Neruda Gabriela Mistral Michelle Bachelet

el huracán *hurricane* **la reforma** *reform*

b. Tapen las respuestas. Gana el grupo que más respuestas correctas recuerde.

21 **Suggestion** Point out that the question words are color-coded to the game tiles.

c. Haga con su grupo otras preguntas sobre América Latina y España al grupo contrario.

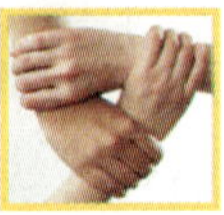

TAREA FINAL

Acontecimientos de la historia

Elaboren una lista con los cinco acontecimientos más importantes de la historia. Para cada acontecimiento, apunten:

- quién participó
- qué pasó
- cuándo aconteció
- dónde estuvieron

Justifiquen la elección y presenten la lista al grupo.

Evalúen las elecciones de otros grupos y voten todos por el acontecimiento más importante.

YO PUEDO...

- Puedo hablar de memorias.
  ¿Qué hacía, dónde estaba y cómo era hace diez años?
- Puedo relacionar momentos pasados.
  Anote los momentos más importantes de su biografía relacionándolos entre sí temporalmente.
- Puedo pedir y dar opinión.
  Comparta con sus compañeros de clase su opinión sobre el personaje más carismático de su país.
- Puedo expresar acuerdo y desacuerdo.
  Cree un diálogo en el que se expresa acuerdo y desacuerdo con las opiniones formuladas en la actividad anterior.
- Puedo expresar recuerdos.
  Anote un recuerdo agradable de algún período en su vida.

GRAMÁTICA FUNCIONAL

Suggestion Use Shel Silverstein's poem *El árbol generoso* to review the preterite and the imperfect.

10B.1 Talk about memories

Preterite, imperfect, and present perfect 5.6

- You know three tenses to talk about the past: the **pretérito indefinido**, the **pretérito imperfecto**, and the **pretérito perfecto**.
- Use the **pretérito perfecto** to talk about past events that are connected to the present.

  Ya **hemos probado** la sopa: está muy rica.
  We've already ***tried*** *the soup: it's very tasty.*

- Use the **pretérito indefinido** to describe completed actions in the past. Also use the **pretérito indefinido** if the actions occurred during a specific period of time.

  La familia de Eduardo **viajó** a Brasil el año pasado.
  Eduardo's family ***traveled*** *to Brazil last year.*

- Use the **pretérito indefinido** for a series of completed actions.

  Me **levanté,** me **vestí** y **preparé** el desayuno.
  I ***got up, got dressed,*** *and* ***prepared*** *breakfast.*

- Use the **pretérito imperfecto** to describe habitual or repeated actions in the past, or to provide the background details.

  Estaba aburrido y no **tenía** planes. Por eso, **acepté** su invitación.
  I ***was bored*** *and* ***didn't have*** *plans, so I* ***accepted*** *his invitation.*

- These two tenses are often used together when one action interrupts another action in progress. Use the **pretérito indefinido** for the action that interrupts the other.

  Tomás **leía** el periódico cuando **sonó** el teléfono.
  Tomás ***was reading*** *the newspaper when the telephone* ***rang.***

- Use the **pretérito imperfecto** to describe simultaneous actions in the past with **mientras** (*while*). Use the preterite with **mientras** when an action interrupts an ongoing action.

  Gabriela **miraba** la televisión **mientras** Julián **cocinaba**.
  Gabriela ***watched*** *television* ***while*** *Julián* ***cooked.***

  Toni **llegó** mientras yo **miraba** la tele.
  Toni ***arrived*** *while* ***I was watching*** *TV.*

- Always use the **pretérito imperfecto** when describing age, weather, time of day, and physical and emotional states.

  Eran las dos de la tarde, **hacía** calor y **tenía** mucha sed.
  It was *two o'clock,* ***it was*** *hot out, and* ***I was*** *very thirsty.*

- To form the past progressive, use the imperfect of **estar** + [*present participle*].

  Guillermo **estaba charlando** con Elisa cuando empezó a llover.
  Guillermo ***was talking*** *with Elisa when it started to rain.*

10B.2 Relate past events

antes/después de + [*infinitive/noun*] 10.3, 10.10

- Use the prepositions **antes de** (*before*) and **después de** (*after*) before infinitives and nouns.

  Juan Carlos fue rey **antes de** aprobarse la Constitución.
  Juan Carlos became king ***before*** *the Constitution was approved.*

  Después de la muerte de Franco, empezó la democracia.
  After *Franco's death, democracy began.*

Suggestion Help students visualize this concept. Draw these events on a time line: **Muerte de Franco - 20/11/1975; Juan Carlos - Rey - 22/11/1975 Constitución - 06/12/1978**

Suggestion Give a visual aspect to this grammar presentation by having volunteers act out the example sentences for interrupted actions, simultaneous actions, and the past progressive.

¡Póngalo en práctica!

G1 Complete los párrafos con la forma correcta de los verbos.

Hoy (1) ...he ido / fui... (yo, ir) al barrio donde (2) ...nací... (yo, nacer) y (3) ...he visto / vi... (yo, ver) a uno de mis vecinos. Cuando mi familia y yo (4) ...dejamos... (dejar) el barrio, yo (5) ...tenía... (tener) 18 años. Mis padres (6) ...vivieron... (vivir) ahí por más de veinte años.

La caída del Muro de Berlín en 1989 (7) ...fue... (ser) un acontecimiento histórico muy importante. Yo (8) ...era... (ser) muy joven, pero recuerdo que la gente (9) ...estaba... (estar) muy emocionada. Cuando (10) ...llegó... (llegar) la noticia, mi familia y yo (11) ...estábamos... (estar) cenando. Un amigo de mis padres nos (12) ...llamó... (llamar) y mi familia entera (13) ...dejó... (dejar) de comer para ir a ver las primeras imágenes por televisión.

G2 Complete las oraciones con las formas correctas de los verbos en el pretérito indefinido o el pretérito imperfecto.

1. Natalia ...dormía... (dormir) cuando ...sonó... (sonar) la alarma.
2. Los hombres ...hablaban... (hablar) en el bar mientras ...tomaban... (tomar) café.
3. Cuando ...empezó... (empezar) la democracia en España, Javier ...tenía... (tener) doce años.
4. Yo ...preparé... (preparar) las maletas, ...tomé... (tomar) el taxi y ...llegué... (llegar) al aeropuerto a tiempo.

G3 Complete las oraciones sobre la vida de José usando **antes de** y **después de**.

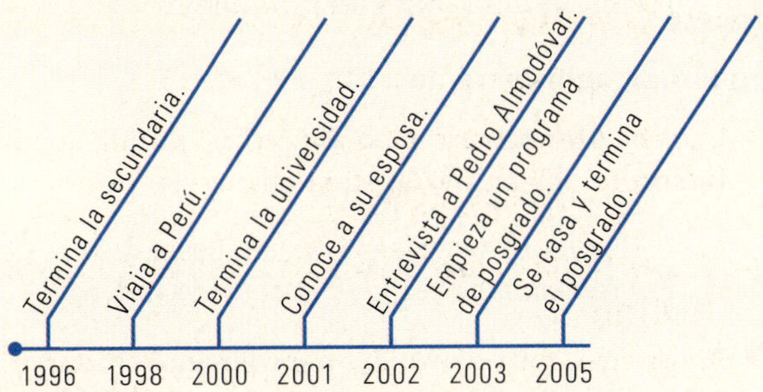

1. José viajó a Perú ...después de... terminar la secundaria.
2. Conoció a su esposa ...después de... la universidad.
3. ...Antes de... entrevistar a Almodóvar, terminó la universidad.
4. Se casó ...después de... empezar el posgrado.

Practice more at **vhlcentral.com.**

10B

GRAMÁTICA FUNCIONAL

10B.3 Ask for and give opinions

creer/opinar + que; para mí/en mi opinión 10.15, 12.8

- Use the verbs **creer** (*to think, to believe*) and **opinar** (*to think*) to ask for and express opinions. These verbs are often followed by the conjunction **que** (*that*). **Creer** and **opinar** are regular **-er** and **-ar** verbs, respectively.

¿Qué **opinas**?
*What **do you think**?*

¿**Crees que** es difícil vivir en otro país?
***Do you think** it is difficult to live in another country?*

- To introduce a personal opinion, say **para mí** (*for me*) or **en mi opinión** (*in my opinion*).

En mi opinión, Diego Maradona jugaba mejor que Pelé.
***In my opinion,** Diego Maradona played better than Pelé.*

10B.4 Express agreement and disagreement

(no) estar de acuerdo; (no) tener razón; (no) ser verdad; también, tampoco 11.2

- To agree or disagree with a statement or idea, use a form of **(no) estar de acuerdo** (*to [not] agree*), **(no) tener razón** (*to [not] be right*), or **(no) ser verdad** (*to [not] be true*).

—Picasso es el mejor pintor de la historia.
—**Estoy de acuerdo.**
—*Picasso is the best painter in history.*
—***I agree.***

- Use **también** to agree with an affirmative statement and **tampoco** to add information to a negative statement. If **tampoco** precedes the verb, the word **no** is not used.

Yo estoy de acuerdo **también**.
*I agree, **too**.*

No estoy de acuerdo **tampoco**.
*I don't agree **either**.*

Tampoco estoy de acuerdo.
*I don't agree **either**.*

G5 Expansion Have students get together in small groups and ask each other's opinions about events on campus. The other group members should agree or disagree.

10B.5 Talk about what you remember

recordar, acordarse de 5.1.1, 5.7.1

- Use the verb **recordar** (*to remember*) to talk about memories. **Recordar** has an **o→ue** stem change.

Recuerdo muy bien el viaje a Costa Rica.
***I remember** the trip to Costa Rica very well.*

Suggestion Ask students to recall their earliest childhood memories.

- A synonym for **recordar** is **acordarse. Acordarse** also has an **o→ue** stem change and it is used reflexively. It is used with the preposition **de**.

Me acuerdo de muchas cosas de mi infancia.
***I remember** many things from my childhood.*

¡Póngalo en práctica!

G4 Complete la conversación.

¿Qué (1) ...opináis... (vosotros, opinar) de la entrada del euro en España? ¿Creéis (2) ...que... es positivo?

(3) ...Creo... (yo, creer) que sí.

Pues en mi (4) ...opinión..., ha traído muchos problemas.

(5) ...Para... mí, es muy positivo.

G5 Complete la conversación.

- Creo que Gabriel García Márquez es el mejor autor latinoamericano del siglo XX. Y tú, Julio, ¿(1) ...estás... de acuerdo?
- Sí, creo que (2) ...tienes... razón. Yo (3) ...también... pienso que escribe muy bien. ¿Qué opinas, Alba?
- Yo no estoy de (4) ...acuerdo... . Para mí, hay otros escritores más talentosos.
- ¡(5) ...Es... verdad! Julio Córtazar es un escritor excelente, por ejemplo, y me encanta la poesía de Mario Benedetti. Yo (6) ...tampoco... estoy de acuerdo con ustedes.

G6 Complete las oraciones con la forma correcta de **recordar** y **acordarse** en el presente.

1. ¿...Te acuerdas... (acordarse, tú) del profesor Álvarez de la secundaria?
2. Siempre ...recordamos... (recordar, nosotros) el maravilloso viaje a Portugal.
3. Martín ...se acuerda... (acordarse) del fin de la dictadura en Argentina.
4. Los estudiantes ...se acuerdan... (acordarse) del primer día del colegio.
5. Nunca ...recuerdo... (recordar, yo) las fechas de cumpleaños de mis amigos.

Practice more at **vhlcentral.com.**

VOCABULARIO

Imágenes de la memoria

las elecciones	*elections*
el entusiasmo	*enthusiasm*
la generación	*generation*
el hecho	*event*
la memoria	*memory*
el milenio	*millennium*
la moneda	*currency*
la muerte	*death*
el Muro de Berlín	*Berlin Wall*
el optimismo	*optimism*
el/la periodista	*journalist, reporter*
el Premio Nobel	*Nobel Prize, Nobel laureate*
el/la testigo	*witness*
el torneo	*tournament*
la Unión Europea	*European Union*
dejar de	*to stop, to cease*
derribar	*to knock down, to demolish*
desaparecer (zc)	*to disappear*
morir (o:ue)	*to die*
votar	*to vote*
decisivo/a	*decisive, crucial*
democrático/a	*democratic*
emocionado/a	*excited*
emocionante	*exciting; moving*

Chile en la memoria

En mi opinión...	*In my opinión, . . .*
no puede olvidarse	*cannot be forgotten*
Bélgica	*Belgium*
el/la compatriota	*fellow countryman/ countrywoman*
la decepción	*disappointment*
el desacuerdo	*disagreement*
la esperanza	*hope*
la nostalgia	*homesickness; nostalgia*
la tormenta	*storm*
la tristeza	*sadness*
estar de acuerdo	*to agree*
estar en paz	*to be at peace*
recordar (o:ue)	*to remember*
ser verdad	*to be true*
tener razón	*to be right*
vivir afuera	*to live abroad*
amargo/a	*bitter; painful*
tampoco	*not . . . either, neither*

Jorge Edwards

el/la crítico/a literario/a	*literary critic*
la dictadura	*dictatorship*
el encuentro	*encounter*
el golpe de estado	*coup d'état*
el miedo	*fear*
la narrativa	*fiction*
la nota de prensa	*press release*
el piano de cola	*grand piano*
el poema	*poem*
el/la poeta/la poetisa	*poet*
el/la representante	*representative*
el soneto	*sonnet*
abandonar	*to quit*
colaborar	*to collaborate*
exiliarse	*to go into exile*
recordar (o:ue)	*to remember*
relacionarse	*to run in the same circles*
representar	*to represent*
cuyo/a	*whose*
nasal	*nasal*

Tell students that **la poeta** and **la poetisa** can both be used to refer to a female poet.

Variación léxica

el *boom* ⟷ el auge ⟷ el éxito

los Juegos Olímpicos ⟷ las Olimpíadas ⟷ las Olimpiadas

la nostalgia ⟷ la morriña (*fam., Esp.*)

vivir afuera (*Amér. L.*) **⟷ vivir fuera** (*Esp.*) **⟷ vivir en el extranjero**

Estrategias

1 Ganar tiempo mientras pensamos

Lección 9A

Every language has certain words and expressions its speakers use to "buy time" while they are thinking. Learning the expressions used in Spanish will help you gain fluency, as well as maintaining the interest of the person with whom you are speaking.

1 Suggestion Remind students to also make eye contact and use gestures to communicate more effectively.

- En parejas, cada uno representa el papel de la ficha. Intercambien los papeles después.

Estudiante A	Estudiante B
Objetivo: Pensar en una anécdota y responder a las preguntas de su compañero/a.	**Objetivo:** Preguntar a su compañero/a por una anécdota que ha vivido. Hacer preguntas constantemente y mostrar interés.

2 Llamar la atención

Lección 9B

Use expressions such as **Perdona** (*fam.*) or **Perdone** (*form.*) to politely get someone's attention.

- Relacione las columnas.

Perdona,...
Perdone,...

Perdone,... ¿me trae la cuenta, por favor?
Perdona,... ¿qué hora tienes?
Perdone,... ¿me permite pasar?
Perdona/e,... ¿está ocupado este asiento?
Perdona,... ¿me prestas tu bolígrafo un momento?

3 Añadir información a una conversación

Lección 10A

Expressions such as **por cierto** or **a propósito** are used to add related information or to change topics of conversation.

- Lea lo que dice esta persona y añada información a la conversación.

3 Luis Sepúlveda is a Chilean writer, political activist, journalist, and film director. His most recent novel is ***La sombra de lo que fuimos*** (2009).

Ayer estaba en el trabajo y empezó a dolerme una muela; llamé al dentista y... ....

He leído una novela muy buena de un escritor chileno —se llama Luis Sepúlveda y... ....

4 Minimizar el desacuerdo

Lección 10B

Part of polite conversation is being able to express disagreement without offending the person you are speaking with. Use expressions such as **bueno; vale; depende;** or **sí, claro, pero** to soften the force of your opinions and give a cooperative tone to the conversation.

- Esta persona está un poco enfadada. Minimice su desacuerdo y ayúdela a sentirse más relajada en la conversación.
  - "No estoy de acuerdo, una sopa de ajo no es lo mejor para curar el resfriado." ....
  - "No comparto tu opinión: si llueve, no podemos hablar de buen tiempo." ....
  - "Mi opinión es que los periódicos tienen demasiada publicidad." ....
  - "La memoria nunca es objetiva, en absoluto." ....

Competencias

1 Expansion To challenge students, have them repeat the activity with the preterite and present perfect forms.

CONJUGAR VERBOS

1 Escriba la forma verbal del pretérito imperfecto para cada verbo en la persona indicada. Compare sus respuestas con las de su compañero/a.

1 estudiar (nosotros)	2 estar (yo)	3 hacer (tú)	4 compartir (vosotros)	5 ser (nosotros)	6 ir (ustedes)
estudiábamos	estaba	hacías	compartíais	éramos	iban
7 compartir (él)	8 conocer (vosotros)	9 estar (ellas)	10 ir (ella)	11 ser (yo)	12 hacer (usted)
compartía	conocíais	estaban	iba	era	hacía

INDICAR EL CAMINO

2 Imagine que está en el lugar que indica la cruz (**X**) del mapa. Pregunte a un(a) compañero/a cómo ir a tres establecimientos. Luego intercambien papeles. Recuerden practicar el uso de **tú** y **usted**.

1. Frutería
2. Locutorio
3. Estanco
4. Panadería
5. Quiosco
6. Agencia de lotería

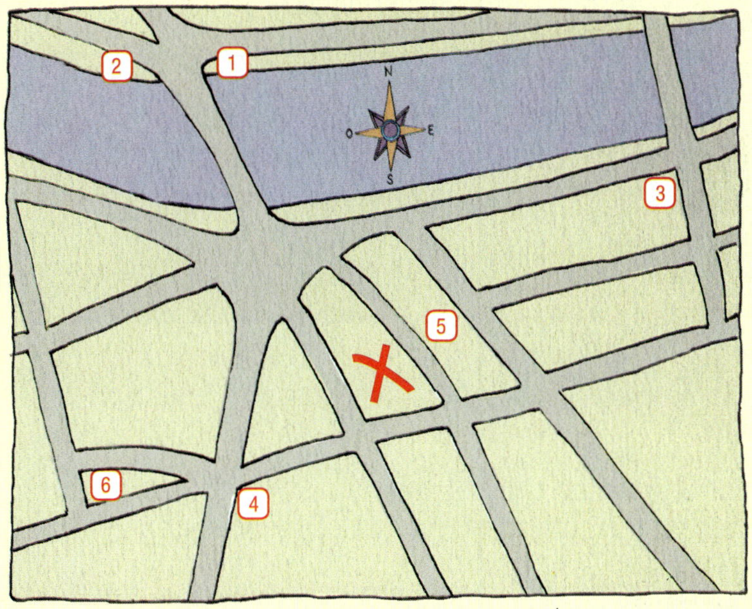

DESCRIBIR SÍNTOMAS Y DOLENCIAS, PEDIR Y DAR CONSEJOS

3 Imagine que se encuentra mal y está en un consultorio. Describa sus síntomas y las posibles causas. Después cambie su descripción con la de un(a) compañero/a y proponga remedios adecuados.

Modelo: *Me encuentro mal hoy. Me duele...*

3 Suggestion Have students peer-edit their descriptions.

CONTAR ANÉCDOTAS

4 ¿Pretérito indefinido o pretérito imperfecto? Complete la conversación con la forma correcta del verbo.

4 Suggestion Have volunteers act out the conversation for the class.

- ¿Sabes qué me (1) pasó (pasar) el otro día?
- ¿Qué te (2) pasó (pasar)?
- (3) Estaba (Estar) en la puerta del auditorio porque (4) quería (querer) escuchar el concierto de Julieta Venegas. (5) Llevaba (Llevar) casi una hora en la cola para sacar la entrada. Y cuando me (6) tocó (tocar) a mí, (7) se acabaron (acabarse) las entradas.
- ¿De verdad?
- (8) Estaba (Estar) muy triste porque (9) tenía (tener) muchas ganas de escucharla. De repente, la persona que (10) estaba (estar) parada delante de mí en la cola (11) recibió (recibir) una llamada al celular y (12) tuvo (tener) que irse. Pero antes, (13) se acercó (acercarse) a mí y me (14) regaló (regalar) su entrada. (15) Era (Ser) para la primera fila. Increíble, ¿no?
- ¡Sí, increíble!

Flash CULTURA

Estrategia

Note-taking

When watching a video, you can take notes to help you remember what you saw. Good notes are short sentences and key words: pay attention to the main points. From the title, you can infer the topic of this episode of Flash Cultura. Focus on that, and have a clean sheet of paper ready!

Vocabulario útil

acompañar *to go with*
ser atendido/a *to be seen (by a doctor)*
chocar *to crash*
la cita previa *scheduled appointment*
golpeado/a *beaten up*
la guardia *Emergency Room*
estar de guardia *to be on duty*
gratuito/a *free (of charge)*
grave *serious*
lastimado/a *injured*
la tos *cough*

Estrategia

Interjections

Interjections are short exclamations, words, or phrases typical of spoken language, and often used to express emotion or a reaction. Many interjections have meanings that can vary depending on context and intonation, and also depending on the country. For example, as a warning you might hear ¡Cuidado! or ¡Ojo! in any Spanish-speaking country, but you wouldn't hear **Híjole** outside of Mexico, or **Jolín** outside of Spain (both are used to express surprise). To express encouragement, you should use ¡Dale! in Argentina, but ¡Sale! in Mexico, and ¡Venga! in Spain.

La salud

Ya ha leído sobre los cuidados necesarios para la salud y ha aprendido cómo opinar y expresar su acuerdo o desacuerdo. Este episodio de Flash Cultura muestra un aspecto del sistema de salud en Argentina que puede llevar a una reflexión sobre el tema.

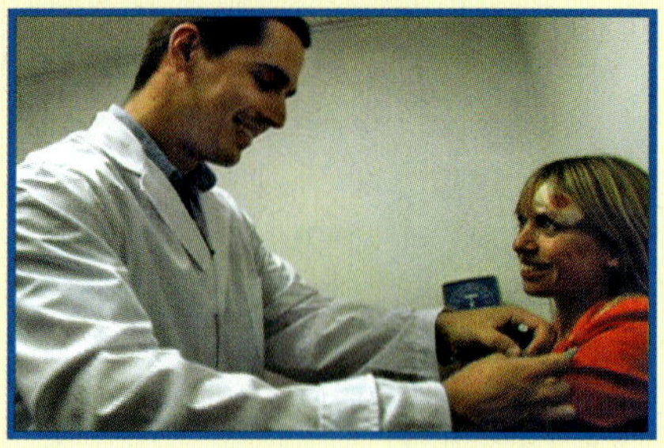

1. ¿Qué opina del sistema de salud de su país? ¿Conoce el sistema de salud de algún otro país? ¿Cree que la atención de la salud es un derecho de todos los ciudadanos? ¿Por qué?

2. Mire este episodio de **Flash Cultura**. Preste atención a los puntos más importantes. ¿Qué cosas encuentra sorprendentes o distintas de su experiencia?

Encourage students to identify similarities and differences between their experiences with health care and the Argentine system depicted in the video. What are the advantages of each system?

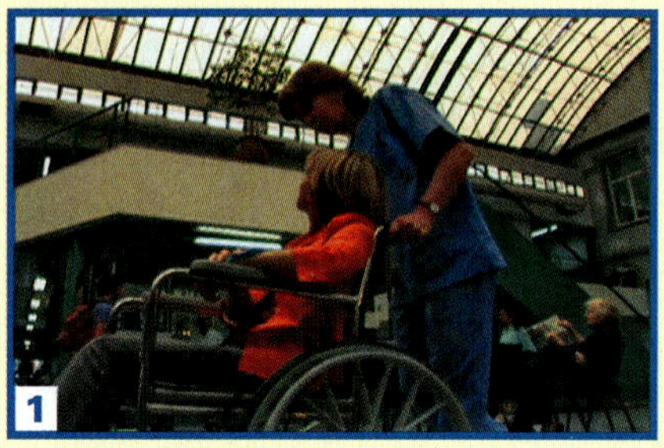

1 **Aquí siempre hay médicos que están de guardia las 24 horas, noche y día.**

2 **¡No cuesta nada! Nuestro sistema de salud es público.**

3. Indique en la lista los pasos que son necesarios y los que no lo son para recibir atención en un hospital público de Argentina.

Sí	No	
✓		1. Enfermarse o tener un accidente
✓		2. Ir a un hospital público
	✓	3. Ser argentino/a
	✓	4. Tener cita previa con un doctor
✓		5. Dar los datos personales en recepción
✓		6. Sacar turno con un número
	✓	7. Conocer al doctor Corbo
✓		8. Esperar en la Sala de Guardia

4. En parejas, escriban una conversación entre un turista que sufrió un accidente (pueden elegir el país) y una persona que le aconseja qué hacer.

Modelo:
- *Usted está lastimado: tiene que ir a un hospital.*
- *No quiero gastar dinero, y por cierto, no me duele mucho...*

Estrategia A more universal way to express surprise could be **¡Vaya!**

Practice more at **vhlcentral.com.**

Audio: Activities, Vocabulary
Video: *Flash Cultura*

Unidad 11

José Carlos, encantado de ayudarlo

Lección 11A

DE VIAJE

Lección 11B

INICIATIVAS

Héctor y Gabriela, propietarios de Patagonia Natural

Machu Picchu: encanto y misterio

AVANCE

11A DE VIAJE

Cambiar de aires

VIAJA

Especial Semana Santa

VIAJA
TE RECOMIENDA LOS MEJORES LUGARES

Sal de casa,
ve a un lugar especial
y haz una pausa en tu vida.

1 

Parque Nacional Volcán Arenal, Costa Rica

2 

hotel + avión + espectáculo de tango
Precios reducidos a grupos

3 

Con la garantía de Paradores de Turismo de España

Recomendar

- **Haz** una pausa y **sal** de la rutina. **Ven** y disfruta del sol.
- ¿**Me recomiendas** ir al mar o a la montaña?
- **Yo te recomiendo** tranquilidad.

11A.1 Affirmative imperative: irregular **tú** forms
recomendar + [*infinitive/noun*]

Vocabulario

1

el cambio de aires *change of scenery*
boricua *Puerto Rican*
el Parador de Turismo de España *state run hotel in a Spanish historic building*
el encanto *charm*
puertorriqueño/a *Puerto Rican*
el ecoturismo, la garantía, el eslogan

¡OJO!

Puerto Ricans (**puertorriqueños/as**) often refer to themselves as **boricuas** (both males and females) or **borinqueños/as**. These words are derived from **Borinquen**, the Taino name for the island before the arrival of Columbus.

1 a. Observe los anuncios y elija un eslogan para cada uno. Compare sus propuestas con las de su compañero/a. 1: Ven a la naturaleza./Siente la aventura. 2: Pon ritmo de tango a tus vacaciones. 3: Da un paseo por la historia.

Siente la aventura.
Disfruta del sol boricua.
Vive el encanto del mar desde adentro.
Ven a la naturaleza.
Da un paseo por la historia.
Pon ritmo de tango a tus vacaciones.

b. ¿Ha visitado estos lugares u otros similares? ¿Qué opción le parece más interesante?

2 a. Localice los imperativos irregulares en los textos de esta página y relaciónelos con estos infinitivos.

1. salir: sal
2. dar: da
3. venir: ven
4. ir: ve
5. poner: pon
6. hacer: haz

b. Cree su propio eslogan con alguno de los verbos anteriores. Piense en un hotel, una ciudad, una región o un espectáculo.
2b Expansion Have students create slogans for key places in your region.

3 Pregunte a su compañero/a por sus gustos y hábitos de viaje, y recomiéndele un destino de los anteriores o algún otro.

Modelo: *Si te gusta visitar ciudades, ve a... / te recomiendo ir a...*

Tell students that many Taino words were incorporated into Spanish and subsequently into English, such as **hamaca**/*hammock*, **huracán**/*hurricane*, and **barbacoa**/*barbecue*.

Información hotel

Dirección: Avenida Rosario 234

Desayuno 7:00-10:00 h

Cena 20:00-24:00 h

Información actividades

Salida del hotel: 21:30 h

Espectáculo de tango: sábado 22:00 h

Información vuelos

Llegada a Buenos Aires vuelo AA 956

Salida de Buenos Aires vuelo AA 957

Recepción en el aeropuerto: 14:30 h

Llegada al hotel: 15:15 h

Transmitir palabras de otros

- "Ya tengo los pasajes."
- Marta **dice/ha dicho que** ya tiene los pasajes.
- "¿Cuándo quieren viajar? ¿Pueden viajar en septiembre?"
- En la agencia de viajes **me han preguntado cuándo** queremos viajar y **si** podemos viajar en septiembre.

11A.2 Reported speech

Vocabulario

4
- la recepción *pick up*
- la llegada *arrival*
- la salida *departure; exit*

5
- el equipaje *baggage*

6
- en regla *in order; valid*
- favorecer (zc) *to favor*
- los ingresos *income*
- el PIB (producto interior bruto) *GDP (Gross Domestic Product)*
- **la ausencia**

El turismo en Latinoamérica

El turismo es una industria muy importante que ha favorecido a la economía de Latinoamérica. Los países que reciben mayores ingresos por turismo en la región son: República Dominicana (50% de su PIB), Argentina (8,1% de su PIB), México (6,2% de su PIB) y Brasil (3,7% de su PIB).

4 Observe las notas de la guía turística. ¿A qué viaje de la página anterior corresponde? al viaje 2

5 a. Escuche a la guía. ¿En qué momento del viaje se encuentran, al principio o al final? al principio

b. Escuche de nuevo y marque lo que ha dicho la guía. **Suggestion** Remind students that with the present perfect, the past participle is invariable.

Ha dicho que...		Ha preguntado...	
el hotel no está muy lejos.	☑	si tenemos los pasaportes a mano.	☐
vamos todos juntos en ómnibus al hotel.	☑	si queremos ir al espectáculo de tango.	☑
el equipaje llega mañana.	☐	cuándo queremos cenar.	☐

6 Transmita estos mensajes a su compañero/a.

En su ausencia ha llamado: Carlos Herrero
Mensaje: ¿Cuándo tienes vacaciones?

En su ausencia ha llamado: Marta
Mensaje: He comprado ya los pasajes de avión.

En su ausencia ha llamado: Alejandro
Mensaje: Tengo el pasaporte en regla. ¿Y tú?

6 Sample answers: Ha llamado Carlos Herrero y ha preguntado cuándo tienes vacaciones. Ha llamado Marta y ha dicho que ya ha comprado los pasajes de avión. Ha llamado Alejandro y ha dicho que tiene el pasaporte en regla. Ha preguntado si tienes el pasaporte en regla tú también.

MI EXPERIENCIA

7 ¿Qué viaje recuerda con especial cariño? Recomiéndeselo a su compañero/a. Cuente al grupo la recomendación de su compañero/a.

GUIÓN DE TRABAJO

- Te recomiendo... → **Lugar:** mar, montaña
- Ve... Haz... Reserva... → **Transporte:** avión... / **Alojamiento:** hotel, parador...
- → Mi compañero/a ha dicho que... (hay un lugar...)

Most tourists visit the Dominican Republic for its beaches, but a growing number are opting to explore the country's mountains and wildlife, which has contributed to the popularity of ecotourism. The majority of tourists come from Europe, and about 25 percent are from the U.S. or Canada.

Practice more at **vhlcentral.com.**

SAM: Actividades pp. 223–225

Experiencias de viaje

LIBRO DE QUEJAS

Lugar y fecha

En: Ponce, Puerto Rico   Fecha: 26 de junio

Datos del cliente

1.er apellido: Suárez   2.° apellido: Abiega   Nombre: Laura

D.N.I.: 51065258   Dirección: C/ Pozas 23, Bilbao, España

Datos del establecimiento

Nombre: Hotel Playas Doradas   Dirección: 111 Calle Villa, Ponce 00733, Puerto Rico

Motivo de la queja

En primer lugar, el hotel está cerca del aeropuerto y hay mucho ruido. Hemos pedido una habitación con vistas al mar y nos han dado una con vistas... ¡al aparcamiento! La atención al cliente me parece pésima. Después, la piscina no está abierta y el jardín está en obras, y por último, el restaurante no tiene menú infantil y en general la comida no es buena. ¡En un hotel de cuatro estrellas! ¡Es increíble!

Suggestion For variety, you may want to introduce other adjectives that are cognates, such as **terrible, horrible,** and **fabuloso/a.**

Expresar protestas

- ¿Qué te parece este hotel?
- No es muy bueno. Las instalaciones me parecen **muy malas** y el servicio es **pésimo**.

11A.3 **estar/parecer + bien/mal**
estar/parecer + bueno/a, malo/a, pésimo/a

Vocabulario

8

el libro de quejas *complaint form*
la instalación *facility*
la queja *complaint*
la vista *view*
el aparcamiento *parking lot*
pésimo/a *dreadful*
estar en obras *to be under construction*
el hotel de cuatro estrellas *four-star hotel*

Estrategia

Ordenar la información

En primer lugar, la habitación es pequeña, **después**, no hay servicio de habitaciones y **por último**, la piscina está cerrada.

8 a. Observe los documentos de las dos páginas. ¿En cuál expresa la cliente opiniones negativas y en cuál positivas? opiniones negativas: en el libro de quejas opiniones positivas: en el cuestionario de satisfacción

b. Lea el libro de quejas y marque qué le parece mal a la cliente.

1. atención al cliente	✓	5. tranquilidad	✓
2. situación	✓	6. habitaciones	✓
3. instalaciones	✓	7. restaurante	✓
4. seguridad	☐	8. calidad/precio	✓

8b Expansion Ask students to rearrange the list in order of greatest to least importance for them. Then have them compare their list with a partner's.

9 a. Escuche esta conversación en la terraza de un bar. ¿Por qué protesta el cliente? Numere sus intervenciones. Protesta porque le han cobrado el pan.

- Me parece pésimo. 3
- Esto no está bien. 2
- Creo que hay un error en la cuenta. 1
- Quiero el libro de quejas. 4

b. ¿Qué le parece la forma en que reacciona el cliente?

10 Elija una de estas situaciones y complete el libro de quejas.

Restaurante La Perdiz. Menorca
Ha esperado una hora la comida.
La comida es mala.
La cuenta tiene errores.

Hotel La Playa. República Dominicana
La habitación es muy pequeña.
El aire acondicionado no funciona.
Hay muchos mosquitos.

Datos del cliente

Nombre: ______ Apellidos: ______

Datos del establecimiento

Nombre: ______ Lugar: ______

Motivo de la queja

En primer lugar,
Después,
Por último,

10 Expansion Tell students to imagine that the hotel or restaurant manager called the customer to make amends. Have them write the dialogue of their telephone conversation.

Suggestion Have students use the questionnaire categories to rate the typical service of a few major domestic airlines.

Cuestionario de satisfacción **Grandes Vuelos**

SERVICIOS	Muy bueno/a	Bastante bueno/a	No muy bueno/a	Nada bueno/a
la reserva en línea			X	
la facturación		X		
la puntualidad	X			
el personal	X			
la comida	X			

¡AYÚDENOS A MEJORAR!

Expresar satisfacción

- ¿Están contentos con el servicio?
- Sí, estamos encantados.
- ¡Qué bien! ¡Me alegro de saberlo!

11A.4 **estar contento/a, encantado/a alegrarse (de) ¡qué + [*adjective/adverb*]!**

Vocabulario

9
la protesta *complaint*
protestar *to complain*
el error

10
el aire acondicionado *air conditioning*

11
mejorar *to improve*
la facturación *check-in*
la puntualidad *punctuality*
el personal *staff*
la compañía aérea *airline*
la puntuación *score, evaluation*
estar encantado/a *to be delighted*
alegrarse (de) *to be glad (that)*
contento/a *happy*
la satisfacción

12
el/la viajero/a *traveler*
el retraso *delay*

14
rural

Ask students if they have ever filed a complaint with a store or other business. How was the complaint addressed? Was the issue resolved?

11 a. Lea el cuestionario y fíjese en los servicios de esta compañía aérea. ¿Cuáles le parecen más importantes? ¿Puede añadir otros?

b. Observe la puntuación que dio el viajero en el cuestionario de satisfacción y marque con cuáles de estas opiniones coincide. con la tercera opinión: la puntualidad, el personal y la comida

1. "Estoy encantado. ¡El servicio de reserva en línea es muy bueno!"
2. "El único problema, la facturación. Hay que esperar mucho."
3. "Me alegro de haber elegido esta compañía. Estoy muy contento con la puntualidad y el personal, y el menú es estupendo. ¡Qué bien!"

12 ¿Cómo reacciona usted ante estas situaciones?

1. Está probando una comida muy buena en un restaurante. ¡ Qué rico !
2. Está visitando un monumento muy bello. ¡ Qué bonito !
3. Su vuelo no tiene retraso. ¡ Qué bien !

¡Qué bonito! • ¡Qué bien! • ¡Qué rico!

13 Recuerde su último viaje en avión y complete el cuestionario de satisfacción según su experiencia.

14 ¿Usted consulta guías, páginas Web o revistas para viajeros? ¿Alguna vez siguió una recomendación que no coincidía con la realidad?

MI EXPERIENCIA

15 Elaboren un cuestionario con los aspectos más importantes de un viaje y pidan a sus compañeros que lo completen.

GUIÓN DE TRABAJO

¿Qué te parece más importante de un viaje? → Primero..., después..., por último...

¿Con qué viajes estás más contento/a? → Yo estoy encantado/a con las casas rurales...

Practice more at **vhlcentral.com.**

SAM: Actividades pp. 226–228

11A

José Carlos, encantado de ayudarlo

En esta ocasión hablamos con José Carlos Segura Prados, empleado del mes en el Hotel El Convento, ubicado en San Juan, Puerto Rico.

¿Está contento con la mención de "Mejor empleado del mes"?
Estoy encantado, pero todo mi equipo es fantástico. Este premio es para todos.

José Carlos Segura Prados, 37 años. Jefe del Departamento de Recepción.

Háblenos del hotel. Es un edificio muy elegante y también parece muy antiguo...
Efectivamente. ¡Se empezó a construir en 1646! Fue un convento carmelita hasta fines de 1903. Comenzó a funcionar como hotel en el año 1962.

¿Y qué ofrece El Convento?
Nuestras claves son el entorno histórico y la atención personalizada. Además, ofrecemos habitaciones lujosas, cuatro restaurantes, un gimnasio, una biblioteca, una playa privada, piscina... En fin, ¡muchas cosas!

¿Lo mejor y lo peor de su trabajo?
El trato con el público. Es gratificante y también difícil. Son las dos caras de la misma moneda.

¿Recuerda algún momento especial?
Sí, claro, ¡muchos! Nuestro hotel es un lugar especial para mucha gente porque aquí han celebrado momentos importantes... Estamos encantados de poder contribuir a esa alegría.

Dar la bienvenida y expresar buenos deseos

¡Bienvenida a casa!

¡Bienvenidos a El Convento!

Le(s) damos la bienvenida a nuestro hotel.

Le(s) deseo una feliz estancia.

11A.5 bienvenido/a(s); desear

Vocabulario

16

ubicado/a *located*
carmelita *Carmelite*
el entorno *environment, surroundings*
lujoso/a *luxurious*
gratificante *rewarding*
el convento, personalizado/a

18

la bienvenida *welcome*
dar la bienvenida *to welcome*
desear *to wish*
¡Feliz estancia! *Have a nice stay!*
la estancia *stay*
¡Bienvenido(s)/a(s)! *Welcome!*

16 a. ¿Sabe qué es un convento? ¿Conoce alguno?

b. Lea la entrevista con José Carlos Segura. ¿Qué tiene de especial el hotel donde trabaja? Sample answer: Antes era un convento carmelita.

17 a. ¿Hay algo que ha dicho José Carlos que le ha llamado la atención?

Modelo: *Ha dicho que...*

17b Explain that **caras** means *faces*, but also can refer to *side* or *face* in a figurative sense.

b. Localice esta expresión en el texto. ¿Qué cree que significa?

"Son las dos caras de la misma moneda." Sample answer: Las mejores y las peores experiencias de su trabajo tienen que ver con el trato con los clientes.

18 a. Anote esta información de José Carlos.

José Carlos Segura Prados; Jefe del Departamento de Recepción; Hotel El Convento

- nombre y apellidos
- puesto de trabajo
- lugar de trabajo

b. Fíjese en la tarjeta del hotel. ¿Dónde se encuentran normalmente estas tarjetas? Marque las expresiones para dar la bienvenida y expresar buenos deseos. Relaciónelas con estas equivalentes. en la habitación del hotel

- ¡Feliz estancia! Le desea una feliz estancia.
- ¡Bienvenido! Le da la bienvenida.

c. Piense en qué situaciones puede usar estas expresiones.

¡Felicitaciones! • ¡Buen viaje! • ¡Felicidades! • ¡Felices vacaciones!

19 Escuche este mensaje de José Carlos. ¿Qué tipo de mensaje es? ¿Qué dice? Possible answer: Es un mensaje de bienvenida. Dice que, en nombre de todo el equipo del Hotel El Convento, nos da la bienvenida, que están encantados de tenernos con ellos y que nos desean una feliz estancia en San Juan.

El Yunque is also home to **el coquí,** a small frog native to Puerto Rico. **El Yunque** is the only tropical rain forest in the U.S. National Forest System.

Vocabulario

20

- la orquídea *orchid*
- el hongo *mushroom*
- incluir (y) *to include*
- el fuerte *fort*
- la fortaleza *fortress*
- el rincón *spot, place*
- con antelación *in advance*
- el descuento (del ...%) *(a . . . %) discount*
- sanjuanero/a (*P.R.*) *from San Juan*
- janguear (*fam., P.R.*) *to hang out*
- **fluorescente**

23

- restaurar *to restore*
- albergar *to accommodate*
- el/la peregrino/a *pilgrim*
- el alojamiento *accommodations*
- **el hostal**

OPINIÓN

¿Cómo se siente en los hoteles?

¿Qué le gusta encontrar en un alojamiento?

Help students to see the English influence in the verb **janguear**. Similar slang words with English influence include **gufear** (*to goof around*), **flirtear** (*to flirt*), and **flipar** (*to flip out*).

23 Explain that Spanish **paradores** usually have fine dining on-site. Puerto Rico also maintains a system of **paradores,** but these are family owned and operated inns with 15–75 rooms, located outside the San Juan metro area.

- **Expansion** You may wish to refer students to page 316 (Lesson 13A) for additional information about **El Camino de Santiago.**

20 Observe los anuncios que hay en la recepción del Hotel El Convento.

Ecoturismo: El Yunque
A solo una hora de San Juan hay un verdadero paraíso tropical: El Yunque. En este bosque de 100 km² vas a encontrar unas 240 especies de árboles, 50 clases de orquídeas, hongos fluorescentes, animales exóticos y otras maravillas de la naturaleza. Ideal para los amantes del trekking.

El Viejo San Juan
Recorre el distrito histórico de la capital de Puerto Rico. El paseo incluye el Fuerte San Felipe del Morro, La Fortaleza, la Catedral, la Casa de los Contrafuertes y muchos rincones fuera del circuito habitual. Haz tu reserva con antelación. Con este cupón recibirás un descuento del 10%.

La noche sanjuanera
¿Quieres divertirte esta noche? Puedes ir a los bares y discotecas de Isla Verde. O quizás prefieres visitar los hoteles de Condado. Si lo que estás buscando es *janguear* como un verdadero boricua, debes ir a la Placita de Santurce. Hay una fiesta abierta todos los fines de semana. ¡Ven!

21 a. Transmita uno de los anuncios a su compañero/a.

Modelo: *El anuncio dice que...*

b. ¿Qué propuesta es más interesante para usted? ¿Por qué?

22 Piense en un(a) amigo/a o familiar a quien le pueda interesar alguna de las propuestas del Hotel El Convento y envíe un correo electrónico para transmitirle el anuncio. Explique por qué le parece interesante.

Modelo: *Mamá, he encontrado este anuncio en mi hotel...*

23 Lea el texto e indique si las afirmaciones son verdaderas (**V**) o falsas (**F**).

La Red de Paradores de Turismo

Una de las maneras más interesantes de conocer España es a través de la Red de Paradores de Turismo. Hay construcciones modernas pero también castillos, palacios, conventos y otros edificios históricos restaurados.

Entre los paradores más conocidos está el Hostal de los Reyes Católicos, ubicado cerca de la catedral de Santiago (Galicia). Es el hotel más antiguo del mundo y también uno de los más lujosos. Nació como Hospital Real en 1499 para albergar a los peregrinos que visitaban Santiago. Más de 500 años después, continúa recibiendo a viajeros de todo el mundo.

	V	F
1. La Red de Paradores de Turismo ofrece alojamiento a peregrinos.	☐	✓
2. Los paradores siempre son edificios antiguos restaurados.	☐	✓
3. El Hostal de los Reyes Católicos se construyó hace 500 años.	✓	☐

Practice more at **vhlcentral.com.**

SAM: Actividades pp. 229–232

24 Fíjense en la imagen que ilustra el juego. Hagan un círculo y piensen en una anécdota breve. Una persona transmite la información a su compañero/a y así sucesivamente. ¿Cuál es el mensaje final?

24 Suggestion Help students to see that this is a game of *Telephone.*

robar *to steal*

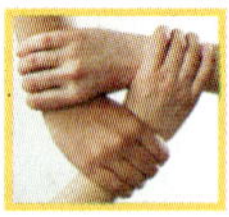

TAREA FINAL

Nuestros viajes favoritos

Piense en los lugares más especiales que ha conocido. Lleve a la clase fotografías o información que conserva de ellos.

Recomiende estos lugares a sus compañeros y hábleles de ellos.

Preparen entre todos un álbum de viaje de estos lugares.

Suggestion If students have souvenirs such as ticket stubs or postcards, encourage them to include those documents as well.

YO PUEDO...

- Puedo expresar recomendaciones.
  Recomiende una actividad de interés en su ciudad o región.
- Puedo transmitir palabras o información de otros.
  Transmita las palabras de Laura: "El profesor no puede venir mañana."
- Puedo expresar protestas y quejas.
  Piense en una experiencia de viaje negativa y exprese sus protestas.
- Puedo expresar satisfacción.
  Piense que está de vacaciones en el hotel donde trabaja José Carlos y su experiencia es muy positiva. Exprese satisfacción.
- Puedo dar la bienvenida y expresar buenos deseos.
  Imagine que da la bienvenida a un(a) compañero/a que hace tiempo que no ha ido a la clase de español.

GRAMÁTICA FUNCIONAL

269

11A.1 Give recommendations

Affirmative imperative: irregular **tú** forms 5.18.3a
recomendar + [*infinitive/noun*] 5.1.1, 5.10, 6.2.4

- Use the imperative to give strong suggestions or recommendations. In 8A.4 and 9B.2, you learned regular **tú** commands. Several common verbs have irregular **tú** commands.

DAR	DECIR	HACER	IR	PONER	SALIR	SER	TENER	VENIR
da	di	haz	ve	pon	sal	sé	ten	ven

Haz la tarea. *Do the homework.*
Sé bueno. *Be good.*
Di la verdad. *Tell the truth.*

- To make recommendations, use [*indirect object pronoun*] + **recomendar** + [*infinitive/noun*]. **Recomendar** has an **e→ie** stem change.

Te **recomiendo** ir. *I recommend that you go.*
Le **recomiendo** el hotel. *I recommend the hotel.*

11A.2 Communicate other people's words

Reported speech 12.10 **decir** 5.1.2

- Use **el estilo indirecto** (*indirect discourse*) to tell what another person has said. Use verbs such as **decir**, **comentar**, **explicar**, and **preguntar** in the present or the present perfect.

DIRECT SPEECH	REPORTED SPEECH
Declaration:	**decir/explicar + que +** [*present tense*]
"Hay una habitación libre."	Dice/Ha dicho **que hay** una habitación libre. *He says/said **that there is** a room available.*
Information question:	**preguntar + qué/cuándo/dónde...** + [*present tense*]
"¿Dónde está el museo?"	Pregunta/Ha preguntado **dónde está** el museo. *She asks/asked **where** the museum **is**.*
Yes-or-no question:	**preguntar + si +** [*present tense*]
"¿Tenéis habitaciones libres?"	Pregunta/Ha preguntado **si tenemos** habitaciones libres. *He asks/asked **if we have** rooms available.*

- When reporting a question, be sure to include the written accent on the adverbs **qué** (*what*), **cuándo** (*when*), **dónde** (*where*), etc.

Silvia me ha preguntado **cuándo** llegará Felipe.
*Silvia asked me **when** Felipe will arrive.*

- Often it is necessary to change the person of the verb when relaying information in reported speech. Use an indirect object pronoun to indicate to whom the speaker is talking.

"¿**Queréis** ir?"→(Me) Pregunta si **queremos** ir.
*"Do you **want** to go?"→He's asking (me) if **we want** to go.*

- **Decir** (*to say, to tell*) is an irregular verb. Its past participle is **dicho**.

DECIR			
(yo)	**digo**	(nosotros/as)	decimos
(tú)	dices	(vosotros/as)	decís
(usted, él, ella)	dice	(ustedes, ellos/as)	dicen

G1 Expansion Have students work in pairs and write a conversation between a mother and her child, using at least six of the irregular **tú** comands from **11A.1.** Have volunteers role-play their conversations for the class.

¡Póngalo en práctica!

G1 Complete la conversación entre dos amigos con la forma correcta del verbo.

Voy a hacer un viaje a Puerto Rico. César, ¿qué me (1) recomiendas (recomendar)?

(2) Ve (Ir) a la playa, (3) haz (hacer) excursiones y (4) pon (poner) ritmo a tu viaje.

Para moverme por la isla ¿me (5) recomiendas (recomendar) ir en carro o en autobús?

Te (6) recomiendo (recomendar) el autobús. Después de tu viaje, ¡(7) ven (venir) a verme para contarme cómo lo pasaste!

G2 Transforme las oraciones al estilo indirecto.

1. "Hay varios hoteles cerca de la playa."
   Me ha explicado/explica (explicar) que hay varios hoteles cerca de la playa.
2. "¿Queréis una habitación con vistas al mar?"
   Me ha preguntado/pregunta (preguntar) si queremos una habitación con vistas al mar.
3. "¿Cuándo queréis la reserva?"
   Me ha preguntado/pregunta (preguntar) cuándo queremos la reserva.
4. "Pueden hacer muchas excursiones interesantes."
   Me ha dicho/dice (decir) que podemos hacer muchas excursiones interesantes.
5. "¿A qué hora empieza el espectáculo?"
   Me ha preguntado/pregunta (preguntar) a qué hora empieza el espectáculo.
6. "Queremos reservar una habitación doble."
   Me han dicho/dicen que quieren una habitación doble.

G2 Expansion Bring in quotes from recent news articles and have students restate them for a partner, using reported speech. Their partner should react to each piece of news.

Practice more at **vhlcentral.com.**

11A

GRAMÁTICA FUNCIONAL

You may wish to explain that **ser** + [*adjective*] is used to describe the inherent qualities of an object, while **estar** + [*adjective*] is used to give a more subjective opinion. Ex. **La comida es buena.** (good quality); **La comida está buena.** (tasty)

11A.3 Express objection

estar/parecer + bien/mal; estar/parecer + bueno/a, malo/a, pésimo/a 5.11.1, 11.1

- Use **estar** and **parecer** (*to seem*) to express a positive or negative judgment. With **parecer**, use the construction [*indirect object pronoun*] + **parece(n)** + [*adjective/adverb*].

  El servicio **me parece bueno,** pero las instalaciones **me parecen malas.**
  *The service **seems good**, but the facilities **seem bad** (to me).*

- Use the adverbs **bien** and **mal** to describe an event or situation when using an infinitive.

  Me parece/Está mal cerrar la piscina si hace calor.
  ***It's not right to close** the pool if it's hot out.*

- Use adjectives such as **bueno/a, malo/a,** and **pésimo/a** when assessing objects or experiences. Remember that adjectives must agree in gender and number with the nouns they modify.

  La comida **está buena,** pero los camareros **me parecen pésimos.**
  *The food **is good**, but I think the waitstaff **is awful.***

11A.4 Express satisfaction

estar contento/a, encantado/a 5.8.2
alegrarse de 5.7.1, 5.10 **¡Qué + [*adjective/adverb*]!** 12.5

- Use **estar contento/a** and **estar encantado/a** to describe positive emotions. Use these expressions followed by **con** + [*noun*] to tell what makes the person happy.

  Los clientes **están** muy **contentos** con la excursión.
  *The clients **are** very **happy** with the excursion.*

- Use the reflexive verb **alegrarse** (*to be happy/glad*) on its own or followed by **de** + [*infinitive*].

¡**Me alegro** mucho!	¡**Me alegro de** saberlo!
*I **am** so **happy**!*	*I **am glad** to hear it!*

- Use the exclamation **¡qué** + [*adjective/adverb*]! to express an opinion.

¡**Qué** interesante!	¡**Qué** bien!	¡**Qué** guapa!
How interesting!	*That's great!*	*How pretty!*

Suggestion Divide the class into small groups. Have students take turns sharing some good news or experiences that they have had recently. The group members should react appropriately.

11A.5 Welcome someone and wish them well

bienvenido/a(s); desear with object pronouns 6.2.4

- The adjective **bienvenido/a** (*welcome*) must agree with the gender of the person or people whom you are welcoming. Alternatively, use the construction [*indirect object pronoun*] + **dar** + **la bienvenida.**

¡**Bienvenidas,** chicas!	**Les damos la bienvenida.**
***Welcome,** girls!*	***We welcome you.***

- Use the verb **desear** (*to wish*) with an indirect object pronoun to wish someone well.

  Te deseo un buen viaje.
  I hope you have a good trip.

Suggestion Have students draft a letter to the student newspaper, airing complaints about the university. Have them use the phrases from **11A.3.**

¡Póngalo en práctica!

G3 Complete la conversación.

¿Qué te (1)...parece... el hotel?

El hotel no me gusta. La información de esta guía es (2)...mala... porque no es real. Me parece (3)...mal... dar información falsa. ¡No (4)...está... bien mentir a la gente!

¡Qué pena! Y las instalaciones, ¿qué tal?

Me (5)...parecen... bastante malas. No hay servicio de habitaciones y no podemos usar la piscina. Hay un restaurante, pero la comida (6)...es/está... mala.

¡Qué lástima! No me (7)...parece... bien pasar las vacaciones en un hotel tan malo.

G4 Complete las oraciones de forma lógica.

1. Los turistas están encantados (estar encantado) con el nuevo hotel en el centro.
2. • Mañana nos vamos de vacaciones al Caribe.
   ▪ ¡...Qué... bien!
3. Norma ...se alegra... (alegrarse) de viajar a Buenos Aires para su trabajo.
4. Estamos muy contentos con la comida del hotel. ¡...Qué... rica!
5. Me alegro ...de... conocer tantos lugares interesantes en este viaje.
6. Mis padres estaban encantados ...con... su habitación con vistas al mar.
7. María ...está contenta... (estar contento) con el hotel que le recomendé.
8. Los niños ...se alegran... (alegrarse) de estar de vacaciones esta semana.

G5 Escriba oraciones completas.

1. bienvenido / hotel / Sr. García
   Bienvenido al hotel, Sr. García.
2. nosotros / dar / bienvenida / estudiantes nuevos
   Nosotros les damos la bienvenida a los estudiantes nuevos.
3. a ti / desear (yo) / unas felices vacaciones
   (Yo) te deseo unas felices vacaciones.
4. bienvenido / Barcelona / Camila y Ramón
   Bienvenidos a Barcelona, Camila y Ramón.

Practice more at **vhlcentral.com.**

VOCABULARIO

Cambiar de aires

la ausencia	*absence*
el cambio de aires	*change of scenery*
el ecoturismo	*ecoturism*
el encanto	*charm*
el equipaje	*baggage*
el eslogan	*slogan*
la garantía	*guarantee; warranty*
los ingresos	*income*
la llegada	*arrival*
el Parador de Turismo de España	*state run hotel in Spanish historic building*
el PIB (producto interior bruto)	*GDP (Gross Domestic Product)*
la recepción	*pick up*
la salida	*departure; exit*
favorecer (zc)	*to favor*
boricua	*Puerto Rican*
puertorriqueño/a	*Puerto Rican*
en regla	*in order; valid*

Experiencias de viaje

el aire acondicionado	*air conditioning*
el aparcamiento	*parking lot*
la compañía aérea	*airline*
el error	*error, mistake*
la facturación	*check-in*
el hotel de cuatro estrellas	*four-star hotel*
la instalación	*facility*
el libro de quejas	*complaint form*
el personal	*staff*
la protesta	*complaint*
la puntuación	*score, evaluation*
la puntualidad	*punctuality*
la queja	*complaint*
el retraso	*delay*
la satisfacción	*satisfaction*
el/la viajero/a	*traveler*
la vista	*view*
alegrarse (de)	*to be glad (that)*
estar en obras	*to be under construction*
estar encantado/a	*to be delighted*
mejorar	*to improve*
protestar	*to complain*
contento/a	*happy*
pésimo/a	*dreadful*
rural	*rural*

José Carlos

¡Bienvenido(s)/a(s)!	*Welcome!*
¡Feliz estancia!	*Have a nice stay!*
el alojamiento	*accommodations*
la bienvenida	*welcome*
el convento	*convent*
el descuento (del ...%)	*(a . . . %) discount*
el entorno	*environment, surroundings*
la estancia	*stay*
la fortaleza	*fortress*
el fuerte	*fort*
el hongo	*mushroom*
el hostal	*hostel*
la orquídea	*orchid*
el/la peregrino/a	*pilgrim*
el rincón	*spot, place*
albergar	*to accommodate*
dar la bienvenida	*to welcome*
desear	*to wish*
incluir (y)	*to include*
janguear (*fam., P.R.*)	*to hang out*
restaurar	*to restore*
carmelita	*Carmelite*
fluorescente	*fluorescent*
gratificante	*rewarding*
lujoso/a	*luxurious*
personalizado/a	*personalized*
sanjuanero/a (*P.R.*)	*from San Juan*
ubicado/a	*located*
con antelación	*in advance*

Successful Language Learning Remind students that when learning a language, it is essential to study every day. For vocabulary, encourage them to study in small increments of time (for example, 15 or 20 minutes) several times a day, rather than dedicating a full hour. Explain that studying this way will help students better retain the vocabulary and also it may be easier for them to find time to study.

Variación léxica

el aparcamiento (*Esp.*) ⟷ **el estacionamiento** (*Amér. L.*) ⟷ **el parqueadero** (*Bol., Col.*) ⟷ **el parking** (*Esp.*)

con antelación ⟷ **con anticipación**

facturar (el equipaje) ⟷ **registrar (el equipaje)** (*Amér. L.*)

el libro de quejas ⟷ **la hoja de reclamaciones** (*Esp.*)

la queja ⟷ **el reclamo** ⟷ **la reclamación** (*Esp.*)

el PIB (producto interior bruto) ⟷ **el PBI (producto bruto interno)**

ubicado/a ⟷ **situado/a**

11B INICIATIVAS

Suggestion Have students think of famous people who have "recycled" themselves by choosing a new profession.

Pasión y profesión

Mi afición, mi trabajo: ¿es posible?

¿Es usted feliz en su trabajo?

No siempre es fácil cambiar de profesión, pero hay opciones creativas. Su afición puede ser una alternativa. Un talento escondido puede servir para empezar un nuevo proyecto laboral. ¿Le gusta la moda? ¿Ha pensado en trabajar como diseñador?

Nunca pensamos en nuestras aficiones como un medio de vida, pero son las cosas que más nos gusta hacer, y las que mejor hacemos.

Para María, Jorge y Javier, su afición es ahora su trabajo, y son ejemplos de que es posible reciclarse profesionalmente.

María, antes ama de casa, trabaja desde hace un año en su propia tienda de ropa. "Siempre me ha gustado la moda, es mi pasión, pero no pensaba en ella como un trabajo."

Jorge antes era profesor de historia. Su afición, el senderismo, es ahora su trabajo: vive en Puntarenas, Costa Rica, y es guía en el Parque Nacional Carara. "La decisión no fue fácil, pero ha valido la pena."

Presentar un contraargumento

- ¿Cambiar de profesión? Es muy difícil.
- Tienes razón, **pero** no es imposible.
- Estoy de acuerdo, **pero** hay que intentarlo.

11B.1 **pero**

Vocabulario

①
pero *but*
la afición *liking, hobby*
el/la diseñador(a) (de moda) *(fashion) designer*
el medio de vida *way of life*
reciclar(se) *to recycle (oneself)*
el senderismo *hiking*
valer (lg) la pena *to be worth it*
el talento

②
el submarinismo *scuba diving*
el/la biólogo/a marino/a *marine biologist*

1 a. Fíjese en el título del reportaje y las fotos. ¿Qué entiende usted por "reciclaje profesional"?

b. Lea el artículo. ¿Qué aficiones tienen estas personas que ahora son su trabajo? la moda, el senderismo, la fotografía

2 a. Relacione las siguientes aficiones con una profesión.

submarinismo → biólogo/a marino/a
moda → diseñador(a)
senderismo → guía
arte → propietario/a de una tienda de artesanía

b. Haga una lista de sus aficiones y posibles empleos alternativos.

3 a. Lea estas reacciones al texto y relacione cada frase con la terminación apropiada.

1. "Creo que es bastante difícil ...c...
2. "Yo creo que los estudios son importantes, ...a...
3. "Creo que las empresas prefieren a personas jóvenes, ...b...

a. pero la experiencia es fundamental."
b. pero últimamente valoran mucho la experiencia de la gente mayor."
c. pero no imposible convertir una afición en una profesión."

b. ¿Es posible convertir una afición en una profesión? Hable con un(a) compañero/a de las ventajas y desventajas.

Modelo: *Yo creo que no es fácil, pero es posible. Si tú...*

3b Suggestion Ask students to consider salary when answering this question. Ask them which is more desirable for them: a low-paying job that they truly enjoy, or a well-paying job that they do not.

Javier ya no trabaja como asesor financiero. Empezó a tomar fotos hace unos años y sigue con ello. Es fotógrafo profesional. "Cambié de vida. Ya no gano tanta plata, pero soy más feliz."

CURRÍCULUM VÍTAE

DATOS PERSONALES

Nombre: Javier Ezequiel Farías
Dirección: 25 de Mayo 677
(C1002ABM) Buenos Aires
Correo electrónico: javierito@mimail.com
Lugar de nacimiento: Montevideo

Explain that **UBA** stands for **Universidad de Buenos Aires.**

ESTUDIOS

marzo 1995 – diciembre 2000 Estudios de Administración de Empresas en la UBA
marzo 2001 – diciembre 2003 Máster en Relaciones Internacionales
marzo 2004 – diciembre 2006 Máster en Márketing
abril 2009 – noviembre 2010 Curso de fotografía profesional

EXPERIENCIA PROFESIONAL

agosto 2006 – octubre 2010 Asesor financiero en OCA-Internacional, Montevideo
septiembre 2010 Reportaje fotográfico en la revista *Trabajo argentino*

IDIOMAS

Dominio del inglés
Conocimientos de italiano y francés

Hablar de cambios

- ¿Has **cambiado de** ciudad/casa?
- No, **sigo** allí.
- ¿**Ya no** trabajas?
- Sí, pero **he cambiado** de trabajo.

11B.2 cambiar de, seguir, ya no

Vocabulario

4
el currículum (vítae) *résumé*
el/la asesor(a) *advisor*
financiero/a *financial*
seguir (e:i) *to go on, to keep (on)*
el/la fotógrafo/a *photographer*
ganar *to earn*
la plata (*fam., Amér. L.*) *money*
el lugar de nacimiento *birthplace*
la experiencia profesional *professional experience*
las Relaciones Internacionales *International Relations*
fotográfico/a

5
volver (o:ue) a... *to do . . . again*
aficionado/a *amateur*
trabajar como *to work as*

6
escondido/a *hidden*

4 a. Lea el currículum de Javier. ¿Cuál es su experiencia laboral? ¿Y su formación académica?

Modelo: *De 1995 a 2000 estudió en la universidad...*

b. ¿En qué parte del currículum aparece esta información? lugar de nacimiento, idiomas, experiencia profesional

de dónde es | qué lenguas habla | dónde ha trabajado

5 a. Javier se presenta a una entrevista de trabajo. Escuche la entrevista y diga qué trabajo solicita. fotógrafo

b. Vuelva a escuchar el audio y señale los datos correctos.

1. Javier sigue en Montevideo. ☐
2. Ha cambiado de ciudad. ☑
3. Ya no trabaja como asesor financiero. ☑
4. Su primer trabajo fue de fotógrafo. ☐

c. ¿Y usted, ha cambiado algo en su vida en los últimos cinco años?

Modelo: *Ya no tomo clases de guitarra, pero sigo jugando al fútbol.*

MI EXPERIENCIA

5c **Suggestion** Have students explain why they stopped doing the activity.

6 Cuente a su compañero/a los cambios que ha habido en sus costumbres y aficiones. Escuche a su compañero/a y busque su talento escondido.

GUIÓN DE TRABAJO

¿Qué has cambiado de tu vida? → He cambiado de trabajo dos veces... / Ya no vivo en... / Sigo en mi empresa.

Creo que tu talento escondido es... → pero... → necesitas formación. / tienes que ser constante.

Practice more at **vhlcentral.com.**

SAM: Actividades pp. 233–235

Cartas al director

Encourage students to refer to the words and expressions they learned in **Lesson 4B** to discuss housing.

DIARIO DE SEVILLA

CARTAS AL DIRECTOR

Mi mujer y yo estamos buscando piso desde hace dos años, pero es difícil porque los precios son altísimos. Ahora vivimos en un piso de alquiler, pero preferimos comprar, y ¿ha visto los anuncios de minipisos que publica su periódico? Son pisos pequeñísimos a precios muy altos. Si un piso de 30 metros cuadrados es tan caro, la vivienda de nuestros sueños es imposible. ¿Cuándo van a bajar los precios?

Eduardo Pérez y Ana Díaz, Alcalá de Guadaíra

Las Rosas

Pisos modernísimos en el centro, con todas las comodidades. ¡Ven a visitarnos!

VENTA

35 m²
salón-cocina
1 baño
1 dormitorio

Expresar valoraciones en grado máximo

- Las viviendas son **pequeñísimas**.
- Sí, y son **muy muy caras**.
- Sí, encontrar un piso económico es **superdifícil**.

11B.3 **-ísimo/a, super-..., muy muy...**

Vocabulario

(7)
altísimo/a *excessive; very high*
de alquiler *rental*
el minipiso *tiny apartment*
pequeñísimo/a *tiny*
la vivienda *home; housing*

(8)
superdifícil *extremely difficult*

(9)
u *or (before a word beginning with* o *or* ho*)*
incomodísimo/a *extremely uncomfortable*

Estrategia

Mostrar interés en la conversación

- Los pisos son carísimos.
- Sí, la verdad que sí. Mi piso tiene 25 m² y ha costado muchísimo.
- ¿Sí? ¿En serio?

7 Lea la carta al director de un periódico español. ¿Por qué se escribe este tipo de cartas a los periódicos? ¿En su país es igual? ¿Por qué escriben Ana y Eduardo? Sample answer: Para expresar opiniones o quejas de los lectores.
Sample answer: Ana y Eduardo escriben porque quieren comprar un piso y todas las ofertas son de pisos pequeños y caros.

8 a. Escriba la forma superlativa de los adjetivos, siguiendo el modelo.

1. moderno/a: *modernísimo/a*
2. caro/a: carísimo/a
3. bueno/a: buenísimo/a
4. cómodo/a: comodísimo/a
5. fácil: facilísimo/a
6. alto/a: altísimo/a

b. Observe estas formas más coloquiales y anote un adjetivo en grado superlativo (*-ísimo/a*) equivalente.

El piso es **muy muy** pequeño. ...pequeñísimo...

Es **super**difícil encontrar casa. ...dificilísimo...

9 Describa las imágenes. Utilice los adjetivos del recuadro u otros.

grandísimo/a • pequeñísimo/a • carísimo/a • (in)comodísimo/a

10 a. Escuche cómo describen Ana y Eduardo la situación de la vivienda y explíquelo. La situación es superdifícil. Los precios son altísimos. El alquiler es muy caro.

- La situación es...
- Los precios son...
- El alquiler es...

b. ¿Cuál es su alternativa? Comprar una casa en un pueblo lejos de la ciudad.

c. Vuelva a escuchar el diálogo y señale las expresiones para mostrar interés en la conversación.

Sí, ya... ☑ ¿No? ☐ ¿De verdad? ☑ ¿Sí? ¿En serio? ☑ ¿Y qué? ☐

11 Piense en la situación de Ana y Eduardo. ¿Conoce a alguien con el mismo problema? ¿Hay también dificultades para encontrar vivienda en su región?

INMOBILIARIA SU CASA

¿Dónde le encantaría vivir?
¿Cómo es la casa de sus sueños?

- con varios baños ☐
- con terraza ☐
- bien comunicada ☐
- cerca del trabajo ☐
- cerca de supermercados ☐
- al lado de una zona verde ☐
- en una zona tranquila ☐
- en el centro ☐

Formular deseos

- ¿Dónde **te gustaría** vivir?
- **Me gustaría** vivir en una casa con jardín. ¿Y a ustedes?
- **Nos encantaría** vivir en el campo, pero a los niños no.

11B.4 **me, te, le... gustaría/ encantaría** + [*infinitive*]

Vocabulario

(12)
la inmobiliaria *real-estate agency*

(14)
el hogar *home*
la falta *lack*
el empleo *employment*

(15)
las afueras *outskirts*

Vivienda propia

Según datos del Consejo de la Juventud de España, aún viven con sus padres el 30% de los jóvenes españoles de entre 30 y 35 años, el 65% de los que tienen entre 25 y 29, y el 93% de los que tienen entre 18 y 25 años. Las principales causas son la falta de empleo estable y el alto costo de las viviendas.

12 Mire las fotos del anuncio. ¿Como es su vivienda ideal?

13 a. Complete el cuestionario de la inmobiliaria. Elija los tres aspectos más importantes para usted. Añada otros si lo necesita.

b. Pregunte a su compañero/a por sus preferencias. **13b Suggestion** Have students explain their preferences.

Modelo: *A mí me gustaría vivir cerca del centro, ¿y a ti?*

c. Pongan en común sus preferencias y hagan una lista de los aspectos más populares de los estudiantes en la clase.

- A muchos les encantaría...
- A algunos les gustaría...

14 Lea la nota sobre la vivienda propia en España. ¿Cómo es en su país? ¿Es habitual comprar o alquilar? ¿Cuándo forman los jóvenes su hogar propio?

MI EXPERIENCIA

14 Suggestion Ask students if they would like to buy or rent, and if they would like to live very close to other family members.

15 Haga su hipótesis y piense dónde le gustaría vivir a su compañero/a.

GUIÓN DE TRABAJO

Yo creo que a Donatella le gustaría vivir en un barco porque...

¿Un barco? No, es incomodísimo. Me gustaría vivir en...

un apartamento grandísimo.
una casa en las afueras.
un estudio en el centro....

¿En serio?

Tell students the popular phrase **En España hay que vivir de los padres hasta que se pueda vivir de los hijos.** Ask them to explain what it means.

Practice more at **vhlcentral.com.**

SAM: Actividades pp. 236–238

11B

Héctor y Gabriela, propietarios de Patagonia Natural

Héctor Varela y Gabriela Bettini, sonrientes en la posada que es también su hogar

Estamos con Héctor y Gabriela, un matrimonio porteño que hace cinco años decidió abrir una posada acá, en El Calafate. ¿Por qué decidieron dejar Buenos Aires?

Bueno, yo trabajaba en una empresa, pero me quedé desocupado hace siete años y en Buenos Aires no encontraba trabajo. Es dificilísimo si tenés más de cuarenta años, así que decidimos abrir nuestro propio negocio, que es también nuestra casa.

Ya no viven en una gran ciudad. ¿Cómo es vivir aquí en la Patagonia?

Es un lugar inhóspito a veces, aunque la ciudad puede serlo mucho más... No, en serio, es lindísimo acá.

En primer lugar, tenemos la vida que queremos. Además, mi esposa y yo seguimos haciendo las cosas que nos gustan... leer, sacar fotos, pasear, practicar deportes... y sobre todo disfrutar de la naturaleza. La verdad, encontramos nuestro sitio en el mundo.

Gabriela, ¿decoró la casa personalmente? *Sí, sí...*

La vi y es muy linda. El *living* es impresionante. ¿Es decoradora profesional?

No, en absoluto. Siempre me gustó la decoración, pero allá en Buenos Aires no tenía tiempo... ni espacio. Nuestro departamento era muy chico. Acá fue facilísimo tener ideas. Solo es cuestión de paciencia.

¿Pueden contarles a nuestros lectores qué ofrece su posada?

Tenemos un paisaje espectacular y además organizamos excursiones. Por ejemplo, mañana vamos a ir al Parque Nacional Los Glaciares con cinco turistas. Y pasado mañana vamos a recorrer el bosque petrificado La Leona. ¡Son dos paseos fantásticos!

Suggestion Have students make a two-column chart and take notes on the couple's life before and after their life-changing move. Ask students to speculate what aspects of city life Héctor and Gabriela might miss.

Añadir información

Tenemos la vida que queremos.
Además, acá es lindísimo, **sobre todo** por el paisaje.

11B.5 además, sobre todo

Vocabulario

16

- el matrimonio *married couple*
- la posada *bed & breakfast*
- desocupado/a *unemployed*
- inhóspito/a *inhospitable*
- encontrar (o:ue) *to find*
- el sitio *place*
- lindo/a *lovely; pretty; nice*
- chico/a (*Amér. L.*) *small*
- espectacular *spectacular*
- pasado mañana *the day after tomorrow*
- petrificado/a *petrified*
- **el/la decorador(a), el glaciar**

16 a. Fíjese en el título del artículo. ¿Qué puede ser Patagonia Natural?

b. Lea la entrevista y piense por qué son Héctor y Gabriela los protagonistas de la lección. ¿Cuál es su historia personal?

c. Escriba un resumen de los motivos que llevaron a Héctor y a Gabriela a vivir en la Patagonia. Use expresiones como **además** y **sobre todo**.

17 a. ¿Sabe el significado de estas palabras del habla argentina? Escriba un equivalente.

1. acá: aquí	3. allá: allí	5. lindo: bonito
2. esposa: mujer	4. chico: pequeño	6. tenés: tienes

b. ¿Qué otras formas del habla argentina reconoce?
Possible answers: sacar fotos, living, departamento

18 a. Escuche la publicidad y marque en el mapa los lugares que nombra.
el Lago Argentino y el glaciar Perito Moreno

b. Escuche otra vez. ¿Qué sonido le llama la atención? ¿Le gusta cómo suena?

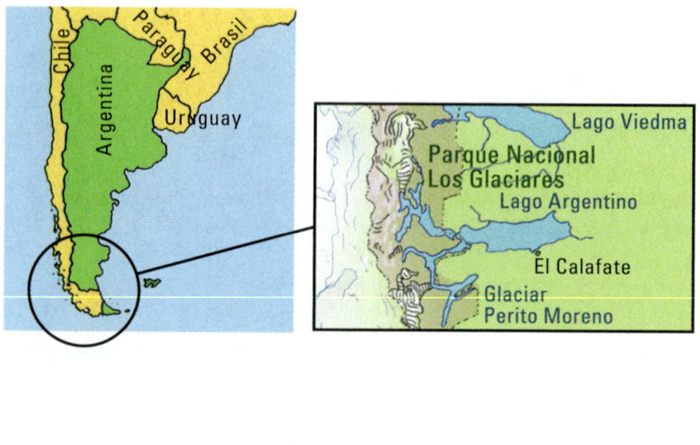

¡OJO!

In the dialect spoken in Argentina and Uruguay (known as Rioplatense Spanish), **vos** replaces **tú** as the second-person singular pronoun (**voseo**). The pronoun **vos** has its own set of verb conjugations. Therefore, in this dialect, people say **vos tenés** instead of **tú tienes**. Although the **voseo** is also used in other countries, such as Paraguay, Bolivia, Chile, Colombia, Guatemala, Ecuador, and Nicaragua, in those places its use is normally limited to informal contexts.

Vocabulario

19

explorar *to explore*
el Patrimonio Mundial *World Heritage*
el manto de hielo *ice sheet*
la riqueza *richness*
la inmensidad *immensity*
No se pierda... *Don't miss . . .*
el valle, la civilización, el continente, extraordinario/a

Tell students that **el continente antártico** is also called **la Antártida**.

OPINIÓN

¿Le gustaría vivir en otro lugar muy diferente de donde vive ahora? ¿Dónde? ¿Por qué?

CAMBIE DE AIRES

¿Le gustaría hacer un viaje diferente? Lo invitamos a explorar un lugar mágico entre lagos, ríos, montañas, valles y bosques, lejos de la civilización: el Parque Nacional Los Glaciares, declarado Patrimonio Mundial por la UNESCO en 1981.

Está ubicado al sudoeste de la provincia de Santa Cruz, justo en la frontera con Chile, y tiene una superficie de 7178 km². Allí se pueden ver los enormes glaciares que forman el manto de hielo más grande después del continente antártico. Uno de ellos es el Perito Moreno, famoso por estar continuamente en movimiento.

Pero ese no es el único atractivo del parque; también va a poder apreciar las altísimas cumbres del monte Fitz Roy (3405 m) y del cerro Torre (3105 m), la extraordinaria riqueza de la flora y de la fauna, y la inmensidad del lago Argentino y el lago Viedma. No se pierda esta experiencia única. ¡Lo esperamos!

Perito Moreno is growing rather than receding, despite concerns about global warming.

19 Lea el artículo sobre el Parque Nacional Los Glaciares, ubicado en la Patagonia argentina. Haga una lista de los adjetivos usados y subraye los de grado superlativo. diferente, mágico, nacional, mundial, enormes, grande, antártico, famoso, único, altísimas, extraordinaria, única

20 Haga a su compañero/a cinco preguntas sobre el texto y responda también a las de su compañero/a.

Modelo: *¿Has estado en la Patagonia? ¿Y en Argentina? ¿Recuerdas un alojamiento especial?*

21 ¿Le gustaría a usted desarrollar un proyecto similar al de Héctor y Gabriela? Escríbales un correo electrónico y pregunte lo que le gustaría saber.

> Estimados Héctor y Gabriela:
> He sabido de la existencia de su posada y les escribo porque me gustaría desarrollar un proyecto...
>
> Saludos cordiales,

22 a. Héctor organiza excursiones por la región. Escuche a Héctor en una de estas excursiones. ¿Qué lugar describe? ¿Le gustaría visitar ese lugar?
el glaciar Perito Moreno

b. ¿Conoce algún otro lugar en América Latina muy especial para usted? ¿Qué lugares de América Latina le gustaría conocer? Busque información en Internet y coméntela con sus compañeros.

22b **Suggestion** Survey the class to find out how many different places students would like to visit and which was the most popular.

Practice more at **vhlcentral.com.**

SAM: Actividades pp. 239–244

23 Observen estas dos series de imágenes e indiquen cómo ha cambiado la vida de Héctor y Gabriela. Utilicen las estructuras que han aprendido en la unidad.

seguir • ya no... • cambiar de

23 Suggestion Have students consult the two-column charts they made while reading the interview.

Antes

Ahora

TAREA FINAL

La vivienda de sus sueños

Realicen una encuesta en la clase para saber los deseos del grupo en cuanto a vivienda.

En parejas, piensen en una promoción inmobiliaria según las respuestas de la mayoría de la clase.

- características de la vivienda
- localización
- precio

Realicen el plano de la vivienda y redacten un anuncio con las características principales.

Presenten al grupo su proyecto. ¿Qué vivienda responde mejor a los deseos de la clase?

YO PUEDO...

- **Puedo presentar un contraargumento.**

  Conecte estas dos ideas sobre encontrar trabajo:
  Es difícil. No es imposible. Es difícil, pero no es imposible.

- **Puedo hablar de cambios en la vida.**

  Piense en sus actividades recientes, actividades que han cambiado, que ya no hace o que siguen igual. Escriba cinco oraciones sobre ellas.

- **Puedo expresar valoraciones en grado máximo.**

  Diga de otra manera que México, D.F. es muy grande y muy lindo. México, D.F. es grandísimo y lindísimo.

  Suggestion Have students restate the superlatives, using the word **ciudad** (Es **una ciudad grandísima y lindísima**).

- **Puedo formular deseos.**

  Nombre tres cosas que le gustaría hacer ahora mismo.

- **Puedo añadir información.**

  Complete con su opinión la situación de la vivienda en su ciudad.
  La situación de la vivienda es...
  Además...
  Sobre todo...

GRAMÁTICA FUNCIONAL

11B.1 Present a counterargument

pero 12.8

- Use the conjunction **pero** (*but*) to introduce information that contrasts with previous information.

Me dedico a la fotografía, **pero** no tengo formación.
*I work in photography, **but** I do not have a degree.*

Marta estudia Economía, **pero** también le interesa la pintura.
*Marta studies Economics, **but** she's also interested in painting.*

11B.2 Talk about changes

cambiar de, seguir 5.1.1, 5.1.2
ya no 11.2

- Use **cambiar de** + [*noun*] to expresses change.

Marcelo **cambió de trabajo** el mes pasado.
*Marcelo **changed jobs** last month.*

- Use **seguir** + [*adverbial phrase*] to express the idea that someone continues to do something.

Sigo con mi trabajo.
*I **am still** at my job.*

- Use **seguir** + [*present participle*] to express a continued action.

Carina **sigue trabajando** en el banco.
*Carina **is still working** at the bank.*

- **Ya no** (*no longer;* [*not*] *anymore*) signals that an action has ended.

Ramiro **ya no** trabaja en el restaurante.
*Ramiro does **not** work at the restaurant **anymore**.*

11B.3 Express the highest degree

The absolute superlative 4.5

- The absolute superlative (**el superlativo absoluto**) describes a quality without making reference to other people or things. It is equivalent to adding *extremely*, *super*, or *very* to an adjective in English. You learned the relative superlative to distinguish one among many in 9A.4.

Fue un viaje **carísimo**, pero valió la pena.
*It was a **really expensive** trip, but it was worth it.*

- To form the absolute superlative, drop the final vowel of the adjective (if there is one) and add **-ísimo/a(s)**.

Suggestion Have students describe the accommodations, food, and professors at the university, using the absolute superlative.

¡Póngalo en práctica!

G1 Empareje el comienzo de cada oración con el final apropiado.

b	1. Quiero vivir en el centro,	a. pero no tengo experiencia de administración.
d	2. No tienes formación en la fotografía,	b. pero los apartamentos allí son muy caros.
a	3. Me gustaría abrir una posada,	c. pero no ganas suficiente para pagar un alquiler.
c	4. Te gustaría salir de la casa de tus padres,	d. pero has hecho varias exposiciones.

G2 Complete la conversación con la expresión **ya no** o con la forma correcta de **cambiar** o **seguir**.

- ¡Cuánto tiempo sin verte, Benjamín! ¿Qué tal estás? ¿(1) Sigues trabajando en la inmobiliaria?
- No, (2) ya no trabajo allí. (3) Cambié de trabajo. Abrí mi propio negocio. ¿Y tú? ¿(4) Sigues en el banco?
- Sí, (5) sigo allí, pero (6) ya no estoy tanto tiempo en la oficina; ahora viajo mucho.
- ¡Qué bien! Me alegro mucho. A veces es necesario (7) cambiar de vida o de trabajo. Ahora que tengo mi propio negocio, (8) ya no viajo tanto como antes, pero ahora tengo menos estrés.

G2 Expansion Have students tell a partner three things they continue doing and three things they no longer do, since starting to study at the university level.

G3 Escriba el adjetivo correspondiente a cada superlativo relativo.

1. suaves	suavísimos
2. llena	llenísima
3. grande	grandísimo
4. cómodo	comodísimo
5. rica	riquísima
6. modernas	modernísimas

Practice more at **vhlcentral.com.**

GRAMÁTICA FUNCIONAL

Suggestion You may want to also explain the formation of superlative forms of **joven** and **trabajador(a) (jovencísimo/a, trabajadorcísimo/a)**.

pequeño/a	→	pequeñísimo/a
grande	→	grandísimo/a
difícil	→	dificilísimo/a

La nueva casa en la playa es **grandísima**.
The new beach house is very big.

- The **-ísimo/a(s)** ending always carries an accent mark, so an adjective that already has a written accent will undergo a change in pronunciation.
- Note that adjectives like **grande** and **difícil** have only one singular form, but they have distinct masculine and feminine forms in the absolute superlative.
- Words whose stem ends in **-c**, **-g**, or **-z** undergo a spelling change to preserve the original pronunciation of the adjective:

rico	→	riquísimo
largo	→	larguísimo
feliz	→	felicísimo

- In colloquial language, other superlative constructions are used, such as **muy muy** (*very, very; really*) and **super-** (*super, extremely*).

Es **super**difícil encontrar un apartamento en este barrio.
*It is **extremely** difficult to find an apartment in this neighborhood.*

11B.4 Express wishes

me, te, le... gustaría/encantaría + [*infinitive*] 5.17.3

- Use the conditional construction [*indirect object pronoun*] + **gustaría/encantaría** + [*infinitive*] to express wishes. You have already seen **me gustaría** + [*infinitive*] used as an expression of courtesy in 6B.4.

A muchos **les encantaría** vivir en un edificio moderno.
Y a ti, ¿qué **te gustaría**?
*Many people **would love** to live in a modern building.*
*And you, what **would you like**?*

11B.5 Add information

además, sobre todo 11.3

- Use the adverbs **además** (*furthermore; besides; as well*) to add information, and **sobre todo** (*above all; especially*) to both add and highlight information.

El apartamento es grandísimo y **además** está muy cerca del centro.
*The apartment is extremely big and **furthermore** it is very close to the center.*

Los parques de Madrid son muy bonitos, **sobre todo** en primavera.
*The parks in Madrid are very pretty, **especially** in spring.*

¡Póngalo en práctica!

G4 Complete las oraciones con el superlativo absoluto.

1. Los apartamentos en ese edificio nuevo son ....carísimos.... (caro).
2. La comida en el restaurante de la esquina siempre está ....riquísima.... (rico).
3. El examen que tenemos mañana va a ser ....facilísimo.... (fácil).
4. Héctor y Gabriela están ....contentísimos.... (contento) con su nueva posada en la Patagonia.
5. Mi tía vende ropa ....elegantísima.... (elegante) en un negocio en el centro.
6. La profesora de historia del arte es ....inteligentísima.... (inteligente).
7. Estoy leyendo un libro ....interesantísimo.... (interesante) sobre personas que cambian de vida y de profesión.
8. El paisaje de la Patagonia es ....bellísimo.... (bello).

G5 Complete las oraciones.

- ¿Dónde (1)....te/le gustaría.... (gustar) vivir?
- Me (2)....encantaría.... (encantar) vivir en una casa con jardín.

A mí (3)....me encantaría.... (encantar) ir de vacaciones a España, pero a mi marido (4)....le gustaría.... (gustar) ir a México.

G6 Complete el párrafo con **además** y **sobre todo**.

Ahora vivimos en el campo. Nos gusta estar aquí. (1)....Además.... la vida aquí es más fácil. Pero (2)....sobre todo.... nos gusta lo que hacemos. Abrimos una posada y nos gusta recibir visitas de todo el mundo. Es interesante el trabajo y (3)....además / sobre todo.... podemos trabajar y vivir en la misma casa. ¡No extrañamos para nada la vida de la ciudad!

Suggestion Ask students where they would like to travel after graduation.

Practice more at **vhlcentral.com.**

VOCABULARIO

Pasión y profesión

la afición	*liking, hobby*
el/la asesor(a)	*advisor*
el/la biólogo/a marino/a	*marine biologist*
el currículum (vítae)	*résumé*
el/la diseñador(a) (de moda)	*(fashion) designer*
la experiencia profesional	*professional experience*
el/la fotógrafo/a	*photographer*
el lugar de nacimiento	*birthplace*
el medio de vida	*way of life*
la plata (*fam., Amér. L.*)	*money*
las Relaciones Internacionales	*International Relations*
el senderismo	*hiking*
el submarinismo	*scuba diving*
el talento	*talent*
ganar	*to earn*
reciclar(se)	*to recycle (oneself)*
seguir (e:i)	*to go on, to keep (on)*
trabajar como	*to work as*
valer (lg) la pena	*to be worth it*
volver (o:ue) a...	*to do . . . again*
aficionado/a	*amateur*
escondido/a	*hidden*
financiero/a	*financial*
fotográfico/a	*photographic*
pero	*but*

Cartas al director

las afueras	*outskirts*
el empleo	*employment*
la falta	*lack*
el hogar	*home*
la inmobiliaria	*real-estate agency*
el minipiso	*tiny apartment*
la vivienda	*home; housing*
altísimo/a	*excessive; very high*
de alquiler	*rental*
incomodísimo/a	*extremely uncomfortable*
pequeñísimo/a	*tiny*
superdifícil	*extremely difficult*
u	*or (before a word beginning with* **o** *or* **ho***)*

Language Note In Spanish, the word **o** (*or*) changes to **u** when it appears before a word that begins with the /o/ sound; this includes words that begin with **ho-**, such as **hostal, hotel,** and **hombre**.

Héctor y Gabriela

No se pierda...	*Don't miss . . .*
la civilización	*civilization*
el continente	*continent*
el/la decorador(a)	*decorator*
el glaciar	*glacier*
la inmensidad	*immensity*
el manto de hielo	*ice sheet*
el matrimonio	*married couple*
el Patrimonio Mundial	*World Heritage*
la posada	*bed & breakfast*
la riqueza	*richness*
el sitio	*place*
el valle	*valley*
encontrar (o:ue)	*to find*
explorar	*to explore*
chico/a (*Amér. L.*)	*small*
desocupado/a	*unemployed*
espectacular	*spectacular*
extraordinario/a	*extraordinary*
inhóspito/a	*inhospitable*
lindo/a	*lovely; pretty; nice*
petrificado/a	*petrified*
pasado mañana	*the day after tomorrow*

Variación léxica

continuamente ⟷ **constantemente**

encontrar ⟷ **hallar**

pequeñísimo/a ⟷ **minúsculo/a** ⟷ **diminuto/a**

la plata (*fam., Amér. L.*) ⟷ **el dinero** ⟷ **la marmaja** (*fam., Col.* y *Méx.*) ⟷ **el pisto** (*fam., Amér. C.*) ⟷ **la pasta** (*fam., Esp.*) ⟷ **la lana** (*fam., Méx.*)

quedar desocupado/a (*Amér. L.*) ⟷ **quedarse en paro** (*Esp.*) ⟷ **quedar desempleado/a**

valer la pena ⟷ **merecer** (zc) **la pena** (*Esp.*)

Vocabulario útil

la altura *height*
el apunamiento *altitude sickness*
la caminata *trek*
el Camino Inca *Inca Trail*
el campamento *campsite*
el/la excursionista *hiker*
a pie *on foot*
el recorrido *route*
reservar *to make a reservation*
la subida *climb*
el viaje *trip*

Estrategia

Make a chart

When reading a text, start by identifying the general organization of the reading. Use a chart to write down each event or topic mentioned. You will find different chronological sequences in this reading, all of them providing information about the Inca Trail. Make three columns: one for Larry's trip, one for the history of the Inca Empire, and one for events in the present, so you don't miss any details.

LECTURA

El Camino Inca

Larry se levanta muy temprano, desarma° el campamento, desayuna y comienza su día. Ayer, él y su grupo caminaron siete millas (once kilómetros) hasta una altura de 9700 pies (2956 metros); hoy, los excursionistas deben recorrer otras siete millas hasta casi 14000 pies (4267 metros), todo el tiempo con mochilas° de cincuenta libras (veintidós kilos y medio) a la espalda. Para otros puede resultar dificilísimo completar este recorrido, pero Larry está haciendo el viaje de su vida: el Camino Inca.

Entre 1438 y 1533, durante el apogeo° del poderoso imperio incaico, los incas construyeron una compleja red° de caminos por los Andes que llevaban hasta Cuzco, la capital del imperio. Actualmente, cientos de miles de turistas viajan a Perú todos los años para recorrer los caminos que aún existen y disfrutar de paisajes espectaculares.

1 a. Discuta con un(a) compañero/a: ¿Qué clase de viajes prefiere hacer en sus vacaciones? ¿Alguna vez ha ido a acampar? ¿Le interesan las antiguas civilizaciones? ¿Por qué? ¿Cuáles son los lugares más extraños del mundo sobre los que ha oído hablar o leído?

b. Hagan juntos una lista de tres recomendaciones para un amigo que va de excursión a las montañas (qué llevar, etc.).

Modelo: *Te recomiendo...*

2 Complete las oraciones con el vocabulario de la lista.

1. A Machu Picchu puedes subir en pocas horas en tren o en autobús, pero llegar hasta lo alto de la montaña ___a pie___ es más emocionante.
2. Los ___excursionistas___ recorren el ___Camino Inca___ en cuatro días, acompañados de guías especializados que organizan los ___campamentos___ y las comidas.
3. No se puede hacer el ___viaje___ a Machu Picchu en cualquier momento: es necesario ___reservar___ lugar con anticipación.
4. La ___caminata/subida___ comienza en un puente colgante y termina en la entrada de Machu Picchu.
5. Es importante tener un buen estado físico para resistir las dificultades del terreno; además, la gran ___altura___ puede producir ___apunamiento___, con dolor de cabeza y mareos.

2 Expansion Have students write the questions that would elicit these statements.

El apunamiento is also known as **el soroche**.

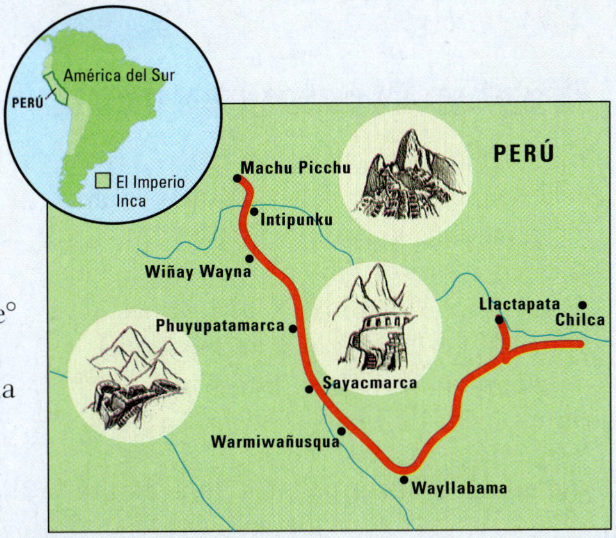

Ruta de cuatro días

El famoso Camino Inca va desde Cuzco hasta la antigua ciudad de montaña Machu Picchu. Muchos visitantes hacen un itinerario guiado de cuatro días, que comienza en un puente colgante° sobre el Río Urubamba y termina en Intipunku, la entrada a Machu Picchu. Los guías organizan los campamentos y las comidas para los viajeros, y también una estancia° de una noche en un hostal durante el recorrido.

Para conservar el Camino Inca, el Instituto Nacional de Cultura de Perú limita a quinientos por día el número de visitantes a pie. Quienes hacen el viaje deben reservar su lugar con anticipación y necesitan un buen estado físico para soportar las dificultades del terreno y la altitud, que genera apunamiento. Las abundantes lluvias° en enero de 2010 provocaron graves inundaciones°: ocho personas murieron y tres mil quinientos turistas fueron evacuados en helicópteros hacia Cuzco. Puentes, caminos y la vía férrea° quedaron dañados° y se suspendieron los viajes durante un tiempo. Afortunadamente el 1.° de abril de 2010 se reabrió Machu Picchu a los turistas de todo el mundo que esperan visitarla.

desarma *breaks down* **mochilas** *backpacks* **apogeo** *height* **red** *network* **puente colgante** *suspension bridge* **estancia** *stay* **abundantes lluvias** *heavy rains* **inundaciones** *floods* **vía férrea** *railway track* **dañados** *damaged*

► Destinos populares

- Las playas del Parque Nacional Manuel Antonio (Costa Rica) ofrecen la oportunidad de nadar y luego caminar por el bosque tropical°.
- Teotihuacán (México). Desde la época de los aztecas, aquí se celebra el equinoccio° de primavera en la Pirámide del Sol.
- Puerto Chicama (Perú), con sus olas° de cuatro kilómetros de largo°, es un destino para surfistas expertos.
- Tikal (Guatemala). Aquí puedes ver las maravillas de la selva° y ruinas de la civilización maya.
- Las playas de Rincón (Puerto Rico) son ideales para descansar y observar a las ballenas°.

bosque tropical *rainforest* **equinoccio** *equinox* **olas** *waves* **de largo** *in length* **selva** *jungle* **ballenas** *whales*

Suggestion If possible, bring in images of the places mentioned in **Destinos populares.**

Estrategia

Writing a speech

A speech must be engaging, entertaining, clear, and concise. To write a speech, begin by establishing who you are, what your purpose is, and whom the speech is for (i.e., that you are a hotel manager welcoming guests). You might include jokes, anecdotes, interesting facts, examples, or quotations to grab the audience's attention and make your point. At the end, remember to include a conclusion to remind listeners of your main purpose. When speaking in a formal setting in Spanish, remember to address your listeners using **ustedes.**

(3) Con un(a) compañero/a, elijan uno de los lugares que se mencionan en la unidad y armen una presentación de bienvenida a un grupo de turistas. Organicen un discurso, usando *En primer lugar..., después..., por último....* Pueden seguir este esquema:

3 Suggestion Have pairs present their speeches to the class.

1. Presentación personal y bienvenida a los visitantes: agradezcan su presencia allí.
2. Mencionen la ocasión: vacaciones, fiesta, luna de miel, reinauguración (Machu Picchu), etc., y señalen por qué es el lugar indicado para eso.
3. Hablen del lugar y de sus beneficios: playas, ruinas arqueológicas, posibilidad de hacer deportes, etc. Pueden añadir que algo ha cambiado recientemente (remodelación del hotel, construcción de un centro comercial, etc.), usando: **Además, actualmente... Sobre todo ahora, con la nueva...**
4. Finalicen con buenos deseos para la visita.

PROYECTO

Para participar en un concurso de viajes, debe escribir sobre su viaje soñado. Escriba un texto breve contando por qué desearía ir a ese lugar, cómo supo que existía (si alguien le contó o lo vio en un programa de televisión, un libro, etc.), cómo le han dicho que es y qué espera encontrar allí. Luego, presente su descripción a la clase.

Estrategia

Summarizing

As you are watching a video, try to organize and repeat back in your own words what has been said. State only the important points. Try to summarize as you go (don't wait until the end, or you may lose track!).

Vocabulario útil

el borde *brink*
la bruma *mist*
la ciudadela *citadel*
contratar *to hire*
la cordillera *mountain range*
el depósito *warehouse*
evitar *to prevent*
la intrepidez *fearlessness*
labrado/a *carved*
la orilla *bank*
perdido/a *lost*
la sangre *blood*
tallado/a *carved*

Estrategia

The word *cool* is common in English; but if you look it up in a bilingual dictionary, chances are you'll find **fresco**. In Spanish, you can use the words **genial**, **estupendo**, **fenomenal**, **bueno**, or **buenísimo**, but expressions used in certain countries also convey a similar meaning. In Mexico, you can say **¡Qué chido! ¡Qué padre!** (or **¡Padrísimo!**); in Argentina, you might say **¡Qué copado!** or **¡Qué bárbaro!**; in Spain, **¡Qué guay!**; in Perú, Colombia, Venezuela, Chile, and Ecuador **¡Qué bacán!**; and in many Caribbean countries you would hear **¡Qué chévere!** Just remember that slang is time-sensitive and expressions are updated all the time.

Flash Cultura

Machu Picchu: encanto y misterio

Ya ha leído sobre gente que quiere pasear, hacer deportes, ver bellos paisajes y tomar fotos; algunos lo hacen viajando, otros deciden convertir eso en su forma de vida. Este episodio de **Flash Cultura** nos lleva a uno de los lugares más hermosos del mundo que ofrece todo esto y más: las ruinas incas de Machu Picchu en Perú.

1. ¿Le gustaría hacer un viaje de aventura? ¿Qué cosas pueden ser difíciles o peligrosas en un viaje a un lugar lejano? ¿Adónde no iría nunca? ¿Por qué?

2. Mire este episodio de **Flash Cultura**. Aunque opinan distintas personas, hay un solo tema principal y todo lo que dicen añade información sobre ese tema. Preste atención y apunte la nueva información que aprende. ¿Qué es lo más importante de Machu Picchu?

Successful Language Learning Tell students that in addition to **a pie**, there are several other expressions they can use that have to do with movement and legs or feet, such as **en cuatro patas** (*on all fours*), **de pie** (*standing*), **de puntillas/en puntas de pie** (*on one's tiptoes*), or **en cuclillas** (*crouching*).

1

Aún hoy es asombroso ver cómo lograron construir en la cima de la montaña...

Suggestion After watching the episode of **Flash Cultura**, you may ask students what other great civilizations they know in the world; encourage them to research important sites in Central and South America.

2

Esta cultura quechua hizo muchas grandes obras...

3. Indique qué oraciones son **verdaderas** y cuáles son **falsas**. Corrija las falsas.

   1. Machu Picchu fue descubierta hace solo cien años. Verdadero.
   2. En quechua, significa "símbolo inca". Falso. Significa "ciudad vieja".
   3. No sabemos por qué la ciudad fue abandonada. Verdadero.
   4. Machu Picchu fue aislada por la conquista española. Falso. La ciudad se salvó de los españoles porque estaba aislada en la montaña.
   5. En la ciudadela no hay dos bloques de piedra iguales. Verdadero.
   6. Todas las construcciones son religiosas. Falso. Hay un sector religioso.

4. En parejas, escriban una conversación: una persona desea hacer un viaje para conocer una antigua civilización, pero el/la empleado/a de la agencia de turismo desea venderle un viaje a otra parte.

Modelo:
- *Me encantaría conocer Atenas. Me han dicho que es preciosa.*
- *Los hoteles están muy caros, es superruidosa y además no es buena época porque hace mucho calor. Le recomiendo pensar en algo diferente...*

Practice more at **vhlcentral.com**.

Audio: Activities, Vocabulary
Video: *Flash Cultura*

Unidad 12

Ricardo Hernández, padre cien por ciento

Lección 12A

SEGUNDA OPORTUNIDAD

Lección 12B

SIN LÍMITES

Marifé, vendedora de ilusiones

Las relaciones personales

AVANCE

12A SEGUNDA OPORTUNIDAD

Vida en común

Querida Matilde:

He conocido a una chica en la universidad. Me encanta porque es divertida, inteligente, culta, responsable, realista y muy atractiva. Es pelirroja y tiene los ojos verdes... El problema es que ella tiene novio, pero no está contenta con su relación. ¿Qué puedo hacer? Gracias por tu ayuda.

Antonio

El consultorio de Matilde

Hola, Matilde:

Quiero hacerte una consulta. En la residencia de estudiantes donde vivo hay un chico que me gusta mucho. Se llama Rafa, es muy simpático, cariñoso, alegre, siempre está de buen humor y es muy optimista. Físicamente es mi tipo: es moreno, alto, guapo... Pero yo soy muy tímida y no sé qué hacer para invitarlo a salir. Espero tu consejo.

Eva

Describir el carácter y el aspecto físico

- ¿Cómo es tu novio?
- Bueno, pues es inteligente, cariñoso y un poco pesimista. Físicamente es bajo, moreno, tiene los ojos negros y usa gafas.

12A.1 ser, tener, usar

Vocabulario

1

el consultorio *advice column*
culto/a *educated*
pelirrojo/a *red-haired*
hacer una consulta *to ask somebody's advice*
la residencia de estudiantes *dorm*
cariñoso/a *affectionate*
de buen/mal humor *in a good/bad mood*
moreno/a *dark-haired, brunet(te)*
alto/a *tall*
tímido/a *shy*
inteligente, responsable, realista, atractivo/a, optimista, el tipo

2

el carácter *character, personality*
el aspecto físico *physical appearance*
pesimista

1 Fíjese en el título de esta sección de la revista y en la imagen. ¿Cuál es el tema? Lea los textos. ¿Por qué escriben a Matilde?
consultas sobre relaciones amorosas; porque quieren consejos

2 a. En las consultas hay descripciones del carácter y del aspecto físico. Anote los adjetivos. **2a Expansion** Have pairs talk about what characteristics are most appealing to them in a mate, and in a friendship.

Carácter: *divertido/a*
inteligente, culto/a, responsable, realista, simpático/a, cariñoso/a, alegre, optimista, tímido/a

SER

Aspecto físico: *atractivo/a*
pelirrojo/a, moreno/a, alto/a, guapo/a

b. Clasifique los adjetivos anteriores por sus terminaciones.

-o/a	*divertido/a*	-e		-ista	

-o/a: divertido/a, culto/a, simpático/a, cariñoso/a, tímido/a, atractivo/a, pelirrojo/a, moreno/a, alto/a, guapo/a; **-e:** inteligente, responsable, alegre; **-ista:** realista, optimista

3 ¿Cómo es físicamente su pareja real o la persona de sus sueños? ¿Y de carácter?

¿Es...

pelirrojo/a? rubio/a?

¿Es...

alto/a? bajo/a?

¿Tiene los ojos...
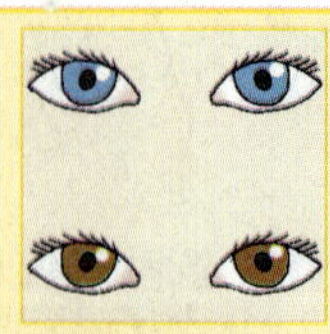
azules? castaños?

¿Tiene el pelo...

blanco y liso? moreno y rizado?

¿Usa... ¿Tiene...

gafas? barba y bigote?

¿Tiene el pelo...

largo? corto?

You may want to give students alternative words for these eye colors: **celeste** for *blue* and **(color) café** for *brown*.

You may want to point out that in many Spanish-speaking countries, **moreno/a** is used to refer to someone with dark skin, and **rubio/a** may be used to talk about someone with light brown hair.

La historia de Eva continúa: comienza a salir con Rafa, se gradúa, y junto con dos amigas alquila su primer apartamento.

FIESTA DE INAUGURACIÓN

de nuestro apartamento

viernes 5 de septiembre a las 9 h

Queridos amigos:

Después de nuestra graduación, hemos dejado la casa de nuestros padres y hemos alquilado un apartamento para las tres en el centro. Estamos muy ilusionadas (...y un poco asustadas también).

Otra buena noticia: nuestro apartamento tiene balcón con vista a la calle. Queremos inaugurarlo con ustedes. ¡Los esperamos!

Eva, Laura y Daniela

Estamos muy preocupados: ahora que tienen un apartamento en el centro, ¿van a olvidar a sus amigos?

¡Felicidades! ¡Estamos encantados con esta decisión!

Lucía y Juanma

¡Felicitaciones, amigas!
Estoy muy contento con la noticia, pero un poco enfadado porque no puedo celebrarlo con ustedes. Tengo que trabajar ese día.

¡Mis mejores deseos!

Pedro

Expresar el estado de ánimo

- ¿Cómo te sientes?
- Estoy un poco asustada pero muy ilusionada.

12A.2 sentirse (e→ie), estar

Vocabulario

3

- **rubio/a** *blond(e)*
- **bajo/a** *short*
- **castaño/a** *brown*
- **liso/a** *straight*
- **rizado/a** *curly*
- **la barba** *beard*
- **el bigote** *mustache*
- **largo/a** *long*
- **corto/a** *short*

4

- **graduarse** (*Amér. L.*) *to graduate*
- **la inauguración** *housewarming party*
- **ilusionado/a** *excited*
- **asustado/a** *frightened*
- **inaugurar** *to open; to inaugurate*
- **preocupado/a** *worried*
- **enfadado/a** *angry*

6

- **triste** *sad*

7

- **el estado de ánimo** *state of mind, mood*

8

- **actualmente** *at the moment*

---

4 Fíjese en la invitación y en las felicitaciones. ¿Qué celebran? ¿Existe la misma costumbre en su país? la inauguración del apartamento que alquilan Eva, Laura y Daniela

5 ¿Cómo se sienten Eva, Laura y Daniela? ¿Y sus amigos?

5 Eva, Laura y Daniela están muy ilusionadas y un poco asustadas. Pedro está muy contento pero un poco enfadado. Juanma y Lucía están muy preocupados y encantados.

		🙂	☹
Eva, Laura y Daniela Pedro Juanma y Lucía	ESTAR	contento/a(s) ilusionado/a(s) encantado/a(s) de buen humor	enfadado/a(s) preocupado/a(s) asustado/a(s) de mal humor

6 Escuche la conversación entre Eva y una amiga. ¿Verdadero o falso?

	V	F
1. Eva se siente asustada.	☐	☑
2. Eugenia está triste porque no tiene pareja.	☐	☑
3. Eva está muy ilusionada.	☑	☐
4. Las dos amigas están muy contentas.	☑	☐

7 a. ¿Cómo está usted de ánimo ahora? ¿Por qué? ¿Y sus compañeros?

b. ¿En qué situaciones se siente contento/a? ¿Y enfadado/a?

MI EXPERIENCIA

Suggestion Bring in magazine images or personal photos that show people with a variety of facial expressions. As you hold up each one, have the class state the person's mood.

8 Piense en una persona muy querida por usted. Descríbala.

GUIÓN DE TRABAJO

¿Quién es?	¿Cómo es físicamente? ¿Y de carácter?	¿Cómo cree que se siente actualmente?
Es mi amigo/a...	Es alto/a... Tiene el pelo rubio... Usa gafas...	Creo que está muy contento/a porque...

Practice more at vhlcentral.com.

SAM: Actividades pp. 245–247

Relaciones personales

FOTONOVELA

1 Adela busca de nuevo el amor y decide escribir un anuncio.

Me llamo Adela. Soy una mujer independiente y optimista. Vivo en Monterrey y quiero conocer a un hombre para una relación seria, enamorarme y casarme.
Celular 8113208982

2 Norberto llama...

3 Y empiezan a salir y conocerse...

Hablar de relaciones personales

Mi hermana Juana **se enamoró y se casó**, pero no **se llevaban bien** y un año más tarde **se separaron**. Ahora **sale con** César.

12A.3 **enamorarse, separarse, llevarse bien/mal**

Vocabulario

9

la fotonovela *photo story*
enamorarse *to fall in love*
regiomontano/a *born in Monterrey*
divorciarse *to get divorced*
el/la ex esposo/a *ex-husband/wife*
llevarse bien/mal *to get along/not to get along*
salir con alguien *to go out with somebody*
separarse *to split up, to separate*
independiente, serio/a

Estrategia

Cerrar una cita

- Lucía, ¿vienes el sábado a la cena?
- Sí, claro.
- **Entonces**, hasta el sábado.
- **De acuerdo, nos vemos.**

11b Suggestion Provide these dialogue lines on strips of paper for students to arrange in the correct order.

9 a. ¿Qué le sugiere el título "Fotonovela"? ¿Alguna vez ha leído una fotonovela?

b. Lea esta fotonovela y resuma qué ocurre.
Una mexicana divorciada busca novio a través de un anuncio que pone en un periódico.

c. ¿En qué orden suelen pasar estas acciones?

divorciarse 5 casarse 3 salir con alguien 1
enamorarse 2 separarse 4

9c Expansion Prepare descriptions about celebrities' lives, using these verbs. Read each description aloud for the class, who will guess the identity of the famous person.

10 Complete la ficha de Adela.

Nombre: *Adela*
Lugar de residencia: Monterrey
Estado civil: Divorciada
Otra información: Es independiente y optimista. Tiene un hijo.

11 a. Escuche la primera llamada telefónica de esta pareja. ¿Cuál es la historia sentimental de cada uno de ellos? Márquelo en el recuadro.

	Se enamoró.	Se casó.	Se separó.	Tuvo una relación seria.	Se divorció.
Norberto	✓			✓	
Adela	✓	✓	✓		✓

b. Escuche el final de la conversación y ordene las frases.

- De acuerdo, nos vemos el jueves. Adiós, Adela. 5
- Muy bien, a las 19:00 h en el Faro del Comercio y ¿damos un paseo? 2
- Entonces, hasta el jueves, Norberto. 4
- Sí, es un lugar precioso. 3
- Muy bien, ¿el jueves a las 19:00 h? 1

c. Fíjese en cómo indican que cierran una cita. ¿Se hace de la misma forma en su lengua? "Entonces, hasta el jueves, Norberto."; "De acuerdo, nos vemos el jueves. Adiós, Adela."

4

5

FIN

Valorar la importancia y expresar afecto

- ¿Qué es importante en una relación?
- Para mí, **es importante llevarse** bien. ¿Y para ti?
- **Es importante** el amor, quererse... ¿**Me quieres**?
- Sí, **te quiero** mucho. **Estoy enamorada de** ti.

12A.4 **es importante** + [*noun/infinitive*] **estar enamorado/a de, te quiero**

Vocabulario

(12)
estar enamorado/a (de) *to be in love (with)*

(14)
el afecto *affection*
querer (e:ie) a alguien *to love someone*
el hombre/la mujer de mi vida *the man/woman of my dreams*

Suggestion Have pairs of students write a brief dialogue between a famous couple from history or literature, using the expressions of affection presented on this page. Encourage creativity. Have a few volunteers role-play their conversations for the class.

12 Lea la fotonovela de esta página. ¿Cómo sigue la historia de amor?

Son buenos amigos. ☐ Se enamoran. ☑ Se casan. ☐

13 ¿Qué es importante para Adela en la vida y en una pareja?

Es importante su hijo, disfrutar de la vida y tener salud. Y en una pareja es importante estar enamorados.

Es importante... estar enamorados/la moda/su carrera profesional/su hijo/viajar/disfrutar de la vida/tener salud.

14 Fíjese en las formas para expresar afecto y ordene la conversación entre dos amigas con estas frases.

Chat
Chatear Editar Ver Acciones Contacto Ayuda
A:

Patri dice: (1) Estoy muy enamorada de Luis.
Sara dice: Pero ¿(2) realmente lo quieres?
Patri dice: (3) Sí, lo quiero muchísimo. Es el hombre de mi vida.
Sara dice: (4) Bueno, si estás tan enamorada de él, ¿por qué no se lo dices?
Patri dice: (5) No puedo. Creo que Luis quiere a otra mujer.

Enviar

- ¿realmente lo quieres?
- Bueno, si estás tan enamorada de él
- No puedo. Creo que Luis quiere a otra mujer.
- Estoy muy enamorada de Luis.
- Sí, lo quiero muchísimo. Es el hombre de mi vida.

MI EXPERIENCIA

15 ¿Qué es importante para usted? Compártalo con sus compañeros.

GUIÓN DE TRABAJO

¿Qué es importante para ti...

...en la vida?
...en una relación?

Es importante el amor, la salud, quererse...

Practice more at **vhlcentral.com.**

SAM: Actividades pp. 248–250

12A

Ricardo Hernández, padre cien por ciento

Asociación Mexicana de Padres de Familia Separados

Boletín informativo N.° 61, junio

La Asociación Mexicana de Padres de Familia Separados is a non-profit organization that was started by divorced parents who were suffering many divorce-related issues, such as unenforced custody agreements, parental alienation, etc.

Mi nombre es Ricardo Hernández, estoy divorciado y vivo en México, D.F. Mi hijo Néstor tiene siete años y vive con su mamá desde que nos separamos hace cuatro años. Me llevo bien con mi ex esposa y tenemos una buena comunicación. Es muy importante ser respetuoso entre padres separados porque esto ayuda a los hijos. Normalmente paso todos los fines de semana y las vacaciones con Néstor.

La vida me dio una segunda oportunidad y el año pasado me enamoré de Virginia, una mujer muy buena, inteligente, cariñosa y muy alegre. Hace seis meses que salimos y estoy muy contento. Mi hijo se lleva muy bien con ella y, por eso, para mí ahora es muy importante tener custodia compartida. Mi ex esposa está de acuerdo y también cree que es importante compartir la custodia. Hoy quiero compartir esta decisión con ustedes a través de este boletín, ¡estoy muy emocionado!

Les envío una foto de Néstor; es del fin de semana pasado. Como ven, nos parecemos mucho; es alto y tiene el pelo negro, como yo, ¡pero es más guapo!

Hoy es el tercer domingo de junio, Día del Padre en México. ¡Felicidades a todos!

Since 1970, the divorce rate in Mexico has increased tenfold. Ask students why they think this is so.

Ricardo Hernández, 37 años. Padre de Néstor.

Hablar de parecidos

- ¿Te pareces a tu padre o a tu madre?
- Físicamente **me parezco** mucho **a** mi madre pero en el carácter **soy como** mi padre.

12A.5 **parecerse (zc) a ser/tener... como**

Vocabulario

16

cien por ciento *one hundred percent*
respetuoso/a *respectful*
la custodia compartida *joint custody*
parecerse (zc) a alguien *to look like somebody*
el parecido *resemblance*
la asociación, separado/a, el divorcio

Suggestion You may want to introduce the terms **el padrastro, la madrastra,** and **el/la hijastro/a.**

16 a. Observe la foto. ¿Qué relación tienen? ¿En qué se nota? Son padre e hijo. Sample answer: Se nota en el aspecto físico (el color del pelo, los ojos...). Se parecen.

b. Esta asociación quiere ayudar a los padres separados. ¿Por qué Ricardo es un ejemplo para ellos? Lea el texto. Sample answer: Porque quiere la custodia compartida, porque se lleva bien con su ex esposa y eso ayuda a su hijo.

c. ¿Hay alguna asociación como esta en su país? ¿Conoce a algún padre o a alguna madre en esta situación?

17 a. Lea la carta de Ricardo. ¿Qué sabe de su vida?

Lugar de residencia: México, D.F. Estado civil: Divorciado
Relaciones personales: Sale con Virginia.
Estado de ánimo hoy: Está muy emocionado.

b. ¿Qué día escribe Ricardo la carta? ¿Qué se celebra ese día? ¿Cuándo es el Día del Padre en su país? el tercer domingo de junio; el Día del Padre

18 Escuche a Néstor que felicita a su padre en el Día del Padre. ¿Cómo lo hace? ¿Qué le dice al final? a través de un programa de radio; ¡Felicidades, papi! ¡Te quiero mucho! ¡Eres el mejor papá del mundo!

19 a. Mire la foto de Ricardo y su hijo. ¿Se parece Néstor a su padre?

b. ¿A quién se parece usted en el físico y en el carácter? ¿Y su compañero/a?

Vocabulario

20

el nombre de pila *first name*
el/la primogénito/a *firstborn*
en el ámbito familiar *among family*
o bien *or otherwise*
el diminutivo *diminutive, nickname*
el/la tocayo/a *namesake*
el doble apellido *two last names*

22

el/la chamaquito/a (*dim. de* el/la chamaco/a) (*Amér. L.*) *kid, youngster*
azteca *Aztec*
el aimara *Aymara*
el aguacate *avocado*
el cacahuate (*Méx.*) *peanut*
el chicle *(chewing) gum*
el/la cuate/a (*fam., Méx.*) *friend, pal*
el náhuatl

23

el romanticismo *romanticism*
el amor (no) correspondido *(un)requited love*

20 Suggestion Explain that when a woman gets married, her name does not officially change, but in social settings she may use her husband's surname, with or without the word **de**. (Ex: Clara Sánchez de Hernández)

20 Expansion Have students introduce themselves to each other, using the Hispanic naming convention.

22a Cacahuate is used in Mexico and **cacahuete** in Spain; **maní** is the term used in the rest of the Spanish-speaking world.

20 a. Lea el texto. ¿De qué trata?
tradiciones relacionadas con los nombres de pila y los apellidos en el mundo hispano

En el mundo hispano es común usar el nombre de pila del padre cuando hay que elegir un nombre para el primogénito, o hijo mayor. Para diferenciar a uno del otro en el ámbito familiar, se suele aclarar "padre" o "hijo" después del nombre, o bien referirse al hijo con diminutivos como Carlitos o Anita. Fuera del ámbito familiar, hay otra tradición que ayuda a diferenciar entre los tocayos. En España y en Latinoamérica también es común tener doble apellido, es decir, un apellido compuesto por el primer apellido del padre y el de la madre, en ese orden. De este modo, Néstor, hijo de Ricardo Hernández Perlera y Clara Sánchez Uribe, se llama Néstor Hernández Sánchez. Esta tradición europea traída a América por los españoles se usa actualmente en muchos países, como Chile, Colombia, México, Perú y Venezuela.

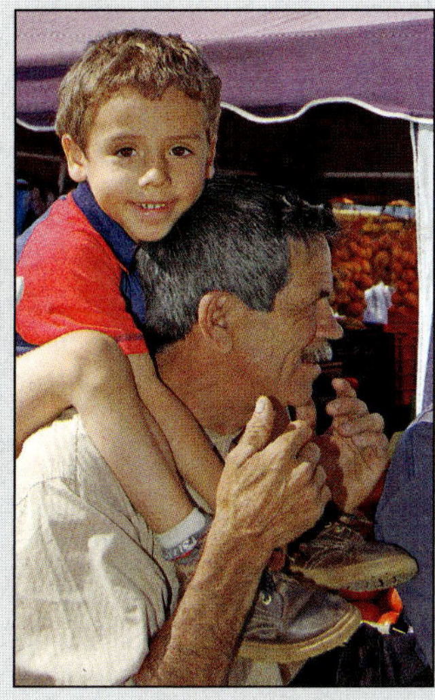

b. Complete las oraciones que resumen el texto anterior. Sample answers:

1. En el mundo hispano, cuando se elige el nombre de pila de un primogénito a veces se usa el nombre de pila del padre.
2. Si en una misma familia el padre y el hijo se llaman Adolfo, quizás los familiares se refieren al hijo como "Adolfo hijo" o "Adolfito".
3. El doble apellido está formado por el apellido del padre y el apellido de la madre, en ese orden.
4. Alejandro González Iñárritu es un famoso director de cine mexicano. Según la tradición descrita en el texto, puede deducir que el apellido de su padre es González y el de su madre es Iñárritu.

21 Escriba qué es importante para usted en las relaciones entre padres e hijos.

Para mí, es importante...

22 a. Lea el texto sobre el náhuatl. ¿Cuál es el origen de esta lengua? ¿Dónde se habla? Es una lengua azteca. Se habla en México y en otros países de Centroamérica.

Una de las palabras que Ricardo podría usar para referirse a su hijo es *chamaquito*, un nahuatlismo habitual en la lengua coloquial de México y otros países de Centroamérica y del Caribe. El náhuatl es una lengua azteca, y es la cuarta lengua indígena de América por el número de personas que la hablan, después del quechua, el aimara y el guaraní.
El español tiene numerosos nahuatlismos: *aguacate*, *cacahuate*, *chamaco*, *chicle*, *chile*, *chocolate*, *cuate*, *guacamole*, *tomate*, *coyote*, *cacao*, *chipotle*, *tequila*, etc.

b. ¿Cuáles de estas palabras existen también en su lengua?

Practice more at vhlcentral.com.

SAM: Actividades pp. 251–254

23 a. Gustavo Adolfo Bécquer fue el máximo protagonista del romanticismo español. Escribió memorables poemas de amor que publicó en sus *Rimas*. Lea el siguiente poema de este autor y marque de qué tema trata.

- [ ] el amor correspondido
- [x] el amor no correspondido

b. ¿Cómo son físicamente y de carácter las dos primeras mujeres con las que habla el poeta? Use los adjetivos del recuadro en su descripción. La primera mujer es morena y apasionada. La segunda mujer es rubia y tierna.

tierna	apasionada	morena	rubia

c. ¿A cuál de las tres mujeres elige el poeta? Hable con su compañero/a sobre por qué el poeta elige a esa mujer. a la tercera

RIMA XI

—Yo soy ardiente°, yo soy morena,
yo soy el símbolo de la pasión,
de ansia de goces° mi alma está llena.
¿A mí me buscas?
—No es a ti; no.

—Mi frente° es pálida°, mis trenzas° de oro°,
puedo brindarte° dichas sin fin°.
Yo de ternura° guardo un tesoro.
¿A mí me llamas?
—No; no es a ti.

—Yo soy un sueño°, un imposible,
vano fantasma° de niebla y luz°;
soy incorpórea°, soy intangible:
No puedo amarte.
—¡Oh, ven; ven tú!

ardiente *passionate* **goces** *pleasures* **frente** *forehead* **pálido/a** *pale* **trenzas** *braids* **de oro** *golden* **brindarte** *give you* **dichas sin fin** *endless happiness* **ternura** *tenderness* **sueño** *dream* **fantasma** *ghost* **niebla y luz** *fog and light* **incorpórea** *without a body*

BÉCQUER, Gustavo Adolfo (1836–1870)

23 Suggestions
- Guide students to see that this poem consists of a "dialogue" between the poetic voice and different types of love.
- Have three volunteers read aloud the verses spoken by the women, while a fourth student reads the lines spoken by the poetic voice.

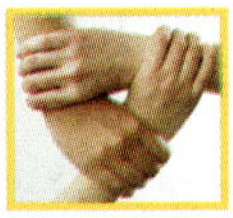

TAREA FINAL

Reglas para una buena vida en común

Pregunte a su compañero/a qué cosas son importantes para la vida en común.

Hagan una lista común entre todos y decidan cuáles son los diez principios más importantes.

Es importante...

1. comunicarse.

2. el respeto.

3. ...

Escriban en una hoja sus principios. Las pueden pegar en la pared de la clase y también en su propia casa.

YO PUEDO...

- Puedo describir el carácter y el aspecto físico de una persona.
  Describa el carácter y el aspecto físico de un(a) amigo/a suyo/a.
- Puedo expresar el estado de ánimo.
  Imagine que hoy es el aniversario de una fecha importante para usted. ¿Es una ocasión feliz o triste? Describa su estado de ánimo.
- Puedo hablar de relaciones personales.
  Piense en un familiar y describa la relación que los une.
- Puedo valorar la importancia de algo y expresar afecto.
  Señale qué es importante para tener una buena relación y piense en una forma de expresar afecto o amor.
- Puedo hablar de parecidos.
  Busque parecidos entre uno de sus compañeros y una persona famosa o familiar.

GRAMÁTICA FUNCIONAL

12A.1 Describe personality and physical traits

ser, tener, usar 4.1, 5.1.1, 5.1.2, 5.8.2

- Use **ser** + (**muy/un poco**) + [*adjective*] to describe people's personality and physical traits.

  Leonardo **es** divertido pero un poco tímido.
  *Leonardo **is** a fun guy, but he is a bit shy.*

  Es muy atractivo, moreno y alto.
  *He **is** very attractive, dark-haired, and tall.*

- As you saw in **2A.4**, adjectives must agree with the noun that they modify. Adjectives that end in **-e** and adjectives that end in **-ista** do not have distinct masculine and feminine forms.

  Emilio es **responsable** y **optimista**; Adriana también es **responsable** y **optimista**.
  *Emilio is **responsible** and **optimistic**; Adriana is also **responsible** and **optimistic**.*

- Use **tener** + **el pelo/los ojos** + [*adjective*] to describe people's appearance. To say that someone wears glasses, use the verb **usar**.

  Marisa **tiene** los ojos verdes y **usa** gafas.
  *Marisa **has** green eyes and **wears** glasses.*

Tell students that they can also use the verb **llevar** to talk about wearing glasses.

12A.2 Express mood

sentirse, estar 5.1.1, 5.1.2, 5.7.1

- Use **sentirse** to talk about feelings and states of mind. To ask someone how he/she feels, say **¿Cómo se/te siente(s)? Sentirse** is a reflexive verb that undergoes an **e→ie** stem change.

  Elena **se siente** de buen humor.
  *Elena **is** in a good mood.*

SENTIRSE			
(yo)	me siento	(nosotros/as)	nos sentimos
(tú)	te sientes	(vosotros/as)	os sentís
(usted, él, ella)	se siente	(ustedes, ellos/as)	se sienten

- Also use **estar** + [*adjective*] to talk about people's feelings.

  Alejandro y Susana **están** muy ilusionados y un poco nerviosos.
  *Alejandro y Susana **are** very excited and a bit nervous.*

12A.3 Talk about personal relationships

enamorarse, separarse, llevarse bien/mal 5.7.1, 11.1

- Use the verbs **enamorarse, casarse, separarse, divorciarse,** and **llevarse bien/mal** to talk about personal relationships.

  Los padres de Candela **se divorciaron**.
  *Candela's parents **got divorced**.*

- **Enamorarse, separarse,** and **divorciarse** are used with the preposition **de**, and **casarse** and **llevarse bien/mal** are used with **con** when you explicitly mention the other person in the relationship.

  Leonor **se enamoró de** Sebastián y **se casó con** él en 2003.
  *Leonor **fell in love with** Sebastián and **married** him in 2003.*

¡Póngalo en práctica!

G1 Complete la conversación. Use cada palabra solamente una vez.

rubio	pesimista	tiene
usa	simpático	pelo

¿Cómo es Enrique?

Es muy (1) simpático pero un poco (2) pesimista

¿Y físicamente?

Es (3) rubio, (4) tiene los ojos azules y (5) usa gafas. Hace mucho tiempo que tiene el (6) pelo largo.

G2 Complete las oraciones con la forma correcta de **sentirse** o **estar**, o con la forma correcta del adjetivo.

1. Mañana es tu cumpleaños; ¿cómo te sientes (sentirse)?
2. Josefina está muy enfadada (enfadado) porque tiene que trabajar todo el día.
3. ¡Enhorabuena a los dos! ¿Cómo os sentís / se sienten (sentirse)?
4. Benjamín y Sofía están (estar) muy contentos.
5. Hoy Héctor está (estar) de muy mal humor.
6. Estoy muy ilusionada, pero un poco asustada (asustado) antes de hacer el viaje.

G2 Expansion Have pairs of students tell each other where they go or what they do when they feel a certain way. Ex: **Cuando estoy de mal humor, salgo a correr en el parque.**

G3 Complete las conversaciones.

- ¿Qué sabes de nuestra compañera Isabel?
- Sé que se (1) enamoró de un chico mexicano muy guapo y (2) se casó (3) con él.

- ¿Sabes si Elena se separó (4) de su marido?
- Sí, ellos no se llevaban (5) bien, así que (6) se divorciaron el año pasado.

Practice more at **vhlcentral.com.**

GRAMÁTICA FUNCIONAL

12A.4 Assess importance and express affection

es importante + [*noun/infinitive*] 5.12.3
estar enamorado/a de; te quiero 5.8.2, 6.2.1

- Use **es importante** + [*noun/infinitive*] to talk about what is important.

  En una relación, **es importante** llevarse bien.
  *In a relationship, **it is important** to get along well.*

- Use **estar enamorado/a (de)** (*to be in love [with]*) to describe someone who has fallen in love.

  Carlos **está enamorado de** Liliana.
  *Carlos **is in love with** Liliana.*

- Use the prepositional pronouns **mí, ti, él, ella, usted, nosotros/as, vosotros/as, ustedes,** or **ellos/as** after **de** to refer to the person who is loved.

  Tomás está enamorado **de mí,** y yo estoy enamorada **de él.**
  *Tomás is in love **with me,** and I am in love **with him.***

- Use **querer a alguien** (*to love someone*) to express feelings of love. You can also use a direct object pronoun before **querer** in this construction. Direct object pronouns are used when a person directly receives the action of the verb.

singular		plural	
me	*me*	**nos**	*us*
te	*you* (fam.)	**os**	*you* (fam., Esp.)
lo	*you* (m., form.); *him*	**los**	*you* (m.; form.); *them* (m.)
la	*you* (f., form.); *her*	**las**	*you* (f., form.); *them* (f.)

Te quiero, Lucía. Estoy enamorado de ti.
***I love you,** Lucía. I am in love with you.*

12A.5 Talk about resemblances

parecerse a 5.7.1 **ser/tener... como** 5.1.2

- To talk about resemblances, use the reflexive verb **parecerse (a)**. **Parecerse** undergoes a **c→zc** spelling change in the **yo** form. The other forms follow the regular conjugation pattern for **-er** verbs.

- As with **de**, use prepositional pronouns after the preposition **a** in this construction.

  Me parezco a mi hermana. — Ella se parece **a mí**.
  ***I look like** my sister.* — *She looks like **me**.*

- Use **nos parecemos** to say *we resemble each other*.

  Mis hermanos y yo **nos parecemos** mucho.
  *My siblings and I **resemble each other** quite a lot.*

- Use **ser como** (*to be like*) to talk about resemblances and similarities. Use the construction **tener** + [*noun*] + **como** to compare physical characteristics.

  Eres como tu padre. — **Tienes** los ojos **como** tu madre.
  *You **are like** your father.* — *You have your mother's eyes.*

¡Póngalo en práctica!

G4 Complete la conversación de manera lógica.

hablar llevarse quiero tener

Para ti, ¿qué es importante en una relación?

Para mí, es importante la comunicación y (1) llevarse bien.

Para mí, es importante (2) tener tiempo para estar juntos y decirle a mi pareja que la (3) quiero. También es importante (4) hablar de los problemas.

G5 Complete las oraciones con el pronombre correcto.

1. Manuel quiere mucho a Patricia. Está enamorado de ella.
2. Mi novia dice que está enamorada de mí. Yo también la quiero.
3. • ¿Me quieres, Dolores?
   ▪ Sí, Emilio, te quiero. Estoy enamorada de ti.
4. Claudio y Ana tienen once nietos y los quieren mucho.
5. Dalia quiere casarse con su novio; está totalmente enamorada de él.

G6 Complete las conversaciones.

- • ¿A quién (1) te pareces?
- ▪ Físicamente me (2) parezco muchísimo a mi padre, pero en el carácter soy (3) como mi madre.
- • Daniela (4) se parece mucho a su abuela, ¿no?
- ▪ Sí, (5) tiene la nariz como ella.
- • Mario y yo nos (6) parecemos a nuestro padre. Los dos tenemos el pelo (7) como él.
- ▪ Sí, también (8) son como él porque son alegres, inteligentes y trabajadores.

G5 Expansion Have students work in pairs to write a dramatic scene from a soap opera, using expressions and pronouns from **12A.4**. Then, in groups of four, have them act out their scenes.

G6 Expansion Ask students to write a brief physical description of a friend or relative, including what celebrity he or she most resembles. Have students read their descriptions aloud in small groups.

Practice more at **vhlcentral.com.**

VOCABULARIO

Vida en común

el aspecto físico	*physical appearance*
la barba	*beard*
el bigote	*mustache*
el carácter	*character, personality*
el consultorio	*advice column*
el estado de ánimo	*state of mind, mood*
la inauguración	*housewarming party*
la residencia de estudiantes	*dorm*
el tipo	*type*
graduarse (*Amér. L.*)	*to graduate*
hacer una consulta	*to ask somebody's advice*
inaugurar	*to open; to inaugurate*
alto/a	*tall*
asustado/a	*frightened*
atractivo/a	*attractive*
bajo/a	*short*
cariñoso/a	*affectionate*
castaño/a	*brown*
corto/a	*short*
culto/a	*educated*
enfadado/a	*angry*
ilusionado/a	*excited*
inteligente	*intelligent*
largo/a	*long*
liso/a	*straight*
moreno/a	*dark-haired, brunet(te)*
optimista	*optimistic*
pelirrojo/a	*red-haired*
pesimista	*pessimistic*
preocupado/a	*worried*
realista	*realistic*
responsable	*responsible*
rizado/a	*curly*
rubio/a	*blond(e)*
tímido/a	*shy*
triste	*sad*
actualmente	*at the moment*
de buen/mal humor	*in a good/bad mood*

Relaciones personales

el afecto	*affection*
el/la ex esposo/a	*ex-husband/wife*
la fotonovela	*photo story*
el hombre/la mujer de mi vida	*the man/woman of my dreams*
divorciarse	*to get divorced*
enamorarse	*to fall in love*
estar enamorado/a (de)	*to be in love (with)*
llevarse bien/mal	*to get along/not to get along*
querer (e:ie) a alguien	*to love someone*
salir con alguien	*to go out with somebody*
separarse	*to split up, to separate*
independiente	*independent*
regiomontano/a	*born in Monterrey*
serio/a	*serious*

Ricardo Hernández

cien por ciento	*one hundred percent*
en el ámbito familiar	*among family*
o bien	*or otherwise*
el aguacate	*avocado*
el aimara	*Aymara*
el amor (no) correspondido	*(un)requited love*
la asociación	*association*
el cacahuate (*Méx.*)	*peanut*
el/la chamaquito/a (*dim. de* **el/la chamaco/a**) (*Amér. L.*)	*kid, youngster*
el chicle	*(chewing) gum*
el/la cuate/a (*fam., Méx.*)	*friend, pal*
la custodia compartida	*joint custody*
el diminutivo	*diminutive, nickname*
el divorcio	*divorce*
el doble apellido	*two last names*
el náhuatl	*Nahuatl*
el nombre de pila	*first name*
el parecido	*resemblance*
el/la primogénito/a	*firstborn*
el romanticismo	*romanticism*
el/la tocayo/a	*namesake*
parecerse (zc) a alguien	*to look like somebody*
azteca	*Aztec*
respetuoso/a	*respectful*
separado/a	*separated*

Variación léxica

cien por ciento ↔ **ciento por ciento** (*Amér. L.*) ↔ **cien por cien** (*Esp.*)

enfadado/a (*Esp.*) ↔ **enojado/a**

graduarse (*Amér. L.*) ↔ **licenciarse** (*Esp.*) ↔ **recibirse** (*Arg., Chile*) ↔ **terminar la carrera**

liso/a ↔ **lacio/a**

el maní ↔ **el cacahuate** (*Méx.*) ↔ **el cacahuete** (*Esp.*)

rizado/a ↔ **chino/a** (*Méx.*) ↔ **colocho/a** (*Amér. C.*) ↔ **enrulado/a** (*Arg.*) ↔ **crespo/a**

simpático/a ↔ **majo/a** (*Esp.*)

12B SIN LÍMITES

Aldeas Infantiles SOS is an international non-profit that, since 1949, has helped children in 132 countries.

Cimientos was founded in 1997 with the ideal of promoting education in order to eliminate the vicious cycle of poverty, lack of skills, and social exclusion.

Voluntarios

MÉDICOS SIN FRONTERAS

Médicos Sin Fronteras colaborará en proyectos de salud en más de sesenta países.

The NGO **Médicos Sin Fronteras** was established in Paris in 1971 by a group of doctors and journalists.

Aldeas Infantiles SOS

Aldeas Infantiles SOS ofrecerá una familia y un hogar estable a miles de niños en todo el mundo.

cimientos

A partir de ahora, Cimientos repartirá más becas escolares entre niños y jóvenes de pocos recursos en Argentina.

Hablar de compromisos futuros

Médicos Sin Fronteras **llegará** a sesenta países.

Aldeas Infantiles SOS **ofrecerá** ayuda a miles de niños.

Cimientos **repartirá** más becas escolares en Argentina a partir de ahora.

12B.1 Simple future (regular forms)
a partir de...

Vocabulario

1

- el/la voluntario/a *volunteer*
- la salud *health*
- estable *stable, dependable*
- a partir de *from, starting*
- repartir *to distribute*
- la beca (escolar) *scholarship*
- los recursos *resources, means*
- el derecho *right*
- la campaña *campaign*
- a favor de *in favor of*
- el/la enfermero/a *nurse*
- el tratamiento *treatment*
- la vacuna *vaccine*
- el compromiso *commitment*
- **defender (e:ie), la crisis, futuro/a**

3

- **la emergencia**

1 Lea los carteles de las organizaciones no gubernamentales (ONG) y relaciónelos con estas afirmaciones. ¿Conoce estas ONG? ¿Existen estas u otras parecidas en su país?

1. Cimientos ..b..
2. Médicos Sin Fronteras ..c..
3. Aldeas Infantiles SOS ..a..

a. Defiende los derechos de los niños en todo el mundo.
b. Ofrece educación de calidad en lugares sin recursos. Organiza campañas a favor de la educación.
c. Sus médicos y enfermeros ayudan en zonas de crisis. Ofrecen tratamiento médico, vacunas y alimento.

2 Fíjese en las formas de **colaborar** y complete las series que faltan del futuro simple.

COLABORAR	colaboraré, colaborarás, colaborará, colaboraremos, colaboraréis, colaborarán
OFRECER	ofreceré, ofrecerás, ofrecerá, ofreceremos, ofreceréis, ofrecerán
REPARTIR	repartiré, repartirás, repartirá, repartiremos, repartiréis, repartirán

2 Suggestion Draw attention to the box **Hablar de compromisos futuros,** read through the examples, and point out that the boldfaced verbs all take the same ending. Then have students complete the chart.

3 a. ¿En qué otros proyectos colaborarán estas organizaciones en el futuro? Exprese estos proyectos usando el futuro simple.

1. Dar formación profesional a jóvenes. *Cimientos dará formación...*
2. Enviar médicos a zonas de guerra. Médicos Sin Fronteras enviará médicos a zonas de guerra.
3. Recoger y repartir medicinas. Médicos Sin Fronteras recogerá y repartirá medicinas.
4. Crear aldeas infantiles y dar una nueva familia a muchos niños. Aldeas Infantiles SOS creará aldeas infantiles y dará una nueva familia a muchos niños.
5. Abrir hospitales de emergencia. Médicos sin fronteras abrirá hospitales de emergencia.

b. ¿Conoce otras ONG o asociaciones de voluntarios en su país, ciudad o barrio? Explique a sus compañeros lo que hacen.

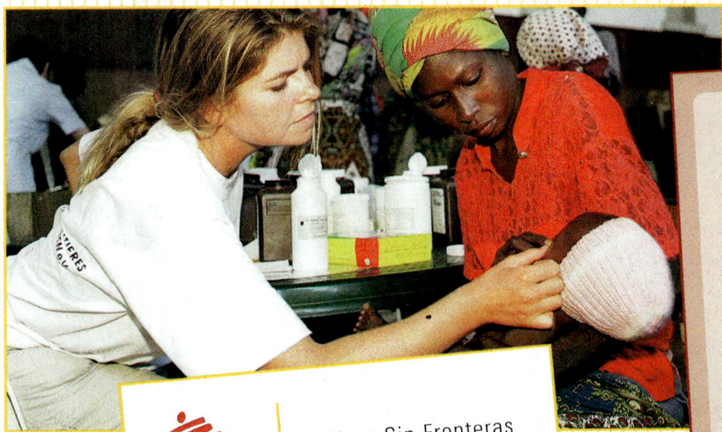

Médicos Sin Fronteras

Paula Fernández

Puerto Príncipe,
lunes 3 de octubre

Hoy ha sido un día muy largo. En este trabajo lo difícil es saber cuándo parar... Es que nuestra labor de atención médica a veces no es suficiente y eso es frustrante. Es lo malo de este trabajo. Lo bueno es que ves el resultado del esfuerzo día a día.

Hace semanas que no hablo con mi madre... tengo que llamarla más. Lo más importante es la familia. A veces lo olvido.

A partir de ahora, llamaré más a casa y estaré más en contacto. Intentaré pasar más tiempo con ellos.

Expresar valoraciones

Lo importante es la familia.
Lo bueno es que me gusta mi trabajo.
Lo difícil es tener tiempo para todo.
Lo malo son los horarios.

12B.2 lo bueno/malo... es/son

Vocabulario

4

Puerto Príncipe *Port-au-Prince*
la labor *work, task*
frustrante *frustrating*
lo malo/bueno *the bad/good thing*
el resultado *result*
estar en contacto *to be in touch*

8

asumir *to assume, to take*
dejar de fumar *to quit smoking*
el último minuto *the last minute*
ahorrar *to save*

4 Lea el diario de Paula. ¿En qué organización de las anteriores trabaja Paula? ¿En qué país? ¿Qué compromisos personales de futuro tiene?

Médicos Sin Fronteras. Haití. Llamará más a su casa y estará más en contacto. Intentará pasar más tiempo con su familia.

5 ¿Cómo valora Paula su trabajo y su vida? Complete las frases.

1. Lo difícil... es saber cuándo parar.
2. Lo bueno... es que ves el resultado.
3. Lo malo... es que la labor a veces no es suficiente y eso es frustrante.
4. Lo más importante... es la familia.

6 ¿Cómo valora usted su carrera/trabajo? Compare sus respuestas con las de su compañero/a.

Modelo: • *Lo bueno de mi carrera/trabajo es...* • *Lo malo es...*

7 Escuche la llamada de Paula a su madre y marque sus intenciones.

1. Llamará más a su madre. ✓
2. Recordará el cumpleaños de su hermano. ✓
3. Volverá a casa en enero. ☐

7 Have volunteers share promises they have made to their parents or other friends and family members.

MI EXPERIENCIA

8 Y usted, ¿cuál de estos u otros compromisos asume más frecuentemente? ¿Y su compañero/a? Valore estas acciones.

GUIÓN DE TRABAJO

pasar más tiempo con mi familia/
dejar de fumar/practicar más deporte/
trabajar menos/no dejarlo todo para el último minuto/
organizar mejor mi tiempo/
aprender a cocinar/ahorrar...

Yo siempre digo: "A partir de ahora, practicaré más deporte."

Yo también; lo importante es tener tiempo.

Practice more at vhlcentral.com.

SAM: Actividades 255–257

Hablar de deseos personales

Deseo encontrar un trabajo.
Quiero integrarme en la sociedad.
Espero lograr mi independencia.

12B.3 **querer, desear, esperar** + [*infinitive*]

Vocabulario

9

el congreso *conference*
la igualdad *equality*
sordo/a *deaf*
desear *to wish*
esperar *to hope; to wait for*
lograr *to achieve, to attain*
la barrera *barrier*
integrarse *to be integrated; to fit into*
la independencia

10

la rueda de prensa *press conference*
sufrir *to suffer*
la marginación *marginalization*
discapacitado/a *disabled*
el grupo marginado *marginalized group*
estar adaptado/a *to be adapted*
la discapacidad *disability*
quería decir... *I meant...*

Estrategia

Tomar la palabra

- Perdón, quería decir que lo importante es informar a la sociedad.
- Sí, y además...
- Una cosa más...

Querer es poder

CONGRESO PARA LA IGUALDAD

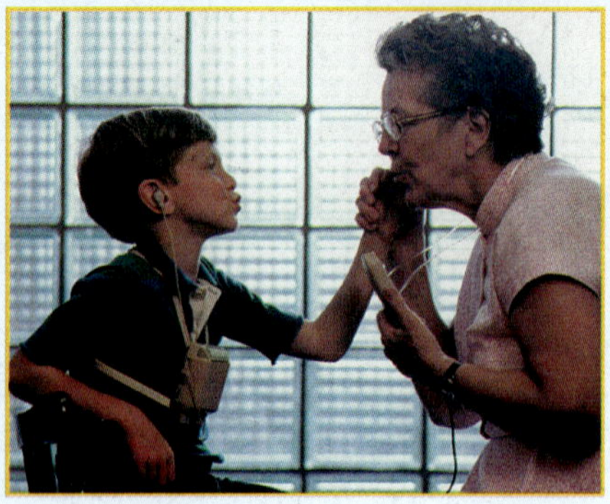

Mercedes es sorda y trabaja como profesora en una escuela para niños sordos: "Quiero ayudar a estos niños."

Marta Torre, abogada: "Quiero ser independiente. Deseo ayudar a mis hijos y espero lograrlo. Lo malo son las barreras físicas."

9 ¿Qué significa la expresión *querer es poder*? ¿Y para estas personas? ¿Qué desean y esperan? Sample answer: Si alguien desea lograr algo, encontrará la manera de hacerlo.

10 a. Primero, lea esta lista. Luego, escuche la rueda de prensa con los organizadores del congreso e indique qué temas mencionan.

- La marginación de personas discapacitadas ✓
- Otros grupos marginados en la sociedad ✓
- Los edificios públicos no están adaptados a personas con discapacidades. ☐
- Informar a la sociedad de sus problemas ✓
- El gobierno no da suficiente ayuda económica a las familias. ☐
- Hay muchas personas marginadas. ✓

b. Escuche de nuevo y diga en qué orden se mencionan en el audio estas expresiones para tomar el turno de palabra.

- Perdón, quería decir que... 2
- Una cosa más... 3
- Sí, y además... 1

11 Mire esta viñeta. ¿A qué tipo de persona critica el personaje de la imagen? ¿Cree que hay motivos para esta crítica? ¿Por qué?

SENDRA

12 Y usted, ¿qué cosas desea en su vida? Compare su respuesta con la de su compañero/a.

12 Suggestion Have students tell the class about their partner's wishes. Write some common desires on the board.

Miguel Sanz, carpintero: "Deseo tener un trabajo como el resto de la gente. Quiero integrarme a la sociedad."

MANIFIESTO DE LOS PARTICIPANTES

Queremos integrarnos a la sociedad y por eso pedimos:

1. la aceptación de la sociedad
2. la eliminación de barreras físicas y mentales en pueblos y ciudades
3. puestos de trabajo para personas con discapacidades
4. ayuda económica para nuestras familias
5. escuelas con programas especiales de integración para nuestros hijos

Hacer peticiones y expresar consecuencias

Queremos puestos de trabajo y **por eso pedimos** medidas de integración.

12B.4 **pedir** (e→i)
por eso

Vocabulario

13

el manifiesto *manifesto*
pedir (e:i) *to ask for*
la aceptación *acceptance*
el puesto de trabajo *job*
el/la carpintero/a *carpenter*
el resto de *the rest of*
la petición *request*
la consecuencia *consequence*
la eliminación, mental, la integración

14

el/la gobernante *ruler, leader*

15

el/la portavoz *spokesperson*

13 Lea el manifiesto del congreso y clasifique las peticiones de los participantes.

trabajo	educación	ciudad/pueblo	sociedad	familia
3	5	2	1	4

14 Relacione las partes de la izquierda con las de la derecha para formar oraciones lógicas. Obtendrá un resumen del manifiesto de los participantes.

El gobierno los representa — por eso — piden compromiso a los gobernantes.
Participar es formar parte — por eso — pedimos la participación.
Quiero ser independiente — por eso — pido la eliminación de barreras.

15 Imagine que es portavoz del congreso. Formule con su compañero/a otras peticiones.

15 Suggestion Help students brainstorm ideas by having them think of problems, and then invent possible solutions.

15 Expansion Have students write a letter to the school newspaper, outlining their petitions.

MI EXPERIENCIA

16 Exprese sus deseos y peticiones personales. Compártalos con sus compañeros y juntos hagan peticiones para sus deseos comunes.

GUIÓN DE TRABAJO

¿Qué quieres/deseas/esperas? → de la sociedad/ de la vida/ del trabajo...

¿Qué piden? → de la sociedad/ de la vida/ del trabajo...

Deseamos encontrar un trabajo,... → por eso... → pedimos el apoyo del gobierno.

Practice more at **vhlcentral.com.**

SAM: Actividades 258–260

Marifé, vendedora de ilusiones

The Spanish government granted ONCE permission to run the **cupón** lottery in order to finance its programs, which meet the needs of Spain's visually impaired citizens. More than 23,000 blind or disabled people sell the **cupón**; it is the largest source of employment for Spain's blind.

Marifé en su puesto de la ONCE junto a su marido

Entrevista a Marifé Cester

En este número de nuestra revista hemos seleccionado a Marifé Cester con motivo de su décimo aniversario como vendedora del cupón del sorteo de la ONCE en la Plaza de San Justo, en el casco viejo de Salamanca.

Ciega desde los once años, su discapacidad no le ha impedido hacer una vida completamente normal. Está casada con Manuel y es madre de dos hijos.

Marifé, gracias a la ONCE encontraste en la venta del cupón una forma de mantener a tu familia y ser independiente. ¿Puedes hacer balance de tu trabajo?

Me encanta: soy independiente, no tengo jefe, y me gusta el trato con el público. Lo malo es que estoy muy poco con mi familia, pero me encanta mi trabajo. Espero seguir con este trabajo muchos años más.

Marifé, ¿cómo te imaginas los próximos diez años?

Intentaré trabajar menos y estaré más con mi familia. Buscaré una persona para las tardes.

Día a día Marifé vende el cupón de la ONCE con la misma ilusión que sus clientes cuando le piden: "¡Uno para esta noche, Marifé!". Ella siempre contesta: "¡Mucha suerte y buen día!".

Expresar buenos deseos

- Colaboraré con una ONG en otro país.
- Ah, ¡buen viaje y buena suerte!

12B.5 **buen viaje**
buena/mucha suerte

Vocabulario

(17)

la ilusión *hope; happiness*
con motivo de *on the occasion of*
décimo/a *tenth*
el cupón *(lottery) ticket*
el sorteo *lottery, drawing*
el casco viejo *historic neighborhood*
la ONCE *Spanish National Organization of the Blind*
ciego/a *blind*
impedir (e:i) *to prevent; to stop*
hacer balance de *to take stock of*
el/la jefe/a *boss*
el trato *interaction*
la sigla *initial letter; acronym*
nacional

17 Observe la fotografía. ¿Sabe qué significan las siglas *ONCE*? Construya el nombre completo.

Ciegos | Organización | Españoles | Nacional

O<u>rganización</u> N<u>acional</u> de C<u>iegos</u> E<u>spañoles</u>

18 ¿Qué cree que significa el título "vendedora de ilusiones"? ¿Qué relación cree que tiene con la ONCE? Lea la entrevista y compruebe sus hipótesis.

19 ¿Qué cree Marifé que es lo bueno y lo malo de su trabajo? Haga una lista de los compromisos de Marifé para el futuro. lo bueno: es independiente, no tiene jefe, le gusta el trato con el público; lo malo: poco tiempo con la familia

20 a. ¿Qué les dice a sus clientes nuestra protagonista para expresar buenos deseos? ¡Mucha suerte y buen día!

b. Asocie estas expresiones con los contextos correspondientes. ¿Cuándo se usa cada una? En parejas, hagan una lista.

¡Buen viaje! | ¡Adiós, mucha suerte!

21 Observe el cupón y escuche el anuncio de la ONCE. ¿Cuál es el premio? treinta y cinco mil euros

Vocabulario

22

el/la perro/a guía *guide dog*
el/la educador(a) *trainer (of dogs)*
educar *to train; to educate*
irse *to leave*
pedir (e:i) permiso *to ask permission*
el/la cachorro/a *puppy*
a cambio *in return*
verdadero/a *real*

24

el/la deportista *athlete*
la medalla *medal*
el bronce *bronze*
el/la pintor(a) *painter*
el/la atleta *track-and-field athlete*
el oro *gold*
la plata *silver*
los Juegos Paralímpicos *Paralympic Games*

25

el socorro *help*
el atentado *attack; offense*

OPINIÓN

¿Existe alguna organización similar a la ONCE en su país?

¿Juega habitualmente a la lotería?

¿Ha ganado algún premio alguna vez?

¡OJO!

ONCE is an initialism, or **sigla**, that stands for **Organización Nacional de Ciegos Españoles**. Note that **la sigla** is either an acronym or each of the initials that make up an acronym, while **el siglo** refers to a century. What is the difference in meaning for these pairs: **la derecha/el derecho**; **la libra/el libro**?

22 Jacobo y Belén. • Son educadores de perros. • Para guiar a las personas ciegas. • Educarán a Lola durante doce meses. • En la Fundación ONCE del Perro Guía (FOPG).

Perros guía

Aquí está Lola, una futura perra guía de la ONCE, con sus educadores, Jacobo y Belén.

"Queremos educar a una gran perra guía."

"Somos educadores de Lola, no sus dueños. Sabemos que Lola se irá."

"Lo bueno es que podemos llevarnos a Lola al trabajo. Tuvimos que pedir permiso, pero es una perra muy buena y nunca hemos tenido ningún problema."

Jacobo y Belén son los educadores de Lola, una cachorra de la Fundación ONCE del Perro Guía (FOPG). Jacobo nos contó cómo empezó su interés por los perros guía. "Queríamos tener un perro, pero por nuestro trabajo y tipo de vida no podíamos. Descubrimos la opción que ofrece la ONCE y lo intentamos." La ONCE paga todos los gastos de Lola; a cambio, Belén y Jacobo educan a la cachorra.

"Educar a Lola no es fácil pero es una labor de voluntariado muy gratificante: sabemos que ayudará a alguien."

Después de doce meses, Lola volverá al centro y empezará su verdadera educación como perro guía. Estará de seis a ocho meses más y se graduará para ayudar a una persona ciega. Lola será sus ojos. ¡Buena suerte, Lola!

22 Lea el texto y haga estas preguntas a su compañero/a.

- ¿Quiénes son?
- ¿Qué hacen?
- ¿Para qué?
- ¿Cómo?
- ¿Dónde?

23 Elija una de estas categorías y escriba una petición.

Quiero...
por eso...

- trabajo
- educación
- sociedad

23 Expansion Have students who chose the same category get together in groups and combine their petitions into a list to be presented to the class.

24 ¿Conoce a estos personajes? Relaciónelos con la información. Elija el más interesante para usted y busque más información en Internet. ¿Conocen a alguien con una discapacidad y con una vida autónoma?

1 Jorge Luis Borges

2 Saúl Mendoza

3 Francisco de Goya

4 Nilda Gómez López

- 4 Deportista puertorriqueña, medalla de bronce en tiro en los Juegos Paralímpicos de Beijing 2008.
- 3 Pintor español sordo.
- 2 Atleta mexicano, medallas de oro y plata en los Juegos Paralímpicos de Atenas 2004.
- 1 Escritor argentino ciego.

24 Ask students if they are familiar with any other famous Spanish speakers with disabilities, such as Puerto Rican singer Jose Feliciano.

Practice more at vhlcentral.com.

SAM: Actividades pp. 261–266

25 a. Fíjese en los eslóganes de estas ONG. ¿Qué le sugieren? Relaciónelos con las categorías del recuadro.

educación • asuntos sociales • política • voluntariado • medio ambiente

Cruz Roja: Tu ayuda vale mucho para el socorro ante desastres.	Amnistía Internacional: Defendemos los derechos humanos en todo el mundo.	Asociación Conciencia: Educando jóvenes para una sociedad democrática.
voluntariado	política	educación

25 Expansion Write slogans from other entities on the board and have students guess the organization.

Greenpeace: Para proteger y defender activamente el planeta de los atentados que se cometen contra la naturaleza.	Desarrollo y asistencia: Tú tienes mucho. Muchos no tienen nada. Por eso da. Porque merece la pena.
medio ambiente	asuntos sociales

b. Piensen en la labor que realiza cada una de estas ONG. ¿Con cuál desearían colaborar? ¿Por qué? ¿Cómo colaborarían? Elija una de estas organizaciones y busque oportunidades para colaborar con ella en su región.

TAREA FINAL

Nuestra ONG

- Haga una lista de las ONG y asociaciones que conoce. Busque ideas en Internet o hable con un club o asociación de voluntariado de su universidad.
- Explique a su compañero/a la labor que realizan estas ONG o asociaciones.
- Compartan y elijan las ideas más interesantes para crear su propia ONG o asociación.
- Elijan un eslogan y unas siglas.
- Presenten su ONG o asociación a la clase. Expliquen a sus compañeros la labor que realizarán en el futuro.

YO PUEDO...

- **Puedo hablar de mis compromisos para el futuro.**
  Piense en algo que quiere cambiar de su vida y escriba los compromisos para hacerlo.
- **Puedo expresar valoraciones.**
  Piense qué es lo bueno y qué es lo malo de: su trabajo, sus estudios, su ciudad...
- **Puedo hablar de deseos personales.**
  Escriba tres deseos personales.
- **Puedo hacer peticiones y expresar consecuencia.**
  Describa una situación y, como consecuencia de esta, exprese una petición.
- **Puedo expresar buenos deseos.**
  Un(a) compañero/a se va de viaje. ¿Qué le dice al despedirse?

GRAMÁTICA FUNCIONAL

Suggestion Have students write down five academic goals they have for the next semester, using the future tense. Have them compare lists with a partner.

12B.1 Talk about future commitments

The simple future (regular forms) 5.16.2a
a partir de... 10.2

- To express actions and events in the future, such as anticipated plans or objectives, use the simple future (**el futuro simple**).

La universidad **ofrecerá** más clases de noche este año.
*The university **will offer** more classes at night this year.*

- In 6B.1, you learned to use **ir + a +** [*infinitive*] to talk about what someone is going to do in the near future. Use the **futuro simple** to express a firm intention for the future.

- For regular verbs, the endings of the **futuro simple** are added to the infinitive. The endings are the same for **-ar**, **-er**, and **-ir** verbs.

	TRABAJAR	SER	VIVIR
(yo)	trabajar**é**	ser**é**	vivir**é**
(tú)	trabajar**ás**	ser**ás**	vivir**ás**
(usted, él, ella)	trabajar**á**	ser**á**	vivir**á**
(nosotros/as)	trabajar**emos**	ser**emos**	vivir**emos**
(vosotros/as)	trabajar**éis**	ser**éis**	vivir**éis**
(ustedes, ellos/as)	trabajar**án**	ser**án**	vivir**án**

Trabajaremos juntos para resolver el problema.
*We **will work** together to solve the problem.*

- Note that all **futuro simple** endings have a written accent except the **nosotros/as** form.

Ellos **irán** de viaje y nosotros **nos quedaremos** en casa.
They will take a trip and we will stay home.

12B.2 Express opinions

lo bueno/lo malo... es/son 3.3.1

- To assess something based on its general characteristics, use **lo** with the masculine singular form of an adjective. Say **lo** + [*adjective*] + **es** followed by a singular noun or an infinitive.

Lo bueno es tener un horario flexible.
***The good thing is** having a flexible schedule.*

Lo importante es la familia.
***The important thing is** family.*

- Use **lo** + [*adjective*] + **son** followed by a plural noun.

Lo malo son las grandes distancias.
*The long distances **are the bad part**.*

- With a conjugated verb, use **lo** + [*adjective*] + **es** + **que**.

Lo difícil es que no tengo tiempo para todo.
***The difficult part is that** I don't have time for everything.*

Suggestion Give the class a variety situations (Ex: **estudiar en otro país, ser político/a,** etc.) and have them react using statements with **lo.**

¡Póngalo en práctica!

G1 Escriba la forma correcta del futuro simple.

1. defender (yo) defenderé
2. pedir (ustedes) pedirán
3. esperar (vosotros) esperaréis
4. desear (tú) desearás
5. educar (ellas) educarán
6. lograr (Juan) logrará
7. compartir (tú y yo) compartiremos
8. ver (usted) verá

G2 Complete las oraciones con la forma correcta del futuro simple.

Quiero hacer algo por la sociedad. He decidido que (1) colaboraré (colaborar) con una ONG.

La empresa ha prometido que a partir de este año (2) subirá (subir) los salarios a los trabajadores. A cambio, los trabajadores (3) serán (ser) eficaces y (4) cumplirán (cumplir) los objetivos.

Este año muchas ONG (5) trabajarán (trabajar) en zonas de catástrofe. Las organizaciones (6) llevarán (llevar) comida, agua y medicamentos a los más afectados.

Nosotros hemos decidido poner más atención al estudio. Por eso, (7) iremos (ir) con más frecuencia a la biblioteca y (8) estudiaremos (estudiar) juntos.

G2 Expansion Have students write a description of what they will do upon graduation. Collect the papers, shuffle them, and read the descriptions aloud for the class to guess the person's identity.

G3 Complete los diálogos.

- ¿Qué es (1) lo importante en la vida?
- Lo (2) importante es la salud.

- ¿Qué es lo bueno y lo malo de tu trabajo?
- Lo bueno (3) es que me gusta. Lo malo (4) son los horarios.

- ¿Qué es lo mejor y lo peor de vivir en otro país?
- Lo mejor (5) es poder aprender cosas nuevas todos los días. Lo peor es (6) que no puedo viajar muy frecuentemente a mi país.

Practice more at **vhlcentral.com.**

GRAMÁTICA FUNCIONAL

12B.3 Talk about desires and hopes

querer/desear/esperar + [*infinitive*] 5.10

- Use the verbs **querer, desear,** and **esperar** followed by an infinitive to express hopes and desires.

> **Quiero ir** de vacaciones pronto.
> ***I want to go*** *on vacation soon.*
>
> **Esperamos verte** de nuevo.
> ***We hope to see*** *you again.*

Suggestion Remind students that **querer** and **pedir** are "boot" verbs.

- **Querer** has the stem change **e→ie,** as you learned in 3B.6. **Desear** and **esperar** are regular **-ar** verbs.

12B.4 Make requests and express consequences

pedir 5.1.1 **por eso** 12.8

- Use the verb **pedir** (*to ask for*) + [*noun*] to make requests. **Pedir** has an **e→i** stem change.

> **Pido** la participación de todos.
> ***I ask for*** *everyone's participation.*

PEDIR			
(yo)	pido	(nosotros/as)	pedimos
(tú)	pides	(vosotros/as)	pedís
(usted, él, ella)	pide	(ustedes, ellos/as)	piden

- Note that no preposition is used between **pedir** and the noun in Spanish. Other common verbs that require a preposition in English but not in Spanish include **buscar** (*to look for*) and **esperar** (*to wait for*).

> Estoy buscando las llaves; espérame.
> *I'm looking* ***for*** *the keys; wait* ***for*** *me!*

- To show consequences, use **por eso** (*that's why; therefore*).

> Queremos ayudas económicas y programas especiales, **por eso** pedimos el compromiso del gobierno.
> *We want economic assistance and special programs;* ***that's why*** *we are asking for a commitment from the government.*

12B.5 Express well wishes

buen viaje, buena/mucha suerte 4.6

- To wish someone a good trip, say **buen viaje.** To wish someone luck, say **buena/mucha suerte.**

> —Mañana tengo una entrevista.
> —¡**Mucha suerte!**
> —*I have an interview tomorrow.*
> —***Good luck!***

G6 Expansion Continue the activity by naming places or people and having students give an appropriate phrase. Ex: **un aeropuerto (¡Buen viaje!); un camarero (¡Buen provecho!)**

- The adjective **bueno** drops the final vowel **-o** in front of a singular masculine noun. Another example of this shortened adjective is in the expression **buen provecho** (*Bon appetit!*).

- When **bueno** is followed by a feminine noun or a plural noun, it is not shortened: **buena suerte; buenos días; buenas noches.**

¡Póngalo en práctica!

G4 Escriba oraciones completas según las pistas.

1. (yo) querer / aprender / español
   Quiero aprender español.
2. (nosotros) esperar / tener / buena salud
   Esperamos tener buena salud.
3. Paola / desear / mejorar / sus notas
   Paola desea mejorar sus notas.
4. Raúl y Mónica / querer / encontrar / trabajos interesantes
   Raúl y Mónica quieren encontrar trabajos interesantes.
5. Florencia / desear / estudiar / física
   Florencia desea estudiar física.

G5 Complete las oraciones con **por eso** o la forma correcta de **pedir**.

- ¿Qué quieres de tu trabajo?
- Quiero un trabajo interesante; (1) por eso (2) pido proyectos participativos y creativos. Y vosotros, ¿qué queréis?

Queremos puestos de trabajo dignos para todos y (3) por eso (4) pedimos la eliminación de barreras físicas y mentales.

- Los ciudadanos quieren una ciudad limpia; (5) por eso (6) piden más recursos. ¿Qué más pueden (7) pedir ?
- Es importante la participación de todos; (8) por eso hay que ir a votar.

G6 Responda a cada situación con una expresión de buenos deseos.

1. —Mañana tengo un examen.
   —¡Buena/Mucha suerte!
2. —Me voy de vacaciones mañana.
   —¡Buen viaje!
3. —Voy a dar una presentación esta semana en mi trabajo.
   —¡Buena/Mucha suerte!
4. —Voy a comer una ensalada.
   —¡Buen provecho!
5. —Son las once de la noche y me voy.
   —¡Buenas noches!

Practice more at **vhlcentral.com.**

VOCABULARIO

Voluntarios

a favor de	*in favor of*
lo malo/bueno	*the bad/good thing*
la beca (escolar)	*scholarship*
la campaña	*campaign*
el compromiso	*commitment*
la crisis	*crisis*
el derecho	*right*
la emergencia	*emergency*
el/la enfermero/a	*nurse*
la labor	*work, task*
Puerto Príncipe	*Port-au-Prince*
los recursos	*resources, means*
el resultado	*result*
la salud	*health*
el tratamiento	*treatment*
el último minuto	*the last minute*
la vacuna	*vaccine*
el/la voluntario/a	*volunteer*
ahorrar	*to save*
asumir	*to assume, to take*
defender (e:ie)	*to defend*
dejar de fumar	*to quit smoking*
estar en contacto	*to be in touch*
repartir	*to distribute*
estable	*stable, dependable*
frustrante	*frustrating*
futuro/a	*future*
a partir de	*from, starting*

Querer es poder

el resto de	*the rest of*
quería decir...	*I meant . . .*
la aceptación	*acceptance*
la barrera	*barrier*
el/la carpintero/a	*carpenter*
el congreso	*conference*
la consecuencia	*consequence*
la discapacidad	*disability*
la eliminación	*elimination*
el/la gobernante	*ruler, leader*
el grupo marginado	*marginalized group*
la igualdad	*equality*
la independencia	*independence*
la integración	*integration*
el manifiesto	*manifesto*
la marginación	*marginalization*
la petición	*request*
el/la portavoz	*spokesperson*
el puesto de trabajo	*job*
la rueda de prensa	*press conference*
desear	*to wish*
esperar	*to hope; to wait for*
estar adaptado/a	*to be adapted*
integrarse	*to be integrated; to fit into*
lograr	*to achieve, to attain*
pedir (e:i)	*to ask for*
sufrir	*to suffer*
discapacitado/a	*disabled*
mental	*mental*
sordo/a	*deaf*

Marifé

con motivo de	*on the occasion of*
el atentado	*attack; offense*
el/la atleta	*track-and-field athlete*
el bronce	*bronze*
el/la cachorro/a	*puppy*
el casco viejo	*historic neighborhood*
el cupón	*(lottery) ticket*
el/la deportista	*athlete*
el/la educador(a)	*trainer (of dogs)*
la ilusión	*hope; happiness*
el/la jefe/a	*boss*
los Juegos Paralímpicos	*Paralympic Games*
la ONCE	*Spanish National Organization of the Blind*
el oro	*gold*
la medalla	*medal*
el/la perro/a guía	*guide dog*
el/la pintor(a)	*painter*
la plata	*silver*
la sigla	*initial letter; acronym*
el socorro	*help*
el sorteo	*lottery, drawing*
el trato	*interaction*
educar	*to train; to educate*
hacer balance de	*to take stock of*
impedir (e:i)	*to prevent; to stop*
irse	*to leave*
pedir (e:i) permiso	*to ask permission*
ciego/a	*blind*
décimo/a	*tenth*
nacional	*national*
verdadero/a	*real*
a cambio	*in return*

Variación léxica

la barrera ⟷ **el obstáculo**

el/la educador(a) (de perros) ⟷ **el/la adiestrador(a)** ⟷ **el/la entrenador(a)**

los Juegos Paralímpicos ⟷ **las Paralimpíadas** (*Amér. L.*) ⟷ **las Paralimpiadas**

la marginación ⟷ **la exclusión**

el/la perro/a guía ⟷ **el/la perro/a lazarillo**

la rueda de prensa ⟷ **la conferencia de prensa**

Successful Language Learning Remind students that when they are studying vocabulary, they should be sure to take the time to listen to each word and repeat its pronunciation.

Estrategias

1 Ordenar la información

Lección 11A

Organizing information in order helps your reader better understand your message and improves communication.

- Escriba las expresiones del recuadro en la postal de la derecha.

Por último
En primer lugar
Después

1 Expansion Have students write a brief e-mail to a friend, explaining three things they did or saw on a trip or outing they took. Have them use the expressions from the box to organize their sentences.

¡Hola, familia!

¿Cómo están? Hemos pasado unos días de vacaciones por el norte de España. (1) ....En primer lugar,.... *pasamos unos días en Asturias y visitamos Oviedo. (2)* ....Después,.... *fuimos a Bilbao y estuvimos en el Guggenheim, ¡es espectacular! (3)* ....Por último,.... *pasamos dos noches en el Parador Sos del Rey Católico y también hicimos senderismo en los Pirineos. ¡Se lo recomiendo!*

Un beso,

Sara

2 Mostrar interés en la conversación

Lección 11B

Every language has certain expressions used to react or to keep a conversation going. These expressions will help you maintain the natural flow of conversation.

2 Suggestion Have students complete this activity orally in pairs. Encourage them to use intonation and emotion in their reactions.

- Reaccione. Suggested answers:

"Este año vamos a Nicaragua de vacaciones."
....¿Sí?....

"Quiero tener ocho hijos."
....¿En serio?....

"He ganado 6 000 000 de euros en la lotería."
....¿De verdad?....

3 Cerrar una cita

Lección 12A

Use these expressions to confirm a date or appointment. They can soften the force of a statement and ease the flow of conversation.

- Vuelva a escuchar el audio de la Actividad 11a de la Lección 12A y marque qué expresiones de cierre ha escuchado.

Entonces, ... ✓

De acuerdo, nos vemos. ✓

Vale, hasta la próxima. ☐

4 Tomar la palabra

Lección 12B

When you want to interrupt someone or "take the floor", you will need to use the appropriate expressions in Spanish. Knowing these expressions will help you express yourself more naturally and effectively, and will ease communication. They will help you develop greater confidence in Spanish.

- Inicie una conversación con su compañero/a sobre el tema 1. Interrúmpalo/la durante sus explicaciones y tome la palabra para preguntarle por el tema 2. Tome de nuevo la palabra e introduzca el tema 3.

1 Usted quiere saber el teléfono de un(a) compañero/a.
2 Quiere preguntarle a su compañero/a si conoce un restaurante argentino en su ciudad.
3 Desea saber de otros lugares donde se habla español en su ciudad.

Competencias

1 Expansion Have students give three recommendations to a partner, who will take notes. Then have students get together with another partner and report on the recommendations.

TRANSMITIR PALABRAS DE OTROS

1 Vuelva a escribir estas oraciones siguiendo el modelo. No olvide usar las palabras entre paréntesis. Suggested answers:

Modelo: *¿Conocen un restaurante bueno? Me gusta la comida latina. (Ana / preguntar / decir)*
Ana ha preguntado si conocemos un restaurante bueno. Dice que le gusta la comida latina.

1. Te recomiendo viajar a Puerto Rico. Es un lugar maravilloso.
   (María / recomendar / decir) María me ha recomendado viajar a Puerto Rico. Dice que es un lugar maravilloso.
2. Si te quieres quedar en ese hotel, te recomiendo hacer la reserva con antelación.
   (Jorge / decir / deber) Jorge ha dicho que si quiero quedarme en ese hotel, debo hacer la reserva con antelación.
3. ¿Dónde está el libro de quejas? Esta agencia de viajes es pésima.
   (Eduardo / preguntar / decir) Eduardo ha preguntado dónde está el libro de quejas. Dice que esta agencia de viajes es pésima.

FORMULAR DESEOS, EXPRESAR VALORACIONES EN GRADO MÁXIMO Y EXPRESAR UN CONTRAARGUMENTO

2 Complete las oraciones con palabras del recuadro. Exprese los adjetivos en grado máximo y los verbos en el condicional. Es posible usar algunas palabras más de una vez. Suggested answers:

famoso/a mucho/a incómodo/a fácil gustar difícil grande encantar caro/a

1. • Me encantaría/gustaría vivir en una casa grandísima.
   ■ A mí también, pero es facilísimo limpiar un apartamento pequeño.
2. • Me gustaría/encantaría viajar por todo el mundo.
   ■ Sí, pero es carísimo.
3. • Me encantaría/gustaría ser un(a) cantautor(a) famosísimo/a.
   ■ ¿A quién no? Pero es dificilísimo.
4. • Me gustaría/encantaría vivir en las afueras.
   ■ Sí, pero es incomodísimo. Debes viajar muchísimo.

2 Expansion Ask students to write a few additional cloze mini-dialogues. Have them exchange papers with a classmate and complete the sentences.

DESCRIBIR EL CARÁCTER Y EL ASPECTO FÍSICO

3 Relacione cada adjetivo con su opuesto. Luego use estos adjetivos y otros que aprendió en la **Lección 12A** para describir una de las personas de las fotos. Su compañero/a adivina quién es.

1. alto/a b	a. moreno/a
2. de buen humor f	b. bajo/a
3. largo/a g	c. rizado/a
4. liso/a c	d. pesimista
5. optimista d	e. alegre
6. rubio/a a	f. de mal humor
7. triste e	g. corto/a

HABLAR DE COMPROMISOS FUTUROS

4 Complete la conversación con un verbo de la lista en la forma correcta del futuro simple.

buscar dejar llamar organizar pasar

• Gustavo, ¿cuándo (1) pasaremos más tiempo juntos? Viajas mucho por trabajo, incluso los fines de semana...
■ Pronto, querida. Mi jefe me ha prometido que (2) buscará a otra persona para encargarse de algunos viajes. De esa manera, yo (3) dejaré de trabajar tantas horas y (4) organizaré mejor mi tiempo libre.
• ¿Y (5) llamarás más a tus padres? Hace varias semanas que no hablas con ellos...

Flash Cultura

Estrategia

Organizing questions

When watching a video, start by trying to identify the main topic and the type of information provided. **A causa de** (*because of*), **por (lo cual/lo tanto)** (*therefore*), **porque** (*because*), **debido a** (*due to, since*), **así que** (*so, therefore*), signal cause-and-effect relationships. Ask **¿por qué?** to find the cause(s) and **¿Cuál es el resultado?** to identify the effect(s).

Vocabulario útil

el amor a primera vista *love at first sight*
antiguamente *in the past*
el callejón *alley*
la campanada *stroke (bell)*
la carretera *road*
los celos *jealousy*
la confluencia *junction*
frenético *frantic*
...y pico *over*
las uvas *grapes*

Estrategia

Changing the topic

When you need to change topics or end a conversation, you can use filler words to soften an abrupt transition. Some common expressions include **(pues) eso...**, **(pues) nada...**, or **en fin...**

3 Suggestion To challenge students, have them cover the second column and complete the sentences in a logical manner.

Las relaciones personales

Ya ha visto cómo el amor y las relaciones sentimentales son esenciales no solo en nuestra vida de cada día sino también para planear el futuro. En este episodio de **Flash Cultura** podrá ver cómo las personas se relacionan y disfrutan del tiempo libre en Madrid.

1 Converse con un(a) compañero/a: Durante los fines de semana, ¿se reúne con sus amigos? ¿Le parece importante tener muchos amigos? ¿Cree que es posible enamorarse a primera vista?

2 Mire el video. Preste atención al entrevistador. ¿Cuál es el tema principal?

1 Suggestion For the last question, have students share anecdotes about people that they know who fell in love at first sight.

...grandes y chicos... van a la plaza a reunirse...

Tell students that a synonym for **amor a primera vista** is **flechazo**, meaning the arrow shot by Cupid that makes the victim fall instantly in love.

Las plazas son lo más romántico del mundo...

3 Una la primera columna (**causas**) con la segunda (**consecuencias**).

1. Los españoles comen doce uvas el 31 de diciembre... c	a. para amar a alguien hay que conocerlo.
2. Muchas crisis en las parejas se producen por... d	b. conoces a mucha gente distinta.
3. El amor a primera vista es imposible porque... a	c. para dar la bienvenida al Año Nuevo.
4. En Madrid hay un ritmo frenético y por eso... b	d. culpa de los celos, sobre todo al comienzo.

4 En parejas, imaginen que están en una plaza observando a la gente alrededor. Uno describe personajes conocidos y el otro adivina quién es.

Modelo:
- *¡Mira! Ese hombre es parecido a ese actor... rubio, alto...*
- *¿Quién...? ¿Robert Redford?*

Practice more at **vhlcentral.com.**

Audio: Activities, Vocabulary
Video: *Flash Cultura*

Unidad 13

Nelson Morales y Edgar Hugo Torrico, bienvenidos a bordo

Lección 13A

AVENTURAS COTIDIANAS

Lección 13B

MUNDO TECNOLÓGICO

Cristina Rubio, asesora laboral

Inventos argentinos

AVANCE

13A AVENTURAS COTIDIANAS

Señores pasajeros

¿Podría decirme cuál es el mostrador de facturación de Air Europa?

¿Puede decirme dónde es la entrega de equipaje?

¿Sabe si el avión de Aerolíneas Argentinas viene con retraso?

¿Le importaría confirmarme la sala de llegada del vuelo 1200 de Aeroméxico?

¿Sabe dónde está la puerta de embarque C-13?

¿Podría decirme si sale algún vuelo de Iberia a Santiago de Cuba?

13A.1 Point out that these are polite expressions used in the **usted** form; however, explain that equivalent **tú** forms may also be used.

Pedir y confirmar información

- ¿Podría decirme dónde está el mostrador de Iberia?
- ¿Le importaría confirmarme si ha llegado ya el vuelo...?

13A.1 **¿Sabe/Puede/Podría/ Le importaría decirme... + si/dónde/cuándo...?**

Vocabulario

(1)

señores pasajeros *passengers:/ladies and gentlemen:*

el mostrador de facturación *check-in desk*

la entrega de equipaje *baggage claim*

con retraso *delayed*

¿Le importaría...? *Would you mind . . . ?*

la sala de llegada *arrival lounge/ area*

la puerta de embarque *boarding gate*

salir *to depart*

confirmar

1 Lea las preguntas frecuentes de los viajeros e identifique los lugares del aeropuerto que se mencionan. Relacione después estos lugares con las imágenes.

1. *mostrador de facturación*
2. puerta de embarque
3. entrega de equipaje
4. sala de llegada

2 Complete las preguntas con las palabras del recuadro. Luego, relaciónelas con las respuestas. Represente las conversaciones con un(a) compañero/a.

cuándo • cuál • dónde • quién • si

1. ¿Puede decirme ...cuál... es la terminal de Air Europa? _c_
2. ¿Le importaría confirmarme ...si... ya ha llegado el vuelo IB 3200? _e_
3. ¿Podría decirme ...dónde... están los carritos? _d_
4. ¿Le importaría decirme ...quién... es el responsable? _a_
5. ¿Sabe ...cuándo... llega el vuelo de Quito? _b_

a. Sí, el señor Rodríguez, supervisor de facturación.
b. Sí, a las 17:00 h.
c. Sí, la terminal 2.
d. Sí, detrás de la cafetería.
e. Sí, acaba de llegar.

3 Pida información a su compañero/a sobre estos puntos.

3 Suggestion To simplify, work with the class to brainstorm a list of words and phrases that can be used in this activity.

IB 3200 Frankfurt Salida 13:20		**PUERTA DE EMBARQUE A-22**	**T4**

Aeropuertos del mundo hispano

Algunos de los aeropuertos internacionales más frecuentados del mundo hispano son el Benito Juárez (MEX) en México, D.F.; El Dorado (BOG), Bogotá; Comodoro Arturo Merino Benítez (SCL), Santiago de Chile; Jorge Chávez (LIM), Lima; y el de Ezeiza, Ministro Pistarini, (EZE), en Buenos Aires. En España son importantes los aeropuertos de Barajas (MAD) en Madrid y El Prat (BCN) en Barcelona.

Vocabulario

2

el carrito *trolley*

el/la responsable *person in charge*

la terminal, el/la supervisor(a)

4

el altavoz *speaker*

la observación *remark*

el destino *destination*

el embarque *boarding*

procedente de *arriving from*

el origen, cancelado/a

5

la tarifa *fare*

la frecuencia

6

la hora de llegada *arrival time*

la hora de embarque *boarding time*

la hora de salida *departure time*

la facturación *check-in*

el control de pasaportes *passport control; immigration*

el control de equipaje *baggage screening*

el cambio de dinero *foreign currency exchange*

las divisas *foreign currency*

el andén *platform*

la confirmación

¡OJO!

Use **¿Dónde está?** to ask for the location of objects or places. Use **¿Dónde es?** to ask where an event or action occurs. **¿Dónde es el control de pasaportes? = ¿Dónde controlan los pasaportes?**

4 Suggestion Before playing the audio, have students look at the charts and identify the information they will be listening for.

4 Escuche la información anunciada por los altavoces del aeropuerto y anótela en los paneles informativos. Pida confirmación a su compañero/a.

HORA	VUELO	ORIGEN	LLEGADA	SALA	OBSERVACIÓN
10:30	LH 2120	BERLÍN	10:30	C	
15:15	VY 1420	ROMA	16:35	C	RETRASO

HORA	VUELO	DESTINO	EMBARQUE	PUERTA	OBSERVACIÓN
9:30	EJ 3443	LAS PALMAS	9:00	A 10	
10:35	AE 1700	CANCÚN	10:00	B 35	CANCELADO

5 ¿Avión o tren? En parejas, elijan una opción cada uno. Pregunte a su compañero/a por la información de su opción de viaje y después responda a las preguntas de su compañero/a.

ESTUDIANTE A

VUELO MADRID-BARCELONA (IBERIA)

Origen: Madrid-Barajas **Destino:** Barcelona-El Prat
Duración: 1 hora, 10 minutos
Tarifas: desde 100 euros (ida y vuelta)
Horario:

lunes a viernes	06:30 a 22:45 h (cada 20 minutos)
sábados y domingos	08:00 a 22:45 h (menor frecuencia)

ESTUDIANTE B

AVE MADRID-BARCELONA (RENFE)

Origen: Madrid-Puerta de Atocha **Destino:** Barcelona-Sants
Duración: 2 horas, 38 minutos
Tarifas: desde 100 euros (ida y vuelta)
Horario:

lunes a viernes	05:45 a 21:00 h (cada hora)
sábados y domingos	06:15 a 22:00 h (menor frecuencia)

MI EXPERIENCIA

5 AVE, which stands for **Alta Velocidad Española,** is a high-speed train service. The service is operated by the Spanish state railway system **RENFE (Red Nacional de Ferrocarriles Españoles).**

6 En parejas, imaginen que van a hacer un viaje. Elijan uno de los medios de transporte y representen las conversaciones más frecuentes de un viaje.

GUIÓN DE TRABAJO

ANTES DE VIAJAR

¿Podría/Puede confirmarme...
a qué hora sale el próximo vuelo/tren a...?
a qué hora llega el próximo vuelo/tren de...?
la hora de embarque/salida de...?

→ El próximo vuelo/tren sale/llega a las...

EN EL AEROPUERTO/ EN LA ESTACIÓN

¿Dónde es la entrega de equipaje, la facturación, el control de pasaportes/ equipaje, el cambio de dinero (divisas)?
¿Dónde está la puerta/el andén/la terminal...?

→ Vaya a...

Practice more at **vhlcentral.com.**

SAM: Actividades pp. 267–269

Suggestion Read through the **Ojo** note with the class; then write cloze sentences on the board for volunteers to complete: **¿Dónde** .... **la facturación? ¿Dónde** .... **los mostradores de facturación? (es; están)**

Rincones escondidos

1 Parque Baconao

2 Santiago de Cuba

3 Trinidad

Enviar Chat Adjuntar Agenda Tipo de letra Colores Borrador

De: Pilar López
Para: Damián Gutiérrez
Asunto: Te recomiendo Cuba.

Fotos de Cuba

¡Hola, Damián!
Sé que estás preparando un viaje y he pensado en escribirte para recomendarte un lugar: ¡Ve a Cuba! Hace una semana volví de allí y ¡ya tengo nostalgia! Es que fue un viaje increíble. Como el año pasado estuvimos en La Habana, esta vez visitamos otros rincones de Cuba y decidimos no organizar nada. No teníamos hotel y solo sabíamos la fecha del pasaje de vuelta. Primero volamos a la capital y allí alquilamos un carro para ir a Trinidad y a Santiago de Cuba.

Para volver tomamos el tren de Santiago a La Habana. Fue un viaje larguísimo. Estábamos a mitad de viaje y se averió el tren, pero nos pareció una experiencia maravillosa compartir 18 horas (avería incluida) con cubanos, ¡te lo recomiendo! Yo en tu lugar, no viajaría con un viaje organizado, e iría a otros lugares que no son tan turísticos, por ejemplo Trinidad. Este lugar nos trasladó al pasado; nos encantó su arquitectura colonial y había muchos carros de los años 50, preciosos. La ciudad de Santiago es más grande y más urbana, y tiene una catedral hermosa. Los días que pasamos en el Parque Baconao fueron maravillosos. ¡El paisaje me pareció espectacular! Había mar y montaña, y nos bañamos en la cascada El Saltón. Fue estupendo. Las playas cubanas son únicas; te las recomiendo.

Nos alojamos en casas particulares y no en hoteles. Los cubanos me parecieron muy hospitalarios. Yo que tú, no iría a hoteles tampoco. Comimos en muchos paladares (pequeños restaurantes en casas de cubanos). Me parecieron excelentes y nada caros; yo en tu lugar comería siempre en ellos. A propósito, la comida cubana es riquísima, te la recomiendo. En el viaje conocimos a muchos cubanos y sin duda, lo mejor de Cuba es su gente: ¡Son fantásticos! Bueno, llámame un día y te enseño más fotos con un mojito.

Un beso, Pilar

Explain that **mojitos** are made of rum, lime, sugar, sparkling water, and fresh mint leaves.

Describir un viaje

- ¿Cómo te **fue** en Cuba?
- El vuelo **fue** muy largo, pero las vacaciones **fueron** fantásticas.

13A.2 Review: Preterite/Imperfect
Preterite to give opinions

7 Fíjese en las fotografías. ¿De dónde pueden ser? Lea el correo y escriba el nombre de los lugares que muestran las fotos.

8 a. ¿Qué cuenta Pilar sobre su viaje? ¿Qué experiencias vivieron ella y sus amigos y dónde estaban en esos momentos? Escriba un resumen.

b. ¿Cuáles fueron las etapas del viaje? ¿Qué medios de transporte utilizaron?
viaje a La Habana, en avión; viaje a Trinidad y a Santiago de Cuba, en carro; viaje de regreso de Santiago de Cuba a La Habana, en tren

9 a. ¿Cómo describe Pilar su viaje a Cuba? Complete las oraciones con palabras del recuadro.

maravilloso/a • increíble • hospitalario/a
excelente • estupendo/a • espectacular

1. El viaje a Cuba fue ......increíble......
2. El viaje en tren fue una experiencia ......maravillosa......
3. El baño en la cascada El Saltón fue ......estupendo......
4. El paisaje de Cuba le pareció ......espectacular......
5. Los cubanos le parecieron muy ......hospitalarios......
6. Los paladares le parecieron ......excelentes......

9b Suggestion If students do not have many travel experiences, encourage them to describe one from film or television.

b. ¿Qué tiene este viaje de particular? ¿Ha hecho usted un viaje similar? ¿Adónde? Cuénteselo a su compañero/a.

Vocabulario

7

preparar un viaje *to organize a trip*
recomendar (e:ie) (un lugar) *to recommend (a place)*
el rincón *corner; spot*
averiarse *to break down*
el viaje organizado *package tour*
trasladar *to transport*
hermoso/a *lovely*
bañarse *to go for a swim*
alojarse *to stay*
la casa particular *private home*
hospitalario/a *hospitable*

10 Vuelva a leer el correo electrónico. ¿Qué le recomienda Pilar a Damián sobre estos temas? Relacione las columnas.

1. "Te lo recomiendo." ...c...
2. "Yo que tú, no iría a hoteles." ...a...
3. "Yo en tu lugar, comería siempre en ellos." ...b...

a. alojarse en casas particulares
b. comer en paladares
c. viajar en tren

11 Complete las oraciones con las palabras y expresiones del recuadro.

pedíría • viajaría • te lo recomiendo • se la recomiendo

1. Yo en tu lugar, ...viajaría...... a México en enero.
2. Alojarse en hoteles de cinco estrellas es carísimo; no ...te lo recomiendo... .
3. Yo que tú ......pediría...... una revista a la auxiliar de vuelo.
4. Esta aerolínea es muy buena; ...se la recomiendo... .

12 Escriba el nombre de las ciudades que visitó Pilar. Después escuche el audio y escriba las ciudades que les recomienda la agencia a los novios. ¿Qué tipo de viaje le parece más atractivo? Recomiende su opción a su compañero/a.

Itinerario de Pilar: La Habana, Trinidad, Santiago de Cuba; Itineraro de la agencia de viajes: Santiago de Cuba, La Habana, Varadero, Trinidad

13 a. Lea de nuevo el correo de Pilar. ¿Qué expresiones usa para dar una explicación? es que, como

b. Explique a su compañero/a el motivo de estas situaciones. Use las expresiones **como** y **es que** en su explicación.

Modelo: *Como no oí el despertador, he perdido el tren.*

Situaciones

1. Ha perdido el vuelo.
2. No ha reservado los billetes de avión.
3. Ha pedido un cambio de asiento.
4. Han cancelado su vuelo.

Motivos

a. Sabe que no hay problemas de plazas.
b. Está nevando mucho.
c. No oyó el despertador.
d. Ahora está demasiado cerca del baño.

MI EXPERIENCIA

14 Pregunte a sus compañeros cómo prefieren pasar las vacaciones.

GUIÓN DE TRABAJO

¿Qué tipo de viajes te gusta hacer?
¿Qué destinos prefieres?
¿Cómo fue el último viaje que hiciste?

Me gustaría hacer el mismo viaje.
¿Qué me recomiendas?
¿Por qué?

Me gusta...
Prefiero ir a la montaña/al mar...
En mi último viaje fui a...

Although **azafato** is a valid term, many native speakers who use **azafata** for females prefer the term **auxiliar de vuelo** for males.

Practice more at **vhlcentral.com.**

SAM: Actividades pp. 270–272

Recomendar

- ¿Conoces Cuba?
- Te la recomiendo; yo que tú iría allí de vacaciones.
- ¿Alguna vez ha visitado las playas dominicanas?
- Sí, se las recomiendo. Son hermosas.

13A.3 **(no) te lo recomiendo**
yo que tú / yo en tu lugar + [*conditional*]

Vocabulario *cont.*

enseñar *to show*
el mojito *traditional Cuban cocktail*
el/la cubano/a, excelente

11

el/la auxiliar de vuelo *flight attendant*

12

el viaje de novios *honeymoon*
proponer (ng) *to propose, to suggest*
apuntarse a *to sign up for*

13

perder (e:ie) un vuelo *to miss a flight*
reservar los billetes *to book the tickets*
el cambio de asiento *seat change*
la(s) plaza(s) *seat(s)*
demasiado *too*

Estrategia

Dar una explicación

Como ya conocía La Habana, esta vez fuimos a otras ciudades. **Es que** me gusta conocer nuevos lugares.

¡OJO!

The neutral terms usually used to refer to flight attendants in Spanish-speaking countries are **auxiliar de vuelo** or **tripulante de cabina de pasajeros** (**TCP**). These professionals are also known as **aeromozos/as** in most of Latin America. In Argentina and Spain, however, the most widespread term is **azafato/a**, a word of Arabic origin that was used to refer to some of the attendants of the Queen of Spain.

Nelson y Edgar, bienvenidos a bordo

Suggestion Before they read the interview, have students state their opinions about the positive and negative aspects of working as a flight attendant.

Nelson Morales y Edgar Hugo Torrico, Jefes de cabina de AeroSur, la aerolínea boliviana

Estamos con Nelson Morales y Edgar Hugo Torrico, dos jefes de cabina de AeroSur. Hoy cumplen 10 años en la empresa...

NELSON *¡Exacto! Comenzamos como tripulantes de cabina de pasajeros el mismo día. Los dos estábamos muy nerviosos, pero nos dábamos ánimo y así nos hicimos amigos. Ahora tenemos diferentes trayectos, pero cuando hacemos escala en la misma ciudad intentamos almorzar o tomar un café juntos.*

¿Y por qué eligieron esta profesión?

EDGAR *Porque nos encanta. Es fantástico poder viajar por todo el mundo, conocer otras culturas... ¡Es una aventura diaria! Nelson y yo somos psicólogos, meseros, recepcionistas, enfermeros, bomberos, limpiadores... Nunca te aburres. ¡Se lo recomiendo a todo el mundo!*

Parece ser el trabajo ideal. ¿Tiene algún aspecto negativo?

NELSON *A veces debemos mostrar nuestra cara menos amable con peticiones como: "¿Podría regresar a su asiento?" o "¿Le importaría apagar su celular?" Es que una de las mayores responsabilidades para los tripulantes de cabina es la seguridad.*

EDGAR *Además, es una profesión sin horarios que da muchas satisfacciones, pero también exige sacrificios. Es que a veces estás de mal humor o extrañas a tu familia, y aún así debes sonreír.*

¿Y cómo es para sus familias tenerlos casi siempre lejos?

NELSON *Bueno, en mi caso es un poco más fácil porque soy soltero. Voy a visitar a mis padres y a mis hermanos cada vez que vuelo a Lima. Para Edgar es un poco más complicado...*

EDGAR *Así es. A veces estoy de viaje varias semanas y extraño mucho a mi señora y a mis hijas, que viven en La Paz. Pero las llamo por teléfono todos los días. Por suerte ellas comprenden que esta es mi vocación y me apoyan.*

Muchas gracias, caballeros. ¡Que tengan un feliz vuelo!

Desear buen viaje

¡Que tengan un feliz vuelo y que disfruten a bordo!

13A.4 **que tengan/disfruten...**

Vocabulario

(15)

- **a bordo** *on board*
- **el/la jefe/a de cabina** *purser*
- **cumplir** *to reach; to fulfill*
- **dar ánimo** *to offer encouragement*
- **el trayecto** *route*
- **hacer escala** *to stop over*
- **diario/a** *everyday, daily*
- **el/la mesero/a** (*Amér. L.*) *waiter/waitress*
- **la petición** *request*
- **el asiento** *seat*
- **la seguridad** *safety*
- **exigir (j) sacrificios** *to require sacrifices*
- **extrañar** (*Amér. L.*) *to miss*

15a Son jefes de cabina. Su profesión consiste en hacer el vuelo más cómodo y seguro. Comenzaron como tripulantes de cabina de pasajeros el mismo día y se hicieron amigos.

15 a. Observe el título y la foto. ¿En qué consiste la profesión de Nelson y Edgar? Lea la entrevista. ¿Qué tienen en común los dos protagonistas?

15b **Suggestion** Ask students to think of other professions in which one has to fulfill a variety of functions.

b. Haga una lista de las tareas que tienen los auxiliares de vuelo. Relacione las tareas con las funciones que Edgar menciona. ¿Está de acuerdo con él?
psicólogo, mesero, recepcionista, enfermero, bombero, limpiador

16 a. ¿Qué peticiones menciona Nelson en la entrevista? Relacione ahora estas peticiones con las imágenes. ¿Podría regresar a su asiento? ¿Le importaría apagar su celular?

Compruebe [2] Apague [3] Abróchese [1]

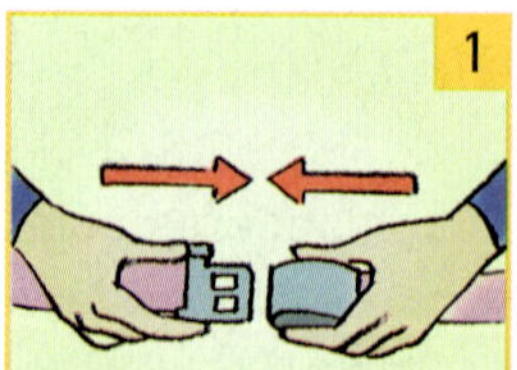
1 ... el cinturón de seguridad.

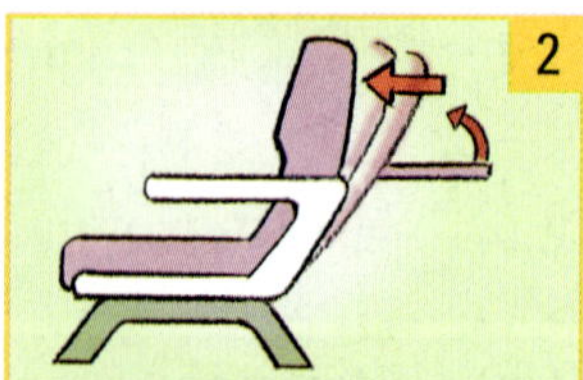
2 ... que el respaldo de su asiento esté en posición vertical y su mesa plegada.

3 ... el celular y los aparatos electrónicos.

b. Marque las oraciones que se pueden usar para desear un buen vuelo.

- ¡Bienvenidos! [ ]
- ¡Les deseamos un feliz vuelo! [✓]
- ¡Que tengan un buen viaje! [✓]
- ¡Que tengan suerte! [ ]

Vocabulario *cont.*

sonreír (e:i) *to smile*
apoyar *to support*
el caballero *gentleman*
¡Que tengan un feliz vuelo! *Have a good flight!*
¡Que disfruten a bordo! *Enjoy your flight!*

16
comprobar (o:ue) *to check*
abrocharse *to fasten*
el cinturón de seguridad *seatbelt*
el respaldo del asiento *seat back*
vertical *upright*
plegado/a *folded*

17
el ómnibus (*Arg.*) *bus*
(semi-)cama *(semi-)sleeper*
amabilísimo/a *very friendly*
la gaseosa (*Amér. L.*) *soda*
al horno *baked*
exquisito/a *delicious*
retirar *to remove*
el estuche *case*
la pantalla *screen*
abrigarse *to wrap up*
la frazada (*Amér. L.*) *blanket*
hacer fila *to get/wait in line*
árido/a

19
la aerolínea abanderada *national airline*
nacional *domestic*
privatizado/a

OPINIÓN

¿Cree que la calidad del servicio que ofrecen las aerolíneas refleja la cultura del país que representan? ¿Por qué?

18 Suggestion Tell students to re-read the story on this page to get ideas, but encourage them to be creative and original with their stories.

17 a. Lea este artículo sobre la experiencia de viajar en un ómnibus de larga distancia en Argentina. ¿Alguna vez hizo un viaje largo en autobús? Comente sus experiencias con un(a) compañero/a.

UNA EXPERIENCIA DE LARGA DISTANCIA

Son las 19:45 en Buenos Aires. Es hora de subir al ómnibus de larga distancia para recorrer los 1300 kilómetros que me separan de Puerto Madryn, provincia de Chubut, en la Patagonia argentina. No me gusta mucho la idea de viajar durante 17 horas, pero un amigo me dijo que pasan rápido en un ómnibus cama. Una azafata amabilísima me ofrece unos chocolates, me pregunta si quiero beber vino, agua, jugo o alguna gaseosa, y me deja el menú. Decido que voy a cenar carne al horno con papas y una ensalada de fruta. Otras opciones eran un plato vegetariano o una cena *kosher*. Pienso que sería una buena idea lavarme las manos. Cuando regreso del baño, la mesa ya está lista. Disfruto de la exquisita cena mientras escucho música. Cuando termino, la azafata retira los platos. Luego me pasa un estuche con al menos diez DVD para que elija una película, y me ofrece un licor o un café. Le digo que así estoy bien y enciendo la pantalla. Cuando termina la película, me lavo los dientes, coloco mi asiento en posición horizontal, me abrigo con la frazada que me dieron y me quedo dormido.

Me despierto varias horas más tarde. Ya no hay tráfico ni luces brillantes. El paisaje es árido, casi desértico, y no veo ninguna ciudad en el horizonte. Aparece otra azafata que me pregunta si dormí bien y si quiero tomar el desayuno. Me ofrece té o café con leche, y unas galletas. ¡Qué suerte que elegí un ómnibus cama y no uno semi-cama, o uno tradicional! Estoy muy descansado. Enciendo el radio y escucho que afuera hace mucho frío. Busco mi computadora portátil y me conecto a Internet. Justo cuando respondo mi último correo, la azafata me dice que estamos llegando a destino. Guardo mis cosas, me pongo de pie y hago fila para bajar. La verdad es que mi amigo tenía razón, el viaje pasó rápido, ya estoy en Puerto Madryn. Tomo un taxi y me dirijo al hotel. Acaban de comenzar mis vacaciones.

b. Conteste las preguntas.

17a Expansion Have students imagine that they took this trip; ask them to rate the following aspects in order of the most important to the least important: entertainment, service, sleeping arrangements, food.

1. ¿Qué le preocupaba al autor acerca de su viaje? Era un viaje de 17 horas.
2. ¿Qué servicios ofrecía el ómnibus? Sample answer: servicio de azafata, cena, baño, música, películas, cafetería, frazada, desayuno, radio, Internet
3. ¿Qué diferencia hay entre un ómnibus cama y un ómnibus tradicional? Sample answer: El asiento del ómnibus cama se puede colocar en posición horizontal para dormir.

c. ¿Le gustaría hacer un viaje en ómnibus cama? ¿Cuáles son sus ventajas?

18 Escriba un breve relato sobre un viaje imaginario muy largo en un ómnibus tradicional o semi-cama.

19 a. ¿Sabe qué es una *aerolínea de bandera*? Lea el artículo.

En algunos países el estado es propietario, total o parcial, de una de las aerolíneas que funcionan en su territorio. Esas aerolíneas reciben el nombre de *abanderadas* o *de bandera*, y generalmente son las encargadas de todos los vuelos nacionales. Algunas de estas empresas han sido privatizadas, pero todavía representan a sus países. Entre las más conocidas del mundo hispanoamericano están Aerolíneas Argentinas, Cubana de Aviación e Iberia.

b. ¿Conoce otras aerolíneas de bandera? Busque en Internet los nombres de otras tres aerolíneas latinoamericanas. ¿Qué países representan?

Practice more at **vhlcentral.com.**

SAM: Actividades pp. 273–276

20 a. Lea los avisos sobre tres rutas turísticas.

EL FIN DEL MUNDO

¿Le gustaría ver los mismos paisajes, escuchar los mismos sonidos y tener las mismas sensaciones que el famoso navegante Magallanes°? ¡Esta es su oportunidad! Puede hacerlo en un moderno catamarán, en un histórico barco de madera o en un romántico velero°. Descubrirá los misterios del canal Beagle, el archipiélago de las islas Bridges, el faro° del fin del mundo y una reserva natural con 3000 pingüinos. ¿Se lo va a perder?

UNA NOCHE BIEN "CHIVA"

¿Alguna vez has bailado en un autobús abierto, sin ventanillas y sin puertas? ¡Te lo recomendamos! Ven a Cartagena y da un paseo en una chiva° colombiana ambientada como discoteca, con luces, humo° y pista de baile°. Puedes tomar algo mientras escuchas música y recorres los barrios más divertidos de la ciudad. ¡Pasarás una noche única e inolvidable°!

Chivas are also known as **escaleras,** since they traditionally have a ladder to the roof, where passengers' belongings or merchandise are stored. These brightly painted buses were first introduced in Colombia in the early 20th century and remain a symbol of rural Colombian culture.

EL CAMINO DE SANTIAGO

Cada año, muchísimos peregrinos recorren a pie los caminos° de toda Europa para visitar los restos° del apóstol° Santiago. De todos los caminos, el más popular es el *Camino francés*. Te invitamos a recorrerlo este verano... ¡en bici! Partiremos de Roncesvalles y viajaremos por todo el norte de España hasta llegar a la maravillosa basílica°. Son 744 kilómetros de desafíos°, alegrías y muchísimo pedaleo°. ¡Acompáñanos!

El Camino ends at Santiago de Compostela's famous cathedral, where St. James's remains are said to be kept in a silver coffer.

Magallanes *Magellan* **velero** *sailing ship* **faro** *lighthouse* **chiva (*Col.*)** *country bus* **humo** *smoke* **pista de baile** *dance floor* **inolvidable** *unforgettable* **caminos** *paths* **restos** *remains* **apóstol** *apostle* **basílica** *basilica* **desafíos** *challenges* **pedaleo** *pedaling*

b. Elija uno de los anuncios turísticos y escriba un correo electrónico a un amigo para recomendarle el viaje.

20b Suggestions
- Have students review the expressions on page 313.
- If needed, have students research more about the chosen destination.

TAREA FINAL

El mejor destino para un viaje

- Piense en sus viajes favoritos y escriba un breve relato.
- Pongan en común sus relatos y en pequeños grupos elijan un lugar para recomendar al resto de la clase.
- Piensen en el medio de transporte en el que van a hacer el viaje y en el itinerario que quieren proponer. Expliquen los motivos de su elección.
- Compartan sus opiniones y decidan cuáles son los tres mejores destinos.

YO PUEDO...

- Puedo pedir y confirmar información.
  Busque una agencia de viajes especializada en viajes al Caribe. Infórmese si hay aeropuerto en un lugar que elija y confirme los datos que conoce.
- Puedo describir experiencias pasadas.
  Hable de un viaje muy especial y describa los distintos aspectos (alojamiento, comida, gente, etc.).
- Puedo recomendar algo a alguien.
  Recomiende a su compañero/a un lugar de vacaciones que usted conoce bien.
- Puedo desear buen viaje.
  Su profesor(a) vuela mañana; deséele un buen viaje.

GRAMÁTICA FUNCIONAL

Suggestion Have pairs of students write a conversation between a new student on campus and a person at the information desk, using these expressions.

13A.1 Ask for and confirm information

¿Sabe + si/dónde/cuándo...?
¿Puede/Podría/Le importaría + [*infinitive*] + si/dónde/cuándo...? 5.13, 5.17, 5.17.1, 5.17.2, 12.8

- There are several ways to politely request and confirm information in Spanish.

  ¿**Podría decirme cómo** llegar al control de pasaportes?
  Could you tell me how to get to the passport check?

  ¿**Sabes si** ya empezaron el embarque del vuelo 417?
  Do you know if they've already started boarding flight 417?

- To make a polite request for information, transform an information question using the constructions **¿Sabe(n)** (*Do you know*) + [*question*]?, **¿Puede(n) decirme** (*Can you tell me*) + [*question*]?, or **¿Le(s) importaría decirme** (*Would you mind telling me*) + [*question*]?

¿Dónde está el baño? *Where is the bathroom?*	¿**Sabe** dónde está el baño? ¿**Puede decirme** dónde está el baño? ¿**Le importaría decirme** dónde está el baño?

- Remember to always use a written accent on question words such as **cómo, cuándo, dónde,** etc.
- To politely confirm information, transform a yes-or-no question using the constructions **¿Sabe(n) + si** (*if, whether*) + [*question*]?, **¿Puede(n) decirme + si** + [*question*]?, or **¿Le(s) importaría decirme + si** + [*question*]?

¿Llegó el vuelo 302? *Did flight 302 arrive?*	¿**Sabe si** llegó el vuelo 302? ¿**Puede decirme si** llegó el vuelo 302? ¿**Le importaría decirme si** llegó el vuelo 302?

- In addition to **decir**, you can use other reporting verbs such as **confirmar** and **explicar** in this construction.
- To make a more formal request, use the conditional form **¿Podría(n)...?** (*Could you . . . ?*) instead of **¿Puede(n)...?** (*Can you . . . ?*).

13A.2 Describe a trip

Review of past tenses: use of the preterite to give opinions 5.2.3, 5.4.3, 5.6, 5.8.2, 5.11.1

- Use the **pretérito indefinido** of the verbs and constructions **ser, parecer** + [*adjective*], and **gustar/encantar** in order to give opinions about a past experience.

  El viaje **fue** increíble.
  *The trip **was** incredible.*

  El hotel **nos pareció** muy bonito.
  ***We thought** that the hotel was very nice.*

  Nos encantó hacer una visita guiada de la ciudad.
  ***We loved** taking a guided tour of the city.*

¡Póngalo en práctica!

G1 Complete la conversación entre Paula y el responsable del quiosco de información.

¿(1)......Puede/Podría...... (Poder, usted) confirmarme la hora de salida del vuelo 5544?

Sí, a las 19:45 h.

¿(2)......Sabe...... (Saber, usted) cuál es la puerta de embarque?

Sí, es la puerta 22.

Gracias, y ¿puede decirme (3)......cómo...... llegar hasta allí?

Sí, tiene que seguir el pasillo a la derecha hasta el fondo.

Le hago una última pregunta. ¿Le importaría decirme (4)......cuándo/a qué hora...... llega el vuelo de Ciudad de Guatemala?

Sí. Tiene prevista su llegada a las 18:00 h.

G1 Expansion Have volunteers read the dialogue aloud.

G2 Suggestion For each item, have students identify why either tense was used.

G2 Complete las oraciones con la forma correcta del verbo en el **pretérito indefinido** o el **pretérito imperfecto.**

- ¿Cómo te (1)......fue...... (ir) en Perú, Antonio? ¿En qué parte del país (2)......estuviste...... (estar)?
- En Cuzco, cerca de Machu Picchu. (3)......Fue...... (Ser) una experiencia estupenda. Las ruinas nos (4)......parecieron...... (parecer) increíbles, pero el alojamiento no nos (5)......gustó...... (gustar) mucho. (6)......Estaba...... (Estar) muy lejos del centro. Eso (7)......fue...... (ser) lo único malo. Lo bueno es que (8)......había...... (haber) gente de todo el mundo.

Practice more at **vhlcentral.com.**

13A

GRAMÁTICA FUNCIONAL

Suggestion Have pairs of students take turns asking each other where they do various activities in the community (Ex: **comer comida japonesa, comprar champú**). They should either express agreement with their partner's preference (**¿Ah, sí? Yo también...**), or make a recommendation using the expressions from **13A.3**.

13A.3 Make recommendations

(no) te lo recomiendo 6.8
yo que tú/yo en tu lugar + [*conditional*] 5.17, 5.17.1

- Use the **e→ie** stem-changing verb **recomendar** to give recommendations.

  ¿Viajar a Costa Rica? **Te lo recomiendo.**
  *Traveling to Costa Rica? **I recommend it (to you).***

- Use the indirect object pronoun **te** followed by the neuter pronoun **lo** (*it*) to refer to general actions or ideas without relating them to a specific object or concrete example. When referring to a specific place or thing, use a direct object pronoun that agrees with this object (**lo, la, los, las**).

  Las empanadas son riquísimas. Te **las** recomiendo.
  *The empanadas are delicious. I recommend **them** (to you).*

- To make the same recommendation in a formal setting, use the **usted** form of the indirect object pronoun and say **Se lo/la/los/las recomiendo.**

- To say what you would do, use the construction **yo que tú/usted** or **yo en tu/su lugar** (*if I were you*) + [*conditional*].

  Yo que tú viajaría a Buenos Aires.
  ***If I were you, I would travel** to Buenos Aires.*

- The conditional (**condicional simple**) is a one-word tense equivalent to the English *would* + [*verb*].

  Yo en su lugar **iría** en coche y **evitaría** el tren.
  *If I were you, **I would go** by car and **I'd avoid** the train.*

- Form the conditional of regular verbs by adding the conditional endings to the infinitive. Note that all forms carry a written accent. The endings are the same for **-ar**, **-er**, and **-ir** verbs.

	VIAJAR	COMER	IR
(yo)	viaj**aría**	com**ería**	**iría**
(tú)	viaj**arías**	com**erías**	**irías**
(usted, él, ella)	viaj**aría**	com**ería**	**iría**
(nosotros/as)	viaj**aríamos**	com**eríamos**	**iríamos**
(vosotros/as)	viaj**aríais**	com**eríais**	**iríais**
(ustedes, ellos/as)	viaj**arían**	com**erían**	**irían**

13A.4 Wish someone a good trip

que tenga(n)/disfrute(n) 5.21.1, 14.26

- To tell someone to have a good trip, say **¡Buen viaje!** (*Have a good trip!/Bon voyage!*). If the person is traveling on an airplane, say **¡Feliz vuelo!** (*Have a good flight!*).

- You can also use the following expressions: **¡Que tenga(n) un feliz vuelo!** (*Hope you have a good flight!*) and **¡Que disfrute(n) del viaje!** (*Hope you enjoy your trip!*).

Tell students that a traditional greeting for pilgrims on **El Camino de Santiago** is **¡Buen camino!**

G3 Expansion Have pairs of students write mini-dialogues using the answers, but with different direct objects. Ex: **¿Me recomiendas la aerolínea de bandera? No, no te la recomiendo. ¿Por qué? Ah, porque no hay vuelos directos. Todos hacen escala.**

¡Póngalo en práctica!

G3 Escriba la recomendación correcta según las pistas.

Modelo: esta empresa / a usted
Se la recomiendo.

1. esa playa / a ti Te la recomiendo.
2. ese hotel / a usted Se lo recomiendo.
3. los plátanos fritos / a ti Te los recomiendo.
4. las clases de salsa / a usted Se las recomiendo.
5. este postre / a ti Te lo recomiendo.
6. esa excursión / a usted Se la recomiendo.

G4 Complete la conversación.

- Quiero viajar a las islas Canarias en agosto, ¿qué opinan?
- No te (1) lo recomiendo; hay muchísimos turistas. Viaja en invierno; es la época ideal. Yo que (2) tú en agosto (3) iría (ir) a los Pirineos.
- ¡Ah! ¡El sur de Portugal! ¡Es espectacular! Te lo (4) recomiendo. Yo en tu (5) lugar, (6) viajaría (viajar) allí.

G5 Escriba la forma correcta del condicional.

1. yo, comprar	compraría
2. Delfina, hablar	hablaría
3. nosotros, leer	leeríamos
4. tú, descansar	descansarías
5. vosotros, estudiar	estudiaríais
6. los profesores, dar	darían
7. ustedes, alquilar	alquilarían
8. yo, recomendar	recomendaría

G5 Expansion Have students write a sentence for each verb form.

G6 Complete las oraciones.

Señores pasajeros, gracias por volar con nosotros. En nombre de toda la tripulación, que (1) tengan un feliz vuelo y (2) que disfruten del viaje.

- Mañana salimos para el Caribe.
- (3) ¡Buen viaje!/¡Feliz vuelo!/¡Que tengan un feliz vuelo!/¡Que disfruten del viaje!

Practice more at **vhlcentral.com.**

VOCABULARIO

Señores pasajeros

¿Le importaría...?	*Would you mind . . . ?*
señores pasajeros	*passengers:/ladies and gentlemen:*
el altavoz	*speaker*
el andén	*platform*
el cambio de dinero	*foreign currency exchange*
el carrito	*trolley*
la confirmación	*confirmation*
el control de equipaje	*baggage screening*
el control de pasaportes	*passport control; immigration*
el destino	*destination*
las divisas	*foreign currency*
el embarque	*boarding*
la entrega de equipaje	*baggage claim*
la facturación	*check-in*
la frecuencia	*frequency*
la hora de embarque	*boarding time*
la hora de llegada	*arrival time*
la hora de salida	*departure time*
el mostrador de facturación	*check-in desk*
la observación	*remark*
el origen	*origin*
la puerta de embarque	*boarding gate*
el/la responsable	*person in charge*
la sala de llegada	*arrival lounge/area*
el/la supervisor(a)	*supervisor*
la tarifa	*fare*
la terminal	*terminal*
confirmar	*to confirm*
salir (lg)	*to depart*
cancelado/a	*cancelled*
procedente de	*arriving from*
con retraso	*delayed*

Rincones escondidos

el/la auxiliar de vuelo	*flight attendant*
el cambio de asiento	*seat change*
la casa particular	*private home*
el/la cubano/a	*Cuban person*
el mojito	*tradicional Cuban cocktail*
la(s) plaza(s)	*seat(s)*
el rincón	*corner; spot*
el viaje de novios	*honeymoon*
el viaje organizado	*package tour*
alojarse	*to stay*
apuntarse a	*to sign up for*
averiarse	*to break down*
bañarse	*to go for a swim*
enseñar	*to show*
perder (e:ie) un vuelo	*to miss a flight*
preparar un viaje	*to organize a trip*
proponer (ng)	*to propose, to suggest*
recomendar (e:ie) (un lugar)	*to recommend (a place)*
reservar los billetes	*to book the tickets*
trasladar	*to transport*
excelente	*excellent*
hermoso/a	*lovely*
hospitalario/a	*hospitable*
demasiado	*too*

Nelson y Edgar

a bordo	*on board*
¡Que disfruten a bordo!	*Enjoy your flight!*
¡Que tengan un feliz vuelo!	*Have a good flight!*
la aerolínea abanderada	*national airline*
el asiento	*seat*
el caballero	*gentleman*
el cinturón de seguridad	*seatbelt*
el estuche	*case*
la frazada (*Amér. L.*)	*blanket*
la gaseosa (*Amér. L.*)	*soda*
el/la jefe/a de cabina	*purser*
el/la mesero/a (*Amér. L.*)	*waiter/waitress*
el ómnibus (*Arg.*)	*bus*
la pantalla	*screen*
la petición	*request*
el respaldo del asiento	*seat back*
la seguridad	*safety*
el trayecto	*route*
abrigarse	*to wrap up*
abrocharse	*to fasten*
apoyar	*to support*
comprobar (o:ue)	*to check*
cumplir	*to reach; to fulfill*
dar ánimo	*to offer encouragement*
exigir (j) sacrificios	*to require sacrifices*
extrañar (*Amér. L.*)	*to miss*
hacer escala	*to stop over*
hacer fila	*to get/wait in line*
retirar	*to remove*
sonreír (e:i)	*to smile*
amabilísimo/a	*very friendly*
árido/a	*arid*
(semi-)cama	*(semi-)sleeper*
diario/a	*everyday, daily*
nacional	*domestic*
exquisito/a	*delicious*
plegado/a	*folded*
privatizado/a	*privatized*
vertical	*upright*
al horno	*baked*

Variación léxica

el/la auxiliar de vuelo ⟷ **el/la azafato/a** (*Arg., Esp.*) ⟷ **el/la tripulante de cabina de pasajeros** (*Amér. L.*)

la entrega de equipaje ⟷ **la recogida de equipajes** (*Esp.*) ⟷ **el retiro de equipaje** (*Arg.*)

extrañar (*Amér. L.*) ⟷ **echar de menos** (*Esp.*)

la frazada (*Amér. L.*) ⟷ **la manta** (*Esp.*) ⟷ **la cobija** (*Amér. L.*)

hacer fila ⟷ **hacer cola**

nacional ⟷ **interno/a** ⟷ **de cabotaje** (*Arg.*)

el viaje de novios ⟷ **la luna de miel**

13B

Suggestion Read the blog title aloud and explain the play on words with **sobrevivir** and **vivir**.

MUNDO TECNOLÓGICO

¿Imprescindibles?

@ Cómopodíamossobrevivirsinellos.com

INICIO | ACERCA DE... | CONTACTO | ARCHIVO | ENLACES | FOTOS | VIDEOS

¿Cómo podíamos (sobre)vivir antes sin ellos?

3 ***iPod*** Este pequeño aparato que se puede llevar en el bolsillo fue una revolución porque permitía escuchar música en todas partes, no ocupaba espacio y tenía mucha capacidad. Cambió nuestro modo de escuchar música. A pesar de todo, algunos nostálgicos prefieren el disco de vinilo o el CD porque permiten escuchar música en compañía y sin tanto aislamiento social. ¡Imprescindible en muchos momentos de placer!

1 **GPS** Los primeros se construyeron en los años ochenta; sin embargo, no empezaron a fabricarse en serie en los coches hasta principios del siglo XXI. Llegas antes a tu destino y ya no tienes las típicas tensiones del viaje o de si vas a llegar o no. Aunque hay quienes prefieren no usarlos porque son una causa de distracción, sin duda son imprescindibles para muchos.

1

2

3

4

4 ***Wi-Fi*** Aunque al principio no era fácil encontrar lugares desde donde conectarse a Internet sin cables, finalmente se transformó en moneda corriente en aeropuertos, hoteles, universidades, empresas y hogares. A pesar de ofrecer menor seguridad y velocidad, hoy es imprescindible porque es sinónimo de movilidad y libertad.

Suggestion Take a quick survey of the class to find out which of these devices they use.

2 **Teléfono inteligente** Al principio tenía menos capacidad y solo lo usábamos para hablar. Ahora puedes escuchar música, guardar canciones y fotos, enviar correos... A pesar de ser muy útil, tiene su lado malo. Ahora estamos siempre localizables. ¿Han mejorado realmente nuestras vidas? ¿Son tan imprescindibles un *iPhone* o un *BlackBerry*?

Describir situaciones y causas en el pasado

- ¿Por qué **compraste** el GPS?
- **Porque** siempre **me perdía**.

13B.1 Review of past tenses
porque + [*imperfect*]

Vocabulario

1

- **imprescindible** *indispensable*
- **sobrevivir** *to survive*
- **el bolsillo** *pocket*
- **tener capacidad** *to have (storage) capacity*
- **ocupar espacio** *to take up space*
- **a pesar de todo** *despite it all*
- **el disco de vinilo** *vinyl record*
- **el aislamiento** *isolation*
- **sin embargo** *however*

1 Observe las imágenes. ¿Qué tecnologías muestran? Lea el blog y relacione las imágenes con las descripciones. ¿Cuál de estas u otras tecnologías es imprescindible para usted? ¿Cómo y por qué empezó a usarla?
1. GPS, 2. teléfono inteligente, 3. iPod, 4. *Wi-Fi*

2 El dominio del inglés como lengua internacional de la ciencia, la tecnología y las comunicaciones lleva a la utilización de muchas palabras de ese idioma en español. Describa para qué sirven estas tecnologías.

- red Wi-Fi
- *iPhone*
- *iPod*
- navegador GPS

3 Relacione estos acontecimientos con sus causas.

1. Mi empresa me dio un teléfono inteligente ..d..
2. Empecé a usar una red Wi-Fi ..c..
3. Pensé que el GPS era más seguro ..a..
4. Me pareció bien tener un *iPod* ..b..

a. porque no tenías que mirar un plano.
b. porque puedes guardar música y muchas cosas más.
c. porque podía estar conectado siempre, tanto en el jardín de casa como en un bar.
d. porque necesitaban poder localizarme siempre.

4 Con su compañero/a, nombre otros dos aparatos tecnológicos sin los cuales no se puede (sobre)vivir en la actualidad. Expliquen su utilidad y describan cómo era la vida sin ellos en el pasado.

Relacionar ideas contrarias

- A pesar de no necesitar el GPS, lo compré. Aunque era un poco caro, valió la pena.
- Es un poco caro; sin embargo, es útil.

13B.2 **a pesar de, aunque, sin embargo**

Vocabulario ***cont.***

aunque *although*
ser moneda corriente *to be common*
la velocidad *speed*
la movilidad *mobility*
fabricar en serie *to mass produce*
la libertad *freedom*
el teléfono inteligente *smartphone*
guardar (canciones/fotos) *to save/store (songs/photos)*
el lado malo *bad side*
estar localizable *to be reachable*
la distracción, la revolución, la tecnología

2

la red Wi-Fi *Wi-Fi network*
el navegador GPS *GPS*

3

estar conectado/a *to be connected (to the Internet)*
localizar *to get hold of, to locate*

5

la ventaja *advantage*
el inconveniente *drawback*

6

el reproductor de MP3 *MP3 player*
la red social *social network*
la diversidad *diversity*
la pobreza *mediocrity*
estar acostumbrado/a a *to be used to*
la abreviatura *abbreviation*
la vocal *vowel*
el código *code*
la taquigrafía *stenography*
sintetizar

7

el lector de libros electrónicos *e-reader*

5 a. Busque en el blog las ventajas y los inconvenientes de estas tecnologías.

	Ventajas	Inconvenientes
1. red Wi-Fi	*movilidad y libertad siempre*	*menor seguridad y velocidad*
2. teléfono inteligente	muy útil	estar siempre localizable
3. *iPod*	escuchar música en todas partes, no ocupa espacio, gran capacidad	aislamiento social
4. navegador GPS	llegar antes al destino, no hay tensiones de viaje	causa de distracción

b. Compare las ventajas y los inconvenientes y forme oraciones.

- red Wi-Fi: A pesar de ser...
- teléfono inteligente: Aunque...
- *iPod*: ...; sin embargo,...
- navegador GPS: A pesar de todo,...

6 Lea los intercambios sobre algunos avances tecnológicos. Dé su propio punto de vista relacionando las ideas contrarias con **aunque, sin embargo** y **a pesar de**. ¿Qué opina su compañero/a? **Expansion** Have students choose one of the quotes and debate the issue in groups.

Modelo: *Aunque es cierto que..., creo que... porque...*

Internet, los *iPod* y los reproductores de MP3 provocan el aislamiento social. De hecho, muchos jóvenes pasan horas y horas en su habitación frente a una computadora.

El acceso a redes sociales en Internet y en los celulares aumenta el número y la diversidad de contactos de la gente. La comunicación más habitual con familiares y amigos sigue siendo en persona.

Otro problema es la pobreza lingüística de los estudiantes. Acostumbrados a sintetizar los mensajes, usan un lenguaje con muchas abreviaturas, y sin comas, acentos ni vocales.

Cada uno sabe en qué contexto debe utilizar uno u otro código. En los SMS y en los correos electrónicos, este lenguaje permite ahorrar tiempo y dinero. Es una nueva forma de taquigrafía.

MI EXPERIENCIA

7 Hable con sus compañeros sobre la última novedad tecnológica que comenzó a usar. ¿Por qué la usa? Señale sus ventajas e inconvenientes.

GUIÓN DE TRABAJO

¿Qué nuevo aparato tecnológico has empezado a usar últimamente? → Un GPS. Un *iPod*. Un lector de libros electrónicos.

¿Por qué? → Empecé a usarlo/la porque... | podía... no tenía que... necesitaba...

¿Es útil? → Aunque...; sin embargo,... A pesar de ser... Sí, mucho. A pesar de todo, antes vivíamos sin ellos.

Para mí es imprescindible un teléfono inteligente.

Practice more at **vhlcentral.com.**

SAM: Actividades pp. 277–279

13B

Contrast the use of **Solo** in the first box and **sola** in the second box. Have a volunteer explain the difference in usage.

¿Un buen equipo?

contador

Ramón: Es serio y metódico. Su jefe está encantado con él, pero sus compañeros piensan que es un poco aburrido. Solo hay una cosa que no le gusta de su trabajo: las horas extras.

analista de *marketing*

Rosa: Dinámica e innovadora. A veces es demasiado impaciente, sobre todo con su jefe, que por cierto es su ex. Quiere abrir su propia empresa porque prefiere trabajar sola.

ejecutiva de ventas

Olga: No soporta la desorganización. Aunque es un poco tímida, le gusta trabajar en equipo, sobre todo con Rosa. Es muy ordenada y puntual.

director

Jaume: Es el ex de Rosa. Es un gran comunicador y muy bromista, aunque sus bromas solamente le parecen divertidas a él. Le encanta su trabajo. Sus empleados piensan que es un tirano.

Expresar posesión

- Mis compañeros de trabajo son estupendos, ¿y **los tuyos**?
- **Los míos** también.

13B.3 Possessive adjectives and pronouns

Vocabulario

8

- el/la contador(a) (*Amér. L.*) *accountant*
- serio/a *serious; reliable*
- solo/solamente *only*
- el/la analista de *marketing* *marketing analyst*
- sobre todo *above all*
- por cierto *incidentally*
- el/la ejecutivo/a de ventas *sales executive*
- ordenado/a *orderly, neat*
- ser un(a) gran comunicador(a) *to be a great communicator*
- bromista *fond of joking*
- el/la tirano/a *tyrant*
- **metódico/a, innovador/a, impaciente, puntual**

9

- discutir *to argue*
- hacer horas extras *to do overtime*
- comprensivo/a *understanding*
- No te preocupes. *Don't worry.*
- Te entiendo perfectamente. *I understand you perfectly.*
- No pasa nada. *Everything is OK.*
- estar motivado/a *to be motivated*
- desagradable *unkind*
- Siento verte así. *I'm sorry to see you like this.*

8 Lea las descripciones y subraye los adjetivos que indican cómo son estas personas. ¿Cree que su perfil es adecuado a su puesto?

8 Expansion As a class, come up with two additional adjectives that might describe each person.

9 a. Escuche las conversaciones y complete la información. Lea de nuevo las descripciones si es necesario.

	¿Quién habla?	¿De qué hablan?
Conversación 1	Rosa y un amigo	del trato del jefe de Rosa en la empresa
Conversación 2	Jaume y una amiga	del trato de los empleados y compañeros de trabajo en la empresa de cada uno

b. ¿Coinciden las opiniones de los empleados y de su jefe? Vuelva a escuchar las conversaciones y elija la opción correcta en cada caso. No.

1

- ¿En tu/tuya empresa tenéis que hacer horas extras?
- No, en mi/mía empresa no.
- Nuestro jefe es un tirano. El vuestro/vuestra es más comprensivo. Yo con el mío/mi, además, no me llevo bien.
- Bueno, Rosa, no te preocupes.
- Quiero tener mi empresa, con mis ideas, no las suyas/sus.
- Te entiendo perfectamente.

2

- ¡Hola, Jaume! ¿Cómo estás?
- Bien, vengo de la oficina.
- ¿A estas horas? ¡Es tardísimo!
- Sí, pero no pasa nada. Mis/Mi empleados están muy motivados y quieren hacer horas extras. Y tú, ¿qué tal en tu/tuyo nuevo trabajo?
- No muy bien, mis compañeros son un poco desagradables.
- Siento verte así, no todas las empresas tienen tan buenos empleados como los míos/mis.

10 Entreviste a un(a) compañero/a de su grupo, acerca de su familia y sus intereses. Luego comente los resultados con el grupo, siguiendo el modelo.

Modelo:
- *Mi hermana tiene catorce años, pero la suya tiene doce. /*
- *Su hermana tiene doce años, pero la mía tiene catorce.*

Cuestionario:

1. ¿Cuántos años tiene tu hermano/a?
2. ¿Cómo se llaman tus padres?
3. ¿Quién es la persona más bromista de tu familia?
4. ¿Cómo te llevas con tus vecinos?
5. ¿Cuál es tu clase más divertida?

Consolar y animar

- Siento oír eso/verte así.
- Gracias.
- No te preocupes, no pasa nada.
- Estoy cansada de trabajar horas extras.
- ¡Ánimo! Te entiendo perfectamente porque me pasa algo similar.

13B.4 **siento** + [*infinitive*] **te entiendo, no pasa nada, no te preocupes, ¡Ánimo!**

Vocabulario

12

Siento oír eso. *I'm sorry to hear that.*

13

únicamente *only*

el contrato de trabajo *employment contract*

14

la igualdad *equality*

el título *degree*

el puesto directivo *managerial position*

15

habilitar *to qualify*

la perspectiva *prospect*

Estrategia

Destacar una información

En mi empresa tenemos vacaciones **solo/solamente** en agosto.
Trabajo en equipo, **sobre todo** con Ana y Nacho.

La mujer en el trabajo

Según la Organización Internacional del Trabajo (OIT), en 2008, el 40,5 por ciento de los empleados mundiales eran mujeres (frente a un 39,9 por ciento en 1998). Las áreas principales donde trabajan son la agricultura, la industria y el sector servicios. Sin embargo, aún hay discriminación, como menores salarios y falta de acceso a puestos directivos.

11 Piense en dos o tres características de su mejor amigo/a y compárelas con las de su compañero/a.

Modelo: • *Mi mejor amigo/a es...* • *El/La mío/a...*

12 Relacione estas expresiones del diálogo con la función que tienen.

¡Ánimo! • No te preocupes./No pasa nada.
Siento verte así. • Te entiendo perfectamente.

Cuando quieres expresar...

1. que has vivido algo similar: Te entiendo perfectamente.
2. que sientes la situación: Siento verte así.
3. calma o tranquilidad: No te preocupes./No pasa nada.
4. energía o fuerza moral: ¡Ánimo!

13 a. Lea las descripciones de la página anterior y anote expresiones equivalentes a las siguientes.

únicamente: solo/solamente   especialmente: sobre todo

b. Cree un diálogo a partir de una de estas situaciones. Su compañero/a intenta consolarlo y animarlo usando las expresiones anteriores.

13b Expansion Have volunteers act out their situations for the class.

- Solo tienes una semana de vacaciones en marzo y tus amigos tienen dos.
- Tiene un contrato de trabajo de solamente veinte horas, pero trabaja cuarenta horas.
- No se lleva bien con su familia, sobre todo con su hermano pequeño.

14 a. En el mundo académico actual hay una mayor igualdad entre hombres y mujeres que en el pasado. El número de mujeres que obtienen un título universitario es igual o superior al de los hombres. ¿Cómo es la situación en las diferentes carreras que ofrece su universidad?

b. Lea la nota de la izquierda sobre la presencia de la mujer en el mercado laboral. ¿Por qué cree que es así?

14b Suggestion Have students consider the role of women in families and how this might affect their career.

MI EXPERIENCIA

15 Piense en la carrera que está estudiando. Compárela con las carreras que siguen sus compañeros.

GUIÓN DE TRABAJO

¿Qué carrera estás estudiando?	Medicina/Derecho/Economía/...
¿Por qué elegiste esa carrera?	..., y sobre todo porque...
¿Qué empleo esperas conseguir con ese título?	Mi título me habilita para trabajar en/de... ¿Y el tuyo?

Remind students that the adjective **solo/a** means *alone*, whereas the adverb **solo** means *only* and is invariable. Tell students that they may see the adverb **sólo** spelled with a written accent mark. Current usage dictates that the written accent is required only in cases of ambiguity. Ex.: **Juan va a hacer sólo un examen.**

Practice more at **vhlcentral.com.**

SAM: Actividades pp. 280–282

Cristina Rubio, asesora laboral

Suggestion Ask students to think of examples of poor working environments from film or television (Ex: *The Office, Office Space*) and have them explain how Cristina's programs might help.

www.coachingporcristina.mx

En la empresa hay que tener psicología

A pesar de estar casi la mitad de nuestras vidas en el trabajo, no prestamos atención a los aspectos emocionales que condicionan nuestra actitud, nuestra motivación y nuestra forma de relacionarnos con los demás: identificar cuál es la tuya te puede ayudar a ser más eficaz.

Después de muchos años de experiencia como psicóloga, me especialicé en el área de *coaching* para empresas porque cuando era terapeuta encontraba muchos casos de conflicto y estrés emocional que tenían su origen en el trabajo y el ambiente laboral. Como en todos los ámbitos de nuestra vida, en la empresa "hay que tener psicología". ¿Qué significa esto? Comprender tus necesidades y las de los demás para saber manejarlas.

¿Cuál es la labor de *coaching*?

La labor de *coaching* se dirige a equipos que quieren ser eficaces, desarrollar habilidades concretas y conseguir sus objetivos. Los aspectos más humanos, como la calidad de las relaciones personales y el nivel de satisfacción personal del equipo, es decir, un buen ambiente laboral, son fundamentales para sentirnos realizados profesionalmente.

Un objetivo triple: persona, empresa y entorno afectivo.

El objetivo es triple. Por un lado, ayudo a las personas a sentirse realizadas a través del programa **"Tus emociones son las mías"**. La empatía es una de las bases fundamentales de la inteligencia emocional en la resolución de conflictos: solo comprendiendo las necesidades y, sobre todo, las motivaciones del otro, podemos buscar soluciones.

Por otro, asesoro a los departamentos de Recursos Humanos de las empresas para crear estructuras organizativas y equipos de trabajo eficaces con el programa **"Las alegrías de tus empleados son las tuyas"**, porque sólo un empleado feliz es un empleado motivado.

Y por último, con el programa **"La estabilidad de tu entorno es la tuya"**, contribuyo a la mejora de la interacción de los equipos de trabajo.

CRISTINA RUBIO
Coaching para empresas
Boulevard Díaz Ordaz 140,
Monterrey, 64650 (México)
Licenciada en Psicología y Economía
Máster en Gestión de Recursos Humanos

Estructurar la información

Por un lado, queremos ayudar a las personas; **por otro,** buscamos mejorar el rendimiento de las empresas.

13B.5 **por un lado/una parte... por otro/otra...**

Vocabulario

16

el/la asesor(a) laboral *labor consultant*
casi *almost*
relacionarse *to interact*
eficaz *efficient*
el ambiente laboral *work atmosphere*

16 a. Observe los datos de la tarjeta de nuestra protagonista. ¿A qué se dedica? ¿Cuál es su formación? Es asesora laboral y se dedica a actividades de *coaching* para empresas. Es licenciada en Psicología y Economía, y tiene un Máster en Gestión de Recursos Humanos.

b. ¿Qué tipo de servicios cree que ofrece el *coaching* para empresas? Lea la página web de Cristina para comprobarlo. ¿Qué opina de estos servicios?

17 a. ¿Cuáles son los programas que ofrece Cristina y cuál es su triple objetivo? "Tus emociones son las mías"; "Las alegrías de tus empleados son las tuyas"; "La estabilidad de tu entorno es la tuya". Triple objetivo: persona, empresa y entorno afectivo.

b. ¿Qué aspectos pueden influir en el trabajo? Organice la información usando la construcción **Por un lado, ...; por otro,....**

18 ¿Qué cree que significa la expresión "hay que tener psicología"? Compare sus ideas con las de su compañero/a. ¿Cree que la psicología nos ayuda a ser más eficaces en el trabajo? Sample answer: Tener habilidad para manejar los problemas y las relaciones interpersonales.

19 Imagine un servicio de *coaching* para su universidad. ¿Qué tipo de persona lo dirige? ¿Qué objetivos tiene? ¿A través de qué medios se comunica con los estudiantes? ¿Aprovecha las nuevas tecnologías? ¿Cuáles?

19 **Expansion** Have pairs discuss other areas of life in which it helps to "use psychology."

Vocabulario *cont.*

comprender *to understand*
la necesidad *need*
manejar *to manage*
la labor *task*
sentirse realizado/a *to feel fulfilled*
el entorno afectivo *emotional environment*
por un lado/por una parte *on the one hand*
por otro lado/por otra parte *on the other hand*
asesorar *to advise*
los Recursos Humanos (RR.HH.) *Human Resources (HR)*
el equipo de trabajo *working team*
la gestión *management*
el rendimiento *performance*
la actitud, la satisfacción personal, la empatía, la inteligencia emocional, la resolución de conflictos, la estabilidad

20
la bolsa de trabajo *employment center*
la pasantía de verano *summer internship*
la solicitud *application*
No dude en... *Don't hesitate to . . .*
el/la orientador(a) profesional *career counselor*
excluyente *a must, required*
a convenir *to be agreed upon*
hacer clic *to click*
el/la pasante *intern*
el/la candidato/a *applicant*
el dominio *command*
la carta de presentación *cover letter*
reunir los requisitos *to meet the requirements*
postularse *to apply*
el resultado

20 a. Lea estos anuncios que la bolsa de trabajo de su universidad ha enviado por correo electrónico. ¿Cuáles son algunas ventajas de hacer una pasantía de verano?

Mensaje nuevo

Enviar | Chat | Adjuntar | Agenda | Tipo de letra | Colores | Borrador

De: Raúl Vázquez
Para:
Asunto: Pasantías de verano

BOLSA DE EMPLEO

Para obtener más información sobre alguna de estas pasantías de verano o si necesita ayuda con el proceso de solicitud, no dude en escribirme.

Raúl Vázquez Peña
Orientador profesional

Buscamos estudiantes de las carreras de Recursos Humanos o Psicología (excluyente) para colaborar como auxiliares en la selección de personal. Las tareas principales serán: atención telefónica, lectura y clasificación de currículum vítae y asistencia a los entrevistadores. Se requiere una personalidad metódica, ordenada y analítica. Horario a convenir. Haz clic aquí para enviar tu solicitud.

Invitamos a estudiantes de Economía con un excelente desempeño° académico a trabajar en nuestro departamento de auditoría° interna. Los estudiantes seleccionados participarán en proyectos que requieren orientación a los resultados, trabajo bajo presión° y atención al detalle, así como capacidad para trabajar en equipo. Los pasantes trabajarán un promedio° de ocho horas diarias. ¡Te esperamos! Inscríbete con tu currículum vítae por Internet.

Ofrecemos pasantías para estudiantes universitarios interesados en trabajar con la comunidad latina. Los candidatos seleccionados darán clases de computación° en español. Deberán tener una actitud positiva, buenas habilidades interpersonales y el deseo de ayudar a la comunidad. Se requiere excelente dominio de computación y un buen nivel de español. De 16 a 20 horas a la semana. Envía tu carta de presentación y tu currículum vítae.

desempeño *performance* **auditoría** *auditing* **bajo presión** *under pressure* **promedio** *average* **computación** *computing*

b. Comente con su compañero/a cuál de estos trabajos le resulta más interesante. ¿Qué requisitos deben reunir los candidatos para ese puesto? ¿Cree que usted podría postularse? ¿Por qué?

20b **Suggestion** Also ask students which internship they would be most qualified for and why.

21 Escriba el anuncio para una oferta de empleo. Describa las responsabilidades del puesto y el tipo de candidato que se busca (formación, personalidad, etc.).

22 a. Lea el texto sobre el español de los negocios. ¿Qué palabras extranjeras se usan regularmente en inglés?
Sample answer: nombres de comidas: tacos, tortilla, paella, etc.

En el español de los negocios y la tecnología, a menudo se usan palabras que proceden de otros idiomas, especialmente del inglés, como *blog, web, link, online* o *coaching, mailing, marketing, master, freelance*... Algunas tienen una adaptación gráfica al español, como "máster" y otras tienen un equivalente muy usado, como "enlace" (*link*), "mercadeo" (*marketing*) o "autónomo" (*freelance*).

22a **Suggestion** For each loanword in English, have students identify the language of origin.

b. ¿Conoce más palabras similares a estas en español? Compártalas con sus compañeros.

Practice more at **vhlcentral.com.**

SAM: Actividades pp. 283–288

23 a. ¿Cuáles cree que son las principales motivaciones para permanecer en un empleo? Elija las tres más importantes para usted.

- el dinero
- la satisfacción con el trabajo
- conseguir un ascenso°
- la relación con jefes y/o compañeros
- otros...

b. Lea estos datos sobre la satisfacción con el trabajo y coméntelos con sus compañeros.

23a Encourage students to consider both internal factors, such as personal relationships and job satisfaction, and external factors, such as the economy and the labor market.

La satisfacción con el trabajo: principal motivación para permanecer en un empleo

Según una encuesta que se realizó a 7508 trabajadores de América del Norte, Europa y Asia

En América del Norte, la satisfacción con el trabajo también es el factor que más anima a los trabajadores a querer permanecer en un empleo (33%), seguido de buenas condiciones laborales, como horarios flexibles, poco tiempo de viaje al trabajo, etc. (15%).

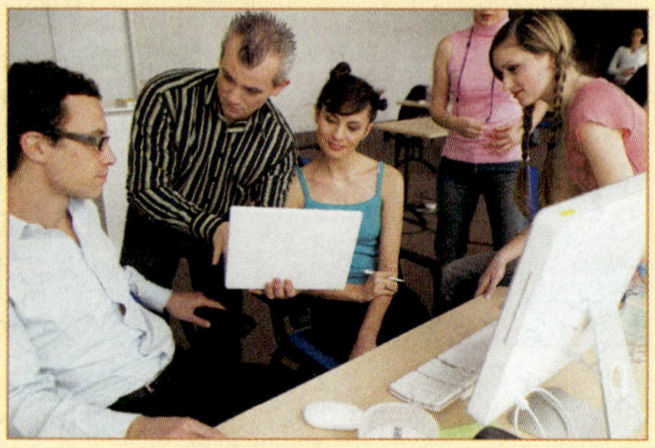

El dinero no es lo que más influye a la hora de dar un giro a la vida laboral. Aquellos que dijeron que, de poder elegir, no permanecerían en su trabajo actual es porque sienten que su carrera está estancada° (30%), no les gusta su trabajo ni desarrollan todo su potencial (25%), o no se llevan bien con su jefe (18%).

conseguir un ascenso *to get a promotion* **estancado/a** *stuck*

c. ¿Está de acuerdo con los resultados? Si no lo está, ¿cuáles cree que son las principales motivaciones entre sus amigos y familiares?

TAREA FINAL

Encuesta de ambiente laboral

Tome notas sobre los factores que favorecen la relación con los compañeros de trabajo y mejoran el ambiente laboral.

Compare sus notas con las de su compañero/a y elaboren preguntas a partir de sus notas. Elijan las mejores preguntas y anótenlas en una tarjeta.

Hagan una puesta en común con la clase y coloquen todas las preguntas en la pizarra. Hagan la encuesta a sus compañeros.

YO PUEDO...

- **Puedo describir circunstancias en el pasado.**
  Cuente cómo se comunicaba la gente sin celular y sin computadora.
- **Puedo relacionar ideas contrarias.**
  Complete esta oración:
  La gente antes no tenía celular; sin embargo *se comunicaba sin problemas.*
- **Puedo expresar posesión.**
  Mi celular es pequeño, el suyo *(de Sara), no.*
- **Puedo consolar y animar.**
  Diga todas las expresiones que sabe para expresar consuelo y dar ánimo.
- **Puedo estructurar la información.**
  ¿Qué piensa usted que se debe hacer cuando hay conflictos laborales?
- *Por una parte...*

GRAMÁTICA FUNCIONAL

13B.1 Describe situations and causes in the past

Review of past tenses: **porque** + [*imperfect*] 5.2.3, 5.4.3, 5.6

- To describe situations and causes in the past, use the **pretérito imperfecto**. Use **porque** (*because*) to express a cause with the construction [*result*] + **porque** + [*cause (imperfect)*].

  Empecé a usar un teléfono inteligente **porque podía** tenerlo todo en un solo aparato.
  *I started to use a smartphone **because I was able to** have everything in just one device.*

- In order to begin a sentence by stating the cause, use **como** (*since/as*) + [*cause (imperfect)*], + [*result*].

  Como tenía mucho sueño ayer por la tarde, dormí una siesta.
  ***As I was** very tired yesterday afternoon, I took a nap.*

13B.2 Relate opposing ideas

a pesar de, aunque, sin embargo 12.11

- Use **aunque** (*although, even though*) to relate opposing ideas. Use the construction **Aunque** [*clause*], + [*clause*].

  Aunque cuesta un poco más, la conexión rápida vale la pena.
  ***Although** it costs a bit more, the fast connection is worth it.*

- **Aunque** can also be used in the middle of a sentence, in the construction [*clause*] + **aunque** [*clause*].

  Ayer nos perdimos **aunque** usamos el nuevo GPS.
  *Yesterday we got lost **even though** we used the new GPS.*

- Use **a pesar de** + [*infinitive/noun*] to express *despite* or *in spite of*.

  A pesar de tener mucha música en mi *iPod*, siempre escucho las diez mismas canciones.

  ***In spite of having** a lot of music on my iPod, I always listen to the same ten songs.*

- Use **a pesar de todo** (*in spite of everything*) before a clause to express an idea that opposes what was stated or implied earlier.

  Internet genera inconvenientes de seguridad. También genera adicción. **A pesar de todo**, es una herramienta muy beneficiosa.

  *The Internet creates problems of security and confidentiality. It's also addictive. **In spite of all that**, it is a very beneficial tool.*

- To express *however*, use **sin embargo** + [*clause*].

  Los nuevos celulares son complicados. **Sin embargo**, nos permiten realizar muchas funciones.
  *The new cell phones are complicated. **However**, they allow us to perform many functions.*

Suggestion Have students work in small groups to create an ad for a technological device or service, using the expressions from **13B.2**.

¡Póngalo en práctica!

G1 Complete las oraciones con la forma correcta del verbo en el pretérito indefinido o el pretérito imperfecto.

1. Leila ....estudió.... (estudiar) psicología en la universidad porque le ....interesaba.... (interesar) la mente humana.
2. Damián y Sergio ....viajaron.... (viajar) a España el verano pasado porque ....tenían.... (tener) que hacer investigación para sus tesis doctorales.
3. Como siempre ....trabajábamos.... (nosotros, trabajar) hasta tarde, ...empezamos.... (nosotros, empezar) a pedir pizza con mucha frecuencia.
4. Carlos ....compró.... (comprar) un GPS porque no le ....gustaba.... (gustar) usar un plano.

G1 Expansion Have students write three additional sentences about their own experiences.

G2 Elija el final más lógico para cada oración.

1. Aunque me gustaría comprar el nuevo *iPhone*, ...c....
2. A pesar de ser una herramienta útil, ...a....
3. Prefiero compartir las noticias importantes en persona; sin embargo, ...d....
4. La red Wi-Fi nos permite estar conectados sin cables, ...b....

a. el GPS puede ser una distracción para el conductor.
b. aunque a veces hay problemas de conectividad.
c. el celular que tengo funciona perfectamente.
d. las videoconferencias me permiten hablar con amigos que viven lejos.

G3 Complete las oraciones con las expresiones **aunque, a pesar de (todo)** y **sin embargo**.

1. ....A pesar de.... los precios bajos, decidí no comprar una agenda electrónica porque prefiero usar una agenda de papel.
2. Con el celular estamos localizables las 24 horas del día, ...aunque.... no siempre lo queremos.
3. Las computadoras portátiles son fáciles de transportar; ....sin embargo.... también son fáciles de romper.
4. La televisión genera muchas controversias. ....A pesar de todo / Sin embargo...., puede utilizarse con fines educativos.
5. ....A pesar de.... ampliar las conexiones, Internet también provoca aislamiento.
6. ....Aunque.... puedo hacer llamadas con mi celular, prefiero mandar mensajes de texto.

Practice more at **vhlcentral.com.**

13B

GRAMÁTICA FUNCIONAL

G4 Expansion Reverse the activity by giving possessive pronouns and having students give the correct possessive adjective plus a possible noun.

13B.3 Express possession

Possessive adjectives and pronouns 8.2

- Use possessive adjectives with nouns to express possession. You learned possessive adjectives in 5B.2.

  Mis hermanos viven en Barcelona.
  My siblings live in Barcelona.

- Use a possessive pronoun in place of [*possessive adjective*] + [*noun*] to express *mine, yours, his,* etc. Possessive pronouns agree in number and gender with the nouns they replace.

	singular		plural	
(yo)	**el mío**	**la mía**	**los míos**	**las mías**
(tú)	**el tuyo**	**la tuya**	**los tuyos**	**las tuyas**
(usted, él, ella)	**el suyo**	**la suya**	**los suyos**	**las suyas**
(nosotros/as)	**el nuestro**	**la nuestra**	**los nuestros**	**las nuestras**
(vosotros/as)	**el vuestro**	**la vuestra**	**los vuestros**	**las vuestras**
(ustedes, ellos/as)	**el suyo**	**la suya**	**los suyos**	**las suyas**

Mi celular ya no funciona bien. ¿Te gusta **el tuyo**?
*My cell phone does not work well anymore. Do you like **yours**?*

- Use the possessive pronoun with the corresponding definite article (**el, la, los, las**).

13B.4 Offer consolation and encouragement

siento + [*infinitive*], te entiendo, ¡ánimo! 5.13, 7.4, 14.26

- To console someone, say **te entiendo** (*I understand [you]*), **no pasa nada** (*it's no problem*), or **no te preocupes** (*don't worry*).
- Another way to console someone is with the construction **siento** + [*infinitive*] (*I am sorry . . .*).

  Siento oír eso. — *I am sorry to hear that.*
  Siento verte tan triste. — *I'm sorry to see you're so sad.*

- Use **eso** (*that*) to refer to an unidentified or unspecified noun, situation, or concept. You will learn more about **eso** and neuter demonstrative pronouns in 15B.
- To offer encouragement or to cheer someone up, use expressions such as ¡Ánimo! (*Cheer up!*), ¡Venga! (*Come on!*), ¡Anímate! (*Go for it!/Cheer up!*), or ¡Dale! (*Come on!*). The use of these expressions varies according to country or region.

13B.5 Organize information

por un lado/una parte... por otro/otra 14.1

- To structure an argument with more than one idea, use the construction **por un lado/una parte... por otro (lado)/otra (parte)** (*on the one hand . . . on the other*).

  Por un lado, me gusta tu propuesta; **por otro,** me gustaría agregar un detalle más.
  ***On the one hand,** I like your proposal; **on the other,** I would like to add one more detail.*

- Pay attention to agreement in this construction; always use the pairs **lado/otro** and **parte/otra**.

¡Póngalo en práctica!

G4 Escriba el pronombre posesivo correspondiente.

Modelo: mi tío *el mío*

1. nuestro jefe el nuestro
2. tus responsabilidades las tuyas
3. su empresa la suya
4. nuestros problemas los nuestros
5. mis vacaciones las mías

G5 Complete las oraciones con la forma apropiada del adjetivo o pronombre posesivo según las pistas.

1. Ese es Antonio; es el jefe de Susana, y también es su (de ella) amigo.
2. • Mis compañeros son estupendos. ¿Y los tuyos (de ti)?
   ■ Los míos también.
3. • Nuestra oficina está en el centro. ¿Y la vuestra (de vosotros)?
   ■ La nuestra también.
4. • Mi (de mí) hermana se llama Celia. ¿Y la tuya (de ti)?
   ■ La mía se llama Beatriz.

G6 Expansion Have students write three additional mini-dialogues for a classmate to complete.

G6 Complete los diálogos con expresiones de consuelo y de ánimo.

- • No estoy contento con mi trabajo.
  ■ No te (1) preocupes, seguro que encuentras una solución.
- • He tenido un conflicto con mis compañeros de trabajo y estoy preocupado.
  ■ Te (2) entiendo, pero estas cosas pasan. Ya se va a resolver el problema.
- • Tengo que dar una presentación mañana en el trabajo y estoy muy nerviosa.
  ■ (3) ¡Ánimo/Anímate! Seguro que te sale bien.
- • No voy a poder terminar este proyecto para mañana.
  ■ No (4) pasa nada, estamos todos atrasados.

G7 Complete las oraciones.

1. Tener un buen clima laboral beneficia por un lado al trabajador, que se siente más cómodo y satisfecho, y por otro (lado) a la empresa, porque aumenta la eficacia.
2. Hay muchos factores que contribuyen a un buen clima laboral. Por una parte, es importante tener una buena relación con tus compañeros, y por otra, la satisfacción personal con tu trabajo.

Suggestion Name controversial people or topics from recent headlines and have the class react using the expressions from **13B.5**.

Practice more at **vhlcentral.com.**

VOCABULARIO

¿Imprescindibles?

la abreviatura	*abbreviation*
el aislamiento	*isolation*
el bolsillo	*pocket*
el código	*code*
el disco de vinilo	*vinyl record*
la distracción	*distraction*
la diversidad	*diversity*
el inconveniente	*drawback*
el lado malo	*bad side*
el lector de libros electrónicos	*e-reader*
la libertad	*freedom*
la movilidad	*mobility*
el navegador GPS	*GPS*
la pobreza	*mediocrity*
la red social	*social network*
la red Wi-Fi	*Wi-Fi network*
el reproductor de MP3	*MP3 player*
la revolución	*revolution*
la taquigrafía	*stenography*
la tecnología	*technology*
el teléfono inteligente	*smartphone*
la velocidad	*speed*
la ventaja	*advantage*
la vocal	*vowel*
estar acostumbrado/a a	*to be used to*
estar conectado/a	*to be connected (to the Internet)*
estar localizable	*to be reachable*
fabricar en serie	*to mass produce*
guardar (canciones/ fotos)	*to save/store (songs/photos)*
localizar	*to get hold of, to locate*
ocupar espacio	*to take up space*
ser moneda corriente	*to be common*
sintetizar	*to synthesize*
sobrevivir	*to survive*
tener capacidad	*to have (storage) capacity*
imprescindible	*indispensable*
a pesar de todo	*despite it all*
aunque	*although*
sin embargo	*however*

Variación léxica

el/la contador(a) (*Amér. L.*) ⟷ **el/la contable** (*Esp.*)

hacer clic ⟷ **pinchar** (*Esp.*)

la pasantía ⟷ **la práctica**

la red Wi-Fi ⟷ **la red inalámbrica**

¿Un buen equipo?

No pasa nada.	*Everything is OK.*
No te preocupes.	*Don't worry.*
Siento oír eso.	*I'm sorry to hear that.*
Siento verte así.	*I'm sorry to see you like this.*
Te entiendo perfectamente.	*I understand you perfectly.*
el/la analista de *marketing*	*marketing analyst*
el/la contador(a) (*Amér. L.*)	*accountant*
el contrato de trabajo	*employment contract*
el/la ejecutivo/a de ventas	*sales executive*
la igualdad	*equality*
la perspectiva	*prospect*
el puesto directivo	*managerial position*
el/la tirano/a	*tyrant*
el título	*degree*
discutir	*to argue*
estar motivado/a	*to be motivated*
habilitar	*to qualify*
hacer horas extras	*to do overtime*
ser un(a) gran comunicador(a)	*to be a great communicator*
bromista	*fond of joking*
comprensivo/a	*understanding*
desagradable	*unkind*
impaciente	*impatient*
innovador(a)	*innovative*
metódico/a	*methodical*
ordenado/a	*orderly, neat*
puntual	*punctual*
serio/a	*serious; reliable*
por cierto	*incidentally*
sobre todo	*above all*
solo/solamente	*only*
únicamente	*only*

Cristina Rubio

a convenir	*to be agreed upon*
No dude en...	*Don't hesitate to. . .*
la actitud	*attitude*
el ambiente laboral	*work atmosphere*
el/la asesor(a) laboral	*labor consultant*
la bolsa de trabajo	*employment center*
el/la candidato/a	*applicant*
la carta de presentación	*cover letter*
el dominio	*command*
la empatía	*empathy*
el entorno afectivo	*emotional environment*
el equipo de trabajo	*working team*
la estabilidad	*stability*
la gestión	*management*
la inteligencia emocional	*emotional intelligence*
la labor	*task*
la necesidad	*need*
el/la orientador(a) profesional	*career counselor*
el/la pasante	*intern*
la pasantía de verano	*summer internship*
los Recursos Humanos (RR.HH.)	*Human Resources (HR)*
el rendimiento	*performance*
la resolución de conflictos	*conflict resolution*
el resultado	*result*
la satisfacción personal	*personal satisfaction*
la solicitud	*application*
asesorar	*to advise, to act as consultant to*
comprender	*to understand*
hacer clic	*to click*
manejar	*to manage*
postularse	*to apply*
relacionarse	*to interact*
reunir los requisitos	*to meet the requirements*
sentirse realizado/a	*to feel fulfilled*
eficaz	*efficient*
excluyente	*a must, required*
casi	*almost*
por un lado/por una parte	*on the one hand*
por otro lado/ por otra parte	*on the other hand*

Juan José Millás es un escritor y periodista español nacido en Valencia en 1946. Empezó a estudiar Filosofía y Letras pero abandonó la universidad al tercer año y se dedicó a leer y escribir mientras trabajaba de diferentes cosas, entre ellas como administrativo en Iberia, la compañía aérea española. Es autor de muchas novelas y artículos periodísticos. Creó el *articuento*, un género literario a medio camino entre° el cuento y el artículo periodístico, en el que un hecho cotidiano puede convertirse en un evento fantástico que permite observar la realidad de forma crítica.

a medio camino entre *halfway between*

Vocabulario útil

la broma pesada *practical joke*
la casilla *box*
el engaño *deception*
la partida *departure*
la pesadilla *nightmare*
rellenar *to fill out*
solicitar *to request*

Estrategia

Recognize the purpose of a text

When reading a text, ask yourself questions about its purpose and intent: Is the text literary or technical, informational or journalistic? If it is a narrative, is it factual or fictional? What's the story about? Why are you reading this text? How does it fit with what you are studying? Asking yourself these questions before, during, and after you read can help you clarify and understand the text.

LECTURA

FORMULARIOS

Juan José Millás

Al despertar, vi que la azafata había dejado sobre el brazo de mi asiento el formulario° que era preciso° rellenar para entrar en el país al que nos dirigíamos. El resto del pasaje dormía en medio de la penumbra°, pues era de noche y solo permanecían encendidas° las luces que indicaban la situación de los baños y las que en los bajos de los asientos delimitaban el pasillo°. Comencé a rellenar el formulario y todo fue bien hasta que debajo de la línea en la que se solicitaba la fecha de nacimiento encontré otra donde había que anotar la de la muerte°. Sobrecogido°, levanté el rostro y vi avanzar a una azafata en medio de aquella atmósfera espectral. Por favor, le dije en voz baja cuando llegó a mi altura, ¿qué hay que poner en esta casilla? ¿Usted qué cree?, respondió ella observándome con ironía, como si me estuviera haciendo el ingenuo°.

Suponiendo entonces que me había sorprendido° la muerte mientras dormía, puse la fecha en la que había salido de Madrid, y en la que aún nos encontrábamos. Luego rellené el resto del formulario, tumbé° el respaldo del asiento, cerré los ojos y di un par de cabezadas°. Me despertó el ajetreo° de las azafatas, que comenzaban a servir el desayuno. Las ventanas estaban abiertas (había amanecido) y las luces encendidas. Vi el formulario, pero preferí (por miedo, supongo) no comprobar si lo de la casilla de la muerte había sido una alucinación. Llegué a destino, entregué el impreso en el control de policía, tomé un taxi, fui al hotel, hice en aquella ciudad lo que se esperaba de mí° y regresé a casa con regalos en la maleta. Mis rutinas son

1 Hable con un(a) compañero/a. ¿Cuál es la pregunta más extraña o difícil que tuvo que contestar? ¿Alguna vez confundió la realidad con un sueño (o una pesadilla [*nightmare*])? ¿Qué opina de las bromas pesadas? ¿Lo engañaron alguna vez? ¿Se considera una persona realista o inclinada a la fantasía?

2 Marque la opción correcta.

2 Suggestion Have students complete this activity in pairs and locate the passage(s) in the text that corresponds to each answer.

1. Cuando la azafata deja el formulario, el pasajero está ....
   (a.) dormido b. despierto c. distraído
2. Lo raro del formulario es ....
   a. todo (b.) una pregunta c. el color
3. Al leer el formulario, el pasajero queda ....
   a. indiferente b. aterrorizado (c.) sorprendido
4. La azafata responde al pasajero con ....
   a. amabilidad (b.) ironía c. asombro
5. Él supone que ....
   a. es una broma pesada (b.) murió mientras dormía c. está loco
6. Rellena la casilla con la fecha de ....
   (a.) su partida b. su cumpleaños c. su llegada
7. Al despertarse, el pasajero .... el formulario.
   a. relee b. olvida (c.) entrega
8. A partir de ese momento, sus rutinas ....
   (a.) son las mismas b. son diferentes c. desaparecen
9. Él tiene la sensación de que todo ....
   a. sigue igual (b.) es diferente c. fue un sueño

desde entonces las de siempre, mi relación con las personas y con el trabajo también. Todo sigue igual, pero de algún modo misterioso todo es diferente, como si, en vez de vivir, imitara° la vida que llevaba antes del viaje. No es desagradable, solo raro.

Suggestion Have students reread the last two sentences and discuss any out-of-body experiences they have had.

formulario *form* **era preciso** *it was necessary* **penumbra** *semi-darkness* **encendidas** *turned on* **pasillo** *aisle* **la muerte** *death* **Sobrecogido** *Startled* **como si me estuviera haciendo el ingenuo** *as though I were playing dumb* **me había sorprendido** *had surprised me* **tumbé** *I reclined* **di un par de cabezadas** *I had a nap* **ajetreo** *activity* **lo que se esperaba de mí** *what was expected of me* **como si... imitara** *as though . . . I were imitating*

► **Astronautas hispanos**

Arnaldo T. Méndez, piloto de la Fuerza Aérea Cubana, fue el primer latinoamericano en llegar al espacio. Fue seleccionado para el programa soviético Interkosmos y viajó en la nave rusa *Soyuz 38* con Yuri Romanenko en 1980.

Franklin L. Chang-Díaz, físico e ingeniero costarricense°, fue el primer astronauta latino de la NASA, con siete viajes al espacio, tres caminatas espaciales y 1606 horas fuera de la órbita terrestre. Cree que el ser humano vivirá en lugares como la Luna, los planetas o puntos del espacio entre la Tierra y su satélite, donde se podrían establecer colonias.

José Hernández es un californiano de ascendencia mexicana que decidió ser astronauta cuando escuchó la historia de Chang-Díaz: "Era alguien como yo, con los mismos problemas de manejo° del inglés, y si él pudo yo también lo haría", contó. En 2009 formó parte de la tripulación del transbordador espacial° *Discovery* en una misión de 14 días en la Estación Espacial Internacional (EEI).

costarricense *Costa Rican* **manejo** *use* **transbordador espacial** *space shuttle*

Estrategia

Writing an incident report

When writing a report, remember that the main purpose is to provide information so that others who were not present at the time can make a decision or take action. An **incident report** or **accident report** is meant to record details or document an unusual event (a medical emergency, destruction of property, etc.). The report must be free from judgmental statements, sarcasm, biases, or condescending comments. It must include date, time, and location, and a description of the context as well as of the actual incident in detail. Be as specific as possible.

3

a. Una persona quiere comprar un pasaje a la Luna y el/la empleado/a de un agencia de turismo trata de explicar al cliente que no es posible, pero este insiste (puede ser una broma, una cámara oculta de un programa de televisión, un caso de locura, etc.). En parejas, armen la conversación. Luego, representen la escena frente a la clase.

b. La AEXA (Agencia Espacial Mexicana) planea organizar viajes turísticos al espacio. En parejas, preparen una presentación del proyecto.

- Elijan el lugar del cosmos para promocionar y expliquen tiempo y condición del viaje.
- Presenten la nave y a los astronautas que la guían.
- Expliquen qué hace único este viaje (valoración de la experiencia, razones para hacerlo, etc.).
- Recomienden el viaje.

Proyecto Ask students to share their reports in small groups and discuss how it is possible to have differing impartial reports. Have groups select the most unbiased report and share it with the class.

PROYECTO

Escriba un informe sobre el episodio del formulario en el vuelo de Madrid. Puede seguir esta estructura:

1. Descripción del incidente: contar qué pasó, cuándo y dónde.
2. Análisis del contexto: las circunstancias en las que se produjo.
3. Explicar la causa del evento: ¿por qué pasó? Si no se sabe, puede utilizar la frase: "Hasta el momento, se desconocen las causas del incidente."
4. Recomendación final: ¿qué se puede hacer para prevenir incidentes como este?

Estrategia

Asking questions

When watching a video, use questions to orient your viewing. Look at the title of the episode and think of questions you could ask using **qué, quién, dónde, cómo, cuándo, por qué**, etc. For example, since the title of this **Flash Cultura** is *Inventos argentinos,* you may ask from the start: **¿Cuáles son? ¿Quiénes los inventaron?**, etc. Write down your questions and check back afterwards.

Vocabulario útil

- el invento *invention*
- la birome (*Arg.*) *ballpoint pen*
- en funcionamiento *running*
- el dulce de leche (*Arg.*) *caramel spread*
- el frasco *bottle*
- las huellas dactilares *fingerprints*
- la jeringa descartable *disposable syringe*
- la masa (cruda) *(raw) dough*
- la pluma *fountain pen*
- el/la porteño/a *person from Buenos Aires*
- el relleno *filling*
- la sangre *blood*
- la tinta *ink*

Estrategia

Making excuses

In Spanish, when you need to make excuses or apologize, you might say: **Lo siento, Perdón, Discúlpame,** or **Te/Le pido disculpas/perdón.** If you were unaware of certain customs or prohibitions, you might say: **Yo no sabía/entendí/soy de aquí.,** or **No fue mi intención.**

Flash CULTURA

Inventos argentinos

Ya ha visto que en la vida moderna estamos rodeados de avances tecnológicos que nos resultan imprescindibles para viajar, trabajar y funcionar en las cosas de todos los días. En este episodio de **Flash Cultura** conocerá los inventos argentinos que cambiaron el mundo del siglo XX.

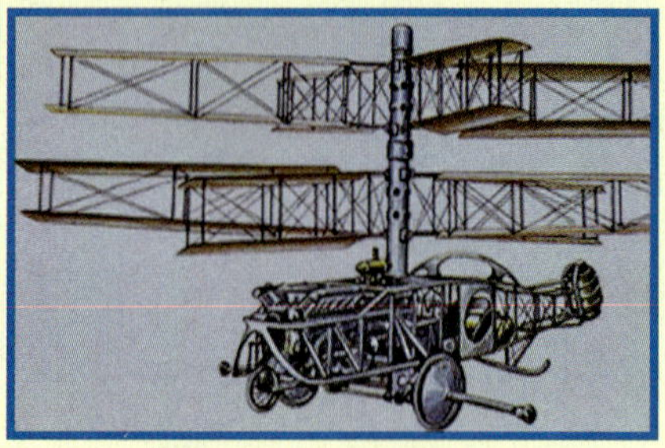

1. Converse con un(a) compañero/a. ¿Qué inventos del siglo XX conoce? ¿Cuál de los inventos modernos es el más importante para su vida? ¿Cuál le resulta imprescindible? ¿Qué cree que hace falta inventar en el mundo actual? ¿Le gustaría inventar algo?

2. Mire el video y haga las preguntas necesarias para reunir la información fundamental: qué es, para qué sirve, quién lo inventó, etc.

1 **Buenos Aires sigue siendo la capital de un país de pioneros e innovadores.**

1 Expansion Have students write a description of their invention and include drawings, if possible. Have students present their inventions to groups of four, who will vote for their favorite one.

2 **El semáforo especial permite, mediante sonidos, avisarles a los ciegos o no videntes cuándo pueden cruzar la calle.**

3. Complete las oraciones sobre los inventos argentinos.
   1. El colectivo para el transporte en la ciudad fue creado por dos ....porteños.......... a principios del siglo XX.
   2. Un inmigrante húngaro llamado Biro inventó la ....birome.......... .
   3. Las ....huellas dactilares.......... fueron idea de un policía argentino para identificar a las personas.
   4. Hay inventos argentinos que salvan la vida de personas en todo el mundo como las transfusiones de ....sangre.........., el *by-pass* y las ....jeringas descartables.......... .
   5. El tango y el ....dulce de leche.......... son inventos esenciales para la cultura de los argentinos.

4. En parejas, escriban una conversación en la que opinan sobre los beneficios y perjuicios de ciertos inventos.

4 Expansion Have pairs act out their conversations in groups of six.

Modelo:
- *Aunque los colectivos son muy útiles para el transporte público, también contaminan el ambiente. Creo que sería mejor usar bicicletas.*
- *Es cierto. Sin embargo, los colectivos son más rápidos...*

Audio: Activities, Vocabulary
Video: *Flash Cultura*

Unidad 14

Acacio Maye Ocomo, una vida en el mar

Lección 14A

UN IDIOMA COMÚN

Lección 14B

PROGRAMAS DE SIEMPRE

Macarena Berlín, *Hablar por hablar*

La comida latina

AVANCE

14A

UN IDIOMA COMÚN

Un mundo en movimiento

ESTA SEMANA Mis viajes a Guinea Ecuatorial

Mario Segura

Mi primera visita fue en el año 1995. Era mi quinto viaje por tierras africanas y tenía curiosidad por conocer un país hispanohablante en África. Pero ¿realmente era hispanohablante? Llegabas a un sitio y te decían *m'bolo* en fang, en otro *tuë a lövari*, en bubi, en el siguiente algo en ndowe, que son algunas de las otras lenguas que se hablan en este país, pero siempre me contestaban con "hola" y una sonrisa cuando los saludaba en español.

En mi segunda visita me quedé un mes y me fascinó su folclore y sus gentes. Casi siempre estaba en la calle, solía ir cada día al mercado y charlaba con los vendedores. La gente era siempre muy amable y me invitaba a comer en su casa. Su hospitalidad es un rasgo de identidad.

De vez en cuando tenía el placer de disfrutar de alguna de sus costumbres y ceremonias.

Los ecuatoguineanos combinan sus raíces africanas con la influencia española, y la tradición católica convive con muchas tradiciones espirituales como la danza *abira*, un ritual que celebran los curanderos para expulsar a los malos espíritus.

Adoro esta tierra, y ¡espero volver pronto!

Hablar de situaciones y acciones habituales en el pasado

En África **solía conocer** a personas interesantes. **De vez en cuando iba** a alguna expedición y...

14A.1 Use of the imperfect: **solía** + [*infinitive*] Time markers

Vocabulario

1

- **un mundo en movimiento** *a world in motion*
- **quinto/a** *fifth*
- **africano/a** *African*
- **hispanohablante** *Spanish-speaking*
- **fascinar** *to captivate*
- **casi siempre** *almost always*
- **soler (o:ue)** *to usually do something*
- **cada día** *each day*
- **charlar** *to chat*
- **el rasgo** *characteristic*
- **de vez en cuando** *from time to time*
- **ecuatoguineano/a** *from Equatorial Guinea*
- **convivir con** *to coexist with*
- **espiritual** *spiritual*
- **la convivencia** *coexistence*
- **el/la curandero/a** *folk healer*

1 a. ¿Qué sabe usted sobre Guinea Ecuatorial? Lea la crónica de Mario Segura, viajero en África. Haga preguntas a su compañero/a sobre estos temas que aparecen en el texto.

- los idiomas que se hablan en Guinea Ecuatorial
- la convivencia de culturas y religiones diferentes
- el carácter de la gente

1 Suggestion To simplify, read through the bulleted items and help students brainstorm the appopriate question words.

b. ¿Qué otras preguntas tiene sobre Guinea Ecuatorial? Haga una lista de tres preguntas y busque sus respuestas en Internet. En grupos de cuatro, compartan sus averiguaciones.

2 ¿Qué solía hacer Mario durante su estancia en Guinea Ecuatorial? ¿Qué situaciones describe? ¿Cuál le parece a usted más interesante? ¿Por qué?

- (Casi) siempre...
- Cada día...
- De vez en cuando...

2 Casi siempre estaba en la calle. Cada día solía ir al mercado, charlaba con los vendedores, la gente lo invitaba a comer en sus casas. De vez en cuando disfrutaba de costumbres y ceremonias.

3 Piense en un viaje especial y diferente que hizo, y explique a sus compañeros qué solía hacer.

Modelo: *Hace un tiempo viví diez meses en Sudamérica. Casi siempre me alojaba en posadas o en casas particulares. Solía hacer las compras en pequeños mercados.*

3 Suggestion If students have not traveled much, have them talk about what they used to do at a friend or family member's house. Alternatively, have students research a Spanish-speaking country or region and write about a virtual trip they took.

Expresar orden y grado

Era mi **quinto** viaje por tierras africanas. La **primera** vez que vine a Guinea Ecuatorial...

14A.2 Ordinal numbers

Vocabulario *cont.*

expulsar *to expel*

el folclore, la hospitalidad, la ceremonia, el ritual

4

el recurso económico *economic resource*

la industria petrolera *oil industry*

la industria de servicios *service industry*

el petróleo *oil*

el recurso natural *natural resource*

el oro *gold*

explotar *to exploit*

cuarto/a *fourth*

el producto interior bruto (PIB) *gross domestic product (GDP)*

tercero/a *third*

la riqueza *wealth*

la mezcla *mix*

primero/a *first*

el uranio, el turismo

5

la lengua materna *mother tongue*

el África (*f.*) subsahariana *Sub-Saharan Africa*

la lengua oficial *official language*

7

destacable *noteworthy*

fa tela
mulapu
nkiel
elotoo
nkobo

Lenguas de Guinea Ecuatorial

Los ecuatoguineanos hablan sus lenguas maternas africanas, y el español se utiliza en el trabajo, en la escuela y en la administración. Guinea Ecuatorial es el único país del África subsahariana que tiene el español como lengua oficial, además del francés y del portugués.

Spanish has been an official language of Equatorial Guinea since 1844. In 1964, the country became independent of Spain. Spanish is rarely used in spontaneous daily interactions between the country's inhabitants. Portuguese was added as an official language in 2007.

4 a. Lea esta información sobre Guinea Ecuatorial y enumere los recursos económicos del país por orden de importancia. primero: industria petrolera, segundo: recursos naturales, tercero: turismo

- industria petrolera
- turismo
- recursos naturales

Antes del descubrimiento de petróleo en 1995, sus recursos naturales eran principalmente la madera, el uranio y el oro, pero no estaban explotados. Ahora es el cuarto productor de petróleo de África y su producto interior bruto es el tercero más alto del mundo, aunque esta riqueza no ha llegado a todos los ecuatoguineanos.

El turismo es el otro gran potencial de este país en el corazón de África: sus playas, su clima tropical, su vegetación exuberante, su folclore, el calor de sus gentes y una atractiva mezcla de culturas, invitan a un viaje diferente.

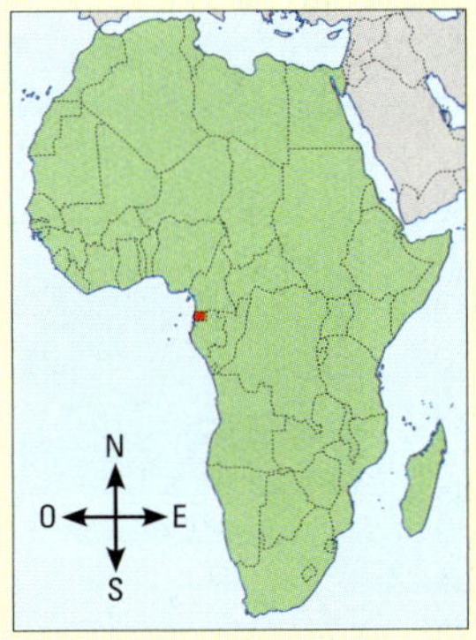

b. ¿Qué puesto ocupa Guinea Ecuatorial como productor de petróleo en África? ¿Y su producto interior bruto a nivel mundial? cuarto; tercero

5 Lea la nota sociocultural sobre las lenguas de Guinea Ecuatorial. ¿En su comunidad se hablan varios idiomas? ¿Cuáles, y en qué contexto?

6 Observe las gráficas sobre el PIB de Bolivia y de España. Luego conteste las preguntas y compare sus respuestas con las de su compañero/a.

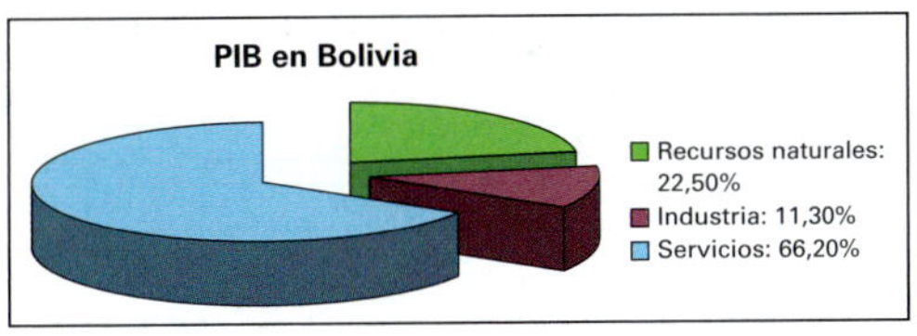

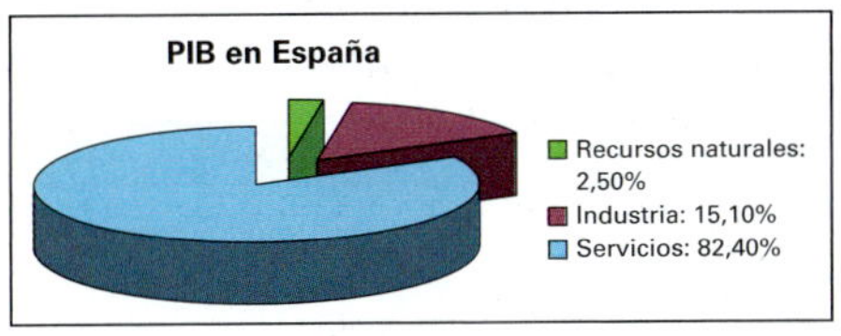

a. ¿Cuál es el segundo recurso económico de Bolivia? ¿Y el tercero? recursos naturales; industria

b. ¿Qué diferencia hay entre la industria en España y en Bolivia? Possible answer: La industria está más desarrollada en España. En Bolivia, la industria es el tercer recurso económico y en España es el segundo.

c. Los recursos naturales son muy importantes para el PIB de Bolivia. ¿Esto le parece algo positivo o negativo? ¿Por qué?

MI EXPERIENCIA

7 Cuando era pequeño/a, ¿estuvo en un país o región interesante? Describa qué solía hacer allí. ¿Qué le pareció destacable? Comente estos aspectos.

GUIÓN DE TRABAJO

Cuando era pequeño/a, solía ir a / me gustaba...

¿Y qué solías hacer allí?
¿Qué cosas hacías cada día?
¿Qué te pareció interesante?

Cada día solía...
Siempre/De vez en cuando...
Me pareció interesante, en primer lugar..., en segundo lugar...

Practice more at **vhlcentral.com.**

SAM: Actividades pp. 289–291

Intercambios

miredsocial.com

Inicio Perfil Amigos Bandeja de entrada Mandy

Fotos **Mandy (Baviera) Alemania**

Muro Información Fotos

Mis compañeros

La catedral de Santa Isabel en Malabo

Mis idiomas:
Alemán, inglés y español

Mi país favorito:
Guinea Ecuatorial, por la gente, el folclore, el clima cálido...

Mi sueño:
Trabajar en Guinea Ecuatorial en proyectos de cooperación internacional

Mis audios:
Entrevista en la radio de la facultad ¡Nuevo!

Mi vida académica en fechas:

- Marzo de 2009: llegada a Malabo. Decidí estudiar un tiempo en Guinea Ecuatorial porque había sido una colonia española en el corazón de África. Además, la universidad de Alcalá había organizado un programa de intercambio con la UNGE (Universidad Nacional de Guinea Ecuatorial).
- Septiembre de 2008: mudanza a Alcalá de Henares (España). Nunca antes había visto tantas fiestas de estudiantes.
- Mayo de 2007: primer viaje sola por Europa: España, Francia, Italia... Un mes antes había aprobado el bachillerato, mi último paso antes de la universidad. Hasta ese momento había pensado en estudiar medicina, pero cambié al español.

MIS MENSAJES

Hola, guapa: No sabía que querías estudiar medicina.

Creía que en Guinea Ecuatorial hablaban francés.

Yo pensaba que Alcalá era muy aburrido, pero ¡no es así!

Hablar de acciones anteriores a una acción pasada

Antes de venir a España ya **había estudiado** español.

14A.3 Past perfect

Vocabulario

8

la bandeja de entrada *inbox*
el perfil *profile*
el programa de intercambio *exchange program*
la vida académica *academic life*
la mudanza *move*
aprobar (o:ue) *to pass*
el bachillerato *high school studies*
la colonia

9

el/la comerciante *storekeeper*
el/la tenista *tennis player*
la formación profesional *professional training*

8 Fíjese en las fotos y en el perfil de esta estudiante de intercambio. ¿Utiliza usted alguna red social? ¿Qué había hecho Mandy antes de estos acontecimientos?

- primer viaje por Europa — Había aprobado el bachillerato.
- viaje a Alcalá — Había viajado por Europa.
- viaje a Guinea Ecuatorial — Había vivido en Alcalá.

9 a. Complete las oraciones con la forma correcta de cada verbo.

1. Antes de ir a Guinea Ecuatorial, Mandy ya ....había estudiado.... (estudiar) español.
2. Tres semanas antes del examen, nosotros ya ....habíamos leído.... (leer) todos los libros.
3. Cuando viajasteis por Latinoamérica, ¿vosotros ya ....habíais aprobado.... (aprobar) el bachillerato?
4. Antes de ser comerciante, yo ....había decidido.... (decidir) ser tenista.
5. Cuando llegamos a tu casa, tú ya ....habías salido.... (salir).
6. Antes de tomar clases de guitarra, ustedes ....habían tomado.... (tomar) clases de piano.

b. Lea estos acontecimientos y cuéntele a su compañero/a qué había hecho usted antes.

terminar el instituto/ estudios	viajar a un país hispanohablante	participar en un curso de español

Modelo: *Antes de terminar el instituto, ya había aprendido idiomas.*

9b Expansion Have students make a time line of their partner's life events. Their partner should verify the accuracy of the time line.

Expresar desconocimiento

No sabía que en Guinea Ecuatorial se hablaba español.

Pensaba que había sido una colonia francesa.

14A.4 **no sabía que, creía que, pensaba que...**

Vocabulario

11

llamar la atención *to catch one's attention*

el volumen *volume*

¿Cómo? *What?; Excuse me?*

12

fomentar *to encourage*

cursar *to study*

incentivar *to encourage*

el perfeccionamiento *improvement*

transfronterizo/a *cross-border*

la beca ERASMUS *ERASMUS scholarship*

la solicitud *application*

validar, el respeto, la tolerancia

Estrategia

Pedir repetición

- He aprendido ndowe.
- ¿Perdona?
- Ndowe: es una lengua bantú.
- Ban... ¿cómo?

¡OJO!

ERASMUS is an acronym of the program's official name in English: *European Region Action Scheme for the Mobility of University Students*, or **Plan de Acción de la Comunidad Europea para la Movilidad de Estudiantes Universitarios**.

12 The Dutch humanist Desiderius Erasmus Roterodamus (1466–1536), was a philosopher, Catholic priest, and theologian.

13 **Expansion** Tell students to imagine that they are several years in the future and have just gotten married. Ask them to write a list of the things that they had done before marrying and share with a partner.

10 Un amigo no sabía que Mandy quería estudiar Medicina. Otro amigo creía que en Guinea Ecuatorial hablaban francés. Otro pensaba que Alcalá era muy aburrido.

10 Vuelva a leer el perfil de Mandy. ¿Qué información era nueva para sus amigos de la red? ¿Aprendió algo usted? Comenten estos temas en parejas.

- la UNGE
- diferencias culturales
- Guinea Ecuatorial
- lenguas en Guinea

11 a. Escuche la entrevista que le hacen a Mandy y ordene los acontecimientos.

Modelo: *Antes de vivir en Alcalá de Henares, ya había viajado por Europa.*

A. ....2.... vivir en Alcalá de Henares ....1.... viajar por Europa

B. ....1.... estudiar en Alemania ....2.... estudiar en España

C. ....2.... venir a España ....1.... estudiar español

b. Escuche de nuevo. Fíjese en los recursos para pedir repetición y complete los fragmentos de la entrevista.

- Cuéntanos, Mandy, ¿qué es lo que más te ha llamado la atención en Alcalá?
- Sin duda, el volumen de las conversaciones.
- ....Perdona...., ¿el volumen?

- Aunque no solo se habla español, también muchas otras lenguas como el fang, el bubi o el annobonés...
- ¿ ....Cómo.... ? ¿Qué lenguas dices?

12 a. Lea este texto sobre un programa de intercambio de estudiantes.

LA GENERACIÓN ERASMUS

ERASMUS se creó en 1987 para fomentar la integración de los jóvenes universitarios europeos, quienes pueden cursar materias de su carrera en otras universidades europeas y validarlas en la propia. Ya han participado 1,7 millones de jóvenes. Además, en 2004 se creó ERASMUS Mundus con el objetivo de integrar a jóvenes profesionales de todo el mundo. Estos programas de intercambio cultural no solo incentivan el perfeccionamiento académico y el estudio de idiomas, también buscan crear una sociedad global basada en el respeto y la tolerancia. Además, abren el mercado laboral y permiten el nacimiento de grandes amistades transfronterizas.

b. ¿En qué consiste el programa de becas ERASMUS? ¿Quiénes pueden participar? ERASMUS es un programa de becas que permite a los estudiantes cursar materias en otras universidades y validarlas en la propia. Pueden participar los estudiantes universitarios europeos.

c. ¿Qué opina acerca de este tipo de programas de intercambio? ¿Le gustaría presentar una solicitud para participar en alguno? ¿Por qué?

12c Ask students if they know of any other international scholarship or fellowship programs.

MI EXPERIENCIA

13 ¿Qué cosas habían hecho ustedes antes de empezar la universidad? Hagan una lista y compárenlas. ¿Qué información les resulta sorprendente?

GUIÓN DE TRABAJO

¿Qué habías hecho antes de empezar la universidad?

Antes de empezar la universidad, yo...
había estudiado...
había vivido en...
había viajado...

Perdona, no sabía que habías...
¿Cómo? Pensaba que...

Practice more at vhlcentral.com.

SAM: Actividades pp. 292–294

Equatorial Guinea has an estimated 600 million barrels of crude oil. The per capita income rose from $600 in 1998 to $10,000 in 2007. However, President Obiang, who has been in power since 1979, has been criticized by some for lack of transparency with regard to oil revenues. In 2010, he pledged reforms that will bring more stability and transparency to his regime.

Acacio Maye Ocomo, una vida en el mar

ORO NEGRO

Es lunes por la mañana y hace dos días el precio del barril de petróleo en la Bolsa de Nueva York llegó a los 74 dólares. Fue un buen día para Guinea Ecuatorial. El desarrollo del sector energético de este país es imparable. Tiene la renta per cápita más alta de África, pero la vida de la mayoría no ha mejorado.

Acacio Maye Ocomo trabaja como ingeniero en una de las plataformas petroleras más importantes del país en el golfo de Guinea. La demanda laboral en este sector ha crecido mucho.

"Si eres ecuatoguineano, es una buena alternativa para vivir bien aquí", explica Acacio. "Trabajo en el mar desde hace seis años. El primer año fue el más duro. Había vuelto a Guinea Ecuatorial después de estudiar ingeniería en España y fue muy difícil al principio. Si trabajas en una plataforma en el mar, pasas mucho tiempo solo. Al principio no tenía muchos días libres y solía quedarme en la plataforma, solía pasar el día en el exterior, leía y contemplaba los atardeceres en el mar.

En la plataforma convivíamos personas de los cinco continentes. Yo pensaba que no era posible entenderse con gente tan diferente, pero estaba equivocado. De vez en cuando podía haber algún malentendido, pero si la relación con tus compañeros es buena, son como una segunda familia. El tercer año cambié de compañía y, por tanto, de compañeros. Fue como volver a empezar. Ahora llevo en esta plataforma dos años, y he conocido a Nora, mi mujer. Trabaja como ingeniera también y es australiana. Nora y yo queremos formar una familia. Si seguimos aquí unos años más, ahorraremos para empezar en otra parte" nos cuenta Acacio, siempre con la sonrisa en los labios y muy esperanzado.

Acacio Maye Ocomo en la plataforma petrolera donde trabaja

Expresar condiciones posibles

Si quieres trabajar en Guinea Ecuatorial, **es** una alternativa segura.

Si repartimos los recursos, la situación **será** mejor para todos.

14A.5 **si** + [*present*], [*present/simple future*]

Vocabulario

(14)

el oro negro *black gold*
el barril de petróleo *oil barrel*
el desarrollo *development*
el sector energético *energy sector*
imparable *unstoppable*
la renta per cápita *per capita income*
la plataforma petrolera *oil rig*
la demanda laboral *labor demand*
duro/a *hard*
el día libre *day off*
el atardecer *dusk*
equivocado/a *mistaken*
el malentendido *misunderstanding*

14 Lea el título de este artículo y observe la foto del protagonista. ¿Qué cree que es el "oro negro"? Después lea el reportaje y anote los datos más interesantes de la vida de este protagonista. Pregúntele a su compañero/a.
El oro negro es el petróleo.

15 Busque en el texto estos términos económicos y relaciónelos con su significado.

1. renta per cápita ...c...
2. sector energético ...b...
3. demanda laboral ...a...

a. necesidad de empleos
b. área económica relacionada con la producción de energía
c. renta nacional dividida por el número de habitantes de un país

16 ¿Qué solía hacer Acacio cuando empezó a trabajar en una plataforma? ¿Qué creía el protagonista antes de convivir con sus compañeros?
Possible answer: Solía quedarse en la plataforma. Solía pasar el día en el exterior. Leía y contemplaba los atardeceres en el mar. Creía que no era posible entenderse con gente tan diferente.

17 Fíjese en estas oraciones que aparecen en el texto y complételas.

1. Si trabajas en una plataforma en el mar, ...pasas mucho tiempo solo...... .
2. Si la relación con tus compañeros es buena, ...son como una segunda familia...... .
3. Si seguimos aquí unos años más, ...ahorraremos para empezar en otra parte...... .

18 Piense en situaciones posibles que pueden suceder en estos trabajos y compare sus ideas con las de su compañero/a.

- pescador(a)
- domador(a) de leones
- astronauta

Modelo: *Si eres pescador...*

18 Suggestion Have students state which profession they find the most interesting and explain why.

¿PROFESIONES COMUNES?

farero/a

Son profesiones particulares, lugares a veces privilegiados donde vivir, en ocasiones fuera de la sociedad.

"Hace más de 10 años que me dedico a esto y me encanta, pero sé que es una profesión en extinción. La tecnología sustituye al hombre."

Estos oficios son únicos porque permiten un encuentro con la naturaleza y con nosotros mismos. Y si algo nos da tantas satisfacciones, el esfuerzo vale la pena.

"Todos los días debo levantarme tempranísimo y salir a trabajar. Paso mucho tiempo solo, y a veces hace frío o llueve, pero soy feliz. Este oficio es una tradición familiar y estoy orgulloso de formar parte de ella."

pescador

guarda forestal

Hay profesiones que condicionan el lugar donde vives, profesiones que te alejan de la sociedad y de tu familia durante mucho tiempo y suponen grandes responsabilidades.

"Si preservamos nuestros espacios naturales, protegeremos el medio ambiente. Por eso no me molestan los sacrificios. Sé que estoy ayudando al planeta."

Vocabulario *cont.*

esperanzado/a *hopeful*
el continente
18
suceder *to happen*
el/la pescador(a) *fisherman/fisherwoman*
el/la domador(a) de leones *lion tamer*
19
el/la farero/a *lighthouse keeper*
el/la guarda forestal *forest ranger*
sustituir (y) *to substitute*
el oficio *trade*
valer (lg) la pena *to be worth it*
condicionar *to determine*
la extinción, la responsabilidad, la satisfacción
20
la revuelta *revolt*
la minoría *minority*
la ascendencia *ancestry*

OPINIÓN

¿Qué opina de la vida de nuestro protagonista?

¿Le gustaría vivir en una plataforma petrolera?¿Por qué?

19 a. Lea estos fragmentos de un artículo sobre trabajos en lugares alejados de los centros urbanos. ¿A qué profesiones corresponden estos testimonios? Anote las profesiones en la imagen adecuada.

pescador(a) • farero/a • científico/a • guarda forestal

b. ¿Qué profesión le parece más interesante? ¿Cuál le gustaría experimentar y por qué? Con su compañero/a, hagan una lista de otras profesiones y lugares poco comunes donde vivir o trabajar.

19b **Suggestion** Alternatively, have pairs write descriptions of uncommon professions for another pair to guess.

20 Aquí tiene algunos datos sobre Guinea Ecuatorial. Clasifíquelos. ¿Recuerda alguno más? Compare sus respuestas con las de sus compañeros.

○ historia ○ recursos ○ política ○ población

- Guinea Ecuatorial es el cuarto exportador de petróleo en África y el segundo proveedor de España. ......recursos......
- Hay tres países con el nombre de Guinea: Guinea, Guinea Bissau y Guinea Ecuatorial. ......geografía......
- Se independizó en el año 1968 después de las primeras revueltas independentistas de 1967. ......historia......
- Con unos 600 000 habitantes, es el único país hispanohablante con mayoría negra. La minoría blanca (1%) son los blancos europeos de ascendencia española. ......población......

Practice more at **vhlcentral.com.**

SAM: Actividades pp. 295–298

21 a. Lea estos fragmentos del libro *Ekomo* (1985) de la escritora ecuatoguineana María Nsue. ¿Cuáles de estos temas trata la autora? ¿Con qué temas asocia usted África? ¿Y sus compañeros? folclore, tradición, modernidad, religión, magia, personalidad de un pueblo

folclore • tradición • modernidad • religión • naturaleza • magia • personalidad de un pueblo

21a **Suggestion** To aid comprehension, encourage students to draw a simple picture to represent each paragraph.

Nfumbá'a, el africano de hoy, hombre del mañana, tras° estar dos lluvias en Europa dejó su tradición encerrada entre los libros; dejó allí su personalidad y sus creencias° africanas, y el ser° sin continente regresó a su pueblo con un disfraz° de europeo pero sin el europeo dentro. [...]

El poblado [...] estaba lleno de gente de las aldeas vecinas que habían acudido° al oír que aquella noche se iba a ejecutar nuestra danza. [...]

Las notas del tambor° llegaron a mis oídos. La danza daba comienzo. [...] Me convertí en los sonidos del tam-tam. Vibré°, vibré y vibré al son de sus sonidos. Mi espíritu se escapó del cuerpo y voló [...].

NSUE, María: *Ekomo*. Madrid, Ediciones Sial, 2008

María Nsue nació en 1945 en una familia de etnia fang. Emigró con sus padres a España cuando tenía ocho años, y allí realizó sus estudios y empezó su carrera literaria. Volvió a Guinea Ecuatorial y trabajó en el Ministerio de Educación y Cultura. Años después decidió instalarse en Madrid. Ekomo es la primera novela publicada por una mujer ecuatoguineana.

tras *after* **creencias** *beliefs* **el ser** *being* **disfraz** *disguise* **acudido** *attended* **tambor** *drum* **vibré** *I vibrated*

b. ¿Qué cree que quiere decir la autora con estas frases?
Possible answers: el africano actual; con ropa y hábitos de europeo; después de dos años en Europa

- "el africano de hoy"
- "con un disfraz de europeo pero sin el europeo dentro"
- "tras estar dos lluvias en Europa"

c. Lea los datos autobiográficos de la autora. ¿Qué relación encuentra con su obra? Possible answer: Es africana, emigró a Europa, estudió y comenzó a trabajar allí, regresó a Guinea...

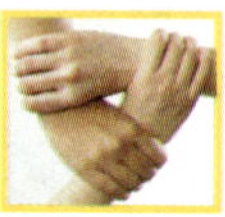

TAREA FINAL

Intercambio cultural en red

Busque datos sobre un país o una región que le interese: lenguas, fiestas, cultura, tradiciones, etc. Escriba una historia en el pasado relacionada con alguno de estos temas.

Comparta su historia con sus compañeros y participen en una red de intercambio cultural para estudiantes. ¿Qué sabían o pensaban de estos temas?

Decidan qué quieren conseguir en esta red y en qué orden: intercambio de información cultural, música, chatear con otros estudiantes, etc.

Emphasize that students may choose a non-Spanish-speaking country or region.

YO PUEDO...

- Puedo hablar de situaciones y acciones habituales en el pasado.
  Piense en un momento de su vida en el pasado y en qué solía hacer.
- Puedo expresar orden y grado.
  Anote con letra estos números ordinales y complete la serie.
  1.° primero 2.° segundo 3.° tercero 4.° cuarto
  5.° quinto , sexto, séptimo, octavo, noveno, décimo
- Puedo hablar de acciones anteriores a una acción pasada.
  Cuente qué idiomas había estudiado antes de aprender español.
- Puedo expresar desconocimiento.
  Diga qué cosas no sabía antes de estudiar esta lección.
- Puedo expresar condiciones posibles.
  Complete la oración.
  Si vives en un país extranjero...

GRAMÁTICA FUNCIONAL

14A.1 Talk about past situations and habitual actions

Use of the imperfect: **solía** + [*infinitive*], **(casi) siempre, de vez en cuando, cada día** 5.15, 5.4.3, 5.6, 12.12

- Use a form of the verb **soler** in the **pretérito imperfecto** to talk about habitual actions in the past. When used in the imperfect, **soler** + [*infinitive*] expresses the idea of *used to*.

  Solía comer en ese restaurante cuando vivía en este barrio.
  *I **used to eat** in that restaurant when I lived in this neighborhood.*

- [*Imperfect of* **soler**] + [*infinitive*] expresses the same idea as **normalmente** + [*imperfect*]; **solía estudiar** = **normalmente estudiaba** (*I usually studied*).

- Other expressions of frequency that often signal the use of the **pretérito imperfecto** include **(casi) siempre** [*(almost) always*], **de vez en cuando** (*from time to time*), and **cada día/mes** (*every day/month*).

  Cuando vivía en Perú, solía dar un paseo **cada día** y **casi siempre** quedaba con mis amigos.
  *When I lived in Peru, I used to take a walk **every day** and I **almost always** made plans to meet with my friends.*

  De vez en cuando íbamos al cine.
  ***Sometimes** we would go to the movies.*

- You have learned other uses of the **pretérito imperfecto** in 9A.1 and 13B.1 and you have seen the **pretérito imperfecto** compared with the **pretérito indefinido** in 9B.3 and 10B.1.

14A.2 Express order and degree

Ordinal numbers 13.2

- Use ordinal numbers (**números ordinales**) to represent a position in a sequence. These numbers are equivalent to *first, second, third,* etc.

primer, primero/a (1.er/1.o/1.a)	**sexto/a** (6.o/6.a)
segundo/a (2.o/2.a)	**séptimo/a** (7.o/7.a)
tercer, tercero/a (3.er/3.o/3.a)	**octavo/a** (8.o/8.a)
cuarto/a (4.o/4.a)	**noveno/a** (9.o/9.a)
quinto/a (5.o/5.a)	**décimo/a** (10.o/10.a)

- Ordinal numbers are adjectives and must agree with the noun they modify.

  Juan empezó a estudiar francés en el **sexto** grado.
  *Juan began studying French in the **sixth** grade.*

- The shortened forms **primer** and **tercer** are used in front of singular masculine nouns. These forms are abbreviated as 1.er and 3.er, respectively.

  Estaba nervioso el **primer** día de clase.
  *He was nervous on the **first** day of class.*

- Use the abbreviated forms 1.a, 2.a, etc. when referring to the feminine forms.

Suggestion Tell students to write five statements about things they used to do, using expressions of frequency. Three sentences should be true and two false. Then have students share their sentences in small groups and guess which statements are false.

¡Póngalo en práctica!

G1 Complete el párrafo con los verbos en el pretérito imperfecto.

Cuando (1) ....era.... (yo, ser) pequeña, (2) ....vivía.... (yo, vivir) con mis padres en Guinea Ecuatorial. Ellos (3) ....trabajaban.... (trabajar) en una empresa de exportación de madera. Nosotros (4) ....teníamos.... (tener) una casa en el centro de Malabo. (5) ....Solía.... (Yo, soler) jugar con mis hermanos en la calle, pues siempre (6) ....hacía.... (hacer) buen tiempo. La gente (7) ....era.... (ser) muy amable y siempre (8) ....ayudaba.... (ayudar) con las necesidades de sus vecinos.

G2 Complete la conversación de forma lógica.

- Cuando eras pequeño, ¿(1) ....solías.... ir a la piscina?
- Sí, iba (2) ....cada mes...., excepto en diciembre.
- ¿Y por qué no ibas en diciembre?
- Porque mis hermanos y yo (3) ....solíamos.... pasar diciembre con los abuelos. ¿Y tú?
- Yo iba a la piscina sólo de (4) ....vez.... en (5) ....cuando.... No me gusta nadar.
- ¿O sea que no hacías nada de deporte?
- En realidad, mis amigos y yo bajábamos a la plaza (6) ....cada.... día después de clases para jugar al fútbol.

G3 Expansion Have students write four sentences about their own lives, using ordinal numbers.

G3 Complete las oraciones con los números ordinales.

1. España es el ....primer.... (1.er) productor de aceite de oliva del mundo.
2. Paco ha ganado el ....tercer.... (3.er) premio en el concurso. Es la ....primera.... (1.a) vez que gana y está muy contento.
3. Nigeria fue el ....segundo.... (2.o) productor de petróleo de África en 2008.
4. Juana es la ....quinta.... (5.a) hermana de una familia de ocho.
5. Vivimos en el ....noveno.... (9.a) piso del edificio.
6. Cuando terminamos el ....séptimo.... (7.o) grado, viajamos a Córdoba.

G4 Escriba la frase correspondiente según el modelo.

Modelo: 3 / productor
el tercer productor

1. 2 / clase — la segunda clase
2. 7 / planta — la séptima planta
3. 4 / lugar — el cuarto lugar
4. 1 / página — la primera página
5. 5 / país — el quinto país
6. 8 / viaje — el octavo viaje

Practice more at **vhlcentral.com.**

GRAMÁTICA FUNCIONAL

Point out that unlike in English, the adverb (**ya**) should not be placed between the auxiliary verb (**había**) and the past participle.

14A.3 Talk about actions prior to a past action

The past perfect 5.5, 11.6

- To talk about actions that happened before another past action or event, use the past perfect (**pretérito pluscuamperfecto**). The **pretérito pluscuamperfecto** is formed with the imperfect of the verb **haber** + [*past participle*].

Antes de vivir en Guinea Ecuatorial, Mariano ya **había viajado** por Europa.
*Before living in Equatorial Guinea, Mariano **had** already **traveled** through Europe.*

Remind students that these past participle forms are invariable.

	HABER	+ [*past participle*]
(yo)	había	hablado comido vivido
(tú)	habías	
(usted, él, ella)	había	
(nosotros/as)	habíamos	
(vosotros/as)	habíais	
(ustedes, ellos/as)	habían	

- The **pretérito pluscuamperfecto** is frequently used with the adverb **ya** (*already*) to emphasize that one action or event occurred prior to another.

14A.4 Express that something is unknown

Use of the imperfect: **no sabía que/creía que/pensaba que** 5.4.3

- Use the imperfect in constructions such as **no sabía que, creía que,** and **pensaba que** to express ignorance about a subject.

No sabía que había intercambios entre universidades.
*I **didn't know** that there **were** exchanges among universities.*

- The verb in the second clause of the sentence is also used in the imperfect.

Yo creía que **vivías** en el centro.
*I thought **you lived** downtown.*

14A.5 Express possible conditions

si + [*present*], [*present/simple future*] 12.9

- To express a possible situation in the present or the future, use the construction **si** + [*present*], [*present/simple future*].

Si viajas al extranjero, **aprendes** la lengua y la cultura de otros países.
***If you travel** abroad, **you learn** the language and culture of other countries.*

- You can also switch the order of the clauses with no comma in between; just be sure that the condition (the *if*-clause) begins with **si**.

Viajaremos a Costa Rica este verano **si ahorramos** suficiente dinero.
*We'll travel to Costa Rica this summer **if we save** enough money.*

¡Póngalo en práctica!

G5 Complete las oraciones con la forma correcta del pretérito pluscuamperfecto.

1. Antes de trabajar en la fábrica, Mariano ...había sido... (ser) camarero.
2. Cuando terminé la carrera de historia en 1999, ya ...había empezado... (empezar) arqueología.
3. Antes de viajar a Guinea Ecuatorial, Flavia y Óscar ya ...habían ido... (ir) a España.
4. Cuando vinimos a Guinea Ecuatorial, ya ...habíamos estudiado... (estudiar) español.
5. Antes de ir a Nueva York, vosotros ...habíais vivido... (vivir) en Los Ángeles.
6. Mariana ya me ...había dicho... (decir) que no podía ir a la clase, pero me llamó de nuevo para avisarme.
7. Cuando llegamos a casa de Ana, ella ya ...había salido... (salir).
8. Antes de aceptar la oferta, Raúl ...había consultado... (consultar) con varios expertos.

G5 Expansion Ask students to write a few impressions that they had at the beginning of this course, about Spanish, classmates, or the professor. Have them share their sentences with a partner.

G6 Complete las oraciones con el pretérito imperfecto.

1. Los estudiantes no ...sabían... (saber) que el fang era una lengua bantú.
2. ...Pensaba... (Yo, pensar) que sabía español cuando viajé a España, pero aprendí muchas expresiones nuevas.
3. • ¿Sabíais que en Guinea Ecuatorial se hablaba español?
   ▪ No, nosotros ...pensábamos... (pensar) que se hablaba otro idioma.
4. Joaquín ...creía... (creer) que ese libro iba a ser aburrido, pero le gustó mucho.

G7 Complete las oraciones.

1. Si ...viajas... (tú, viajar) a Guinea Ecuatorial el año que viene, ...podrás... (tú, poder) practicar español.
2. Si ...trabajas... (tú, trabajar) en el extranjero, ...conocerás/conoces... (tú, conocer) a muchas personas interesantes.
3. Si ...aprendes... (tú, aprender) la lengua del país, ...te integrarás/te integras... (tú, integrarse) sin problemas.
4. Si ...tengo... (yo, tener) vacaciones, te ...visitaré... (yo, visitar) en julio.
5. Mi hermano ...puede/podrá... (él, poder) ir también si ...termina... (él, terminar) de escribir su tesis.

Practice more at **vhlcentral.com.**

VOCABULARIO

14A

Un mundo en movimiento

un mundo en movimiento	*a world in motion*
el África (f.) subsahariana	*Sub-Saharan Africa*
la ceremonia	*ceremony*
la convivencia	*coexistence*
el/la curandero/a	*folk healer*
el folclore	*folklore*
la hospitalidad	*hospitality*
la industria de servicios	*service industry*
la industria petrolera	*oil industry*
la lengua materna	*mother tongue*
la lengua oficial	*official language*
la mezcla	*mix*
el oro	*gold*
el petróleo	*oil*
el producto interior bruto (PIB)	*gross domestic product (GDP)*
el rasgo	*characteristic*
el recurso económico	*economic resource*
el recurso natural	*natural resource*
la riqueza	*wealth*
el ritual	*ritual*
el turismo	*tourism*
el uranio	*uranium*
charlar	*to chat*
convivir con	*to coexist with*
explotar	*to exploit*
expulsar	*to expel*
fascinar	*to captivate*
soler (o:ue)	*to usually do something*
africano/a	*African*
cuarto/a	*fourth*
destacable	*noteworthy*
ecuatoguineano/a	*from Equatorial Guinea*
espiritual	*spiritual*
hispanohablante	*Spanish-speaking*
primero/a	*first*
quinto/a	*fifth*
tercero/a	*third*
cada día	*each day*
casi siempre	*almost always*
de vez en cuando	*from time to time*

Intercambios

¿Cómo?	*What?, Excuse me?*
el bachillerato	*high school studies*
la bandeja de entrada	*inbox*
la beca ERASMUS	*ERASMUS scholarship*
la colonia	*colony*
el/la comerciante	*storekeeper*
la formación profesional	*professional training*
la mudanza	*move*
el perfeccionamiento	*improvement*
el perfil	*profile*
el programa de intercambio	*exchange program*
el respeto	*respect*
la solicitud	*application*
el/la tenista	*tennis player*
la tolerancia	*tolerance*
la vida académica	*academic life*
el volumen	*volume*
aprobar (o:ue)	*to pass*
cursar	*to study*
fomentar	*to encourage*
incentivar	*to encourage*
llamar la atención	*to catch one's attention*
validar	*to validate*
transfronterizo/a	*cross-border*

Acacio Maye Ocomo

la ascendencia	*ancestry*
el atardecer	*dusk*
el barril de petróleo	*oil barrel*
el continente	*continent*
la demanda laboral	*labor demand*
el desarrollo	*development*
el día libre	*day off*
el/la domador(a) de leones	*lion tamer*
la extinción	*extinction*
el/la farero/a	*lighthouse keeper*
el/la guarda forestal	*forest ranger*
el malentendido	*misunderstanding*
la minoría	*minority*
el oficio	*trade*
el oro negro	*black gold*
el/la pescador(a)	*fisherman/ fisherwoman*
la plataforma petrolera	*oil rig*
la renta per cápita	*per capita income*
la responsabilidad	*responsibility*
la revuelta	*revolt*
la satisfacción	*satisfaction*
el sector energético	*energy sector*
condicionar	*to determine*
suceder	*to happen*
sustituir (y)	*to substitute*
valer (lg) la pena	*to be worth it*
duro/a	*hard*
equivocado/a	*mistaken*
esperanzado/a	*hopeful*
imparable	*unstoppable*

Variación léxica

aburrido/a ⟷ **aguado/a** (*fam., Ven. y Ecu.*) ⟷ **monse** (*fam., Per.*) ⟷ **fome** (*fam. Chi.*)

la convivencia ⟷ **la coexistencia** ⟷ **la cohabitación**

el día libre ⟷ **el día de descanso** ⟷ **el día franco** (*Arg.*)

el folclore ⟷ **el folklore**

fomentar ⟷ **promover** ⟷ **incentivar**

hispanohablante ⟷ **hispanoparlante** ⟷ **de habla hispana**

validar ⟷ **homologar**

Suggestion Have pairs of students select a column of vocabulary and play *Hangman*, using the words from that list.

14B

Suggestion After reviewing the Web page, survey the class to find out which decade they prefer. Ask them to discuss whether they remember the same elements of pop culture, or if they cherish different ones. You may also wish to talk about world events that marked that decade and perhaps shaped some of the movies, music, and shows that were popular.

PROGRAMAS DE SIEMPRE

La mejor década

@ www.lamejordecada.com

FORO LA MEJOR DÉCADA

El programa de televisión ***La mejor década*** nos recuerda la música que escuchábamos cuando éramos jóvenes, los actores que admirábamos cuando íbamos al cine o nuestros programas de televisión favoritos. ¿Qué recuerda usted, amigo internauta y telespectador, de las últimas tres décadas? Defienda en esta página web su década favorita.

Recuerdo que cuando pasaban la serie *Dallas* en la tele, no había nadie por la calle, y ¿quién no ha visto la película *E.T.*? Cuando tenía 16 años, me enamoré del cantante Prince y también escuchaba a The Police o Madonna (¡durante un año me estuve vistiendo como ella!). Sin duda, ¡es la década ganadora!

Ana 82

Cuando compré mi primer LP de U2 ¡no sabía nada de inglés!, pero me encantaba su música y todavía me gusta, hoy los he estado escuchando. En la tele veíamos *Friends*, ¡una serie muy divertida! Mi hermano estaba loco por *Los Simpson*. Y películas… ¡muchas! *La vida es bella* de Roberto Benigni, y más: *Thelma y Louise*, *Todo sobre mi madre* de Almodóvar, etc. Yo defiendo esta década.

Fibi

¡La primera década del siglo XXI, sin duda! Empezamos un nuevo milenio y eso es único. También se estrenó *Harry Potter*. Me aprendí de memoria todas las películas, ¡no podía dejar de verlas! Además, creo que todos quedamos fascinados con *Lost*, (¡qué sorpresa el final!), nos volvimos investigadores con *CSI* y lloramos con las canciones del grupo musical Coldplay. Definitivamente: ¡la mejor década!

Y2K

Situar hechos pasados

Cuando era pequeña, no **teníamos** cable en casa…

Cuando instalaron el cable, ya no **vivía** con mis padres.

14B.1 **cuando** + [*imperfect*]/[*preterite*]

Vocabulario

1

el/la telespectador(a) *television viewer*
la página web *Web page*
pasar la serie de televisión *to broadcast the television series*
la serie de televisión *television series*
ganador(a) *winning*
estrenarse *to premiere*
aprender de memoria *to memorize*
fascinado/a *fascinated*
llorar *to cry*

1 Observe la página web del programa *La mejor década* y lea los mensajes del foro. ¿Qué décadas (los 80, 90 ó 00) recuerdan y defienden? Complete la ficha.

	Década	Película	Serie de televisión	Grupo musical
Ana 82	los 80	*E.T.*	*Dallas*	Prince, The Police y Madonna
Fibi	los 90	*La vida es bella, Thelma y Louise, Todo sobre mi madre*	*Friends, Los Simpson*	U2
Y2K	del 2000	*Harry Potter*	*Lost, CSI*	Coldplay

2 ¿Conoce usted las referencias de esas décadas que comentan en el foro? Participe en el foro con su recuerdo y después coméntelo con su compañero/a.

Modelo:
- *Cuando tenía 13 años, a mí también me gustaba Coldplay.*
- *Yo compré todos sus CD y esta semana he visto un DVD de su último concierto.*

3 Pida información a su compañero/a sobre estos temas.

¿Qué hacías…? — cuando tenías 15 años…

¿Qué te gustaba…? — cuando terminaste la escuela primaria…

¿Qué pasó…? — cuando…

Hablar de acciones pasadas en desarrollo

- ¿Qué hicieron ayer?
- **Estuvimos durmiendo** la siesta toda la tarde.

14B.2 **estar** (*past tense*) + [*present participle*]

Vocabulario *cont.*

el grupo musical *band, music group*
el sitio web *Web site*
la década, admirar, instalar, el/la investigador(a)

5

el/la aficionado/a *fan*
revivir *to relive*
el espectáculo *show*

6

la letra *lyrics*
a mediados de los 60 *in the mid-sixties*
la clase media *middle class*
incansable *tireless*
plantearse preguntas *to question, to ask oneself questions*
la historieta *comic strip*
brillante

Mafalda

Este simpático personaje del humorista Quino (Joaquín Salvador Lavado) es una niña muy inteligente que vive en Argentina a mediados de los 60 y principios de los 70. Forma parte de una típica familia de clase media y de un curioso grupo de amigos. Luchadora social incansable, siempre se plantea preguntas y hace comentarios brillantes sobre la actualidad de su país y del mundo. La historieta se publicó en los periódicos de 1964 a 1973 y ya ha sido traducida a 26 idiomas.

4 **Maná** is a popular Mexican rock band that has been making albums for over 20 years. They have won numerous awards, including three Grammys.

4 Conteste las preguntas. ¡Sea creativo/a!

Modelo:
- *¿Qué escuchaba cuando iba al instituto?*
- *Cuando iba al instituto estaba todo el día escuchando* Maná.

1. ¿Qué estaba haciendo tu hermana cuando llegamos?
   Cuando llegamos, mi hermana estaba...
2. ¿Qué serie de televisión estuviste mirando este último año?
   Este último año estuve mirando...
3. ¿Qué estuvisteis estudiando en la clase de español?
   En la clase de español estuvimos estudiando...
4. ¿Qué estaban buscando nuestros compañeros en la biblioteca?
   Nuestros compañeros estaban buscando...

5 Fíjese en la foto y complete el comentario de este aficionado. ¿Ha visto usted un concierto de alguno de sus grupos favoritos? ¿Y su compañero/a?

Cuando U2 dio su último concierto en Barcelona yo fui el primero de la fila. Al día siguiente, estuve en casa ....escuchando.... (escuchar) la radio y ....mirando.... (mirar) la tele durante todo el día para revivir el maravilloso espectáculo. Aunque habíamos estado ....esperando.... (esperar) durante horas, valió la pena.

6 Fíjese en la viñeta. ¿Qué música le gusta a Mafalda? ¿Le parece necesario entender la letra de las canciones? ¿O piensa que es suficiente con disfrutar de la melodía? Coméntelo con su compañero/a.

entendés (*voseo*) *you understand* **perro** *dog* **guau** *woof*

6 **Suggestion** Ask students if they like any songs in a language they don't know, and what they like about them.

MI EXPERIENCIA

7 Elija con su compañero/a un año, descríbanlo y defiendan su opinión en clase.

GUIÓN DE TRABAJO

En el año 1995, 2000, 2005, 2010,
¿cuántos años tenías?
¿qué música...?
¿qué película...?
¿qué programas...?
¿qué recuerdos...?
¿qué estabas haciendo...?

→

solía...
tenía...
escuchaba...
miraba...
En el año...
estaba...

Practice more at **vhlcentral.com.**

SAM: Actividades pp. 299–301

14B Remind students that Francisco Franco was in power until his death in 1975; during his rule, society was tightly controlled. A democratic constitution was enacted in 1978.

Cuéntame cómo pasó

Cuéntame cómo pasó

Es una serie de televisión española que durante muchos años ha sido y es líder de audiencia. Aunque se empezó a transmitir en 2001, la ficción se inicia en 1968 y muestra un retrato de la sociedad española a través de una familia de clase media, los Alcántara, que vive día a día la transformación de la España franquista en una democracia moderna. Los españoles recuerdan con esta serie lo del pluriempleo de sus padres, lo que representó la llegada de la tele al hogar, que se convirtió en un miembro más de la familia; lo de la emigración al resto de Europa; lo que contaban los abuelos; y más tarde la llegada de la democracia. En definitiva, representa la vida durante una transición democrática.

Transmitir mensajes

Carlos: "Mañana voy a tu casa."

- Carlos me **comentó** ayer **que** hoy **venía** a mi casa.

14B.3 Indirect discourse: reporting verbs

Vocabulario

8

contar (o:ue) *to tell*
ser líder de audiencia *to be the highest rated*
el retrato *portrait*
día a día *day by day*
franquista *Francoist*
el pluriempleo *having more than one job, moonlighting*
la transición democrática *democratic transition*
la transformación, la democracia, la ficción

9

el capítulo *episode*
preguntar *to ask*
explicar *to explain*
comentar *to mention*
el sueldo *salary*
el/la publicista *publicist*
guatemalteco/a *Guatemalan*
hondureño/a *Honduran*

Point out the usage of **los Alcántara**, as well as **Los Simpson** on page 344. Show students that to refer to a family (*the Joneses, the Simpsons*), they should use the plural definite article **los**, followed by the last name, in its singular form: **los Jones**, **los Simpson**.

8 a. Observe la foto. ¿Qué tipo de familia representa? ¿De qué época? ¿Por qué aparece la tele en la foto familiar? Lea el texto y compruebe. Sample answers: una familia española de clase media; de la década de los 60; porque es como un miembro más de la familia

b. ¿Cómo cree que son los personajes de la serie? Coméntelo con su compañero/a.

9 a. Lea las descripciones de lo que dijeron los personajes en los primeros capítulos de la serie. ¿Quién dijo qué? Relacione las columnas.

1. Antonio preguntó a su familia por qué nunca cenaban todos juntos.
2. Toni le explicó a su hermana Inés que a sus padres los habían educado así, pero que ahora era diferente.
3. Mercedes preguntó cuándo le habían dicho que traían la televisión.
4. Inés le comentó a su madre que era necesario otro sueldo, que muchas chicas ya trabajaban y que era normal.

¿Por qué nunca cenamos todos juntos?

Es necesario otro sueldo. Muchas chicas ya trabajan, es normal.

A papá y a mamá los educaron así, pero ahora es diferente.

¿Cuándo te han dicho que traen la televisión?

b. Transforme las oraciones de estilo directo al estilo indirecto. Use los verbos *preguntar*, *decir* y *comentar*. Sample answers:

Modelo: María: "Mi hermana quiere ser publicista."
María comentó que su hermana quería ser publicista.

1. Pablo: "La semana pasada vi un musical muy divertido."
Pablo dijo que la semana pasada había visto un musical muy divertido.
2. Cristina: "Tengo mucho sueño porque hoy me he levantado a las 6 de la mañana." Cristina comentó que tenía mucho sueño porque se había levantado a las 6 de la mañana.
3. Teresa: "¿Qué solían hacer ustedes durante las vacaciones cuando eran niños?"
Teresa preguntó qué solíamos hacer durante las vacaciones cuando éramos niños.
4. Marcelo: "La mamá de mi mejor amigo es guatemalteca y el papá es hondureño." Marcelo comentó que la mamá de su mejor amigo era guatemalteca y el papá era hondureño.
5. Analía: "¿Quieren cenar en casa? Mi marido va a preparar empanadas."
Analía preguntó si queríamos cenar en su casa y dijo que su marido iba a preparar empanadas.

9b Expansion Have pairs of students take turns reporting on what was said during a recently aired TV episode, using **preguntar, decir,** and **comentar.**

Los años 60

En España en los 60 tuvo lugar una gran transformación económica y social. La explosión turística, el éxodo rural y la emigración al resto de Europa, junto con las inversiones extranjeras, facilitaron la salida de la posguerra y la entrada en una sociedad de consumo. La ilusión de muchos era comprar un pequeño piso, un coche SEAT 600 y un televisor y tener unas pequeñas vacaciones en la costa.

Referirse a un tema

- ¿Sabes **lo que** dijo Toni ayer?
- Dijo que **lo de** casarse no tenía sentido.

14B.4 **lo que** + [*verb*], **lo de** + [*noun/infinitive*]

Estrategia

Controlar el contacto

- ¿Sigues la serie *Cuéntame*?
- No, no tengo tiempo, el trabajo, las clases... Me gusta más la radio, ¿sabes?

Vocabulario

(10)
anterior *previous*
el éxodo *exodus*
la inversión *investment*
la posguerra *postwar period*
la explosión

(11)
tratar *to be about*

(15)
emitir la serie *to broadcast the (television) series*

Have students reread the last sentence of the cultural sidebar. Did Americans have similar goals during a particular decade? (the 50s)

10 Imagine con su compañero/a una conversación entre estos personajes de la serie sobre el tema propuesto. Reproduzcan el diálogo a sus compañeros.

Mercedes empieza a trabajar.

Modelo:
- Mercedes: *Antonio, quiero empezar a trabajar.*
- Antonio: ...

En el anterior capítulo Mercedes le dijo a Antonio que quería empezar a trabajar y entonces Antonio le dijo que...

11 a. Lea de nuevo el texto sobre la serie. ¿Qué temas trata?
lo del pluriempleo
lo que representó la llegada de la tele

Trata lo de...	• el pluriempleo.
Trata lo que...	• representó la llegada de la tele.
	• la emigración al resto de Europa.
	• contaban nuestros abuelos.

lo de la emigración a Europa
lo que contaban nuestros abuelos

b. ¿Era lo mismo en su país en esa época? ¿Qué vivieron sus padres y sus abuelos en esa época? **11b Suggestion** Make a list on the board of the defining elements of the 60s and early 70s in the U.S.

Modelo: *Mi madre cuenta que...*

12 Escuche la publicidad de la serie en la radio. ¿Qué es lo de la hija de los Alcántara? Sample answer: Que quería viajar a París y su madre no supo qué contestar.

13 Escuche de nuevo el audio y señale qué palabra se usa para controlar el contacto en la conversación. ¿Sabes?

○ Mira... ○ ¿Sabes? ○ Ya... ○ ¿Perdona?

14 ¿Hay alguna serie como *Cuéntame cómo pasó* en su país? ¿Cree que tendría éxito en otro país? Sample answer: *The Wonder Years*

MI EXPERIENCIA

15 Seleccione su serie de televisión favorita (de ahora o de hace años) o una película para contársela a sus compañeros.

GUIÓN DE TRABAJO

Mi serie favorita es....
Cuando era pequeño/a, siempre miraba...
La mejor película que he visto es...

¿De qué trata?
¿Quiénes son los personajes?
¿Qué canal la emite?

Trata...
Los personajes...
En el último capítulo pasó...
Entonces el protagonista dijo/comentó/preguntó...

Practice more at **vhlcentral.com.**

SAM: Actividades pp. 302–304

Macarena Berlín, *Hablar por hablar*

La periodista madrileña no quería dejar su programa de radio en Cadena Dial, pero en febrero de 2009, cuando le ofrecieron dirigir el programa de radio *Hablar por hablar* de la Cadena Ser—líder de la noche—, aceptó. Desde 1989, de lunes a viernes de 01:30 a 04:00 h, miles de personas escuchan cada noche las historias que otros oyentes cuentan a través de las líneas telefónicas del programa. Muchas veces la solución inmediata llega a través de otra llamada o por medio de los "chatines": redactores espontáneos que, a través de un chat, mandan sus comentarios a las historias. En Colombia, Radio Caracol, emisora hermana de la Cadena Ser, también emite su *Hablar por hablar*.

Macarena Berlín, locutora de radio

ENTREVISTA A MACARENA EN EL BLOG DE LOS CHATINES:

Macarena, cuando te acuestas cada día, ¿piensas en las personas que llaman al programa? [...]
Procuro desconectar antes de dormir, pero a veces es inevitable no recordar esa llamada que te ha tocado el corazón.

¿Echas de menos los programas que estabas haciendo?
Yo entiendo la vida como un camino con etapas. Cada aventura es una nueva y fascinante, así que no te permite extrañar la anterior.

¿Te ha costado adaptarte al horario de la noche?
Como ya llevaba unos años de noche, la verdad es que no.

¿Con qué tipo de periodismo identificas tu profesión?
Con el que no traspasa los límites del respeto.

¿Crees que el hilo conductor que mueve el programa es el morbo, el insomnio, la empatía o simplemente la curiosidad?
La empatía, seguro... todos hemos vivido conflictos alguna vez.

Suggestion Ask students to talk about the advantages and disadvantages of Macarena's current job.

Expresar intenciones no realizadas

- ¿Querías cambiar de trabajo?
- Sí, pensaba cambiar de trabajo, **pero** me ofrecieron un nuevo proyecto y me quedé.

14B.5 **quería/pensaba** + [*infinitive*] **pero** + [*verb*]

Vocabulario

16

hablar por hablar *to talk for the sake of it*
la cadena de radio *radio network*
el/la oyente *listener*
a través de *through*
por medio de *by means of*
espontáneo/a *impromptu*
la emisora *radio station*
procurar *to try*
echar de menos (*Esp.*) *to miss*
costar (o:ue) *to be difficult*
traspasar *to cross, to go beyond*
el hilo *thread*
el morbo *morbid interest*
el insomnio

18

el testimonio

16 a. ¿Sabe lo que significa la expresión *hablar por hablar*? Después de conocer a nuestra protagonista y su programa, seleccione la definición adecuada. ¿Cree que es una expresión positiva? Coméntelo con sus compañeros.
Possible answer: Es más bien negativa, pues no se piensa lo que se dice.

Decir algo sin fundamento. ☑ | Hablar mucho. ☐ | Hablar sin escuchar. ☐

b. ¿Qué tipo de programa es *Hablar por hablar*? ¿De qué trata?
Possible answer: Un consultorio. Trata de los problemas de la gente que llama, y son los oyentes los que opinan y aconsejan.

17 Lea la entrevista a Macarena Berlín. Marque verdadero (V) o falso (F).

	V	F
1. Macarena pensaba dirigir en 1989 *Hablar por hablar*, pero empezó en televisión.	☐	☑
2. La locutora dice que siempre extraña sus anteriores programas.	☐	☑
3. No fue difícil para Macarena adaptarse al horario de la noche.	☑	☐

18 a. Antes de escuchar la llamada titulada "Mercedes comienza a trabajar mañana después de 22 años", piense en los motivos de la llamada.

- ¿Cuál cree que es su testimonio?
- ¿Cree que Mercedes quería hacer algo en su pasado que al final no hizo?

b. Ahora escuche. ¿Por qué está Mercedes nerviosísima? ¿Cómo reacciona Macarena? ¿Qué dice Mercedes para comprobar que Macarena la escucha? Sample answers: Porque vuelve a trabajar después de 22 años. Macarena dice que es normal. ¿Sabes?

19 Mercedes no quería dejar su profesión, pero, por diferentes motivos, tuvo que hacerlo. ¿Hay algo que usted (no) quería o pensaba hacer en los últimos años pero (no) hizo? Coméntelo con su compañero/a.

Modelo: *Pensaba hacer un curso de..., pero...*

19 Suggestion Encourage students to describe how their life might be different if they had (not) done it.

Vocabulario

20

la finalidad *purpose*
enganchar *to get someone hooked*
la cita *appointment, date*
el cansancio *tiredness*
de paso *in the process*
solidarizarse (con) *to support someone*
veterano/a

22

los contenidos *content*
el sueño *dream*
el formato

23

el choque cultural *culture shock*
el reportaje *article*
el/la costarricense *person from Costa Rica*
chocar *to surprise; to collide*

OPINIÓN

¿Conoce algún programa como *Hablar por hablar*?

¿Qué finalidad tiene un programa así?

21 Expansion Have a volunteer take on the role of Macarena and host a show. Students should "phone" in their comments, or they can submit them in chat form to you, Macarena's assistant on the show. Have the rest of the class play the role of callers.

20 El programa *Hablar por hablar* tiene un blog que sirve de comunicación entre los oyentes, los "chatines" y Macarena. Lea lo que escribe esta persona y enumere los motivos por los que *Hablar por hablar* "engancha". ¿Se le ocurre alguno más? Sample answers:

@hablarporhablar.com

pucelana dijo:

¡Hola, chatines!

¡Qué buena idea la de este blog! Yo no siempre puedo conectarme al chat, pero escucho el programa desde hace nueve años, o sea que soy veterana. No falto ningún día a la cita con la radio aunque a veces me quedo dormida de puro cansancio. Lo escucho todos los días, cosa que con el chat no puedo y lo siento porque hay gente fantástica que está deseando ayudar a los demás y, de paso, a sí mismos. Por alguna razón este programa engancha tanto. Unas veces, porque nos solidarizamos con quien llama, otras porque nos recuerda aquella ocasión en que a nosotros también nos ocurrió algo parecido... y que nadie pudo darnos un consejo, otras por hablar con el chatín con el que has llegado a tener una cierta amistad... y también por escuchar la música que ponen [...]. Un saludo especial a todos [...].

Adiós y gracias.

- Porque nos solidarizamos con quien llama
- Porque nos recuerda aquella ocasión en que a nosotros también nos ocurrió algo parecido
- Por hablar con el chatín
- Por escuchar la música que ponen

21 Imagínese que usted es un "chatín" y escriba un comentario para Mercedes.

@hablarporhablar.com

22 Lea este texto. ¿Por qué se emite *Hablar por hablar* en Colombia? ¿Qué es lo que cambia de un programa a otro? Sample answer: Son emisoras hermanas; pertenecen al Grupo Unión Radio. Cambian los contenidos propios de cada país.

Colombia

Caracol Radio, una de las cadenas de radio más prestigiosas de América Latina, forma parte del Grupo Prisa Radio, el mismo grupo al que pertenece la Cadena Ser de España, y son "emisoras hermanas". Por eso, algunos programas tienen el mismo formato en los dos países, pero se producen con contenidos propios en cada país. Patricia Pardo es "la Macarena colombiana": de lunes a jueves dirige el programa *Hablar por hablar* de 23:30 a 2:00 de la mañana. En este espacio, los oyentes comparten sus historias, sus sueños, lo que les preocupa o lo que les alegra en la vida... y Patricia, sobre todo, los escucha. Todo con acento colombiano.

Practice more at **vhlcentral.com.**

SAM: Actividades pp. 305–310

23 a. Lea el texto y complete el mapa de ideas en una hoja aparte.

@ choquecultural.com

INICIO | ACERCA DE... | CONTACTO | ARCHIVO | ENLACES | FOTOS | VIDEOS

Choque cultural

¡Hola a todos! Bienvenidos a *Choque cultural*, mi blog sobre viajes. Cada semana publicaré fotos, videos y reportajes de los diferentes lugares del mundo que he conocido. Quizás se pregunten quién soy y cómo es que he estado en tantos sitios. Me presentaré: Mi nombre es Rita y soy una guía de turismo costarricense. Gracias a mi trabajo he tenido la suerte de visitar muchísimos países y de conocer diferentes culturas, costumbres y tradiciones. Ahora quiero compartir con ustedes lo que más me gusta y lo que más me choca de todos esos destinos. Abróchense los cinturones y ¡buen viaje!

Chicago, Estados Unidos — Montevideo, Uruguay — Cuzco, Perú — Fez, Marruecos — Río de Janeiro, Brasil

CHOQUE CULTURAL

- ¿Qué es?
- ¿De qué trata?
- ¿Quién lo escribe?
- ¿Qué cree que es un choque cultural?

b. ¿Conoce alguna de las ciudades de las imágenes? Piense en un "choque cultural" que puede producirse para usted en alguno de estos sitios u otros y coméntelo con la clase.

c. ¿Cree que Internet es un buen medio para conocer otras culturas? ¿Qué tipo de conocimiento cultural solo se puede aprender "en directo"? 23c **Suggestion** Ask students what cultural elements might be lacking when exploring a culture via the Internet.

TAREA FINAL

Las imágenes de una década

Decidan, en grupos pequeños, qué década quieren presentar y qué tipo de secciones va a tener la presentación: música, cine, series de televisión, anuncios, programas de radio, de deporte, etc.

Recojan imágenes, noticias y declaraciones de los personajes más significativos de esa década. Anoten también sus recuerdos sobre estos programas.

Seleccionen las declaraciones para transmitirlas a sus compañeros. Digan también qué les llamó la atención y por qué.

Desarrollen una presentación con las noticias, las imágenes y las declaraciones más representativas e interesantes. **Suggestion** Encourage students to use personal photographs or mementos, if possible.

YO PUEDO...

- **Puedo situar hechos pasados.**
  ¿Qué recuerdos tiene de su infancia? ¿Qué hacía cuando era joven?
- **Puedo hablar de acciones pasadas en desarrollo.**
  Termine estas oraciones.
  Ayer estaba vistiéndome cuando...
  Durante todo el día he estado...
- **Puedo transmitir mensajes.**
  Cuéntele a su compañero/a algo que le dijeron ayer.
- **Puedo referirme a un tema.**
  Coméntele a su compañero/a algo referido a un tema de esta lección.
- **Puedo expresar intenciones no realizadas.**
  ¿Hay algo que quería hacer y no hizo, o algo que no iba a hacer y finalmente hizo?

GRAMÁTICA FUNCIONAL

14B.1 Give ages and have volunteers say what they did or what happened to them at a particular age. Ex: **Cuando tenía seis años, mis abuelos me llevaron a Disneyworld.**

14B.1 Situate past events

cuando + [*imperfect / preterite*] 5.2.3, 5.6, 12.12

- Use **cuando** with either the **pretérito imperfecto** or the **pretérito indefinido** to describe when events occurred in the past. Use the **pretérito imperfecto** to refer to a habitual action or situation.

  Cuando Paula **trabajaba** en el restaurante, tomaba el autobús todos los días.
  *When Paula **worked** at the restaurant, she took the bus every day.*

- Always use the **pretérito imperfecto** to refer to age with **tener**.

  Cuando tenía 18 años, viajé a Europa por primera vez.
  ***When I was** 18 years old, I traveled to Europe for the first time.*

- Use **cuando** with the **pretérito indefinido** to refer to a specific, completed action.

  Cuando terminé la secundaria, mis padres me regalaron una cámara.
  ***When I finished** high school, my parents gave me a camera.*

14B.2 Talk about past actions in progress

estar (*past tense*) + [*present participle*]; Irregular present participles 5.14.2, 5.15

- Use a past form of the verb **estar** + [*present participle*] to describe an ongoing action in the past.

  Pedro **estaba cocinando** cuando escuchó la noticia por la radio.
  *Pedro **was cooking** when he heard the news on the radio.*

- You can use the **pretérito perfecto**, the **pretérito indefinido**, or the **pretérito imperfecto** in this construction. You learned the differences between these three tenses in 10B.1.

- You learned the regular forms of the present participle (**el gerundio**) in 7A.3. Remember that if the stem of an **-er** or **-ir** verb ends in a vowel, the present participle ends in **-yendo** (e.g., **traer→trayendo**).

- Stem-changing **-ir** verbs also undergo a change to form the present participle. Verbs with an **e→ie** stem change in the present tense undergo an **e→i** stem change to form the present participle. Verbs with an **o→ue** stem change in the present tense undergo an **o→u** stem change to form the present participle.

e→i	pref**e**r**ir**→pref**i**r**iendo**	d**e**cir, v**e**nir, p**e**dir, v**e**stir...
o→u	d**o**rmir→d**u**rmiendo	p**o**der, m**o**rir...

Evo estaba **durmiendo** la siesta cuando llegamos a la casa.
*Evo was **taking a nap** when we arrived at the house.*

G3 **Expansion** Write a list of times on the board and have pairs of students ask each other what they were doing yesterday at each hour.

¡Póngalo en práctica!

G1 Complete las oraciones con el pretérito indefinido y/o el pretérito imperfecto.

1. Cuando ......era...... (yo, ser) pequeño, siempre ......jugaba...... (yo, jugar) afuera con mis amigos después del colegio.
2. Anoche cuando tú y Gabriela ...llegasteis/llegaron... (llegar) a la fiesta, los otros invitados ya ......estaban...... (estar) ahí.
3. Cuando Miguel ......estudiaba...... (estudiar) en la universidad, ...vivía...... (vivir) en una residencia estudiantil.
4. Cuando ......teníamos...... (nosotros, tener) cinco años, ...se estrenó...... (estrenarse) *Parque Jurásico*.
5. Cuando ......nació...... (nacer) mi hermana menor, mis abuelos me ......llevaron...... (llevar) al hospital a conocerla.
6. Cuando Javier y Luis ......empezaron...... (empezar) a estudiar inglés en la academia, no ......se conocían...... (conocerse).

G2 Complete las oraciones con la forma correcta del progresivo pasado. Suggested answers:

- Sr. Pérez, ¿(1)......ha estado yendo...... (ir) a las reuniones de este mes?
- No, pero ayer (2)......estuve leyendo...... (leer) las actas de todas las reuniones durante cuatro horas.

- ¿Qué hicieron tus hermanos ayer, Susana?
- Nada especial, (3)...estuvieron escuchando... (escuchar) la radio toda la tarde.

Cuando Pepe (4)......estaba preparando...... (preparar) la comida, comenzó el programa.

Últimamente yo (5)......he estado estudiando...... (estudiar) en el café de la esquina.

Anoche Julio y yo (6)......estuvimos mirando...... (mirar) el partido de fútbol hasta las once.

G3 Conteste las preguntas con la forma correcta del verbo entre paréntesis.

1. ¿Qué estabas haciendo ayer a las ocho? (dormir)
   - ......Estaba durmiendo......
2. ¿Qué estabais haciendo tú y tus amigas ayer a las siete? (vestirse)
   - ......Nos estábamos vistiendo...... para la fiesta.
3. ¿Qué estaba haciendo Juan? (traer)
   - ......Estaba trayendo...... unos libros y se cayó.
4. ¿Qué estuvieron haciendo tus primos ayer? (mirar)
   - ......Estuvieron mirando...... la tele todo el día.

Practice more at **vhlcentral.com.**

GRAMÁTICA FUNCIONAL

14B.3 Convey messages

Indirect discourse: reporting verbs 5.6, 12.10

- Use indirect discourse (**el estilo indirecto**) to report what another person has said. Reporting verbs, or verbs that are used to relate someone else's speech, include **decir, comentar, explicar,** and **preguntar**.
- In 11A.2, you learned to use indirect discourse in the present tense. This chart shows the transformation of the main verb when using reporting verbs in the past tenses.

Direct discourse "...."	→	Indirect discourse **explicó/decía/comentó que...**
presente		**pretérito imperfecto**
pretérito perfecto		**pretérito pluscuamperfecto**
pretérito imperfecto		**pretérito imperfecto**
pretérito indefinido		**pretérito indefinido** **pretérito pluscuamperfecto**

Gloria: "El mes pasado **fui** tres veces al cine."
Gloria **me comentó que** el mes pasado **fue/había ido** tres veces al cine.
Gloria: *"Last month **I went** to the movies three times."*
*Gloria **told me that** she **went/had gone** to the movies three times last month.*

14B.4 Refer to a topic

lo de + [*noun/infinitive*], lo que + [*verb*] 3.3.2, 5.13

- Use **lo de** + [*noun/infinitive*] or **lo que** + [*conjugated verb*] to refer to a topic in a general sense.

¿Sabes **lo que dijo** el ministro de Cultura? Dijo que **lo de ir** al cine gratis a partir de los 65 años no será posible.
*Do you know **what** the Minister of Culture **said**? He said that **the thing about going** to the movies for free if you are 65 or older is not going to be possible.*

14B.5 Express unfulfilled intentions

quería/pensaba + [*infinitive*], pero + [*verb*] 5.4.3, 12.8

- Use the **pretérito imperfecto** of **querer** or **pensar** + [*infinitive*] to express intentions that were not fulfilled.

Pensábamos organizar una fiesta sorpresa.
***We were planning on organizing** a surprise party.*

- To express the condition or event that caused the plan to change, use **pero** + [*conjugated verb*].

Yo quería estudiar medicina, **pero** al final **hice** periodismo.
*I wanted to study medicine, **but** in the end **I studied** journalism.*

- Note that **poder** and **querer** have slightly different meanings in affirmative and negative statements in the preterite.

afirmativo	**pude**	*I succeeded*	**quise**	*I tried (to)*
negativo	**no pude**	*I failed (to)*	**no quise**	*I refused (to)*

Suggestion Have students write four sentences about their own lives, using **(no) poder** and **(no) querer.**

¡Póngalo en práctica!

G4 Transforme las afirmaciones y preguntas al estilo indirecto.

1. "¿Te acuerdas de las canciones de Abba?"
   Andrés me preguntó si
   me acordaba de las canciones de Abba
2. "Antes había menos programas de televisión."
   Mi madre dijo que antes
   había menos programas de televisión
3. "¿Cuándo te fuiste de vacaciones?"
   Mi jefe me preguntó cuándo
   me fui/me había ido de vacaciones
4. "Esta mañana he visto a un viejo amigo."
   Mi compañero de cuarto me comentó ayer que
   había visto a un viejo amigo
5. "Me encanta la música hip-hop."
   Domingo me contó que
   le encantaba la música hip-hop
6. "Hemos viajado a Panamá cinco veces."
   Laura y Juan me comentaron que
   habían viajado a Panamá cinco veces.

G4 Expansion Bring in simple quotes from current events and/or famous quotes from history. Read each one aloud and have students identify who said them, using reported speech.

G5 Complete las oraciones con **lo que** o **lo de**.

- ¿Sabes (1) lo de la hermana de Isa? Me han dicho que (2) lo que nos contaba de su novio era mentira.
- Sí, y (3) lo de irse a vivir a Jamaica también.

- ¿Piensas que es cierto (4) lo que Felipe nos dijo ayer?
- ¿(5) Lo de la tormenta de granizo en verano? Sí, creo que sí.

G6 Complete las conversaciones con **pero** o la forma adecuada de **querer** o **pensar**.

- Dolores, ¿no (1) querías (tú, querer) ir ayer a la exposición del Museo del Prado?
- Sí, (2) pensaba (pensar) ir, (3) pero al final no fui.

- Santiago y Víctor, ¿(4) pensabais/pensaban (pensar) trabajar en la biblioteca durante el verano?
- Sí, (5) queríamos (querer) trabajar allí, (6) pero no conseguimos el trabajo.

G7 Reescriba las oraciones con **poder** o **querer**.

1. Me fue imposible abrir la puerta. No pude abrir la puerta.
2. Le pidieron escribir una canción y dijo que no. No quiso escribir una canción.
3. ¡Qué bien! Terminaste la investigación. Pudiste terminar la investigación.

Practice more at **vhlcentral.com.**

VOCABULARIO

La mejor década

a mediados de los 60	*in the mid-sixties*
el/la aficionado/a	*fan*
la clase media	*middle class*
la década	*decade*
el espectáculo	*show*
el grupo musical	*band, music group*
el/la investigador(a)	*investigator*
la historieta	*comic strip*
la letra	*lyrics*
la página web	*Web page*
la serie de televisión	*television series*
el sitio web	*Web site*
el/la telespectador(a)	*television viewer*
admirar	*to admire*
aprender de memoria	*to memorize*
estrenarse	*to premiere*
instalar	*to install*
llorar	*to cry*
pasar la serie de televisión	*to broadcast the television series*
plantearse preguntas	*to question, to ask oneself questions*
revivir	*to relive*
brillante	*brilliant, smart*
fascinado/a	*fascinated*
ganador(a)	*winning*
incansable	*tireless*

Cuéntame cómo pasó

el capítulo	*episode*
la democracia	*democracy*
el éxodo	*exodus*
la explosión	*explosion*
la ficción	*fiction*
la inversión	*investment*
el pluriempleo	*having more than one job, moonlighting*
la posguerra	*postwar period*
el/la publicista	*publicist*
el retrato	*portrait*
el sueldo	*salary*
la transformación	*transformation*
la transición democrática	*democratic transition*
comentar	*to mention*
contar (o:ue)	*to tell*
emitir la serie	*to broadcast the (television) series*
explicar	*to explain*
preguntar	*to ask*
ser líder de audiencia	*to be the highest rated*
tratar	*to be about*
anterior	*previous*
franquista	*Francoist*
guatemalteco/a	*Guatemalan*
hondureño/a	*Honduran*
día a día	*day by day*

Macarena Berlín

hablar por hablar	*to talk for the sake of it*
la cadena de radio	*radio network*
el cansancio	*tiredness*
el choque cultural	*culture shock*
la cita	*appointment, date*
los contenidos	*content*
el/la costarricense	*person from Costa Rica*
la emisora	*radio station*
la finalidad	*purpose*
el formato	*format*
el hilo	*thread*
el insomnio	*insomnia*
el morbo	*morbid interest*
el/la oyente	*listener*
el reportaje	*article*
el sueño	*dream*
el testimonio	*testimony*
veterano/a	*veteran*
chocar	*to surprise; to collide*
costar (o:ue)	*to be difficult*
echar de menos (*Esp.*)	*to miss*
enganchar	*to get someone hooked*
procurar	*to try*
solidarizarse (con)	*to support someone*
traspasar	*to cross, to go beyond*
espontáneo/a	*impromptu*
veterano/a	*veteran*
a través de	*through*
de paso	*in the process*
por medio de	*by means of*

Variación léxica

el capítulo ⟷ **el episodio**

fascinado/a ⟷ **deslumbrado/a** ⟷ **encantado/a**

pasar la serie de televisión ⟷ **poner/echar la serie de televisión** (*Esp.*)

el sueldo ⟷ **la paga** ⟷ **el salario**

el/la telespectador(a) ⟷ **el/la televidente** (*Amér. L.*)

Estrategias

1 Dar una explicación

Lección 13A

Explaining the reasoning behind a situation can help people understand you better. Expressions such as **es que** and **como** are used to introduce an explanation.

1 Suggestion Have students share their explanations with the class, who will vote for the most original one.

- Busque la mejor explicación para estas situaciones y piense en otras.

Situación	Explicación	
Usted no ha hecho los deberes.	Su gato está enfermo y ha tenido que ir al veterinario con él.	En su oficina hay mucho trabajo. Ha tenido que hacer horas extras.
Ha llegado tarde a la clase de español.	No hay sitio en la calle para estacionar el coche.	¿...?
Ha olvidado el cumpleaños de su mejor amigo/a.		

2 Destacar una información

Lección 13B

Emphasizing a particular piece of information with expressions such as **solo/solamente** (*only*) or **sobre todo** (*especially*) will help you communicate more effectively.

- Relacione estos elementos.

En el trabajo, Paula se lleva mal con todos, pero...	solo/solamente	una semana en Navidad.
Nunca tenemos vacaciones en invierno,...	sobre todo	20 horas.
Tengo un contrato de trabajo de...		con su jefe.
No quiero trabajar por las mañanas,...		por mis estudios.

3 Pedir repetición

Lección 14A

It's important to be able to ask for repetition when you do not understand something. Use expressions such as **¿Perdona?/¿Perdone?** and **¿Cómo?** to ask for repetition.

- Lea uno de estos textos a su compañero/a. Su compañero/a interrumpe cuando no entiende algo.

Estudiante A

Mi amigo Ndongo es ecuatoguineano. En su casa hablan el bubi, que es una de las lenguas que se hablan en Guinea Ecuatorial, además del español, que es una de las lenguas oficiales.

Estudiante B

Cuando llegué a casa de mi amiga, Petra me dijo *m'bolo*. Es el saludo fang, una de las lenguas que se hablan en Guinea Ecuatorial.

4 Controlar el contacto

Lección 14B

Use expressions such as **¿Sabes?/¿Sabe?** to check comprehension and ensure fluent conversation.

- Complete este diálogo con la palabra adecuada.

• ¿Vas mucho al cine?
• Pues no, nunca tengo tiempo. Estudio dos carreras y encima trabajo, ...¿sabes?... Prefiero comprarme las películas en DVD y así las veo cuando quiero.

mira	sí, ya...
¿sabes?	¿perdona?

- En parejas, preparen una conversación con otra de las expresiones para controlar el contacto.

Competencias

PEDIR Y CONFIRMAR INFORMACIÓN, DESCRIBIR UN VIAJE, RECOMENDAR

1 Imagine que va a una agencia de viajes y su compañero/a es la persona que debe orientarlo/la. Escriban una conversación acerca de un viaje que hará a un lugar que su compañero/a ya ha visitado.

Modelo: • *Buenos días, ¿en qué puedo ayudarlo/la?*
• *Buenos días. Me gustaría saber...*

1 Suggestion Tell students to start by picking a destination and brainstorming vocabulary and phrases for their conversation.

CONECTAR IDEAS CONTRARIAS

2 Con su compañero/a, hable sobre las ventajas y los inconvenientes de usar una computadora portátil y una computadora de escritorio. Usen las palabras del recuadro para relacionar las ideas contrarias.

a pesar de • aunque • sin embargo

EXPRESAR POSESIÓN

3 Complete la conversación con los adjetivos y pronombres posesivos correspondientes.

- ¿Te conté que estoy buscando empleo?
- ¿Y (1) tu anterior trabajo? ¿No te gustaba?
- No era el trabajo en sí lo que me afectaba; era (2) mi jefe.
- Por suerte, yo me llevo bien con el (3) mío. ¿Qué pasó?
- Después de cinco años aconsejándole sobre todo, desde una buena escuela para (4) sus hijos hasta la corbata que debía ponerse para (5) sus reuniones, he puesto punto final. (6) Sus problemas se estaban convirtiendo en los (7) míos.

HABLAR DE SITUACIONES HABITUALES EN EL PASADO, Y EXPRESAR DESCONOCIMIENTO Y SITUACIONES POSIBLES

4 Lucía escribió un testimonio acerca de su infancia, pero tiene algunas dudas con los tiempos verbales. ¿Puede ayudarla?

Cuando era pequeña, solía (1) **almorzar/almorzaba** en la casa de mi abuela después de la escuela. Me (2) **gustar/gustaba** acompañarla en la cocina cada día. Recuerdo que una vez (3) **preparaba/preparó** empanadas. Yo nunca las (4) **pruebo/había probado** y me encantaron. (5) **Pensaba/Pienso** que era una comida que mi abuela había inventado. No sabía que (6) **era/fue** un plato típico argentino. Algunos años más tarde (7) **encontraré/encontré** la receta en un blog de cocina. Las primeras no me (8) **salieron/saldrán** bien, pero la quinta docena que (9) **preparé/había preparado** fue exquisita. Si (10) **quisieron/quieren** les enseño a hacerlas.

SITUAR HECHOS PASADOS, HABLAR DE ACCIONES PASADAS EN DESARROLLO, EXPRESAR INTENCIONES NO REALIZADAS Y TRANSMITIR MENSAJES

5 Complete las oraciones y luego transmítalas en estilo indirecto.

Modelo: "Cuando era pequeño *iba* (ir) al parque todos los días."
Pedro *dijo que cuando era pequeño iba al parque todos los días.*

1. "Estoy cansada porque estuve (estar) estudiando toda la semana."
   Clara dijo/comentó que estaba cansada porque había estado estudiando toda la semana.
2. "¿Ustedes cuándo fueron (ir) a un partido de fútbol por última vez?"
   Juan y Esteban preguntaron cuándo habíamos ido a un partido de fútbol por última vez.
3. "Cuando tu mamá tenía (tener) 10 años, no había (haber) teléfonos inteligentes."
   Tomás comentó/dijo que cuando mi mamá tenía 10 años no había teléfonos inteligentes.
4. "¿Sabéis lo que comentó (comentar) la profesora el otro día?"
   Yo pregunté si sabíais lo que había comentado la profesora el otro día.

5 Suggestion Tell students to first read through the questions and choose the correct tense; then have them conjugate the verbs in parentheses. Finally, have them rewrite the questions using indirect discourse.

Flash CULTURA

Estrategia

Brainstorming

Before watching this **Flash Cultura** episode, brainstorm about the topic mentioned in the title, **La comida latina**, and list related Spanish words you already know about food, drinks, restaurants, how to order, saying thank you, asking for information, expressing what you like and dislike, etc.

Vocabulario útil

- **abarcar** *to encompass, to cover*
- **blando/a** *soft, tender*
- **confeccionar** *to make*
- **en cada esquina** *on every corner*
- **molido/a** *ground*
- **picado/a** *chopped; ground*
- **probar (o:ue)** *to taste*
- **¡Buen provecho!** *Enjoy your meal!*
- **rallar** *to grate*
- **la rebanada** *slice*
- **sin remedio/no hay remedio** *hopeless*
- **sabroso/a** *tasty*

Estrategia

Same food, different name

There are several Spanish names for vegetables and fruits depending on the region you are in. So you could ask for **el aguacate** (*avocado*) or **la fresa** (*strawberry*) in Mexico, Venezuela, or Spain; but you would have to say **la palta** and **la frutilla** in Argentina, Chile, Paraguay, and Uruguay. Pay close attention to the regional usage notes listed in this text and other dictionaries.

La comida latina

Ya ha leído sobre cómo las distintas culturas influyen en las personas y se convierten en parte de su historia, sea en Guinea Ecuatorial o en España. Este episodio de **Flash Cultura** muestra uno de los aspectos esenciales de la cultura hispana: la comida, presente con sus platos tradicionales en la ciudad de Los Ángeles.

1 Hable con un(a) compañero/a. ¿Ha probado platos de distintos países? ¿Cuál es su favorito? ¿Qué piensa que debe ofrecer un restaurante de comida típica de su país en el extranjero?

2 Mire el video. ¿Cuánto sabía sobre la comida latina antes de verlo? Y ahora, ¿qué cosas nuevas aprendió?

Successful Language Learning: Tell students about the many expressions with the word **boca** that exist in Spanish: **a pedir de boca** means *just perfect*, **en boca de todos** is *something that everybody knows*, and **quedarse con la boca abierta** is *to be flabbergasted.*

1 **Hay quienes aseguran que el taco es la hamburguesa del siglo XXI.**

2 **En los últimos años... también hay más lugares donde podemos comprar productos hispanos.**

3 Complete las oraciones con la opción correcta.

1. Un taco americano lleva carne
   a. molida. b. rallada.
2. El ingrediente fundamental de la comida mexicana es el
   a. aguacate. b. chile.
3. El cortadito es la versión cubana del
   a. licor de café. b. café espresso.
4. Inca Kola es una bebida de
   a. Perú. b. México.
5. Para condimentar una comida latina se necesitan
   a. cocos. b. especias.

3 Suggestion To challenge students, ask them to close their texts and present these items as cloze sentences.

4 Con un(a) compañero/a, represente una conversación en la que comenta las sorpresas que tuvo al visitar Los Ángeles.

4 Expansion Have students role-play their conversations for the class.

Modelo:
- *Antes de ir a Los Ángeles, no había probado nunca los tamales. Son muy ricos.*
- *¿Hay tamales en Los Ángeles? Pensaba que era comida mexicana...*

Practice more at **vhlcentral.com.**

Audio: Activities, Vocabulary
Video: *Flash Cultura*

Unidad 15

Evaristo Acebedo, Casa Vera

Lección 15A

DE LA MADRE TIERRA

Lección 15B

REBELDES CON CAUSA

Marina Sánchez, un genio de los números

Las alpacas

AVANCE

15A DE LA MADRE TIERRA

¿Qué comeremos?

Expresar probabilidad

¿**Habrá** algún producto de alimentación 100% natural o **tendrán** todos conservantes?

15A.1 Review of simple future
Simple future: irregular forms

Vocabulario

①
la frambuesa *raspberry*
el conservante *preservative*
el cacao en polvo *cocoa powder*
seco/a *dry*
la agricultura ecológica *organic farming*
el hidrato de carbono *carbohydrate*
la grasa *fat*
el tomate frito *tomato sauce*
el aceite de oliva virgen extra *extra virgin olive oil*
endulzar *to sweeten*
cocido/a *cooked*
espolvorear *to sprinkle*
la mermelada, el ingrediente, la proteína, el gluten, el colorante, vegetariano/a

②
la etiqueta *label*
la conservación *preservation*
el consumo *consumption*

Tomate frito is a pureed sauce made with fried tomatoes, garlic, onion, salt, and sugar.

1. Fíjese en la imagen y relacione los productos con las descripciones.

- Se usa sobre los platos de pasta. 4
- Es fruta cocida en azúcar. 1
- Sirve para endulzar el café. 3
- Se espolvorea sobre el tiramisú. 2

2. Lea la información que ofrecen las etiquetas y clasifíquela. ¿Qué información le interesa a usted y por qué? **Suggestion** Help students to see the word **polvo** in the verb **espolvorear**.

Composición	frambuesas,... azúcar, conservante, tomate, aceite de oliva virgen extra, sal, etc.
Conservación y consumo	conservar en un lugar fresco y seco, ... consumir preferentemente antes de
Información nutricional	proteínas,... hidratos de carbono, grasas, lípidos
Origen	agricultura ecológica

3. Escuche esta conversación entre dos clientes en un supermercado. Complete las dudas que tienen y escriba el infinitivo correspondiente.

saber • querer • poner • venir
decir • haber • hacer • poder

1. ¿De dónde vendrán? (las frutas) venir
2. Lo pondrá en la etiqueta. (el origen) poner
3. ¿Podremos encontrar esta información? poder
4. ¿Quién lo sabrá? saber
5. ¿Cómo harán estos alimentos? hacer
6. ¿Habrá algún dependiente? haber
7. ¿Querrán atendernos? querer
8. Me dirán que si... decir

Hacer sugerencias

- Lo mejor sería leer la etiqueta.
- Lo mejor es la confianza en el producto.

15A.2 **lo mejor es/sería** + [*infinitive/noun*]

Vocabulario *cont.*

la información nutricional *nutritional information*
la composición

3

la galleta *cookie*

4

la certeza *certainty*
el suflé

6

el producto fresco *fresh food*
el envase de plástico *plastic container*
el envase reciclable *recyclable container*
el contenedor *(recycling) container*
celíaco/a

7

el producto ecológico *organic product*

8

la leche entera *whole milk*
la leche descremada en polvo *powdered skim milk*
el jarabe *syrup*
apto/a para *appropriate/safe for*
bajo/a en calorías *low-calorie*
la fecha de caducidad *expiration date*
artificial

INGREDIENTES: leche entera, azúcar, leche descremada en polvo, jarabe de glucosa, cacao en polvo, estabilizantes, emulsionantes, colorantes, aromatizantes artificiales.

4 Complete el diálogo con el futuro simple de probabilidad.

- Invité a Carlos y a Graciela a cenar.
- Hay que preparar algo especial para Graciela, ¿no?
- Sí, pero no recuerdo qué. ¿...Será... (Ser) vegetariana?
- Sí, alguna vez me dijo que no come carne ni pescado.
- ¿...Podrá... (Poder) comer queso? Así le preparamos un suflé...
- Sí. ¿...Tendrá... (Tener) problema si los demás comemos un asado?

5 Escuche la conversación de nuevo y anote las sugerencias sobre estos temas.

- ¿Tendrán gluten estas galletas? • Yo creo que sí, pero... lo mejor es mirar en la etiqueta.
- ¿Habrá algún dependiente por aquí? • No sé, yo creo que... lo mejor sería llamar al teléfono de atención al cliente.

6 Elija una situación y escriba un correo electrónico a la tienda de alimentación donde lo compró con sus dudas y sugerencias como consumidor.

Compra un producto fresco, pero no tiene etiqueta y no sabe si tiene algún conservante.

Es celíaco. Compra un producto que cree que no tiene gluten, pero en la etiqueta no encuentra ninguna información.

Compra un producto en un envase de plástico. Lleva el símbolo de envase reciclable, pero no sabe en qué contenedor reciclar el envase.

7 a. ¿Qué cree que significan estos símbolos? Revise las etiquetas de los envases de la actividad 1 y relacione.

vegetariano [3] comercio justo [2] producto ecológico [5] envase reciclable [1] sin gluten [4]

b. Ordene de mayor a menor importancia, para usted, la información que aportan estos símbolos y comente su opinión con su compañero/a.

7 Make sure that students are familiar with celiac disease, which involves an intestinal reaction to wheat gluten.

MI EXPERIENCIA

8 Fíjese en los datos que aparecen en el envase de helado. Comparta con la clase sus dudas y sugerencias sobre este y otros productos.

GUIÓN DE TRABAJO

Composición
Información nutricional

Conservación y consumo
Origen

¿Será un producto bajo en calorías?
¿Qué fecha de caducidad tendrá?
¿Será ecológico?

→ Lo mejor es/sería...

Practice more at vhlcentral.com.

SAM: Actividades pp. 311–313

Mucho sabor

De: info@supermercadosveracruz.mx
Para: ana.rodriguez.pelaez@micorreo.mx
Asunto: Próxima apertura Supermercados Veracruz

SUPERMERCADOS VERACRUZ

¡Su mercado natural!

Estimado cliente:

SUPERMERCADOS VERACRUZ le ofrece la calidad de nuestros productos ecológicos, recogidos directamente de la tierra, sin conservantes ni colorantes, con todo su sabor y sus nutrientes. Queremos que nuestros productos le aporten todo lo mejor. Deseamos preservar el medio ambiente y que disfrute del sabor más auténtico de los alimentos. Queremos evitar el uso de pesticidas y ofrecer el alimento en su estado puro. Esperamos que asista a la apertura de nuestra nueva tienda y que disfrute de las promociones especiales. Ojalá que **SUPERMERCADOS VERACRUZ** cumpla con sus expectativas y mejore su alimentación y su salud.

Atentamente,

SUPERMERCADOS VERACRUZ, su mercado natural

Suggestion Ask students to think of local natural foods markets. Do they have similar products and goals?

Queremos potenciar el consumo de los alimentos naturales.
Queremos vender productos de calidad a buen precio.
Queremos cumplir con las necesidades y peticiones del consumidor.

Hablar de objetivos

Espero que nuestros productos aporten mucha calidad.

15A.3 **esperar/querer/desear que** + [*subjunctive*]
Present subjunctive: regular forms

Vocabulario

9

- la apertura *opening*
- el sabor *flavor, taste*
- recogido/a *picked*
- aportar *to provide*
- preservar *to preserve*
- evitar *to avoid*
- asistir (a) *to attend*
- Ojalá *I/We wish*
- cumplir con *to meet*
- la expectativa *expectation*
- potenciar *to foster*
- el alimento natural *natural food*
- el/la consumidor(a) *consumer*

9 ¿Qué tipo de empresa envía este correo? ¿Qué la distingue de otras empresas? ¿Cuáles son sus objetivos en relación con estos temas?
Es un supermercado. Sample answer: Sus productos son naturales y ecológicos.

- medio ambiente
- sabor de los alimentos
- apertura de tienda

Modelo: *Desean preservar el medio ambiente y quieren que sus productos le aporten al cliente todo lo mejor.* Quieren preservar el medio ambiente y que el cliente disfrute del sabor más auténtico de los alimentos. Esperan que el cliente asista a la apertura de su nueva tienda.

10 Fíjese en la gráfica y complete las oraciones.

SUPERMERCADOS VERACRUZ
quiere/espera/desea

potenciar el consumo
vender productos de calidad
cumplir con las necesidades del consumidor

que EL CLIENTE/CONSUMIDOR...
consuma (consumir) productos naturales.
compre (comprar) productos de calidad.
vea (ver) sus necesidades satisfechas.

11 Añada más objetivos a este correo publicitario y haga una lista con su compañero/a. ¿Qué desean las empresas de sus clientes? ¿Y los clientes de las empresas?

Modelo: *Las empresas, por ejemplo las ecológicas, desean que sus clientes...*

Expresar esperanza

- ¡Ojalá que vendáis mucho!
- A ver si es verdad.

15A.4 **ojalá (que)** + [*subjunctive*]
a ver si + [*indicative*]

Estrategia

Suavizar una opinión
Yo diría que no tienes razón.

Vocabulario *cont.*

el nutriente, el pesticida, la promoción

10

consumir

12

el/la productor(a) *producer*
bajar *to go down*

15

la cola *line*
la demanda *demand*
envasado/a *packaged*
el alimento transgénico *transgenic food*
el reciclaje *recycling*

16

conquistar *to captivate*

14c Expansion Have students pick five problems at school and solutions and draft a letter to the school newspaper.

Los productos envasados son la mejor opción.

Los alimentos transgénicos son malos para la salud.

Las campañas de reciclaje no son necesarias.

12a Expansion Have pairs of students write one additional sentence for each person in the chain. Have pairs read their sentences aloud for the class to guess.

12 a. En la cadena de consumo, el productor, la empresa y el consumidor tienen sus propios intereses. ¿A quién cree que pertenecen estas esperanzas?
Ojalá que vendamos mucho: empresa; A ver si bajan los precios: consumidor; A ver si llueve: productor; Ojalá este año el tiempo mejore: productor

Ojalá que vendamos mucho. | A ver si bajan los precios. | A ver si llueve... | Ojalá este año el tiempo mejore.

b. ¿Qué espera usted como consumidor(a) de los productores y de las empresas?

13 Lea esta conversación. ¿Cómo se expresa el desacuerdo con una opinión?
Yo diría que...

13 Expansion Ask students if they or anyone they know is a locavore (**locávoro/a**)—someone who only eats food produced within a range of 150 kilometers.

Queremos que las ventas aumenten con las exportaciones...

Yo diría que lo mejor es vender y consumir en tu región. Es más barato para el cliente y mejor para la región.

14 a. Complete la encuesta que su universidad hace a los estudiantes.

Queremos que nuestros servicios mejoren todo el tiempo. Por eso, son bienvenidas todas tus opiniones, quejas y sugerencias.

- Comida • Ambiente • Calidad de servicio • Relación calidad/precio

Lo que más me gusta: ....
Lo que menos me gusta: ....

b. Compare sus respuestas con las de sus compañeros de grupo. Exprese y justifique su desacuerdo con las opiniones que son diferentes.

Modelo: *Yo diría que las largas colas no son el principal problema...*

c. Con el grupo, propongan soluciones para los aspectos negativos de la cafetería. Usen expresiones como *Ojalá...* o *A ver si...* Escríbanlas.

Modelo: *A ver si ponen más empleados en las horas de más demanda.*

15 ¿Y usted qué diría? Exponga su opinión a la clase sobre las afirmaciones de la columna a la izquierda y sus esperanzas al respecto.

MI EXPERIENCIA

16 Formen tres grupos, uno por cada integrante de la cadena de consumo. Cada grupo define sus objetivos particulares y luego hacen una puesta en común.

GUIÓN DE TRABAJO

¿Qué desean los productores?	Los productores deseamos que aumenten las exportaciones. Ojalá que...
¿Qué esperan las empresas?	Las empresas esperamos que se incrementen las ventas. A ver si...
¿Qué quieren los consumidores?	Los consumidores queremos que los alimentos cumplan con los estándares básicos de calidad y seguridad...

Practice more at **vhlcentral.com.**

SAM: Actividades pp. 314–316

Evaristo Acebedo, propietario de Casa Vera

Evaristo Acebedo, Casa Vera

Latino de honor

Ask students if they know of local organizations that distribute food to people in need. Ask them if they or anyone they know has volunteered there.

Evaristo Acebedo, un hombre muy conocido y querido por toda la comunidad latina de Miami, es, en este número de COMUNIDAD LATINA, nuestro **LATINO DE HONOR.** Evaristo dirige con éxito desde 1990 CASA VERA, una tienda dedicada a los productos de alimentación latinos.

Evaristo empezó su negocio importando y vendiendo productos típicos de su país de origen, Cuba, y de otros países del Caribe. De personalidad emprendedora, poco tiempo después de haber llegado a los Estados Unidos, vio la oportunidad en Miami y la aprovechó: "Decidí probar porque aquí la comunidad latina es muy importante. Hay mucha población cubana, mexicana... Yo creo que es necesario conocer las características de la zona antes de abrir un negocio."

Sus productos tuvieron una excelente acogida, así que pronto amplió el negocio para ofrecer productos imprescindibles a la hora de preparar muchos de los platos de toda América Latina: harina de maíz, picantes y adobos, arroces para todos los gustos, crema de coco, frijoles, gandules, etc.

Hoy su tienda es un referente en Miami, no solo para los latinos. "Es importante que los estadounidenses descubran nuestros productos y que vean que hay más cosas que los tacos o el arroz con frijoles."

Pero no todo es negocio en su vida. Evaristo colabora también, junto con su esposa Lidia, de origen dominicano, en el proyecto solidario "Comida y amor", que reparte productos de alimentación y platos de comida a personas sin recursos: "Es necesario ser conscientes de que no todos tenemos los mismos medios económicos. No queremos que nadie pase hambre por aquí."

Expresar necesidad

Es necesario importar los productos más conocidos y **que** la gente **acceda** a ellos fácilmente.

Es importante ser solidarios y **que** la gente de pocos recursos no **pase** hambre.

15A.5 **es necesario/importante** + [*infinitive*]/**que** + [*subjunctive*]

Vocabulario

17

- el número *issue*
- aprovechar *to take advantage*
- la acogida *acceptance*
- abrir un negocio *to open a business*
- ampliar un negocio *to expand a business*
- la harina de maíz *cornmeal*
- los picantes *hot spices*
- el adobo *marinade*
- el coco *coconut*
- el frijol *bean*
- el gandul *pigeon pea*
- sin recursos *in need*
- los medios *means*
- pasar hambre *to go hungry*

17 a. Lea el artículo sobre Evaristo. ¿Qué tipo de publicación es *Comunidad latina*? ¿Dónde se publica y por qué? Destaque tres factores por los que los editores han considerado "Latino de honor" a este emprendedor cubano.

b. ¿Qué es Casa Vera? ¿Qué productos vende? ¿Cómo empezó y se desarrolló? ¿Conoce algún negocio similar en su ciudad?

c. Haga una lista con su compañero/a donde expresen esperanzas positivas para Evaristo y su negocio.

Modelo: *Ojalá que...*

18 a. ¿Cuál es la opinión de Evaristo sobre las siguientes cuestiones? ¿Qué necesidades expresa?

abrir un negocio | los estadounidenses | las personas sin recursos

b. ¿Qué tipo de negocio le parece más interesante? ¿Cuáles de estas categorías cree que sería necesario o importante considerar antes de abrir ese negocio? ¿Por qué? Comparta sus opiniones con el resto de la clase.

Modelo: *Es necesario hacer una investigación de mercado y que nuestros potenciales consumidores nos cuenten acerca de sus gustos y preferencias.*

18b Expansion Have students write a simple business plan and present it to the class.

investigación de mercado | público | ubicación | inversión inicial | productos de calidad | higiene | estrategias de *marketing* | servicio al cliente | paciencia y dedicación

Vocabulario *cont.*

importar

(18)

la investigación de mercado *market research*
el gusto *taste, liking*
la ubicación *location*
la higiene *hygiene*
la paciencia *patience*
la dedicación

(19)

reunir *to collect*
el recetario *recipe collection*
la elaboración *production*
nutritivo/a *nutritious*
la materia prima *raw material*
el toque *touch*
el trigo *wheat*
la costumbre *habit*
sabroso/a *tasty*
el utensilio

(21)

la piña *pineapple*
el melocotón *peach*
el aguacate *avocado*
la fresa *strawberry*
el albaricoque *apricot*
la alcachofa *artichoke*

OPINIÓN

¿Cuáles son los productos de alimentación típicos de la gastronomía de su comunidad? ¿Es popular la gastronomía de su país o comunidad en el mundo? ¿Por qué?

20 Expansion Have groups of students take turns reading their recipes aloud. The other group members have to identify the dish.

19 a. Observe las imágenes y haga hipótesis sobre el contenido del texto. ¿Qué tienen en común los productos de las fotos? Después lea el texto y compruebe sus predicciones. Los cuatro son ingredientes básicos en la alimentación.

CHEFS contra el HAMBRE

Chefs contra el hambre es un proyecto que pertenece a la "Iniciativa América Latina y Caribe sin Hambre" de la Organización para la Alimentación y la Agricultura (FAO, por sus siglas en inglés). El objetivo es reunir en un libro recetas que se pueden elaborar con los ingredientes más básicos y con utensilios de cocina sencillos. Se invita a los chefs y amantes de la cocina a compartir sus recetas. Quieren potenciar la elaboración de recetas ricas, nutritivas y económicas, además de enseñar a utilizar y enriquecer los alimentos. La iniciativa espera que los habitantes de los países con menor variedad de materias primas mejoren sus hábitos alimenticios y disfruten de los alimentos con un buen toque de sabor.

maíz

trigo

arroz

papas

b. ¿Cuáles son los objetivos de esta iniciativa? ¿Quién participa y a quién va dirigida? ¿Cómo propone la FAO conseguir estos objetivos?

Modelo: *La "Iniciativa América Latina y Caribe sin Hambre" desea/espera/quiere...*

c. Busque en el texto palabras relacionadas con estos términos. costumbre: hábito; sabroso: rico; productos: alimentos, ingredientes, materias primas; preparar: elaborar; plato: receta

costumbre • sabroso • productos • preparar • plato

20 Piense en un alimento básico de su comunidad y escriba una receta que quiere compartir. **20 Suggestion** Remind students to use **usted** commands in their recipes.

21 a. Algunas frutas y verduras reciben diferentes nombres en los países del mundo hispano. Busque las palabras del recuadro en un diccionario y escríbalas al lado de su sinónimo de la lista.

durazno • damasco • palta • alcaucil • ananá • frutilla

piña = ananá
melocotón = durazno
aguacate = palta
fresa = frutilla
alcachofa = alcaucil
albaricoque = damasco

b. ¿Encuentran otro nombre para alguna de estas frutas y verduras?

c. Busque más ejemplos como los anteriores con su grupo y compártanlos con el resto de la clase.

Practice more at **vhlcentral.com.**

SAM: Actividades pp. 317–320

22 a. Mire las fotos y describa lo que ve. ¿Qué tipo de ceremonia cree que se está celebrando? Luego lea el texto sobre la Pachamama y compruebe sus respuestas.

La fiesta de la Pachamama

Explain that, at its height, the Incan Empire covered present-day Peru, Ecuador, Bolivia, and parts of Colombia and Chile.

La adoración a la Pachamama, o Madre Tierra, es un legado° del imperio incaico° que sobrevive con fuerza entre los pueblos del noroeste de Argentina, el norte de Chile y las regiones andinas de Bolivia y Perú. Muchas son las ceremonias en honor de la Pachamama, pero el homenaje° principal se celebra durante el mes de agosto, en especial el primer día del mes. Aunque en otras épocas las ceremonias se hacían solamente en los hogares, éstas han ganado protagonismo y ahora es común realizar una fiesta para toda la comunidad.

De acuerdo con el rito, es importante agradecer° a la Pachamama por los bienes° recibidos durante el año transcurrido° y entregarle todo lo que no se quiere que falte el año entrante°. Familias y vecinos se reúnen entonces para cavar un pozo° en la tierra. Luego "alimentan" a la Madre Tierra enterrando° una olla de barro° con semillas° de maíz, cordero°, papas, yerba, gaseosas, etc. A continuación se tapa el pozo con una piedra.

Nadie falta a esta cita. Mayores y niños de todas las edades se hacen presentes° en el lugar y continúan la celebración comiendo, bebiendo, y festejando con música y coplas°. También es costumbre realizar una procesión y elegir a la representante de la Madre Tierra entre las ancianas° de mayor edad.

legado *heritage* **incaico** *Incan* **homenaje** *tribute* **agradecer** *to thank* **bienes** *goods* **transcurrido** *that passed* **entrante** *coming* **cavar un pozo** *dig a hole* **enterrando** *by burying* **olla de barro** *clay pot* **semillas** *seeds* **cordero** *lamb* **se hacen presentes** *participate* **coplas** *popular folk songs* **ancianas** *old women*

b. ¿Qué es la fiesta de la Pachamama? ¿Dónde y cuándo se celebra? ¿En qué consiste la celebración?

c. ¿Conoce alguna tradición similar en su comunidad? 22c Students may mention Earth Day activities.

d. La fiesta de la Pachamama tiene su origen en el respeto por la tierra. Con sus compañeros, piense en otras maneras de respetar a nuestra Madre Tierra.

Modelo: *Es necesario que aprendamos a no ensuciar ni contaminar la tierra con nuestras actividades.*

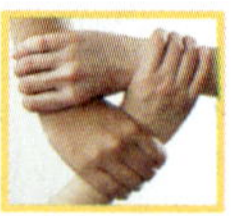

TAREA FINAL

Un negocio en el extranjero

Formen pequeños grupos y seleccionen los productos que quieren vender, el país y el lugar donde quieren abrir el negocio.

Piensen en las probabilidades de mercado, fijen los objetivos del proyecto, las esperanzas y las necesidades.

Expongan su proyecto al grupo y voten por el mejor proyecto o incluso una fusión de varios proyectos.

YO PUEDO...

- Puedo expresar probabilidad.
  Ha recibido una llamada de un número desconocido. Exprese probabilidad.
- Puedo hacer sugerencias.
  Sugiera una solución para la situación mencionada arriba.
- Puedo hablar de objetivos.
  Anote los objetivos que tiene usted para este curso.
- Puedo expresar esperanza.
  Exprese algo que espera que le suceda a uno de sus compañeros.
- Puedo expresar necesidad.
  ¿Qué es necesario para tener éxito en un negocio?

GRAMÁTICA FUNCIONAL

Suggestion Name famous people and have the class make conjectures about where they are and what they are doing at this moment.

15A.1 Express probability

Review of simple future; irregular simple future 5.16.2b, 5.16.2c

- Use the **futuro simple** to express conjecture or probability.

¿Qué hora **será**?	**Serán** las ocho.
I wonder what time it is.	*It is probably about eight.*

- Note that this usage does not imply a future meaning. English words and expressions that convey this idea include *I wonder, I bet, may be, might,* and *probably.*
- Use the future of **estar** + [*present participle*] to make conjectures about what is happening at that moment.

¿De qué **estarán hablando**?
*What **must they be talking** about?*

Estarán planeando la fiesta sorpresa para Paula.
***I bet they're planning** Paula's surprise party.*

- You learned the regular forms of the **futuro simple** in 12B.1. Some common verbs have irregular stems.

decir	→	dir-		
haber	→	habr-		
hacer	→	har-		é
poder	→	podr-		ás
poner	→	pondr-	+	á
querer	→	querr-		emos
saber	→	sabr-		éis
salir	→	saldr-		án
tener	→	tendr-		
venir	→	vendr-		

- Irregular future forms use the same set of endings as regular forms. Remember that all forms except for the **nosotros/as** form carry a written accent.

El avión **saldrá** para San Salvador dentro de dos horas; **tendremos** que darnos prisa.
*The airplane **will leave** for San Salvador in two hours; **we'll have** to hurry up.*

- The future form of **hay** (*there is/are*) is **habrá** (*there will be*).

Dicen que mañana **habrá** una tormenta.
*They say that **there will be** a storm tomorrow.*

15A.2 Make suggestions

lo mejor es/sería + [*infinitive/noun*] 3.3.1, 5.8.3, 5.13

- Use **lo mejor es/sería** + [*infinitive/noun*] to make suggestions.

Lo mejor es el pan casero.
*Home-made bread **is the best**.*

Lo mejor sería cultivar nuestros propios productos.
***It would be best** to grow our own produce.*

G4 Expansion Ask students to write several suggestions about places, things, and activities on campus. Have them read their list to a partner, who will agree or refute the suggestions.

¡Póngalo en práctica!

G1 Escriba la forma correcta de cada verbo en el futuro simple.

1. tú, salir	saldrás
2. Gael, hacer	hará
3. nosotros, poder	podremos
4. vosotros, saber	sabréis
5. ellas, querer	querrán
6. yo, venir	vendré
7. usted, poner	pondrá
8. Nina y Ramón, decir	dirán

G2 Complete la conversación con el futuro simple.

¿Estos frijoles (1) tendrán (tener) conservantes?

No sé. ¿(2) Estará (Estar) esa información en la etiqueta?

No, no dice nada en la etiqueta. ¿No (3) habrá (haber) algún teléfono de información para preguntarlo?

G3 Complete las oraciones usando el futuro simple.

1. ¿De dónde vendrán (venir) estos tomates?
2. Esta salsa, ¿ podrá (poder) usarse fría, o tendré (tener, yo) que calentarla?
3. ¿ Querrán (Querer) cenar todos en casa mañana?
4. ¿ Sabrá (saber) Julia preparar los platos tradicionales que pensamos servir?

G4 Complete los diálogos.

- Lo mejor de la tienda (1) es el chocolate negro.
- Sí, (2) lo mejor sería comprar varios paquetes.

- Lo (3) mejor es tomar una bebida fría en la playa.
- Tienes razón, lo mejor (4) sería ir al supermercado antes de salir para la costa; así compramos algunas.

- (5) Lo mejor es poder comer verduras locales.
- Sí, lo mejor (6) sería encontrar una granja dónde conseguirlas.

Practice more at **vhlcentral.com.**

GRAMÁTICA FUNCIONAL

15A.3 Talk about objectives

esperar/querer/desear + [*subjunctive*]; Regular present subjunctive 5.20.1, 5.21.1

- Use the subjunctive (**el subjuntivo**) to express desires and hopes with the verbs **esperar, querer,** and **desear.**

  Quiero que **ustedes ayuden** con los quehaceres domésticos.
  *I want **you to help** with the household chores.*

- Except for commands, all of the verb forms you have learned up until now have been in the indicative mood (**el indicativo**), which is used to state facts and express actions. The subjunctive is used to express will and influence, among many other uses that you will learn in subsequent lessons.

- To form the present subjunctive (**presente del subjuntivo**), start with the **yo** form of the present indicative, drop the **-o** ending, and replace it with the endings of the **presente del subjuntivo.**

	TRABAJAR	VENDER	ASISTIR
(yo)	trabaj**e**	vend**a**	asist**a**
(tú)	trabaj**es**	vend**as**	asist**as**
(usted, él, ella)	trabaj**e**	vend**a**	asist**a**
(nosotros/as)	trabaj**emos**	vend**amos**	asist**amos**
(vosotros/as)	trabaj**éis**	vend**áis**	asist**áis**
(ustedes, ellos/as)	trabaj**en**	vend**an**	asist**an**

- The endings of the **presente del subjuntivo** for **-ar** verbs (except for the first-person singular conjugation) coincide with the endings of **-er** and **-ir** verbs in the present indicative. Likewise, the endings of the present subjunctive for **-er** and **-ir** verbs coincide with the endings of **-ar** verbs in the present indicative, with the exception of the first-person singular conjugation.

  -ar → -e
  -er/-ir → -a

- The subjunctive is used in sentences with two subjects and two verbs. Sentences that use the subjunctive have a main clause and a subordinate clause.

  MAIN CLAUSE | **SUBORDINATE CLAUSE**
  Mi mamá quiere **que yo hable** con el supervisor.
  *My mom wants **me to speak** with the supervisor.*

- Use the infinitive in sentences with only one subject.

  Mi mamá quiere **hablar** con el supervisor.
  *My mom wants **to speak** with the supervisor.*

- Use the conjunction **que** (*that*) to connect the two clauses in the sentence.

  El gerente quiere **que** hablemos más con los clientes.
  The manager wants us to speak more with the clients.

- Note that the word *that* is often omitted in the English translation.

  Espero **que** nos lleven a un restaurante vegetariano.
  I hope (that) they take us to a vegetarian restaurant.

G5 Expansion Provide students with sentence starters that elicit the subjunctive and have them complete the sentences logically.

¡Póngalo en práctica!

G5 Empareje el comienzo de cada oración con el final correcto.

d	1. Espero que tú	a. llame a todos los productores esta semana.
e	2. Deseamos que vosotros	b. festejemos la Nochebuena en su casa.
a	3. El gerente quiere que Marcos	c. colaboren en este proyecto.
b	4. Mis abuelos quieren que mis hermanos y yo	d. te mejores pronto.
c	5. La profesora quiere que ustedes	e. lo paséis bien en vuestras vacaciones.

G6 Complete las oraciones con la forma correcta del verbo (infinitivo o presente del subjuntivo).

Quiero (1) comunicarme (comunicarse) con nuestros clientes y que nuestros clientes (2) valoren (valorar) nuestros productos.

Sí, las empresas esperamos (3) promocionar (promocionar) nuestros productos y que los clientes (4) compren (comprar) con frecuencia.

Los consumidores esperamos que los productores (5) trabajen (trabajar) bien y que las empresas (6) vendan (vender) buenos productos.

Queremos que las empresas (7) usen (usar) más ingredientes naturales porque queremos que nuestros hijos (8) estén (estar) sanos.

El propietario del negocio desea (9) anunciar (anunciar) la apertura de su tienda en la calle Mayor el próximo 7 de octubre. Espera que todos (10) pasen (pasar) por la tienda para ver las ofertas.

Suggestion Emphasize that the subjunctive cannot appear in a sentence without **que** (the only exception is with **Ojalá**). Suggest to students that when they are practicing subjunctive verb conjugation, they should always say the verb form preceded by **que,** so that it becomes second nature.

Practice more at **vhlcentral.com.**

GRAMÁTICA FUNCIONAL

15A.4 Express hope

ojalá que + [*subjunctive*];
a ver si + [*indicative*] 5.20.1, 5.21.1, 11.5

- Always use the **subjunctive** with the interjection **ojalá (que)**. **Ojalá (que)** means *I/We hope* or *I/We wish* and its form is invariable.

Ojalá (que) recibamos buenas ofertas.	**Espero que recibamos** buenas ofertas.

I hope (that) we receive good offers.

Ojalá lleguemos antes de las siete.
I hope we get there before seven.

- Use the **indicative** with the construcion **a ver si** (*let's see if*). **A ver si** is used in colloquial language.

A ver si recibimos buenas ofertas.
Let's see if we receive good offers.

A ver si llegamos antes de las siete.
Let's see if we get there before seven.

15A.5 Express necessity

es necesario + [*infinitive*];
es necesario + **que** + [*subjunctive*] 5.8.4, 5.20.1, 5.21.6

- Use **es necesario** (*it is necessary*) + [*infinitive*] to express necessity in a general sense.

Es necesario aumentar nuestras ventas.
It is necessary to increase our sales.

Es necesario bajar los precios.
It is necessary to reduce prices.

- Use **es necesario** + **que** + [*subjunctive*] to express what a specific person or group needs to do.

Es necesario que nuestras ventas **aumenten**.
It is necessary that our sales increase.

Es necesario que las empresas de alimentos **bajen** los precios.
It is necessary that food companies reduce prices.

- **Es necesario que** is an impersonal expression that always requires the use of the **subjunctive**. Other examples of impersonal expressions that are always used with the subjunctive include **es importante que**, **es esencial que**, and **es imprescindible que.**

Es importante que escuchemos las opiniones de los demás.
It is important that we listen to the opinions of others.

Es esencial que las empresas **usen** ingredientes frescos.
It is essential that companies use fresh ingredients.

Es imprescindible que trates con respeto a los clientes.
It is essential that you treat clients with respect.

Suggestion Ask students to write a list of what students of Spanish need to do in order to succeed in class. Tell them to use the infinitive in some statements and the subjunctive in others.

¡Póngalo en práctica!

G7 Complete las oraciones.

1. ¡...Ojalá... que vendamos todo el cacao!
2. A ver si ...es... (ser) verdad.
3. Ojalá me ...llamen... (llamar) del trabajo al que me postulé.
4. A ver si ...podemos... (nosotros, poder) terminar el proyecto a tiempo.
5. Ojalá que ...ganemos... (nosotros, ganar) el partido mañana.
6. ¡Ojalá que ...deje... (dejar) de llover!

G7 Expansion Have students write a few additional statements about current world events.

G8 Complete las conversaciones usando el infinitivo o el presente del subjuntivo.

Yo creo que es absolutamente necesario (1)...leer... (leer) con atención las etiquetas de los productos.

Sí, pero es necesario también que las etiquetas (2)...transmitan... (transmitir) la información con claridad.

• • • • •

Si quieres sacar una buena nota, es necesario (3)...dedicar... (dedicar) mucho tiempo al estudio.

Claro que sí, pero también es importante que los estudiantes (4)...participen... (participar) mucho en la clase.

• • • • •

Es importante que (5)...comamos... (nosotros, comer) bien.

También es importante (6)...hacer... (hacer) ejercicio para sentirse bien.

Practice more at **vhlcentral.com.**

15A

GRAMÁTICA FUNCIONAL

SÍNTESIS

Mire las fotografías y escriba un diálogo corto para cada una, usando el vocabulario indicado.

Suggestion Explain that the speakers in the dialogues do not necessarily need to be those pictured.

1. 

ojalá	variado	compartir	compañeros de trabajo

- ______________________________
- ______________________________
- ______________________________
- ______________________________

2. 

vendrán	alimentos	supermercado	consumir

- ______________________________
- ______________________________
- ______________________________
- ______________________________

3. 

espero que	fruta	mercado	sabor

- ______________________________
- ______________________________
- ______________________________
- ______________________________

4. 

a ver si	conservantes	fresco	gluten

- ______________________________
- ______________________________
- ______________________________
- ______________________________

Expansion Have students act out their dialogues for the class.

VOCABULARIO

¿Qué comeremos?

el aceite de oliva virgen extra	*extra virgin olive oil*
la agricultura ecológica	*organic farming*
el cacao en polvo	*cocoa powder*
la certeza	*certainty*
el colorante	*colorant, coloring*
la composición	*composition*
la conservación	*preservation*
el conservante	*preservative*
el consumo	*consumption*
el contenedor	*(recycling) container*
el envase de plástico	*plastic container*
el envase reciclable	*recyclable container*
la etiqueta	*label*
la fecha de caducidad	*expiration date*
la frambuesa	*raspberry*
la galleta	*cookie*
el gluten	*gluten*
la grasa	*fat*
el hidrato de carbono	*carbohydrate*
la información nutricional	*nutritional information*
el ingrediente	*ingredient*
el jarabe	*syrup*
la leche descremada en polvo	*powdered skim milk*
la leche entera	*whole milk*
la mermelada	*marmalade, jam*
el producto ecológico	*organic product*
el producto fresco	*fresh food*
la proteína	*protein*
el suflé	*soufflé*
el tomate frito	*tomato sauce*
endulzar	*to sweeten*
espolvorear	*to sprinkle*
apto/a para	*appropriate/safe for*
artificial	*artificial*
bajo/a en calorías	*low-calorie*
celíaco/a	*celiac*
cocido/a	*cooked*
seco/a	*dry*
vegetariano/a	*vegetarian*

Mucho sabor

Ojalá	*I/We wish*
el alimento natural	*natural food*
el alimento transgénico	*transgenic food*
la apertura	*opening*
la cola	*line*
el/la consumidor(a)	*consumer*
la demanda	*demand*
la expectativa	*expectation*
el nutriente	*nutrient*
el pesticida	*pesticide*
el/la productor(a)	*producer*
la promoción	*promotion*
el reciclaje	*recycling*
el sabor	*flavor; taste*
aportar	*to provide*
asistir (a)	*to attend*
bajar	*to go down*
conquistar	*to captivate*
consumir	*to consume*
cumplir con	*to meet*
evitar	*to avoid*
potenciar	*to foster*
preservar	*to preserve*
envasado/a	*packaged*
recogido/a	*picked*

Evaristo Acebedo

la acogida	*acceptance*
el adobo	*marinade*
el aguacate	*avocado*
el albaricoque	*apricot*
la alcachofa	*artichoke*
el coco	*coconut*
la costumbre	*habit*
la dedicación	*dedication*
la elaboración	*production*
la fresa	*strawberry*
el frijol	*bean*
el gandul	*pigeon pea*
el gusto	*taste, liking*
la harina de maíz	*cornmeal*
la higiene	*hygiene*
la investigación de mercado	*market research*
la materia prima	*raw material*
los medios	*means*
el melocotón	*peach*
el número	*issue*
la paciencia	*patience*
los picantes	*hot spices*
la piña	*pineapple*
el recetario	*recipe collection*
el toque	*touch*
el trigo	*wheat*
la ubicación	*location*
el utensilio	*utensil*
abrir un negocio	*to open a business*
ampliar un negocio	*to expand a business*
aprovechar	*to take advantage*
importar	*to import*
pasar hambre	*to go hungry*
reunir	*to collect*
nutritivo/a	*nutritious*
sabroso/a	*tasty*
sin recursos	*in need*

Variación léxica

el aguacate ↔ **la palta** (*C. S., Bol., Per.*)

el albaricoque ↔ **el damasco** (*C. S.*) ↔ **el chabacano** (*Méx.*)

la alcachofa ↔ **el alcaucil** (*Arg., Uru.*)

el azúcar moreno ↔ **el azúcar negro** (*Arg.*) ↔ **la panela** (*Col.*)

el durazno (*Amér. L.*) ↔ **el melocotón** (*Esp.*)

la fecha de caducidad ↔ **la fecha de vencimiento**

la fresa ↔ **la frutilla** (*C. S., Bol.*)

el maíz ↔ **el choclo** (*Amér. S.*) ↔ **el elote** (*Méx.*)

la piña ↔ **el ananá** (*Arg., Uru.*)

Suggestion Ask students if they have said or overheard similar arguments in their households. Then ask the class if they think that these types of conflict are universal, or if they are found in one type of society or segment of the population more than others.

15B REBELDES CON CAUSA

No me entienden

No entiendo a mis hijos... ¿Te entendían tus padres a ti? ¿Cuántas veces has dicho o te han dicho que...?

1 ¡Me molesta que siempre tengan que decidir sobre todo lo que hago!

4 ¡Mis padres no me entienden!

2 ¡No me gusta que salgas hasta tan tarde!

5 ¡No soporto que me digáis siempre lo que tengo que hacer!

3 ¿Qué tenemos que hacer para que nos hagas caso con tus estudios?

6 ¡Es ridículo que te enojes! ¡Te lo decimos por tu bien y para que estés bien!

Suggestion Have volunteers read the comments aloud. Encourage them to use emotion and gestures.

JORNADAS DE LA FAMILIA

Expresar disgusto y enfado

- A mí **me molesta** que mis padres **controlen** mi vida.
- Mis padres **no soportan** que **salga** siempre con mis amigos.

15B.1 **no gustar / molestar / no soportar** + **que** + [*subjunctive*]

Vocabulario

1

molestar *to bother*
hacer caso (a alguien) *to pay attention (to somebody)*
no soportar *to not stand*
por tu bien *for your own good*
la campaña de conciliación *conciliation campaign*
el disgusto *upset; trouble*
rebelde, ridículo/a, controlar, terrible

2

generacional *generational*
la norma *rule*
la falta de comunicación *lack of communication*

1 Fíjese en el cartel de esta campaña de conciliación. ¿Cuál es el tema? ¿Cuál cree que es el objetivo? ¿Qué tipo de institución cree que promueve esta campaña? Possible answers: los conflictos entre padres e hijos; promover la comunicación entre padres e hijos; una organización especializada en la familia

2 Lea los comentarios en el cartel y marque los conflictos generacionales (entre padres e hijos) que se tratan.

- [ ] los estudios
- [x] la hora de llegar a casa
- [x] las normas
- [ ] la ropa
- [ ] las fiestas
- [x] la falta de comunicación

3 a. Busque en el cartel frases en las que se expresa disgusto y enfado. ¿Quién dice cada frase, los padres o los hijos?
1 Me molesta...; 2 No me gusta...; 5 No soporto...; 6 Es ridículo... los hijos (1, 4, 5), los padres (2, 3, 6)

b. Elija un tema de la Actividad 2 y escriba otras oraciones frecuentes en los conflictos entre padres e hijos. Compare sus oraciones con las del grupo.

4 ¿Cree que estos u otros conflictos generacionales siempre han existido y existirán? ¿Qué puede significar la expresión "rebeldes con causa"?
Sample answer: La expresión "rebeldes con causa" es un guiño a la película protagonizada por James Dean y conocida en español como *Rebelde sin causa*. Se utiliza para referirse a las personas que tienen una causa justificada para su rebeldía.

en mi opinión • yo creo que • yo pienso que • es ridículo que

Expresar finalidad

- Te hemos inscrito en una academia **para que aprendas...**
- Sí, y **para que** no nos **digas** que no te ayudamos con tus estudios.

15B.2 **para que** + [*subjunctive*]

Expresar condiciones

Con tal de que me llames al llegar, te dejo el coche.

15B.3 **con tal (de) que, en caso (de) que, sin que** + [*subjunctive*]

Vocabulario

(5)

inscribir (a alguien en algo) *to enroll (somebody in something)*

la actividad extraescolar *extracurricular activity*

hoy en día *nowadays*

el/la adolescente *teenager*

los deberes *homework*

desarrollar *to develop*

la academia

(6)

el instituto *high school*

aceptar *to accept*

pretender *to try to*

aún *still, yet*

desperdiciar *to waste*

(7)

retrasarse *to be late*

(8)

la escuela bilingüe *bilingual school*

la escuela pública *public school*

la escuela privada *private school*

el comedor *dining hall*

7 Suggestion Alternatively, give each pair a different, specific context on which to base their conversation. Have pairs act out their situations in groups of six and vote for the funniest, most creative, etc.

5 Muchos padres inscriben a sus hijos en actividades extraescolares (deporte, música, etc.). Lea la opinión de una psicóloga escolar al respecto. ¿Coincide usted con esta opinión? ¿Y su compañero/a?

Los padres quieren que los hijos hagan actividades extraescolares para que tengan una formación completa. Hoy en día hay mucha oferta: deportes, música, idiomas, informática... pero son niños o adolescentes, y una parte muy importante de su formación debe ser el juego. Los chicos salen de la escuela a las cinco de la tarde, pero no llegan a casa hasta las siete u ocho. Solo tienen tiempo para hacer los deberes y cenar. Yo recomiendo reducir estas actividades a dos tardes por semana, y respetar los gustos del niño o adolescente para que se desarrolle de una manera más natural.

6 a. Muchas veces, padres e hijos tienen distintos puntos de vista sobre el mismo tema. Macarena quiere buscar trabajo cuando termine el instituto y Sandra, su mamá, quiere que vaya a la universidad. Lea los testimonios.

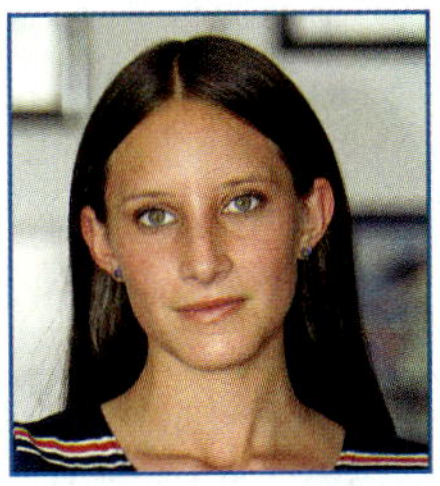

"Me molesta que mi mamá no acepte que ya soy mayor. Pretende decirme lo que tengo que hacer sin que yo opine. Dice que es por mi bien, pero en realidad quiere vivir mi vida. Yo quiero tomar mis propias decisiones, no soporto que me dé órdenes. En caso de que necesite ayuda, se la voy a pedir."

"Macarena piensa que es una mujer adulta, pero aún es una niña. No sé qué hacer para que me escuche. Yo le doy consejos para que no tenga los mismos problemas que yo tuve. Le permitiré que tome algunas decisiones por su cuenta con tal de que continúe sus estudios. Es ridículo que desperdicie su potencial."

b. ¿Qué le parece esta situación? ¿A usted le pasó algo parecido alguna vez? Comente sus experiencias con su compañero/a.

7 Con su compañero/a, escriban una posible conversación entre Sandra y Macarena. Asegúrense de usar todas las expresiones del recuadro.

con tal (de) que • sin que • en caso (de que)
no gustar • para que • molestar

8 ¿Para qué cree que inscriben los padres a sus hijos en estas escuelas?

bilingües | públicas/privadas | con comedor | con actividades extraescolares

MI EXPERIENCIA

9 Comparta con el grupo qué conflictos puede haber entre padres e hijos.

GUIÓN DE TRABAJO

¿Qué problemas puede haber entre padres e hijos? → A los padres/hijos... no les gusta que... les molesta que...

¿Se le ocurre alguna solución? → Creo que.... con tal (de) que... en caso de que... sin que...

Practice more at **vhlcentral.com.**

SAM: Actividades pp. 321–323

El proceso de independizarse

Para padres e hijos

Suggestion Have pairs of students choose one of the **consultas** and draft a response, giving the person at least three pieces of advice.

Consultas

Comenzar la universidad es uno de los acontecimientos más esperados y temidos por todos: los gastos y también los miedos de padres e hijos ante el gran cambio hacen que recibamos muchas consultas. Hemos seleccionado algunas de las preocupaciones más frecuentes:

"Este año comienzo la universidad lejos de casa. Estoy muy contenta porque estudiaré una carrera que me interesa mucho y porque estaré con casi todos mis amigos. Pero me preocupa que mis padres no me dejen independizarme. ¡Mi mamá ya está pensando en visitarme todos los fines de semana!"

—Micaela, Los Ángeles

"Este año termino el colegio. Me gustaría estudiar música, pero temo que mis padres se opongan. Ellos quieren que sea médico, igual que mi padre y mi abuelo. El problema es que la medicina no me interesa para nada... No sé cómo decirles que me dejen decidir a mí sin herirlos."

—Claudio, San Francisco

"Tengo una hija adolescente que pronto viajará a otra ciudad para comenzar la universidad y me preocupa su adaptación. Me da miedo que no se alimente bien y que no descanse lo suficiente. No quiero sobreprotegerla, pero no creo que esté lista para organizarse sola. Estoy pensando en llamarla todos los días para asegurarme de que esté bien."

—Susana, Sacramento

"Mi esposa y yo siempre quisimos darle lo mejor a nuestro hijo. Estamos orgullosos: es un chico simpático, deportista y estudioso. Pero nos preocupa que cuando termine la escuela no podamos pagarle una educación universitaria. Daríamos todo con tal de que él pueda cumplir sus sueños, pero esto está fuera de nuestro alcance."

—Pablo, San Diego

Expresar temor y preocupación

- **Me preocupa que** no **tengamos** tiempo para nuestros hijos.
- **A mí me da miedo que** los niños no **quieran** estudiar.
- **Temo que** mi hija no **pueda** estudiar por falta de dinero.

15B.4 **preocupar / dar miedo / temer + que +** [*subjunctive*]

Vocabulario

(10)

independizarse *to become independent*
el gasto *expense*
oponerse (ng) *to object*
herir (e:ie) *to hurt*
sobreproteger (j) *to overprotect*

10 Fíjese en el título de la revista *Para padres e hijos*. ¿Qué implica ser padres hoy en día? ¿Qué diferencias hay entre ser padres de niños pequeños y ser padres de adolescentes?

11 a. Observe las fotos. ¿Qué le llama la atención? Lea el consultorio de la revista. ¿Qué les preocupa a los padres y a los adolescentes de la universidad? ¿Coinciden?

- [x] gasto económico
- [ ] transporte
- [x] carrera universitaria
- [x] alimentación y descanso
- [ ] integración
- [x] independencia

b. ¿Usted o algún amigo ha tenido las mismas preocupaciones o los mismos conflictos? ¿Qué solución encontró?

12 a. Expresen sus preocupaciones y temores sobre los siguientes temas.

Costo de la educación | Elección de la universidad | Elección de la carrera

Modelo: *A mí me preocupa...*
A algunos padres les preocupa...

b. ¿Qué otros temas educativos le preocupan a usted?

Expresar extrañeza

- Me sorprende que los padres no comprendan a sus hijos.
- A mí me parece raro que los padres no lo intenten.

15B.5 **sorprender / extrañar / parecer raro + que + [*subjunctive*]**

Estrategia

Reforzar argumentos

- Me preocupa que no vengan.
- Desde luego. Ya es tarde.
- Efectivamente.

Vocabulario *cont.*

cumplir sus sueños *to make his/her dreams come true*
estar fuera del (de nuestro) alcance *to be beyond one's means*

13

parecer (zc) raro *to think something is odd*
sorprender *to surprise*
extrañar *to surprise*
exagerar *to exagerate*

15

la deserción universitaria *university drop-outs*

16

la calificación *grade*
la nota *grade*
el suspenso *failure*
el aplazo *failure*
la escala *scale*

17

efectivamente *indeed*

Las notas

En el mundo hispano, las calificaciones escolares en la secundaria suelen ser numéricas. En Argentina, Colombia, España, México y Uruguay, por ejemplo, 1–3 es suspenso o aplazo, 4–5 es regular, 6–7 es bueno 8–9 es muy bueno, y 10 es sobresaliente o excelente. En otros países, la escala es diferente: En Cuba, Guatemala y Honduras, va del 1 al 100; en Ecuador y Venezuela, del 1 al 20; en Bolivia y Chile, del 1 al 7; y en Paraguay, del 1 al 5. En Puerto Rico, se califica con letras, de la A (excelente) a la F (aplazo).

13 a. Algunos de los participantes han dirigido sus dudas a un sociólogo del programa de radio *Para padres e hijos*. Escuche las consultas. ¿Qué les sorprende a los participantes? Marque verdadero (V) o falso (F).

	V	F
1. A Micaela no le sorprende la reacción de sus padres.	☐	☑
2. Al sociólogo no le extraña que los padres de Micaela la quieran cuidar.	☑	☐
3. Al sociólogo le parece raro que Susana esté preocupada por su hija.	☐	☑

b. ¿Qué le sorprende a usted de estas consultas?

14 Vuelva a escuchar el audio y anote las expresiones que se usan para reforzar lo que dice el interlocutor. ¿Cuáles son? ¿Expresan acuerdo o desacuerdo?

efectivamente, desde luego
Expresan acuerdo.

15 Suggestion Ask students to discuss Argentina's dropout rate and cost of study, and if they believe there could be a correlation.

15 a. Observe la tabla de datos sobre las universidades públicas de Argentina, España y los Estados Unidos.

	¿Cuánto cuesta por año estudiar en una universidad pública?	¿Cuántos estudiantes hay por cada profesor?	¿Cuánto duran las carreras?	¿Cuál es el porcentaje de deserción universitaria?
Argentina	$0	19	5–6 años	60%
España	2500–3500 €	12	4–5 años	25%
Estados Unidos	$50 000	14,1	4 años	35%

b. Comente con su compañero/a los datos que le parecen raros o que le sorprenden.

Modelo:
- *A mí me sorprende que la universidad sea gratuita en Argentina.*
- *Desde luego. Yo no lo sabía.*

16 Lea la nota sociocultural sobre los sistemas de calificaciones. ¿Cuál es el equivalente en su país?

16 Suggestion Ask students which grading method they prefer.

MI EXPERIENCIA

17 ¿Qué le preocupa o le parece raro de las universidades de su país? Con la clase, hagan una puesta en común.

GUIÓN DE TRABAJO

¿Qué opinas/te preocupa/ te parece raro/te sorprende? → Opino que... / Me preocupa que... / Me parece raro que... / Me sorprende que...

de las universidades / de los gastos de educación / de las notas → Porque pienso que... / Porque creo que...

Desde luego. / Efectivamente. / (No) Estoy de acuerdo.

Practice more at **vhlcentral.com.**

SAM: Actividades pp. 324–326

Marina Sánchez, un genio de los números

Marina Sánchez es una de las finalistas de la Olimpiada Matemática de Centroamérica y El Caribe, en la que participan más de 40 estudiantes de secundaria o bachillerato de 15 países de la región. Todos ellos ganaron medallas en las olimpiadas nacionales de sus respectivos países. Marina es una de las representantes de la República Bolivariana de Venezuela y hemos hablado con ella.

Suggestion Draw attention to the title. Explain that nouns referring to people usually match the gender of the person (Ex: **Julia es maestra; Pedro es enfermero**); however, some nouns, such as **el genio**, are invariable due to the word's etymology. Give students these additional examples: **la estrella, el ángel, el personaje, el miembro.**

Hola, Marina, ¿es la primera vez que te presentas a este concurso?
No, qué va. Ya me he presentado dos veces, pero esta es la primera vez que llego a la final.

¿Piensas que este tipo de concursos son solo para cerebritos?
No pienso eso, ¡qué va! Es una oportunidad para que nos interesemos más por las matemáticas. Me molesta que piensen que solo les interesa a los cerebritos.

¿Qué harás si ganas el concurso?
Bueno, mis padres me han dado permiso para que haga un viaje a España.

Supongo que las matemáticas son tu asignatura favorita, ¿no?
No son las mátemáticas, sino la física. Aunque también me gustan mucho las ciencias sociales. Y bueno, el profe de Tecnología es muy chévere, y también me gusta esa asignatura. A veces es un poco aburrida, pero sirve para que comprendamos el mundo que nos rodea.

¿Y qué asignaturas te gustan menos?
Lengua y literatura, por ejemplo, no me gusta, pero bueno, por lo menos sirve para que leamos un poco más.

¿Y en tu tiempo libre? Imagino que no te dedicas a resolver ecuaciones y que prefieres salir con tus amigos, ¿no?
Desde luego, en mi tiempo libre prefiero divertirme con mis amigos.

¿Y qué te gustaría hacer en el futuro? ¿Piensas estudiar matemáticas en la universidad?
No, ¡para nada!, me gustaría estudiar alguna carrera técnica como informática o ingeniería.

Mañana es la final. ¿Estás nerviosa o te preocupa algo?
Me da miedo quedarme en blanco, pero no, no me preocupa mucho.

Marina Sanchéz, estudiante

Suggestion Ask students to share experiences they have had at academic competitions.

Enfatizar opiniones

- ¡Qué va! No pienso eso.
- No me gustan las matemáticas sino la física.
- ¿Qué dices? ¡Para nada!
- No me gusta la informática, pero me parece importante.

15B.6 **¡qué va!, no pienso eso, no... sino..., no... pero**

Vocabulario

18

el bachillerato *high school (studies)*
el/la cerebrito *nerd*
la asignatura *school subject*
Matemáticas *Math*

18 a. ¿Qué cree que es una "olimpiada matemática"? ¿Cuántos años cree que tiene nuestra protagonista? Lea la entrevista y compruebe. Es un concurso de matemáticas entre colegios a nivel local, provincial, regional, nacional o internacional. Marina tiene 15 ó 16 años.

b. ¿Por qué participa Marina en esta olimpiada? ¿Qué le gusta, le molesta, le preocupa?

19 ¿De qué manera enfatiza Marina sus opiniones? ¿Qué estructuras utiliza en estas situaciones?

- Para decir que una afirmación no es cierta. no pienso eso, ¡qué va!, ¡para nada!
- Para dar la alternativa cierta. no... sino...

20 a. Fíjese en las asignaturas que se nombran en el texto y en las de la lista. Piense en un equivalente en su país y diga para qué cree que se estudian.

EDUCACIÓN SECUNDARIA
Biología y Geología
Educación plástica y visual
Música
Química
Educación ético-cívica
Educación física
Lengua extranjera

Modelo:
- *Lengua y literatura sirve para que leamos un poco más.*
- *Yo no pienso eso, pienso que sirve para...*

b. ¿Estudian las mismas asignaturas los estudiantes de esta edad en su país? Compare con sus compañeros. ¿Qué otras asignaturas propondría usted?

Adriana escribe cartas a Nick, miembro de los *Backstreet Boys*, contándole todo lo que le pasa. *Maldita adolescente* es una novela que trata sobre la necesidad de sentirse querido y la importancia de buscar ilusiones nuevas cada día.

Vocabulario *cont.*

Física *Physics*
Ciencias sociales *Social Studies*
Tecnología *Technology*
Lengua y literatura *Language and Literature*
estudiar una carrera *to study a degree*
la ingeniería *engineering*
quedarse en blanco *to draw a blank*
el genio, la ecuación

(20)

Educación plástica y visual *Art*
Química *Chemistry*
Educación ético-cívica *Civics*
Educación física *Physical Education*
la lengua extranjera *foreign language*
Biología, Geología

(21)

eufórico/a *euphoric*

OPINIÓN

¿Conoce otros concursos como las olimpiadas matemáticas? ¿Para qué sirven?

¿Marina le parece una adolescente "típica"?

21a Suggestion Have one or two volunteers read the passage aloud. Encourage them to adopt the tone of a young teen girl who is excited about shopping.

21 a. Lea la carta que escribe Adriana, la protagonista de la novela *Maldita adolescente*. ¿A quién le dirige la carta? ¿Por qué está tan contenta?

EVERYBODY

¡Bien, Nick, lo conseguí! Estoy tan contenta que no paro de bailar y cantar "Everybody". Mi hermano dice que estoy loca y que soy una maldita° adolescente, pero me da igual°, estoy eufórica. Me voy de compras con Sandra y con Carmen, a ver si tengo más suerte que con mi madre. Por fin ha accedido a darme la pasta° para que me compre yo la ropa, ¡lo que le ha costado! De verdad, no la entiendo. Se pasa el día° diciendo lo importante que es para una mujer ser independiente y tener su propio dinero y patatín y patatán°, y luego quiere controlar cada cosa que entra en mi armario. Fue papá quien le dijo por teléfono que me diera la pasta ["dale el dinero"]. "¡A saber lo que se compra!", respondió ella. Pero papá le dijo que si era mayor para cuidar de mis hermanos, también lo era para elegir mi propia ropa. ¡Yabadabadúuu! ¡Papi for president! [...]

- ¡Adriana!
- ¡Ya vooooooy!

Te dejo, Nick, me llama mi hermano. Seguro que mis amigas están abajo esperándome. [...]

MENÉNDEZ, María: *Maldita adolescente*. Madrid, Ediciones SM, 2009.

maldita *darn* **me da igual** *I don't care* **pasta** *money* **Se pasa el día** *She spends all day* **patatín y patatán** *this and that*

b. ¿Tiene algún conflicto esta adolescente? ¿Con quién y por qué? ¿Hay algo que no entiende o le molesta?

c. Subraye las expresiones o palabras del texto que relaciona con un lenguaje coloquial. ¿Conoce otra forma de expresar lo mismo?

22 Escriba un breve texto sobre las aficiones, el carácter y los gustos de su grupo de amigos. **22 Suggestion** Collect students' descriptions, shuffle them, and read them aloud for the class, who will try to guess the identity of the student.

23 Lea la información sobre el sistema educativo español y compárelo con el de su país. ¿A qué edad empiezan los niños el colegio? ¿Piensa que esa es la edad apropiada? ¿Para qué edades es obligatoria la educación?

La educación infantil es voluntaria, aunque la mayoría de los padres llevan a sus hijos al colegio a los tres años. La escuela infantil ayuda a los padres en la educación de sus hijos y potencia sus capacidades y su relación con otros niños. La educación primaria y secundaria son obligatorias.

- Educación infantil (0–6 años)
- Educación primaria (6–12 años)
- Educación secundaria obligatoria (ESO) (12–16 años)
- Educación secundaria no obligatoria: Bachillerato (16–18 años) Ciclos formativos (16–18 años)
- Educación superior, universidad (18–21 años)

Practice more at **vhlcentral.com.**

SAM: Actividades pp. 327–332

24 Suggestion Have students read through the testimonies and underline the positive and negative feelings of each student.

24 Lea acerca de las esperanzas y los miedos de tres estudiantes. ¿Algo le sorprende? Comente con su compañero/a si han sentido lo mismo alguna vez.

24 Expansion Have students choose one of the students and write another testimony from his/her perspective, written five years from now.

"Hoy he recibido la carta de aceptación de mi futura universidad. ¡No puedo creerlo! Estoy muy ilusionada con la vida universitaria: el campus, los profesores, los otros estudiantes, las fiestas... Lo único que me preocupa es no poder conseguir empleo. Mis padres me ayudarán con la universidad, pero yo debo pagar los otros gastos."

"En unos meses terminaré la carrera de medicina y estoy muy orgulloso de mis logros°. Tuve algunas dificultades y en varias ocasiones pensé en dejar los estudios, pero ahora veo que mi esfuerzo valió la pena. Me preocupa que no pueda pagar mi préstamo estudiantil°... ¡es mucho dinero!"

"Estoy estudiando dirección de cine; es mi vocación. Cuando era pequeña, miraba las mismas películas muchas veces para intentar descubrir cómo las hacían. Me encanta esta carrera, pero sé que no será fácil encontrar empleo inmediatamente. Temo que deba regresar a casa de mis padres cuando termine la universidad."

logro *achievement* **préstamo estudiantil** *student loan*

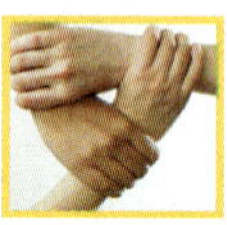

TAREA FINAL

Conversaciones entre padres e hijos

Hagan dos grupos en clase. Uno son los padres y el otro, los hijos.

Preparen una lista de los conflictos que tienen con el otro grupo y expónganlos.

Elijan los temas más interesantes y representen conversaciones entre padres e hijos en la clase.

Voten y elijan la mejor representación.

YO PUEDO...

- Puedo expresar disgusto y enfado.
  Diga cuatro cosas que no soporta.
- Puedo expresar finalidad.
  ¿Para qué cree usted que los padres inscriben a sus hijos en actividades extraescolares?
- Puedo expresar temor y preocupación.
  ¿Cuáles cree usted que son las principales preocupaciones sobre la educación universitaria?
- Puedo expresar extrañeza.
  En esta unidad ha aprendido mucho sobre varios sistemas escolares. Diga qué le extraña o le parece raro de estos sistemas.
- Puedo enfatizar opiniones.
  ¿Piensa que el costo de la educación en su país es demasiado alto?

GRAMÁTICA FUNCIONAL

15B.1 Express displeasure and annoyance

no gustar/molestar/no soportar + que + [*subjunctive*];
Irregular subjunctive forms 5.11.1, 5.20.2

- Use **no gustar** (*not to like*)/**molestar** (*to bother*) + **que** + [*subjunctive*] to express disapproval. **Gustar** and **molestar** are used with indirect object pronouns.

  No me gusta que la gente **hable** durante la película.
  I don't like that people talk during the movie.

- **No soportar** (*to be unable to stand*) + **que** + [*subjunctive*] is another verb of emotion that triggers the subjunctive in the subordinate clause.

  No soporto que mis padres me **pregunten** si tengo deberes o no.
  I can't stand that my parents ask me whether I have homework or not.

- In the examples above, the two clauses in each sentence have different subjects. If the subject of the two verbs in a sentence is the same, use the infinitive of the second verb.

  different subjects
  No soportamos que vivas tan lejos de casa.
  We can't stand that you live so far away from home.

  same subject
  No soporto vivir tan lejos de casa.
  I can't stand to live so far away from home.

- Use the subjunctive in the subordinate clause with expressions such as **es ridículo que** (*it is ridiculous that*) and **es terrible que** (*it is terrible that*). In **15A.5** you learned about other impersonal expressions that require the subjunctive in the subordinate clause.

  Es ridículo que tenga que estar en casa a las ocho de la noche.
  It is ridiculous that I have to be home by eight.

- As you learned in **15A.3**, most forms of the present subjunctive are based on the **yo** form of the present indicative. If a verb has an irregular **yo** form in the present indicative, this spelling will be carried throughout all forms in the present subjunctive.

HACER (ha**g**o)	→	ha**g**a, ha**g**as, ha**g**a, ha**g**amos, ha**g**áis, ha**g**an
TENER (ten**g**o)	→	ten**g**a, ten**g**as, ten**g**a, ten**g**amos, ten**g**áis, ten**g**an
SALIR (sal**g**o)	→	sal**g**a, sal**g**as, sal**g**a, sal**g**amos, sal**g**áis, sal**g**an
DECIR (di**g**o)	→	di**g**a, di**g**as, di**g**a, di**g**amos, di**g**áis, di**g**an

Quiero que me **digas** la verdad.
*I want you to **tell** me the truth.*

Suggestion Have students write three sentences expressing what they don't like about their living situation (on- or off-campus) and share them with a partner.

Suggestion Ask students to create cues for three additional dehydrated sentences from the perspective of a group of professors.

Additional verbs with irregular **yo** forms include **caer**, **caber**, **oír**, **poner**, **traer**, **valer**, **venir**, **seguir**.

¡Póngalo en práctica!

G1 Empareje el comienzo de cada oración con el final apropiado.

b	1. A Julián no le gusta que sus compañeros de cuarto	a. salgas la noche antes de un examen.
d	2. Marisa no soporta que su hermana	b. dejen la ropa tirada en el piso.
a	3. Es ridículo que tú	c. diga que no somos responsables.
c	4. Nos molesta que la gente	d. use su ropa sin pedirle permiso.
e	5. Es terrible que tú y Gonzalo	e. tengáis que volver a escribir las monografías.

G2 Complete las oraciones con el indicativo o el subjuntivo de los verbos indicados.

1. No ...soporto... (soportar) que mis padres me ...digan... (decir) lo que tengo que hacer.
2. No me ...gusta... (gustar) que ...tengamos... (nosotros, tener) deberes para el fin de semana.
3. A los padres de Sara les ...molesta... (molestar) que ella ...salga... (salir) durante la semana.
4. ...Es... (Ser) ridículo que los estudiantes no ...hagan... (hacer) proyectos grupales más a menudo.
5. Me gusta que mis estudiantes ...hagan... (hacer) actividades extraescolares, pero no soporto que por culpa de estas actividades no ...terminen... (terminar) la tarea.

G3 Escriba oraciones sobre lo que a usted no le gusta. Siga el modelo.

Modelo: no gustar / los niños / hacer tarea los fines de semana.
No me gusta que los niños hagan tarea los fines de semana.

1. no soportar / mis padres / llamar todos los días
   No soporto que mis padres me llamen todos los días.
2. no gustar / mis compañeros / tener más tiempo libre que yo No me gusta que mis compañeros tengan más tiempo libre que yo.
3. molestar / mi vecino / hacer tanto ruido
   Me molesta que mi vecino haga tanto ruido.
4. no soportar / mi hermana / usar mi celular
   No soporto que mi hermana use mi celular.

Practice more at **vhlcentral.com.**

GRAMÁTICA FUNCIONAL

15B.2 Express purpose

para que + [*subjunctive*] 5.20, 5.21.2, 12.6

- Use the subjunctive after **para que** (*so that*) to express purpose.

  Mis padres me inscribieron en un programa **para que estudie** más.
  My parents enrolled me in a program ***so that I study*** *more.*

  Te recomiendo este libro **para que aprendas** español.
  I recommend this book ***so that you learn*** *Spanish.*

- Note that the two verbs in the examples above have different subjects. If both verbs refer to the same person, use the construction **para** + [*infinitive*].

  Estudio español **para viajar**.
  I am studying Spanish ***in order to travel****.*

  Esteban trabaja los fines de semana **para pagar** sus estudios.
  Esteban works on weekends ***to pay for*** *his studies.*

Suggestion Write sentence starters (Ex: **Voy a terminar la carrera con tal de que...**) on the board and have students complete them with information from their own lives.

15B.3 Express conditions

con tal (de) que, en caso (de), sin que 5.21.8

- Always use the subjunctive with the conjunctions **con tal (de) que** (*provided that*) and **en caso (de) que** (*in case [that]*). Note that the preposition **de** is optional in the first two conjunctions.

  Te dejo salir esta noche **con tal de que termines** toda la tarea.
  I will let you go out tonight ***provided that you finish*** *all your homework.*

  Te presto mi diccionario **en caso de que lo necesites**.
  I'll lend you my dictionary ***in case you need it****.*

- When the subject of the two verbs is the same, you can use **con tal de** and **en caso de** + [*infinitive*]. In this case **de** is required.

  Con tal de aprobar el examen, voy a estudiar toda la noche.
  In order to pass *the exam, I will study all night.*

  Cómprate un sándwich **en caso de tener hambre** esta tarde.
  Buy yourself a sandwich ***in case you get hungry*** *this afternoon.*

- Always use the subjunctive with the conjunction **sin que** (*without*).

  Siempre ayudo a mis padres **sin que me lo pidan**.
  I always help my parents ***even if they don't ask*** *me to.*

- Use **sin** + [*infinitive*] when the subject of the two verbs is the same.

  Nunca tomo el coche **sin pedir** permiso antes.
  I never take the car ***without asking for*** *permission first.*

¡Póngalo en práctica!

G4 Complete las oraciones con el infinitivo o el presente del subjuntivo.

1. Inscribimos a nuestros hijos en una academia para que ...recuperen... (ellos, recuperar) las asignaturas.
2. No, no te voy a comprar un celular para que ...hables... (tú, hablar) todo el día con tus amigos.
3. Voy a estudiar para ...poder... (yo, poder) viajar con todos mis compañeros a la playa al final del semestre.
4. Germán ha comprado una bicicleta para ...llegar... (Germán, llegar) más rápido a la universidad.
5. He decidido estudiar con mis amigos para que ...preparemos... (nosotros, preparar) juntos el examen.
6. Mis padres me han regalado una computadora portátil para que ...tenga... (yo, tener) la posibilidad de trabajar en muchos sitios.

G5 Complete la conversación.

- Tu papá y yo te permitimos salir con tus amigos mañana por la noche con tal de que (1) ...hagas... (hacer) los quehaceres domésticos. También tienes que mantener tu celular encendido en caso de que (2) ...necesitemos... (nosotros, necesitar) llamarte.
- Está bien, pero siempre permiten que salga Florencia sin que (3) ...termine... (terminar) toda su tarea, y no me parece justo.
- Florencia ya terminó la secundaria, es una situación distinta. Terminaste la tarea para mañana, ¿no?
- Bueno, tengo que estudiar un poco más para mi examen de biología.
- Entonces, te dejamos salir mañana con tal de que (4) ...estudies... para tu examen hoy por la noche. Y no te olvides de los quehaceres domésticos.

G6 Empareje las frases para formar oraciones completas.

1. Te ayudo con tal de que ...c...
2. No me importa no salir con mis amigos hoy con tal de ...a...
3. Pedí una pizza en caso de ...b...
4. Estudié el subjuntivo en caso de que ...d...

a. aprobar el examen mañana.
b. tener hambre mientras estudio.
c. tú me ayudes mañana.
d. tenga que usarlo en el examen.

G6 Suggestion To challenge students, have them cover the lettered phrases and complete the sentences logically.

Practice more at **vhlcentral.com.**

GRAMÁTICA FUNCIONAL

G8 Expansion Have students write a few questions about current events, using **preocupar** and **dar miedo**. Then have them interview a classmate and report back on any common fears or worries they have.

15B.4 Express fear and concern

preocupar/dar miedo + que + [*subjunctive*];
Irregular subjunctive forms 5.11.1, 5.20, 5.21.1

- Use **preocupar** (*to worry*) and **dar miedo** (*to scare*) + **que** + [*subjunctive*] to express fear and concern. These expressions are used with indirect object pronouns.

(a mí)	me		
(a ti)	te		
(a usted/él/ella)	le	preocupa	+ **que** +
(a nosotros/as)	nos	da miedo	[*subjunctive*]
(a vosotros/as)	os		
(a ustedes, a ellos/as)	les		

Me preocupa que mis hijos no **quieran** estudiar.
It worries me that *my children do not* ***want*** *to study.*

Nos da miedo que nuestros hijos **vivan** lejos de casa.
It scares us that *our children* ***live*** *far from home.*

- If the main verb and **preocupar/dar miedo** refer to the same subject, use an infinitive after **preocupar/dar miedo**.

Me da miedo cambiar de colegio.
It scares me to change *schools.*

Nos preocupa no encontrar trabajo.
It worries us that we may not find *work.*

- Use the subjunctive with the verb of emotion **temer** (*to fear, to be afraid*) + **que** when **temer** and the verb that follows it have different subjects.

Temo que mis compañeros no **coloboren** en el proyecto.
I am afraid that *my classmates won't* ***collaborate*** *on the project.*

- Use the infinitive after **temer** if the subject is the same.

Temo no aprobar el examen de Química.
I am afraid I won't pass *the Chemistry exam.*

- In 15B.1, you learned the present subjunctive of several verbs with irregular **yo** forms. If an **-ar** or **-er** verb has a stem change in the present indicative, this change will be carried throughout all forms in the **subjunctive**, with the exception of the **nosotros/as** and **vosotros/as** forms.

PENSAR (p**ie**nso)	→	p**ie**nse, p**ie**nses, p**ie**nse, pensemos, penséis, p**ie**nsen
PODER (p**ue**do)	→	p**ue**da, p**ue**das, p**ue**da, podamos, podáis, p**ue**dan
QUERER (qu**ie**ro)	→	qu**ie**ra, qu**ie**ras, qu**ie**ra, queramos, queráis, qu**ie**ran

- **-Ir** stem-changing verbs maintain the present indicative stem change, but they also show a second stem change in the **nosotros/as** and **vosotros/as** forms. This is the same stem change that occurs in the present participle.

PREFERIR (pref**ie**ro)	→	pref**ie**ra, pref**ie**ras, pref**ie**ra, pref**i**ramos, pref**i**ráis, pref**ie**ran
DORMIR (d**ue**rmo)	→	d**ue**rma, d**ue**rmas, d**ue**rma, d**u**rmamos, d**u**rmáis, d**ue**rman

¡Póngalo en práctica!

G7 Escriba la forma correcta del verbo en el presente del subjuntivo.

1. Alicia, sentir	sienta
2. nosotros, dormir	durmamos
3. los aviones, volar	vuelen
4. yo, poder	pueda
5. vosotros, mentir	mintáis
6. tú, cerrar	cierres
7. nosotros, confesar	confesemos
8. la profesora, recomendar	recomienda

G8 Complete las oraciones con la forma apropiada del verbo indicado.

Ema (1) ...teme... (temer) que a sus invitados no les (2) ...guste... (gustar) la comida que preparó.

A los profesores les (3) ...preocupa... (preocupar) que sus estudiantes no (4) ...lean... (leer) el material antes de ir a la clase.

¿Te (5) ...da miedo... (dar miedo) (6) ...empezar... (empezar) la universidad?

A Consuelo le (7) ...preocupa... (preocupar) que sus amigos no (8) ...sigan... (seguir) en contacto.

G9 Elija la opción que tiene el mismo significado.

1. No sé si voy a aprobar el examen y esto me da miedo. ...b...
   a. Me da miedo que no apruebes el examen.
   b. Me da miedo no aprobar el examen.

2. Vas a volver tarde y eso me preocupa. ...a...
   a. Me preocupa que vuelvas tarde.
   b. Me preocupa volver tarde.

3. Quieres ir a acampar con tus amigos y eso nos preocupa. ...a...
   a. Nos preocupa que quieras ir a acampar con tus amigos.
   b. Nos preocupa acampar con tus amigos.

4. Nunca me dices adónde vas y eso me molesta. ...b...
   a. Me molesta decirte adónde voy.
   b. Me molesta que no me digas adónde vas.

Practice more at **vhlcentral.com.**

GRAMÁTICA FUNCIONAL

Suggestion Give students cloze sentences that use **pero** and **sino** and have them complete each one with information from their lives. Ex: **Mi compañero/a de cuarto es** .... **pero** .... **A mis padres no les preocupa** .... **sino** ....

15B.5 Express surprise

sorprender/extrañar/parecer raro + [*subjunctive*] 5.11.1, 5.20, 5.21.1

- Use the subjunctive with the verbs **sorprender** (*to surprise*), **extrañar** (*to surprise*), and **parecer raro** (*to seem strange*) to express surprise. These verbs are used with indirect object pronouns.

  Me sorprende que prefieran un colegio privado.
  I am surprised that they prefer a private school.

  A Javier **le extraña que no quieras** venir a la fiesta.
  *Javier **thinks it's odd that you don't want to** come to the party.*

- As with other verbs of emotion, use the subjunctive if the verbs in the sentence have different subjects. If both verbs have the same subject, use the infinitive for the second verb.

  Me parece raro usar uniforme.
  ***It seems strange to me to wear** a uniform.*

15B.6 Emphasize opinions

¡qué va!, no pienso eso; no... sino; pero vs. sino 7.4, 12.8

- To stress your disagreement with a statement, say **no pienso eso, pienso que...** (*I don't think so, I think that . . .*).
- Use **¡qué va!** (*no way!/come on!*) to express disagreement about a stated idea. **¡Qué va!** is a very informal expression. Other similar expressions include **¿qué dices?** (*what are you talking about?*) and **para nada** (*not in the least; not at all*). Both expressions are used in informal conversations.

  - ¿Piensas que debería pedir disculpas?
  - No, **para nada**. Sólo dijiste la verdad.

  - *Do you think that I should apologize?*
  - *No, **not at all**. You just told the truth.*

- Use **no... sino** (*no/not . . . but/but rather*) to present an alternative idea to an idea that has already been stated or implied.

  No hemos pedido carne, **sino** pescado.
  *We didn't order meat, **but** fish.*

- Although **pero** and **sino** both mean *but*, they are used in different situations. **Sino** is used when the first part of a sentence is negative and the second part contradicts it. **Sino** can often be translated as *but rather* or *on the contrary*. In all other cases, use **pero** to mean *but*.

  Manuel **no** viajará a la ciudad esta noche, **sino** que tomará el tren por la mañana.
  *Manuel will **not** travel to the city tonight, **but rather** will take the train in the morning.*

  Manuel quiere volver a la ciudad lo antes posible, **pero** prefiere dormir una noche más en el hotel.
  *Manuel wants to return to the city as soon as possible, **but** he prefers to sleep in the hotel one more night.*

¡Póngalo en práctica!

G10 Complete las conversaciones.

- Nos (1)...extraña... (extrañar) que los padres (2)...acepten... (aceptar) la nueva situación.
- Sí, a nosotros también nos (3)...parece... (parecer) raro que los niños no (4)...tengan... (tener) clase por la tarde.

- ¿Te (5)...sorprende... (sorprender) que algunos profesores (6)...permitan... (permitir) el uso de computadoras portátiles en la clase?
- No, ya no me (7)...extraña... (extrañar) (8)...ver... (ver) el uso de tecnología en el aula.

Suggestion Tell the class to imagine that they are Spanish students who have recently arrived to spend a semester at your school. Have students work in small groups and write a conversation about what they think is surprising and strange about university life in the U.S.

G11 Complete las conversaciones.

¿Crees que a los estudiantes no les interesan las asignaturas de ciencias (1)...sino... las de letras?

No, ¡qué (2)...va...! No (3)...pienso... (pensar) eso. Pienso que depende de gustos.

• • • • •

Para ti, ¿es importante que los estudiantes (4)...tomen... (tomar) clases en todas las disciplinas posibles antes de elegir una carrera universitaria?

No, para (5)...nada..., no pienso (6)...eso... Creo que algunos estudiantes empiezan la universidad con una idea muy clara de la carrera que quieren elegir en sus estudios.

• • • • •

Creo que lo importante a la hora de buscar un trabajo no es la experiencia que uno tiene, (7)...sino... el interés que uno muestra en la entrevista.

¿Qué (8)...dices...? En mi opinión, la experiencia es fundamental.

Practice more at **vhlcentral.com.**

VOCABULARIO

No me entienden

hoy en día	*nowadays*
por tu bien	*for your own good*
la academia	*academy*
la actividad extraescolar	*extracurricular activity*
el/la adolescente	*teenager*
la campaña de conciliación	*conciliation campaign*
el comedor	*dining hall*
los deberes	*homework*
el disgusto	*upset; trouble*
la escuela bilingüe	*bilingual school*
la escuela privada	*private school*
la escuela pública	*public school*
la falta de comunicación	*lack of communication*
el instituto	*high school*
la norma	*rule*
aceptar	*to accept*
controlar	*to control*
desarrollar	*to develop*
desperdiciar	*to waste*
hacer caso (a alguien)	*to pay attention (to somebody)*
inscribir (a alguien en algo)	*to enroll (somebody in something)*
molestar	*to bother*
pretender	*to try to*
retrasarse	*to be late*
no soportar	*to not stand*
generacional	*generational*
rebelde	*rebel*
ridículo/a	*ridiculous*
terrible	*terrible*
aún	*still, yet*

El proceso de independizarse

estar fuera del (de nuestro) alcance	*to be beyond one's (our) means*
el aplazo	*failure*
la calificación	*grade*
la deserción universitaria	*university drop-outs*
la escala	*scale*
el gasto	*expense*
la nota	*grade*
el suspenso	*failure*
cumplir (sus) sueños	*to make his/her dreams come true*
exagerar	*to exagerate*
extrañar	*to surprise*
herir (e:ie)	*to hurt*
independizarse	*to become independent*
oponerse (ng)	*to object*
parecer (zc) raro	*to think something is odd*
sobreproteger (j)	*to overprotect*
sorprender	*to surprise*
efectivamente	*indeed*

Marina Sánchez

quedarse en blanco	*to draw a blank*
la asignatura	*school subject*
el bachillerato	*high school (studies)*
Biología	*Biology*
el/la cerebrito	*nerd*
Ciencias sociales	*Social Studies*
la ecuación	*equation*
Educación ético-cívica	*Civics*
Educación física	*Physical Education*
Educación plástica y visual	*Art*
Física	*Physics*
el genio	*genius*
Geología	*Geology*
la ingeniería	*engineering*
la lengua extranjera	*foreign language*
Lengua y literatura	*Language and Literature*
Matemáticas	*Math*
Química	*Chemistry*
Tecnología	*Technology*
estudiar una carrera	*to study for a degree*
eufórico/a	*euphoric*

Variación léxica

la asignatura ⟷ **la materia** (*Amér. L.*)

el/la cerebrito (*fam., Amér. L.*) ⟷ **el empollón/la empollona** (*fam., Esp.*) ⟷ **el/la traga** (*fam., Arg.*) ⟷ **el/la ñoño/a** (*fam., Amér. L.*)

inscribir (a alguien en algo) ⟷ **apuntar (a alguien en algo)** (*Esp.*) ⟷ **anotar (a alguien en algo)** (*Arg.*)

El poeta chileno **Pablo Neruda** (1904–1973) siempre apreció la buena mesa, y prueba de eso son sus odas dedicadas a frutas y verduras, como *Oda a la cebolla*, *Oda a la alcachofa*, *Oda al tomate*, *Oda a la papa* y *Oda a la manzana*. En 1971, Neruda recibió el Premio Nobel de Literatura.

Vocabulario útil

agregar *to add*
apreciar *to value, to esteem*
el asado *roast*
asesinar *to murder*
la buena mesa *fine dining*
la cebolla *onion*
desatarse *to break, to run wild*
hervir (e:ie) *to boil*
el hueso *pit*
el injerto *graft*
la verdura/hortaliza *vegetable*

Estrategia

Figurative language

Figurative language, which uses imagery, shouldn't be interpreted in a literal sense. The writer or speaker appeals to the reader's imagination with comparisons, describing something through metaphors (the implicit comparison between two objects that have something in common), personifications (which attribute human qualities to objects), hyperbole (strong exaggeration), etc. You can find figurative language in poems, songs, advertising, and even in everyday language.

LECTURA

Oda al tomate

Pablo Neruda

1 Converse con un(a) compañero/a.

1. ¿Qué comida no falta nunca en...?
   a. el Día de Acción de Gracias
   b. Navidad
   c. Halloween
   d. el Día de San Valentín
2. ¿Qué estado de los Estados Unidos se relaciona con estos alimentos?
   a. chile y frijoles
   b. manzanas
   c. queso
   d. maíz
3. Proponga un alimento que merece su mes/día nacional y cuándo sería.

1 Suggestion Have students explain why this food deserves to be honored.

2 Después de leer el poema *Oda al tomate*, elija la opción que corresponde.

1. ¿Qué quiere decir "la calle se llenó de tomates"?
   a. Se cultivan tomates en la calle.
   (b.) Han comenzado a vender tomates en la calle.
2. ¿Qué significa "en diciembre se desata el tomate"?
   (a.) Diciembre es la estación del tomate.
   b. En diciembre los tomates se rompen.
3. ¿A qué se refiere el poeta con "debemos asesinarlo"?
   a. El tomate no es bueno para la salud y hay que evitarlo.
   (b.) Hay que cortar el tomate para comerlo.
4. Cuando el poeta dice "¡vamos!, ¡ya es hora!" se refiere a que...
   a. es el tiempo ideal para comprar tomates.
   (b.) es la hora de ir a comer.

La calle
se llenó de tomates,
mediodía,
verano,
la luz
se parte
en dos
mitades°
de tomate,
corre
por las calles
el jugo.
En diciembre
se desata
el tomate,
invade
las cocinas,
entra por los almuerzos
se sienta
reposado
en los aparadores°,
entre los vasos,
las mantequilleras,
los saleros azules.
Tiene
luz propia,
majestad benigna.
Debemos, por desgracia,
asesinarlo:
se hunde°
el cuchillo
en su pulpa viviente°,
es una roja
víscera,
un sol
fresco,
profundo,
inagotable°,
llena las ensaladas
de Chile,
se casa alegremente
con la clara cebolla,
y para celebrarlo
se deja
caer°
aceite,
hijo
esencial del olivo,
sobre sus hemisferios
entreabiertos°,
agrega
la pimienta
su fragancia,
la sal su magnetismo:
son las bodas
del día,
el perejil°
levanta
banderines,
las papas
hierven vigorosamente,
el asado
golpea°
con su aroma
en la puerta,
es hora!
vamos!
y sobre
la mesa, en la cintura°
del verano,
el tomate,
astro° de tierra
estrella
repetida
y fecunda,
nos muestra
sus circunvoluciones°,
sus canales,
la insigne plenitud°
y la abundancia
sin hueso,
sin coraza°,
sin escamas° ni
espinas°,
nos entrega
el regalo
de su color fogoso°
y la totalidad de
su frescura°.

se parte... *splits in half* **aparadores** *sideboards* **se hunde** *buries/sinks* **viviente** *living* **inagotable** *inexhaustible* **se deja caer** *is poured* **entreabiertos** *half-open* **perejil** *parsley* **golpea** *knocks* **cintura** *waist* **astro** *star* **circunvoluciones** *circumvolutions* **insigne plenitud** *distinguished fullness* **coraza** *shell* **escamas** *scales* **espinas** *bones* **fogoso** *passionate* **frescura** *freshness*

Suggestion Before they read the poem, have students scan the poem for cognates. Discuss the meanings with students. Also go over words that are in the same family as words students already know, such as **mantequillera**.

Estrategia

Odes

Have you ever read an ode before? An ode celebrates a person, a place, or a thing, usually identified in the title. Ancient Greeks and Romans wrote odes to praise athletes, champions, memorable places, victory at war, and celebrations, but modern odes have evolved to praise the most simple things in everyday life; some odes include a subtle sense of humor.

Suggestion Have students exchange odes with a partner for peer-editing. Then, have them read their odes aloud in small groups.

3 En parejas, hagan comparaciones siguiendo estos pasos. Luego escriban oraciones completas y compártanlas con la clase.

1. Elija un objeto cualquiera.
2. Anote alguna característica de ese objeto.
3. Para cada característica, busque otro objeto que la comparta.

Objeto 1	Característica	Objeto 2
Luna	brillante	moneda

PROYECTO

Escriba una oda a un objeto, animal, lugar o persona.

Paso 1: Decida cuál es el objeto que va a retratar en su oda y haga una lista de las palabras que pueden describirlo.

Paso 2: Escriba frases sobre las cualidades únicas del objeto que eligió.

Paso 3: Explique su preferencia e interés por ese objeto.

Paso 4: Revise todo lo que escribió: tache las repeticiones y desarrolle algunas comparaciones que hagan más vívida la descripción.

Paso 5: Elija las dos oraciones con más fuerza y ubique una al comienzo y la otra al final de su oda. Ordene las oraciones restantes como mejor le parezca. ¡Y no se preocupe por la rima!

Flash CULTURA

Estrategia

Make predictions

Before watching this Flash Cultura episode, make some guesses about what you will learn about animals, farms, native cultures, climates, old traditions, etc. Then, watch the video and check your predictions. Don't worry if your predictions weren't accurate. The purpose of making predictions is to access prior knowledge in order to make it easier to take in new information.

Vocabulario útil

afilar *to sharpen*
esquilar *to shear*
la gama *range*
la hebra de hilo *thread*
la joroba *hump*
la mascota *pet*
la manta *blanket*
tejer *to weave*
la tela *fabric*
la temporada *season*
teñir (e:i) *to dye*

Estrategia

Word origin

In everyday Spanish there are many words from ancient languages spoken by native peoples of the Americas. For example, **alpaca** comes from Aymara, and **llama**, **vicuña**, and **guanaco** come from Quechua. Many words for food come from Quechua, Guaraní, and Nahuatl. Can you find some examples?

4 **Expansion** Have a few pairs act out their conversations for the class.

Las alpacas

Ya ha aprendido sobre la producción de alimentos orgánicos y la educación de los niños. Este episodio de **Flash Cultura** muestra cómo en la región andina del Perú existe una industria ecológica que da trabajo a miles de personas: la cría de la alpaca, un animal que los incas consideraban digno de un rey.

1 ¿Alguna vez tuvo una mascota o intentó cultivar alguna planta? ¿Existe algún conocimiento que se transmite de generación en generación en su familia?

2 Mire este episodio de **Flash Cultura** y preste atención a las distintas etapas y condiciones del proceso para la cría de alpacas. ¿Es diferente o parecido a lo que imaginaba?

La alpaca posee una de las fibras más finas del mundo.

Successful Language Learning: Remind students to be on the lookout for false cognates. Ask students to define the word **fábrica**. Does it have any relation with the word **tela**?

Esta preciosa fibra cuenta con la gama de colores naturales más grande del mundo.

3 Relacione los elementos de las dos columnas para formar oraciones.

1. Algunas personas en Perú tienen alpacas para que ...d...	a. antes de la temporada de lluvia.
2. Para que las niñas puedan formar parte de sus comunidades, es necesario que ...b...	b. aprendan a tejer.
3. Lo mejor es esquilar a las alpacas ...a...	c. se transforme en una hebra de hilo.
4. Es necesario girar la fibra para que ...c...	d. les den buena suerte.

4 Con un(a) compañero/a invente un diálogo entre un(a) vendedor(a) de una tienda de mascotas y un(a) cliente que busca su mascota ideal.

Modelo:
- *No soporto los pelos largos y me molesta mucho que las mascotas tengan olor. ¿Habrá una mascota para mí?*
- *Lo mejor para usted sería una tortuga (turtle).*

4 **Suggestion** Ask students if they or anyone they know has an exotic pet; have them describe the animal.

Audio: Activities, Vocabulary
Video: *Flash Cultura*

Unidad 16

Ingrid Betancourt, una luchadora

Lección 16A

EMBAJADORES DE LA PAZ

Lección 16B

TÍPICOS TÓPICOS

Estela y Mario, publicistas

Puerto Rico, ¿nación o estado?

AVANCE

16A EMBAJADORES DE LA PAZ

Compromiso de todos

FORMULARIO DE ADHESIÓN
MARCHA MUNDIAL POR LA PAZ Y LA NO VIOLENCIA

La Marcha Mundial por la Paz y la No Violencia es una propuesta de movilización social en la que participan más de 100 países. La verdadera fuerza de esta marcha nace de la adhesión y del compromiso de todos.

Suggestion Besides ending wars and dismantling nuclear arms, the **Marcha** aims to eliminate all forms of violence— "physical, economic, racial, religious, cultural, sexual, and psychological." Ask students if any of these types of violence are present in their country or region.

MARCHA MUNDIAL POR LA PAZ Y LA NO-VIOLENCIA

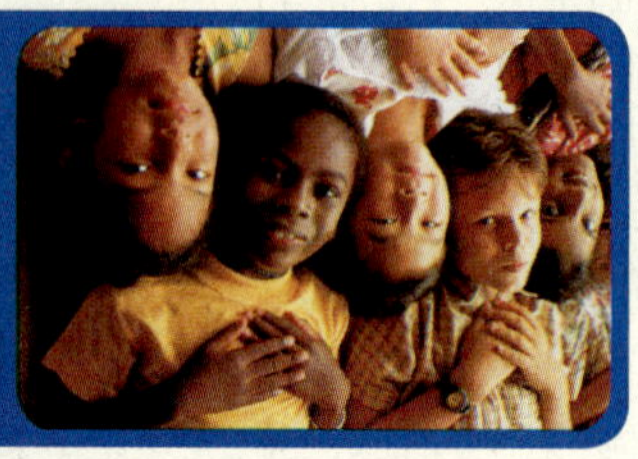

Suggestion Before going through the reading, have students scan the form for cognates and underline them.

Me adhiero a la MARCHA MUNDIAL POR LA PAZ Y LA NO VIOLENCIA porque:

1 Creo que las armas nucleares deben desaparecer en todo el mundo y que debemos reducir progresivamente las armas convencionales. 2 No creo que ningún ejército deba invadir otro territorio. 3 Me parece que el respeto de los derechos humanos y la firma de tratados de no agresión entre países son imprescindibles para la paz. 4 Dudo que las guerras sean el camino o den la solución para resolver conflictos. 5 Pienso que los gobiernos deben renunciar a la guerra como medio para resolverlos.

Y además porque rechazo toda forma de violencia.

Exponer una opinión

- Pienso que la paz mundial es posible.
- Pues yo no creo que sea fácil conseguirla.

16A.1 **creer/pensar/parecer que** + [*indicative*]
no creer que + [*subjunctive*]

Vocabulario

1
adherirse (e:ie) *to join*
el formulario *form*
la adhesión *support*
la paz *peace*
la no violencia *non-violence*
la movilización social *social demonstration*
la fuerza *strength, power*

3
los derechos humanos *human rights*
el ejército *army*

1 ¿Ha oído hablar de la Marcha Mundial por la Paz y la No Violencia? Lea la introducción de este formulario de adhesión y coméntelo con su compañero/a.

2 Elabore una definición de la palabra "adhesión" con su compañero/a y compártala con la clase. Possible answers: Unión. Apoyar una idea u opinión.

3 a. Fíjese en estas palabras y expresiones. ¿Qué cree que significan? Escriba una definición o explicación en español. ¿Qué relación tienen con la paz?

PAZ

derechos humanos · invasiones territoriales · violencia · armas nucleares · ejércitos · compromiso · guerras

b. ¿Qué opiniones se exponen en la adhesión a la Marcha Mundial sobre los temas de la actividad anterior? ¿Qué opina usted? ¿Y su compañero/a?

Modelo: *Yo también pienso que... / No creo que...*

Mostrar escepticismo

Dudo que haya paz sin la unión y el apoyo de todas las naciones.

16A.2 **dudar que** + [*subjunctive*]

Vocabulario *cont.*

el arma nuclear *nuclear weapon*
la firma *signing; signature*
el tratado *treaty*
dudar *to doubt*
el gobierno *government*
renunciar (a) *to give up, to relinquish*
rechazar *to reject*
la marcha, reducir, convencional, invadir, el territorio, la agresión

4

el/la pacifista, el/la dictador(a)

5

firmar *to sign*
hacer falta *to be necessary*
convencer (z) *to convince*
de un día para el otro *overnight*

6

sobre la base de *based upon*
la unidad popular *unity of the people*
el consenso

7

el/la escultor(a) *sculptor*
la justicia social *social justice*

8

el desastre, el pretexto

Premios Nobel

¿Qué tienen en común un arquitecto argentino, un político costarricense y una líder indígena guatemalteca? El Premio Nobel de la Paz. Adolfo Pérez Esquivel lo recibió en 1980 por su defensa de los derechos humanos. Óscar Arias Sánchez lo obtuvo en 1987 por su participación en los procesos de paz en América Central. Por último, Rigoberta Menchú fue premiada en 1992 por dedicar su vida a la lucha por los derechos de los indígenas.

"De la paz se debe esperar todo, de la guerra, nada más que desastre." (Simón Bolívar)

"El pretexto para todas las guerras: conseguir la paz." (Jacinto Benavente)

"La violencia es el miedo a los ideales de los demás." (Mahatma Gandhi)

4 Fíjese en estos comentarios que muestran escepticismo sobre la Marcha Mundial. Encuentre en el formulario de adhesión otras frases que expresan escepticismo. No creo que..., Dudo que...

Dudo que los pacifistas consigan algo con la Marcha Mundial.

Yo dudo que logremos la paz mientras haya dictadores en el mundo.

5 a. Complete los diálogos con la forma correcta de los verbos. Luego compruebe sus respuestas con las de su compañero/a.

- ¡Hola! Te invito a firmar este formulario de adhesión a la Marcha Mundial por la Paz y la No Violencia.
- Seguro. ¿Dónde firmo? Pienso que (1) es (ser) una causa maravillosa.
- Desde luego. Nosotros creemos que todos (2) debemos (deber) unirnos para luchar por la paz.
- ¿Todos? Dudo que todos (3) quieran (querer) la paz.
- Pues pienso que (4) hace (hacer) falta convencerlos.
- Creo que (5) tienes (tener) razón.

- Buenos días, señora. La invito a firmar este formulario.
- ¿De qué se trata?
- Se trata de una marcha por la paz mundial. Pensamos que (6) es (ser) importante que todos juntos reclamemos a los gobiernos el fin de las guerras.
- Pues yo no creo que eso (7) sea (ser) posible de un día para el otro. Pienso que a veces las guerras (8) ayudan (ayudar). No me parece que la paz se (9) logre (lograr) sólo con buenos deseos. Perdone, pero dudo que la marcha (10) sirva (servir) de algo.

b. ¿Y usted qué opina de la marcha? ¿Está de acuerdo o en desacuerdo? Comente su opinión con su compañero/a.

6 Lea esta cita del argentino Adolfo Pérez Esquivel. ¿Qué duda, piensa y no cree Pérez Esquivel?

"La paz no nos la van a regalar, incluso podemos decir que la paz no es ausencia de conflicto. La paz se logra sobre la base de entender lo vital de la unidad popular, del consenso y del respeto a la diversidad."

Adolfo Pérez Esquivel was incarcerated for 14 months during Argentina's dirty war; while in detention, he was awarded the Pope John XXIII Peace Memorial. In 1999 he received the Pacem en Terris Peace and Freedom Award.

Adolfo Pérez Esquivel, Premio Nobel de la Paz

7 Comente con su compañero/a su opinión sobre el Premio Nobel de la Paz. ¿Cuál es su significado? ¿Le parece importante? ¿Por qué? La nota de la izquierda hace referencia a tres ganadores de ese premio. ¿Los conoce?

MI EXPERIENCIA

8 Exponga su opinión o manifieste escepticismo ante la guerra u otros conflictos a partir de las citas de la izquierda. Coméntelas con el grupo.

GUIÓN DE TRABAJO

¿Qué piensa/cree acerca de...?

OPINIÓN
(No) Creo que...
(No) Pienso que...
(No) Me parece que...

ESCEPTICISMO
Dudo que...

Jacinto Benavente was a Spanish dramatist who won the Nobel Prize for Literature in 1922.

Practice more at vhlcentral.com.

SAM: Actividades pp. 333–335

Debate social

1

Colombia estará a la cabeza del turismo latinoamericano
Se pondrá en marcha un ambicioso plan para estimular la llegada de visitantes a los tres principales destinos turísticos de Colombia: Cartagena, Santa Marta y la isla de San Andrés.

2

La iniciativa "Mil grullas por la Paz" se celebrará como en años anteriores en Rosario (Argentina)
Esta original iniciativa intentará sensibilizar por la paz a la población en general y a los niños en particular. En cuanto a la proyección internacional, este año Chile también participará en la convocatoria.

3

La Secretaría de Inclusión de El Salvador propondrá nuevas políticas sociales y culturales
Con respecto a los grupos más desfavorecidos: niños, jóvenes y mujeres, anunció que habrá medidas especiales.

4

Perú tendrá un crecimiento del 7% anual durante los próximos 15 años
Un aprovechamiento más racional de sus enormes recursos naturales será la clave.

Transmitir información

- "**Mañana saldrá** la Marcha por la Paz."
- Ayer uno de los organizadores **confirmó que** la Marcha por la Paz **saldría hoy**.

16A.3 Indirect discourse (Future-Conditional)

Vocabulario

9

- **estar a la cabeza** *to lead*
- **poner en marcha** *to set in motion*
- **la grulla** *crane*
- **sensibilizar** *to sensitize*
- **la convocatoria** *call (to action)*
- **la secretaría** *ministry, department*
- **la política** *policy*
- **desfavorecido/a** *underprivileged*
- **anunciar** *to announce*
- **la medida** *measure, step*
- **el crecimiento** *growth*
- **el aprovechamiento** *exploitation*
- **enorme** *huge*
- **la clave** *key*
- **el titular** *headline*
- **la sensibilización** *sensitization*

el debate, ambicioso/a, estimular, racional

9 Fíjese en las imágenes y lea los titulares. Relaciónelos con estas palabras clave.

2 sensibilización   4 recursos naturales   1 destinos turísticos   3 plan social

10 a. Escuche el programa de radio. ¿De qué país es? ¿Qué tipo de programa es?
Colombia; informativo sobre noticias de actualidad

b. Escuche de nuevo a la locutora de radio que habla de estas noticias de actualidad y emparéjelas con el titular de arriba al que se refiere.

- La Oficina de Prensa del Ministerio de Transporte de Colombia informó que se pondría en marcha... 1
- El ministro de Economía peruano declaró que su país tendría... 4
- La asociación argentina CHICOS confirmó que un año más el proyecto intentaría sensibilizar... y añadieron que Chile participaría... 2
- El presidente de El Salvador anunció que la Secretaría de Inclusión propondría... 3

10 Expansion Show short clips from recent online news broadcasts. Have students rephrase the items, using reported speech.

11 Imagine que usted trabaja como locutor(a) en un programa de radio y debe transmitir estos titulares. Use los sustantivos del recuadro **A** y los verbos del recuadro **B** como ayuda.

Modelo: *Los coordinadores confirmaron que la marcha comenzaría a las 10 h.*

"La marcha comenzará a las 10 de la mañana."
"Haremos una campaña electoral."
"Iniciaremos las negociaciones de paz."
"Aumentaremos los sueldos."
"Además, estaremos buscando voluntarios."
"Nuestra lucha continuará."

A	B
coordinadores	informar
director(a)	añadir
gobierno	declarar
ministros	confirmar
pacifista	anunciar
presidente/a	afirmar

11 Suggestion Remind students that all conditional forms carry a written accent.

Estrategia

Introducir un tema

En cuanto a la economía, el Ministerio anunció nuevas medidas.

Con respecto a las conversaciones de paz, hoy hubo grandes avances.

Vocabulario

(10)

la oficina de prensa *press office*
el ministerio *ministry, department*
informar *to inform*
declarar *to declare; to state*
el/la ministro/a, el/la presidente/a, confirmar

(11)

el/la locutor(a) *announcer*
añadir *to add*
afirmar *to assert*
la campaña electoral *electoral campaign*
el/la coordinador(a)

(12)

los líderes mundiales *world leaders*
en cuanto a *as for*
con respecto a *regarding*
la multinacional

(13)

la política *politics*

(14)

la desigualdad *inequality*
el analfabetismo *illiteracy*
el nivel *level*
el derecho *right*
caritativo/a *charitable*
eliminar

(15)

indiscutible *indisputable*

14a Possible answers: El coordinador declaró que eliminarían las desigualdades entre niños y niñas en la enseñanza. El coordinador confirmó que reducirían el analfabetismo de adultos en un 50%. El coordinador anunció que mejorarían la calidad de la educación en todos los niveles. El coordinador afirmó que lucharían para que todas las personas reciban preparación para la vida activa.

12 ¿Qué titulares le gustaría leer en la prensa? Complete con su compañero/a los siguientes titulares con noticias futuras.

12 Point out that **multinacional** takes a feminine article because it is the shorter version of **la compañía/empresa multinacional.**

- Los líderes mundiales anunciaron que...
- El/La presidente/a de la multinacional... dijo que...
- El/La jefe/a de prensa de la ONG... confirmó que...

13 Coméntele a su compañero/a sus planes en cuanto a estos temas. Después imagine que ha pasado un día y transmita a la clase la información que su compañero/a le dijo ayer.

familia | trabajo | aficiones | cambios | iniciativas

Modelo:
- *Continuaré con mi afición a la política.*
- *Iris me dijo ayer que continuaría con su afición a la política, y en cuanto al trabajo...*

14 a. Lea con su compañero/a los objetivos que menciona uno de los coordinadores de la Campaña Mundial por la Educación. Luego túrnense para transformar las oraciones al estilo indirecto.

"Lograremos la enseñanza primaria universal y gratuita."
"Eliminaremos las desigualdades entre niños y niñas en la enseñanza."
"Reduciremos el analfabetismo de adultos en un 50%."
"Mejoraremos la calidad de la educación en todos los niveles."
"Lucharemos para que todas las personas reciban preparación para la vida activa."

Modelo: *El coordinador afirmó que lograrían la enseñanza primaria universal y gratuita.*

b. Lea la viñeta cómica de Mafalda. ¿Qué duda expresa su amigo Felipe sobre la educación?

© Joaquín Salvador Lavado (QUINO) Toda Mafalda — Ediciones de La Flor, 1993

Modelo: *Felipe duda que...*

14b Possible answer: Felipe duda que alguna persona "sienta compasión" por los niños y les quite el derecho a la educación, así que tendrá que seguir yendo a la escuela.

MI EXPERIENCIA

15 Busque en el periódico de hoy cinco noticias interesantes y coméntelas con sus compañeros.

15 **Suggestion** Encourage the class to react to what their classmates report, using impersonal expressions and the subjunctive.

GUIÓN DE TRABAJO

El/La ministro/a de...
El/La presidente/a de...
El/La cantante...
El/La escritor(a)...

→ informó / añadió / declaró / confirmó / anunció / afirmó → que...

Practice more at **vhlcentral.com.**

SAM: Actividades pp. 336-338

Ingrid Betancourt, una luchadora

Ingrid Betancourt, política colombiana

"Nuestro mundo debe cambiar y cada uno de nosotros debe romper la maldición de su propia indiferencia."

Ingrid Betancourt, política colombiana secuestrada durante más de seis años por las Fuerzas Armadas Revolucionarias de Colombia (FARC), recibió en 2008 el Premio Príncipe de Asturias de la Concordia.

En el discurso que pronunció en la ceremonia, afirmó que no se sentiría totalmente libre ni feliz mientras tenga compañeros presos en la selva.

Estos son algunos fragmentos de su discurso en la entrega del premio:

"Tengo la profunda convicción que cuando hablamos, estamos cambiando el mundo."

"Las guerrillas de Colombia deben oír desde aquí las voces de quienes reclamamos la libertad de todos los colombianos."

"Desde Asturias, hacemos un desgarrador llamado a nuestros pueblos hermanos en toda América Latina, para que impidan que el secuestro se generalice en nuestro continente. Pedimos que la droga que se produce en Colombia y en otras regiones no pueda transitar por los territorios de nuestras geografías, porque con la riqueza que genera se alimenta el terrorismo y se incrementa el secuestro. Pedimos que todos nuestros pueblos detengan el tráfico de armas porque esas mismas armas se utilizan en contra de nuestra población para quitar la vida y la libertad de nuestros seres queridos."

Explain that **FARC** is a Marxist-Leninist revolutionary guerrilla organization. It is the largest and oldest insurgent group in the Americas, and it funds its activities through kidnappings and the drug trade.

Pedir algo por una razón

Pedimos que los secuestrados **queden** libres **porque** la libertad **es** un derecho.

16A.4 **pedir que** + [*subjunctive*] **porque** + [*indicative*]

Vocabulario

16

- el/la luchador(a) *fighter*
- el/la político/a *politician*
- el/la secuestrado/a *kidnapping victim*
- las fuerzas armadas *armed forces*
- la concordia *harmony*
- el discurso *speech*
- libre *free*
- el/la preso/a *prisoner*
- la selva *jungle*
- la libertad *freedom*
- desgarrador(a) *heartrending*
- impedir (e:i) *to prevent*
- el secuestro *kidnapping*
- la droga *drug(s)*
- la riqueza *wealth*
- el tráfico de armas *arms trade*
- quitar *to take away*
- romper *to break*
- la maldición *curse*

16 a. ¿Conoce a la protagonista? Comente con su compañero/a lo que sabe de ella.

b. ¿Conoce el conflicto que existe en Colombia? ¿Qué cree que puede ayudar a resolverlo?

c. Lea la cita a pie de foto y la introducción al artículo. ¿Por qué cree que es una luchadora? ¿Por qué recibió el Premio Príncipe de Asturias de la Concordia? Possible answers: Por haber sobrevivido su secuestro. Le dieron el premio por luchar contra la corrupción política (la violencia terrorista) y en favor de una solución pacífica del conflicto con las FARC.

17 a. En la ceremonia de entrega del Premio Príncipe de Asturias, Ingrid Betancourt dio un discurso. ¿Sobre qué habló? Lea los fragmentos del discurso y marque los temas.

- libertad ✓
- terrorismo ✓
- educación ☐
- derechos humanos ✓
- cambio climático ☐
- turismo en Colombia ☐
- inmigración ☐
- guerra ✓
- FARC ✓
- droga ✓

b. ¿Qué pidió Ingrid Betancourt sobre la droga y por qué? Imagine otras posibles peticiones de Betancourt en el resto de su discurso.
Possible answer: Pidió que la droga que se produce en Colombia y en otras regiones no pueda transitar por los territorios de América Latina.

18 Imagine que usted es embajador(a) de la paz. ¿Qué pide? ¿Por qué? Comparta sus ideas con su compañero/a.

Modelo: *Pido que... porque...*

18 Expansion Have pairs pick one or two of their petitions and draft proposed solutions to the problem.

Vocabulario *cont.*

la convicción, la guerrilla, el terrorismo, la indiferencia

(18)

el/la embajador(a) de la paz *ambassador for peace*

(19)

el/la diplomático/a *diplomat*
afiliarse *to join*
el caciquismo *despotism*
el partido político *political party*
liberar *to set free*
las letras *literature*
denunciar, la corrupción, el/la candidato/a

(20)

pacífico/a *peaceful*
la defensa *defense*

(21)

la casualidad *coincidence*

(23)

el pueblo indígena *native people*
la lengua nativa *native language*
el/la mestizo/a *person of mixed race*
el/la gitano/a *gypsy*

Desde 1981, la Fundación Príncipe de Asturias organiza cada año una ceremonia en Oviedo, España, para entregar los Premios Príncipe de Asturias. Es un reconocimiento a las personas, instituciones o grupos de trabajo que se hayan destacado en las siguientes categorías: Artes, Comunicación y Humanidades, Letras, Deportes, Ciencias Sociales, Investigación Científica y Técnica, Cooperación Internacional y Concordia.

20 Suggestion Have students make their descriptions anonymous. Ask students to read them aloud for the class to identify the famous person.

You may want to point out that **caciquismo** is derived from the word **cacique**, which is an Arawak word meaning *chief*. Since becoming incorporated into Spanish, it has acquired other meanings, such as *boss* or *tyrant*.

19 a. Lea algunos datos adicionales de la biografía de Ingrid Betancourt.

1961	Nació el 25 de diciembre de 1961 en Bogotá. Hija del político Gabriel Betancourt, ministro de Educación, y de Yolanda Pulecio, política colombiana.
1983	Estudió Comercio Exterior y Relaciones Internacionales en el Instituto de Estudios Políticos de París. Ese mismo año se casó con el diplomático Fabrice Delloye (con quien tuvo dos hijos) y obtuvo la doble nacionalidad francesa y colombiana.
1989	Regresó a Colombia. Se afilió al Partido Liberal para denunciar la corrupción y el caciquismo.
1994	Hizo su primera campaña política.
1997	Se casó con el publicista Juan Carlos Lecompte.
1998	Fundó el Partido Verde Oxígeno, ecologista y progresista, y se presentó como candidata en las elecciones legislativas de Colombia.
1998–2001	Fue miembro del Senado de Colombia.
2001	Renunció a su cargo como senadora y se presentó como candidata a la presidencia.
2002	Durante la campaña electoral, ella y su asesora Clara Rojas visitaron una zona de actividad guerrillera, y las FARC las secuestraron.
2008	El ejército colombiano liberó a Ingrid Betancourt el 2 de julio.
2008	Recibió el Premio Príncipe de Asturias de la Concordia.

b. Destaque tres fechas significativas para usted de la biografía y explique a su compañero/a por qué las eligió.

c. ¿Cree que Ingrid Betancourt podría ser "embajadora de la paz"? ¿Por qué?

Modelo: *A mí me parece...*

20 Escriba algunos datos significativos de la biografía de una persona conocida por sus acciones pacifistas o por la defensa de los derechos humanos. Después comparta su biografía con la clase y exponga su opinión.

21 Escuche lo que narra Diana sobre los acentos y las expresiones en Colombia. Después, indique si las oraciones son verdaderas (V) o falsas (F).

	V	F
1. Diana dice que en su país las diferencias en los acentos y en las expresiones son muy marcadas.	✓	
2. Natalia, la prima de Diana, vive en Manizales.		✓
3. En Colombia, encontrar a alguien "de chepa" es encontrarlo de casualidad.	✓	
4. A Natalia la invitaron a comer postre.		✓
5. "Estar como un postre" significa ponerse lindo/a.	✓	
6. Diana piensa que Colombia es un país sin diversidad.		✓

Practice more at **vhlcentral.com.**

SAM: Actividades pp. 339–342

22 a. ¿Qué sabe de la diversidad cultural colombiana? Lea el texto. ¿Cómo interpreta el título "Colombia, Colombias"? ¿Qué información ofrecen estas imágenes? ¿Qué culturas conviven en Colombia?

Colombia, COLOMBIAS

El Ministerio de Cultura de Colombia organiza todos los años muchos eventos este día, el 21 de mayo: Día de la Diversidad Cultural y Día Nacional de la Afrocolombianidad.

En Colombia conviven:

- 87 pueblos indígenas
- 65 lenguas nativas (wayuunaiki, lenguas makú, guahibo, etc.)
- más de 10 millones de afrocolombianos
- 30 millones de mestizos
- 25000 raizales
- 12000 gitanos
- gran número de inmigrantes de diferentes lugares (sirios, libaneses, japoneses, chinos y europeos, entre otros)

Colombia

21 de mayo Día Mundial de la Diversidad Cultural y Día Nacional de la Afrocolombianidad

b. ¿Qué diversidad cultural hay en su región? Comparta sus conocimientos con la clase.

22b Suggestion Also ask students to describe any cultural manifestations or celebrations.

TAREA FINAL

Manifiesto por...

Elijan el tema de su manifiesto (la paz, la educación, los derechos humanos...).

Redacten entre todos la introducción (motivo, quién firma el manifiesto, etc.).

En parejas, redacten dos o tres oraciones con sus opiniones.

Léanlas y hagan una lista común con toda la clase. Añadan sus peticiones en cuanto al tema de su manifiesto.

Elaboren una presentación con todas las frases. Añadan fotos o dibujos, y la firma de todos.

YO PUEDO...

- Puedo exponer una opinión.

  Opine con una oración afirmativa y otra negativa sobre un tema de actualidad.

  - *Creo que... No creo que...*

- Puedo mostrar escepticismo.

  Lea esta afirmación y exprese escepticismo.
  "El hombre podrá vivir en la Luna."

- Puedo transmitir información.

  Transmita estas afirmaciones que escuchó ayer.

  Meteorólogo: "El fin de semana hará muy buen tiempo."

  Profesor: "La próxima semana habrá un examen."

- Puedo pedir algo por una razón.

  Exprese una petición a la clase y diga por qué.

GRAMÁTICA FUNCIONAL

Suggestion You may also wish to present the subjunctive of **saber: sepa, sepas, sepa, sepamos, sepáis, sepan.**

16A.1 Express an opinion

creer/pensar/parecer que + [*indicative*];
no creer que + [*subjunctive*] 5.21.4
Irregular subjunctive forms 5.20.2

- To express an opinion, use **creer/pensar/parecer que** + [*indicative*]. Use an indirect object pronoun with **parecer que**.

> **Me parece que** el desarme nuclear **es** importante para lograr la paz mundial.
> *I think that nuclear disarmament **is** important in order to achieve world peace.*

- Use the **subjunctive** with the constructions **no creer/no pensar/no parecer que**. Statements with these constructions convey uncertainty or doubt.

> **No creo que** el desarme nuclear **sea** posible.
> ***I don't think that** nuclear disarmament **is** possible.*

- (No) **creer/pensar/parecer** + [*infinitive*] can be used if the verb that follows has the same subject.

> **No creo que pueda ir** a la fiesta mañana. Estoy enfermo.
> **No creo poder ir** a la fiesta mañana. Estoy enfermo.
> ***I don't think I can go** to the party tomorrow. I'm sick.*

- You have learned the formation of the regular present subjunctive forms, as well as the present subjunctive of stem-changing verbs and verbs with irregular **yo** forms. Some verbs are irregular in the present subjunctive.

DAR	ESTAR	SER	IR
dé	esté	sea	vaya
des	estés	seas	vayas
dé	esté	sea	vaya
demos	estemos	seamos	vayamos
deis	estéis	seáis	vayáis
den	estén	sean	vayan

> No creo que el profesor nos **dé** más tiempo para escribir el trabajo.
> *I don't think that the professor **will give** us more time to write the paper.*

16A.2 Show skepticism

dudar que + [*subjunctive*] 5.20, 5.21.4

- To show skepticism, use **dudar que** + [*subjunctive*].

> **Dudamos que** nos **den** una oportunidad.
> ***We doubt that** they **will give** us an oppoortunity.*

- The construction **dudar de que** + [*subjunctive*] is also correct.

> **Dudo de que** Mario **quiera** venir.
> ***I doubt (that)** Mario **wants** to come.*

- If both **dudar** and the verb that follows have the same subject, you can use the construction **dudar** + [*infinitive*].

> **Dudo que pueda** ir. / **Dudo poder** ir.
> ***I doubt I can** go.*

¡Póngalo en práctica!

G1 Complete las conversaciones.

- Creo que te van a (1) ...dar... (dar) el premio.
- ¿De verdad? No creo que me lo (2) ...den... (dar); hay mucha gente cualificada.

- Creo que iremos a la marcha para la paz mañana. ¿Piensan (3) ...ir... (ir) ustedes?
- No, no creo que (4) ...vayamos... (ir); no solemos ir a las marchas.

- Llamé a Juan Cruz, pero no contestó. No me parece que (5) ...esté... (estar) en casa.
- Entonces creo que (6) ...voy... (ir) a llamar a César para ver si me puede ayudar.

- No creo que (7) ...vayamos... (nosotros, ir) a la fiesta mañana porque todavía estamos un poco resfriados.
- Creo que (8) ...deben... (ustedes, deber) descansar.

- ¿Crees (9) ...poder... (poder) terminar el proyecto escolar?
- Sí, pero no creo que Marta lo (10) ...termine... (terminar).

G2 Empareje el comienzo de la oración con el final apropiado.

c	1. No creo que nosotros	a. es importante eliminar la desigualdad social.
d	2. Rosa no cree	b. estén preparados para el debate.
e	3. A Leticia no le parece que	c. podamos ir al evento del candidato.
a	4. Creo que	d. poder ayudar con el discurso.
b	5. Cecilia no cree que sus compañeros	e. sea buena idea poner en marcha el plan.

G3 Complete las conversaciones.

- ¿Dudas que la paz (1) ...sea... (ser) posible?
- Sí, y Elena también duda que los gobiernos (2) ...den... (dar) la respuesta y (3) ...estén... (estar) comprometidos con la paz.
- ✦ Yo también dudo que lo (4) ...hagan... (hacer).

- Dudo que la nueva iniciativa (5) ...tenga... (tener) resultados positivos. Hay mucha violencia en esta ciudad.
- Sí, todos dudamos que (6) ...cambie... la situación.

Suggestion Divide the class into small groups. Bring in Spanish-language tabloids and distribute one to each group. Have them read the headlines and react to them, using **dudar que.**

Practice more at **vhlcentral.com.**

GRAMÁTICA FUNCIONAL

16A.3 Convey information

Indirect discourse: future-conditional 12.10
Simple future and conditional: irregular forms 5.16.2b, 5.17.2

- Use indirect discourse (**el estilo indirecto**) to report what another person has said. When the direct speech is given in the **futuro simple**, use the **condicional** in indirect speech.

"**Estudiaremos** los resultados."
Ayer nos informaron que **estudiarían** los resultados.

*"**We will study** the results."*
*Yesterday they informed us that **they would study** the results.*

- You have seen the use of indirect discourse in 11A.2 and 14B.3, and you have learned the use of the reporting verbs **decir, comentar, explicar,** and **preguntar**. Other reporting verbs include **informar, declarar, añadir, confirmar, anunciar,** and **afirmar**.

- Several verbs have irregular forms in the **futuro simple** and the **condicional**. You learned the regular forms in 12B.1 and 13A.3, and the irregular forms of the **futuro simple** in 15A.1. The same verbs that have irregular forms in the **futuro simple** are also irregular in the **condicional**. The endings of irregular and regular verbs in the **condicional** are the same.

	Direct discourse	→		Indirect discourse
Infinitive	**Simple future**	**Reporting verb**		**Conditional**
haber	**habr**á	informó	+ que	**habr**ía
hacer	**har**á	declaró		**har**ía
poder	**podr**á	añadió		**podr**ía
salir	**saldr**á	confirmó		**saldr**ía
tener	**tendr**á	anunció		**tendr**ía
poner	**pondr**á	afirmó		**pondr**ía

"Mañana **saldremos** para Montevideo."
Gabriel me confirmó que **saldrían** para Montevideo al día siguiente.

*"**We will leave** for Montevideo tomorrow."*
*Gabriel confirmed to me that **they would leave** for Montevideo the following day.*

16A.4 Request something for a reason

pedir que + [*subjunctive*], **porque** + [*indicative*] 5.20, 5.21.1, 12.6

- Use the subjunctive with **pedir** (*to ask [for]*) + **que** to make a request. To give a reason, use **porque** + [*indicative*].

Pedimos que los gobiernos **renuncien** a la violencia **porque** no **es** la solución de ningún conflicto.
*We ask that governments **renounce** violence **because it is** not the solution to any conflict.*

Te **pido que escuches** lo que tengo que decir **porque es** importante estar bien informado.
*I **ask you to listen** to what I have to say **because it is** important to be well informed.*

Suggestion Ask students to anonymously write one thing that they will do in their free time before the next class. Collect the papers and have students guess who wrote them, using reported speech. Ex: **Jugaré en el torneo de tenis. (Alicia afirmó que jugaría en el torneo.)**

¡Póngalo en práctica!

G4 Escriba la forma correcta del verbo en el condicional.

1. Lourdes, hacer	haría
2. Néstor y yo, salir	saldríamos
3. ustedes, poner	pondrían
4. vosotros, tener	tendríais
5. tú, poder	podrías
6. una razón, haber	habría

G5 Transforme estas declaraciones y preguntas al estilo indirecto.

1. "Este año no tendré vacaciones hasta septiembre."
   Mi padre nos confirmó que este año no tendría vacaciones hasta septiembre
2. "Pondremos en marcha un plan contra la crisis."
   El ministro de Economía afirmó que pondrían en marcha un plan contra la crisis
3. "Mañana haré una fiesta."
   Mi compañero de trabajo me dijo que hoy haría una fiesta
4. "Podremos entregar la nueva propuesta antes del viernes."
   El gerente declaró que podrían entregar la nueva propuesta antes del viernes
5. "La universidad extenderá la convocatoria hasta el próximo viernes."
   La profesora anunció que la universidad extendería la convocatoria hasta el próximo viernes
6. "Habrá otro debate la semana que viene."
   El locutor añadió que habría otro debate la semana que viene

G5 Expansion Have students explain what others ask of them and why by completing cloze sentences. Ex: **Mis padres piden .... porque .... Los profesores piden .... porque ....**

G6 Complete las oraciones.

Pedimos que nos (1) den (ellos, dar) una explicación porque no lo (2) entendemos (nosotros, entender). Os pido que, por favor, (3) vayáis (vosotros, ir) a la Marcha Mundial, (4) porque es importante el compromiso de todos.

El profesor nos pide que (5) preparemos (nosotros, preparar) unas preguntas para hacerle al candidato que viene a la clase mañana porque (6) quiere (él, querer) que todos participemos.

Clara me pide que le (7) ayude (yo, ayudar) con los titulares desde la oficina de prensa porque (8) está (ella, estar) muy ocupada hoy.

Practice more at **vhlcentral.com.**

VOCABULARIO

Compromiso de todos

la adhesión	support
la agresión	aggression
el arma nuclear	nuclear weapon
el consenso	consensus
los derechos humanos	human rights
el desastre	disaster
el/la dictador(a)	dictator
el ejército	army
el/la escultor(a)	sculptor
la firma	signing; signature
el formulario	form
la fuerza	strength, power
el gobierno	government
la justicia social	social justice
la marcha	march
la movilización social	social demonstration
la no violencia	non-violence
el/la pacifista	pacifist
la paz	peace
el pretexto	pretext
el territorio	territory
el tratado	treaty
la unidad popular	unity of the people
adherirse (e:ie)	to join
convencer (z)	to convince
dudar	to doubt
firmar	to sign
hacer falta	to be necessary
invadir	to invade
rechazar	to reject
reducir (zc)	to reduce
renunciar (a)	to give up, to relinquish
convencional	conventional
de un día para el otro	overnight
sobre la base de	based upon

Variación léxica

aumentar el sueldo ⟷ subir el sueldo

la convicción ⟷ la certeza ⟷ el convencimiento

la petición ⟷ el pedido

el pretexto ⟷ la excusa ⟷ la justificación

regalar ⟷ obsequiar

Debate social

estar a la cabeza	to lead
poner en marcha	to set in motion
el analfabetismo	illiteracy
el aprovechamiento	exploitation
la campaña electoral	electoral campaign
la clave	key
la convocatoria	call (to action)
el/la coordinador(a)	coordinator
el crecimiento	growth
el debate	debate
el derecho	right
la desigualdad	inequality
la grulla	crane
los líderes mundiales	world leaders
el/la locutor(a)	announcer
la medida	measure, step
el ministerio	ministry, department
el/la ministro/a	minister, secretary
la multinacional	multinational (firm)
el nivel	level
la oficina de prensa	press office
la política	policy; politics
el/la presidente/a	president
la secretaría	ministry, department
la sensibilización	sensitization
el titular	headline
afirmar	to assert
anunciar	to announce
añadir	to add
confirmar	to confirm
declarar	to declare; to state
eliminar	to eliminate
estimular	to stimulate
informar	to inform
sensibilizar	to sensitize
ambicioso/a	ambitious
caritativo/a	charitable
desfavorecido/a	underprivileged
enorme	huge
indiscutible	indisputable
racional	rational
en cuanto a	as for
con respecto a	regarding

Ingrid Betancourt

el caciquismo	despotism
el/la candidato/a	candidate
la casualidad	coincidence
la concordia	harmony
la convicción	conviction
la corrupción	corruption
la defensa	defense
el/la diplomático/a	diplomat
el discurso	speech
la droga	drug(s)
el/la embajador(a) de la paz	ambassador for peace
las fuerzas armadas	armed forces
el/la gitano/a	gypsy
la guerrilla	guerrilla
la indiferencia	indifference
la lengua nativa	native language
las letras	literature
la libertad	freedom
el/la luchador(a)	fighter
la maldición	curse
el/la mestizo/a	person of mixed race
el partido político	political party
el/la político/a	politician
el/la preso/a	prisoner
el pueblo indígena	native people
la riqueza	wealth
el/la secuestrado/a	kidnapping victim
el secuestro	kidnapping
la selva	jungle
el terrorismo	terrorism
el tráfico de armas	arms trade
afiliarse	to join
denunciar	to denounce
impedir (e:i)	to prevent
liberar	to set free
quitar	to take away
romper	to break
desgarrador(a)	heartrending
libre	free
pacífico/a	peaceful

16B TÍPICOS TÓPICOS

Point out the expression **100 × 100** and explain that **×** stands for **por**.

Publicidad hasta en el café

No se lo tome solo.

¡TÓMESELO EN BUENA COMPAÑÍA!

CAFÉ ANTIGUA

Se lo garantizamos: nuestro café es 100 × 100 orgánico. Nuestros expertos se lo compran directamente a la población maya del departamento de Sacatepéquez, en Guatemala.

No se confunda, no ahorre en calidad. Exíjala. No lo olvide. Es mejor que consuma productos certificados. Invite a sus amigos: ¡saboréenlo y disfrútenlo juntos!

¡DESPERTAOS CON CHOCOLATE BUEN DÍA Y EMPEZAD EL DÍA CON ENERGÍA!

Consejos para papás y mamás:

Tomad Chocolate Buen Día a la taza o comedlo con pan. Dádselo a vuestros hijos en el desayuno o en la merienda y... ¡tomáoslo con ellos! ¡No os lo perdáis!

Animar a la acción y dar consejo

No lo olvide: Es mejor que consuma productos certificados.

Desayunad chocolate. Es pura energía.

16B.1 Affirmative and negative imperative
es mejor que + [*subjunctive*]

Vocabulario

(1)
el tópico *cliché*
la publicidad *advertising*
en buena compañía *in good company*
confundirse *to become confused*
ahorrar *to save*
exigir (j) *to demand*
certificado/a *certified*
saborear *to savor*
la merienda *(afternoon) snack*
perdérselo (e:ie) *to miss out*
el estado de ánimo *mood*

(3)
el eslogan

1 Observe la publicidad y complete el mapa de ideas asociado con el café.

gustos
solo o con leche
lugares
personas

estados de ánimo
expresiones, palabras...
otros

2 a. Lea los anuncios y seleccione las frases que animan a la acción. ¿Qué le sugieren? ¿Le parecen anuncios eficaces?

Modelo:
- *"No se lo tome solo." Me gusta porque...*
- *"Es mejor que..."*

b. Localice los verbos en imperativo de los anuncios, observe su formación y complete la tabla.

	Imperativo afirmativo (+)	Imperativo negativo (–)
tú	toma	no tomes
usted	tome	no tome
vosotros/as	tomad	no toméis
ustedes	tomen	no tomen

3 ¿Café, chocolate, té o alguna otra infusión? ¿Usted cómo se lo toma y cuándo? Pregunte a su compañero/a.

Modelo: *Yo prefiero café, y me lo tomo...*

4 Cree con su compañero/a otras oraciones y eslóganes que animen a tomar estos productos.

4 Suggestion Ask students whether fair trade or organic coffee, chocolate, and tea are important to them.

Vocabulario

5

sentirse (e:ie) como en casa *to feel at home*

el pico *peak, mountain*

6

devolver (o:ue) *to return*

la diferencia *difference (in price)*

probar (o:ue) *to taste*

la fragancia *fragrance, perfume*

el crucero *cruise*

8

provenir (e:ie) de *to come from*

un tercio *a third*

Referirse a personas u objetos conocidos

- Le he comprado este paquete de café. ¿Dónde **se lo** dejo?
- Déjemelo aquí mismo. Ahora **se lo** pago.

16B.2 **me, te, se... + lo/la...**

El café

Además de ser un producto de consumo básico, el café es casi un ritual en muchos países hispanos, donde la gente queda para tomarlo o invita a un café a sus amigos o familiares.
La mayor parte de la producción mundial de café proviene de Latinoamérica, especialmente de Brasil, Colombia, Guatemala, Honduras y México. Brasil es el principal productor mundial de café y el mayor exportador, con cerca de un tercio del mercado global.

9 Expansion Write a list of brand-name products on the board and have groups of students write new slogans for them. Have groups share the slogans with the class, who will vote for the most creative, humorous, effective, etc.

5 Escuche los anuncios publicitarios y relacione cada uno con el eslogan correspondiente.

- Siéntate a nuestra mesa y siéntete como en casa. 2
- No lo piense más: haga su diseño, díganoslo y se lo llevamos a casa. 3
- Venid a la naturaleza, vividla. 1

6 a. Fíjese en estas oraciones de los anuncios presentados en esta lección. ¿A qué se refieren? Nuestro café es 100 x 100 orgánico; chocolate Buen Día; el mueble; la calidad

Se lo garantizamos. | **Dádselo** en el desayuno. | **Se lo** llevamos a casa. | Exíja**la**.

b. Relacione las diferentes versiones (con y sin pronombres) de los mismos eslóganes.

1. Si encuentra algo más barato, le devolvemos la diferencia. ....c....
2. Hasta que no prueben estos yogures, no saben lo que se pierden. ....b....
3. Conozca la nueva fragancia. Le recomiendo la experiencia. ....d....
4. Subid vuestra mejor foto y ganad un crucero por el Caribe. ....a....

a. Subidla y ganáoslo.
b. Hasta que no los prueben, no lo saben.
c. Si lo encuentra más barato, se la devolvemos.
d. Conózcala. Se la recomiendo.

7 Observe la viñeta cómica. ¿Es habitual una situación así en su cultura?

7 Suggestion Have three volunteers read the comic aloud. Then ask the class what **lo** might stand for (**el café**).

8 a. Lea la nota. ¿Es también para usted un ritual tomar café?

b. Piense en un producto conocido por la clase y hable de él a sus compañeros sin decir el nombre. Sus compañeros adivinan qué es.

Modelo: *Antes de acostarme, la tomo tibia para dormir mejor. (la leche)*

MI EXPERIENCIA

9 Cree eslóganes para animar a sus compañeros a adoptar hábitos de vida saludables. Comparen los eslóganes de toda la clase y elijan los más eficaces. **9 Expansion** Have students write a script for a public service announcement, using their slogan.

GUIÓN DE TRABAJO

¿Qué hábitos saludables puedo incorporar en mi vida diaria?

Compra frutas y verduras. Cómelas todos los días.

Aprende a relajarte. No lo olvides: tu salud es lo primero.

Es mejor que camines en vez de tomar el autobús.

Practice more at **vhlcentral.com.**

SAM: Actividades pp. 343–345

Usos y costumbres

El Salvador
De los países de Centroamérica, El Salvador es el más pequeño y el más densamente poblado. La gente habla español y, en menor medida, el náhuatl. El plato típico es la pupusa, o tortilla de maíz que se come rellena con queso, frijoles fritos u otros ingredientes. La moneda es el dólar estadounidense, y se exportan café, azúcar y camarones. El 6 de agosto se celebra la tradicional "Bajada", que es la fiesta nacional más importante. Ese día la gente que vive al pie del volcán y en las poblaciones vecinas baja a la ciudad a venerar al patrono de la república y participar en la procesión por las calles de la capital.

La Bajada is the culminating event in a week-long celebration known as the **fiestas agostinas**, which celebrate the Divine Savior, the country's patron saint.

Atracciones turísticas
- Con sus 300 kilómetros de costa a lo largo del océano Pacífico y sus altísimas olas, El Salvador es uno de los destinos favoritos en Latinoamérica para los surfistas.
- En el pueblo de Ilobasco se elaboran artesanías con arcilla y cerámica pintada a mano. Igual de famosas son las "sorpresas", o pequeñas piezas de cerámica en cuyo interior se representan escenas de la vida diaria.
- En el Parque Nacional Montecristo hay orquídeas, monos araña, pumas, quetzales y tucanes. Se le conoce también como El Trifinio porque está ubicado donde se unen las fronteras de Guatemala, Honduras y El Salvador.

Hablar sobre usos y costumbres
- En El Salvador, el 6 de agosto **se celebra** una de las fiestas nacionales más importantes. Ese día **los salvadoreños veneran** al santo patrono de la república.
- ¿Y qué **hace la gente**?

16B.3 **se** + [*3rd-person verb*]
la gente...
3rd-person plural verb

Vocabulario
(10)
- densamente *densely*
- poblado/a *populated*
- relleno/a *stuffed, filled*
- el camarón *shrimp*
- el/la patrono/a *patron saint*
- la procesión *procession*
- turístico/a *tourist*
- la ola *wave*
- el/la surfista *surfer*
- la arcilla *clay*
- el/la mono/a araña *spider monkey*
- el tucán *toucan*
- cuyo/a *whose*
- el uso *custom*
- **venerar, la orquídea**

10 a. Lea el texto sobre El Salvador. ¿Dónde es posible encontrar este tipo de artículos? Sample answers: enciclopedia, revista de turismo, manual de geografía, etc.

b. ¿Por qué puede ser importante conocer los usos y costumbres de un país?

c. Relacione estos términos con su significado.

1. densamente ...c...
2. náhuatl ...e...
3. procesión ...a...
4. surfista ...d...
5. ubicado ...b...

a. marcha de personas que realizan un recorrido religioso
b. situado
c. con muchos habitantes en poco espacio
d. persona que practica el surf
e. lengua indígena

11 Busque en el texto esta clase de información sobre los usos y costumbres de El Salvador. gastronomía: pupusa; lenguas: español y náhuatl; fiestas: el 6 de agosto, la Bajada; turismo: surf, artesanía en arcilla, Parque Nacional Montecristo; comercio: se exportan café, azúcar y camarones

gastronomía | lenguas | fiestas | turismo | comercio

11 Suggestion Alternatively, write these categories on the board. Have students read the article twice. Then have them close their books and complete the activity.

Modelo: *En El Salvador, la gente come... Se habla...*

12 Elija dos lugares especiales para usted y anote sus usos y costumbres. Después comparta la información con sus compañeros sin decirles el nombre de los lugares. ¿Adivinaron de qué lugares se trataba?

LUGAR	Se habla...	Se come...	Se celebra...	Son...	La gente...

Hacer comparaciones

- ¿Es el país más interesante para visitar?
- No, es **igual de** interesante **que** todos. Todos los países son **igual de** interesantes. Para el verdadero viajero, la costa es **igual que** la sierra y el lago es **igual que** el volcán.

16B.4 igual (de + [*adjective*]) + que

Vocabulario

13

- comunicativo/a *communicative*
- el sedentarismo *sedentary lifestyle*
- ocultar *to hide*
- congelado/a *frozen*
- complejo/a *complex*
- **anticuado/a, el grupo étnico**

14

- extenso/a *vast*
- bello/a *beautiful*
- homogéneo/a *homogeneous*

16

- cosmopolita *cosmopolitan*

¡OJO!

Note that **igual** is invariable in the comparative structure **igual de** + [*adjective*] + **que**. As with all adverbs, it does not agree in number with the preceding noun. Examples: **Su población es igual de homogénea que la de Honduras** and **Sus platos típicos son igual de deliciosos que los de otros países de Centroamérica.**

Estrategia

Atenuar las generalizaciones

No todos los argentinos son de Buenos Aires.
Centroamérica tiene unas playas maravillosas, pero eso no es todo.

15 Suggestion Begin by brainstorming with the class a list of stereotypes that foreigners might say about people from this country.

13a Expansion Have students work in pairs and discuss their opinions on these comparisons.

13 a. Escriba oraciones para comparar la información dada.

Modelo: *mi ciudad / cara / la tuya*
Mi ciudad es igual de cara que la tuya.

1. los hombres / comunicativos / las mujeres
2. el sedentarismo / peligroso / otros malos hábitos
3. ocultar la verdad / mentir
4. la verdura congelada / nutritiva / la verdura fresca / ¿?
5. todas las lenguas del mundo / complejas

1. Los hombres son igual de comunicativos que las mujeres. 2. El sedentarismo es igual de peligroso que otros malos hábitos. 3. Ocultar la verdad es igual que mentir. 4. ¿La verdura congelada es igual de nutritiva que la verdura fresca? 5. Todas las lenguas del mundo son igual de complejas.

b. Con su compañero/a, elija uno de estos temas para continuar haciendo comparaciones.

Modelo: *Mi celular tiene menos funciones que los nuevos teléfonos inteligentes, pero es igual de útil si tengo que hacer una llamada.*

profesiones | nacionalidades o grupos étnicos | empresas o productos

14 Fíjese en los datos y compare estos dos países centroamericanos.

Costa Rica es más turístico y menos extenso que Nicaragua. Nicaragua está más poblada que Costa Rica. Son países igual de bellos y la gente es igual de hospitalaria.

Costa Rica	Nicaragua
interesante +	interesante +
turístico + +	turístico +
extenso –	extenso +
poblado –	poblado +
bello +	bello +
hospitalario +	hospitalario +

Modelo: *Costa Rica es igual de interesante que Nicaragua.*
Costa Rica es más turístico que...

15 Piense en su país y los tópicos más frecuentes en relación con él. ¿Encuentra alguna generalización que desee atenuar?

No todos los españoles duermen la siesta. | No todos los argentinos bailan el tango. | En México se comen tacos, pero eso no es todo.

MI EXPERIENCIA

15 Expansion Continue the activity by having students talk about generalizations that exist about people from their city or region.

16 ¿Cuál es más atractiva: la vida en una ciudad cosmopolita o la vida en un pueblo de montaña? Compare con el grupo y describa los usos y costumbres de cada estilo de vida.

GUIÓN DE TRABAJO

¿Crees que la vida en una ciudad es más atractiva que la vida en un pueblo?

No, es menos atractiva.
En la ciudad, la gente vive...
Se viaja... y se come...
La gente que vive en la ciudad está acostumbrada a...
¿Tú qué opinas?

Para mí es igual de atractiva. Simplemente se trata de dos cosas diferentes.

Practice more at **vhlcentral.com.**

SAM: Actividades pp. 346–348

Estela y Mario, publicistas

MIRADOR: ESCUELA DE MARKETING Y PUBLICIDAD

MIRADOR: Estela y Mario, antiguos alumnos de nuestra escuela, ¿en qué están trabajando ahora mismo?

MARIO: *Estamos a punto de lanzar una campaña para dar a conocer una nueva bebida.*

ESTELA: *Es un encargo muy amplio que incluye el diseño de la botella, la etiqueta y la campaña de promoción propiamente dicha que vendrá después.*

MIRADOR: ¿Pueden anticiparnos algún detalle?

MARIO: *Se trata de una bebida muy especial y muy guatemalteca. No podemos decir más. El trabajo es muy lindo y el desafío es enorme, parecido al que hice en Managua, de donde soy oriundo, cuando me contrataron junto a otros publicistas para encontrar la marca país, o sea, el logo representativo del país.*

ESTELA: *De hecho, los objetivos son iguales que los de marca país. Buscamos representar a Guatemala de cara al turismo y la exportación.*

MARIO: *Estamos trabajando con los colores y sus símbolos: el amarillo para la autenticidad, el morado para el misticismo, el verde claro para la diversidad, el rojo para la evolución y el verde oscuro para la cercanía.*

MIRADOR: ¿Qué le dirían a los alumnos de nuestra escuela que están a punto de terminar sus estudios este año?

ESTELA: *No tengan miedo y sean honestos. La valentía y la honestidad son las fuerzas más poderosas de la tierra.*

Point out the comparison **los objetivos son iguales que los de...** and explain that **iguales** is used as an adjective here, so therefore it is plural.

Estela Salvador y Mario Martínez, redactores, publicistas y productores gráficos

Hablar sobre un suceso próximo

Estamos a punto de terminar el proyecto.

16B.5 **estar a punto de** + [*infinitive*]

Vocabulario

17

lanzar una campaña *to launch a campaign*
dar a conocer *to make known*
el encargo *job, assignment*
el diseño *design*
la campaña de promoción *promotional campaign*
propiamente dicho/a *per se*
oriundo/a *native*
la marca *brand*
morado/a *purple*
claro/a *light*
oscuro/a *dark*
la cercanía *proximity*
la valentía *courage*

17 a. ¿Cómo se imagina usted la profesión de un publicista? ¿Qué habilidades se necesitan para esta profesión?

b. Lea la entrevista a estos publicistas. ¿En qué consiste su proyecto? ¿Qué le parece la idea? Anote ideas sobre estos temas.
Es una campaña publicitaria para dar a conocer una nueva bebida.

- elementos gráficos
- producto
- objetivos
- valores

18 a. ¿En qué fase del proyecto están Estela y Mario? Señale verdadero (V) o falso (F).

	V	F
1. Estela y Mario están a punto de lanzar su campaña.	✓	☐
2. Están a punto de terminar la campaña de promoción.	☐	✓
3. Están a punto de empezar el diseño.	☐	✓

b. Dé sus propios consejos y sugerencias a Estela y a Mario acerca de la campaña en la que están trabajando. Use algunas de estas expresiones.

- Es mejor que...
- Les recomiendo...
- Tienen que...
- Lo mejor es/sería...
- En su lugar, yo...
- ¿Por qué no...?

Modelo: *Es mejor que la publicidad apele a las emociones del consumidor.*

19 Piense en un proyecto que está a punto de comenzar o finalizar, o en las decisiones que está a punto de tomar. Coménteselo al grupo.

Vocabulario *cont.*

el/la publicista, anticipar, el logo, el símbolo, la autenticidad

18

apelar *to appeal*

20

feria *(trade) fair*
tener lugar *to be held*
el certamen *contest*
el cóctel *cocktail*
el jurado *panel of judges*
tener en cuenta *to take into account*
la gama *range*
compuesto/a por *made up of*
la guinda *wild cherry*
el durazno *peach*
el aroma *aroma, scent*
creciente *growing*
así como *as well as*

22

geográfico/a

23

el dinamismo

¡OJO!

To be made up of translates as **estar compuesto/a por** or **componerse de**. Note the preposition used in each case, since they are not interchangeable. Examples: **La mayor parte del cuerpo humano está compuesta por agua** or **La mayor parte del cuerpo humano se compone de agua.**

OPINIÓN

¿La publicidad nos aclara o nos confunde?

¿Cuál cree que sería el mejor símbolo para representar a su país?

Opinión Have the class discuss advertising and whether all advertising involves some measure of deceit.

20a **Suggestion** Read aloud the first sentence of the article and explain that Roman numerals are often used to express ordinal numbers (XI = **undécimo/a**).

20 a. ¿Qué productos asocia con estos países? Luego lea el texto e identifique el producto y el país del que trata. ¿Coincide con las ideas que tenía? ¿Conocía este producto? bebida Xelateca (Guatemala)

- Alemania
- Italia
- Guatemala
- China
- España
- Cuba
- México
- Colombia

En el marco de° la XI Feria Alimentaria de Guatemala, tuvo lugar la final del certamen para elegir la bebida nacional. El premio fue para "Xelateca", un cóctel destinado a representar al país dentro y fuera de sus fronteras.

El jurado tuvo en cuenta para su elección el costo de elaboración, sabor e ingredientes representativos de Guatemala, y los sorprendió el uso creativo de las frutas nativas y la amplia gama de sabores.

La bebida ganadora está compuesta por agua de guinda, jarabe de azúcar, jugo de limón y durazno. Su sabor evoca aromas de selvas, lagos y volcanes. Todo esto y mucho más en una botella.

María Urzua, ganadora del concurso junto a su bebida: "Xelateca"

El proyecto surge de la iniciativa de un creciente grupo de países de la región centroamericana, firmemente decididos a proyectar su imagen en el extranjero a través de símbolos e imágenes fácilmente reconocibles e identificables.

Queda ahora por delante un largo camino para dar a conocer al mercado estos nuevos productos, así como el de hacerse un hueco° en el imaginario colectivo°, al lado de la margarita, el mate, el pisco... ¡Salud!

En el marco de *Within the framework of* **hacerse un hueco** *to make a place for itself* **el imaginario colectivo** *collective imagination*

b. Subraye los ingredientes de esta bebida.¿Le parece una bebida apetitosa? ¿Qué ingredientes son típicos de la ciudad o región?
agua de guinda, jarabe de azúcar, jugo de limón y durazno, entre otros ingredientes

21 Escriba tres eslóganes publicitarios para dar a conocer la bebida "Xelateca" y promocionar Guatemala. Luego compare con el grupo y elijan el mejor eslogan.

20a **Suggestion** After students read the last sentence, ask them if they are familiar with the other drinks mentioned and in what country or countries they are popular (**la margarita - México; el mate - Argentina, Uruguay, Paraguay; el pisco - Perú, Chile**).

22 a. Lea el texto. ¿Cuál es el origen de los nombres de los países que se mencionan? Ecuador: posición geográfica; Bolivia: Simón Bolívar; Colombia: Cristóbal Colón; Guatemala: náhuatl *quauhtlemallan* (bosque, lugar de muchos árboles); Chile: aimara *tili* (fin del mundo)

¿De dónde provienen los nombres de los países latinoamericanos? A veces, el origen no es difícil de adivinar, como ocurre con Ecuador, cuyo nombre revela su posición geográfica. En otros casos, el nombre es una derivación de un apellido. Por ejemplo, Bolivia debe su denominación a Simón Bolívar, el libertador del país, mientras que Colombia lleva ese nombre en honor a quien descubrió América, Cristóbal Colón (*Colombo* en italiano). El origen de otros países es más difícil de deducir a simple vista. Guatemala proviene del náhuatl *quauhtlemallan*, que significa "bosque, lugar de muchos árboles". En el caso de Chile existen diferentes teorías; una de ellas es que el nombre viene del aimara *tili*, que significa "fin del mundo".

b. Investigue el origen del nombre de otro país latinoamericano. Explíquelo.

Practice more at **vhlcentral.com.**

SAM: Actividades pp. 349–354

23 a. Lea el texto y estos eslóganes publicitarios de varios países latinoamericanos. ¿Qué elementos destaca cada país? Relacione estos conceptos con los eslóganes y coméntelo con el grupo.

Sample answers: Cuba: cultura; Honduras: naturaleza; Guatemala: historia

> Igual que en el mundo de los negocios, los países compiten entre sí como productos y crean también su propio eslogan, que los caracteriza y diferencia para potenciar su imagen y atraer el turismo y las inversiones.

naturaleza • cultura • historia • comida • fiestas

CUBA
Explore nuestra riqueza cultural

COLOMBIA:
el riesgo es que te quieras quedar.

Honduras:
Un país pequeño, tres grandes mundos
Naturaleza tropical • Renacimiento Maya Creación Caribeña

Nicaragua...
única... ¡original!

El Salvador
¡Impresionante!

Costa Rica
Sin ingredientes artificiales

Playas *hermosas.*
Fiestas *impresionantes.*
Frutas *exóticas.*
Así es **PANAMÁ.**

República Dominicana
Lo tiene todo

Bienvenido a
Guatemala,
corazón del mundo maya.

23b Expansion Ask students to work in groups and create one new logo or symbol for their country and one for their region.

b. Los países también crean su propio logo, la marca país, como esta de Argentina. Busque marcas o símbolos que identifican a otros países o sus distintas regiones y cuente al grupo qué conceptos transmiten y por qué son populares.

Argentina

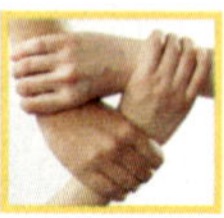

TAREA FINAL

Una campaña publicitaria

- Seleccionen un país o una región y un producto que lo/la caracterice.
- Piensen en los valores más positivos de ese país y producto, y compárenlos para seleccionar el más adecuado.
- Diseñen un buen eslogan y seleccionen una o más imágenes representativas.
- Elijan la mejor campaña para exponerla en el tablero de anuncios del departamento de español.

YO PUEDO...

- Puedo animar a la acción.
  Escriba tres eslóganes para animar a hacer más deporte.
- Puedo referirme a personas u objetos conocidos.
  El CD ...te lo... he dejado al lado de la computadora. No es necesario que ...me... lo devuelvas; es para ti, ...te lo... regalo. No ...me... des las gracias.
- Puedo hablar sobre usos y costumbres.
  Describa algún grupo profesional muy estereotipado para que sus compañeros puedan identificarlo.
- Puedo hacer comparaciones.
  Compare dos productos que ha visto en esta lección.
- Puedo expresar la proximidad de un suceso.
  Diga dos cosas que está a punto de hacer.

GRAMÁTICA FUNCIONAL

Suggestion Give students a situation (Ex: aboard an airplane, in computer class) and have pairs write a series of commands that one would hear in that context.

16B.1 Encourage and give advice

Affirmative and negative commands 5.18, 5.19
es mejor que + [*subjunctive*] 5.8.3, 5.21.5

- Use the imperative (**el imperativo**) to give instructions and advice. Regular affirmative **tú** commands have the same form as the **usted/él/ella** form of the present indicative. Affirmative **usted** commands coincide with the present form of the subjunctive.

	TOMAR
(tú)	tom**a**
(usted)	tom**e**

G2 Suggestion Go over items 5 and 6 and emphasize that the **vosotros/as** commands do not have any stem change.

- The affirmative **vosotros/as** command is formed by dropping the **-r** from the infinitive and adding a **-d**. Affirmative **ustedes** commands coincide with the present form of the subjunctive.

	TOMAR	BEBER	CONSUMIR
(vosotros/as)	toma**d**	bebe**d**	consumi**d**
(ustedes)	tom**en**	beb**an**	consum**an**

- With affirmative commands, attach the reflexive pronoun to the end of the verb. When the command has two or more syllables, add a written accent to maintain the original stress.
- In affirmative **vosotros/as** commands, the **-d** is dropped when the reflexive pronoun **os** is added to the end of the verb.

Levantaos.	Callaos.
Get up.	*Be quiet.*

- All other pronouns are added directly to the end of affirmative commands. Add a written accent if necessary to maintain the original pronunciation of the command.

Leedlo.	Míreme.
Read it.	*Look at me.*

- All forms of the negative imperative coincide with the conjugation of the present subjunctive.

	TOMAR	BEBER	CONSUMIR
(tú)	no tom**es**	no beb**as**	no consum**as**
(usted)	no tom**e**	no beb**a**	no consum**a**
(vosotros/as)	no tom**éis**	no beb**áis**	no consum**áis**
(ustedes)	no tom**en**	no beb**an**	no consum**an**

- Place object and reflexive pronouns in front of the verb with negative commands.

No **se sienten** allí, por favor.	No **le prestes** ese libro.
Do not sit there, please.	*Don't lend him that book.*

- Always use the subjunctive with the construction **es mejor que**.

Es **mejor que leas** las instrucciones.
*It is **better that you read** the instructions.*

G4 Expansion Have students repeat the activity in pairs. Have them take turns converting the commands into **usted** or **ustedes** commands.

¡Póngalo en práctica!

G1 Complete la tabla con la forma correcta del imperativo.

	afirmativo	negativo
1. hablar, tú	habla	no hables
2. poner, usted	ponga	no ponga
3. escribir, vosotros	escribid	no escribáis
4. creer, ustedes	crean	no crean
5. estudiar, tú	estudia	no estudies
6. bailar, ustedes	bailen	no bailen

G2 Complete las oraciones.

No (1) compre (usted, comprar) el café allí. Lo venden muy caro. Es mejor que lo (2) compre (comprar) en otro sitio.

No te lo (3) pienses (tú, pensar) dos veces. Decide tú y no se lo (4) digas (tú, decir) a nadie.

(5) Despertaos (Vosotros, despertarse) con alegría y (6) comenzad (vosotros, comenzar) bien el día.

(7) Abran (Ustedes, abrir) los libros y (8) lean (ustedes, leer) la primera página, por favor.

G3 Reescriba las oraciones usando el imperativo con un pronombre.

Modelo: Quiero que termines la tarea.
Termínala.

1. Quiero que preparen el almuerzo. Prepárenlo.
2. Es necesario que estudiéis las lecciones. Estudiadlas.
3. No quiero que comas los postres. No los comas.
4. Te pido que te despiertes. Despiértate.
5. Es mejor que usted lea el capítulo. Léalo.
6. No quiero que miréis las fotografías. No las miréis.

G4 Escriba lo contrario de estas oraciones.

Modelo: Dale su diccionario.
No le des su diccionario.

1. Regálale un libro. No le regales un libro.
2. Dime la verdad. No me digas la verdad.
3. Sal de aquí. No salgas de aquí.
4. No le hables. Háblale.
5. Dame ese libro. No me des ese libro.
6. No le prestes tu carro. Préstale tu carro.
7. No le tomes una foto. Tómale una foto.
8. Véndeselo. No se lo vendas.

Practice more at vhlcentral.com.

16B

GRAMÁTICA FUNCIONAL

Suggestion As an auditory activity, read aloud sentences to the class and have them write down the appropriate command form, using pronouns when possible. Ex: **Juanita, debes llevarle las bebidas al señor Cruz. (Juanita, llévaselas.)**

16B.2 Refer to known people or objects

Double pronouns 5.18.6, 5.19.2, 6.3

- When using direct object pronouns with either indirect object pronouns or reflexive pronouns, always place the indirect object pronoun or reflexive pronoun first. Place both pronouns before the verb.

  ¿Te gusta el libro? **Te lo** compro.
  Do you like the book? I will buy ***it for you.***

- In infinitive constructions and progressive tenses, the pronouns can be placed before the conjugated verb or attached to the end of the infinitive or present participle.

  Te lo quiero comprar. / Quiero comprár**telo**.
  I want to buy ***it for you.***

  Me las está preparando. / Está preparándo**melas**.
  He's making ***them for me.***

- When third-person indirect object pronouns (**le, les**) are combined with third-person direct object pronouns (**lo, la, los, las**), the indirect object pronoun is changed: **le/les → se.**

  A mi hermana le encanta el flan. **Se** lo voy a preparar mañana.
  My sister loves flan. I am going to make it ***for her*** *tomorrow.*

Mando	**la carta**	**a mi amiga.**	**→**	**Se la mando.**
	↓	↓		
	la	le	le + la →	se la

Order of pronouns:
1st: **me, te, le/se, nos, os, les/se** (indirect object and reflexive)
2nd: **lo, la, los, las** (direct object)

- In affirmative commands, the pronouns are attached to the end of the verb, as you have seen in **16B.1**. The same order of pronouns is maintained with commands, and **le/les** changes to **se** when used with a direct object pronoun.

  Mándaselo. / *Send it to him/her/them.*
  Regáleselos. / *Give them to him/her/them.*

- Add a written accent in order to maintain the original pronunciation of the command.

- With the exception of the reflexive pronoun **os**, all pronouns can be directly added to affirmative **vosotros/as** commands. Remember that the **vosotros/as** command loses the final **-d** when used with the reflexive pronoun **os**, as you have seen in **16B.1**.

  Mandádmelos. / *Send them to me.*
  Ponéoslas. / *Put them on.*

- As you have seen in **16B.1**, pronouns must be placed in front of negative commands. The same order of pronouns is maintained, and **le/les** is changed to **se** if used with direct object pronouns.

  No me los mandes. / *Don't send them to me.*
  No se lo digan. / *Don't tell (it to) him/her/them.*

¡Póngalo en práctica!

G5 Complete las conversaciones.

Me gustaría comprar este libro. ¿(1) Me (2) lo puede cobrar ya? Es que tengo mucha prisa.

Aquí tiene, ¿quiere que (3) se (4) lo envuelva?

Sí, por favor, (5) se (6) lo voy a regalar a mi hermano.

• • • • •

A mi madre le encantaría esta cámara.

¡Cómprasela!

Sí, tienes razón, (7) se (8) la voy a comprar.

• • • • •

Necesito enviar estos paquetes a mis primos antes de sus cumpleaños.

¿Cómo (9) se (10) los quiere enviar?

Por correo prioritario, por favor, así llegan más rápido.

G6 Transforme los mandatos afirmativos en mandatos negativos y viceversa.

Modelo: No se lo des.
Dáselo.

1. Coméoslos. No os los comáis.
2. No se lo olvide. Olvídeselo.
3. No se los mandes. Mándaselos.
4. Dádnoslos. No nos los deis.
5. Regálesela. No se la regale.
6. Prepárenselo. No se lo preparen.
7. No me lo digan. Díganmelo.
8. Recuérdamelo. No me lo recuerdes.

G6 Suggestion To simplify, first have students read through the verbs and identify whether they are **vosostros/as, usted,** or **ustedes** commands.

Practice more at **vhlcentral.com.**

GRAMÁTICA FUNCIONAL

Note that for simplicity, the impersonal and passive uses of **se** are presented together in this lesson.

16B.3 Talk about habits and customs

se + [*3rd-person verb form*]; **la gente...**; 3rd-person plural verb 3.4, 6.7

- Use the construction **se** + [*third-person verb*] to make impersonal statements.

  Se vive bien ahí.
  One lives well there. / People live well there.

- When the object of the verb is a person, use the preposition **a** and a third-person singular verb form.

  En Guatemala **se respeta** mucho **a** los ancianos.
  *In Guatemala, the elderly **are well respected**.*

- With objects or things, the verb can be singular or plural. The verb must agree with the subject.

  Se usa el picante.
  *Hot sauce **is used**.*

  Se exportan muchas materias primas.
  *Many raw materials **are exported**.*

- Use **la gente** (*people*) to refer to a group of people in general terms. **La gente** is a singular noun that requires a singular article. Note that this noun also requires the third-person singular verb form.

  La gente es amable.
  ***People** are friendly.*

  A **la gente** le gusta hablar.
  ***People** like to talk.*

- You can also say **los/las** + [*plural noun*] to make generalizing statements. Use the third-person plural verb form with this construction.

  Los centroamericanos hablan varias lenguas.
  ***Central Americans** speak several languages.*

16B.4 Make comparisons

igual de/que 12.7

- Use **igual de** + [*adjective*] + **que** (*as ... as*) to make comparisons.

  Tu país es **igual de bello que** el mío.
  *Your country is **as beautiful as** mine.*

- You can also express this equivalence with **igual de** + [*plural adjective*].

  Estela y Mario son **igual de trabajadores**.
  *Estela and Mario are **equally hard-working**.*

- Use **igual que** (*the same as*) to compare two things without specifying the characteristic being compared.

  La costa es igual de turística que el interior.
  The coast is as touristy as the interior.

  La costa es **igual que** el interior.
  *The coast is **the same as** the interior.*

Suggestion Work with the class to create a list of ten generalizations about life in this country.

¡Póngalo en práctica!

G7 Complete la conversación.

En muchos pueblos pequeños, la gente (1) es (ser) muy simpática y (2) está (estar) siempre dispuesta a ayudarte.

Sí, (3) se/la gente vive de otra manera en las áreas rurales, más relajada. En las ciudades modernas (4) se vive (vivir) muy deprisa. (5) Se come (Comer) rápido y la gente (6) tiene (tener) otro ritmo de vida. (7) Se pierden (Perder) muchas buenas costumbres.

Sí, en los pueblos pequeños (8) la gente no tiene tanta prisa.

G8 Reescribe las oraciones usando **se**.

Modelo: Aquí la gente habla dos idiomas.
Aquí se hablan dos idiomas.

1. Aquí la gente toma mucho café.
   Aquí se toma mucho café.
2. En Paraguay la gente habla guaraní.
   En Paraguay se habla guaraní.
3. En Uruguay la gente toma mate en todos lados.
   En Uruguay se toma mate en todos lados.
4. En el Caribe la gente toma muchos jugos.
   En el Caribe se toman muchos jugos.

G9 Complete las oraciones.

- Para mí, el café más barato es el más sabroso.
- No estoy de acuerdo. Todos los cafés son (1) igual de ricos. El más barato es igual (2) que el más caro.

  Tu hermana es (3) igual de simpática (4) que tú.

  La torta de chocolate que hace Guadalupe es igual (5) de rica (6) que la que hacía mi abuela.

  Mi primo y yo somos igual (7) de inteligentes, pero no somos igual (8) de trabajadores.
- ¡Esta película es igual (9) que todas las comedias románticas!
- No es cierto. No es (10) igual de optimista y no tiene un final feliz.

Suggestion Have the class choose two universities and create a list of criteria to compare. Then have them work in pairs to form the comparisons.

Practice more at **vhlcentral.com.**

16B.5 Talk about an imminent event

estar a punto de + [*infinitive*] 5.15

- Use the construction **estar a punto de** (*to be about to*) + [*infinitive*] to tell that an action is imminent.

Estoy **a punto de salir.**	La peli **está a punto de empezar.**
I ***am about to go out.***	*The movie* ***is about to begin.***

- Use **estar** in a past tense to indicate an event that was imminent in the past.

  Diego **estaba a punto de volver** a su casa cuando Gisela llegó al restaurante.
  Diego ***was about to return*** *home when Gisela arrived at the restaurant.*

¡Póngalo en práctica!

G10 Complete las conversaciones.

- Hola, ¿Marta?
- Hola, (1) ...estaba... (yo, estar) a punto de llamarte.
- Y yo estoy a (2) ...punto... de llegar, por eso te llamo.

- (3) ...Estoy... a punto (4) ...de... terminar esta novela. Me gusta muchísimo.
- Menos mal que me lo dices, (5) ...estaba... a punto de preguntarte si te gustó el final.

G10 Expansion Have students write an original dialogue using this expression at least twice.

Practice more at **vhlcentral.com.**

SÍNTESIS

Expansion Have students work in pairs and combine their dialogues. Have volunteers read them aloud for the class.

Mire las fotografías y escriba un diálogo corto para cada una, usando el vocabulario indicado.

1. 

igual de	la gente	se vive	bello

- ______
- ______
- ______
- ______

2. 

se venden	está a punto de	turístico	costumbres

- ______
- ______
- ______
- ______

3. 

no compres	marca	gente	se

- ______
- ______
- ______
- ______

VOCABULARIO

Publicidad hasta en el café

en buena compañía	*in good company*
el crucero	*cruise*
la diferencia	*difference (in price)*
el eslogan	*slogan*
el estado de ánimo	*mood*
la fragancia	*fragrance, perfume*
la merienda	*(afternoon) snack*
el pico	*peak, mountain*
la publicidad	*advertising*
un tercio	*a third*
el tópico	*cliché*
ahorrar	*to save*
confundirse	*to become confused*
devolver (o:ue)	*to return*
exigir (j)	*to demand*
perdérselo (e:ie)	*to miss out*
probar (o:ue)	*to taste*
provenir (e:ie) de	*to come from*
saborear	*to savor*
sentirse (e:ie) como en casa	*to feel at home*
certificado/a	*certified*

Usos y costumbres

la arcilla	*clay*
el camarón	*shrimp*
el grupo étnico	*ethnic group*
el/la mono/a araña	*spider monkey*
la ola	*wave*
la orquídea	*orchid*
el/la patrono/a	*patron saint*
la procesión	*procession*
el sedentarismo	*sedentary lifestyle*
el/la surfista	*surfer*
el tucán	*toucan*
el uso	*custom*
ocultar	*to hide*
venerar	*to venerate*
anticuado/a	*antiquated*
bello/a	*beautiful*
complejo/a	*complex*
comunicativo/a	*communicative*
congelado/a	*frozen*
cosmopolita	*cosmopolitan*
cuyo/a	*whose*
extenso/a	*vast*
homogéneo/a	*homogeneous*
poblado/a	*populated*
relleno/a	*stuffed, filled*
turístico/a	*tourist*
densamente	*densely*

Estela y Mario

propiamente dicho/a	*per se*
el aroma	*aroma, scent*
la autenticidad	*authenticity*
la campaña de promoción	*promotional campaign*
la cercanía	*proximity*
el certamen	*contest*
el cóctel	*cocktail*
el dinamismo	*dynamism*
el diseño	*design*
el durazno	*peach*
el encargo	*job, assignment*
la feria	*(trade) fair*
la gama	*range*
la guinda	*wild cherry*
el jurado	*panel of judges*
el logo	*logo*
la marca	*brand*
el/la publicista	*publicist*
el símbolo	*symbol*
la valentía	*courage*
anticipar	*to anticipate*
apelar	*to appeal*
dar a conocer	*to make known*
lanzar una campaña	*to launch a campaign*
tener en cuenta	*to take into account*
tener lugar	*to be held*
claro/a	*light*
compuesto/a por	*made up of*
creciente	*growing*
geográfico/a	*geographic*
morado/a	*purple*
oriundo/a	*native*
oscuro/a	*dark*
así como	*as well as*

Variación léxica

celebrarse ⟷ **tener lugar**

el certamen ⟷ **el concurso**

el eslogan ⟷ **el lema**

extenso/a ⟷ **vasto/a**

oriundo/a ⟷ **nativo/a**

provenir ⟷ **proceder**

la publicidad ⟷ **la propaganda**

¡Salud! ⟷ **¡Chinchín!** (*fam.*)

el/la surfista ⟷ **el/la tablista** (*Per., Col.*)

tener en cuenta ⟷ **tomar en cuenta**

Estrategias

1 Suggestion Have students compare their dialogues in pairs.

1 Suavizar una opinión

Lección 15A

Use expressions of courtesy such as **Yo diría que...** (*I'd say that . . .*) to soften your opinions. This will allow you to give your opinion without forcing it on another person. Sample answers:

○ **Lea los diálogos e introduzca la estrategia en las frases en las que considere necesario.**

- Yo siempre hago las compras en el supermercado. Es más cómodo.
- Pero los productos no son tan frescos como en el mercado.

Pero yo diría que los productos no son tan frescos como en el mercado.

- Hay que promocionar este producto con una idea ecológica.
- ¿Un coche? ¿Y cómo vamos a hacerlo?

Yo diría que hay que promocionar este producto con una idea ecológica.

- Las tiendas deben permanecer abiertas el mayor tiempo posible.
- ¿Y abrir también los domingos? ¡Es demasiado!

Yo diría que las tiendas deben permanecer abiertas el mayor tiempo posible. Yo diría que es demasiado.

2 Reforzar argumentos

Lección 15B

Expressions such as **efectivamente** (*exactly; indeed*) and **desde luego** (*of course*) will help you show that you are very much in agreement, and will show empathy towards the person you are speaking with.

○ **Complete los diálogos empleando alguna de estas palabras o expresiones.**

efectivamente • desde luego • pero • también • no

- ...Desde luego/Efectivamente..., la paz se construye con el compromiso de todos nosotros.
- Sí, ...pero... también hay que tomar decisiones políticas.

- La fecha de caducidad de esta mermelada es de la semana pasada.
- Sí, yo ...también... lo he visto. ...Desde luego..., hay que leer las etiquetas con atención.

- Si en casa no hay colaboración con la labor de la escuela, ...no... se va a conseguir nada.
- Los padres tienen que apoyar a los profesores y no ir en su contra.

3 Introducir un tema

Lección 16A

Expressions such as **en cuanto a** (*as for*) and **con respecto a** (*regarding*) will help you control the direction of a conversation with naturalness and fluency. **3 Suggestion** Encourage students to incorporate the expressions from Activities 1 and 2 when stating their opinions and replying to others'.

○ **Converse con sus compañeros con relación a los temas propuestos e introduzca sus ideas.**

el costo de la educación | **el proceso de independizarse** | **los conflictos generacionales**

4 Atenuar las generalizaciones

Lección 16B

Use expressions such as **no todos los** + [*noun*] (*not all . . .*) or **eso no es todo** (*that's not all*) to refute a generalization or contradict stereotypes.

○ **Observe las siguientes generalizaciones y busque argumentos para matizarlas.**

- Todos los productos envasados llevan fecha de caducidad.
- Todos los adolescentes tienen problemas en su desarrollo.
- Los anuncios siempre tratan de venderte algo.

Competencias

EXPRESAR PROBABILIDAD

1 Reaccione ante estas situaciones usando el futuro para expresar probabilidad.

Modelo: *Su compañero/a no vino al curso de español.*
(estar / enfermo) *Estará enfermo* .

1. No está seguro/a del origen de un producto.
   (ser / importado) ¿ Será importado ?
2. Suena el timbre de su casa a la medianoche.
   (quién / venir / a estas horas) ¿ Quién vendrá a estas horas ?
3. Le sorprende ver pocos clientes en un negocio céntrico.
   (por qué / haber / tan poca gente) ¿ Por qué habrá tan poca gente ?
4. No encuentra el símbolo de "reciclable" en un envase.
   (poder / reciclarse) ¿ Se podrá reciclar ?
5. Acaba de colgar con su madre y vuelve a sonar el teléfono.
   (qué / querer / ahora) ¿ Qué querrá ahora ?
6. Lee la etiqueta de un alimento para saber su composición.
   (tener / conservantes) ¿ Tendrá conservantes ?

EXPRESAR TEMOR, FINALIDAD, EXTRAÑEZA, DISGUSTO Y ENFADO

2 Amanda quiere pasar las vacaciones con su novio y su madre no está de acuerdo. Escriba con su compañero/a un diálogo entre ellas. Usen todas las expresiones del recuadro. **2 Expansion** Have pairs act out their dialogues for the class.

importante	esperar	extrañar	necesario	soportar
molestar	querer	preocupar	dar miedo	sorprender

EXPONER UNA OPINIÓN, MOSTRAR ESCEPTICISMO, TRANSMITIR INFORMACIONES

3 Lea este reportaje sobre una marcha por la paz. Imagine que es un(a) periodista que debe transmitir la información pero que se opone a la manifestación.

> Esta tarde comenzará la marcha por la paz en Bogotá. Pediremos la libertad de los secuestrados y el cese de los enfrentamientos armados. Pensamos que la única manera de que el gobierno y las FARC se pongan de acuerdo es por medio del diálogo.

Modelo: *En cuanto a las noticias políticas, los organizadores confirmaron que la marcha comenzaría esta tarde. Pero yo no creo que...*

3 Expansion Have students write the dialogue of an interview between the journalist and one of the demonstrators.

ANIMAR A LA ACCIÓN

4 Escriba una oración imperativa con pronombre para cada una de estas sugerencias.

Modelo: *Tiene que acompañar sus recetas con aceite de oliva.*
Acompáñelas con aceite de oliva.

1. Tienen que comprar este libro de cocina pronto porque se agota. Cómprenlo pronto porque se agota.
2. No tiene que dejar de comer frutas y verduras. No deje de comerlas.
3. Tienes que consumir productos frescos. Consúmelos.
4. Tenéis que beber este jugo refrescante bien frío. Bebedlo bien frío.

Flash CULTURA

Estrategia

Play-acting

When watching a video, try to picture yourself in the situation featured. In this **Flash Cultura** episode you will find different people giving their opinions about independence and statehood. Go through the possible conversation in your mind: What's your opinion on that issue? What would you reply?

Vocabulario útil

la aduana *customs*
el buzón *mailbox*
la estadidad *statehood*
el partido *game*
la patria *homeland*
permanecer (zc) *to remain*
las relaciones exteriores *foreign relations*

Estrategia

A **gentilicio**, or *demonym*, is the name given to the people from a particular city, region, or country. Some **gentilicios** are easy to predict, like **montevideano** (from the city of Montevideo); some others are less obvious, like **boricua** that derives from the Taino name for Puerto Rico, **Borikén**; the people from the island are also called **puertorriqueños/as**. Don't forget that, unlike English, in Spanish, **gentilicios** are lowercase.

Puerto Rico, ¿nación o estado?

Ya ha leído sobre la lucha por la libertad como derecho de todos los seres humanos y también sobre la búsqueda de identidad en países de habla hispana. Este episodio de **Flash Cultura** se ocupa de la importancia del debate político que toca estos dos temas en la isla de Puerto Rico.

1 ¿Qué opina de la libertad y la igualdad como derechos? ¿Qué cosas son menos importantes y se pueden negociar? ¿Lee habitualmente los diarios para conocer la situación política de su país? ¿Conversa con sus amigos o familia sobre esos temas? ¿Le parece divertido discutir sobre política?

2 Mire el episodio de **Flash Cultura** y escuche lo que dicen los entrevistados; preste atención a cómo lo dicen, mientras imagina qué diría usted en esa situación.

1 **El debate se ha convertido en el deporte nacional de Puerto Rico.**

Suggestion Give students a few demonyms in English from different cities in this country. Then have them read the **Estrategia.**

2 **Creo que Puerto Rico necesita soberanía para tomar sus propias decisiones.**

3 Ordene las características de Puerto Rico en la columna adecuada.

Como estado libre asociado	Como territorio de Estados Unidos
1, 4, 5, 7	2, 3, 6, 8

1. Se habla español.
2. La moneda es el dólar.
3. No hace falta visa para entrar a EE.UU.
4. No se vota para presidente de EE.UU.
5. Se pagan sólo impuestos locales.
6. Funciona el servicio de correos de EE.UU.
7. No se pagan impuestos federales.
8. Tiene un representante en el Congreso de EE.UU.

3 Suggestion Alternatively, present these items orally as true/false statements.

4 En parejas, escriban la conversación entre un(a) visitante que comenta sus impresiones sobre la ciudad y un lugareño/a que le explica la otra cara de las cosas.

Modelo:
- *Me parece que aquí la gente está siempre feliz.*
- *No todos los habitantes son igual de felices.*

Practice more at **vhlcentral.com.**

Unidad 17

Audio: Activities, Vocabulary
Video: *Flash Cultura*

Salvador Moncada, ciencia para la vida

Lección 17A

EL FUTURO POR DELANTE

Lección 17B

AFICIONES COMUNES

Amanda y Rubén, la vida es un tango

Lo mejor de Argentina

AVANCE

17A

Point out the use of the accent mark on **o** (*or*) between numerals in the phrase **50 ó 100 años**. Tell students that the accent is often included over **o** between numerals to avoid confusion with **0**.

EL FUTURO POR DELANTE

Dentro de cien años...

Si observamos las nuevas tendencias, pensaremos en un futuro muy tecnológico. ¿Qué novedades vendrán? ¿Cuáles harán nuestra vida más fácil? ¿Cómo será nuestra vida dentro de 50 ó 100 años? ¿Podemos saberlo con antelación? Son muchos los que se han hecho estas preguntas. En este número recordamos algunas de las más **famosas predicciones de las últimas décadas** y nos atrevemos con **predicciones de un futuro probable**.

FAMOSAS PREDICCIONES DE LAS ÚLTIMAS DÉCADAS

- "La TV no llegará muy lejos. La gente no querrá mirar todas las noches una caja de madera."
  Darryl Zanuck, productor de la 20th Century Fox, 1946
- "Podremos enviar el correo por misil antes de llegar a la Luna."
  Arthur Summerfield, director general del Servicio Postal de EE.UU., 1959
- "No habrá necesidad de tener una computadora en cada casa."
  Ken Olsen, fundador de Digital Equipment Corporation, 1977
- "Dentro de dos años no sabremos qué es el spam."
  Bill Gates, Fundador de Microsoft, 2004
- "El *iPod* nunca tendrá éxito."
  Alan Sugar, fundador de Amstrad, 2005

PREDICCIONES DE UN FUTURO PROBABLE

- Tal vez las computadoras estén dentro de nuestro cuerpo.
- A lo mejor habrá una moneda electrónica común.
- Seguro que los libros serán electrónicos y no de papel.
- Puede que se hablen muy pocos idiomas, cuatro o cinco como mucho.
- Es muy probable que haya profesiones que se desarrollen a distancia, por ejemplo, la medicina.
- Quizá dentro de cien años nos comunicaremos con la mente.

Hacer predicciones

- ¿Cuáles **serán** las lenguas del futuro?
- **Dentro de** algún tiempo **se hablarán** menos lenguas.

17A.1 Simple future of irregular verbs **dentro de**

Vocabulario

1

- dentro de *in, within*
- la tendencia *trend*
- la novedad *innovation*
- hacer la vida más fácil *to make life easier*
- con antelación *ahead of time*
- atreverse *to dare*
- tal vez *maybe*
- a lo mejor *maybe*
- quizá(s) *perhaps*
- el avance *breakthrough*
- **el futuro, tecnológico/a, la predicción, probable**

1 a. Lea la introducción de este artículo sobre avances tecnológicos. ¿Qué es una predicción? Possible answers: Decir antes. Anunciar un hecho con antelación.

b. Lea el texto "Famosas predicciones de la historia". ¿Conoce a las personas citadas? ¿Qué le parece curioso de estas predicciones? ¿Qué tienen en común? Ninguna se ha cumplido.

2 Fíjese en los dibujos y en los dos usos de *dentro de*. ¿Con cuál de las preposiciones que ya ha aprendido se puede reemplazar *dentro de*? en

1

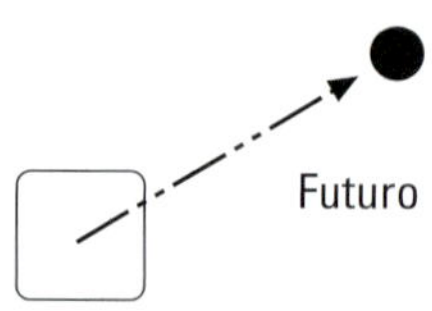

2

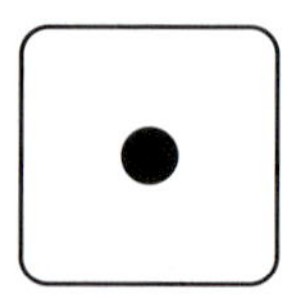

(1) **Dentro de** cien años puede que las computadoras estén...

(2) ...**dentro de** nuestros cuerpos.

3 Seleccione tres de estos temas y haga sus predicciones. Compare sus predicciones con las de su compañero/a.

3 Suggestion Have students react to their partners' predictions, using phrases such as **dudo que**.

- Medicina
- Comunicación
- Trabajo
- Lenguas
- Tecnología

Modelo: *Dentro de... años...*

Suggestion Explain that **quizá** and **quizás** are used interchangeably. However, due to phonetics, there is a tendency to use **quizá** when the following word begins with a consonant (**quizá llueva**) and **quizás** when the word that follows begins with a vowel (**quizás abran hoy**).

Expresar probabilidad

- Es muy probable que los médicos trabajen a distancia.
- Sí, seguro que lo harán.

17A.2 **es probable que** + [*subjunctive*]
a lo mejor + [*indicative*]

Vocabulario

5

desechable *disposable*
Marte (*m.*) *Mars*
la cura *cure*

6

enterarse de *to find out (about)*
el cargo *position*
estar en manos de alguien *to be under someone's control*
¡Pero, hombre/mujer! *Come on!*
amargarle la vida a alguien *to make someone's life miserable*

¡OJO!

Although the meaning of the expression **a lo mejor** is similar to that of **tal vez** or **quizá**, this expression is always followed by verbs in the indicative mood.

6 Expansion Have students work in pairs. Ask them to write a dialogue between two friends who are discussing a prediction. Have them end the dialogue with the same line as the *Mafalda* comic (**¡Vos siempre tratando de amargarle la vida a uno!**). Have volunteers role-play their conversations for the class.

7 Suggestion If needed, simplify by giving students categories within which to make predictions.

4 Lea el texto "Predicciones de un futuro probable". ¿En qué se diferencian las predicciones de ambos textos de la página anterior? ¿Qué predicciones le parecen más y menos probables? ¿Coincide con su compañero/a?

5 a. Lea estas predicciones para dentro de diez años. Marque las oraciones en las que se usa el subjuntivo.

- [ ] Seguro que todos los objetos de uso diario serán desechables.
- [x] Tal vez algunos seres humanos puedan vivir en Marte.
- [x] Puede ser que dejemos de usar petróleo para producir energía.
- [ ] A lo mejor todos los alimentos serán transgénicos.
- [x] Quizá se terminen todos los conflictos armados.
- [x] Es posible que se encuentre la cura a todas las enfermedades.
- [x] Es probable que todos podamos trabajar desde casa.

b. Clasifique las expresiones de probabilidad anteriores. Answers may vary.

Más probable	Menos probable
es probable que, a lo mejor, seguro que, tal vez/quizá + [*indicativo*]	es posible que, puede (ser) que, tal vez/quizá + [*subjuntivo*]

c. ¿Qué piensa que es probable, posible o seguro que pase dentro de diez años? Comente sus predicciones con su compañero/a. ¿Están de acuerdo o en desacuerdo?

6 Observe la viñeta cómica de *Mafalda* sobre el futuro. ¿Cuáles son las predicciones de Felipe? ¿Qué le parece probable que suceda en un mundo gobernado por niños? Possible answer: Dentro de treinta años los niños harán cosas y ocuparán cargos.

MI EXPERIENCIA

7 Comparta con el grupo algunas predicciones para un futuro lejano.

GUIÓN DE TRABAJO

¿Cómo será el mundo dentro de 100/200/300 años?

Puede (ser) que...	Seguro que...
Es probable que...	Tal vez / Quizá...
Es posible que...	A lo mejor...

Practice more at **vhlcentral.com.**

SAM: Actividades pp. 355–357

Ciencia con conciencia

XII Feria Internacional de Educación, Ciencia y Tecnología

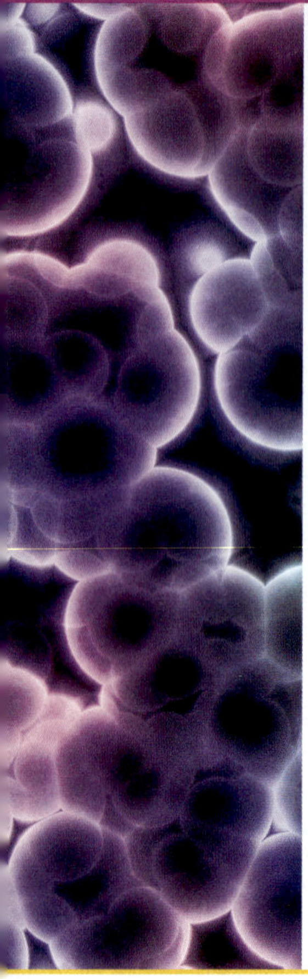

Es obvio que todos nos beneficiamos de los avances de la ciencia. Sin embargo, no estamos seguros de que los investigadores reciban toda la ayuda que necesitan. Por eso, cada año organizamos en Lima, Perú, la Feria Internacional de Educación, Ciencia y Tecnología, CIENTEC. El objetivo de esta feria es crear un espacio para que los investigadores puedan tratar problemas y necesidades relacionados con su profesión. Queremos promover las actividades de investigación que respeten la naturaleza y que permitan a las generaciones futuras vivir en un mundo donde haya paz, equidad y un desarrollo sostenible.

Por otro lado, es evidente que detrás de cada gran científico hay un niño curioso. Sin embargo, no está demostrado que nuestros jóvenes reciban suficientes incentivos para formar parte del mundo científico. Por eso hemos creado dos programas dirigidos a ellos:

- Programa Internacional Minicientíficos: Queremos estimular el interés de los niños de 7 a 11 años por la ciencia y los experimentos. Por lo tanto, hemos creado una serie de actividades interactivas cuyo objetivo es el descubrimiento y la experimentación: talleres, cursos, excursiones, campamentos, concursos, etcétera.
- Programa Internacional Evaluador Joven: Intentamos promover el uso del método científico entre los estudiantes para complementar su formación, y fomentar la apreciación y comprensión de la ciencia. De este modo, estarán mejor preparados para responder a las necesidades del mundo actual.

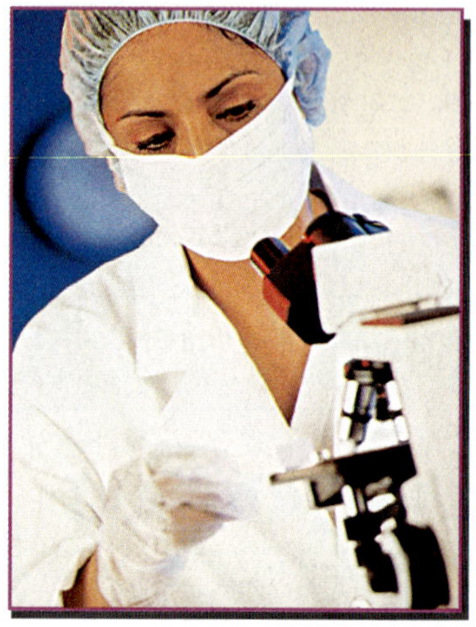

Estamos seguros de que le gustará participar, así que lo invitamos a recorrer esta exposición interactiva y descubrir la ciencia con otros ojos. Lo esperamos del 15 al 19 de noviembre en el Club de la Unión, Plaza de Armas, Lima.

Expresar certeza y evidencia

- Es evidente que la energía solar es ecológica.
- Sí, pero no está demostrado que sea más económica.

17A.3 **no estar seguro/a de que** + [*subjunctive*]
estar seguro/a de que + [*indicative*]

Vocabulario

8

el/la investigador(a) *researcher*
la investigación *research*
la equidad *fairness*
sostenible *sustainable*
demostrar (o:ue) *to prove*
el incentivo *encouragement*
el descubrimiento *discovery*
el método científico *scientific method*
descubrir *to discover*
evidente *obvious, clear*
obvio/a *obvious*

8 a. Fíjese en el título "Ciencia con conciencia". ¿Qué le sugiere la relación entre las palabras *ciencia* y *conciencia*? ¿De qué cree que tratará el texto?

b. Lea el folleto de la feria y busque en el texto expresiones equivalentes a estas.

- Es verdad/cierto que... es obvio, es evidente, estamos seguros de que
- No es verdad/cierto que... no estamos seguros de que, no está demostrado que

c. Observe los ejemplos del texto y seleccione la opción correcta.

8c Expansion For each of the expressions given (**Es obvio que; No estamos seguros de que**), ask the class to write two statements that might be overheard by students on your campus.

- Con **frases afirmativas** se usa **indicativo/subjuntivo.**
  Es obvio que todos nos **beneficiamos/beneficiemos** de los avances de la ciencia.
  Es evidente que detrás de cada gran científico **hay/haya** un niño curioso.
- Con frases negativas se usa **indicativo/subjuntivo**.
  No estamos seguros de que los investigadores **reciben/reciban** toda la ayuda que necesitan.
  No está demostrado que nuestros jóvenes **reciben/reciban** suficientes incentivos.

9 ¿Alguna vez ha estado en una feria como la que se describe? ¿Le pareció interesante? ¿Por qué? ¿Qué opina de los programas para fomentar el interés de los niños y jóvenes por la ciencia? Coméntelo con la clase.

9 Suggestion Have the class consider other ways in which interest in science is cultivated at an early age, such as science museums.

Vocabulario *cont.*

la conciencia, el experimento, interactivo/a, la experimentación, la apreciación

(10)

cómodo/a *convenient*
móvil *mobile*
abundante *plentiful*
resistente *strong, tough*
renovable *renewable*
comunitario/a *communal*
rápido/a *quick, fast*
fiable *reliable*
libre *free*
la seguridad *security*
el/la alarmista *alarmist*

inmediato/a, ecológico/a, universal, la privacidad

(11)

así (es) que *so*
por lo tanto *therefore*
por eso *therefore*

Estrategia

Expresar consecuencia

No está claro que el teléfono celular sea seguro, pero no está demostrado que sea peligroso, **así (es) que / por lo tanto** no seas alarmista.

Crear conciencia con ciencia

Es el lema de la Feria Nacional Infantil y Juvenil de Experimentación Científica, organizada por el Consejo Hondureño de Ciencia, Tecnología e Innovación, que tiene como objetivo motivar vocaciones científicas y tecnológicas, y crear mayor interés y conciencia sobre la importancia de la ciencia en nuestra vida diaria.

12 Expansion Challenge students to think of a time of their day-to-day existence that is *not* touched by science.

10 Algunos avances científicos están muy presentes en nuestra vida diaria y a veces hay debate sobre su utilidad y sus (des)ventajas. Comente con su compañero/a qué sabe sobre los avances representados en las fotos.

el teléfono celular

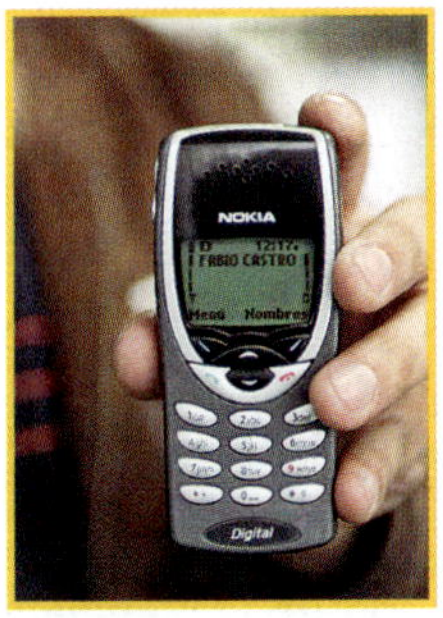

+ cómodo, móvil, inmediato...
− ¿peligro para la salud?

los alimentos transgénicos

+ abundantes, resistentes, baratos...
− ¿saludables?

la energía nuclear y la energía solar

+ sostenible, abundante, renovable...
− ¿ecológica? ¿económica?

Internet

+ universal, comunitario, rápido...
− ¿fiable, libre? ¿privacidad, seguridad?

11 a. Encuentre en el texto de la página anterior estos conectores y escriba las frases que unen.

Estamos seguros de que le gustará participar	... *así (es) que...*	lo invitamos a recorrer esta exposición interactiva.
Queremos estimular el interés de los niños de 7 a 11 años por la ciencia y los experimentos.	... *por lo tanto...*	hemos creado una serie de actividades interactivas...

b. Anote alguna consecuencia de su conversación de la Actividad 10.

12 Lea la nota de la izquierda. ¿Cuál es el objetivo del evento que se describe? Y usted, ¿cómo está presente la ciencia en su vida?

Motivar vocaciones científicas y tecnológicas, y crear mayor interés y conciencia sobre la importancia de la ciencia en nuestra vida diaria.

MI EXPERIENCIA

13 Expansion With the class, build a time line of important scientific breakthroughs on the board. Then, as a group, select the top five or top ten.

13 Seleccionen un avance científico importante y decisivo para todo el mundo. Describan por qué es importante y qué consecuencias tiene en sus vidas.

GUIÓN DE TRABAJO

¿Cuál crees que es el avance científico más importante? → Es evidente/obvio que... Estoy seguro/a de que...

¿Qué consecuencias tuvo? → así que... por eso... por lo tanto...

Practice more at **vhlcentral.com.**

SAM: Actividades pp. 358–360

17A

Salvador Moncada, ciencia para la vida

Quark   Número 12

Salvador Moncada, científico

Salvador Moncada (Tegucigalpa, 1944), investigador y científico hondureño. Ha dedicado gran parte de su carrera a la investigación farmacéutica. Ha patentado diez nuevos fármacos y ha publicado más de 700 artículos en diferentes revistas científicas de prestigio internacional. Es uno de los 25 científicos más citados del mundo.

Entrevista a Salvador Moncada

El científico e investigador Salvador Moncada nos habla del papel de la ciencia en la sociedad actual. A Salvador Moncada le preocupa la modernización de la ciencia.

1 *"La inversión en ciencia y tecnología va a redundar a medio o largo plazo en beneficios para la sociedad, en creación de riqueza, de empleo, y en mejores condiciones de vida."*

El doctor Moncada se expresa abiertamente sobre la comunidad a la que pertenece y afirma que:

3 *"Los científicos muchas veces no se llevan su tiempo para explicar a la sociedad qué es lo que están haciendo y por qué lo están haciendo."*

Sobre la aplicación de la ciencia en la vida, Moncada añade que:

2 *"El científico debería estar interesado en las posibilidades de aplicación práctica de la ciencia y empezar a pensar 'Bueno, voy a hacer esto, pero ¿con qué fin?'. Estamos en un momento en que la cuestión está en saber cómo cerrar la brecha para lograr que el conocimiento básico se torne en conocimiento productivo."*

1 *"Los científicos también debemos tener una conciencia y una responsabilidad hacia lo que se está haciendo."*

2 *"La comunidad científica debería comunicar mucho más y participar mucho más en la discusión general de la sociedad de por qué se hace investigación."*

3 *"La comunidad científica debe vivir en sociedad."*

Salvador Moncada is Honduran-British. He is married to Princess Marie-Esméralda of Belgium; they and their children reside in London. Moncada was knighted in 2010 for services to Science.

Vocabulario

(14)
redundar en *to benefit*
abiertamente *openly, frankly*
a corto/medio/largo plazo *in the short/medium/long term*
estar interesado/a en *to be interested in*
cerrar (e:ie) la brecha *to close the gap*
tornarse *to become*
farmacéutico/a *pharmaceutical*
patentar *to patent*
el fármaco *medicine*
citado/a *cited, quoted*
la modernización
(15)
la modernidad *modernity*
(16)
dominar *to prevail, to stand out*
el campo científico *scientific field*
rezagado/a *falling behind*
la infraestructura

Expresar continuidad

Sigue habiendo muy buenos científicos hispanos, pero muchos de ellos **siguen sin volver** a sus países.

17A.4 **seguir** + [*present participle*]
seguir sin + [*infinitive*]

14 a. Observe el título de la página. ¿Quién cree que es nuestro protagonista y por qué cree usted que es el protagonista de esta lección?

b. Lea los datos de su biografía y señale sobre qué aspectos informa.

- ☑ profesión
- ☑ carrera profesional
- ☑ país de origen
- ☑ edad
- ☐ premios
- ☑ campo de investigación
- ☐ domicilio
- ☑ los académicos

15 a. Fíjese ahora en las citas del texto a la derecha. ¿Cuáles cree que son los principales temas de la entrevista? Lea después todo el texto e identifique a qué cita se refiere cada uno de estos tres temas.

[2] Comunidad científica   [1] Responsabilidad de los científicos   [3] Ciencia y sociedad

b. ¿Con qué temas se relaciona la ciencia en esta entrevista? Busque información en el texto para justificar su respuesta.

- ☑ modernidad
- ☐ cultura
- ☑ comunidad científica
- ☑ comunicación
- ☑ sociedad
- ☐ industria
- ☑ investigación
- ☐ otros

16 a. Escuche este fragmento de una entrevista sobre Salvador Moncada y complete esta cita del investigador. ¿A qué región del mundo se refiere la conversación? América Latina

"Sigue ...perdiendo... científicos y sigue ...sin crear... la infraestructura necesaria para mantener los científicos en sus países."

b. Reformule estas frases con las estructuras anteriores.

- Antes no se invertía en ciencia. Ahora tampoco se invierte en ciencia.
  Se sigue sin invertir en ciencia.
- Antes la ciencia estaba lejos de la sociedad. Ahora también.
  La ciencia sigue estando lejos de la sociedad.

16a **Suggestion** Have students read the quote again. Write the expression **fuga de cerebros** on the board and tell them that this is the phenomenon that is described in the quote. Ask the class to guess the English equivalent (*brain drain*).

Vocabulario

(17)

controlar *to check*
la fase *stage*
medir (e:i) *to measure*
la sangre *blood*
el pinchazo *prick*
inyectarse *to give oneself an injection*
desarrollar *to develop*
suministrar *to administer*
la bomba *pump*
denominarse *to be called*
bilbaíno/a *from Bilbao (Spain)*
lo más... posible *as... as possible*
ajustado/a a *adapted to*
la jeringa *syringe*
la diabetes, la glucosa, el chip, diabético/a, la dosis, la insulina, el organismo

(19)

el ácido *acid*
cardiovascular

(20)

conmemorar *to commemorate*
el sistema inmunológico *immune system*
el/la discípulo/a *disciple*
la humanidad *humankind*
la salsa golf *sauce similar to Thousand Island dressing*
la capa de ozono *ozone layer*
el metabolismo

OPINIÓN

¿La ciencia es una prioridad en nuestra sociedad?

¿Es el desarrollo científico un avance? ¿En qué sentido?

17 a. Lea este artículo. ¿Qué descubrimiento describe? ¿Qué aplicación tendrá en la vida diaria?

Las personas con diabetes podrán controlar los niveles de glucosa con un chip

El chip, en fase de investigación, medirá el nivel de azúcar en la sangre y mandará un aviso al teléfono celular del paciente y a su centro médico.

Las personas diabéticas podrán olvidarse de los pinchazos diarios para medir el nivel de azúcar y de inyectarse la dosis de insulina que necesitan.
Un gran equipo de investigadores de ocho países europeos está desarrollando un sensor subcutáneo (un chip instalado debajo de la piel) que controlará el nivel de azúcar de los pacientes. Cada 10 ó 15 minutos podrá transmitir esos datos al teléfono celular del paciente y al centro médico, y podrá incluso suministrar la dosis necesaria de insulina en cada momento a través de unas bombas de insulina que el paciente llevará también dentro de su cuerpo.
El proyecto, denominado Paul Cezanne, está coordinado en España por el investigador del Instituto de Microelectrónica de Barcelona —Consejo Superior de Investigaciones Científicas (CSIC)—, Carlos Domínguez. Este profesor bilbaíno explica que el proyecto quiere "desarrollar un sensor lo más ajustado posible a las necesidades de los pacientes" para "mejorar su calidad de vida".

b. Busque en el texto las palabras que se ajustan a cada definición.

1. Enfermedad que produce un exceso de glucosa en la sangre: diabetes
2. Persona que padece diabetes: diabético/a
3. Azúcar presente en el organismo: glucosa
4. Hormona para tratar la diabetes: insulina
5. Dar algo que se necesita: suministrar
6. Introducir en el cuerpo un líquido a través de una jeringa: inyectar

17 Suggestion Survey the class to find out if they or anyone they know has diabetes. Have them discuss how this new technology would help that person. Then ask the class if they think there is anyone that might not be well served by this chip, and why (Ex: an elderly person might not own a cell phone).

c. Haga una lista de otros inventos (reales o imaginarios) que podrían mejorar la calidad de vida de las personas diabéticas.

18 Piense en un avance científico que haya cambiado su vida. ¿Tiene consecuencias negativas? ¿Cómo se podría perfeccionar?

18 Suggestion Have students write their descriptions without identifying the scientific breakthrough by name. Then have them read aloud their descriptions in small groups. Their classmates should try to identify the breakthrough.

19 Observe la foto. ¿Para qué se usa este medicamento? Lea el texto y encuentre su relación con el doctor Moncada.

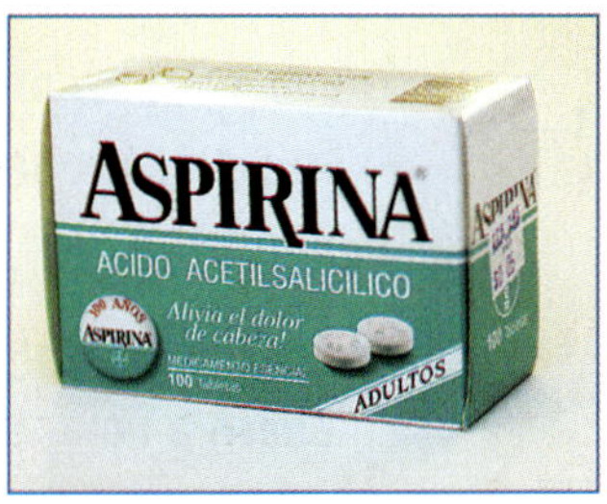

Las investigaciones sobre el ácido acetilsalicílico y el óxido nítrico han llevado al doctor Moncada a las puertas del Nobel en dos ocasiones porque revolucionaron el tratamiento de las enfermedades cardiovasculares. Fue en 1987 cuando Salvador Moncada publicó los resultados de sus investigaciones, que renovaron la utilidad de la aspirina para tratar las enfermedades cardiovasculares.

19 Suggestion Ask students if they know how aspirin helps prevent cardiovascular problems. (It inhibits the formation of blood clots, which increase the risk of heart attack and stroke.)

Practice more at **vhlcentral.com.**

SAM: Actividades pp. 361–364

20 a. En los 110 años de historia del Premio Nobel, estos cuatro científicos latinoamericanos han sido premiados por sus aportes a las ciencias. ¿Los conoce?

Bernardo Alberto Houssay (1887–1971) recibió el Premio Nobel de Fisiología y Medicina en 1947 por sus estudios sobre el metabolismo del azúcar en el cuerpo y su relación con la diabetes. En honor de este gran médico argentino, el día de su nacimiento se conmemora el Día del Investigador Científico en su país.

César Milstein (1927–2002), biólogo argentino, recibió el Premio Nobel de Fisiología y Medicina en 1984 por sus investigaciones sobre el sistema inmunológico humano. Por motivos políticos, debió mudarse a Inglaterra en 1963, aunque viajaba a Argentina con frecuencia. En 2010 se estrenó un documental sobre su vida, filmado por Ana Fraile, su sobrina nieta: *Un fueguito: La historia de César Milstein.*

Luis Federico Leloir (1906–1987), discípulo de Houssay, recibió el Premio Nobel de Química en 1970 gracias a sus descubrimientos sobre la biosíntesis de los carbohidratos. Además de sus importantes descubrimientos científicos, este brillante investigador argentino hizo otro gran aporte a la humanidad: inventó la salsa golf.

José Mario Molina nació en 1943 y es un ingeniero químico mexicano. En 1995, se convirtió en el primer estudioso del medio ambiente en recibir el Premio Nobel de Química. Fue por sus investigaciones sobre la formación y la descomposición de la capa de ozono. ¿Un dato curioso? Cuando era pequeño, quería ser músico.

b. Comente con su compañero/a cuál de los descubrimientos de estos científicos le parece el más interesante. Describa por qué y qué consecuencias tiene para la humanidad.

c. En total, quince latinoamericanos han recibido el Premio Nobel. Busque información en español sobre uno de ellos y preséntela al resto de la clase.

TAREA FINAL

Una exposición científica

Elabore una lista de avances científicos con aplicación en la vida diaria.

Seleccionen los mejores, los más útiles y positivos.

Elaboren un cartel con fotos de estos avances y todas sus conclusiones para dar una presentación.

YO PUEDO...

- Puedo hacer predicciones.
  Escriba tres predicciones sobre el futuro con sus correspondientes plazos.
- Puedo expresar probabilidad.
  Exprese las probabilidades con relación a su propio futuro.
- Puedo expresar certeza y evidencia.
  Exprese sus certezas sobre esta oración:
  La energía solar es ecológica y económica.
- Puedo expresar continuidad.
  ¿Qué cosas sigue haciendo desde que empezó a estudiar español? ¿Qué cosas sigue sin hacer?

GRAMÁTICA FUNCIONAL

17A.1 Make predictions

Simple future of irregular verbs 5.16.2b
dentro de 5.16.2d, 10.6

- Use the **simple future** to make predictions about the future. You have learned regular and irregular forms of the **futuro simple** in 12B.1 and 15A.1.

  En el año 2050, muchas personas **sabrán** hablar más de dos idiomas.
  *In the year 2050, many people **will know how** to speak more than two languages.*

- As you are studying irregular forms of the **futuro simple**, it may help to group stems into three categories. Remember that these verbs undergo the same stem changes in the **condicional**.

PONER **SALIR** **TENER** **VENIR**	pon**d**ré sal**d**ré ten**d**ré ven**d**ré	add a **d**
PODER **QUERER** **SABER**	podré querré sabré	take away an **e**
DECIR **HACER**	**dir**é **har**é	stem change

- The future form of **hay** is **habrá**.
- Use **dentro de** (*in, within*) + [*length of time*] to talk about the future.

  Dentro de cincuenta años, **habrá** muchos avances en la medicina.
  ***Within** fifty year's time, **there will be** many advances in medicine.*

17A.2 Express probability

es probable que + [*subjunctive*] 5.8.5, 5.20, 5.21.7
a lo mejor + [*indicative*] 11.5

- Use the subjunctive with the expressions **es (poco/muy/ bastante) probable/posible que** and **puede (ser) que** to express probability.

  Es muy probable que tengamos más vacunas.
  ***It is very likely that we will have** more vaccines.*

- Use **tal vez** (*maybe*) and **quizá(s)** (*perhaps*) with the indicative in order to indicate a greater degree of probability. These expressions may also be used with the subjunctive to indicate a lesser degree of probability.

  Tal vez vamos al museo mañana.
  Tal vez vayamos al museo mañana.
  ***Maybe we will go** to the museum tomorrow.*

- Always use the indicative with **a lo mejor**.

Suggestion Point out that the **lo** in **a lo mejor** is invariable.

  A lo mejor los niños **empezarán** a estudiar lenguas extranjeras a una edad más temprana.
  ***Perhaps** children **will begin** to study foreign languages at an earlier age.*

¡Póngalo en práctica!

G1 Complete la conversación.

- (1) Dentro de 55 años, yo (2) tendré (tener) 75 años y (3) estaré (estar) jubilada.
- ¿Y crees que (4) haremos (nosotros, hacer) la misma vida que ahora?
- Creo que (5) podremos (nosotros, poder) viajar más y en todas las casas (6) habrá (haber) robots.
- Sí, a lo mejor (7) vendrán/vienen (venir) otros avances técnicos y no (8) tendremos/ tenemos (nosotros, tener) que trabajar tantas horas.

G2 Son las ocho de la mañana. ¿Dentro de cuánto tiempo hará Mario estas cosas?

Modelo: 12 h, ir a la tienda
Dentro de cuatro horas irá a la tienda.

1. 14 h, estudiar francés
   Dentro de seis horas estudiará francés.
2. 16 h, llamar a Carlos
   Dentro de ocho horas llamará a Carlos.
3. 19 h, salir con María
   Dentro de once horas saldrá con María.
4. 21 h, hacer la tarea
   Dentro de trece horas hará la tarea.
5. 23 h, poner la tele
   Dentro de quince horas pondrá la tele.

Suggestion Emphasize that using the indicative or subjunctive with **tal vez** and **quizá(s)** depends on the perspective of the speaker and the degree of probability that is being expressed.

G3 Complete las oraciones.

- A lo mejor (1) se descubre/ se descubrirá (descubrirse) pronto un medicamento contra el cáncer.
- Sí, puede ser que lo (2) veamos (ver) nosotros mismos.

- Es muy posible que (3) sea (ser) así, aunque quizá (4) pasa/pase (pasar) algún tiempo todavía.
- Tal vez no (5) tenemos/tengamos (nosotros, tener) que esperar tanto tiempo. Es seguro que en el campo de la medicina (6) hay (haber) avances importantes todos los años.

- El otro día la hermana de Federico nos habló del semestre que pasó en París. Quizás yo también (7) estudie (estudiar) en una universidad extranjera.
- Es seguro que muchos estudiantes (8) deciden (decidir) estudiar en otro país por un semestre. Es una oportunidad muy buena de aprender otras lenguas y conocer otras culturas.

Practice more at **vhlcentral.com.**

GRAMÁTICA FUNCIONAL

Suggestion Have students create a two-column chart with the labels **Indicativo** and **Subjuntivo**. Tell them to classify the expressions from **17A.2** and **17A.3** in the appropriate column(s).

- Always use the indicative with the impersonal expression **es seguro que**.

  Es seguro que más personas **tendrán** acceso a Internet.
  It is a sure thing that more people will have Internet access.

- The present subjunctive form of **hay** is **haya**.

  Quizás **haya** menos conflictos internacionales en el futuro.
  Maybe there will be fewer international conflicts in the future.

17A.3 Express certainty and evidence

(no) estar seguro/a de que, (no) es evidente que, (no) está claro/demostrado que + [*indicative/subjunctive*] 5.8.2, 5.8.6, 5.21.4b

- Use the indicative in affirmative sentences with the expressions **estar seguro/a de que** (*to be sure that*), **es evidente que** (*to be evident that*), and **está claro/demostrado que** (*it is clear/proven that*), as these expressions indicate certainty.

  Estamos totalmente **seguros de que** dentro de cien años todos los libros **serán** digitales.
  We are completely sure that all books will be digital within a hundred years.

- Use the subjunctive with these same expressions in negative statements, as they convey doubt.

  No está demostrado que dentro de cien años **podamos** viajar a otros planetas.
  It is not proven that we will be able to travel to other planets within a hundred years.

17A.4 Express continuity

seguir + [*present participle*]; **seguir sin** + [*infinitive*] 5.13, 5.15

- Use **seguir** + [*present participle*] to express continuity of an action.

  Siguen investigando los efectos de la nueva medicina.
  They are still investigating the effects of the new medicine.

  Afirman que **sigue bajando** el riesgo de contraer gripe A.
  They state that the risk of contracting Type-A flu keeps declining.

- Use **seguir sin** + [*infinitive*] to express the continuity of an unfulfilled action.

  Sigo sin visitar la exposición.
  I still have not visited the exposition.

  Aunque me lo explicaron, **sigo sin entender** cómo funciona este experimento.
  Even though they explained it to me, I still don't understand how this experiment works.

Suggestion Have students work in small groups and mention what things have continued to be the same at your university since last semester. Then have them discuss what elements of society/politics are still the same from the last presidential administration to the current one.

¡Póngalo en práctica!

G4 Escriba oraciones completas para hacer predicciones en el futuro.

1. quizá / Joaquín / hacerse médico
   Quizá Joaquín se hace/haga médico.
2. a lo mejor / nosotros / desarrolla / la vacuna
   A lo mejor nosotros desarrollaremos/desarrollamos la vacuna.
3. es posible que / el gobierno / aumentar / su apoyo
   Es posible que el gobierno aumente su apoyo.

G5 Complete las oraciones.

- Es evidente que los países (1) tienen (tener) que invertir en ciencia y tecnología.
- Sí, aunque no está claro que los descubrimientos (2) sean (ser) propiedad exclusiva de un país.
- Está completamente demostrado que la tecnología (3) ayuda (ayudar) a muchas personas, pero que también (4) puede (poder) causar problemas.
- Sí, por ejemplo, está claro que Internet (5) ofrece (ofrecer) muchos beneficios, pero no es evidente que (6) sea (ser) la mejor forma de informarse ni de comunicarse.
- Desde luego. Estoy segura de que (7) hay (haber) muchas cosas que se comunican mejor en persona.

G6 Complete las oraciones.

- La ciencia (1) sigue avanzando en la investigación, pero sigue sin (2) dar (dar) una buena solución.
- En los próximos años los científicos (3) seguirán intentándolo.
- El restaurante sigue (4) preparando (preparar) comida muy rica, pero todavía no tiene muchos clientes.
- ¿Sigue (5) sin tener una página web? Los dueños tienen que (6) seguir pensando en cómo atraer a más clientes.

G7 Complete las oraciones de forma lógica con el gerundio o con **sin** + [*infinitivo*].

1. ¡Qué problema! Sigo sin entender (entender) cómo funciona esta máquina.
2. Los científicos siguen investigando/sin investigar (investigar) la causa de la explosión en el laboratorio.
3. El ingeniero sigue esperando (esperar) los materiales. Aún no han llegado.
4. El director del laboratorio sigue sin contratar (contratar) nuevos científicos. Quiere hacer todo el trabajo solo.

Practice more at **vhlcentral.com.**

VOCABULARIO

Dentro de cien años...

amargarle la vida a alguien	*to make someone's life miserable*
con antelación	*ahead of time*
estar en manos de alguien	*to be under someone's control*
hacer la vida más fácil	*to make life easier*
¡Pero, hombre/mujer!	*Come on!*
el avance	*breakthrough*
el cargo	*position*
la cura	*cure*
el futuro	*future*
Marte (*m.*)	*Mars*
la novedad	*innovation*
la predicción	*prediction*
la tendencia	*trend*
atreverse	*to dare*
enterarse de	*to find out (about)*
desechable	*disposable*
probable	*probable*
tecnológico/a	*technological*
a lo mejor	*maybe*
quizá(s)	*perhaps*
tal vez	*maybe*
dentro de	*in, within*

Variación léxica

desechable ↔ **descartable** (*Arg.*)

la fase ↔ **la etapa**

la jeringa ↔ **la jeringuilla** (*Esp.*)

medio plazo ↔ **mediano plazo** (*C.S.*)

quizá ↔ **quizás**

Ciencia con conciencia

el/la alarmista	*alarmist*
la apreciación	*appreciation*
la conciencia	*conscience*
el descubrimiento	*discovery*
la equidad	*fairness*
la experimentación	*experimentation*
el experimento	*experiment*
el incentivo	*encouragement*
la investigación	*research*
el/la investigador(a)	*researcher*
el método científico	*scientific method*
la privacidad	*privacy*
la seguridad	*security*
demostrar (o:ue)	*to prove*
descubrir	*to discover*
abundante	*plentiful*
cómodo/a	*convenient*
comunitario/a	*communal*
ecológico/a	*ecological*
evidente	*obvious, clear*
inmediato/a	*immediate*
interactivo/a	*interactive*
fiable	*reliable*
libre	*free*
móvil	*mobile*
obvio/a	*obvious*
rápido/a	*quick, fast*
renovable	*renewable*
resistente	*strong, tough*
sostenible	*sustainable*
universal	*universal*
así (es) que	*so*
por eso	*therefore*
por lo tanto	*therefore*

Salvador Moncada

a corto/medio/largo plazo	*in the short/medium/ long term*
lo más... posible	*as... as possible*
el ácido	*acid*
la bomba	*pump*
el campo científico	*scientific field*
la capa de ozono	*ozone layer*
el chip	*chip*
la diabetes	*diabetes*
el/la discípulo/a	*disciple*
la dosis	*dose*
el fármaco	*medicine*
la fase	*stage*
la glucosa	*glucose*
la humanidad	*humankind*
la infraestructura	*infrastructure*
la insulina	*insulin*
la jeringa	*syringe*
el metabolismo	*metabolism*
la modernidad	*modernity*
la modernización	*modernization*
el nivel	*level*
el organismo	*organism*
el pinchazo	*prick*
la salsa golf	*sauce similar to Thousand Island dressing*
la sangre	*blood*
el sistema inmunológico	*immune system*
cerrar (e:ie) la brecha	*to close the gap*
conmemorar	*to commemorate*
controlar	*to check*
denominarse	*to be called*
desarrollar	*to develop*
dominar	*to prevail, to stand out*
estar interesado/a en	*to be interested in*
inyectarse	to give oneself an injection
medir (e:i)	*to measure*
patentar	*to patent*
redundar en	*to benefit*
suministrar	*to administer*
tornarse	*to become*
ajustado/a a	*adapted to*
bilbaíno/a	*from Bilbao (Spain)*
cardiovascular	*cardiovascular*
citado/a	*cited, quoted*
diabético/a	*diabetic*
farmacéutico/a	*pharmaceutical*
rezagado/a	*falling behind*
abiertamente	*openly, frankly*

Suggestion Encourage students to write sentences using the words from **Variación léxica**.

17B AFICIONES COMUNES

¿Bailas conmigo?

Suggestion If possible, bring in a sample of each type of music in this list. Play the samples and have students try to identify the name in Spanish.

TRES PASOS

TRAE A OTRA PERSONA CONTIGO Y APRENDAN A BAILAR JUNTOS. ¡NO TE LO PIERDAS!

oferta del mes 2 × 1

"A mí me divierte mucho bailar con mi amiga, pero me aburre bailar un solo ritmo y que siempre hagamos los mismos pasos. Por eso vinimos a la escuela. Ven tú también a aprender con nosotros. En clase lo pasamos muy bien."
Miguel

Para todas las edades y niveles

"Desde que he aprendido en Tres pasos, ya no me aburre el baile. Ahora me divierte bailar y que mi mujer y yo bailemos juntos. Gracias al baile, nos entendemos mejor."
Luis

"Lo paso muy bien con mis compañeros de baile. Me río mucho con ellos y nos llevamos de maravilla. A través del baile también nos comunicamos."
Irene

CLASES DE BAILE DE SALÓN

sevillanas	tango	merengue	cumbia
vals	salsa	pasodoble	chachac

Expresar diversión y aburrimiento

- Me divierte bailar contigo y me río mucho.
- Yo también lo paso muy bien, pero me aburre que siempre bailemos lo mismo.

17B.1 **reírse, pasarlo bien**
divertir/aburrir + [*infinitive*]/
que + [*subjunctive*]
conmigo, contigo...

Vocabulario

1

- el paso (de baile) *(dance) step*
- el baile de salón *ballroom dance*
- las sevillanas (*pl.*) *popular dance originated in Seville*
- el vals *waltz*
- el pasodoble *Spanish march-like dance*
- la cumbia *dance typical of the Caribbean coast of Colombia*
- el chachachá *cha-cha*
- divertir(se) (e:ie) *to amuse/to have fun*
- aburrir(se) *to bore/to get bored*

1 Fíjese en el folleto de esta escuela de baile y relacione alguno de los bailes de la lista con las imágenes. ¿Conoce el resto de los bailes? ¿Qué representa el nombre de la escuela? Sample answers: foto 1: salsa; foto 2: tango; "Paso" es un movimiento del pie y los bailes consisten en dar dos, tres o más pasos hacia un lado u otro.

2 a. Lea los comentarios de los alumnos de la escuela y complete las oraciones.

REÍRSE / PASARLO BIEN → Me río. / Lo paso bien.

CONmigo
CONtigo.

b. ¿Qué le aburre a Miguel? ¿Qué le divierte a Luis?

Miguel:
"Me aburre bailar un solo ritmo"
"Me aburre que siempre hagamos los mismos pasos"

Luis:
"Me divierte bailar"
"Me divierte que mi mujer y yo bailemos juntos"

3 a. ¿Con qué asocia la palabra *bailar*? Complete el mapa de ideas y coméntelo con su compañero/a.

bailar → *celebraciones* .... / .... *música*

b. ¿Es el baile una afición popular en su región? ¿Cuáles son los bailes más populares? Y a usted, ¿qué actividades le divierten y cuáles le aburren?

3 Suggestion Discuss when and where people usually dance in this country. Is it part of family gatherings, parties on college campuses, etc.?

Expresar acciones recíprocas

- ¿**Se tutean** en la escuela de baile?
- Sí, **nos tuteamos** todos.

17B.2 Reciprocal verbs

Vocabulario *cont.*

el ritmo *rhythm*
pasarlo bien *to have a good time*
reírse (e:i) *to laugh*
de maravilla *wonderfully*
el aburrimiento *boredom*
el merengue

5

tutearse *to use the* tú *form of address*
enfadarse *to get angry*
abrazarse *to hug each other*
besarse *to kiss each other*
enojarse *to get angry*
quererse (e:ie) *to love each other*
saludarse *to greet each other*

6

escribirse *to write to each other*
mirarse *to look at each other*
contarse (o:ue) *to tell each other*

7

cantar *to sing*

¡OJO!

The preposition **con** followed by **mí** or **ti** forms **conmigo** and **contigo**. This rule does not apply to the preposition **sin**. So you should say, for example, **Vino conmigo; no quiso ir sin mí.**

Bailes

Los bailes son la expresión de los gustos populares de sus países de origen. La salsa en Colombia, Cuba y Puerto Rico; la cumbia en Colombia; el merengue y la bachata en la República Dominicana; el tango en Argentina y Uruguay; y las sevillanas, el flamenco y el pasodoble en España.

4 Fíjese en cómo influye el baile en las relaciones personales de estos alumnos. Lea las siguientes oraciones y explíquelas. Possible answers: Luis entiende a su mujer y ella lo entiende a él. Irene se comunica con sus compañeros de baile y ellos se comunican con ella.

Modelo: *Luis entiende a...*

- "Gracias al baile nos entendemos mejor." ¿Quién entiende a quién?
- "A través del baile también nos comunicamos." ¿Quién se comunica con quién?

5 a. Escuche a una pareja que va a la escuela Tres pasos. Marque verdadero (V) o falso (F). ¿Qué baile eligen finalmente? un curso de vals y otro de bailes latinos

	V	F
1. La pareja y la secretaria de la escuela se tutean.	✓	
2. Los alumnos de los cursos se abrazan y se besan en clase.		✓
3. La pareja se entiende bien.	✓	

b. Fíjese en estas acciones recíprocas. Decida si cada una debe usar **nos, os** o **se**. Luego complete las oraciones.

5b Suggestion First, have students read the sentences and underline the subject in each one. Then have them go through the items a second time and pick the appropriate pronoun.

1. Mi hermano y yo ...nos... queremos mucho.
2. ¿...Os... entendéis tú y tus padres?
3. Peter y María ...se... comunican en inglés.
4. Los buenos amigos siempre ...se... ayudan en tiempos difíciles.
5. Mi abuela y yo ...nos... llevamos bien.
6. Los estudiantes y el profesor ...se... saludan al comienzo de la clase.

6 Piense en qué situaciones realiza usted estas acciones recíprocas y compártalo con su compañero/a.

escribirse • besarse • abrazarse • mirarse • saludarse
quererse • contarse algo • comunicarse en español

Modelo: *Mi amiga alemana y yo nos escribimos una vez al mes.*

MI EXPERIENCIA

7 Averigüe con qué aficiones o actividades lo pasa bien o se aburre su compañero/a y con quién se entiende mejor para hacerlas.

GUIÓN DE TRABAJO

¿Te divierte tocar un instrumento?	No, me aburre mucho tocar. Me aburre que sea necesario practicar tanto para tocar bien.
¿Con qué/quién lo pasas bien?	Me divierte... y me río mucho con...
¿Quién comparte esa afición contigo?	Mi pareja/mejor amiga/hermano... Nos entendemos/llevamos/comunicamos muy bien.

Suggestion Have students work in pairs. Ask them to create a dance school for your community and write a radio ad for the school.

Practice more at **vhlcentral.com.**

SAM: Actividades pp. 365–367

Buena comunicación

Compruebe el grado de afinidad que tiene con sus amigos, familiares, compañeros de trabajo...

GUSTOS

1. Le gusta que sus amigos, familiares...
   a. sean divertidos, cuenten chistes, se rían mucho.
   b. sean personas serias e intelectuales.
   c. expresen su estado de ánimo en cada momento.
   d. sean honestos y le digan siempre la verdad.

2. Le gusta que...
   a. tengan el mismo gusto por el arte, la literatura, etc.
   b. sean aficionados del mismo equipo de fútbol.
   c. miren los mismos programas de televisión.
   d. tengan gustos diferentes de los suyos.

INTERESES

3. Cuando sale a divertirse, no le interesa que sus amigos...
   a. le hablen de política.
   b. le hagan preguntas personales.
   c. le cuenten sus problemas.
   d. estén mirando el celular constantemente.

4. Le interesa que...
   a. le recomienden libros, música, películas...
   b. le cuenten dónde están las mejores ofertas.
   c. lo/la pongan al día sobre los últimos chismes.
   d. le propongan hacer viajes juntos.

PREFERENCIAS

5. En su cumpleaños prefiere que...
   a. le preparen alguna sorpresa.
   b. nadie lo recuerde.
   c. le hagan regalos prácticos, como ropa, algo para la cocina, etc.
   d. sus familiares salgan con usted a cenar.

6. Ante la opción de quedarse en casa un sábado, le gusta más que...
   a. le propongan ir a un centro comercial.
   b. lo/la inviten a un restaurante y a ver una película.
   c. le organicen una excursión.
   d. lo/la llamen para salir a pasear por la ciudad.

Resultados: cuente el número de respuestas iguales.
6 respuestas = Son totalmente afines. 5 = Son muy afines. 4 = Son bastante afines. 3 = Comparten algunos intereses.
2 = No son muy afines. 1 = Tienen muy poco en común. 0 = No son nada afines.

Expresar gustos, intereses y preferencias

- En un restaurante, ¿le gusta que le recomienden un menú?
- No, prefiero que no me digan nada.

17B.3 **gustar/interesar** + **que** + [*subjunctive*]; **preferir** + **que** + [*subjunctive*]

Vocabulario

8
contar (o:ue) chistes *to tell jokes*
decir la verdad *to tell the truth*
poner (a alguien) al día *to update (someone)*
el chisme *piece of gossip*
la sorpresa *surprise*
ser afín *to have a lot in common*
la afinidad, intelectual, invitar

10
la cualidad *characteristic, feature*

8 Haga el test y compare sus resultados con los de su compañero/a. ¿Tienen gustos, intereses y preferencias comunes?

9 Subraye las formas verbales de las respuestas del test. Después complete la tabla de verbos.

	indicativo	subjuntivo
CONTAR RECORDAR	(yo) cuento recuerdo	(yo) cuente recuerde
RECOMENDAR	recomiendo	recomiende
DECIR HACER PONER PROPONER SALIR	digo hago pongo propongo salgo	diga haga ponga proponga salga

10 Basándose en el test, describa con tres cualidades su personalidad. Sus compañeros adivinan cuáles son sus gustos, intereses y preferencias.

11 Añada otra opción para cada situación del test y comparta las opciones adicionales con un(a) compañero/a.

11 Expansion Ask the class if this test would work to determine compatibility in a romantic relationship. If not, have them modify it or add questions so that it suits partners in a romantic relationship.

Estrategia

Reforzar una negación

- A Pepa no le gusta que le hagan regalos.
- Es verdad. **No** le gusta **nada**.

Reaccionar de forma negativa

Me molesta que me haya mentido.

Me preocupa que no hayas aprobado el examen.

Me decepciona que hayas reaccionado así.

Me entristece que hayan decidido no venir.

17B.4 **me molesta/preocupa/decepciona/entristece + que +** [*subjunctive*]
Present perfect subjunctive

Vocabulario

14

molestar *to bother, to annoy*

mentir (e:ie) *to lie*

decepcionar *to disappoint*

entristecer (zc) *to sadden*

postergar *to postpone*

preocupar *to worry*

17

el rendimiento *performance*

12 Suggestion Remind students that River Plate is an Argentinean team. Often they are referred to simply as **River**.

12 a. Ordene el diálogo de estas dos personas que hablan sobre el fútbol.

2 A mí tampoco, no me gusta nada el fútbol.

3 Pero como eres argentino seguro que te interesa más que gane River Plate.

1 A mí no me interesa nada que gane o pierda un equipo de fútbol, ¿y a ti?

4 No es verdad. No me interesa nada.

b. Observe cómo se refuerza una negación. Por cierto, ¿a usted le interesa el fútbol? ¿Hay algún deporte que no le gusta nada?

13 Exprese la reacción de estas personas ante los sucesos que se mencionan.

Modelo: *Mi amigo llegó una hora tarde.*
(molesta) Me molesta que haya llegado una hora tarde.

1. *Te olvidaste de mi cumpleaños.*
   (decepciona) Me decepciona que te hayas olvidado de mi cumpleaños.
2. *Mis padres postergaron su viaje.*
   (entristece) Me entristece que hayan postergado su viaje.
3. *Mi novio leyó mi correo electrónico.*
   (molesta) Me molesta que haya leído mi correo electrónico.
4. *Mis hermanos no llamaron desde que salieron esta mañana.*
   (preocupa) Me preocupa que no hayan llamado todavía.

14 a. Fíjese en la viñeta cómica. ¿Tienen estas personas algún interés común? Coméntelo con su compañero/a. ¿Hay buena comunicación en esta familia?
ver la televisión

b. Comente con su compañero/a qué intereses comparten ustedes con sus respectivas familias.

15 Escriba lo que le gusta, lo que le interesa y lo que prefiere en relación con estos temas y compare con su compañero/a. Añada otros temas si lo desea.

- los deportes
- los viajes
- la política

MI EXPERIENCIA

16 Expansion Also share your likes, interests, and preferences about teaching Spanish. Have students identify those that combine well with their own.

16 Hable con su compañero/a y descubra sus gustos, intereses y preferencias sobre el aprendizaje del español.

GUIÓN DE TRABAJO

¿Cuáles son tus gustos, intereses y preferencias sobre la manera de aprender español?

Me interesa más que me enseñen palabras argentinas (o cubanas, etc...).
Prefiero que me den deberes para hacer en casa.
Me gusta que el profesor nos recomiende música en español.

¿Qué aspectos te preocupan sobre tu rendimiento en el curso al que estás asistiendo?

Me preocupa que todavía no haya aprendido a usar bien el subjuntivo.

Practice more at **vhlcentral.com.**

SAM: Actividades pp. 368–370

17B

Amanda y Rubén, la vida es un tango

Amanda Roa y Rubén Sosa ganaron el concurso de tango para parejas maduras que se celebró en la plaza Dorrego del barrio porteño de San Telmo, en Buenos Aires.

Amanda, ¿desde cuándo baila tango?

Empecé de joven. Recién llegada de Paraguay, conocí a Rubén y él me enseñó. Me divierte bailar, la paso bien y creo que no lo hago mal.

¿Y usted, Rubén, siempre bailó tango?

Era jovencito y la gente me decía: "Pibe, vos sos muy bueno en esto del tango, no podés seguir bailando gratarola", y así empecé. La pasé bien pero, realmente, nunca viví solo de bailar.

¿Cuántos años llevan casados?

(Amanda) *Mirá, 15 años nomás. Pero nos conocemos desde hace 43 años. Rubén fue mi primer novio, pero nos separamos. Después de más de 20 años nos vimos un día casualmente cuando él iba manejando y yo, en colectivo.*

Amanda y Rubén, en el último tango ganador del concurso

Como Rubén es muy buen bailarín, me enamoré otra vez al volver a ser su pareja de tango. Nos llevamos rebién y nos amamos profundamente.

¿Cuál es su tango favorito?

(Rubén) Volver, *siempre volvemos al primer amor.*

(Amanda) *Sí,* Volver, *y me gusta más que lo cante una voz masculina. La versión de Carlos Gardel, por ejemplo, es buenísima.*

Además del tango, ¿tienen otras aficiones comunes?

(Rubén) *Sí, casi todas. Nos entendemos muy bien. Somos hinchas de Boca Juniors, y nos divierte mucho ir a la cancha. También somos buenos cocineros. Solemos organizar cenas con amigos; preferimos que vengan a casa y pasarla bien acá.*

(Amanda) *Rubén hace unos asados muy ricos y yo soy buena con las empanadas. Bueno, digamos que se pueden comer…*

Gracias por atendernos y ¡felicitaciones a los dos!

Suggestion Read aloud Amanda's last statement and point out that she is using this phrase to show modesty about her skills.

Hablar de habilidades

- ¿Eres bueno para el baile?
- No lo hago mal. Soy bueno con los ritmos latinos. Además, tomo clases particulares con Verónica. Ella es muy buena profesora.

17B.5 **ser bueno/a en/para/con + [*noun*]**
ser + buen(a)/mal(a) + [*noun*]
no lo hago (nada) mal

Vocabulario

17

maduro/a *mature*
porteño/a *of/from the city of Buenos Aires*
recién *just*
pasarla bien (*Amér. L.*) *to have a good time*
ser bueno/a (en algo) *to be good (at something)*
ser malo/a (en algo) *to be bad (at something)*
el/la pibe/a (*Arg.*) *young boy/girl*
gratarola (*C. S.*) *for free*
nomás *only*
casualmente *by chance*
manejar (*Amér. L.*) *to drive*
el colectivo (*Arg.*) *bus*

17 Mire a la pareja de la foto. ¿Qué están haciendo y dónde? ¿Cree que son solo pareja de baile o también en la vida real? Lea la entrevista y compruebe.
Están bailando tango en una plaza de Buenos Aires (Argentina).
• Son pareja de baile y también en la vida real.

18 ¿Cuál es el motivo de la entrevista? ¿Qué relación tiene esta pareja con el tango? ¿Desde cuándo? Ganaron el concurso de tango para parejas maduras de la plaza Dorrego de San Telmo (Buenos Aires). • Se divierten con el tango, la pasan bien. • Amanda empezó cuando llegó de Paraguay; Rubén baila desde joven.

19 ¿Cuáles son las aficiones de Amanda y Rubén? ¿Qué dicen de sus habilidades? bailar: Rubén dice que es muy bueno y Amanda dice que no lo hace mal; el fútbol: Les divierte ir a la cancha; cocinar: Rubén hace buenos asados y Amanda es muy buena con las empanadas.
- bailar: *Rubén dice que es muy bueno y Amanda dice que...*
- ...

20 ¿En qué es usted bueno/a? ¿Y su compañero/a?

Modelo: • *¿Eres bueno en la cocina?*
• *No lo hago nada mal.*

21 Fíjese en estas palabras y expresiones típicas del habla argentina que aparecen en el texto. ¿Qué significan? Escriba un equivalente y diga si conoce otros ejemplos de argentinismos.

1. pasarla bien .... pasarlo bien
2. pibe .... chico
3. vos sos .... tú eres
4. podés .... puedes
5. gratarola .... gratis
6. mirá .... mire
7. nomás .... solamente
8. manejando .... conduciendo
9. colectivo .... autobús
10. rebién .... muy bien
11. acá .... aquí
12. felicitaciones .... enhorabuena/felicidades

22 ¿Conoce usted a parejas que comparten una misma pasión como el baile? ¿Son buenos en lo que hacen?

Language Notes Draw attention to the word **gratarola** and explain that this is a **lunfardo** word derived from **gratis**. Students will learn about **lunfardo** on page 427. Point out the word **rebién** and explain that **re-** is a shortened version of the prefix **requete-**, which is used to emphasize the quality of something. **Requete-** is used in most countries, whereas **re-** is only primarily in Argentina. Then point out the phrase **ser hincha de** and tell students that **hincha** is a masculine and feminine noun (**el hincha, la hincha**).

Vocabulario *cont.*

rebién (*fam., Arg.*) *very well*
ser hincha de *to be a supporter of*
la cancha (*Amér. L.*) *sports field*
acá *here*
la clase particular *private lesson*

23

el bandoneón *type of accordion*
el/la bandoneonista *bandoneón player*
criticar *to criticize*
el sello discográfico *record label*
editar *to release (music)*
más tarde *later*
la banda sonora *sound track*
el/la ciudadano/a ilustre *distinguished citizen*
el porqué *reason*
contemporáneo/a, el/la enemigo/a

25

la jerga *slang, jargon*
carecer (de) *to lack*
el cuerpo *body*
el delito *crime*

26

la sabiduría *wisdom*
alejados/as entre sí *far from each other*
la estrofa *stanza*
la frente *forehead*
agarrar *to grab*
tener canas *to have gray hair*
apenado/a *sad*
el dialecto, diferenciarse de

OPINIÓN

¿Cree que bailar favorece la buena comunicación?

¿Hay edad para el baile, para aprender un idioma, para el amor...?

25 Suggestion Explain that one common characteristic of **lunfardo** is the word play known as **vesre** (derived from **al revés**), or reversal of syllables. Give students **lunfardo** words and have them work in pairs to guess their meaning. Ex: **gotán (tango), gomías (amigos), feca con chele (café con leche)**

23 a. ¿Sabe quién era Astor Piazzolla? ¿En qué cree que fue bueno? Lea el artículo y compruebe. Fue uno de los músicos argentinos más importantes: innovó el tango. • Fue bueno en el arte de componer tangos y bandas sonoras para películas, también con el bandoneón.

Astor Piazzolla (Mar del Plata, 1921; Buenos Aires; 1992), compositor y bandoneonista argentino, es uno de los músicos de tango más importantes.

En los años 50 y 60, Piazzolla introdujo una nueva forma de hacer tango. Por entonces, fue muy criticado por los tangueros clásicos. Para ellos, estas composiciones no eran tango. Piazzolla respondió con una nueva definición: "Es música contemporánea de Buenos Aires." Sus obras no se escuchaban en la radio, y los sellos discográficos no editaban su música.

"Sí, es cierto, soy un enemigo del tango; pero del tango como ellos lo entienden. [...] Si todo ha cambiado, también debe cambiar la música de Buenos Aires."

PIAZZOLLA, Astor: *En Revista Antena Buenos Aires, 1954.*

Más tarde, lo reconocieron intelectuales y músicos de todo el mundo.

En sus últimos diez años, escribió más de 300 tangos y unas 50 bandas sonoras de películas. Dio conciertos en Europa y América. Buenos Aires lo nombró "ciudadano ilustre."

Su música no se parece a ninguna otra: es, simplemente, Piazzolla.

b. ¿Qué título resume mejor la trayectoria de Astor Piazzolla? Proponga otro título adecuado.

"Piazzolla, único" "Otra idea del tango" "..................................."

c. Lea el texto y asocie la visión que Piazzolla tenía del tango con alguna de estas palabras. Explique el porqué de su elección a su compañero/a.
Suggested answers: innovación, cambio, modernidad

innovación • cambio • adaptación • tradición • modernidad • respeto

24 Piense en un(a) artista que conoce y escriba un breve texto sobre sus habilidades.

25 a. ¿Sabe qué es el lunfardo? Compruebe en el texto. Es un habla que procede de los inmigrantes italianos que vivían en Buenos Aires y Montevideo en la segunda mitad del siglo XIX.

El lunfardo es inseparable del tango. No se trata de un idioma, un dialecto ni una jerga, porque carece de gramática propia. El lunfardo es un conjunto de palabras (aproximadamente 5000) referidas a las distintas partes del cuerpo, la comida, la bebida, el dinero, la ropa, el delito, etc. Nace durante la segunda mitad del siglo XIX en Buenos Aires y Montevideo gracias a la inmigración italiana, aunque también tiene influencias de otros idiomas como el gallego, el francés, el portugués, el quechua y el guaraní, entre otros. Muchas palabras y expresiones del lunfardo ya son de uso habitual, por ejemplo: *morfar* (comer), *laburar* (trabajar), *mango* (dinero), *guita* (dinero). La cantidad y los términos de lunfardo que se utilizan dependen del hablante y de la persona con quien este se comunica, ya que muchas palabras del lunfardo son vistas como vulgares.

b. ¿Ha escuchado alguna de estas palabras en tangos o de personas argentinas? ¿Qué significa la oración "Laburo noche y día, pero no tengo un mango"? Trabajo noche y día, pero no tengo dinero.

Practice more at **vhlcentral.com.**

SAM: Actividades pp. 371–376

26 a. ¿Para qué es bueno el tango según Mario Benedetti? para el contacto y la comunicación entre las personas, para conocerse

"Es virtualmente imposible que, después de varios tangos, dos cuerpos no empiecen a conocerse. En esa sabiduría, en ese desarrollo del contacto se diferencia el tango de otros pasos de baile que mantienen a los bailarines alejados entre sí [...]. El abrazo del tango es sobre todo comunicación."

BENEDETTI, Mario: *La borra del café*. Madrid, Punto de Lectura, 2007.

b. Lea ahora el fragmento del tango *Volver* y relacione las estrofas con las emociones e ideas siguientes: nostalgia, tristeza y paso del tiempo. Después relacione las palabras señaladas con su significado.

Volver,
con la frente **marchita**[1],
las nieves del tiempo
platearon[2] mi sien.

Sentir, que es un **soplo**[3] la vida,
que veinte años no es nada,
que **febril**[4] la mirada,
errante[5] en las sombras,
te busca y te nombra.

Vivir,
con el alma **aferrada**[6]
a un dulce recuerdo,
que lloro otra vez.

Música: Carlos Gardel
Versos: Alfredo Le Pera

3 Espacio muy breve de tiempo.

5 Que va de un lugar a otro.

1 Sin vitalidad.

6 Agarrada fuertemente.

2 Tener canas en el pelo. Envejecer.

4 Inquieta, apenada.

26c **Suggestion** If having students sing the lyrics, try to play the music in the background.

c. Con su grupo, ahora busque en Internet los versos de otro tango, como *Mi Buenos Aires querido, El día que me quieras* o *Balada para un loco.* Compártalos con el resto de la clase y luego cántelos. Comente con sus compañeros qué emociones le produjo escuchar esos versos.

TAREA FINAL

Test de afinidad

En parejas, piensen en dos preguntas para conocer las aficiones de sus compañeros.

Hagan una lista común con las preguntas de todos.

Háganse el test unos a otros.

Hagan el balance de aficiones de la clase. ¿Comparten muchas?

Suggestion Encourage students to use different questions than those in the test on page 424.

YO PUEDO...

- **Puedo expresar diversión y aburrimiento.**
  ¿Qué le aburre y qué le divierte cuando está en una fiesta? ¿Con quién se ríe?
- **Puedo expresar acciones recíprocas.**
  Cuente todo lo que hacen recíprocamente usted y su mejor amigo/a.
- **Puedo expresar gustos, intereses y preferencias.**
  Nombre algo que le gusta, algo que le interesa y algo que prefiere de su clase de español.
- **Puedo hablar de habilidades.**
  Piense en alguien cercano a usted. ¿En qué es bueno/a esta persona?

GRAMÁTICA FUNCIONAL

You may wish to teach students the verb **sonreír** (*to smile*) at this point, and explain that it follows the same conjugation pattern as **reír**.

17B.1 Express delight and boredom

reírse, pasarlo bien, divertir/aburrir + [*infinitive*]/**que** + [*subjunctive*] 5.7.1, 5.20, 6.4, 6.8 **conmigo, contigo** 6.6, 10.4

- Use the reflexive verb **reírse** (*to laugh*) to express delight. **Reírse** is an irregular verb.

REÍRSE			
(yo)	me **río**	(nosotros/as)	nos **reímos**
(tú)	te **ríes**	(vosotros/as)	os reís
(usted, él, ella)	se **ríe**	(ustedes, ellos/as)	se **ríen**

Me río mucho con mis amigos.
I laugh a lot with my friends.

- Use the expression **pasarlo bien** (*to have a good time*) to describe having fun. The expression **pasarla bien**, more common in Latin America than in Spain, is also correct.

¿Lo has pasado bien?
Have you had a good time?

- Use [*indirect object pronoun*] + **divertir** (*to have a good time, to enjoy*)/**aburrir** (*to get bored*) + **que** + [*subjunctive*] to express delight and boredom.

(a mí)	me		
(a ti)	te		
(a usted, él, ella)	le	divierte	+ que +
(a nosotros/as)	nos	aburre	[*subjunctive*]
(a vosotros/as)	os		
(a ustedes, ellos/as)	les		

A Mónica **le aburre que** su pareja siempre **baile** salsa.
*It bores Mónica that her partner always **dances** salsa.*

- As you have seen, the subjunctive is used with many expressions when a sentence has two verbs with different subjects. If the two verbs refer to the same person, use an infinitive after **divertir/aburrir**.

Me divierte leer. *I enjoy reading.*

Les aburre leer el periódico. *They get bored when they read the paper.*

¡OJO! **Divertir** and **aburrir** can also be used reflexively.

No nado porque **me aburro**. *I don't swim because **I get bored**.*

Me divierto cuando nado. *I have fun when I swim.*

- When used with the preposition **con**, the pronouns **yo** and **tú** take the forms **conmigo** and **contigo**. In all other cases, subject pronouns are used with the preposition **con**.

Lo paso muy bien **contigo**.
*I have a good time **with you**.*

Viviana se ríe mucho **con ellos**.
*Viviana laughs a lot **with them**.*

Suggestion Point out that **divertir(se)** is an **e:ie** stem-changing verb.

¡Póngalo en práctica!

G1 Complete las conversaciones.

Anoche fui a un salón de baile y (1)...lo pasé... (yo, pasarlo) fenomenal: bailé salsa, tango y (2)...me reí... (yo, reírse) mucho con unos chicos muy graciosos.

A mí, en cambio, no me divierte mucho (3)...bailar... (bailar).

• • • • •

¿(4)...Te divierte... (Divertir, tú) cocinar (5)...conmigo... (tú y yo)?

Sí, pero me aburre que tú lo (6)...hagas... (hacer) todo.

• • • • •

Me divierte (7)...ir... (ir) al cine para ver comedias con mis amigos.

A mí también me gustan las comedias, pero me divierte que mis amigos y yo (8)...alquilemos... (alquilar) películas para verlas juntos en casa.

G2 Una las frases para formar oraciones lógicas.

1. ¡Cállate! Me aburre ...b...
2. Me divierte mucho ...c...
3. Nos aburrimos mucho ...a...
4. A mi hermano y a mí nos divierte que ...d...

a. cuando vamos a la ópera.
b. que hables tanto.
c. ir al teatro.
d. papá se vista de Santa Claus.

G3 Complete el párrafo con las palabras y expresiones de la lista.

le aburre | conmigo | río | venga | me divierte

Me (1)...río... mucho cuando mi hermano se viste de payaso (*clown*). ¡Es tan divertido! También (2)...me divierte... mucho que (3)...venga... al parque (4)...conmigo... . Sé qué a él (5)...le aburre... ir al parque, pero lo hace por mí.

Practice more at **vhlcentral.com.**

GRAMÁTICA FUNCIONAL

17B.2 Express reciprocal actions

Reciprocal verbs 5.7.2, 6.4

- Use reciprocal verbs (**verbos recíprocos**) to express a shared or reciprocal action between two or more people or things. Reciprocal verbs are only conjugated in plural forms and are accompanied by the plural reflexive pronouns (**nos, os, se**).

  Marisela y Jorge **se quieren** mucho.
  Marisela and Jorge ***love each other*** *a lot.*

  Se hablan todos los días y **se ven** cuatro veces por semana.
  They talk to each other *every day and* ***they see each other*** *four times a week.*

- The reflexive pronoun is understood as *(to) each other* or *(to) one another*. When a verb is reciprocal, you can add **el uno al otro/la una a la otra** (*each other*) or **mutuamente** (*mutually*) to make this idea explicit.

  Mi vecina y yo **nos saludamos** todos los días.
  My neighbor and I ***greet each other*** *every day.*

  Os entendéis muy bien **el uno al otro**.
  You understand each other *very well.*

You may wish to explain that structures with other prepositions, such as **el uno con el otro** or **el uno por el otro**, are possible, depending on the preposition used with the main verb.

- Examples of other reciprocal verbs include **abrazarse** (*to hug each other*), **amarse** (*to love each other*), **besarse** (*to kiss each other*), **encontrarse** (*to meet*), **escribirse** (*to write to each other*), **mirarse** (*to look at each other*), and **darse la mano** (*to shake hands*).

  Raúl y Maribel **se miraron a los ojos**.
  Raúl and Maribel ***looked each other in the eye.***

G5 Expansion Have students use their imagination to write two additional sentences for each photo. Ex: **Las mujeres: Se tutean. La pareja: Se entienden muy bien.**

- Use the verb **tutearse** to talk about the use of the familiar form **tú** in conversation. Synonymous expressions include **darse del tú** and **tratarse de tú**.

  Nos tuteamos.
  We use the **tú** *form with each other.*

¡OJO!

Context is important to distinguish reciprocal verbs from plural reflexive verbs. For example, note the difference in meaning between these two sentences:

Nos llamamos una vez por semana.
We call each other *once a week.*

Nos llamamos Armando y Estela.
Our names *are Armando and Estela.*

¡Póngalo en práctica!

G4 Complete las oraciones.

- Vosotros, ¿cómo (1) ...os... saludáis en Argentina?
- (2) ...Nos... besamos también.

Mis padres (3) ...se... quieren (el uno al otro) como el primer día.

Mi amiga Marisa vive en Buenos Aires, pero (4) ...nos... escribimos casi todos los días.

Los primos de Graciela (5) ...se... visitan (el uno al otro) con frecuencia.

Cristián y yo (6) ...nos... encontramos en un café antes de la clase de historia para estudiar juntos.

G5 ¿Qué hacen las personas de las fotos?

Suggested answers:

1. Se abrazan./Se saludan.

2. Se besan.

3. Se hablan.

4. Se dan la mano./Se saludan.

G6 Complete las oraciones con la forma correcta del verbo recíproco.

1. En el trabajo, mis compañeros y yo ...nos tuteamos... (tutearse).
2. Los primos de Gisela siempre ...se mandan... (mandarse) tarjetas de cumpleaños.
3. Enrique y yo decidimos ...encontrarnos... (encontrarse) en la entrada del museo para ver juntos la nueva exposición.
4. Vosotros ...os llamáis... (llamarse) casi todos los días, ¿no?
5. Camila y José Luis ...se aman... (amarse) mucho y se van a casar el año que viene.
6. Anoche en la fiesta de despedida, Paloma y Nicolás ...se abrazaron... (abrazarse) antes de salir.

Suggestion You may also want to introduce the verbs **odiarse** and **(no) aguantarse**. Then ask students to write brief descriptions of famous people, using reciprocal verbs. Divide the class into small groups and have students read their descriptions aloud for their classmates to guess who is being described. Ex: **Son actores. Antes se amaban, pero ahora se odian. Cuando se ven en la alfombra roja, no se hablan. (Jennifer Aniston y Brad Pitt)**

Practice more at **vhlcentral.com.**

GRAMÁTICA FUNCIONAL

17B.3 Express tastes, interests, and preferences

gustar/interesar + que + [*subjunctive*]; preferir + que + [*subjunctive*];
Irregular subjunctive forms 5.11.1, 5.20, 5.21.1c

- Use **gustar/interesar + que +** [*subjunctive*] to express likes and interests when the verbs in the sentence have different subjects. Use these verbs with indirect object pronouns.

  Me gusta que mis amigos me **llamen** si van a llegar tarde.
  I like my friends to call me if they are going to arrive late.

- Use the infinitive with **gustar/interesar** if both verbs in the sentence refer to the same person.

  No me gusta contar mis historias de viajes.
  I don't like to tell stories about my trips.

- Use the construction **preferir + que +** [*subjunctive*] to talk about preferences.

  Prefiero que vayamos de compras más tarde.
  I prefer that we go shopping later.

  Prefiero ir al gimnasio después de la clase.
  I prefer to go to the gym after class.

- As you learned in **15B.4**, **-ar** and **-er** verbs with a stem change in the **yo** form of the present indicative reflect the same stem change in the present subjunctive, except for the **nosotros/as** and **vosotros/as** forms.

CONTAR (**cue**nto)	→	**cue**nte, **cue**ntes, **cue**nte, contemos, contéis, **cue**nten (*similar verbs:* recordar, volver, poder)
RECOMENDAR (recom**ie**ndo)	→	recom**ie**nde, recom**ie**ndes, recom**ie**nde, recomendemos, recomendéis, recom**ie**nden (*similar verbs:* querer, preferir)

- As you learned in **15B.1**, if the verb has an irregular **yo** form in the present, this spelling is used in all forms in the subjunctive.

PONER (pon**go**)	→	pon**ga**, pon**gas**, pon**ga**, pon**gamos**, pon**gáis**, pon**gan** (*similar verbs:* proponer, hacer)

17B.4 Express dislikes and reproach

molestar/preocupar + que + [*subjunctive*]; decepcionar/ entristecer + que + [*subjunctive*] 5.11.1, 5.21.1d
Present perfect subjunctive 5.22.1

- Use **molestar/preocupar** (*to bother/to concern; to worry*) to express dislikes and concerns. Use **decepcionar/entristecer** (*to disappoint; to sadden*) to express reproach or disappointment. These verbs are followed by **que** + [*subjunctive*] when the verbs in the sentence have different subjects. Use these verbs with indirect object pronouns, and use the infinitive when both verbs in the sentence refer to the same person.

  Me molesta que la gente **fume** cuando estoy comiendo.
  It bothers me if people smoke when I am eating.

  Me decepciona que no me **llames**.
  It disappoints me that you don't call.

  Me preocupa tener que leer tanto para mañana.
  It worries me to have to read so much for tomorrow.

¡Póngalo en práctica!

G7 Complete las oraciones.

Me gusta que mis amigos (1) sean (ser) divertidos y me gusta (2) pasarlo (yo, pasarlo) bien con ellos.

Me interesa que (3) volvamos (nosotros, volver) a este lugar en algún momento.

Me gusta que mi familia y yo (4) podamos (poder) comunicarnos.

- ¿Os interesa que os (5) proponga (yo, proponer) otra opción?
- Sí, preferimos que nos (6) hagas (tú, hacer) otra propuesta mejor.

G8 Complete las oraciones.

1. Eva prefiere (preferir) que vosotros le recomendéis (recomendar) un restaurante menos caro.
2. A Juan Carlos le interesa (interesar) alquilar (alquilar) un apartamento en Barcelona durante el verano.
3. ¿Te gusta (gustar) que tus hermanos te llamen (llamar) por Skype?
4. No me gusta (gustar) que mis padres me digan (decir) lo que debería hacer.

G9 Elija la opción correcta para completar cada oración.

1. Nos molesta que **llegar/llegues** a casa tan tarde.
2. Me preocupa no **poder/pueda** pagar las facturas.
3. A mi madre le decepciona que mi hermano no **ser/sea** abogado.
4. Me entristece no **verte/te vea** más a menudo.
5. ¿No te molesta **salir/salgas** sin paraguas con este tiempo?
6. Nos preocupa que la abuela ya no **reírse/se ría** como antes.

Suggestion Ask students to write a description about their likes, interests, and preferences. Collect the papers, shuffle them, and read each one aloud for the class to guess who it is.

Practice more at **vhlcentral.com.**

GRAMÁTICA FUNCIONAL

- Use the present perfect subjunctive (**pretérito perfecto de subjuntivo**) in order to comment on past events. The **pretérito perfecto de subjuntivo** is used to refer to past events that in some way act upon the present.

 Me decepciona que no me **hayas llamado**.
 *It disappoints me that you **haven't called**.*

- The **pretérito perfecto de subjuntivo** is formed with the present subjunctive of the verb **haber** + [*past participle*]. The verb **haber** is irregular in the present subjunctive. You have learned regular past participles in **6A.4** and irregular past participles in **7B.4**.

HABER			
(yo)	**haya**	(nosotros/as)	**hayamos**
(tú)	**hayas**	(vosotros/as)	**hayáis**
(usted, él, ella)	**haya**	(ustedes, ellos/as)	**hayan**

 Me molesta que no me **hayáis ayudado** con la limpieza.
 *It bothers me that you **didn't help** me with the cleaning.*

17B.5 Talk about skills and abilities

ser bueno/a en/para/con + [*noun*] 5.8.7, 10.4, 10.12, 10.15
no lo hago (nada) mal 11.1 **ser buen(a)/mal(a)** + [*noun*]

- Use **ser bueno/a** or **malo/a** + **en/para/con** to talk about someone's or something's abilities. Use **en/para** + [*discipline*] and **con** + [*a specific thing*].

 Luisa **es muy buena en** matemáticas/**para** el diseño/**con** las cuentas.
 *Luisa **is very good at** math/**at** design/**at** calculations.*

- Use **(nada) mal** as an adverb of manner to describe something that someone does well.

 Me gusta jugar al tenis y no lo hago **nada mal**.
 *I like playing tennis and I play **pretty well**.*

- Use the construction **ser buen(a)/mal(a)** + [*noun*] to describe someone's skill in a specific role.

 Andrés **es buen pintor**.
 *Andrés **is a good painter**.*

- When **bueno/a** or **malo/a** are placed after the noun, the adjective emphasizes the good or bad qualities of the individual's personal characteristics, instead of highlighting the abilities of the person.

 Es **buena profesora**.
 *She is **a good teacher**. (She is good at her profession.)*

 Es una **profesora buena**.
 *She is **a good teacher**. (She is a teacher and a good person.)*

¡Póngalo en práctica!

G10 **Complete las oraciones con la forma correcta del verbo en el pretérito perfecto de subjuntivo.**

1. No soporto que mis amigos no me ....hayan dicho.... (decir) si vienen a la fiesta o no.
2. A David le parece raro que Candelaria no lo ....haya llamado.... (llamar).
3. Nos preocupa que no ....hayas leído.... (tú, leer) el manual de instrucciones.
4. A los profesores les extraña que ....hayamos decidido.... (nosotros, decidir) estudiar en la cafetería.
5. No creo que nuestro equipo ....haya ganado.... (ganar).
6. Pía no está totalmente segura de que sus compañeros ....hayan ido.... (ir) a la biblioteca.

G11 **Complete las oraciones. Use el pretérito perfecto de subjuntivo en la segunda cláusula.**

1. Nos ....decepciona.... (decepcionar) que Teo y Lucas todavía no ....hayan llegado.... (llegar).
2. Me ....entristece.... (entristecer) que mi hermano ....haya olvidado.... (olvidar) mi cumpleaños otra vez.
3. A Uriel le ....molesta.... (molestar) que no ....hayáis hecho.... (vosotros, hacer) la tarea para hoy.

G12 **Complete las conversaciones.** Suggested answers:

(1)....Soy.... (Yo, ser) bueno (2)....para.... la cocina, sobre todo (3)....con.... los postres, pero no sé bailar. ¿Y tú?

A mí me gusta bailar. Sí, creo que (4)....soy.... (ser) buena (5)....para.... el baile. No lo (6)....hago.... (yo, hacer) mal. Y en la universidad, ¿cómo te va?

En general, soy bueno (7)....en.... las ciencias, pero las humanidades me cuestan un poco más.

Para mí es lo contrario: historia es mi materia preferida. Tengo un (8)....buen.... profesor este semestre; explica muy bien el material.

Suggestion Point out that using **no... (nada) mal** is a subtle way to talk about one's own skills.

Practice more at **vhlcentral.com.**

VOCABULARIO

¿Bailas conmigo?

el aburrimiento	*boredom*
el baile de salón	*ballroom dance*
el chachachá	*cha-cha*
la cumbia	*dance typical of the Caribbean coast of Colombia*
el merengue	*merengue*
el paso (de baile)	*(dance) step*
el pasodoble	*typical Spanish march-like dance*
el ritmo	*rhythm*
las sevillanas (*pl.*)	*popular dance originated in Seville*
el vals	*waltz*
abrazarse	*to hug each other*
aburrir	*to bore*
aburrirse	*to get bored*
besarse	*to kiss each other*
cantar	*to sing*
contarse (o:ue)	*to tell each other*
divertir (e:ie)	*to amuse*
divertirse (e:ie)	*to have fun*
enfadarse	*to get angry*
enojarse	*to get angry*
escribirse	*to write to each other*
mirarse	*to look at each other*
pasarlo bien	*to have a good time*
quererse (e:ie)	*to love each other*
reírse (e:i)	*to laugh*
saludarse	*to greet each other*
tutearse	*to use the* **tú** *form of address*
de maravilla	*wonderfully*

Buena comunicación

la afinidad	*afinity*
el chisme	*piece of gossip*
la cualidad	*characteristic, feature*
el rendimiento	*performance*
la sorpresa	*surprise*
contar (o:ue) chistes	*to tell jokes*
decepcionar	*to disappoint*
decir la verdad	*to tell the truth*
entristecer (zc)	*to sadden*
invitar	*to invite*
mentir (e:ie)	*to lie*
molestar	*to bother, to annoy*
poner (a alguien) al día	*to update (someone)*
postergar	*to postpone*
preocupar	*to worry*
ser afín	*to have a lot in common*
intelectual	*intellectual*

Variación léxica

aquí ⟷ **acá** (*Amér. L.*)

el chisme ⟷ **el cotilleo** (*Esp.*)

nomás (*Amér. L.*) ⟷ **no más** ⟷ **solamente**

pasarlo bien/mal ⟷ **pasarla bien/mal** (*Amér. L.*) ⟷ **pasárselo bien/mal** (*Esp.*)

el/la pibe/a (*Arg.*) ⟷ **el/la chamaco/a** (*Méx.*) ⟷ **el/la chaval(a)** (*Esp.*)

muy bien ⟷ **rebién** (*fam., Arg.*)

Amanda y Rubén

la banda sonora	*sound track*
el bandoneón	*type of accordion*
el/la bandoneonista	**bandoneón** *player*
la cancha (*Amér. L.*)	*sports field*
el/la ciudadano/a ilustre	*distinguished citizen*
la clase particular	*private lesson*
el colectivo	*bus*
el cuerpo	*body*
el delito	*crime*
el dialecto	*dialect*
el/la enemigo/a	*enemy*
la estrofa	*stanza*
la frente	*forehead*
la jerga	*slang, jargon*
el/la pibe/a (*Arg.*)	*young boy/girl*
el porqué	*reason*
la sabiduría	*wisdom*
el sello discográfico	*record label*
agarrar	*to grab*
carecer (de)	*to lack*
criticar	*to criticize*
diferenciarse de	*to differentiate from*
editar	*to release (music)*
manejar (*Amér. L.*)	*to drive*
pasarla bien (*Amér. L.*)	*to have a good time*
ser bueno/a (en algo)	*to be good (at something)*
ser hincha de	*to be a supporter of*
ser malo/a (en algo)	*to be bad (at something)*
tener canas	*to have gray hair*
alejados/as entre sí	*far from each other*
apenado/a	*sad*
contemporáneo/a	*contemporary*
maduro/a	*mature*
porteño/a	*of/from the city of Buenos Aires*
acá	*here*
casualmente	*by chance*
gratarola (*C. S.*)	*for free*
más tarde	*later*
nomás	*only*
rebién (*fam., Arg.*)	*very well*
recién	*just*

La escritora española **Cristina Fernández Cubas** (1945–) estudió periodismo y derecho en Barcelona. Durante los últimos treinta años ha escrito cuentos, novelas y obras de teatro y ha viajado por todo el mundo. Vivió en ciudades como El Cairo, París, Berlín y Lima. Su obra ha sido traducida a diez idiomas y actualmente es un referente muy importante para los escritores de relatos breves.

Vocabulario útil

- la abadesa *abbess*
- alcanzar a ver *to catch a glimpse of*
- la celosía *lattice*
- el convento de clausura *cloistered convent*
- el encierro *seclusion*
- la fachada *façade*
- habitualmente *normally, usually*
- impedir (e:i) *to stop, to hinder*
- la monja *nun*
- no le interesa lo más mínimo *he/she couldn't care less*

Estrategia

Visualizing

When reading a text, pay attention to the details and descriptions: use your five senses to create images in your mind reflecting the ideas in the text. These images will help you go deeper into the text and make the world of the story come alive in your mind while you are reading, much as if you were watching a movie. Imagine what characters look like, how they walk and talk, where the story takes place, what time of the day it is, etc.

LECTURA

El viaje

Cristina Fernández Cubas

Un día la madre de una amiga me contó una curiosa anécdota.

Estábamos en su casa, en el barrio antiguo de Palma de Mallorca, y desde el balcón interior, que daba a° un pequeño jardín, se alcanzaba a ver la fachada del vecino convento de clausura. La madre de mi amiga solía visitar a la abadesa; le llevaba helados para la comunidad y conversaban durante horas a través de la celosía. Estábamos ya en una época en que las reglas de clausura eran menos estrictas de lo que fueron antaño°, y nada impedía a la abadesa, si así lo hubiera deseado°, que interrumpiera en más de una ocasión su encierro y saliera al mundo.

1 Suggestion For the second question, tell students to imagine that they do not have Internet access.

1. Converse con un(a) compañero/a: Imagine que no puede salir de su casa. ¿Qué haría? ¿Cómo conocería el mundo exterior? ¿Alguna vez estuvo de visita en un convento o monasterio? ¿Cuál sería para usted el viaje más largo?

2. Empareje elementos de las columnas para formar oraciones y completar el relato.

1. La autora escuchó esta historia de boca ___e___	a. esta mujer conversaba horas con la abadesa.
2. Desde el balcón de su casa se alcanza a ver ___f___	b. se presentó en la puerta de la casa de su vecina.
3. La mujer habitualmente llevaba ___h___	c. agradeció a la dueña de la casa y se marchó.
4. A través de la celosía, ___a___	d. ha vuelto a salir del encierro de su convento.
5. Hacía casi treinta años que ___i___	e. de la madre de una amiga que vive en Palma.
6. Una mañana, la abadesa ___b___	f. la fachada de un convento de clausura.
7. Ella pidió permiso para ___j___	g. el convento se veía muy bonito.
8. Después de observar en silencio, dijo que ___g___	h. helados a la comunidad de monjas.
9. Con mucha alegría, la abadesa ___c___	i. la abadesa no salía de su encierro.
10. Supuestamente, la abadesa no ___d___	j. contemplar su convento desde el balcón.

2 Suggestion To challenge students, have them cover the second column with a sheet of paper and complete the sentences from memory.

Pero ella se negaba en redondo°. Llevaba casi treinta años entre aquellas cuatro paredes y las llamadas del exterior no le interesaban lo más mínimo.

Por eso la señora de la casa creyó que estaba soñando° cuando una mañana sonó el timbre° y una silueta oscura se dibujó° al trasluz° en el marco de la puerta°. "Si no le importa", dijo la abadesa tras los saludos de rigor°, "me gustaría ver el convento desde fuera". Y después, en el mismo balcón en el que fue narrada la historia se quedó unos minutos en silencio. "Es muy bonito", concluyó. Y, con la misma alegría con la que había llamado a la puerta, se despidió y regresó al convento.

Creo que no ha vuelto a salir, pero eso ahora no importa. El viaje de la abadesa me sigue pareciendo, como entonces, uno de los viajes más largos de todos los viajes largos de los que tengo noticias.

Suggestion Ask students if they think that the abbess thought for a long time about the decision to leave, or if it was a whim.

daba a *looked onto* **antaño** *in the past* **si así...** *if she had wanted to* **se negaba en redondo** *refused point blank* **soñando** *dreaming* **timbre** *door bell* **se dibujó** *was outlined* **al trasluz** *against the light* **marco de la puerta** *door frame* **los saludos de rigor** *the usual greetings*

Estrategia

Narrative writing

"A story should have a beginning, a middle, and an end... but not necessarily in that order." This deceptively simple quote from film director Jean-Luc Godard has long helped writers approach the task of narration. Keep this concept in mind as you plan your writing. Notice, for example, in *El viaje*, that the beginning of the narrative—a visit with a friend's mother—occurs at a point in time after the actions of the plot—the abbess's visit—have already ended.

Estrategia Have the class give examples of books or movies that present the story "out of order." Ex: *Pulp Fiction*

3 Converse con un(a) compañero/a.

1. ¿Qué cree que pensaron los vecinos al ver a la abadesa por la calle? ¿Y las otras monjas del convento: le reprocharon su salida o quisieron imitarla? ¿Les pareció divertido o escandaloso?
2. Imagine un final diferente: cuando la abadesa ve el convento desde el balcón, toma una decisión importante: ¿cuál es y qué hace después?

4

PROYECTO

Busque algún monumento importante de un país hispanohablante e investigue los datos principales sobre su historia:

- ubicación geográfica
- época de construcción
- motivo por el cual se construyó
- significado

Luego escriba su descripción en un relato: puede ser desde el punto de vista de alguien que lo ve por primera vez, o de un(a) enamorado/a que espera a su novio/a allí, etc. Siga estos pasos:

1. Describa físicamente el monumento y su reacción personal al conocerlo.
2. Visualice sus sensaciones y sus emociones (miedo, sorpresa, etc.) y anótelas.
3. Para que el lector pueda relacionarse con el relato, identifique el tema del monumento y subraye por qué es importante.
4. Elija el punto de vista más adecuado para su historia (primera o tercera persona) y escríbala.

Estrategia

Using prior knowledge

Before, during, and after watching a video, consider what you already know about that particular topic. This will improve your comprehension. Before watching this **Flash Cultura** episode, think: What do you know about Argentina? (What have you read or heard about it, have you been there, etc.?)

Vocabulario útil

ajetreado/a *hectic*
a las apuradas *in a hurry*
chupar *to suck*
la estancia *ranch*
la parrilla *grill*
reconocido/a *renowned*
la tertulia *roundtable (discussion)*

Estrategia

Understanding cultural rituals

In Argentina, Uruguay, or Paraguay, sharing **mate** is a symbol of interpersonal relationships. **Mate** is traditionally drunk in family gatherings or with friends and is part of everyday life; discussions, love quarrels, and confessions are sealed with a **mate**. To be invited to share **mate** is an invitation to friendship, so beware! Rejecting it or making faces at the prospect of sharing the **bombilla** with other people might be offensive. What other customs and rituals have you learned about that at first struck you as odd?

4 Expansion Tell the class to imagine that one week has gone by. Have them present a phone conversation between the two friends, in which they discuss how the gift was received, etc.

Flash CULTURA

Lo mejor de Argentina

Ya ha leído sobre cómo las pasiones son el motor de la vida: puede ser una pasión por buscar la verdad o por disfrutar de las cosas que nos hacen felices. En este episodio de **Flash Cultura** descubrirá algunas de las pasiones esenciales de los argentinos.

1. ¿Qué le apasiona? (actividades, ideas...) ¿A qué no renunciaría nunca? ¿Le gustan las cosas exóticas o prefiere las tradicionales? ¿Qué tradiciones conserva? ¿Se siente más atraído/a por el pasado, el presente o el futuro?

2. Mientras mira el episodio de **Flash Cultura**, tenga en mente: ¿Qué sabe sobre el tango, el mate, el asado? ¿Qué idea tiene de los argentinos?

1 **...en el corazón del barrio de San Telmo... se puede disfrutar de una de las cosas que más les gustan a los argentinos: el tango.**

2 **...a nadie se le ocurriría tomar café de la taza de otra persona... ¡pero el mate es para compartir!**

3. Indique si estas oraciones son verdaderas o falsas. Después, con un(a) compañero/a, corrija las falsas.

   1. En Buenos Aires existen muchos cafés. Verdadero.
   2. El Tortoni está en las afueras de la ciudad. Falso. Está en el centro de Buenos Aires.
   3. Borges prefería tomar submarinos. Falso. Borges prefería tomar agua tónica.
   4. Carlos Gardel fue un famoso escritor. Falso. Gardel fue cantante de tangos.
   5. El bandoneón es un instrumento importante para el tango. Verdadero.
   6. El asado necesita de mucho tiempo para cocinarse. Verdadero.
   7. El mate se hace con café. Falso. El mate se hace con la yerba mate.
   8. En Argentina se come mucha carne. Verdadero.

4. Con un(a) compañero/a, escriba un diálogo entre una persona que le quiere hacer un regalo a su novio/a y un(a) amigo/a que le da consejos.

   Modelo:
   - *Estoy seguro de que un CD de tango es un buen regalo.*
   - *Pero a ella no le gusta nada bailar...*

Audio: Activities, Vocabulary
Video: *Flash Cultura*

Unidad 18

Rafa Nadal, un número uno

Lección 18A

NUEVOS RETOS

Lección 18B

MEJOR IMPOSIBLE

Marián Rico, ¡pura vida!

Palacios del arte

AVANCE

18A NUEVOS RETOS

Al límite

Retos deportivos

¿Quién es para usted el deportista que ha superado el reto deportivo más difícil?

Iván Vallejo decidió ser montañista a los 8 años.

Iván Vallejo es un montañista ecuatoriano al que admiro mucho. Es un gran deportista para quien es necesario superarse día a día. Es el primer sudamericano que logró escalar todos los ochomiles (las 14 montañas más altas del mundo) sin auxilio de oxígeno. Además, es ingeniero químico y da conferencias sobre la realización de metas. ¡Es increíble todo lo que hace!

Esteban Rodríguez, Mendoza

Yo estoy impresionada con Andoni Rodelgo y Alice Goffart. Son dos deportistas para los que las adversidades no existen. Hace un tiempo, dieron la vuelta al mundo en bicicleta. Recorrieron aproximadamente 44 000 kilómetros en tres años, tres meses y tres días. Ahora quieren repetir la experiencia con su pequeña hija, Maia. ¡Es increíble la energía que tienen! Nada es imposible para ellos.

Julia Fernández, Quito

Andoni y **Alice** recorrieron tres continentes con sus bicicletas.

Identificar

Es un montañista ecuatoriano **que** ha superado muchos retos y **para el que** no existen retos imposibles.

Son deportistas **a los que** admiro.

18A.1 [*preposition*] + **quien/el, la, los, las + que**

Vocabulario

1

- **el reto deportivo** *sport challenge*
- **el/la deportista** *sportsman, sportswoman*
- **superar retos** *to overcome challenges*
- **el/la montañista** *mountain climber*
- **superarse** *to outdo oneself*
- **sudamericano/a** *South American*
- **escalar** *to climb (a mountain)*
- **el auxilio** *help*
- **la meta** *goal*
- **estar impresionado/a** *to be impressed*
- **la adversidad** *setback*

1 Observe las fotos de estos deportistas. ¿Qué deportes practican? Relacione después los nombres de los deportes y los deportistas. montañismo y ciclismo

tenis	atletismo	gimnasia	natación
ciclismo	Fórmula 1	maratón	montañismo

1 Expansion For each word, have students list one or two related words. Ex: **ciclista: bicicleta**

1. atleta: *atletismo*
2. nadador(a): natación
3. piloto: Fórmula 1
4. montañista: montañismo
5. corredor(a): maratón
6. ciclista: ciclismo
7. tenista: tenis
8. gimnasta: gimnasia

2 Lea el artículo de la revista de deporte y resuma los datos más sorprendentes acerca de estos deportistas.

Modelo: *Iván Vallejo es un montañista que... para quien...*

3 Complete las oraciones con las expresiones del recuadro.

3 Suggestion To challenge students, have them cover the word bank.

del que • para el que • que • con los que • a quien

1. Es el atleta ...que... ha batido el récord en los 110 metros.
2. ¡No sabes todos los desafíos ...con los que... se enfrentaron estos ciclistas!
3. Hoy he conocido al deportista guatemalteco ...del que... todos hablan.
4. Es un montañista ...para el que... no hay retos imposibles.
5. Es una deportista formidable y una persona ...a quien/que... admiro mucho.

Expresar admiración

- Admiro a Rafa Nadal. **Estoy impresionado con** su juego. ¡**Es increíble cómo** juega!
- Yo **admiro a** Ricardo Abad. ¡**Es sorprendente que haya corrido** 6000 km en 150 días!

18A.2 **admirar a**
estar impresionado/a con
es increíble cómo
es increíble/sorprendente/ impresionante/admirable que + [*subjunctive*]

Vocabulario *cont.*

dar la vuelta al mundo *to go around the world*
el atletismo *track and field*
la gimnasia *gymnastics*
el ciclismo *cycling*
el montañismo *mountain climbing*
el/la atleta *track and field athlete*
el/la nadador(a) *swimmer*
el/la corredor(a) *runner*
el oxígeno, la Fórmula 1, el maratón, el/la ciclista, el/la gimnasta, el/la piloto

2
sorprendente *surprising*

3
batir un récord *to break a record*
enfrentarse a *to face*

4
el Polo Norte *North Pole*
cruzar *to cross*
el océano *ocean*
el bote de remos *row boat*
ascender (e:ie) *to climb*

¿Alpinismo o andinismo?

El montañismo de altura recibe nombres específicos según el lugar en que se practica. Por eso, se llama *alpinismo* en los Alpes y *andinismo* en los Andes. La principal diferencia entre los *alpinistas* y los *andinistas* es el número de metros sobre el nivel del mar que deben ascender: hasta 5000 en Europa y de 5000 a 7000 en América.

4 Mire las fotos y lea las informaciones. Haga preguntas a su compañero/a como en el ejemplo.

Fátima del Ángel Palacios

Fátima del Ángel se convirtió en la primera latinoamericana en llegar al Polo Norte.

Ricardo Abad

Corrió 150 maratones (6000 km) en 150 días.

Juan Carlos Sagastume

Cruzó el océano Atlántico en un bote de remos: 5280 km en 64 días, 13 horas y 17 minutos.

Modelo: *¿Quién es el que corrió 150 maratones en 150 días?*

5 Complete las opiniones de los lectores. Luego, elija al deportista de la lección que más le impresiona a usted y explique a su compañero/a por qué.

1. Esteban admira mucho a Iván porque...
2. Julia está impresionada con Andoni y Alice porque...
3. Yo admiro a... porque...

5 Expansion Have students talk about what athletes they admire at their own university (or another school).

6 Escuche las llamadas de otros lectores de la revista y complete las oraciones.

1. Joaquín está impresionado con Fátima del Ángel por sus expediciones al Polo Norte y al desierto del Sahara.
2. Amélie piensa que es increíble que Andoni y Alice hayan hecho algo así.
3. María Elena admira a Juan Carlos por todos sus logros.

6 Suggestion Before playing the audio, have students read through the sentences.

7 Lea las oraciones y elija la forma correcta de cada verbo.

1. Es sorprendente que Ricardo **corra/haya corrido** 6000 km en cinco meses.
2. Es increíble que Juan Carlos **pueda/haya podido** superar todos esos desafíos y que además **tenga/haya tenido** su propia empresa.
3. Es impresionante que Andoni y Alice **decidan/hayan decidido** viajar de España a Bélgica en bicicleta con su pequeña hija.
4. Me parece admirable que Fátima del Ángel **sea/haya sido** una deportista tan completa.

MI EXPERIENCIA

8 Piense en un(a) deportista o equipo que ha superado algún reto especial y explique a sus compañeros quién es, qué ha hecho y por qué lo/la admira.

GUIÓN DE TRABAJO

¿A qué deportista o equipo admiras? → Admiro a... / Estoy impresionado/a con...

¿Por qué? → Porque es increíble/ sorprendente/ impresionante/admirable... → que haya.... / que sea... / cómo...

Practice more at **vhlcentral.com.**

SAM: Actividades pp. 377–379

Nuevos aires

Suggestion Have students read through the tab headings and identify the English loanwords (**kayak, rafting**), and one that is influenced by English (**puenting**).

www.vivelaaventura.ar

VIVE LA AVENTURA EN MENDOZA

ala delta | buceo | cabalgata | canotaje | ciclismo | escalada | esquí | kayak | parapente | *puenting* | *rafting* | ***tirolesa***

Gracias a su particular geografía, Mendoza es un lugar excelente para dejar salir al aventurero que todos llevamos dentro. ¡Después de que practiques un deporte de aventura, serás otro! Las opciones son infinitas.

TIROLESA

Practicar tirolesa es una experiencia apasionante. Consiste en deslizarse de un punto a otro en el aire con la ayuda de cables de acero y un arnés. ¿Te animas? Ven a divertirte con nosotros. Tenemos todo el equipo y guías bilingües especializados.

Información importante:

- El plazo de inscripción es del 1 al 10 de cada mes. Puedes reservar tu lugar en línea en cualquier momento.
- Salida en colectivo a las 8:00 h (hay que presentarse 15 minutos antes de que salga el colectivo).
- Llegada a Potrerillos a las 10:00 h.
- Después de que tengamos una charla de seguridad, comienza la aventura. El recorrido es de 1400 metros y se divide en 6 etapas.
- La actividad termina a las 13:00 h. Almorzaremos asado y daremos un paseo.
- Regresaremos a las 17:00 h, después de una ronda de mate.

Language Note Point out the term **ala delta** and explain that **ala** is similar to the words **ave** and **agua**: it is a feminine noun, but it takes the definite article **el**.

Relacionar acontecimientos

Tenemos que presentarnos 15 minutos **antes de que salga** el autobús.

La aventura comenzará **después de que tengamos** una charla de seguridad.

18A.3 **antes/después de que** + [*subjunctive*]

Vocabulario

9

el/la aventurero/a *adventurer*
el ala delta *hang glider*
la cabalgata *horseback riding*
la escalada *climbing*
el parapente *paragliding*
el *puenting* *bungee jumping*
el canotaje *canoeing*
la tirolesa *zip lining*
deslizarse *to glide*
el acero *steel*

9 a. Observe la página web de una empresa que organiza actividades deportivas en Mendoza, Argentina. ¿Quién organiza en su pueblo o ciudad ese tipo de actividades?

- ☐ los clubes privados
- ☐ la universidad
- ☐ el ayuntamiento
- ☐ otros...

b. ¿En qué tipo de deportes se especializa esta empresa? ¿Le gustaría practicar alguno? deportes de aventura

10 Fíjese en la información sobre los horarios y marque la opción correcta.

1. La actividad comienza **antes**/**después** de que se sirva el asado.
2. Hay que inscribirse para practicar tirolesa **antes**/**después** del día 10 de cada mes.
3. **Antes**/**Después** de dar un paseo, tomarán mate.
4. Tendrán la charla de seguridad **antes**/**después** de la llegada a Potrerillos.

11 Haga preguntas a su compañero/a sobre las actividades.

Modelo: • *¿Cuándo hay que presentarse en el colectivo?*
• *Quince minutos antes de que salga el colectivo.*

Vocabulario *cont.*

el arnés *harness*
el equipo *equipment*
el plazo de inscripción *enrollment period*
antes de que *before*
después de que *after*
infinito/a, el *rafting*

13

la brújula *compass*
la mochila *backpack*
el casco *helmet*
la tienda de campaña *tent*
los guantes *gloves*
el bastón *pole*
descender (e:ie) *to descend*
la pendiente *slope*

Estrategia

Intensificar

Nadó **kilómetros y kilómetros** completamente solo.

Nuevos deportes

El ser humano siempre intenta superar desafíos. Por eso, no es extraño que surjan nuevos deportes extremos como el surf volcánico. Este deporte se practica en el Cerro Negro, un volcán de 730 metros de alto que está ubicado en Nicaragua. Desde 2005, unos 10 000 surfistas han descendido con sus tablas por una pendiente de 500 metros a una velocidad de hasta 80 km por hora.

12 ¿Qué va a hacer después de la clase de español? ¿Y antes de que termine? Con sus compañeros, forme oraciones que relacionen acontecimientos.

Modelo:
- *Antes de que termine la clase, haremos esta actividad.*
- *Después de que entreguemos el ejercicio, el/la profesor(a)...*

13 a. Mire las fotos. ¿Qué objetos reconoce? Relacione con flechas.

brújula | botas de trekking | mochila | casco

tienda de campaña | guantes | gafas | bastones

b. Lea la publicidad de esta tienda. ¿Por qué se repiten las palabras señaladas?
para intensificar

> Practicar deportes de aventura no es fácil. Necesitas **horas y horas** de entrenamiento y un buen equipo. Tú pon la dedicación, nosotros ponemos todo lo demás.

14 a. Relacione estos eslóganes con las imágenes y anote el nombre de los deportes.

14a Expansion Have students work in pairs. Tell them to take turns describing one of the objects listed. Their partner will guess what it is. Ex: **Usamos esto para guardar las cosas. Se lleva en la espalda. (la mochila)**

"Vuela y vuela como un pájaro" [3] ala delta

"Metros y metros de montaña para ti" [1] escalada/montañismo

"Más y más océano frente a tus ojos" [2] buceo

1

2

3

b. En parejas, decidan cuál es la actividad deportiva más interesante de la lección y creen un eslogan publicitario.

14b Suggestion Have pairs read aloud their slogans and have the class identify what they are advertising.

MI EXPERIENCIA

15 Elija una actividad y escriba un breve programa o calendario. Informe al grupo y pregúntense por otros programas de actividades.

GUIÓN DE TRABAJO

¿Cuál es el plazo de inscripción? ¿Cómo se forman los grupos?	Antes de (que)... Después de que sepamos el número de personas inscritas...
¿Qué equipo necesito? ¿Qué entrenamiento previo necesito?	Para este deporte necesitas... El entrenamiento que necesitas...

Practice more at **vhlcentral.com.**

SAM: Actividades pp. 380–382

Rafa Nadal, un número uno

¿Cómo es Rafael Nadal antes de salir a la cancha y después de que millones de personas sigan sus partidos?

El deportista más joven que ha recibido el Premio Príncipe de Asturias y el ídolo de millones de aficionados por su carisma y su valía personal, nació el 3 de junio de 1986 en Manacor, Mallorca. De pequeño era uno de esos niños que decía "Cuando sea mayor, seré futbolista". Sin embargo, su tío y entrenador Toni Nadal vio que Rafa tenía buenas cualidades físicas para el tenis. Para Rafa Nadal, los entrenamientos con su tío han sido decisivos. "Me exige mucho, supongo que por ser de mi familia. Él me ha enseñado a ser deportista, y sobre todo a ser mejor persona."

Dice mucho sobre su carácter esta anécdota que cuenta su tío de un torneo en el que Rafa, que tenía siete años entonces, jugaba contra un tenista de catorce. Toni le dijo a su sobrino: "Si veo que te da una paliza descomunal, tú no te preocupes, que yo haré llover y pararemos el partido". El cielo estaba nublado y el partido empezó. Rafael perdía 3-0, pero con siete años Rafael ya era muy luchador y tenía una confianza verdaderamente ciega en sí mismo; así que empezó a remontar el partido. En ese momento empezó a llover y se paró el partido. Después de cinco minutos, Rafael se acercó a su tío y le dijo: "Toni, puedes parar la lluvia cuando quieras, ¡creo que puedo ganar!"

Rafa Nadal, en la final del Abierto de Australia

Suggestion Ask students if they have seen Nadal play. Have volunteers say what they admire about him.

Hablar de retos futuros

Cuando sea mayor, seré futbolista.

18A.4 **cuando** + [*subjunctive*]

Vocabulario

(16)

- la cancha *court*
- el partido *match*
- la valía *value, worth*
- el/la entrenador(a) *coach*
- el entrenamiento *training*
- el torneo *tournament*
- la paliza *thrashing*
- descomunal *massive*
- la confianza *confidence*
- remontar *to surmount*
- ganar torneos *to win tournaments*
- **el ídolo, el carisma, decisivo/a**

(18)

- estar seguro/a de sí mismo/a *to be self-confident*

16 Mire la imagen. ¿Qué sabe sobre el protagonista de esta unidad?

ganar torneos | Mallorca (España) | ....

Modelo: *Rafa Nadal es un tenista que....*

17 a. Lea el artículo sobre Rafael Nadal. ¿Qué relación profesional tiene con su tío Toni? ¿Por qué Toni es tan importante para el deportista?
Es su entrenador. Possible answer: Es un ejemplo como deportista y como persona.

b. ¿Qué decía Rafael cuando era pequeño? ¿Quería ser tenista? ¿Qué retos tenía para el futuro? ¿Y usted qué decía cuando era pequeño/a?

Modelo: *Cuando sea mayor...* seré futbolista.

18 a. Qué nos dice la anécdota de Rafa y su tío sobre la personalidad de este deportista? Busque expresiones equivalentes a estas. 18a Seguro de sí mismo: Tenía una confianza verdaderamente ciega en sí mismo. Bueno para el tenis: Tenía buenas cualidades físicas para el tenis. Constante: Luchador.

seguro de sí mismo • bueno para el tenis • constante

b. ¿Qué diferencia hay entre estas frases? ¿Cuál de ellas le parece indicada para Rafael Nadal? Possible answer: "Cuando llegue a número uno..." es mucho más optimista que "Si llego a número uno...".

- **Si llego** a número uno...
- **Cuando llegue** a número uno...

18b **Expansion** Have students complete these phrases with information from their own lives.

19 Exprese retos futuros en relación a estos temas con mayor o menor optimismo.

conseguir el trabajo de mis sueños | dar la vuelta al mundo | tener más tiempo libre

Muy optimista: *Cuando termine...*   No tan optimista: *Si termino...*

Vocabulario

(20)

los Juegos Panamericanos *Pan-American Games*
llevar a cabo *to carry out*
competir (e:i) *to compete*
celebrar *to take place*
posponer (ng) *to put off*
la Segunda Guerra Mundial *World War II*
ininterrumpidamente *uninterruptedly*
fortalecer (zc) *to strengthen*
el lema *motto*
incorporar *to include*
el círculo, el emblema

(22)

la leyenda *legend*
el/la beisbolista *baseball player*
el béisbol *baseball*
el/la boxeador(a) *boxer*
el/la lanzador(a) de disco *discus thrower*
el/la nadador(a) de sincronizada *synchronized swimmer*

(23)

hípico/a *equestrian*
la pelota *ball*
el asa (*f.*) *handle*
el aro *hoop*
el/la contrincante *opponent*
el/la pato/a *duck*
lanzar *to throw*
la pólvora *gunpowder*
atrapar *to catch*
la cesta *basket*
el frontón *jai-alai court*
la raqueta

OPINIÓN

¿Cuáles son, en su opinión, las cualidades que debe tener un deportista para triunfar?

Suggestion Point out that **posponer** is a synonym of the more formal word **postergar**, which students learned in Lesson 17B.

20 a. Lea el texto sobre los Juegos Panamericanos. Luego haga una lista de los datos que más le llaman la atención.

LOS JUEGOS PANAMERICANOS

Los Juegos Panamericanos están entre los acontecimientos deportivos más importantes del mundo. La Organización Deportiva Panamericana (ODEPA) los lleva a cabo cada cuatro años, siempre un año antes de los Juegos Olímpicos. Allí compiten miles de atletas de 42 naciones de América del Norte, América Central, Sudamérica y el Caribe.

RIO 2007

Los primeros Juegos Panamericanos se celebraron en Buenos Aires en 1951. Originariamente iban a realizarse en el año 1942, pero se pospusieron por la Segunda Guerra Mundial. Desde entonces, se han celebrado ininterrumpidamente.

Además de promover el desarrollo deportivo, el objetivo de estos juegos es fortalecer la unión y la amistad entre los pueblos. Por eso, el lema de la ODEPA, "América, Espírito, Sport, Fraternité", incorpora cuatro de los idiomas más usados en las Américas: español, portugués, inglés y francés. Además, en su emblema se ven cinco círculos de colores (azul, rojo, blanco, amarillo y verde). Al menos uno de esos colores aparece en cada bandera nacional de los países participantes.

b. ¿Qué cree que significa la expresión "llevar a cabo" en el texto? Piense en otros tres casos en los que se podría usar esta expresión. realizar

21 ¿Qué acontecimiento deportivo le resulta especialmente interesante? Escriba una crónica breve. **21 Suggestion** If some students are not interested in watching or playing sports, encourage them to write a critique about a famous sporting event.

22 ¿Conoce a estas leyendas del deporte? ¿Con qué deporte los asocia?

beisbolista [2] boxeador [3] lanzadora de disco [1]
tenista [4] nadadora de sincronizada [5]

Yarelis Barrios 1

Cuba

Sammy Sosa 2

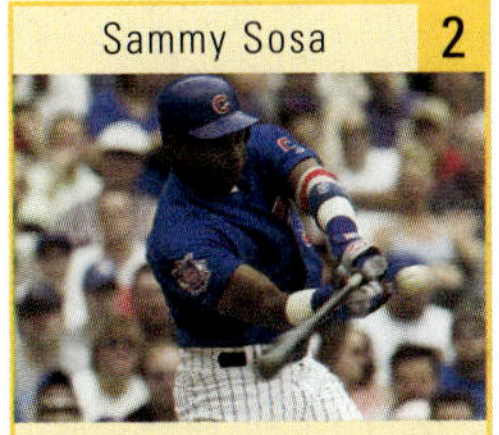

República Dominicana

Oscar de la Hoya 3

EE.UU.

Juan Martín del Potro 4

Argentina

Gemma Mengual 5

España

Practice more at **vhlcentral.com.**

SAM: Actividades pp. 383–386

23a Suggestion Tell students that **gaucho** can be considered a loose equivalent of the term cowboy. Traditionally, **gauchos** herded cattle on the vast **estancias** (ranches), and were excellent horsemen and hunters.

23 a. ¿Qué deportes asocia con Argentina, Colombia y España? Si su respuesta es "fútbol" o "béisbol", lo invitamos a conocer deportes tradicionales de esos tres países hispanohablantes.

El *pato* es un deporte hípico que se ha practicado en Argentina por 400 años. Los jugadores de un equipo deben pasarse una pelota con asas unos a otros hasta lograr introducirla en el aro de sus contrincantes. El nombre del deporte se debe a que, en un principio, los gauchos argentinos usaban un pato vivo en lugar de una pelota.

El *tejo* es el deporte nacional de Colombia. Es un deporte muy antiguo, ya que lo practicaban los indígenas antes de la llegada de Colón. En la actualidad, los jugadores deben lanzar un disco (tejo) e introducirlo en un círculo metálico (bosín) en cuyos bordes se colocan "mechas" (pequeñas bolsas con pólvora). Gana el jugador que hace explotar más mechas.

El *jai alai*, o cesta punta, es un deporte de origen vasco parecido al *squash*. En lugar de raqueta, los jugadores usan una cesta para atrapar la pelota y lanzarla contra un frontón. Para practicarlo, es conveniente usar casco: ¡la pelota puede alcanzar una velocidad de hasta 250 kilómetros por hora!

b. ¿Qué deportes asocia con su ciudad/estado/región? ¿Por qué? ¿Alguna vez los ha visto ser jugados? Comente su experiencia con sus compañeros.

TAREA FINAL

Revista deportiva

En parejas, elijan un deporte y busquen información sobre deportistas y eventos deportivos relacionados, récords, etc.

Escriban un artículo o crónica deportiva breve con la información que han seleccionado. Incluyan imágenes.

Compartan y clasifiquen los artículos y elaboren entre todos una revista deportiva.

Suggestion Encourage the class to come up with a title for the magazine.

YO PUEDO...

- **Puedo identificar.**
  Identifique a un(a) deportista que admira.
- **Puedo expresar admiración.**
  Explique por qué admira a este/a u otros deportistas.
- **Puedo relacionar acontecimientos.**
  Después de que ......pase...... (pasar) el verano, jugaremos al tenis en cancha cubierta.
- **Puedo hablar de retos futuros.**
  Cuando ...vaya de vacaciones... (ir de vacaciones) , ...

GRAMÁTICA FUNCIONAL

18A.1 Identify someone or something

[*preposition*] + **quien / el, la, los, las + que** 3.1.2, 6.9

- Use a preposition followed by the relative pronouns (**pronombres relativos**) **quien** (*who; whom; that*) or **el, la, los, las + que** (*that; which; who*) to identify someone or something already mentioned in the sentence.

  Nadia es la amiga **con quien/con la que** hice tirolesa.
  Nadia is the friend ***with whom*** *I went zip-lining.*

- Use **que** by itself when no preposition is present.

  Es un deportista **que** ha corrido 150 maratones.
  He is an athlete ***who*** *has run 150 marathons.*

- **Que** and **quien** both introduce a clause that refers to an antecedent (something or someone already mentioned in the sentence).

- The antecedent of the pronoun **que** can be a person or thing, while the antecedent of **quien** can only be a person. Use **quien** after a preposition or the personal **a**.

  Es un deportista **a quien** admiro.
  Es un deportista **que** admiro.
  He is an athlete ***whom*** *I admire.*

- The construction [*preposition*] + **el, la, los, las** + **que** may also be used in place of [*preposition*] + **quien**. The definite article must match the antecedent in both gender and number.

  Son **las tenistas a las que** más me gusta ver jugar.
  Son **las tenistas a quienes** más me gusta ver jugar.
  They are ***the tennis players that*** *I like best to watch play.*

Es **un alpinista para el que** no hay retos imposibles.
Es **un alpinista para quien** no hay retos imposibles.
He is ***a mountain climber for whom*** *there are no impossible challenges.*

- Note that **que** and **quien** do not carry a written accent in these constructions.

¡OJO! In English, relative pronouns are sometimes optional. In Spanish, relative pronouns are never omitted.

Es la deportista **que** más me gusta.
She is the athlete ***(that)*** *I like best.*

Suggestion Explain that **quien** is often used in nonrestrictive clauses. Ex: **Mi amiga, quien vive en Montevideo, viene a visitarme.**

Suggestion Have students write five sentences about their families. Tell them to use a different relative pronoun in each sentence.

¡Póngalo en práctica!

G1 Complete las oraciones con el pronombre relativo correcto: **que** o **quien**.

1. La escaladora vasca Edurne Pasaban es la única ...que... ha alcanzado todos los ochomiles.
2. Rafael Nadal es uno de los deportistas a ...quien... más admiran los españoles.
3. Manu Ginóbili es un jugador de básquetbol argentino ...que... juega en la NBA.
4. Diego Forlán es un jugador de fútbol uruguayo para el ...que... ganar el Balón de Oro en el Mundial de Sudáfrica 2010 no fue imposible.
5. Antonio Abertondo es un nadador ...que... cruzó el canal de la Mancha.
6. Miguel Indurain es un ciclista ...que... ha ganado carreras en varios países.

G2 Empareje las frases para formar oraciones completas.

1. El jugador	b	4. Las deportistas	c
2. El equipo	d	5. La deportista	e
3. Los entrenadores	a		

a. que toman más riesgos son los que ganan más torneos.
b. al que le dieron el premio fue contratado por un equipo europeo.
c. a quienes eligieron para el equipo fueron las que entrenaron todo el invierno.
d. que perdió ante el Barça es el segundo en la liga.
e. a la que le interesa el periodismo tiene oportunidades de trabajo después de los Juegos Olímpicos.

G3 Combine las oraciones usando pronombres relativos. Suggested answers:

Modelo: El jugador tiene solo dieciocho años. El jugador marcó el último gol.
El jugador que tiene solo dieciocho años marcó el último gol.

1. A la montañista le gusta superar retos. La montañista ascendió el Aconcagua.
   La montañista a quien le gusta superar retos ascendió el Aconcagua.
2. El ciclismo es un deporte divertido. El ciclismo atrae a deportistas de todas las edades.
   El ciclismo es un deporte divertido que atrae a deportistas de todas las edades.
3. La brújula está en la mochila. La mochila está en la tienda de campaña.
   La brújula está en la mochila que está en la tienda de campaña.
4. Gabriel es un nadador. Para Gabriel, es muy importante intentar batir un récord.
   Gabriel es un nadador para quien es muy importante intentar batir un récord.

Practice more at **vhlcentral.com.**

GRAMÁTICA FUNCIONAL

Suggestion Tell pairs of students to pretend that they are sports commentators that are working together at a major sporting event. Have them role-play their commentary of the event.

18A.2 Express admiration

admirar a, estar impresionado/a con 5.8.2
es increíble cómo/que + [*verb*] 5.8.8
Use of present perfect subjunctive 5.22.2

- Use the verb **admirar** (*to admire*) to express admiration for a person. Remember to use the personal **a**.

  ¿A qué deportista **admiras**?
  *What athlete **do you admire**?*

  Admiro a Iván Vallejo.
  ***I admire** Iván Vallejo.*

- Use the construction **estar impresionado/a con** (*to be impressed with/by*) to show admiration for someone or something.

  Estoy impresionada con su valentía.
  ***I am impressed with** his courage.*

- Use the construction **es increíble cómo** (*it is incredible how*) + [*verb*] to express admiration for an action or event. This construction does not use the subjunctive.

  Es increíble cómo escala Iván Vallejo.
  ***It is incredible how** Iván Vallejo **climbs**.*

  Es increíble cómo anotó ese gol.
  ***It's amazing how he scored** that goal.*

- Remember to use a written accent on **cómo** in this construction.

- Use the **presente de subjuntivo** with the construction **es increíble/impresionante/sorprendente** (*to be incredible/ impressive; astonishing/surprising*) + **que** to express astonishment about an event in the present.

  Es **impresionante que juegue** tan bien.
  *It is **amazing that he plays** so well.*

  Es **sorprendente que** el béisbol **sea** tan popular en Japón.
  *It's **surprising that** baseball **is** so popular in Japan.*

- Use the **pretérito perfecto de subjuntivo** with the construction **es increíble/impresionante/sorprendente + que** to express astonishment about a past event.

Es impresionante que hayan escalado tantas montañas altas.
***It is impressive that they have climbed** so many tall mountains.*

Es **increíble que haya participado** en tres Juegos Olímpicos.
*It's **incredible that she has participated** in three Olympic Games.*

¡Póngalo en práctica!

G4 Complete las oraciones.

1. ¡Es increíble ...cómo... entrenan los deportistas de élite!
2. Estoy impresionada ...con... el nuevo equipo de mi ciudad.
3. ...Admiro... (yo, admirar) a Lionel Messi porque es un gran futbolista y un buen deportista.
4. Admiro mucho ...a... esta deportista.
5. Es increíble cómo ...dedica... (dedicar) su vida al deporte.
6. Estoy impresionado ...con... ella.
7. Es sorprendente que ella ...haya podido... (poder) ganar la medalla de oro cuando sólo tenía veinte años.
8. Es increíble que los atletas olímpicos ...hayan dedicado... (dedicar) tantos años de su infancia a entrenar.

G5 Complete las oraciones para que transmitan las mismas ideas que las originales. Suggested answers:

1. Admiro a la escaladora española.
   Estoy impresionado ...con la escaladora española...
2. Es increíble cómo el equipo ha ganado tantos torneos.
   Es increíble que el equipo ...haya ganado tantos torneos...
3. Es impresionante cómo los deportistas profesionales siempre tratan de superarse.
   Es impresionante que los deportistas profesionales siempre ...traten de superarse...
4. Estamos impresionados con este boxeador.
   Admiramos ...a este boxeador...
5. Es increíble que Carolina y Héctor vayan al gimnasio todos los días.
   Es increíble cómo Carolina y Héctor ...van al gimnasio todos los días...

G6 Empareje las oraciones para formar mini-conversaciones.

1. Admiro mucho al jugador nuevo en el equipo de fútbol. ...e...
2. ¿Qué pensáis del torneo? ...c...
3. Es sorprendente que el nadador haya podido cruzar el río en tan poco tiempo. ...d...
4. Es increíble que Ricardo y Luisa hayan decidido hacer *puenting*. ...a...
5. Es impresionante que haya tantas personas interesadas en correr maratones en los últimos años. ...b...

a. Me dijeron que querían superar este reto tan difícil.
b. Sí, parece que es una meta personal de muchas personas correr uno.
c. Estamos impresionados con todos los equipos este año.
d. Tienes razón. Creo que batió un récord.
e. Sí, es increíble cómo juega. Yo también lo admiro.

Practice more at vhlcentral.com.

GRAMÁTICA FUNCIONAL

18A.3 Relate events to one another

antes/después de que + [*subjunctive*] 5.13, 5.20, 5.21.3a, 12.12
Spelling changes in the present subjunctive 5.20.2

- Use **antes de que** (*before*) and **después de que** (*after*) to relate events in time. Use these constructions in sentences that have verbs with different subjects. Always use the subjunctive after **antes de que**.

  Antes de que vayamos al partido, quiero pasar por la casa de un amigo.
  Before we go *to the game, I want to stop by my friend's house.*

- Use the subjunctive after **después de que** to relate anticipated events in the future.

  Después de que lleguen todos, vamos a ir al estadio.
  After *everyone* ***arrives***, *we are going to go to the stadium.*

- If both events occurred in the past, use **después de que** + [*indicative*].

  Después de que terminó el torneo, volvimos a la universidad en autobús.
  After *the tournament* ***ended***, *we returned to the university by bus.*

- If the sentence has only one subject, use **antes/después de** + [*noun/infinitive*] to compare two events in time.

  Antes de hacer montañismo, tenemos que conseguir el equipo adecuado.
  Before doing *mountaineering, we have to get the proper equipment.*

  Después del campeonato, Gonzalo dejó de entrenar los fines de semana.
  After the championship, *Gonzalo stopped training on the weekends.*

- Verbs that end in **-car, -gar,** and **-zar** have spelling changes in all forms of the present subjunctive in order to maintain the original pronunciation of the verb stem.

PRACTICAR (c→qu)	→	practi**que**, practi**ques**, practi**que**, practi**que**mos, practi**qué**is, practi**quen**
ENTREGAR (g→gu)	→	entre**gue**, entre**gues**, entre**gue**, entre**gue**mos, entre**gué**is, entre**guen**
EMPEZAR (z→c)	→	empie**ce**, empie**ces**, empie**ce**, empe**ce**mos, empe**cé**is, empie**cen**

No podéis inscribiros después de que **empiece** el torneo.
You can't register after the tournament ***begins***.

Es importante que **practiques** antes de que comience el campeonato.
It's important that ***you practice*** *before the championship begins.*

Suggestion Have students talk about their day up until this point, using **antes/después de +** [*infinitive/noun*] and **antes/después de que +** [*indicative*]. Then have them talk about tonight's plans, using **antes/después de +** [*infinitive/noun*] and **antes/después de que +** [*subjunctive*].

¡Póngalo en práctica!

G7 Complete las oraciones.

1. Los atletas tienen que prepararse antes de que las olimpiadas empiecen (empezar).
2. Después de que terminen (terminar) las competiciones, los atletas seguirán con sus entrenamientos.
3. Tienes que inscribirte antes de que llegue (llegar) el día del torneo.
4. Después de que practiquéis (vosotros, practicar) montañismo, vamos a empezar a entrenar para el triatlón.
5. Antes de que prueben (ustedes, probar) el montañismo, tienen que informarse de las mejores rutas.
6. Después de que volvimos (nosotros, volver) del campeonato, nuestro entrenador nos habló de cómo mejorar nuestro rendimiento.
7. Antes de que comience (comenzar) el verano, los atletas aprovechan los días menos calurosos de la primavera para entrenar más horas.
8. Después de que entrenamos (nosotros, entrenar) por tres horas, empezó a llover.

G8 Complete la tercera oración para que trasmita las mismas ideas.

Modelo: **Voy al gimnasio a las 8:00 de la mañana. La clase de español empieza a las 10:30.**
Antes de que *empiece la clase de español, voy al gimnasio.*

1. El instructor va a llegar pronto. Después, vamos a hacer *rafting*.
   Después de que llegue el instructor, vamos a hacer *rafting*.
2. Arturo y Paula encontraron un sitio en el camping a las 4:00 de la tarde. A las 4:15, armaron su tienda de campaña.
   Después de encontrar un sitio en el camping, Arturo y Paula armaron la tienda de campaña.
3. Rosario habló con la otra entrenadora a las 3:30 de la tarde. El equipo empezó a entrenar a las 4:00.
   Después de que Rosario habló con la otra entrenadora, el equipo empezó a entrenar.
4. Roberto sale a correr a las 7:00 de la mañana. El diario llega a su puerta a las 6:00 de la mañana.
   Antes de que Roberto salga a correr, el diario llega a su puerta.
5. El plazo de inscripción cierra el 25 de octubre. Después de esa fecha, tenéis que pedir un permiso especial para poder participar.
   Después de que cierre el plazo de inscripción, tenéis que pedir un permiso especial para poder participar.

Practice more at **vhlcentral.com.**

18A

GRAMÁTICA FUNCIONAL

18A.4 Talk about future challenges

cuando + [*subjunctive*] 5.20, 5.21.3b, 12.12

- Use the subjunctive with **cuando** to refer to a pending action or event in the future. Use the present subjunctive in the clause that follows **cuando** to refer to any action that has not yet occurred.

  Cuando me jubile, viajaré más.
  ***When I retire**, I will travel more.*

  Cuando era pequeña siempre decía: "**Cuando sea** mayor, seré futbolista."
  *When I was young I always said: "**When I am** older, I will be a soccer player."*

- Use **cuando** + [*present indicative*] to talk about a habitual action in the present.

  Cuando viajo, me gusta escribir en mi diario.
  ***When I travel**, I like to write in my diary.*

- Use **cuando** + [*preterite*] to refer to a completed action in the past.

  Cuando llegamos al hotel, estábamos muy cansados.
  ***When we arrived** at the hotel, we were very tired.*

- Use **cuando** + [*imperfect*] to talk about a habitual past action. In 14B.1, you learned to use **cuando** with either the preterite or the imperfect to situate past events.

  Cuando era pequeño, mi familia vivía en las afueras de la ciudad.
  ***When I was** young, my family lived outside the city.*

¡Póngalo en práctica!

G9 Complete las oraciones.

1. Iremos a ver un partido de tenis cuando ....queráis.... (vosotros, querer).
2. Cuando ....tenga.... (yo, tener) tiempo, escribiré un blog sobre deporte.
3. Cuando mi hermana ....está.... (estar) cansada durante la tarde, le gusta dormir la siesta.
4. Cuando Benjamín ....jugaba.... al fútbol en la secundaria, su posición preferida era de mediocampista.
5. Me gustaría trabajar en un canal de televisión cuando ....termine.... (terminar) mis estudios.
6. Cuando ....llegamos.... (nosotros, llegar) a la fiesta de cumpleaños, ya habían servido la tarta.
7. Te llamaré cuando ....llegue.... (yo, llegar) a casa.
8. Cuando ....empiece.... (empezar) el partido, voy a tomar un descanso del estudio.
9. Cuando ....era.... (ser) pequeño, David jugaba al fútbol todos los días.
10. Nos gustaría conocer Chichén Itzá cuando ....vayamos.... (ir) a México.

Suggestion Write a series of phrases on the board that begin with **Cuando** (Ex: **Cuando me gradúe... Cuando era niño/a...**). Have students complete them logically.

Practice more at **vhlcentral.com.**

SÍNTESIS

Expansion Have students who wrote dialogues work in pairs and synthesize their conversations. Then have them act them out for the class. For students who wrote paragraphs, have them work together to combine what they wrote; have volunteers read their paragraphs aloud for the class.

Mire las fotografías y escriba un diálogo o párrafo corto para cada una, usando el vocabulario indicado.

1. 

el reto	es increíble cómo	el montañismo	antes (de) que

- ________
- ________
- ________
- ________

2. 

el futbolista	cuando sea	entrenar	estoy impresionado/a con

- ________
- ________
- ________
- ________

VOCABULARIO

Al límite

la adversidad	*setback*
el/la atleta	*track and field athlete*
el atletismo	*track and field*
el auxilio	*help*
el bote de remos	*row boat*
el ciclismo	*cycling*
el/la ciclista	*cyclist*
el/la corredor(a)	*runner*
el/la deportista	*sportsman, sportswoman*
la Fórmula 1	*Formula 1*
la gimnasia	*gymnastics*
el/la gimnasta	*gymnast*
el maratón	*marathon*
la meta	*goal*
el montañismo	*mountain climbing*
el/la montañista	*mountain climber*
el/la nadador(a)	*swimmer*
el océano	*ocean*
el oxígeno	*oxygen*
el/la piloto	*pilot*
el Polo Norte	*North Pole*
el reto deportivo	*sport challenge*
ascender (e:ie)	*to climb*
batir un récord	*to break a record*
cruzar	*to cross*
dar la vuelta al mundo	*to go around the world*
enfrentarse a	*to face*
escalar	*to climb (a mountain)*
estar impresionado/a	*to be impressed*
superar retos	*to overcome challenges*
superarse	*to outdo oneself*
sorprendente	*surprising*
sudamericano/a	*South American*

Nuevos aires

el acero	*steel*
el ala delta	*hang glider*
el arnés	*harness*
el/la aventurero/a	*adventurer*
el bastón	*pole*
la brújula	*compass*
la cabalgata	*horseback riding*
el canotaje	*canoeing*
el casco	*helmet*
el equipo	*equipment*
la escalada	*climbing*
los guantes	*gloves*
la mochila	*backpack*
el parapente	*paragliding*
la pendiente	*slope*
el plazo de inscripción	*enrollment period*
el *puenting*	*bungee jumping*
el *rafting*	*rafting*
la tienda de campaña	*tent*
la tirolesa	*zip-lining*
descender (e:ie)	*to descend*
deslizarse	*to glide*
infinito/a	*infinite*
antes de que	*before*
después de que	*after*

Suggestion Have students create a three-column chart with the labels **Deportes, Equipo** (*Equipment*), and **Personas.** Have them write as many words from the vocabulary as they can in each category.

Rafa Nadal

el aro	*hoop*
el asa (*f.*)	*handle*
el béisbol	*baseball*
el/la beisbolista	*baseball player*
el/la boxeador(a)	*boxer*
la cancha	*court*
el carisma	*charisma*
la cesta	*basket*
el círculo	*circle*
la confianza	*confidence*
el/la contrincante	*opponent*
el emblema	*emblem*
el/la entrenador(a)	*coach*
el entrenamiento	*training*
el frontón	*jai-alai court*
el ídolo	*idol*
los Juegos Panamericanos	*Pan-American Games*
el/la lanzador(a) de disco	*discus thrower*
el lema	*motto*
la leyenda	*legend*
el/la nadador(a) de sincronizada	*synchronized swimmer*
la paliza	*thrashing*
el partido	*match*
el/la pato/a	*duck*
la pelota	*ball*
la pólvora	*gunpowder*
la raqueta	*racket*
la Segunda Guerra Mundial	*World War II*
el torneo	*tournament*
la valía	*value, worth*
atrapar	*to catch*
celebrar	*to take place*
competir (e:i)	*to compete*
estar seguro/a de sí mismo/a	*to be self-confident*
fortalecer (zc)	*to strengthen*
ganar torneos	*to win tournaments*
incorporar	*to include*
lanzar	*to throw*
llevar a cabo	*to carry out*
posponer (ng)	*to put off*
remontar	*to surmount*
decisivo/a	*decisive*
descomunal	*massive*
hípico/a	*equestrian*
ininterrumpidamente	*uninterruptedly*

Variación léxica

la adversidad ⟷ **el percance** ⟷ **el contratiempo** ⟷ **el revés**

la cancha ⟷ **la pista** (*Esp.*)

el/la contrincante ⟷ **el/la oponente** ⟷ **el/la adversario/a** ⟷ **el rival**

hípico/a ⟷ **ecuestre**

el montañista ⟷ **el/la montañero/a**

el *rafting* ⟷ **el balsismo**

la tienda de campaña ⟷ **la carpa** (*Amér. L.*)

la tirolesa ⟷ **el canopy**

18B MEJOR IMPOSIBLE

Acontecimientos de la vida

Expresar sentimientos

- Me puse triste cuando te marchaste y hoy me alegro de que estés aquí.
- Me da pena que no vengan.

18B.1 **alegrarse de que** + [*subjunctive*]; **ponerse triste** + **cuando/si** + [*indicative*]/**al** + [*infinitive*]

Vocabulario

①
dar pena *to upset*
alegrarse de *to be glad that*
la jubilación *retirement*
ponerse contento/a *to become happy*
ponerse triste *to become sad*
marcharse *to leave, to go away*
el Día de la Madre *Mother's Day*
cumplir años de casados *to have one's wedding anniversary*
el Año Nuevo *New Year*
las bodas de plata *silver wedding anniversary*

1 a. Lea las tarjetas de felicitación y hable con su compañero/a de estos temas.
Possible answers:
Tarjeta 1: ¿Quiénes se alegran? ¿De qué se alegran? sus compañeros de trabajo; de que pueda disfrutar de su jubilación con salud
Tarjeta 2: ¿Qué acontecimiento celebran? 25 años de casados; sus bodas de plata
Tarjeta 3: ¿Cuándo se ponen tristes las madres? ¿Cuándo se ponen contentas? cuando sus hijos se marchan; cuando sus hijos están cerca
Tarjeta 4: ¿Qué empiezan juntos? ¿De qué se alegra? un año nuevo; de que empiecen juntos el año

b. ¿Qué sentimientos le producen a usted normalmente estos acontecimientos?

Modelo: *Me alegro de que un matrimonio celebre sus bodas de plata.*

2 Complete el diálogo con la forma correcta de los verbos del recuadro.

tener	alegrar	estar	pensar	ponerse	acordarse

2 Expansion Have volunteers role-play the conversation for the class.

MARTÍN: ¡Hola, Paola! ¡Feliz cumpleaños!
PAOLA: Ah, bueno. Gracias.
MARTÍN: ¿No ...te alegra... cumplir años?
PAOLA: No, para nada. ¡ ...Me pongo... triste cuando ...pienso... que soy un año más vieja!
MARTÍN: Bueno, alégrate de que ...estés... sana, ...tengas... un buen trabajo y tu familia esté bien. ¡Alégrate también de que ...me haya acordado... de que hoy es tu cumpleaños!

3 ¿Escribe usted este tipo de felicitaciones? ¿En qué otras ocasiones felicita a sus familiares, compañeros o amigos? ¿Y su compañero/a?

Felicitar y expresar deseos

- ¡Felicidades! ¡Que seas muy feliz!
- ¡Gracias, igualmente!

18B.2 **felicidades, feliz** + [*noun*] **que** + [*subjunctive*]

Vocabulario

2

el cumpleaños *birthday*
cumplir años *to have one's birthday*
acordarse (o:ue) de *to remember*

5

la fiesta de quince años *fifteenth birthday party*
la graduación

¡OJO!

¡Felicitaciones!, **¡Felicidades!**, and **¡Enhorabuena!** are synonyms. However, there are slight differences in meaning: **felicitaciones** and **enhorabuena** are more often used to commemorate an achievement, whereas **felicidades** has a more general meaning and does not imply a particular achievement on the part of the recipient. Note that **enhorabuena** is more frequently used in Spain and **felicitaciones** is commonly used in Latin America.

4 Escuche estas felicitaciones y anote el número de la conversación correspondiente en la imagen.

4 Suggestion Explain that the stork (**la cigüeña**) myth exists in nearly all of Europe; the concept was brought to the Americas by the Europeans.

5 Marque cómo se felicita en cada ocasión.

	¡Felicitaciones! ¡Felicidades! ¡Enhorabuena!	¡Feliz cumpleaños!	¡Feliz Día de...!	¡Feliz Navidad! ¡Felices fiestas!
aniversario (boda, negocio)	✓			
boda	✓			
conseguir algo: trabajo, premio	✓			
cumpleaños	✓	✓		
Día del Padre/de la Madre/de San Valentín	✓		✓	
graduación	✓		✓	
nacimiento	✓			
Navidad	✓			✓
quince años	✓	✓		

6 Lea la viñeta cómica. ¿Entiende el chiste? Coméntelo con su compañero/a. ¿Cómo se felicita el cumpleaños en su lengua?

6 Suggestion Have volunteers read the comic aloud. Ask for other volunteers to offer other variations for the punch line (Ex: **Por eso lo digo...**).

7 ¿Qué cree que puede celebrar su compañero/a pronto? Investigue a través de preguntas y felicítelo/a.

Modelo: *¿Tu cumpleaños es este mes?*

MI EXPERIENCIA

8 ¿Qué le produce a su compañero/a sentimientos de alegría? ¿Y de tristeza? Compártanlo con el grupo. Elijan un acontecimiento y felicítense.

GUIÓN DE TRABAJO

¿Qué te alegra? ¿Qué te pone contento/a? →	Me alegra que... Me pone contento/a cuando/si... →	los logros personales los cumpleaños las celebraciones el inicio/fin de las vacaciones
¿Qué te da pena? ¿Qué te pone triste? →	Me da pena que... Me pone triste que... →	el inicio/fin del curso el invierno el verano las despedidas

Practice more at **vhlcentral.com.**

SAM: Actividades pp. 387–389

Suggestion Before going through the web page, have students scan it for cognates and underline them.

Celebraciones a la carta

eventoscostarica.cr

Eventos Costa Rica

Inicio

Eventos
- Bodas
- Quince años
- Despedidas de soltero/a
- Bautizos
- Aniversarios
- Cumpleaños
- Graduaciones
- Jubilaciones
- Fiestas de empresas

Menús

Galería de fotos

Contacto

¡Es una excelente idea que nosotros le planifiquemos y organicemos su celebración como usted la ha soñado!

Realizamos toda clase de eventos especiales: su boda, la fiesta de cumpleaños de su esposo/a, los quince años de su hija, el bautizo del bebé, la graduación de sus hijos, la despedida de soltera de su mejor amiga... ¿No es una buena idea que usted disfrute de cada uno de estos momentos al máximo? Para ello nosotros nos ocupamos de todos los detalles.

Disponemos de salones con una decoración exquisita, terraza al aire libre con vista panorámica y piscina. Nuestra experiencia y profesionalidad le garantiza que es una excelente idea dejarlo todo en nuestras manos. Sus invitados se sentirán cómodos, se divertirán, comerán rico y se llevarán un hermoso recuerdo de ese día. Nuestro servicio puede incluir: coordinadores, maestros de ceremonias, decoración especial, música, limusina, *catering* de calidad, pasteles y mucho más; en definitiva, todo lo que necesita.

En resumen, si quiere disfrutar de un evento bien organizado, en un lugar mágico, contáctenos y solicite ya su cotización sin compromiso. Estamos al alcance de su teléfono o computadora, y nos ponemos a sus órdenes.

¡Si tiene un sueño, hágalo realidad con nosotros!

Evaluar ideas

- ¿Es una buena idea celebrar mi cumpleaños?
- Sí, **es una excelente idea que** puedas disfrutar de tu día.

18B.3 **(no) es (una) buena idea** + [*infinitive*]/**que** + [*subjunctive*]

Vocabulario

9

- **la despedida de soltero/a** *bachelor(ette) party*
- **el bautizo** *baptism*
- **planificar** *to plan*
- **ocuparse de los detalles** *to take care of the details*
- **el salón de fiestas** *function hall*
- **disponer (ng) de** *to have (at one's disposal)*
- **el/la invitado/a** *guest*
- **el/la maestro/a de ceremonias** *master of ceremonies*
- **el pastel** *cake*
- **en definitiva** *all in all*

9 a. La palabra "evento" se usa para referirse a una fiesta o celebración. ¿Cuántas celebraciones se le ocurren en un minuto? Anótelas y compare con su compañero/a. ¿Están todas las que aparecen en esta página web?

b. Lea el texto y marque verdadero (V) o falso (F).

	V	F
1. Eventos Costa Rica es un salón de fiestas.	☐	☑
2. Todas las celebraciones se realizan en una terraza con piscina.	☐	☑
3. Eventos Costa Rica solo organiza celebraciones familiares.	☐	☑
4. El pedido de cotización no genera ninguna obligación.	☑	☐
5. Eventos Costa Rica ofrece servicio de transporte para los invitados.	☑	☐

10 a. Relacione las columnas.

¿Es buena idea...	me organicen la despedida de soltera? ¡Nos vamos a reír mucho!
¿No es una excelente idea que mis amigas...	organizar una fiesta de graduación?

b. Elija un evento y anote sus propuestas para celebrarlo. Evalúe las propuestas de su compañero/a.

11 ¿Cómo valora usted este tipo de empresas? ¿Ha celebrado o ha asistido a algún evento organizado por una empresa como Eventos Costa Rica?

Expresar condiciones posibles

Si puede, llámeme.

18B.4 **si** + [*present*], [*imperative*]

Vocabulario *cont.*

en resumen *in short*
la cotización *estimate*
ocurrirse *to think of*
la limusina, el evento, la celebración, mágico/a

15

rescatar *to rescue*
derramarse *to shed*
matar *to kill*
la espada *sword*
devorar, la rosa

Estrategia

Resumir en ideas principales

- **En resumen,** si usted quiere sorprender a sus invitados, contáctenos.
- Sí, **en definitiva,** somos su mejor opción.

Diada de Sant Jordi

El 23 de abril se celebra el Día del Libro para conmemorar la muerte de Miguel de Cervantes, William Shakespeare e Inca Garcilaso de la Vega. Ese día también se recuerda a San Jorge, patrono de Cataluña. Según la leyenda, un dragón iba a devorar a una princesa, pero San Jorge la rescató y mató al dragón con su espada. Donde se derramó la sangre del dragón, creció un rosal de rosas rojas. Por eso, todos los años, los catalanes intercambian rosas y libros en la **Diada de Sant Jordi** (*Día de San Jorge* en catalán).

Expansion Ask students to describe any other legends with which they are familiar.

12 ¿Qué nos sugiere Eventos Costa Rica si queremos celebrar un evento?

Si quiere disfrutar de un evento bien organizado,... → contáctenos y solicite su cotización sin compromiso.

Si tiene un sueño,... → hágalo realidad con nosotros.

13 a. Piense en posibles condiciones para estas oraciones.

1. Si *vas a casarte*, vístete como una reina.
2. Si quieres una boda especial, ...
3. Si .... celebrar la mejor fiesta de los quince, ...
4. Si quiere sorprender a sus invitados, ...
5. Si .... despedida de soltero/a, ...

13a Expansion Have students compare their answers in pairs.

b. Usted quiere hacer una fiesta de cumpleaños e invitar a mucha gente. Piense en los problemas que pueden surgir. Cuénteselos a su compañero/a para que le dé una solución.

Modelo:
- *No tengo mucho espacio en casa.*
- *Si no tienes mucho espacio, celébralo en un restaurante.*

14 Lea de nuevo el texto de presentación de Eventos Costa Rica y resuma el contenido en dos ideas principales.

- En resumen, esta empresa...
- En definitiva, ...

15 Lea la nota sobre la Diada de Sant Jordi. En su país, ¿hay alguna celebración como la que se describe? Escriba un pequeño reportaje sobre ella.

15 Suggestion Remind students of Barcelona architecture that they have seen; **Casa Batlló**, with its scaled roof, appears to represent the legend of **Sant Jordi**.

MI EXPERIENCIA

16 Pregúntele a su compañero/a cuál es la celebración que más le gusta. ¿Qué valora a la hora de prepararla y celebrarla? ¿Qué condiciones pueden favorecer la celebración? En resumen, ¿qué es lo principal?

GUIÓN DE TRABAJO

¿Cuál es la celebración que más te gusta? → La celebración que más me gusta es... / Las celebraciones que más me gustan son... → la Navidad / las bodas / los cumpleaños / las fiestas de la empresa / San Valentín / otras

¿Qué te parece importante para prepararla? → Es una buena idea... / No es mala idea... / Si (no) tengo dinero...

En resumen... / En definitiva...

Practice more at **vhlcentral.com.**

SAM: Actividades pp. 390–392

18B

Marián Rico, ¡pura vida!

Suggestion Ask the class what flowers they think sell the most in this country and what the most popular occasions are.

Marián Rico, florista de Costa Rica

Marián Rico es una joven tica que trabaja como florista en San José. Su país es uno de los grandes exportadores de flores, especialmente a los EE.UU. Hoy vuelve a trabajar después de la cita anual con Iberiada, un evento que durante una semana reúne a floristas de diferentes países de América Latina y de España.

Marián, ¿fue interesante el encuentro?

Sí, fue muy interesante. Este tipo de encuentros nos permite conocer tendencias y volver a ver a compañeros floristas. Es una excelente idea que se organicen estos eventos.

Veo que le gusta su trabajo de florista, ¿le va bien?

¡Pura vida! Me alegro de que mi gran pasión sea mi trabajo.

¿Venden flores solo en San José?

No, no, acá hacemos arreglos florales para entregar en cualquier parte del país. También trabajamos mucho con empresas que organizan todo tipo de eventos y celebraciones.

¿Qué flores se venden más y en qué fechas?

Nuestra flor nacional, la orquídea; también los arreglos de rosas y flores variadas. Depende de la estación; por ejemplo, los claveles o los tulipanes ahora vuelven a venir... Hay muchas ocasiones para regalar flores, pero el día que más flores se venden es el 14 de febrero, Día de San Valentín. También el Día de la Madre (15 de agosto) o en Navidad.

Dicen que las flores hablan...

Sí, las flores tienen un lenguaje propio, muestran nuestros sentimientos de alegría, amor, amistad o incluso tristeza. Si quiere felicitar a una persona o mostrarle su afecto, ¡dígaselo con flores!

Muchas gracias, Marián.

Con gusto. Vuelva a visitarme cuando quiera.

Indicar acciones que se repiten

Las rosas rojas son la mejor opción para **volver a enamorar** a tu pareja.

18B.5 **volver a** + [*infinitive*]

Vocabulario

17

¡Pura vida! (*C. R.*) *Great!*
el/la tico/a (*fam.*) *Costa Rican*
el/la exportador(a) *exporter*
el arreglo floral *flower arrangement*
el clavel *carnation*
el tulipán *tulip*
mostrar (o:ue) afecto *to show affection*
Con gusto. *You're welcome.*
el/la florista

19

la tarjeta de visita *business card*

17 a. Mire la foto de Marián Rico. ¿A qué se dedica? ¿Qué está haciendo en la imagen? Lea la entrevista. ¿De qué habla Marián? Ordene los temas según aparecen. Es florista. Esta preparando un ramo de flores.

- 5 sentimientos que expresan las flores
- 4 fechas de mayor venta
- 3 flores más vendidas
- 1 congreso de Iberiada
- 2 lugares donde envían flores

b. ¿Ha escuchado alguna vez la expresión *¡Pura vida!*? Localícela en el texto. ¿Qué cree que significa? Escenifique una conversación con su compañero/a y utilícela.

18 a. ¿Qué piensa Marián sobre la flores? ¿Por qué dice *Dígaselo con flores*?
Piensa que las flores tienen un lenguaje propio y muestran nuestros sentimientos.
Possible answer: Porque a veces comunicamos mejor nuestros sentimientos con flores que con palabras.

b. ¿Qué flores se venden más y cuándo? Complete esta intervención de Marián. la orquídea, los arreglos de rosas y flores variadas; Las ventas dependen de la estación, pero el día que más se vende es el Día de San Valentín.
"Ahora los claveles o los tulipanes ...vuelven a venir..."

c. Localice en el texto la estructura *volver a*... e indique qué significado tiene.
vuelve a trabajar, volver a ver, vuelven a venir, vuelva a visitarme, vuelva a vernos pronto (en la tarjeta)
○ siempre ◉ otra vez ○ nunca más

19 a. ¿A quién va dirigida la frase *Vuelva a vernos pronto* de la tarjeta de visita de la tienda? ¿Qué mensaje transmite? a sus clientes; se los espera y serán bienvenidos

b. ¿Qué quiere volver a hacer usted pronto? ¿Y su compañero/a?

19b **Expansion** Ask students to think about any regrets they have, and to express them using **no volver a** + [*infinitive*].

Possible answers: para representar su identidad; porque es la flor más cultivada en el país, porque crece en todo el territorio, por elección de los habitantes

20 a. Lea este texto. ¿Por qué los países eligen una "flor nacional"? ¿Cuáles son algunos de los motivos por los que se elige una flor en particular?

Los países tienen diferentes símbolos que representan su identidad: banderas, escudos, himnos, etc. Muchos países de América Latina también tienen una "flor nacional".

La orquídea guaria morada es la flor nacional y la más cultivada de Costa Rica. Los indios y los primeros colonizadores la apreciaban, y a las mujeres indígenas les gustaba adornarse la cabeza con sus grandes flores moradas.

La flor que actualmente representa a la República Dominicana es la rosa de Bayahibe, pero no siempre fue así. En 1957, el estado dominicano eligió la caoba como flor y árbol nacional. Sin embargo, muchos dominicanos no estaban de acuerdo con esa decisión. Por eso, en 2010 se estableció que la rosa de Bayahibe sería la flor nacional.

Argentina y Uruguay tienen la misma flor nacional: el ceibo. En el caso de Argentina, la decisión se tomó en el año 1942 después de una serie de encuestas entre los habitantes. Debido a la diversidad de climas y relieves, era imposible encontrar una flor que se pudiera cultivar en todo el territorio. Los uruguayos, en cambio, optaron por esa flor debido a que crece naturalmente en todos sus departamentos.

b. Hable con sus compañeros sobre la flor de su estado o región. Si ya hay una flor, ¿está usted de acuerdo con la elección? Si no, ¿qué opción propondría?

21 Elija la flor que más le gusta y descríbala. Exprese los sentimientos que le produce. ¿Le gusta regalarlas o que se las regalen? ¿En qué ocasiones?

Mi flor preferida es...

22 ¿Ha oído hablar del "lenguaje de las flores"? Lea el texto. ¿Qué flor le parece más apropiada para regalar a una madre? ¿Y a su pareja? ¿Por qué?

Las flores tienen un lenguaje propio. Cada tipo de flor tiene un significado y su color puede expresar diferentes sentimientos. Por ejemplo, las margaritas blancas representan la inocencia y la pureza. Las amarillas, en cambio, son una sutil declaración de amor. En el caso de las rosas, el color rosado claro simboliza admiración y simpatía, mientras que el amarillo indica alegría y agradecimiento.

Vocabulario

20

- el escudo *coat of arms*
- el himno *anthem*
- el/la colonizador(a) *colonizer*
- apreciar *to appreciate*
- adornar(se) *to decorate*
- la caoba *mahogany tree*
- el ceibo *coral tree*
- la encuesta *survey*
- el relieve *relief, geographical feature*
- **la identidad, optar**

22

- expresar un sentimiento *to express a feeling*
- la margarita *daisy*
- la pureza *purity*
- sutil *subtle*
- la declaración de amor *declaration of love*
- rosado/a *pink*
- simbolizar *to represent*
- la simpatía *friendliness*
- **la inocencia**

OPINIÓN

¿Compra habitualmente flores? ¿Por qué?

Si regala flores, ¿en qué ocasiones lo hace?

22 Expansion Ask students if they have any other associations with certain flowers or colors. Do they agree with the symbolism described here?

Practice more at **vhlcentral.com.**

SAM: Actividades pp. 393–398

23 a. El Año Nuevo se celebra con costumbres diferentes según las culturas. Fíjese en las fotos. ¿Qué elementos le llaman la atención? ¿Qué pueden representar? Lea el texto y compruebe sus predicciones.

23a Suggestion Remind students that Christmas falls during the summer in Argentina and Chile.

23a Expansion Have students research other rituals or beliefs related to luck in Spanish-speaking countries.

Para cenar, los venezolanos hacen **hallacas**, que son pasteles de maíz rellenos. Muchos latinoamericanos comen carne de cerdo° para tener abundancia durante el nuevo año. En Argentina quedan muchas tradiciones europeas; por eso, a pesar del calor, comen nueces°, turrones° y platos más propios de invierno. En Chile comen lentejas.

En España y algunos países de América Latina, se comen **doce uvas**° con las campanadas° del reloj que anuncian el nuevo año. Hay que comer una con cada campanada para tener suerte en los doce meses siguientes.

¡FELIZ AÑO NUEVO!

En Costa Rica, encontrar en Año Nuevo una pequeña **flor silvestre**° llamada Santa Lucía, significa suerte. Si se mete en el billetero°, no faltará dinero.

En Ecuador, Colombia, México, Venezuela, Argentina y otros países de América Latina, para recibir el Año Nuevo se quema° el **"Año Viejo"** (un muñeco de cartón°, telas...).

carne de cerdo *pork* **nueces** *walnuts* **turrones** *nougat candy* **flor silvestre** *wildflower* **billetero** *wallet* **uvas** *grapes* **se quema** *is burned* **muñeco de cartón** *cardboard dummy*

b. ¿Cómo se celebra el Año Nuevo en su cultura? ¿Existe algún ritual? ¿Hay una comida típica o tradición especial? Piense en otras celebraciones importantes y comparta con la clase.

TAREA FINAL

Organizar una celebración

- Piensen en ocasiones (día del español, fin de curso, graduación, cumpleaños del/de la profesor(a)...) para organizar una celebración y hagan una lista.
- Decidan entre todas las propuestas cuál van a celebrar.
- Evalúen ideas de organización (*es una buena idea que cada pareja se ocupe de...*) y repartan tareas. Señalen condiciones para la realización de las tareas.
- Si necesitan una tarjeta de felicitación, háganla.
- Si ya tienen todo organizado, ¡celebren su fiesta!

YO PUEDO...

- Puedo expresar sentimientos.
  Diga qué le da pena y de qué se alegra en estos momentos: ¿Cuándo se pone más contento/a, al empezar o al terminar un proyecto?
- Puedo felicitar.
  Hoy es el Día del Estudiante de Español. Felicite a su compañero/a.
- Puedo evaluar ideas.
  Piense en alguna de las ideas que ha escuchado referidas a la celebración de eventos y evalúela.
- Puedo expresar condiciones.
  Complete la oración.
  Si quieres aprender español, ...
- Puedo indicar acciones que se repiten.
  Describa dos cosas que hace todos los años en septiembre o en diciembre.

GRAMÁTICA FUNCIONAL

18B.1 Express feelings

alegrarse de/dar pena + **que** + [*subjunctive*] 5.7.1, 5.20, 5.21.1d, 6.4
ponerse triste 5.7.3, 6.4
cuando/si + [*indicative*]/**al** + [*infinitive*] 5.13, 12.12

- Use **alegrarse de** (*to be happy*) + **que** + [*subjunctive*] to express what makes someone happy. **Alegrarse** is a reflexive verb.

  Nos alegramos de que hayas venido.
  We are happy that you came.

  Se alegra de que puedas venir a visitarlo.
  ***He is glad you can come** to visit him.*

- Use [*indirect object pronoun*] + **da pena que** + [*subjunctive*] to express sadness.

  Nos da pena que te vayas.
  It saddens us that you are leaving.

  Le da pena que no puedas venir a visitarlo.
  ***He is sad you can't** come to visit him.*

- Use the subjunctive with these two constructions when the two verbs in a sentence refer to different people. As you have seen in previous lessons, if both verbs refer to the same person, use an infinitive after **alegrarse de** or **dar pena**.

  Me alegro de estar aquí.
  ***I am happy to be** here.*

  Me da pena no poder ir.
  ***I'm sad I can't** go.*

- Use the reflexive verb **ponerse** (*to become*) with an adjective (**triste, alegre**) to express a change in a subject's mood that is usually considered to be temporary.

  Me puse muy triste cuando recibí la noticia.
  ***I became very sad** when I got the news.*

  Mi abuela **se pone alegre** cuando vamos a visitarla.
  *My grandmother **is happy** when we go visit her.*

- Use **al** + [*infinitive*] to refer to a specific moment when something happens or happened.

  Mi perro se pone muy contento **al verme**.
  *My dog becomes happy **upon seeing** me (**when/if he sees** me).*

- Express a similar idea with **cuando/si** + [*indicative*].

  Mi perro se pone muy contento **cuando** me **ve**.
  *My dog becomes happy **when he sees** me.*

  Se pone muy triste **si me voy**.
  *He gets very sad **if I leave**.*

G2 Expansion Have students write a series of mini-conversations that might be overheard at their house.

Suggestion Have pairs of students take turns making statements using the expressions from **18B.1**. Their partner should restate it, using a different expression with similar meaning. Ex: **Me dio pena perderme la fiesta. (Me puse triste al perderme la fiesta.)**

¡Póngalo en práctica!

G1 Complete las oraciones.

1. Dafne ....se alegra........ (alegrarse) de que su abuela ....se sienta........ (sentirse) mejor.
2. A Alejandro ....le da pena........ (dar pena) que no ....podamos........ (poder, nosotros) ir a su fiesta de jubilación.
3. Mis primos siempre ....se ponen contentos........ (ponerse contento) cuando ....vamos........ (ir, nosotros) a la casa de sus padres para cenar.
4. Anoche ....te pusiste........ (ponerse, tú) triste al ....oír........ (oír) la canción que te hizo pensar en tu ex novio.

G2 Complete las conversaciones.

- ¿Te alegras de que nos (1)........veamos........ (ver) pronto?
- Sí, ayer me puse muy contento cuando mi madre me (2)........dijo........ (decir) que vendrías a la boda.

- ¿No os da pena que (3)........termine........ (terminar) el verano?
- Sí, yo me pongo triste al (4)........pensar........ (pensar) que pronto vendrá el otoño.

- Me alegro de que (5)........hayan podido........ (poder) venir a la fiesta.
- ¡Muchas gracias por habernos invitado! Lo pasamos muy bien y nos da pena (6)........tener........ que irnos temprano.

- Al (7)........llegar........ (llegar) al apartamento, me puse contenta porque la cena estaba preparada.
- Me alegro de que (8)........te lleves........ (llevarse) bien con tu compañera de cuarto. ¡Qué simpática que es!

G3 Empareje el comienzo de la oración con el final apropiado.

1. Siempre me pongo muy contento	b
2. Candela se puso un poco triste	a
3. Verónica y Paula se alegran de que	d
4. Me da pena que	c
5. Mis compañeros de piso se pusieron muy contentos	e

a. al terminar la novela porque le había gustado mucho.
b. cuando hablo con un viejo amigo.
c. no me hayan invitado a la fiesta.
d. a su jefa le haya gustado su propuesta.
e. cuando vieron que había limpiado la cocina.

Practice more at **vhlcentral.com.**

18B

GRAMÁTICA FUNCIONAL

18B.2 Offer congratulations and best wishes

felicidades, enhorabuena, feliz + [*noun*], **que** + [*subjunctive*] 5.20, 5.21.1, 14.26

- Say **felicidades, felicitaciones,** or **enhorabuena** to congratulate someone. All three expressions can mean *congratulations*, but **felicitaciones** is used more frequently in Latin America and **enhorabuena** is more common in Spain.

  ¡**Felicitaciones** por tu graduación!
  ***Congratulations** on your graduation!*

  ¡**Enhorabuena** por el premio!
  ***Congratulations** on the prize!*

- **Felicitaciones** or **enhorabuena** are more often used to congratulate someone on a more significant, unique accomplishment, while the more general **felicidades** can be used to mean *congratulations, happy birthday,* and *happy holidays.*

- Use the construction **feliz** + [*noun*] to give well wishes, as in **¡Feliz cumpleaños!** (*Happy birthday!*) and **¡Feliz Día de la Madre!** (*Happy Mother's Day!*). Use **felices** with plural nouns.

¡**Feliz** Año Nuevo!	¡**Felices** fiestas!
Happy New Year!	*Happy holidays!*

- Say **igualmente** (*likewise; the same to you*) to return the greeting.

  Gracias, **igualmente. ¡Felices fiestas!**
  *Thanks, **the same to you. Happy holidays!***

- Use the subjunctive in set phrases that take **que** + [*subjunctive*].

¡**Que** lo **pasen** bien!	¡Que **vuelvan** pronto!
Have a good time!	***Come back** soon!*

18B.3 Evaluate ideas

(no) es (una) buena idea + [*infinitive*] / **que** + [*subjunctive*] 5.8.9, 5.13, 5.20, 5.21.5

- Use **(no) es (una) buena idea** + [*infinitive*] / **que** + [*subjunctive*] to assess an idea. Use the infinitive to assess an idea in general terms or **que** + [*subjunctive*] when there is a specified subject. Note that other adjectives can be substituted for **buena**.

  Es buena idea celebrar los cumpleaños infantiles en un parque.
  ***It is a good idea to celebrate** childrens' birthdays at a park.*

  No es una buena idea que siempre **llegues** tarde al trabajo.
  *It's not a good idea for you **to** always **arrive** late to work.*

- As in English, use the negative question in order to ask another person to confirm your idea.

  ¿No es una excelente idea que pasemos la Nochevieja en Buenos Aires?
  ***Isn't it an excellent idea for us to spend** New Year's Eve in Buenos Aires?*

Suggestion Point out the lack of a written accent on **Que**. Tell students that they could think of this expression as *May you/we/they...*

Suggestion Have pairs of students take turns proposing plans for the weekend, using **(no) es una buena idea...** Tell them to decide on a plan.

¡Póngalo en práctica!

G4 Complete los diálogos.

- ¡(1) Feliz Navidad!
- Gracias, (2) igualmente; y si no nos vemos en los próximos días, ¡Feliz Año Nuevo!

- Empiezo un nuevo trabajo mañana.
- ¡(3) Felicitaciones / Enhorabuena ! ¡Te deseo mucha suerte!

- ¡(4) Feliz cumpleaños! ¡(5) Que cumplas muchos más!
- ¡Muchas gracias!

- Hoy es nuestro aniversario.
- ¡(6) Felicidades !

- ¡(7) Feliz Día de San Valentín!
- Gracias, (8) igualmente .

G5 Empareje las dos partes de estas conversaciones.

- 1. Feliz Año Nuevo! d
- 2. Mañana festejo mi jubilación. a
- 3. ¡Feliz cumpleaños! e
- 4. La semana que viene mi esposa y yo festejamos nuestras bodas de plata. b
- 5. El viernes salimos para la costa. c
- a. ¡Felicitaciones! Sé que usted trabajó muchos años en la empresa.
- b. ¡Felicidades!
- c. ¡Que lo pasen muy bien!
- d. ¡Igualmente!
- e. Muchas gracias. ¿Te puedes creer que ya cumplo veinte años?

G6 Complete las oraciones.

- ¿Qué opinas? ¿No es una buena idea (1) hacer (hacer) una fiesta y (2) celebrar (celebrar) juntos nuestros cumpleaños?
- No, es mejor idea que cada uno (3) haga (hacer) su propia fiesta y así nos divertimos dos días.

- ¿Es buena idea que (4) salgamos (nosotros, salir) temprano para la playa mañana?
- Creo que sí, pero no es buena idea (5) salir (salir) muy tarde.

- ¿No es buena idea que (6) organicemos (nosotros, organizar) una fiesta de Año Nuevo?
- No sé, es mucho trabajo planificar una fiesta de ese tipo. En mi opinión, es mejor idea (7) ir (ir) con todos nuestros amigos a la plaza y (8) festejar (festejar) juntos.

Practice more at **vhlcentral.com.**

GRAMÁTICA FUNCIONAL

G7 Expansion Eliminate the second part of each sentence, leaving only the **si** clause. Have students provide alternate endings.

18B.4 Express possible conditions

si + [*present indicative*], [*imperative*] 5.18.1, 12.9, 5.19.1

- Use the construction **si** + [*present indicative*], [*imperative*] to make a suggestion or give a command with a condition.

  Si me **quieres** localizar la semana que viene, **llámame** al celular porque estaré de viaje.
  *If **you want** to reach me next week, **call me** on my cellular phone because I will be on a trip.*

- If the sentence starts with **si** + [*verb*], use a comma after the verb. If the **si** clause comes at the end of the sentence, you don't need a comma.

  Si me necesitas, llámame.
  If you need me, call me.

  Llámame si me necesitas.
  Call me if you need me.

- Remember to use the correct imperative form (**tú**, **usted**, **vosotros/as**, or **ustedes**) for the person or group you are addressing.

  Si quieren viajar a Buenos Aires para Año Nuevo, **hagan** la reserva ya.
  *If you want to travel to Buenos Aires for New Year's, **make** your reservations now.*

  No invitéis a mucha gente si no queréis molestar a los vecinos.
  ***Don't invite** a lot of people if you don't want to bother the neighbors.*

- Remember that indirect object, direct object, and reflexive pronouns may also be used with command forms. You learned how to use direct object pronouns with either indirect object pronouns or reflexive pronouns in 16B.2.

  Si vienes a mi boda, **confírmamelo** con antelación.
  ***If you are coming** to my wedding, **let me know (it)** in advance.*

  Si van a armar una fiesta sorpresa, **no se lo digan** a Eduardo.
  *If you're going to throw a surprise party, **don't tell** Eduardo.*

- You have already learned other constructions with **si** clauses. In 8A.3, you learned to propose plans with **si** + [*present indicative*], [*present indicative*].

  Si quieres, podemos ir al cine más tarde.
  ***If you want, we can** go to the movies later.*

- In 14A.5, you learned to express a possible situation in the present or the future with the construction **si** + [*present*], [*present/simple future*].

  Si estudias español, **tendrás** muchas oportunidades laborales.
  ***If you study** Spanish, **you will have** many job opportunities.*

Suggestion Write a series of **si** clauses on the board (Ex: **Si mi familia gana la lotería...**). Have students complete them logically.

¡Póngalo en práctica!

G7 **Complete las oraciones.**

Si (1) vais (vosotros, ir) a la fiesta de cumpleaños del hijo de Ana y Pedro, (2) decídnoslo (a nosotros, decir, lo) para que vayamos juntos.

Sr. Montejo, si (3) hay (haber) reunión el jueves, por favor, (4) mándeme (mandar a mí) un mensaje.

Si (5) piensan (ustedes, pensar) salir hasta tarde, (6) llámenme (llamar a mí).

Si te (7) gusta (gustar) el vestido, (8) cómpralo / cómpratelo (comprarlo).

G8 **Complete las oraciones con el imperativo.**

1. Si tienes tiempo después de clase, llámame (llamar a mí).
2. Si terminas el arreglo floral en una hora, llévalo (llevar, lo) a la iglesia.
3. Si usted consigue pasajes a un buen precio, pase (pasar) el Año Nuevo en Barcelona.
4. Si ustedes terminan su tarea a tiempo, salgan (salir) con sus amigos.
5. Si no llueve, festejad (festejar) vuestra graduación con un evento al aire libre.
6. Si usted va a la casa de sus abuelos en Navidad, salúdelos (saludar, ellos) de mi parte.

G9 **Empareje el comienzo de cada oración con el final apropiado.**

1. Si conocen una buena panadería para conseguir un pastel de cumpleaños,	d
2. Si se te ocurren más ideas para la despedida de soltera de Isabel,	a
3. Si decidís pasar las fiestas en la costa,	e
4. Si ves a Matías,	b
5. Si no le gusta el arreglo floral,	c

a. llámame porque me estoy ocupando de los detalles.
b. dile que la fiesta de los 15 años de su prima es el próximo sábado.
c. llámenos enseguida y se lo podemos cambiar.
d. por favor, denme la dirección.
e. llamadnos, así nos vemos.

Practice more at **vhlcentral.com.**

GRAMÁTICA FUNCIONAL

18B.5 Indicate repeated actions

volver a + [*infinitive*] 5.15

- Use the construction **volver a** + [*infinitive*] to express the repetition of an action.

  Siempre es bonito **volver a ver** a los amigos de la infancia.
  *It is always nice **to see** childhood friends **again**.*

- The verb **volver** can be used in different tenses in this construction.

  ¿Cuándo **volverás a ofrecer** el curso de español?
  *When **will you offer** the Spanish course **again**?*

- Other constructions that express repeated actions include **otra vez**, **de nuevo**, **nuevamente**, and **una vez más**.

  ¡Qué alegría verte **de nuevo**!
  *It's so great to see you **again**!*

¡Póngalo en práctica!

G10 Complete las oraciones.

- ¿Cómo puedo volver a (1)......ver...... (ver) a tu compañera de cuarto?
- Un día, cuando (2)......volvamos...... (nosotras, volver) a salir juntas, te aviso.

Ayer (3)......volví...... (yo, volver) a escuchar un CD de mi grupo preferido.

Ezequiel siempre (4)......vuelve...... (volver) a contar los mismos chistes.

¡Cuidado! No quiero que (5)......vuelvas...... (tú, volver) a caerte.

(6)......Vuelvo...... (Yo, volver) a pensar en mi infancia cuando oigo esa canción.

Practice more at **vhlcentral.com.**

SÍNTESIS

Suggestion Have students work in groups to write an ad using **volver a + [*infinitive*]** and at least one of the other expressions such as **otra vez.**

Mire las fotografías y escriba un diálogo o párrafo corto para cada una, usando el vocabulario indicado.

1. 

pastel	cumplir	felicidades	alegrarse de

- ______
- ______
- ______
- ______

2. 

feliz	acordarse	florista	simbolizar

- ______
- ______
- ______
- ______

3. 

aniversario	volver a	cuando	si

- ______
- ______
- ______
- ______

VOCABULARIO

Acontecimientos de la vida

el Año Nuevo	*New Year*
las bodas de plata	*silver wedding anniversary*
el cumpleaños (*invar.*)	*birthday*
el Día de la Madre	*Mother's Day*
la fiesta de quince años	*fifteenth birthday party*
la graduación	*graduation*
la jubilación	*retirement*
acordarse (o:ue) de	*to remember*
alegrarse de	*to be glad that*
cumplir años	*to have one's birthday*
cumplir años de casados	*to have one's wedding anniversary*
dar pena	*to upset*
marcharse	*to leave, to go away*
ponerse contento/a	*to become happy*
ponerse triste	*to become sad*

Celebraciones a la carta

en definitiva	*all in all*
en resumen	*in short*
el bautizo	*baptism*
la celebración	*celebration*
la cotización	*estimate*
la despedida de soltero/a	*bachelor(ette) party*
la espada	*sword*
el evento	*event*
el/la invitado/a	*guest*
la limusina	*limousine*
el/la maestro/a de ceremonias	*master of ceremonies*
el pastel	*cake*
la rosa	*rose*
el salón de fiestas	*function hall*
derramarse	*to shed*
devorar	*to devour*
disponer (ng) de	*to have (at one's disposal)*
matar	*to kill*
ocuparse de los detalles	*to take care of the details*
ocurrirse	*to think of*
planificar	*to plan*
rescatar	*to rescue*
mágico/a	*magic*

Marián Rico

Con gusto.	*You're welcome.*
¡Pura vida! (*C.R.*)	*Great!*
el arreglo floral	*flower arrangement*
la caoba	*mahogany tree*
el ceibo	*coral tree*
el clavel	*carnation*
el/la colonizador(a)	*colonizer*
la declaración de amor	*declaration of love*
la encuesta	*survey*
el escudo	*coat of arms*
el/la exportador(a)	*exporter*
el/la florista	*florist*
el himno	*anthem*
la identidad	*identity*
la inocencia	*innocence*
la margarita	*daisy*
la pureza	*purity*
el relieve	*relief, geographical feature*
la simpatía	*friendliness*
la tarjeta de visita	*business card*
el/la tico/a (*fam.*)	*Costa Rican*
el tulipán	*tulip*
adornar(se)	*to decorate*
apreciar	*to appreciate*
expresar un sentimiento	*to express a feeling*
mostrar (o:ue) afecto	*to show affection*
optar	*to opt, to choose*
simbolizar	*to represent*
rosado/a	*pink*
sutil	*subtle*

Variación léxica

el billetero ↔ la billetera ↔ la cartera

la cotización ↔ el presupuesto

dar pena ↔ apenar

ponerse triste ↔ entristecerse (zc)

el/la tico/a (*fam.*) ↔ el/la costarricense

Estrategias

1 Expresar consecuencia

Lección 17A

Expressions that show consequence, such as **así (es) que** (*so*) or **por lo tanto** (*therefore*), help you bring ideas together and express a natural conclusion to an intervention.

- Termine estas oraciones con una consecuencia.

"En el futuro, todos los profesionales podrán trabajar desde casa, ...
...."

"Es muy probable que los robots hagan el trabajo de muchas personas, ...
...."

"Está claro que el idioma español se habla cada día más, ...
...."

2 Reforzar una negación

2 Expansion Have students write two additional statements about children's dislikes.

Lección 17B

Unlike in English, multiple negative words can, and should, be used together in Spanish to reinforce the negation (**no... nada**). Using negative expressions correctly will help you express yourself with greater fluency.

- Refuerce la negación de estas oraciones, así como lo haría un hispanohablante. Piense en otras situaciones y emplee este recurso.

A los niños no les gusta que les prohíban ver la tele.	A los niños no les gusta nada que les prohíban ver la tele.
No les divierte ver las películas de mayores.	A los niños no les divierte nada ver las películas de mayores.

3 Intensificar

3 Expansion Have students write a conversation between two students who are complaining about how busy they are.

Lección 18A

Spanish uses repeated words in order to add intensity and subjectiveness to speech.

- Piense que ha realizado estas acciones y reformule las frases añadiendo intensidad a la acción.

caminar 20 horas	hacer frío durante todo el invierno	escribir cien páginas cada día
caminar horas y horas	hacer frío durante días y días/hacer frío un día y otro día y otro día/ hacer frío durante meses y meses	escribir páginas y páginas cada día

4 Resumir ideas principales

Lección 18B

In a conversation, it can be helpful to sum up the main ideas and call attention to the most important concepts. To do so, use expressions such as **en resumen** (*in short*) or **en definitiva** (*all in all*). Sometimes what follows is not just a summary, but also a personal conclusion or assessment.

- Resuma lo que dice esta persona.

El sábado es la boda de Juan y Ana, pero ese día tengo otra fiesta, no tengo mucha relación con ellos y...	....

Competencias

HACER PREDICCIONES, EXPRESAR PROBABILIDAD, EXPRESAR CONTINUIDAD

1 Haga predicciones sobre un futuro cercano. Su compañero/a deberá expresar la probabilidad de que eso suceda.

Modelo: • *Dentro de cinco años habrá una moneda única en todo el mundo.*
• *Me parece poco probable que sea así. Seguro seguirá habiendo...*

EXPRESAR RECIPROCIDAD

2 Describa las acciones que muestran las fotos. Use **nos, os** o **se**. 1. Daniel y Virginia se besan; 2. Andrea y yo nos abrazamos; 3. Vosotros os saludáis.

1 

(Daniel y Virginia / besarse)

2 

(Andrea y yo / abrazarse)

3 

(vosotros / saludarse)

EXPRESAR REPROCHE, EXPRESAR SENTIMIENTOS

3 Alicia ha estado muy ocupada últimamente y no ha tenido tiempo para sus familiares y amigos. Complete los comentarios de algunos de ellos. **3 Expansion** Have students write Alicia's responses to these statements. Have her offer excuses and explanations for letting these people down.

1. Me molesta que no ....te hayas dado cuenta.... (darse cuenta) de que me corté el pelo.
2. Me pone triste que no ....te hayas acordado.... (acordarse) de mi cumpleaños.
3. Me decepciona que ....te hayas olvidado.... (olvidarse) de ir a nuestra clase de baile.

IDENTIFICAR, EXPRESAR ADMIRACIÓN, RELACIONAR ACONTECIMIENTOS, HABLAR SOBRE RETOS FUTUROS, FELICITAR

4 Complete esta conversación con la forma correcta de los verbos.

VICENTE: ¿Sabes lo que me (1)....dijo.... (decir) mi nieto? Que cuando (2)....sea.... (ser) mayor, (3)....será.... (ser) un aventurero como Iván Vallejo.

CAMILA: ¿Cómo quién?

VICENTE: Iván Vallejo. Es un montañista ecuatoriano al que (4)....admira.... (admirar) mucho.

CAMILA: ¿Y por qué?

VICENTE: Porque (5)....está.... (estar) impresionado con sus logros. La verdad, ¡(6)....es.... (ser) increíble lo que (7)....puede/ha podido.... (poder) hacer!

CAMILA: Ya veo. ¿Y cuándo te lo (8)....dijo.... (decir)?

VICENTE: Ayer, después de (9)....ver.... (ver) un documental sobre la vida del deportista.

CAMILA: ¡Felicitaciones! (10)....Tienes.... (Tener) un nieto muy decidido.

Estrategia

Synthesizing

When watching a video, try to synthesize what you see and hear (not to be mistaken with summarizing: see Unit 11, page 284). Synthesizing involves putting together new facts and images with your prior knowledge, opinions, feelings, and experiences and coming up with a new idea or concept. When watching this **Flash Cultura** episode, try to reorganize the topic and generate your own explanation, adding your personal take.

Vocabulario útil

alargado/a *elongated*
alucinante *amazing*
ceder *to hand over*
el lienzo *canvas*
la muestra *exhibition*
la planta *floor (of a building)*
polémico/a *controversial*
el primer plano *foreground*
el tamaño *size*

Estrategia

Using the verb *dar*

Dar is one of the most versatile verbs in Spanish and it is used in a number of expressions, such as **darse cuenta** (*to realize*) or **dar por sentado** (*to take for granted*). One of the meanings of **dar** is *to cause* or *produce*: **me da asco** (*it makes me sick*), **me da miedo** (*it scares me*). There are hundreds of feelings you can express in Spanish with **dar**. Try it with **envidia, rabia, confianza, frío, vergüenza, alegría.**

Flash Cultura

Palacios del arte

Ya ha visto que la vida está llena de ocasiones para celebrar: triunfos en el deporte, logros en el trabajo, eventos familiares, un nuevo año o simplemente el amor y la amistad. Este episodio de **Flash Cultura** prueba que el arte imita a la vida y muestra cómo lo hace grandiosamente en los famosos museos del Triángulo Dorado de Madrid.

1 ¿Prefiere el arte antiguo o el moderno? ¿Cree que el arte es aburrido mientras que el espectáculo es divertido? ¿Admira a algún artista? ¿Opina que las tendencias, en el arte como en la moda, vuelven a repetirse?

2 Mire el episodio de **Flash Cultura**. ¿Qué generalizaciones puede hacer sobre el tema? ¿Qué idea o reflexión se le ocurre? ¿Cuál es su opinión?

1 **Los grises, los negros dan una sensación de horror...**

2 **Otra corta caminata y llegamos al Museo Thyssen. Las pinturas de este museo provienen de una extraordinaria colección privada...**

3 Complete estas oraciones con la opción correcta.

1. El Paseo del Prado es una
   a. plaza. (b.) calle. c. galería.
2. Uno de los pintores españoles más famosos es
   a. Diego de la Vega. b. Darío Blasco. (c.) Diego Velázquez.
3. De la modelo del cuadro *La maja vestida* de Goya se desconoce
   a. la nacionalidad. b. la edad. (c.) la identidad.
4. El Museo Reina Sofía fue construido como
   (a.) hospital. b. palacio. c. hotel.
5. El *Guernica* de Picasso es un cuadro muy
   a. antiguo. (b.) grande. c. colorido.

3 Suggestion Alternatively, complete this activity orally in class and provide the items as true/false statements.

4 Con un(a) compañero/a, converse sobre las tres cosas/lugares/personas que más admira. Comente por qué son importantes para usted.

Modelo:
- *Una persona a la que admiro mucho es... /Antes de morirme quiero ver el cuadro de...*
- *Es increíble cómo puede... Me alegro de que vuelva a...*

4 Expansion Have students imagine that they are meeting up with the person they most admire. Ask them to write the conversation that transpires.

Practice more at **vhlcentral.com.**

Apéndice

Verb Conjugation Tables

This list includes the infinitive of verbs introduced as active vocabulary in **PROTAGONISTAS**, as well as other common verbs. Each verb is followed by a model verb conjugated on the same pattern. The number in parentheses indicates where in the verb tables, pages **A4–A11**, you can find the conjugated forms of the model verb. Many of these verbs can be used reflexively. To check the verb conjugation, use the tables on pages **A4–A11**. For placement of reflexive pronouns, see page **A12**.

abandonar like hablar (1)
abonar like hablar (1)
abrazarse like cruzar (37)
abrigarse like llegar (41)
abrir like vivir (3) *except* **p. p.** is **abierto**
abrocharse like hablar (1)
aburrirse like vivir (3)
acariciar like hablar (1)
aceptar like hablar (1)
acompañar like hablar (1)
aconsejar like hablar (1)
acordarse (o:ue) like contar (24)
acostarse (o:ue) like contar (24)
actualizar like cruzar (37)
actuar like graduar (40)
adaptar like hablar (1)
adivinar like hablar (1)
admirar like hablar (1)
adoptar like hablar (1)
adornar like hablar (1)
afectar like hablar (1)
afiliarse like hablar (1)
afirmar like hablar (1)
agarrar like hablar (1)
agrupar like hablar (1)
ahorrar like hablar (1)
albergar like llegar (41)
alegrarse like hablar (1)
almorzar (o:ue) like contar (24) *except* **(z:c)** before **e**
alojarse like hablar (1)
amargar like llegar (41)
ampliar like hablar (1)
añadir like vivir (3)
anotar like hablar (1)
anticipar like hablar (1)
anunciar like hablar (1)
apagar like llegar (41)
apelar like hablar (1)
aportar like hablar (1)
apoyar like hablar (1)
apreciar like hablar (1)
aprender like comer (2)
aprobar (o:ue) like contar (24)
aprovechar like hablar (1)
apuntarse like hablar (1)
arreglar like hablar (1)
ascender (e:ie) like entender (27)
asesorar like hablar (1)
asistir like vivir (3)
asumir like vivir (3)
asustar like hablar (1)
atender (e:ie) like entender (27)
atrapar like hablar (1)
atreverse like comer (2)
averiarse like enviar (39)
averiguar like hablar (1) *except* **(u:ü)** before **e**
ayudar like hablar (1)
bailar like hablar (1)
bajar like hablar (1)
bañarse like hablar (1)
batir like vivir (3)
beber like comer (2)
besar like hablar (1)
buscar like tocar (43)
calcular like hablar (1)
cambiar like hablar (1)
caminar like hablar (1)
cansarse like hablar (1)
cantar like hablar (1)
cargar like llegar (41)
casarse like hablar (1)
celebrar like hablar (1)
cenar like hablar (1)
cerrar (e:ie) like pensar (30)
charlar like hablar (1)
chatear like hablar (1)
chocar like tocar (43)
clasificar like tocar (43)
clavar like hablar (1)
cocinar like hablar (1)
colaborar like hablar (1)
coleccionar like hablar (1)
colocar like tocar (43)
comentar like hablar (1)
comenzar (e:ie) like empezar (26)
comer (2)
compaginar like hablar (1)
comparar like hablar (1)
compartir like vivir (3)
competir (e:i) like pedir (29)
completar like hablar (1)
componer (ng) like poner (15)
comprar like hablar (1)
comprender like comer (2)
comprobar (o:ue) like contar (24)
conciliar like hablar (1)
condicionar like hablar (1)
conducir (zc) (6)
confirmar like hablar (1)
confundirse like vivir (3)
conjugar like llegar (41)
conmemorar like hablar (1)
conocer (zc) (35)
conquistar like hablar (1)
conseguir (e:i) like seguir (32)
conservar like hablar (1)
construir (y) like destruir (38)
consumir like vivir (3)
contar (o:ue) (24)
contestar like hablar (1)
controlar like hablar (1)
convencer (z) like vencer (44)
convenir (ng) like venir (22)
convertir (e:ie) like sentir (33)
convivir like vivir (3)
correr like comer (2)
costar (o:ue) like contar (24)
crecer (zc) like conocer (35)
creer (36)
criticar like tocar (43)
cruzar (37)
cuidar like hablar (1)
cultivar like hablar (1)
cumplir like vivir (3)
cursar like hablar (1)
dar (7)
decepcionar like hablar (1)
decidir like vivir (3)
decir (g) (e:i) (8)
declarar like hablar (1)
dedicar like tocar (43)
defender (e:ie) like entender (27)
dejar like hablar (1)
demostrar (o:ue) like contar (24)
denominarse like hablar (1)
denunciar like hablar (1)
depender like comer (2)
derramar like hablar (1)
derribar like hablar (1)
desaparecer (zc) like conocer (35)
desarrollar like hablar (1)
desayunar like hablar (1)
descansar like hablar (1)
descender (e:ie) like entender (27)
desconectarse like hablar (1)
describir like vivir (3)
descubrir like vivir (3) *except* **p. p.** is **descubierto**
desear like hablar (1)
deslizar like cruzar (37)
desperdiciar like hablar (1)
despertar (e:ie) like pensar (30)
despertarse (e:ie) like pensar (30)
devolver (o:ue) like volver (34)
devorar like hablar (1)
dibujar like hablar (1)
diferenciarse like hablar (1)
dirigir (j) like proteger (42)
discutir like vivir (3)
diseñar like hablar (1)
disfrutar like hablar (1)
divertirse (e:ie) like sentir (33)
divorciarse like hablar (1)
doler (o:ue) like volver (34)
dominar like hablar (1)
dormir (o:ue) (25)
ducharse like hablar (1)
dudar like hablar (1)
echar like hablar (1)
editar like hablar (1)
educar like tocar (43)
egresar like hablar (1)
elaborar like hablar (1)
elegir (j) (e:i) like pedir (29) *except* **(g:j)** before **a** and **o**
eliminar like hablar (1)
emitir like vivir (3)
empezar (e:ie) (26)
enamorarse like hablar (1)
encantar like hablar (1)
encender (e:ie) like entender (27)
encontrar (o:ue) like contar (24)
encontrarse (o:ue) like contar (24)
endulzar like cruzar (37)
enfadarse like hablar (1)
enfrentarse like hablar (1)
enganchar like hablar (1)
enojarse like hablar (1)
enseñar like hablar (1)
entender (e:ie) (27)
enterarse like hablar (1)
entrar like hablar (1)
entretenerse (ng) (e:ie) like **tener** (20)
entristecer (zc) like conocer (35)
enviar (39)
escalar like hablar (1)
escenificar like tocar (43)
escribir like vivir (3) *except* **p. p.** is **escrito**
escuchar like hablar (1)
esperar like hablar (1)
espolvorear like hablar (1)
establecer (zc) like conocer (35)
estar (9)
estimular like hablar (1)
estrenar like hablar (1)
estudiar like hablar (1)
evitar like hablar (1)
exagerar like hablar (1)
exigir (j) like proteger (42)
exiliarse like hablar (1)
explicar like tocar (43)
explorar like hablar (1)
exponer (ng) like poner (15)
exportar like hablar (1)

expresar like hablar (1)
expulsar like hablar (1)
extrañar like hablar (1)
fabricar like tocar (43)
faltar like hablar (1)
fascinar like hablar (1)
favorecer (zc) like conocer (35)
fijarse like hablar (1)
financiar like hablar (1)
firmar like hablar (1)
flexibilizar like cruzar (37)
fomentar like hablar (1)
formar like hablar (1)
fortalecer (zc) like conocer (35)
fumar like hablar (1)
funcionar like hablar (1)
ganar like hablar (1)
garantizar like cruzar (37)
girar like hablar (1)
graduarse (40)
guardar like hablar (1)
gustar like hablar (1)
haber (10)
habilitar like hablar (1)
hablar (1)
hacer (11)
heredar like hablar (1)
herir (e:ie) like sentir (33)
imaginar like hablar (1)
impedir (e:i) like pedir (29)
importar like hablar (1)
imprimir like vivir (3) *except* **p. p.** is **impreso** or **imprimido**
inaugurar like hablar (1)
incentivar like hablar (1)
incluir (y) like destruir (38)
incorporar like hablar (1)
independizarse like cruzar (37)
informar like hablar (1)
inscribir like vivir (3)
instalar like hablar (1)
integrarse like hablar (1)
intercambiar like hablar (1)
interesar like hablar (1)
interpretar like hablar (1)
invadir like vivir (3)
invitar like hablar (1)
inyectar like hablar (1)
ir (12)
jugar (u:ue) (28)
lanzar like cruzar (37)
lavar like hablar (1)
leer like creer (36)
levantarse like hablar (1)
liberar like hablar (1)
limitar like hablar (1)
limpiar like hablar (1)
llamar like hablar (1)
llamarse like hablar (1)
llegar (41)
llevar like hablar (1)
llorar like hablar (1)
llover (o:ue) like volver (34)
localizar like cruzar (37)
lograr like hablar (1)
madrugar like llegar (41)
mandar like hablar (1)
manejar like hablar (1)
mantener (ng) (e:ie) like tener (20)
maquillarse like hablar (1)
marcar like tocar (43)
marcharse like hablar (1)
matar like hablar (1)
medir (e:i) like pedir (29)
mejorar like hablar (1)
mencionar like hablar (1)
meter like comer (2)
mirar like hablar (1)
molestar like hablar (1)
montar like hablar (1)
morir (o:ue) like dormir (25) *except* **p. p.** is **muerto**
mostrar (o:ue) like contar (24)
mudarse like hablar (1)
nacer (zc) like conocer (35)
nadar like hablar (1)
navegar like llegar (41)
nevar (e:ie) like pensar (30)
nombrar like hablar (1)
observar like hablar (1)
obtener (ng) (e:ie) like tener (20)
ocultar like hablar (1)
ocupar like hablar (1)
ocurrir like vivir (3)
ofrecer (zc) like conocer (35)
oír (13)
olvidar like hablar (1)
oponerse (ng) like poner (15)
optar like hablar (1)
ordenar like hablar (1)
organizar like cruzar (37)
parar like hablar (1)
parecer (zc) like conocer (35)
participar like hablar (1)
pasar like hablar (1)
pasear like hablar (1)
patentar like hablar (1)
pedir (e:i) (29)
pelar like hablar (1)
pensar (e:ie) (30)
perder (e:ie) like entender (27)
perdonar like hablar (1)
permitir like vivir (3)
pertenecer (zc) like conocer (35)
pintar like hablar (1)
planificar like tocar (43)
plantearse like hablar (1)
poder (o:ue) (14)
poner (ng) (15)
posponer (ng) like poner (15)
postergar like llegar (41)
postular like hablar (1)
potenciar like hablar (1)
practicar like tocar (43)
preguntar like hablar (1)
preocupar like hablar (1)
preparar like hablar (1)
presentar like hablar (1)
preservar like hablar (1)
prestar like hablar (1)
pretender like comer (2)
probar (o:ue) like contar (24)
procurar like hablar (1)
programar like hablar (1)
pronunciar like hablar (1)
proponer (ng) like poner (15)
proteger (j) (42)
protestar like hablar (1)
provenir (ng) (e:ie) like venir (22)
quedar like hablar (1)
quemar like hablar (1)
querer (e:ie) (16)
quererse (e:ie) (16)
realizar like cruzar (37)
rechazar like cruzar (37)
recibir like vivir (3)
reciclar like hablar (1)
recoger (j) like proteger (42)
recomendar (e:ie) like pensar (30)
recordar (o:ue) like contar (24)
recorrer like comer (2)
redactar like hablar (1)
reducir (zc) like conducir (6)
redundar like hablar (1)
reencontrar (o:ue) like contar (24)
reformular like hablar (1)
regalar like hablar (1)
regatear like hablar (1)
regresar like hablar (1)
reír (31)
relacionar like hablar (1)
rellenar like hablar (1)
remontar like hablar (1)
rendir (e:i) like pedir (29)
renunciar like hablar (1)
repartir like vivir (3)
repetir (e:i) like pedir (29)
representar like hablar (1)
rescatar like hablar (1)
reservar like hablar (1)
respetar like hablar (1)
respirar like hablar (1)
responder like comer (2)
restaurar like hablar (1)
resumir like vivir (3)
retirar like hablar (1)
reunir like vivir (3) *except* **reú-** in the present (all sing. forms and 3rd person pl.)
revisar like hablar (1)
revivir like vivir (3)
rodar (o:ue) like contar (24)
rodear like hablar (1)
romper like comer (2) *except* **p. p.** is **roto**
saber (17)
saborear like hablar (1)
salir (lg) (18)
saludar like hablar (1)
salvar like hablar (1)
seguir (g) (e:i) (32)
seleccionar like hablar (1)
señalar like hablar (1)
sensibilizar like cruzar (37)
sentir (e:ie) (33)
separarse like hablar (1)
ser (19)
servir (e:i) like pedir (29)
significar like tocar (43)
simbolizar like cruzar (37)
sintetizar like cruzar (37)
sobreproteger (j) like proteger (42)
sobrevivir like vivir (3)
soler (o:ue) like poder (14)
solicitar like hablar (1)
solidarizarse like cruzar (37)
solucionar like hablar (1)
sonreír like reír (31)
soportar like hablar (1)
sorprender like comer (2)
subir like vivir (3)
subrayar like hablar (1)
suceder like comer (2)
sufrir like vivir (3)
sujetar like hablar (1)
suministrar like hablar (1)
superar like hablar (1)
surgir (j) like proteger (42)
sustituir (y) like destruir (38)
tachar like hablar (1)
tapear like hablar (1)
tener (ng) (e:ie) (20)
terminar like hablar (1)
tocar (43)
tomar like hablar (1)
tornarse like hablar (1)
trabajar like hablar (1)
traducir (zc) like conducir (6)
traer (ig) (21)
transformar like hablar (1)
transportar like hablar (1)
trasladar like hablar (1)
traspasar like hablar (1)
tratar like hablar (1)
trotar like hablar (1)
tutearse like hablar (1)
usar like hablar (1)
utilizar like cruzar (37)
vacunar like hablar (1)
valer (lg) like salir (18) *except* **-er** verb and **tú** imperative is **vale**
validar like hablar (1)
vender like comer (2)
venerar like hablar (1)
venir (ng) (e:ie) (22)
ver (23)
vestirse (e:i) like pedir (29)
viajar like hablar (1)
visitar like hablar (1)
vivir (3)
volar (o:ue) like contar (24)
volver (o:ue) (34)
votar like hablar (1)

Verb Conjugation Tables

Regular verbs: simple tenses

	Infinitive	INDICATIVE					SUBJUNCTIVE		IMPERATIVE
		Present	Imperfect	Preterite	Future	Conditional	Present	Past	
1	hablar **Participles:** hablando hablado	hablo hablas habla hablamos habláis hablan	hablaba hablabas hablaba hablábamos hablabais hablaban	hablé hablaste habló hablamos hablasteis hablaron	hablaré hablarás hablará hablaremos hablaréis hablarán	hablaría hablarías hablaría hablaríamos hablaríais hablarían	hable hables hable hablemos habléis hablen	hablara hablaras hablara habláramos hablarais hablaran	habla tú (no hables) hable Ud. hablemos hablad (no habléis) hablen Uds.
2	comer **Participles:** comiendo comido	como comes come comemos coméis comen	comía comías comía comíamos comíais comían	comí comiste comió comimos comisteis comieron	comeré comerás comerá comeremos comeréis comerán	comería comerías comería comeríamos comeríais comerían	coma comas coma comamos comáis coman	comiera comieras comiera comiéramos comierais comieran	come tú (no comas) coma Ud. comamos comed (no comáis) coman Uds.
3	vivir **Participles:** viviendo vivido	vivo vives vive vivimos vivís viven	vivía vivías vivía vivíamos vivíais vivían	viví viviste vivió vivimos vivisteis vivieron	viviré vivirás vivirá viviremos viviréis vivirán	viviría vivirías viviría viviríamos viviríais vivirían	viva vivas viva vivamos viváis vivan	viviera vivieras viviera viviéramos vivierais vivieran	vive tú (no vivas) viva Ud. vivamos vivid (no viváis) vivan Uds.

All verbs: compound tenses

PERFECT TENSES											
INDICATIVE								SUBJUNCTIVE			
Present Perfect		Past Perfect		Future Perfect		Conditional Perfect		Present Perfect		Past Perfect	
he has ha hemos habéis han	hablado comido vivido	había habías había habíamos habíais habían	hablado comido vivido	habré habrás habrá habremos habréis habrán	hablado comido vivido	habría habrías habría habríamos habríais habrían	hablado comido vivido	haya hayas haya hayamos hayáis hayan	hablado comido vivido	hubiera hubiera hubiera hubiéramos hubierais hubieran	hablado comido vivido

PERFECT TENSES					
INDICATIVE				SUBJUNCTIVE	
Present Progressive	**Past Progressive**	**Future Progressive**	**Conditional Progressive**	**Present Progressive**	**Past Progressive**
estoy estás está estamos estáis están } hablando, comiendo, viviendo	estaba estabas estaba estábamos estabais estaban } hablando, comiendo, viviendo	estaré estarás estará estaremos estaréis estarán } hablando, comiendo, viviendo	estaría estarías estaría estaríamos estaríais estarían } hablando, comiendo, viviendo	esté estés esté estemos estéis estén } hablando, comiendo, viviendo	estuviera estuvieras estuviera estuviéramos estuvierais estuvieran } hablando, comiendo, viviendo

Irregular verbs

		INDICATIVE					SUBJUNCTIVE		IMPERATIVE
	Infinitive	**Present**	**Imperfect**	**Preterite**	**Future**	**Conditional**	**Present**	**Past**	
4	caber **Participles:** cabiendo cabido	**quepo** cabes cabe cabemos cabéis caben	cabía cabías cabía cabíamos cabíais cabían	**cupe** **cupiste** **cupo** **cupimos** **cupisteis** **cupieron**	**cabré** **cabrás** **cabrá** **cabremos** **cabréis** **cabrán**	**cabría** **cabrías** **cabría** **cabríamos** **cabríais** **cabrían**	**quepa** **quepas** **quepa** **quepamos** **quepáis** **quepan**	**cupiera** **cupieras** **cupiera** **cupiéramos** **cupierais** **cupieran**	cabe tú (no **quepas**) **quepa** Ud. **quepamos** cabed (no **quepáis**) **quepan** Uds.
5	caer **Participles:** **cayendo** **caído**	**caigo** caes cae caemos caéis caen	caía caías caía caíamos caíais caían	caí **caíste** **cayó** **caímos** **caísteis** **cayeron**	caeré caerás caerá caeremos caeréis caerán	caería caerías caería caeríamos caeríais caerían	**caiga** **caigas** **caiga** **caigamos** **caigáis** **caigan**	**cayera** **cayeras** **cayera** **cayéramos** **cayerais** **cayeran**	cae tú (no **caigas**) **caiga** Ud. (no **caiga**) **caigamos** caed (no **caigáis**) **caigan** Uds.
6	conducir (c:zc) **Participles:** conduciendo conducido	**conduzco** conduces conduce conducimos conducís conducen	conducía conducías conducía conducíamos conducíais conducían	**conduje** **condujiste** **condujo** **condujimos** **condujisteis** **condujeron**	conduciré conducirás conducirá conduciremos conduciréis conducirán	conduciría conducirías conduciría conduciríamos conduciríais conducirían	**conduzca** **conduzcas** **conduzca** **conduzcamos** **conduzcáis** **conduzcan**	**condujera** **condujeras** **condujera** **condujéramos** **condujerais** **condujeran**	conduce tú (no **conduzcas**) **conduzca** Ud. (no **conduzca**) **conduzcamos** conducid (no **conduzcáis**) **conduzcan** Uds.

		INDICATIVE					SUBJUNCTIVE		IMPERATIVE
	Infinitive	**Present**	**Imperfect**	**Preterite**	**Future**	**Conditional**	**Present**	**Past**	
7	dar **Participles:** dando dado	**doy** das da damos **dais** dan	daba dabas daba dábamos dabais daban	**di** **diste** **dio** **dimos** **disteis** **dieron**	daré darás dará daremos daréis darán	daría darías daría daríamos daríais darían	**dé** des **dé** demos **deis** den	**diera** **dieras** **diera** **diéramos** **dierais** **dieran**	da tú (no des) **dé** Ud. demos dad (no **deis**) den Uds.
8	decir (e:i) **Participles:** **diciendo** **dicho**	**digo** **dices** **dice** decimos decís **dicen**	decía decías decía decíamos decíais decían	**dije** **dijiste** **dijo** **dijimos** **dijisteis** **dijeron**	**diré** **dirás** **dirá** **diremos** **diréis** **dirán**	**diría** **dirías** **diría** **diríamos** **diríais** **dirían**	**diga** **digas** **diga** **digamos** **digáis** **digan**	**dijera** **dijeras** **dijera** **dijéramos** **dijerais** **dijeran**	**di** tú (no **digas**) **diga** Ud. **digamos** decid (no **digáis**) **digan** Uds.
9	estar **Participles:** estando estado	**estoy** **estás** **está** estamos estáis **están**	estaba estabas estaba estábamos estabais estaban	**estuve** **estuviste** **estuvo** **estuvimos** **estuvisteis** **estuvieron**	estaré estarás estará estaremos estaréis estarán	estaría estarías estaría estaríamos estaríais estarían	**esté** **estés** **esté** estemos estéis **estén**	**estuviera** **estuvieras** **estuviera** **estuviéramos** **estuvierais** **estuvieran**	**está** tú (no **estés**) **esté** Ud. estemos estad (no estéis) **estén** Uds.
10	haber **Participles:** habiendo habido	**he** **has** **ha** **hemos** habéis **han**	había habías había habíamos habíais habían	**hube** **hubiste** **hubo** **hubimos** **hubisteis** **hubieron**	**habré** **habrás** **habrá** **habremos** **habréis** **habrán**	**habría** **habrías** **habría** **habríamos** **habríais** **habrían**	**haya** **hayas** **haya** **hayamos** **hayáis** **hayan**	**hubiera** **hubieras** **hubiera** **hubiéramos** **hubierais** **hubieran**	
11	hacer **Participles:** haciendo **hecho**	**hago** haces hace hacemos hacéis hacen	hacía hacías hacía hacíamos hacíais hacían	**hice** **hiciste** **hizo** **hicimos** **hicisteis** **hicieron**	**haré** **harás** **hará** **haremos** **haréis** **harán**	**haría** **harías** **haría** **haríamos** **haríais** **harían**	**haga** **hagas** **haga** **hagamos** **hagáis** **hagan**	**hiciera** **hicieras** **hiciera** **hiciéramos** **hicierais** **hicieran**	**haz** tú (no **hagas**) **haga** Ud. **hagamos** haced (no **hagáis**) **hagan** Uds.
12	ir **Participles:** **yendo** **ido**	**voy** **vas** **va** **vamos** **vais** **van**	**iba** **ibas** **iba** **íbamos** **ibais** **iban**	**fui** **fuiste** **fue** **fuimos** **fuisteis** **fueron**	**iré** **irás** **irá** **iremos** **iréis** irán	**iría** **irías** **iría** **iríamos** **iríais** irían	**vaya** **vayas** **vaya** **vayamos** **vayáis** **vayan**	**fuera** **fueras** **fuera** **fuéramos** **fuerais** **fueran**	**ve** tú (no **vayas**) **vaya** Ud. **vamos** (no **vayamos**) **id** (no **vayáis**) **vayan** Uds.
13	oír (y) **Participles:** **oyendo** **oído**	**oigo** **oyes** **oye** **oímos** oís **oyen**	oía oías oía oíamos oíais oían	oí **oíste** **oyó** **oímos** **oísteis** **oyeron**	oiré oirás oirá oiremos oiréis oirán	oiría oirías oiría oiríamos oiríais oirían	**oiga** **oigas** **oiga** **oigamos** **oigáis** **oigan**	**oyera** **oyeras** **oyera** **oyéramos** **oyerais** **oyeran**	**oye** tú (no **oigas**) **oiga** Ud. **oigamos** **oíd** (no **oigáis**) **oigan** Uds.

	Infinitive	INDICATIVE					SUBJUNCTIVE		IMPERATIVE
		Present	Imperfect	Preterite	Future	Conditional	Present	Past	
14	poder (o:ue) **Participles:** **pudiendo** podido	**puedo** **puedes** **puede** podemos podéis **pueden**	podía podías podía podíamos podíais podían	**pude** **pudiste** **pudo** **pudimos** **pudisteis** **pudieron**	**podré** **podrás** **podrá** **podremos** **podréis** **podrán**	**podría** **podrías** **podría** **podríamos** **podríais** **podrían**	**pueda** **puedas** **pueda** podamos podáis **puedan**	**pudiera** **pudieras** **pudiera** **pudiéramos** **pudierais** **pudieran**	**puede** tú (no **puedas**) **pueda** Ud. podamos poded (no podáis) **puedan** Uds.
15	poner **Participles:** poniendo **puesto**	**pongo** pones pone ponemos ponéis ponen	ponía ponías ponía poníamos poníais ponían	**puse** **pusiste** **puso** **pusimos** **pusisteis** **pusieron**	**pondré** **pondrás** **pondrá** **pondremos** **pondréis** **pondrán**	**pondría** **pondrías** **pondría** **pondríamos** **pondríais** **pondrían**	**ponga** **pongas** **ponga** **pongamos** **pongáis** **pongan**	**pusiera** **pusieras** **pusiera** **pusiéramos** **pusierais** **pusieran**	**pon** tú (no **pongas**) **ponga** Ud. **pongamos** poned (no **pongáis**) **pongan** Uds.
16	querer (e:ie) **Participles:** queriendo querido	**quiero** **quieres** **quiere** queremos queréis **quieren**	quería querías quería queríamos queríais querían	**quise** **quisiste** **quiso** **quisimos** **quisisteis** **quisieron**	**querré** **querrás** **querrá** **querremos** **querréis** **querrán**	**querría** **querrías** **querría** **querríamos** **querríais** **querrían**	**quiera** **quieras** **quiera** queramos queráis **quieran**	**quisiera** **quisieras** **quisiera** **quisiéramos** **quisierais** **quisieran**	**quiere** tú (no **quieras**) **quiera** Ud. queramos quered (no queráis) **quieran** Uds.
17	saber **Participles:** sabiendo sabido	**sé** sabes sabe sabemos sabéis saben	sabía sabías sabía sabíamos sabíais sabían	**supe** **supiste** **supo** **supimos** **supisteis** **supieron**	**sabré** **sabrás** **sabrá** **sabremos** **sabréis** **sabrán**	**sabría** **sabrías** **sabría** **sabríamos** **sabríais** **sabrían**	**sepa** **sepas** **sepa** **sepamos** **sepáis** **sepan**	**supiera** **supieras** **supiera** **supiéramos** **supierais** **supieran**	sabe tú (no **sepas**) **sepa** Ud. **sepamos** sabed (no **sepáis**) **sepan** Uds.
18	salir **Participles:** saliendo salido	**salgo** sales sale salimos salís salen	salía salías salía salíamos salíais salían	salí saliste salió salimos salisteis salieron	**saldré** **saldrás** **saldrá** **saldremos** **saldréis** **saldrán**	**saldría** **saldrías** **saldría** **saldríamos** **saldríais** **saldrían**	**salga** **salgas** **salga** **salgamos** **salgáis** **salgan**	saliera salieras saliera saliéramos salierais salieran	**sal** tú (no **salgas**) **salga** Ud. **salgamos** salid (no **salgáis**) **salgan** Uds.
19	ser **Participles:** siendo sido	**soy** **eres** **es** **somos** **sois** **son**	**era** **eras** **era** **éramos** **erais** **eran**	**fui** **fuiste** **fue** **fuimos** **fuisteis** **fueron**	seré serás será seremos seréis serán	sería serías sería seríamos seríais serían	**sea** **seas** **sea** **seamos** **seáis** **sean**	**fuera** **fueras** **fuera** **fuéramos** **fuerais** **fueran**	**sé** tú (no **seas**) **sea** Ud. **seamos** sed (no **seáis**) **sean** Uds.
20	tener (e:ie) **Participles:** teniendo tenido	**tengo** **tienes** **tiene** tenemos tenéis **tienen**	tenía tenías tenía teníamos teníais tenían	**tuve** **tuviste** **tuvo** **tuvimos** **tuvisteis** **tuvieron**	**tendré** **tendrás** **tendrá** **tendremos** **tendréis** **tendrán**	**tendría** **tendrías** **tendría** **tendríamos** **tendríais** **tendrían**	**tenga** **tengas** **tenga** **tengamos** **tengáis** **tengan**	**tuviera** **tuvieras** **tuviera** **tuviéramos** **tuvierais** **tuvieran**	**ten** tú (no **tengas**) **tenga** Ud. **tengamos** tened (no **tengáis**) **tengan** Uds.

	Infinitive	INDICATIVE Present	Imperfect	Preterite	Future	Conditional	SUBJUNCTIVE Present	Past	IMPERATIVE
21	traer **Participles:** **trayendo** **traído**	**traigo** traes trae traemos traéis traen	traía traías traía traíamos traíais traían	**traje** **trajiste** **trajo** **trajimos** **trajisteis** **trajeron**	traeré traerás traerá traeremos traeréis traerán	traería traerías traería traeríamos traeríais traerían	**traiga** **traigas** **traiga** **traigamos** **traigáis** **traigan**	**trajera** **trajeras** **trajera** **trajéramos** **trajerais** **trajeran**	 trae tú (no **traigas**) **traiga** Ud. **traigamos** traed (no **traigáis**) **traigan** Uds.
22	venir (e:ie) **Participles:** **viniendo** venido	**vengo** **vienes** **viene** venimos venís vienen	venía venías venía veníamos veníais venían	**vine** **viniste** **vino** **vinimos** **vinisteis** **vinieron**	**vendré** **vendrás** **vendrá** **vendremos** **vendréis** **vendrán**	**vendría** **vendrías** **vendría** **vendríamos** **vendríais** **vendrían**	**venga** **vengas** **venga** **vengamos** **vengáis** **vengan**	**viniera** **vinieras** **viniera** **viniéramos** **vinierais** **vinieran**	 **ven** tú (no **vengas**) **venga** Ud. **vengamos** venid (no **vengáis**) **vengan** Uds.
23	ver **Participles:** viendo **visto**	**veo** ves ve vemos **veis** ven	**veía** **veías** **veía** **veíamos** **veíais** **veían**	**vi** viste **vio** vimos visteis vieron	veré verás verá veremos veréis verán	vería verías vería veríamos veríais verían	**vea** **veas** **vea** **veamos** **veáis** **vean**	viera vieras viera viéramos vierais vieran	 ve tú (no **veas**) **vea** Ud. **veamos** ved (no **veáis**) **vean** Uds.

Stem-changing verbs

	Infinitive	INDICATIVE Present	Imperfect	Preterite	Future	Conditional	SUBJUNCTIVE Present	Past	IMPERATIVE
24	contar (o:ue) **Participles:** contando contado	**cuento** **cuentas** **cuenta** contamos contáis **cuentan**	contaba contabas contaba contábamos contabais contaban	conté contaste contó contamos contasteis contaron	contaré contarás contará contaremos contaréis contarán	contaría contarías contaría contaríamos contaríais contarían	**cuente** **cuentes** **cuente** contemos contéis **cuenten**	contara contaras contara contáramos contarais contaran	 **cuenta** tú (no **cuentes**) **cuente** Ud. contemos contad (no contéis) **cuenten** Uds.
25	dormir (o:ue) **Participles:** **durmiendo** dormido	**duermo** **duermes** **duerme** dormimos dormís **duermen**	dormía dormías dormía dormíamos dormíais dormían	dormí dormiste **durmió** dormimos dormisteis **durmieron**	dormiré dormirás dormirá dormiremos dormiréis dormirán	dormiría dormirías dormiría dormiríamos dormiríais dormirían	**duerma** **duermas** **duerma** **durmamos** **durmáis** **duerman**	**durmiera** **durmieras** **durmiera** **durmiéramos** **durmierais** **durmieran**	 **duerme** tú (no **duermas**) **duerma** Ud. **durmamos** dormid (no **durmáis**) **duerman** Uds.
26	empezar (e:ie) (z:c) **Participles:** empezando empezado	**empiezo** **empiezas** **empieza** empezamos empezáis **empiezan**	empezaba empezabas empezaba empezábamos empezabais empezaban	**empecé** empezaste empezó empezamos empezasteis empezaron	empezaré empezarás empezará empezaremos empezaréis empezarán	empezaría empezarías empezaría empezaríamos empezaríais empezarían	**empiece** **empieces** **empiece** **empecemos** **empecéis** **empiecen**	empezara empezaras empezara empezáramos empezarais empezaran	**empieza** tú (no **empieces**) **empiece** Ud. **empecemos** empezad (no **empecéis**) **empiecen** Uds.

		INDICATIVE					SUBJUNCTIVE		IMPERATIVE
	Infinitive	Present	Imperfect	Preterite	Future	Conditional	Present	Past	
27	entender (e:ie) **Participles:** entendiendo podido	**entiendo** **entiendes** **entiende** entendemos entendéis **entienden**	entendía entendías entendía entendíamos entendíais entendían	entendí entendiste entendió entendimos entendisteis entendieron	entenderé entenderás entenderá entenderemos entenderéis entenderán	enter dería enter derías enter dería enter deríamos enter deríais enter derían	**entienda** **entiendas** **entienda** entendamos entendáis **entiendan**	entendiera entendieras entendiera entendiéramos entendierais entendieran	**entiende** tú (no **entiendas**) **entienda** Ud. entendamos entended (no entendáis) **entiendan** Uds.
28	jugar (u:ue) (g:gu) **Participles:** jugando jugado	**juego** **juegas** **juega** jugamos jugáis **juegan**	jugaba jugabas jugaba jugábamos jugabais jugaban	**jugué** jugaste jugó jugamos jugasteis jugaron	jugaré jugarás jugará jugaremos jugaréis jugarán	jugar'a jugar'as jugar'a jugar'amos jugar'ais jugar'an	**juegue** **juegues** **juegue** **juguemos** **juguéis** **jueguen**	jugara jugaras jugara jugáramos jugarais jugaran	**juega** tú (no **juegues**) **juegue** Ud. **juguemos** jugad (no **juguéis**) **jueguen** Uds.
29	pedir (e:i) **Participles:** **pidiendo** pedido	**pido** **pides** **pide** pedimos pedís **piden**	pedía pedías pedía pedíamos pedíais pedían	pedí pediste **pidió** pedimos pedisteis **pidieron**	pediré pedirás pedirá pediremos pediréis pedirán	pedir'a pedir'as pedir'a pedir'amos pedir'ais pedir'an	**pida** **pidas** **pida** **pidamos** **pidáis** **pidan**	**pidiera** **pidieras** **pidiera** **pidiéramos** **pidierais** **pidieran**	**pide** tú (no **pidas**) **pida** Ud. **pidamos** pedid (no **pidáis**) **pidan** Uds.
30	pensar (e:ie) **Participles:** pensando pensado	**pienso** **piensas** **piensa** pensamos pensáis **piensan**	pensaba pensabas pensaba pensábamos pensabais pensaban	pensé pensaste pensó pensamos pensasteis pensaron	pensaré pensarás pensará pensaremos pensaréis pensarán	pensaría pensarías pensaría pensaríamos pensaríais pensarían	**piense** **pienses** **piense** pensemos penséis **piensen**	pensara pensaras pensara pensáramos pensarais pensaran	**piensa** tú (no **pienses**) **piense** Ud. pensemos pensad (no penséis) **piensen** Uds.
31	reír (e:i) **Participles:** **riendo** **reído**	**río** **ríes** **ríe** **reímos** reís **ríen**	reía reías reía reíamos reíais reían	reí **reíste** **rio** **reímos** **reísteis** **rieron**	reiré reirás reirá reiremos reiréis reirán	reiría reirías reiría reiríamos reiríais reirían	**ría** **rías** **ría** **riamos** **riáis** **rían**	**riera** **rieras** **riera** **riéramos** **rierais** **rieran**	**ríe** tú (no **rías**) **ría** Ud. **riamos** **reíd** (no **riáis**) **rían** Uds.
32	seguir (e:i) (gu:g) **Participles:** **siguiendo** seguido	**sigo** **sigues** **sigue** seguimos seguís **siguen**	seguía seguías seguía seguíamos seguíais seguían	seguí seguiste **siguió** seguimos seguisteis **siguieron**	seguiré seguirás seguirá seguiremos seguiréis seguirán	seguiría seguirías seguiría seguiríamos seguiríais seguirían	**siga** **sigas** **siga** **sigamos** **sigáis** **sigan**	**siguiera** **siguieras** **siguiera** **siguiéramos** **siguierais** **siguieran**	**sigue** tú (no **sigas**) **siga** Ud. **sigamos** seguid (no **sigáis**) **sigan** Uds.
33	sentir (e:ie) **Participles:** **sintiendo** sentido	**siento** **sientes** **siente** sentimos sentís **sienten**	sentía sentías sentía sentíamos sentíais sentían	sentí sentiste **sintió** sentimos sentisteis **sintieron**	sentiré sentirás sentirá sentiremos sentiréis sentirán	sentiría sentirías sentiría sentiríamos sentiríais sentirían	**sienta** **sientas** **sienta** **sintamos** **sintáis** **sientan**	**sintiera** **sintieras** **sintiera** **sintiéramos** **sintierais** **sintieran**	**siente** tú (no **sientas**) **sienta** Ud. **sintamos** sentid (no **sintáis**) **sientan** Uds.

	Infinitive	INDICATIVE Present	Imperfect	Preterite	Future	Conditional	SUBJUNCTIVE Present	Past	IMPERATIVE
34	volver (o:ue) **Participles:** volviendo **vuelto**	**vuelvo** **vuelves** **vuelve** volvemos volvéis **vuelven**	volvía volvías volvía volvíamos volvíais volvían	volví volviste volvió volvimos volvisteis volvieron	volveré volverás volverá volveremos volveréis volverán	volvería volverías volvería volveríamos volveríais volverían	**vuelva** **vuelvas** **vuelva** volvamos volváis **vuelvan**	volviera volvieras volviera volviéramos volvierais volvieran	**vuelve** tú (no **vuelvas**) **vuelva** Ud. volvamos volved (no volváis) **vuelvan** Uds.

Verbs with spelling changes only

	Infinitive	INDICATIVE Present	Imperfect	Preterite	Future	Conditional	SUBJUNCTIVE Present	Past	IMPERATIVE
35	conocer (c:zc) **Participles:** conociendo conocido	**conozco** conoces conoce conocemos conocéis conocen	conocía conocías conocía conocíamos conocíais conocían	conocí conociste conoció conocimos conocisteis conocieron	conoceré conocerás conocerá conoceremos conoceréis conocerán	conocería conocerías conocería conoceríamos conoceríais conocerían	**conozca** **conozcas** **conozca** **conozcamos** **conozcáis** **conozcan**	conociera conocieras conociera conociéramos conocierais conocieran	conoce tú (no **conozcas**) **conozca** Ud. **conozcamos** conoced (no **conozcáis**) **conozcan** Uds.
36	creer (y) **Participles:** **creyendo** **creído**	creo crees cree creemos creéis creen	creía creías creía creíamos creíais creían	creí **creíste** **creyó** **creímos** **creísteis** **creyeron**	creeré creerás creerá creeremos creeréis creerán	creería creerías creería creeríamos creeríais creerían	crea creas crea creamos creáis crean	**creyera** **creyeras** **creyera** **creyéramos** **creyerais** **creyeran**	cree tú (no creas) crea Ud. creamos creed (no creáis) crean Uds.
37	cruzar (z:c) **Participles:** cruzando cruzado	cruzo cruzas cruza cruzamos cruzáis cruzan	cruzaba cruzabas cruzaba cruzábamos cruzabais cruzaban	**crucé** cruzaste cruzó cruzamos cruzasteis cruzaron	cruzaré cruzarás cruzará cruzaremos cruzaréis cruzarán	cruzaría cruzarías cruzaría cruzaríamos cruzaríais cruzarían	**cruce** **cruces** **cruce** **crucemos** **crucéis** **crucen**	cruzara cruzaras cruzara cruzáramos cruzarais cruzaran	cruza tú (no **cruces**) **cruce** Ud. **crucemos** cruzad (no **crucéis**) **crucen** Uds.
38	destruir (y) **Participles:** **destruyendo** destruido	**destruyo** **destruyes** **destruye** destruimos destruís **destruyen**	destruía destruías destruía destruíamos destruíais destruían	destruí destruiste **destruyó** destruimos destruisteis **destruyeron**	destruiré destruirás destruirá destruiremos destruiréis destruirán	destruiría destruirías destruiría destruiríamos destruiríais destruirían	**destruya** **destruyas** **destruya** **destruyamos** **destruyáis** **destruyan**	**destruyera** **destruyeras** **destruyera** **destruyéramos** **destruyerais** **destruyeran**	**destruye** tú (no **destruyas**) **destruya** Ud. **destruyamos** destruid (no **destruyáis**) **destruyan** Uds.
39	enviar **Participles:** enviando enviado	**envío** **envías** **envía** enviamos enviáis **envían**	enviaba enviabas enviaba enviábamos enviabais enviaban	envié enviaste envió enviamos enviasteis enviaron	enviaré enviarás enviará enviaremos enviaréis enviarán	enviaría enviarías enviaría enviaríamos enviaríais enviarían	**envíe** **envíes** **envíe** enviemos enviéis **envíen**	enviara enviaras enviara enviáramos enviarais enviaran	**envía** tú (no **envíes**) **envíe** Ud. enviemos enviad (no enviéis) **envíen** Uds.

	Infinitive	INDICATIVE					SUBJUNCTIVE		IMPERATIVE
		Present	Imperfect	Preterite	Future	Conditional	Present	Past	
40	graduar **Participles:** graduando graduado	**gradúo** **gradúas** **gradúa** graduamos graduáis **gradúan**	graduaba graduabas graduaba graduábamos graduabais graduaban	gradué graduaste graduó graduamos graduasteis graduaron	graduaré graduarás graduará graduaremos graduaréis graduarán	graduaría graduarías graduaría graduaríamos graduaríais graduarían	**gradúe** **gradúes** **gradúe** graduemos graduéis **gradúen**	graduara graduaras graduara graduáramos graduarais graduaran	**gradúa** tú (no **gradúes**) **gradúe** Ud. graduemos graduad (no graduéis) **gradúen** Uds.
41	llegar (g:gu) **Participles:** llegando llegado	llego llegas llega llegamos llegáis llegan	llegaba llegabas llegaba llegábamos llegabais llegaban	**llegué** llegaste llegó llegamos llegasteis llegaron	llegaré llegarás llegará llegaremos llegaréis llegarán	llegaría llegarías llegaría llegaríamos llegaríais llegarían	**llegue** **llegues** **llegue** **lleguemos** **lleguéis** **lleguen**	llegara llegaras llegara llegáramos llegarais llegaran	llega tú (no **llegues**) **llegue** Ud. **lleguemos** llegad (no **lleguéis**) **lleguen** Uds.
42	proteger (g:j) **Participles:** protegiendo protegido	**protejo** proteges protege protegemos protegéis protegen	protegía protegías protegía protegíamos protegíais protegían	protegí protegiste protegió protegimos protegisteis protegieron	protegeré protegerás protegerá protegeremos protegeréis protegerán	protegería protegerías protegería protegeríamos protegeríais protegerían	**proteja** **protejas** **proteja** **protejamos** **protejáis** **protejan**	protegiera protegieras protegiera protegiéramos protegierais protegieran	protege tú (no **protejas**) **proteja** Ud. **protejamos** proteged (no **protejáis**) **protejan** Uds.
43	tocar (c:qu) **Participles:** tocando tocado	toco tocas toca tocamos tocáis tocan	tocaba tocabas tocaba tocábamos tocabais tocaban	**toqué** tocaste tocó tocamos tocasteis tocaron	tocaré tocará tocarás tocaremos tocaréis tocarán	tocaría tocarías tocaría tocaríamos tocaríais tocarían	**toque** **toques** **toque** **toquemos** **toquéis** **toquen**	tocara tocaras tocara tocáramos tocarais tocaran	toca tú (no **toques**) **toque** Ud. **toquemos** tocad (no **toquéis**) **toquen** Uds.
44	vencer (c:z) **Participles:** venciendo vencido	**venzo** vences vence vencemos vencéis vencen	vencía vencías vencía vencíamos vencíais vencían	vencí venciste venció vencimos vencisteis vencieron	venceré vencerás vencerá venceremos venceréis vencerán	vencería vencerías vencería venceríamos venceríais vencerían	**venza** **venzas** **venza** **venzamos** **venzáis** **venzan**	venciera vencieras venciera venciéramos vencierais vencieran	vence tú (no **venzas**) **venza** Ud. **venzamos** venced (no **venzáis**) **venzan** Uds.
45	esparcir (c:z) **Participles:** esparciendo esparcido	**esparzo** esparces esparce esparcimos esparcís esparcen	esparcía esparcías esparcía esparcíamos esparcíais esparcían	esparcí esparciste esparció esparcimos esparcisteis esparcieron	esparciré esparcirás esparcirá esparciremos esparciréis esparcirán	esparciría esparcirías esparciría esparciríamos esparciríais esparcirían	**esparza** **esparzas** **esparza** **esparzamos** **esparzáis** **esparzan**	esparciera esparcieras esparciera esparciéramos esparcierais esparcieran	esparce tú (no **esparzas**) **esparza** Ud. **esparzamos** esparcid (no **esparzáis**) **esparzan** Uds.
46	extinguir (gu:g) **Participles:** extinguiendo extinguido o **extinto**	**extingo** extingues extingue extinguimos extinguís extinguen	extinguía extinguías extinguía extinguíamos extinguíais extinguían	extinguí extinguiste extinguió extinguimos extinguisteis extinguieron	extinguiré extinguirás extinguirá extinguiremos extinguiréis extinguirán	extinguiría extinguirías extinguiría extinguiríamos extinguiríais extinguirían	**extinga** **extingas** **extinga** **extingamos** **extingáis** **extingan**	extinguiera extinguieras extinguiera extinguiéramos extinguierais extinguieran	extingue tú (no **extingas**) **extinga** Ud. **extingamos** extinguid (no **extingáis**) **extingan** Uds.

Reflexive verbs: simple tenses

- In all simple indicative and subjunctive tenses, the reflexive pronoun is placed before the conjugated verb. In the imperative, the reflexive pronoun is attached to the verb in affirmative commands, but precedes the verb in negative commands.

Infinitive	SIMPLE INDICATIVE TENSES	SIMPLE SUBJUNCTIVE TENSES	IMPERATIVE
casarse	**me** caso	**me** case	
	te casas	**te** cases	cása**te** tú (no **te** cases)
	se casa	**se** case	cáse**se** Ud. (no **se** case)
	nos casamos	**nos** casemos	casémo**nos** (no **nos** casemos)
	os casáis	**os** caséis	casa**os** (no **os** caséis)
	se casan	**se** casen	cásen**se** Uds. (no **se** casen)

Reflexive verbs: compound tenses

- In all compound tenses, the reflexive pronoun is placed before the conjugated verb.

Infinitive	COMPOUND INDICATIVE TENSES	COMPOUND SUBJUNCTIVE TENSES
casarse	**me** he casado	**me** haya casado
	te has casado	**te** hayas casado
	se ha casado	**se** haya casado
	nos hemos casado	**nos** hayamos casado
	os habéis casado	**os** hayáis casado
	se han casado	**se** hayan casado

Glossary of Grammatical Terms

ADJECTIVE A word that modifies, or describes, a noun or pronoun.

muchos libros | un hombre **rico**
many books | *a **rich** man*

Demonstrative adjective An adjective that specifies which noun a speaker is referring to.

esta fiesta | **ese** chico
***this** party* | ***that** boy*

aquellas flores
***those** flowers*

Possessive adjective An adjective that indicates ownership or possession.

su mejor vestido | Este es **mi** hermano.
***her** best dress* | *This is **my** brother.*

Stressed possessive adjective A possessive adjective that emphasizes the owner or possessor.

un libro **mío** | una amiga **tuya**
*a book **of mine*** | *a friend **of yours***

ADVERB A word that modifies, or describes, a verb, adjective, or another adverb.

Pancho escribe **rápidamente**.
*Pancho writes **quickly**.*

Este cuadro es **muy** bonito.
*This picture is **very** pretty.*

ANTECEDENT The noun to which a pronoun or dependent clause refers.

El **libro** que compré es interesante.
The book that I bought is interesting.

Le presté cinco dólares a **Diego**.
I loaned Diego five dollars.

ARTICLE A word that points out a noun in either a specific or a non-specific way.

Definite article An article that points out a noun in a specific way.

el libro | **la** maleta
***the** book* | ***the** suitcase*

los diccionarios | **las** palabras
***the** dictionaries* | ***the** words*

Indefinite article An article that points out a noun in a general, non-specific way.

un lápiz | **una** computadora
***a** pencil* | ***a** computer*

unos pájaros | **unas** escuelas
***some** birds* | ***some** schools*

CLAUSE A group of words that contains both a conjugated verb and a subject, either expressed or implied.

Main (or Independent) clause A clause that can stand alone as a complete sentence.

Pienso ir a cenar pronto.
I plan to go to dinner soon.

Subordinate (or Dependent) clause A clause that does not express a complete thought and therefore cannot stand alone as a sentence.

Trabajo en la cafetería **porque necesito dinero para la escuela**.
*I work in the cafeteria **because I need money for school**.*

Adjective clause A dependent clause that functions to modify or describe the noun or direct object in the main clause. When the antecedent is uncertain or indefinite, the verb in the adjective clause is in the subjunctive.

Queremos contratar al candidato **que mandó su currículum ayer**.
*We want to hire the applicant **who sent his résumé yesterday**.*

¿Conoce un buen restaurante **que esté cerca del teatro**?
*Do you know of a good restaurant **that's near the theater**?*

Adverbial clause A dependent clause that functions to modify or describe a verb, an adjective, or another adverb. When the adverbial clause describes an action that has not yet happened or is uncertain, the verb in the adverbial clause is usually in the subjunctive.

Llamé a mi mamá **cuando me dieron la noticia**.
*I called my mom **when they gave me the news**.*

El ejército está preparado **en caso de que haya un ataque**.
*The army is prepared **in case there is an attack**.*

Noun clause A dependent clause that functions as a noun, often as the object of the main clause. When the main clause expresses will, emotion, doubt, or uncertainty, the verb in the noun clause is in the subjunctive (unless there is no change of subject).

José sabe **que mañana habrá un examen**.
*José knows **that tomorrow there will be an exam**.*

Luisa dudaba **que la acompañáramos**.
*Luisa doubted **that we would go with her**.*

COMPARATIVE A grammatical construction used with nouns, adjectives, verbs, or adverbs to compare people, objects, actions, or characteristics.

Tus clases son **menos interesantes** que las mías.
*Your classes are **less interesting** than mine.*

Como **más frutas** que verduras.
*I eat **more fruits** than vegetables.*

CONJUGATION A set of the forms of a verb for a specific tense or mood, or the process by which these verb forms are presented.

PRETERITE CONJUGATION OF **CANTAR**:

cant**é**	cant**amos**
cant**aste**	cant**asteis**
cant**ó**	cant**aron**

CONJUNCTION A word used to connect words, clauses, or phrases.

Susana es de Cuba **y** Pedro es de España.
*Susana is from Cuba **and** Pedro is from Spain.*

No quiero estudiar, **pero** tengo que hacerlo.
*I don't want to study, **but** I have to.*

CONTRACTION The joining of two words into one. The only contractions in Spanish are **al** and **del**.

Mi hermano fue **al** concierto ayer.
*My brother went **to the** concert yesterday.*

Saqué dinero **del** banco.
*I took out money **from the** bank.*

DIRECT OBJECT A noun or pronoun that directly receives the action of the verb.

Tomás lee **el libro**. **La** pagó ayer.
*Tomás reads **the book**. She paid **it** yesterday.*

GENDER The grammatical categorizing of certain kinds of words, such as nouns and pronouns, as masculine, feminine, or neuter.

MASCULINE
articles **el, un**
pronouns **él, lo, mío, este, ese, aquel**
adjective **simpático**

FEMININE
articles **la, una**
pronouns **ella, la, mía, esta, esa, aquella**
adjective **simpática**

IMPERSONAL EXPRESSION A third-person expression with no expressed or specific subject.

Es muy importante. **Llueve** mucho.
It's very important. ***It's raining** hard.*

Aquí **se habla** español.
*Spanish **is spoken** here.*

INDIRECT OBJECT A noun or pronoun that receives the action of the verb indirectly; the object, often a living being, to or for whom an action is performed.

Eduardo **le** dio un libro **a Linda**.
*Eduardo gave a book **to Linda**.*

La profesora **me** puso una C en el examen.
*The professor gave **me** a C on the test.*

INFINITIVE The basic form of a verb. Infinitives in Spanish end in **-ar**, **-er**, or **-ir**.

hablar	correr	abrir
to speak	***to run***	***to open***

INTERROGATIVE An adjective or pronoun used to ask a question.

¿**Quién** habla? ¿**Cuántos** compraste?
***Who** is speaking?* ***How many** did you buy?*

¿**Qué** piensas hacer hoy?
***What** do you plan to do today?*

MOOD A grammatical distinction of verbs that indicates whether the verb is intended to make a statement or command, or to express doubt, emotion, or condition contrary to fact.

Imperative mood Verb forms used to make commands.

Di la verdad. **Caminen** ustedes conmigo.
***Tell** the truth.* ***Walk** with me.*

¡**Comamos** ahora! ¡**No** lo **hagas**!
***Let's eat** now!* ***Don't do** it!*

Indicative mood Verb forms used to state facts, actions, and states considered to be real.

Sé que **tienes** el dinero.
***I know** that **you have** the money.*

Subjunctive mood Verb forms used principally in subordinate (dependent) clauses to express wishes, desires, emotions, doubts, and certain conditions, such as contrary-to-fact situations.

Prefieren que **hables** en español.
*They prefer that **you speak** in Spanish.*

NOUN A word that identifies people, animals, places, things, and ideas.

hombre	gato
man	***cat***
México	**casa**
Mexico	***house***
libertad	**libro**
freedom	***book***

NUMBER A grammatical term that refers to singular or plural. Nouns in Spanish and English have number. Other parts of a sentence, such as adjectives, articles, and verbs, also have number.

SINGULAR	PLURAL
una cosa ***a*** *thing*	**unas** cosas ***some*** *things*
el profesor ***the*** *professor*	**los** profesores ***the*** *professors*

PASSIVE VOICE A sentence construction in which the recipient of the action becomes the subject of the sentence. Passive statements emphasize the thing that was done or the person that was acted upon. They follow the pattern [*recipient*] + **ser** + [*past participle*] + **por** + [*agent*].

ACTIVE VOICE:
Juan **entregó** la tarea.
Juan ***turned in*** *the assignment.*

PASSIVE VOICE:
La tarea **fue entregada por** Juan.
The assignment ***was turned in by*** *Juan.*

PAST PARTICIPLE A past form of the verb used in compound tenses. The past participle may also be used as an adjective, but it must then agree in number and gender with the word it modifies.

Han **buscado** por todas partes.
They have ***searched*** *everywhere.*

Yo no había **estudiado** para el examen.
I hadn't ***studied*** *for the exam.*

Hay una ventana **abierta** en la sala.
There is an ***open*** *window in the living room.*

PERSON The form of the verb or pronoun that indicates the speaker, the one spoken to, or the one spoken about. In Spanish, as in English, there are three persons: first, second, and third.

PERSON	SINGULAR	PLURAL
1st	**yo** *I*	**nosotros/as** *we*
2nd	**tú, usted** *you*	**vosotros/as, ustedes** *you*
3rd	**él, ella** *he, she*	**ellos, ellas** *they*

PREPOSITION A word or words that describe(s) the relationship, most often in time or space, between two other words.

Anita es **de** California.
Anita is ***from*** *California.*

La chaqueta está **en** el carro.
The jacket is ***in*** *the car.*

PRESENT PARTICIPLE In English, a verb form that ends in *-ing*. In Spanish, the present participle ends in **-ndo**, and is often used with **estar** to form a progressive tense.

Está **hablando** por teléfono ahora mismo.
He is ***talking*** *on the phone right now.*

PRONOUN A word that takes the place of one or more nouns.

Demonstrative pronoun A pronoun that takes the place of a specific noun.

Quiero **esta**.
I want ***this one****.*

¿Vas a comprar **ese**?
Are you going to buy ***that one****?*

Juan prefirió **aquellos**.
Juan preferred ***those*** *(over there).*

Object pronoun A pronoun that functions as a direct or indirect object of the verb.

Te digo la verdad.
I'm telling ***you*** *the truth.*

Me lo trajo Juan.
Juan brought ***it to me****.*

Possessive pronoun A pronoun that functions to show ownership or possession. Possessive pronouns are preceded by a definite article and agree in gender and number with the nouns they replace.

Perdí mi libro. ¿Me prestas **el tuyo**?
I lost my book. Will you loan me ***yours****?*

Las clases suyas son aburridas, pero **las nuestras** son buenísimas.
Their classes are boring, but ***ours*** *are great.*

Prepositional pronoun A pronoun that functions as the object of a preposition. Except for **mí, ti,** and **sí**, these pronouns are the same as subject pronouns. The adjective **mismo/a** may be added to express *myself, himself*, etc. After the preposition **con**, the forms **conmigo, contigo,** and **consigo** are used.

¿Es **para mí**?
Is this ***for me****?*

Juan habló **de ella**.
Juan spoke ***about her****.*

Iré **contigo**.
I will go ***with you****.*

Se lo regaló **a sí mismo**.
He gave it ***to himself****.*

Reflexive pronoun A pronoun that indicates that the action of a verb is performed by the subject on itself. These pronouns are often expressed in English with *-self*: *myself, yourself*, etc.

Yo **me bañé**.
I ***took a bath****.*

Elena **se acostó**.
Elena ***went to bed****.*

Relative pronoun A pronoun that connects a subordinate clause to a main clause.

El edificio **en el cual** vivimos es antiguo.
*The building **that** we live in is ancient.*

La mujer **de quien** te hablé acaba de renunciar.
*The woman **(whom)** I told you about just quit.*

Subject pronoun A pronoun that replaces the name or title of a person or thing, and acts as the subject of a verb.

Tú debes estudiar más.
***You** should study more.*

Él llegó primero.
***He** arrived first.*

SUBJECT A noun or pronoun that performs the action of a verb and is often implied by the verb.

María va al supermercado.
***María** goes to the supermarket.*

(Ellos) Trabajan mucho.
***They** work hard.*

Esos libros son muy caros.
***Those books** are very expensive.*

SUPERLATIVE A grammatical construction used to describe the most or the least of a quality when comparing a group of people, places, or objects.

Tina es **la menos simpática** de las chicas.
*Tina is **the least pleasant** of the girls.*

Tu coche es **el más rápido** de todos.
*Your car is **the fastest** one of all.*

Los restaurantes en Calle Ocho son **los mejores** de todo Miami.
*The restaurants on Calle Ocho are **the best** in all of Miami.*

Absolute superlatives Adjectives or adverbs combined with forms of the suffix **-ísimo/a** in order to express the idea of *extremely* or *very*.

¡Lo hice **rapidísimo**!
*I did it **so fast**!*

Ella es **jovencísima**.
*She is **very, very young**.*

TENSE A set of verb forms that indicates the time of an action or state: past, present, or future.

Compound tense A two-word tense made up of an auxiliary verb and a present or past participle. In Spanish, there are two auxiliary verbs: **estar** and **haber**.

En este momento, **estoy estudiando**.
*At this time, **I am studying**.*

El paquete no **ha llegado** todavía.
*The package **has** not **arrived** yet.*

Simple tense A tense expressed by a single verb form.

María **estaba** mal anoche.
*María **was** ill last night.*

Juana **hablará** con su mamá mañana.
*Juana **will speak** with her mom tomorrow.*

VERB A word that expresses actions or states of being.

Auxiliary verb A verb used with a present or past participle to form a compound tense. **Haber** is the most commonly used auxiliary verb in Spanish.

Los chicos **han** visto los elefantes.
*The children **have** seen the elephants.*

Espero que **hayas** comido.
*I hope you **have** eaten.*

Reflexive verb A verb that describes an action performed by the subject on itself and is always used with a reflexive pronoun.

Me compré un carro nuevo.
***I bought myself** a new car.*

Pedro y Adela **se levantan** muy temprano.
*Pedro and Adela **get (themselves) up** very early.*

Spelling-change verb A verb that undergoes a predictable change in spelling, in order to reflect its actual pronunciation in the various conjugations.

practicar	**c→qu**	practi**c**o	practi**qué**
dirigir	**g→j**	diri**g**í	diri**j**o
almorzar	**z→c**	almor**z**ó	almor**cé**

Stem-changing verb A verb whose stem vowel undergoes one or more predictable changes in the various conjugations.

entender	**(e:ie)**	ent**ie**ndo
pedir	**(e:i)**	p**i**den
dormir	**(o:ue, u)**	d**ue**rmo, d**u**rmieron

Grammar Reference

This grammar reference organizes all of the grammatical structures presented in **PROTAGONISTAS** by part of speech. The lozenges next to each topic show you which lessons teach these structures in their communicative context.

Table of Contents

1 Pronunciation, Intonation, and Spelling (Pronunciación, entonación y ortografía)

1.1 The alphabet (**El alfabeto**) U0

- The Spanish alphabet is comprised of 29 letters and contains three special letters: **ñ**, which comes after **n**, and **ch** and **ll**, which come after **c** and **l**, respectively.

letter	name of letter	sound (international phonetic alphabet)	sound (in relation to English)	examples
a	a	[a]	• like the *a* in *father*, but shorter	**A**n**a**, t**a**p**a**s, **a**diós
b	be	[b] [β]	• like the English hard *b* when at the beginning of a word • like a soft *b* with no equivalent in English in all other positions	**B**arcelona, **b**eso L2A, L5A Ro**b**erto, escri**b**ir
c	ce	[k] [θ] [Esp.]* [s] [Amér. L.]*	• before **a, o,** or **u**, like the *c* in *car* • in parts of Spain, like the *th* in *think* when before **e** or **i** • in Latin America, like the *s* in *sit* when before **e** or **i**	**C**arlos, **c**osa, **c**urso L1A, L4B **c**inco, Bar**c**elona L1A, L5B ha**c**er, co**c**ina
ch	che	[tʃ]	• like the *ch* in *chair*	o**ch**o, no**ch**e, **Ch**ile L3A
d	de	[d] [ð]	• when at the beginning of a word, similar to the *d* in *dog*, but softer • in all other positions, a softer sound similar to the English *th* in *there*	**d**ónde, **d**ormir ma**d**re, Ma**d**ri**d**, ciuda**d** L6B
e	e	[ɛ]	• like the *e* in *they*, but shorter	P**e**dro, **e**spañol
f	efe	[f]	• like the English *f*	ca**f**é, **F**élix, ga**f**as
g	ge	[g] [x]	• like the *g* in *girl* • before **e** or **i**, similar to the English *h*	**g**amba, ten**g**o, **g**ustar L1A, L3B Mi**g**uel, **G**uernica a**g**enda, **g**imnasia L1A, L3B
h	hache		• The Spanish **h** is always silent.	**h**otel, **h**ola
i	i	[i]	• like the *ee* in *beet*, but shorter	h**i**jo, Fr**i**da
j	jota	[x]	• similar to the *h* in *his*	**j**ulio, ro**j**o L3B relo**j** L6B
k	ka (ca)	[k]	• like the *k* in *key*; this letter is rarely used in Spanish	**k**ilo, **k**ilómetro L4B
l	ele	[l]	• like the *l* in *lake*	**l**ámpara, hospita**l**
ll	elle	[j] [Amér. L.]* [ʒ] [R. P.] [ʎ] [Esp.]*	• like the *y* in *yes* • in Argentina and Uruguay, like the *sh* in *shoe* • in some areas of Spain, like a continuous *lj* sound	Sevi**ll**a, **ll**amada L3A
m	eme	[m]	• like the *m* in *home*	**M**aría, A**m**érica
n	ene	[n]	• like the *n* in *nice*	bue**n**o, A**n**a

letter	name of letter	sound (international phonetic alphabet)	sound (in relation to English)	examples
ñ	eñe	[ɲ]	• much like the *ny* in *canyon*	mañana, España L3A
o	o	[o]	• like the *o* in *tone*, but shorter	dónde, hola
p	pe	[p]	• like the *p* in *top*, but softer; no air is expelled from the mouth	paella, España, playa L5A, L6A
q	cu	[k]	• like the *k* in *key*; *q* is always followed by *u* in Spanish	querer, pequeño L4B
r	ere	[r]	• a sound similiar to the *dd* in *ladder* when in the middle or at the end of a word, but the tongue touches the roof of the mouth behind the teeth	bar, mercado, carácter L4A
	erre	[rr]	• when at the beginning of a word, after the consonants **l**, **n**, and **s**, or in the combination **rr,** a strong trilled sound that does not exist in English	barrio, rastro, restaurante L4A
s	ese	[s]	• like the *s* in *summer*	queso, Sevilla, ese
t	te	[t]	• shorter than the English *t;* no air is expelled from the mouth	tiempo, Marta L6A
u	u	[u]	• like the *oo* in *room*, but shorter	uno, Perú
v	ve (uve)	[b] [β]	• like the English hard *b* when at the beginning of a word • a soft *b* with no equivalent in English in all other positions	viaje, vino L2A, L5A Javier, por favor
w	doble ve (uve doble)	[w]	• like the *w* in *web* or the Spanish *b/v*; this letter is found only in foreign words	*web cam* L6B
x	equis	[ks] [s]*	• pronounced like an English *x* • in some Spanish-speaking areas, like an aspirated *s*; in others, like a weak *h*	taxi, exacto explicar, extranjero
y	i griega (ye)	[i] [j]* [ʒ] [R. P.]*	• when at the end of a word, like the *ee* in beet, but shorter • when at the beginning or in the middle of a word, like the *y* in *yes* • in Argentina and Uruguay, like the *sh* in *shoe* when at the beginning or in the middle of a word	hay, voy, soy, y yo, mayo
z	zeta (ceta)	[θ] [Esp.]* [s] [Amér. L.]*	• in parts of Spain, pronounced like the *th* in *think* • in Latin America, pronounced like the *s* in *sit*	Zaragoza L5B Venezuela, azúcar

*As noted, the pronunciation of **c**, **z**, **ll**, and **y** varies between Latin America (**Amér. L.**), the **Rioplatense** region (**R. P.**), and parts of Spain (**Esp.**); the pronunciation of **x** also varies in some Spanish-speaking countries.

1.2 Spoken stress and written accents (**Entonación y acento ortográfico**) L2B

- The next-to-last syllable is stressed in most Spanish words.

  postre, **chu**rro, pa**ta**ta, **ta**pa

- Words ending in a consonant (all but **n** and **s**) are stressed on the last syllable.

  cami**nar**, re**loj**, ver**dad**

- When a word does not follow these rules, the stressed syllable carries a written accent mark.

  ja**món**, al**bón**digas, a**zú**car

- A written accent mark is also used to differentiate between monosyllabic words that are spelled the same but have different meanings.

el	**él**	**té**	te
the	*he*	*tea*	*you*

- All interrogative pronouns are written with an accent.

  ¿cu**á**ndo? ¿c**ó**mo? ¿qui**é**n? ¿qu**é**? ¿d**ó**nde?

1.3 Linking

- The sound and rhythm of spoken Spanish is influenced by linking, in which two syllables are merged into one. This phenomenon mainly occurs when a word that ends in a vowel is followed by a word that begins with a vowel: L1B, L3A

  Me llamo‿Eladio. Soy de‿Argentina. Vivo‿en Córdoba.

- When identical vowel sounds appear together, they are pronounced like one long vowel.

  mi‿hijo una clase‿excelente

- Two identical consonants together sound like a single consonant.

  con‿Natalia sus‿sobrinos las‿sillas

- Also, a consonant at the end of a word is linked with the vowel at the beginning of the next word.

  es‿ingeniera mis‿abuelos sus‿hijos

1.4 Upper and lower case letters (**Mayúsculas y minúsculas**) U0

- In Spanish, upper case letters are used less often than in English. Upper case letters are used for proper nouns naming people, countries, cities, and provinces, as well as for the first word in a sentence.

  Es **C**armen **A**breu, de la **R**epública **D**ominicana.

  ¡**H**ola! **Me** llamo **S**alma **H**ayek.

- Unlike in English, upper case letters are not used in Spanish for days of the week, months, or adjectives of nationality and religion. L1B, L3A

  Alejandra, mi amiga **boliviana**, llega el primer **miércoles** de **junio**.
  *Alejandra, my **Bolivian** friend, arrives on the first **Wednesday** in **June**.*

1.5 Question marks and exclamation points (**Signos de interrogación y exclamación**) U0

- Question marks (**¿ ?**) and exclamation points (**¡ !**) precede and follow questions and exclamations, respectively.

  ¿Cómo se escribe**?** **¡**Buenos días**!** **¡**Hola**!**, **¿**qué tal**?**

2 Nouns (Sustantivos) L1A

2.1 Gender (El género) L1A, L3A

- Spanish nouns have gender and are considered either masculine or feminine. Often the ending of the word indicates its gender.

masculine		feminine	
-o	banc**o**, muse**o**, puebl**o**	**-a**	comid**a**, isl**a**, paell**a**
-r	amo**r**, ba**r**, ma**r**	**-ión**	canc**ión**, profes**ión**
-l	hospita**l**, hote**l**, so**l**	**-ad, -ud**	ciud**ad**, sal**ud**

- Nouns ending in **-e** can be either masculine or feminine.

masculine		feminine	
-e	nombr**e**, restaurant**e**, tomat**e**	**-e**	clas**e**, madr**e**, noch**e**

- Some important exceptions:

masculine	feminine
(el) dí**a**, map**a**, sof**á**, clim**a**, idiom**a**, problem**a**, av**ión**, cam**ión**	(la) flo**r**, man**o**, radi**o**

- Other important distinctions:

masculine		feminine	
Days of the week	el martes, el lunes	Letters	la b, la a
Numbers	el uno, el dos	Telling time	la una, las dos
Place names that do not end in **-a***	Quito es muy bonit**o**. Perú es montaños**o**. **El** Amazonas es enorme.	Place names that end in an unaccented **-a**	Barcelona es muy bonit**a**. España es montaños**a**.

*Note that it is appropriate to use the feminine article with any city name.

- Names of professions: L1B

masculine		feminine	
-o	médic**o**, ingenier**o**	**-a**	médic**a**, ingenier**a**
-ero	camarer**o**, panader**o**	**-era**	camarer**a**, panader**a**
-or	profes**or**, pint**or**	**-ora**	profes**ora**, pint**ora**
-ista	dent**ista**, period**ista**	**-ista**	dent**ista**, period**ista**
-nte	estudia**nte**, canta**nte**	**-nte**	estudia**nte**, canta**nte**

- Note that many professions ending in **-ista** or **-nte** can refer to both men and women. In these cases, the article also agrees with the person's gender, e.g., **el** estudiante, **la** dentista. Some nouns ending in **-nte**, such as **dependiente/a** and **presidente/a,** do have a distinct feminine form.

2.2 Formation of the plural (**El plural**) L1B, L2A

singular		plural	
Ending in a vowel	cas**a**, coch**e**, camarer**o**	**+ -s**	casa**s**, coche**s**, camarero**s**
Ending in a consonant	hospita**l**, me**s**, profeso**r**, tre**n**	**+ -es**	hospital**es**, mes**es**, profesor**es**, tren**es**
Ending in **-s** (after an unstressed vowel)	(el) lunes, (la) crisis	No change	(los) lunes, (las) crisis

- When the final syllable of a noun carries a written accent in the singular form, the written accent is dropped in the plural.

  la nación — **las naciones**
  the nation — *the nations*

- When a singular noun ends in **-z**, change the **z** to **c** before adding **-es**.

  el lápiz — **los lápices**
  the pencil — *the pencils*

3 Articles (Los artículos) L1A

3.1 Definite articles (**Los artículos determinados**) L2A

- Definite articles, equivalent to *the* in English, identify specific nouns.

	singular	plural
masculine	**el** carro	**los** carros
feminine	**la** plaza	**las** plazas

- The masculine definite article **el** is used with the singular form of feminine nouns that begin with a stressed **a**, such as **agua**, **alma**, or **área**. Feminine adjectives are still used with these words, and plural forms of these nouns take feminine articles.

  el aula — **un** aula — **las** aulas — **el** agua frí**a**
  the classroom — *a classroom* — *the classrooms* — *the cold water*

3.1.1 el/la de + [*noun*]; el/la que + [*verb*] L9B

- Use the construction **el/la** + [*noun*] + **de +** [*noun*] or **el/la** + [*noun*] + **que +** [*verb*] to refer to a person based on another point of reference.

  El (señor) de la frutería se llama Antonio.
  The man from *the fruit stand is named Antonio.*

  Magdalena es **la (señora) que** tiene el estanco.
  Magdalena is ***the woman who*** *has the tobacconist shop.*

- The noun between the article and **de/que** can be omitted. Remember to use the contraction **del** when **de** appears before the masculine definite article **el**.

  La del quiosco es mi amiga Juana.
  The girl (The one) *from the kiosk is my friend Juana.*

  Los de la panadería son ecuatorianos.
  The people *from the bakery are Ecuadorean.*

  El que vive en esa casa es Pedro.
  The one who *lives in that house is Pedro.*

3.1.2 [*preposition*] + [*definite article*] + que L18A

- In a relative clause (**cláusula relativa**), the construction [*definite article*] + **que** refers to the noun that is the object of the clause. The article must match the corresponding noun in gender and number.

  Es **una deportista a la que** admiro.
  *She is **an athlete whom** I admire.*

  Son **profesionales para los que** no hay retos imposibles.
  *They are **professionals for whom** there are no impossible challenges.*

3.2 Indefinite articles (Los artículos indeterminados) L1A, L2A

- Indefinite articles, equivalent to *a*, *an*, *one*, or *some* in English, identify unspecified nouns.

	singular	plural
masculine	**un** pueblo	**unos** pueblos
feminine	**una** montaña	**unas** montañas

⚠ The plural forms of the indefinite article, **unos** and **unas**, are used to indicate approximate amounts.

  Medellín tiene **unos** barrios bonitos.
  *Medellín has **some** pretty neighborhoods.*

  Tengo **unas** postales de Santiago de Chile.
  *I have **some** postcards from Santiago, Chile.*

- Note the difference in meaning when the indefinite article is omitted.

  Medellín tiene barrios bonitos.
  Medellín has pretty neighborhoods.

3.3 The neuter article lo (El artículo neutro *lo*)

3.3.1 lo + [*adjective*] L12B, L15A

- Use the neuter article **lo** to form a noun phrase from an adjective or an adverb.

  Lo bueno es que gano mucho; **lo malo** es que siempre estoy de viaje.
  ***The good thing** is that I earn a lot; **the bad thing** is that I am always traveling.*

  Para mí, **lo más importante** es la familia.
  *For me, **the most important thing** is family.*

  Lo mejor sería consumir productos ecológicos.
  ***The best thing** would be to eat organic produce.*

3.3.2 lo de + [*noun/infinitive*]; lo que + [*verb*] L14B

- To refer to a topic that has already been alluded to, use **lo de** + [*noun/infinitive*] or **lo que** + [*verb*].

  El último capítulo trataba sobre **lo de** la hija de los Alcántara... **lo de** irse a Londres con su novio.
  *The last episode was about **the thing with** the Alcántaras' daughter . . . **the thing about** going to London with her boyfriend.*

  ¿Es verdad **lo que** me contaste ayer?
  *Is **what** you told me yesterday true?*

3.4 Generalizing (Generalizar) L16B

- When referring to a group of people in general terms, use **la gente** (*people*). **La gente** is a singular noun and requires a singular article. Note that this noun also requires the third-person singular verb form.

  La gente es muy amable.
  ***People are** really nice.*

- Another way to refer to a group of people in general terms is **la mayoría** (*the majority; most people*). When **la mayoría** is followed by **de** + [*plural noun*], the verb can agree with **mayoría** (singular) or with the other noun (plural).

  La mayoría de los estudiantes **habla(n)** un poco de español.
  ***Most** students **speak** a little Spanish.*

- The plural verb must be used with the verbs **ser, estar,** and **parecer**.

  La mayoría de los profesores **son** latinoamericanos.
  ***The majority** of the professors **are** Latin American.*

- You can also use **los/las** + [*plural noun*] to make generalizing statements. Use the third-person plural verb form with this construction.

  Los actores son personas abiertas.
  ***Actors are** outgoing people.*

4 Adjectives (Los adjetivos) L1B, L2A

- An adjective always agrees with the corresponding noun in both gender and number, even when the noun and the adjective are found in separate sentences.

  Granada es un**a** ciudad fantástic**a**. Está llen**a** de impresionantes monumentos históricos.
  Granada is a fantastic city. It is full of impressive historic monuments.

4.1 Gender (El género) L2A, L12A

- As with nouns, the gender of adjectives is often signaled by the final letter. Some adjectives have distinct masculine and feminine forms; most adjectives ending in **-e**, **-ista**, or a consonant use the same form for masculine and feminine.

masculine		feminine	
-o	divertid**o**, content**o**	**-a**	divertid**a**, content**a**
-e	responsabl**e**, trist**e**	**-e**	responsabl**e**, trist**e**
-consonant	feliz	*-consonant*	feliz
-ista	optim**ista**	**-ista**	optim**ista**

- You have seen that the ending **-ista** is used in certain nouns (**taxista**, **periodista**). In adjectives, this ending remains unchanged when describing both masculine and feminine nouns.

  Clara es siempre muy optim**ista**.
  Clara is always very optimistic.

  Su novio Pedro es pesim**ista**.
  Her boyfriend Pedro is pessimistic.

⚠ Adjectives that describe colors and end in **-o** change to the ending **-a** in the feminine form: blanc**o/a**, negr**o/a**, etc. As with all adjectives, adjectives of color that end in **-e** or a consonant, such as **verde**, **azul**, **marrón**, and **gris**, can be masculine or feminine. In addition, some nouns, such as **café**, **rosa**, and **naranja,** can be used as invariable adjectives. L3B

⚠ Note that the adjectives **otro/a** and **medio/a** are used without an indefinite article.

Otra botella de agua, por favor. L2B
***Another** bottle of water, please.*

¿Me da **medio** kilo de tomates? L4A
*Would you give me a **half** kilogram of tomatoes?*

- Nationalities L1B

masculine		feminine	
-o	italian**o**	**-a**	italian**a**
-*consonant*	alemán españo**l**	-*consonant* + **a**	aleman**a** españo**la**

⚠ Note that the written accent on the final syllable of adjectives of nationality such as **alemán** or **inglés** is dropped when **-a** is added to form the feminine: **alemana, inglesa**.

⚠ For adjectives of nationality that end in an accented **í**, such as **paquistaní** or **marroquí**, form the plural by adding **-es**: **paquistaníes, marroquíes**.

4.2 The plural (El plural) L2A

singular		plural	
Ending in a vowel	simpátic**o**, típic**a**, important**e**	+ **s**	simpático**s**, típica**s**, importante**s**
Ending in a consonant	internaciona**l**, popula**r**	+ **es**	internacional**es**, popular**es**

4.3 Position of adjectives (Posición de los adjetivos) U0, L1B

- In Spanish, the adjective is usually placed after the noun it modifies:

  La medicina es una profesión **interesante**.
  Medicine is an ***interesting*** *profession.*

- Adjectives used in greetings are placed in front of the noun:

  Buenos días, **buenas** tardes, **buenas** noches.
  Good *morning,* ***good*** *afternoon,* ***good*** *night.*

4.4 The comparative and the superlative (El comparativo y el superlativo)

4.4.1 Regular forms (Las formas regulares) L6A, L9A

- Form regular comparatives and superlatives using **más** (*more*) and **menos** (*less*).

	comparative	superlative
interesante(s)	**más interesante(s)**	**el/la más interesante** **los/las más interesantes**
	menos interesante(s)	**el/la menos interesante** **los/las menos interesantes**
divertido/a(s)	**más divertido/a(s)**	**el más divertido** **la más divertida** **los más divertidos** **las más divertidas**
	menos divertido/a(s)	**el menos divertido** **la menos divertida** **los menos divertidos** **las menos divertidas**

Para mí, **los** programas **más divertidos** son los concursos. **Los menos divertidos** son las noticias.
In my opinion, game shows are ***the most entertaining*** *TV programs.* ***The least entertaining ones*** *are the news broadcasts.*

4.4.2 Irregular forms (Las formas irregulares) L6A, L9A

	comparative	superlative
bueno/a	**mejor**	**el/la mejor**
malo/a	**peor**	**el/la peor**
grande	**mayor**	**el/la mayor**
pequeño/a	**menor**	**el/la menor**
joven	**menor**	**el/la menor**
viejo/a	**mayor**	**el/la mayor**

El perro es **el mejor** amigo del hombre.
*Dog is man's **best** friend.*

Para mí, el lunes es **el peor** día de la semana.
*In my opinion, Monday is **the worst** day of the week.*

4.4.3 Comparisons of equality (El comparativo de igualdad) L8B

- Comparisons of equality are formed with the construction **tan/tanto... como...**
- **Tan** precedes adjectives and adverbs and always remains unchanged.

Aquí la vida no es **tan** fácil **como** en Europa.
*Life here is not **as** easy **as** in Europe.*

Viajar en el tren de alta velocidad es casi **tan** rápido **como** viajar en avión.
*Traveling on the high-speed train is almost **as** fast **as** traveling by plane.*

- **Tanto** can be used alone or in front of a noun, in which case it needs to agree in both gender and number.

¡Esa canción me gusta **tanto**!
*I like that song **so much**!*

Aquí hay **tantas** panaderías **como** en mi barrio.
*There are **as many** bakeries here **as** in my neighborhood.*

- Comparisons of equality with verbs are formed by placing **tanto como** after the verb. Note that in this construction **tanto** does not change in number or gender.

Mi hermana ya gana **tanto como** yo.
*My sister already earns **as much as** I do.*

4.5 The absolute superlative (El superlativo absoluto) L11B

- The absolute superlative describes a quality without making reference to other people or things. It is equivalent to *extremely*, *super*, or *very*.
- To form the absolute superlative, drop the final vowel of the adjective (if there is one) and add **-ísimo/a(s)**. The ending always carries a written accent mark.

pequeño/a(s)	pequeñísimo/a(s)
caro/a(s)	carísimo/a(s)
grande(s)	grandísimo/a(s)
fácil(es)	facilísimo/a(s)

- Note these spelling changes that are necessary to preserve the original pronunciation of the adjective:

ri**co** → ri**qu**ísimo

lar**go** → lar**gu**ísimo

feli**z** → feli**c**ísimo

- In colloquial language, other superlative constructions are used, such as **muy muy** and the prefix **super-**.

  Esta película es **muy muy buena**.
  *This movie is **really good**.*

  Este sofá es **supercómodo**.
  *This sofa is **super comfortable**.*

4.6 Shortened adjectives (**El adjetivo apocopado**) L12B

- The adjectives **bueno** and **grande** are shortened to **buen** and **gran** before a singular masculine noun. Note that the adjective is not shortened when used with feminine or plural nouns or when used after the noun.

¡**Buen** viaje! (*masc. sing.*) *Have a **good** trip!*	un **gran** libro *a **great** book*
¡**Buena** suerte! (*fem. sing.*) ***Good** luck!*	un libro **grande** *a **big** book*

⚠ Note that there are slight differences in meaning when the adjective is placed before or after the noun.

5 Verbs (Los verbos)

- Spanish verbs are classified into three groups, according to their endings:

  -ar verbs: hablar, trabajar, tomar...

  -er verbs: aprender, beber, comer...

  -ir verbs: vivir, escribir, compartir...

5.1 The present (**El presente**)

5.1.1 Regular verbs (Verbos regulares) L1B, L2A, L2B, L3B

	-ar verbs (trabajar)	-er verbs (aprender)	-ir verbs (vivir)
(yo)	trabaj**o**	aprend**o**	viv**o**
(tú)	trabaj**as**	aprend**es**	viv**es**
(usted, él, ella)	trabaj**a**	aprend**e**	viv**e**
(nosotros/as)	trabaj**amos**	aprend**emos**	viv**imos**
(vosotros/as)	trabaj**áis**	aprend**éis**	viv**ís**
(ustedes, ellos/as)	trabaj**an**	aprend**en**	viv**en**

- Stem-changing verbs (**Verbos con cambio en la raíz**) L2B, L3B, L4A, L4B, 10B, L11A, L12A, L12B

	e > ie (querer)	o > ue (poder)	e > i (servir)
(yo)	qu**ie**ro	p**ue**do	s**i**rvo
(tú)	qu**ie**res	p**ue**des	s**i**rves
(usted, él, ella)	qu**ie**re	p**ue**de	s**i**rve
(nosotros/as)	queremos	podemos	servimos
(vosotros/as)	queréis	podéis	servís
(ustedes, ellos/as)	qu**ie**ren	p**ue**den	s**i**rven

⚠ The **nosotros/as** and **vosotros/as** forms of these verbs do not have changes in the stem vowel.

  Yo qu**ie**ro ir al cine, pero vosotras qu**e**réis salir a cenar.
  I want to go to the movies, but you want to go out to dinner.

⚠ Some verbs have irregular forms in the first-person singular conjugation in order to maintain the original pronunciation of the verb stem, e.g., **g → j**: **recoger (recojo)** or **gu → g**: **seguir (sigo)**.

5.1.2 Irregular verbs (Verbos irregulares) L3B, L4A, L6B, L11A, L11B

- Certain verbs undergo changes in the first-person singular form (**Cambios en la primera persona del singular**).

The following verbs are irregular in the first-person singular form (**yo**).

	infinitive	first-person singular (present)	
-g-	hacer poner salir	ha**g**o pon**g**o sal**g**o	L3A, L4A
-y	dar estar	do**y** esto**y**	
-zc-	conocer	cono**zc**o	L5B, L7A
	saber	**sé**	L6B
	ver	**veo**	

- Stem-changing verbs with irregular **yo** forms (**Verbos mixtos**) L2A, L3B, L12A

These stem-changing verbs are also irregular in the first-person singular form.

	-g- + e > ie	
	tener	**venir**
(yo) (tú) (usted, él, ella) (nosotros/as) (vosotros/as) (ustedes, ellos/as)	ten**g**o t**ie**nes t**ie**ne tenemos tenéis t**ie**nen	ven**g**o v**ie**nes v**ie**ne venimos venís v**ie**nen

- Fully irregular verbs (**Verbos totalmente irregulares**) L1A, L1B, L3A, L3B, L6B, L12A

	ser	ir	haber
(yo) (tú) (usted, él, ella) (nosotros/as) (vosotros/as) (ustedes, ellos/as)	soy eres es somos sois son	voy vas va vamos vais van	he has ha hemos habéis han

! In the present tense, the verb **haber** is principally used in the form **hay**, which is impersonal and invariable. Use **hay** to express both *there is* and *there are* in Spanish. The conjugated present-tense forms of **haber** are only used as auxiliary verbs, such as in the formation of the present perfect: **He trabajado**. L3A

5.2 The preterite (**El pretérito indefinido**) L5A, L5B, L8B, L9B, L10B

5.2.1 Regular forms (Las formas regulares) L5A

	-ar verbs (**terminar**)	**-er** verbs (**nacer**)	**-ir** verbs (**vivir**)
(yo)	termin**é**	nac**í**	viv**í**
(tú)	termin**aste**	nac**iste**	viv**iste**
(usted, él, ella)	termin**ó**	nac**ió**	viv**ió**
(nosotros/as)	termin**amos**	nac**imos**	viv**imos**
(vosotros/as)	termin**asteis**	nac**isteis**	viv**isteis**
(ustedes, ellos/as)	termin**aron**	nac**ieron**	viv**ieron**

- ¿Cuándo **terminaste** los estudios?
- *When **did you finish** your studies?*
- **Terminé** en 1999.
- ***I finished** in 1999.*
- ¿Dónde **naciste**?
- *Where **were you born**?*
- **Nací** en Montevideo y **viví** allí veinte años.
- ***I was born** in Montevideo and **I lived** there for twenty years.*

⚠ The endings of **-er** and **-ir** verbs are identical in the preterite.

⚠ In **-ar** and **-ir** verbs, the conjugations of the first-person plural (**nosotros/as**) are identical in the present and in the preterite: **hablamos** (present) - **hablamos** (preterite); **abrimos** (present) - **abrimos** (preterite).

⚠ In the preterite, the spoken stress always falls on the first vowel of the the verb ending. In the regular forms of this tense, the root does not carry the stressed syllable. This pronunciation pattern is characteristic of the preterite: **hablé, hablaste, habló, hablamos, hablasteis, hablaron; vendí, vendiste, vendió, vendimos, vendisteis, vendieron; abrí, abriste, abrió, abrimos, abristeis, abrieron.**

5.2.2 Irregular forms (Las formas irregulares) L5B, L8B

	ser	**ir**	**dar**
(yo)	fui	fui	di
(tú)	fuiste	fuiste	diste
(usted, él, ella)	fue	fue	dio
(nosotros/as)	fuimos	fuimos	dimos
(vosotros/as)	fuisteis	fuisteis	disteis
(ustedes, ellos/as)	fueron	fueron	dieron

⚠ The forms of the verbs **ser** and **ir** are identical in the preterite. Use context to determine their meaning.

Camila **fue** a la fiesta anoche.
*Camila **went** to the party last night.*

Jorge **fue** periodista del diario universitario por varios años.
*Jorge **was** a reporter for the university newspaper for several years.*

- The endings for **dar** in the preterite are the same as the regular preterite endings for **-er** and **-ir** verbs, but there are no written accent marks. The preterite of the verb **ver** follows a similiar pattern (**vi**, **viste**, **vio**, etc.).
- A number of other verbs have irregular forms in the preterite. These verbs can be divided into three categories (**u**-stem, **i**-stem, and **j**-stem), according to the stem change that the verb undergoes in the preterite.

	tener (**u**-stem)	**venir** (**i**-stem)	**decir** (**j**-stem)
(yo)	tuv**e**	vin**e**	dij**e**
(tú)	tuv**iste**	vin**iste**	dij**iste**
(usted, él, ella)	tuv**o**	vin**o**	dij**o**
(nosotros/as)	tuv**imos**	vin**imos**	dij**imos**
(vosotros/as)	tuv**isteis**	vin**isteis**	dij**isteis**
(ustedes, ellos/as)	tuv**ieron**	vin**ieron**	dij**eron**

⚠ The endings of these verbs are the regular preterite endings of **-er** and **-ir** verbs, except for the **yo** and **usted** forms. Note that these two endings do not have written accents.

- These verbs are irregular in the preterite and undergo similar stem changes to **tener, venir,** and **decir**.

infinitive	**u**-stem	preterite forms
poder	pud-	pude, pudiste, pudo, pudimos, pudisteis, pudieron
poner	pus-	puse, pusiste, puso, pusimos, pusisteis, pusieron
saber	sup-	supe, supiste, supo, supimos, supisteis, supieron
estar	estuv-	estuve, estuviste, estuvo, estuvimos, estuvisteis, estuvieron

infinitive	**i**-stem	preterite forms
querer	quis-	quise, quisiste, quiso, quisimos, quisisteis, quisieron
hacer	hic-	hice, hiciste, hi**z**o, hicimos, hicisteis, hicieron

⚠ Note that the third-person singular preterite form of **hacer** undergoes a **c→z** spelling change: **hizo.**

- Preterite verbs with **j**-stems, like **decir**, omit the letter **i** in the ending of the **ustedes/ellos/ellas** form.

infinitive	**j**-stem	preterite forms
traer	traj-	traje, trajiste, trajo, trajimos, trajisteis, tra**je**ron
conducir	conduj-	conduje, condujiste, condujo, condujimos, condujisteis, condu**je**ron
traducir	traduj-	traduje, tradujiste, tradujo, tradujimos, tradujisteis, tradu**je**ron

Todos **trajeron** comida o bebidas a la fiesta.
*Everyone **brought** food or drinks to the party.*

⚠ Most verbs that end in **-cir** follow the pattern of **j**-stem verbs in the preterite. For example, **producir → produje, produjiste,** etc.

⚠ In the first- and third-person singular forms of irregular verbs in the preterite, the accent falls on the root and not the ending: **hice, hizo, vine, vino, quise**...

- The preterite form of **hay** (*inf.* **haber**) is **hubo** (*there was; there were*).

Hubo una tormenta muy fuerte el sábado por la noche.
***There was** a very strong storm on Saturday night.*

- *See the verb tables on pp. A4–A11 for the full conjugations of irregular verb patterns.*

5.2.3 Use of the preterite (El uso del pretérito indefinido) L5A, L5B, L8B, L10B, L13A, L13B, L14B

- The preterite is used to talk about finished actions and events in the past.

El mes pasado **viajé** a Puerto Rico. Ahí **conocí** a mucha gente y **me divertí** mucho.
*Last month **I traveled** to Puerto Rico. **I met** a lot of people there and **I had** a lot of **fun**.*

- The preterite is often used with time expressions that specify the moment in the past: **anoche, ayer, el otro día, la semana pasada, el mes pasado, hace dos años, el año pasado, en 1990**, etc.

El 28 de junio de 1982, Manuela terminó la universidad.
*Manuela graduated from college **on June 28, 1982**.*

En 1988, celebró su boda.
***In 1988**, she got married.*

Hace un mes, Manuela y Carolina abrieron la tienda.
*Manuela and Carolina opened the shop **a month ago**.*

- The preterite is also used in order to comment on or evaluate an experience in the past.

Mi viaje a la Patagonia **fue** increíble. Me **gustó** mucho el paisaje y la gente me **pareció** muy amable.
*My trip to Patagonia **was** incredible. I really **liked** the scenery and the people **seemed** really friendly.*

5.3 The present perfect (El pretérito perfecto) L6A, L7B, L10B

- The present perfect is formed with the present of the verb **haber** and the past participle of the main verb.

	haber	+ [*past participle*]
(yo)	he	
(tú)	has	habl**ado**
(usted, él, ella)	ha	com**ido**
(nosotros/as)	hemos	dorm**ido**
(vosotros/as)	habéis	
(ustedes, ellos/as)	han	

¿**Has viajado** a Europa alguna vez?
***Have you** ever **traveled** to Europe?*

- ¿**Has tomado** ya un café?
- No, todavía no.
- ***Have you had** a cup of coffee yet?*
- *No, not yet.*

5.3.1 The past participle (El participio pasado)

• **-ar** verbs: **-ado**	**hablar** → **hablado** **trabajar** → **trabajado** **estudiar** → **estudiado** **estar** → **estado**	**Has trabajado** mucho. ***You have worked** a lot.*

• **-er** and **-ir** verbs: **-ido**	**comer** → **comido** **vender** → **vendido** **dormir** → **dormido** **ir** → **ido**	**He vendido** mi coche. ***I have sold** my car.*

⚠ The past participles of **-er** and **-ir** verbs whose stems end in **-a**, **-e**, or **-o** have an accent mark on the **i** of the **-ido** ending.

infinitive	past participle
caer	caído
creer	creído
leer	leído
oír	oído
reír	reído
traer	traído

5.3.2 Irregular past participles (Los participios pasados irregulares) L7B

infinitive	past participle
abrir	abierto
cubrir	cubierto
decir	dicho
escribir	escrito
hacer	hecho
morir	muerto
poner	puesto
romper	roto
ver	visto
volver	vuelto

- ¿Qué **has hecho** esta tarde?
  *What **have you done** this afternoon?*
- **He escrito** un ensayo para la clase de sociología y **he visto** a mis padres.
  ***I wrote** en essay for sociology class and **I saw** my parents.*

5.3.3 Placement of direct object pronouns (La posición de los pronombres de objeto directo) L7B

- The present perfect is comprised of the verb **haber** + [*past participle*]. These two components always appear together and cannot be separated by another word. When an object pronoun is used, it is placed before the conjugated form of **haber**.

  - ¿**Has puesto** la mesa?
  - *Sí,* **la he puesto**.
  - ***Have you set** the table?*
  - *Yes, **I have set it**.*

  - ¿**Habéis visto** a Juan?
  - *No, no* **lo hemos visto** *todavía.*
  - ***Have you seen** Juan?*
  - *No, **we have** not **seen him** yet.*

5.3.4 Use of the present perfect (El uso del pretérito perfecto) L6A, L10B

- The present perfect is used to refer to past events that in some way act upon the present, either because the consequences of the past action affect the present or because the past action has taken place within a time period that has not ended.

  ¿**Has llamado** a Carla?
  ***Have you called** Carla?*

- The present perfect is frequently used with the adverb **ya** (*already*).

  ¿**Ya han terminado** la tarea?
  ***Have you already finished** the homework?*

⚠ In some Latin American countries, the present perfect is seldom used, and the preterite is used instead. In Spain, the present perfect is frequently used to refer to events in the recent past.

5.4 The imperfect (**El pretérito imperfecto**) L9A

5.4.1 Regular forms (Las formas regulares)

	-ar verbs	**-er** verbs	**-ir** verbs
	HABL**AR**	TEN**ER**	VIV**IR**
(yo)	habl**aba**	ten**ía**	viv**ía**
(tú)	habl**abas**	ten**ías**	viv**ías**
(usted, él, ella)	habl**aba**	ten**ía**	viv**ía**
(nosotros/as)	habl**ábamos**	ten**íamos**	viv**íamos**
(vosotros/as)	habl**abais**	ten**íais**	viv**íais**
(ustedes, ellos/as)	habl**aban**	ten**ían**	viv**ían**

De niño, **vivía** en Córdoba con mis abuelos.
*As a child, **I lived** in Córdoba with my grandparents.*

Teníamos una casa muy bonita.
***We had** a very nice house.*

⚠ The first- and third-person singular forms are the same in all conjugations of the imperfect.

⚠ Additionally, the endings of **-er** and **-ir** verbs in the imperfect are the same.

5.4.2 Irregular forms (Las formas irregulares) 9A.2

	ser	**ir**
(yo)	**era**	**iba**
(tú)	**eras**	**ibas**
(usted, él, ella)	**era**	**iba**
(nosotros/as)	**éramos**	**íbamos**
(vosotros/as)	**erais**	**ibais**
(ustedes, ellos/as)	**eran**	**iban**

Cuando **era** más joven, **iba** a conciertos de rock.
*When **I was** younger, **I used to go** to rock concerts.*

5.4.3 Use of the imperfect (El uso del pretérito imperfecto) L9A, L9B, L10B, L13A, L13B, L14A, L14B

The imperfect is used to:

- speak about habitual or repeated actions in the past

  Cuando **estudiaba, compartía** un apartamento con dos compañeros. **Estaba** siempre con ellos y **teníamos** un grupo de música.
  *When **I was** a student, **I shared** an apartment with two roommates. **I was** with them all the time and **we had** a band.*

- describe situations or contexts in the past

  Era de noche, **hacía** mucho calor y yo **no podía** dormir.
  ***It was** night, **it was** very hot, and **I couldn't** sleep.*

- describe the context and the circumstances of a past event

  Esta mañana **estaba** en casa; por eso he recibido la noticia.
  ***I was** at home this morning, so I received the news.*

  En 2008 voté por primera vez. **Tenía** 18 años.
  *In 2008 I voted for the first time. **I was** 18 years old.*

  Estábamos en Mallorca cuando llegó la noticia.
  ***We were** in Mallorca when the news arrived.*

- compare the past and the present

  Yo antes **era** muy inseguro. Ahora sé lo que quiero.
  ***I used to be** very insecure. Now I know what I want.*

  Hace 10 años **vivía** todavía en casa de mis padres. Hoy vivo con mi esposa.
  *Ten years ago **I** still **lived** with my parents. Now I live with my wife.*

- express ignorance on a subject

  No **sabía** que en Guinea Ecuatorial hablaban español. **Pensaba** que se hablaban otros idiomas.
  ***I didn't know** that they spoke Spanish in Equatorial Guinea. **I thought** that they spoke other languages.*

- express intentions that were not realized

  Yo **quería** estudiar sociología, pero al final estudié derecho.
  *I **wanted** to study sociology, but I ended up studying law.*

5.5 The past perfect (El pretérito pluscuamperfecto) L14A

5.5.1 Conjugation (Conjugación)

- The past perfect is formed with the imperfect of the verb **haber** and the past participle of the main verb.

	haber	+ [*past participle*]
(yo)	había	
(tú)	habías	hablado
(usted, él, ella)	había	tenido
(nosotros/as)	habíamos	vivido
(vosotros/as)	habíais	
(ustedes, ellos/as)	habían	

5.5.2 Use of the past perfect (El uso del pretérito pluscuamperfecto)

- The past perfect is used to express a past action that occurred before a previous past action.

  Cuando llegué, el tren ya **había salido**.
  *When I arrived, the train **had** already **left**.*

5.6 Contrasting past verb tenses (Contraste de los tiempos del pasado)

L9B, L10B, L13A, L13B, L14A, L14B

- Present perfect (**El pretérito perfecto**)

  Use the present perfect to speak about past events that influence the present. When this tense is used, either the consequences of the past event reach into the present, or the time expression refers to a period of time that is not yet over.

  ¿**Has estado** en Costa Rica alguna vez?
  ***Have you** ever **been** to Costa Rica?*

  No, **todavía no he estado**.
  *No, **I haven't been there yet**.*

  Hoy **he aprendido** muchas cosas.
  ***I have learned** many things today.*

- Preterite (**El pretérito indefinido**)

  Use the preterite to narrate past actions that belong to a period of time that is over. When narrating past events, time expressions such as **de repente** and **(y) entonces** can signal the use of the preterite.

  Fui a México hace dos años.
  I went *to Mexico two years ago.*

  Apagaron las luces del teatro, y entonces **empezó** la función.
  The lights in the theater ***were shut off****, and then the show* ***began****.*

- The use of the present perfect and the preterite also depends on factors such as the point of view of the speaker and the differences among different Spanish-speaking countries. In most countries in Latin America, the use of the present perfect is limited and the preterite is preferred.

  Este año **estuve** en España. (*Latin American Spanish*)
  Este año **he estado** *en España. (Iberian Spanish)*
  I was *in Spain this year. /* ***I have been*** *to Spain this year.*

- Imperfect (**El pretérito imperfecto**)

  Use the imperfect to describe past situations and causes that establish the background details to the main action. This tense is often used along with other past tenses.

  Como **llovía** mucho, no salimos.
  Because ***it was raining*** *a lot, we didn't go out.*

  Ayer no fui a trabajar porque **estaba** enferma.
  I didn't go to work yesterday because ***I was*** *sick.*

- Past perfect (**El pretérito pluscuamperfecto**)

  This tense expresses an action in the past that occurred before another past action.

  Antes de aprender español, **había estudiado** francés.
  Before learning Spanish, ***I had studied*** *French.*

5.7 Reflexive verbs (**Verbos reflexivos**)

5.7.1 Reflexive pronouns (Pronombres reflexivos) U0, L7A, L10B, L11A, L12A, L17B, L18B

- A reflexive verb is made up of a form of the verb and the reflexive pronoun.

	llamarse
(yo)	**me** llamo
(tú)	**te** llamas
(usted, él, ella)	**se** llama
(nosotros/as)	**nos** llamamos
(vosotros/as)	**os** llamáis
(ustedes, ellos/as)	**se** llaman

- With a reflexive verb, the subject both performs and receives the action of the verb.

  Me lavo la cara.
  I wash *my face.*

  Nos despertamos a las siete y media.
  We wake up *at seven-thirty.*

- Note the difference in meaning when the verb is not reflexive.

  Siempre **lavo los platos** después de cenar.
  I always ***wash the dishes*** *after dinner.*

  Claudia **despierta a su hermano** por la mañana.
  Claudia ***wakes up her brother*** *in the morning.*

Note that the definite article is generally used to refer to parts of the body or clothing in conjunction with reflexive verbs.

Te pones **el** abrigo.
*You put on **your** coat.*

Ella se lava **las** manos.
*She washes **her** hands.*

Reflexive verbs in Spanish do not always translate to a reflexive meaning in English.

- ¿Cómo **te sientes**? — *How **do you feel**?*
- **Me siento** mejor, gracias. — ***I feel** better, thank you.*
- **Me alegro.** — ***I am glad.***

- Reflexive verbs are frequently used to talk about relationships and emotions.

Me separé de mi ex, pero **nos llevamos** bien.
***I broke up** with my ex, but **we get along** well.*

Mi hijo **se parece** mucho a los dos.
*My son **looks** a lot **like** both of us.*

Me alegro de que te jubiles, aunque **nos lo hemos pasado** muy bien contigo.
***I am happy** that you are retiring, although **we have had a good time** with you.*

Se ríe mucho con sus compañeros de baile. Les divierte bailar.
***She laughs** a lot with her dance partners. They have a good time dancing.*

5.7.2. Reciprocal verbs (Verbos recíprocos) L17B

- Reciprocal verbs are only conjugated in plural forms and are accompanied by the plural reflexive pronouns (**nos, os, se**). These verbs express a shared or reciprocal action between two or more people or things. When a verb is reciprocal, the phrase **el uno al otro/a la otra** can be added to the sentence, and the pronoun is understood as *(to) each other* or *(to) one another.*

María y Carlos **se abrazan.** (María abraza a Carlos y Carlos abraza a María.)
*María and Carlos **hug each other.** (María hugs Carlos and Carlos hugs María.)*

Mi hermana y yo **nos llamamos** todos los días.
*My sister and I **call each other** every day.*

5.7.3 Pronominal verb of change: *ponerse* (Verbo pronominal de cambio) L18B

- The pronominal verb **ponerse** is conjugated with the reflexive pronouns **me, te, se, nos, os,** and **se** and can be followed by an adverb (**muy, un poco**) and/or an adjective (**triste, alegre**). **Ponerse** expresses a change in a subject's mood that is usually considered to be temporary. When used with an adjective, the verb is often translated into English as *to become.*

Mi madre **se puso** muy contenta al verme.
*My mother **became** very happy when she saw me.*

Nos ponemos un poco tristes cuando nos despedimos.
***We get** a little sad when we say good-bye to each other.*

5.8 ser/estar

5.8.1 Comparison of uses L1A, L1B, L2A, L2B, L3A, L3B, L5B

ser	estar
Used to identify: L1A • names and identity **Soy** Eva. ***I am*** *Eva. (My name is Eva.)* • nationality L1B **Soy** polaca. **Soy** de Varsovia. ***I am*** *Polish.* ***I am*** *from Warsaw.* • profession L1B Antonio **es** arquitecto. *Antonio* ***is*** *an architect.* María **es** médica. *María* ***is*** *a doctor.* • characteristics of people and things (descriptions) L1B, L2A Sevilla **es** una ciudad muy bonita. *Seville* ***is*** *a very pretty city.* Sevilla **es** la capital de Andalucía. *Seville* ***is*** *the capital of Andalucía.* • time L3A ¿Qué hora **es**? **Son** las tres de la tarde. *What time* ***is it****?* ***It is*** *3 o'clock in the afternoon.*	**Used to identify:** • geographical and relative location L2A, L3B ¿Dónde **está** Sevilla? *Where* ***is*** *Seville?* Sevilla **está** en el sur de España. *Seville* ***is*** *in the south of Spain.* Los CD **están** a la derecha del despertador. *The CDs* ***are*** *to the right of the alarm clock.* • marital status L5B ¿**Está** usted casada? ***Are you*** *married?* No, **estoy** soltera. *No,* ***I am*** *single.* • tastes of food and drinks L2B El pulpo **está** muy rico. *The octopus* ***is*** *very good.*

5.8.2 ser/estar + [*adjective*] L1B, L4B, L10A, L11A, L12A, L13A

ser + [*adjective*]	estar + [*adjective*]
• expresses characteristics Emilio **es** una persona **optimista**. *Emilio* ***is*** *an* ***optimistic*** *person.* Carmen **es** un poco **tímida**. *Carmen* ***is*** *a bit* ***shy****.* **Son** muy **simpáticos**. ***They are*** *very* ***nice****.*	• expresses physical or mental states **Estamos contentos** con la casa nueva. ***We are happy*** *with the new house.* Ángel **está** muy **enamorado** de ella. *Ángel* ***is*** *quite* ***in love*** *with her.* Mi padre **está enfermo**. **Está resfriado**. *My father* ***is sick****.* ***He has a cold****.*

- With negative adjectives, **un poco** can soften the negative impact.

  Pedro es muy amable, pero **un poco** pesimista.
  Pedro is very friendly, but he is ***a bit*** *pessimistic.*

- **Estar** + [*adjective*] is normally used to express a temporary state experienced by the subject of the sentence, while **ser** + [*adjective*] is normally used to express an inherent characteristic. L11A

  La paella **es** un plato **típico** de Valencia. La paella que han servido hoy **está** muy **rica**.
  Paella ***is*** *a* ***typical*** *Valencian dish. The paella they served today* ***is*** *very* ***tasty****.*

- Use the construction **estar impresionado/a con** + [*noun*] to express admiration. L18A

  Estoy impresionado con las aventuras de esta alpinista.
  I am impressed by *the adventures of this mountain climber.*

- **Estar seguro/a de que** and **está demostrado que** are used to express certainty and evidence in affirmative statements. Use these constructions in negative sentences with the subjunctive. (See **5.21**) L17A

  Estoy (completamente) **seguro de que** esta técnica **ayuda** a las personas.
  ***I am** (completely) **sure that** this technique **helps** people.*

  Está demostrado que esta técnica **ayuda** a las personas.
  ***It has been shown that** this technique **helps** people.*

  No estamos seguros de que los avances de la ciencia **representen** una mejora.
  ***We are not sure that** scientific advances **have made** improvements.*

  No está demostrado que sea un invento original.
  ***It has not been shown to be** an original invention.*

5.8.3 es mejor que + [*subjunctive*], lo mejor es/sería + [*infinitive/noun*] L15A, L16B

- Use the verb **ser** with these constructions to make suggestions. (See **5.21**)

  Lo mejor es consumir productos frescos.
  ***It is best** to eat fresh produce.*

  Es mejor que leas la etiqueta.
  ***It is better that you read** the label.*

  Lo mejor son las marcas conocidas.
  *The most well-known brands **are the best**.*

- When used with a noun, the verb agrees in number.

  Lo mejor **es el precio**.
  *The best thing **is the price**.*

  Lo mejor **son los conservantes naturales**.
  ***Natural preservatives are** the best.*

- Use **ser** in the conditional to make polite suggestions.

  Lo mejor **sería** usar envases reciclables.
  *It **would be** best to use recyclable containers.*

  Lo mejor **sería** un modelo de etiqueta único.
  *A unique label **would be** best.*

5.8.4 es necesario + [*infinitive*] / que + [*subjunctive*] L15A

- Use the infinitive when describing necessity in a general or global sense.

  Es necesario conocer los productos típicos de cada país.
  ***It is necessary to become familiar with** each country's typical products.*

- Use the subjunctive when describing what a specific person or group needs to do. (See **5.21**)

  Es necesario que ustedes **conozcan** nuestros productos.
  ***It is necessary** for you **to become familiar with** our products.*

5.8.5 es probable/posible que + [*subjunctive*] L17A

- Probability can be gauged through the use of adjectives of degree, such as **muy**, **poco**, and **bastante**. (See **5.21**)

  Es poco probable que desaparezcan los libros.
  ***It is hardly** probable that books will disappear.*

  Es bastante posible que sea verdad.
  ***It is fairly** possible that it is true.*

  Es muy probable que tengas razón.
  ***It is very** probable that you are right.*

5.8.6 (no) es evidente que + [*indicative/subjunctive*] L17A

- Use the indicative to express certainty and evidence, and the subjunctive to express lack of certainty and evidence. (See **5.21**)

  Es evidente que **hay** una solución.
  It is evident *that* ***there is*** *a solution.*

  No es evidente que los móviles **sean** malos para la salud.
  It is not evident that *cell phones* ***are*** *bad for your health.*

5.8.7 ser bueno/a, malo/a en/para/con + [*noun*] L17B

- Express someone's or something's ability with **ser + bueno/a, malo/a + en/para/con**. Use **en/para** + [*discipline*] and **con** + [*a specific thing*].

  Es muy **buena para** la música y bastante **mala en** matemáticas.
  She is *very* ***good at*** *music and pretty* ***bad at*** *math.*

  Sí, **es malo para** las relaciones públicas, pero **es bueno con** las cuentas.
  Yes, ***he is bad at*** *public relations, but* ***he is good at*** *calculations.*

5.8.8 es increíble cómo + [*verb in the indicative*] L18A

- Use this construction to express admiration.

  Es increíble cómo recorrió en bicicleta tantos lugares de Sudamérica.
  It's incredible how she traveled through *so many places in South America by bicycle.*

5.8.9 (no) es (una) buena idea + [*infinitive*] / que + [*subjunctive*] L18B

- Use this construction to assess an idea in general terms (with the infinitive) or a concrete way (with the subjunctive). (See **5.21**)

  No es una buena idea contratar una empresa de eventos.
  It is not a good idea to hire *an event-planning service.*

  Es una excelente idea que celebres tu cumpleaños en la piscina.
  It is an excellent idea for you to celebrate *your birthday at the pool.*

5.9 hay/estar L2A, L3B, L4B

hay	estar
• Expresses the existence of something. **Hay** is a form of the verb **haber**. This form is used in the present and it is invariable. ¿Qué **hay** en esta calle? L3B *What* ***is there*** *on this street?* **Hay** una librería y una zapatería. ***There is*** *a bookstore and a shoestore.*	• Expresses the location or position of an object or person. Lupe **está** en México. L2A *Lupe* ***is*** *in Mexico.* ¿Dónde **está** el hotel? **Está** en el centro. *Where* ***is*** *the hotel?* ***It is*** *downtown.*
Hay can be followed by: • a noun without an article L3B En mi barrio **no hay** parque. ***There isn't*** *a park in my neighborhood.* • [*indefinite article*] + [*noun*] L3B Cerca de mi apartamento **hay** un colegio. ***There is*** *a school near my apartment.* • plural noun with no article En el barrio **hay** bares y tiendas. L3B ***There are*** *bars and shops in the neighborhood.* • [*number*] + [*noun*] En este barrio **hay** dos mercados. L3B ***There are*** *two markets in this neighborhood.*	**Estar** can be used with: • [*definite article*] + [*singular noun*] L3B ¿Dónde **está** el bolígrafo? Está en la mesa. *Where* ***is*** *the pen? It is on the table.* • [*preposition*] + [*noun*] L4B El metro **está** a cinco minutos. *The subway* ***is*** *five minutes away.* • [*definite article*] + [*plural noun*] Los estudiantes **están** en el bar. *The students* ***are*** *at the bar.* • proper nouns El Rastro **está** en Madrid. L3B *El Rastro* ***is*** *in Madrid.*

5.10 Verbs used with an infinitive (**Verbos con infinitivo**)

- Many verbs are regularly used in combination with other verbs. In these constructions, the second verb is used in the infinitive.

ir a L6A	¿Qué **vas a hacer** este verano? *What are you **going to do** this summer?*
poder L3B, L7B	**No podemos jugar**. ***We can't play**.*
saber L8A	Irene ya **sabe nadar**. *Irene already **knows how to swim**.*
empezar a L9B	**Empecé a trabajar** en Caracas. ***I started working** in Caracas.*
tener que L6A, L10A	Juan **tiene que estudiar**. *Juan **has to study**.*
hay que L10A	**Hay que solucionar** muchos problemas. ***We need to fix** a lot of problems.*
recomendar L11A	**Te recomiendo ir** a un buen hotel. ***I recommend that you go** to a good hotel.*
alegrarse de L11A	**Me alegro** mucho **de oírte**. ***I am** very **happy to hear from you**.*
querer L3B, L8B, L12B	**Quiero ir** de vacaciones a Costa Rica. ***I want to go** on vacation to Costa Rica.*
esperar L12B	**Esperamos tener** muchos invitados. ***We hope to have** many guests.*
desear L12B	**Deseo tener** un trabajo interesante. ***I want to have** an interesting job.*

⚠ **Saber de** + [*noun*] means to know about something or to possess certain knowledge.

Ella **sabe** mucho **de** computadoras.
*She **knows** a lot **about** computers.*

⚠ **Empezar a** indicates the beginning of an action or an event. L9B

Todos los días **empiezo a** trabajar a las 8:00 de la mañana.
*Every day **I start** working at 8:00 in the morning.*

Este año **empiezo a** estudiar japonés.
*This year **I will start to** study Japanese.*

Esta semana **empezamos a** pintar la casa.
*This week **we start** painting the house.*

- The preterite of **empezar** is generally used to talk about past actions or events.

En 2005 **empecé a** estudiar.
***I started** studying in 2005.*

⚠ **Quería**, the imperfect form of **querer**, is a polite way to express a request. L3B

Quería un perfume.
***I wanted** a perfume.*

Quería información sobre los precios de habitaciones en agosto. L6B
***I wanted** information about the prices of rooms in August.*

5.11 **Gustar** and similar verbs (**Gustar y verbos semejantes**)

- Use **gustar** with indirect object pronouns (**me, te, le, nos, os, les**).

  Gustar must agree with the subject of the sentence. When the subject is an infinitive, use the third-person singular form, **gusta**. L4A

  Me gusta la ciudad.
  I like the city.

  No **me gustan** los edificios modernos.
  I don't like modern buildings.

  Nos gusta leer el periódico por la mañana.
  We like to read the newspaper in the morning.

⚠ Although constructions with **gustar** are roughly equivalent to the English expression *to like*, note that the object that is liked is the subject of the Spanish sentence with **gustar** and the person who likes the object is expressed through the indirect object pronoun.

- Use **mucho** with **gustar** to express different degrees of preference.

  ¿**Te gusta** tu barrio?
  Do you like your neighborhood?

  Sí, **me gusta** mucho.
  Yes, I like it a lot.

- Use **me gustaría** + [*infinitive*] to express a desire or request information. **Gustaría** is the conditional form of **gustar**. L6B

  Me gustaría ir a Cuba de vacaciones.
  ***I would like to go** to Cuba on vacation.*

  Hola, buenos días. **Me gustaría reservar** una habitación.
  *Hello, good morning. **I would like to reserve** a room.*

5.11.1 Verbs with indirect object pronouns (Verbos con pronombres de objeto indirecto)

L7A, L11A, L13A, L15B, L17B, L18B

- Verbs such as **encantar**, **molestar**, **interesar**, and **preocupar** express pleasure or displeasure, surprise, concern, or other feelings. These verbs are frequently used with indirect object pronouns in similar constructions to **gustar**. The verb **dar** can also be used with indirect object pronouns in certain constructions. When used with indirect object pronouns, these verbs are conjugated in the third-person singular or plural forms, depending on the subject.

(A mí)	**me**	gusta(n)	[*infinitive*] [*singular or plural noun*] **que** + [*subjunctive*]
(A ti)	**te**	molesta(n)	
(A usted, a él, a ella)	**le**	da(n) miedo/pena	
(A nosotros/as)	**nos**	divierte(n)	
(A vosotros/as)	**os**	aburre(n)	
(A ustedes, a ellos/as)	**les**	parece(n)	

- Use **a mí, a ti**, etc., for emphasis or clarification.

  A mis hijos **les encantan** los videojuegos.
  *My children **love** videogames.*

  No me interesa la política.
  *Politics **do not interest me**.*

  ¿Qué **te parece** el hotel?
  *What **do you think** of the hotel?*

  ¿**Os interesa** estar en forma?
  ***Are you interested** in getting in shape?*

  Me preocupa mucho la economía actual.
  *The current economy **worries me**.*

  Me parece horrible.
  ***I think it is** horrible.*

- If a subordinate clause has a different subject than the sentence's main clause, use the subjunctive in the subordinate clause. (See **5.21**)

  Me molesta que la gente **llegue** tarde a clase.

  ***It bothers me that** people **arrive** late to class.*

5.11.2 doler L10A

- The verb **doler** is conjugated in the third person. Use **doler** in the singular or plural form in order to agree with the subject, the part of the body that hurts. As with the previous list of verbs (**5.11.1**), use **doler** with indirect object pronouns.

  (A mí) **me duele** la cabeza.
  *My head **hurts**.*

  (A mí) **me duelen** los pies.
  *My feet **hurt**.*

  (A ella) **le duele** la garganta.
  *Her throat **hurts**.*

5.12 Third-person verb forms (**Verbos en tercera persona**)

5.12.1 se + [*third-person verb form*] L7B

- Use **se puede** + [*infinitive*] to express what can or cannot be done, or what is or is not permitted.

  En un pueblo **se puede** jugar en la calle.
  *In a small town, **one can** play in the street.*

  Aquí **no se puede** fumar.
  *Smoking **is not permitted** here.*

- Use **se dice** to ask for or give a translation.

  - ¿Cómo **se dice** "hello" en español?
  - **Se dice** *"hola"*.
  - *How do you say "hello" in Spanish?*
  - ***You say**, "hola".*

- Use **se escribe** to ask for or provide a spelling.

  "Hola" **se escribe** con *hache.*
  *"Hola" **is written** with an* h.

- Use **se habla(n)** to ask or tell what languages are spoken in a certain place. L1B

  En México **se habla** español.
  *Spanish **is spoken** in Mexico.*

5.12.2 Impersonal third-person verb forms used in weather expressions (Verbos impersonales de fenómenos meteorológicos en tercera persona) L10A

- Use the verbs **llover** (*to rain*) and **nevar** (*to snow*) in the third-person singular.

  Hoy **llueve** mucho.
  ***It's raining** a lot today.*

  Siempre **nieva** en enero.
  ***It** always **snows** in January.*

- Use the third-person singular form of **hacer** in many common expressions about the weather.

  Hace sol.
  It is sunny.

  Hace mal tiempo.
  The weather is bad.

  Hace calor.
  It's hot.

  Hace buen tiempo.
  The weather is good.

  Hace frío.
  It's cold.

  Hace 30 °C.
  It's 30°C.

5.12.3 Ser L12A

- The verb **ser** is used in the third person in many impersonal constructions, such as **es importante** + [*noun/infinitive*].

Es importante tener buenos amigos.
***It is important to have** good friends.*

Es importante la amistad.
Friendship is important.

- Other adjectives that can be used in this construction include **interesante**, **imprescindible**, **difícil**, **fácil**, etc.

5.12.4 Hace L5A, L8B

- Use the third-person singular form of **hacer**, **hace**, to express *ago*.

Hace dos años, abrí la tienda.
*I opened the store two years **ago**.*

5.13 The infinitive (El infinitivo)

- Use **podría/puede** + [*infinitive*] in polite requests. L13A

¿**Podría confirmarme** la hora de llegada de este tren, por favor?
***Could you confirm** the arrival time of this train **for me**, please?*

- Alternatively, make polite requests using the construction **le importaría** + [*infinitive*].

¿**Le importaría decirme** dónde está la Terminal 2?
***Would you mind telling me** where Terminal 2 is?*

- **Sentir** + [*infinitive*] is used to offer consolation. L13B

Siento oír eso.
***I am sorry to hear** that.*

- Use **lo de** + [*infinitive*] to refer to a topic or matter that has been mentioned previously. (See **3.3**) L14B

¿Te han comentado **lo de quedar** mañana?
*Have they told you **about getting together** tomorrow?*

- Use **es mejor +** [*infinitive*] or **lo mejor es/sería** + [*infinitive*] to make suggestions. (See **5.8.3** and **5.21**) L15A

Lo mejor es consumir de forma responsable.
***It is best to consume** in a responsible way.*

Lo mejor sería tener buena información.
***It would be best to have** good information.*

- Use **seguir sin** + [*infinitive*] to express the continuity of an unrealized action. (See **5.15**) L17A

Siguen sin descubrir ningún remedio eficaz.
***They still have not discovered** an effective remedy.*

- Use **antes/después de** + [*noun/infinitive*] to compare two events temporally. (See **5.21**) L18A

Antes de convertirse en deportista, trabajaba como mecánico.
***Before becoming** an athlete, he worked as a mechanic.*

Después de ganar la medalla de oro, se jubiló.
***After winning** the gold medal, he retired.*

Después de la medalla de oro, se jubiló.
***After the** gold **medal**, he retired.*

- Use **(no) es (una) buena/mala/excelente idea** + [*infinitive*] to assess an idea. (See **5.21**) L18B

Es una buena idea enviar tarjetas de invitación.
***It is a good idea to send** invitations.*

- Use **al** + [*infinitive*] to relate two simultaneous events. This structure is equivalent to **cuando** + [*conjugated verb in the indicative*]. L18B

  Se puso triste **al terminar** la fiesta. (Se puso triste **cuando terminó** la fiesta.)
  *He became sad **when** the party **ended**.*

  Al enterarse de la noticia, se puso triste.
  ***Upon hearing** the news, he became sad.*

5.14 The present participle (El gerundio) L7A, L14B

5.14.1 estar + [*present participle*]

- Form the present progressive with a present-tense form of the verb **estar** followed by the present participle. Regular verbs form the present participle with these endings:

-ar → **-ando**
-er → **-iendo**
-ir → **-iendo**

	estar	+ *present participle*
(yo) (tú) (usted, él, ella) (nosotros/as) (vosotros/as) (ustedes, ellos/as)	estoy estás está estamos estáis están	habl**ando** aprend**iendo** escrib**iendo**

- Use the construction **estar** + [*present participle*] to describe actions and events that are in progress, or to express the development of an action.

  - ¿Qué haces? / ¿Qué **estás haciendo**?
  - **Estoy jugando** con mi hijo.
  - *What **are you doing**?*
  - ***I am playing** with my son.*

  - ¿Qué hacen las chicas?
  - **Están haciendo** deporte.
  - *What are the girls doing?*
  - *They **are playing** sports.*

- Use a past tense form of **estar** with the present participle to talk about actions that were in progress in the past.

  Estuvo llamando toda la mañana.
  ***She was calling** all morning.*

- This structure is also used to describe actions that began in the past and continue in the present.

  Últimamente **estoy estudiando** idiomas.
  *Lately **I've been studying** languages.*

  Hemos estado comprando los regalos de Navidad.
  ***We have been buying** Christmas presents.*

- In colloquial language, the present participle can be used without **estar** as a short answer. L14B

  - ¿Qué hiciste el fin de semana?
  - Nada especial, en casa **leyendo** y **viendo** la tele.

  - *What did you do this weekend?*
  - *Nothing special, at home **reading** and **watching** TV.*

5.14.2 Irregular forms of the present participle (Las formas irregulares del gerundio) L14B

- There is a group of verbs with irregular present participles. They are **-ir** verbs with an **e** or an **o** in the root, which change to **i** and **u**, respectively. This group also includes the verb **poder**, whose present participle is **pudiendo**.

	present participle
e-ir: PREFERIR (e → i)	pref**i**riendo
o-ir: DORMIR (o → u)	d**u**rmiendo

- When the stem of an **-er** or **-ir** verb ends in a vowel, the present participle ends in **-yendo**.

infinitive	present participle
ir	**y**endo
leer	le**y**endo
oír	o**y**endo

* For more irregular present participles, see the verb tables on pages A4–A11.

5.15 Verbal periphrases (**Perífrasis verbales**)

- Verbal periphrases are constructions consisting of a verb followed by an infinitive, present, or past participle.
- **Soler** + [*infinitive*] is used to express habitual actions. L14A

  Suelo trabajar por la noche. (**Normalmente trabajo** por la noche.)
  ***I usually work** at night.*

- Use **estar** + [*present participle*] to express the development of an action. L14B

  Ayer **estuve leyendo** toda la tarde.
  ***I was reading** all afternoon yesterday.*

- Use **estar a punto de** + [*infinitive*] to express that an action is imminent. L16B

  Estamos a punto de cenar.
  We are about to have dinner.

- Use **seguir** + [*present participle*] to express a continuous action. L17A

  Hace un mes empecé a buscar trabajo y **sigo buscando** trabajo en mi especialidad.
  *I started to look for work a month ago and **I am still looking for** a job in my specialty.*

- Use **seguir sin** + [*infinitive*] to express the continuity of an unrealized action. L17A

  Sigo sin trabajar en mi especialidad.
  ***I am still not working** in my specialty.*

- Use **volver a** + [*infinitive*] to express the repetition of an action. L18B

  Nací en Buenos Aires, pasé mi juventud en Bariloche y de mayor **volví a vivir** en la capital.
  *I was born in Buenos Aires, I grew up in Bariloche, and when I was older **I lived** in the capital **again**.*

5.16 The future (**El futuro**)

5.16.1 ir a + [*infinitive*] (El futuro próximo) L6B

	ir	+ a + [*infinitive*]
(yo)	voy	a estudiar
(tú)	vas	a volver
(usted, él, ella)	va	a dormir
(nosotros/as)	vamos	
(vosotros/as)	vais	
(ustedes, ellos/as)	van	

- This construction is generally used with time expressions that indicate that an event will occur in the immediate future, such as **esta tarde, este año, el próximo año, la semana que viene**, etc.

¿Qué **vas a hacer** estas vacaciones?
*What **are you going to do** during vacation?*

Voy a viajar. Todavía no sé si **voy a ir** a Caracas.
***I am going to travel**. I still don't know if **I am going to go** to Caracas.*

El próximo mes **voy a hacer** un viaje a Ecuador.
*Next month **I am going to take** a trip to Ecuador.*

5.16.2 The simple future (El futuro simple)

5.16.2a Regular forms (Las formas regulares) L12B

	-ar verbs	-er verbs	-ir verbs
	HABL**AR**	APREND**ER**	ABR**IR**
(yo)	hablar**é**	aprender**é**	abrir**é**
(tú)	hablar**ás**	aprender**ás**	abrir**ás**
(usted, él, ella)	hablar**á**	aprender**á**	abrir**á**
(nosotros/as)	hablar**emos**	aprender**emos**	abrir**emos**
(vosotros/as)	hablar**éis**	aprender**éis**	abrir**éis**
(ustedes, ellos/as)	hablar**án**	aprender**án**	abrir**án**

- The endings of the simple future tense are added to the infinitive of the verb. The endings are the same for **-ar, -er,** and **-ir** verbs.

Paula **llamará** más a su familia.
*Paula **will call** her family more.*

Volverá a casa en enero.
***She will return** home in January.*

A partir de ahora **estaremos** más a menudo en contacto.
*From now on **we will be** in contact more often.*

- The simple future expresses actions and events in the future, such as anticipated plans or objectives.

Médicos Sin Fronteras **abrirá** más hospitales de emergencia en África.
*Doctors Without Borders **will open** more emergency hospitals in Africa.*

Aldeas Infantiles SOS **dará** información profesional a más jóvenes en Sudamérica.
*SOS Children's Villages **will provide** professional information to more young people in South America.*

5.16.2b Irregular forms (Las formas irregulares) L15A, L16A, L17A

infinitive	stem	future forms
decir	dir-	diré, dirás, dirá, diremos, diréis, dirán
hacer	har-	haré, harás, hará, haremos, haréis, harán
poner	pondr-	pondré, pondrás, pondrá, pondremos, pondréis, pondrán
salir	saldr-	saldré, saldrás, saldrá, saldremos, saldréis, saldrán
tener	tendr-	tendré, tendrás, tendrá, tendremos, tendréis, tendrán
venir	vendr-	vendré, vendrás, vendrá, vendremos, vendréis, vendrán
haber	habr-	habré, habrás, habrá, habremos, habréis, habrán
poder	podr-	podré, podrás, podrá, podremos, podréis, podrán
querer	querr-	querré, querrás, querrá, querremos, querréis, querrán
saber	sabr-	sabré, sabrás, sabrá, sabremos, sabréis, sabrán

5.16.2c Use of the simple future (**El uso del futuro simple**) L15A, L17A

Use the simple future:

- to express commitments or planned objectives

  Este año **estudiaré** español.
  *This year **I will study** Spanish.*

- to express probability or supposition about the present

  Estas galletas **tendrán** muchos conservantes.
  *These cookies **must have** a lot of preservatives.*

  ¿**Vendrán** de España estas naranjas?
  ***I wonder if** these oranges **come** from Spain.*

- to make predictions about the future

  Dentro de poco tiempo, los libros **serán** digitales.
  *In a very short time, books **will come** in digital form.*

  En el futuro, **habrá** menos lenguas que ahora.
  *In the future **there will be** fewer languages than there are now.*

5.16.2d Time expressions (**Marcadores temporales**) L17A

- Use **dentro de** followed by a period of time to refer to the future.

  Dentro de 50 años, los seres humanos vivirán en la Luna.
  ***In 50 years' time**, humans will live on the moon.*

  Dentro de muy poco, todos tendremos algún libro electrónico.
  ***Within a short period of time**, we will all have some kind of electronic book.*

5.17 Simple conditional (**Condicional simple**) L13A, L16A

- The simple conditional is formed by adding the conditional endings to the infinitive. The endings are the same for **-ar**, **-er**, and **-ir** verbs.

5.17.1 Regular forms (Las formas regulares)

	-ar verbs	**-er** verbs	**-ir** verbs
	GAN**AR**	V**ER**	SERV**IR**
(yo)	ganar**ía**	ver**ía**	servir**ía**
(tú)	ganar**ías**	ver**ías**	servir**ías**
(usted, él, ella)	ganar**ía**	ver**ía**	servir**ía**
(nosotros/as)	ganar**íamos**	ver**íamos**	servir**íamos**
(vosotros/as)	ganar**íais**	ver**íais**	servir**íais**
(ustedes, ellos/as)	ganar**ían**	ver**ían**	servir**ían**

⚠ Note that the conditional endings coincide with the imperfect endings for **-er** and **-ir** verbs.

5.17.2 Irregular forms (Las formas irregulares) L13A, L16A

- The verbs that have irregular forms in the conditional are the same verbs that have irregular forms in the future tense, and the same irregular stems are used. (See **5.16.2b**) To form the conditional of these verbs, add the endings used with regular verbs to the irregular stems.

infinitive	stem	conditional forms
decir	dir-	diría, dirías, diría, diríamos, diríais, dirían
hacer	har-	haría, harías, haría, haríamos, haríais, harían
poner	pondr-	pondría, pondrías, pondría, pondríamos, pondríais, pondrían
salir	saldr-	saldría, saldrías, saldría, saldríamos, saldríais, saldrían
tener	tendr-	tendría, tendrías, tendría, tendríamos, tendríais, tendrían
venir	vendr-	vendría, vendrías, vendría, vendríamos, vendríais, vendrían
haber	habr-	habría, habrías, habría, habríamos, habríais, habrían
poder	podr-	podría, podrías, podría, podríamos, podríais, podrían
querer	querr-	querría, querrías, querría, querríamos, querríais, querrían
saber	sabr-	sabría, sabrías, sabría, sabríamos, sabríais, sabrían

5.17.3 Use of the simple conditional (El uso del condicional simple) L10A, L11B, L13A

- Use **poder** and **importar** in the second- or third-person conditional to ask for information in a polite way.

  ¿**Podrías** decirme qué hora es?
  Could you *tell me what time it is?*

  ¿**Le importaría** confirmarme la salida de mi vuelo?
  Would you mind *confirming the departure of my flight for me?*

- Use the conditional form **debería** to ask for or give advice.

  - No puedo dormir. ¿Qué **debería** hacer?
  - **Deberías** trabajar menos y descansar más.
  - *I can't sleep. What* ***should I*** *do?*
  - ***You should*** *work less and rest more.*

- Use the expressions **yo que tú / yo en tu lugar** with the conditional to make recommendations.

  Yo que tú, viajaría a Cuba.
  If I were you, *I would travel to Cuba.*

  Yo en tu lugar alquilaría un coche.
  If I were you, *I would rent a car.*

- Use the conditional constructions [*indirect object pronoun*] + **gustaría/encantaría** + [*infinitive*] to express desires.

(a mí)	me	gustaría/encantaría + [*infinitive*]
(a ti)	te	
(a usted, a él, a ella)	le	
(a nosotros/as)	nos	
(a vosotros/as)	os	
(a ustedes, a ellos/as)	les	

  - ¿Dónde **te gustaría vivir**?
  - **Me encantaría vivir** en Andalucía.

  - *Where* ***would you like to live****?*
  - ***I would love to live*** *in Andalucía.*

- Use the conditional to make suggestions with the construction **lo mejor +** [*conditional*]. L15A

  Lo mejor sería consumir productos frescos.
  It would be best *to consume fresh products.*

5.18 The affirmative imperative (**El imperativo afirmativo**)

5.18.1 Use of the imperative (El uso del imperativo) L8A, L9B, L10A, L11A, L16B, L18B

- Use the imperative to give instructions.

  Añade miel a la receta.
  ***Add** honey to the recipe.*

- Use the imperative to give commands or advice.

  ¡**Empezad** el día con nuestro chocolate Buen día!
  ***Start** the day with our Buen día hot chocolate!*

  Si quieres quedar, **llámame** esta semana.
  *If you want to make plans, **call me** this week.*

5.18.2 Regular forms (Las formas regulares)

5.18.2a Singular commands (**Mandatos singulares**) L8A, L9B

	-ar verbs	**-er** verbs	**-ir** verbs
	TOM**AR**	COM**ER**	ABR**IR**
(tú)	tom**a**	com**e**	abr**e**
(usted)	tom**e**	com**a**	abr**a**

Toma la primera calle a la derecha.
***Take** the first street on the right.*

Gire a la izquierda.
***Turn** left.*

- Affirmative **tú** commands (familiar commands) usually have the same form as the third-person form of the present indicative. Affirmative **usted** commands (formal commands) coincide with the present form of the subjunctive. (See **5.20**) **Usted** commands are formed by dropping the final **-o** of the **yo** form of the present indicative. For **-ar** verbs, add **-e**; for **-er** and **-ir** verbs, add **-a**.
- The imperative undergoes the same stem changes as verbs in the present tense.

	seguir	**cerrar**	**contar**
(tú)	s**i**gue	c**ie**rra	c**ue**nta
(usted)	s**i**ga	c**ie**rre	c**ue**nte

Sigue todo recto.
***Continue** straight ahead.*

Cierra la ventana, por favor.
***Close** the window, please.*

5.18.2b Plural commands (**Mandatos plurales**) L16B, L18B

- The affirmative **vosotros/as** command is formed by dropping the **r** from the infinitive and adding a -**d**.

	-ar verbs	**-er** verbs	**-ir** verbs
	AHORR**AR**	BEB**ER**	CONSUM**IR**
(vosotros/as)	ahorra**d**	bebe**d**	consumi**d**

- The **ustedes** command is formed by dropping the final **-o** of the **yo** form in the present tense and adding the appropriate ending. For **-ar** verbs, add **-en**; for **-er** and **-ir** verbs, add **-an**.

	-ar verbs	-er verbs	-ir verbs
(ustedes)	AHORR**AR** ahorr**en**	BEB**ER** beb**an**	CONSUM**IR** consum**an**

- Stem-changing verbs include the stem change in the **ustedes** command.

	seguir	cerrar	contar
(ustedes)	s**i**gan	c**ie**rren	c**ue**nten

5.18.3 Irregular forms (Las formas irregulares)

5.18.3a Singular commands (**Mandatos singulares**) L9B, L11A

- Irregular affirmative **tú** commands:

	decir	hacer	ir	poner	salir	ser	tener	venir
(tú)	**di**	**haz**	**ve**	**pon**	**sal**	**sé**	**ten**	**ven**

Ve a la playa, **haz** excursiones y **ven** a visitarme.
__Go__ to the beach, __do__ some day trips, and __come__ visit me.

- Irregular **usted** commands:

	dar	estar	ir	saber	ser
(usted)	**dé**	**esté**	**vaya**	**sepa**	**sea**

Sea puntual, por favor.
__Be__ punctual, please.

- Verbs ending in **-car, -gar,** and **-zar** have a spelling change in the formal command forms.

sa**car**	**c → qu**	sa**que**(n)
ju**gar**	**g → gu**	jue**gue**(n)
almor**zar**	**z → c**	almuer**ce**(n)

5.18.3b Plural commands (**Mandatos plurales**)

- **Vosotros** commands have no irregular forms.
- The same verbs that have irregular **usted** commands have irregular **ustedes** commands. L16B

	dar	estar	ir	saber	ser
(ustedes)	**den**	**estén**	**vayan**	**sepan**	**sean**

5.18.4 Commands with reflexive verbs (El imperativo de los verbos reflexivos) L10A

5.18.4a Singular commands (**Mandatos singulares**) L10A

- With affirmative commands, attach the reflexive pronoun to the end of the verb.

	ducharse	levantarse	acostarse
(tú)	dúcha**te**	levánta**te**	acuésta**te**
(usted)	dúche**se**	levánte**se**	acuéste**se**

Acuéstate pronto.
Go to bed *soon.*

⚠ When a reflexive pronoun is attached to an affirmative command that has two or more syllables, an accent mark is added to maintain the original stress.

5.18.4b Plural commands (**Mandatos plurales**) L16B

- In affirmative **vosotros/as** commands, the **-d** is dropped when the reflexive pronoun **os** is added to the end of the verb.

Poned + **os** → **Poneos** los abrigos.
Put on *your coats.*

- In affirmative **ustedes** commands, attach the reflexive pronoun to the end of the imperative form of the verb. As in singular commands, a written accent is added to maintain the original pronunciation of the verb.

Lávense las manos antes de cenar.
Wash *your hands before dinner.*

5.18.5 The imperative with direct object pronouns (El imperativo con pronombres de objeto directo)

5.18.5a Singular commands (**Mandatos singulares**) L10A

- As with all pronouns, direct object pronouns (**lo, la, los, las**) are attached to the end of affirmative commands.

	tomar	comer	poner	hacer
(tú)	tóma**lo**	cóme**la**	pon**lo**	haz**la**
(usted)	tóme**los**	cóma**las**	pónga**los**	hága**las**

- Es bueno comer fruta, ¿no?
- Sí, sí, **cómela** varias veces al día.
- *It is good to eat fruit, isn't it?*
- *Yes, yes,* ***eat it*** *several times a day.*

⚠ A written accent is placed on the verb in order to maintain the original stress after the pronoun is attached.

5.18.5b Plural commands (**Mandatos plurales**) L16B

- In affirmative **vosotros/as** commands, attach direct object pronouns directly to the imperative form. The final **-d** is not dropped.

Leedlo.	**Probadlas.**
Read it.	*Try them.*

- Direct object pronouns are also attached to affirmative **ustedes** commands.

Pónganlo sobre la mesa.
Put it *on the table.*

5.18.6 The imperative with direct and indirect object pronouns (El imperativo con pronombres de objeto directo e indirecto) L16B

- In affirmative commands, the pronouns are attached to the end of the verb. When both direct and indirect object pronouns are used, the indirect object pronoun is always placed before the direct object pronoun. Remember that **le/les** changes to **se** if it precedes **lo/la/los/las**. A written accent is added in order to preserve the original pronunciation of the verb.

5.18.6a Singular commands (**Mandatos singulares**)

	dar	escribir
(tú) (usted)	dá**melo** dé**melo**	escríbe**melo** escríba**melo**

Dámelo.
Give it to me.

5.18.6b Plural commands (**Mandatos plurales**)

	dar	escribir
(vosotros/as) (ustedes)	dád**melo** dén**melo**	escribíd**melo** escríban**melo**

Escribídmelo.
Write it for me.

5.19 Negative commands (**El imperativo negativo**)

5.19.1 Formation of the negative imperative L16B, L18B

- All forms of the negative imperative coincide with the conjugation of the present subjunctive.

	NEGATIVE IMPERATIVE		
	-ar verbs	**-er** verbs	**-ir** verbs
	OLVID**AR**	CRE**ER**	CONSUM**IR**
(tú)	no olvid**es**	no cre**as**	no consum**as**
(usted)	no olvid**e**	no cre**a**	no consum**a**
(vosotros/as)	no olvid**éis**	no cre**áis**	no consum**áis**
(ustedes)	no olvid**en**	no cre**an**	no consum**an**

No olvidéis la tarea para mañana.
Don't forget *the homework for tomorrow.*

5.19.2 Use of the negative imperative with pronouns L16B

- Object and reflexive pronouns must be placed in front of the verb when used with negative commands.

No la olvidéis.
Don't forget it.

- If indirect and direct object pronouns are used together, place the indirect object pronoun in front of the direct object pronoun. Note that **le/les** must be changed to **se** if used before **lo/la/los/las**.

No se lo digan (a ellos).
Don't tell (it to) them.

5.20 Present subjunctive (**Presente del subjuntivo**) L15A, L15B, L16A, L17A, L17B, L18A, L18B

5.20.1 Regular forms (Las formas regulares)

	-ar verbs	**-er** verbs	**-ir** verbs
	TRABAJ**AR**	VEND**ER**	VIV**IR**
(yo)	trabaj**e**	vend**a**	viv**a**
(tú)	trabaj**es**	vend**as**	viv**as**
(usted, él, ella)	trabaj**e**	vend**a**	viv**a**
(nosotros/as)	trabaj**emos**	vend**amos**	viv**amos**
(vosotros/as)	trabaj**éis**	vend**áis**	viv**áis**
(ustedes, ellos/as)	trabaj**en**	vend**an**	viv**an**

- The endings of the present subjunctive for **-ar** verbs (except for the first-person singular conjugation) coincide with the endings of **-er** and **-ir** verbs in the present indicative. Likewise, the present subjunctive endings for **-er** and **-ir** verbs coincide with the endings of **-ar** verbs in the present indicative, with the exception of the first-person singular conjugation.

-ar → **-e**
-er, -ir → **-a**

⚠ Note that in the present subjunctive, the **yo** form of regular verbs is the same as the third-person singular form (**usted, él, ella**).

5.20.2 Irregular forms (Las formas irregulares) L15B, L16A, L17A, L17B, L18A

- Verbs with an irregular **yo** form in the present indicative show the same irregularity in all forms of the present subjunctive. **-ar** and **-er** verbs that undergo a stem change in the **yo** form of the present indicative maintain the same stem change in the present subjunctive (e→ie: qu**ie**ro, o→ue: c**ue**nto), with the exception of the **nosotros/as** and **vosotros/as** forms. In addition, verbs ending in **-car, -gar,** and **-zar** have a spelling change in all forms of the present subjunctive in order to maintain the original pronunication.

	hacer (-go)	**pensar** (e:ie)	**contar** (o:ue)	**educar** (c:qu)	**entregar** (g:gu)	**comenzar** (e:ie) (z:c)
(yo)	ha**g**a	p**ie**nse	c**ue**nte	edu**que**	entre**gue**	com**ie**n**ce**
(tú)	ha**g**as	p**ie**nses	c**ue**ntes	edu**que**s	entre**gue**s	com**ie**n**ce**s
(usted, él, ella)	ha**g**a	p**ie**nse	c**ue**nte	edu**que**	entre**gue**	com**ie**n**ce**
(nosotros/as)	ha**g**amos	pensemos	contemos	edu**que**mos	entre**gue**mos	comen**ce**mos
(vosotros/as)	ha**g**áis	penséis	contéis	edu**qué**is	entre**gué**is	comen**cé**is
(ustedes, ellos/as)	ha**g**an	p**ie**nsen	c**ue**nten	edu**que**n	entre**gue**n	com**ie**n**ce**n

- **-ir** stem-changing verbs undergo the same stem changes in the subjunctive as they do in the present indicative, but the **nosotros/as** and **vosotros/as** forms also have a stem change. The unstressed **e** changes to **i**, while the unstressed **o** changes to **u**.

	pedir (e:i)	**sentir** (e:ie)	**dormir** (o:ue)
(yo)	p**i**da	s**ie**nta	d**ue**rma
(tú)	p**i**das	s**ie**ntas	d**ue**rmas
(usted, él, ella)	p**i**da	s**ie**nta	d**ue**rma
(nosotros/as)	p**i**damos	s**i**ntamos	d**u**rmamos
(vosotros/as)	p**i**dáis	s**i**ntáis	d**u**rmáis
(ustedes, ellos/as)	p**i**dan	s**ie**ntan	d**ue**rman

- These verbs have irregular forms in the present subjunctive.

	dar	estar	ir	saber	ser
(yo)	dé	esté	vaya	sepa	sea
(tú)	des	estés	vayas	sepas	seas
(usted, él, ella)	dé	esté	vaya	sepa	sea
(nosotros/as)	demos	estemos	vayamos	sepamos	seamos
(vosotros/as)	deis	estéis	vayáis	sepáis	seáis
(ustedes, ellos/as)	den	estén	vayan	sepan	sean

- The present subjunctive of the impersonal verb **haber** is **haya**.
- See the verb tables on pages A4–A11 for more irregular verbs.

5.21 Use of the subjunctive (**El uso del subjuntivo**)

5.21.1 Use of the subjunctive to express desires, requests, interests, and feelings (Para expresar deseos, peticiones, intereses y sentimientos)

- The subjunctive is used in sentences with two subjects and two verbs. L15B

  (Yo) quiero que **(tú)** salgas.
  I *want* ***you*** *to leave.*

- Use the infinitive when two verbs in a sentence refer to the same subject.

  (Yo) quiero salir.
  I *want to leave.*

a) With verbs such as **desear, querer,** and **esperar** L15A

Deseo que Fernando **asista** a la reunión.
I want *Fernando* ***to attend*** *the meeting.*

Queremos que todos **trabajen** contentos.
We want *everyone* ***to work*** *happily.*

¿**Espera usted que** los productos **se vendan** en países extranjeros?
Do you hope that *the products* ***will be sold*** *in foreign countries?*

- Use the subjunctive in set phrases that take **que** + [*subjunctive*]. L13A, L18B

  ¡**Que tengan** un buen viaje!
  Have *a good trip!*

  ¡**Que te mejores**!
  (I hope you) ***Feel better****!*

- The subjunctive is always used with the interjection **ojalá (que)**. **Ojalá** (**que**) means *I hope* or *I wish.* L15A

  ¡**Ojalá (que) tenga** éxito su negocio!
  I hope (that) *your business* ***is*** *successful!*

b) With the verb **pedir** L16A

Ingrid Betancourt **pide que haya** paz en Colombia y en toda América Latina.
Ingrid Betancourt ***asks for*** *peace in Colombia and in all of Latin America.*

c) With verbs such as **gustar, interesar,** and **preferir** L17B

(A mí) **no me interesa que** la gente me **cuente** su vida.
I am not interested in *people* ***telling*** *me about their lives.*

Prefiero que me **inviten** a una excursión que a cenar.
I prefer that *people* ***invite*** *me on a trip rather than out to dinner.*

d) To express feelings L15B

- Express displeasure and annoyance using verbs and expressions such as **molestar, no gustar,** or **no soportar**. L15B, L17B

A Juliana **no le gusta que** le **digan** lo que tiene que hacer.
Juliana ***does not like being told*** *what to do.*

A mi hijo **le molesta que** el profesor le **haga** repetir los ejercicios.
It bothers *my son* ***that*** *the teacher* ***makes*** *him repeat exercises.*

No soporto que mis alumnos no **escuchen** en clase.
I can't stand *the fact that my students don't* ***listen*** *in class.*

- Express fear and concern using verbs such as **preocupar** and **dar miedo**. L15B

Me preocupa que la educación en ese colegio no **sea** buena.
It concerns me that *the education at that school* ***is*** *not good.*

Nos da miedo que vuelva a casa tarde.
We're afraid that he will return *home late.*

- Express surprise using verbs and expressions such as **sorprender, extrañar,** and **parecer raro**. L15B

Me sorprende que no te **guste** este colegio.
I am surprised that *you don't* ***like*** *this school.*

A Miguel **le extraña que** tantos padres **lleven** a sus hijos a ese colegio.
Miguel ***is surprised that*** *so many parents* ***send*** *their children to that school.*

Nos parece raro que un pueblo tan grande **tenga** solo un colegio.
It seems strange to us that *a town of that size* ***has*** *only one school.*

- Express disappointment using verbs such as **decepcionar** and **entristecer**. L17B

Nos decepciona que no **estudies** los fines de semana.
It disappoints us that *you don't* ***study*** *on the weekends.*

Me entristece que no **llames** con frecuencia.
It saddens me that *you don't* ***call*** *often.*

- Express happiness and sadness using expressions such as **alegrarse de** and **dar pena**. L18B

Me alegro de que te jubiles con salud.
I am glad that you are retiring *in good health.*

Nos da pena que te vayas.
It makes us sad *to see* ***you go****.*

- Express delight and boredom using verbs such as **divertir** and **aburrir**. L17B

Le divierte mucho **que haya** baile todos los sábados.
He enjoys *the fact* ***that there is*** *a dance every Saturday.*

Me aburre que siempre **escuchemos** la misma música.
It bores me that we *always* ***listen*** *to the same music.*

5.21.2 Use of the subjunctive to express purpose (Para expresar finalidad) L15B

- Use the subjunctive with **para que** if the sentence has clauses with different subjects.

Mis hijos quieren un teléfono celular **para que** sus amigos los **puedan** llamar durante el día.
*My children want a cell phone **so that** their friends **can** call them during the day.*

5.21.3 Use of the subjunctive to compare two events temporally (Para relacionar temporalmente dos hechos) L18A

a) With the phrases **antes de que / después de que**

- Use the subjunctive if the sentence has clauses with different subjects.

Tenemos que prepararlo todo **antes de que vengan** los invitados.
*We have to prepare everything **before** the guests **arrive**.*

Podemos quedar para cenar **después de que termine el partido**.
*We can arrange to have dinner **after the game ends**.*

b) To compare two events temporally with **cuando** L18A

- Use the indicative if the clause that follows **cuando** refers to habitual actions in the present or completed actions in the past.

Cuando era joven, me gustaba mucho salir por la noche.
***When I was young**, I really enjoyed going out at night.*

Estábamos mirando el noticiero **cuando** mi tío **llamó**.
*We were watching the newscast **when** my uncle **called**.*

- Use the subjunctive to refer to a pending action in the future with **cuando**.

Cuando llegue a la cima de la montaña, pensaré en vosotros.
***When I arrive** at the top of the mountain, I will think of you.*

5.21.4 Use of the subjunctive to express opinion, certainty, evidence, or skepticism (Para expresar opinión, certeza, evidencia y escepticismo)

- The indicative is used in statements that express certainty or belief.

Creo que Pablo **viene** mañana.
***I think that** Pablo **is coming** tomorrow.*

- The subjunctive is used in statements that convey uncertainty or doubt.

No creo que Pablo **venga** mañana.
***I don't think that** Pablo **is coming** tomorrow.*

- The subjunctive is not used in simple sentences (with one conjugated verb).

Pablo **viene** mañana.
*Pablo **is coming** tomorrow.*

Pablo **no viene** mañana.
*Pablo **is not coming** tomorrow.*

a) With verbs such as **creer, pensar,** or **parecer** L16A

No creo que la paz **se logre** sin trabajo.
***I don't think that** peace **can be achieved** without effort.*

No nos parece que la guerra **sea** una solución.
***We don't think that** war **is** a solution.*

No pienso que eso **sea** imposible.
***I don't think that** it **is** impossible.*

b) No estar (totalmente/muy) seguro de/claro/demostrado que; no ser evidente/obvio que; dudar que L16A, L17A

No estoy totalmente seguro de que mi empresa **invierta** dinero en ese proyecto.
I am not totally sure that *my company* ***will invest*** *money in that project.*

No está demostrado que las computadoras **sean** perjudiciales para la salud.
It is not proven that *computers* ***are*** *dangerous to your health.*

No es evidente que la enfermedad **se transmita.**
It is not clear that *the disease* ***is transmitted****.*

c) Always use the subjunctive with the expression **dudar que.** L16A

Dudo que la paz **sea** una realidad sin el compromiso de todos.
I doubt that *peace* ***can be*** *a reality without the commitment of everyone.*

5.21.5 Use of the subjunctive to express assessments (Para expresar valoraciones): (no) *es (una) buena/mala idea que* and *es mejor que* L16B, L18B

- Use these expressions with the subjunctive to assess an idea in a specific or concrete way.
- Use these expressions with an infinitive to assess an idea in general terms.

En general **es una buena idea ir de vacaciones** a la playa, pero creo que esta vez **es mejor que vayamos a la montaña**.
Generally, ***it is a good idea to vacation*** *at the beach, but I think that this time* ***it is better that we go to the mountains****.*

5.21.6 Use of the subjunctive to express necessity (Para expresar necesidad) L15A

- Use the subjunctive to express necessity or influence in a specific or concrete way.

Es necesario que tu empresa lance una campaña publicitaria.
It is necessary that your company launch *a publicity campaign.*

- Use the infinitive to express necessity or influence in general terms.

Para vender, **es necesario conocer** el mercado.
In order to sell, ***it is necessary to be familiar with*** *the market.*

5.21.7 Use of the subjunctive to express probability (Para expresar probabilidad) L17A

- The subjunctive is always used with these expressions: **es (poco/muy/bastante) probable/posible que; puede (ser) que.**

Es poco probable que haya vida en otros planetas.
It is not very likely that there is *life on other planets.*

Puede (ser) que algún día **descubran** una vacuna contra el cáncer.
It is possible that *one day* ***they will discover*** *a vaccine for cancer.*

- **Tal vez** and **quizá(s)** can be used with the indicative in order to indicate a greater degree of probability or with the subjunctive to indicate greater uncertainty. The forms **quizá** and **quizás** are both correct.

Tal vez son hermanos. (more probable)
Tal vez sean hermanos. (less probable)
Maybe they are *brothers/siblings.*

Quizás hay una solución. (more probable)
Quizás haya una solución. (less probable)
Perhaps there is *a solution.*

- **A lo mejor** is always used with the indicative.

A lo mejor en el futuro se hablan solo dos o tres lenguas.
In the future ***perhaps*** *only two or three languages will be spoken.*

5.21.8 Use of the subjunctive to express conditions (Para expresar condiciones) L15B

- Use the subjunctive with the conjunctions **con tal (de) que, en caso (de) que,** and **sin que**. Note that the use of the preposition **de** is optional in the first two conjunctions.

  Te permito salir con tus amigos **con tal de que** me **ayudes** con la cena.
  I will let you go out with your friends ***provided that you help*** *me with dinner.*

  Voy a llevar mi celular **en caso de que** mis padres **necesiten** llamarme.
  I am going to take my cell phone ***in case*** *my parents* ***need*** *to call me.*

  Quiero planear una fiesta sorpresa **sin que** mi amiga **se entere**.
  I want to plan a surprise party ***without*** *my friend* ***finding out.***

5.22 Present perfect subjunctive (**Pretérito perfecto de subjuntivo**)

5.22.1 Conjugation (Conjugación) L17B

- The present perfect subjunctive is composed of the present subjunctive of the verb **haber** + [*past participle*]. The verb **haber** is irregular in the present subjunctive. As in the indicative mood, the past participle does not change in form depending on the subject; only the form of **haber** changes.

	haber	+ [*past participle*]
(yo)	**haya**	hablado tenido vivido
(tú)	**hayas**	
(usted, él, ella)	**haya**	
(nosotros/as)	**hayamos**	
(vosotros/as)	**hayáis**	
(ustedes, ellos/as)	**hayan**	

5.22.2 Use of the present perfect subjunctive (El uso del pretérito perfecto de subjuntivo) L18A

- As in the indicative mood, the present perfect subjunctive is used to refer to past events that in some way relate to or influence the present. The present perfect subjunctive is often used when expressing present reactions to past events.

  Me sorprende que **hayas tenido** dificultades en la clase de historia.
  It surprises me that ***you have had/you had*** *difficulties in history class.*

- Use the present perfect subjunctive in a dependent clause when the verb in the main clause is in the present and the dependent clause refers to an action or state in the past.

6 Pronouns (Los pronombres)

6.1 Subject pronouns (**Los pronombres de sujeto**) L1A, L1B

- Subject pronouns replace the name or title of a person who acts as the subject of a verb. Note that, unlike in English, subject pronouns are often omitted in Spanish, because verb conjugations generally indicate the subject of the verb.

	singular		plural	
first person	**yo**	*I*	**nosotros** **nosotras**	*we* (m., m. + f.) *we* (f.)
second person	**tú**	*you* (fam.)	**vosotros** **vosotras**	*you* (m., m. + f.; fam.) *you* (f., fam.)
	usted	*you* (form.)	**ustedes**	*you* (form./fam.)
third person	**él** **ella**	*he* *she*	**ellos** **ellas**	*they* (m., m. + f.) *they* (f.)

⚠ When referring to a group of mixed gender, use the masculine plural forms **nosotros, vosotros,** and **ellos**. Use the feminine forms **nosotras, vosotras,** and **ellas** only when all members of the group are female.

⚠ Personal pronouns are used for emphasis or to contrast one person with another. They are also sometimes used in a short answer that does not contain a verb.

• Buenos días, ¿qué desean?	• *Good morning, what would you like?*
▪ **Yo**, un café con leche.	▪ ***For me**, a coffee with milk.*
• ¿Y **usted**?	• *And **you**?*
✦ **Yo**, un té.	✦ ***For me**, a cup of tea.*

⚠ In Latin America, **ustedes** is used in place of **vosotros/as** to address a group in an informal setting. In addition, some regions of Latin America, particularly Argentina and Uruguay, use **vos** instead of **tú**.

6.2 Object pronouns (**Los pronombres de objeto**) L3B, L4A

- Spanish has both stressed and unstressed object pronouns. Unstressed object pronouns are used along with a verb and may be accompanied by a stressed object pronoun for emphasis. Stressed object pronouns are used with a preposition. Unstressed object pronouns are divided into direct and indirect object pronouns.

6.2.1 Direct object pronouns (Los pronombres de objeto directo) L3B, L12A

- Direct object pronouns replace direct object nouns, which directly receive the action of the verb. Third-person direct object pronouns are used when the direct object noun has already been mentioned.

singular		plural	
me	*me*	**nos**	*us*
te	*you* (fam.)	**os**	*you* (fam.)
lo	*you* (m., form.); *him*; *it* (m.)	**los**	*you* (m., m. + f.; form.); *them* (m., m. + f.)
la	*you* (f., form.); *her*, *it* (f.)	**las**	*you* (f., form.); *them* (f.)

Quería esa camisa. ¿**La** puedo ver?
*I wanted that shirt. Can I see **it**?*

Queríamos esos zapatos. ¿**Los** podemos ver?
*We wanted those shoes. Can we see **them**?*

Debo llamar a mi tía porque hoy es su cumpleaños. Voy a llamar**la**.
*I should call my aunt because today is her birthday. I am going to call **her**.*

⚠ The **personal a** must be used whenever the direct object is a person. It is not needed when the direct object pronoun is used.

Vi **a** Susi. *I saw Susi.*
La vi. *I saw her.*

6.2.2 Indirect object pronouns (Los pronombres de objeto indirecto) L4A

- An indirect object is a noun or pronoun that answers the question *to whom* or *for whom* an action is done. An indirect object pronoun and the noun to which it refers are frequently used in the same sentence in order to emphasize and clarify to whom the pronoun refers.

singular		plural	
me	*(to, for) me*	**nos**	*(to, for) us*
te	*(to, for) you* (fam.)	**os**	*(to, for) you* (fam.)
le	*(to, for) you* (form.); *(to, for) him, her*	**les**	*(to, for) you* (form.); *(to, for) them*

Juan **me** presta su libro de texto.
*Juan lends **me** his textbook.*

Le doy la tarjeta a mi abuela.
I give the card to my grandmother.

6.2.3 Stressed object pronouns (Los pronombres tónicos de objeto) L4A

- Stressed object pronouns, or prepositional pronouns, have the same forms as the subject pronouns, except for **mí** and **ti**. These pronouns act as the object of a preposition and are often used with the preposition **a** to clarify the person or group that is receiving the action of the verb. They can also be used with other prepositions.

a mí	**a él**	**a vosotros/as**
a ti	**a ella**	**a ustedes**
a usted	**a nosotros/as**	**a ellos/as**

⚠ Note that **mí** carries a written accent in order to differentiate it from the possessive adjective **mi**.

- ¿Os gusta el teatro? — *Do you like the theater?*
- **A mí** me encanta. — ***I** love it.*
- **A mí** no me gusta mucho. — ***I** don't like it very much.*

Enrique se sienta **delante de mí** en la clase de biología.
*Enrique sits **in front of me** in biology class.*

⚠ Unstressed object pronouns are used with a verb (**me** gusta, **nos** gusta, **me** toca...), but stressed object pronouns may be used alone.

- El barrio me gusta, ¿y **a ti**? — *I like the neighborhood, and **you**?*
- **A mí** no me gusta mucho. — ***I** don't like it very much.*

⚠ Often an indirect or direct object appears at the beginning of a sentence and is then repeated, immediately before the verb, in the form of an unstressed pronoun.

A Rosa le gusta vivir en el centro.
***Rosa** likes living downtown.*

¿**A ti te** gustan los mercados tradicionales?
*Do **you** like traditional markets?*

⚠ **Tocar** is used with indirect object pronouns to indicate whose turn is next.

- ¿**A quién le** toca? — ***Whose** turn is it?*
- **Me** toca **a mí**. — *It is **my** turn.*

6.2.4 Placement of object pronouns (La posición de los pronombres de objeto)

L7B, L8B, L10A, L11A, L16B

- Object pronouns are always placed before the conjugated verb.

- ¿**Me** ayudas? — *Will you help **me**?*
- Claro que **te** ayudo. — *Of course I'll help **you**.*

Le recomiendo este hotel.
*I recommend this hotel **to you**.*

- When a conjugated verb is followed by an infinitive or the present participle, the object pronoun may be placed before the conjugated verb or attached to the infinitive or present participle. If the pronoun is attached to a present participle, add an accent mark to maintain the original stress.

¿**Te** puedo ayudar? / ¿Puedo ayudar**te**?
*Can I help **you**?*

Te estoy escribiendo un mensaje. / Estoy escribiéndo**te** un mensaje.
*I am writing a message **to you**.*

Object pronouns are also attached to affirmative commands. Sometimes an accent mark is needed to maintain the original stress.

Llámame.	Avísenos.
Call ***me***.	*Let* ***us*** *know.*

6.3 Using direct and indirect pronouns together (**La posición y combinación de los pronombres de objeto directo e indirecto**) L16B

- The indirect object pronoun (**me, te, le, nos, os, les**) or reflexive pronoun (**me, te, se, nos, os**) is placed before a direct object pronoun. When third-person indirect object pronouns (**le, les**) are combined with third-person direct object pronouns (**lo, la, los, las**), the indirect object pronoun changes to **se**. Both object pronouns can be added to the end of an infinitive or present participle, in which case a written accent is added to maintain the original spoken stress.

  Quiero mandar**le** esta postal a Marina. **Se la** quiero **mandar**. / Quiero **mandársela**.
  I want to send this postcard ***to Marina****. I want to* ***send it to her****.*

  Voy a dar**te** mi libro. **Te lo** voy a **dar**. / Voy a **dártelo**.
  I am going to give ***you*** *my book. I am going to* ***give it to you****.*

6.4 Reflexive and reciprocal constructions (**Estructuras reflexivas y recíprocas**) L17B, L18B

- Reflexive verbs are used with the reflexive pronouns **me, te, se, nos, os,** and **se**.

  Me río mucho contigo.
  I laugh *a lot with you.*

  Nos pusimos muy contentos con la noticia.
  It made us *very happy to hear the news.*

- Reciprocal actions are expressed using the plural reflexive pronouns **nos, os,** and **se**.

  Mi hermano y yo **nos queremos** mucho.
  My brother and I ***love each other*** *a lot.*

  Diego y Jimena **se abrazan**.
  Diego and Jimena ***hug each other****.*

6.5 Indefinite pronouns and adjectives (**Los adjetivos y pronombres indefinidos**) L2B, L3A, L8A, L9A

- **algo/nada** L2B
  - ¿Desea **algo** más? — *Would you like* ***anything*** *else?*
  - No, gracias, **nada** más. — *No, thank you,* ***nothing*** *else.*

- **otro/a** L2B

  Camarero, por favor, **otra** botella de agua.
  Waiter, ***another*** *bottle of water, please.*

⚠ Do not use an indefinite article with **otro/a**.

  Otro café, por favor.
  Another *coffee, please.*

- **todo/a (s)** L3A

todo el día	**todos** los días	**todos** los viernes
all *day long*	***every*** *day*	***every*** *Friday*

- **alguien/nadie** L8A
  - ¿Hay **alguien** en la oficina? — *Is* ***anyone*** *in the office?*
  - No, en este momento **no** hay **nadie**. — *No, at this moment there isn't* ***anyone*** */* ***no one*** *is there.*

- **alguno/a; algún/ninguno/a; ningún** L9A

  - ¿Hay **algún** documental en la tele?
  - Sí, creo que hay **alguno**.
  - No, **no** hay **ninguno**.

  - *Are there **any** documentaries on television?*
  - *Yes, I think there is **one**.*
  - *No, there aren't **any**.*

⚠ **Alguno/a** and **ninguno/a** can be used with or without nouns. In front of a masculine singular noun, drop the final **-o**.

  - ¿No hay **ningún** debate esta noche?
  - No, no hay **ninguno**.
  - Sí, creo que hay **alguno**.

  - *Aren't there **any** debates tonight?*
  - *No, there aren't **any**.*
  - *Yes, I think there is **one**.*

6.6 Pronouns and the preposition **con** (**Pronombres y la preposición *con***) L17B

- Use the personal subject pronouns with the preposition **con**, except with **yo** and **tú**, which take the forms **conmigo** and **contigo**.

  Lola no quiere bailar **conmigo** ni **contigo**; solo baila **con él**.
  *Lola does not want to dance **with me** or **with you**; she only dances **with him**.*

  - ¿Vienes **conmigo** al cine mañana?
  - No, lo siento, he quedado **con mis amigos**.

  - *Are you coming **with me** to the movies tomorrow?*
  - *No, I'm sorry, I made plans **with my friends**.*

6.7 Impersonal contructions with **se** + [*third-person verb form*] (**Construcciones impersonales**) L16B

- The construction **se** + [*third-person verb form*] is used in impersonal statements equivalent to the English passive voice. As always, the verb must agree with the subject (singular or plural).

  En Argentina **se celebra** la Navidad en verano.
  En Argentina **se celebran** las Navidades en verano.
  *Christmas **is celebrated** in the summer in Argentina.*

- **Se** + [*third-person singular verb form*] is also used to express an unspecified or general subject, often expressed as *one*, *people*, *they*, or *you* in English.

  En este restaurante **se come** bien.
  *In this restaurant, **one eats/you eat** well.*

- The third-person plural verb form can also be used to make general statements.

  Los españoles no siempre **duermen** la siesta.
  *Spaniards do not always **take** an afternoon nap.*

6.8 The neuter pronoun **lo** (**El pronombre neutro *lo***) L13A, L16B, L17B

- The pronoun **lo** is used to refer to actions or ideas in general, without being related to a specific object or concrete example. It forms part of some expressions, such as **pasarlo bien/mal** (*to have a good/bad time*).

  Yo suelo viajar sola. Te **lo** recomiendo.
  *I often travel alone. I recommend **it** to you.*

  Nos vemos mañana a las 22:30 h, no **lo** olvide.
  *See you tomorrow at 10:30 p.m., don't forget (**it**).*

  Ayer estuvimos bailando y **lo** pasamos muy bien.
  We were dancing yesterday and we had a good time.

6.9 Relative pronouns (**Los pronombres relativos**) L18A

- Relative pronouns **que** (*that; which; who*) and **quien** (*who; whom; that*) introduce a relative clause that refers to an antecedent, i.e., something or someone already mentioned in the sentence. The antecedent of the pronoun **que** can be a person or thing, while the antecedent of **quien** can only be a person. **Quien** is often used after a preposition or the personal **a**.

  Es un deportista **que** ha ganado muchos campeonatos.
  *He is an athlete **who** has won many championships.*

  Es un deporte **que** tiene muchos aficionados.
  *It is a sport **that** has many fans.*

  Es un deportista **a quien** admiro.
  *He is an athlete **whom** I admire.*

7 Demonstratives (Demostrativos)

7.1 Demonstrative adjectives (**Los adjetivos demostrativos**) L3B

- Demonstrative adjectives precede the nouns they modify and agree with them in both gender and number. They designate objects or people situated at varied distances from the speaker.

singular		plural		
masculine	**feminine**	**masculine**	**feminine**	
este	**esta**	**estos**	**estas**	*this; these*
ese	**esa**	**esos**	**esas**	*that; those*
aquel	**aquella**	**aquellos**	**aquellas**	*that; those (over there)*

- ¿**Este** libro de **aquí** es de arte?
- No, **ese** libro de **ahí** es de arte.

- *Is **this** book **here** about art?*
- *No, **that** book **there** is about art.*

7.2 Demonstrative pronouns (**Los pronombres demostrativos**) L3B

- Demonstrative pronouns are identical to their corresponding demonstrative adjectives.

  - ¿Piensas que este vestido es el mejor?
  - No, prefiero **ese**.

  - *Do you think that this dress is the best?*
  - *No, I prefer **that one**.*

⚠ Note that in case of ambiguity, demonstrative pronouns are written with an accent mark to distinguish them from demonstrative adjectives.

7.3 Use of demonstrative adjectives and pronouns (**Uso de los adjetivos y pronombres demostrativos**)

- The use of each category of demonstrative adjectives and pronouns is determined by the distance between the speaker or the listener and the person or thing referenced by the speaker.

  este (*this*): close to the speaker
  ese (*that*): can be close to the listener, farther from the speaker
  aquel (*that . . . over there*): far from both the speaker and the listener

7.4 Neuter demonstrative pronouns (**Los pronombres demostrativos neutros**) L13B, L15B

- The three neuter demonstrative pronouns, **esto, eso,** and **aquello**, are used to refer to unidentified or unspecified nouns, situations, and concepts.

  Siento oír **eso**.
  *I am sorry to hear **that**.*

  ¿Y **esto** te parece bien?
  *And **this** seems OK to you?*

8 Possessive adjectives and pronouns (Los adjetivos y pronombres posesivos)

8.1 Possessive adjectives (**Los adjetivos posesivos**) L2A, L5B

singular	plural	
mi	**mis**	*my*
tu	**tus**	*your* (fam.)
su	**sus**	*your* (form.), *his, her, its*
nuestro/a	**nuestros/as**	*our*
vuestro/a	**vuestros/as**	*your* (fam.)
su	**sus**	*your* (form.), *their*

- Possessive adjectives indicate possession and they agree in both gender and number with the nouns that they modify, i.e., the person or object that is possessed.

mi barrio	**mi** ciudad	**mis** libros	**mis** clases
my *neighborhood*	***my*** *city*	***my*** *books*	***my*** *classes*

¿Dónde viven **vuestros** hermanos?
Where do ***your*** *siblings live?*

⚠ **Su** and **sus** have multiple meanings (*your, his, her, its, their*). To avoid confusion, you can use the construction [*article*] + [*noun*] + **de** + [*subject pronoun/name*].

su abuelo	***his/her/your/their*** *grandfather*
el abuelo de **él/ella**	*his/her grandfather*
el abuelo de **usted/ustedes**	*your grandfather*
el abuelo de **ellos/ellas**	*their grandfather*
el abuelo de **Ernesto**	*Ernesto's grandfather*

8.2 Possessive pronouns (**Los pronombres posesivos**) L13B

singular		plural		
masculine	feminine	masculine	feminine	
mío	**mía**	**míos**	**mías**	*my, (of) mine*
tuyo	**tuya**	**tuyos**	**tuyas**	*your, (of) yours*
suyo	**suya**	**suyos**	**suyas**	*your, (of) yours; his,(of) his; her, (of) hers; its*
nuestro	**nuestra**	**nuestros**	**nuestras**	*our, (of) ours*
vuestro	**vuestra**	**vuestros**	**vuestras**	*your, (of) yours*
suyo	**suya**	**suyos**	**suyas**	*your, (of) yours; their, (of) theirs*

- Possessive pronouns agree in both gender and number with the thing that is possessed.
- The possessive pronoun is used with an article in order to take the place of a noun that has already been mentioned.

  - Mi empresa es muy grande, ¿y **la tuya**? — *My company is very big, and* ***yours****?*
  - **La mía** no. — ***Mine*** *isn't.*

- The possessive pronoun can be used without an article in order to state the identity of the owner.

  - ¿De quién es este libro? — *Whose book is this?*
  - Es **mío**. — *It is* ***mine****.*

⚠ Note that these words can also be used as adjectives when placed after the corresponding nouns. Ex. **ese libro mío** (*that book of mine*).

9 Interrogative Pronouns (Los pronombres interrogativos)

- In Spanish, all interrogative pronouns carry a written accent.

¿Cómo?	¿**Cómo** se escribe "hola"? U0, L1A ***How** do you spell "hola"?*
¿Quién?	¿**Quién** es? L1A ***Who** is it?*
¿Dónde?	¿**Dónde** está Granada? L2A ***Where** is Granada?*
¿Adónde?	¿**Adónde** fuiste el año pasado? L2A ***Where** did you go last year?*
¿De dónde?	¿**De dónde** es usted? L1A ***Where** are you from?*
¿Cuánto/a?	¿**Cuánto** es? L2B ***How much** is it?*
¿Cuántos/as?	¿**Cuántos** dormitorios tiene tu apartamento? L4B ***How many** rooms does your apartment have?*
¿Por qué?	¿**Por qué** no trabajas menos? L6A ***Why** don't you work less?*
¿Qué + [*verb*]?	¿**Qué** significa "carne"? U0, L2B ***What** does "carne" mean?* ¿**Qué** es eso? L1A ***What** is that?*
¿Qué + [*noun*]?	¿**Qué** hora es? L3A ***What** time is it?* ¿**Qué** apartamentos te gustan? L4B ***Which** apartments do you like?*
¿Cuál(es)?	¿**Cuál** es de alquiler? L4B ***Which (one)** is for rent?* ¿**Cuáles** tienen piscina? ***Which (ones)** have a pool?*
¿Qué tal?	¿**Qué tal?** U0 ***How are you?*** (informal)
¿Cuándo?	¿**Cuándo** naciste tú? L5A ***When** were you born?*

10 Prepositions (Las preposiciones)

10.1 a

• time indications	• ¿**A** qué hora vas a la biblioteca? L3A ▪ **A** las siete. • *What time are you going to the library?* ▪ ***At** seven o'clock.* La biblioteca abre de diez **a** ocho. L5A *The library is open from ten **to** eight.*
• place indications, directions	• ¿**A**dónde vas? ▪ Voy **al** trabajo. L3A, L6B • *Where are you going?* ▪ *I am going **to** work.*
• distance, location	Está **a** 100 kilómetros de aquí. L2A *It is 100 kilometers from here.* • ¿Quería ver el pañuelo **a la derecha del** marco? L3A ▪ No, no. Me interesa el que está **a la izquierda del** marco, **al lado de** la lámpara. • *Did you want to see the scarf **to the right** of the picture frame?* ▪ *No, no. I'm interested in the one **to the left** of the frame, **next to** the lamp.*
• with a direct object (people)	• ¿Conoces **a** Laura? L5B, L7B ▪ No, no la conozco. • *Do you know Laura?* ▪ *No, I don't know her.*
• indirect object	**A** María no le gusta el barrio. L4A, L7A, L12A *María does not like the neighborhood.*

⚠ Remember to use the contraction **al** when **a** is followed by the masculine singular article **el**: **a** + **el** = **al.**

10.2 a partir de

A partir de ahora practicaré más deporte. L12B
***From** now **on** I will play more sports.*

A partir de mañana dejaré de trabajar tanto.
***Starting** tomorrow, I will stop working so much.*

10.3 antes de

Antes de retirarse, Indurain ganó el Tour de Francia cinco veces. L10B
***Before** retiring, Indurain won the Tour de France five times.*

10.4 con U0, L17B

- When used with the preposition **con** (*with*), the pronouns **yo** and **tú** take the forms **conmigo** and **contigo**. In all other cases, use subject pronouns with the preposition **con**.

  ¿Quieres que vaya **contigo** al médico?
  *Do you want me to go **with you** to the doctor?*

- **Con** is also used in the construction **ser bueno/malo con** (*to be good/bad at*) + [*a specific thing*] to express ability.

  Verónica es muy buena **con** la videoconsola.
  *Verónica is very good **at** the video game console.*

10.5 de

• time indications	Son las cinco **de** la tarde. L3A *It is five o'clock* ***in*** *the afternoon.* David nació el 14 **de** febrero **de** 1995. L5A *David was born on February 14th, 1995.* 15 **de** mayo **de** 2005 *May 15, 2005* El museo abre **de** diez a ocho. L3A *The museum is open* ***from*** *ten to eight.* **De** 2003 a 2004 viajé por Asia. L5A ***From*** *2003 to 2004, I traveled throughout Asia.*
• place indications: origin	Ana es **de** Bogotá. L1A *Ana is* ***from*** *Bogotá.* Vamos **de** Madrid a San Sebastián. L6B *We are going* ***from*** *Madrid to San Sebastián.*
• place indications: in prepositional phrases	Sevilla está cerca **de** Córdoba. L2A *Sevilla is close to Córdoba.* El bolígrafo está debajo **del** sofá. L3B *The pen is under the sofa.*
• to order food at a restaurant	**De** primero, las lentejas con chorizo. ***As*** *a first course, lentils with chorizo.* L2B
• indicating quantity	Un kilo **de** queso, por favor. L4A *A kilogram* ***of*** *cheese, please.*
• to indicate possession or belonging	los días **de** la semana L3A *the days* ***of*** *the week* Dolores es la madre **de** Manuel. L5B *Dolores is Manuel's mother.*
• **ser** + **de** to describe material	La mesa es **de** vidrio. L8A *The table is made (out)* ***of*** *glass.* Los pañuelos son **de** papel. *The handkerchiefs are made (out)* ***of*** *paper.*

10.6 dentro de L17A

- Use **dentro de** + [*length of time*] to talk about the future.

  Dentro de unos años no habrá teléfonos fijos.
  Within/In *a few years there will be no home telephone lines.*

- **Dentro de** may also be used to refer to location in space. When used with this meaning, **dentro de** is translated in English as *in* or *inside*.

  Dentro de la mochila está el libro.
  The book is ***inside*** *the backpack.*

10.7 desde

• time indications: a certain moment	• ¿**Desde** cuándo conoces a Eva? L5B, L8B ▪ **Desde** 1992. • *How long have you known Eva?* ▪ ***Since** 1992.* Tengo vacaciones **desde** el 15 de agosto hasta el 10 de septiembre. *I have vacation **from** August 15th to September 10th.*

10.8 desde hace

• time indications: interval	• ¿Desde cuándo vivís en Cádiz? ▪ **Desde hace** tres años. L5B • *How long have you lived in Cádiz?* ▪ ***For** three years.*

10.9 desde que + [*verb*]

Desde que me jubilé, vivo en Sevilla. L8B
***Since** I retired, I live in Seville.*

10.10 después de

El Muro de Berlín se derribó 37 años **después de** su construcción. L10B
*The Berlin Wall was brought down 37 years **after** its construction.*

10.11 durante L8B

Viví en Bogotá **durante** cinco años.
*I lived in Bogotá **for** five years.*

10.12 en

• time indications	**En** julio Manuela abrió la tienda. L5A *Manuela opened the store **in** July.*
• place indications	Granada está **en** el sur de España. L1B, L2A, L3B *Granada is **in** the south of Spain.* Normalmente desayuno **en** casa. *I usually have breakfast **at** home.*
• means of transportation	Voy a París **en** tren. L6B *I go to Paris **by** train.*
• in the construction **ser bueno/malo en** + [*discipline*], to express ability	No soy bueno **en** deportes. L17B *I am not good **at** sports.*

10.13 entre

• place indications	El bolígrafo está **entre** el libro y el teléfono. L3B *The pen is **between** the book and the phone.*

⚠ The preposition **entre** can mean both *between* and *among*.

Entre todas las personas aquí presentes, nadie estuvo en Asia.

***Among** all the people here, no one has been to Asia.*

10.14 hasta

• time expressions	**Hasta** hoy no he tenido tiempo para escribirte. L8B *I haven't had time to write to you **until** today.* Desde 1990 **hasta** 2005, Emilio vivió en Buenos Aires. *From 1990 **to** 2005, Emilio lived in Buenos Aires.*
• expression of farewell	¡**Hasta** luego! U0 *See you later!*

10.15 para L4B, L8A, L10B, L17B

• the recipient of something *(for)*	La postal es **para** ti. *The postcard is **for** you.*
• purpose: + [*infinitive*] *(in order to)*	Estudio español **para** viajar a Uruguay. *I am studying Spanish **in order to** travel to Uruguay.*
• purpose: + [*noun*] *(for, used for)*	Este libro es **para** la clase de ciencia. *This book is **for** science class.*
• destination *(toward, in the direction of)*	Mañana salimos **para** Buenos Aires. *We are leaving **for** Buenos Aires tomorrow.*
• deadline *(by, for)*	Tengo que terminar este proyecto **para** el jueves. *I have to finish this project **by** Thursday.*
• comparison with others or an opinion *(for, considering)*	**Para** ser extranjero, habla muy bien el inglés. ***For** a foreigner, he speaks English very well.* **Para** mí, eso es positivo. ***For** me, that is a positive thing.*
• in the employ of *(for)*	Marcos trabaja **para** el gobierno. *Marcos works **for** the government.*
• in the construction **ser bueno/malo para** + [*discipline*] *(at)*	Soy muy bueno **para** las matemáticas. *I am very good **at** math.*

10.16 por L3A, L6B

• duration of an action *(for, during, in)*	**Por** la tarde no trabajo; **por** la mañana, sí. *I don't work **in** the afternoon, but I do **in** the morning.* Fuimos de vacaciones **por** un mes. *We went on vacation **for** a month.*
• general location, direction *(around, through, along, by)*	Vamos a Barcelona y pasamos **por** Tarragona. *We are going to Barcelona and we will pass **through** Tarragona.* Caminamos **por** el río. *We walked **along** the river.*
• means by which something is done *(by, by way of, by means of)*	Compramos productos **por** Internet. *We buy products online.* Ayer hablé con mi hermano **por** teléfono. *Yesterday I spoke with my brother **by** (on the) phone.*

por *cont.*	
• reason or motive for an action *(because of, on account of, on behalf of)*	Lo hice **por** ti. *I did it **for** you (for your sake).* Joaquín está nervioso **por** el examen. *Joaquín is nervous **because of** the exam.*
• object of a search *(for, in search of)*	Tuve que volver a casa **por** mi billetera. *I had to return home **for** my wallet.*
• exchange or substitution *(for, in exchange for)*	Le pagué 50 dólares **por** la mesa. *I paid him $50 **for** the table.* Muchas gracias **por** tu ayuda. *Thank you very much **for** your help.*
• unit of measurement *(per, by)*	Matías manejaba a 100 kilómetros **por** hora. *Matías was driving at 100 kilometers **per** hour.*

10.17 Prepositions and prepositional phrases of place (Las preposiciones y locuciones preposicionales de lugar) L3B, L9B

a la derecha de	*to the right of*	**delante de**	*in front of*
a la izquierda de	*to the left of*	**detrás de**	*behind of*
al final de	*at the end of*	**en**	*in*
al lado de	*next to*	**encima de**	*on top of*
debajo de	*underneath*	**enfrente de**	*across from*

- Perdone, ¿hay un café por aquí?
- **Al final de** esta calle, **al lado del** *gimnasio, hay un café.*

- *Excuse me, is there a café around here?*
- ***At the end of** this street, **next to** the gym there is a café.*

11 Adverbs (Los adverbios) L7A

- Adjectives modify nouns and agree with them in both gender and number (**el coche rápido**), whereas adverbs modify verbs, adjectives, or other adverbs and are invariable (**va rápidamente**, **va muy rápidamente**).
- One group of adverbs is formed by adding **-mente** to the feminine form of the corresponding adjective, much like the English ending *-ly*.

adjective	adverb
actual	actualmente
último/a	últimamente
activo/a	activamente
especial	especialmente
general	generalmente

Actualmente estoy escribiendo un libro.
***Currently**, I am writing a book.*

Últimamente a Javier le interesa la política internacional.
***Lately** Javier is interested in international politics.*

Generalmente la gente se habla de *tú*, **especialmente** los compañeros de trabajo.
***Generally** people address each other as* tú, ***especially** co-workers.*

11.1 Adverbs of manner (**Adverbios de modo**) L11A, L12A, L17B

- Some adverbs have their own forms. These are some common adverbs.

así	*like this; so*
bien	*well*
despacio	*slowly*
fatal	*terribly* (informal)
mal	*badly*
mejor	*better*
nada mal	*not bad at all* (informal)
peor	*worse*
regular	*so-so*

Hablo **bien** inglés, pero hablo muy **mal** francés.
*I speak English **well**, but I speak French very **badly**.*

¿Es correcto **así**?
*Is it correct **like this**?*

Hable más **despacio**, por favor.
*Speak more **slowly**, please.*

- Lorenzo hace **muy bien** el asado.
- Sí, no lo hace **nada mal**.

- *Lorenzo prepares barbecue **very well**.*
- *Yes, he doesn't do **a bad job at all**.*

11.2 Adverbs of affirmation and negation (**Adverbios de afirmación y negación**) L8A, L10B, L11B

- Adverbs of affirmation

sí	*yes*
claro	*clearly*
también	*too, also, as well*

- Yo estoy de acuerdo. ¿Y tú?
- Yo **también**.

- *I agree. Do you?*
- *I do, **too**.*

- Adverbs of negation

no	*no; not*
nunca	*never*
tampoco	*neither, not . . . either*
ya no	*no longer, (not) anymore*

- No estoy de acuerdo.
- Yo **tampoco**.

- *I don't agree.*
- *I don't **either**.*

- ¿**Ya no** trabajas?
- No, dejé de trabajar el año pasado.

- *You don't work **anymore**?*
- *No, I stopped working last year.*

11.3 Adverbs of inclusion (**Adverbios de inclusión**) L11B

además	*furthermore; besides; as well*
sobre todo	*above all*

El apartmento es muy bonito y **además** tiene mucha luz.
*The apartment is pretty and it has a lot of light **as well**.*

11.4 Adverbs of quantity (**Adverbios de cantidad**) L2A, L2B, L6A, L8A

algo	*somewhat*
aproximadamente	*approximately*
bastante	*enough; rather*
mucho	*a lot*
muy	*very*
nada	*not at all*
poco	*little; not much; not very*
un poco	*a little (bit)*

Me gusta **mucho**.
*I like it **a lot**.*

Ávila está **bastante** cerca.
*Ávila is **rather** close.*

Esos muebles son **poco** funcionales.
*That furniture is **not very** functional.*

El sofá es **muy** cómodo.
*The sofa is **very** comfortable.*

El pulpo está **un poco** salado, pero muy rico.
*The octopus is **a little** salty, but very good.*

No estoy **nada** de acuerdo.
*I don't agree **at all**.*

11.5 Adverbial phrases and adverbs of doubt (**Locuciones adverbiales y adverbios de duda**) L7B, L15A, L17A

a lo mejor	*maybe, perhaps*
a ver si	*let's see if*
quizá(s)	*maybe, perhaps*
tal vez	*maybe, perhaps*

A lo mejor el nuevo producto tiene éxito en el mercado.
***Maybe** the new product will be successful in the market.*

A ver si el año que viene tenemos mejor tiempo.
***Let's see if** we have better weather next year.*

Quizá(s) Clara no ha llegado todavía.
***Perhaps** Clara hasn't arrived yet.*

Tal vez la ciencia encuentre pronto una respuesta.
***Maybe** science will find an answer soon.*

11.6 Adverbs of time (**Adverbios de tiempo**) L5A, L6A, L9B, L14A, L18A

ahora	*now*
anoche	*last night*
anteayer	*the day before yesterday*
antes	*before, earlier*
antes de (que)	*before*
ayer	*yesterday*
de repente	*suddenly*
después	*after; then; afterward*
después de (que)	*after*
entonces	*then*
hoy	*today*
luego	*later (on); afterward; next; then*
mañana	*tomorrow*
primero	*first*
tarde	*late*
todavía	*still; yet* (in negative phrases)
ya	*already* (in affirmative phrases and questions); *anymore* (in negative phrases)

Antes practicaba karate; **ahora** practico baloncesto.
__Before,__ I practiced karate; __now__ I play basketball.

Antes de tener computadora, **ya** navegaba por Internet.
__Before__ I had a computer, I __already__ surfed the Internet.

Anoche salí con amigos.
__Last night__ I went out with friends.

Ayer fuimos al cine.
__Yesterday__ we went to the movies.

Estábamos en la cocina cuando **de repente** se apagó la luz.
We were in the kitchen when the light __suddenly__ went out.

Recibirán el premio **después de que** ganen el campeonato.
They will receive the prize __after__ winning the championship.

Hoy vamos al concierto.
__Today__ we are going to the concert.

Mañana ellos van al cine.
They are going to the movies __tomorrow__.

Inés viene **más tarde**.
Inés is coming __later__.

Primero trabajé en Berlín, **luego** volví a España y **después** trabajé en una organización no gubernamental.
__First__ I worked in Berlin, __afterwards__ I returned to Spain, and __then__ I worked in a non-governmental organization.

- ¿**Ya** has hecho los deberes?
- No, **todavía** no los he hecho.

- *Have you done the homework __already__?*
- *No, I haven't done it __yet__.*

11.7 Adverbs of place (**Adverbios de lugar**) L2A, L3B

cerca	*near, close*	**a la derecha**	*to/on the right*
lejos	*far*	**debajo**	*under; underneath*
aquí	*here*	**al lado**	*next to; beside*
ahí	*there*	**detrás**	*behind*
allí	*there; over there*	**delante**	*in front*
a la izquierda	*to/on the left*	**encima**	*on top*

- ¿La casa de Pedro está **cerca**?
- Sí, está **aquí al lado, detrás** del supermercado.

- *Is Pedro's house **close**?*
- *Yes, it's **right near here, behind** the supermarket.*

11.8 Adverbs and expressions of frequency (**Adverbios y expresiones de frecuencia**) L2B, L6A

a veces	*sometimes*
bastante	*enough; rather; quite; quite a lot*
casi nunca	*almost never*
mucho	*a lot*
nada	*(not) at all*
normalmente	*normally; usually*
nunca	*never*
siempre	*always*
una vez al mes	*once a month*

Siempre desayuno en casa.
*I **always** have breakfast at home.*

A veces cenamos afuera.
***Sometimes** we go out to dinner.*

Normalmente como un menú del día en un restaurante.
*I **usually** order the set menu in a restaurant.*

- Yo voy **mucho** al cine, ¿y tú?
- Voy **bastante**.

- *I go to the movies **a lot**, and you?*
- *I go **quite a lot**.*

- ¿Vais **mucho** de viaje?
- No **mucho, una vez al mes**.

- *Do you go on trips **a lot**?*
- *Not **a lot**, **once a month**.*

Nunca voy al cine.
*I **never** go to the movies.*

Casi nunca veo la televisión.
*I **almost never** watch television.*

No duermo **nada** últimamente. Estoy un poco preocupado.
*I don't sleep **at all** lately. I am a little worried.*

11.9 Adverbs of exclusion (**Adverbios de exclusión**) L13B

solo	*only*
solamente	*only*

Solo uno de los países hispanohablantes está en África.
Only *one Spanish-speaking country is in Africa.*

⚠ The word **solo** is both a masculine singular adjective meaning *alone* or *lonely* and an adverb meaning *only*. In cases where the meaning of the word **solo** could be ambiguous, add a written accent to the adverb, **sólo**.

Marcos va **solo** al cine.
Marcos goes to the movies ***alone****.*

Marcos va **sólo** al cine.
Marcos ***only*** *goes to the movies.*

12 The Sentence (La oración)

12.1 The affirmative sentence (**La oración afirmativa**) L1A

subject	+ verb	+ complement
Pedro *Pedro*	es *is*	de Málaga. *from Málaga.*

⚠ In Spanish, subject pronouns are rarely used because the verb conjugation reveals the subject.

- ¿De dónde eres?
- Soy de Caracas.

- *Where are* ***you*** *from?*
- ***I*** *am from Caracas.*

- The **usted** and **ustedes** forms are exceptions, because it is necessary to differentiate this form from the third-person forms **él/ella** or **ellos/ellas.**

¿De dónde es **usted**?
Where are ***you*** *from?*

12.2 The negative sentence (**La oración negativa**) L1A, L6A

- In a negative sentence, place **no** before the verb.

No entiendo.
I do ***not*** *understand.*

Analía **no** es de España.
Analía is ***not*** *from Spain.*

- ¿Eres de León?
- **No**, **no** soy de León; soy de Toledo.

- *Are you from León?*
- ***No****, I am* ***not*** *from León. I am from Toledo.*

12.3 The double negative (**La doble negación**) L6A, L8A

- If **nada**, **nadie**, **nunca**, or **ni... ni** are used after the verb, place **no** before the verb.

⚠ Note that, unlike in English, all indefinite words in a negative sentence must be negative.

No hemos visto **nada**.
We have ***not*** *seen* ***anything****.*

No oigo a **nadie**.
I do ***not*** *hear* ***anyone****.*

No he estado **nunca** en Dinamarca.
I have ***never*** *been in Denmark.*

No me gusta **ni** el cine **ni** el teatro.
I ***don't*** *like the movies* ***or*** *the theater.*

- The first **ni** may be omitted.

- Yo estudio francés y bailo tango. ¿Y tú?
- Yo **no** estudio francés **ni** bailo tango, pero leo mucho.

- *I study French and dance tango. What about you?*
- *I* ***don't*** *study French* ***or*** *dance tango, but I read a lot.*

12.4 The interrogative sentence (La oración interrogativa) UO, L1A

- The syntax of an interrogative sentence without an interrogative pronoun is the same as an affirmative sentence. They can only be distinguished by the intonation and punctuation.

Eres de Venezuela. *You are from Venezuela.*	¿Eres de Venezuela? *Are you from Venezuela?*

- If an interrogative pronoun is used, place the verb before the subject.

¿De dónde es Andrea? *Where is Andrea from?*	¿Cómo se llama usted? *What is your name?*

12.5 The exclamatory sentence (La oración exclamativa) L11A

¡**Qué** + [*noun*]!	¡Qué casualidad! *What a coincidence!*
¡**Qué** + [*adjective*]!	¡Qué interesante! *How interesting!*
¡**Qué** + [*adverb*]!	¡Qué bien! *Great!*

12.6 Clauses of purpose and cause (La cláusula de propósito y la cláusula causal)

- **The causal conjunction** L6B, L16A

  These conjunctions specify the cause of an action.

  Voy a Caracas **porque** tengo amigos allí.
  I am going to Caracas ***because*** *I have friends there.*

- **The conjunction of purpose** L4B
- Use **para** + [*infinitive*] to express purpose.

  Saber lenguas es bueno **para viajar**.
  Knowing languages is good ***for traveling****.*

- Use **servir para** + [*infinitive*] to describe the function of an object.

• ¿**Para qué sirve** este aparato?	• *What is this machine* ***for****?*
▪ Es muy práctico; **sirve para hacer** pan en casa.	▪ *It is very practical;* ***it is for making*** *bread at home.*

- Use **para que** + [*subjunctive*] to express purpose or intention in sentences with two verbs with different subjects. 15B

  Te voy a dar unos ejercicios **para que aprendas** las formas del subjuntivo.
  I'm going to give you some exercises ***so that you learn*** *the forms of the subjunctive.*

12.7 The comparative sentence (La oración comparativa) L3A, L6A, L8B, L16B

igual de + [*adjective*] + **que**	*as . . . as*
igual que	*the same as*
más + [*adjective/adverb/noun*] + **que**	*more/(-er) . . . than*
menos + [*adjective/adverb/noun*] + **que**	*less/(-er) . . . than*
tan + [*adjective/adverb*] + **como**	*as . . . as*
tanto(s) + [*noun*] + **como**	*as much/many . . . as*
[*verb*] + **tanto como**	*as much as*

Mi país es **igual de bello que** el tuyo.
*My country is **as beautiful as** yours.*

Mi acento es **igual que** el tuyo.
*My accent is **the same as** yours.*

¡Trabajas **más** horas **que** yo!
*You work **more** hours **than** I (do).*

Este restaurante es **menos** caro **que** aquel.
*This restaurant is **less** expensive **than** that one.*

Leo **más** rápido **que** mi hermano.
*I read **faster than** my brother.*

Mi jefa no es **tan** amable **como** la vuestra.
*My boss is not **as** friendly **as** yours.*

Tengo **tantos** libros **como** tú.
*I have **as many** books **as** you (do).*

Ella no habla **tanto como** él.
*She does not talk **as much as** he (does).*

⚠ When using **más/menos** with a number, use the preposition **de** instead of **que** to make the comparison. L3A

Mi compañera de cuarto tiene **más de** cien libros.
*My roommate has **more than** one hundred books.*

12.8 Conjunctions (**Las conjunciones**) L10B, L11B, L12B, L13A, L14B, L15B

- Conjunctions are words used to connect words, clauses, or phrases.

Coordinating conjunctions	
y	Juan está enfermo **y** no puede ir a trabajar. *Juan is sick **and** cannot go to work.*
pero	Es difícil, **pero** no imposible. *It is difficult, **but** not impossible.*
no... sino	**No** me llamo Carlos, **sino** Tomás. *My name is not Carlos, **but** (rather) Tomás.*
Subordinating conjunctions	
que	Creo **que** esta es una buena oportunidad. *I think **that** this is a good opportunity.* • ¿Crees **que** es difícil vivir en otro país? ▪ Creo **que** sí. • *Do you think (**that**) it is difficult to live in another country?* ▪ *I think so.*
si + [*indirect question*]	¿Podría decirme **si** está abierta la farmacia? *Could you tell me **whether** the pharmacy is open?*
Subordinating adverbial conjunctions	
por eso	Quiero un trabajo digno; **por eso** hago una petición formal. *I want a decent job; **that's why** I am making a formal request.*

- The conjunction **si** introduces an interrogative phrase.
- A phrase introduced by **sino** presents information that opposes the information in the previous phrase.
- In Spanish, the verbs **creer**, **opinar**, and **pensar** are often used with the conjunction **que**.

12.9 The conditional sentence (La oración condicional) L8A, L14A, L18B

Possible conditions:

- **si** + [*present indicative*], [*present indicative*]

  Si conoces la lengua de un país, **es** más fácil integrarse.
  If you know *a country's language,* ***it is*** *easier to become integrated.*

- **si** + [*present indicative*], [*simple future*]

  Si vienes a mi país, **conocerás** muchos sitios interesantes.
  If you come *to my country,* ***you will see*** *many interesting places.*

- **si** + [*present indicative*], [*imperative*]

  Si tiene tiempo, **llámenos**.
  If you have *time,* ***call us***.

12.10 Indirect discourse (Estilo indirecto) L11A, L14B, L16A

- Indirect discourse, or reported speech, refers to a sentence that reports what another person has said. The following verbs are often used to relate someone else's statement or question: **decir, comentar, explicar, preguntar, añadir, informar, declarar, confirmar, anunciar,** and **afirmar**.

  Dice que quiere una habitación doble.
  She says *she wants a double room.*

  Preguntó si la habitación tenía balcón.
  She asked *if the room had a balcony.*

- If the main clause of a sentence using indirect speech is conjugated in the present or the present perfect, the verb in the subordinate clause is conjugated in the present.

Direct speech	Indirect speech: Present	Indirect speech: Present perfect
"El hotel no **está** muy lejos." *"The hotel* ***is*** *not very far."*	Ramón **dice que** el hotel no **está** muy lejos. *Ramón* ***says that*** *the hotel* ***is*** *not very far.*	Ramón **ha dicho que** el hotel no **está** muy lejos. *Ramón* ***has said that*** *the hotel* ***is*** *not very far.*
"¿Para cuándo **quiere** la reserva?" *"When* ***do you want*** *the reservation for?"*	Ella **pregunta para cuándo quiero** la reserva. *She* ***asks/is asking when I want*** *the reservation for.*	Ella **ha preguntado para cuándo quiero** la reserva. *She* ***asked when I want*** *the reservation for.*
"¿**Podéis** viajar en octubre?" *"****Can you*** *travel in October?"*	Manuela **pregunta si podemos** viajar en octubre. *Manuela* ***asks/is asking if we can*** *travel in October.*	Manuela **ha preguntado si podemos** viajar en octubre. *Manuela* ***asked if we can*** *travel in October.*

- If the verb reporting the message is in the past tense, follow these tense correlations.

Direct speech	Indirect speech
Present "¿**Conoces** a Manu Chao?" *"**Do you know** Manu Chao?"*	**Imperfect** Margarita me preguntó si **conocía** a Manu Chao. *Margarita asked me if **I knew** Manu Chao.*
Present perfect "**He estado** en Mallorca." *"**I have been** to Mallorca."*	**Past perfect** María me dijo que **había estado** en Mallorca. *María told me that **she had been** to Mallorca.*
Imperfect "La situación económica **era** muy grave." *"The economic situation **was** very serious."*	**Imperfect** La gente comentaba que la situación económica **era** muy grave. *People commented that the economic situation **was** very serious.*
Preterite "Yo también **viví** en Hamburgo." *"**I** also **lived** in Hamburg."*	**Preterite/Past perfect** Peter me confirmó que él también **vivió/había vivido** en Hamburgo. *Peter confirmed to me that he also **lived/had lived** in Hamburg.*
Simple future "**Saldremos** mañana a las 20:00 h." *"**We will leave** tomorrow at 8:00 p.m."*	**Conditional** Ayer nos informaron que **saldríamos** hoy a las 20:00 h. *Yesterday they informed us that **we would leave** today at 8:00 p.m.*

12.11 Conjunctions of concession (**Conjunciones concesivas**) L13B

- **aunque** [*clause*] + [*clause*] / [*clause*] + **aunque** [*clause*]

  Aunque no tenía celular, era muy fácil contactar con él.
  ***Even though** he did not have a cell phone, it was very easy to contact him.*

  Era muy fácil contactar con él **aunque** no tenía celular.
  *It was very easy to contact him, **even though** he did not have a cellular phone.*

- **a pesar de todo**

  Sabía que era necesario tener celular. **A pesar de todo,** no se lo compró nunca.
  *He knew that it was necessary to have a cellular phone. **In spite of/Despite everything,** he never bought himself one.*

- **a pesar de** + [*infinitive/noun*]

  A pesar de los avances tecnológicos, yo prefiero los medios tradicionales de comunicación.
  ***In spite of/Despite advances in technology,** I prefer traditional means of communication.*

  No me gusta el celular **a pesar de ser** útil para algunas cosas.
  *I don't like cell phones, **even though** they are useful for some things.*

- [*clause*] + **sin embargo** + [*clause*]

  No uso mucho la computadora; **sin embargo**, me gusta mucho navegar por Internet.
  *I don't use the computer much; **however**, I really like to surf the Web.*

12.12 Expressions of frequency (**Expresiones de frecuencia**) L6A, L14A, L14B

- Expressions of frequency are often used with the imperfect in order to speak about habitual actions and situations in the past. L14A

(casi) siempre	*(almost) always*
de vez en cuando	*from time to time*
cada día/mes	*every day/month*

Cuando estaba estudiando, Federico **siempre se acostaba** tarde.
*When he was studying, Federico **always went to bed** late.*

Cuando Natalia estuvo trabajando en aquella empresa, **se levantaba cada día** a las cinco.
*When Natalia was working at that company, **she got up every day** at five o'clock.*

Cuando era pequeña, **de vez en cuando iba** al cine con mi hermana mayor.
*When I was young, **I went** to the movies with my older sister **from time to time**.*

- **cuando** + [*imperfect*/*preterite*] L14B

Cuando iba a la escuela, no me gustaba aprender idiomas.
***When I went** to school, I didn't like learning languages.*

Cuando terminé mis estudios, empecé a trabajar aquí.
***When I finished** my studies, I started working here (at that moment).*

- Use **al** + [*infinitive*] to refer to a specific moment in time. L18B

Me quito los zapatos **al volver** (cuando vuelvo) a casa.
*I take off my shoes **upon returning** (when I return) home.*

- **antes/después de +** [*infinitive/noun*] L10B

Antes de las Olimpiadas, muchas personas no sabían dónde estaba Barcelona.
***Before the Olympic Games**, many people did not know where Barcelona was.*

Después de pasar mis primeras vacaciones en España, decidí aprender español.
***After spending** my first vacation in Spain, I decided to study Spanish.*

- **antes de que / después de que** + [*subjunctive*] L18A

Antes de que pase el verano, iré de vacaciones.
***Before** the summer **ends**, I will go on vacation.*

- **cuando** + [*subjunctive*] (to refer to the future) L18A

Cuando termine la película, llamaré a mi madre.
***When** the movie **finishes**, I will call my mother.*

- **dentro de** + [*length of time*] (to refer to the future) L17A

Dentro de un mes dejaré de trabajar.
***Within one month's time**, I will stop working.*

13 Numbers and Quantifiers (Los adjetivos numerales y los cuantificadores)

13.1 Cardinal numbers (**Los números cardinales**) L1A, L1B, L2A, L4B

L1A, L1B

0 cero	10 diez	20 veinte	30 treinta
1 uno/a	11 once	21 veintiuno/a	31 treinta y uno/a
2 dos	12 doce	22 veintidós	32 treinta y dos
3 tres	13 trece	23 veintitrés	33 treinta y tres
4 cuatro	14 catorce	24 veinticuatro	34 treinta y cuatro
5 cinco	15 quince	25 veinticinco	[...]
6 seis	16 dieciséis	26 veintiséis	40 cuarenta
7 siete	17 diecisiete	27 veintisiete	50 cincuenta
8 ocho	18 dieciocho	28 veintiocho	60 sesenta
9 nueve	19 diecinueve	29 veintinueve	70 setenta
			80 ochenta
			90 noventa

L2A, L4B

100 cien	500 quinientos/as	2 000 dos mil
101 ciento uno	600 seiscientos/as	10 000 diez mil
153 ciento cincuenta y tres	700 setecientos/as	20 000 veinte mil
200 doscientos/as	800 ochocientos/as	100 000 cien mil
201 doscientos/as uno/a	900 novecientos/as	200 000 doscientos/as mil
299 doscientos/as noventa y nueve	1 000 mil	1 000 000 un millón
300 trescientos/as	1 001 mil uno/a	2 000 000 dos millones
400 cuatrocientos/as	1 549 mil quinientos/as cuarenta y nueve	

⚠ For numbers that end in **-uno**, use **-un** before masculine nouns and **-una** before feminine nouns.

⚠ Numbers between 200 and 900 also have feminine forms to agree with feminine plural nouns: doscient**os** coch**es**, doscient**as** cas**as**.

⚠ **Mil** is invariable: **mil** coches, **mil** casas.

⚠ Only the last two digits (tens and ones) are joined by **y**: mil treinta **y** seis (1036). In the numbers 16–19 and 21–29, the digits are joined as one word by **i**: diec**i**ocho (18), veint**i**cuatro (24).

⚠ The term **cien** is used in counting and when not followed by a lesser number. When it is followed by a lesser number, **ciento** is used: **ciento veinticinco** (125).

13.2 Ordinal numbers (**Los números ordinales**) L5A, L14A

- Ordinal numbers are used to indicate the order or sequence.

  Ella conoció a su mejor amiga en el **primer** grado.
  *She met her best friend in **first** grade.*

- They are also used to give order to an argument.

  En **primer** lugar, en **segundo** lugar... por último.
  *In the **first** place, in the **second** place . . . lastly.*

1.º primero/a, primer	*first*
2.º segundo/a	*second*
3.º tercero/a, tercer	*third*
4.º cuarto/a	*fourth*
5.º quinto/a	*fifth*
6.º sexto/a	*sixth*
7.º séptimo/a	*seventh*
8.º octavo/a	*eighth*
9.º noveno/a	*ninth*
10.º décimo/a	*tenth*

- **Primero** and **tercero** have shortened forms when they are used before singular masculine nouns: **primer** and **tercer**.

  Juan es el **primer** hijo de Manolita y el **tercer** nieto de sus abuelos.
  *Juan is Manolita's **first** son and his grandparents' **third** grandchild.*

13.3 Other quantifiers (**Otros cuantificadores**) L3A

- Quantifiers are words that indicate quantity.

  Todos/as los/las alumnos/as hablan español.
  ***All the** students speak Spanish.*

  Casi todos/as practican en casa.
  ***Almost all (of them)** practice at home.*

  La mayoría (**de** los alumnos) conoce algún país hispanohablante.
  ***The majority** (**of** the students) have been to a Spanish-speaking country.*

  Varios/as son amigos/as.
  ***Several (of them)** are friends.*

  Solo uno/a ha estado en Chile.
  ***Only one** has been to Chile.*

  Cada persona conoce sus preferencias.
  ***Each person** knows his or her preferences.*

- When **la mayoría** is followed by **de** + [*plural noun*], the verb can agree with **mayoría** (singular) or with the other noun (plural).

  La mayoría de los estudiantes estudia(n) español.
  ***The majority of the students** study Spanish.*

- The plural form must be used with the verbs **ser**, **estar**, and **parecer**.

  La mayoría de los profesores **son** latinoamericanos.
  ***The majority** of the professors **are** Latin American.*

14 Strategies For Improving Communication (Estrategias para mejorar la comunicación)

14.1 Discourse connectors (**Conectores del discurso**) L13B

- Expressions such as **por un lado... por otro** and **por una parte... por otra** help to structure discourse.

  Son muchas cosas. **Por un lado** el trabajo, los alumnos; **por otro**, la familia, los niños, la casa...
  *There are many things. **On the one hand**, work, the students; **on the other**, family, the children, the house . . .*

14.2 Giving examples (**Dar ejemplos**) L7A

- **por ejemplo**

  Me interesan mucho las ciudades peruanas, **por ejemplo**, Lima, Cuzco...
  *Peruvian cities interest me very much. **For example**, Lima, Cuzco . . .*

14.3 Generalizing and clarifying (**Generalizar y matizar**) L7B

generalmente **en general** **especialmente**	**Generalmente/En general** la gente no come muchas verduras, **especialmente** la gente joven. ***Generally/In general** people do not eat a lot of vegetables, **especially** young people.*

14.4 Introducing an explanation and encouraging (**Introducir una explicación y animar**) L8A

mira	• ¿Me puedes ayudar, por favor? ▪ **Mira**, ahora no tengo tiempo, pero más tarde sí. • *Can you help me, please?* ▪ ***Look**, I don't have time now, but I can later on.*
venga	• Estoy muy cansado. ▪ ¡**Venga**! ¡Ya casi hemos llegado! • *I am very tired.* ▪ ***Come on**! We are almost there!*

⚠ **Venga** is primarily used in Spain. Other expressions such as **vamos** or **dale** can be used in similar contexts.

14.5 Reformulating ideas (**Reformular**) L8B

o sea **es decir**	¿Usted no puede encontrar otro momento para hablar conmigo sobre mi trabajo? **O sea**, me gustaría hacerle unas preguntas. **Es decir**, quería preguntarle si me podría dar unos consejos sobre mi trabajo. *You don't have any other time to talk to me about my paper? **I mean**, I would like to ask you some questions. **That is**, I wanted to ask you if you could give me some advice about my paper.*

14.6 Buying time while one is thinking (**Ganar tiempo mientras pensamos**) L9A

pues no sé... **bueno...**	• ¿A qué hora cierra el supermercado? ▪ **Pues no sé... bueno...** creo que a las nueve. • *What time does the supermarket close?* ▪ ***Well, I don't know . . . well . . .*** *I think at nine o'clock.*
pues... **a ver...**	• ¿Qué ciudad es la capital de Chile? ▪ Mmmm... **a ver, pues...** ¡Santiago! • *What city is the capital of Chile?* ▪ *Mmmm . . .* ***let's see, um*** *. . . Santiago!*
¿cómo era?	• ¿Conoces esa canción que te digo? ▪ Pues sí, **a ver... ¿cómo era?** • *Do you know that song I'm talking about?* ▪ *Well yes,* ***let's see . . . how did it go?***
entonces **es que**	• **Bueno**, **entonces**, vamos al cine mañana, ¿no? ▪ No puedo, **es que** tengo mucha tarea. • ***Well, then,*** *we are going to the movies tomorrow, right?* ▪ *I can't,* ***the thing is,*** *I have a lot of homework.*

- These interjections fall into different grammatical categories (conjunctions, adjectives, adverbs) and they are always invariable. They are used to join ideas and to fill gaps in communication. Other expressions include ¡**Anda ya**! (*Come on!/Oh my!*) and ¿**De verdad**? (*Really?*).

14.7 Calling someone's attention (**Llamar la atención**) L9B

perdona	**Perdona**, ¿sabes dónde hay una farmacia? ***Excuse me****, do you know where there is a pharmacy?*
perdone	**Perdone**, ¿puede ayudarme? Me he perdido. ***Excuse me****, can you help me? I am lost.*

⚠ **Perdona** is the familiar (**tú**) command and **perdone** is the formal (**usted**) command.

14.8 Asking for repetition (**Pedir repetición**) L14A

perdona	• Yo viví un tiempo en Guinea Ecuatorial. ▪ ¿**Perdona**? • *I lived in Equatorial Guinea for a while.* ▪ ***Pardon me****?*
¿cómo?	• La capital de Guinea Ecuatorial es Malabo. ▪ ¿**Cómo**? • *The capital of Equatorial Guinea is Malabo.* ▪ ***Sorry****?*

14.9 Adding information in a conversation (**Añadir información en una conversación**) L10A

por cierto	**Por cierto**, la semana pasada vi a María. ***By the way***, *I saw María last week.*
a propósito	**A propósito**, ¿desde cuándo no hablas con ella? ***Incidentally***, *how long has it been since you have spoken with her?*

14.10 Minimizing disagreement (**Minimizar el desacuerdo**) L10B

pero (depende)	Es verdad que es difícil estar lejos de casa, **pero depende**... siempre se puede volver. *It is true that it is hard to be away from home,* ***but it depends*** *. . . you can always go back.*
pero (bueno)	El trabajo es difícil, **pero bueno**, a mí me gusta. *The job is difficult,* ***but you know***, *I like it.*
claro que... pero	**Claro que** cambiar de trabajo es una buena idea, **pero** la situación es difícil. ***Of course*** *changing jobs is a good idea,* ***but*** *the situation is difficult.*

14.11 Softening an opinion (**Suavizar una opinión**) L15A

yo diría que	**Yo diría que** hay que consumir más frutas y verduras. ***I would say that*** *you should eat more fruits and vegetables.*

14.12 Putting information in order (**Ordenar la información**) L5A, L11A

en primer lugar **después** **por último**	**En primer lugar**, el apartamento es pequeño, **después**, es muy oscuro y, **por último**, no tiene muebles. ***First of all***, *the apartment is small,* ***next***, *it is very dark, and* ***lastly***, *it does not have any furniture.*

14.13 Showing interest in the conversation (**Mostrar interés en la conversación**) L11B

sí, la verdad que sí	• Los alquileres en Barcelona son muy caros. ▪ **Sí, la verdad que sí.** • *Rents in Barcelona are very expensive.* ▪ ***Yes, you're right.***
¿sí?, ¿en serio?	• Álvaro se casa en mayo. ▪ **¿Sí?, ¿en serio?** • *Álvaro is getting married in May.* ▪ ***Really? Seriously?***

14.14 Confirming a plan (**Cerrar una cita**) L12A

entonces **de acuerdo** **nos vemos**	• **Entonces** vamos al cine el lunes a las siete, ¿no? ▪ Sí. • **De acuerdo**. ¡**Nos vemos**! • ***So*** *we are going to the movies on Monday at seven o'clock, right?* ▪ *Yes.* • ***OK. See you (then)!***

14.15 Taking the floor (**Tomar la palabra**) L12B

Perdón, quería decir que... **Sí, y además** **Una cosa más**	• **Perdón, quería decir que** los apartamentos en este edificio son muy caros. ▪ **Sí, y además** son muy pequeños. ✦ **Una cosa más**: no hay espacio suficiente para una pareja con hijos. • ***Pardon me, I meant to say that*** *the apartments in this building are very expensive.* ▪ ***Yes, and furthermore*** *they are very small.* ✦ ***One more thing****: there is not enough space for a couple with children.*

14.16 Giving an explanation (**Dar una explicación**) L13A

como	**Como** mi esposo conoce mis gustos, nos compró pasajes a Costa Rica para nuestras vacaciones. ***As/Since*** *my husband knows my preferences, he bought us tickets to Costa Rica for our vacation.*
es que	**Es que** me encanta este país. ***It's just that (the reason is that)*** *I love this country.*

14.17 Emphasizing a piece of information (**Destacar una información**) L13B

solo/solamente	Aunque a Isabel le encanta la música, **solo/solamente** ha asistido a dos conciertos. *Although Isabel loves music, she has* ***only*** *attended two concerts.*
sobre todo	A María José le gustan mucho los deportes, **sobre todo** los de aventura. *María José likes sports,* ***above all*** *adventure sports.*

14.18 Maintaining contact (**Controlar el contacto**) L14B

¿sabes?	Ella necesita más ayuda, **¿sabes?** *She needs more help, **you know?***

14.19 Reinforcing arguments (**Reforzar argumentos**) L15B

desde luego	**Desde luego**, ser adolescente no es fácil. ***Of course**, being an adolescent is not easy.*
efectivamente	**Efectivamente**, no lo es. ***Indeed**, it is not.*

14.20 Bringing up a topic (**Introducir un tema**) L16A

en cuanto a	**En cuanto a** la marcha por la paz, no hay novedades. ***With respect to** the peace march, there are no new developments.*

14.21 Diminishing generalizations (**Atenuar las generalizaciones**) L16B

no todos los...	**No todos los** caribeños viven cerca de la playa. ***Not all** Caribbeans live close to the beach.*
Eso no es todo.	Y **eso no es todo**. Hay muchos otros estereotipos que tampoco son ciertos. *And **that's not all**. There are many other stereotypes that aren't true either.*

14.22 Expressing consequences (**Expresar consecuencias**) L17A

así (es) que	La ciencia tiene soluciones, **así (es) que** vamos a esperar. *Science has solutions, **so** we are going to wait.*
por lo tanto	Los estudios no son concluyentes. **Por lo tanto**, no hay razón de alarma. *The studies are not conclusive. **Therefore**, there is no reason for alarm.*

14.23 Reinforcing a negation (**Reforzar una negación**) L17B

no... nada	A Ricardo **no** le gusta **nada** que le llamen por la mañana temprano. *Ricardo does **not** like it **at all** when people call him early in the morning.*

14.24 Intensifying meaning (**Intensificar**) L18A

repeating the word and using the conjunction *y*	Este deportista ha ganado **premios y premios**. *This athlete has won **prizes upon prizes**.*

14.25 Summarizing main ideas (**Resumir ideas principales**) L18B

en resumen	**En resumen**, no tienen fecha para la celebración. ***In short**, they do not have a date for the celebration.*
en definitiva	Sí, **en definitiva**, ese es el problema. *Yes, **in short**, that is the problem.*

14.26 Fixed expressions (**Expresiones lexicalizadas**)

- To express disagreement in a colloquial manner: **¡Qué va!** L15B
  - ¿Tienes mucha tarea? — *Do you have a lot of homework?*
  - **¡Qué va!** Solo de matemáticas. — ***No, not really.** Only math.*

- To express wishes: L13A, L18B

  Que te mejores pronto. ***Feel better soon.***
  Que tengan un buen viaje. ***Have a nice trip.***
  Que sean felices. ***May you be happy.***

- To console: L13B

  Te entiendo. ***I understand.***
  No pasa nada. *(There's)* ***No problem.***
  No te preocupes. ***Don't worry.***

Glossary

This glossary contains the active vocabulary words and expressions taught in each lesson of **PROTAGONISTAS**, as well as other useful vocabulary. A numeral following an entry indicates the lesson where the word or expression is introduced.

Note on alphabetization

For purposes of alphabetization, **ch** and **ll** are not treated as separate letters, but **ñ** still follows **n**. Therefore, in this glossary you will find that **añadir**, for example, appears after **anuncio**.

Abbreviations used in this glossary

adj.	adjective	*f.*	feminine	*pl.*	plural
adv.	adverb	*fam.*	familiar	*prep.*	preposition
art.	article	*form.*	formal	*pron.*	pronoun
conj.	conjunction	*interrog.*	interrogative	*sing.*	singular
contrac.	contraction	*loc.*	phrase	*v.*	verb
exp.	expression	*m.*	masculine		

Español-Inglés

A

a *prep.* at; to; **¿A qué hora...?** *exp.* At what time...? **3A; a bordo** *loc. adv.* on board **13A; a cambio** *loc. adv.* in return **12B; a cambio de** *loc. adv.* in exchange for **8A; a convenir** *exp.* to be agreed upon **13B; a favor de** *loc. adv.* in favor of **12B; a finales del siglo XIX** *loc. adv.* towards the end of the 19th century **8B; a la derecha** *loc. adv.* (to the) right **9B; a la derecha de** *loc. adv.* to the right of **3B; a la izquierda** *loc. adv.* (to the) left **9B; a la izquierda de** *loc. adv.* to the left of **3B; a la venta** *loc. adv.* for sale **4B; a largo plazo** *loc. adv.* in the long term **9A; a mediados de los 60** *loc. adv.* in the mid sixties **14B; a partir de** *loc. prep.* from, starting **12B; a pesar de (que)** *conj.* despite **6B; a principios del siglo XX** *loc. adv.* at the beginning of the 20th century **8B; a propósito** *conj.* incidentally; by the way **10A; a tiempo** *loc. adv.* in/on time **7B; a través de** *loc. prep.* through **14B; a tu servicio** *loc. adv.* at your service **7B; a veces** *loc. adv.* sometimes **2B; a ver** *exp.* let's see... **6A; amor a distancia** *m.* long-distance love **6B; cuidar (a/de) alguien** *v.* to take care of someone **5B; dedicarse a (hacer) algo** *v.* to do something (for a living) **7A; desde/de... hasta/a...** *loc. prep.* from... until/to **8B; día a día** *m.* daily life **7A; día a día** *loc. adv.* day by day **14B; estar a... kilómetros de...** *loc. adv.* to be... kilometers from... **2A; estar dirigido/a a** *v.* to be aimed at **6A; gracias a** *loc. prep.* thanks to... **5B; ir a trabajar** *v.* to go to work **3A; jugar a la lotería** *v.* to play the lottery **9B; llegar a casa** *v.* to arrive home **3A; llevar a cabo** *v.* to carry out **18A; llevar a los niños al colegio** *v.* to take the kids to school **3A; Me toca a mí.** *exp.* It's my turn. **4A; parecerse a alguien** *v.* to look like somebody **12A; paseo a caballo** *m.* horseback ride **6B; reparto a domicilio** *m.* home delivery **7B; ser sensible a** *v.* to be sensitive to **10A; una vez a la semana** *loc. adv.* once a week **6A**

abanderado/a: aerolínea abanderada *f.* national airline **13A**

abandonar *v.* to leave; to give up **7B**

abandonar *v.* to quit **10B**

abanico *m.* (hand-held) fan **3B**

abiertamente *adv.* openly, frankly **17A**

abierto/a *adj.* open **3A**

abogado/a *m./f.* lawyer **1B**

abonar *v.* to fertilize **8A**

abrazarse *v.* to hug each other **17B**

abrazo *m.* hug **2A**

abreviatura *f.* abbreviation **13B**

abrigarse *v.* to wrap up **13A**

abril *m.* April **1B; el 13 de abril** *m.* April 13 **3A**

abrir *v.* open **3A; abrir un negocio** *v.* to open a business **15A**

abrocharse *v.* to fasten **13A**

abuela *f.* grandmother **5B**

abuelo *m.* grandfather **5B**

abuelos *m.* grandparents **5B**

abundante *adj.* plentiful **17A**

aburrido/a *adj.* boring **1B**

aburrimiento *m.* boredom **17B**

aburrir *v.* to bore **17B**

aburrirse *v.* to get bored **17B**

acá *adv.* here **6B**

academia *f.* academy **15B**

académico/a: vida académica *f.* academic life **14A**

acariciar *v.* to caress **9A**

aceite *m.* oil **8A; aceite de oliva** *m.* olive oil **2B; aceite de oliva virgen extra** *m.* extra virgin olive oil **15A**

aceituna *f.* olive **2B**

acento: con acento *loc. adv.* with an accent **0**

aceptación *f.* acceptance **12B**

aceptar *v.* to accept **15B**

acero *m.* steel **18A; cable de acero** *m.* steel cable **18A**

ácido *m.* acid **17A**

ácido acetilsalicílico *m.* aspirin **17A**

acogida *f.* acceptance **15A**

acompañado/a: sentirse acompañado/a *v.* to feel accompanied **9A**

acompañar *v.* to keep company **9A**

acondicionado/a *adj.* equipped **6B; aire acondicionado** *m.* air conditioning **11A**

aconsejar *v.* to advise **6A**

acontecimiento *m.* event **5A**

acordarse de *v.* to remember **18B**

acostarse *v.* to go to bed **7A**

acostumbrado/a: estar acostumbrado/a a *v.* to be used to **13B**

actitud *f.* attitude **13B**

actividad *f.* activity **0; actividad extraescolar** *f.* out-of-school activity **15B; actividad laboral** *f.* job **7B**

activo/a *adj.* active **5A**

acto: acto de fe *m.* matter of faith **8A**

actor *m.* actor **1A**

actriz *f.* actress **1A**

actuación *f.* acting **5A**

actualidad: en la actualidad *loc. adv.* today; nowadays **8B**

actualizar *v.* to update **7B**

actualmente *adv.* currently, at the moment **7A**

actuar *v.* to act **5A**

acuerdo: estar de acuerdo *v.* to agree **5B**

adaptado/a: estar adaptado *v.* to be adapted **12B**

adaptarse *v.* to adapt **10A**

adecuado/a *adj.* appropriate; suitable **5B**

además *adv.* in addition **2A**

adherirse *v.* to join **16A**

adhesión *f.* support **16A**

Adiós. *exp.* Good-bye. **0**

adivinar *v.* guess **0**

administración *f.* administration **8A**

administrativo/a *adj.* administrative **7B**

admirar *v.* to admire **14B**

adobo *m.* marinade **15A**

adolescente *m.* y *f.* adolescent, teenager **9A**

adopción *f.* adoption **5B**

adoptar *v.* to adopt **5B**

adornar(se) *v.* to decorate **18B**

adversidad *f.* setback **18A**

aéreo/a: compañía aérea *f.* airline **11A**

aerolínea *f.* airline **13A; aerolínea abanderada** *f.* national airline **13A**

aeropuerto *m.* airport **0**

afectar *v.* to affect **10A**

afectivo/a: entorno afectivo *m.* emotional environment **13B**
afecto *m.* affection **12A**
afecto *m.* affection **18B; mostrar afecto** *v.* to show affection **18B**
afición *f.* liking, hobby **11B**
aficionado/a *adj.* amateur **11B**
aficionado/a *m./f.* fan **14B**
afiliarse *v.* to join, to become a member **16A**
afín: ser afín *v.* to have a lot in common **17B**
afinidad *f.* affinity **17B**
afirmar *v.* to assert **16A**
África *f.* Africa **14A; el África subsahariana (f.)** *f.* Sub-Saharan Africa **14A**
africano/a *adj.* African **14A**
afuera: vivir afuera *v.* to live abroad **10B**
afueras *f.* outskirts **11B**
agarrar *v.* to grab **17B**
agasajado/a *m./f.* guest of honor **18B**
agencia *f.* agency **4B; agencia de lotería** *f.* lottery ticket booth **9B; agencia de viajes** *f.* travel agency **4B**
agenda: agenda semanal *f.* (weekly) planner **3A**
agosto *m.* August **3A**
agradable *adj.* pleasant **2A**
agresión *f.* aggression **16A**
agricultor(a) *m./f.* farmer **7B**
agricultura *f.* agriculture **15A; agricultura ecológica** *f.* organic farming **15A**
agromercado *m.* produce market **4A**
agrónomo/a: (ingeniero/a) agrónomo/a *m./f.* agronomist **7A**
agrupar *v.* group, organize **0**
aguacate *m.* avocado **12A**
ahorrar *v.* to save **12B**
ahorros *m.* savings **8B**
aimara *m.* Aymara **12A**
aire *m.* air **7B; aire acondicionado** *m.* air conditioning **11A; al aire libre** *loc. adv.* outdoors **3A; cambio de aires** *m.* change of scenery **11A**
aislamiento *m.* isolation **13B**
ajo *m.* garlic **8A**
ajustado/a a *adj.* adjusted to, adapted to **17A**
al *contrac.* (contraction of **a + el**); **al aire libre** *loc. adv.* outdoors **3A; al horno** *loc. adv.* baked **13A; al lado de** *loc. adv.* next to **3B; al mismo tiempo** *loc. adv.* at the same time **7A; al parecer** *loc. adv.* apparently **8B; dos veces al mes** *loc. adv.* twice a month **6A; llevar a los niños al colegio** *v.* to take the kids to school **3A; poner al día** *v.* to bring up to date **7B; tres veces al año** *loc. adv.* three times a year **3A**
ala: ala delta *m.* hang glider **18A**
alarmista *m. y f.* alarmist **17A**
albaricoque *m.* apricot **15A**
alberca *f.* pool **5B**
albergar *v.* to accommodate **11A**
albergue *m.* hostel **6B**
albóndiga *f.* meatball **2B**
álbum *m.* album **5B**
alcachofa *f.* artichoke **15A**
alcance: estar fuera de (nuestro) alcance *exp.* to be beyond (one's) means **15B**
aldea *f.* village **9A**
alegrarse (de) *v.* to be glad (that) **11A**
alegre *adj.* bright **4B**
alegre *adj.* happy **5B**
alejado/a: alejados entre sí *loc. adv.* far from each other **17B**
alemán *m.* German **1B**
alemán/alemana *adj.* German **1B**
alergia *f.* allergy **10A**
alfombra *f.* carpet **4B**
algo *pron.* something **2B; ¿Algo más?** *exp.* Anything else? **2B; dedicarse a (hacer) algo** *v.* to do something (for a living) **7A; estar haciendo algo** *v.* to be doing something **7A; hacer algo en casa** *v.* to do something at home **3A**
algodón *m.* cotton **9A**
alguien *pron.* someone **5B; cuidar (a/de) alguien** *v.* to take care of someone **7A**
algún *adj.* some, any **9A**
alguno/a *adj.* some, any **9A**
algunos/as *pron.* some **5A**
alimentación: tienda de alimentación *f.* grocery store **4A; producto de alimentación** *m.* food product **15A**
alimento *m.* food **2B; alimento natural** *m.* natural food **15A; alimento transgénico** *m.* transgenic food **15A**
allá *adv.* there **6B**
allí *adv.* there **2A**
alma (f.) *f.* soul **6A**
almorzar *v.* to eat lunch **2B**
alojamiento *m.* accommodation **6B**
alojarse *v.* to stay **13A**
alquiler *m.* rental; rent **4B; de alquiler** *adj.* rental **11B**
alrededor *adv.* around **8A**
altavoz *m.* speaker **13A**
altísimo/a *adj.* excessive, very high **11B**
alto/a *adj.* high; tall **8A; temporada alta** *f.* peak season **4B**
alumno/a *m./f.* student **0**
amabilísimo/a *adj.* very friendly **13A**
amargar: amargarle la vida a alguien *exp.* to upset somebody **17A**
amargo/a *adj.* bitter; painful **10B**
amarillo/a *adj.* yellow **3B; fiebre amarilla** *f.* yellow fever **10A**
Amazonas *m.* Amazon River **5A**
ambicioso/a *adj.* ambitious **16A**
ambiente *m.* atmosphere **2A; ambiente laboral** *m.* work atmosphere **13B; medio ambiente** *m.* environment **4B**
ámbito: ámbito familiar *m.* among family **12A;** *m./f.* friend
amigos/as salir (con amigos) *v.* to go out (with friends) **3A**
amistad *f.* friendship **5B**
amo/a de casa *f.* homemaker **1B**
amor *m.* love **6B; amor a distancia** *m.* long-distance love **6B; amor correspondido** *m.* requited love **12A; amor no correspondido** *m.* unrequited love **12A; declaración de amor** *f.* declaration of love **18B**
ampliar: ampliar un negocio *v.* to expand a business **15A**
amueblado/a *adj.* furnished **4B**
analfabetismo *m.* illiteracy **16A**
analgésico *m.* painkiller **10A**
analista: analista de marketing *m. y f.* marketing analyst **13B**
ananá *m.* pineapple **15A**
anaranjado/a *adj.* orange **3B**
ancho/a *adj.* wide **4B**
andar: ¡Anda ya! *exp.* Come on! **9B**
andén *m.* platform **13A**
anécdota *f.* anecdote **9B**
animal *m.* animal **7B**
anímico/a: estado anímico *m.* state of mind **10A**
ánimo: estado de ánimo *m.* state of mind, mood **12A; dar ánimo** *v.* to offer encouragement **13A**
aniversario *m.* anniversary **5A**
anoche *adv.* last night **5A**
anotar *v.* write down **0**
antelación: con antelación *loc. adv.* in advance, ahead of time **11A**
anterior *adj.* previous **14B**
antes *adv.* before **0**
antes *m.* before; the past **9A; antes de que** *conj.* before **18A**
antibiótico *m.* antibiotic **10A**
anticipar *v.* to anticipate **16B**
anticuado/a *adj.* antiquated **16B**
antigüedad *f.* antique **4A**
antiguo/a *adj.* old **2A**
anunciar *v.* to announce **16A**
anuncio *m.* ad(vertisement) **0**
añadir *v.* to add **0**
año *m.* year **2B; Año Nuevo** *m.* New Year **18B; cumplir 15 años** *v.* to turn 15 years old **5A; cumplir años** *v.* to have one's birthday **18B; cumplir años de casados** *v.* to be one's wedding anniversary **18B; este año** *loc. adv.* this year **6A; fiesta de quince años** *f.* fifteenth birthday party **18B; los años 60** *m.* the sixties **8B; tres veces al año** *loc. adv.* three times a year **3A; una persona de 80 años** *f.* an 80-year-old person **3A**
apagado/a: luz apagada *f.* lights off **6A**
apagar *v.* to put out **7A**
aparato *m.* device **4B**
aparcamiento *m.* parking lot **11A**
apartamento *m.* apartment **4B**
apelar *v.* to appeal **16B**
apellido *m.* last name **1B; doble apellido** *m.* two last names **12A**
apenado/a *adj.* sad **17B**
apertura *f.* opening **15A**
aplazo *m.* failure **15B**
aportar *v.* to provide **15A**
apoyar *v.* to support **13A**
apreciación *f.* appraisal, assessment **17A**
apreciar *v.* to appreciate **18B**
aprender *v.* to learn **3A; aprender de memoria** *v.* to memorize **14B; aprender español** *v.* to learn Spanish **3A**
aprobar *v.* to pass **14A**
aprovechamiento *m.* exploitation **16A**
aprovechar *v.* to take advantage **15A**
aproximadamente *adv.* approximately **3A**
apto/a para *adj.* appropriate/safe for **15A**
apuntarse a *v.* to sign up for **13A**

araña *f.* spider; **mono/a araña** *m./f.* spider monkey **16B**
árbol *m.* tree; **árbol genealógico** *m.* family tree **5B**
archivo *m.* file **7B**
arcilla *f.* clay **16B**
Argentina *f.* Argentina **0**
argentino/a *adj.* Argentine
árido/a *adj.* arid **13A**
arma *f.* weapon; **arma nuclear** *f.* nuclear weapon **16A; tráfico de armas** *m.* arms trade **16A**
armado/a: fuerzas armadas *f.* armed forces **16A**
armario *m.* closet **4B**
arnés *m.* harness **18A**
aro *m.* hoop **18A**
aroma *m.* aroma, scent **16B**
arquitecto/a *m./f.* architect **1A**
arquitectura *f.* architecture **8A**
arreglar *v.* to repair **7B**
arreglo: arreglo floral *m.* flower arrangement **18B**
arroz *m.* rice **2B; arroz con verduras** *m.* rice with vegetables **2B**
arte *m.* art **3B; obra de arte** *f.* work of art **8A**
artesanía *f.* crafts **3B**
artificial *adj.* artificial **15A**
asa (f.) *f.* handle **18A**
asado *m.* barbecue **1A**
ascendencia *f.* ancestry **14A**
ascender *v.* to climb **18A**
asequible *adj.* affordable **6B**
asesor(a) *m./f.* advisor **11B; asesor(a) laboral** *m./f.* labor consultant **13B**
asesorar *v.* to advise, to act as consultant to **13B**
así *adv.* like this, this way; **así (es) que** *conj.* so **17A; así como** *conj.* as well as **16B; Siento verte así.** *exp.* I'm sorry to see you like this. **13B**
asiento *m.* seat **13A; cambio de asiento** *m.* seat change **13A; respaldo del asiento** *m.* seat back **13A**
asignatura *f.* school subject **15B**
asistencia: asistencia sanitaria *f.* health care **10A**
asistir (a) *v.* to attend **15A**
asociación *f.* association **12A**
aspecto *m.* aspect **7B; aspecto físico** *m.* physical appearance **12A**
aspirina *f.* aspirin **10A**
asumir *v.* to assume, to take **12B**
asustado/a *adj.* frightened **12A**
asustar *v.* to frighten **7A**
atardecer *m.* dusk **14A**
atención *f.* attention; **llamar la atención** *v.* to catch one's attention **14A; poner atención (a)** *v.* pay attention (to) **0**
atender *v.* to attend to **7A**
atender to see (a patient), to examine **10A**
atentado *m.* attack; offense **12B**
Atentamente, *exp.* Sincerely, **6B**
atleta *m. y f.* track-and-field athlete **12B**
atletismo *m.* track and field **18A**
atractivo/a *adj.* attractive **12A**
atractivos *m.* attractions **4B**
atrapar *v.* to catch **18A**
atreverse *v.* to dare **17A**
audiencia *f.* audience; **ser líder de audiencia** *v.* to be the highest rated **14B**
aún *adv.* still, yet **15B**
aunque *conj.* although **13B**
ausencia *f.* absence **11A**
autenticidad *f.* authenticity **16B**
auténtico/a *adj.* authentic **4A**
auto *m.* car **6B**
autoayuda *f.* self-help **6A**
autobús *m.* bus **4B**
autosuficiente *adj.* self-sufficient **7B**
auxiliar *m. y f.* assistant **7B; auxiliar de vuelo** *m. y f.* flight attendant **13A**
auxilio *m.* help **18A**
avance *m.* breakthrough **17A**
avenida *f.* avenue **2A**
aventura *f.* adventure **5B**
aventurero/a *m. y f.* adventurer **18A**
aventurero/a *adj.* adventurous **9A**
averiarse *v.* to break down **13A**
averiguar *v.* find out **0**
avión *m.* plane **6B; pasaje de avión** *m.* plane ticket **6B**
ayer *adv.* yesterday **5A**
ayuda *f.* help **5B; pedir ayuda** *v.* to ask for help **5B**
ayudar *v.* to help **5B**
ayuntamiento *m.* city hall **2A**
azteca *adj.* Aztec **12A**
azúcar *m.* sugar **0**
azul *adj.* blue **3B**

B

bacalao: bacalao en salsa *m.* cod with sauce **2B**
bachillerato *m.* high school **15B**
bachillerato *m.* high school studies **14A**
bailaor(a) *m./f.* flamenco dancer **7A**
bailar *v.* to dance **6A**
bailarín *m.* dancer **7A**
bailarina *f.* dancer **7A**
baile *m.* dance; ball **5A; baile de salón** *m.* ballroom dance **17B; baile flamenco** *m.* flamenco dance **7A; paso de baile** *m.* step **17B**
baja: baja por maternidad *f.* maternity leave **7B**
bajar *v.* to go down **15A**
bajo/a *adj.* low **4A;** short **12A; bajo/a en calorías** *adj.* low-calorie **15A**
balance: hacer balance de *v.* to take stock of **12B**
balcón *m.* balcony **4B**
baleares: Islas Baleares *f.* Balearic Islands **4B**
banana *f.* banana **15A**
bancario/a: transferencia bancaria *f.* bank transfer **7B**
banco *m.* bank **0**
banco *m.* bench **0**
banda: banda sonora *f.* sound track **17B**
bandeja *f.* tray; **bandeja de entrada** *f.* inbox **14A**
bandera *f.* flag **8B**
bandoneón *m.* type of accordion **17B**
bandoneonista *m. y f.* bandoneón player **17B**
banquete *m.* reception **5A**
bañarse *v.* to swim, to go for a swim **10A**
baño *m.* bathroom **4B; darse un baño** *v.* to take a bath **10A**
bar *m.* bar, café **0**
barato/a *adj.* cheap **4B**
barba *f.* beard **12A**
bárbaro *adj.* great **11B**
barco *m.* boat, ship; **en barco** *loc. adv.* by boat **5A**
barrera *f.* barrier **12B**
barril: barril de petróleo *m.* oil barrel **14A**
barrio *m.* neighborhood **1A**
base: sobre la base de *loc. prep.* based upon **16A**
bastante *adv.* quite a bit/lot **5B**
bastón *m.* pole **18A**
basura *f.* garbage **8A; comida basura** *f.* junk food **10A**
bata *f.* robe **5A**
batería *f.* battery **7B**
batir *v.* to beat **8A; batir un récord** *v.* to break a record **18A**
bautizo *m.* baptism **5B**
bazar *m.* bazaar **8B**
beber *v.* to drink **2B**
bebida *f.* beverage **2B**
beca *f.* scholarship **8B; beca (escolar)** *f.* scholarship **12B; beca ERASMUS** *f.* ERASMUS scholarship **14A**
béisbol *m.* baseball **18A**
beisbolista *m./f.* baseball player **18A**
Bélgica *f.* Belgium **10B**
belleza *f.* beauty **4B**
bello/a *adj.* beautiful **16B**
Berlín: Muro de Berlín *m.* Berlin Wall **10B**
besarse *v.* to kiss each other **17B**
beso *m.* kiss **2A**
biblioteca *f.* library **1A; biblioteca ambulante** *f.* traveling library **9A**
bici *f.* bike (bicycle) **6B**
bicicleta *f.* bike (bicycle) **6B**
bien *adv.* well **1A; bien comunicado/a** *loc. adv.* easily accessible **4B; Estoy bien.** *exp.* I'm OK. **7B; llevarse bien/mal** *v.* to get along/not to get along **12A; o bien** *conj.* or otherwise **12A; pasarla bien** *v.* to have a good time **17B; pasarlo bien** *v.* to have a good time **17B; por tu bien** *exp.* for your own good **15B**
bienestar *m.* well-being **6A**
bienvenida *f.* welcome **11A; dar la bienvenida** *v.* to welcome **11A**
Bienvenido/a(s) *exp.* Welcome! **11A**
bigote *m.* mustache **12A**
bilbaíno/a *adj.* from Bilbao **17A**
bilingüe *adj.* bilingual **18A; escuela bilingüe** *f.* bilingual school **15B**
billete *m.* ticket **6B; comprar (billetes de) lotería** *v.* to buy lottery tickets **9B; reservar los billetes** *v.* to book the tickets **13A**
billetero *m.* wallet **18B**
biografía *f.* biography **5A**
biología *f.* biology **1B**
biólogo/a biologist; **biólogo/a marino/a** *m./f.* marine biologist **11B**
blanco/a *adj.* white **3B; quedarse en blanco** *exp.* to go blank **15B**
blando/a *adj.* soft **9A**

blog *m.* blog **3A**
bloqueado/a *adj.* locked; blocked **7B**
boca *f.* mouth **9A**
boda *f.* wedding **5A; bodas de plata** *f.* silver wedding anniversary **18B**
bolígrafo *m.* ballpoint pen **3B**
Bolivia *f.* Bolivia **0**
bollería *f.* pastries **2B**
bolsa *f.* bag; sack **4A; bolsa de comercio** *f.* stock exchange **3A; bolsa de trabajo** *f.* employment center **13B**
bolsillo *m.* pocket **13B**
bolso *m.* bag **3B**
bomba *f.* pump **17A**
bombero/a *m./f.* firefighter **7A**
bonito/a *adj.* pretty **2A**
bordo: a bordo *loc. adv.* on board **13A; ¡Que disfruten a bordo!** *exp.* Enjoy your flight! **13A**
boricua *adj.* Puerto Rican **11A**
bosque *m.* forest **5A; bosque virgen** *m.* virgin forest **6B**
bota *f.* boot **3B**
bote: bote de remos *m.* rowing boat **18A**
botella *f.* bottle **2B**
botiquín *m.* firs-aid kit **10A**
botón *m.* button **4B**
boxeador(a) *m./f.* boxer **18A**
Brasil *m.* Brazil **1A**
brazo *m.* arm **10A; del brazo** *loc. adv.* arm in arm **5A**
brecha: cerrar la brecha *v.* to close the gap **17A**
bricolage *m.* do-it-yourself **8A**
brillante *adj.* bright **9A**
brillante *adj.* brilliant, smart **14B**
brócoli *m.* broccoli **15A**
bromista *adj.; m. y f.* fond of joking **13B**
bronce *m.* bronze **12B**
brújula *f.* compass **18A**
bruto/a: producto interior bruto (PIB) *m.* gross domestic product (GDP) **11A, 14A**
bueno *exp.* well... **2A; ¿Bueno?** *exp.* Hello? **6B**
bueno/a *adj.* good; **¡Buen provecho!** *exp.* Enjoy your meal. **8A; buen tiempo** *m.* good weather **2A; Buenas noches.** *exp.* Good evening/night. **0; Buenas tardes.** *exp.* Good afternoon. **0; Buenas.** *exp.* Hi. **0; Buenos días.** *exp.* Good morning. **0; Buenos días.** *exp.* Hello. **0; de buen/mal humor** *loc. adv.* in a good/bad mood **12A; en buena compañía** *loc. adv.* in good company **16B; hace buen/mal tiempo** *v.* there is good/bad weather **10A; lo malo/bueno** *m.* the bad/good thing **12B; ser bueno/a (en algo)** *v.* to be good (at something) **17B**
burro/a *m.* donkey **0**
buscar *v.* to look for **1B**

C

cabalgata *f.* horse riding **18A**
caballero *m.* gentleman **13A**
caballo *m.* horse **6B; paseo a caballo** *m.* horseback ride **6B**
cabaña *f.* cabin **6B**
cabeza *f.* head **10A; estar a la cabeza** *exp.* to lead **16A**
cabina: jefe/a de cabina *m./f.* purser **13A**
cable *m.* cable, wire; **cable de acero** *m.* steel cable **18A**
cabo: llevar a cabo *v.* to carry out **18A**
cacahuate *m.* peanut **12A**
cacao: cacao en polvo *m.* cocoa powder **15A**
cachorro/a *m./f.* puppy **12B**
caciquismo *m.* despotism **16A**
cada *adj.* each; **cada día** *loc. adv.* each day **14A**
cadena *f.* chain; network; **cadena de radio** *f.* radio network **14B**
caducidad: fecha de caducidad *f.* expiration date **15A**
café *m.* coffee **0; café solo** *m.* black coffee **2B**
cafeína *f.* caffeine **2B**
cafetería *f.* café; cafeteria **1B**
caja *f.* box **8A**
cajero/a *m./f.* cashier **1B**
cajón *m.* drawer **8A**
calamares *m.* calamari, squid **2B**
calcular *v.* calculate **0**
calendario *m.* calendar, schedule **3A**
calidad *f.* quality; **calidad de vida** *f.* quality of life **2A**
calificación *f.* grade **15B**
callado/a *adj.* silent; **estar callado/a** *v.* to be silent, not to talk **9A**
calle *f.* street **2A**
calor *m.* heat **2A; hacer frío/calor** *v.* to be cold/hot **10A; tener frío/calor** *v.* to be cold/hot **10A**
calorías *f. pl.* calories; **bajo/a en calorías** *adj.* low-calorie **15A**
calzado *m.* shoes **10A**
cama *f.* bed **4B; (semi-)cama** *adj.* (semi-) sleeper **13A; cama de matrimonio** *f.* double bed **4B; hacer la cama** *v.* to make the bed **3A**
cámara *f.* camera; **cámara web** *f.* webcam **6B**
camarero/a *m./f.* waiter/waitress **2B**
camarógrafo/a *m./f.* cameraman/camerawoman **9A**
camarón *m.* shrimp **16B**
cambiar *v.* to change **7B;**
cambiar de casa *v.* to move **5A; cambiar de trabajo** *v.* to change jobs **7B; cambiar de vida** *v.* to change one's life **7B**
cambio *m.* change; **a cambio** *loc. adv.* in return **12B; a cambio de** *loc. adv.* in exchange for **8A; cambio de aires** *m.* change of scenery **11A; cambio de asiento** *m.* seat change **13A; cambio de dinero** *m.* foreign currency exchange **13A**
caminar *v.* to walk **5B; caminar sin rumbo fijo** *v.* to wander aimlessly **17B**
camión *m.* truck **7A**
camionero/a *m./f.* truck driver **7A**
camisa *f.* shirt **3B**
camiseta *f.* T-shirt **3B**
campamento *m.* campsite **6B**
campana *f.* bell **18B**
campanada *f.* peal of a bell **18B**
campaña *f.* campaign **12B; campaña de conciliación** *f.* conciliation campaign **15B; campaña de promoción** *f.* promotional campaign **16B; campaña electoral** *f.* electoral campaign **16A; lanzar una campaña** *v.* to launch a campaign **16B; tienda de campaña** *f.* tent **18A**
campesino/a *m./f.* peasant **9A**
camping *m.* campsite **6B**
campo *m.* country(side) **3A; campo científico** *m.* scientific field **17A**
Canadá *m.* Canada **0**
canadiense *adj.* Canadian **1B**
canal *m.* channel **9A**
canas: tener canas *v.* to have gray hair **17B**
cancelado/a *adj.* cancelled **13A**
cancha *f.* court **18A** sports field **17B**
canción *f.* song **7A**
candidato/a *m./f.* applicant **13B**
candidato/a *m./f.* candidate **16A**
canotaje *m.* canoeing **18A**
cansado/a *adj.* tired **6A**
cansancio *m.* tiredness **14B**
cansarse de (algo) *v.* to get tired/bored of (something) **9B**
cantante *m. y f.* singer **5A**
cantar *v.* to sing **17B**
cantautor(a) *m./f.* singer-songwriter **7A**
cantidad *f.* quantity **4A**
caoba *f.* mahogany tree **18B**
capa: capa de ozono *f.* ozone layer **17A**
capacidad: tener capacidad *v.* to have (storage) capacity **13B**
capital *f.* capital **2A**
capítulo *m.* episode **14B**
cara *f.* face **5A**
caracol *m.* escargot, snail **2B**
carácter *m.* atmosphere **4A**
carácter *m.* character, personality **12A**
caravana: caravana de coches *f.* motorcade **5A**
carbono: hidrato de carbono *m.* carbohydrate **15A**
cardiovascular *adj.* cardiovascular **17A**
carecer (de) *v.* to lack **17B**
cargar *v.* to load; to carry **9A**
cargo *m.* position **17A**
Caribe: mar Caribe *m.* Caribbean Sea **4B**
caribeño/a *adj.* Caribbean **4B**
cariñoso/a *adj.* affectionate **12A**
carisma *m.* charisma **18A**
caritativo/a *adj.* charitable **16A**
carmelita *adj.* Carmelite **11A**
carne *f.* meat **2B; carne de cerdo** *f.* pork **18B**
caro/a *adj.* expensive **3B**
carpa *f.* tent **9A**
carpintería *f.* carpentry **8A**
carpintero/a *m./f.* carpenter **12B**
carrera *f.* major, career **1B; estudiar una carrera** *v.* to study for a degree **15B**
carrito *m.* trolley **13A**
carro *m.* car **5A**
carta *f.* letter; **carta al director/a la directora** *f.* letter to the editor **2A; carta de presentación** *f.* letter of introduction **13B**

cartel *m.* poster **0**
casa *f.* house **4B; cambiar de casa** *v.* to move **5A; casa particular** *f.* private home **13A; en casa** *loc. adv.* at home **2B; ensalada de la casa** *f.* house salad **2B; hacer algo en casa** *v.* to do something at home **3A; hora de llegar a casa** *f.* time somebody has to be home **15B; llegar a casa** *v.* to arrive home **3A; sentirse como en casa** *v.* to feel at home **16B**
casado/a *adj.* married **5B; cumplir años de casados** *v.* to be one's wedding anniversary **18B**
casarse *v.* to get married **8B**
cascada *f.* waterfall **6B**
casco *m.* helmet **18A; casco viejo** *m.* historic neighborhood **12B**
casi *adv.* almost **13B; casi nunca** *loc. adv.* hardly ever **6A; casi siempre** *loc. adv.* almost always **14A**
casilla *f.* (check) box **0**
caso: hacer caso (a alguien) *v.* to pay attention (to somebody) **15B**
castaño/a *adj.* brown **12A**
castillo *m.* castle **6B**
casualidad *f.* coincidence **16A**
casualmente *adv.* by chance **17B**
catalán *m.* Catalan **1B**
catedral *f.* cathedral **2A**
católico/a *adj.* Catholic **5A**
ceibo *m.* coral tree **18B**
celebración *f.* celebration **18B**
celebrar *v.* to celebrate **5A**
celebrar *v.* to take place **18A**
celebrarse *v.* to be held **4A**
celeste *adj.* light blue **9A**
celíaco/a *adj.* celiac **15A**
celular: (teléfono) celular *m.* cell phone **1B**
cenar *v.* to eat supper **2B**
central *f.* main office **2A**
céntrico/a *adj.* in the centre of town **7B**
centro *m.* center, downtown **1A; centro comercial** *m.* shopping mall **2A**
cerámica: hacer cerámica *f.* to do pottery **6A**
cerca de *prep.* near **2A**
cercanía *f.* proximity **16B**
cerdo *m.* pig; **carne de cerdo** *f.* pork **18B**
cereales *m.* cereal **2B**
cerebrito *m./f.* nerd **15B**
ceremonia *f.* ceremony **14A; maestro/a de ceremonias** *m./f.* master of ceremonies **18B**
cerilla *f.* match **8A**
cerrar *v.* to close; **cerrar la brecha** *v.* to close the gap **17A**
certamen *m.* contest **16B**
certeza *f.* certainty **15A**
certificado/a *adj.* certified **16B**
cerveza *f.* beer **2B**
cesta *f.* basket **7B, 18A**
ceviche *m.* marinated seafood dish **1A**
chachachá *m.* cha-cha **17B**
chamaco/a *m./f.* kid, youngster **12A**
chamaquito/a (dim. de chamaco/a) *m./f.* kid, youngster **12A**
chaqueta *f.* jacket **3B**
charla (fam.) *f.* conversation **9A**
charlar *v.* to chat **14A**
chat *m.* chat room **3A**
chatear *v.* to chat (on the Internet) **6B**
Chau. *exp.* Bye. **0**
cheque *m.* check; **cheque-regalo** *m.* gift-voucher **3B**
chicle *m.* chewing gum **9B**
chico/a *adj.* small **11B**
Chile *m.* Chile **0**
chimenea *f.* chimney **8B**
chino *m.* Chinese **1B**
chino/a *adj.* Chinese **1B, 4A**
chip *m.* chip **17A**
chisme *m.* piece of gossip **17B**
chiste *m.* joke **5B; contar chistes** *v.* to tell jokes **17B**
chocar *v.* to surprise; to collide **14B**
choclo *m.* corn **15A**
chocolate *m.* chocolate **0**
choque *m.* collision; **choque cultural** *m.* culture shock **14B**
chorizo *m.* sausage, chorizo **2B**
churros *m.* churros **2B**
cibercafé *m.* Internet café **4A**
ciclismo *m.* cycling **18A**
ciclista *m. y f.* cyclist **18A**
ciego/a *adj.* blind **12B**
cien: cien por ciento *adj.* one hundred percent **12A**
ciencia *f.* science **6A; ciencias políticas** *f.* political science **1B; Ciencias sociales** *f.* Social Studies **15B**
científico/a *adj.* scientific; **campo científico** *m.* scientific field **17A; método científico** *m.* scientific method **17A**
ciento: cien por ciento *adj.* one hundred percent **12A**
cierto/a *adj.* right, true; **por cierto** *loc. adv.* by the way, incidentally **10A**
cine *m.* movie theater **3A**
cinturón *m.* belt **8A; cinturón de seguridad** *m.* seatbelt **13A**
circulación *f.* circulation **10A**
círculo *m.* circle **18A**
cita *f.* appointment, date **14B**
citado/a *adj.* cited, quoted **17A**
ciudad *f.* city **0; Ciudad de Guatemala** *f.* Guatemala City **0; Ciudad de Panamá** *f.* Panama City **0**
ciudadano/a *m./f.* citizen **8B; ciudadano/a ilustre** *m./f.* distinguished citizen **17B**
cívico/a: Educación ético-cívica *f.* Citizenship Education **15B**
civil: estado civil *m.* marital status **5B; guerra civil** *f.* civil war **8B**
civilización *f.* civilization **11B**
claro *exp.* of course **1B**
claro/a *adj.* light **16B**
clase *f.* class **1B; (el resto de) la clase** *f.* (the rest of) the class **0; clase de música** *f.* music class **3A; clase media** *f.* middle class **14B; clase particular** *f.* private lesson **17B; dar clases (de algo)** *v.* to give [subject] classes **8A; fuera de clase** *loc. adv.* outside of class **3A; tener clase** *v.* to have class **3A**
clásico *m.* classic **9A**
clásico/a *adj.* classic **4B, 7A**
clasificar *v.* classify **0**
clavar *v.* to nail down **8A**
clave *f.* key **6A; lugar clave** *m.* landmark **4A**
clavel *m.* carnation **18B**
clavo *m.* nail **8A**
clic: hacer clic *v.* to click **13B**
cliente *m. y f.* client **2A**
clima *m.* climate **2A**
clínica *f.* clinic **10A**
coche *m.* car **3A; caravana de coches** *f.* motorcade **5A; ir en coche** *v.* to go by car **3A**
cocido/a *adj.* cooked **15A**
cocina *f.* cooking **8A**
cocina *f.* kitchen **4B; receta (de cocina)** *f.* recipe **8A**
cocinar *v.* to cook **3A**
coco *m.* coconut **15A**
cóctel *m.* cocktail **16B**
código *m.* code **13B**
col *f.* cabbage **15A**
cola *f.* line (waiting) **15A; piano de cola** *m.* grand piano **10B**
colaborar *v.* to collaborate **10B**
colaborar *v.* to participate **3A**
colección *f.* collection **3B**
coleccionar *v.* to collect **9B**
colectivo/a *adj.* collective **8A**
colectivo *m.* bus **17B**
colega *m. y f.* colleague **7B**
colegio *m.* school **3A; llevar a los niños al colegio** *v.* to take the kids to school **3A**
colocar *v.* to place **9B**
Colombia *f.* Colombia **0**
colombiano/a *adj.* Colombian **3B**
colonia *f.* colony **14A**
colonial: zona colonial *f.* colonial area **3A**
colonizador(a) *m./f.* colonizer **18B**
color *m.* color **3B; ¿De qué color?** *exp.* What color? **3B**
colorante *m.* colorant **15A**
comedor *m.* dining hall **15B;** dining room **4B; salón-comedor** *m.* living room-dining room **4B**
comentar *v.* to discuss **0;** to mention **14B**
comenzar *v.* to begin, to start **8B**
comer *v.* to eat lunch, to eat **2B**
comercial: centro comercial *m.* shopping mall **2A**
comerciante *m./f.* storekeeper **14A**
comercio *m.* commerce **8B; bolsa de comercio** *f.* stock exchange **3A; comercio justo** *m.* fair trade **3B**
cómic *m.* comic book **9B**
cómics *m.* comics **7A**
comida *f.* food **1A; comida basura** *f.* junk food **10A**
como *conj.* as, like; **así como** *conj.* as well as **16B; sentirse como en casa** *v.* to feel at home **16B; tan/tanto... como** *conj.* as much/many... as **8B; tanto ... como** *conj.* both ... and **7A; trabajar como** *v.* to work as **11B**
cómo *interrog.* how **0, 1A; ¿Cómo?** *exp.* What?, Excuse me? **14A; ¿Cómo es?** *exp.* What is it like? **4B; ¿Cómo es...?** *exp.* What is... like? **2A; ¿Cómo se dice...?** *exp.* How do you say...? **6B; ¿Cómo se escribe...?** *exp.* How do you spell...? **1A; ¿Cómo vas?** *exp.* How are you going there? **6B**
comodidades *f. pl.* comforts **7B**
cómodo/a *adj.* comfortable **2A;** convenient **17A**

compaginar *v.* to combine **7A**
compañero/a *m./f.* classmate, colleague, partner **2B; compañero/a de trabajo** *m./f.* coworker **5B**
compañía *f.* company; **(hacer) compañía** *v.* (to keep) company **7A; compañía aérea** *f.* airline **11A; en buena compañía** *loc. adv.* in good company **16B**
comparar *v.* compare **0**
compartido/a *adj.* shared; **custodia compartida** *f.* joint custody **12A**
compartir *v.* to share **5A**
compatible *adj.* compatible **5B**
compatriota *m. y f.* fellow countryman/countrywoman **10B**
competencia *f.* competence; ability **2**
competir *v.* to compete **18A**
complejo/a *adj.* complex **16B**
complementos *m.* accessories **3B**
completar *v.* complete **0**
completo/a *adj.* complete **9A**
componer *v.* to compose **7A**
composición *f.* composition **15A**
comprar *v.* to buy **3B; comprar (billetes de) lotería** *v.* to buy lottery tickets **9B**
compras: hacer las compras *v.* to go grocery shopping **3A; lista de compras** *f.* shopping list **4A**
comprender *v.* to understand **13B**
comprensivo/a *adj.* understanding **13B**
comprobar *v.* to check, to verify **13A**
compromiso *m.* commitment **5A**
compuesto/a por *adj.* made up of **16B**
computadora *f.* computer **4B**
común *adj.* common, ordinary; **punto común** *m.* point in common **5B**
comunicación *f.* communication **3B; falta de comunicación** *f.* lack of communication **15B; medios de comunicación** *m.* media **9A**
comunicado/a: bien comunicado/a *loc. adv.* easily accessible **4B**
comunicador(a) *m./f.* communicator **13B**
comunicativo/a *adj.* communicative **16B**
comunidad *f.* community **1A; comunidad inmigrante** *f.* immigrant community **8B**
comunitario/a *adj.* communal **17A**
con *prep.* with; **¿Con qué frecuencia?** *exp.* How often? **3A; arroz con verduras** *m.* rice with vegetables **2B; con acento** *loc. adv.* with an accent **0; con antelación** *loc. adv.* in advance, ahead of time **11A; con encanto** *loc. adv.* charming **6B; Con gusto.** *exp.* You're welcome. **18B; con motivo de** *exp.* on the occasion of **12B; con respecto a** *loc. prep.* regarding **16A; con retraso** *loc. adv.* delayed **13A; con tarjeta** *loc. adv.* with a credit card **3B; contar con** *v.* to include **9A; salir (con amigos)** *v.* to go out (with friends) **3A**
conciencia *f.* conscience **17A**
concierto *m.* concert **1A; dar un concierto** *v.* to give a concert **7A**
conciliación: campaña de conciliación *f.* conciliation campaign **15B**
conciliar *v.* to reconcile **6A**
concordia *f.* harmony **16A**
concretamente *adv.* specifically **7B**
concreto/a: en concreto *loc. adv.* in particular **7B**
condicionar *v.* to determine **14A**
conducir *v.* to drive **7A**
conectado/a *adj.* connected (to the Internet) **13B**
conexión: estar en conexión *v.* to be connected **6A**
confianza *f.* confidence **18A; tener confianza en** *v.* to trust in **5B**
confirmación *f.* confirmation **13A**
confirmar *v.* to confirm **6B**
confitería *f.* café **4A**
conflicto *m.* conflict **7A; conflicto generacional** *m.* generational conflict **15B; resolución de conflictos** *f.* conflict resolution **13B**
confundirse *v.* to become confused **16B**
congelado/a *adj.* frozen **16B**
congreso *m.* conference **12B**
conjugar *v.* conjugate **0**
conmemorar *v.* to commemorate **17A**
conocer *v.* to meet; to know (people) **5A; dar a conocer** *v.* to make known **16B**
conocido/a *adj.* known; **más conocido/a** *adj.* best-known **4A**
conquistar *v.* to conquest, to captivate **15A**
consciente: hacer consciente *v.* to make aware **3B**
consecuencia *f.* consequence **12B**
conseguir *v.* to get; to obtain **4A**
consejo *m.* piece of advice **6A**
consenso *m.* consensus **16A**
conservación *f.* preservation **15A**
conservante *m.* preservative **15A**
conservar *v.* to keep **8A**
construir *v.* build **0**
construir *v.* create **0**
consulta: hacer una consulta *v.* to ask somebody's advice **12A**
consultas *f.* questions **6B**
consultorio *m.* advice column **12A**
consultorio *m.* problem page; (medical) practice **10A**
consumidor(a) *m./f.* consumer **3B**
consumir *v.* to consume **15A**
consumo *m.* consumption **3B**
contacto *m.* touch, contact **17B; estar en contacto** *v.* to be in touch **12B**
contador(a) *m./f.* accountant **13B**
contar *v.* to tell **14B; contar chistes** *v.* to tell jokes **17B; contar con** *v.* to include **9A**
contarse *v.* to tell each other **17B**
contemporáneo/a *adj.* contemporary **3B**
contenedor *m.* recycling container **15A**
contenidos *m.* content **14B**
contento/a *adj.* happy **11A; ponerse contento/a** *v.* to be happy **18B**
contestar *v.* answer **0**
contigo *prep. + pron.* with you **5A**
continente *m.* continent **11B**
contrato *m.* contract; **contrato de trabajo** *m.* employment contract **13B**
contrincante *m. y f.* opponent **18A**
control *m.* control; **control de equipaje** *m.* baggage screening **13A; control de pasaportes** *m.* passport control; immigration **13A**
controlar *v.* to check **17A**
controlar *v.* to control **15B**
convencer *v.* to convince **16A**
convencional *adj.* conventional **16A**
convenir: a convenir *loc. adv.* to be agreed upon **13B**
convento *m.* convent **6B**
conversación *f.* conversation **1B**
convertirse (en) *v.* to become **7A**
convicción *f.* conviction **16A**
convivencia *f.* coexistence **14A**
convivir con *v.* to coexist with **14A**
convocatoria *f.* call (to action) **16A**
coordinador(a) *m./f.* coordinator **16A**
corazón *m.* heart **2A; revista del corazón** *f.* gossip magazine **9B**
corbata *f.* tie **3B**
coreano *m.* Korean **1B**
coreano/a *adj.* Korean **1B**
correcto/a *adj.* correct **0**
corredor(a) *m./f.* runner **18A**
correo *m.* mail; **correo electrónico** *m.* e-mail **4B**
correr *v.* to run; **correr un maratón** *v.* to run a marathon **18A**
correspondido/a: amor (no) correspondido *m.* (un)requited love **12A**
corriente: ser moneda corriente *v.* to be common **13B**
corrupción *f.* corruption **16A**
corto/a *adj.* short **12A; a corto/medio/largo plazo** *loc. adv.* short/medium/long term **17A**
cosa *f.* thing **4A**
cosmopolita *adj.* cosmopolitan **16B**
costa *f.* coast **4B**
Costa Rica *f.* Costa Rica **0**
costar *v.* to be difficult **14B;** to cost **4A; ¿Cuánto cuestan...?** *exp.* How much do... cost? **4A**
costarricense *adj.* Costa Rican **14B**
costarricense *m. y f.* Costa Rican **14B**
costumbre *f.* habit **15A**
cotización *f.* estimate **18B**
crecer *v.* to grow **7B**
crecer *v.* to grow up **9B**
creciente *adj.* growing **16B**
crecimiento *m.* growth **16A**
crédito *m.* credit, loan; **pedir un crédito** *v.* to ask for a loan **5B**
creer *v.* to believe; **Creo que sí/no.** *exp.* I think so/not. **7B**
crema *f.* cream; **crema de leche** *f.* cream **15A; crema solar protectora** *f.* sunscreen **10A**
crisis *f.* crisis **12B**
criticar *v.* to criticize **17B**
crítico/a *m./f.* critic; **crítico/a literario/a** *m./f.* literary critic **10B**
cromo (de fútbol) *m.* (soccer) trading card **9B**
cronológicamente *adv.* chronologically **5B**
cruasán *m.* croissant **2B**
crucero *m.* cruise **16B**
cruzar *v.* to cross **18A**
cuadrado/a *adj.* square; **metros cuadrados (m2)** *m.* square meters **4B**
cuál *interrog.* what, which; **¿Cuál es tu número de teléfono?** *exp.* What is your phone number? **1B; ¿cuál(es)?** *interrog.* which one(s)? **4B; ¿Cuáles...?** *interrog.* Which...? **4B**
cualidad *f.* characteristic, feature **17B**
cuando *conj.* when

cuándo *interrog.* When…? **0**
cuanto: en cuanto a *conj.* as for **16A**
cuánto/a *interrog.* how much; **¿Cúanto es?** *exp.* How much is it? **2B; ¿Cuánto tiempo (hace)…?** *exp.* How long have/has? **8B; cuántos/as** *interrog.* how many **4B**
cuarto/a *adj.* fourth **14A**
cuate/a (fam.) *m./f.* friend, pal **12A**
Cuba *f.* Cuba **0**
cubano/a *m./f.* Cuban person **13A**
cuenta *f.* account; bill **2B; tener en cuenta** *v.* to take into account **16B**
cuento *m.* short story **9B**
cuero *m.* leather **8A**
cuerpo *m.* body **6A**
cuestionario *m.* questionnaire **6A**
cuidar: cuidar (a/de) alguien *v.* to take care of someone **5B**
cultivar *v.* to grow; to cultivate **7B**
culto/a *adj.* educated **12A**
culto: lugar de culto *m.* place of worship **8A**
cultural *adj.* cultural **6A; choque cultural** *m.* culture shock **14B; política cultural** *f.* cultural policy **16A**
cumbia *f.* dance typical of the Caribbean coast of Colombia **17B**
cumpleaños (invar.) *m.* birthday **5A**
cumplir *v.* to reach; to fulfill **13A; cumplir (sus) sueños** *v.* to make (his/her) dreams come true **15B; cumplir 15 años** *v.* to turn 15 years old **5A; cumplir años** *v.* to have one's birthday **18B; cumplir años de casados** *v.* to be one's wedding anniversary **18B; cumplir con** *v.* to meet **15A**
cupón *m.* (lottery) ticket **12B**
cura *f.* cure **17A**
curandero/a *m./f.* folk healer **14A**
curioso/a *adj.* curious; **objeto curioso** *m.* curiosity; nicknack **4A**
currículum (vítae) *m.* résumé **11B**
cursar *v.* to study **14A**
curso *m.* class, course **3A**
custodia: custodia compartida *f.* joint custody **12A**
cuyo/a *pron.* whose **10B**

D

dado: tiren el dado *exp.* roll the die **10A**
dar *v.* to give **4A; ¡Dale!** *exp.* Come on! **8A; dar a conocer** *v.* to make known **16B; dar ánimo** *v.* to offer encouragement **13A; dar clases (de algo)** *v.* to give [subject] classes **8A; dar la bienvenida** *v.* to welcome **11A; dar la vuelta** *v.* to flip; to turn over **8A; dar la vuelta al mundo** *v.* to go around the world **18A; dar pena** *v.* to upset **18B; dar un concierto** *v.* to give a concert **7A; dar un ejemplo** *v.* to give an example **7A; dar un paseo** *v.* to take a walk **6A; darse un baño** *v.* to take a bath **10A; Me da/pone…** *exp.* I'd like… **4A**
datos *m. pl.* data, information **0**
de *prep.* of; **¿De qué color?** *exp.* What color? **3B; ¿De qué talla?** *exp.* What size? **3B; ¿De verdad?** *exp.* Really? **9B; a cambio de** *loc. adv.* in exchange for **8A; a favor de** *loc. adv.* in favor of **12B; a la derecha de** *loc. adv.* to the right of **3B; a la izquierda de** *loc. adv.* to the left of **3B; a partir de** *loc. prep.* from, starting **12B; a pesar de (que)** *conj.* despite **6B; al lado de** *loc. adv.* next to **3B; alegrarse de** *v.* to be glad that **18B; antes de que** *conj.* before **18A; aprender de memoria** *v.* to memorize **14B; cambiar de trabajo** *v.* to change jobs **7B; cambiar de vida** *v.* to change one's life **7B; con motivo de** *exp.* on the occasion of **12B; de alquiler** *adj.* rental **11B; de buen/mal humor** *loc. adv.* in a good/bad mood **12A; de hecho** *exp.* in fact **7A; de la mañana** *loc. adv.* a.m.; in the morning **3A; de la noche** *loc. adv.* p.m.; in the evening/night **3A; de la tarde** *loc. adv.* p.m.; in the afternoon **3A; de maravilla** *loc. adv.* wonderfully **17B; de nuevo** *loc. adv.* again **0; de paso** *loc. adv.* in the process **14B; de repente** *loc. adv.* suddenly **9B; de vez en cuando** *loc. adv.* from time to time **14A; debajo de** *loc. prep.* under **3B; dejar de fumar** *v.* to quit smoking **12B; delante de** *loc. prep.* in front of **3B; dentro de** *loc. prep.* in, within **17A; depender (de)** *v.* to depend (on) **10A; desde/de… hasta/a…** *loc. adv.* from… until/to **8B; después de que** *conj.* after **18A; detrás de** *loc. prep.* behind **3B; día de la semana** *m.* day of the week **3A; el resto de** *m.* the rest of **12B; en vías de desarrollo** *adj.* developing **3B; encima de** *loc. prep.* on (top of) **3B; estar a… kilómetros de…** *loc. adv.* to be… kilometers from… **2A; estar de acuerdo** *v.* to agree **5B; estar de vacaciones** *v.* to be on vacation **7B; estar de viaje** *v.* to be away **7A; estar fuera de (nuestro) alcance** *exp.* to be beyond (one's) means **15B; estar seguro/a de sí mismo/a** *v.* to be self-confident **18A; hablarse de tú/usted** *v.* to address somebody as **tú/usted 7B; horarios de trabajo** *m.* work schedules **3A; mayor de** *adj.* older than **9A; por medio de** *loc. prep.* by means of **14B; procedente de** *loc. adv.* arriving from **13A; rodeado/a de** *loc. adv.* surrounded by **6B; salir de** *v.* to leave **3A; sobre la base de** *loc. prep.* based upon **16A; Yo soy de Madrid.** *exp.* I'm from Madrid. **1A**
debajo: debajo de *loc. prep.* under **3B**
debate *m.* debate **16A**
deberes *m.* homework **15B**
década *f.* decade **14B**
decepción *f.* disappointment **10B**
decepcionar *v.* to disappoint **17B**
decidir *v.* to decide **6A**
décimo/a *adj.* tenth **12B**
decir *v.* to say, to tell **7A; ¡No me digas!** *exp.* You don't say! **9B; ¿Cómo se dice...?** *exp.* How do you say…? **0; ¿Diga?** *exp.* Hello? **6B; ¿Dígame?** *exp.* Hello? **6B; decir la verdad** *v.* to tell the truth **17B; es decir** *exp.* in other words **8B; quería decir** *exp.* I meant… **12B**
decisivo/a *adj.* crucial, decisive **10B**
declaración: declaración de amor *f.* declaration of love **18B**
declarar *v.* to state **16A**
decoración *f.* decoration **3B**
decorador(a) *m./f.* decorator **11B**
dedicación *f.* dedication **15A**
dedicar *v.* to dedicate **6A**
dedicarse: dedicarse a (hacer) algo *v.* to do something (for a living) **7A; ¿A qué te dedicas?** *exp.* What do you do (for work)? **1B**
defender *v.* to defend **12B**
defensa *f.* defense **16A**
definitiva/a: en definitiva *loc. adv.* all in all **18B**
dejar *v.* to quit; to give up, to leave **5A, 7B; dejar de** *v.* to stop, to cease **10B; dejar de fumar** *v.* to quit smoking **12B**
del *contrac.* of the **3B; a finales del siglo XIX** *loc. adv.* towards the end of the 19th century **8B; del brazo** *loc. adv.* arm in arm **5A; descuento (del …%)** *m.* (a …%) discount **11A; menú del día** *m.* fixed-price menu **2B**
delante: delante de *loc. prep.* in front of **3B**
delfín *m.* dolphin **5A**
delito *m.* crime **17B**
delta: ala delta *m.* hang glider **18A**
demanda *f.* demand **15A; demanda laboral** *f.* labor demand **14A**
demasiado *adv.* too **13A**
democracia *f.* democracy **14B**
democrático/a *adj.* democratic **10B; transición democrática** *f.* democratic transition **14B**
demostrar *v.* to prove **17A**
denominarse *v.* to be called **17A**
densamente *adv.* densely **16B**
dentista *m. y f.* dentist **10A**
dentro: dentro de *loc. prep.* in **17A**
denunciar *v.* to denounce **16A**
depender (de) *v.* to depend (on) **10A**
deporte *m.* sport(s) **3A; hacer deporte** *v.* to exercise **3A; zapatillas (de deporte)** *f.* running shoes; sneakers **3B**
deportista *m. y f.* athlete **12B;** sportsman/sportswoman **18A**
deportivo/a *adj.* sporting **6A; reto deportivo** *m.* sport challenge **18A**
derecha *f.* right; **a la derecha** *loc. adv.* (to the) right **9B; a la derecha de** *loc. adv.* to the right of **3B**
derecho *m.* right **3B; derechos humanos** *m.* human rights **16A; hecho/a y derecho/a** *exp.* all grown-up **9A**
derramarse *v.* to shed **18B**
derribar *v.* to knock down, demolish **10B**
desacuerdo *m.* disagreement **10B; estar en desacuerdo** *v.* to disagree **5B**
desagradable *adj.* unkind **13B**
desaparecer *v.* to disappear **10B**
desarrollar *v.* to develop **15B**
desarrollo *m.* development **14A; en vías de desarrollo** *adj.* developing **3B**
desastre *m.* disaster **16A**
desayunar *v.* to eat breakfast **2B**
desayuno *m.* breakfast **2B**
descafeinado *m.* decaf coffee **2B**
descansar *v.* to rest **5B**

descanso *m.* rest **3A**
descender *v.* to descend **18A**
descomunal *adj.* massive **18A**
desconectarse *v.* to disconnect (oneself) **7B**
descremado/a: leche descremada en polvo *f.* powdered skim milk **15A**
describir *v.* describe **0**
descubrimiento *m.* discovery **17A**
descubrir *v.* to discover, to learn **17A**
descuento *m.* discount **6A; descuento (del ...%)** *m.* (a ...%) discount **11A**
desde *prep.* since; from **2A; desde entonces** *loc. adv.* since then **7A; desde hace** *loc. prep.* for (and until now) **5B; desde niño(s)/a(s)** *loc. adv.* since childhood **8B; desde pequeño/a** *loc. adv.* since childhood **5B; desde que** *conj.* since **8B; desde/de... hasta/a...** *loc. prep.* from... until/to **8B**
desear *v.* to wish **11A; ¿Qué desean tomar?** *exp.* What would you like (to have)? **2B**
desechable *adj.* disposable **17A**
deserción: deserción universitaria *f.* university drop-outs **15B**
desértico/a *adj.* desert-like **5A**
desfavorecido/a *adj.* underprivileged **16A**
desgarrador(a) *adj.* heartrending **16A**
desigualdad *f.* inequality **16A**
desinfectante *m.* disinfectant **10A**
deslizarse *v.* to glide **18A**
desocupado/a *adj.* unemployed **11B**
despacio *adv.* slowly **10A; Más despacio, por favor.** *exp.* Slower, please. **0**
despedida *f.* leave-taking **0; despedida de soltero/a** *f.* bachelor(ette) party night **18B**
desperdiciar *v.* to waste **15B**
despertador *m.* alarm clock **3B**
despertar *v.* to wake up, to awaken; **despertar la inquietud** *v.* to stir up interest **9A**
despertarse *v.* to wake up **7A**
después *adv.* after **0; después de que** *conj.* after **18A**
destacable *adj.* noteworthy **14A**
destacado/a *adj.* notable **5A**
destino *m.* destination **13A; destinos turísticos** *m.* tourist destinations **4B**
desventaja *f.* disadvantage **9B**
detalle *m.* detail; **ocuparse de los detalles** *v.* to take care of the details **18B**
detrás: detrás de *loc. prep.* behind **3B**
devolución *f.* return **9A**
devolver *v.* to return **16B**
devorar *v.* to devour **18B**
día *m.* day; **Buenos días.** *exp.* Good morning. **0; cada día** *loc. adv.* each day **14A; de un día para el otro** *loc. adv.* overnight **16A; día a día** *m.* daily life **7A; día a día** *loc. adv.* day by day **14B; Día de la Madre** *m.* Mother's Day **18B; día de la semana** *m.* day of the week **3A; día festivo** *m.* holiday **3A; día libre** *m.* day off **14A; el otro día** *loc. adv.* the other day **9B; hoy en día** *loc. adv.* nowadays **15B; menú del día** *m.* fixed-price menu **2B; poner (a alguien) al día** *v.* to update **17B; poner al día** *v.* to bring up to date **7B; todo el día** *loc. adv.* all day **6A; todos los días** *loc. adv.* every day **3A**
diabetes *f.* diabetes **17A**
diabético/a *adj.* diabetic **17A**
dialecto *m.* dialect **17B**
diálogo *m.* dialogue **0**
diario *m.* diary; journal **5A**
diario/a *adj.* daily, everyday **13A; rutina diaria** *f.* daily routine **3A**
diarrea *f.* diarrhea **10A**
dibujar *v.* draw **0**
dibujo *m.* drawing **3B**
dicho/a: propiamente dicho *exp.* per se **16B**
diciembre *m.* December **3A**
dictador(a) *m./f.* dictator **16A**
dictadura *f.* dictatorship **10B**
dieta *f.* diet **7B**
diferencia *f.* difference (in price) **16B**
diferenciarse de *v.* to differentiate from **17B**
diferente *adj.* different **2A**
difícil *adj.* hard; difficult **7A**
dificultad *f.* difficulty **6B**
digital *adj.* digital **9B**
digno/a *adj.* decent; worthy **3B**
diminutivo *m.* diminutive, nickname **12A**
dinamismo *m.* dynamism **16B**
dinero *m.* money **6B; cambio de dinero** *m.* foreign currency exchange **13A**
Dios *m.* God **8A**
diplomático/a *m./f.* diplomat **16A**
dirección *f.* address
directivo/a *m./f.* manager **8B; puesto directivo** *m.* managerial position **13B**
directo/a: en directo *loc. adv.* live **4A**
director(a) *m./f.* director **1A; carta al director/a la directora** *f.* letter to the editor **2A**
dirigido/a: estar dirigido/a a *v.* to be aimed at **6A**
dirigir *v.* to run; to manage **6A**
discapacidad *f.* disability **12B**
discapacitado/a *adj.* disabled **12B**
discípulo *m.* disciple **17A**
disco *m.* album **7A; disco de vinilo** *m.* vinyl record **13B; tienda de discos** *f.* music store **3B**
disco: lanzador(a) de disco *m./f.* discus thrower **18A**
discográfico/a: sello discográfico *m.* record label **17B**
discoteca *f.* disco, night club **2A**
discurso *m.* speech **16A**
discutir *v.* to argue **13B**
diseñador(a) *m./f.* designer **3B; diseñador(a) (de moda)** *m./f.* (fashion) designer **11B**
diseñar *v.* to design **0**
diseño *m.* design **4B; diseño gráfico** *m.* graphic design **7A**
disfrutar *v.* to enjoy **4A; ¡Que disfruten a bordo!** *exp.* Enjoy your flight! **13A**
disgusto *m.* disgust **15B**
dispensador *m.* dispenser **9B**
disponer *v.* to have (at one's disposal) **18B**
distancia *f.* distance **2A; amor a distancia** *m.* long-distance love **6B**
distinto/a *adj.* different **4A**
distracción *f.* distraction **13B**
diversidad *f.* diversity **7A**
diversión *f.* fun **6A**
diverso/a *adj.* various **5B**
divertido/a *adj.* fun **1B**
divertir *v.* to amuse **17B**
divertirse *v.* to have fun **17B**
divisas *f.* foreign currency **13A**
divorciado/a *adj.* divorced **5B**
divorciarse *v.* to get divorced **12A**
divorcio *m.* divorce **12A**
divulgación: divulgación médica *f.* popularization of medicine **17A**
DNI (Documento Nacional de Identidad) *m.* national identity card **3A**
doble *m.* double **2B; doble apellido** *m.* two last names **12A; habitación doble** *f.* double room **6B**
docena *f.* dozen **4A; media docena** *f.* half a dozen **4A**
doctor(a) *m./f.* doctor **10A**
documental *m.* documentary **9A**
dolencia *f.* ailment **10A**
doler *v.* to hurt, to ache **10A**
dolor *m.* pain **10A**
domador(a): domador(a) de leones *m./f.* lion tamer **14A**
doméstico/a *adj.* home; **objetos domésticos** *m.* furnishings **4B; servicio doméstico** *m.* domestic service **8B**
domicilio *m.* home address **2A; reparto a domicilio** *m.* home delivery **7B**
dominar *v.* to prevail, to stand out **17A**
domingo *m.* Sunday **3A**
dominical: suplemento dominical *m.* Sunday supplement **9B**
dominio *m.* command **13B**
donación *f.* donation **9A**
dónde *interrog.* where **1A; ¿De dónde eres?** *exp.* Where are you from? **1A; ¿De dónde es usted?** *exp.* Where are you from? **1A; ¿Dónde está...?** *exp.* Where is...? **2A**
dorada *f.* sea bream (type of fish) **2B**
dormir *v.* to sleep; **dormir la siesta** *v.* to take a nap **6A**
dormitorio *m.* bedroom **4B**
dos *adj.* two; **dos veces al mes** *loc. adv.* twice a month **6A; hace dos meses** *loc. adv.* two months ago **5A; los/las dos** *pron.* both **6B**
dosis *f.* dose **17A**
droga *f.* drug(s) **16A**
ducharse *v.* to shower **7A**
dudar *v.* to doubt **16A; No dude en...** *exp.* Don't hesitate to... **13B**
dueño/a *m./f.* owner **8B**
dulce *m.* candy, sweet **2B**
dulce *adj.* sweet **2B**
duración *f.* duration **6B**
durazno *m.* peach **16B**
duro/a *adj.* hard; tough **7B**
DVD *m.* DVD **9B; película en DVD** *f.* movie on DVD **4B**

E

e *conj.* and (before i or hi + consonant) **1B**
echar: echar de menos *v.* to miss **14B**
ecológico/a *adj.* ecological, organic **17A**
ecológico/a organic **7B; agricultura ecológica** *f.* organic farming **15A; producto ecológico** *m.* organic product **15A**

economía *f.* Economics **1B**
económico/a *adj.* affordable **2B; prensa económica** *f.* financial press **3A; recurso económico** *m.* economic resource **14A**
ecoturismo *m.* ecotourism **11A**
ecuación *f.* equation **15B**
Ecuador *m.* Ecuador **0**
ecuatoguineano/a *adj.* from Equatorial Guinea **14A**
edad *f.* age **4A**
edición: edición especial *f.* special edition **3B**
edificio *m.* building **2A**
editar *v.* to edit; to release **7A**
editar *v.* to release (music) **17B**
educación *f.* education **8A; Educación ético-cívica** *f.* Citizenship Education **15B; Educación física** *f.* Physical Education **15B; Educación plástica y visual** *f.* Art **15B**
educador(a) *m./f.* trainer (of dogs) **12B**
educar *v.* to train; to educate **12B**
efectivamente *adv.* indeed **15B**
efectivo/a: en efectivo *loc. adv.* cash **3B**
efecto *m.* effect **6A**
eficaz *adj.* efficient **13B**
egresar *v.* to graduate **9A**
ejecutivo/a: ejecutivo/a de ventas *m./f.* sales executive **13B**
ejemplo *m.* example **0; dar un ejemplo** *v.* to give an example **7A**
ejercicio *m.* exercise **10A; hacer ejercicio** *v.* to exercise; to work out **6A**
ejército *m.* army **16A**
el *art.* the (*m., sing.*) **2A**
él *pron.* he **1A; él es...** *exp.* He is... **0**
El Salvador *m.* El Salvador **0**
el/la turista *m. y f.* tourist **1B**
elaboración *f.* production **15A**
elaborar *v.* to create, to make **0**
elástico/a: goma elástica *f.* rubber band **8A**
elecciones *f.* elections **10B**
electoral: campaña electoral *f.* electoral campaign **16A**
electricidad *f.* electricity **8A**
electrodoméstico *m.* appliance **8A**
electrónico/a *adj.* electronic; **correo electrónico** *m.* e-mail **4B; lector de libros electrónicos** *m.* e-reader **13B**
elegante *adj.* elegant **4B**
elegir *v.* choose **7A; ¿Qué ... eliges?** *exp.* What... do you choose? **1A**
eliminación *f.* elimination **12B**
eliminar *v.* to eliminate **16A**
ella *pron.* she **1A; ella es...** *exp.* She is... **0**
ellos/as *pron.* they **1B**
embajada *f.* embassy **10A**
embajador(a): embajador(a) de la paz *m./f.* ambassador for peace **16A**
embargo: sin embargo *conj.* however **5A**
embarque *m.* boarding **13A; hora de embarque** *f.* boarding time **13A; puerta de embarque** *f.* boarding gate **13A**
emblema *m.* emblem **18A**
emergencia *f.* emergency **12B**
emigración *f.* emigration **8B**
emigrante *m. y f.* emigrant **8B**
emisora *f.* radio station **14B**
emitir: emitir la serie *v.* to broadcast the TV series **14B**
emocionado/a *adj.* excited **10B**
emocionante *adj.* exciting, moving **10B**
empanada *f.* empanada **17B**
empatía *f.* empathy **13B**
empezar *v.* to start **5A**
empleado/a *m./f.* employee **3A**
empleo *m.* employment **11B**
emprendedor(a) *adj.* enterprising **8B**
empresa *f.* company **6A**
empresario/a *m./f.* business person **8B; mujer empresaria** *f.* business woman **5A**
en *prep.* in; **bacalao en salsa** *m.* cod with sauce **2B; convertirse en** *v.* to become **7A; de vez en cuando** *loc. adv.* from time to time **14A; en barco** *loc. adv.* by boat **5A; en casa** *loc. adv.* at home **2B; en concreto** *loc. adv.* in particular **7B; en cuanto a** *loc. prep.* as for **16A; en definitiva** *loc. adv.* all in all **18B; en directo** *loc. adv.* live **4A; en efectivo** *loc. adv.* cash **3B; en equipo** *loc. adv.* as a team **7A; en especial** *loc. adv.* especially **7B; en general** *loc. adv.* generally **4A; en la actualidad** *loc. adv.* today; nowadays **8B; en línea** *loc. adv.* online **9B; En mi opinión, ...** *exp.* In my opinion, ... **10B; En parejas/grupos** *loc. adv.* In pairs/groups **0; en regla** *loc. adv.* in order; valid **11A; en resumen** *loc. adv.* in short **18B; en vías de desarrollo** *adj.* developing **3B; entrar en** *v.* to enter **3A; especializado/a en** *adj.* specializing in **2B; estar en conexión** *v.* to be connected **6A; estar en contacto** *v.* to be in touch **12B; estar en desacuerdo** *v.* to disagree **5B; estar en forma** *v.* to be fit, in (good) shape **7A; estar en manos de alguien** *exp.* to be under someone's control **17A; estar en obras** *v.* to be under construction **11A; estar en paz** *v.* to be at peace **10B; estar interesado/a en** *v.* to be interested in **17A; hacer algo en casa** *v.* to do something at home **3A; hoy en día** *loc. adv.* nowadays **15B; ir en coche** *v.* to go by car **3A; ir en...** *v.* to go by (means of transportation) **6B; No dude en...** *exp.* Don't hesitate to... **13B; participar en** *v.* to participate in **3A; película en DVD** *f.* movie on DVD **4B; quedarse en blanco** *exp.* to go blank **15B; tener confianza en** *v.* to trust in **5B**
enamorado/a (de) *adj.* in love with **2A; estar enamorado/a (de)** *v.* to be in love (with) **12A**
enamorarse *v.* to fall in love **12A**
encantado/a *adj.* delighted **11A; Encantado/a.** *exp.* Pleased to meet you. **0**
encantar *v.* to love; to get a kick out of **5B**
encanto *m.* charm **11A; con encanto** *loc. adv.* charming **6B**
encargo *m.* job, assignment **16B**
encender *v.* to turn on **4B**
encima: encima de *loc. prep.* on (top of) **3B**
encontrar *v.* to find **4A**
encontrarse *v.* to be; to feel **10A**
encontrarse *v.* to be; to feel **10A**
encuentro *m.* meeting, encounter **6A; punto de encuentro** *m.* meeting point **9A**
encuesta *f.* survey **18B**
endulzar *v.* to sweeten **15A**
enemigo/a *m./f.* enemy **17B**
energético/a: sector energético *m.* energy sector **14A**
energía *f.* energy **7A**
enero *m.* January **5A**
enfadado/a *adj.* angry **12A**
enfadarse *v.* to get angry **17B**
enfermedad *f.* illness **10A**
enfermero/a *m./f.* nurse **12B**
enfermo/a *adj.* sick **5B**
enfrentarse a *v.* to face **18A**
enganchar *v.* to get someone hooked **14B**
enojarse *v.* to get angry **17B**
enorme *adj.* huge **16A**
ensalada *f.* salad; **ensalada de la casa** *f.* house salad **2B**
ensayo *m.* rehearsal **7A**
enseñanza *f.* teaching **7A**
enseñar *v.* to show; to teach **5B, 13A**
entender *v.* to understand; **No entiendo.** *exp.* I don't understand. **0; Te entiendo perfectamente.** *exp.* I understand you perfectly. **13B**
enterarse de *v.* to find out (about) **17A**
entero/a: leche entera *f.* whole milk, full-cream milk **15A**
entonces *adv.* then **9B**
entonces *conj.* then; so **7A; desde entonces** *loc. adv.* since then **7A**
entorno *m.* environment, surroundings **11A; entorno afectivo** *m.* emotional environment **13B**
entrada *f.* arrival (time) **6A**
entrada *f.* ticket **7B; bandeja de entrada** *f.* inbox **14A**
entrar en *v.* to enter **3A**
entre *prep.* between **2A; alejados entre sí** *loc. adv.* far from each other **17B**
entrega *f.* delivery **7B; entrega de equipaje** *f.* baggage claim **13A**
entrenador(a) *m./f.* coach **18A**
entrenamiento *m.* training **18A**
entretenerse *v.* to amuse oneself **9A**
entretenimiento *m.* entertainment **8B**
entrevista *f.* interview **3A**
entristecer *v.* to make sad **17B**
entusiasmo *m.* enthusiasm **10B**
envasado/a *adj.* packaged **15A**
envase *m.* container; **envase de plástico** *m.* plastic container **15A; envase reciclable** *m.* recyclable container **15A**
enviar *v.* to send **7B**
época *f.* time of year **6B**
época *f.* time, period **9A**
equidad *f.* fairness **17A**
equilibrado/a *adj.* balanced **7B**
equilibrio *m.* balance **6A**
equipaje *m.* baggage **11A; control de equipaje** *m.* baggage screening **13A; entrega de equipaje** *f.* baggage claim **13A**
equipo *m.* equipment **14A;** *m.* team; **en equipo** *loc. adv.* as a team **7A; equipo de trabajo** *m.* working team **13B**
equivocado/a *adj.* mistaken **14A**
ERASMUS: beca ERASMUS *f.* ERASMUS scholarship **14A**

error *m.* mistake **11A**
escala *f.* scale **15B; hacer escala** *v.* to stop over **13A**
escalada *f.* climbing **18A**
escalar *v.* to climb (a mountain) **18A**
escaparate *m.* shop window **3B**
escenificar *v.* to role-play **0**
escocés/escocesa *adj.* Scottish **7B**
escondido/a *adj.* hidden **6B**
escribir *v.* write **0; ¿Cómo se escribe...?** *exp.* How do you spell...? **0**
escribirse *v.* to write to each other **17B**
escritor(a) *m./f.* writer **1A**
escuchar *v.* listen **0; escuchar la radio** *v.* to listen to the radio **2A**
escudo *m.* coat of arms **18B**
escuela *f.* school **3B; escuela bilingüe** *f.* bilingual school **15B; escuela primaria** *f.* elementary school **9A; escuela privada** *f.* private school **15B; escuela pública** *f.* public school **15B**
escultor(a) *m./f.* sculptor **16A**
ese/a *adj., pron.* that
esfuerzo *m.* effort **8A**
eslogan *m.* slogan **11A**
eso *pron.* that; **por eso** *conj.* therefore **17A; Siento oír eso.** *exp.* I'm sorry to hear that. **13B**
esos/as *adj., pron.* those
espacio *m.* space, room; **ocupar espacio** *v.* to take up space **13B**
espada *f.* sword **18B**
espalda *f.* back **10A**
España *f.* Spain **0**
español *m.* Spanish **1B; aprender español** *v.* to learn Spanish **3A**
español/a *adj* Spanish
especial *adj.* special **2B; edición especial** *f.* special edition **3B; en especial** *loc. adv.* especially **7B**
especialista *m. y f.* specialist **10A**
especializado/a en *adj.* specializing in **2B**
especialmente *adv.* specially **7A**
espectacular *adj.* spectacular **11B**
espectáculo *m.* show **4A**
espejo *m.* mirror **9A**
esperanza *f.* hope **10B**
esperanzado/a *adj.* hopeful **14A**
esperar *v.* to hope; to wait for **12B**
espíritu *m.* spirit **6A**
espiritual *adj.* spiritual **14A**
espolvorear *v.* to sprinkle **15A**
espontáneo/a *adj.* impromptu **14B**
esposo/a *f.* husband/wife **5B; ex esposo/a** *m./f.* ex-husband/wife **12A**
esquí *m.* skiing **1A**
estabilidad *f.* stability **13B**
estable *adj.* stable, dependable **12B**
establecer *v.* to establish **6A**
establecimiento *m.* store; establishment **9B**
estación *f.* station **4A; estación (del año)** *f.* season **10A**
estado *m.* state **5B; estado anímico** *m.* state of mind **10A; estado civil** *m.* marital status **5B; estado de ánimo** *m.* state of mind, mood **12A; estado físico** *m.* physical condition **10A; golpe de estado** *m.* coup d'état **10B**
Estados Unidos (EE.UU.) *m.* United States (U.S.A.) **0**
estadounidense *adj.* American **1B**
estancia *f.* ranch **3A**; stay **11A; ¡Feliz estancia!** *exp.* Have a nice stay! **11A**
estanco *m.* tobacconist's **9B**
estándar *adj.* standard **7B**
estar *v.* to be; **¿dónde está...?** *exp.* where is...? **2A; ¿Está Carmen?** *exp.* Is Carmen in? **6B; ¿Qué tal está(n)...?** *exp.* How is/are...? **2B; estar a la cabeza** *exp.* to lead **16A; estar a... kilómetros de...** *loc. adv.* to be... kilometers from... **2A; estar acostumbrado/a a** *v.* to be used to **13B; estar adaptado** *v.* to be adapted **12B; estar callado/a** *v.* to be silent, not to talk **9A; estar conectado/a** *v.* to be connected (to the Internet) **13B; estar de acuerdo** *v.* to agree **5B, 10B; estar de vacaciones** *v.* to be on vacation **7B; estar de viaje** *v.* to be away **7A; estar dirigido/a a** *v.* to be aimed at **6A; estar en conexión** *v.* to be connected **6A; estar en contacto** *v.* to be in touch **12B; estar en desacuerdo** *v.* to disagree **5B; estar en forma** *v.* to be fit, in (good) shape **7A; estar en manos de alguien** *exp.* to be under someone's control **17A; estar en obras** *v.* to be under construction **11A; estar en paz** *v.* to be at peace **10B; estar enamorado/a (de)** *v.* to be in love (with) **12A; estar encantado/a** *v.* to be delighted **11A; estar fuera de (nuestro) alcance** *exp.* to be beyond (one's) means **15B; estar haciendo algo** *v.* to be doing something **7A; estar ilusionado/a** *v.* to be excited **12A; estar impresionado/a** *v.* to be impressed **18A; estar interesado/a en** *v.* to be interested in **17A; estar localizable** *v.* to be reachable **13B; estar motivado/a** *v.* to be motivated **13B; estar pendiente de** *v.* to be waiting for, to be attentive **17B; estar resfriado/a** *v.* to have a cold **10A; estar seguro/a de sí mismo/a** *v.* to be self-confident **18A; Estoy bien.** *exp.* I'm OK. **7B**
este *m.* east **2A**
este/a *adj., pron.* this; **esta semana** *loc. adv.* this week **6A; este año** *loc. adv.* this year **6A; este mes** *loc. adv.* this month **6A**
estilo *m.* style **4B**
estimado/a *adj.* dear **6B; Estimados señores:** *exp.* Dear sirs, **6B**
estimulante *adj.* stimulating **6A**
estimular *v.* to stimulate **16A**
estómago *m.* stomach **10A**
estos/as *adj., pron.* these
estrategia *f.* Strategy **1**
estrella *f.* star **5A; hotel de cuatro estrellas** *m.* four-star hotel **11A**
estrenarse *v.* to premiere **14B**
estrés *m.* stress **3A**
estresante *adj.* stressful **1B**
estrofa *f.* stanza **17B**
estuche *m.* case **13A**
estudiante *m./f.* student; **residencia de estudiantes** *m.* dorm **12A**
estudiar *v.* study **1B; estudiar una carrera** *v.* to study for a degree **15B**
estudio *m.* studio apartment **4B**
estudios *m. pl* studies **5A**
estupendo/a *adj.* wonderful **6B**
etapa *f.* stage **9A**
ético/a: Educación ético-cívica *f.* Citizenship Education **15B**
etiqueta *f.* label **15A**
étnico/a: grupo étnico *m.* ethnic group **16B**
eufórico/a *adj.* euphoric **15B**
euro *m.* euro; **Son 9 euros.** *exp.* It's 9 euros. **2B**
europeo/a *adj.* European **6A; Unión Europea** *f.* European Union **10B**
euskera *m.* Basque (language) **1B**
evaluador(a) *m./f.* critic, appraiser **17A**
evento *m.* event **18B**
evidente *adj.* obvious, clear **17A**
evitar *v.* to avoid **15A**
evolución *f.* evolution **16B**
ex *prep.* former, ex; **ex esposo/a** *m.* ex-husband/wife **12A**
exacto/a *adj.* exact **6A**
exagerar *v.* to exaggerate **15B**
excelente *adj.* excellent **13A**
excluyente *adj.* a must, required **13B**
excursión *f.* excursion **6A**
exigir *v.* to demand **16B; exigir sacrificios** *v.* to require sacrifices **13A**
exiliarse *v.* to go into exile **10B**
exilio *m.* exile **8B**
exitoso/a *adj.* successful **5A**
éxodo *m.* exodus **14B**
exótico/a *adj.* exotic **4A**
expectativa *f.* expectation **15A**
experiencia *f.* experience **4B; experiencia profesional** *f.* professional experience **11B; Mi experiencia** *exp.* My experience **0**
experimentación *f.* experimentation **17A**
experimento *m.* experiment **17A**
explicar *v.* to explain **14B**
explorar *v.* to explore **11B**
explosión *f.* explosion **14B**
explotar *v.* to exploit **14A**
exponer *v.* to display, to post **0**
exportador(a) *m./f.* exporter **18B**
exportar *v.* to export **7B**
exposición *f.* exhibition **6A**
expresar: expresar un sentimiento *v.* to express a feeling **18B**
expulsar *v.* to expel **14A**
exquisito/a *adj.* delicious **13A**
exquisito/a *adj.* exquisite **18B**
extensión *f.* area **6B**
extenso/a *adj.* vast **16B**
extinción *f.* extinction **14A**
extra *adj.* extra; **aceite de oliva virgen extra** *m.* extra virgin olive oil **15A; hacer horas extras** *v.* to do overtime **13B**
extraescolar: actividad extraescolar *f.* extracurricular activity **15B**
extranjero/a *adj.* foreign **2A; lengua extranjera** *f.* foreign language **15B**
extrañar *v.* to miss **13A**
extrañar *v.* to surprise **15B**
extrañeza *f.* surprise, astonishment **15B**
extraordinario/a *adj.* extraordinary **11B**
extremo/a *adj.* extreme **18A**

F

fábrica *f.* factory **8B**
fabricar *v.* to manufacture; **fabricar en serie** *v.* to mass produce **13B**
fácil *adj.* easy **6B; hacer la vida más fácil** *exp.* to make life easier **17A**
factor *m.* factor **6A**
facturación *f.* check-in **11A; mostrador de facturación** *f.* check-in desk **13A**
falda *f.* skirt **3B**
falso/a: ¿Verdadero o falso? *adj.* false **0**
falta *f.* lack **11B; falta de comunicación** *f.* lack of communication **15B; hacer falta** *v.* to be necessary **16A**
faltar *v.* to miss, to lack; **que faltan** *adj.* missing **0**
familia *f.* family **2A; la Familia Real** *f.* the royal family **4B; médico/a de familia** *m./f.* family doctor **10A**
familiar *m.* relative **5B; ámbito familiar** *m.* among family **12A**
famoso/a *adj.* famous **2A**
fantástico/a *adj.* fantastic **2A**
farero/a *m./f.* lighthouse keeper **14A**
farmacéutico/a *adj.* pharmaceutical **17A**
fármaco *m.* medicine **17A**
fascinado/a *adj.* fascinated **14B**
fascinar *v.* to captivate **14A**
fase *f.* stage **17A**
fauna *f.* fauna
fauna *f.* fauna; **observación de flora y fauna** *f.* wildlife viewing **6B**
favor *m.* favor; **a favor de** *loc. adv.* in favor of **12B; Más despacio, por favor.** *exp.* Slower, please. **0; por favor** *exp.* please **2B**
favorecer *v.* to favor **11A**
favorito/a *m./f.* favorite **9B**
fax *m.* fax **7B**
fe *f.* faith; **acto de fe** *m.* matter of faith **8A**
febrero *m.* February **5A**
fecha *f.* date **5A; fecha de caducidad** *f.* expiration date **15A**
Felicidades *exp.* Congratulations **5A**
felicitación: tarjeta de felicitación *f.* greeting card **5A**
Felicitaciones *exp.* Congratulations! **6A**
feliz *adj.* happy **5A; ¡Feliz estancia!** *exp.* Have a nice stay! **11A; ¡Que tengan un feliz vuelo!** *exp.* Have a good flight! **13A**
femenino/a *adj.* feminine **0**
feo/a *adj.* ugly **3B**
feria *f.* fair (trade) **16B**
ferry: tomar el ferry *v.* to take the ferry **3A**
festivo/a: día festivo *m.* holiday **3A**
fiable *adj.* reliable **17A**
fibra *f.* fiber **10A**
ficción *f.* fiction **14B**
fiebre *f.* fever **10A; fiebre amarilla** *f.* yellow fever **10A**
fiesta *f.* festival **2A; fiesta de quince años** *f.* fifteenth birthday party **18B; fiesta popular** *f.* town festival **6A; salón de fiestas** *m.* reception room **18B**
fijarse en *v.* look at **0**
fijo/a: caminar sin rumbo fijo *v.* to wander aimlessly **17B**
fila: hacer fila *v.* to get in line **13A**
Filadelfia *f.* Philadelphia **1A**
filete: filete de ternera *m.* filet of veal **2B**
filosofía *f.* philosophy **5A; Filosofía y Letras** *f.* Arts **5A**
fin *m.* end; **fin de semana** *m.* weekend **2B; los fines de semana** *loc. adv.* (on) weekends **5B; por fin** *exp.* at last **10A**
final *m.* end, ending **0; a finales del siglo XIX** *loc. adv.* towards the end of the 19th century **8B**
finalidad *f.* purpose **14B**
finalista *m. y f.* finalist **9B**
financiar *v.* to finance **4B**
financiero/a *adj.* financial **11B**
finanzas *f., pl.* finance; **mundo de las finanzas** *m.* world of finance **3A**
finca *f.* farm **8B**
fiordo *m.* fjord **6B**
firma *f.* signing; signature **16A**
firmar *v.* to sign **16A**
Física *f.* Physics **15B**
físico/a *adj.* physical **6A; aspecto físico** *m.* physical appearance **12A; Educación física** *f.* Physical Education **15B; estado físico** *m.* physical condition **10A**
flamenco/a: baile flamenco *m.* flamenco dance **7A**
flan *m.* flan (custard) **2B**
flexibilidad: flexibilidad horaria *f.* schedule flexibility **6A**
flexibilizar *v.* to make flexible **6A**
flexible: jornada flexible *f.* flexible workday **6A**
flor *f.* flower; **ramo de flores** *m.* bunch of lowers **18B**
flora: observación de flora y fauna *f.* wildlife viewing **6B**
floral: arreglo floral *m.* flower arrangement **18B**
florista *m. y f.* florist **18B**
floristería *f.* florist's **9B**
flotante *adj.* floating **9A**
fluorescente *adj.* fluorescent **11A**
folclore *m.* folklore **14A**
folleto *m.* brochure, pamphlet **0**
fomentar *v.* to encourage **14A**
forestal: guarda forestal *m. y f.* forest ranger **14A**
forma *f.* shape; **estar en forma** *v.* to be fit, in (good) shape **7A**
formación *f.* education **6A; formación profesional** *f.* professional training **14A**
formar *v.* to create, to form **0**
formato *m.* format **14B**
Fórmula 1 *f.* Formula 1 **18A**
formulario *m.* form **16A**
foro *m.* forum **1B**
fortalecer *v.* to strengthen **18A**
fortaleza *f.* fortress **11A**
fortuna: hacer fortuna *v.* to make fortune **8B**
foto *f.* photo **0; pie de foto** *m.* caption **5A; tomar fotos** *v.* to take pictures **6B**
fotocopiadora *f.* photocopier **7B**
fotografía *f.* photograph **1B**
fotográfico/a *adj.* photographic **11B**
fotógrafo/a *m./f.* photographer **11B**
fotonovela *f.* photo story **12A**
fragancia *f.* fragrance, perfume **16B**
frambuesa *f.* raspberry **15A**
francés *m.* French **1B**
francés/francesa *adj.* French **1B**
franquista *adj.* Francoist **14B**
frasco *m.* jar **8A**
frase *f.* phrase **0**
frazada *f.* blanket **13A**
frecuencia *f.* frequency **13A; ¿Con qué frecuencia?** *exp.* How often? **3A**
frecuente *adj.* common **2B**
frente *f.* forehead **17B**
fresa *f.* strawberry **15A**
fresco/a *adj.* fresh; **producto fresco** *m.* fresh food **15A**
frigorífico *m.* refrigerator **7B**
frijol *m.* bean **4A**
frío *m.* cold **2A; hacer frío/calor** *v.* to be cold/hot **10A; tener frío/calor** *v.* to be cold/hot **10A**
frito/a *adj.* fried; **patatas fritas** *f.* potato chips **4A; tomate frito** *m.* tomato sauce **15A**
frontera *f.* border **7A**
frontón *m.* jai-alai court **18A**
frustrante *adj.* frustrating **12B**
fruta *f.* fruit **2B**
frutería *f.* fruit shop **9B**
frutero/a *m./f.* fruit seller **9B**
fuego *m.* heat; fire **8A**
fuera *adv.* out **2B; estar fuera de (nuestro) alcance** *exp.* to be beyond (one's) means **15B; fuera de clase** *loc. adv.* outside of class **3A**
fuerte *m.* fort **11A**
fuerza *f.* strength, power **16A; fuerzas armadas** *f.* armed forces **16A**
fumar *v.* to smoke; **dejar de fumar** *v.* to quit smoking **12B**
función *f.* function **4B**
funcional *adj.* functional **4B**
funcionar *v.* to function, to work **7B**
fundador(a) *m./f.* founder **4B**
fútbol *m.* soccer **1A**
futuro *m.* future **8B**
futuro/a *adj.* future **12B**

G

gafas *f.* glasses **3B; gafas de sol** *f.* sunglasses **3B**
gallego *m.* Galician (language) **1B**
galleta *f.* cookie **2B**
gama *f.* range **16B**
gamba *f.* shrimp **2B**
ganador(a) *adj.* winning **14B**
ganar *v.* to earn **11B**
ganar to win **5A; ganar torneos** *v.* to win tournaments **18A**
gandul *m.* pigeon pea **15A**
garaje *m.* garage **4B**
garantía *f.* guarantee; warranty **11A**
garantizar *v.* to guarantee **3B**
garganta *f.* throat **10A**
gaseosa *f.* soda **13A**
gasto *m.* expense **15B**
gastronomía *f.* gastronomy; cuisine **4B**
gastronómico/a *adj.* culinary, gastronomic **2B**
genealógico/a: árbol genealógico *m.* family tree **5B**
generación *f.* generation **10B**
generacional *adj.* generational **15B**

general: en general *loc. adv.* generally **4A**
generalmente *adv.* generally **7B**
genético/a: manipulación genética *f.* genetic modification **7B**
genial *adj.* great **6B**
genio *m. y f.* genius **15B**
gente *f.* people **2A; hablar con la gente** *v.* to talk to people **2A; mi gente** *exp.* my folks **5B**
geográfico/a *adj.* geographic **16B**
Geología *f.* Geology **15B**
gestión *f.* management **13B**
gimnasia *f.* gymnastics **18A; hacer gimnasia** *v.* to exercise **10A**
gimnasio *m.* gym **3A**
gimnasta *m. y f.* gymnast **18A**
girar *v.* to turn **9B**
gitano/a *m./f.* gypsy **16A**
glaciar *m.* glacier **11B**
glucosa *f.* glucose **17A**
gluten *m.* gluten **15A**
gobernante *m./f.* ruler, leader **12B**
gobierno *m.* government **16A**
golf *m.* golf **1A; salsa golf** *f.* thousand-island dressing **17A**
golpe *m.* blow; **golpe de estado** *m.* coup d'état **10B**
goma *f.* rubber; **goma elástica** *f.* rubber band **8A**
gordo *m.* jackpot; first prize **9B**
gordo/a *adj.* fat **9B**
gorro *m.* cap **10A**
gota *f.* drop **2B**
GPS: navegador GPS *m.* GPS **13B**
gracias *f. pl.* thanks; **¡Gracias!** *exp.* Thank You! **0; gracias a** *loc. prep.* thanks to… **5B; Nada más, gracias.** *exp.* Nothing else, thanks. **2B**
gracioso/a *adj.* funny **9A**
graduación *f.* graduation **18B**
graduarse *v.* to graduate **12A**
gráfico/a: diseño gráfico *m.* graphic design **7A**
grande *adj.* big **4B; gran** *adj.* great **5B; ser un(a) gran comunicador(a)** *v.* to be a great communicator **13B**
grasa *f.* fat **15A**
gratarola *adv.* for free **17B**
gratificante *adj.* rewarding **11A**
gratuito/a *adj.* free (of charge) **9B**
gris *adj.* gray **3B**
grulla *f.* crane **16A**
grupo *m.* group; **En parejas/grupos** *loc. adv.* In pairs/groups **0; grupo étnico** *m.* ethnic group **16B; grupo marginado** *m.* marginalized group **12B; grupo musical** *m.* music group/band **14B**
guacamole *m.* guacamole **1A**
guantes *m.* gloves **18A**
guapo/a *adj.* good-looking **9A**
guaraní *m.* Guarani **1B**
guarda: guarda forestal *m. y f.* forest ranger **14A**
guardar *v.* to keep, to put away **8A;** *v.* to save **7B**
guardar (canciones/fotos) *v.* to save/store (songs/photos) **13B**
guardería *f.* day care **5B**
guatemalteco/a *adj.* Guatemalan **2A**
gubernamental: ONG (organización no gubernamental) *f.* NGO (non-governmental organization) **5A**
guerra *f.* war **8B; guerra civil** *f.* civil war **8B; Segunda Guerra Mundial** *f.* World War II **18A**
guerrilla *f.* guerrilla **16A**
guía *f.* guide(book) **1B; el/la guía turístico/a** *m. y f.* (tour) guide **1B; perro/a guía** *m. y f.* guide dog **12B**
guinda *f.* wild cherry **16B**
Guinea Ecuatorial *f.* Equatorial Guinea **0**
guitarra *f.* guitar **8A**
guitarrista *m. y f.* guitarist **7A**
gustar *v.* to like; to please **4A**
gusto *m.* taste, liking **15A; Con gusto.** *exp.* You're welcome. **18B; Mucho gusto.** *exp.* Pleased to meet you. **0**

H

habano: puro habano *m.* Cuban cigar **3B**
haber: ¡No hay problema! *exp.* No problem! **7B**
habilidad *f.* ability **8A**
habilitar *v.* to qualify **13B**
habitación *f.* room **4B; habitación doble** *f.* double room **6B; habitación individual** *f.* single room **6B**
habitante *m. y f.* inhabitant **2A**
hábito *m.* habit **7A**
hablar *v.* to speak **1B; ¿Qué lenguas hablas?** *exp.* What languages do you speak? **1B; hablar con la gente** *v.* to talk to people **2A; hablar por hablar** *v.* to talk for the sake of it **14B; se habla(n)** *v.* is/are spoken **1B**
hablarse: hablarse de tú/usted *v.* to address somebody as **tú/usted 7B**
hace *v.* ago **5A:** hace dos meses *loc. adv.* **two months ago 5A**
hacer *v.* to do, to make **3A; ¿Cuánto tiempo (hace)…?** *exp.* How long have/has? **8B; ¿Qué tiempo hace?** *exp.* What's the weather like? **10A; dedicarse a (hacer) algo** *v.* to do something (for a living) **7A; desde hace** *loc. prep.* for (and until now) **5B; estar haciendo algo** *v.* to be doing something **7A; hace 30 °C de temperatura** *v.* the temperature is 30 °C **10A; hace buen/mal tiempo** *v.* there is good/bad weather **10A; hace dos meses** *loc. adv.* two months ago **5A; hacer algo en casa** *v.* to do something at home **3A; hacer balance de** *v.* to take stock of **12B; hacer caso (a alguien)** *v.* to pay attention (to somebody) **15B; hacer cerámica** *v.* to do pottery **6A; hacer clic** *v.* to click **13B; hacer compañía** *v.* to keep company **7A; hacer consciente** *v.* to make aware **3B; hacer deporte** *v.* to exercise; to work out **3A; hacer escala** *v.* to stop over **13A; hacer falta** *v.* to be necessary **16A; hacer fila** *v.* to get in line **13A; hacer fortuna** *v.* to make fortune **8B; hacer frío/calor** *v.* to be cold/hot **10A; hacer gimnasia** *v.* to exercise **10A; hacer horas extras** *v.* to do overtime **13B; hacer la cama** *v.* to make the bed **3A; hacer la vida más fácil** *exp.* to make life easier **17A; hacer las compras** *v.* to go grocery shopping **3A; hacer las maletas** *v.* to pack **8B; hacer realidad** *v.* to make something happen **8B; hacer sol** *v.* to be sunny **10A; hacer una consulta** *v.* to ask somebody's advice **12A**
hacerse *v.* to become **8B; hacerse vegetariano/a** *v.* to become a vegetarian **7B**
hambre *f.* hunger
hambre: tener hambre *v.* to be hungry; **pasar hambre** *v.* to go hungry **15A**
harina *f.* flour **15A; harina de maíz** *f.* cornmeal **15A**
hasta *prep.* until; **desde/de… hasta/a…** *loc. prep.* from… until/to **8B; Hasta la vista.** *exp.* See you later. **0; Hasta mañana.** *exp.* See you tomorrow. **0**
hebreo *m.* Hebrew **7A**
hecho *m.* event **10B; de hecho** *exp.* in fact **7A**
hecho/a hecho/a y derecho/a *exp.* all grown-up **9A**
hectárea *f.* hectare **6B**
helado *m.* ice cream **2B**
hepatitis *f.* hepatitis **10A**
heredar *v.* to inherit **9B**
herida *f.* injury **10A**
herir *v.* to hurt **15B**
hermano/a *m./f.* brother/sister **5A**
hermanos *m.* siblings **5B**
hermoso/a *adj.* lovely **13A**
hielo *m.* ice **2B; manto de hielo** *m.* ice sheet **11B**
hierba *f.* herb **6A**
higiene *f.* hygiene **15A**
hijo/a *m./f.* son/daughter **5A; tener un hijo** *v.* to have a child **8B**
hilo *m.* thread **14B**
himno *m.* anthem **18B**
hincha *m./f.* supporter, fan; **ser hincha de** *v.* to be a supporter of **17B**
hip-hop *m.* hip-hop **1A**
hípico/a *adj.* equestrian **18A**
hispanohablante *adj.* Spanish-speaking **14A**
historia *f.* history **1B**
historia story **5A**
histórico/a *adj.* historic **6B**
historieta *f.* comic strip **14B**
hogar *m.* home **8A**
hoja *f.* sheet; leaf **0, 8A**
Hola *exp.* Hello./Hi. **0; ¿Hola?** *exp.* Hello? **6B**
hombre *m.* man **3B; ¡Pero, hombre/mujer!** *exp.* Come on! **17A; el hombre/la mujer de mi vida** *exp.* the man/woman of my dreams **12A**
homogéneo/a *adj.* homogeneous **16B**
Honduras Honduras **0**
hondureño/a *adj.* Honduran **14B**
hongo *m.* mushroom **11A**
hora ¿A qué hora…? *exp.* At what time…? **3A; ¿Qué hora es?** *exp.* What time is it? **3A; hacer horas extras** *v.* to do overtime **13B; hora de embarque** *f.* boarding time **13A; hora de llegada** *f.* time of arrival **13A; hora de llegar a casa** *f.* time somebody has to be home **15B; hora de salida** *f.* departure time **13A**

horario/a: flexibilidad horaria *f.* schedule flexibility **6A**
horarios *m.* schedules **3A; horarios de trabajo** *m.* work schedules **3A**
horizonte *m.* horizon **8B**
horno *m.* oven; **al horno** *adj.* baked **13A**
horrible *adj.* horrible **2A**
hortaliza *f.* vegetable **7B**
hospital *m.* hospital **1B**
hospitalario/a *adj.* hospitable **13A**
hospitalidad *f.* hospitality **14A**
hostal *m.* hostel **11A**
hotel *m.* hotel **0; hotel de cuatro estrellas** *m.* four-star hotel **11A**
hotelero/a *m./f.* hotel manager **4B**
hour *f.* hour
hoy *adv.* today **6A; hoy en día** *loc. adv.* nowadays **15B**
hueso *m.* bone **9A**
huevo *m.* egg **2B**
humanidad *f.* humankind **17A; Patrimonio de la Humanidad** *m.* World Heritage (Site) **8A**
humano/a: derechos humanos *m.* human rights **16A; Recursos Humanos (RR.HH.)** *m.* Human Resources (HR) **13B; ser humano** *m.* human being **8A**
humor: de buen/mal humor *loc. adv.* in a good/bad mood **12A**

I

ida: ida y vuelta *exp.* round-trip **6B**
idea *f.* idea **4B**
ideal *adj.* ideal **2A; vivienda ideal** *f.* ideal home **4B**
identidad *f.* identity **18B; DNI (Documento Nacional de Identidad)** *m.* national identity card **3A**
idioma *m.* language **1B**
ídolo *m.* idol **18A**
iglesia *f.* church **2A**
igualdad *f.* equality **8B**
ilimitado/a *adj.* unlimited **8A**
ilusión *f.* hope **12B**
ilusionado/a *adj.* excited **12A; estar ilusionado/a** *v.* to be excited **12A**
ilustre: ciudadano/a ilustre *m./f.* distinguished citizen **17B**
imagen *f.* picture, image **1A**
imaginar *v.* to imagine **5B; imaginarse que…** *v.* imagine that… **0**
impaciente *adj.* impatient **13B**
imparable *adj.* unstoppable **14A**
impedir *v.* to prevent; to stop **12B**
impermeable *m.* raincoat **10A**
importante *adj.* important **2A**
importar *v.* to import **15A; ¿Le importaría...?** *exp.* Would you mind…? **13A**
imprescindible *adj.* indispensable **13B**
impresionado/a *adj.* impressed **18A; estar impresionado/a** *v.* to be impressed **18A**
impresionante *adj.* impressive **5A**
impresora *f.* printer **7B**
imprimir *v.* to print **7B**
impuesto *m.* tax **4B**
inauguración *f.* housewarming party **12A**
inaugurar *v.* to open; to inaugurate **12A**
incansable *adj.* tireless **14B**
incendio *m.* fire **7A**
incentivar *v.* to encourage **14A**
incentivo *m.* encouragement **17A**
incluido/a: IVA incluido *loc. adv.* tax included **2B**
incluir *v.* to include **11A**
inclusión (social) *f.* social inclusion **16A**
incomodísimo/a *adj.* extremely uncomfortable **11B**
inconveniente *m.* drawback **13B**
incorporar *v.* to include **18A**
incorrecto/a *adj.* incorrect **0**
increíble *adj.* incredible **5B; ¡Increíble!** *exp.* Unbelievable! **9B**
independencia *f.* independence **12B**
independiente *adj.* independent **12A**
independizarse *v.* to become independent **15B**
India *f.* India **6A**
indiferencia *f.* indifference **16A**
indígena *adj.; m. y f.* indigenous, native **1B; pueblo indígena** *m.* native people **16A**
indio/a *adj.* Indian **4A**
individual: habitación individual *f.* single room **6B**
industria *f.* industry; **industria de servicios** *f.* service industry **14A; industria petrolera** *f.* oil industry **14A**
industrial *adj.* industrial **8B**
infancia *f.* childhood **9A**
infantil: moda infantil *f.* children's fashion **3B**
infección *f.* infection **10A**
infinito/a *adj.* infinite **18A**
influyente *adj.* influential **7A**
información *f.* information; **información nutricional** *f.* nutritional information **15A**
informado/a *adj.* informed **9B**
informar *v.* to inform, to tell **16A**
informática *f.* computer science **1B**
informático/a: técnico/a informático/a *m./f.* computer technician **1B**
informativo *m.* news (program) **9A**
infraestructura *f.* infrastructure **17A**
infusión *f.* infusion **6A**
ingeniería *f.* engineering **8A**
ingeniero/a *m./f.* engineer **1B; (ingeniero/a) agrónomo/a** *m./f.* agronomist **7A**
inglés *m.* English **1B**
inglés/inglesa *adj.* English **1B**
ingrediente *m.* ingredient **15A**
ingresos *m.* income **11A**
inhóspito/a *adj.* inhospitable **11B**
ininterrumpidamente *adv.* uninterruptedly **18A**
inmediato/a *adj.* immediate **17A**
inmensidad *f.* immensity **11B**
inmigrante *m. y f.* immigrant **5B**
inmigrante *adj., m. y f.* immigrant; **comunidad inmigrante** *f.* immigrant community **8B**
inmobiliaria *f.* real-estate agency **4B**
inmunológico/a: sistema inmunológico *m.* immune system **17A**
innovador(a) *adj.* innovative **13B**
inocencia *f.* innocence **18B**
inolvidable *adj.* unforgettable **5B**
inquietud *f.* interest **9A; despertar la inquietud** *v.* to stir up interest **9A**
inscribir (a alguien en algo) *v.* to enroll **15B**
inscripción: plazo de inscripción *m.* enrollment period **18A**
insomnio *m.* insomnia **14B**
insoportable *adj.* unbearable **2A**
instalación *f.* facility **11A**
instalar *v.* to install **14B**
instituto *m.* high school **15B**
insulina *f.* insulin **17A**
integración *f.* integration **12B**
integrarse *v.* to be integrated; to fit into **12B**
intelectual *adj.* intellectual **17B**
inteligencia: inteligencia emocional *f.* emotional intelligence **13B**
inteligente *adj.* intelligent **12A; teléfono inteligente** *m.* smartphone **13B**
intenso/a *adj.* intense **3A**
interactivo/a *adj.* interactive **17A**
intercambiar *v.* to exchange **8A**
intercambio *m.* exchange **1B; programa de intercambio** *m.* exchange program **14A**
interés *m.* interest **1A**
interesado/a: estar interesado/a en *v.* to be interested in **17A**
interesante *adj.* interesting **1B; ¡Qué interesante!** *exp.* How interesting! **1B**
interesar *v.* to be of interest **7A**
interior: producto interior bruto (PIB) *m.* gross domestic product (GDP) **11A, 14A**
internacional *adj.* international **1B; proyección internacional** *f.* international projection **16A; Relaciones Internacionales** *f.* International Relations **11B; Salón Internacional de la Moda** *m.* International Fashion Fair **3B**
internauta *m. y f.* internet user **6A**
Internet: navegar por Internet *v.* to surf the Internet **6A**
interpretación *f.* performance **5A**
interpretar *v.* to perform **7A**
invadir *v.* to invade **16A**
invasión: invasión territorial *f.* territorial invasion **16A**
inversión *f.* investment **14B**
investigación *f.* research **8B; investigación de mercado** *f.* market research **15A**
investigador(a) *m./f.* investigator **14B;** researcher **17A**
invierno *m.* winter **2A**
invitado/a *m./f.* guest **18B**
invitar *v.* to invite **17B**
inyectarse *v.* to give oneself an injection **17A**
ir *v* to go; **¿Cómo vas?** *exp.* How are you going there? **6B; ir a trabajar** *v.* to go to work **3A; ir en coche** *v.* to go by car **3A; ir en…** *v.* to go by (means of transportation) **6B; ir mal** *v.* to go wrong **7B**
irse *v.* to leave **12B**
isla *f.* island **1A; Islas Baleares** *f.* Balearic Islands **4B**
italiano *m.* Italian **1B**
italiano/a *adj.* Italian **1B**
IVA: IVA incluido *loc. adv.* tax included **2B**
izquierda *f.* left; **a la izquierda** *loc. adv.* (to the) left **9B; a la izquierda de** *loc. adv.* to the left of **3B**

J

jabón *m.* soap **8A**
jamón *m.* ham **0; jamón serrano** *m.* Serrano ham **2B**
janguear (fam.) *v.* to hang out **11A**
japonés *m.* Japanese **1B**
jarabe *m.* syrup **15A**
jardín *m.* yard **4B**
jardinería *f.* gardening **8A**
jazz *m.* jazz **7A**
jeans *m.* jeans **3B**
jefe/a *m./f.* boss **12B; jefe/a de cabina** *m./f.* purser **13A**
jerga *f.* jargon **17B**
jeringa *f.* syringe **17A**
jornada: jornada flexible *f.* flexible workday **6A**
joven (pl. jóvenes) *adj.; m. y f.* young **2A; el/la joven hecho/a y derecho/a** *exp.* all grown-up **9A**
jóvenes *m.* young people **2A**
jubilación *f.* retirement **18B**
jubilado/a *adj.* retired **5B**
judío/a *m./f.* Jew **7A**
juego *m.* game **0; Juegos Panamericanos** *m.* Pan-American Games **18A; Juegos Paralímpicos** *m.* Paralympic Games **12B**
jueves *m.* Thursday **3A**
jugar *v.* to play **7A; jugar a la lotería** *v.* to play the lottery **9B**
jugo *m.* juice; **jugo de naranja** *m.* orange juice **2B**
juguete *m.* toy **8B**
juguetería *f.* toy store **9B**
julio *m.* July **3A**
jungla *f.* jungle **5A**
junio *m.* June **5A**
juntos/as *adj.* together **5A**
jurado *m.* panel of judges **16B**
justicia: justicia social *f.* social justice **16A**
justo/a: comercio justo *m.* fair trade **3B**
juvenil *adj.* for young people **7A**
juventud *f.* youth **9A**

K

karate *m.* karate **3A**
kayak *m.* kayak **6B**
kilo *m.* kilogram **4A; medio kilo** *m.* half a kilogram **4A**
kilómetro *m.* kilometer **2A; estar a... kilómetro(s) de...** *loc. adv.* to be... kilometers from... **2A**
kínder *m.* kindergarten **5B**

L

la *art.* the (*f., sing.*) **2A**
La Habana *f.* Havana **0**
labor *f.* work, task **12B**
laboral *adj.* working **7B; actividad laboral** *f.* job **7B; ambiente laboral** *m.* work atmosphere **13B; asesor(a) laboral** *m./f.* labor consultant **13B; demanda laboral** *f.* labor demand **14A**
lado *m.* side; **al lado de** *m.* next to **3B; lado malo** *m.* bad side **13B; por otro lado** *loc. adv.* on the other hand **13B; por un lado** *loc. adv.* on the one hand **13B**
lago *m.* lake **6B**
lámpara *f.* lamp **3B**
lancha *f.* boat **9A**
lanzador(a) de disco *m./f.* discus thrower **18A**
lanzador(a) de disco *m./f.* discus thrower **18A**
lanzar *v.* to throw **18A; lanzar una campaña** *v.* to launch a campaign **16B**
largo/a *adj.* long **12A; a corto/medio/largo plazo** *loc. adv.* short/medium/long term **17A; a largo plazo** *loc. adv.* in the long term **9A**
las *art.* the (*f., pl.*) **2A**
latino/a: referente latino *m.* Hispanic icon **1A**
lavar *v.* to wash; **lavar los platos** *v.* to do the dishes **5A**
leche *f.* milk **0; crema de leche** *f.* cream **15A; leche descremada en polvo** *f.* powdered skim milk **15A; leche entera** *f.* whole milk, full-cream milk **15A**
lector(a): lector de libros electrónicos *m.* e-reader **13B**
Lectura *f.* Reading **1**
leer *v.* read **0**
legumbres *f.* legumes **2B**
lejos de *prep.* far from **2A**
lema *m.* motto **3B**
lengua *f.* tongue, language; **lengua extranjera** *f.* foreign language **15B; lengua materna** *f.* mother tongue **14A; lengua nativa** *f.* native language **16A; lengua oficial** *f.* official language **14A; Lengua y literatura** *f.* Language and Literature; Reading **15B; ¿Qué lenguas hablas?** *exp.* What languages do you speak? **1B**
lenteja *f.* lentil **2B; lentejas con chorizo** *f.* lentils with chorizo sausage **2B**
lento/a *adj.* slow **7B**
león/leona *m./f.* lion/lioness; **domador(a) de leones** *m./f.* lion tamer **14A**
letra *f.* letter; lyrics **7A**
letras *f.* literature **16A**
levantarse *v.* to get up **7A**
leyenda *f.* legend **18A**
liberar *v.* to free **16A**
libertad *f.* freedom **13B**
libre *adj.* free **16A; al aire libre** *loc. adv.* outdoors **3A; día libre** *m.* day off **14A; tiempo libre** *m.* free time **5B**
librería *f.* bookstore **3B**
libro *m.* book **0; lector de libros electrónicos** *m.* e-reader **13B; libro de quejas** *m.* complaint form **11A**
licencia *f.* license **2A; licencia por maternidad** *f.* maternity leave **7B**
líder *m. y f.* leader; **líderes mundiales** *m. y f.* world leader **16A; ser líder de audiencia** *v.* to be the highest rated **14B**
limitar *v.* to limit **6A**
limpiar *v.* to clean **3A**
limusina *f.* limousine **18B**
lindo/a *adj.* lovely; pretty; nice **11B**
línea *f.* line **4A; en línea** *loc. adv.* online **9B**
lípido *m.* lipid **15A**
liso/a *adj.* straight **12A**
lista *f.* list **0; lista de compras** *f.* shopping list **4A**
literario/a: crítico/a literario/a *m./f.* literary critic **10B**
literatura *f.* literature **1B; Lengua y literatura** *f.* Language and Literature; Reading **15B**
llamada *f.* call **3A; llamada de teléfono** *f.* telephone call **3A**
llamar *v.* to call; **llamar la atención** *v.* to catch one's attention **14A**
llamar(se) *v.* to be named **0; (Él/Ella) se llama...** *exp.* His/Her name is... **0; ¿Cómo se llama?** *exp.* What is your name? **0; ¿Cómo te llamas?** *exp.* What is your name? **0; Yo me llamo...** *exp.* My name is... **0**
llegada *f.* arrival **11A; hora de llegada** *f.* time of arrival **13A; sala de llegada** *f.* arrival lounge **13A**
llegar *v.* to arrive **3A; hora de llegar a casa** *f.* time somebody has to be home **15B; llegar a casa** *v.* to arrive home **3A**
llevar *v.* to take **5B;** *v.* to wear **3B; llevar a cabo** *v.* to carry out **18A; llevar a los niños al colegio** *v.* to take the kids to school **3A; llevar un negocio** *v.* to run a business **9B; llevar una vida...** *v.* to lead a... life **10A; llevarse bien/mal** *v.* to get along/not to get along **12A**
llorar *v.* to cry **14B**
llover *v.* to rain **10A**
lluvia *f.* rain **6A**
lo *art.;* **lo malo/bueno** *m.* the bad/good thing **12B; lo más... posible** *m.* as... as possible **17A; lo mejor** *m.* the best (thing) **4B; Lo siento.** *exp.* I'm sorry. **3B**
localizable: estar localizable *v.* to be reachable **13B**
localizar *v.* to find, to locate **0**
localizar to get hold of, to locate **13B**
loco/a *adj.* crazy **7B**
locutor(a) *m./f.* announcer **16A**
locutorio *m.* call center; Internet café **8B**
logo *m.* logo **16B**
lograr *v.* to achieve **8A**
lograr to manage **5B**
Londres London **1A**
los *art.* the (*m. pl.*) **2A; los/las dos** *pron.* both **6B**
Los Ángeles *m.* Los Angeles **1A**
lotería *f.* lottery; **agencia de lotería** *f.* lottery ticket booth **9B; comprar (billetes de) lotería** *v.* to buy lottery tickets **9B; jugar a la lotería** *v.* to play the lottery **9B; vendedor(a) de lotería** *m./f.* lottery ticket seller **9B**
luchador(a) *adj.; m./f.* fighter **5A**
luego *adv.* later, then **0; Hasta luego.** *exp.* See you later. **0**
lugar *m.* place **2A; lugar clave** *m.* landmark **4A; lugar de culto** *m.* place of worship **8A; lugar de nacimiento** *m.* birthplace **11B; tener lugar** *v.* to be held **16B**
lujoso/a *adj.* luxurious **11A**
lunes *m.* Monday **3A**
lunfardo *m.* Buenos Aires slang **17B**
luz *f.* light; **luz apagada** *f.* lights off **6A**

M

maceta *f.* flowerpot **8A**
madera *f.* wood **8A**
madre *f.* mother; **Día de la Madre** *m.* Mother's Day **18B; madre trabajadora** *f.* working mother **7B**
madrugar *v.* to get up early **7A**
maduro/a *adj.* mature **17B**
maestro/a *m./f.* master; teacher **6A; maestro/a de ceremonias** *m./f.* master of ceremonies **18B**
magacín *m.* news and talk show **9A**
mágico/a *adj.* magic/a **18B**
maíz *m.* corn **2B; harina de maíz** *f.* cornmeal **15A**
mal *adv.* badly; **ir mal** *v.* to go wrong **7B; llevarse bien/mal** *v.* to get along/not to get along **12A; menos mal** *exp.* thank goodness **10A**
maldición *f.* malediction **16A**
malentendido *m.* misunderstanding **14A**
maleta *f.* suitcase **8B; hacer las maletas** *v.* to pack **8B**
mallorca *f.* Puerto-Rican pastry **1A**
malo/a *adj.* bad; **de buen/mal humor** *loc. adv.* in a good/bad mood **12A; hace buen/mal tiempo** *exp.* there is good/bad weather **10A; lado malo** *m.* bad side **13B; lo malo/bueno** *m.* the bad/good thing **12B; ser malo/a (en algo)** *exp.* to be bad (at something) **17B**
mamá (*fam.*) *f.* mom **5B**
manazas *m. y f.* clumsy person **8A**
mandar *v.* to send **7B**
manejar *v.* to manage **13B**
manejar *v.* to drive **17B**
manera *f.* way **5A**
manifiesto *m.* manifesto **12B**
manipulación: manipulación genética *f.* genetic modification **7B**
manitas *m. y f.* handyman/handywoman **8A**
mano *f.* hand **8A; estar en manos de alguien** *v.* to be under someone's control **17A; manos a la obra** *exp.* (Let's) Get to work! **8A**
mantener *v.* to keep **5B**
mantenimiento *m.* maintenance **4B**
mantequilla *f.* butter **2B**
manto: manto de hielo *m.* ice sheet **11B**
manzana *f.* apple **4A**
manzanilla *f.* chamomile tea **10A**
mañana *adv.* tomorrow **0; de la mañana** *loc. adv.* a.m.; in the morning **3A; Hasta mañana.** *exp.* See you tomorrow. **0; pasado mañana** *loc. adv.* the day after tomorrow **11B; por la mañana** *loc. adv.* in the morning **3A**
mapa *m.* map **4B**
maquillarse *v.* to put makeup on **7A**
mar *m.* sea; **mar Caribe** *m.* Caribbean Sea **4B**
maratón *m.* marathon **18A; correr un maratón** *v.* to run a marathon **18A**
maravilla *f.* wonder; **de maravilla** *loc. adv.* wonderfully **17B**
maravilloso/a *adj.* wonderful **5A**
marca *f.* brand **3B**
marcar *v.* to check off, to mark **0**
marcha *f.* march **16A**
marcha: poner en marcha *exp.* to set in motion **16A**
marcharse *v.* to leave, to go away **18B**
marco *m.* picture frame **3B**
margarita *f.* daisy **18B**
marginación *f.* marginalization **12B**
marginado/a: grupo marginado *m.* marginalized group **12B**
marido *m.* husband **5B**
marino/a: biólogo/a marino/a *m./f.* marine biologist **11B**
marketing: analista de marketing *m. y f.* marketing analyst **13B**
marrón *adj.* brown **3B**
marroquí *adj.* Moroccan **4A**
Marte *m.* Mars **17A**
martes *m.* Tuesday **3A**
marzo *m.* March **5A**
más *adj., adv., pron.* more; **¿Algo más?** *exp.* Anything else? **2B; el/la más/menos** *m./f.* the most/least **9A; hacer la vida más fácil** *exp.* to make life easier **17A; lo más... posible** *m.* as... as possible **17A; más conocido/a** *adj.* best-known **4A; más que** *adj.* more than **3A; más tarde** *loc. adv.* later **17B; Nada más, gracias.** *exp.* Nothing else, thanks. **2B**
masculino/a *adj.* masculine **0**
masía (Cataluña) *f.* country house **7B**
matar *v.* to kill **18B**
mate *m.* mate **6A**
mate: yerba mate *f.* mate (infusion) **3B**
Matemáticas *f.* Math **15B**
materia: materia prima *f.* raw material **15A**
material *m.* material **8A**
maternidad *f.* maternity; **baja por maternidad** *f.* maternity leave **7B; licencia por maternidad** *f.* maternity leave **7B**
materno/a: lengua materna *f.* mother tongue **14A**
matrimonio *m.* marriage **5B;** married couple **11B; cama de matrimonio** *f.* double bed **4B**
mayo *m.* May **2A**
mayor *adj.* older **9A; las personas mayores** *f. pl.* the elderly **6A**
mayoría *f.* most, majorityy **5B**
me *pron.* me, to me; **¡No me digas!** *exp.* You don't say! **9B; Me da/pone...** *exp.* I'd like... **4A; Me toca a mí.** *exp.* It's my turn. **4A; Yo me llamo...** *exp.* My name is... **0**
mecánica *f.* mechanics **8A**
mecánico/a *adj.; m./f.* mechanic **7B; taller (mecánico)** *m.* repair shop **7B**
medalla *f.* medal **12B**
mediados: a mediados de los 60 *loc. adv.* in the mid sixties **14B**
medicación *f.* medication **10A**
medicamento *m.* medicine **10A**
medicina *f.* medicine **10A**
médico/a *m./f.* doctor **1B; divulgación médica** *f.* popularization of medicine **17A; médico/a de familia** *m./f.* family doctor **10A**
medida *f.* measure, step **16A**
medio *m.* means; **medio ambiente** *m.* environment **4B; medio de transporte** *m.* means of transportation **4A; medio de vida** *m.* way of life **11B; medios** *m.* means **15A; medios de comunicación** *m.* media **9A; por medio de** *loc. prep.* by means of **14B**
medio/a *adj.* mean, average; half; **a corto/medio/largo plazo** *loc. adv.* short/medium/long term **17A; clase media** *f.* middle class **14B; media docena** *f.* half a dozen **4A; medio kilo** *m.* half a kilogram **4A**
medir *v.* to measure **17A**
meditación *f.* meditation **6A**
mejor *adv.* better **6A; a lo mejor** *loc. adv.* maybe **17A; el/la mejor/peor** *m./f.* the best/worst **9A; lo mejor** *m.* the best (thing) **4B**
mejorar *v.* to improve **6A**
melocotón *m.* peach **15A**
memoria *f.* memory **10B; aprender de memoria** *f.* to memorize **14B**
memorias *f.* memoirs; memories **5B**
mencionar *v.* mention **0**
menos *adv.* less **6A; echar de menos** *v.* to miss **14B; el/la más/menos** *m./f.* the most/least **9A; menos mal** *exp.* thank goodness **10A; menos que** *adj.* less than **3A**
mensajería *f.* messenger company **7B**
mental *adj.* mental **12B**
mente *f.* mind **6A**
menú: menú del día *m.* fixed-price menu **2B**
mercado *m.* market **0; investigación de mercado** *f.* market research **15A**
merengue *m.* merengue **17B**
merienda *f.* (afternoon) snack **16B**
mermelada *f.* jam, marmalade **2B**
mes *m.* month; **dos veces al mes** *loc. adv.* twice a month **6A; el mes pasado** *loc. adv.* last month **5A; el próximo mes** *loc. adv.* next month **5B; este mes** *loc. adv.* this month **6A; hace dos meses** *loc. adv.* two months ago **5A**
mesa *f.* table **3B**
mesero/a *m./f.* waiter/waitress **13A**
mestizo/a *m./f.* person of mixed race **16A**
meta *f.* goal **18A**
metabolismo *m.* metabolism **17A**
metal *m.* metal **8A**
meter *v.* to put **8A**
metódico/a *adj.* methodical **13B**
método: método científico *m.* scientific method **17A**
metro *m.* meter; subway **0; metros cuadrados (m2)** *m.* square meters **4B**
mexicano/a *adj.* Mexican **2B**
México *m.* Mexico **0; México, D.F.** *m.* Mexico City **2A**
mezcla *f.* mix **14A**
mi *adj.* my **2A**
miedo *m.* fear **10B**
miel *f.* honey **7B**
miembro *m.* member **5A**
miércoles *m.* Wednesday **3A**
migración *f.* migration **8B**
migrante: población migrante *m.* migrant population **8B**
milenio *m.* millennium **10B**
miles *m.* thousands **6B**
millón *m.* million **8B**
minipiso *m.* tiny apartment **11B**

ministerio *m.* ministry, department **16A**
ministro/a *m./f.* minister **16A**
minoría *f.* minority **14A**
minuto *m.* minute **1A; último minuto** *m.* last minute **12B**
mirar *v.* to look at; to watch **6A; Mira...** *v.* Look... **8A**
mirarse *v.* to look at each other **17B**
misa *f.* Mass **5A**
misil *m.* missile **17A**
misión *f.* mission **10A**
mismo/a *adj.* same; **al mismo tiempo** *loc. adv.* at the same time **7A; estar seguro/a de sí mismo/a** *v.* to be self-confident **18A; tiempo para uno/a mismo/a** *m.* time for oneself **3A**
misticismo *m.* mysticism **16B**
mochila *f.* backpack **9A**
moda *f.* fashion **3B; diseñador(a) (de moda)** *m./f.* (fashion) designer **11B; moda infantil** *f.* children's fashion **3B; Salón Internacional de la Moda** *m.* International Fashion Fair **3B**
modelo *m. y f.* (fashion) model **3B;** *m.* model **0**
moderado/a *adj.* moderate **6B**
modernidad *f.* modernity **17A**
modernización *f.* modernization **17A**
moderno/a *adj.* modern **2A**
mojito *m.* traditional Cuban cocktail **13A**
molestar *v.* to bother, to annoy **15B**
momento *m.* moment **5A**
moneda *f.* coin **0**
moneda *f.* currency **10B; ser moneda corriente** *exp.* to be common **13B**
mono/a *m./f.* monkey; **mono/a araña** *m./f.* spider monkey **16B**
montaña *f.* mountain **3A**
montañismo *m.* mountain climbing **18A**
montañista *m. y f.* mountain climber **18A**
montar *v.* to assemble **8A**
montar to ride **9A**
monumento *m.* monument **1A**
morado/a *adj.* purple **16B**
morbo *m.* morbid interest **14B**
moreno/a *adj.* dark-haired, brunet(te) **12A**
morir *v.* to die **10B**
mosquito *m.* mosquito **10A**
mostrador: mostrador de facturación *m.* check-in desk **13A**
mostrar *v.* show **0; mostrar afecto** *v.* to show affection **18B**
motivado/a: estar motivado/a *v.* to be motivated **13B**
motivo: con motivo de *exp.* on the occasion of **12B**
móvil *adj.* mobile **17A**
movilidad *f.* mobility **13B**
movilización: movilización social *f.* social demonstration **16A**
movimiento: un mundo en movimiento *exp.* a world in motion **14A**
MP3: reproductor de MP3 *m.* MP3 player **13B**
mucho *adv.* a lot **2A, 6A**
mucho/a *adj.; pron.* a lot, much **2A**
mudanza *f.* move **14A**
mudarse *v.* to move (from home) **7B**
mueble *m.* piece of furniture **8A**
muela *f.* molar **10A**
muerte *f.* death **10B**
mujer *f.* woman; wife **3A; ¡Pero, hombre/mujer!** *exp.* Come on! **17A; el hombre/la mujer de mi vida** *exp.* the man/woman of my dreams **12A; mujer empresaria** *f.* business woman **5A**
multimedia (invar.) *adj.* multimedia **9B**
multinacional *f.* multinational (firm) **16A**
mundial *adj.* global; worldwide **7B; líderes mundiales** *m. y f.* world leader **16A; Patrimonio Mundial** *m.* World Heritage **11B; Segunda Guerra Mundial** *f.* World War II **18A**
mundo *m.* world **4A; dar la vuelta al mundo** *v.* to go around the world **18A; mundo de las finanzas** *m.* world of finance **3A; un mundo en movimiento** *exp.* a world in motion **14A**
muñeco *m.* figure **18B**
muro *m.* wall; **Muro de Berlín** *m.* Berlin Wall **10B**
museo *m.* museum **0**
música *f.* music **1A; clase de música** *m.* music class **3A**
musical *adj.* musical; **grupo musical** *m.* music group **14B**
músico/a *m./f.* musician **3A**
muy *adv.* very **2A; muy bien** *adv.* very well **1A**

N

nacer *v.* to be born **5A**
nacimiento *m.* birth **5A; lugar de nacimiento** *m.* birthplace **11B**
nacional *adj.* domestic **13A;** national **12B; DNI (Documento Nacional de Identidad)** *m.* national identity card **3A; parador nacional** *m.* state-run hotel in Spanish historic building **6B**
nacionalidad *f.* nationality **1B**
nada *adv.* at all **8A; Nada más, gracias.** *exp.* Nothing else, thanks. **2B; No pasa nada.** *exp.* Everything is OK. **13B**
nadador(a) *m./f.* swimmer **18A; el/la nadador(a) de sincronizada** *m./f.* synchronized swimmer **18A**
nadar *v.* to swim **5A**
nadie *pron.* nobody; anybody **8A**
nado *m.* swimming; **nado sincronizado** *m.* synchronized swimming **18A**
náhuatl *m.* Nahuatl **12A**
naranja *f.* orange **2B; jugo de naranja** *m.* orange juice **2B; zumo de naranja** *m.* orange juice **2B**
nariz *f.* nose **9A**
narrativa *f.* fiction **10B**
nasal *adj.* nasal **10B**
natación *f.* swimming **10A**
nativo/a *adj.* native; **lengua nativa** *f.* native language **16A**
natural *adj.* fresh **2B; alimento natural** *m.* natural food **15A; recurso natural** *m.* natural resource **14A**
naturaleza *f.* nature **4B**
navegador: navegador GPS *m.* GPS **13B**
navegar *v.* to sail; **navegar por Internet** *v.* to surf the Internet **6A**
Navidad *f.* Christmas **5B**
necesidad *f.* need **13B**
negativo/a *adj.* negative **2B**
negocio *m.* business; store **7B; abrir un negocio** *v.* to open a business **15A; ampliar un negocio** *v.* to expand a business **15A; viaje de negocios** *m.* business trip **3A**
negro/a *adj.* black **3B; oro negro** *m.* black gold **14A**
nervioso/a *adj.* nervous **10A**
nevar *v.* to snow **10A**
Nicaragua *f.* Nicaragua **0**
nieto/a *m./f.* grandson/granddaughter **5B**
nietos *m.* grandchildren **5B**
ningún *adj.* no **9A**
ninguno/a *adj.* no, none **9A**
niño/a *m./f.* boy/girl **3A; desde niño(s)/a(s)** *loc. adv.* since childhood **8B; llevar a los niños al colegio** *v.* to take the kids to school **3A**
nítrico: óxido nítrico *m.* nitric oxide **17A**
nivel *m.* level **16A**
no *adv.* no, not **1A; ¡No hay problema!** *exp.* No problem! **7B; ¡No me digas!** *exp.* You don't say! **9B; ¿Por qué no...?** *exp.* Why don't you...? **6A; amor (no) correspondido** *m.* (un)requited love **12A; Creo que sí/no.** *exp.* I think so/not. **7B; No pasa nada.** *exp.* Everything is OK. **13B; no puede olvidarse** *v.* cannot be forgotten **10B; No se pierda...** *exp.* Don't miss... **11B; No se puede...** *exp.* You/One can't... **7B; No te preocupes.** *exp.* Don't worry. **13B; todavía no** *loc. adv.* not yet **6A; no soportar** *v.* not to be able to stand **15B; no violencia** *f.* non-violence **16A**
n.º (número) *m.* number **2A**
Nobel: Premio Nobel *m.* Nobel Prize, Nobel laureate **10B**
noche *f.* night; **Buenas noches.** *exp.* Good evening/night. **0; de la noche** *loc. adv.* p.m.; in the evening/night **3A; pasar la noche** *v.* to spend the night **6B; por la noche** *loc. adv.* in the evening; at night **3A**
nocturno/a: vigilante nocturno/a *m./f.* night security guard **3A**
nomás *adv.* only **17B**
nombrar *v.* name **0**
nombre *m.* name **1B; nombre de pila** *m.* first name **12A**
norma *f.* rule **15B**
normalmente *adv.* normally **2B**
norte *m.* north **2A**
nos *pron.* us; **¡Nos vemos!** *exp.* See you! **0**
nosotros/as *pron.* we **1B**
nostalgia *f.* homesickness, nostalgia **10B**
nota *f.* grade **15B;** note **4A; nota de prensa** *f.* press release **10B**
noticia *f.* news **4A**
novedad *f.* innovation **17A**
noviembre *m.* November **5A**
novio/a *m./f.* boyfriend/girlfriend **5A;** groom/bride **5A; novios** *m.* sweethearts **6B; viaje de novios** *m.* honeymoon **13A**
nublado/a *adj.* cloudy **10A**
nuclear: arma nuclear *f.* nuclear weapon **16A**
Nueva Orleans *f.* New Orleans **1A**
Nueva York *f.* New York **1A**
nuevo/a: Año Nuevo *m.* New Year **18B**

nuez *f.* nut **18B**
número *m.* issue **15A; number 0; ¿Cuál es tu número de teléfono?** *exp.* What is your phone number? **1B; nº** *m.* number **2A**
nunca *adv.* never **6A; casi nunca** *loc. adv.* hardly ever **6A**
nutricional: información nutricional *f.* nutritional information **15A**
nutriente *m.* nutrient **15A**
nutritivo/a *adj.* nutritious **15A**

O

o *conj.* or; **o bien** *exp.* or otherwise **12A; o sea** *exp.* that is **8B**
objetivo *m.* goal; objective **3B**
objeto *m.* object **3B; objeto curioso** *m.* curiosity; nicknack **4A; objetos domésticos** *m.* furnishings **4B**
obligación *f.* obligation **5B**
obra *f.* work (of art), piece; **manos a la obra** *exp.* (Let's) Get to work! **8A; obra de arte** *f.* work of art **8A**
obras *f. pl.* construction **2A; estar en obras** *v.* to be under construction **11A**
obrero/a *m./f.* worker **8B**
observación *f.* remark **13A; observación de flora y fauna** *f.* wildlife viewing **6B**
observar *v.* to observe **0**
obtener *v.* to get, to obtain **0**
obvio *adj.* obvious **17A**
océano *m.* ocean **18A**
ocio *m.* leisure **6A**
ocultar *v.* to hide **16B**
ocupado/a *adj.* busy **2A**
ocupar *v.* to spend; to take up **5B; ocupar espacio** *v.* to take up space **13B**
ocuparse: ocuparse de los detalles *v.* to take care of the details **18B**
ocurrirse *v.* to think of **18B**
oeste *m.* west **2A**
oficial *adj.* official; **lengua oficial** *f.* official language **14A**
oficina *f.* office **6A; oficina de prensa** *f.* press office **16A**
oficio *m.* trade **14A**
ofrecer *v.* to offer **4B**
oído *m.* ear; hearing **10A; ser todo/a oidos** *exp.* to be all ears **9A**
oír: Siento oír eso. *exp.* I'm sorry to hear that. **13B**
Ojalá. *exp.* I/We wish. **15A**
ojo *m.* eye **9A; ¡Ojo!** *exp.* Be careful! **0**
ola *f.* wave **16B**
oliva: aceite de oliva virgen extra *m.* extra virgin olive oil **15A; aceite de oliva** *m.* olive oil **2B**
olvidar *v.* to forget **5B; no puede olvidarse** *exp.* cannot be forgotten **10B**
ómnibus *m.* bus **13A**
ONCE *f.* Spanish National Organization of the Blind **12B**
ONG (organización no gubernamental) *f.* NGO (non-governmental organization) **5A**
opinión *f.* opinion; **En mi opinión, ...** *exp.* In my opinion, ... **10B**
oponerse *v.* to object **15B**
oportunidad *f.* opportunity **8B**
optar *v.* to choose **18B**
optimismo *m.* optimism **10B**
optimista *adj.* optimistic **12A**
oración *f.* sentence **0**
ordenado/a *adj.* orderly, neat **13B**
ordenador *m.* computer **7B**
ordenar *v.* put in order **0**
orgánico/a *adj.* organic **7B**
organismo *m.* organism **17A**
organización *f.* organization **3B; ONG (organización no gubernamental)** *f.* NGO (non-governmental organization) **5A**
organizado/a: viaje organizado *m.* package tour **13A**
organizar *v.* to organize **6A**
orgulloso/a *adj.* proud **2A**
orientador(a): orientador(a) profesional *m./f.* career counselor **13B**
oriental *adj.* oriental **6A**
origen *m.* origin **1A, 13A**
original *adj.* original **3B**
orilla *f.* shore **6B**
oriundo/a *adj.* native **16B**
oro *m.* gold **12B; oro negro** *m.* black gold **14A**
orquídea *f.* orchid **11A**
oscuro/a *adj.* dark **16B**
otoño *m.* fall **10A**
otro/a *adj.* other; **de un día para el otro** *loc. adv.* overnight **16A; otra vez** *loc. adv.* again **0; por otro lado/por otra parte** *loc. adv.* on the other hand **13B**
Ottawa *f.* Ottawa **1A**
óxido *m.* oxide **17A; óxido nítrico** *m.* nitric oxide **17A**
oxígeno *m.* oxygen **18A**
oyente *m. y f.* listener **14B**
ozono: capa de ozono *f.* ozone layer **17A**

P

paciencia *f.* patience **15A**
paciente *m. y f.* patient **10A**
pacífico/a *adj.* peaceful **16A**
pacifista *m. y f.* pacifist **16A**
padres *m.* parents **5B**
paella *f.* paella **1A**
página *f.* page **0; página web** *f.* Web page **14B**
pago *m.* payment **7B**
país *m.* country **0; país receptor** *m.* host country **8B; País Vasco** *m.* Basque Country **1B**
paisaje *m.* landscape **6B**
palabra *f.* word **0**
paliza *f.* thrashing **18A**
paludismo *m.* malaria **10A**
pan *m.* bread **2B**
panadería *f.* bakery **8B**
Panamá *m.* Panama **0**
panameño/a *adj.* Panamanian **2A**
panamericano/a: Juegos Panamericanos *m.* Pan-American Games **18A**
panorámico/a *adj.* panoramic **18B**
pantalla *f.* screen **13A**
pantalones *m.* pants **3B**
pañuelo *m.* scarf; handkerchief **3B**
papa *f.* potato **2B**
papá (fam.) *m.* dad **5B**
papel *m.* paper; **papel de** *m.* role of **5B**
papelería *f.* stationery store **9B**
paquete *m.* package **4A**
paquistaní *adj.* Pakistani **4A**
par *m.* pair **5A**
para *prep.* for; **¿Para qué sirve?** *exp.* What is it used for? **4B; apto/a para** *adj.* appropriate/safe for **15A; de un día para el otro** *loc. adv.* overnight **16A; servir para...** *v.* to be good for... **4B; tiempo para uno/a mismo/a** *m.* time for oneself **3A**
parador: parador nacional *m.* state-run hotel in Spanish historic building **6B; Parador de Turismo de España** *m.* state-run hotel in Spanish historic building **11A**
paraguas *m.* umbrella **3B**
Paraguay *m.* Paraguay **0**
paraíso *m.* paradise **4B**
paralímpico/a: Juegos Paralímpicos *m.* Paralympic Games **12B**
parapente *m.* paragliding **18A**
parar *v.* to stop **3A**
parásito *m.* parasite **8A**
parecer *v.* to seem **5B; al parecer** *loc. adv.* apparently **8B; parecer raro** *v.* to think something is odd **15B**
parecerse: parecerse a alguien *v.* to look like somebody **12A**
parecido *m.* resemblance **12A**
pareja *f.* couple; partner **5B; En parejas/grupos** *loc. adv.* In pairs/groups **0**
parque *m.* park **2A**
párrafo *m.* paragraph **0**
parte: por otra parte *loc. adv.* on the other hand **13B**
participar en *v.* to participate in **3A**
particular *adj.* particular; private; **casa particular** *f.* private home **13A; clase particular** *f.* private lesson **17B**
partido *m.* match **18A; partido político** *m.* political party **16A**
partir: a partir de *loc. prep.* from, starting **12B**
pasado/a *adj.* last **5A; el mes pasado** *loc. adv.* last month **5A; la semana pasada** *loc. adv.* last week **5A; pasado mañana** *loc. adv.* the day after tomorrow **11B**
pasaje *m.* ticket; **pasaje de avión** *m.* plane ticket **6B**
pasajero/a *m./f.* passenger; **señores pasajeros** *exp.* ladies and gentlemen, passengers **13A**
pasante *m. y f.* intern **13B**
pasantía *f.* internship; **pasantía de verano** *f.* summer internship **13B**
pasaporte *m.* passport; **control de pasaportes** *m.* passport control; immigration **13A**
pasar *v.* to happen **8B; ¿Qué pasa?** *exp.* What's up? **0; No pasa nada.** *exp.* Everything is OK. **13B; pasar hambre** *v.* to go hungry **15A; pasar la noche** *v.* to spend the night **6B; pasar la serie de televisión** *v.* to broadcast the television series **14B; pasar las vacaciones** *v.* to spend one's vacation **4B; pasar por** *v.* to go via **6B; pasarlo/a bien** *v.* to have a good time **17B**

pasatiempo *m.* pastime **7A**
pasear *v.* to go for a walk **3A**
paseo *m.* path, walkway **2A; dar un paseo** *v.* to take a walk **6A; paseo a caballo** *m.* horseback ride **6B**
pasivo/a *adj.* passive **6A**
paso *m.* step; **de paso** *loc. adv.* in the process **14B; paso de baile** *m.* step **17B**
pasodoble *m.* typical Spanish march-like dance **17B**
pasta *f.* pasta **2B**
pastel *m.* cake **18B**
pata *f.* paw **5A**
Patagonia *f.* Patagonia **6B**
patata *f.* potato **2B; patatas fritas** *f.* potato chips **4A**
patentar *v.* to patent **17A**
pato/a *m./f.* duck **18A**
patrimonio *m.* heritage; **Patrimonio de la Humanidad** *m.* World Heritage (Site) **8A; Patrimonio Mundial** *m.* World Heritage **11B**
patrono/a *m./f.* patron saint **16B**
paz *f.* peace **2A; embajador(a) de la paz** *m./f.* ambassador for peace **16A; estar en paz** *v.* to be at peace **10B**
pedido *m.* order; request **7B**
pedir *v.* to ask for **12B; pedir ayuda** *v.* to ask for help **5B; pedir permiso** *v.* to ask permission **12B; pedir un crédito** *v.* to ask for a loan **5B**
peine *m.* comb **8A**
Pekín *m.* Beijing **1B**
pelar *v.* to peel **8A**
película *f.* movie **1A; película en DVD** *f.* movie on DVD **4B; ver películas** *v.* to watch movies **3A**
peligroso/a *adj.* dangerous **10A**
pelirrojo/a *adj.* red-haired **12A**
pelo *m.* hair **9A**
pelota *f.* ball **18A**
peludo/a *adj.* furry **9A**
peluquería *f.* hair salon **8B**
pena *f.* sadness; shame; **dar pena** *v.* to upset **18B; valer la pena** *v.* to be worth it **11B**
pendiente *f.* slope **18A; estar pendiente de** *v.* to be waiting for, to be attentive **17B**
pensar (de/en) *v.* to think (of/about) **4A**
pepino *m.* cucumber **8A**
pequeñísimo/a *adj.* tiny **11B**
pequeño/a *adj.* small **4B; desde pequeño/a** *loc. adv.* since childhood **5B**
per cápita: renta per cápita *f.* per capita income **14A**
perder *v.* to lose **7B; perder un vuelo** *v.* to miss a flight **13A**
perderse *v.* to miss **16B**
perderse: No se pierda… *v.* Don't miss… **11B**
perdonar: Perdona, … *exp.* Excuse me, … **5A; perdone (form.)** *exp.* excuse me **9B**
peregrino/a *m./f.* pilgrim **11A**
perfeccionamiento *m.* improvement **14A**
perfectamente: Te entiendo perfectamente. *exp.* I understand you perfectly. **13B**
perfecto/a *adj.* perfect **2A**
perfil *m.* profile **14A**
perfume *m.* perfume **3B**
perfumería *f.* perfume/cosmetics shop **3B**
periferia *f.* suburbs **2A**
periódico *m.* newspaper **7A**
periodista *m. y f.* journalist, reporter **10B**
permiso *m.* permission; **pedir permiso** *v.* to ask permission **12B**
permitir *v.* to allow **6B**
pero *conj.* but **2A; ¡Pero, hombre/mujer!** *exp.* Come on! **17A**
perro/a *m./f.* dog; **perro/a guía** *m./f.* guide dog **12B**
persona *f.* person **1B; las personas mayores** *f.* the elderly **6A; una persona de 80 años** *f.* an 80-year-old person **3A**
personaje *m.* character, important figure **1A**
personal *adj.* personal **3B; satisfacción personal** *f.* personal satisfaction **13B**
personal *m.* staff **11A**
personalizado/a *adj.* personalized **11A**
perspectiva *f.* prospect **13B**
pertenecer *v.* to belong **3B**
Perú *m.* Peru **0**
pesar: a pesar de todo *loc. adv.* despite it all **13B**
pesar: a pesar de (que) *conj.* despite **6B**
pescado *m.* fish **2B; sopa de pescado** *f.* fish soup **2B**
pescador(a) *m./f.* fisherman/fisherwoman **14A**
pesimista *adj.* pessimistic **12A**
pésimo/a *adj.* dreadful **11A**
pesticida *m.* pesticide **15A**
petición *f.* request **12B**
petrificado/a *adj.* petrified **11B**
petróleo *m.* oil **14A; barril de petróleo** *m.* oil barrel **14A**
petrolero/a *adj.* oil; **industria petrolera** *f.* oil industry **14A; plataforma petrolera** *f.* oil rig **14A**
piano *m.* piano **8A; piano de cola** *m.* grand piano **10B**
PIB (producto interior bruto) *m.* GDP (Gross Domestic Product) **11A, 14A**
pibe/a *m./f.* young boy/girl **17B**
picante *adj.* spicy **2B; picantes** *m.* hot spices **15A**
picazón *f.* itch **10A**
pie *m.* foot **10A; pie de foto** *m.* caption **5A**
piel *f.* skin **10A**
pierna *f.* leg **10A**
pila: nombre de pila *m.* first name **12A**
piloto *m. y f.* pilot **18A**
pimiento *m.* (bell) pepper **2B**
pinchazo *m.* prick **17A**
pintar *v.* to paint **6A**
pintor(a) *m./f.* painter **12B**
pintura *f.* painting **3A**
piña *f.* pineapple **15A**
pirámide *f.* pyramid **2A**
piscina *f.* swimming pool **3A**
piso *m.* floor, story **8A**
placer *m.* pleasure **5B**
plan: plan social *m.* social plan **16A**
planificar *v.* to plan **18B**
plano *m.* plan **8A**
planta *f.* plant **8A**
plantearse: plantearse preguntas *v.* to question, to ask oneself questions **14B**
plástico *m.* plastic **8A**
plástico/a *adj.* plastic; **Educación plástica y visual** *f.* Art **15B; envase de plástico** *m.* plastic container **15A**
plata *f.* silver **12B**
plata (fam.) *f.* money **11B; bodas de plata** *f.* silver wedding anniversary **18B**
plataforma: plataforma petrolera *f.* oil rig **14A**
plato *m.* dish; plate **8A; lavar los platos** *v.* to do the dishes **5A; plato principal** *m.* main course **2B; primer plato** *m.* first course **2B**
playa *f.* beach **1A**
plaza seat **13A**
plaza square **1B**
plazo *m.* term, period; **a corto/medio/largo plazo** *loc. adv.* short/medium/long term **17A; a largo plazo** *loc. adv.* in the long term **9A; plazo de inscripción** *m.* enrollment period **18A**
plegado/a *adj.* folded **13A**
pluriempleo *m.* having more than one job, moonlighting **14B**
población *f.* population **2A; población migrante** *f.* migrant population **8B**
poblado/a *adj.* populated **16B**
pobreza *f.* poverty **13B**
poco/a *adj.* little **2B**
poco: un poco *loc. adv.* a little **2B**
pocos/as *adj.* few **2A**
poder *v.* to be able to; **¿Los puedo ver?** *v.* Can I see them? **3B; no puede olvidarse** *v.* cannot be forgotten **10B; Yo puedo…** *v.* I can… **0**
poderse: No se puede… *v.* You/One can't… **7B**
poema *m.* poem **10B**
poeta/poetisa *m./f.* poet **10B**
policía *f.* police **0**
polideportivo *m.* sports center **2A**
políglota *adj.* multilingual, polyglot **1B**
política *f.* policy **6A;** politics **16A; ciencias políticas** *f.* political science **1B; política cultural** *f.* cultural policy **16A; política social** *f.* social policy **16A**
político/a *m./f.* politician **16A**
político/a: partido político *m.* political party **16A**
Polo Norte *m.* North Pole **18A**
polvo *m.* powder; **cacao en polvo** *m.* cocoa powder **15A; leche descremada en polvo** *f.* powdered skim milk **15A**
pólvora *f.* gunpowder **18A**
poner *v.* to put **4A; Me da/pone…** *v.* I'd like… **4A; poner (a alguien) al día** *v.* to update **17B; poner al día** *v.* to bring up to date **7B; poner atención (a)** *v.* pay attention (to) **0; poner en marcha** *exp.* to set in motion **16A**
ponerse: ponerse triste *v.* to be sad **18B**
ponerse: ponerse contento/a *v.* to be happy **18B**
popular *adj.* popular **2B; fiesta popular** *f.* town festival **6A; unidad popular** *f.* unity of the people **16A**
por *prep.* for, by; **¿Por qué no…?** *exp.* Why don't you? **6A; ¿Por qué…?** *interrog.* Why…? **6A; baja por maternidad** *f.* maternity leave **7B; cien por ciento** *adj.*

one hundred percent **12A; hablar por hablar** *v.* to talk for the sake of it **14B; licencia por maternidad** *f.* maternity leave **7B; Más despacio, por favor.** *exp.* Slower, please. **0; navegar por Internet** *v.* to surf the Internet **6A; pasar por** *v.* to go via **6B; por tu bien** *exp.* for your own good **15B; por cierto** *exp.* by the way, incidentally **10A; por eso** *conj.* therefore **17A; por favor** *exp.* please **2B; por fin** *exp.* at last **10A; por la mañana** *loc. adv.* in the morning **3A; por la noche** *loc. adv.* in the evening; at night **3A; por la tarde** *loc. adv.* in the afternoon **3A; por lo tanto** *conj.* therefore **17A; por medio de** *loc. prep.* by means of **14B; por otro lado/por otra parte** *loc. adv.* on the other hand **13B; por un lado/por una parte** *loc. adv.* on the one hand **13B; por vocación** *loc. adv.* by vocation **7A**

porción *f.* serving **15A**

porqué *m.* reason **17B**

portada *f.* cover **3B**

portavoz *m. y f.* spokesperson **12B**

porteño/a *adj.* of/from the city of Buenos Aires **17B**

Portugal *m.* Portugal **1A**

portugués *m.* Portuguese **1B**

portugués/portuguesa *adj.* Portuguese **1B**

posada *f.* bed & breakfast **11B**

posguerra *f.* postwar period **14B**

posibilidad *f.* possibility **6A**

posible *adj.* possible **4A; lo más... posible** *m.* as... as possible **17A**

positivo/a *adj.* positive **2B**

posponer *v.* to put off **18A**

postal *f.* postcard **9B**

póster *m.* poster **4A**

postergar *v.* to postpone **17B**

postre *m.* dessert **2B**

postularse *v.* to apply **13B**

potenciar *v.* to foster **15A**

practicar *v.* practice **0; practicar tirolesa** *v.* to go zip-lining **18A**

práctico/a *adj.* practical **3B**

prado *m.* meadow **9A**

precio *m.* price **4A**

precioso/a *adj.* lovely **2A**

predicción *f.* prediction **17A**

preferido/a *adj.* favorite **3B**

pregunta *f.* question **0; plantearse preguntas** *v.* to question, to ask oneself questions **14B**

preguntar *v.* to ask **14B**

premio *m.* award; prize **2B; Premio Nobel** *m.* Nobel Prize, Nobel laureate **10B**

prenda *f.* garment **3B**

prensa *f.* press **9B; nota de prensa** *f.* press release **10B; oficina de prensa** *f.* press office **16A; prensa económica** *f.* financial press **3A; prensa rosa** *f.* gossip press **9B; rueda de prensa** *f.* press conference **12B**

preocupación *f.* worry; concern **7A**

preocupado/a *adj.* worried **12A**

preocupar *v.* to worry; to concern **7A; No te preocupes.** *exp.* Don't worry. **13B**

preparar *v.* to make; to prepare **7A; preparar un viaje** *v.* to organize a trip **13A**

presencia *f.* presence **8B**

presentación: carta de presentación *f.* letter of introduction **13B**

presentar *v.* to introduce, to present **0**

preservar *v.* to preserve **15A**

presidente/a *m./f.* president **16A**

presión *f.* pressure **4B**

preso/a *m./f.* prisoner **16A**

prestar *v.* to lend **9A**

prestigioso/a *adj.* prestigious **10A**

pretender *v.* to try to **15B**

pretexto *m.* pretext **16A**

prevención *f.* prevention **10A**

primario/a: escuela primaria *f.* elementary school **9A**

primavera *f.* spring **10A**

primero/a *adj.* first **14A; primer +** *m.*: **primer plato** *m.* first course **2B**

primo/a *m./f.* cousin **5B; materia prima** *f.* raw material **15A**

primogénito/a *m./f.* firstborn **12A**

principal *adj.* main **4B; plato principal** *m.* main course **2B**

príncipe *m.* prince; **Puerto Príncipe** *m.* Port-au-Prince **12B**

principio: a principios del siglo XX *loc. adv.* at the beginning of the 20th century **8B**

privacidad *f.* privacy **17A**

privado/a *adj.* private **4B; escuela privada** *f.* private school **15B**

privatizado/a *adj.* privatized **13A**

privilegiado/a *adj.; m./f.* lucky person **2A**

probabilidad *f.* probability **15A**

probable *adj.* probable **17A**

probablemente *adv.* probably **4A**

probar *v.* to taste **16B; probar suerte** *v.* to try one's luck **5A**

problema *m.* problem **2A; ¡No hay problema!** *exp.* No problem! **7B**

procedencia *f.* origin **8B**

procedente: procedente de *adj.* arriving from **13A**

procesión *f.* procession **16B**

procurar *v.* to try to **14B**

productividad *f.* productivity **6A**

producto *m.* product **3B; producto de alimentación** *m.* food product **15A; producto ecológico** *m.* organic product **15A; producto fresco** *m.* fresh food **15A; producto interior bruto (PIB)** *m.* gross domestic product (GDP) **11A, 14A**

productor(a) *m./f.* producer **3B, 15A**

profesión *f.* profession **1B**

profesional *m. y f.* professional **3A**

profesional *adj.* professional **2B; experiencia profesional** *f.* professional experience **11B; formación profesional** *f.* professional training **14A; orientador(a) profesional** *m./f.* career counselor **13B**

profesionalidad *f.* professionalism **2B**

profesor(a) *m./f.* teacher **1B**

programa *m.* program **9A; programa de intercambio** *m.* exchange program **14A; programa de radio** *m.* radio program **3A**

programar *v.* to plan **3A**

promoción *f.* graduating class **9A; promotion 9B; campaña de promoción** *f.* promotional campaign **16B**

pronóstico *m.* weather forecast **9A**

pronto *adv.* soon **0; Hasta pronto.** *exp.* See you soon. **0**

pronunciar *v.* pronounce **0**

propiamente: propiamente dicho *exp.* per se **16B**

propiedad *f.* property **6A**

propietario/a *m./f.* owner **8B**

proponer *v.* to propose, to suggest **13A**

propósito: a propósito *exp.* incidentally; by the way **10A**

Protagonistas *m. y f.* Protagonists **0**

protector(a): crema solar protectora *f.* sunscreen **10A**

proteger *v.* to protect **3B**

proteína *f.* protein **15A**

protesta *f.* protest **11A**

protestar *v.* to complain **11A**

provecho: ¡Buen provecho! *exp.* Enjoy your meal. **8A**

provenir de *v.* to come from **16B**

provincia *f.* province **7B**

próximo/a: el próximo mes *loc. adv.* next month **5B**

proyección: proyección internacional *f.* international projection **16A**

proyecto *m.* project **4B**

prueba *f.* test **0**

psicología *f.* psychology **6A**

psicólogo/a *m./f.* psychologist **1B**

publicidad *f.* advertisement **6B;** *f.* advertising **16B**

publicista *m. y f.* publicist **14B**

público/a: escuela pública *f.* public school **15B**

pueblo *m.* town **1A; pueblo indígena** *m.* native people **16A**

puente *m.* long weekend **6B**

puenting *m.* bungee jumping **18A**

puerta *f.* door; **puerta de embarque** *f.* boarding gate **13A**

Puerto Príncipe *m.* Port-au-Prince **12B**

Puerto Rico *m.* Puerto Rico **0**

puertorriqueño/a *m./f.* Puerto Rican **1A**

pues *exp.* well **6A**

puesto *m.* job; position **4B;** stand (in a market) **4A; puesto de trabajo** *m.* job **12B; puesto directivo** *m.* managerial position **13B**

pulpo *m.* octopus **2B**

pulsera: reloj de pulsera *m.* wristwatch **3B**

punto *m.* point; **punto en común** *m.* point in common **5B; punto de encuentro** *m.* meeting point **9A**

puntuación *f.* score, evaluation **11A**

puntual *adj.* punctual **13B**

puntualidad *f.* punctuality **11A**

pupusa *f.* Salvadoran filled tortilla **8B**

pupusería *f.* store where pupusas are sold **8B**

pureza *f.* purity **18B**

puro/a *adj.* pure **7B; ¡Pura vida!** *exp.* Great! **18B; puro habano** *m.* Cuban cigar **3B**

Q

que *rel. pron.* that; **¡Que disfruten a bordo!** *exp.* Enjoy your flight! **13A; ¡Que tengan un feliz vuelo!** *exp.* Have a good flight! **13A; antes de que** *conj.* before **18A; así (es) que** *conj.* so **17A;**

Creo que sí/no. *exp.* I think so/not. **7B; desde que** *conj.* since **8B; después de que** *conj.* after **18A; más que** *adj.* more than **3A; menos que** *adj.* less than **3A; tener que** *v.* to have to **6A**
qué *interrog.* what **0, 1A; ¡Qué interesante!** *exp.* How interesting! **1B; ¡Qué tiempos!** *exp.* Those were the days! **5B; ¿A qué hora...?** *exp.* At what time...? **3A; ¿Con qué frecuencia?** *exp.* How often? **3A; ¿De qué color?** *exp.* What color? **3B; ¿De qué talla?** *exp.* What size? **3B; ¿Para qué sirve?** *exp.* What is it used for? **4B; ¿Qué ... eliges?** *exp.* What... do you choose? **1A; ¿Qué desean tomar?** *exp.* What would you like (to have)? **2B; ¿Qué es?** *exp.* What is it? **1A; ¿Qué hora es?** *exp.* What time is it? **3A; ¿Qué tal está(n)...?** *exp.* How is/ are...? **2B; ¿Qué te/le pasa?** (*fam./form.*) *exp.* What's wrong? **10A; ¿Qué tiempo hace?** *exp.* What's the weather like? **10A**
quechua *m.* Quechua **1B**
quedar *v.* to arrange (to) **8A**
quedarse *v.* to stay **8B; quedarse en blanco** *exp.* to go blank **15B**
queja *f.* complaint **11A; libro de quejas** *m.* complaint form **11A**
quemar *v.* to burn **18B**
querer *v.* to want **3B; querer a alguien** *v.* to love someone **12A; quería decir** *exp.* I meant... **12B**
quererse *v.* to love each other **17B**
queso *m.* cheese **2B**
quién *interrog.* who **1A; ¿Quién es?** *exp.* Who is it? **1A**
química *f.* chemistry **1B**
químico/a *m./f.* chemist **8B**
quince: fiesta de quince años *f.* fifteenth birthday party **18B**
quinceañera *f.* fifteen-year-old girl **5A**
quinto/a *adj.* fifth **14A**
quiosco *m.* kiosk **9B**
quiosquero/a *m./f.* kiosk attendant **9B**
quitar *v.* to take away **16A**
quizá(s) *adv.* perhaps **17A**

R

ración *f.* portion **2B**
racional *adj.* rational **16A**
radio *f.* radio **4B; cadena de radio** *f.* radio network **14B; escuchar la radio** *v.* to listen to the radio **2A; programa de radio** *m.* radio program **3A**
rafting *m.* rafting **18A**
ramo *m.* bunch **9B; ramo de flores** *m.* bunch of lowers **18B**
rápido/a *adj.* quick, fast **17A**
raqueta *f.* racket **18A**
raro/a *adj.* strange, odd; **parecer raro** *v.* to think something is odd **15B**
rasgo *m.* characteristic **14A**
ratón *m.* mouse **7B**
razón *f.* reason; **tener razón** *v.* to be right **10B**
real: la Familia Real *f.* the royal family **4B**
realidad *f.* reality; **hacer realidad** *v.* to make something happen **8B**
realista *adj.* realistic **12A**
realizado/a: sentirse realizado/a *v.* to feel fulfilled **13B**
realizar *v.* to do; to perform **5A**
rebaja *f.* discount **3B**
rebelde *adj.* rebel **15B**
rebién (fam.) *adv.* very well **17B**
recepción *f.* pick up **11A**
receptor(a): país receptor *m.* host country **8B**
receta (de cocina) *f.* recipe **8A**
recetario *m.* recipe collection **15A**
rechazar *v.* to reject **16A**
recibir *v.* receive **2B**
reciclable: envase reciclable *m.* recyclable container **15A**
reciclado/a *adj.* recycled **8A**
reciclaje *m.* recycling **15A**
reciclarse *v.* to recycle (oneself) **11B**
recién *adv.* just **17B**
recoger *v.* to pick up, to collect **5B**
recogido/a *adj.* picked **15A**
recomendación *f.* recommendation **6A**
recomendado/a *adj.* recommended **4A**
recomendar (un lugar) *v.* to recommend (a place) **13A**
recompensa *f.* reward **8B**
récord: batir un récord *v.* to break a record **18A**
recordar *v.* to remember **5A**
recorrer *v.* to cover (a distance) **9B**
recorrer *v.* to travel **5A**
recto/a *adj.* straight **9B**
recuadro *m.* box **0**
recuerdo *m.* memory **5B**
recurso *m.* resource, means **12B; recurso económico** *m.* economic resource **14A; Recursos Humanos (RR.HH.)** *m.* Human Resources (HR) **13B; recurso natural** *m.* natural resource **14A; sin recursos** *loc. adv.* in need **15A**
Recursos Humanos (RR.HH.) *m., pl.* Human Resources (HR) **13B**
red *f.* network **9A; red social** *f.* social network **13B; red Wi-Fi** *f.* Wi-Fi network **13B**
redactar *v.* write **0**
reducir *v.* to reduce **16A**
redundar en *v.* to give good results; to benefit **17A**
reencontrar *v.* to meet again **9A**
reencuentro *m.* reunion **6B**
referente: referente latino *m.* Hispanic icon **1A**
reformular *v.* to restate **8B**
refresco *m.* soft drink; soda **4A**
refrigerador *m.* refrigerator **8A**
regalarse *v.* to give oneself a present **6B**
regalo *m.* present **3B; cheque-regalo** *m.* gift-voucher **3B; tienda de regalos** *f.* gift shop **3B**
regatear *v.* to haggle; to bargain **4A**
regiomontano/a *adj.* born in Monterrey **12A**
regla: en regla *loc. adv.* in order; valid **11A**
regresar *v.* to go back, to return **8B**
regular *adv.* so-so **8A**
Reino Unido *m.* United Kingdom **8B**
reír *v.* to laugh **6A**
reírse *v.* to laugh **17B**
relación *f.* relationship **5B; Relaciones Internacionales** *f.* International Relations **11B**
relacionar *v.* to match, to relate **0**
relacionarse *v.* to interact **13B**
relacionarse *v.* to run in the same circles **10B**
relajación *f.* relaxation **6A**
relajado/a *adj.* relaxed **3A**
relajante *adj.* relaxing **6A**
relieve *m.* relief, geographical feature **18B**
religión *f.* religion **8A**
religioso/a *adj.* religious **8A**
rellenar *v.* fill in **0**
relleno/a *adj.* stuffed, filled (with food) **16B**
reloj *m.* clock; watch **3A; reloj (de pulsera)** *m.* (wrist)watch **3B**
remedio *m.* remedy, cure **10A**
remo: bote de remos *m.* rowing boat **18A**
remolacha *f.* beet **15A**
remontar *v.* to surmount **18A**
rendimiento *m.* performance **13B**
rendir *v.* to perform **6A**
renovable *adj.* renewable **17A**
renta: renta per cápita *f.* per capita income **14A**
renunciar a *v.* to give up, to relinquish **16A**
repartir *v.* to deliver **7B**
repartir *v.* to distribute **12B**
reparto: reparto a domicilio *m.* home delivery **7B**
repelente *m.* repellent **10A**
repetir *v.* repeat **0**
reportaje *m.* report; article **14B**
reportero/a *m./f.* reporter **7B**
representante *m. y f.* representative **10B**
representar *v.* to represent **10B**
representar *v.* to role-play **0**
reproductor(a): reproductor de MP3 *m.* MP3 player **13B**
República Dominicana *f.* Dominican Republic **0**
requisito: reunir los requisitos *v.* to meet the requirements **13B**
rescatar *v.* to rescue **18B**
reseña *f.* summary; review **9A**
reserva *f.* reservation **6B**
reservar *v.* to make a reservation **6B**
reservar *v.* to set aside **6A; reservar los billetes** *v.* to book the tickets **13A**
resfriado/a: estar resfriado/a *v.* to have a cold **10A**
residencia: residencia de estudiantes *f.* dorm **12A**
resistente *adj.* strong, tough **17A**
resolución: resolución de conflictos *f.* conflict resolution **13B**
respaldo: respaldo del asiento *m.* seat back **13A**
respecto: con respecto a *loc. prep.* regarding **16A**
respetar *v.* to respect **8A**
respeto *m.* respect **14A**
respetuoso/a *adj.* respectful **12A**
respirar *v.* to breathe **7B**
responder *v.* answer **0**
responsabilidad *f.* responsibility **9A**
responsable *m. y f.* person in charge **13A**
responsable *adj.* responsible **3B**
respuesta *f.* answer **0**
restaurante *m.* restaurant **0**
restaurar *v.* to restore **11A**
resto *m.* rest; **el resto de** *m.* the rest of **12B; el resto de la clase** *m.* the rest of the class **0**

resultado *m.* result **12B**
resumen *m.* summary; **en resumen** *exp.* in short **18B**
resumir *v.* summarize **0**
retirar *v.* to remove **13A**
reto *m.* challenge; **reto deportivo** *m.* sport challenge **18A; superar retos** *v.* to overcome challenges **18A**
retraso *m.* delay **11A; con retraso** *loc. adv.* delayed **13A**
retrato *m.* portrait **14B**
reunión *f.* meeting **7B**
reunir *v.* to collect **15A**
reunir *v.* to gather **0; reunir los requisitos** *v.* to meet the requirements **13B**
reunir(se) *v.* to meet; to gather **6A**
revisar *v.* review **0**
revista *f.* magazine **9B; revista del corazón** *f.* (gossip) magazine **9B**
revivir *v.* to relive **14B**
revolución *f.* revolution **13B**
revuelta *f.* revolt **14A**
rezagado/a *adj.* falling behind **17A**
rico/a *adj.* rich **7A**
rico/a *adj.* tasty **2B**
ridículo/a *adj.* ridiculous **15B**
riesgo *m.* risk **7A**
rincón *m.* corner; spot **13A**
rincón *m.* spot, place **11A**
río *m.* river **3A**
riqueza *f.* richness **11B**
riqueza *f.* wealth **14A**
ritmo *m.* rhythm **17B; ritmo de vida** *m.* pace of life **3A**
rito *m.* ritual **6A**
ritual *m.* ritual **14A**
rizado/a *adj.* curly **12A**
rodar *v.* to shoot, to film **9B**
rodeado/a de *loc. adv.* surrounded by **6B**
rodear *v.* circle **0**
rojo/a *adj.* red **3B**
romanticismo *m.* romanticism **12A**
romántico/a *adj.* romantic **2A**
romper *v.* to break **16A**
ropa *f.* clothes, clothing; **tienda de ropa** *f.* clothing store **3B**
rosa *f.* rose **18B; prensa rosa** *f.* gossip press **9B**
rosado/a *adj.* pink **18B**
rosca: tapa de rosca *f.* screw top **8A**
rubio/a *adj.* blond(e) **12A**
rueda: rueda de prensa *f.* press conference **12B**
ruido *m.* noise **2A**
ruinas *f.* ruins **2A**
rumbo: caminar sin rumbo fijo *v.* to wander aimlessly **17B**
rural *adj.* rural **11A**
ruta *f.* route **6B**
rutina *f.* routine **7A; rutina diaria** *f.* daily routine **3A**

S

sábado *m.* Saturday **3A**
saber *v.* to know; **saber (algo) (de)** *v.* to know (something) (about) **8A**
sabiduría *f.* wisdom **17B**
sabor *m.* flavor; taste **15A**
saborear *v.* to savor **16B**
sabroso/a *adj.* tasty **15A**
sacrificio: exigir sacrificios *v.* to require sacrifices **13A**
sal *f.* salt **8A**
sala *f.* ward **10A; sala de llegada** *f.* arrival lounge/area **13A**
salado/a *adj.* salty **2B**
salchicha *f.* sausage **4A**
Sale *exp.* Come on! **8A**
salida *f.* departure, exit **6A; hora de salida** *f.* departure time **13A**
salir *v.* to depart **13A; salir (con amigos)** *v.* to go out (with friends) **3A; salir con alguien** *v.* to go out with somebody **12A; salir de** *v.* to leave **3A**
salón *m.* living room **4B; baile de salón** *m.* ballroom dance **17B; salón de fiestas** *m.* reception room **18B; Salón Internacional de la Moda** *m.* International Fashion Fair **3B; salón-comedor** *m.* living room-dining room **4B**
salsa *f.* salsa **1A; bacalao en salsa** *m.* cod with sauce **2B; salsa golf** *f.* thousand-island dressing **17A**
salud *f.* health **7A**
saludarse *v.* to greet each other **17B**
saludo *m.* greeting **0**
salvadoreño/a *adj.* Salvadoran **8B**
salvar *v.* to save, to rescue **9B**
salvavidas (*invar.*) *m. y f.* lifeguard **10A**
sándwich *m.* sandwich **2B**
sangre *f.* blood **17A**
sanitario/a: asistencia sanitaria *f.* health care **10A**
sanjuanero/a *adj.* from San Juan **11A**
sano/a *adj.* healthy **5B;** *adj.* saint; **Semana Santa** *f.* Easter; Holy Week **5A**
sartén *f.* frying pan **8A**
satisfacción *f.* satisfaction **11A; satisfacción personal** *f.* personal satisfaction **13B**
sección *f.* section **8B**
seco/a *adj.* dry **15A**
secretaría *f.* ministry, department **16A**
secretario/a *m./f.* secretary **1B**
sector *m.* sector **8B; sector energético** *m.* energy sector **14A**
secuestrado/a *m./f.* kidnap victim **16A**
secuestro *m.* kidnap victim **16A**
sede *f.* headquarters **9A**
sedentarismo *m.* sedentary lifestyle **16B**
seguir *v.* to continue, to go on, to keep going **9B**
Segunda Guerra Mundial *f.* World War II **18A**
seguridad *f.* safety **13A**
seguridad security **17A; cinturón de seguridad** *m.* seatbelt **13A**
seguro/a *adj.* sure, safe; **estar seguro/a de sí mismo/a** *v.* to be self-confident **18A; Seguro que...** *exp.* I'm sure (that)... **9A**
seleccionar *v.* select **0**
sello *m.* stamp; **sello discográfico** *m.* record label **17B**
selva *f.* jungle **16A**
semana *f.* week **2B; día de la semana** *m.* day of the week **3A; esta semana** *loc. adv.* this week **6A; fin de semana** *m.* weekend **2B; la semana pasada** *loc. adv.* last week **5A; los fines de semana** *loc. adv.* (on) weekends **5B; Semana Santa** *f.* Easter; Holy Week **5A; una vez a la semana** *loc. adv.* once a week **6A**
semanal: agenda semanal *f.* (weekly) planner **3A**
semi: semi-cama *adj.* semi-sleeper **13A**
senderismo *m.* hiking **11B**
sensibilización *f.* sensitization **16A**
sensibilizar *v.* to sensitize **16A**
sensible *adj.* sensitive; **ser sensible a** *v.* to be sensitive to **10A**
sentimiento *m.* feeling; **expresar un sentimiento** *v.* to express a feeling **18B**
sentir *v.* to feel; **Lo siento.** *exp.* I'm sorry. **3B; sentirse acompañado/a** *v.* to feel accompanied **9A; sentirse como en casa** *v.* to feel at home **16B; sentirse realizado/a** *v.* to feel fulfilled **13B; Siento oír eso.** *exp.* I'm sorry to hear that. **13B; Siento verte así.** *exp.* I'm sorry to see you like this. **13B**
señalar *v.* indicate **0**
señor(a) *m./f.* sir/madam **6B; Estimados señores:** *exp.* Dear sirs, **6B**
señorita *f.* young lady; Miss **0**
separado/a *adj.* separated **12A**
separarse *v.* to split up, to separate **12A**
septiembre *m.* September **5A**
ser *v.* to be **1A; ¿Cómo es?** *exp.* What is it like? **4B; ¿Cómo es...?** *exp.* What is... like? **2A; ¿Cuánto es?** *exp.* How much is it? **2B; ¿Qué es?** *exp.* What is it? **1A; ¿Qué hora es?** *exp.* What time is it? **3A; ¿Quién es?** *exp.* Who is it? **1A; es posible** *v.* it's possible **4A; o sea** *exp.* that is **8B; ser afín** *v.* to have a lot in common **17B; ser bueno/a (en algo)** *v.* to be good (at something) **17B; ser hincha de** *v.* to be a supporter of **17B; ser humano** *m.* human being **8A; ser líder de audiencia** *v.* to be the highest rated **14B; ser malo/a (en algo)** *v.* to be bad (at something) **17B; ser moneda corriente** *exp.* to be common **13B; ser sensible a** *v.* to be sensitive to **10A; ser todo/a oidos** *exp.* to be all ears **9A; ser un(a) gran comunicador(a)** *v.* to be a great communicator **13B; ser verdad** *v.* to be true **10B; Son 9 euros.** *exp.* It's 9 euros. **2B; Yo soy de Madrid.** *exp.* I'm from Madrid. **1A; Yo soy...** *exp.* I am... **0**
serie *f.* series; **emitir la serie** *v.* to broadcast the TV series **14B; fabricar en serie** *v.* to mass produce **13B; pasar la serie de televisión** *v.* to broadcast the television series **14B; serie de televisión** *f.* television series **14B**
serio/a *adj.* serious, grave **12A, 17A;** *adj.* serious; reliable **13B**
serrano/a: jamón serrano *m.* Serrano ham **2B**
servicio *m.* service; **a tu servicio** *loc. adv.* at your service **7B; servicio doméstico** *m.* domestic service **8B; Servicios Sociales** *m.* Social Services **5B; industria de servicios** *f.* service industry **14A**
servir para *v.* to be good for... **4B; ¿Para qué sirve?** *exp.* What is it used for? **4B**
sevillanas *f.* popular dance originated in Seville **17B**

sí *adv.* yes **1A; alejados entre sí** *loc. adv.* far from each other **17B; Creo que sí/no.** *exp.* I think so/not. **7B; estar seguro/a de sí mismo/a** *v.* to be self-confident **18A**
siempre *adv.* always **2B; casi siempre** *loc. adv.* almost always **14A; para siempre** *loc. adv.* forever **8B**
siesta *f.* nap **6A; dormir la siesta** *v.* to take a nap **6A**
sigla *f.* initial letter; acronym **12B**
siglo *m.* century; **a finales del siglo XIX** *loc. adv.* towards the end of the 19th century **8B; a principios del siglo XX** *loc. adv.* at the beginning of the 20th century **8B**
significar *v.* to mean; **¿Qué significa...?** *exp.* What does... mean? **0**
siguiente *adj.* following/next... **0**
silencio *m.* silence **6A**
silla *f.* chair **4B**
sillón *m.* armchair **4B**
silvestre *adj.* wild **18B**
simbolizar *v.* to represent **18B**
símbolo *m.* symbol **8A**
simpatía *f.* friendliness **2B**
simpático/a *adj.* nice **2A**
sin *prep.* without; **caminar sin rumbo fijo** *v.* to wander aimlessly **17B; sin embargo** *conj.* however **5A; sin embargo** *conj.* however **13B; sin recursos** *adj.* in need **15A**
sincronizada: el/la nadador(a) de sincronizada *m./f.* synchronized swimmer **18A**
sintetizar *v.* to synthesize **13B**
síntoma *m.* symptom **10A**
sistema *m.* system; **sistema inmunológico** *m.* immune system **17A**
sitio *m.* place **11B;** *m.* room; space **9B; sitio web** *m.* website **14B**
sobre *prep.* on, about; **sobre la base de** *loc. prep.* based upon **16A; sobre todo** *loc. adv.* above all **13B**
sobreproteger *v.* to overprotect **15B**
sobrevivir *v.* to survive **13B**
sobrino/a *m./f.* nephew/niece **18A**
social *adj.* social **6A; Ciencias sociales** *f.* Social Studies **15B; justicia social** *f.* social justice **16A; movilización social** *f.* social demonstration **16A; plan social** *m.* social plan **16A; política social** *f.* social policy **16A; red social** *f.* social network **13B; Servicios Sociales** *m.* Social Services **5B**
sociedad *f.* society **9A**
socorro *m.* help **12B**
sofá *m.* sofa **4B**
sol *m.* sun **4B; gafas de sol** *f.* sunglasses **3B; hacer sol** *v.* to be sunny **10A; tomar el sol** *v.* to sunbathe **10A**
solar: crema solar protectora *f.* sunscreen **10A**
soler *v.* to usually do something **14A**
solicitar *v.* to request **4A**
solicitud *f.* application **13B**
solidarizarse (con) *v.* to support someone **14B**
solo/a *adj.* alone **7A; café solo** *m.* black coffee **2B**
solo/solamente *adv.* only **13B**
soltero/a *adj.* single **5B; despedida de soltero/a** *f.* stag/hen night **18B**
solucionar *v.* to solve **10A**
soneto *m.* sonnet **10B**
sonoro/a: banda sonora *f.* sound track **17B**
sonreír *v.* to smile **13A**
sonrisa *f.* smile **10A**
sopa *f.* soup; **sopa de pescado** *f.* fish soup **2B**
sordo/a *adj.* deaf **12B**
sorprendente *adj.* surprising **18A**
sorprender *v.* to surprise **15B**
sorpresa *f.* surprise **17B**
sorteo *m.* draw **9B;** *m.* lottery, drawing **12B**
soso/a *adj.* bland, lacking salt **2B**
sostenible *adj.* sustainable **17A**
souvenir *m.* souvenir **4A**
Sr./Sra. *m./f.* Mr./Mrs. **2A**
su *adj.* your/his/her/its **2A**
subir *v.* to climb **5A**
submarinismo *m.* scuba diving **11B**
subrayar *v.* underline **0**
subsahariana: el África subsahariana (f.) *f.* Sub-Saharan Africa **14A**
subte *m.* subway **4A**
subterráneo *m.* subway **4A**
suceder *v.* to happen **14A**
sudamericano/a *adj.* South American **18A**
sueldo *m.* salary **14B**
sueldo *m.* wage(s) **3B**
sueño *m.* dream **8B; cumplir (sus) sueños** *v.* to make (his/her) dreams come true **15B**
suerte *f.* (good) luck **8B; probar suerte** *v.* to try one's luck **5A**
suéter *m.* sweater **3B**
suficiente *adj.* enough **6A**
suflé *m.* soufflé **15A**
sufrir *v.* to suffer **12B**
sujetar *v.* to hold **8A**
sumario *m.* table of contents **1B**
suministrar *v.* to administer **17A**
superar: superar retos *v.* to overcome challenges **18A**
superarse *v.* to outdo (oneself) **18A**
superdifícil *adj.* extremely difficult **11B**
superficie *f.* area **2A**
supervisor(a) *m./f.* supervisor **13A**
suplemento: suplemento dominical *m.* Sunday supplement **9B**
sur *m.* south **2A**
surfista *m. y f.* surfer **16B**
surgir *v.* to come up **15A**
suspenso *m.* failure **15B**
sustituir *v.* to substitute **14A**
sutil *adj.* subtle **18B**

T

tabla *f.* chart, table **0**
tachar *v.* cross out **0**
taco *m.* taco **2B**
taichí *m.* tai chi **8A**
tailandés *m.* Thai **7A**
Tailandia Thailand **7A**
talento *m.* talent **11B**
talla *f.* size **3B; ¿De qué talla?** *exp.* What size? **3B**
taller *m.* workshop; **taller mecánico** *m.* repair shop **7B**
también *adv.* as well, too **1B**
tampoco *adv.* not . . . either, neither **10B**
tan *adv.* so; **tan/tanto... como** *conj.* as much/many... as **8B**
tanto *adv.* so much
tanto/a *adj.* so much
tanto/a(s) *adj.* as many **8B**
tanto: tan/tanto... como *conj.* as much/many... as **8B; tanto ... como** *conj.* both ... and **7A**
tapa *f.* tapa **2B; tapa de rosca** *f.* screw top **8A**
tapear *v.* to eat tapas **2B**
tapiz (pl. tapices) *m.* tapestry **3B**
taquigrafía *f.* stenography **13B**
tarde *f.* afternoon; *adv.* late **7A; Buenas tardes.** *exp.* Good afternoon. **0; de la tarde** *loc. adv.* p.m.; in the afternoon **3A; más tarde** *loc. adv.* later **17B; por la tarde** *loc. adv.* in the afternoon **3A**
tarea *f.* homework **0**
tarifa *f.* fare **13A**
tarjeta *f.* card; **con tarjeta** *loc. adv.* with a credit card **3B; tarjeta de felicitación** *f.* greeting card **5A; tarjeta de visita** *f.* business card **18A**
taxi *m.* taxi **0**
taza *f.* coffee cup, mug **2B**
te *pron.* you, to you
té *m.* tea **2B**
teatro *m.* theater **1A**
técnico/a: técnico/a informático/a *m./f.* computer technician **1B**
tecnología *f.* technology **8A**
tecnológico/a *adj.* technological **17A**
tela *f.* (piece of) cloth; fabric **8A**
tele *f.* television **3A**
telefonía *f.* telephone service **9B**
teléfono *m.* telephone; **¿Cuál es tu número de teléfono?** *exp.* What is your phone number? **1B; llamada de teléfono** *f.* (telephone) call **3A; teléfono celular** *m.* cell phone **1B; teléfono inteligente** *m.* smartphone **13B**
telenovela *f.* soap opera **5A**
telespectador(a) *m./f.* television viewer **14B**
televidente *m.* TV viewer **9A**
televisión *f.* television **3A; pasar la serie de televisión** *v.* to broadcast the television series **14B; serie de televisión** *f.* television series **14B**
televisor *m.* television (set) **4B**
temperatura *f.* temperature **10A; hace 30 °C de temperatura** *v.* the temperature is 30 °C **10A**
temporada: temporada alta *f.* peak season **4B**
temporalmente *adv.* temporarily **8B**
temprano *adv.* early **7A**
tendencia *f.* tendency, trend **17A**
tener *v.* to have **2A; ¡Que tengan un feliz vuelo!** *exp.* Have a good flight! **13A; tener canas** *v.* to have gray hair **17B; tener capacidad** *v.* to have (storage) capacity **13B; tener clase** *v.* to have class **3A; tener confianza en** *v.* to trust in **5B; tener en cuenta** *v.* to take into account **16B; tener frío/calor** *v.* to be cold/hot **10A; tener lugar** *v.* to be held **16B; tener que** *v.* to have to **6A; tener razón** *v.* to be right **10B; tener un hijo** *v.* to have a child **8B; tiene** *v.* it has **2A**

tenis *m.* tennis **1A**
tenista *m. y f.* tennis player **14A**
tenso/a *adj.* tense **10A**
terapia *f.* therapy **3A**
tercero/a *adj.* third **14A**
tercio *m.* a third **16B**
termas *f.* hot springs **6B**
terminación *f.* ending **0**
terminal *f.* terminal **13A**
terminar *v.* to end **3A**
ternera: filete de ternera *m.* filet of veal **2B**
terraza *f.* balcony **4B**
terrible *adj.* terrible **15B**
territorial: invasión territorial *f.* territorial invasion **16A**
territorio *m.* territory **16A**
terrorismo *m.* terrorism **16A**
tertulia *f.* roundtable; talk show **9A**
tesoro *m.* treasure **10A**
test *m.* test **1A**
testigo *m. y f.* witness **10B**
testimonio *m.* testimony **8B**
tetería *f.* tea room **8B**
texto *m.* reading, textbook **0**
tía *f.* aunt **5B**
tico/a (fam.) *adj.; m./f.* Costa Rican **18B**
tiempo *m.* time **3A**; weather **10A; ¡Qué tiempos aquellos!** *exp.* Those were the days! **5B; ¿Cuánto tiempo (hace)...?** *exp.* How long have/has? **8B; ¿Qué tiempo hace?** *exp.* What's the weather like? **10A; a tiempo** *loc. adv.* in/on time **7B; al mismo tiempo** *loc. adv.* at the same time **7A; buen tiempo** *m.* good weather **2A; hace buen/mal tiempo** *v.* there is good/bad weather **10A; tiempo libre** *m.* free time **5B; tiempo para uno/a mismo/a** *m.* time for oneself **3A**
tienda *f.* store **2A; tienda de alimentación** *f.* grocery store **4A; tienda de campaña** *f.* tent **18A; tienda de discos** *f.* music store **3B; tienda de regalos** *f.* gift shop **3B; tienda de ropa** *f.* clothing store **3B**
tierno/a *adj.* affectionate **9A**
tierra *f.* land, dirt **9A**
tímido/a *adj.* shy **12A**
tío *m.* uncle **5B**
típico/a *adj.* typical **2A**
tipo *m.* type **12A**
tirano/a *m./f.* tyrant **13B**
tiren el dado *exp.* roll the dice **10A**
tirolesa *f.* zip lining **18A; practicar tirolesa** *v.* to go zip-lining **18A**
titular *m.* headline, title **16A**
título *m.* degree **13B**
tocar *v.* to touch; **¿A quién le toca?** *exp.* Whose turn is it? **4A; Me toca a mí.** *exp.* It's my turn. **4A; tocar (un instrumento)** *v.* to play (an instrument) **8A**
tocayo/a *m./f.* namesake **12A**
todavía *adv.* still; **todavía no** *loc. adv.* not yet **6A**
todo *pron.* all, everything **2A, 4A; a pesar de todo** *loc. adv.* despite it all **13B; sobre todo** *loc. adv.* above all **13B**
todo/a *adj.* all; **ser todo/a oidos** *exp.* to be all ears **9A; todo el día** *loc. adv.* all day **6A; todos los días** *loc. adv.* every day **3A; todo recto** *loc. adv.* straight ahead
Toledo *m.* Toledo **1A**
tolerancia *f.* tolerance **14A**
tomar *v.* to take **9B; ¿Qué desean tomar?** *exp.* What would you like (to have)? **2B; tomar el ferry** *v.* to take the ferry **3A; tomar el sol** *v.* to sunbathe **10A; tomar fotos** *v.* to take pictures **6B**
tomate *m.* tomato **4A; tomate frito** *m.* tomato sauce **15A**
tópico *m.* topic; cliché **16B**
toque *m.* touch **15A**
tormenta *f.* storm **10B**
tornarse *v.* to become **17A**
torneo *m.* tournament **10B; ganar torneos** *v.* to win tournaments **18A**
tortilla *f.* (Mexican) tortilla; **tortilla española** *f.* Spanish potato omelet **2B**
tostada *f.* toast **2B**
trabajador(a) *adj.; m./f.* worker **3A; madre trabajadora** *f.* working mother **7B**
trabajar *v.* to work **1B; ir a trabajar** *v.* to go to work **3A; trabajar como** *v.* to work as **11B**
trabajo *m.* job **1B;** *m.* work **2A; bolsa de trabajo** *m.* employment center **13B; cambiar de trabajo** *m.* to change jobs **7B; compañero/a de trabajo** *m.* coworker **5B; contrato de trabajo** *m.* employment contract **13B; equipo de trabajo** *m.* working team **13B; horarios de trabajo** *m.* work schedules **3A; puesto de trabajo** *m.* job **12B; trabajo voluntario** *m.* volunteer work **7A**
trabalenguas *m.* tongue-twister **6A**
tradición *f.* tradition **2B**
tradicional *adj.* traditional **4A**
traducir *v.* to translate **7A**
traer *v.* to bring **7B**
tráfico *m.* traffic **2A; tráfico de armas** *m.* arms trade **16A**
traje *m.* suit **3B**
tranquilidad *f.* peace, tranquility **2A**
tranquilo/a *adj.* calm, quiet **2A**
transferencia: transferencia bancaria *f.* bank transfer **7B**
transformación *f.* transformation **14B**
transformar *v.* transform **0**
transfronterizo/a *adj.* cross-border **14A**
transgénico/a: alimento transgénico *m.* transgenic food **15A**
transición: transición democrática *f.* democratic transition **14B**
transparente *adj.* transparent **9A**
transportar *v.* to transport **7A**
transporte *m.* transportation; **medio de transporte** *m.* means of transportation **4A**
trasladar *v.* to transport **13A**
traspasar *v.* to cross, to go beyond **14B**
tratado *m.* treaty **16A**
tratamiento *m.* treatment **12B**
tratar *v.* to be about **14B**
trato *m.* interaction **12B**
trayecto *m.* route **13A**
trekking *m.* hiking **6B**
tren *m.* train **6B**
tres *adj.* three; **tres veces al año** *loc. adv.* three times a year **3A**
trigo *m.* wheat **15A**
triste *adj.* sad **12A; ponerse triste** *v.* to be sad **18B**
tristeza *f.* sadness **10B**
trompeta *f.* trumpet **7A**
trotamundos *m. y f.* globetrotter **9A**
trotar *v.* to trot **9A**
trovador(a) *m./f.* troubadour **7A**
truco *m.* trick **8A**
tu *adj.* your; **a tu servicio** *loc. adv.* at your service **7B**
tú *pron.* you (*sing. fam.*) **1A; ¿Y tú?** *exp.* And you? **1A; hablarse de tú/usted** *v.* to address somebody as **tú/usted 7B**
tucán *m.* toucan **16B**
tulipán tulip **18B**
turismo *m.* tourism **14A**
turístico/a *adj.* tourist **16B; destinos turísticos** *m.* tourist destinations **4B; el/la guía turístico/a** *m./f.* tour guide **1B**
turrón *m.* nougat candy **18B**
tutearse *v.* to use the **tú** form of address **17B**
tuteo *m.* use of **tú 7B**
TV *f.* TV **9A**

U

u *conj.* or (before a word beginning with **o** or **ho**) **11B**
ubicación *f.* location **15A**
ubicado/a *adj.* located **11A**
últimamente *adv.* lately **7A**
último/a *adj.* last **5A**
último/a último minuto *m.* last minute **12B**
un(a) *art.* a, an **1A; por un lado/por una parte** *loc. adv.* on the one hand **13B; un poco** *loc. adv.* a little **2B; una vez a la semana** *loc. adv.* once a week **6A**
únicamente *adv.* only **13B**
único/a *adj.* unique **2A**
unidad *f.* unit, unity; **unidad popular** *f.* unity of the people **16A**
unión: Unión Europea *f.* European Union **10B**
universal *adj.* universal **17A**
universidad *f.* university **2A**
universitario/a *adj.; m./f.* college student **2A; deserción universitaria** *f.* university drop-outs **15B**
universo *m.* universe **9B**
uno/a *adj. y pron.* one; **tiempo para uno/a mismo/a** *m.* time for oneself **3A**
uranio *m.* uranium **14A**
Uruguay *m.* Uruguay **0**
uruguayo/a *adj.* Uruguayan **7A**
usar *v.* use **0**
uso *m.* custom **16B**
usted *pron.* you (*sing. form.*) **1A; ¿De dónde es usted?** *exp.* Where are you from? **1A; ¿Y usted?** *exp.* And you? **0; hablarse de tú/usted** *v.* to address somebody as **tú/usted 7B**
ustedes *pron.* you (*pl. form.*) **1A**
utensilio *m.* utensil **15A**
útil *adj.* useful **9A**
utilizar *v.* use **0**
uva *f.* grape **18B**

V

vaca *f.* cow **0**
vacaciones *f.* vacation **3A; estar de vacaciones** *v.* to be on vacation **7B; pasar las vacaciones** *v.* to spend one's vacation **4B**

vacío/a *adj.* empty **4B**
vacuna *f.* vaccine **12B**
vacunar *v.* to vaccinate **10A**
Vale *exp.* OK **2B**
valentía *f.* courage **16B**
valer: valer la pena *v.* to be worth it **11B**
valerse *v.* to be self-sufficient **5B**
valía *f.* value, worth **18A**
validar *v.* to validate **14A**
valle *m.* valley **11B**
vals *m.* waltz **17B**
variado/a *adj.* assorted **7B**
variedad *f.* variety **7A**
vasco/a *adj.* Basque **18A**
vecino/a *m./f.* neighbor **4A**
vegetación *f.* vegetation **6B**
vegetariano/a *adj.* vegetarian **15A; hacerse vegetariano/a** *v.* to become a vegetarian **7B**
vela *f.* candle **5A**
velocidad *f.* speed **13B**
vendedor(a) *m./f.* salesperson; **vendedor(a) de lotería** *m./f.* lottery ticket seller **9B**
vender *v.* to sell **8B**
venerar *v.* to venerate **16B**
Venezuela *f.* Venezuela **0**
Venga *exp.* Come on! **8A**
venir *v.* to come **3B**
venta *f.* sale **4B; a la venta** *loc. adv.* for sale **4B; ejecutivo/a de ventas** *m./f.* sales executive **13B**
ventaja *f.* advantage **9B**
ver *v.* to see **3B; ¿Los puedo ver?** *exp.* Can I see them? **3B; a ver** *exp.* let's see… **6A; Siento verte así.** *exp.* I'm sorry to see you like this. **13B; ver películas** *v.* to watch movies **3A**
verano *m.* summer **2A; pasantía de verano** *f.* summer internship **13B**
verdad: ¿De verdad? *exp.* Really? **9B; ¿verdad?** *exp.* right? **4A; decir la verdad** *v.* to tell the truth **17B; …,la verdad** *exp.* to tell you the truth **2A; ser verdad** *v.* to be true **10B**
verdadero/a *adj.* real **12B; ¿Verdadero o falso?** *exp.* True or false? **0**
versión *f.* version **9B**
verde *adj.* green **3B**
verduras *f.* vegetables **2B; arroz con verduras** *m.* rice with vegetables **2B**
vereda *f.* rural neighborhood **9A**
verse: ¡Nos vemos! *exp.* See you! **0**
vertical *adj.* upright **13A**
vestido *m.* dress **3B**
vestirse *v.* to get dressed **7A**
veterano/a *adj.* veteran **14B**
veterinario/a *m./f.* veterinarian **3A**
vez *f.* time **3A; a veces** *loc. adv.* sometimes **2B; de nuevo; otra vez** *loc. adv.* again **0; de vez en cuando** *loc. adv.* from time to time **14A; dos veces al mes** *loc. adv.* twice a month **6A; tal vez** *loc. adv.* maybe **17A; tres veces al año** *loc. adv.* three times a year **3A; una vez a la semana** *loc. adv.* once a week **6A**
vía: en vías de desarrollo *adj.* developing **3B**
viajar *v.* to travel **3A**
viaje *m.* trip **3B; agencia de viajes** *f.* travel agency **4B; estar de viaje** *v.* to be away **7A; preparar un viaje** *v.* to organize a trip **13A; viaje de negocios** *m.* business trip **3A; viaje de novios** *m.* honeymoon **13A; viaje organizado** *m.* package tour **13A**
viajero/a *m./f.* traveler **11A**
vida *f.* life; **¡Pura vida!** *exp.* Great! **18B; amargarle la vida a alguien** *exp.* to upset somebody **17A; calidad de vida** *f.* quality of life **2A; cambiar de vida** *v.* to change one's life **7B; el hombre/la mujer de mi vida** *exp.* the man/woman of my dreams **12A; hacer la vida más fácil** *exp.* to make life easier **17A; llevar una vida…** *v.* to lead a… life **10A; medio de vida** *m.* way of life **11B; ritmo de vida** *m.* pace of life **3A; vida académica** *f.* academic life **14A**
vidrio *m.* (pane of) glass **8A**
viejo/a *adj.* old **5B; casco viejo** *m.* historic neighborhood **12B**
viernes *m.* Friday **3A**
vigilante: vigilante nocturno/a *m. y f.* night security guard **3A**
vinilo: disco de vinilo *m.* vinyl record **13B**
vino *m.* wine **2B**
viñeta (cómica) *f.* cartoon **0**
violencia: no violencia *f.* non-violence **16A**
virgen *adj.* virgin; **aceite de oliva virgen extra** *m.* extra virgin olive oil **15A; bosque virgen** *m.* virgin forest **6B**
visita: tarjeta de visita *f.* business card **18A**
visitante *m. y f.* visitor **8B**
visitar *v.* to visit **4A**
vista *f.* view **11A; Hasta la vista.** *exp.* See you later. **0**
visual: Educación plástica y visual *f.* Art **15B**
vital *adj.* vital **7A**
Viva *exp.* ¡Viva! **2A**
vivienda *f.* home; housing **11B; vivienda ideal** *f.* ideal home **4B**
vivir *v.* to live **2A; vivir afuera** *v.* to live abroad **10B**
vocación *f.* vocation **7A; por vocación** *loc. adv.* by vocation **7A**
vocal *f.* vowel **13B**
volar *v.* to fly **5A**
volcán *m.* volcano **6B**
volumen *m.* volume **14A**
voluntario/a *m./f.* volunteer **12B; trabajo voluntario** *m.* volunteer work **7A**
volver *v.* to come back **6B**
volver *v.* to go back, to return **8B**
volver a *v.* to do … again **11B**
vosotros/as *pron.* you (*pl. fam.*) **1B**
votar *v.* to vote **10B**
voz (pl. voces) *f.* voice **6A**
vuelo *m.* flight **6B; ¡Que tengan un feliz vuelo!** *exp.* Have a good flight! **13A; auxiliar de vuelo** *m. y f.* flight attendant **13A; perder un vuelo** *v.* to miss a flight **13A**
vuelta *f.* turn; **dar la vuelta** *v.* to flip; to turn over **8A; dar la vuelta al mundo** *v.* to go around the world **18A; ida y vuelta** *exp.* round-trip **6B**

W

web *f.* web; **cámara web** *f.* webcam **6B; página web** *f.* Web page **14B; sitio web** *m.* website **14B**
Wi-Fi: red Wi-Fi *f.* Wi-Fi network **13B**

Y

y *conj.* and **0; hecho/a y derecho/a** *exp.* all grown-up **9A; ida y vuelta** *exp.* round-trip **6B; observación de flora y fauna** *f.* wildlife viewing **6B**
ya *adv.* already **6A; ¡Anda ya!** *exp.* Come on! **9B**
yerba: yerba mate *f.* mate (infusion) **3B**
yo *pron.* I **1A; Yo soy…** *exp.* I am… **0**
yoga *m.* yoga **3A**
yogur *m.* yogurt **2B**
yuca *f.* yucca **4A**

Z

zapatería *f.* shoe store **3B**
zapatillas (de deporte) *f.* running shoes; sneakers **3B**
zapato *m.* shoe **3B**
zona *f.* region **5A; zona colonial** *f.* colonial area **3A**
zumo *m.* juice **2B; zumo de naranja** *m.* orange juice **2B**

English-Spanish

A

a un(a) *art.* **1A: (a ...%) discount** descuento (del ...%) *m.* **11A: a little** un poco *loc. adv.* **2B: a lot** mucho *adv.* **2A, 6A: half a dozen** media docena *f.* **4A: half a kilogram** medio kilo *m.* **4A: once a week** una vez a la semana *loc. adv.* **6A: quite a bit/lot** bastante *adv.* **5B: three times a year** tres veces al año *loc. adv.* **3A: twice a month** dos veces al mes *loc. adv.* **6A**
a.m. de la mañana *loc. adv.* **3A**
abbreviation abreviatura *f.* **13B**
ability competencia *f.* **2:** habilidad *f.* **8A**
about sobre *prep.* **: to be about** tratar *v.* **14B: to know (something) (about)** saber (algo) (de) *v.* **8A**
above: above all sobre todo *loc. adv.* **13B**
abroad: to live abroad vivir afuera *v.* **10B**
absence ausencia *f.* **11A**
academic: academic life vida académica *f.* **14A**
academy academia *f.* **15B**
accent acento *m.* **0: with an accent** con acento *loc. adv.* **0**
accept aceptar *v.* **15B**
acceptance aceptación *f.* **12B:** acogida *f.* **15A**
accessible: easily accessible bien comunicado/a *loc. adv.* **4B**
accessories complementos *m. pl.* **3B**
accommodate albergar *v.* **11A**
accommodations alojamiento *m.* **6B**
accompanied: to feel accompanied sentirse acompañado/a *v.* **9A**
accordion (type of) bandoneón *m.* **17B**
account cuenta *f.* **: to take into account** tener en cuenta *v.* **16B**
accountant contador(a) *m./f.* **13B**
ache doler *v.* **10A**
achieve lograr *v.* **8A:** conseguir *v.* **4A**
acid ácido *m.* **17A**
acronym sigla *f.* **12B**
act actuar *v.* **5A: acting** actuación *f.* **5A**
active activo/a *adj.* **5A**
activity actividad *f.* **0: extracurricular activity** actividad extraescolar *f.* **15B**
actor actor *m.* **1A**
actress actriz *f.* **1A**
ad anuncio *m.* **4B**
adapt adaptarse *v.* **10A**
adapted adaptado/a *adj.* **12B: adapted to** ajustado/a a *adj.* **17A**
add añadir *v.* **4A**
address dirección *f.* **: home address** domicilio *m.* **2A: to address somebody as tú** hablarse de tú *v.* **7B: to use the tú form of address** tutearse *v.* **17B: to address somebody as usted** hablarse de usted *v.* **7B**
adjusted ajustado/a *adj.* **17A**
administer suministrar *v.* **17A**
administration administración *f.* **8A**
administrative administrativo/a *adj.* **7B**
admire admirar *v.* **14B**
adolescent adolescente *m. y f.* **9A**
adopt adoptar *v.* **5B**
adoption adopción *f.* **5B**
advance: in advance con antelación *loc. adv.* **11A**
advantage ventaja *f.* **9B: to take advantage** aprovechar *v.* **15A**
adventure aventura *f.* **5B**
adventurer aventurero/a *m. y f.* **18A**
adventurous aventurero/a *adj.* **9A**
advertisement publicidad *f.* **6B:** anuncio *m.* **4B**
advertising publicidad *f.* **16B**
advice consejos *m. pl.* **6A: advice column** consultorio *m.* **12A: to ask somebody's advice** hacer una consulta *v.* **12A**
advise aconsejar *v.* **6A:** asesorar *v.* **13B**
advisor asesor(a) *m./f.* **11B**
affect afectar *v.* **10A**
affection afecto *m.* **12A: to show affection** mostrar afecto *v.* **18B**
affectionate cariñoso/a *adj.* **12A:** tierno/a *adj.* **9A**
affinity afinidad *f.* **17B**
affordable asequible *adj.* **6B:** económico/a *adj.* **2B**
Africa África *f.* **14A: Sub-Saharan Africa** África subsahariana *f.* **14A**
African africano/a *adj.* **14A**
after después *adv.* **0:** después de que *conj.* **18A: the day after tomorrow** pasado mañana *loc. adv.* **11B**
afternoon tarde *f.* **0: Good afternoon.** Buenas tardes. *exp.* **0: in the afternoon** de la tarde *loc. adv.* **3A: in the afternoon** por la tarde *loc. adv.* **3A**
again de nuevo; otra vez *loc. adv.* **0: to do ... again** volver a *v.* **11B: to meet again** reencontrar *v.* **9A**
age edad *f.* **4A**
agency agencia *f.* **4B: real-estate agency** inmobiliaria *f.* **4B, 11B: travel agency** agencia de viajes *f.* **4B**
aggression agresión *f.* **16A**
ago hace *v.* **5A: two months ago** hace dos meses *loc. adv.* **5A**
agree estar de acuerdo *v.* **5B, 10B: to be agreed upon** a convenir *loc. adv.* **13B**
agriculture agricultura *f.* **15A**
agronomist (ingeniero/a) agrónomo/a *m./f.* **7A**
ahead: ahead of time con antelación *loc. adv.* **11A: straight ahead** todo recto *loc. adv.*
ailment dolencia *f.* **10A**
aimed: to be aimed at estar dirigido/a a *v.* **6A**
air aire *m.* **7B: air conditioning** aire acondicionado *m.* **11A**
airline compañía aérea *f.* **11A:** aerolínea *f.* **13A: national airline** aerolínea abanderada *f.* **13A**
airport aeropuerto *m.* **0**
alarm: alarm clock despertador *m.* **3B**
alarmist alarmista *m. y f.* **17A**
album álbum *m.* **5B:** disco *m.* **7A**
all todo *pron.* **2A: above all** sobre todo *loc. adv.* **13B: all day** todo el día *loc. adv.* **6A: all grown-up** joven hecho/a y derecho/a *exp.* **9A: all in all** en definitiva *loc. adv.* **18B: at all** nada *adv.* **8A: despite it all** a pesar de todo *loc. adv.* **13B: to be all ears** ser todo/a oídos *exp.* **9A**
allergy alergia *f.* **10A**
allow permitir *v.* **6B**
almost casi *adj.* **13B: almost always** casi siempre *loc. adv.* **14A**
alone solo/a *adj.* **7A**
along: to get along/not to get along llevarse bien/mal *v.* **12A**
already ya *adv.* **6A**
although aunque *conj.* **13B**
always siempre *adv.* **2B: almost always** casi siempre *loc. adv.* **14A**
amateur aficionado/a *adj.* **11B**
Amazon River Amazonas *m.* **5A**
ambassador embajador(a) *m./f.* **16A: ambassador for peace** embajador(a) de la paz *m./f.* **16A**
ambitious ambicioso/a *adj.* **16A**
American estadounidense *adj.* **1B: South American** sudamericano/a *adj.* **18A**
among entre *prep.* **2A: among family** en el ámbito familiar *m.* **12A**
amuse divertir *v.* **17B: to amuse oneself** entretenerse *v.* **9A**
an un(a) *art.* **1A**
analyst: marketing analyst analista de *marketing m. y f.* **13B**
ancestry ascendencia *f.* **14A**
and y *conj.* **0:** e (before **i** or **hi** + consonant) *conj.* **1B: both ... and** tanto ... como *conj.* **7A**
anecdote anécdota *f.* **9B**
angry enfadado/a *adj.* **12A: to get angry** enfadarse *v.*, enojarse *v.* **17B**
animal animal *m.* **7B**
anniversary aniversario *m.* **5A: silver wedding anniversary** bodas de plata *f. pl.* **18B: to have one's wedding anniversary** cumplir años de casados *v.* **18B**
announce anunciar *v.* **16A**
announcer locutor(a) *m./f.* **16A**
annoy molestar *v.* **15B**
answer respuesta *f.* **0:** contestar *v.* **0:** responder *v.* **0**
anthem himno *m.* **18B**
antibiotic antibiótico *m.* **10A**
anticipate anticipar *v.* **16B**
antiquated anticuado/a *adj.* **16B**
antique antigüedad *f.* **4A**
any algún *adj.* **9A:** alguno/a *adj.* **9A**
anybody alguien *pron.*, **(in negative statements)** nadie *pron.* **8A**
anybody alguien *pron.*, **(in negative statements)** nadie *pron.* **8A**
anything algo *pron.* **2B: Anything else?** ¿Algo más? *exp.* **2B**
apartment apartamento *m.* **4B: tiny apartment** minipiso *m.* **11B**
apparently al parecer *loc. adv.* **8B**
appeal apelar *v.* **16B**
appearance: physical appearance aspecto físico *m.* **12A**
apple manzana *f.* **4A**
appliance electrodoméstico *m.* **8A**
applicant candidato/a *m./f.* **13B**
application solicitud *f.* **13B**
apply postularse *v.* **13B**
appointment cita *f.* **14B**

appraisal apreciación *f.* **17A**
appraiser evaluador(a) *m./f.* **17A**
appreciate apreciar *v.* **18B**
appreciation apreciación *f.* **17A**
appropriate adecuado/a *adj.* **5B**: apto/a *adj.* **15A**
approximately aproximadamente *adv.* **3A**
apricot albaricoque *m.* **15A: April 13** el 13 de abril *m.* **3A**
April abril *m.* **1B**
architect arquitecto/a *m./f.* **1A**
architecture arquitectura *f.* **8A**
area extensión *f.* **6B**: superficie *f.* **2A**: área *f.* **: the colonial area** zona colonial *f.* **3A**
Argentina Argentina *f.* **0**
Argentine argentino/a *adj.*
argue discutir *v.* **13B**
arid árido/a *adj.* **13A**
arm brazo *m.* **10A: arm in arm** del brazo *loc. adv.* **5A**
armchair sillón *m.* **4B**
armed: armed forces fuerzas armadas *f.* **16A**
arms armas *f. pl.* **16A: arms trade** tráfico de armas *m.* **16A: coat of arms** escudo *m.* **18B**
army ejército *m.* **16A**
aroma aroma *m.* **16B**
around alrededor *adv.* **8A: to go around the world** dar la vuelta al mundo *v.* **18A**
arrange (to meet) quedar *v.* **8A**
arrangement: flower arrangement arreglo floral *m.* **18B**
arrival llegada *f.* **11A: arrival lounge** sala de llegada *f.* **13A: arrival time** entrada *f.* **6A: time of arrival** hora de llegada *f.* **13A**
arrive llegar *v.* **3A: to arrive home** llegar a casa *v.* **3A: arriving from** procedente de *adj.* **13A**
Art Educación plástica y visual *f.* **15B**
art arte *m.* **3B: work of art** obra de arte *f.* **8A**
article reportaje *m.* **14B**
Arts Filosofía y letras *f.* **5A**
artichoke alcachofa *f.* **15A**
artificial artificial *adj.* **15A**
as: as a team en equipo *loc. adv.* **7A: as many** tantos/as *adv.* **8B: as much/many... as** tan/tanto... como *conj.* **8B: as well as** así como *conj.* **16B: as... as possible** lo más... posible *m.* **17A: to work as** trabajar como *v.* **11B: as for** en cuanto a *loc. prep.* **16A: as well** también *adv.* **1B**
aside: to set aside reservar *v.* **6A**
ask preguntar *v.* **0: to ask for** pedir *v.* **12B: to ask for a loan** pedir un crédito *v.* **5B: to ask for help** pedir ayuda *v.* **5B: to ask oneself questions** plantearse preguntas *v.* **14B: to ask permission** pedir permiso *v.* **12B: to ask somebody's advice** hacer una consulta *v.* **12A**
aspect aspecto *m.* **7B**
aspirin aspirina *f.* **10A**: ácido acetilsalicílico *m.* **17A**
assemble montar *v.* **8A**
assert afirmar *v.* **16A**
assessment apreciación **17A**
assignment encargo *m.* **16B**
assistant auxiliar *m. y f.* **7B**
association asociación *f.* **12A**
assorted variado/a *adj.* **7B**
assume asumir *v.* **12B**
astonishment extrañeza *f.* **15B**
at en *prep.* **2B: at all** nada *adv.* **8A: at home** en casa *loc. adv.* **2B: at last** por fin *exp.* **10A: at night** por la noche *loc. adv.* **3A: at the beginning of the 20th century** a principios del siglo XX *loc. adv.* **8B: at the moment** actualmente *adv.* **12A: at the same time** al mismo tiempo *loc. adv.* **7A: At what time...?** ¿A qué hora...? *exp.* **3A: at your service** a tu /suservicio *loc. adv.* **7B: to be aimed at** estar dirigido/a a *v.* **6A: to be at peace** estar en paz *v.* **10B**
athlete deportista *m. y f.* **12B: track-and-field athlete** atleta *m. y f.* **12B, 18A**
atmosphere ambiente *m.* **2A**: carácter *m.* **4A: work atmosphere** ambiente laboral *m.* **13B**
attack atentado *m.* **12B**
attain lograr *v.* **12B**
attend asistir (a) *v.* **15A: attend to** atender *v.* **7A**
attendant: flight attendant auxiliar de vuelo *m. y f.* **13A: kiosk attendant** quiosquero/a *m./f.* **9B**
attention atención *f.* **0: pay attention to** poner atención a *v.* **0: to catch one's attention** llamar la atención *v.* **14A: to pay attention (to somebody)** hacer caso (a alguien) *v.* **15B**
attentive: to be attentive estar pendiente de *v.* **17B**
attitude actitud *f.* **13B**
attraction atractivo *m.* **4B**
attractive atractivo/a *adj.* **12A**
August agosto *m.* **3A**
aunt tía *f.* **5B**
authentic auténtico/a *adj.* **4A**
authenticity autenticidad *f.* **16B**
avenue avenida *f.* **2A**
avocado aguacate *m.* **12A**
avoid evitar *v.* **15A**
award premio *m.* **2B**
aware consciente *adj.* **3B: to make aware** hacer consciente *v.* **3B**
away: to be away estar de viaje *v.* **7A**
Aymara aimara *m.* **12A**
Aztec azteca *adj.* **12A**

B

bachelor(ette): bachelor(ette) party despedida de soltero/a *f.* **18B**
back espalda *f.* **10A: seat back** respaldo del asiento *m.* **13A: to come back** volver *v.* **6B**
backpack mochila *f.* **9A**
bad malo/a *m.* **10A: bad side** lado malo *m.* **13B: in a bad mood** de mal humor *loc. adv.* **12A: the bad thing** lo malo *m.* **12B: there is bad weather** hace mal tiempo *v.* **10A: to be bad (at something)** ser malo/a (en algo) *exp.* **17B**
bag bolsa *f.* **4A**: bolso *m.* **3B**
baggage equipaje *m.* **11A: baggage claim** entrega de equipaje *f.* **13A: baggage screening** control de equipaje *m.* **13A**
baked al horno *loc. adv.* **13A**
bakery panadería *f.* **8B**
balance equilibrio *m.* **6A**
balanced equilibrado/a *adj.* **7B**
balcony terraza *f.* **4B**: balcón *m.* **4B**
Balearic Islands Islas Baleares *f. pl.* **4B**
ball pelota *f.* **18A**: (dance) baile *m.* **5A**
ballpoint pen bolígrafo *m.* **3B**
ballroom: ballroom dance baile de salón *m.* **17B**
banana banana *f.* **15A**
band grupo musical *m.* **14B: rubber band** goma elástica *f.* **8A**
bandoneón (type of accordion) bandoneón *m.* **17B: bandoneón player** bandoneonista *m. y f.* **17B**
bank banco *m.* **1B: bank transfer** transferencia bancaria *f.* **7B**
baptism bautizo *m.* **5B**
bar bar *m.* **0**
barbecue asado *m.* **1A**
bargain regatear *v.* **4A**
barrel: oil barrel barril de petróleo *m.* **14A**
barrier barrera *f.* **12B**
baseball béisbol *m.* **18A: baseball player** beisbolista *m./f.* **18A**
based: based on sobre la base de *loc. prep.* **16A**
basket cesta *f.* **7B**
basketball baloncesto *m.*
Basque vasco/a *adj.* **18A**: (language) euskera *m.* **1B**
Basque Country País Vasco *m.* **1B**
bath: to take a bath darse un baño *v.* **10A**
bathroom baño *m.* **4B**
battery batería *f.* **7B**
bazaar bazar *m.* **8B**
be encontrarse *v.* **10A**: ser *v.* **1A**: estar *v.* **2A: Be careful!** ¡Ojo! *exp.* **0: How are you?** ¿Qué tal? *exp.* **0: How is/are...?** ¿Qué tal está(n)...? *exp.* **2B: How much is it?** ¿Cúanto es? *exp.* **2B: I am...** (Yo) soy... *exp.* **0: I'm OK.** Estoy bien. *exp.* **7B: I'm sorry.** Lo siento. *exp.* **3B: I'm sure (that)...** Seguro que... *exp.* **9A: Is Carmen there?** ¿Está Carmen? *exp.* **6B: It's 9 euros.** Son 9 euros. *exp.* **2B: It's my turn.** Me toca a mí. *exp.* **4A: it's possible** es posible *loc. adv.* **4A: it's sunny** hace sol *v.* **10A: to be a great communicator** ser un(a) gran comunicador(a) *v.* **13B: to be a supporter of** ser hincha de *v.* **17B: to be about** tratar *v.* **14B: to be adapted** estar adaptado/a *v.* **12B: to be aimed at** estar dirigido/a a *v.* **6A: to be all ears** ser todo/a oídos *exp.* **9A: to be at peace** estar en paz *v.* **10B: to be away** estar de viaje *v.* **7A: to be bad (at something)** ser malo/a (en algo) *v.* **17B: to be beyond (our) means** estar fuera de (nuestro) alcance *exp.* **15B: to be born** nacer *v.* **5A: to be cold/hot** tener frío/calor *v.* **10A: to be cold/hot** (weather) hace frío/calor *v.* **10A: to be common** ser moneda corriente *exp.* **13B: to be self-confident** estar seguro/a de sí mismo/a *v.* **18A: to be connected** estar en conexión *v.* **6A: to be delighted** estar encantado/a *v.* **11A: to be difficult** costar

v. 14B: **to be doing something** estar haciendo algo *v.* 7A: **to be excited** estar ilusionado/a *v.* 12A: **to be glad (that)** alegrarse (de) *v.* 11A: **to be good (at something)** ser bueno/a (en algo) *v.* 17B: **to be good for** servir para *v.* 4B: **to be happy** ponerse contento/a *v.* 18B: **to be held** celebrarse *v.* 4A: **to be impressed** estar impresionado/a *v.* 18A: **to be in (good) shape** estar en forma *v.* 7A: **to be in love (with)** estar enamorado/a (de) *v.* 12A: **to be under someone's control** estar en manos de alguien *exp.* 17A: **to be in touch** estar en contacto *v.* 12B: **to be integrated** integrarse *v.* 12B: **to be interested in** estar interesado/a en *v.* 17A: **to be of interest** interesar *v.* 7A: **to be on vacation** estar de vacaciones *v.* 7B: **to be reachable** estar localizable *v.* 13B: **to be right** tener razón *v.* 10B: **to be sad** ponerse triste *v.* 18B: **to be self-sufficient** valerse *v.* 5B: **to be sensitive to** ser sensible a *v.* 10A: **to be silent** estar callado/a *v.* 9A: **to be the highest rated** ser líder de audiencia *v.* 14B: **to be true** ser verdad *v.* 10B: **to be under construction** estar en obras *v.* 11A: **to be waiting for** estar pendiente de *v.* 17B: **to be worth it** valer la pena *v.* 11B: **to be... kilometers from...** estar a... kilómetros de... *loc. adv.* 2A: **What is it like?** ¿Cómo es? *exp.* 4B: **What is it used for?** ¿Para qué sirve? *exp.* 4B: **What is it?** ¿Qué es? *exp.* 1A: **What time is it?** ¿Qué hora es? *exp.* 3A: **where is...?** ¿dónde está...? *exp.* 2A: **Who is it?** ¿Quién es? *exp.* 1A: **I'm from Madrid.** Yo soy de Madrid. *exp.* 1A: **to be called** denominarse *v.* 17A: **to be motivated** estar motivado/a *v.* 13B: **to be used to** estar acostumbrado/a a *v.* 13B: **What's the weather like?** ¿Qué tiempo hace? *exp.* 10A

beach playa *f.* 1A

bean frijol *m.* 4A

beard barba *f.* 12A

beat batir *v.* 8A

beautiful bello/a *adj.* 16B

beauty belleza *f.* 4B

because porque *conj.*

become convertirse en *v.* 7A: hacerse *v.* 8B: tornarse *v.* 17A: **to become a vegetarian** hacerse vegetariano/a *v.* 7B: **to become confused** confundirse *v.* 16B: **to become independent** independizarse *v.* 15B: **to become sad** ponserse triste *v.* 18B: **to join, to become a member** afiliarse *v.* 16A

bed cama *f.* 4B: **bed & breakfast** posada *f.* 11B: **double bed** cama de matrimonio *f.* 4B: **to go to bed** acostarse *v.* 7A: **to make the bed** hacer la cama *v.* 3A

bedroom dormitorio *m.* 4B

beer cerveza *f.* 2B

beet remolacha *f.* 15A

before antes *adv.* 9A: antes de que *conj.* 18A: antes *m.* 9A

begin comenzar *v.* 8B: empezar *v.* 5A

beginning: at the beginning of the 20th century a principios del siglo XX *loc. adv.* 8B

behind detrás de *loc. prep.* 3B: **falling behind** rezagado/a *adj.* 17A

Beijing Pekín *m.* 1B

being: human being ser humano *m.* 8A

Belgium Bélgica *f.* 10B

bell campana *f.* 18B: **peal of a bell** campanada *f.* 18B

belong pertenecer *v.* 3B

belt cinturón *m.* 8A

bench banco *m.* 0

benefit redundar en *v.* 17A

Berlin Wall Muro de Berlín *m.* 10B

best mejor *adj., adv.* 4A: **best-known** más conocido/a *adj.* 4A: **the best** el/la mejor *m./f.* 9A: **the best (thing)** lo mejor *m.* 4B

better mejor *adv.* 6A

between entre *prep.* 2A

beverage bebida *f.* 2B

beyond: to be beyond (one's) means estar fuera de (nuestro) alcance *exp.* 15B

bicycle bicicleta *f.* 6B

big grande *adj.* 4B

bike bici(cleta) *f.* 6B

Bilbao: from Bilbao bilbaíno/a *adj.* 17A

bilingual bilingüe *adj.* 18A: **bilingual school** escuela bilingüe *f.* 15B

bill cuenta *f.* 2B

biography biografía *f.* 5A

biologist biólogo/a *m./f.* 11B: **marine biologist** biólogo/a marino/a *m./f.* 11B

biology biología *f.* 1B

birth nacimiento *m.* 5A

birthday cumpleaños *m.* 5A: **fifteenth birthday party** fiesta de quince años *f.* 18B: **to have one's birthday** cumplir años *v.* 18B

birthplace lugar de nacimiento *m.* 11B

bit: quite a bit/lot bastante *adv., pron.* 5B

bitter amargo/a *adj.* 10B

black negro/a *adj.* 3B: **black coffee** café solo *m.* 2B: **black gold** oro negro *m.* 14A

bland soso/a *adj.* 2B

blank: to draw a blank quedarse en blanco *v.* 15B

blanket frazada *f.* 13A

blind ciego/a *adj.* 12B

blocked bloqueado/a *adj.* 7B

blog blog *m.* 3A

blond(e) rubio/a *adj.* 12A

blood sangre *f.* 17A

blue azul *adj.* 3B: **light blue** celeste *adj.* 9A

board: on board a bordo *loc. adv.* 13A

boarding embarque *m.* 13A: **boarding gate** puerta de embarque *f.* 13A: **boarding time** hora de embarque *f.* 13A

boat lancha *f.* 9A: **by boat** en barco *loc. adv.* 5A: **row boat** bote de remos *m.* 18A

body cuerpo *m.* 6A

Bolivia Bolivia *f.* 0

bone hueso *m.* 9A

book libro *m.* 0: **comic book** cómic *m.* 9B: **to book the tickets** reservar los billetes *v.* 13A

bookstore librería *f.* 3B

boot bota *f.* 3B

booth: lottery ticket booth agencia de lotería *f.* 9B

border frontera *f.* 7A

bore aburrir *v.* 17B

bored: to get bored aburrirse *v.* 17B: **to get tired/bored of (something)** cansarse de (algo) *v.* 9B

boredom aburrimiento *m.* 17B

boring aburrido/a *adj.* 1B

boss jefe/a *m./f.* 12B

both los/las dos *pron.* 6B: **both ... and** tanto ... como *conj.* 7A

bother molestar *v.* 15B, 17B

bottle botella *f.* 2B

bouquet ramo *m.* 9B

box caja *f.* 8A: recuadro *m.* 0

boxer boxeador(a) *m./f.* 18A

boy niño *m.* 3A: **young boy** el pibe *m.* 17B

boyfriend novio *m.* 5A

brand marca *f.* 3B

Brazil Brasil *m.* 1A

Brazilian brasileño/a *adj.*

bread pan *m.* 2B

break romper *v.* 16A: **to break a record** batir un récord *v.* 18A: **break down** averiarse *v.* 13A

breakfast desayuno *m.* 2B: **bed & breakfast** posada *f.* 11B: **to eat breakfast** desayunar *v.* 2B

breakthrough avance *m.* 17A

breathe respirar *v.* 7B

bride novia *m./f.* 5A

bright alegre *adj.* 4B: brillante *adj.* 9A

brilliant brillante *adj.* 14B

bring traer *v.* 7B: **to bring up to date** poner al día *v.* 7B

broadcast emitir *v.* 14B: **to broadcast the television series** pasar la serie de televisión *v.* 14B

broccoli brócoli *m.* 15A

brochure folleto *m.* 0

bronze bronce *m.* 12B

brother hermano *m.* 5A

brown castaño/a *adj.* 12A: (color) café *adj.* 3B: marrón *adj.* 3B

brunet(te) moreno/a *adj.* 12A

Buenos Aires: Buenos Aires slang lunfardo *m.* 17B: **of/from the city of Buenos Aires** porteño/a *adj.* 17B

build construir *v.* 0

building edificio *m.* 2A

bunch ramo *m.* 9B: **bunch of flowers** ramo de flores *m.* 18B

bungee: bungee jumping puenting *m.* 18A

burn quemar *v.* 18B

bus autobús *m.* 4B: colectivo *m.* 17B: ómnibus *m.* 13A

business negocio *m.* 7B: **business card** tarjeta de visita *f.* 18B: **business person** empresario/a *m./f.* 8B: **business trip** viaje de negocios *m.* 3A: **business woman** mujer empresaria *f.* 5A: **to expand a business** ampliar un negocio *v.* 15A: **to open a business** abrir un negocio *v.* 15A

busy ocupado/a *adj.* 2A

but pero *conj.* 2A

butter mantequilla *f.* 2B

button botón *m.* 4B

buy comprar *v.* 3B: **to buy lottery tickets** comprar (billetes de) lotería *v.* 9B

by en, por *prep.* **5A: by boat** en barco *loc. adv.* **5A: by chance** casualmente *adv* **17B: by means of** por medio de *loc. prep.* **14B: by the way** por cierto *exp.* **10A: by vocation** por vocación *loc. adv.* **7A: day by day** día a día *loc. adv.* **14B: surrounded by** rodeado/a de *loc. adv.* **6B: to go by (means of transportation)** ir en... *v.* **6B: to go by car** ir en coche *v.* **3A: by the way** a propósito *exp.* **10A**
Bye. Chau. *exp.* **0**

C

cabbage col *f.* **15A**
cabin cabaña *f.* **6B**
cable cable *m.* **18A: steel cable** cable de acero *m.* **18A**
café confitería *f.* **4A:** cafetería *f.* **1B:** bar *m.* **2B: Internet café** cibercafé *m.* **4A: Internet café** locutorio *m.* **8B**
caffeine cafeína *f.* **2B**
cake pastel *m.* **18B**
calamari calamares *m. pl.* **2B**
calculate calcular *v.* **0**
calendar calendario *m.* **3A**
call llamada *f.* **3A:** (to action) convocatoria *f.* **16A: call center** locutorio *m.* **8B**
calm tranquilo/a *adj.* **2A**
calorie caloría *m.* **15A: low-calorie** bajo en calorías *adj.* **15A**
cameraman/camerawoman camarógrafo/a *m./f.* **9A**
campaign campaña *f.* **12B: conciliation campaign** campaña de conciliación *f.* **15B: electoral campaign** campaña electoral *f.* **16A: promotional campaign** campaña de promoción *f.* **16B: to launch a campaign** lanzar una campaña *v.* **16B**
campsite campamento *m.* **6B: camping** *m.* **6B**
can (to be able to) poder *v.* **3B: Can I see them?** ¿Los puedo ver? *exp.* **3B: I can...** Yo puedo *v.* **0: You/One can't...** No se puede... *v.* **7B**
Canada Canadá *m.* **0**
Canadian canadiense *adj.* **1B**
cancelled cancelado/a *adj.* **13A**
candidate candidato/a *m./f.* **16A**
candle vela *f.* **5A**
candy dulce *m.* **2B; nougat candy** turrón *m.* **18B**
cannot: cannot be forgotten no puede olvidarse *v.* **10B**
canoeing canotaje *m.* **18A**
cap gorro *m.* **10A**
capacity capacidad *f.* **13B: to have (storage) capacity** tener capacidad *v.* **13B**
capita: per capita income renta per cápita *f.* **14A**
capital capital *f.* **2A**
caption pie de foto *m.* **5A**
captivate conquistar *v.* **15A:** conquistar *v.* **15A:** fascinar *v.* **14A**
car auto *m.* **6B:** coche *m.* **3A:** carro *m.* **5B: to go by car** ir en coche *v.* **3A**
carbohydrate hidrato de carbono *m.* **15A**
card tarjeta *f.* **3B: (soccer) trading card** el cromo (de fútbol) *m.* **9B: credit card** tarjeta de crédito *f.* **3B: greeting card** tarjeta de felicitación *f.* **5A: national identity card** DNI *m.* **3A: with a credit card** con tarjeta *loc. adv.* **3B**
cardiovascular cardiovascular *adj.* **17A**
care: day care guardería *f.* **5B: health care** asistencia sanitaria *f.* **10A: to take care of someone** cuidar (a/de) alguien *v.* **5B: to take care of the details** ocuparse de los detalles *v.* **18B**
career carrera *f.* **1B: career counselor** orientador(a) profesional *m./f.* **13B**
caress acariciar *v.* **9A**
Caribbean caribeño/a *adj.* **4B: Caribbean Sea** mar Caribe *m.* **4B**
Carmelite carmelita *adj.* **11A**
carnation clavel *m.* **18B**
carpenter carpintero/a *m./f.* **12B**
carpentry carpintería *f.* **8A**
carpet alfombra *f.* **4B**
carry cargar *v.* **9A:** llevar *v.* **3A: carry out** llevar a cabo *v.* **18A**
cartoon viñeta (cómica) *f.* **0**
case estuche *m.* **13A**
cash en efectivo *loc. adv.* **3B**
cashier cajero/a *m./f.* **1B**
castle castillo *m.* **6B**
Catalan catalán/catalana *adj.* **1B:** catalán *m.* **1B**
catch atrapar *v.* **18A: to catch one's attention** llamar la atención *v.* **14A**
cathedral catedral *f.* **2A**
Catholic católico/a *adj.* **5A**
cease dejar de *v.* **10B**
celebrate celebrar *v.* **5A**
celebration celebración *f.* **18B**
celiac celíaco/a *adj.* **15A**
cell: cell phone (teléfono) celular *m.* **1B**
center centro *m.* **1A: call center** locutorio *m.* **8B: employment center** bolsa de trabajo *m.* **13B: in the center of town** céntrico/a *adj.* **7B**
century siglo *m.* **8B: towards the beginning of the 20th century** a principios del siglo XX *loc. adv.* **8B: towards the end of the 19th century** a finales del siglo XIX *loc. adv.* **8B**
cereal cereales *m. pl.* **2B**
ceremony ceremonia *f.* **14A: master of ceremonies** maestro/a de ceremonias *m./f.* **18B**
certainty certeza *f.* **15A**
certified certificado/a *adj.* **16B**
ceviche (marinated seafood dish) ceviche *m.* **1A**
cha-cha chachachá *m.* **17B**
chair silla *f.* **4B**
challenge reto *m.* **18A: to overcome challenges** superar retos *v.* **18A**
chamomile (tea) manzanilla *f.* **10A**
change cambio *m.* **11A:** cambiar *v.* **7B: change of scenery** cambio de aires *m.* **11A: seat change** cambio de asiento *m.* **13A: to change jobs** cambiar de trabajo *v.* **7B: to change one's life** cambiar de vida *v.* **7B**
channel canal *m.* **9A**
character personaje *m.* **1A:** carácter *m.* **12A**
characteristic cualidad *f.* **17B:** rasgo *m.* **14A**
charisma carisma *m.* **18A**
charitable caritativo/a *adj.* **16A**
charm encanto *m.* **11A**
charming con encanto *loc. adv.* **6B**
chart tabla *f.* **0**
chat charlar *v.* **14A: chat room** chat *m.* **3A: to chat (on the Internet)** chatear *v.* **6B**
cheap barato/a *adj.* **4B**
check comprobar *v.* **13A:** controlar *v.* **17A: check off** marcar *v.* **0**
checkbox casilla *f.* **0**
check-in facturación *f.* **11A: check-in desk** mostrador de facturación *m.* **13A**
cheese queso *m.* **2B**
chemist químico/a *m./f.* **8B**
chemistry química *f.* **1B**
cherry cereza *f.* **: wild cherry** guinda *f.* **16B**
chewing: chewing gum chicle *m.* **9B**
child niño/a *m./f.* **8B**
child: to have a child tener un hijo *v.* **8B**
childhood infancia *f.* **9A: since childhood** desde niño(s)/a(s) *loc. adv.* **8B: since childhood** desde pequeño/a *loc. adv.* **5B**
children: children's fashion moda infantil *f.* **3B**
Chile Chile *m.* **0**
Chilean chileno/a *adj.*
chimney chimenea *f.* **8B**
Chinese chino/a *adj.* **1B:** chino *m.* **1B**
chip chip *m.* **17A: potato chips** patatas fritas *f.* **4A**
chocolate chocolate *m.* **0**
choose elegir *v.* **7A:** optar *v.* **18B: What... do you choose?** ¿Qué... eliges? *exp.* **1A**
chorizo (sausage) chorizo *m.* **2B**
Christmas Navidad *f.* **5B**
chronologically cronológicamente *adv.* **5B**
church iglesia *f.* **2A**
churros churros *m.* **2B**
cigar: Cuban cigar puro habano *m.* **3B**
circle círculo *m.* **18A:** rodear *v.* **0**
circulation circulación *f.* **10A**
cited citado/a *adj.* **17A**
citizen ciudadano/a *m./f.* **8B: distinguished citizen** ciudadano/a ilustre *m./f.* **17B**
city ciudad *f.* **0: city hall** ayuntamiento *m.* **2A**
Civics Educación ético-cívica *f.* **15B**
civil: civil war guerra civil *f.* **8B**
civilization civilización *f.* **11B**
claim: baggage claim entrega de equipaje *f.* **13A**
class clase *f.* **1B:** curso *m.* **3A: graduating class** promoción *f.* **9A: middle class** clase media *f.* **14B: music class** clase de música *f.* **3A: the rest of the class** el resto de la clase *f.* **0: to have class** tener clase *v.* **3A: to give (subject) ... classes** dar clases (de algo) *v.* **8A**
classic clásico/a *adj.* **4B, 7A:** clásico *m.* **9A**
classify clasificar *v.* **0**
classmate compañero/a (de clase) *m./f.* **0**
clay arcilla *f.* **16B**
clean limpio/a *adj.* **3A:** limpiar *v.* **3A**
clear evidente *adj.* **17A**

cliché tópico *m.* **16B**
click hacer clic *v.* **13B**
client cliente *m. y f.* **2A**
climate clima *m.* **2A**
climb ascender *v.* **18A:** subir *v.* **5A:** (a mountain) escalar *v.* **18A**
climber: mountain climber montañista *m. y f.* **18A**
climbing escalada *f.* **18A:** montañismo *m.* **18A**
clinic clínica *f.* **10A**
clock reloj *m.* **3A: alarm clock** despertador *m.* **3B**
close cerrar *v.* **17A: to close the gap** cerrar la brecha *v.* **17A**
closet armario *m.* **4B**
cloth tela *f.* **8A: piece of cloth** tela *f.* **8A**
clothing ropa *f.* **3B: clothing store** tienda de ropa *f.* **3B**
cloudy nublado/a *adj.* **10A**
club: night club discoteca *f.* **2A**
clumsy person manazas *m. y f.* **8A**
coach entrenador(a) *m./f.* **18A**
coast costa *f.* **4B**
coat chaqueta *f.* **3B: coat of arms** escudo *m.* **18B**
cocktail cóctel *m.* **16B**
cocoa cacao *m.* **15A: cocoa powder** cacao en polvo *m.* **15A**
coconut coco *m.* **15A**
cod bacalao *m.* **2B: cod with sauce** bacalao en salsa *m.* **2B**
code código *m.* **13B**
coexist (with) convivir (con) *v.* **14A**
coexistence convivencia *f.* **14A**
coffee café *m.* **0: black coffee** café solo *m.* **2B: coffee cup** taza *f.* **2B: decaf coffee** descafeinado *m.* **2B**
coin moneda *f.* **0**
coincidence casualidad *f.* **16A**
cold frío *m.* **2A: to be cold/hot** tener frío/calor *v.* **10A: to be cold/hot** (weather) hacer frío/calor *v.* **10A: to have a cold** estar resfriado/a *v.* **10A**
collaborate colaborar *v.* **10B**
colleague colega *m. y f.* **7B:** compañero/a *m./f.* **0**
collect coleccionar *v.* **9B:** recoger *v.* **5B:** reunir *v.* **15A**
collection colección *f.* **3B**
collective colectivo/a *adj.* **8A**
college universidad *f.* **2A: college student** universitario *adj.; m./f.* **2A**
collide chocar *v.* **14B**
Colombia Colombia *f.* **0**
Colombian colombiano/a *adj.* **3B**
colonial colonial *adj.* **3A: the colonial area** zona colonial *f.* **3A**
colonizer colonizador(a) *m./f.* **18B**
colony colonia *f.* **14A**
color color *m.* **3B: What color?** ¿De qué color? *exp.* **3B**
colorant colorante *m.* **15A**
coloring colorante *m.* **15A**
column columna *f.*; **advice column** consultorio *m.* **12A**
comb peine *m.* **8A**
combine compaginar *v.* **7A**
come venir *v.* **3B: Come on!** ¡Anda ya! *exp.* **9B: Come on!** ¡Dale!/¡Venga! /¡Sale! *exp.* **8A: Come on!** ¡Pero, hombre/mujer! *exp.* **17A: to come back** volver *v.* **6B: to come from** provenir de *v.* **16B: to make (his/her) dreams come true** cumplir (sus) sueños *v.* **15B: to come up** surgir *v.* **15A**
comfortable cómodo/a *adj.* **2A**
comforts comodidades *f. pl.* **7B**
comic viñeta (cómica) *f.* **0: comic book** cómic *m.* **9B: comic strip** historieta *f.* **14B**
comics cómics *m.* **7A**
command dominio *m.* **13B**
commemorate conmemorar *v.* **17A**
commerce comercio *m.* **8B**
commitment compromiso *m.* **5A**
common frecuente *adj.* **2B: point in common** punto común *m.* **5B: to be common** ser moneda corriente *exp.* **13B: to have a lot in common** ser afín *v.* **17B**
communal comunitario/a *adj.* **17A**
communication comunicación *f.* **3B: lack of communication** falta de comunicación *f.* **15B**
communicative comunicativo/a *adj.* **16B**
communicator: to be a great communicator ser un(a) gran comunicador(a) *v.* **13B**
community comunidad *f.* **1A: immigrant community** comunidad inmigrante *f.* **8B**
company empresa *f.* **6A:** compañía *f.* **7A: (to keep) company** (hacer) compañía *v.* **7A: courier company** mensajería *f.* **7B: in good company** en buena compañía *loc. adv.* **16B: messenger company** mensajería *f.* **7B: to keep company** acompañar *v.* **9A**
compare comparar *v.* **0**
compass brújula *f.* **18A**
compatible compatible *adj.* **5B**
compete competir *v.* **18A**
competence competencia *f.* **2**
complain quejarse *v.* : protestar *v.* **11A**
complaint queja *f.* **11A: complaint form** libro de quejas *m.* **11A**
complete completo/a *adj.* **9A:** completar *v.* **0**
complex complejo/a *adj.* **16B**
compose componer *v.* **7A**
composition composición *f.* **15A**
computer computadora *f.* **4B:** ordenador *m.* **7B: computer science** informática *f.* **1B: computer technician** técnico/a informático/a *m./f.* **1B**
concern preocupación *f.* **7A:** preocupar *v.* **7A**
concert concierto *m.* **1A: to give a concert** dar un concierto *v.* **7A**
conciliation: conciliation campaign campaña de conciliación *f.* **15B**
condition: physical condition estado físico *m.* **10A**
conditioning: air conditioning aire acondicionado *m.* **11A**
conference congreso *m.* **12B: press conference** rueda de prensa *f.* **12B**
confidence confianza *f.* **18A**
confident: to be self-confident estar seguro/a de sí mismo/a *v.* **18A**
confirm confirmar *v.* **6B**
confirmation confirmación *f.* **13A**
conflict conflicto *m.* **7A: conflict resolution** resolución de conflictos *f.* **13B:**
confused confundido/a *adj.* **16B: to become confused** confundirse *v.* **16B**
Congratulations! ¡Felicidades! *exp.* **5A:** ¡Felicitaciones! *exp.* **6A:** ¡Enhorabuena! *exp.* **18B**
conjugate conjugar *v.* **0**
connected: to be connected estar en conexión *v.* **6A to be connected (to the Internet)** estar conectado *v.* **13B**
conscience conciencia *f.* **17A**
consensus consenso *m.* **16A**
consequence consecuencia *f.* **12B**
construction obras *f.* **2A: to be under construction** estar en obras *v.* **11A**
consultant: labor consultant asesor(a) laboral *m./f.* **13B: to act as consultant to** asesorar *v.* **13B**
consume consumir *v.* **15A**
consumer consumidor(a) *m./f.* **3B**
consumption consumo *m.* **3B**
contact contacto *m.* **17B**
container envase *m.* **15A: plastic container** envase de plástico *m.* **15A: recyclable container** envase reciclable *m.* **15A: recycling container** contenedor *m.* **15A**
contemporary contemporáneo/a *adj.* **3B**
content contenido *m.* **14B: table of contents** sumario *m.* **1B**
contest certamen *m.* **16B**
continent continente *m.* **11B**
continue seguir *v.* **9B**
contract: employment contract contrato de trabajo *m.* **13B**
control controlar *v.* **15B: passport control** control de pasaportes *m.* **13A: to be under someone's control** estar en manos de alguien *exp.* **17A**
convenient cómodo/a *adj.* **17A**
convent convento *m.* **6B**
conventional convencional *adj.* **16A**
conversation charla *f.* **9A:** conversación *f.* **1A**
conviction convicción *f.* **16A**
convince convencer *v.* **16A**
cook cocinero/a *m./f.* : cocinar *v.* **3A**
cooked cocido/a *adj.* **15A**
cookie galleta *f.* **2B**
cooking cocina *f.* **8A**
coordinator coordinador(a) *m./f.* **16A**
corn choclo *m.* **15A:** maíz *m.* **2B**
corner rincón *m.* **13A**
cornmeal harina de maíz *f.* **15A**
correct correcto/a *adj.* **0**
corruption corrupción *f.* **16A**
cosmetics: perfume/cosmetics shop perfumería *f.* **3B**
cosmopolitan cosmopolita *adj.* **16B**
cost costar *v.* **4A: How much do... cost?** ¿Cuánto cuestan...? *exp.* **4A**
Costa Rica Costa Rica *f.* **0**
Costa Rican costarricense *adj.* **14B:** tico/a *(fam.) adj.; m./f.* **18B:** costarricense *m. y f.* **14B**
cotton algodón *m.* **9A**
counselor: career counselor orientador(a) profesional *m./f.* **13B**

country país *m.* **0:** (countryside) campo *m.* **3A: country house** masía (*Cataluña*) *f.* **7B: host country** país receptor *m.* **8B**
coup d'état golpe de estado *m.* **10B**
couple pareja *f.* **5B**
courage valentía *f.* **16B**
courier: courier company mensajería *f.* **7B**
course curso *m.* **3A: first course** primer plato *m.* **2B: main course** plato principal *m.* **2B**
court cancha *f.* **18A**
cousin primo/a *m./f.* **5B**
cover portada *f.* **3B:** (a distance) recorrer *v.* **9B: cover letter** carta de presentación *f.* **13B**
cow vaca *f.* **0**
coworker compañero/a de trabajo *m./f.* **5B**
crafts artesanía *f.* **3B**
crane grulla *f.* **16A**
crazy loco/a *adj.* **7B**
cream crema de leche *f.* **15A: ice cream** helado *m.* **2B**
create crear *v.* **0:** construir *v.* **0:** elaborar *v.* **0:** formar *v.* **0**
credit: credit card tarjeta de crédito *f.* **3B: to pay with a credit card** pagar con tarjeta *v.* **3B**
crime delito *m.* **17B**
crisis crisis *f.* **12B**
critic evaluador(a) *m./f.* **17A: literary critic** crítico/a literario/a *m./f.* **10B**
criticize criticar *v.* **17B**
croissant cruasán *m.* **2B**
cross cruzar *v.* **18A:** traspasar *v.* **14B: to cross out** tachar *v.* **0**
cross-border transfronterizo/a *adj.* **14A**
crucial decisivo/a *adj.* **10B**
cruise crucero *m.* **16B**
cry llorar *v.* **14B**
Cuba Cuba *f.* **0**
Cuban cubano/a *adj., m./f.* **13A: Cuban cigar** puro habano *m.* **3B**
cucumber pepino *m.* **8A**
cuisine cocina *f.* **8A:** gastronomía *f.* **4B**
culinary gastronómico/a *adj.* **2B**
cultivate cultivar *v.* **7B**
cultural cultural *adj.* **6A: cultural policy** política cultural *f.* **16A**
culture: culture shock choque cultural *m.* **14B**
cumbia (dance typical of the Caribbean coast of Colombia) cumbia *f.* **17B**
cup: coffee cup taza *f.* **2B**
cure cura *f.* **17A:** remedio *m.* **10A**
curiosity curiosidad *f.* **:** objeto curioso *m.* **4A**
curly rizado/a *adj.* **12A**
currency moneda *f.* **10B: foreign currency** divisas *f. pl.* **13A: foreign currency exchange** cambio de dinero *m.* **13A**
currently actualmente *adv.* **7A**
curse maldición *f.* **16A**
custody: joint custody custodia compartida *f.* **12A**
custom uso *m.* **16B**
cycling ciclismo *m.* **18A**
cyclist ciclista *m. y f.* **18A**

D

dad papá (*fam.*) *m.* **5B**
daily diario/a *adj.* **13A: daily life** día a día *m.* **7A: daily routine** rutina diaria *f.* **3A**
daisy margarita *f.* **18B**
dance baile *m.* **5A:** bailar *v.* **6A: ballroom dance** baile de salón *m.* **17B: flamenco dance** baile flamenco *m.* **7A**
dancer bailarín/bailarina *m./f.* **7A: flamenco dancer** bailaor(a) *m./f.* **7A**
dangerous peligroso/a *adj.* **10A**
dare atreverse *v.* **17A**
dark oscuro/a *adj.* **16B: dark-haired** moreno/a *adj.* **12A**
data datos *m. pl.* **0**
date fecha *f.* **5A:** (appointment) cita *f.* **14B: expiration date** fecha de caducidad *f.* **15A: to bring up to date** poner al día *v.* **7B**
daughter hija *f.* **5A**
day día *m.* **3A: all day** todo el día *loc. adv.* **6A: day by day** día a día *loc. adv.* **14B: day care** guardería *f.* **5B: day of the week** día de la semana *m.* **3A: day off** día libre *m.* **14A: each day** cada día *loc. adv.* **14A: every day** todos los días *loc. adv.* **3A: Mother's Day** Día de la Madre *m.* **18B: the day after tomorrow** pasado mañana *loc. adv.* **11B: the other day** el otro día *loc. adv.* **9B: Those were the days!** ¡Qué tiempos aquellos! *exp.* **5B**
deaf sordo/a *adj.* **12B**
dear estimado/a *adj.* **6B: Dear sirs,** Estimados señores: *exp.* **6B**
death muerte *f.* **10B**
debate debate *m.* **16A**
decade década *f.* **14B**
decaf: decaf coffee descafeinado *m.* **2B**
December diciembre *m.* **3A**
decent digno/a *adj.* **3B**
decide decidir *v.* **6A**
decisive decisivo/a *adj.* **10B**
declaration: of love declaración de amor *f.* **18B**
declare declarar *v.* **16A**
decorate adornar(se) *v.* **18B**
decoration decoración *f.* **3B**
decorator decorador(a) *m./f.* **11B**
dedicate dedicar *v.* **6A**
dedication dedicación *f.* **15A**
defend defender *v.* **12B**
defense defensa *f.* **16A**
degree título *m.* **13B: to study for a degree** estudiar una carrera *v.* **15B**
delay retraso *m.* **11A**
delayed con retraso *loc. adv.* **13A**
delicious exquisito/a *adj.* **13A**
delighted encantado/a *adj.* **11A**
deliver repartir *v.* **7B:** entregar *v.* **7B**
delivery entrega *f.* **7B: home delivery** reparto a domicilio *m.* **7B**
demand demanda *f.* **15A:** exigir *v.* **16B**
demand: labor demand demanda laboral *f.* **14A**
democracy democracia *f.* **14B**
democratic democrático/a *adj.* **10B**
democratic: democratic transition transición democrática *f.* **14B**
demolish derribar *v.* **10B**
demonstration: social demonstration movilización social *f.* **16A**
denounce denunciar *v.* **16A**
dense denso/a *adj.* **16B**
densely densamente *adv.* **16B**
dentist dentista *m. y f.* **10A**
depart salir *v.* **13A**
department secretaría *f.* **16A:** ministerio *m.* **16A**
departure salida *f.* **6A: departure time** hora de salida *f.* **13A**
depend depender *v.* **10A**
dependable estable *adj.* **12B**
descend descender *v.* **18A**
describe describir *v.* **0**
desert desierto *m.* **5A: desert-like** desértico/a *adj.* **5A**
design diseño *m.* **4B:** diseñar *v.* **0: graphic design** diseño gráfico *m.* **7A**
designer diseñador(a) *m./f.* **3B: fashion designer** diseñador(a) de moda *m./f.* **11B**
desk mostrador *m.* **13A: check-in desk** mostrador de facturación *m.* **13A**
despite a pesar de (que) *conj.* **6B: despite it all** a pesar de todo *loc. adv.* **13B**
despotism caciquismo *m.* **16A**
dessert postre *m.* **2B**
destination destino *m.* **13A: tourist destination** destino turístico *m.* **4B**
detail detalle *m.* **18B: to take care of the details** ocuparse de los detalles *v.* **18B**
determine condicionar *v.* **14A**
develop desarrollar *v.* **15B**
developing en vías de desarrollo *adj.* **3B**
development desarrollo *m.* **14A**
device aparato *m.* **4B**
devour devorar *v.* **18B**
diabetes diabetes *f.* **17A**
diabetic diabético/a *adj.* **17A**
dialect dialecto *m.* **17B**
dialogue diálogo *m.* **0**
diarrhea diarrea *f.* **10A**
diary diario *m.* **5A**
dictator dictador(a) *m./f.* **16A**
dictatorship dictadura *f.* **10B**
die morir *v.* **10B**
die: roll the die tiren el dado *exp.* **10A**
diet dieta *f.* **7B**
difference diferencia *f.* **16B**
different diferente *adj.* **2A:** distinto/a *adj.* **4A**
differentiate diferenciarse *v.* **17B**
difficult difícil *adj.* **7A: extremely difficult** superdifícil *adj.* **11B: to be difficult** costar *v.* **14B**
difficulty dificultad *f.* **6B**
digital digital *adj.* **9B**
diminutive diminutivo *m.* **12A**
dine cenar *v.* **2B**
dining: dining hall comedor *m.* **15B: dining room** comedor *m.* **4B: living room-dining room** salón-comedor *m.* **4B**
diplomat diplomático/a *m./f.* **16A**
director director(a) *m./f.* **1A**
dirt tierra *f.* **9A**
disability discapacidad *f.* **12B**
disabled discapacitado/a *adj.* **12B**
disadvantage desventaja *f.* **9B**

disagree estar en desacuerdo *v.* **5B**
disagreement desacuerdo *m.* **10B**
disappear desaparecer *v.* **10B**
disappoint decepcionar *v.* **17B**
disappointment decepción *f.* **10B**
disaster desastre *m.* **16A**
disciple discípulo *m.* **17A**
disco discoteca *f.* **2A**
disconnect (oneself) desconectarse *v.* **7B**
discount rebaja *f.* **3B:** descuento *m.* **6A: (a ...%) discount** descuento (del ...%) *m.* **11A**
discover descubrir *v.* **17A**
discovery descubrimiento *m.* **17A**
discus thrower lanzador(a) de disco *m./f* **17A**
discuss comentar *v.* **0**
disgust disgusto *m.* **15B**
dish plato *m.* **8A: to do the dishes** lavar los platos *v.* **5A**
disinfectant desinfectante *m.* **10A**
dispenser dispensador *m.* **9B**
display exponer *v.* **0**
disposable desechable *adj.* **17A**
distance distancia *f.* **2A: long-distance love** amor a distancia *m.* **6B**
distinguished: distinguished citizen ciudadano/a ilustre *m./f.* **17B**
distraction distracción *f.* **13B**
distribute repartir *v.* **12B**
diversity diversidad *f.* **7A**
diving: scuba diving submarinismo *m.* **11B**
divorce divorcio *m.* **12A: to get divorced** divorciarse *v.* **12A**
divorced divorciado/a *adj.* **5B**
do hacer *v.* **3A:** realizar *v.* **5A: to be doing something** estar haciendo algo *v.* **7A: to do ... again** volver a *v.* **11B: to do something for a living** dedicarse a (hacer) algo *v.* **7A: to do overtime** hacer horas extras *v.* **13B: to do pottery** hacer cerámica *v.* **6A: to do something at home** hacer algo en casa *v.* **3A: to do the dishes** lavar los platos *v.* **5A: to usually do something** soler *v.* **14A: What do you do (for work)?** ¿A qué te dedicas? *exp.* **1B**
doctor doctor(a) *m./f.* **10A:** médico/a *m./f.* **1B: family doctor** médico/a de familia *m./f.* **10A**
documentary documental *m.* **9A**
dog perro/a *m./f.* **12B: guide dog** perro/a guía *m. y f.* **12B**
do-it-yourself bricolaje *m.* **8A**
dolphin delfín *m.* **5A**
domestic nacional *adj.* **13A: domestic service** servicio doméstico *m.* **8B: gross domestic product (GDP)** producto interior bruto (PIB) *m.* **11A, 14A**
Dominican Republic República Dominicana *f.* **0**
donation donación *f.* **9A**
donkey burro *m.* **9A**
dorm residencia de estudiantes *f.* **12A**
dose dosis *f.* **17A**
double doble *m.* **2B: double bed** cama de matrimonio *f.* **4B: double room** habitación doble *f.* **6B**
doubt duda *f.* **16A:** dudar *v.* **16A**
downtown centro *m.* **1A**
dozen docena *f.* **4A: half a dozen** media docena *f.* **4A**
draw sorteo *m.* **9B:** dibujar *v.* **0: to draw a blank** quedarse en blanco *v.* **15B**
drawback inconveniente *m.* **13B**
drawer cajón *m.* **8A**
drawing dibujo *m.* **3B:** sorteo *m.* **12B**
dreadful pésimo/a *adj.* **11A**
dream sueño *m.* **8B:** soñar *v.* **8B: the man/woman of my dreams** el hombre/la mujer de mi vida *exp.* **12A: to make (his/her) dreams come true** cumplir (sus) sueños *v.* **15B**
dress vestido *m.* **3B: to get dressed** vestirse *v.* **7A**
dressing: sauce similar to Thousand Island dressing salsa golf *f.* **17A**
drink bebida *f.* **2B:** beber *v.* **2B: soft drink** refresco *m.* **4A**
drive conducir *v.* **7A:** manejar *v.* **17B**
driver: taxi driver taxista *m. y f.* **2A: truck driver** camionero/a *m./f.* **7A**
drop gota *f.* **2B: university drop-outs** deserción universitaria *f.* **15B**
drug droga *f.* **16A**
dry seco/a *adj.* **15A**
duck pato/a *m./f.* **18A**
duration duración *f.* **6B**
dusk atardecer *m.* **14A**
DVD DVD *m.* **9B: movie on DVD** película en DVD *f.* **4B**
dynamism dinamismo *m.* **16B**

E

each cada *adj.* **14A: each day** cada día *loc. adv.* **14A**
each other: far from each other alejados entre sí *loc. adv.* **17B to greet each other** saludarse *v.* **17B: to hug each other** abrazarse *v.* **17B: to kiss each other** besarse *v.* **17B: to look at each other** mirarse *v.* **17B: to love each other** quererse *v.* **17B: to tell each other** contarse *v.* **17B: to write to each other** escribirse *v.* **17B**
ear (inner) oído *m.* **10A:** (outer) oreja *f.* **10A: to be all ears** ser todo/a oídos *exp.* **9A**
early temprano *adv.* **7A: to get up early** madrugar *v.* **7A**
earn ganar *v.* **11B**
easily: easily accessible bien comunicado/a *loc. adv.* **4B**
east este *m.* **2A**
Easter Semana Santa *f.* **5A**
easy fácil *adj.* **6B: to make life easier** hacer la vida más fácil *v.* **17A**
eat comer *v.* **2B: to eat breakfast** desayunar *v.* **2B: to eat lunch** almorzar *v.* **2B: to eat lunch** comer *v.* **2B: to eat supper** cenar *v.* **2B: to eat tapas** tapear *v.* **2B**
ecological ecológico/a *adj.* **17A:**
economic: economic resource recurso económico *m.* **14A**
economics economía *f.* **1B**
ecotourism ecoturismo *m.* **11A**
Ecuador Ecuador *m.* **0**
Ecuadorian ecuatoriano/a *adj.*
edit editar *v.* **7A**
edition: special edition edición especial *f.* **3B**
editor: letter to the editor carta al director/a la directora *f.* **2A**
educate educar *v.* **12B**
educated culto/a *adj.* **12A**
education educación *f.* **8A:** formación *f.* **6A: Physical Education** Educación física *f.* **15B**
effect efecto *m.* **6A**
efficient eficaz *adj.* **13B**
effort esfuerzo *m.* **8A**
egg huevo *m.* **2B**
eight ocho *adj.* **1A**
eighteen dieciocho *adj.* **1B**
eighty ochenta *adj.* **1B**
either o *conj.* **: not . . . Either** tampoco *adv.* **10B**
El Salvador El Salvador *m.* **0**
elderly: elderly people las personas mayores *f.* **6A**
election elección *f.* **10B**
electoral: electoral campaign campaña electoral *f.* **16A**
electricity electricidad *f.* **8A**
elegant elegante *adj.* **4B**
elementary: elementary school escuela primaria *f.* **9A**
eleven once *adj.* **1A**
eliminate eliminar *v.* **16A**
elimination eliminación *f.* **12B**
else: Anything else? ¿Algo más? *exp.* **2B: Nothing else, thanks.** Nada más, gracias. *exp.* **2B**
e-mail correo electrónico *m.* **4B:** e-mail *m.* **4B**
embassy embajada *f.* **10A**
emergency emergencia *f.* **12B**
emigrant emigrante *m. y f.* **8B**
emigration emigración *f.* **8B**
emotional: emotional environment entorno afectivo *m.* **13B: emotional intelligence** inteligencia emocional *f.* **13B**
empanada empanada *f.* **17B**
empathy empatía *f.* **13B**
employee empleado/a *m./f.* **3A**
employment empleo *m.* **11B: employment center** bolsa de trabajo *f.* **13B: employment contract** contrato de trabajo *m.* **13B**
empty vacío/a *adj.* **4B**
encounter encuentro *m.* **6A**
encourage fomentar *v.* **14A:** incentivar *v.* **14A**
encouragement incentivo *m.* **17A: to offer encouragement** dar ánimos *v.* **13A**
end final *m.* **0:** fin *m.* **:** terminar *v.* **3A: towards the end of the 19th century** a finales del siglo XIX *loc. adv.* **8B**
ending terminación *f.* **0**
enemy enemigo/a *m./f.* **17B**
energy energía *f.* **7A: energy sector** sector energético *m.* **14A**
engineer ingeniero/a *m./f.* **1B**
engineering ingeniería *f.* **8A**
English inglés/inglesa *adj.* **1B:** inglés *m.* **1B**
enjoy disfrutar (de) *v.* **4A: Enjoy your flight!** ¡Que disfruten a bordo! *exp.* **13A: Enjoy your meal.** ¡Buen provecho! *exp.* **8A**

enough suficiente *adj.* **6A**
enroll inscribir *v.* **15B**
enrollment: enrollment period plazo de inscripción *m.* **18A**
enter entrar en *v.* **3A**
enterprising emprendedor(a) *adj.* **8B**
entertainment entretenimiento *m.* **8B**
enthusiasm entusiasmo *m.* **10B**
environment entorno *m.* **11A:** medio ambiente *m.* **4B: emotional environment** entorno afectivo *m.* **13B**
episode capítulo *m.* **14B**
equality igualdad *f.* **8B**
equation ecuación *f.* **15B**
Equatorial Guinea Guinea Ecuatorial *f.* **0: from Equatorial Guinea** ecuatoguineano/a *adj.* **14A**
equestrian hípico/a *adj.* **18A**
equipment equipo *m.* **18A**
equipped acondicionado/a *adj.* **6B**
ERASMUS: ERASMUS scholarship beca ERASMUS *f.* **14A**
e-reader lector de libros electrónicos *m.* **13B**
error error *m.* **11A**
escargot caracol *m.* **2B**
especially en especial *loc. adv.* **7B**
establish establecer *v.* **6A**
establishment establecimiento *m.* **9B**
estate: real-estate agency inmobiliaria *f.* **4B, 11B**
estimate cotización *f.* **18B**
ethnic étnico/a *adj.* **16B: ethnic group** grupo étnico *m.* **16B**
euphoric eufórico/a *adj.* **15B**
euro euro *m.* **2B: It's 9 euros.** Son 9 euros. *exp.* **2B**
Europe Europa *f.*
European europeo/a *adj.* **6A: European Union** Unión Europea *f.* **10B**
evaluation puntuación *f.* **11A**
evening noche *f.* **3A: Good evening.** Buenas noches. *exp.* **0: in the evening** por la noche *loc. adv.* **3A: in the evening** de la noche *loc. adv.* **3A**
event acontecimiento *m.* **5A:** evento *m.* **18B:** hecho *m.* **10B**
ever: hardly ever casi nunca *loc. adv.* **6A**
every: every day todos los días *loc. adv.* **3A**
everyday diario/a *adj.* **13A**
everything todo *pron.* **2A: Everything is OK.** No pasa nada. *exp.* **13B**
evolution evolución *f.* **16B**
ex ex *m. y f.* **12A: ex-husband** ex esposo *m.* **12A: ex-wife** ex esposa *f.* **12A**
exact exacto/a *adj.* **6A**
exaggerate exagerar *v.* **15B**
examine (a patient) atender *v.* **10A**
example ejemplo *m.* **0: to give an example** dar un ejemplo *v.* **7A**
excellent excelente *adj.* **13A**
excessive altísimo/a *adj.* **11B**
exchange intercambio *m.* **1B:** intercambiar *v.* **8A: exchange program** programa de intercambio *m.* **14A: in exchange for** a cambio de *loc. adv.* **8A: stock exchange** bolsa (de comercio) **3A**
excited emocionado/a *adj.* **10B:** ilusionado/a *adj.* **12A**
exciting emocionante *adj.* **10B**
excursion excursión *f.* **6A**
excuse perdonar *v.* **9B: excuse me** perdone (*form.*) *exp.* **9B: Excuse me, ...** Perdona,... *exp.* **5A: Excuse me?** ¿Cómo? *exp.* **14A**
executive ejecutivo/a *m./f.* **13B: sales executive** ejecutivo/a de ventas *m./f.* **13B**
exercise ejercicio *m.* **10A:** hacer deporte *v.* **3A:** hacer ejercicio *v.* **6A:** hacer gimnasia *v.* **10A**
exhibition exposición *f.* **6A**
exile exilio *m.* **8B: to go into exile** exiliarse *v.* **10B**
exit salida *f.* **6A, 11A**
exodus éxodo *m.* **14B**
exotic exótico/a *adj.* **4A**
expand: to expand a business ampliar un negocio *v.* **15A**
expectation expectativa *f.* **15A**
expel expulsar *v.* **14A**
expense gasto *m.* **15B**
expensive caro/a *adj.* **3B**
experience experiencia *f.* **4B: My experience** Mi experiencia *exp.* **0: professional experience** experiencia profesional *f.* **11B**
experiment experimento *m.* **17A**
experimentation experimentación *f.* **17A**
expiration: expiration date fecha de caducidad *f.* **15A**
explain explicar *v.* **14B**
exploit explotar *v.* **14A**
exploitation aprovechamiento *m.* **16A**
explore explorar *v.* **11B**
explosion explosión *f.* **14B**
export exportar *v.* **7B**
exporter exportador(a) *m./f.* **18B**
express expresar *v.* **18B**
exquisite exquisito/a *adj.* **18B**
extinction extinción *f.* **14A**
extra extra *adj.* **15A: extra virgin olive oil** aceite de oliva virgen extra *m.* **15A**
extraordinary extraordinario/a *adj.* **11B**
extreme extremo/a *adj.* **18A**
extremely super- *pref.* **11B:** -ísimo/a *suf.* **11B**
eye ojo *m.* **9A**

F

fabric tela *f.* **8A: piece of fabric** tela *f.* **8A**
face cara *f.* **5A:** enfrentarse *v.* **18A**
facility instalación *f.* **11A**
fact hecho *m.* **7A: in fact** de hecho *exp.* **7A**
factor factor *m.* **6A**
factory fábrica *f.* **8B**
failure aplazo *m.* **15B:** suspenso *m.* **15B**
fair justo/a *adj.* **3B: fair trade** comercio justo *m.* **3B: International Fashion Fair** Salón Internacional de la Moda *m.* **3B:** feria *f.* **16B**
fairness equidad *f.* **17A**
faith fe *f.* **8A: matter of faith** acto de fe *m.* **8A**
fall otoño *m.* **10A:** caerse *v.* **: falling behind** rezagado/a *adj.* **17A: to fall in love** enamorarse *v.* **12A**
false falso/a *adj.* **0: True or false?** ¿Verdadero o falso? *exp.* **0**
family familia *f.* **2A: among family** en el ámbito familiar *m.* **12A: family doctor** médico/a de familia *m./f.* **10A: family tree** árbol genealógico *m.* **5B: the royal family** Familia Real *f.* **4B**
famous famoso/a *adj.* **2A**
fan aficionado/a *m./f.* **14B:** (hand-held) abanico *m.* **3B**
fantastic fantástico/a *adj.* **2A**
far: far from each other alejados entre sí *loc. adv.* **17B:** lejos *adv.* **2A: far from** lejos de *prep.* **2A**
fare tarifa *f.* **13A**
farm finca *f.* **8B**
farmer agricultor(a) *m./f.* **7B**
farming: organic farming agricultura ecológica *f.* **15A**
fascinated fascinado/a *adj.* **14B**
fashion moda *f.* **3B: children's fashion** moda infantil *f.* **3B: fashion designer** diseñador(a) de moda *m./f.* **11B: International Fashion Fair** Salón Internacional de la Moda *m.* **3B**
fast rápido/a *adj.* **17A**
fasten abrocharse *v.* **13A**
fat gordo/a *adj.* **9B:** grasa *f.* **15A**
father padre *m.* **5B**
favor favorecer *v.* **11A: in favor of** a favor de *loc. adv.* **12B**
favorite preferido/a *adj.* **3B:** favorito/a *m./f.* **9B**
fax fax *m.* **7B**
fear miedo *m.* **10B:** tener miedo *v.*
feature (characteristic) cualidad *f.* **17B: geographical feature** relieve *m.* **18B**
February febrero *m.* **5A**
feel encontrarse *v.* **10A:** sentirse *v.* **9A: to feel accompanied** sentirse acompañado/a *v.* **9A: to feel at home** sentirse como en casa *v.* **16B: to feel fulfilled** sentirse realizado/a *v.* **13B**
feeling sentimiento *m.* **18B: to express a feeling** expresar un sentimiento *v.* **18B**
fellow: fellow countryman/countrywoman compatriota *m. y f.* **10B**
feminine femenino/a *adj.* **0: Masculine or feminine?** ¿Masculino o femenino? *adj.* **0**
ferry ferry *m.* **3A: to take the ferry** tomar el ferry *v.* **3A**
fertilize abonar *v.* **8A**
festival fiesta *f.* **2A:** fiesta popular *f.* **6A**
fever fiebre *f.* **10A: yellow fever** fiebre amarilla *f.* **10A**
few pocos/as *adj.* **2A**
fiber fibra *f.* **10A**
fiction ficción *f.* **14B:** narrativa *f.* **10B**
field campo *m.* **17A: scientific field** campo científico *m.* **17A: sports field** cancha *f.* **17B: track and field** atletismo *m.* **18A**
fifteen quince *adj.* **1B: fifteen-year-old girl** quinceañera *f.* **5A**
fifteenth: fifteenth birthday party fiesta de quince años *f.* **18B**
fifth quinto/a *adj.* **14A**
fifty cincuenta *adj.* **1B**
fighter luchador(a) *adj.*; *m./f.* **5A**
figure muñeco *m.* **18B**
file archivo *m.* **7B**

filet: filet of veal filete de ternera *m.* **2B**
fill in rellenar *v.* **0**
filled relleno/a *adj.* **16B**
film rodar *v.* **9B**
finalist finalista *m. y f.* **9B**
finance financiar *v.* **4B: world of finance** mundo de las finanzas *m.* **3A**
financial financiero/a *adj.* **11B: financial press** prensa económica *f.* **3A**
find encontrar *v.* **4A:** localizar *v.* **0: to find out** averiguar *v.* **0: to find out** enterarse de *v.* **17A**
fire fuego *m.* **8A:** incendio *m.* **7A**
firefighter bombero/a *m./f.* **7A**
first primero/a *adj.* **14A: first course** primer plato *m.* **2B: first name** nombre de pila *m.* **12A: first prize** gordo *m.* **9B: first-aid kit** botiquín *m.* **10A: firstborn** primogénito/a *m./f.* **12A**
fish pez *m.* **:** (food) pescado *m.* **2B: fish soup** sopa de pescado *f.* **2B**
fisherman/fisherwoman pescador(a) *m./f.* **14A**
fit: to be fit estar en forma *v.* **7A: to fit into** integrarse *v.* **12B**
five cinco *adj.* **1A**
fixed: fixed-price menu menú del día *m.* **2B**
fjord fiordo *m.* **6B**
flag bandera *f.* **8B**
flamenco: flamenco dance baile flamenco *m.* **7A: flamenco dancer** bailaor(a) *m./f.* **7A**
flan (custard) flan *m.* **2B**
flavor sabor *m.* **15A**
flexibility: schedule flexibility flexibilidad horaria *f.* **6A**
flexible flexible *adj.* **6A: flexible workday** jornada flexible *f.* **6A: to make flexible** flexibilizar *v.* **6A**
flight vuelo *m.* **6B: Enjoy your flight!** ¡Que disfruten a bordo! *exp.* **13A: flight attendant** auxiliar de vuelo *m. y f.* **13A: Have a good flight!** ¡Que tengan un feliz vuelo! *exp.* **13A: to miss a flight** perder un vuelo *v.* **13A**
flip dar la vuelta *v.* **8A**
floating flotante *adj.* **9A**
floor piso *m.* **8A**
florist florista *m. y f.* **18B: florist's shop** floristería *f.* **9B**
flower: bunch of flowers ramo de flores *m.* **18B: flower arrangement** arreglo floral *m.* **18B: flower pot** maceta *f.* **8A: flower shop** floristería *f.* **9B**
fluorescent fluorescente *adj.* **11A**
fly volar *v.* **5A**
folded plegado/a *adj.* **13A**
folk: folk healer curandero/a *m./f.* **14A**
folklore folclore *m.* **14A**
folks: my folks mi gente *exp.* **5B**
following siguiente *adj.* **0**
fond: fond of joking bromista *adj.*; *m. y f.* **13B**
food comida *f.* **1A:** alimentos *m. pl.* **2B: food product** producto de alimentación *m.* **15A: fresh food** producto fresco *m.* **15A: junk food** comida basura *f.* **10A: natural food** alimento natural *m.* **15A: transgenic food** alimento transgénico *m.* **15A**
foot pie *m.* **10A**
for para *prep.* **4B:** por *prep.* **15B: appropriate/safe for** apto/a para *loc. adj.* **15A: as for** en cuanto a *loc. prep.* **16A: for (your) own good** por (tu) bien *loc. adv.* **15B: for free** gratarola *adv.* **17B: for sale** a la venta *loc. adv.* **4B: for young people** juvenil *adj.* **7A: in exchange for** a cambio de *loc. adv.* **8A: time for oneself** tiempo para uno/a mismo/a *m.* **3A: to ask for help** pedir ayuda *v.* **5B: to do something for a living** dedicarse a (hacer) algo *v.* **7A: to go for a walk** pasear *v.* **3A: to talk for the sake of it** hablar por hablar *v.* **14B: What is it used for?** ¿Para qué sirve? *exp.* **4B:** (and until now) desde hace *loc. prep.* **5B**
forces: armed forces fuerzas armadas *m.* **16A**
forecast: weather forecast pronóstico *m.* **9A**
forehead la frente *f.* **17B**
foreign extranjero/a *adj.* **2A: foreign currency** divisas *f.* **13A: foreign currency exchange** cambio de dinero *m.* **13A: foreign language** lengua extranjera *f.* **15B**
forest bosque *m.* **5A: forest ranger** guarda forestal *m. y f.* **14A: virgin forest** bosque virgen *m.* **6B**
forever para siempre *loc. adv.* **8B**
forget olvidar(se) *v.* **5B: cannot be forgotten** no puede olvidarse *v.* **10B**
form formulario *m.* **16A:** formar *v.* **0: complaint form** libro de quejas *m.* **11A**
format formato *m.* **14B**
Formula 1 Fórmula 1 *f.* **18A**
fort fuerte *m.* **11A**
fortress fortaleza *f.* **11A**
fortune: to make fortune hacer fortuna *v.* **8B**
forty cuarenta *adj.* **1B**
forum foro *m.* **1B**
foster potenciar *v.* **15A**
founder fundador(a) *m./f.* **4B**
four cuatro *adj.* **1A: four-star hotel** hotel de cuatro estrellas *m.* **11A**
fourteen catorce *adj.* **1B**
fourth cuarto/a *adj.* **14A**
fragrance fragancia *f.* **16B**
frame marco *m.* **3B**
Francoist franquista *adj.* **14B**
frankly abiertamente *adv.* **17A**
free libre *adj.* **16A: free time** tiempo libre *m.* **5B:** gratuito/a *adj.* **9B**
freedom libertad *f.* **13B: to set free** liberar *v.* **16A**
French francés/francesa *adj.* **1B:** francés *m.* **1B**
frequency frecuencia *f.* **13A**
fresh natural *adj.* **2B:** fresco/a *adj.* **15A: fresh food** producto fresco *m.* **15A**
Friday viernes *m.* **3A**
friend amigo/a *m./f.* **3A:** cuate/a (*fam.*) *m./f.* **12A: to go out with friends** salir con amigos *v.* **3A**
friendliness simpatía *f.* **2B**
friendly simpático/a *adj.* **2B: very friendly** amabilísimo/a *adj.* **13A**
friendship amistad *f.* **5B**
frighten asustar *v.* **7A**
frightened asustado/a *adj.* **12A**
from a partir de (que) *conj.* **12B:** de *prep.* **8B:** desde *prep.* **5B: arriving from** procedente de *loc. adv.* **13A: far from each other** alejados entre sí *loc. adv.* **17B: from San Juan** sanjuanero/a *m./f* **11A: from time to time** de vez en cuando *loc. adv.* **14A: from... until/ to** desde/de... hasta/a *loc. prep.* **8B: to come from** provenir de *v.* **16B: to be... kilometers from...** estar a... kilómetros de... *loc. adv.* **2A**
frozen congelado/a *adj.* **16B**
fruit fruta *f.* **2B: fruit seller** frutero/a *m./f.* **9B: fruit shop** frutería *f.* **9B**
frustrating frustrante *adj.* **12B**
fry freír *v.* **: frying pan** sartén *f.* **8A**
fulfill cumplir *v.* **13A: to feel fulfilled** sentirse realizado/a *v.* **13B**
full-fledged hecho/a y derecho/a *exp.* **9A**
fun divertido/a *adj.* **1B:** diversión *f.* **6A: to have fun** divertirse *v.* **17B**
function función *f.* **4B:** funcionar *v.* **7B: function hall** salón de fiestas *m.* **18B**
functional funcional *adj.* **4B**
funny gracioso/a *adj.* **9A**
furnished amueblado/a *adj.* **4B**
furnishings objetos domésticos *m.* **4B**
furniture: piece of furniture mueble *m.* **8A**
furry peludo/a *adj.* **9A**
future futuro/a *adj.* **12B:** futuro *m.* **8B**

G

Galician gallego *m.* **1B**
game juego *m.* **0: Olympic Games** Juegos Olímpicos *m.* **12B: Pan-American Games** Juegos Panamericanos *m.* **18A: Paralympic Games** Juegos Paralímpicos *m.* **12B**
gap: to close the gap cerrar la brecha *v.* **17A**
garage garaje *m.* **4B**
garbage basura *f.* **8A**
gardening jardinería *f.* **8A**
garlic ajo *m.* **8A**
garment prenda *f.* **3B**
gastronomic gastronómico/a *adj.* **2B**
gastronomy gastronomía *f.* **4B**
gate: boarding gate puerta de embarque *f.* **13A**
gather reunir *v.* **0:** reunirse *v.* **6A**
GDP: gross domestic product (PIB) producto interior bruto *m.* **11A, 14A**
generally generalmente *adv.* **7B:** en general *loc. adv.* **4A**
generation generación *f.* **10B**
generational: generacional *adj.* **15B**
genetic: genetic modification manipulación genética *f.* **7B**
genius genio *m. y f.* **15B**
gentleman caballero *m.* **13A**
geographic geográfico/a *adj.* **16B**
Geology Geología *f.* **15B**
German alemán/alemana *adj.* **1B:** alemán *m.* **1B**

get conseguir *v.* **4A:** obtener *v.* **0: (Let's) Get to work!** manos a la obra *exp.* **8A: to get a kick out of** encantar *v.* **5B: to get along** llevarse bien *v.* **12A: to get angry** enfadarse *v.* **17B: to get angry** enojarse *v.* **17B: to get bored** aburrirse *v.* **17B: to get divorced** divorciarse *v.* **12A: to get dressed** vestirse *v.* **7A: to get in line** hacer fila *v.* **13A: to get married** casarse *v.* **8B: to get someone hooked** enganchar *v.* **14B: to get tired/bored of** cansarse de *v.* **9B: to not get along** llevarse mal *v.* **12A: to get hold of** localizar *v.* **13B: to get up** levantarse *v.* **7A: to get up early** madrugar *v.* **7A**
gift regalo *m.* **3B: gift shop** tienda de regalos *f.* **3B: gift voucher** cheque-regalo *m.* **3B**
girl niña *f.* **3A: fifteen-year-old girl** quinceañera *f.* **5A: young girl** la piba *f.* **17B**
girlfriend novia *m./f.* **5A**
give dar *v.* **4A: to give [subject] classes** dar clases (de algo) *v.* **8A: to give a concert** dar un concierto *v.* **7A: to give an example** dar un ejemplo *v.* **7A: to give good results** redundar en *v.* **17A: to give oneself (a present)** regalarse *v.* **6B: to give oneself an injection** inyectarse *v.* **17A: to give up** abandonar *v.* **7B: to give up** dejar *v.* **5A: to give up** renunciar a *v.* **16A**
glacier glaciar *m.* **11B**
glad alegre *adj.* **11A: to be glad that** alegrarse de *v.* **11A, 18B**
glass vaso *m.* **:** vidrio *m.* **8A: pane of glass** vidrio *m.* **8A**
glasses gafas *f.* **3B: sunglasses** gafas de sol *f.* **3B**
glide deslizarse *v.* **18A: hang glider** ala delta *m.* **18A**
global mundial *adj.* **7B**
globetrotter trotamundos *m. y f.* **9A**
gloves guantes *m. pl.* **18A**
glucose glucosa *f.* **17A**
gluten gluten *m.* **15A**
go ir *v.* **3A: How are you going there?** ¿Cómo vas? *exp.* **6B: to go around the world** dar la vuelta al mundo *v.* **18A: to go back** regresar *v.* **8B: to go back** volver *v.* **8B: to go beyond** traspasar *v.* **14B: to go by (means of transportation)** ir en… *v.* **6B: to go by car** ir en coche *v.* **3A: to go down** bajar *v.* **15A: to go for a swim** bañarse *v.* **10A: to go for a walk** pasear *v.* **3A: to go grocery shopping** hacer las compras *v.* **3A: to go hungry** pasar hambre *v.* **15A: to go into exile** exiliarse *v.* **10B: to go on** seguir *v.* **11B: to go out (with friends)** salir (con amigos) *v.* **3A: to go out with somebody** salir con alguien *v.* **12A: to go to bed** acostarse *v.* **7A: to go to work** ir a trabajar *v.* **3A: to go via** pasar por *v.* **6B: to go wrong** ir mal *v.* **7B: to go away** marcharse *v.* **18B**
goal meta *f.* **18A:** objetivo *m.* **3B**
God Dios *m.* **8A**
gold oro *m.* **12B: black gold** oro negro *m.* **14A**
golf golf *m.* **1A**
good bueno/a *adj.* **0: (good) luck** suerte *f.* **8B: for (your) own good** por (tu) bien *exp.* **15B: Good afternoon.** Buenas tardes. *exp.* **0: Good evening.** Buenas noches. *exp.* **0: Good morning.** Buenos días. *exp.* **0: Good night.** Buenas noches. *exp.* **0: good weather** buen tiempo *m.* **2A: good-looking** guapo/a *adj.* **9A: Have a good flight!** ¡Que tengan un feliz vuelo! *exp.* **13A: in a good mood** de buen humor *loc. adv.* **12A: in good company** en buena compañía *loc. adv.* **16B: the good thing** lo bueno *m.* **12B: there is good weather** hace buen tiempo *exp.* **10A: to be good (at something)** ser bueno/a (en algo) *v.* **17B: to be good for…** servir para… *v.* **4B: to be in (good) shape** estar en forma *v.* **7A: to give good results** redundar en *v.* **17A: to have a good time** pasarla bien *v.* **17B: to have a good time** pasarlo bien *v.* **17B**
Good-bye. Adiós. *exp.* **0**
gossip: piece of gossip chisme *m.* **17B: gossip magazine** revista del corazón *f.* **9B: gossip press** prensa rosa *f.* **9B**
government gobierno *m.* **16A**
governmental: NGO (non-governmental organization) ONG (organización no gubernamental) *f.* **5A**
GPS navegador GPS *m.* **13B**
grab agarrar *v.* **17B**
grade calificación *f.* **15B:** nota *f.* **15B**
graduate egresar *v.* **9A:** graduarse *v.* **12A**
graduating: graduating class promoción *f.* **9A**
graduation graduación *f.* **18B**
grand: grand piano piano de cola *m.* **10B**
grandchildren nietos *m.* **5B**
granddaughter nieta *f.* **5B**
grandfather abuelo *m.* **5B**
grandmother abuela *f.* **5B**
grandparents abuelos *m.* **5B**
grandson nieto *m.* **5B**
grape uva *f.* **18B**
graphic: graphic design diseño gráfico *m.* **7A**
gray gris *adj.* **3B: to have gray hair** tener canas *v.* **17B**
great bárbaro/a *adj.* **11B:** genial *adj.* **6B:** gran (grande) *adj.* **5B: to be a great communicator** ser un(a) gran comunicador(a) *v.* **13B**
Great! ¡Pura vida! *exp.* **18B**
green verde *adj.* **3B**
greet saludar *v.* **17B: to greet each other** saludarse *v.* **17B**
greeting saludo *m.* **0: greeting card** tarjeta de felicitación *f.* **5A**
grocery: grocery store tienda de alimentación *f.* **4A: to go grocery shopping** hacer las compras *v.* **3A**
groom novio *m.* **5A**
gross: gross domestic product (GDP) producto interior bruto (PIB) *m.* **11A, 14A**
group agrupar *v.* **0: ethnic group** grupo étnico *m.* **16B: In pairs/groups** En parejas/grupos *loc. adv.* **0: marginalized group** grupo marginado *m.* **12B: music group** grupo musical *m.* **14B**
grow crecer *v.* **7B:** cultivar *v.* **7B: to grow up** crecer *v.* **9B**
growing creciente *adj.* **16B**
growth crecimiento *m.* **16A**
guacamole guacamole *m.* **1A**
Guarani guaraní *m.* **1B**
guarantee garantía *f.* **11A:** garantizar *v.* **3B**
guard: night security guard vigilante nocturno/a *m./f.* **3A**
Guatemala City Ciudad de Guatemala *f.* **0**
Guatemalan guatemalteco/a *adj.* **2A**
guerrilla guerrilla *f.* **16A**
guess adivinar *v.* **0**
guest invitado/a *m./f.* **18B: guest of honor** agasajado/a *m./f.* **18B**
guide: guide dog perro/a guía *m./f.* **12B: guidebook** guía *f.* **1B: tour guide** guía (turístico) *m. y f.* **1B**
guitar guitarra *f.* **8A**
guitarist guitarrista *m. y f.* **7A**
gum: chewing gum chicle **9B**
gunpowder pólvora *f.* **18A**
gym gimnasio *m.* **3A**
gymnast gimnasta *m. y f.* **18A**
gymnastics gimnasia *f.* **18A**
gypsy gitano/a *m./f.* **16A**

H

habit costumbre *f.* **15A:** hábito *m.* **7A**
haggle regatear *v.* **4A**
hair pelo *m.* **9A: dark-haired, brunet(te)** moreno/a *adj.* **12A: hair salon** peluquería *f.* **8B: red-haired** pelirrojo/a *adj.* **12A: to have gray hair** tener canas *v.* **17B**
half mitad *f.* **: half a dozen** media docena *f.* **4A: half a kilogram** medio kilo *m.* **4A**
hall: city hall ayuntamiento *m.* **2A: dining hall** comedor *m.* **15B: function hall** salón de fiestas *m.* **18B**
ham jamón *m.* **0: Serrano ham** jamón serrano *m.* **2B**
hand mano *f.* **8A: on the other hand** por otro lado/por otra parte *loc. adv.* **13B**
handkerchief pañuelo *m.* **3B**
handle el asa (*f.*) *f.* **18A**
handyman/handywoman manitas *m. y f.* **8A**
hang: hang glider ala delta *m.* **18A: to hang out** janguear (*fam.*) *v.* **11A**
happen pasar *v.* **8B:** suceder *v.* **14A: to make something happen** hacer realidad *v.* **8B**
happiness ilusión *f.* **12B**
happy alegre *adj.* **5B:** contento/a *adj.* **11A:** feliz *adj.* **5A: to become happy** ponerse contento/a *v.* **18B**
hard difícil *adj.* **7A:** duro/a *adj.* **7B**
hardly: hardly ever casi nunca *loc. adv.* **6A**
harmony concordia *f.* **16A**
harness arnés *m.* **18A**
Havana La Habana *f.* **0**
have tener *v.* **2A: Have a good flight!** ¡Que tengan un feliz vuelo! *exp.* **13A: Have a nice stay!** ¡Feliz estancia! *exp.* **11A: How long have/has?** ¿Cuánto tiempo (hace)…? *exp.* **8B: to have (storage) capacity** tener capacidad *v.* **13B: to have a child** tener un hijo *v.* **8B: to have a cold** estar resfriado/a *v.* **10A: to have a good time** pasarla bien

v. **17B: to have a good time** pasarlo bien *v.* **17B: to have a lot in common** ser afín *v.* **17B: to have (at one's disposal)** disponer *v.* **18B: to have class** tener clase *v.* **3A: to have fun** divertirse *v.* **17B: to have gray hair** tener canas *v.* **17B: to have one's birthday** cumplir años *v.* **18B: to have to** tener que *v.* **6A**
he él *pron.* **1A: he is...** él es... *exp.* **0**
head cabeza *f.* **10A**
headline titular *m.* **0**
headquarters sede *f.* **9A**
healer: folk healer curandero/a *m./f.* **14A**
health salud *f.* **7A: health care** asistencia sanitaria *f.* **10A**
healthy sano/a *adj.* **5B**
hear oír *v.* **13B: I'm sorry to hear that.** Siento oír eso. *exp.* **13B**
heart corazón *m.* **2A**
heartrending desgarrador(a) *adj.* **16A**
heat calor *m.* **2A:** fuego *m.* **8A**
Hebrew hebreo *m.* **7A**
hectare hectárea *f.* **6B**
Hello. Buenos días. *exp.* **0:** Hola. *exp.* **0:** (when answering the phone) ¿Diga?; ¿Dígame?; ¿Hola?; ¿Bueno? *exp.* **6B**
helmet casco *m.* **18A**
help ayuda *f.* **5B:** auxilio *m.* **18A:** socorro *m.* **12B:** ayudar *v.* **5B: self-help** autoayuda *f.* **6A: to ask for help** pedir ayuda *v.* **5B**
hepatitis hepatitis *f.* **10A**
her su(s) *adj.* **2A**
herb hierba *f.* **6A**
here aquí *adv.* **3B:** acá *adv.* **6B**
heritage: World Heritage Patrimonio Mundial *m.* **11B: World Heritage (Site)** Patrimonio de la Humanidad *m.* **8A**
hesitate: Don't hesitate to... No dude en... *exp.* **13B**
Hi. Buenas. *exp.* **0:** Hola. *exp.* **0**
hidden escondido/a *adj.* **6B**
hide esconder *v.* **6B:** ocultar *v.* **16B**
high alto/a *adj.* **8A: high school** secundaria *f.*, instituto *m.* **15B: high school studies** bachillerato *m.* **14A: to be the highest rated** ser líder de audiencia *v.* **14B: very high** altísimo *adj.* **11B**
hiking senderismo *m.* **11B:** trekking *m.* **6B**
hip-hop hip-hop *m.* **1A**
his su(s) *adj.* **2A**
Hispanic hispano/a *adj.*
historic histórico/a *adj.* **6B: historic neighborhood** casco viejo *m.* **12B**
history historia *f.* **1B**
hobby afición *f.* **11B**
hold sujetar *v.* **8A: to be held** tener lugar *v.* **16B: to hold** celebrarse *v.* **4A**
holiday día festivo *m.* **3A**
holy: Holy Week Semana Santa *f.* **5A**
home vivienda *f.* **11B:** hogar *m.* **8A: at home** en casa *loc. adv.* **2B: home address** domicilio *m.* **2A: home delivery** reparto a domicilio *m.* **7B: ideal home** vivienda ideal *f.* **4B: private home** casa particular *f.* **13A: time somebody has to be home** hora de llegar a casa *f.* **15B: to arrive home** llegar a casa *v.* **3A: to do something at home** hacer algo en casa *v.* **3A: to feel at home** sentirse como en casa *v.* **16B**
homemaker el amo/a de casa (f) *f.* **1B**
homesickness nostalgia *f.* **10B**
homework tarea *f.* **0:** deberes *m. pl.* **15B**
homogeneous homogéneo/a *adj.* **16B**
Honduran hondureño/a *adj.* **14B**
Honduras Honduras *f.* **0**
honey miel *f.* **7B**
honeymoon viaje de novios *m.* **13A**
honor: guest of honor agasajado/a *adj.* **18B**
hooked: to get someone hooked enganchar *v.* **14B**
hoop aro *m.* **18A**
hope esperanza *f.* **10B:** ilusión *f.* **12B:** esperar *v.* **12B**
hopeful esperanzado/a *adj.* **14A**
horizon horizonte *m.* **8B**
horrible horrible *adj.* **2A**
horse caballo *m.* **6B: horseback ride** paseo a caballo *m.* **6B: horseback riding** cabalgata *f.* **18A**
hospitable hospitalario/a *adj.* **13A**
hospital hospital *m.* **1B**
hospitality hospitalidad *f.* **14A**
host: host country país receptor *m.* **8B**
hostel albergue *m.* **6B:** hostal *m.* **11A**
hot caliente *adj.* **:** calor *m.* **10A: hot spices** picantes *m. pl.* **15A: hot springs** termas *f. pl.* **6B: to be cold/hot** tener frío/calor *v.* **10A: to be cold/hot** (weather) hacer frío/calor *v.* **10A**
hotel hotel *m.* **0: four-star hotel** hotel de cuatro estrellas *m.* **11A: hotel manager** hotelero/a *m./f.* **4B: state-run hotel in Spanish historic building** el parador nacional *m.* **6B: state-run hotel in Spanish historic buildings** Parador de Turismo de España *m.* **11A**
house casa *f.* **4B: country house** masía (*Cataluña*) *f.* **7B: house salad** ensalada de la casa *f.* **2B: housewarming party** inauguración *f.* **12A**
housing vivienda *f.* **11B**
how cómo *interrog.* **1A: How are you going there?** ¿Cómo vas? *exp.* **6B: how interesting!** ¡Qué interesante! *exp.* **1B: How is/are...?** ¿Qué tal está(n)...? *exp.* **2B: How long have/has?** ¿Cuánto tiempo (hace)...? *exp.* **8B: how many?** ¿cuántos/as? *interrog.* **4B: How much is it?** ¿Cúanto es? *exp.* **2B: How often?** ¿Con qué frecuencia? *exp.* **3A**
however sin embargo *conj.* **5A, 13B**
HR: Human Resources (HR) Recursos Humanos (RR.HH.) *m., pl.* **13B**
hug abrazo *m.* **2A:** abrazar *v.* **17B: to hug each other** abrazarse *v.* **17B**
huge enorme *adj.* **16A**
human: human being ser humano *m.* **8A: Human Resources (HR)** Recursos Humanos (RR.HH.) *m.* **13B: human rights** derechos humanos *m.* **16A**
Humanities Filosofía y Letras *f.* **5A**
humankind humanidad *f.* **17A**
hundred: one hundred cien *adj.* **1B: one hundred percent** cien por ciento *adj.* **12A**
hungry: to be hungry tener hambre *v.* **: to go hungry** pasar hambre *v.* **15A**
hurt doler *v.* **10A:** herir *v.* **15B**
husband esposo *m.* **5B:** marido *m.* **5B: ex-husband** ex esposo *m.* **12A**
hygiene higiene *f.* **15A**

I

I yo *pron.* **1A: I think so/not.** Creo que sí/no. *exp.* **7B: I'd like...** Me da/pone... *exp.* **4A: I'm OK.** Estoy bien. *exp.* **7B: I am...** (Yo) soy... *exp.* **0: I meant...** quería decir... *exp.* **12B**
ice hielo *m.* **2B: ice cream** helado *m.* **2B: ice sheet** manto de hielo *m.* **11B**
icon: Hispanic icon referente latino *m.* **1A**
idea idea *f.* **4B**
ideal ideal *adj.* **2A**
identity identidad *f.* **18B: national identity card** DNI *m.* **3A**
idol ídolo *m.* **18A**
ill enfermo/a *adj.* **10A**
illiteracy analfabetismo *m.* **16A**
illness enfermedad *f.* **10A**
image imagen *f.* **1A**
imagine imaginarse *v.* **0**
immediate inmediato/a *adj.* **17A**
immensity inmensidad *f.* **11B**
immigrant inmigrante *m. y f.* **5B: immigrant community** comunidad inmigrante *f.* **8B**
immigration control de pasaportes *m.* **13A**
immune: immune system sistema inmunológico *m.* **17A**
impatient impaciente *adj.* **13B**
import importar *v.* **15A**
important importante *adj.* **2A: important figure** personaje *m. y f.* **1A**
impressed impresionado/a *adj.* **18A**
impressive impresionante *adj.* **5A**
impromptu espontáneo/a *adj.* **14B**
improve mejorar *v.* **6A**
improvement perfeccionamiento *m.* **14A**
in dentro de *loc. prep.* **17A:** en *prep.* **3B: all in all** en definitiva *loc. adv.* **18B: in (good) shape** en forma *loc. adv.* **7A: in a good/bad mood** de buen/mal humor *loc. adv.* **12A: in exchange for** a cambio de *loc. adv.* **8A: in fact** de hecho *exp.* **7A: in favor of** a favor de *loc. adv.* **12B: In my opinion, ...** En mi opinión, ... *exp.* **10B: in need** sin recursos *adj.* **15A: in other words** es decir *exp.* **8B: in particular** en concreto *loc. adv.* **7B: in return** a cambio *loc. adv.* **12B: in short** en resumen *loc. adv.* **18B: in the afternoon** de la tarde *loc. adv.* **3A: in the afternoon** por la tarde *loc. adv.* **3A: in the evening** por la noche *loc. adv.* **3A: in the evening** de la noche *loc. adv.* **3A: in the long term** a largo plazo *loc. adv.* **9A: in the mid sixties** a mediados de los 60 *loc. adv.* **14B: in the process** de paso *loc. adv.* **14B: in time** a tiempo *loc. adv.* **7B: Is Carmen there?** ¿Está Carmen? *exp.* **6B: point in common** punto común *m.* **to be in touch** estar en contacto *v.* **12B: to be interested in** estar interesado/a en *v.* **17A: to fall in love** enamorarse *v.* **12A: to participate in** participar en *v.* **3A: to trust in** tener confianza en *v.* **5B:**

in addition además *adv.* **2A: in advance** con antelación *loc. adv.* **11A: in front of** delante de *loc. prep.* **3B: in love with** enamorado/a de *adj.* **2A: in order** en regla *loc. adv.* **11A: in the morning** de la mañana *loc. adv.* **3A: in the morning** por la mañana *loc. adv.* **3A: specializing in** especializado/a en *adj.* **2B**
inaugurate inaugurar *v.* **12A**
inbox bandeja de entrada *f.* **14A**
incidentally por cierto *conj.* **10A:** a propósito *conj.* **10A**
include contar con *v.* **9A:** incluir *v.* **11A:** incorporar *v.* **18A: tax included** IVA incluido *loc. adv.* **2B**
inclusion: social inclusion inclusión social *f.* **16A**
income ingresos *m.* **11A: per capita income** renta per cápita *f.* **14A**
incorrect incorrecto/a *adj.* **0**
incredible increíble *adj.* **5B**
indeed efectivamente *adv.* **15B**
independence independencia *f.* **12B**
independent independiente *adj.* **12A: to become independent** independizarse *v.* **15B**
India India *f.* **6A**
Indian indio/a *adj.* **4A**
indicate señalar *v.* **0**
indifference indiferencia *f.* **16A**
indigenous indígena *adj. invar.* **1B**
indispensable imprescindible *adj.* **13B**
industrial industrial *adj.* **8B**
industry industria *f.* **14A: oil industry** industria petrolera *f.* **14A: service industry** industria de servicios *f.* **14A**
inequality desigualdad *f.* **16A**
infection infección *f.* **10A**
infinite infinito/a *adj.* **18A**
influential influyente *adj.* **7A**
inform informar *v.* **16A**
information datos *m. pl.* **0: nutritional information** información nutricional *f.* **15A**
informed informado/a *adj.* **9B**
infrastructure infraestructura *f.* **17A**
infusion infusión *f.* **6A: mate** (infusion) yerba mate *f.* **3B**
ingredient ingrediente *m.* **15A**
inhabitant habitante *m.* y *f.* **2A**
inherit heredar *v.* **9B**
inhospitable inhóspito/a *adj.* **11B**
initial: initial letter sigla *f.* **12B**
injection: to give oneself an injection inyectarse *v.* **17A**
injury herida *f.* **10A**
innocence inocencia *f.* **18B**
innovation novedad *f.* **17A**
innovative innovador(a) *adj.* **13B**
insomnia insomnio *m.* **14B**
install instalar *v.* **14B**
insulin insulina *f.* **17A**
integrated: to be integrated integrarse *v.* **12B**
integration integración *f.* **12B**
intellectual intelectual *adj.* **17B**
intelligence inteligencia *f.* **13B: emotional intelligence** inteligencia emocional *f.* **13B**
intelligent inteligente *adj.* **12A**
intense intenso/a *adj.* **3A**
interact relacionarse *v.* **13B**
interaction trato *m.* **12B**
interactive interactivo/a *adj.* **17A**
interest inquietud *f.* **9A:** interés *m.* **1A: morbid interest** morbo *m.* **14B: to be of interest** interesar *v.* **7A: to stir up interest** despertar la inquietud *v.* **9A**
interested: to be interested in estar interesado/a en *v.* **17A**
interesting interesante *adj.* **1B: how interesting!** ¡Qué interesante! *exp.* **1B**
intern pasante *m.* y *f.* **13B**
international internacional *adj.* **1B: International Fashion Fair** Salón Internacional de la Moda *m.* **3B: international projection** proyección internacional *f.* **16A: International Relations** Relaciones Internacionales *f. pl.* **11B**
Internet Internet *m.* **4A: Internet café** cibercafé *m.* **4A: Internet café** locutorio *m.* **8B: Internet user** internauta *m./f.* **6A: to be connected (to the Internet)** estar conectado *v.* **13B: to surf the Internet** navegar por Internet *v.* **6A**
internship: summer internship pasantía de verano *f.* **13B**
interview entrevista *f.* **3A**
introduce presentar *v.* **0**
invade invadir *v.* **16A**
invasion: territorial invasion invasión territorial *f.* **16A**
investigator investigador(a) *m./f.* **14B**
investment inversión *f.* **14B**
invite invitar *v.* **17B**
is: that is o sea *exp.* **8B**
island isla *f.* **1A: Balearic Islands** Islas Baleares *f.* **4B**
isolation aislamiento *m.* **13B**
issue número *m.* **15A**
it lo/la *pron.* **3B: It's my turn.** Me toca a mí. *exp.* **4A: it's possible** es posible *v.* **4A: to be worth it** valer la pena *v.* **11B, 14A: to talk for the sake of it** hablar por hablar *exp.* **14B: What is it like?** ¿Cómo es? *exp.* **4B: What is it used for?** ¿Para qué sirve? *exp.* **4B: What time is it?** ¿Qué hora es? *exp.* **3A: it has** tiene *v.* **2A**
Italian italiano/a *adj.* **1B:** italiano *m.* **1B**
itch picazón *f.* **10A**

J

jacket chaqueta *f.* **3B**
jackpot gordo *m.* **9B**
jai-alai court frontón *m.* **18A**
jam mermelada *f.* **2B**
January enero *m.* **5A**
Japanese japonés *m.* **1B**
jar frasco *m.* **8A**
jargon jerga *f.* **17B**
jazz jazz *m.* **7A**
jeans jeans *m.* **3B**
Jew judío/a *m./f.* **7A**
job actividad laboral *f.* **7B:** puesto (de trabajo) *m.* **4B:** trabajo *m.* **1B:** encargo *m.* **16B: having more than one job** pluriempleo *m.* **14B: to change jobs** cambiar de trabajo *v.* **7B**
join adherirse, afiliarse *v.* **16A**
joint: joint custody custodia compartida *f.* **12A**
joke chiste *m.* **5B: fond of joking** bromista *adj.* **13B: to tell jokes** contar chistes *v.* **17B**
journal diario *m.* **5A**
journalist periodista *m.* y *f.* **10B**
juice: orange juice jugo (*m.*) de naranja, zumo de naranja (*Esp.*) *m.* **2B**
July julio *m.* **3A**
jump: bungee jumping puenting *m.* **18A**
June junio *m.* **5A**
jungle jungla *f.* **5A:** selva *f.* **16A**
junk: junk food comida basura *f.* **10A**
just recién *adv.* **17B**
justice justicia *f.* **16A: social justice** justicia social *f.* **16A**

K

karate karate *m.* **3A**
kayak kayak *m.* **6B**
keep conservar *v.* **8A:** guardar *v.* **8A:** mantener *v.* **5B: to keep company** hacer compañía *v.* **7A: to keep company** acompañar *v.* **9A: to keep on** seguir *v.* **9B: to keep going** seguir *v.* **9B**
keeper: lighthouse keeper farero/a *m./f.* **14A**
key clave *adj.* **6A:** llave *f.* **6A**
kick: to get a kick out of encantar *v.* **5B**
kid chamaquito/a *m./f.* **12A: to take the kids to school** llevar a los niños al colegio *v.* **3A**
kidnapping secuestro *m.* **16A: kidnapping victim** secuestrado/a *m./f.* **16A**
kill matar *v.* **18B**
kilogram kilo *m.* **4A: half a kilogram** medio kilo *m.* **4A**
kilometer kilómetro *m.* **2A: to be... kilometers from...** estar a... kilómetros de... *loc. adv.* **2A**
kindergarten kínder *m.* **5B**
kiosk quiosco *m.* **9B: kiosk attendant** quiosquero/a *m./f.* **9B**
kiss beso *m.* **2A:** besar *v.* **17B: to kiss each other** besarse *v.* **17B**
kit: first-aid kit botiquín *m.* **10A**
kitchen cocina *f.* **4B**
knock down derribar *v.* **10B**
know conocer *v.* **5A:** saber *v.* **8A: best-known** más conocido/a *adj.* **4A: to know (something) (about)** saber (algo) (de) *v.* **8A: to make known** dar a conocer *v.* **16B**
Korean coreano/a *adj.* **1B:** coreano *m.* **1B**

L

label etiqueta *f.* **15A: record label** sello discográfico *m.* **17B**
labor: labor consultant asesor(a) laboral *m./f.* **13B: labor demand** demanda laboral *f.* **14A**
lack falta *f.* **11B:** carecer de *v.* **17B: lack of communication** falta de comunicación *f.* **15B: lacking salt** soso/a *adj.* **2B**
lady: young lady señorita *f.* **0**

lake lago *m.* **6B**
lamp lámpara *f.* **3B**
land tierra *f.* **9A**
landmark lugar clave *m.* **4A**
landscape paisaje *m.* **6B**
language lengua *f.* **1B:** idioma *m.* **1B: foreign language** lengua extranjera *f.* **15B: Language and Literature; Reading** Lengua y literatura *f.* **15B: native language** lengua nativa *f.* **16A: official language** lengua oficial *f.* **14A: What languages do you speak?** ¿Qué lenguas hablas? *exp.* **1B**
last pasado/a *adj.* **5A:** último/a *adj.* **5A: at last** por fin *exp.* **10A: last minute** último minuto *m.* **12B: last month** el mes pasado *m.* **5A: last name** apellido *m.* **1B: last night** anoche *adv.* **5A: last week** la semana pasada *loc. adv.* **5A: two last names** doble apellido *m.* **12A**
late tarde *adv.* **7A: to be late** retrasarse *v.*
lately últimamente *adv.* **7A : to be late** retrasarse *v.*
later luego *adv.* **0:** más tarde *loc. adv.* **17B: See you later.** Hasta luego. *exp.* **0**
laugh reír *v.* **6A:** reírse *v.* **17B**
launch: to launch a campaign lanzar una campaña *v.* **16B**
laureate: Nobel laureate Premio Nobel *m.* **10B**
lawyer abogado/a *m./f.* **1B**
layer: ozone layer capa de ozono *f.* **17A**
lead estar a la cabeza *exp.* **16A: to lead a... life** llevar una vida... *v.* **10A**
leader líder *m. y f.* **16A:** gobernante *m./f.* **12B: world leaders** líderes mundiales *m. y f.* **16A**
leaf hoja *f.* **8A**
learn aprender *v.* **3A:** descubrir *v.* **0: to learn Spanish** aprender español *v.* **3A**
least: the least el/la menos *m./f.* **9A**
leather cuero *m.* **8A**
leave abandonar *v.* **7B:** dejar *v.* **5A:** irse *v.* **12B:** marcharse *v.* **18B:** salir de *v.* **3A: leave-taking** despedida *f.* **0: maternity leave** baja por maternidad *f.* **7B: maternity leave** licencia por maternidad *f.* **7B**
left izquierda *f.* **9B: to the left** a la izquierda *loc. adv.* **9B: to the left of** a la izquierda de *loc. adv.* **3B**
leg pierna *f.* **10A**
legend leyenda *f.* **18A**
legume legumbre *f.* **2B**
leisure ocio *m.* **6A**
lend prestar *v.* **9A**
lentil lenteja *f.* **2B: lentils with chorizo** lentejas with chorizo *f* **2B**
less menos *adv.* **6A: less than** menos que *adj.* **3A**
lesson lección *f.* **0: private lesson** clase particular *f.* **17B**
let permitir *v.* **6B: (Let's) Get to work!** manos a la obra *exp.* **8A: let's see...** a ver... *exp.* **6A**
letter letra *f.* **0:** carta *f.* **2A: cover letter** carta de presentación *f.* **13B: initial letter** sigla *f.* **12B: letter to the editor** carta al director/a la directora *f.* **2A**
level nivel *m.* **16A**
library biblioteca *f.* **1A**
license licencia *f.* **2A**
life vida *f.* **2A: academic life** vida académica *f.* **14A: daily life** día a día *m.* **7A: pace of life** ritmo de vida *m.* **3A: quality of life** calidad de vida *f.* **2A: to change one's life** cambiar de vida *v.* **7B: to lead a... life** llevar una vida... *v.* **10A: to make life easier** hacer la vida más fácil *exp.* **17A: 17A: to make someone's life miserable** amargarle la vida a alguien *exp.*. **17A: way of life** medio de vida *m.* **11B**
lifeguard salvavidas (*invar.*) *m. y f.* **10A**
lifestyle: sedentary lifestyle sedentarismo *m.* **16B**
light claro/a *adj.* **16B:** luz *f.* **: light blue** celeste *adj.* **9A: lights off** luz apagada *f.* **6A**
lighthouse faro *m.* **14A: lighthouse keeper** farero/a *m./f.* **14A**
like gustar *v.* **4A: desert-like** desértico/a *adj.* **5A: I'd like...** Me da/pone... *v.* **4A: I'm sorry to see you like this.** Siento verte así. *exp.* **13B: to look like somebody** parecerse a alguien *v.* **12A: What is it like?** ¿Cómo es? *exp.* **2A, 4B: What would you like (to have)?** ¿Qué desean tomar? *exp.* **2B**
liking afición *f.* **11B:** gusto *m.* **15A**
limit límite *m.* **:** limitar *v.* **6A**
limousine limusina *f.* **18B**
line línea *f.* **4A: to get in line** hacer fila *v.* **to wait in line** hacer fila *v.* **3A:** cola *f.* **15A**
lion león *m.* **14A: lion tamer** domador(a) de leones *m./f.* **14A**
lipid lípido *m.* **15A**
list lista *f.* **0: shopping list** lista de compras *f.* **4A**
listen escuchar *v.* **0: to listen to the radio** escuchar la radio *v.* **2A**
listener oyente *m. y f.* **14B**
literary: literary critic crítico/a literario/a *m./f.* **10B**
literature letras *f.* **16A:** literatura *f.* **1B: Language and Literature** Lengua y Literatura *f.* **15B**
little pequeño/a *adj.* **4B:** poco/a *adv.* **2B: a little** un poco *loc. adv.* **2B**
live en directo *loc. adv.* **4A:** vivir *v.* **2A: Long live...** ¡Viva! *exp.* **2A: to live abroad** vivir afuera *v.* **10B**
living: living room salón *m.* **4B: living room-dining room** salón-comedor *m.* **4B: to do something for a living** dedicarse a (hacer) algo *v.* **7A**
load cargar *v.* **9A**
loan: to ask for a loan pedir un crédito *v.* **5B**
locate localizar *v.* **13B: located** ubicado/a *adj.* **11A**
location ubicación *f.* **15A**
locked bloqueado/a *adj.* **7B**
lodging alojamiento *m.* **6B**
logo logo *m.* **16B**
London Londres *m.* **1A**
long largo/a *adj.* **12A: How long have/has?** ¿Cuánto tiempo (hace)...? *exp.* **8B: in the long term** a largo plazo *loc. adv.* **9A: Long live...** ¡Viva! *exp.* **2A: long term** a largo plazo *loc. adv.* **17A: long weekend** puente *m.* **6B: long-distance love** amor a distancia *m.* **6B**
look: Look, Mira... *v.* **8A: to look at** fijarse en *v.* **0: to look at** mirar *v.* **6A: to look at each other** mirarse *v.* **17B: to look like somebody** parecerse a alguien *v.* **12A: to look for** buscar *v.* **1B**
Los Angeles Los Ángeles *m.* **1A**
lose perder *v.* **7B**
lot: a lot mucho/a *adj.*; *adv.* **2A, 6A: parking lot** aparcamiento *m.* **11A: quite a lot** bastante *adv.* **5B: to have a lot in common** ser afín *v.* **17B**
lottery lotería *f.* **9B:** sorteo *m.* **12B: lottery ticket booth** agencia de lotería *f.* **9B: lottery ticket seller** vendedor(a) de lotería *m./f.* **9B: to buy lottery tickets** comprar (billetes de) lotería *v.* **9B: to play the lottery** jugar a la lotería *v.* **9B**
lounge: arrival lounge sala de llegada *f.* **13A**
love amor *m.* **6B:** encantar *v.* **5B: (un) requited love** amor (no) correspondido *m.* **12A: declaration of love** declaración de amor *f.* **18B: long-distance love** amor a distancia *m.* **6B: to fall in love** enamorarse *v.* **12A: to love each other** quererse *v.* **17B: to love someone** querer a alguien *v.* **12A**
lovely hermoso/a *adj.* **13A:** precioso/a *adj.* **2A:** lindo/a *adj.* **11B**
low bajo/a *adj.* **4A: low-calorie** bajo en calorías *adj.* **15A**
luck suerte *f.* **8B: to try one's luck** probar suerte *v.* **5A**
lucky: lucky person privilegiado/a *adj.*; *m./f.* **2A**
lunch: to eat lunch almorzar *v.* **2B: to eat lunch** comer *v.* **2B**
luxurious lujoso/a *adj.* **11A**
lyrics letra *f.* **7A**

M

madam señora *f.* **6B**
made up of compuesto/a por *adj.* **16B**
magazine revista *f.* **9B: gossip magazine** revista del corazón *f.* **9B**
magic mágico/a *adj.* **18B**
mahogany: mahogany tree caoba *f.* **18B**
main principal *adj.* **4B: main course** plato principal *m.* **2B: main office** central *f.* **2A**
maintenance mantenimiento *m.* **4B**
major (academic) carrera *f.* **1B**
majority mayoría *f.* **5B**
make elaborar *v.* **0:** hacer *v.* **3A:** preparar *v.* **7A: to make (his/her) dreams come true** cumplir (sus) sueños *v.* **15B: to make fortune** hacer fortuna *v.* **8B: to make a reservation** reservar *v.* **6B: to make aware** hacer consciente *v.* **3B: to make flexible** flexibilizar *v.* **6A: to make known** dar a conocer *v.* **16B: to make life easier** hacer la vida más fácil *v.* **17A: to make sad** entristecer *v.* **17B: to make someone's life miserable** amargarle

la vida a alguien *exp.* **17A: to make something happen** hacer realidad *v.* **8B: to make the bed** hacer la cama *v.* **3A**
makeup maquillaje *m.* **7A: to put makeup on** maquillarse *v.* **7A**
malaria paludismo *m.* **10A**
mall: shopping mall centro comercial *m.* **2A**
mallorca (Puerto-Rican pastry) mallorca *f.* **1A**
man hombre *m.* **3B: the man of my dreams** el hombre de mi vida *exp.* **12A**
manage dirigir *v.* **6A:** lograr *v.* **5B:** manejar *v.* **13B**
management gestión *f.* **13B**
manager directivo/a *m./f.* **8B: hotel manager** hotelero/a *m./f.* **4B: managerial position** puesto directivo *m.* **13B**
manifesto manifiesto *m.* **12B**
many muchos/as *adj.* **2A: as many** tantos/as *adj.* **8B: as much/many... as** tan/tanto... como *conj.* **8B: how many?** ¿cuántos/as? *interrog.* **4B**
map mapa *m.* **4B**
marathon maratón *m.* **18A: to run a marathon** correr un maratón *v.* **18A**
march marcha *f.* **16A**
March marzo *m.* **5A**
marginalization marginación *f.* **12B**
marginalized marginado/a *adj.* **12B**
marinade adobo *m.* **15A**
marine marino/a *adj.* **11B: marine biologist** biólogo/a marino/a *m./f.* **11B**
marital: marital status estado civil *m.* **5B**
mark marcar *v.* **0**
market mercado *m.* **0: market research** investigación de mercado *f.* **15A: produce market** agromercado *m.* **4A: stand (in a market)** puesto *m.* **4A**
marketing *marketing m.* **13B: marketing analyst** analista de *maketing m. y f.* **13B**
marmalade mermelada *f.* **2B**
marriage matrimonio *m.* **5B**
married casado/a *adj.* **5B: married couple** matrimonio *m.* **11B: to get married** casarse *v.* **8B**
Mars Marte *m.* **17A**
masculine masculino/a *adj.* **0: Masculine or feminine?** ¿Masculino o femenino? *adj.* **0**
Mass misa *f.* **5A**
mass: to mass produce fabricar en serie *v.* **13B**
massive descomunal *adj.* **18A**
master maestro/a *m./f.* **6A: master of ceremonies** maestro/a de ceremonias *m./f.* **18B**
match cerilla *f.* **8A:** partido *m.* **18A:** relacionar *v.* **0**
mate (infusion) yerba mate *f.* **3B, 6A**
material material *m.* **8A: raw material** materia prima *f.* **15A**
maternity: maternity leave baja por maternidad *f.* **7B:** licencia por maternidad *f.* **7B**
Math Matemáticas *f. pl.* **15B**
matter asunto *m.* **: matter of faith** acto de fe *m.* **8A**
mature maduro/a *adj.* **17B**
May mayo *m.* **2A**
maybe a lo mejor *loc. adv.* **17A:** tal vez *loc. adv.* **17A**
me mí *pron.* **: excuse me** perdone (*form.*) *exp.* **9B: Excuse me, ...** Perdona,... *exp.* **5A**
meadow prado *m.* **9A**
meal comida *f.* **2B: Enjoy your meal.** ¡Buen provecho! *exp.* **8A**
mean significar *v.* **0: What does ... mean?** ¿Qué significa...? *exp.* **0**
means medios *m.* **15A:** recursos *m. pl.* **12B: by means of** por medio de *loc. prep.* **14B: means of transportation** medio de transporte *m.* **4A: to be beyond (one's) means** estar fuera de (nuestro) alcance *exp.* **15B: to go by (means of transportation)** ir en... *v.* **6B**
measure medida *f.* **16A:** medir *v.* **17A**
meat carne *f.* **2B**
meatball albóndiga *f.* **2B**
mechanic mecánico/a *adj.; m./f.* **7B**
mechanics mecánica *f.* **8A**
medal medalla *f.* **12B**
media medios de comunicación *m.* **9A**
medication medicación *f.* **10A**
medicine medicina *f.* **10A:** fármaco *m.* **17A:** medicamento *m.* **10A**
mediocrity pobreza *f.* **13B**
meditation meditación *f.* **6A**
medium: medium term a medio plazo *loc. adv.* **17A**
meet complir con *v.* **15A:** conocer *v.* **5A:** reunir(se) *v.* **6A: Pleased to meet you.** Encantado/a. *exp.* **0: to meet again** reencontrar *v.* **9A: to meet the requirements** reunir los requisitos *v.* **13B**
meeting reunión *f.* **7B:** encuentro *m.* **6A: meeting point** punto de encuentro *m.* **9A**
member miembro *m.* **5A: to become a member** afiliarse *v.* **16A**
memoir memorias *f. pl.* **10B**
memorize aprender de memoria *v.* **14B**
memory memoria *f.* **5B, 10B:** recuerdo *m.* **5B**
mental mental *adj.* **12B**
mention comentar *v.* **14B:** mencionar *v.* **0**
menu menú *m.* **2B: fixed-price menu** menú del día *m.* **2B**
merengue merengue *m.* **17B**
messenger: messenger company mensajería *f.* **7B**
metabolism metabolismo *m.* **17A**
metal metal *m.* **8A**
meter metro *m.* **4B: square meters** metros cuadrados (m2) *m. pl.* **4B**
method método *m.* **17A: scientific method** método científico *m.* **17A**
methodical metódico/a *adj.* **13B**
Mexican mexicano/a *adj.* **2B**
Mexico México *m.* **0**
Mexico City México, D.F. *m.* **2A**
mid a mediados de *loc. adv.* **14B: in the mid-sixties** a mediados de los 60 *loc. adv.* **14B**
middle: middle class clase media *f.* **14B**
migrant: migrant population población migrante *f.* **8B**
migration migración *f.* **8B**
milk leche *f.* **0: skim milk** leche descremada *f.* **15A: whole milk** leche entera *f.* **15A**
millennium milenio *m.* **10B**
million millón *m.* **8B**
mind mente *f.* **6A: state of mind** estado anímico *m.* **10A,: state of mind** estado de ánimo *m.* **12A: Would you mind...?** ¿Le importaría...? *exp.* **13A**
minister ministro/a *m./f.* **16A**
ministry secretaría *f.* **16A:** ministerio *m.* **16A**
minority minoría *f.* **14A**
minute minuto *m.* **1A: last minute** último minuto *m.* **12B**
mirror espejo *m.* **9A**
Miss señorita *f.* **0**
miss echar de menos *v.* **14B:** extrañar *v.* **13A: Don't miss...** No se pierda *exp.* **11B: to miss a flight** perder un vuelo *v.* **13A: to miss out** perdérselo *v.* **16B**
missile misil *m.* **17A**
missing que faltan *adj.* **0**
mission misión *f.* **10A**
mistake error *m.* **11A**
mistaken equivocado/a *adj.* **14A**
misunderstanding malentendido *m.* **14A**
mix mezcla *f.* **14A:** mezclar *v.* **14A**
mobile móvil *adj.* **17A**
mobility movilidad *f.* **13B**
model modelo *m.* **0: fashion model** modelo *m. y f.* **3B**
moderate moderado/a *adj.* **6B**
modern moderno/a *adj.* **2A**
modernity modernidad *f.* **17A**
modernization modernización *f.* **17A**
modification: genetic modification manipulación genética *f.* **7B**
mojito (traditional Cuban cocktail) mojito *m.* **13A**
molar muela *f.* **10A**
mom mamá (*fam.*) *f.* **5B**
moment momento *m.* **5A: at the moment** actualmente *adv.* **12A**
Monday lunes *m.* **3A**
money plata (*fam.*) *f.* **11B:** dinero *m.* **6B**
monkey mono/a *m./f.* **16B: spider monkey** mono/a araña *m./f.* **16B**
Monterrey: born in Monterrey regiomontano/a *m./f.* **12A**
month mes *m.* **5A: last month** el mes pasado *loc. adv.* **5A: next month** el próximo mes *loc. adv.* **5B: this month** este mes *loc. adv.* **6A: twice a month** dos veces al mes *loc. adv.* **6A: two months ago** hace dos meses *loc. adv.* **5A**
monument monumento *m.* **1A**
mood estado de ánimo *m.* **12A: in a good/bad mood** de buen/mal humor *loc. adv.* **12A**
moonlighting pluriempleo *m.* **14B**
morbid: morbid interest morbo *m.* **14B**
more más *adv.* **3A: more than** más que *adj.* **3A**
morning mañana *f.* **3A: Good morning.** Buenos días. *exp.* **0: in the morning** de la mañana *loc. adv.* **3A: in the morning** por la mañana *loc. adv.* **3A**
Moroccan marroquí *adj.* **4A**

Morocco Marruecos *m.*
mosquito mosquito *m.* **10A**
most mayoría *f.* **5B: the most** el/la más *m./f.* **9A**
mother madre *f.* **5B: mother tongue** lengua materna *f.* **14A: Mother's Day** Día de la Madre *m.* **18B: working mother** madre trabajadora *f.* **7B**
motion movimiento *m.* **14A: a world in motion** un mundo en movimiento *exp.* **14A: set in motion** poner en marcha *exp.* **16A**
motorcade caravana de coches *f.* **5A**
motto lema *m.* **3B**
mountain montaña *f.* **3A: mountain climber** montañista *m. y f.* **18A: mountain climbing** montañismo *m.* **18A**
mouse ratón *m.* **7B**
mouth boca *f.* **9A**
move cambiar de casa *v.* **5A:** mudanza *f.* **14A: (from home)** mudarse *v.* **7B**
movie película *f.* **1A: movie on DVD** película en DVD *f.* **4B: movie theater** cine *m.* **3A: to watch movies** ver películas *v.* **3A**
moving emocionante *adv.* **10B**
MP3: MP3 player reproductor de MP3 *m.* **13B**
Mrs. señora (Sra.) *f.* **2A**
much mucho/a *adv.* **2A: as much/many... as** tan/tanto... como *conj.* **8B: How much is it?** ¿Cuánto es? *exp.* **2B**
mug taza *f.* **2B**
multilingual políglota *adj.* **1B**
multimedia multimedia (*invar.*) *adj.* **9B**
multinational multinacional (firm) *f.* **16A**
museum museo *m.* **0**
mushroom hongo *m.* **11A**
music música *f.* **1A: music class** clase de música *f.* **3A: music group** grupo musical *m.* **14B: music store** tienda de discos *f.* **3B**
musician músico/a *m./f.* **3A**
must (to have to; must) deber *v.* **: a must** excluyente *adj.* **13B**
mustache bigote *m.* **12A**
my mi(s) *adj.* **2A:** mío/a(s) *pron.* **: In my opinion, ...** En mi opinión, ... *exp.* **10B: It's my turn.** Me toca a mí. *exp.* **4A: my folks** mi gente *exp.* **5B**
mysticism misticismo *m.* **16B**

N

Nahuatl náhuatl *m.* **12A**
nail clavo *m.* **8A: to nail down** clavar *v.* **8A**
naïveté inocencia *f.* **18B**
name nombre *m.* **1B:** nombrar *v.* **0: first name** nombre de pila *m.* **12A: His/Her name is...** (Él/Ella) se llama *exp.* **0: last name** apellido *m.* **1B: My name is...** (Yo) me llamo... *exp.* **0: two last names** doble apellido *m.* **12A: What is your name?** ¿Cómo se llama? *exp.* **0: What is your name?** ¿Cómo te llamas? *exp.* **0**
namesake tocayo/a *m./f.* **12A**
nap siesta *f.* **6A: to take a nap** dormir la siesta *v.* **6A**
nasal nasal *adj.* **10B**
national nacional *adj.* **12B: national airline** aerolínea abanderada *f.* **13A: national identity card** DNI *m.* **3A**
nationality nacionalidad *f.* **1B**
native oriundo/a *adj.* **16B:** indígena *adj. invar.* **1B: native language** lengua nativa *f.* **16A: native people** pueblo indígena *m.* **16A**
natural natural *adj.* **14A: natural food** alimento natural *m.* **15A: natural resource** recurso natural *m.* **14A**
nature naturaleza *f.* **4B**
near cerca de *prep.* **2A**
neat ordenado/a *adj.* **13B**
necessary necesario/a *adj.* **: to be necessary** hacer falta *v.* **16A**
need necesidad *f.* **13B: in need** sin recursos *loc. adv.* **15A**
negative negativo/a *adj.* **2B**
neighbor vecino/a *m./f.* **4A**
neighborhood barrio *m.* **1A: historic neighborhood** casco viejo *m.* **12B: rural neighborhood** vereda *f.* **9A**
neither tampoco *adv.* **10B**
nephew sobrino *m.* **18A**
nerd cerebrito *m./f.* **15B**
nervous nervioso/a *adj.* **10A**
network red *f.* **9A: radio network** cadena de radio *f.* **14B: social network** red social *f.* **13B: Wi-Fi network** red Wi-Fi *f.* **13B**
never nunca *adv.* **6A**
new nuevo/a *adj.* **1A: New Year** Año Nuevo *m.* **18B**
New Orleans Nueva Orleans *f.* **1A**
New York Nueva York *f.* **1A**
news noticia *f.* **4A: news and talk show** magacín *m.* **9A: news program** informativo *m.* **9A**
newspaper periódico *m.* **7A**
next próximo/a *adj.* **5B:** siguiente *adj.* **0: next month** el próximo mes *m.* **5B: next to** al lado de *loc. adv.* **3B**
NGO (non-governmental organization) ONG (organización no gubernamental) *f.* **5A**
Nicaragua Nicaragua *f.* **0**
Nicaraguan nicaragüense *adj.*
nice simpático/a *adj.* **2A:** lindo/a *adj.* **11B: Have a nice stay!** ¡Feliz estancia! *exp.* **11A**
nicknack objeto curioso *m.* **4A**
nickname diminutivo *m.* **12A**
niece sobrina *f.* **18A**
night noche *f.* **3A: at night** por la noche *loc. adv.* **3A: at night** de la noche *loc. adv.* **3A: Good night.** Buenas noches. *exp.* **0: last night** anoche *adv.* **5A: night club** discoteca *f.* **2A: night security guard** vigilante nocturno/a *m. y f.* **3A: to spend the night** pasar la noche *v.* **6B**
nine nueve *adj.* **1A**
nineteen diecinueve *adj.* **1B**
ninety noventa *adj.* **1B**
nitric oxide óxido nítrico *m.* **17A**
no ningún *adj.* **9A:** no *adv.* **1A:** (none) ninguno/a *adj.* **9A: No problem!** ¡No hay problema! *exp.* **7B**
Nobel Prize Premio Nobel *m.* **10B**
nobody nadie *pron.* **8A**
noise ruido *m.* **2A**
none ninguno/a *pron., adj.* **9A**
non-violence no violencia *f.* **16A**
normally normalmente *adv.* **2B**
north norte *m.* **2A: North Pole** Polo Norte *m.* **18A**
nose nariz *f.* **9A**
nostalgia nostalgia *f.* **10B**
not no *adv.* **1A: Don't worry.** No te preocupes. *exp.* **13B: I think so/not.** Creo que sí/no. *exp.* **7B: not . . . either, neither** tampoco *adv.* **10B: not to be able to stand** no soportar *v.* **15B: not yet** todavía no *loc. adv.* **6A: You/One can't...** No se puede... *exp.* **7B**
notable destacado/a *adj.* **5A**
note nota *f.* **4A**
noteworthy destacable *adj.* **14A**
nothing nada *adv.* **2B: Nothing else, thanks.** Nada más, gracias. *exp.* **2B**
nougat candy turrón *m.* **18B**
November noviembre *m.* **5A**
nowadays en la actualidad *loc. adv.* **8B:** hoy en día *loc. adv.* **15B**
nuclear: nuclear weapon arma nuclear *f.* **16A**
number nº (número) *m.* **2A:** número *m.* **0**
nurse enfermero/a *m./f.* **12B**
nut nuez *f.* **18B**
nutrient nutriente *m.* **15A**
nutritional: nutritional information información nutricional *f.* **15A**
nutritious nutritivo/a *adj.* **15A**

O

object objeto *m.* **3B:** oponerse *v.* **15B**
objective objetivo *m.* **3B**
obligation obligación *f.* **5B**
observe observar *v.* **0**
obtain conseguir *v.* **4A:** obtener *v.* **0**
obvious obvio/a *adj.* **17A:** evidente *adj.* **17A**
occasion ocasión *f.* **: on the occasion of** con motivo de *exp.* **12B**
ocean océano *m.* **18A**
octopus pulpo *m.* **2B**
odd raro/a *adj.* **15B: to think something is odd** parecer raro *v.* **15B**
of de *prep.* **2B: by means of** por medio de *loc. prep.* **14B: day of the week** día de la semana *m.* **3A: filet of veal** filete de ternera *m.* **2B: in favor of** a favor de *loc. adv.* **12B: means of transportation** medio de transporte *m.* **4A: of the** del (= de + el) *contrac.* **3B: on the occasion of** con motivo de *exp.* **12B: on top of** encima de *loc. prep.* **3B: outside of class** fuera de clase *loc. prep.* **3A: piece of advice** consejo *m.* **6A: place of worship** lugar de culto *m.* **8A: the rest of** el resto de *m.* **12B: time of year** época *f.* **6B: to be of interest** interesar *v.* **7A: to get a kick out of** encantar *v.* **5B: to take care of someone** cuidar a/de *v.* **5B, 7A: to the left of** a la izquierda de *loc. adv.* **3B: to the right of** a la derecha de *loc. adv.* **3B: work of art** obra (de arte) *f.* **8A: world of finance** mundo de las finanzas *m.* **3A: of course** claro *exp.* **1B**

off: day off día libre *m.* **14A: lights off** luz apagada *f.* **6A**
offense atentado *m.* **12B**
offer ofrecer *v.* **4B: to offer encouragement** dar ánimos *v.* **13A**
office oficina *f.* **6A: main office** central *f.* **2A: press office** oficina de prensa *f.* **16A**
official oficial *adj.* **14A: official language** lengua oficial *f.* **14A**
often a menudo *loc. adv.* **: How often?** ¿Con qué frecuencia? *exp.* **3A**
oil aceite *m.* **8A:** petróleo *m.* **14A: extra virgin olive oil** aceite de oliva virgen extra *m.* **15A: oil barrel** barril de petróleo *m.* **14A: oil industry** industria petrolera *f.* **14A: oil rig** plataforma petrolera *f.* **14A: olive oil** aceite de oliva *m.* **2B**
OK ¡Vale! *exp.* **2B:** De acuerdo. *exp.* **2B: Everything is OK.** No pasa nada. *exp.* **13B: I'm OK.** Estoy bien. *exp.* **7B**
old antiguo/a *adj.* **2A:** viejo/a *adj.* **5B: an 80-year-old person** una persona de 80 años *f.* **3A: fifteen-year-old girl** quinceañera *f.* **5A**
older mayor *adj.* **9A**
olive aceituna *f.* **2B: extra virgin olive oil** aceite de oliva virgen extra *m.* **15A: olive oil** aceite de oliva *m.* **2B**
on en *prep.* **3B: Come on!** ¡Anda ya! *exp.* **9B: movie on DVD** película en DVD *f.* **4B: on (top of)** encima de *loc. prep.* **3B: on board** a bordo *loc. adv.* **13A: on the occasion of** con motivo de *exp.* **12B: on the other hand** por otro lado/por otra parte *loc. adv.* **13B: on time** a tiempo *loc. adv.* **7B: on weekends** los fines de semana *loc. adv.* **5B: to be on vacation** estar de vacaciones *v.* **7B: to depend on** depender de *v.* **10A: to put makeup on** maquillarse **7A: on the one hand** por un lado/por una parte *loc. adv.* **13B**
once: once a week una vez a la semana *loc. adv.* **6A**
one uno/a *adj.* **1A: on the one hand** por un lado/por una parte *loc. adv.* **13B: one hundred percent** cien por ciento *adj.* **12A: which one(s)?** ¿cuál(es)? *interrog.* **4B: You/One can't...** No se puede... *exp.* **7B**
one hundred cien *adj.* **1B**
oneself uno/a mismo/a *m./f.* **3A: time for oneself** tiempo para uno/a mismo/a *m.* **3A: to amuse oneself** entretenerse *v.* **9A: to outdo oneself** superarse *v.* **18A: to question, to ask oneself questions** plantearse preguntas *v.* **14B**
online en línea *loc. adv.* **9B**
only nomás *adv.* **17B:** solo/solamente *adv.* **13B:** únicamente *adv.* **13B**
open abierto/a *adj.* **3A:** abrir *v.* **3A:** inaugurar *v.* **12A: to open a business** abrir un negocio *v.* **15A**
opening apertura *f.* **15A**
openly abiertamente *adv.* **17A**
opinion opinión *f.* **10B: In my opinion, ...** En mi opinión, ... *exp.* **10B**
opponent contrincante *m.* y *f.* **18A**
opportunity oportunidad *f.* **8B**
opt optar *v.* **18B**
optimism optimismo *m.* **10B**
optimistic optimista *adj.* **12A**
or o *conj.* **: or otherwise** o bien *exp.* **12A:** u (before **o** or **ho**) *conj.* **11B**
orange anaranjado/a *adj.* **3B:** naranja *f.* **2B: orange juice** jugo de naranja *m.* **2B: orange juice** zumo de naranja *m.* **2B**
orchid orquídea *f.* **11A**
order pedido *m.* **7B:** pedir *v.* **7B: in order** en regla *loc. adv.* **11A: put in order** ordenar *v.* **0**
orderly ordenado/a *adj.* **13B**
organic ecológico/a *adj.* **7B:** orgánico/a *adj.* **7B: organic farming** agricultura ecológica *f.* **15A: organic product** producto ecológico *m.* **15A**
organism organismo *m.* **17A**
organization organización *f.* **3B: NGO (non-governmental organization)** ONG (organización no gubernamental) *f.* **5A**
organize agrupar *v.* **0:** organizar *v.* **6A: to organize a trip** preparar un viaje *v.* **13A**
oriental oriental *adj.* **6A**
origin procedencia *f.* **8B:** origen *m.* **1A, 13A**
original original *adj.* **3B**
other otro/a *adj.* **: in other words** es decir *exp.* **8B: on the other hand** por otro lado/por otra parte *loc. adv.* **13B: the other day** el otro día *loc. adv.* **9B**
otherwise or otherwise o bien *conj.* **12A**
Ottawa Ottawa *f.* **1A**
our nuestro/a(s) *adj.* **5B:**
out fuera *adv.* **2B: to get a kick out of** encantar *v.* **5B: to go out** salir *v.* **3A: to go out with somebody** salir con alguien *v.* **12A**
outdo: to outdo oneself superarse *v.* **18A**
outdoors al aire libre *loc. adv.* **3A**
outside fuera *prep.* **3A: outside of class** fuera de clase *loc. adv.* **3A**
outskirts afueras *f. pl.* **11B**
overcome superar *v.* **18A**
overnight de un día para el otro *loc. adv.* **16A**
overprotect sobreproteger *v.* **15B**
overtime horas extras *f. pl.* **13B: to do overtime** hacer horas extras *v.* **13B**
own propio/a *adj.* **: for (your) own good** por (tu/su) bien *loc. adv.* **15B**
owner dueño/a *m./f.* **8B:** propietario/a *m./f.* **8B**
oxygen oxígeno *m.* **18A**
ozone: ozone layer capa de ozono *f.* **17A**

P

p.m. de la noche *loc. adv.* **3A:** de la tarde *loc. adv.* **3A: 6 p.m.** 18:00 h *f.* **1B**
pace: pace of life ritmo de vida *m.* **3A**
pacifist pacifista *m.* y *f.* **16A**
pack hacer las maletas *v.* **8B**
package envase *m.* **15A:** paquete *m.* **4A: package tour** viaje organizado *m.* **13A**
packaged envasado/a *adj.* **15A**
paella (Spanish rice dish) paella *f.* **0**
page página *f.* **0: problem page** consultorio *m.* **10A: Web page** página web *f.* **14B**
pain dolor *m.* **10A**
painful amargo/a *adj.* **10B**
painkiller analgésico *m.* **10A**
paint pintar *v.* **6A**
painter pintor(a) *m./f.* **12B**
painting pintura *f.* **3A**
pair par *m.* **5A: In pairs/groups** En parejas/grupos *loc. adv.* **0**
Pakistani paquistaní *adj.* **4A**
pal cuate/a *(fam.) m./f.* **12A**
pamphlet folleto *m.* **0**
pan: frying pan sartén *f.* **8A**
Panama Panamá *m.* **0**
Panama City Ciudad de Panamá *f.* **0**
Panamanian panameño/a *adj.* **2A**
Pan-American: Pan-American Games Juegos Panamericanos *m.* **18A**
panel: panel of judges jurado *m.* **16B**
panoramic panorámico/a *adj.* **18B**
pants pantalones *m. pl.* **3B**
paradise paraíso *m.* **4B**
parador (state-run hotel in Spanish historic buildings) Parador de Turismo de España *m.* **11A**
paragliding parapente *m.* **18A**
paragraph párrafo *m.* **0**
Paraguay Paraguay *m.* **0**
Paraguayan paraguayo/a *adj.*
Paralympic: Paralympic Games Juegos Paralímpicos *m.* **12B**
parasite parásito *m.* **8A**
parents padres *m. pl.* **5B**
park parque *m.* **2A:** aparcar *v.* **11A**
parking: parking lot aparcamiento *m.* **11A**
participate colaborar *v.* **3A:** participar *v.* **3A**
particular: in particular en concreto *loc. adv.* **7B**
partner pareja *f.* **5B:** compañero/a *m./f.* **2B**
party fiesta *f.* **: bachelor(ette) party** despedida de soltero/a *f.* **18B: fifteenth birthday party** fiesta de quince años *f.* **18B: housewarming party** inauguración *f.* **12A: political party** partido político *m.* **16A**
pasodoble (Spanish march-like dance) pasodoble *m.* **17B**
pass aprobar *v.* **14A:** pasar *v.*
passenger pasajero/a *m./f.* **13A: passengers/ladies and gentlemen** señores pasajeros *exp.* **13A**
passive pasivo/a *adj.* **6A**
passport pasaporte *m.* **13A: passport control** control de pasaportes *m.* **13A**
past antes *m.* **9A:** pasado *m.*
pasta pasta *f.* **2B**
pastime pasatiempo *m.* **7A**
pastries bollería *f.* **2B**
Patagonia Patagonia *f.* **6B**
patent patentar *v.* **17A**
path paseo *m.* **2A**
patience paciencia *f.* **15A**
patient paciente *m.* y *f.* **10A**
patron: patron saint patrono/a *m./f.* **16B**
paw pata *f.* **5A**
pay pagar *v.* **3B: pay attention (to)** poner atención (a) *v.* **0: to pay attention (to somebody)** hacer caso (a alguien) *v.* **15B**
payment pago *m.* **7B**

peace paz *f.* **2A:** tranquilidad *f.* **2A: ambassador for peace** embajador(a) de la paz *m./f.* **16A: to be at peace** estar en paz *v.* **10B**
peaceful pacífico/a *adj.* **16A:** tranquilo/a *adj.* **2A**
peach durazno *m.* **16B:** melocotón *m.* **15A**
peak: peak season temporada alta *f.* **4B**
peal: peal of a bell campanada *f.* **18B**
peanut cacahuate *m.* **12A**
peasant campesino/a *m./f.* **9A**
peel pelar *v.* **8A**
pen bolígrafo *m.* **3B**
people gente *f.* **2A: for young people** juvenil *adj.* **7A: native people** pueblo indígena *m.* **16A: to talk to people** hablar con la gente *v.* **2A: unity of the people** unidad popular *f.* **16A: young people** jóvenes *m. pl.* **2A**
pepper pimienta *f.* **: bell pepper** pimiento *m.* **2B**
per: per capita income renta per cápita *f.* **14A: per se** propiamente dicho/a *exp.* **16B**
percent por ciento *loc. adv.* **11A: (a ...%) discount** descuento (del ...%) *m.* **11A: one hundred percent** cien por ciento *adj.* **12A**
perfect perfecto/a *adj.* **2A**
perfectly: I understand you perfectly. Te entiendo perfectamente. *exp.* **13B**
perform interpretar *v.* **7A:** realizar *v.* **5A:** rendir *v.* **6A**
performance interpretación *f.* **5A:** rendimiento *m.* **13B**
perfume fragancia *f.* **16B:** perfume *m.* **3B: perfume/cosmetics shop** perfumería *f.* **3B**
perhaps quizá(s) *adv.* **17A**
period época *f.* **9A:** período *m.* **: enrollment period** plazo de inscripción *m.* **18A: postwar period** posguerra *f.* **14B**
permission: to ask permission pedir permiso *v.* **12B**
person persona *f.* **1B: an 80-year-old person** persona de 80 años *f.* **3A: business person** empresario/a *m./f.* **8B: person in charge** responsable *m. y f.* **13A: person of mixed race** mestizo/a *m./f.* **16A**
personal personal *adj.* **3B: personal satisfaction** satisfacción personal *f.* **13B**
personality carácter *f.* **12A**
personalized personalizado/a *adj.* **11A**
Peru Perú *m.* **0**
Peruvian peruano/a *adj.*
pessimistic pesimista *adj.* **12A**
pesticide pesticida *m.* **15A**
petrified petrificado/a *adj.* **11B**
pharmaceutical farmacéutico/a *adj.* **17A**
Philadelphia Filadelfia *f.* **1A**
philosophy filosofía *f.* **5A**
phone teléfono *m.* **1B: cell phone** (teléfono) celular *m.* **1B: What is your phone number?** ¿Cuál es tu número de teléfono? *exp.* **1B**
photo foto *f.* **0: photo story** fotonovela *f.* **12A**
photocopier (foto)copiadora *f.* **7B**
photograph fotografía *f.* **1B**
photographer fotógrafo/a *m./f.* **11B**
photographic fotográfico/a *adj.* **11B**
phrase frase *f.* **0**
physical físico/a *adj.* **6A: physical appearance** aspecto físico *m.* **12A: physical condition** estado físico *m.* **10A: Physical Education** Educación física *f.* **15B**
Physics Física *f.* **15B**
piano piano *m.* **8A: grand piano** piano de cola *m.* **10B**
pick up recepción *f.* **11A:** recoger *v.* **5B, 8A**
picked recogido/a *adj.* **15A**
picture imagen *f.* **1A: picture frame** marco *m.* **3B: to take pictures** tomar fotos *v.* **6B**
piece: piece of advice consejo *m.* **6A: piece of furniture** mueble *m.* **8A: piece of gossip** chisme *m.* **17B**
pig cerdo/a *m./f.*
pigeon paloma *f.* **: pigeon pea** gandul *m.* **15A**
pilgrim peregrino/a *m./f.* **11A**
pilot piloto *m. y f.* **18A**
pineapple piña *f.* **15A**
pink rosado/a *adj.* **18B**
place lugar *m.* **2A:** sitio *m.* **11B:** rincón *m.* **11A:** colocar *v.* **9B: place of worship** lugar de culto *m.* **8A: to take place** celebrar *v.* **18A**
plan plano *m.* **8A:** planificar *v.* **18B:** programar *v.* **3A: social plan** el plan social *m.* **16A**
plane avión *m.* **6B: plane ticket** pasaje de avión *m.* **6B**
planner: (weekly) planner agenda semanal *f.* **3A**
plant planta *f.* **8A**
plastic plástico *m.* **8A: plastic container** envase de plástico *m.* **15A**
plate plato *m.* **8A**
platform andén *m.* **13A**
play jugar *v.* **7A: to play the lottery** jugar a la lotería *v.* **9B:** (an instrument) tocar *v.* **8A**
player jugador(a) *m./f.* **: bandoneón player** bandoneonista *m. y f.* **17B: baseball player** beisbolista *m. y f.* **18A: MP3 player** reproductor de MP3 *m.* **13B: soccer player** futbolista *m. y f.* **: tennis player** tenista *m. y f.* **14A**
pleasant agradable *adj.* **2A**
please por favor *exp.* **2B:** gustar *v.* **4A**
pleased: Pleased to meet you. Encantado/a. *exp.* **0: Pleased to meet you.** Mucho gusto. *exp.* **0**
pleasure placer *m.* **5B**
plentiful abundante *adj.* **17A**
pocket bolsillo *m.* **13B**
poem poema *m.* **10B**
poet poeta/poetisa *m./f.* **10B**
point punto *m.* **5B: meeting point** punto de encuentro *m.* **9A: point in common** punto común *m.* **5B**
pole bastón *m.* **18A**
police policía *f.* **0**
policy política *f.* **6A: cultural policy** política cultural *f.* **16A: social policy** política social *f.* **16A**
political político/a *adj.* **1B: political party** partido político *m.* **16A: political science** ciencias políticas *f.* **1B**
politician político/a *m./f.* **16A**
politics política *f.* **16A**
polyglot políglota *adj. invar.* **1B**
pool alberca *f.* **5B:** piscina *f.* **3A, 4B**
popular popular *adj.* **2B**
populated poblado/a *adj.* **16B**
population población *f.* **2A: migrant population** población migrante *m.* **8B**
pork carne de cerdo *f.* **18B**
Port-au-Prince Puerto Príncipe *m.* **12B**
portion ración *f.* **2B**
portrait retrato *m.* **14B**
Portugal Portugal *m.* **1A**
Portuguese portugués/portuguesa *adj.* **1B:** portugués *m.* **1B**
position cargo *m.* **17A:** puesto *m.* **4B: managerial position** puesto directivo *m.* **13B**
positive positivo/a *adj.* **2B**
possibility posibilidad *f.* **6A**
possible posible *adj.* **4A: as... as possible** lo más... posible *m.* **17A: it's possible** es posible *exp.* **4A**
post exponer *v.* **0**
postcard postal *f.* **9B**
poster cartel *m.* **0:** póster *m.* **4A**
postpone postergar *v.* **17B**
postwar: postwar period posguerra *f.* **14B**
potato papa *f.* **2B:** patata *f.* **2B: potato chips** patatas fritas *f.* **4A: Spanish potato omelet** tortilla española *f* **2B**
pottery cerámica *f.* **6A: to do pottery** hacer cerámica *f.* **6A**
poverty pobreza *f.* **13B**
powder polvo *m.* **15A: cocoa powder** cacao en polvo *m.* **15A: powdered skim milk** leche descremada en polvo *f.* **15A**
power fuerza *f.* **16A**
practical práctico/a *adj.* **3B**
practice practicar *v.* **0: medical practice** consultorio *m.* **10A**
prediction predicción *f.* **17A**
premiere estrenarse *v.* **14B**
prepare preparar *v.* **7A**
presence presencia *f.* **8B**
present regalo *m.* **3B:** presentar *v.* **0: to give oneself a present** regalarse *v.* **6B**
preservation conservación *f.* **15A**
preservative conservante *m.* **15A**
preserve preservar *v.* **15A**
president presidente/a *m./f.* **16A**
press prensa *f.* **9B: financial press** prensa económica *f.* **3A: gossip press** prensa rosa *f.* **9B: press conference** rueda de prensa *f.* **12B: press office** oficina de prensa *f.* **16A: press release** nota de prensa *f.* **10B**
pressure presión *f.* **4B**
prestigious prestigioso/a *adj.* **10A**
pretext pretexto *m.* **16A**
pretty bonito/a *adj.* **2A:** lindo/a *adj.* **11B**
prevail dominar *v.* **17A**
prevent impedir *v.* **12B**
prevention prevención *f.* **10A**
previous anterior *adj.* **14B**
price precio *m.* **4A: fixed-price menu** menú del día *m.* **2B**

prick pinchazo *m.* **17A**
print imprimir *v.* **7B**
printer impresora *f.* **7B**
prisoner preso/a *m./f.* **16A**
privacy privacidad *f.* **17A**
private privado/a *adj.* **4B: private home** casa particular *f.* **13A: private lesson** clase particular *f.* **17B: private school** escuela privada *f.* **15B**
privatized privatizado/a *adj.* **13A**
prize premio *m.* **5A: first prize** gordo *m.* **9B: Nobel Prize** Premio Nobel *m.* **10B**
probability probabilidad *f.* **15A**
probable probable *adj.* **17A**
probably probablemente *adv.* **4A**
problem problema *m.* **2A: No problem!** ¡No hay problema! *exp.* **7B: problem page** consultorio *m.* **10A**
process proceso *m.* **: in the process** de paso *loc. adv.* **14B**
procession procesión *f.* **16B**
produce: produce market agromercado *m.* **4A: to mass produce** fabricar en serie *v.* **13B**
producer productor(a) *m./f.* **3B**
product producto *m.* **3B: organic product** producto ecológico *m.* **15A: food product** producto de alimentación *m.* **15A: gross domestic product (GDP)** producto interior bruto (PIB) *m.* **11A, 14A**
production elaboración *f.* **15A**
productivity productividad *f.* **6A**
profession profesión *f.* **1B**
professional profesional *adj.* **2B:** profesional *m.* *y f.* **3A: professional experience** experiencia profesional *f.* **11B: professional training** formación profesional *f.* **14A**
professionalism profesionalidad *f.* **2B**
profile perfil *m.* **14A**
program programa *m.* **9A: exchange program** programa de intercambio *m.* **14A: radio program** programa de radio *m.* **3A**
project proyecto *m.* **4B**
projection: international projection proyección internacional *f.* **16A**
promotion promoción *f.* **9B**
promotional: promotional campaign campaña de promoción *f.* **16B**
pronounce pronunciar *v.* **0**
property propiedad *f.* **6A**
propose proponer *v.* **13A**
prospect perspectiva *f.* **13B**
protagonist protagonista *m.* *y f.* **0**
protect proteger *v.* **3B**
protein proteína *f.* **15A**
protest protesta *f.* **11A**
proud orgulloso/a *adj.* **2A**
prove demostrar *v.* **17A**
provide aportar *v.* **15A**
province provincia *f.* **7B**
proximity cercanía *f.* **16B**
psychologist psicólogo/a *m./f.* **1B**
psychology psicología *f.* **6A**
public público/a *adj.* **15B: public school** escuela pública *f.* **15B**
publicist publicista *m.* *y f.* **14B**
Puerto Rican boricua *adj.* **11A:** puertorriqueño/a *m./f.* **1A**
Puerto Rico Puerto Rico *m.* **0**
pump bomba *f.* **17A**
punctual puntual *adj.* **13B**
punctuality puntualidad *f.* **11A**
puppy cachorro/a *m./f.* **12B**
pupusa (Salvadoran filled tortilla) pupusa *f.* **8B**
pure puro/a *adj.* **7B**
purity pureza *f.* **18B**
purple morado/a *adj.* **16B**
purpose finalidad *f.* **14B**
purser jefe/a de cabina *m./f.* **13A**
put meter *v.* **8A:** poner *v.* **4A: put away** guardar *v.* **8A: put in order** ordenar *v.* **0: put off** posponer *v.* **18A: put out** apagar *v.* **7A: to put makeup on** maquillarse *v.* **7A**
pyramid pirámide *f.* **2A**

Q

qualify habilitar *v.* **13B**
quality calidad *f.* **2A: quality of life** calidad de vida *f.* **2A**
quantity cantidad *f.* **4A**
Quechua quechua *m.* **1B**
question pregunta *f.* **0:** consulta *f.* **6B: to question** plantearse preguntas *v.* **14B**
questionnaire cuestionario *m.* **6A**
quick rápido/a *adj.* **17A**
quiet tranquilo/a *adj.* **2A**
quit abandonar *v.* **10B:** dejar *v.* **5A, 7B: to quit smoking** dejar de fumar *v.* **12B**
quite: quite a bit/lot bastante *adv.* **5B**
quoted citado/a *adj.* **17A**

R

racket raqueta *f.* **18A**
radio radio *f.* **4B: radio network** cadena de radio *f.* **14B: radio program** programa de radio *m.* **3A: radio station** emisora *f.* **14B: to listen to the radio** escuchar la radio *v.* **2A**
rafting rafting *m.* **18A**
rain lluvia *f.* **6A:** llover *v.* **10A**
raincoat impermeable *m.* **10A**
ranch estancia *f.* **3A**
range gama *f.* **16B**
ranger: forest ranger guarda forestal *m.* *y f.* **14A**
raspberry frambuesa *f.* **15A**
rated: to be the highest rated ser líder de audiencia *v.* **14B**
rational racional *adj.* **16A**
raw: raw material materia prima *f.* **15A**
reach cumplir *v.* **13A**
read leer *v.* **0**
reading lectura *f.* **1:** texto *m.* **0**
real verdadero/a *adj.* **12B: real-estate agency** inmobiliaria *f.* **4B**
realistic realista *adj.* **12A**
Really? ¿De verdad? *exp.* **9B**
reason razón *f.* **:** porqué *m.* **17B**
rebel rebelde *adj.* **15B**
receive recibir *v.* **2B**
reception recepción *f.* **:** banquete *m.* **5A: reception room** salón de fiestas *m.* **18B**
recipe receta (de cocina) *f.* **8A: recipe collection** recetario *m.* **15A**
recommend recomendar *v.* **13A**
recommendation recomendación *f.* **6A**
recommended recomendado/a *adj.* **4A**
reconcile conciliar *v.* **6A**
record: record label sello discográfico *m.* **17B: vinyl record** disco de vinilo *m.* **13B**
recycle reciclar *v.* **11B**
recyclable container envase reciclable *m.* **15A**
recycled reciclado/a *adj.* **8A**
recycling reciclaje *m.* **15A**
red rojo/a *adj.* **3B: red-haired** pelirrojo/a *adj.* **12A**
reduce reducir *v.* **16A**
refrigerator frigorífico *m.* **7B:** refrigerador *m.* **8A**
regarding con respecto a *loc. prep.* **16A**
region zona *f.* **5A**
rehearsal ensayo *m.* **7A**
reject rechazar *v.* **16A**
relate relacionar *v.* **0**
relation: International Relations Relaciones Internacionales *f.* **11B**
relationship relación *f.* **5B**
relative familiar *m.* **5B**
relaxation relajación *f.* **6A**
relaxed relajado/a *adj.* **3A**
relaxing relajante *adj.* **6A**
release: press release nota de prensa *f.* **10B:** (music) editar *v.* **7A, 17B**
reliable fiable *adj.* **17A:** serio/a *adj.* **13B**
relief (Geog.) relieve *m.* **18B**
religion religión *f.* **8A**
religious religioso/a *adj.* **8A**
relinquish renunciar a *v.* **16A**
relive revivir *v.* **14B**
remark observación *f.* **13A**
remedy remedio *m.* **10A**
remember acordarse de *v.* **18B:** recordar *v.* **5A**
remove retirar *v.* **13A**
renewable renovable *adj.* **17A**
rent alquiler *m.* **4B**
rental de alquiler *adj.* **11B:** alquiler *m.* **4B**
repair arreglar *v.* **7B: repair shop** taller (mecánico) *m.* **7B**
repeat repetir *v.* **0**
repellent repelente *m.* **10A**
report reportaje *m.* **14B**
reporter periodista *m.* *y f.* **10B:** reportero/a *m./f.* **7B**
represent representar *v.* **10B:** simbolizar *v.* **18B**
representative representante *m.* *y f.* **10B**
request petición *f.* **12B:** pedido *m.* **7B:** solicitar *v.* **4A**
require exigir *v.* **13A: required** excluyente *adj.* **13B: to require sacrifices** exigir sacrificios *v.* **13A**
requirement requisito *m.* **13B: to meet the requirements** reunir los requisitos *v.* **13B**
requited: requited love amor correspondido *m.* **12A**
rescue rescatar *v.* **18B:** salvar *v.* **9B**

research investigación *f.* **8B:** investigar *v.* **8B: market research** investigación de mercado *f.* **15A**
researcher investigador(a) *m./f.* **17A**
resemblance parecido *m.* **12A**
reservation reserva *f.* **6B: to make a reservation** reservar *v.* **6B**
resolution: conflict resolution resolución de conflictos *f.* **13B**
resource recurso *m.* **12B: economic resource** recurso económico *m.* **14A: Human Resources (HR)** Recursos Humanos (RR.HH.) *m.* **13B: natural resource** recurso natural *m.* **14A**
respect respeto *m.* **14A:** respetar *v.* **8A**
respectful respetuoso/a *adj.* **12A**
responsibility responsabilidad *f.* **9A**
responsible responsable *adj.* **3B**
rest descanso *m.* **3A:** descansar *v.* **5B: the rest of** el resto de *m.* **12B**
restate reformular *v.* **8B**
restaurant restaurante *m.* **0**
restore restaurar *v.* **11A**
result resultado *m.* **12B: to give good results** redundar en *v.* **17A**
résumé currículum vítae *m.* **11B**
retire jubilarse *v.*
retired jubilado/a *adj.* **5B**
retirement jubilación *f.* **18B**
return devolución *f.* **9A:** devolver *v.* **16B:** regresar *v.* **8B:** volver *v.* **8B: in return** a cambio *loc. adv.* **12B**
reunion reencuentro *m.* **6B**
review reseña *f.* **9A:** revisar *v.* **0**
revolt revuelta *f.* **14A**
revolution revolución *f.* **13B**
reward recompensa *f.* **8B**
rewarding gratificante *adj.* **11A**
rhythm ritmo *m.* **17B**
rice arroz *m.* **2B: rice with vegetables** arroz con verduras *m.* **2B**
rich rico/a *adj.* **7A**
richness riqueza *f.* **11B**
ride montar *v.* **9A: horseback ride** paseo a caballo *m.* **6B: horseback riding** cabalgata *f.* **18A**
ridiculous ridículo/a *adj.* **15B**
rig: oil rig plataforma petrolera *f.* **14A**
right correcto/a *adj.* **:** derecho *m.* **3B: human rights** derechos humanos *m.* **16A: to be right** tener razón *v.* **10B: to the right** a la derecha *loc. adv.* **9B: to the right of** a la derecha de *loc. adv.* **3B**
right? ¿verdad? *exp.* **4A**
rise aumentar *v.* **5A**
risk riesgo *m.* **7A**
ritual rito *m.* **6A:** ritual *m.* **14A**
river río *m.* **3A: Amazon River** Amazonas *m.* **5A**
robe bata *f.* **5A**
role papel *m.* **5B**
role-play escenificar *v.* **0:** representar *v.* **0**
roll the die tiren el dado *exp.* **10A**
romantic romántico/a *adj.* **2A**
romanticism romanticismo *m.* **12A**
room habitación *f.* **4B:** sitio *m.* **9B: chat room** chat *m.* **3A: dining room** comedor *m.* **4B: double room** habitación doble *f.* **6B: living room** salón *m.* **4B: living room-dining room** salón-comedor *m.* **4B: reception room** salón de fiestas *m.* **18B: single room** habitación individual *f.* **6B**
rose rosa *f.* **18B**
round redondo/a *adj.* **: round-trip** ida y vuelta *exp.* **6B**
roundtable tertulia *f.* **9A**
route ruta *f.* **6B:** trayecto *m.* **13A**
routine rutina *f.* **7A: daily routine** rutina diaria *f.* **3A**
row: row boat bote de remos *m.* **18A**
royal: the royal family la Familia Real *f.* **4B**
rubber band goma elástica *f.* **8A**
ruins ruinas *f.* **2A**
rule norma *f.* **15B**
ruler gobernante *m./f.* **12B**
run correr *v.* **18A:** dirigir *v.* **6A: to run a marathon** correr un maratón *v.* **18A: to run in the same circles** relacionarse *v.* **10B: to run a business** llevar un negocio *v.* **9B**
runner corredor(a) *m./f.* **18A**
running: running shoes zapatillas (de deporte) *f.* **3B**
rural rural *adj.* **11A: rural neighborhood** vereda *f.* **9A**

S

sack bolsa *f.* **4A**
sacrifice el sacrificio *m.* **13A: to require sacrifices** exigir sacrificios *v.* **13A**
sad apenado/a *adj.* **17B:** triste *adj.* **12A: to be sad** ponerse triste *v.* **18B: to make sad** entristecer *v.* **17B**
sadness tristeza *f.* **10B**
safe seguro/a *adj.* **: safe for** apto/a para *adj.* **15A**
safety seguridad *f.* **13A**
saint santo/a *m./f.* **: patron saint** patrono/a *m./f.* **16B**
sake: to talk for the sake of it hablar por hablar *exp.* **14B**
salad ensalada *f.* **2B: house salad** ensalada de la casa *f.* **2B**
salary sueldo *m.* **14B**
sale venta *f.* **4B: for sale** a la venta *loc. adv.* **4B: sales executive** ejecutivo/a de ventas *m./f.* **13B**
salon: hair salon peluquería *f.* **8B**
salsa salsa *f.* **1A**
salt sal *f.* **8A: lacking salt** soso/a *adj.* **2B**
salty salado/a *adj.* **2B**
Salvadoran salvadoreño/a *adj.* **8B**
same mismo/a *adj.* **7A: at the same time** al mismo tiempo *loc. adv.* **7A**
San Juan: from San Juan sanjuanero/a *m./f.* **11A**
sandwich sándwich *m.* **2B**
satisfaction satisfacción *f.* **11A: personal satisfaction** satisfacción personal *f.* **13B**
Saturday sábado *m.* **3A**
sauce salsa *f.* **2B: sauce similar to Thousand Island dressing** salsa golf *f.* **17A: tomato sauce** tomate frito *m.* **15A**
sausage salchicha *f.* **4A: chorizo sausage** chorizo *m.* **2B**
save ahorrar *v.* **12B:** guardar *v.* **7B:** salvar *v.* **9B: to save (songs/photos)** guardar (canciones/fotos) *v.* **13B**
savings ahorros *m. pl.* **8B**
savor saborear *v.* **16B**
say decir *v.* **7A: How do you say...?** ¿Cómo se dice...? *exp.* **0: You don't say!** ¡No me digas! *exp.* **9B**
scale escala *f.* **15B**
scarf pañuelo *m.* **3B**
scenery paisaje *m.* **6B: change of scenery** cambio de aires *m.* **11A**
scent aroma *m.* **16B**
schedule calendario *m.* **3A:** horario *m.* **3A: schedule flexibility** flexibilidad horaria *f.* **6A: work schedule** horario de trabajo *m.* **3A**
scholarship beca (escolar) *f.* **8B, 12B: ERASMUS scholarship** beca ERASMUS *f.* **14A**
school escuela *f.* **3B:** colegio *m.* **3A: bilingual school** escuela bilingüe *f.* **15B: elementary school** escuela primaria *f.* **9A: high school** secundaria *f.*, instituto *m.* **15B high school studies** bachillerato *m.* **15B: private school** escuela privada *f.* **15B: public school** escuela pública *f.* **15B: school subject** asignatura *f.* **15B: to take the kids to school** llevar a los niños al colegio *v.* **3A**
science ciencia *f.* **6A: computer science** informática *f.* **1B: political science** ciencias políticas *f.* **1B**
scientific científico/a *adj.* **17A: scientific field** campo científico *m.* **17A: scientific method** método científico *m.* **17A**
score puntuación *f.* **11A**
Scottish escocés/escocesa *adj.* **7B**
screen pantalla *f.* **13A**
screening: baggage screening control de equipaje *m.* **13A**
screw: screw top tapa de rosca *f.* **8A**
scuba: scuba diving submarinismo *m.* **11B**
sculptor escultor(a) *m./f.* **16A**
sea mar *m.* **4B: Caribbean Sea** mar Caribe *m.* **4B**
sea bream (type of fish) dorada *f.* **2B**
season estación (del año) *f.* **10A: peak season** temporada alta *f.* **4B**
seat plaza *f.* **13A:** asiento *m.* **13A: seat back** respaldo del asiento *m.* **13A: seat change** cambio de asiento *m.* **13A**
seatbelt cinturón de seguridad *m.* **13A**
secretary secretario/a *m./f.* **1B:** ministro/a *m./f.* **16A**
section sección *f.* **8B**
sector sector *m.* **8B: energy sector** sector energético *m.* **14A**
security seguridad *f.* **17A: night security guard** vigilante nocturno/a *m./f.* **3A**
sedentary: sedentary lifestyle sedentarismo *m.* **16B**
see ver *v.* **3B: Can I see them?** ¿Los puedo ver? *exp.* **3B: I'm sorry to see you like this.** Siento verte así. *exp.* **13B: let's see...** a ver... *exp.* **6A: See you later.** Hasta la vista. *exp.* **0: See you tomorrow.** Hasta mañana *exp.* **0: See you!** ¡Nos vemos! *exp.* **0: to see a patient** atender *v.* **10A**

seem parecer *v.* **5B**
select seleccionar *v.* **0**
self: self-help autoayuda *f.* **6A: self-sufficient** autosuficiente *adj.* **7B: to be self-sufficient** valerse *v.* **5B: to be self-confident** estar seguro/a de sí mismo/a *v.* **18A**
sell vender *v.* **8B**
semi-: semi-sleeper semi-cama *adj.* **13A**
send enviar *v.* **7B:** mandar *v.* **7B**
sensitive sensible *adj.* **10A**
sensitization sensibilización *f.* **16A**
sensitize sensibilizar *v.* **16A**
sentence oración *f.* **0**
separate separarse *v.* **12A**
separated separado/a *adj.* **12A**
September septiembre *m.* **5A**
series serie *f* **: television series** serie de televisión *f.* **14B: to broadcast the television series** pasar/emitir la serie de televisión *v.* **14B**
serious serio/a *adj.* **12A, 17A**
Serrano: Serrano ham jamón serrano *m.* **2B**
service servicio *m.* **5B: at your service** a tu/su servicio *loc. adv.* **7B: domestic service** servicio doméstico *m.* **8B: service industry** industria de servicios *f.* **14A: Social Services** Servicios Sociales *m. pl.* **5B: telephone service** telefonía *f.* **9B**
serving porción *f.* **15A**
set: television set televisor *m.* **4B: to set aside** reservar *v.* **6A: set free** liberar *v.* **16A: set in motion** poner en marcha *exp.* **16A**
setback adversidad *f.* **18A**
seven siete *adj.* **1A**
seventeen diecisiete *adj.* **1B**
seventy setenta *adj.* **1B**
sevillana (popular dance originated in Seville) sevillanas *f.* **17B**
shape: to be in (good) shape estar en forma *v.* **7A**
share compartir *v.* **5A**
she ella *pron.* **1A**
shed derramarse *v.* **18B**
sheet: ice sheet manto de hielo *m.* **11B: sheet of paper** hoja (de papel) *f.* **8A**
shirt camisa *f.* **3B**
shock: culture shock choque cultural *m.* **14B**
shoe zapato *m.* **3B: running shoes** zapatillas (de deporte) *f. pl.* **3B: shoe store** zapatería *f.* **3B: shoes** calzado *m.* **10A**
shoot (film) rodar *v.* **9B**
shop tienda *f.* **3B: fruit shop** frutería *f.* **9B: gift shop** tienda de regalos *f.* **3B: perfume/cosmetics shop** perfumería *f.* **3B: repair shop** taller (mecánico) *m.* **7B: shop window** escaparate *m.* **3B: tabaconist shop** estanco *m.* **9B**
shopping: shopping list lista de compras *f.* **4A: shopping mall** centro comercial *m.* **2A: to go grocery shopping** hacer las compras *v.* **3A**
shore orilla *f.* **6B**
short bajo/a *adj.* **12A:** corto/a *adj.* **12A: (in the) short term** a corto plazo *loc. adv.* **17A: in short** en resumen *exp.* **18B: short story** cuento *m.* **9B**
show espectáculo *m.* **4A:** enseñar *v.* **5B:** mostrar *v.* **0: news and talk show** magacín *m.* **9A: talk show** tertulia *f.* **9A: to show affection** mostrar afecto *v.* **18B**
shower ducha *f.* **7A:** ducharse *v.* **7A**
shrimp gamba *f.* **2B:** camarón *m.* **16B**
shy tímido/a *adj.* **12A**
siblings hermanos *m. pl.* **5B**
sick enfermo/a *adj.* **5B**
side lado *m.* **13B: bad side** lado malo *m.* **13B**
sign firmar *v.* **16A: sign up for** apuntarse a *v.* **13A**
signature firma *f.* **16A**
signing firma *f.* **16A**
silence silencio *m.* **6A**
silent: to be silent estar callado/a *v.* **9A**
silver plata *f.* **12B: silver wedding anniversary** bodas de plata *f.* **18B**
since desde que *conj.* **8B:** desde *prep.* **2A: since childhood** desde niño(s)/a(s) *loc. adv.* **8B: since childhood** desde pequeño/a *loc. adv.* **5B: since then** desde entonces *loc. adv.* **7A**
Sincerely, Atentamente, *exp.* **6B**
sing cantar *v.* **17B**
singer cantante *m. y f.* **5A: singer-songwriter** cantautor(a) *m./f.* **7A**
single soltero/a *adj.* **5B: single room** habitación individual *f.* **6B**
sir señor *m.* **6B: Dear sirs,** Estimados señores: *exp.* **6B**
sister hermana *f.* **5A**
six seis *adj.* **1A**
sixteen dieciséis *adj.* **1B**
sixty sesenta *adj.* **1B: in the mid sixties** a mediados de los 60 *loc. adv.* **14B: the sixties** los años 60 *m.* **8B**
size talla *f.* **3B: What size?** ¿De qué talla? *exp.* **3B**
ski esquiar *v.*
skiing esquí *m.* **1A**
skim: skim milk leche descremada *f.* **15A**
skin piel *f.* **10A**
skirt falda *f.* **3B**
sleeper: (semi-)sleeper (semi-)cama *adj.* **13A**
slogan eslogan *m.* **11A**
slope pendiente *f.* **18A**
slow lento/a *adj.* **7B**
slower: Slower, please. Más despacio, por favor. *exp.* **0**
slowly despacio *adv.* **10A**
small chico/a *adj.* **11B:** pequeño/a *adj.* **4B**
smart brillante *adj.* **14B:** listo/a *adj.*
smartphone teléfono inteligente *m.* **13B**
smile sonrisa *f.* **10A:** sonreír *v.* **13A**
smoke fumar *v.* **12B: to quit smoking** dejar de fumar *v.* **12B**
snack: afternoon snack merienda *f.* **16B**
snail caracol *m.* **2B**
sneakers zapatillas (de deporte) *f.* **3B**
snow nieve *f.* **10A:** nevar *v.* **10A**
so entonces *adv.* **7A:** así (es) que *conj.* **17A: I think so/not.** Creo que sí/no. *exp.* **7B**
soap jabón *m.* **8A: soap opera** telenovela *f.* **5A**
soccer fútbol *m.* **1A: soccer player** futbolista *m./f.*
social social *adj.* **6A: social demonstration** movilización social *f.* **16A: social inclusion** inclusión social *f.* **16A: social justice** justicia social *f.* **16A: social network** red social *f.* **13B: social plan** el plan social *m.* **16A: social policy** política social *f.* **16A: Social Services** Servicios Sociales *m.* **5B: Social Studies** Ciencias sociales *f.* **15B**
society sociedad *f.* **9A**
soda gaseosa *f.* **13A:** refresco *m.* **4A**
sofa sofá *m.* **4B**
soft blando/a *adj.* **9A: soft drink** refresco *m.* **4A**
solve solucionar *v.* **10A**
some algún, alguno/a *adj.* **9A:** algunos/as *pron.* **5A**
somebody alguien *pron.* **5B**
someone alguien *pron.* **5B: to take care of someone** cuidar (a/de) alguien *v.* **7A**
something algo *pron.* **2B: to be doing something** estar haciendo algo *v.* **7A: to do something at home** hacer algo en casa *v.* **3A: to do something (for a living)** dedicarse a (hacer) algo *v.* **7A**
sometimes a veces *loc. adv.* **2B**
son hijo *m.* **5A**
song canción *f.* **7A**
sonnet soneto *m.* **10B**
soon pronto *adv.* **0: See you soon.** Hasta pronto *exp.* **0**
sorry: I'm sorry to hear that. Siento oír eso. *exp.* **13B: I'm sorry to see you like this.** Siento verte así. *exp.* **13B: I'm sorry.** Lo siento. *exp.* **3B**
so-so regular *adv.* **8A**
soufflé suflé *m.* **15A**
soul alma *f.* **6A**
sound sonido *m.* **: sound track** banda sonora *f.* **17B**
soup sopa *f.* **2B: fish soup** sopa de pescado *f.* **2B**
south sur *m.* **2A: South American** sudamericano/a *adj.* **18A**
souvenir recuerdo *m.* **5B:** souvenir *m.* **4A**
space espacio *m.* **13B:** sitio *m.* **9B: to take up space** ocupar espacio *v.* **13B**
Spain España *f.* **0**
Spanish español(a) *adj.* **1B:** español *m.* **1B: Spanish-speaking** hispanohablante *adj.* **14A: to learn Spanish** aprender español *v.* **3A: Spanish National Organization for the Blind** ONCE *f.* **12B: Spanish potato omelet** tortilla española *f.* **2B**
speak hablar *v.* **1B: is/are spoken** se habla(n) *v.* **1B: What languages do you speak?** ¿Qué lenguas hablas? *exp.* **1B**
speaker altavoz *m.* **13A**
special especial *adj.* **2B: special edition** edición especial *f.* **3B**
specialist especialista *m. y f.* **10A**
specializing: specializing in especializado/a en *adj.* **2B**
specially especialmente *adv.* **7A**
specifically concretamente *adv.* **7B**
spectacular espectacular *adj.* **11B**
speech discurso *m.* **16A**
speed velocidad *f.* **13B**

spell: How do you spell...? ¿Cómo se escribe? *exp.* **0, 1A**
spend ocupar *v.* **5B:** (money) gastar *v.* **: to spend one's vacation** pasar las vacaciones *v.* **4B: to spend the night** pasar la noche *v.* **6B**
spicy picante *adj.* **2B**
spider araña *f.* **16B: spider monkey** mono/a araña *m./f.* **16B**
spirit espíritu *m.* **6A**
spiritual espiritual *adj.* **14A**
split up separarse *v.* **12A**
spokesperson portavoz *m. y f.* **12B**
sport deporte *m.* **3A: sport challenge** reto deportivo *m.* **18A: sports center** polideportivo *m.* **2A**
sporting deportivo/a *adj.* **6A**
sportsman/woman deportista *m. y f.* **18A**
spot rincón *m.* **11A, 13A**
spring primavera *f.* **10A**
sprinkle espolvorear *v.* **15A**
square plaza *f.* **1B: square meters** metros cuadrados (m2) *m.* **4B**
squid calamares *m. pl.* **2B**
stability estabilidad *f.* **13B**
stable estable *adj.* **12B**
staff personal *m.* **11A**
stage etapa *f.* **9A:** fase *f.* **17A**
stand (in a market) puesto *m.* **4A**
stand: not to be able to stand no soportar *v.* **15B**
stand out dominar *v.* **17A**
standard estándar *adj.* **7B**
stanza estrofa *f.* **17B**
star estrella *f.* **5A, 11A: four-star hotel** hotel de cuatro estrellas *m.* **11A**
start comenzar *v.* **8B:** empezar *v.* **5A**
starting a partir de *conj.* **12B**
state estado *m.* **5B:** declarar *v.* **16A: state of mind** estado anímico *m.* **10A: state of mind** estado de ánimo *m.* **12A: state-run hotel in Spanish historic building** el parador nacional *m.* **6B**
station estación *f.* **4A: radio station** emisora *f.* **14B**
stationery: stationery store papelería *f.* **9B**
status: marital status estado civil *m.* **5B**
stay estancia *f.* **11A:** alojarse *v.* **13A:** quedarse *v.* **8B: Have a nice stay!** ¡Feliz estancia! *exp.* **11A**
steel acero *m.* **: steel cable** cable de acero *m.* **18A**
stenography taquigrafía *f.* **13B**
step medida *f.* **16A:** paso de baile *m.* **17B**
still aún, todavía *adv.* **15B**
stimulate estimular *v.* **16A**
stimulating estimulante *adj.* **6A**
stir: to stir up interest despertar la inquietud *v.* **9A**
stock stock exchange la bolsa (de comercio) *f.* **3A: to take stock of** hacer balance de *v.* **12B**
stomach estómago *m.* **10A**
stop dejar de *v.* **10B:** parar *v.* **3A:** impedir *v.* **12B: to stop over** hacer escala *v.* **13A**
storage: to have (storage) capacity tener capacidad *v.* **13B**
store tienda *f.* **2A:** negocio *m.* **7B:** establecimiento *m.* **9B: clothing store** tienda de ropa *f.* **3B: grocery store** tienda de alimentación *f.* **4A: music store** tienda de discos *f.* **3B: shoe store** zapatería *f.* **3B: stationery store** papelería *f.* **9B: toy store** juguetería *f.* **9B: store where pupusas are sold** pupusería *f.* **8B**
store (songs/photos) guardar (canciones/fotos) *v.* **13B**
storekeeper comerciante *m./f.* **14A**
storm tormenta *f.* **10B**
story historia *f.* **5A:** piso *m.* **8A: photo story** fotonovela *f.* **12A: short story** cuento *m.* **9B**
straight recto/a *adj.* **9B:** (hair) liso/a *adj.* **12A**
strategy estrategia *f.* **0**
strawberry fresa *f.* **15A**
street calle *f.* **2A**
strength fuerza *f.* **16A**
strengthen fortalecer *v.* **18A**
stress estrés *m.* **3A**
stressful estresante *adj.* **1B**
strip: comic strip historieta *f.* **14B**
strong resistente *adj.* **17A:** fuerte *adj.*
student estudiante *m. y f.* **:** alumno/a *m./f.* **0**
studies estudios *m. pl.* **5A: high school studies** bachillerato *m.* **14A: Social Studies** Ciencias sociales *f.* **15B**
studio: studio apartment estudio *m.* **4B**
study cursar *v.* **14A:** estudiar *v.* **1B: to study for a degree** estudiar una carrera *v.* **15B**
stuffed relleno/a *adj.* **16B**
style estilo *m.* **4B**
subject asunto *m.* **: school subject** asignatura *f.* **15B**
Sub-Saharan: Sub-Saharan Africa el África (*f.*) subsahariana *f.* **14A**
substitute sustituir *v.* **14A**
subtle sutil *adj.* **18B**
suburbs periferia *f.* **2A:** afueras *f. pl.*
subway metro *m.* **0:** subte(rráneo) *m.* **4A**
success éxito *m.* **5A**
successful exitoso/a *adj.* **5A**
suddenly de repente *loc. adv.* **9B**
suffer sufrir *v.* **12B**
sugar azúcar *m.* **0**
suggest proponer *v.* **13A**
suit traje *m.* **3B**
suitable adecuado *adj.* **5B**
suitcase maleta *f.* **8B**
summarize resumir *v.* **0**
summary reseña *f.* **9A**
summer verano *m.* **2A: summer internship** pasantía de verano *f.* **13B**
sun sol *m.* **4B**
sunbathe tomar el sol *v.* **10A**
Sunday domingo *m.* **3A: Sunday supplement** suplemento dominical *m.* **9B**
sunny: to be sunny hacer sol *v.* **10A**
sunscreen crema solar protectora *f.* **10A**
supervisor supervisor(a) *m./f.* **13A**
supper cena *f.* **2B: to eat supper** cenar *v.* **2B**
supplement suplemento *m.* **9B**
support adhesión *f.* **16A:** apoyar *v.* **13A: (someone)** solidarizarse (con) *v.* **14B**
supporter: to be a supporter of ser hincha de *v.* **17B**
sure seguro/a *adj.* **9A: I'm sure (that)...** Seguro que... *exp.* **9A**
surf: to surf the Internet navegar por Internet *v.* **6A**
surfer surfista *m. y f.* **16B**
surmount remontar *v.* **18A**
surprise sorpresa *f.* **17B:** extrañeza *f.* **15B:** chocar *v.* **14B:** extrañar *v.* **15B:** sorprender *v.* **15B**
surprising sorprendente *adj.* **18A**
surrounded rodeado/a *adj.* **6B**
surroundings entorno *m.* **11A**
survey encuesta *f.* **18B**
survive sobrevivir *v.* **13B**
sustainable sostenible *adj.* **17A**
sweater suéter *m.* **3B**
sweet dulce *adj.* **2B**
sweeten endulzar *v.* **15A**
sweethearts novios *m. pl.* **6B**
swim bañarse *v.* **10A:** nadar *v.* **5A**
swimmer nadador(a) *m./f.* **18A**
swimming natación *f.* **10A: swimming pool** piscina *f.* **3A**
sword espada *f.* **18A**
symbol emblema *m.* **18A:** símbolo *m.* **8A**
symptom síntoma *m.* **10A**
synchronized: synchronized swimmer nadador(a) de sincronizada *m./f.* **18A: synchronized swimming** nado sincronizado *m.* **18A**
synthesize sintetizar *v.* **13B**
syringe jeringa *f.* **17A**
syrup jarabe *m.* **15A**
system sistema *m.* **17A: immune system** sistema inmunológico *m.* **17A**

T

table mesa *f.* **3B:** tabla *f.* **0: table of contents** sumario *m.* **1B**
taco taco *m.* **2B**
tai chi taichí *m.* **8A**
take asumir *v.* **12B:** llevar *v.* **5B:** tomar *v.* **9B: to take a bath** darse un baño *v.* **10A: to take a nap** dormir la siesta *v.* **6A: to take a walk** dar un paseo *v.* **6A: to take advantage** aprovechar *v.* **15A: to take away** quitar *v.* **16A: to take care of someone** cuidar (a/de) alguien *v.* **5B: to take care of the details** ocuparse de los detalles *v.* **18B: to take into account** tener en cuenta *v.* **16B: to take pictures** tomar fotos *v.* **6B: to take place** celebrar *v.* **18A: to take stock of** hacer balance de *v.* **12B: to take the ferry** tomar el ferry *v.* **3A: to take the kids to school** llevar a los niños al colegio *v.* **3A: to take up** ocupar *v.* **5B: to take up space** ocupar espacio *v.* **13B**
talent talento *m.* **11B**
talk hablar *v.* **2A: news and talk show** magacín *m.* **9A: not to talk** estar callado/a *v.* **9A: talk show** tertulia *f.* **9A: to talk for the sake of it** hablar por hablar *v.* **14B: to talk to people** hablar con la gente *v.* **2A**
tall alto/a *adj.* **8A**
tamer: lion tamer domador(a) de leones *m./f.* **14A**
tapa tapa *f.* **2B: to eat tapas** tapear *v.* **2B**
tapestry tapiz (*pl.* tapices) *m.* **3B**
task labor *f.* **12B**

taste gusto *m.* **15A:** sabor *m.* **15A:** probar *v.* **16B**
tasty rico/a *adj.* **2B:** sabroso/a *adj.* **15A**
tax impuesto *m.* **4B: ecotax** ecotasa *f.* **4B: tax included** IVA incluido *loc. adv.* **2B**
taxi taxi *m.* **0**
tea té *m.* **2B: tea room** tetería *f.* **8B**
teach enseñar *v.* **5B**
teacher maestro/a *m./f.* **6A:** profesor(a) *m./f.* **1B**
teaching enseñanza *f.* **7A**
team equipo *m.* **7A: as a team** en equipo *loc. adv.* **7A: working team** equipo de trabajo *m.* **13B**
technician técnico/a *m./f.* **1B: computer technician** técnico/a informático/a *m./f.* **1B**
technological tecnológico/a *adj.* **17A**
technology tecnología *f.* **8A**
teenager adolescente *m./f.* **9A**
telephone teléfono *m.* **3A: telephone call** llamada (de teléfono) *f.* **3A: telephone service** telefonía *f.* **9B**
television tele *f.* **3A:** televisión *f.* **3A: television series** serie de televisión *f.* **14B: television set** televisor *m.* **4B: television viewer** telespectador(a) *m./f.* **14B: to broadcast a television series** pasar/emitir la serie de televisión *v.* **14B**
tell contar *v.* **14B:** decir *v.* **7A:** informar *v.* **0: to tell each other** contarse *v.* **17B: to tell jokes** contar chistes *v.* **17B: to tell the truth** decir la verdad *v.* **17B: to tell you the truth ...,** la verdad *exp.* **2A**
temperature temperatura *f.* **10A: the temperature is 30°C** hace 30 °C de temperatura *v.* **10A**
temporarily temporalmente *adv.* **8B**
ten diez *adj.* **1A**
tendency tendencia *f.* **17A**
tennis tenis *m.* **1A: tennis player** tenista *m. y f.* **14A**
tense tenso/a *adj.* **10A**
tent carpa *f.* **9A:** tienda de campaña *f.* **18A**
tenth décimo/a *adj.* **12B**
term plazo *m.* **9A: (in the) long term** a largo plazo *loc. adv.* **9A: (in the) medium term** a medio plazo *loc. adv.* **17A: (in the) short term** a corto plazo *loc. adv.* **17A**
terminal terminal *f.* **13A**
terrible terrible *adj.* **15B**
territorial: territorial invasion invasión territorial *f.* **16A**
territory territorio *m.* **16A**
terrorism terrorismo *m.* **16A**
test prueba *f.* **0:** test *m.* **1A**
testimony testimonio *m.* **8B**
text texto *m.* **0**
textbook texto *m.* **0**
Thai tailandés *m.* **7A**
Thailand Tailandia *f.* **7A**
than: less than menos que *adj.* **3A: more than** más que *adj.* **3A: older than** mayor de *adj.* **9A**
thank: Nothing else, thanks. Nada más, gracias. *exp.* **2B: Thank you!** ¡Gracias! *exp.* **0: thank goodness** menos mal *exp.* **10A: thanks to...** gracias a... *loc. prep.* **5B**
that ese/a *adj.* **3A:** que *conj.* **:** eso *pron.* **13B: I'm sorry to hear that.** Siento oír eso. *exp.* **13B: that is** o sea *exp.* **8B: that one** ese/a *pron.* **3A**
the el/la/los/las *art.* **2A**
theater teatro *m.* **1A: movie theater** cine *m.* **3A**
them ellos/as *pron.* **1B:** los/las *pron.* **3B: Can I see them?** ¿Los puedo ver? *exp.* **3B**
then entonces *adv., conj.* **7A, 9B: since then** desde entonces *loc. adv.* **7A**
then... luego... *adv.* **0**
therapy terapia *f.* **3A**
there allá *adv.* **6B:** allí *adv.* **2A: How are you going there?** ¿Cómo vas? *exp.* **6B: there is good/bad weather** hace buen/mal tiempo *v.* **10A: there is/there are** hay *v.* **3B**
therefore por eso *conj.* **17A:** por lo tanto *conj.* **17A**
these estos/as *adj.* **3A: these (ones)** estos/as *pron.* **3A**
they ellos/as *pron.* **1B**
thing cosa *f.* **4A: the bad/good thing** lo malo/bueno *m.* **12B: the best (thing)** lo mejor *m.* **4B**
think pensar *v.* **4A: I think so/not.** Creo que sí/no. *exp.* **7B: to think of/about** pensar de *v.* **4A: to think of/remember** ocurrirse *v.* **18B: to think something is odd** parecer raro *v.* **15B: to think of/about** pensar en *v.* **0**
third tercero/a *adj.* **14A:** tercio *m.* **16B**
thirteen trece *adj.* **1B**
thirty treinta *adj.* **1B**
this este/a *adj.* **3A:** esto *pron.* **: this month** este mes *loc. adv.* **6A: this one** este/a *pron.* **3A: this week** esta semana *loc. adv.* **6A: this year** este año *loc. adv.* **6A**
those esos/as *adj.* **3A: those (ones)** esos/as *pron.* **3A: Those were the days!** ¡Qué tiempos aquellos! *exp.* **5B**
thousands miles *m. pl.* **6B**
thrashing paliza *f.* **18A**
thread hilo *m.* **14B**
three tres *adj.* **1A: three times a year** tres veces al año *loc. adv.* **3A**
throat garganta *f.* **10A**
through a través de *loc. prep.* **14B**
throw lanzar *v.* **18A**
Thursday jueves *m.* **3A**
ticket entrada *f.* **7B:** pasaje *m.* **6B:** billete *m.* **6B: lottery ticket** cupón *m.* **12B: lottery ticket booth** agencia de lotería *f.* **9B: lottery ticket seller** vendedor(a) de lotería *m./f.* **9B: plane ticket** pasaje de avión *m.* **6B: to book the tickets** reservar los billetes *v.* **13A: to buy lottery tickets** comprar (billetes de) lotería *v.* **9B**
tie corbata *f.* **3B**
time época *f.* **9A:** vez (*pl.* veces) *f.* **3A:** tiempo *m.* **3A: ahead of time** con antelación *loc. adv.* **11A: at the same time** al mismo tiempo *loc. adv.* **7A: At what time...?** ¿A qué hora...? *exp.* **3A: boarding time** hora de embarque *f.* **13A: departure time** hora de salida *f.* **13A: free time** tiempo libre *m.* **5B: from time to time** de vez en cuando *loc. adv.* **14A: in/on time** a tiempo *loc. adv.* **7B: three times a year** tres veces al año *loc. adv.* **3A: time for oneself** tiempo para uno/a mismo/a *m.* **3A: time of arrival** hora de llegada *f.* **13A: time of year** época *f.* **6B: time somebody has to be home** hora de llegar a casa *f.* **15B: to have a good time** pasarla bien *v.* **17B: to have a good time** pasarlo bien *v.* **17B: What time is it?** ¿Qué hora es? *exp.* **3A**
tiny pequeñísimo/a *adj.* **11B: tiny apartment** minipiso *m.* **11B**
tired cansado/a *adj.* **6A: to get tired of (something)** cansarse de (algo) *v.* **9B**
tiredness cansancio *m.* **14B**
tireless incansable *adj.* **14B**
title título *m.* **:** titular *v.* **0**
to a *prep.* **: from time to time** de vez en cuando *loc. adv.* **14A: from... until/to** desde/de... hasta/a *loc. prep.* **8B: next to** al lado de *loc. adv.* **3B: thanks to...** gracias a... *loc. prep.* **5B: to be sensitive to** ser sensible a *v.* **10A: to go to bed** acostarse *v.* **7A: to go to work** ir a trabajar *v.* **3A: to take the kids to school** llevar a los niños al colegio *v.* **3A: to the left of** a la izquierda de *loc. adv.* **3B: to the right of** a la derecha de *loc. adv.* **3B**
toast tostada *f.* **2B**
tobacconist: tabaconist shop estanco *m.* **9B**
today hoy *adv.* **6A:** en la actualidad *loc. adv.* **8B**
together juntos/as *adj.* **5A**
Toledo Toledo *f.* **1A**
tolerance tolerancia *f.* **14A**
tomato tomate *m.* **4A: tomato sauce** tomate frito *m.* **15A**
tomorrow mañana *adv.* **5B: See you tomorrow.** Hasta mañana *exp.* **0: the day after tomorrow** pasado mañana *loc. adv.* **11B**
tongue: mother tongue lengua materna *f.* **14A**
tongue-twister trabalenguas *m.* **6A**
too demasiado *adv.* **13A:** también *adv.* **1B**
top: on top of encima de *loc. prep.* **3B: screw top** tapa de rosca *f.* **8A**
topic tópico *m.* **16B**
toucan tucán *m.* **16B**
touch contacto *m.* **17B:** toque *m.* **15A: to be in touch** estar en contacto *v.* **12B**
tough duro/a *adj.* **7B:** resistente *adj.* **17A**
tour: package tour viaje organizado *m.* **13A: tour guide** el/la guía turístico/a *m. y f.* **1B: to do a canopy tour** practicar tirolesa *v.* **18A**
tourism turismo *m.* **14A**
tourist turístico/a *adj.* **16B:** turista *m. y f.* **1B: tourist destination** destino turístico *m.* **4B**
tournament torneo *m.* **10B**
towards hacia *prep.* **: towards the end of the 19th century** a finales del siglo XIX *loc. adv.* **8B**
town pueblo *m.* **1A: in the center of town** céntrico/a *adj.* **7B**
toy juguete *m.* **8B: toy store** juguetería *f.* **9B**

track: sound track banda sonora *f.* **17B: track and field** atletismo *m.* **18A**
track-and-field: track-and-field athlete atleta *m. y f.* **12B**
trade oficio *m.* **14A: arms trade** tráfico de armas *m.* **16A: fair trade** comercio justo *m.* **3B**
trading: (soccer) trading card el cromo (de fútbol) *m.* **9B**
tradition tradición *f.* **2B**
traditional tradicional *adj.* **4A**
traffic tráfico *m.* **2A**
train tren *m.* **6B:** educar *v.* **12B**
trainer (of dogs) educador(a) *m./f.* **12B**
training entrenamiento *m.* **18A: professional training** formación profesional *f.* **14A**
tranquility tranquilidad *f.* **2A**
transfer: bank transfer transferencia bancaria *f.* **7B**
transform transformar *v.* **0**
transformation transformación *f.* **14B**
transgenic: transgenic food alimento transgénico *m.* **15A**
transition: democratic transition transición democrática *f.* **14B**
translate traducir *v.* **7A**
transparent transparente *adj.* **9A**
transport transportar *v.* **7A:** trasladar *v.* **13A**
transportation: means of transportation medio de transporte *m.* **4A**
travel recorrer *v.* **5A:** viajar *v.* **3A: travel agency** agencia de viajes *f.* **4B**
traveler viajero/a *m./f.* **11A**
traveling: traveling library biblioteca ambulante *f.* **9A**
treasure tesoro *m.* **10A**
treatment tratamiento *m.* **12B**
treaty tratado *m.* **16A**
tree árbol *m.* **5B: coral tree** ceibo *m.* **18B: family tree** árbol genealógico *m.* **5B: mahogany tree** caoba *f.* **18B**
trend tendencia *f.* **17A**
trick truco *m.* **8A**
trip viaje *m.* **3B: business trip** viaje de negocios *m.* **3A: round-trip** ida y vuelta *exp.* **6B: to organize a trip** preparar un viaje *v.* **13A**
trolley carrito *m.* **13A**
trot trotar *v.* **9A**
troubadour trovador(a) *m./f.* **7A**
trouble disgusto *m.* **15B**
truck camión *m.* **7A: truck driver** camionero/a *m./f.* **7A**
true cierto/a *adj.* **:** verdadero/a *adj.* **0: to be true** ser verdad *v.* **10B: to make (his/her) dreams come true** cumplir (sus) sueños *v.* **15B: True or false?** ¿Verdadero o falso? *adj.* **0**
trumpet trompeta *f.* **7A**
trust: to trust in tener confianza en *v.* **5B**
truth verdad *f.* **17B: to tell the truth** decir la verdad *v.* **17B: to tell you the truth** ..., la verdad *exp.* **17B**
try intentar *v.* **: to try one's luck** probar suerte *v.* **5A: to try to** pretender *v.* **15B: to try to** procurar *v.* **14B**
T-shirt camiseta *f.* **3B**
tú: to address somebody as tú hablarse de tú *v.* **7B: use of tú** tuteo *m.* **7B: to use the tú form of address** tutearse *v.* **17B**
Tuesday martes *m.* **3A**
tulip tulipán *m.* **18B**
turn girar *v.* **9B: It's my turn.** Me toca a mí. *exp.* **4A: to turn 15 years old** cumplir 15 años *v.* **5A: to turn over** dar la vuelta *v.* **8A: Whose turn is it?** ¿A quién le toca? *exp.* **4A: to turn on** encender *v.* **4B**
TV tele; TV *f.* **9A: 14B: TV viewer** televidente *m.* **9A**
twelve doce *adj.* **1A**
twenty veinte *adj.* **1B**
twice: twice a month dos veces al mes *loc. adv.* **6A**
two dos *adj.* **1A: two last names** doble apellido *m.* **12A: two months ago** hace dos meses *loc. adv.* **5A**
type tipo *m.* **12A**
typical típico/a *adj.* **2A**
tyrant tirano/a *m./f.* **13B**

U

ugly feo/a *adj.* **3B**
umbrella paraguas *m.* **3B**
unbearable insoportable *adj.* **2A**
Unbelievable! ¡Increíble! *exp.* **9B**
uncle tío *m.* **5B**
uncomfortable incómodo/a *adj.* **11B: extremely uncomfortable** incomodísimo/a *adj.* **11B**
under debajo de *loc. prep.* **3B: to be under construction** estar en obras *v.* **11A: to be under someone's control** estar en manos de alguien *exp.* **17A**
underline subrayar *v.* **0**
underneath debajo *adv.* **3B**
underprivileged desfavorecido/a *adj.* **16A**
understand entender *v.* **13B:** comprender *v.* **13B: I don't understand.** No entiendo. *exp.* **0: I understand you perfectly.** Te entiendo perfectamente. *exp.* **13B**
understanding comprensivo/a *adj.* **13B**
unemployed desocupado/a *adj.* **11B**
unforgettable inolvidable *adj.* **5B**
uninterruptedly ininterrumpidamente *adv.* **18A**
union: European Union Unión Europea *f.* **10B**
unique único/a *adj.* **2A**
United Kingdom Reino Unido *m.* **8B**
United States (U.S.A.) Estados Unidos (EE. UU.) *m.* **0**
unity unidad *f.* **16A**
universal universal *adj.* **17A**
universe universo *m.* **9B**
university universidad *f.* **2A: university drop-outs** deserción universitaria *f.* **15B**
unkind desagradable *adj.* **13B**
unlimited ilimitado/a *adj.* **8A**
unrequited: unrequited love amor no correspondido *m.* **12A**
unstoppable imparable *adj.* **14A**
until hasta *prep.* **8B**
up arriba *adv.* **: to bring up to date** poner al día *v.* **7B: What's up?** ¿Qué pasa? *exp.* **0**
update actualizar *v.* **7B:** poner (a alguien) al día *v.* **17B**
upon: based upon sobre la base de *loc. prep.* **16A: to be agreed upon** a convenir *loc. adv.* **13B**
upright vertical *adj.* **13A**
upset dar pena *v.* **18B: to upset somebody** amargarle la vida a alguien *v.* **17A:** disgusto *m.* **15B**
uranium uranio *m.* **14A**
Uruguay Uruguay *m.* **0**
Uruguayan uruguayo/a *adj.* **7A**
us nosotros/as *pron.* **1B: let's see...** a ver... *exp.* **6A**
use usar *v.* **0:** utilizar *v.* **0: What is it used for?** ¿Para qué sirve? *exp.* **4B: use of tú** tuteo *m.* **7B**
useful útil *adj.* **9A**
useless inútil *adj.*
user: Internet user internauta *m. y f.* **6A**
usted: to address somebody as usted hablarse de usted *v.* **7B**
usually normalmente *adv.* **14A: to usually do something** soler *v.* **14A**
utensil utensilio *m.* **15A**

V

vacation vacaciones *f. pl.* **3A: to be on vacation** estar de vacaciones *v.* **7B: to spend one's vacation** pasar las vacaciones *v.* **4B**
vaccinate vacunar *v.* **10A**
vaccine vacuna *f.* **12B**
valid en regla *loc. adv.* **11A**
validate validar *v.* **14A**
valley valle *m.* **11B**
value valía *f.* **18A**
variety variedad *f.* **7A**
various diverso/a *adj.* **5B**
vast extenso/a *adj.* **16B**
veal ternera *f.* **2B: filet of veal** filete de ternera *m.* **2B**
vegetable hortaliza *f.* **7B**
vegetables verduras *f.* **2B**
vegetarian vegetariano/a *adj.* **15A: to become a vegetarian** hacerse vegetariano/a *v.* **7B**
vegetation vegetación *f.* **6B**
venerate venerar *v.* **16B**
Venezuela Venezuela *f.* **0**
Venezuelan venezolano/a *adj.*
version versión *f.* **9**
very muy *adv.* **2A: very friendly** amabilísimo/a *adj.* **13A: very high** altísimo *adj.* **11B: very well** rebién (*fam.*) *adv.* **17B: very well** muy bien *adv.* **1A**
veteran veterano/a *adj.* **14B**
veterinarian veterinario/a *m./f.* **3A**
via: to go via pasar por *v.* **6B**
victim: kidnapping victim secuestrado/a *m./f.* **16A**
view vista *f.* **11A**
viewer: television viewer televidente *m./f.* **9A: television viewer** telespectador(a) *m./f.* **14B**
viewing: wildlife viewing observación de flora y fauna *f.* **6B**
village aldea *f.* **9A**
vinyl: vinyl record disco de vinilo *m.* **13B**
violence violencia *f.* **16A**

virgin: extra virgin olive oil aceite de oliva virgen extra *m.* **15A: virgin forest** bosque virgen *m.* **6B**
visit visitar *v.* **4A**
visitor visitante *m. y f.* **8B**
vital vital *adj.* **7A**
vocation vocación *f.* **7A: by vocation** por vocación *loc. adv.* **7A**
voice voz (*pl.* voces) *f.* **6A**
volcano volcán *m.* **6B**
volume volumen *m.* **14A**
volunteer voluntario/a *m./f.* **12B: volunteer work** trabajo voluntario *m.* **7A**
vote votar *v.* **10B**
voucher: gift voucher cheque-regalo *m.* **3B**
vowel vocal *f.* **13B**

W

wages sueldo *m.* **3B**
wait: to be waiting for estar pendiente de *v.* **17B: to wait for** esperar *v.* **12B:** esperar *v.* **12B: to wait in line** hacer fila *v.* **13A**
waiter camarero *m.* **2B:** mesero *m.* **13A**
waitress camarera *f.* **2B:** mesera *f.* **13A**
wake up despertarse *v.* **7A**
walk caminar *v.* **5B: to go for a walk** pasear *v.* **3A, 5A: to take a walk** dar un paseo *v.* **6A:** pasear *v.* **5B**
walkway paseo *m.* **2A**
wall pared *f.* **: Berlin Wall** Muro de Berlín *m.* **10B**
wallet billetero *m.* **18B**
waltz vals *m.* **17B**
wander: to wander aimlessly caminar sin rumbo fijo *v.* **17B**
want querer *v.* **3B**
war guerra *f.* **8B: civil war** guerra civil *f.* **8B: World War II** Segunda Guerra Mundial *f.*
ward sala *f.* **10A**
warranty garantía *f.* **11A**
waste desperdiciar *v.* **15B**
watch reloj *m.* **3A:** mirar *v.* **6A: to watch movies** ver películas *v.* **3A: wrist watch** reloj de pulsera *m.* **3B**
waterfall cascada *f.* **6B**
wave ola *f.* **16B**
way manera *f.* **5A: by the way** por cierto *conj.* **10A: by the way** a propósito *exp. conj.* **10A: way of life** medio de vida *m.* **11B**
we nosotros/as *pron.* **1B**
wealth riqueza *f.* **14A**
weapon arma *f.* **16A: nuclear weapon** arma nuclear *f.* **16A**
wear llevar *v.* **3B**
weather tiempo *m.* **10A: good weather** buen tiempo *m.* **2A: there is bad weather** hace mal tiempo *exp.* **10A: there is good weather** hace buen tiempo *exp.* **10A: weather forecast** pronóstico *m.* **9A: What's the weather like?** ¿Qué tiempo hace? *exp.* **10A**
Web: Web page página web *f.* **14B: Web site** sitio web *m.* **14B**
webcam cámara web *f.* **6B**
wedding boda *f.* **5A: silver wedding anniversary** bodas de plata *f.* **18B: to have one's wedding anniversary** cumplir años de casados *v.* **18B**
Wednesday miércoles *m.* **3A**
week semana *f.* **2B: day of the week** día de la semana *m.* **3A: Holy Week** Semana Santa *f.* **5A: last week** la semana pasada *loc. adv.* **5A: once a week** una vez a la semana *loc. adv.* **6A: this week** esta semana *loc. adv.* **6A**
weekend fin de semana *m.* **2B: long weekend** puente *m.* **6B: (on) weekends** los fines de semana *loc. adv.* **5B**
weekly semanal *adj.* **3A**
welcome bienvenida *f.* **11A:** dar la bienvenida *v.* **11A: You're welcome.** Con gusto. *exp.* **18B**
Welcome! ¡Bienvenido/a(s)! *exp.* **11A**
well bien *adv.* **1A:** pues *exp.* **6A: as well as** así como *conj.* **16B: very well** muy bien *adv.* **1A: very well** rebién (*fam.*) *adv.* **17B: well-being** bienestar *m.* **6A**
well… bueno… *exp.* **2A**
west oeste *m.* **2A**
what qué *interrog.* **1A: At what time…?** ¿A qué hora…? *exp.* **3A: What color?** ¿De qué color? *exp.* **3B: What is it like?** ¿Cómo es? *exp.* **4B: What is it used for?** ¿Para qué sirve? *exp.* **4B: What is it?** ¿Qué es? *exp.* **1A: What is… like?** ¿Cómo es…? *exp.* **2A: What size?** ¿De qué talla? *exp.* **3B: What time is it?** ¿Qué hora es? *exp.* **3A: What would you like (to have)?** ¿Qué desean tomar? *exp.* **2B: What… do you choose?** ¿Qué… eliges? *exp.* **1A: What's the weather like?** ¿Qué tiempo hace? *exp.* **10A: What's wrong?** ¿Qué te/le pasa? (*fam./form.*) *exp.* **10A**
What? ¿Cómo? *exp.* **14A**
wheat trigo *m.* **15A**
when cuándo *interrog.* **0**
where dónde *interrog.* **1A: Where are you from?** ¿De dónde eres? *exp.* **1A: Where are you from?** ¿De dónde es usted? *exp.* **1A: where is...?** ¿dónde está...? *exp.* **2A**
which: which one(s)? ¿cuál(es)? *interrog.* **4B**
white blanco/a *adj.* **3B**
who quién *interrog.* **1A: Who is it?** ¿Quién es? *exp.* **1A**
whole: whole milk leche entera *f.* **15A**
whose cuyo/a *pron.* **10B**
why por qué *interrog.* **6A: Why don't you…?** ¿Por qué no…? *exp.* **6A**
wide ancho/a *adj.* **4B**
wife esposa *f.* **5B:** mujer *f.* **3A: ex-wife** ex esposa *f.* **12A**
Wi-Fi: Wi-Fi network red Wi-Fi *f.* **13B**
wild silvestre *adj.* **18B: wild cherry** guinda *f.* **16B**
wildlife: wildlife viewing observación de flora y fauna *f.* **6B**
win ganar *v.* **5A: to win tournaments** ganar torneos *v.* **18A**
window ventana *f.* **: shop window** escaparate *m.* **3B**
wine vino *m.* **2B**
winning ganador(a) *adj.* **14B**
winter invierno *m.* **2A**
wisdom sabiduría *f.* **17B**
wish desear *v.* **11A: I/We wish.** Ojalá. *exp.* **15A**
with con *prep.* **2B: with a credit card** con tarjeta *loc. adv.* **3B: with me** conmigo *prep.* + *pron.* **5A: with you** contigo *prep.* + *pron.* **5A**
within dentro de *loc. prep.* **17A**
witness testigo *m. y f.* **10B**
woman mujer *f.* **3A, 5B: business woman** mujer empresaria *f.* **5A: the woman of my dreams** la mujer de mi vida *exp.* **12A**
wonderful estupendo/a *adj.* **6B:** maravilloso/a *adj.* **5A**
wonderfully de maravilla *loc. adv.* **17B**
wood madera *f.* **8A**
word palabra *f.* **0: in other words** es decir *exp.* **8B**
work labor *f.* **12B:** trabajo *m.* **2A:** funcionar *v.* **7B:** trabajar *v.* **1B: to go to work** ir a trabajar *v.* **3A: to work as** trabajar como *v.* **11B: volunteer work** trabajo voluntario *m.* **7A: What do you do (for work)?** ¿A qué te dedicas? *exp.* **1B: work atmosphere** ambiente laboral *m.* **13B: work schedule** horario de trabajo *m.* **3A: to work out** hacer ejercicio *v.* **6A: work of art** obra (de arte) *f.* **8A**
workday: flexible workday jornada flexible *f.* **6A**
worker trabajador(a) *adj.; m./f.* **3A:** obrero/a *m./f.* **8B**
working laboral *adj.* **7B: working mother** madre trabajadora *f.* **7B: working team** equipo de trabajo *m.* **13B**
world mundo *m.* **4A: a world in motion** un mundo en movimiento *exp.* **14A: to go around the world** dar la vuelta al mundo *v.* **18A: World Heritage** Patrimonio Mundial *m.* **11B: World Heritage (Site)** Patrimonio de la Humanidad *m.* **8A: world leaders** líderes mundiales *m. y f. pl.* **16A: world of finance** mundo de las finanzas *m.* **3A**
worldwide mundial *adj.* **7B**
worried preocupdo/a *adj.* **12A**
worry preocupación *f.* **7A:** preocupar *v.* **7A**
worship: place of worship lugar de culto *m.* **8A**
worth valía *f.* **18A: to be worth it** valer la pena *v.* **11B**
worthy digno/a *adj.* **3B**
would: What would you like (to have)? ¿Qué desean tomar? *exp.* **2B: Would you mind…?** ¿Le importaría…? *exp.* **13A**
wrap up abrigarse *v.* **13A**
wrist: wristwatch reloj de pulsera *m.* **3B**
write escribir *v.* **0:** redactar *v.* **0: to write to each other** escribirse *v.* **17B: to write down** anotar *v.* **0**
writer escritor(a) *m./f.* **1A**
wrong equivocado/a *adj.* **: to go wrong** ir mal *v.* **7B**

Y

yard jardín *m.* **4B**
year año *m.* **2B: fifteen-year-old girl** quinceañera *f.* **5A: New Year** Año Nuevo *m.* **18B: this year** este año *loc. adv.* **6A: three times a year** tres veces al año *loc. adv.* **3A: time of year** época *f.* **6B: to turn 15 years old** cumplir 15 años *v.* **5A**

yellow amarillo/a *adj.* **3B: yellow fever** fiebre amarilla *f.* **10A**
yes sí *adv.* **1A**
yesterday ayer *adv.* **5A**
yet aún *adv.* **15B: not yet** todavía no *loc. adv.* **6A**
yoga yoga *m.* **3A**
yogurt yogur *m.* **2B**
you tú (*sing. fam.*) *pron.* **1A:** usted (*sing. form.*) *pron.* **1A:** ustedes (*pl. form.*) *pron.* **1A:** vosotros/as (*pl. fam.*) *pron.* **1B: And you?** ¿Y tú/usted? *exp.* **1A: with you** contigo *pron.* **5A: You/One can't...** No se puede... *exp.* **7B**
young joven (*pl.* jóvenes) *adj.*; *m. y f.* **2A: for young people** juvenil *adj.* **7A: young boy/girl** pibe/a *m./f.* **17B: young people** jóvenes *m.* **2A**
youngster chamaquito/a *m./f.* **12A**
your tu(s) (*sing. fam.*) *adj.* **2A:** su(s) (*form.*) *adj.* **2A:** vuestro/a(s) (*pl. fam.*) *adj.* **5B: at your service** a tu/su servicio *loc. adv.* **7B**
youth juventud *f.* **9A**
yucca yuca *f.* **4A**

Z

zip: zip-lining tirolesa *f.* **18A**

Cultural Index

Note: For a complete listing of grammar topics, see pp. A17–A18.

About the Author

Jan Underwood received her M.A. in Comparative Literature from McGill University in Montreal, Quebec, and her M.A. in Foreign Languages and Literatures (Spanish and French) from Portland State University in Portland, Oregon. She has lived all over the United States and in Mexico, Guatemala, Canada, and France, but for more than 20 years she's made her home in Portland, where she is an instructor of Spanish at Portland Community College. In addition to teaching and writing textbook materials, Ms. Underwood writes fiction; her first novel was published in 2006, and she is currently working on another.

Text Credits

135 © Cristian Dzwonik (Nik)
202 © Andrés Rábago García (El Roto)
298 © Fernando J. Sendra, humorista gráfico argentino.
330 © EL PAÍS S.L. - JUAN JOSÉ MILLÁS
345 © Joaquín Salvador Lavado (QUINO) Toda Mafalda — Ediciones de La Flor, 1993
382 Pablo Neruda. "Oda al tomate", ODAS ELEMENTALES. © Fundación Pablo Neruda, 2010
389 © Joaquín Salvador Lavado (QUINO) Toda Mafalda — Ediciones de La Flor, 1993
413 © Joaquín Salvador Lavado (QUINO) Toda Mafalda — Ediciones de La Flor, 1993
434 © Cristina Fernández Cubas

Photo and Art Credits

All images © Vista Higher Learning unless otherwise noted.

Cover: (t) © Corbis; (mtl) © LeighSmithImages/Alamy; (mtr) María Eugenia Corbo; (mbm) Paula Díez; (mbr) © LWA-Dann Tardif/Corbis; (b) © David Angel/Alamy.

Front Matter: iii (b) © Andresr/Shutterstock; **XXV** (tr) © Ali Burafi.

Preliminary Unit: 1 (tl) © JIM RUYMEN/UPI/Landov; (tr) © David Dell; (cl) © J.D. Dallet/age fotostock; (r) Paula Díez; (bl) © Diego Santacruz, ARCHIVO EL ESPECTADOR, COMUNICAN S.A.; **2** (tl) © Schraps/face to face/Newscom; (tcl) Rafael Ríos; (tcr) © Media Bakery; (r) © Plainpicture RM/age fotostock; (bl) © Agencia El Universal/Newscom; (blc) © Masterfile; (brc) © Cover/Getty Images; **3** (tlc) © SCOTT DALTON/The New York Times/Redux; (tr) © LWA-Dann Tardif/Corbis; (bl) © Cover/Getty Images; (blc) © Exactostock/SuperStock; (brc) © STOCK4B/Getty Images; **4** (tl) © George Shelley/age fotostock; (tcl) © Fundación Once; (tcr) Paula Díez; (bl) © Klaus Tiedge/age fotostock; (brc) © Unión Radio; (br) © Andy Sotiriou/Getty Images; **5** (tcl) © Casa Editorial EL TIEMPO; (tcr) © Don Mason/age fotostock; (r) © Mel Yates/Cultura/Photononstop; (bcl) © bw media photoagentur/age fotostock; (bcr) © Antoine Couvercelle/DPPI/Icon SMI 547/Newscom.

Unit One: 9 (tl) © JIM RUYMEN/UPI/Landov; (bl) Ali Burafi; **10** (tcl) © Album/Newscom; **11** (tl) Katie Wade; (tr) Janet Dracksdorf; **12** (b) © Federico Delicado; **13** (tl) © Javier Larrea/age fotostock; (bc) Martín Bernetti; **14** (tl) © JIM RUYMEN/UPI/Landov; (tcl) © Media Bakery; (tcr) © Max Messerli/age fotostock; (tr) © akg - images/The Image Works; (bcl) José Blanco; (bcr) © ÁNGEL LUIS GARCÍA/El Nuevo Día de Puerto Rico/Newscom; (br) © Ralph A. Ledergerber/Photographers Direct; **15** (tl) Katie Wade; (tr) © Tifonimages/Shutterstock; (tcl) © Schmid, Reinhard; (tcr) Ali Burafi; (cr) Pascal Pernix; (bl) © Foodstories/age fotostock; (br) © Schraps/face to face/Newscom; **16** (tc) Ali Burafi; (cl) Oscar Artavia Solano; (cr) José Blanco; (bc) © Tramonto/age fotostock; (b) Anne Loubet; **20** (t) Olimpia Torres; **21** (t) © Thomas Northcut/Getty Images; **23** (tl) José Blanco; (tc, tr, cl) Janet Dracksdorf; (c, cr) José Blanco; **25** (t) © J.D. Dallet/age fotostock; (b) Paola Ríos; **26** (c) Katie Wade; (br) Martín Bernetti; **30** (t) © Javier Larrea/age fotostock; **32** (t) Paula Díez; (bc) Janet Dracksdorf; (br) © Stephen Coburn/Shutterstock; **33** (c) © Germán Ariel Berra/Shutterstock; (r) © Hans Georg Roth/Corbis; **34** (tr) Ali Burafi.

Unit Two: 35 (t) © David Dell; (c) © J.D. Dallet/age fotostock; (b) Martín Bernetti; **36** (t) © Gg/eStock Photo; **38** (t) © Jose Fuste Raga/Corbis; **39** (tl) Lauren Krolick; (cl) Martín Bernetti; (c) © Javier Larrea/age fotostock; (cr) Darío Eusse Tobón; **40** (t) © David Dell; **41** (t) Rubén Varela; **42** (c) José Blanco; **46** (t) Olimpia Torres; **47** (t) Olimpia Torres; **49** (tr) © Media Bakery; **50** (tl) © J.D. Dallet/age fotostock; **51** (t) © Antonia Santolaya; (c) © Red 2/age fotostock; **52** (t, tc, c, bc, b) Olimpia Torres; **56** (b) © Germán Tejerina; **57** (bc inset) © Mar Ferrero; (br inset) © Tesa González; (b) © Federico Delicado; **58** (t) Martín Bernetti.

Unit Three: 59 (c) © Diego Santacruz, ARCHIVO EL ESPECTADOR, COMUNICAN S.A.; (b) © Allstar Picture Library/Alamy; **60** (t) © Tomeu Ozonas/Photographers Direct; **62** (t) © Getty Images/Digital Vision; **64** (cr) María Eugenia Corbo; **65** (bl) © Marka/age fotostock; (bc) © Karl Weatherly/age fotostock; (br) © Álvaro Leiva/age fotostock; **66** (tl) © Aspen Stock/age fotostock; (tr) © Javier Larrea/age fotostock; (cl) © Noam/Fotolia; (cr) © Andrés Rodríguez/Big Stock Photo; **70** (t) © P. Narayan/age fotostock; **71** (t) © Federico Delicado; (bcl) Martín Bernetti; (bcr) © Felinda/Dreamstime; (br) © Elnur/Dreamstime; (l) © Federico Delicado; **72** (tcr) © Marcos Welsh/age fotostock; (tr) © MAURITIUS IMAGES/LATINSTOCK; **73** (cl) © Javier Larrea/age fotostock; (cr) Pascal Pernix; **74** (t) © Diego Santacruz, ARCHIVO EL ESPECTADOR, COMUNICAN S.A.; **75** (bcl) © Emilio Ereza /Alamy; (br) Katie Wade; **76** (t) Olimpia Torres; (tc, br, bl) Olimpia Torres; **80** (b) © Javier Larrea/age fotostock; **82** (t) © Javier Soriano/AFP/Getty Images; **84** (tr) © Allstar Picture Library/Alamy; (bl) © Staff/MCT/Newscom.

Unit Four: 85 (c) Paula Díez; (b) Oscar Artavia Solano; **86**-87 (t) Katie Wade; **87** (tr) © Federico Delicado; (tc, c, bc, b) © Julio Sánchez; **88** (b) © Teresa Novoa Martínez; **91** (t) Ali Burafi; **95** (b) © Javier Larrea/age fotostock; **96** (t) Martín Bernetti; (c) José Blanco; (b) © Javier Larrea/age fotostock; **98** (t) © L. E. MacDonald; **99** (tl) Ali Burafi; (c) © Bernardita Barriola Caré; (tr) Lauren Krolick; **100** (tl) © Red Cover/Masterfile; (tcl, cl) Paula Díez; (tr) © IPS CO. LTD./Latinstock; (cb) © BILDERDIENST A. HÖHN/LATISTOCK; (cc) © Eduardo Sánchez Gatell/123RF; **101** (tcl) Martín Bernetti; (tcr) © ZTS/Shutterstock; **102** (tl) Paula Díez; (tr) © carolecastelli/123RF; (cr) © Map Resources; **104** (t) © BILDERDIENST A. HÖHN/LATINSTOCK; (bc) Anne Loubet; (b) © Ferico Delicado; **108** (bl) © skodonnell/iStockphoto; **109** (cl) © Federico Delicado; (bc) © Elisanth/ Dreamstime; (bcr) © Margo Harrison/123RF; (br) © bilder/Shutterstock; **110** (t) Oscar Artavia Solano.

Unit Five: 111 (tl) © Schraps/face to face/Newscom; (cr) Rafael Ríos; **112** (l) © Chederros/age fotostock; **113** (tl) © John Van Hasselt/Sygma/Corbis; (tc) © Simeone, Giovanni/Fototeca 9x12; **114** (t) Mónica M. González; (cr) Rossy Llano; (bcr) © Sam Bloomberg-Rissman/age fotostock; (br) © Graziano Arici/age fotostock; (bl) © Media Bakery; **116** (tl) © Schraps/face to face/Newscom; (cr) MIRAMAX/DIMENSION FILMS/THE KOBAL COLLECTION; **117** (tl) © CHEMA MOYA/epa/Corbis; (tc) © Antoine Couvercelle/DPPI/Icon SMI 547/Newscom; (tr) © JIM RUYMEN/ UPI/Landov; (bl) © Dusko Despotovic/Corbis; (bc) © a11/ZUMA Press/Newscom; (br) © Micheline Pelletier/Sygma/Corbis; (ccr) © Rosa Osuna Alcalaya; **118** (tl) © Jaume Gual/age fotostock; **122** (t) © Comstock /Fotosearch; (c) © Corbis; (b) © Andresr/Shutterstock; **124** (t) © Arthur Klonsky/Corbis; (b) © Federico Delicado; **128** (tl) Rafael Ríos; **129** (b) Janet Dracksdorf; **130** (tr) © godfer/Fotolia; (bl) © Cathy Yeulet/Big Stock Photo; (br) © Pixtal/age fotostock; **134** (t) © Cristian G. Dzwonik (Nik); (b) © Daniel Pessah; **135** (t) © Cristian G. Dzwonik (Nik).

Unit Six: 137 (t) © Media Bakery; (c) © Plainpicture RM/age fotostock; **138** (c) © Battroid; **139** (tl) © Lindsay Hebberd/Corbis; (tcl) © aquasolid/ iStockphoto; (cl) © Doco Dalfiano/age fotostock; (cr) © Pete Saloutos/Shutterstock; (tr) © tonobalaguerf/Shutterstock; **141** (t) © Federico Delicado; **142** (t) © Media Bakery; **143** (b) Ali Burafi; **144** (t) © rj lerich/Shutterstock; (tc) © Galyna Andrushko/Shutterstock; (bc) Martín Bernetti; (b) Ali Burafi; **147** (c) Oscar Artavia Solano; **148** (t) Pascal Pernix; **151** (tl) © Federico Delicado; (br) © Marta Montaña; **153** (bl) © Hidalgo & Lopesino/age fotostock; **154** (t) © Plainpicture RM/age fotostock; (b) © StockLite/Shutterstock; **156** (t) © Galyna Andrushko/Shutterstock; (bc) © Pelonmaker/Shutterstock; (b) © Celso Diniz/Shutterstock.

Unit Seven: 163 (t) © EL UNIVERSAL/Newscom; (c) © Masterfile; **164** (tl) © Masterfile/Latinstock; (tmr) © AFP/Getty Images; **165** (tl) © Masterfile/Latinstock; (tr) © Taka/ age fotostock; (cl) © Leo Himsl/ age fotostock; (cr) © Jenny Cundy/Image Source; **166** (tcl) © MAURITIUS IMAGES/Latinstock; (tcr) © Design Pics Inc./Alamy; (tr) © Aspen Stock/age fotostock; (c) Martín Bernetti; (bl) © Federico Delicado; **168** (t) © EL UNIVERSAL/Newscom; **169** (t) © ARCHIVO/Newscom; (c) © SUN/Newscom; (br) © AFP/Getty Images; **170** (cl) © Noam/Fotolia; (cr) © Thomas Northcut/Getty Images; (bl) © Tetra Images/Alamy; **176** (t) © Hagg + Kropp/age fotostock; **177** (t) © Superstock/age fotostock; **178** (t) © Superstock/age fotostock; **180** (t) © Masterfile; **182** (bc) Katie Wade; **186** (t) © PhotoAlto/Alamy.

Unit Eight: 189 (t) © Cover/Getty Images; **191** (tl) © guysal/Shutterstock; (tc) © Jean Dominique Dallet; **192**-193 (tl, tc, tr, c, bl, bcl, bcr, br) Olimpia Torres; **194** (tl) © Cover/Getty Images; (tr) © Cover/Getty Images; **195** (tl) José Blanco; (tr) © Lee Torrens/Shutterstock; (bl) © Heeb Christian/ age fotostock; (bc) © Rob Wilson/Shutterstock; (br) © CORTESÍA/Newscom; **196** (tl, tr, tcl, tcr, cl, cr, bl, br) © Federico Delicado; **200** (t) © CARLOS PEREZ DE ROZAS/EFE/Corbis; **201** (tl) © Getty Images; (tcr) Nicolás Corbo; **202** (tl inset, tcl inset, cl inset, tcr inset, cr inset) © Federico Delicado; (tcl) José Blanco; **203** (tl) © Paul Springett/ Alamy; (tc) © Javier Lizón/EFE/Corbis; **205** (bl, bcl, bcr, br) María Eugenia Corbo; **206** (tr) Katie Wade; (cl) © P.J. Sharpe/Corbis; (c) Darío Eusse Tobón; (cr) Lars Rosen Gunnilstam; (bcl) Katie Wade; **210** (c) © Federico Delicado; **211** (tr) Martín Bernetti.

Unit Nine: 213 (t) © SCOTT DALTON/The New York Times/Redux; **214** (t) © Pablo Corral V/CORBIS; **215** (tl, tc) Teresa Garrido; (tr) María Eugenia Corbo; **216** (tl) Ana Cabezas Martín; **218** (r) © SCOTT DALTON /The New York Times/Redux; **219** (tl) Vanessa Bertozzi; (cr) © Bettmann/ CORBIS; **220** (tl, tcl) Oscar Artavia Solano; (tr) Martín Bernetti; (ccl) © Kuzma/Big Stock Photo; **224** (tr) © JUAN MARTÍN/EFE/Corbis; **225** (tl) Janet Dracksdorf; (tc) © Javier Lizón/EFE/Corbis; (tr) © Federico Delicado; **226** (cl, cr, bl, br) © Federico Delicado; **227** (t) © Federico Delicado; (bl) © EMILIO NARANJO/EFE/Corbis; **229** (cl) © Magical Andes Photography/Photographers Direct; (c) © AP Photo/Paul White; (cr) © Marco Simola Photography/Photographers Direct; **230** (c) © Federico Delicado; (bl) © Magical Andes Photography/Photographers Direct; (bc) © Marco Simola Photography/Photographers Direct; (br) © AP Photo/Paul White; **234** (t) © AP Photo/Jose Luis Magana; **235** (tr) © PictureNet/Corbis.

Unit Ten: 237 (t) © LWA-Dann Tardif/Corbis; (c) © Cover/Getty Images; **238** (t) © Federico Delicado; (c) © Félix Moreno Arrastio; (bcr) Katie Wade; **239** (cl) © Grafton Marshall Smith/CORBIS; (b) © Federico Delicado; **240** (cl, cr) © Federico Delicado; **242** (t) © LWA-Dann Tardif/ Corbis; **243** (tr, cl) Olimpia Torres; **244** (t) © Federico Delicado; (t inset) © Federico Delicado; **248** (tl) © ARCHIVO PARTICULAR/El Tiempo de Colombia/Newscom; (tr) © EFE/Corbis; **249** (tl) (ELECTRONIC IMAGE) AFP PHOTO/Antonio SCORZALOCATION: RIO DE JANEIRO, BRAZILPOST © ANTONIO SCORZA/AFP/Newscom; (tr) © Kyodo /Landov; **250** (tr) Martín Bernetti; (tcr) Rafael Ríos; **252** (t) © Cover/Getty Images; **253** (bl) © TIME & LIFE Images/Getty Images; **256** (b) Martín Bernetti.

Unit Eleven: 261 (t) © Exactostock/SuperStock; (c) © STOCK4B/Getty Images; **262** (tl) Oscar Artavia Solano; (tc) María Eugenia Corbo; **263** (t) María Eugenia Corbo; (b) Ali Burafi; **265** (t) Vanessa Bertozzi; **266** (t) © Exactostock/SuperStock; **267** (tc, tr) José Blanco; **268** (tl, tr) © Federico Delicado; **272** (tl) © Javier Larrea/age fotostock; (tr) Rafael Ríos; **273** (t) © Masterfile/Latinstock; **274** (t) © Federico Delicado; (bl) © Jerry Whaley/ age fotostock; (bcr) © Mikhail Lavrenov/123rf; (br) Janet Dracksdorf; **275** (tcl) Ali Burafi; (tcr) © Harry Neave/Fotolia; (cl) Martín Bernetti; (cr) Anne Loubet; (b) © Fred Goldstein/Fotolia; **276** (t) © STOCK4B/Getty Images; (br) © Federico Delicado; **277** (t) Kathryn Alena Korf; **278** (tl, tcl, tcr, tr, cl, cr) © Federico Delicado; **282** (t) Paola Ríos.

Unit Twelve: 285 (t) © George Shelley/age fotostock; **286** (cl, c, cr, bl, bc, br) © Federico Delicado; **287** (tl) © Andrey Arkusha/Shutterstock; **288** (tl, tc, tr) Paula Díez; **289** (tl, tr) Paula Díez; **290** (t) © George Shelley/age fotostock; **291** (t) Oscar Artavia Solano; **292** (t) © Topham/The Image Works; **296** (tc) © Ulises Rodríguez/EFE/Corbis; (tr) © Fundación Cimientos; (tr) © Sarah Meghan Lee/The Image Works; **297** (t) © Getty Images; **298** (tl) © Nathan Benn/ CORBIS; **299** (t) © Mika/Corbis; **301** (tr) © Getty Images; (bcl) © Graziano Arici/age fotostock; (bcr) © Louisa Gouliamaki/epa/Corbis; (br) © ZUMA Press/Newscom; **307** (bcl) José Blanco; (bcr) © Robert Lerich/Fotolia; (br) Anne Loubet.

Unit Thirteen: 309 (t) Paula Díez; **314** (t) Paula Díez; (bl, bc, br) © Federico Delicado; **316** (tl) Lauren Krolick; (tc) Darío Eusse Tobón; (tr) Katie Wade; **325** (t) © Orange Line Media/Shutterstock; (c) © Sean Prior/Shutterstock; **331** (t) © NuStock/iStock Photo.

Unit Fourteen: 333 (c) © Unión Radio; **334** (r) © Michel Renaudeau/age fotostock; **336** (cl) © AP Photo/Christine Nesbitt; **337** (t) © Klaus Tiedge/age fotostock; **344** (cr) © HANDOUT/KRT/Newscom; (br) © A3803 Jochen Luebke/Newscom; **345** (t) © Yuri Arcurs/Dreamstime; **348** (t) © Unión Radio; **350** (tl) Katie Wade; (tc) © jorisvo/Shutterstock.

Unit Fifteen: 357 (t) © Andy Sotiriou/Getty Images; **359** (c) © Colin Underhill/Alamy; (bl) Paula Díez; **360** (tl) Janet Dracksdorf; (tc) © Sandra Cunningham/Shutterstock; (tr) © eddieberman/iStockphoto; (r) Vanessa Bertozzi; **362** (t) © Andy Sotiriou/Getty Images; **363** (tl) © Oficina Regional de FAO para América Latina y el Caribe; (ccr) Janet Dracksdorf; (b) José Blanco; **364** (tl) © Javier Etcheverry/Alamy; (br) © AIZAR RALDES/AFP/Getty Images; **365** (bl) Katie Wade; **368** (tc) Darío Eusse Tobón; (bc) Gabriela Ferland; **372** (t) © Andresr/Shutterstock; (c) © Getty Images/Digital Vision; **382** (tr) © Pedro León.

Unit Sixteen: 385 (t) © Casa Editorial EL TIEMPO; (c) © Don Mason/age fotostock; **387** (cr) © ROBIN TOWNSEND/EFE/Corbis; **388** (c) © Luis Camacho Arana; **390** (t) © Casa Editorial EL TIEMPO; **391** (l) © KO/The Grosby Group/Newscom; **392** (b) © Gg/age fotostock; **396** (tcr) © Louis Held/age fotosctock; **397** (c) © Federico Delicado; **398** (t) © Guy Motil/Corbis; (b) © Royalty-Free/CORBIS; **400** (t) © Don Mason/age fotostock; 401 (tr) © Courtesy of María Teresa González U.; **406** (t) Lauren Krolick; (c) Ali Burafi; (b) © Javier Larrea/age fotostock; **409** (r) Martín Bernetti.

Unit Seventeen: 414 (tr) © Comstock Photos; (tl) © clearviewstock/Fotolia; **415** (tl) Martín Bernetti; (tr) © YinYang/iStockphoto; (cr) © Ronald Hudson/Big Stock Photo; **416** (t) © Courtesy of Carlos Escobar; **417** (b) Martín Bernetti; **418** (tl) © Bettmann/CORBIS; (tr) © Corbin O'Grady Studio/Photo Researchers,Inc.; (cl) © AP Photo/John Lindsay; (cr) © ANTONIO NAVA/Landov; **420** (b) © Javier Larrea/age fotostock; **422** (tl) © craftvision/iStock; (tc) © Interfoto/age fotostock; **425** (c) © Federico Delicado; **426** (t) © bw media photoagentur/age fotostock; **427** (t) © C.van Zuylen/Lebrecht; **430** (tl) Ali Burafi; (tr) © Pixtal/age fotostock; (bl) Anne Loubet; (br) © Orange Line Media/Shutterstock; **431** (b) Martín Bernetti; **432** (cl) Martín Bernetti; **435** (t) © imagebroker/Alamy.

Unit Eighteen: 437 (t) © Antoine Couvercelle/DPPI/Icon SMI 547/Newscom; (c) © Mel Yates/Cultura/Photononstop; **438** (tl) © CORTESÍA IVAN VALLEJO/El Comercio de Ecuador/Newscom; (tr) © Courtesy of Andoni Rodelgo & Alice Goffart; **439** (tl) Ricardo Abad corriendo por la Bardenas Reales de Navarra © Ivana Gutierrez; (c) © Agencia El Universal/El Universal de México/Newscom; (tr) © Courtesy of Juan Carlos Sagastume; **440** (tl) © Imag'In Pyrénées/Fotolia; (tr) © Kevin Schafer/Alamy; **441** (tc) Janet Dracksdorf; (tr) © Danny Warren/iStock; (l) © Scott B. Rosen/The New York Times/Redux; (bc) © Djmattaar/ Dreamstime; **442** (tr) © Antoine Couvercelle/DPPI/Icon SMI 547/Newscom; **443** (tl) © Staff/MCT/Newscom; (tr) © REUTERS/Donald Miralle/POOL/Landov; (bcl) © ROBERT GHEMENT/epa/Corbis; (bcr) © Chiquilín García/Newscom; (bl) © EMMANUEL DUNAND/AFP/Getty Images/Newscom; (br) © Jun Tsukida/AFLO/Icon SMI 938/Newscom; **444** (tl) © Sol Neelman/Corbis; (tc) © Matteo Prezioso; (tr) © Robert Fried/Alamy; **446** (c) Martín Bernetti; **448** (cl) © rebvt/Shutterstock; **450** (bl) © DreamPictures/Blend; (br) © Botond Horváth/Shutterstock; **451** (b) © Federico Delicado; **452** (tcr) © Jeff Greenberg/age fotostock; **453** (l) © Tolo Balaguer/age fotostock; **454** (t) © Mel Yates/Cultura/Photononstop; **455** (tc) © Elsa Guerrero; (tr) © Garden World Images/age fotostock; (b) Janet Dracksdorf; **456** (tl) © Firofoto food; (bl) © Arco Images GmbH/Alamy; (br) © Francisco Ipanaque/EFE/Corbis; **460** (t) © Cathy Yeulet/Big Stock Photo; (c) © vgstudio/Fotolia; (b) Martín Bernetti; **463** (tl) Oscar Artavia Solano; (tr) Anne Loubet.

End Matter: A141 (t) Katie Wade.